WORD
BIBLICAL
COMMENTARY

WORD
BIBLICAL
COMMENTARY

VOLUME 2

Genesis 16–50

GORDON J. WENHAM

WORD BOOKS, PUBLISHER · DALLAS, TEXAS

Word Biblical Commentary
Genesis 16–50
Copyright © 1994 by Word, Incorporated

Library of Congress Cataloging-in-Publication Data
Main entry under title:

Word biblical commentary.

    Includes bibliographies.
    1. Bible—Commentaries—Collected works.
BS491.2.W67   220.7'7   81–71768
ISBN 0–8499–0201–0 (vol. 2) AACR2

Printed in the United States of America

Scripture quotations in the body of the commentary, unless otherwise indicated, are generally from the Revised Standard Version of the Bible, copyright 1946 (renewed 1973), 1956, and © 1971 by the Division of Christian Education of the National Council of Churches of Christ in the USA and are used by permission. The author's own translation of the Scripture text appears in italic type under the heading *Translation*.

00 01 QPV 12 11 10 9

For John, Mary, Elizabeth, and Christopher
Genesis 33:5

Contents

Author's Preface

It is with a great sense of relief and thankfulness that after fourteen years I have finally reached the end of this commentary. As the author, I am only too aware of its shortcomings. Much more could have been said on nearly every page, but I have tried to resist the modern urge to ever longer commentaries. I think most readers will prefer a manageable volume to an exhaustive one.

The format of this volume is similar to the first. Those looking for a compact overview of my interpretation should read first the *Explanation* section, which sums up the more detailed exegesis of the *Comment* section. Though of course based on a detailed study of the Hebrew text, I have tried to write both sections so that those who do not know the language may follow the argument. Do not be put off by the occasional use of Hebrew words: they are either translated, or the context should make their meanings plain. However, the *Notes* do presuppose some knowledge of Hebrew as they discuss problems of Hebrew grammar and text-critical issues. Like the *Notes*, the *Form/Structure/Setting* sections are intended primarily for scholars and serious students, who wish to enter into the critical debates about the arrangement and growth of the text, issues that often have an important bearing on interpretation. Finally, the bibliographies should, as in the first volume, be seen as supplementary to Westermann's: they do not pretend to be exhaustive. While trying to list fully the more recent scholarly literature on Genesis available to me, I have only cited the most significant earlier publications.

Again I have many people to thank for help in this volume. My colleagues for several terms of sabbatical leave. The British Academy and Tyndale House for research grants. Mrs. Margaret Hardy for typing it. Professor K. A. Kitchen for reading parts of the manuscript, and various students, especially Dr. Y. Endo, P. Barker, C. Bartholomew, and T. Renz for help with checking it. Mrs. Melanie McQuere and Mrs. Terri Gibbs for all their work in preparing it for publication. And last, but not least, my wife and family, for putting up with me writing it.

Cheltenham
July 1993

GORDON J. WENHAM

Editorial Preface

The launching of the *Word Biblical Commentary* brings to fulfillment an enterprise of several years' planning. The publishers and the members of the editorial board met in 1977 to explore the possibility of a new commentary on the books of the Bible that would incorporate several distinctive features. Prospective readers of these volumes are entitled to know what such features were intended to be; whether the aims of the commentary have been fully achieved time alone will tell.

First, we have tried to cast a wide net to include as contributors a number of scholars from around the world who not only share our aims but are in the main engaged in the ministry of teaching in university, college, and seminary. They represent a rich diversity of denominational allegiance. The broad stance of our contributors can rightly be called evangelical, and this term is to be understood in its positive, historic sense of a commitment to Scripture as divine revelation and to the truth and power of the Christian gospel.

Then, the commentaries in our series are all commissioned and written for the purpose of inclusion in the *Word Biblical Commentary*. Unlike several of our distinguished counterparts in the field of commentary writing, there are no translated works, originally written in a non-English language. Also, our commentators were asked to prepare their own rendering of the original biblical text and to use those languages as the basis of their own comments and exegesis. What may be claimed as distinctive with this series is that it is based on the biblical languages, yet it seeks to make the technical and scholarly approach to the theological understanding of Scripture understandable by—and useful to—the fledgling student, the working minister, and colleagues in the guild of professional scholars and teachers as well.

Finally, a word must be said about the format of the series. The layout, in clearly defined sections, has been consciously devised to assist readers at different levels. Those wishing to learn about the textual witnesses on which the translation is offered are invited to consult the section headed *Notes*. If the readers' concern is with the state of modern scholarship on any given portion of Scripture, they should turn to the sections on *Bibliography* and *Form/Structure/Setting*. For a clear exposition of the passage's meaning and its relevance to the ongoing biblical revelation, the *Comment* and concluding *Explanation* are designed expressly to meet that need. There is therefore something for everyone who may pick up and use these volumes.

If these aims come anywhere near realization, the intention of the editors will have been met, and the labor of our team of contributors rewarded.

General Editors: *David A. Hubbard*
Glenn W. Barker†
Old Testament: *John D. W. Watts*
New Testament: *Ralph P. Martin*

Abbreviations

BN	*Biblische Notizen*
BO	*Bibliotheca orientalis*
Brockelmann	C. Brockelmann, *Hebräische Syntax*
BR	*Biblical Research*
BSac	*Bibliotheca Sacra*
BT	*The Bible Translator*
BTB	*Biblical Theology Bulletin*
BWANT	Beiträge zur Wissenschaft vom Alten und Neuen Testament
BZ	*Biblische Zeitschrift*
BZAW	Beihefte zur *ZAW*
CAD	*The Assyrian Dictionary of the Oriental Institute of the University of Chicago*
CAH	*Cambridge Ancient History*
CBQ	*Catholic Biblical Quarterly*
CBQMS	CBQ Monograph Series
ConB	Coniectanea biblica
ConBOT	ConB Old Testament Series
CRAIBL	*Comptes rendus de l'académie des inscriptions et belles-lettres*
CTJ	*Calvin Theological Journal*
CTM	*Concordia Theological Monthly*
CurTM	*Currents in Theology and Mission*
DBSup	*Dictionnaire de la Bible, Supplément*
DBAT	*Dielheimer Blätter zum AT*
DJD	*Discoveries in the Judaean Desert*
EAEHL	*Encyclopedia of Archaeological Excavations in the Holy Land*, ed. M. Avi-Yonah
EI	*Ereș Israel*
EgT	*Eglise et Théologie*
EHS	Europäischen Hochschulschriften
EM	*Encyclopedia Miqrait*
ETL	*Ephemerides theologicae lovanienses*
ETR	*Etudes théologiques et religieuses*
EvQ	*Evangelical Quarterly*
EvT	*Evangelische Theologie*
EWAS	T. Muraoka, *Emphatic Words and Structures in Biblical Hebrew*
ExpTim	*Expository Times*
FOTL	The Forms of the Old Testament Literature
FRLANT	Forschungen zur Religion und Literatur des Alten und Neuen Testaments
GKC	*Gesenius' Hebrew Grammar*, ed. E. Kautzch, tr. A. E. Cowley
GTJ	*Grace Theological Journal*
GTOT	J. Simons, *The Geographical and Topographical Texts of the OT*
GTT	*Gereformeerd Theologisch Tijdschrift*
HAR	*Hebrew Annual Review*
HBT	*Horizons in Biblical Theology*
Hen	*Henoch*
HS	*Hebrew Studies*

HSM	*Harvard Semitic Monographs*
HTR	*Harvard Theological Review*
HUCA	*Hebrew Union College Annual*
IBD	*Illustrated Bible Dictionary*
IDB	*Interpreter's Dictionary of the Bible*, ed. G. A. Buttrick, 4 vols. (Nashville: Abingdon, 1962)
IDBSup	Supplementary volume to *IDB*
IEJ	*Israel Exploration Journal*
IKZ	*Internationale Katholische Zeitschrift*
ILR	*Israel Law Review*
Int	*Interpretation*
ITQ	*Irish Theological Quarterly*
ITS	Innsbrucker theologische Studien
IndTS	*Indian Theological Studies*
IrBS	*Irish Biblical Studies*
ISBE	*International Standard Bible Encyclopedia*, rev., ed. G. W. Bromiley
JAAR	*Journal of the American Academy of Religion*
JANESCU	*Journal of the Ancient Near Eastern Society of Columbia University*
JAOS	*Journal of the American Oriental Society*
JBC	*The Jerome Biblical Commentary*, ed. R. E. Brown et al.
JBL	*Journal of Biblical Literature*
JBR	*Journal of Bible and Religion*
JCS	*Journal of Cuneiform Studies*
JEOL	*Jaarbericht . . . ex oriente lux*
JETS	*Journal of the Evangelical Theological Society*
JJS	*Journal of Jewish Studies*
JNES	*Journal of Near Eastern Studies*
JNSL	*Journal of Northwest Semitic Languages*
Joüon	P. P. Joüon, *Grammaire de l'hébreu biblique* (Rome: Pontifical Biblical Institute, 1947)
JQR	*Jewish Quarterly Review*
JRT	*Journal of Religious Thought*
JSJ	*Journal for the Study of Judaism in the Persian, Hellenistic and Roman Period*
JSOT	*Journal for the Study of the OT*
JSOTSup	*JSOT* Supplement Series
JSS	*Journal of Semitic Studies*
JTS	*Journal of Theological Studies*
JTSoA	*Journal of Theology for Southern Africa*
KB	L. Koehler and W. Baumgartner, *Lexicon in Veteris Testamenti Libros*, 3d ed.
KD	*Kerygma und Dogma*
KS	*Kleine Schriften*
Lambdin	T. O. Lambdin, *Introduction to Biblical Hebrew* (New York: Scribner's, 1971)
LD	Lectio divina
Leš	*Lešonenu*
LingBib	*Linguistica Biblica*

MDOG	*Mitteilungen der deutschen Orient-Gesellschaft*
MGWJ	*Monatsschrift für Geschichte und Wissenschaft des Judentums*
MTZ	*Münchener theologische Zeitschrift*
NBD	*New Bible Dictionary,* ed. J. D. Douglas
NedTT	*Nederlands theologisch tijdschrift*
NERTOT	*Near Eastern Texts Relating to the Old Testament,* ed. W. Beyerlin
NICOT	New International Commentary on the Old Testament
NorTT	*Norsk Teologisk Tidsskrift*
NRT	*La nouvelle revue théologique*
OBO	Orbis Biblicus et Orientalis
OCCL	*Oxford Companion to Classical Literature,* ed. P. Harvey
OLP	*Orientalia loveniensia periodica*
Or	*Orientalia*
OrAnt	*Oriens antiquus*
OTS	*Oudtestamentische Studiën*
PEQ	*Palestine Exploration Quarterly*
PIBA	*Proceedings of the Irish Biblical Association*
POTT	*Peoples of OT Times,* ed. D. J. Wiseman
PWCJS	*Proceedings of the World Congress of Jewish Studies*
RA	*Revue d'Assyriologie*
RB	*Revue biblique*
Rel	*Religion*
ResQ	*Restoration Quarterly*
RevistB	*Revista bíblica*
RevThom	*Revue thomiste*
RHPR	*Revue d'histoire et de philosophie religieuses*
RivB	*Rivista biblica*
RLA	*Reallexicon der Assyriologie*
RTL	*Revue théologique de Louvain*
RTP	*Revue de Théologie et Philosophie*
SBH	F. I. Andersen, *The Sentence in Biblical Hebrew*
SBLMS	SBL Monograph Series
SBLSP	SBL Seminar Papers
SBLSS	SBL Semeia Studies
SBS	Stuttgarter Bibelstudien
SBT	Studies in Biblical Theology
ScEs	*Science et Esprit*
SEÅ	*Svensk exegetisk årsbok*
Sem	*Semitica*
SJLA	Studies in Judaism in Late Antiquity
SJOT	*Scandinavian Journal of the OT*
SJT	*Scottish Journal of Theology*
SR	*Studies in Religion/Sciences religieuses*
ST	*Studia theologica*
StudBT	*Studia Biblica et Theologica*
TA	*Tel Aviv*
TD	*Theology Digest*
TDNT	*Theological Dictionary of the New Testament,* ed. G. Kittel and G. Friedrich

TDOT	*Theological Dictionary of the Old Testament,* ed. G. J. Botterweck and H. Ringgren
TGl	*Theologie und Glaube*
TGUOS	*Transactions of the Glasgow University Oriental Society*
THWAT	*Theologisches Handwörterbuch zum Alten Testament,* ed. E. Jenni and C. Westermann
Them	*Themelios*
TJ	*Trinity Journal*
TLZ	*Theologische Literaturzeitung*
TQ	*Theologische Quartalschrift*
TRE	*Theologische Realenzyklopädie*
TRev	*Theologische Revue*
TRu	*Theologische Rundschau*
TS	*Theological Studies*
TTZ	*Trierer theologische Zeitschrift*
TV	*Theologia Viatorum*
TWAT	*Theologisches Wörterbuch zum Alten Testament,* ed. G. J. Botterweck and H. Ringgren
TynBul	*Tyndale Bulletin*
TZ	*Theologische Zeitschrift*
UF	*Ugarit-Forschungen*
UT	C. H. Gordon, *Ugaritic Textbook*
VE	*Vox Evangelica*
VR	*Vox Reformata*
VT	*Vetus Testamentum*
VTSup	Vetus Testamentum, Supplements
Waltke	B. K. Waltke, "The Samaritan Pentateuch and the Text of the Old Testament," in *New Perspectives on the Old Testament,* ed. J. B. Payne (Waco, TX: Word, 1970) 212–39.
WBC	Word Biblical Commentary
WMANT	Wissenschaftliche Monographien zum Alten und Neuen Testament
WO	*Die Welt des Orients*
WOC	B. K. Waltke and M. O'Connor, *An Introduction to Biblical Hebrew Syntax*
WTJ	*Westminster Theological Journal*
ZA	*Zeitschrift für Assyriologie*
ZAW	*Zeitschrift für die alttestamentliche Wissenschaft*
ZDMG	*Zeitschrift der deutschen morgenländischen Gesellschaft*
ZDPV	*Zeitschrift des deutschen Palästina–Vereins*
ZTK	*Zeitschrift für Theologie und Kirche*

MODERN TRANSLATIONS

AB	Anchor Bible		*According to the*
AV	Authorized Version		*Masoretic Text,* 1917
JB	Jerusalem Bible	KJV	King James Version
JPS	Jewish Publication Society of America, *The Holy Scriptures*	NAB	New American Bible
		NASB	New American Standard Bible

NEB	New English Bible	RSV	Revised Standard
NIV	New International		Version
	Version	RV	Revised Version
REB	Revised English Bible	TEV	Today's English Version

TEXTS, VERSIONS, AND ANCIENT WORKS

G, LXX	Septuagint	*Tg. Onq.*	*Targum Onqelos*
L	Codex Leningradensis,	*Tg. Neof.*	*Targum Neofiti*
	B19a	*Tg. Ps.-J.*	*Targum Pseudo-Jonathan*
MT	Masoretic Text	*Frg. Tg.*	*Fragment-Targum*
NT	New Testament	Vg	Vulgate
OT	Old Testament	α'	Aquila
SamPent	Samaritan Pentateuch	σ'	Symmachus
S	Syriac text	θ'	Theodotion

BIBLICAL AND APOCRYPHAL BOOKS

Old Testament

Gen	Genesis	Cant	Canticles,
Exod	Exodus		Song of Solomon
Lev	Leviticus	Isa	Isaiah
Num	Numbers	Jer	Jeremiah
Deut	Deuteronomy	Lam	Lamentations
Josh	Joshua	Ezek	Ezekiel
Judg	Judges	Dan	Daniel
Ruth	Ruth	Hos	Hosea
1–2 Sam	1–2 Samuel	Joel	Joel
1–2 Kgs	1–2 Kings	Amos	Amos
1–2 Chr	1–2 Chronicles	Obad	Obadiah
Ezra	Ezra	Jon	Jonah
Neh	Nehemiah	Mic	Micah
Esth	Esther	Nah	Nahum
Job	Job	Hab	Habakkuk
Ps(s)	Psalm(s)	Zeph	Zephaniah
Prov	Proverbs	Hag	Haggai
Eccl	Ecclesiastes	Zech	Zechariah
		Mal	Malachi

New Testament

Matt	Matthew	1–2 Cor	1–2 Corinthians
Mark	Mark	Gal	Galatians
Luke	Luke	Eph	Ephesians
John	John	Phil	Philippians
Acts	Acts	Col	Colossians
Rom	Romans	1–2 Thess	1–2 Thessalonians

1–2 Tim	1–2 Timothy	1–2 Pet	1–2 Peter
Titus	Titus	1–2–3 John	1–2–3 John
Phlm	Philemon	Jude	Jude
Heb	Hebrews	Rev	Revelation
Jas	James		

HEBREW GRAMMAR

abs	absolute	hoph	hophal
acc	accusative	impf	imperfect
act	active	impv	imperative
adv acc	adverbial accusative	ind	indicative
aor	aorist	inf	infinitive
apoc	apocopated	juss	jussive
c	common	masc, m	masculine
coh	cohortative	niph	niphal
conj	conjunction	obj	object
consec	consecutive	pass	passive
constr	construct	pf	perfect
def art	definite article	pl	plural
fem, f	feminine	prep	preposition
fut	future	pronom	pronominal
gen	genitive	ptcp	participle
hiph	hiphil	sg	singular
hithp	hithpael	subj	subject

MISCELLANEOUS

Akk.	Akkadian	K	Kethib, "written"
c.	circa	LE	Laws of Eshnunna
chap(s).	chapter(s)	LH	Laws of Hammurabi
CUP	Cambridge University Press	LI	Lipit-Ishtar Laws
		MAL	Middle Assyrian Laws
E	Elohist	MS(S)	manuscript(s)
EA	El-Amarna Letters	n.b.	*nota bene*, note well
ed(s).	editors(s), edited by	P	Priestly Source
ET	English translation	*pace*	with due respect to, but differing from
GE	Gilgamesh Epic		
Gr.	Greek	Q	Qere, to be "read"
Heb.	Hebrew	tr.	translated by
HL	Hittite Laws	UP	University Press
J	Yahwist	viz.	*videlicet*, namely
JE	Yahwist plus the Elohist		

Main Bibliography

COMMENTARIES (quoted by author's name alone)

Aalders, G. C. *Genesis I, II.* 5th ed. Korte verklaring der Heilige Schrift. Kampen: Kok, 1974. **Brueggemann, W.** *Genesis.* Interpretation Commentary. Atlanta: John Knox 1982. **Cassuto, U.** *A Commentary on the Book of Genesis 1–11.* Tr. I. Abrahams. Jerusalem: Magnes, 1961, 1964. **Calvin, J.** *A Commentary on Genesis.* Tr. J. King, 1847. Repr. London: Banner of Truth, 1965. **Coats, G. W.** *Genesis.* FOTL 1. Grand Rapids, MI: Eerdmans, 1983. **Cook, F. C.** *Genesis-Exodus.* Speaker's Bible. London: Murray, 1871. **Davidson, R.** *Genesis 1–11, 12–50.* Cambridge Bible Commentary. Cambridge: CUP, 1973, 1979. **Delitzsch, F.** *A New Commentary on Genesis.* Vols. *1,2.* Tr. S. Taylor. Edinburgh: Clark, 1888; repr. Klock, 1978. **Dillmann, A.** *Die Genesis.* Kurzgefasstes exegetisches Handbuch. 6th ed. Leipzig: Hirzel, 1892. **Driver, S. R.** *The Book of Genesis.* 3rd ed. Westminster Commentary. London: Methuen, 1904. **Ehrlich, A. B.** *Randglossen zur hebräischen Bibel, vol. 1.* Hildesheim: Olms, 1968 (original edition 1908). **Gibson, J. C. L.** *Genesis I, II.* Edinburgh: St. Andrew Press, 1981, 1982. **Gispen, W. H.** *Genesis I–III.* Commentar op het Oude Testament. Kampen: Kok, 1974–83. **Gunkel, H.** *Genesis.* 9th ed. (=3d ed.). Göttingen: Vandenhoeck, 1977 (1910). **Hamilton, V. P.** *The Book of Genesis: Chapters 1–17.* Grand Rapids, MI: Eerdmans, 1990. **Jacob, B.** *Das erste Buch der Tora.* New York: Ktav, 1974 (1934). **Junker, H.** *Das Buch Genesis.* Echter Bibel. 4th ed. Wurzburg: Echter Verlag, 1965. **Keil, C. F.** *The Pentateuch I.* Biblical Commentary. Tr. J. Martin. Repr. Grand Rapids: Eerdmans, n.d. **Kidner, D.** *Genesis: An Introduction and Commentary.* Tyndale OT Commentary. London: Tyndale, 1967. **König, E.** *Die Genesis eingeleitet, übersetzt, erklärt.* Gütersloh: Bertelsman, 1919. **Leibowitz, N.** *Studies in Bereshit.* 4th ed. Jerusalem: World Zionist Organization, 1981. **Procksch, O.** *Die Genesis übersetzt und erklärt.* 2d ed. Leipzig: Deicherische Verlags–buchhandlung, 1924. **Rad, G. von.** *Genesis.* 2nd ed. Tr. J. H. Marks and J. Bowden. London: SCM Press, 1972. **Rashi.** *Pentateuch with Rashi's Commentary.* Tr. M. Rosenbaum and A. M. Silbermann. New York: Hebrew Publishing Company. **Sarna, N. M.** *Genesis.* The JPS Torah Commentary. Philadelphia: Jewish Publication Society, 1989. **Skinner, J.** *A Critical and Exegetical Commentary on Genesis.* ICC. 2d ed. Edinburgh: Clark, 1930. **Speiser, E. A.** *Genesis.* AB. New York: Doubleday, 1969. **Spurrell, G. J.** *Notes on the Text of the Book of Genesis.* 2d ed. Oxford: Clarendon Press, 1896. **Vawter, B.** *On Genesis: A New Reading.* Garden City: Doubleday, 1977. **Weinfeld, M.** *Sefer Bereshit.* Tel-Aviv: Gordon, 1975. **Westermann, C.** *Genesis.* 1–11, 12–36, 37–50. Biblischer Kommentar: Altes Testament. Neukirchen: Neukirchener Verlag, 1974–82. Vols. I, II, III. Tr. J. J. Scullion. London: SPCK, 1984, 1986. (Quotations are usually from Scullion's translation; my own translations are indicated by dual page numbering with German page number first, e.g., 296, ET 217). **Zimmerli, W.** *1. Mose 1–11: Die Urgeschicte.* Zürich: Zwingli, 1967.

OTHER FREQUENTLY CITED WORKS

Aharoni, Y. *The Land of the Bible: A Historical Geography.* Tr. A. F. Rainey. Philadelphia: Westminster, 1967. **Alter, R.** *The Art of Biblical Narrative.* New York: Basic Books, 1981. **Anderson, F. I.** *The Hebrew Verbless Clause in the Pentateuch.* Nashville: Abingdon, 1970. **Blum, E.** *Die Komposition der Vätergeschichte.* WMANT 57. Neukirchen: Neukirchener, 1984. **Clines, D. J. A.** *The Theme of the Pentateuch.* JSOTSup 10. Sheffield: JSOT, 1978. **Dahood, M.** "Northwest Semitic Notes on Genesis." *Bib* 55 (1974) 76–82. **Fishbane, M.** *Text and Texture.* New

York: Schocken, 1979. **Fokkelman, J. P.** *Narrative Art in Genesis.* Amsterdam: van Gorcum, 1975. **Fowler, J. D.** *Theophoric Personal Names in Ancient Hebrew.* JSOTSup 49. Sheffield, JSOT, 1988. **Freedman, D. N.** "Notes on Genesis." *ZAW* 64 (1952) 190–94. **Humphreys, W. L.** *Joseph and His Family: A Literary Study.* Columbia: University of South Carolina, 1988. **Jacob, E.** *Theology of the Old Testament.* Tr. A. W. Heathcote and P. J. Allcock. New York: Harper, 1958. **Kirkpatrick, D.,** ed. *Faith Born in the Struggle for Life.* Tr. L. McCoy. Grand Rapids, MI: Eerdmans, 1988. **Longacre, R. E.** *Joseph: A Story of Divine Providence.* Winona Lake, IN: Eisenbrauns, 1989. **McEvenue, S. E.** *The Narrative Style of the Priestly Writer.* AnBib 50. Rome: Biblical Institute, 1971. **Millard, A. R.,** and **Wiseman, D. J.,** eds. *Essays on the Patriarchal Narratives.* Winona Lake, IN: Eisenbrauns, 1983. **Noth, M.** *Die israelitischen Personennamen im Rahmen der gemeinsemitischen Namengebung.* Stuttgart: Kohlhammer, 1928. **Radday, Y. T.,** and **Shore, H.** *Genesis: An Authorship Study in Computer-Assisted Statistical Linguistics.* Rome: Biblical Institute, 1985. **Redford, D. B.** *A Study of the Biblical Story of Joseph.* VTSup 20. Leiden: Brill, 1970. **Rendsburg, G. A.** *The Redaction of Genesis.* Winona Lake, IN: Eisenbrauns, 1986. **Rendtorff, R.** *Das überlieferungsgeschichtliche Problem des Pentateuch.* BZAW 147. Berlin: de Gruyter, 1976. **Ross, A. P.** *Creation and Blessing.* Grand Rapids, MI: Baker, 1988. **Schmidt, L.** *Literarische Studien zur Josephsgeschichte.* BZAW 167. Berlin: de Gruyter, 1986. **Schmitt, H.-C.** *Die nichtpriesterliche Josephgeschichte.* BZAW 154. Berlin: de Gruyter, 1980. **Seters, J. Van.** *Abraham in History and Tradition.* New Haven: Yale UP, 1975. **Soggin, J. A.** *OT and Oriental Studies.* BibOr 29. Rome: Biblical Institute Press, 1975. **Speiser, E. A.** *Oriental and Biblical Studies.* Ed. J. J. Finkelstein and M. Greenberg. Philadelphia: University of Pennsylvania, 1967. **Sternberg, M.** *The Poetics of Biblical Narrative.* Bloomington: Indiana UP, 1985. **Strus, A.** "La poétique sonore des récits de la Genèse." *Bib* 60 (1979) 1–22. ————. *Nomen-Omen: La stylistique sonore des noms propres dans le Pentateuque.* Rome: Biblical Institute, 1978. **Stuart, D. K.** *Studies in Early Hebrew Meter.* HSM 13. Missoula: Scholars Press, 1976. **Thompson, T. L.** *The Historicity of the Patriarchal Narratives: The Quest for the Historical Abraham.* BZAW 133. Berlin/New York: de Gruyter, 1974. **Vaux, R. de.** *Ancient Israel: Its Life and Institutions.* Tr. J. McHugh. New York: McGraw-Hill, 1961. ————. *The Early History of Israel.* Tr. D. Smith. London/Philadelphia: DLT/Westminster, 1978. **Vergote, J.** *Joseph en Égypte.* Louvain: Publications universitaires, 1959. **Volz, P.,** and **Rudolph, W.** *Der Elohist als Erzähler ein Irrweg der Pentateuchkritik? An der Genesis erläutert.* BZAW 63. Giessen: Töpelmann, 1933. **Weisman, Z.** *From Jacob to Israel.* (Heb.) Jerusalem: Magnes, 1986. **Wellhausen, J.** *Prolegomena to the History of Ancient Israel.* Reprint. Cleveland: World, 1965. **Whybray, R. N.** *The Making of the Pentateuch: A Methodological Study.* JSOTSup 53. Sheffield: JSOT, 1987. **Zohary, M.** *Plants of the Bible.* Cambridge: CUP, 1982.

Introduction

In the *Introduction* to Volume 1 of this series, I surveyed current critical approaches to the book of Genesis as a whole and then looked at some of the special problems raised by Gen 1–11 for the modern reader. Here I shall consider some of the issues raised by the stories of the patriarchs in chaps. 12–50. Limitations of space prevent a full review of modern debate, which has been intense and detailed. What follows is merely an attempt to orient the reader to current discussion and to clarify some of the assumptions that underlie the rest of the commentary.

Historical Setting of the Patriarchs

BIBLIOGRAPHY

Bimson, J. J. "Archaeological Data and the Dating of the Patriarchs." In *Essays on the Patriarchal Narratives*, ed. A. R. Millard and D. J. Wiseman. Leicester: IVP, 1980. 59–92. **Coats, G. W.** *Genesis with an Introduction to Narrative Literature.* Grand Rapids: Eerdmans, 1983. **Dever, W. G.,** and **Clark, W. M.** "The Patriarchal Traditions." In *Israelite and Judaean History,* ed. J. H. Hayes and J. M. Miller. London: SCM Press, 1977. 70–166. **Eichler, B. L.** "Nuzi and the Bible: A Retrospective." In *Dumu-e₂-dub-ba-a. FS Å. W. Sjöberg,* ed. H. Behrens, D. Loding, and M. T. Roth. Philadelphia: Publications of the Samuel Noah Kramer Fund 11. Pennsylvania: University Museum, 1989. 107–19. **Kitchen, K. A.** *The Bible in Its World.* Exeter: Paternoster Press, 1977. **Laessoe, J.** "Literacy and Oral Tradition in Ancient Mesopotamia." In *Studia orientalia Ioanni Pedersen septuagenario . . . dicata.* Munksgaard, Copenhagen, 1953. 205–18. **Luke, J. T.** "Abraham and the Iron Age: Reflections on the New Patriarchal Studies." *JSOT* 4 (1977) 35–47. **Malamat, A.** *Mari and the Early Israelite Experience.* Oxford: British Academy, 1989. **Mazar, A.** *Archaeology and the Land of the Bible.* New York: Doubleday, 1992. **Millard, A. R.** "Abraham." *ABD* 1:35–41. ——— and **Wiseman, D. J.,** eds. *Essays on the Patriarchal Narratives.* Leicester: IVP, 1980. **Rowton, M. B.** "Dimorphic Structure and Topology." *OrAnt* 15 (1976) 17–31. ———. "Dimorphic Structure and the Problem of the ʿapirū-ʿibrîm." *JNES* 35 (1976) 13–20. **Selman, M. J.** "The Social Environment of the Patriarchs." *TynBul* 27 (1976) 114–36. ———. "Comparative Customs and the Patriarchal Age." In *Essays on the Patriarchal Narratives,* ed. A. R. Millard and D. J. Wiseman. Leicester: IVP, 1980. 93–138. **Seters, J. Van.** *Abraham in History and Tradition.* New Haven: Yale UP, 1975. ———. *Prologue to History: The Yahwist as Historian in Genesis.* Louisville: Westminster, 1992. **Talmon, S.** "'400 Jahre' oder 'vier Generationen' (Gen 15:13–15): geschichtliche Zeitangaben oder literarische Motive?" In *Die hebräische Bibel und ihre zweifache Nachgeschichte: FS R. Rendtorff,* ed. E. Blum, C. Macholz, and E. W. Stegemann. Neukirchen: Neukirchener Verlag, 1990. 3–12. **Thompson, T. L.** *The Historicity of the Patriarchal Narratives.* BZAW 133. Berlin: de Gruyter, 1974. **Vaux, R. de.** *The Early History of Israel.* Tr. D. Smith. Philadelphia: Westminster/London: DLT, 1978. **Weeks, N.** "Mari, Nuzi and the Patriarchs." *AbrN* 16 (1975/76). **Westbrook, R.** "The Purchase of the Cave of Machpelah." *ILR* 6 (1971) 29–38.

The chronology of Genesis dates Abraham about 2000 B.C. and his descendants in the following centuries. Between Joseph and the time of Moses, it places

a long interlude of four generations (15:16) or four centuries (15:13; Exod 12:40–41). Whether this chronological framework can be trusted has long been debated, especially since the composition of Genesis occurred long after the events it purports to relate (cf. Wenham, *Genesis 1–15*, xxvi–xlv). The most conservative critic would admit a gap of six to seven centuries between Abraham and the composition of Genesis, while the more radical would double that. Are there any grounds for holding that Gen 12–50 describes historical events and people, or are its stories merely the creation of a gifted novelist?

The New Literary Criticism (cf. Wenham, *Genesis 1–15*, xxxii–xxiv) often sidesteps this question. The new critics tend to be concerned with the final form of the text and the narrator's art as a writer: for them it does not matter very much whether what is described really happened. It is the story that counts: whether it tells exact history or pure fiction is irrelevant. While this commentary owes much to the new criticism, the old historical questions are still valid, even though answers are not easy to find.

An assessment of the historical worth of the patriarchal narratives must take into consideration four issues. First, their character or genre: are they trying to report events? Second, is it possible that reports of patriarchal deeds could have been reliably transmitted to form the written sources of Genesis? Third, can a patriarchal period be identified? Dates suggested for the patriarchal period vary from about 2200 B.C. to 1200 B.C. If we can determine when the patriarchs may have lived, we can then address the final issue: do the accounts of their lifestyle and customs match what we know from external sources? I shall look at these questions in turn.

First, what kind of story are we dealing with in Gen 12–50? Older theories that the stories were originally about astral or Canaanite gods have been abandoned. Nor can the patriarchs be viewed simply as personifications of tribal groups. The Genesis stories are essentially stories about family life: birth, rivalry between wives and siblings, marriage, and death are the dominant interests of these stories. Westermann aptly sums them up: "The whole has the form of a family history over three generations" (2:28). Working within this general framework, Coats has classified every part of Genesis form-critically as report, tale, novella, and so on. This broad consensus about the character of the material in Gen 12–50 clarifies the intentions of the author, but it does not show whether the book gives a reliable account of events.

Comparison with other literature from the ancient Near East shows the unusual, if not unique, quality of the patriarchal story. Apart from royal inscriptions and myths about the gods, oriental narratives about human subjects fall into three main groups. Autobiographies, and occasionally biographies, are written close to the events described and recount events in a straightforward unmiraculous style. The stories of Sinuhe and Wenamun (*ANET,* 18–22, 25–29) fall into this category. Then there are historical legends, such as the epic of Gilgamesh. These deal with historical figures, but they are written centuries later and are full of fantastic deeds, which are clearly the product of imaginative storytellers. Finally, there are purely fictional stories, e.g. "The Three Ox-Drivers of Adab," about people who never existed. K. A. Kitchen (*The Bible in Its World,* 65) observes that the patriarchal narratives fall somewhere between the first and second types of narrative.

"In sober content and mode of expression, they are clearly closest to the first category. . . . They share their third person narrative form with occasional texts of the first category and all texts of the second group, but entirely lack the fantasy-embellishments of the second group." Like the historical legends, the patriarchal stories are written centuries after the events recorded, but unlike them they lack the fantastic details, apart from the great ages of the patriarchs. But even were we to class them as legends, rather than as biographies, oriental parallels would suggest that we are dealing with real historical figures, not make-believe.

The question of the survival of valid historical reminiscence over centuries of oral transmission is more problematic. Ancient historians tend to be very suspicious of oral tradition more than a hundred years old. Can we place any trust in stories that appear to have been handed down by word of mouth for centuries? De Vaux (*The Early History of Israel*, 182) points to the methods of Arab storytellers as giving some reason for holding that the patriarchal stories have not been completely distorted in the retelling. "Nomadic and semi-nomadic Arabs still narrate in their tents the traditions, genealogies and stories of their tribes or families. Both adults and children hear the same stories again and again and whenever the narrator omits or adds something, they correct him at once. Different versions of the same story are often found in different families. Everyone knows the history of his tribe or clan by heart." And this history can cover many centuries. The orally transmitted reminiscences of the Taamira tribe from the Bethlehem area go back four centuries. Mohammed's ancestral history went back seven centuries, while Yemenite tribes traced their genealogy back for ten centuries before the rise of Islam. De Vaux observes that while "these traditions are to some extent credible, they are not entirely reliable" (*Early History*, 183). These parallels certainly show that complicated folk history may be passed down over many generations, so that the relatively simple outline of the Genesis story could have been preserved intact.

Various dates have been proposed for the patriarchal age. The extreme proposals may be quickly dismissed. To date the patriarchs to the Late Bronze Age (fourteenth century B.C.) allows too little time between the entry into Egypt in Joseph's time and the exodus. On the other hand, the proposal to date the patriarchs in the Early Bronze Age (c. 2300 B.C.) rests on rather a narrow basis. It depends on equating the destruction of the towns near Bab edh-dra with that of Sodom and Gomorrah as described in Gen 19. Most modern scholars have preferred to identify the patriarchal age either with Middle Bronze Age I (MB 1), which spans roughly 2200–2000 B.C. or Middle Bronze Age 2 (MB 2), 2000–1700 B.C. MB 1 is an intermediate period between the great urban civilizations of the Early Bronze and MB 2. During MB 1 the cities seem to have been largely abandoned, but the Negeb, the dry and sparsely populated south of Canaan, had quite a number of settlements at this time. This fits in with the activities of Abraham and Isaac, whose main sphere of action seems to have been in the south of the country around Beersheba, Gerar, and Hebron.

Against identifying MB 1 with the patriarchal age is the apparent absence of settlement at some of the major cities visited by them, Dothan, Shechem, Bethel, Hebron, Beersheba (cf. Dever and Clark, *Israelite History*, 99–101). But many sites were rebuilt in MB 2, so that if we place the patriarchs in this era, many of the details of their wanderings make sense.

Bimson ("Archaeological Data," 59–92) has suggested that it may be unnecessary to choose between MB 1 and MB 2, if we admit that the patriarchal period spanned more than a century or so. The Abraham/Isaac stories could fit in MB 1, and the Jacob stories in MB 2. But there are many uncertainties, which make it unwise to be dogmatic. Do the biblical references to a place, e.g., Beersheba, imply there was a town there when the patriarchs visited it? Have archeologists correctly identified the site mentioned in the Bible and been able to excavate there, e.g., Hebron? In our present state of knowledge, we must admit to some uncertainty and take it as likely that the patriarchs lived sometime in the early second millennium.

Finally, does Genesis' picture of patriarchal life match what is known from extrabiblical sources in the early second millennium? This was the subject of heated debate in the 1970s and early 1980s, but more recently the debate has moderated. R. de Vaux (*Early Israel,* 161–266) offers a magisterial discussion of the issues. Some scholars did indeed create parallels between the stories of Genesis and extrabiblical texts where there were none and then on the basis of real or imagined parallels made strong claims for the historicity of Genesis. The studies of Thompson (*Historicity*) and Van Seters (*Abraham in History*) were a salutary reaction to these excesses, but they go too far in belittling the historical accuracy of Genesis and trying to place its customs and ideas in the first millennium. The picture of patriarchal life and religion drawn in Genesis does not fit well with what we know of Israel in 600–500 B.C. But once again we cannot discuss the evidence in detail; we simply point to what conclusions may fairly and reasonably be drawn.

Genesis places Abraham's origins in Ur in southern Iraq. (The epithet "of the Chaldeans" is a later clarificatory gloss.) Ur was a flourishing center long before 2000 B.C., but it is remarkable how many of the biblical names are attested in southern Mesopotamia at this period, e.g., Serug (Abraham's great-grandfather), Nahor (Abraham's brother), Jacob-El (cf. Abraham's grandson). Several names seem to be connected with the worship of the moon, whose god and goddesses were patrons of Ur: they include Laban, Sarah, Milcah, and Terah. No one claims that any of the people named in the nonbiblical texts should be identified with the biblical figures: the evidence simply shows that the patriarchal stories fit the environment in which they are set.

Abraham then moved to Harran in northern Syria (upper Mesopotamia), and it is to this region that he sent his servant to find a wife for Isaac and to which Jacob went for the same purpose. Once again, personal and place names found in this area (e.g., Serug, Terah, Nahor, Jacob) echo those in Genesis. Particularly striking proof of the antiquity of the biblical tradition are names like Ishmael, Isaac, and Jacob, which are Amorite imperfects. De Vaux observes that the names Abraham, Isaac, and Jacob "belong to onomastic types which were well known before the Israelites emerged as a people and, what is more, they appeared in the very regions from which the patriarchs came according to the Bible." "One is bound to conclude that these traditions have a firm historical basis" (*Early History,* 199, 200). More recently A. Malamat (*Mari,* 31) has affirmed that the patriarchal names common to Mari and the OT constitute "a most potent argument in favour of the antiquity of Israel's proto-historical core."

The Amorite background of the patriarchs may explain their close relationship with the Arameans (e.g., Laban's family), who were probably descended from the Amorites who appeared to have settled in this area in the early second millennium (cf. de Vaux, *Early History,* 200–209). Another striking feature of the patriarchs is their lifestyle. They are not bedouin who migrate across deserts on camels, nor are they traders on donkeys, although they own donkeys and keep to the trade routes. Rather, they are seminomadic: they move from place to place when the situation demands it but stay for longish periods in one place making agreements with local townspeople. Their main occupation is keeping flocks and herds, but sometimes they sow and raise crops. Studies by Rowton (*OrAnt* 15 [1976] 17–31) and Malamat (*JNES* 35 [1976] 13–20) suggest that patriarchal society was dimorphic, i.e., a tribal grouping partially settled in towns or villages but partially on the move with their flocks. Such social groupings have doubtless existed throughout Middle Eastern history, but it is striking that the texts from Mari (c. 1700 B.C.), which lies between Ur and Harran, exemplify this type of existence. Not only does patriarchal society seem to be organized like Mari's, but many Mari terms (e.g., pasture land, inheritance, tribes, leaders; cf. Malamat, *Mari,* 33) find parallels in the Bible. While it would be wrong to insist that these parallels demonstrate that the patriarchal age is contemporary with Mari, as dimorphism is a recurrent phenomenon, the differences between patriarchal society and that of the monarchy period in Israel suggest that Genesis enshrines valid historical reminiscence of earlier times.

Finally, since family issues are so prominent in Genesis, it is natural that many customs in Genesis about adoption, marriage, inheritance, and burial have been compared with extrabiblical texts. These texts come from a wide range of periods and locations, and they shed much light on biblical practice; indeed, they show that the accounts in Genesis are true to life and reflect authentically the customs of the ancient Orient. However, some scholars have gone further and attempted to demonstrate close affinities between the record of Genesis and particular Near Eastern texts. Hence, appeal was made to the Nuzi texts to demonstrate that the patriarchs were of Hurrian origin or that the patriarchs lived in about the fourteenth century B.C. But in most instances this overpresses the comparative evidence (cf. Eichler, "Nuzi and the Bible," 107–19). Indeed, in some cases such parallelomania has led to quite false comparisons being made, e.g., in 12:10–20 (wife-sister). More generally, social customs in the ancient Orient changed so slowly that it is difficult to use them for dating purposes. For instance, the dowry was a regular part of marriage arrangements throughout the ancient world, so its mention in Gen 29:24, 29 says nothing about the age of the story.

If social laws and customs are to be used for dating purposes, we must be able to trace their evolution chronologically and geographically across the ancient Near East. A careful attempt to do this has been made by M. J. Selman ("Comparative Customs"; *TynBul* 27 [1976] 114–36). He concludes that "the patriarchal narratives accurately reflect a social and historical setting which belongs to the second and first millennia B.C." ("Comparative Customs," 128). In other words, most of the stories would be perfectly at home at any point in this era. However, he does note three points at which Genesis seems more at home in the second

millennium than later: in its use of the term *rab* for the eldest son in 25:23, in the adoption of a slave as heir in 15:3, and in the adoption by a grandfather of his grandsons in 48:8–20 ("Comparative Customs," 126–27). In a similar comparative study, Westbrook (*ILR* 6 [1971] 38) argues that the law underlying the purchase of land in Gen 23 reflects earlier, not later, custom.

Further discovery may shed light on these and other parallels, showing perhaps their persistence over a wider span of time and area. However, comparative study may be done within the OT itself, and this clearly shows that some of the practices apparently taken for granted by the patriarchs were forbidden by later law. For example, Abraham married his half sister (20:12), which is prohibited in Lev 18:9, 11; 20:17, and Jacob married two sisters (29:21–30), which is banned in Lev 18:18. Judah and Simeon married Canaanites, and Joseph an Egyptian, whereas intermarriage with foreigners was later fiercely condemned (Exod 34:16; Deut 7:3). Isaac and Jacob both change the order of seniority of their descendants in making their will (27; 48:13–20), something prohibited by Deut 21:15–17. If the patriarchal stories were merely the invention of later writers, it is hardly likely that the patriarchs would have been portrayed as flouting the law at so many points. For, whenever these stories were written down, it is certain that they portray the patriarchs as paradigms, the fathers of the nation with whom God related in remarkable ways. These discrepancies between the behavior of the patriarchs and later legal norms clearly suggest that the traditions were old and were preserved despite the moral waywardness of those whose lives were recalled.

A similar picture emerges in the study of patriarchal religion. At many points the beliefs and practices of the patriarchs seem to be at variance with those inculcated in the later books of the Pentateuch or the prophets. This is discussed more fully below. But once again this discrepancy between the witness of Genesis and the other books suggests that Genesis is based on traditions going back to much earlier times.

In his recent authoritative discussion of the archeological evidence, A. Mazar writes, "The patriarchal narrative known to us from the Book of Genesis must have been very old traditions which were orally passed on from generation to generation until they were written for the first time, perhaps during the time of the United Kingdom of David and Solomon. To substantiate this theory and identify the earliest nucleus of these traditions, we should note the many details which do not correspond to the period of the Israelite settlement and monarchy. As is the nature of oral transmission, many features have been added, yet the origin of the traditions might go back as early as MB II" (*Archaeology and the Land of the Bible*, 225–26). What Mazar says about the archeological data in Genesis applies just as aptly to the social and religious data too.

The Egyptian Background to the Joseph Story

BIBLIOGRAPHY

Geyer, J. B. "The Joseph and Moses Narrative: Folk-Tale and History." *JSOT* 15 (1980) 51–61. **Herrmann, S.** *Israels Aufenthalt in Ägypten.* SBS 40. Stuttgart: Katholisches Bibelwerk, 1970. **Humphreys, W. L.** *Joseph and His Family: A Literary Study.* Columbia: University of South Carolina, 1988. **Janssen, J. M. A.** "Egyptological Remarks on the Story of Joseph in

Genesis." *JEOL* 14 (1955/56) 63–72. **Kitchen, K. A.** Review of *The Biblical Story of Joseph* by D. B. Redford. *OrAnt* 12 (1973) 233–42. ―――――. "Some Egyptian and Near Eastern Background to Genesis 12–50." In *He Swore an Oath,* ed. R. S. Hess, P. E. Satterthwaite, and G. J. Wenham. Cambridge: Tyndale House, 1993. 67–92. **Redford, D. B.** *A Study of the Biblical Story of Joseph.* VTSup 20. Leiden: Brill, 1970. **Schulman, A. R.** "On the Egyptian Name of Joseph: A New Approach." In *Studien zur altägyptischen Kultur,* ed. H. Altenmüller and D. Wildung. Hamburg: Buske Verlag, 1975. 2:235–43. **Vergote, J.** *Joseph en Égypte.* Louvain: Publications Universitaires, 1959. ―――――. Review of *The Biblical Story of Joseph* by D. B. Redford. *BO* 29 (1972) 327–30. ―――――. "'Joseph en Égypte': 25 ans après." In *Pharaonic Egypt,* ed. S. Israelit-Groll. Jerusalem: Magnes Press, 1985. 289–306. **Ward, W. A.** "The Egyptian Office of Joseph." *JSS* 5 (1960) 144–50. **Willi-Plein, I.** "Historiographische Aspekte der Josefsgeschichte." *Hen* 1 (1979) 305–31.

It is often argued that the Joseph Story (Gen 37–50) constitutes a discrete, independent unit within Genesis. For reasons explained below (p. 345), I prefer to regard it as the second half of the Jacob story, which begins in 25:19. The Jacob story has been split in two by the insertion of the family history of Esau (36:1–37:1). But though there are many close links in style, theme, and actors between chaps. 25–35 and 37–50, the latter chapters are unique in setting most of the action within Egypt instead of in Canaan or Mesopotamia.

Particularly in chaps. 39–42, Egyptian life and institutions are described in astonishing detail and color. The narrator relishes reporting the exotic customs of the Egyptian court to entertain and instruct his readers. Clearly he was someone well informed about Egypt. Indeed, according to Vergote, he must have had experience living in Egypt, for his knowledge extends to the smallest details (Vergote, *Joseph en Égypte,* 209; cf. Schulman, "Egyptian Name of Joseph," 236). The names of people in the story, Potiphar, Asenath, Zaphenath-Paneah are well-known types of Egyptian names. The rise of Semites to high positions in the Egyptian court is well attested. The description of Joseph's investiture corresponds well with Egyptian paintings of such ceremonies. The dreams are full of authentic Egyptian color: their importance and that of official dream interpreters are also true to life. The comments on land tenure in Egypt, that all land except for the priests' holdings was held by the Pharaoh, is also an apt generalization. Finally, the mummification of Jacob and Joseph is typically Egyptian; and Joseph's age at death, 110, was the ideal span of life in ancient Egypt. Further minor points of correspondence between the story of Joseph and Egyptian life are noted in the studies of Janssen (*JEOL* 14 [1955/56] 63–72), Vergote (*Joseph en Égypte*), Redford (*Biblical Story of Joseph*), de Vaux (*Early History*), and Kitchen ("Some Egyptian") and at appropriate points in the commentary.

But can all these references to Egyptian customs be used to date Joseph's career and the composition of the narrative? Here it is much harder to be dogmatic, because as in other parts of the ancient Near East, society was conservative and Egyptian customs changed very slowly. Thus many features of the Joseph story could fit with what we know of Egyptian life from 2000 B.C. to the Christian era. Furthermore, as in other parts of the patriarchal story, the past is described with the terminology of the narrator's own era. Particularly names of places and peoples seem to have been modernized in Genesis, e.g. Dan (14:14), Ur of the *Chaldeans* (15:7), possibly Philistines (21:32, 34), and Arameans (31:20, 24). These

terms may be, strictly speaking, anachronisms, but they represent the narrator's way of clarifying the story for his contemporary readers, just as a modern writer might describe Babylon as being near Baghdad, although Baghdad did not exist in Nebuchadrezzar's day. Thus, when we read the story of Joseph, we view his career from the standpoint of a later writer, who has described Joseph in terms that made sense to the first readers rather than with the terminology that a contemporary of Joseph would have used. But with these cautions we shall try to suggest a date for Joseph and a date for the composition of the Joseph story.

There is little that enables us to date Joseph firmly. His name, like that of Jacob, Isaac, Ishmael, is an early Amorite one, typical of the early second millennium. Texts from Egypt of this era (the Middle Kingdom) show there were many Asiatic slaves there then, probably brought by slave traders. It is usually thought though that Joseph's rise to power coincided with the Hyksos dynasty c. 1650–1540 B.C., when Semitic chieftains ruled Egypt.

"Into this background Joseph fits perfectly. Like so many others, he was a Semitic servant in the household of an important Egyptian. The royal court is punctiliously Egyptian in etiquette (Gen 41:14; 43:32); yet the Semite Joseph is readily appointed to high office (as in the case of Hūr, perhaps, a little later). The peculiar and ready blend of Egyptian and Semitic elements mirrored in the Joseph-narrative fits the Hyksos period perfectly. Furthermore, the E. Delta is prominent under the Hyksos (Avaris), but not again in Egyptian history until Moses' day" (K. A. Kitchen, *IBD*, 420).

However, Vergote suggests that Joseph should be dated somewhat later in the eighteenth Egyptian dynasty (c. 1550–1300 B.C.), as he observes that famine and Semites settling in the delta and rising to high office are found in many periods. He holds that the titles given to Joseph in 41:40–41 and 45:8 fit the eighteenth dynasty best (Vergote, *Joseph en Égypte*, 98–102, 212). However, in this era the Pharaohs lived in Thebes (330 miles south of Cairo) and Memphis, which does not fit the biblical account so well.

None of these arguments are very cogent, but if we cannot be sure when Joseph lived, we may be confident that he did. As de Vaux observes: "This early tradition must have a historical basis. There is no reason to doubt that a person called Joseph really existed" (*Early History*, 313).

The narrative itself has also been dated very differently by different scholars. Despite accepting the documentary hypothesis, Vergote (*Joseph en Égypte*, 210) maintains that the Ramesside coloring of the narrative is so pronounced that it must have originally been written then, perhaps by Moses. At the other extreme, Redford (*Biblical Story of Joseph*) holds that it was written in about the sixth century B.C. Most writers adopt a mediating position. A date in the reign of Solomon (c. 970–930 B.C.) is often suggested as a possibility in view of his close connections with Egypt.

Once again the problem lies in dating evidence. On the one hand, the evidence is at home in many periods of Egyptian history; on the other, the Ramesside period is much better documented than later eras. The issues here are complicated and can be dealt with adequately only by Egyptologists. Here I can merely set out the arguments in favor of different dates.

Vergote (*Joseph en Égypte*, 203–9) points to names in the Joseph story that apparently originated in the new kingdom era. Potipher(a) belongs to a class of

names that developed in the eighteenth dynasty, though most examples come from later periods. According to Vergote, the same may be said of Joseph's Egyptian name, Zaphenath-Paneah, and his wife's, Asenath. Similarly, the word *Pharaoh* becomes a title for the Egyptian king in this era and the words for "reed grass" (אחו), "magician" (חרטם), and "bow down" (אברך) seem to come into use in this period. Details in the investiture ceremony also seem to reflect customs in about the thirteenth century. Similarly, the phrase "the Land of Rameses" (47:11) fits this era. Vergote admits such practices and terminology may have continued in use later than 1200 B.C., but if Joseph lived long before then, why should the narratives about him reflect thirteenth-century Egyptian practice unless they were first committed to writing about that time?

Whereas Vergote looks for the era in which terms and customs originated as a way of dating the narrative, Redford (*Biblical Story of Joseph*) looks for eras in which they are clearly attested and dates the writing to this period. Since the spice trade is not mentioned until the sixth century, Gen 37 cannot be earlier than that. This appeal to negative evidence, however, proves nothing save that Egyptian records do not tell us everything. However, Redford does contest some of Vergote's specific arguments, e.g., about the term "magicians," Zaphenath-Paneah, and the investiture, which he claims only fit a late composition. But, on closer examination, none of Redford's arguments are conclusive (cf. reviews of Redford by Vergote, *BO* 29 [1972] 327–30, and Kitchen, *OrAnt* 12 [1973] 233–42).

But this is not to accept that Vergote has demonstrated that the Joseph story was first written down in the time of Moses. The evidence he cites is suggestive but not decisive. In fact, Vergote himself points to features within the story in its present form that indicate it was at least revised in Canaan. For example, in Canaan the grain shrivels up in the *east* wind (41:6, 23, 27), whereas in Egypt it is the *south* wind that is hot and drying. Similarly if the title "lord over his house" (45:8) is understood in the Hebrew sense of "prime minister," i.e., the official next to the king, it fits the story better than if it is given its Egyptian meaning, which would suggest that Joseph was a lesser official. These features show that, whenever the Joseph story originated and was first put in writing, its present form at least dates from post-settlement or early monarchy times.

The Chronology of the Patriarchs

BIBLIOGRAPHY

Fokkelman, J. P. "Time and the Structure of the Abraham Cycle." *OTS* 25 (1989) 96–109. **Gevirtz, S.** "The Life Spans of Joseph and Enoch and the Parallelism: *šibᶜātayim-šibᶜîm wĕšibᶜāh*." *JBL* 96 (1977) 570–71. **Hughes, J.** *Secrets of the Times.* JSOTSup 66. Sheffield: Academic Press, 1990. **Labuschagne, C. J.** "The Life Spans of the Patriarchs." *OTS* 25 (1989) 121–27. **Young, D. W.** "On the Application of Numbers from Babylonian Mathematics to Biblical Life Spans and Epochs." *ZAW* 100 (1988) 331–61. ———. "The Influence of Babylonian Algebra on Longevity among the Antediluvians." *ZAW* 102 (1990) 321–35.

Scientifically minded Western readers are perplexed by the ages of the patriarchs. We find it hard to believe that Isaac was 180 years old when he died or that Abraham was 100 when Isaac was born. In otherwise quite sober family tales, the

ages at which the patriarchs marry, give birth to their first child, and die all seem distinctly high.

There are other problems too. Apparently on their deathbeds both Abraham and Isaac give their parting instructions to their servant (chap. 24) or son (chap. 27), but a look at their obituary notices in 25:7 and 35:28 suggests that Abraham lived another thirty-five years and Isaac perhaps another forty-five years. It could be that they did not die as soon as they expected, but 24:55–67 certainly gives the impression that Abraham's servant did not stay long with Laban and that when he returned Abraham was dead.

Furthermore, many of the figures seem to be round numbers: 14, 20, 40, 60, 100 are common. Fourteen years elapsed between the birth of Ishmael and the birth of Isaac (17:24–26). Jacob worked 14 years for Leah and Rachel (29:18, 30). On inclusive reckoning, Joseph was a slave and imprisoned for a total of 14 years (37:2; 41:46). There were 14 years of plenty and famine .in Egypt (41:26–27). Rebekah waited 20 years for the birth of children (25:20, 26). Jacob spent 20 years in Laban's household (31:41). Isaac and Esau both marry at the age of 40 (25:20; 26:34). Joseph was about 40 when his father arrived in Egypt (41:46–47; 45:6). Isaac was 60 when Jacob was born (25:26). Joseph was 30 (half of 60), when he entered Pharaoh's service (41:46). Abraham was 100 at the birth of Isaac (17:17), and 100 years elapsed between his departure from Harran and his death (12:4; 25:7).

The announcement of the birth of Isaac is marked out as specially significant, not simply by the five divine speeches in Gen 17 but by the clustering of chronological detail (16:16; 17:1, 17, 24, 25). This recalls the flood story, which is also marked by its abundance of chronological data (7:6, 11, 17, 24; 8:3, 4, 5, 6, 10, 13, 14). The flood divides world history into two epochs: it marked the end of the old world and the beginning of the new and is therefore chronicled in terms of Noah's life. The birth of Isaac is of similar significance and is therefore carefully dated, too, in terms of his parents' and brother's ages.

Outside Genesis it has long been recognized that Moses' life falls into three periods of 40 years, making a total of 120 years. The 40 years of the wilderness wanderings are often regarded as a round number.

D. W. Young, in studies of Babylonian mathematics (*ZAW* 100 [1988] 331–61; *ZAW* 102 [1990] 321–25), has drawn attention to their use of the sexagesimal (base 60) number system. This he has suggested may explain some of the numbers in the Sumerian king list and the ages of the antediluvian patriarchs. Babylonian mathematicians were very familiar with the fractions of 60, e.g., 40, 30, 20, 15, 12, 10, 6, 5, 4, 3, 2, and did many calculations with them and the squares of these numbers, e.g., $30^2 = 900$, $5^2 = 25$, etc. It is noticeable that many of the prominent numbers in the patriarchal stories seem to be fractions or multiples of 60, e.g., 20, 30, 40, 60, 90, 180, or a square $100 = 10^2$. Gevirtz (*JBL* 96 [1977] 570–71) noted that the ages of Abraham, Isaac, and Jacob at death formed an interesting sequence:

$$
\begin{aligned}
175 \ (\text{Abraham}) &= 7 \times 5^2 \\
180 \ (\text{Isaac}) &= 5 \times 6^2 \\
147 \ (\text{Jacob}) &= 3 \times 7^2
\end{aligned}
$$

The prominence of 7 within Genesis (7 years of plenty/famine, 7 years working for Rachel) may also be related to the sexagesimal system, 7 being the first prime number that is not a factor of 60.

Against the suggestion that the years of the patriarchs should be regarded as round numbers, it could be argued that 17:1 states that Abraham was 99 when God appeared to him. However, if we regard 100 years as a round figure, then all 99 need mean is "one year before Abraham was a hundred years old." This sort of calculation may explain other figures in the narrative that do not appear immediately related to basic numbers in the sexagesimal system.

The Religion of the Patriarchs

BIBLIOGRAPHY

Alt, A. "The God of the Fathers." Tr. by R. A. Wilson from *Der Gott der Väter* (Stuttgart: Kohlhammer, 1929). In *Essays on OT History and Religion*. Garden City: Anchor Books, 1968. 1–100. **Blum, E.** *Die Komposition der Vätergeschichte.* WMANT 57. Neukirchen: Neukirchener Verlag, 1984. **Cazelles, H.** "La religion des Patriarches." *DBSup* 7:141–56. **Cross, F. M.** *Canaanite Myth and Hebrew Epic.* Cambridge, MA: Harvard UP, 1973. **Eissfeldt, O.** "Jahwe, der Gott der Väter." *KS* 4 (1968) 79–91. _____. "Der Kanaanäische El als Geber der den israelitischen Erzvätern geltenden Nachkommenschaft- und Landbesitzverheissungen." *KS* 5. 50–62. **Emerton, J. A.** "The Origin of the Promises to the Patriarchs in the Older Sources of the Book of Genesis." *VT* 32 (1982) 14–32. **Freedman, D. N.** "Who Is like Thee among the Gods?" In *Ancient Israelite Religion: FS F. M. Cross,* ed. P. D. Miller, P. D. Hanson, and S. D. McBride. Philadelphia: Fortress Press, 1987. 315–35. **Haran, M.** "The Religion of the Patriarchs." *ASTI* 4 (1965) 30–55. **Heimerdinger, J.-M.** "The God of Abraham." *VE* 22 (1992) 41–55. **Hoftijzer, J.** *Die Verheissungen an die drei Erzväter.* Leiden: Brill, 1956. **Köckert, M.** *Vätergott und Väterverheissungen.* FRLANT 142. Göttingen: Vandenhoeck & Ruprecht, 1988. **Koch, K.** "*pāḥād yiṣḥaq*—eine Gottesbezeichnung?" In *Werden und Wirken des ATs: FS C. Westermann,* ed. R. Albertz, H.-P. Müller, H. W. Wolff, and W. Zimmerli. Göttingen: Vandenhoeck & Ruprecht, 1980. 107–15. **Maag, V.** "*Malkut Jhwh.*" VTSup 7 (1960) 129–53. **Martin, W. J.** *Stylistic Criteria and the Analysis of the Pentateuch.* London: Tyndale Press, 1953. **Mettinger, T. N. D.** *In Search of God: The Meaning and Message of the Everlasting Names.* Tr. F. H. Cryer. Philadelphia: Fortress Press, 1988. **Moberly, R. W. L.** *The Old Testament of the Old Testament.* Minneapolis: Fortress Press, 1992. **Moor, J. C. de.** *The Rise of Yahwism: The Roots of Israelite Monotheism.* BETL 41. Leuven: Leuven UP, 1990. **Rendtorff, R.** *Das überlieferungsgeschichtliche Problem des Pentateuch.* BZAW 147. Berlin: de Gruyter, 1976. **Seters, J. Van.** "The Religion of the Patriarchs in Genesis." *Bib* 61 (1980) 220–33. **Weidmann, H.** *Die Patriarchen und ihre Religion im Licht der Forschung seit Wellhausen.* FRLANT 94. Göttingen: Vandenhoeck & Ruprecht, 1968. **Wellhausen, J.** *Prolegomena to the History of Ancient Israel.* Reprint. Cleveland: World, 1965. **Wenham, G. J.** "The Religion of the Patriarchs." In *Essays on the Patriarchal Narratives,* ed. A. R. Millard and D. J. Wiseman. Leicester: IVP, 1980. 157–88. **Westermann, C.** *Die Verheissungen an die Väter.* Göttingen: Vandenhoeck & Ruprecht, 1976.

In reviewing the historical setting of the patriarchs and the Egyptian background to the Joseph story, we suggested that we are dealing with old traditions refracted through the lens of a later period. Thus, in describing Abraham's victory over the eastern kings, 14:14 states that he pursued them as far as Dan, a site that was called Laish until centuries after Abraham (Judg 18:29). Similarly, the

Joseph story describes Joseph, who possibly lived in the Hyksos period, in terminology that is no older than the New Kingdom. Something similar is observable in the Genesis account of the religion of the patriarchs: pre-Mosaic religion is described from a post-Mosaic perspective. The author of Genesis, who lived centuries after the patriarchs, describes their religious practices in terms that made sense to the first readers of the book.

This dual focus poses problems for the modern reader, who wants to distinguish the beliefs and practices of the patriarchs themselves from the interpretation of them given by the author of Genesis. How can we know that Genesis is not just reflecting the worship and ideas of the era in which it was written, as opposed to the period in which it sets the patriarchs? Does Genesis simply project back the religious practice and ideals of the monarchy period into the era of the patriarchs? This was, of course, the view of Wellhausen, who wrote: "[W]e attain to no historical knowledge of the patriarchs, but only of the time when the stories about them arose in the Israelite people; this later age is here unconsciously projected, in its inner and its outward features, into hoar antiquity, and is reflected there like a glorified mirage" (*Prolegomena*, 318–19). Wellhausen still has his modern disciples who are completely skeptical about ever knowing anything about the patriarchs and their religion. However, the dominant view this century is that there are some old elements within Genesis that enable us to sketch the basics of patriarchal religion.

This approach, however, does not eliminate the need to distinguish between the narrator's standpoint and earlier tradition. Indeed, the OT points to this distinction. Exod 3:13–15 tells how God first told Moses that his name was Yahweh, the LORD. And Exod 6:3 is even more explicit. "God said to Moses, 'I am the LORD [Yahweh]. I appeared to Abraham, to Isaac and to Jacob, as God Almighty [El Shaddai], but by my name the LORD I did not make myself known to them.'" Here God's revelation to the patriarchs is explicitly contrasted with his revelation to Moses. The patriarchs are said not to have known God as Yahweh, only as El Shaddai: the term "Yahweh" was revealed first to Moses.

The significance of this comment is frequently minimized for two main reasons. First, since Exod 6:2–3 belongs to the latest source P, it cannot be trusted. Second, the similar comment in 3:13–15 (E) also tends to be disregarded, because at numerous points in Genesis the god of the patriarchs is called the LORD (Yahweh). These passages are usually ascribed to J, the earliest of the traditional sources, and they therefore have more credibility than the remarks of E and P.

There have been many attempts to harmonize Exod 6:3 with Genesis by reinterpreting Exodus. For example, some Jewish and Christian commentators hold that "Name" means character, that though the patriarchs knew the word "Yahweh," they did not know the full divine character implied by this name. Others have suggested that the sentence should be read as a question, "Did I not make myself known?" (W. J. Martin), or as an assertative, "Surely I made myself known" (Andersen, *SBH*, 102). But none of these reinterpretations is very convincing (Wenham, "Religion," 177–80), especially if 6:3 is read in the light of 3:13–15 which also indicates that the name Yahweh was new in Moses' time (Moberly, *The OT of the OT*, 21–35). Nor is de Moor's attempt (*The Rise of Yahwism*, 244–47) to prove that Yahweh-Il was a minor deity of patriarchal times convincing,

as he has to ignore the plain sense of Exod 6:3 and posit a purge of Yahwistic names from pre-Mosaic tradition.

It is better with the earliest translators and most critical commentators to take Exod 6:3 in its straightforward meaning and to accept that the patriarchs knew God as El Shaddai and that it was only in the time of Moses that Yahweh came into use. A careful reading of Genesis confirms this view. Unfortunately, in considering the question of the divine names, most scholars have failed to distinguish the words of God in Genesis and the narrator's remarks. When this is done, it is apparent that generally it is the narrator who speaks of God as the LORD, whereas when God describes himself, he calls himself El, or El Shaddai. For example, 17:1 (narrator), "The LORD appeared to Abram, and said to him [God], 'I am El Shaddai.'" This distinction between the terminology used by God himself and by the narrator is most clearly maintained in the Joseph story: in the prose of Gen 37–50, Yahweh is used only in the narrative framework, never in the speeches within the story. Elsewhere the data are more complex, and I have analyzed them more fully in my essay, "Religion of the Patriarchs" (1980). I think it fair to conclude that the author of Genesis held, first, that the patriarchs knew God as El or El Shaddai, not as Yahweh, and, second, that El Shaddai and Yahweh were the same God. Thus, because the narrator believed Yahweh and El were identical, he felt free to interchange "the LORD" and "God" in his own descriptions of the past and even in the speech of the human actors, but in the words of God, he tended to preserve the more historically accurate terminology, "El" or "El Shaddai."

Earlier we argued that the patriarchs should be dated in the early second millennium. It is striking that Genesis should portray them as worshiping El, for in this era El was the head of the Canaanite pantheon, the supreme creator God. He was known as the old, wise, and merciful God. He is king over all other gods. Nothing important in the world can happen without El's permission. He has power over life and death. He is the only God who can bless people with children (de Moor, *Rise of Yahwism,* 69–76). Later in the second millennium (cf. Ugaritic texts) and certainly in the first millennium, El seems to have been displaced by Baal as the most powerful god. Though El still retained his authority as the oldest God, in later times Baal had become the most significant and active deity. Yet in the patriarchal narratives there is no hint of this, unlike Num 25, 1 Kgs 18, or Hosea, where Baal is seen as the arch-rival to Yahweh. In thus portraying El as the God of the patriarchs, Genesis is preserving an old and reliable memory of the religious situation in the early second millennium.

As already observed, many of the personal and place names of the patriarchal era include "El" in them, e.g., Ishmael, Israel, Bethel, Peniel, Bethuel, and it is often surmised that the names Jacob and Isaac are abbreviated "El" names (Jacobel and Isaacel). Often an epithet is attached to "El" in Genesis, El Elyon (14:18–22), El-Roi (16:13), El Olam (21:33), El of Bethel (31:13), El the God of Israel (33:18–20), and attempts have been made to find equivalents to these titles in nonbiblical texts. (For further discussion, see my article "Religion of the Patriarchs," 168–71).

The most common "El" name in Genesis is El Shaddai, often translated "God Almighty." This may be the oldest name for God in Genesis (so T. N. D. Mettinger, *In Search of God,* 67–72). Unfortunately, the meaning and etymology of "Shaddai"

are obscure. Two suggestions have had a wide following. "Shaddai" is related to Akk. *šadû* "mountain," and this refers to the ancient belief that El dwelt on a high mountain, where he presided over the divine council (e.g., Cross, *Canaanite Myth*, 52–56). Another possibility is that it is a modification of an Amorite title for God, *bêl šadê* "lord of the steppe" (R. de Vaux, *Early History*, 276–78), which would be another link between the patriarchs and Amorites (see above).

Genesis never gives an explanation of the epithet "Shaddai," another indication of its antiquity, but the title "El Shaddai" always occurs in Genesis in connection with the promise of descendants (17:1; 28:3; 35:11; 43:14; 48:3; 49:25). This is particularly fitting, for El is the only Canaanite deity who can grant children (de Moor, *Rise of Yahwism*, 69). The title "creator of heaven and earth" (14:19) is also paralleled outside the Bible.

A. Alt, in a very important study, "The God of the Fathers" (1929), made much of the titles in Genesis, such as "the God of Abraham" or "the God of my Father" (e.g., 24:12; 31:5). On the basis of parallels in Nabatean inscriptions, he argued that these sorts of titles were the oldest in Genesis. They represented the piety of nomads, who knew no name for God but simply worshiped the God known to their ancestors. He was a god without a name or attachment to a particular sanctuary, and he was chiefly concerned with the protection of the clan; so promises of progeny and divine assistance would have been central in this sort of religion. Since Alt's theory posits close continuity between patriarchal piety and the description of it in Genesis, it has attracted widespread following.

However, Alt's view has received trenchant criticism down the years, most recently from Köckert (*Vätergott*), and it seems too much to claim that epithets like "God of Abraham/my father" are unique to nomadic religion, or that the patriarchal God was necessarily nameless. As in 49:25, El Shaddai could be simultaneously called "the God of your father." Thus Alt's attempt to discover what was distinctive about patriarchal religion on the basis of titles such as "God of your father" seems misconceived; the "El" names and their Canaanite parallels give a better insight into the differences between patriarchal and later Israelite religion.

Of course, according to the Pentateuch, there was a fundamental continuity between the religion of the patriarchs and post-Mosaic religion. Thus they built altars and offered sacrifice (e.g., 12:7, 8; 13:18; 31:54; 46:1). Sacrifice is rarely mentioned, but the sacrifice of the ram instead of Isaac (22:1–19) does appear to be of cardinal importance and a model for later worship. Abraham and Jacob are both said to have offered tithes (14:20; 28:22) and to have prayed (e.g., chaps. 18, 32). Circumcision was widely practiced by Israel's neighbors. Gen 17 traces its introduction among the Hebrews to Abraham's day, and Gen 34 presupposes its practice in Israel. As de Vaux has argued (*Early History*, 286–87), this is historically quite plausible.

More intriguing are the points of dissimilarity between patriarchal religion and later practice. The absence of reference to Baal or any other Canaanite deities has already been noted. In view of the dominance of Baal in later Canaanite religion, this is a striking testimony to the antiquity of the traditions of Genesis. As Mettinger observes: "It is thus astonishing to note to what degree the patriarchal stories keep silent about Baal. If these texts were really explicable as literary products of the period of the monarchy, this would hardly be the case" (*In Search of God*, 53).

On the other hand, the patriarchs do indulge in worship practices that later generations regarded as improper. They erect pillars, pour libations over them, and plant trees (28:18, 22; 35:14; 21:33), whereas Deut 12:2–3 condemns worship "upon the hills under every green tree" and commends the uprooting of pillars and Asherim. What is more, the patriarchs seem to frequent the great sanctuary sites of Shechem, Bethel, Hebron, and Beersheba, presumably offering their sacrifices at these famous shrines. There is, however, no explicit mention of their worshiping at Jerusalem. Admittedly, Ps 110 appears to identify Salem (Gen 14:18) with Jerusalem, and 2 Chr 3:1 identifies Mount Moriah (Gen 22:2) with the temple mount, but this is not obvious in Genesis itself. Yet from the time of David onwards, Jerusalem was the holy city, and it surely would be expected that, if Genesis were merely the projection of the monarchy period, Jerusalem would have been given a much higher profile and the associations of the patriarchs with other shrines and their suspect practices glossed over.

What is more, from the Mosaic period onward, official Israelite religion was concerned with a strict exclusivism toward other religions, "You shall have no other gods before me," and a devotion to holiness, "You shall be holy to me; for I the LORD am holy" (Exod 20:3; Lev 20:26; cf. Moberly, *The OT of the OT,* 99–103). In contrast, the patriarchs are portrayed as religiously tolerant, apparently worshiping the Canaanite high god El and visiting the local shrines dedicated to him. Though the patriarchs are faithful followers of their God, they generally enjoy good relations with men of other faiths. There is an air of ecumenical bonhomie about patriarchal religion, which contrasts with the sectarian exclusiveness of the Mosaic age and later prophetic demands.

If these contrasts between patriarchal and later religious practice point to the authenticity of the traditions in Genesis, can anything be said about the faith of the patriarchs? They are pre-eminently portrayed as men to whom God spoke and made far-reaching promises. Indeed, as is universally recognized, these promises and their fulfillment are the theme of Genesis and the rest of the Pentateuch. These promises in Genesis are clearly central to the author's understanding of his story. So it is easy to argue, as many do, that these promises are largely, if not entirely, the creation of later editors trying to link the individual tales of the patriarchs into a coherent overarching plan (e.g., Hoftijzer, *Die Verheissungen;* Van Seters, *Bib* 61 [1980] 220–33; Rendtorff, *Problem;* Blum, *Die Komposition*). The promises are the editorial glue that gives unity to what were originally short independent traditions.

Now it is difficult to argue that this could not be the case. We just do not know how far the author of Genesis rewrote and remodeled the traditions that he received. But if the picture of oral transmission among Arab tribesmen may be applied to ancient Israel (see above), clearly Hebrew storytellers would have had much less freedom to adapt and modify material than is often alleged. If everyone knew the stories by heart and corrected the storyteller when he deviated, development of the traditions must have been slow. Furthermore, many of the stories in Genesis make little sense without the promises in them. The promise of descendants is a vital element throughout the Abraham and Jacob stories. Only in the Joseph story does this concern retreat in importance, but this part of Genesis is remarkable for its rare reference to the promises.

Various scholars have tried to show that different aspects of the promises are intrinsic to the story and therefore must rest on ancient tradition. Alt (*The God of the*

Fathers), for example, insisted that the idea of a god protecting his people was intrinsic to a belief in a God of the fathers. Thus, promises of divine presence and protection are likely to be authentic. Westermann argued that the family character of the Genesis stories made it likely that they would be concerned with descendants and land, but only very briefly. Maag (VTSup 7 [1960] 129–53) insisted that the promise of land would be pertinent to nomads on the move. Eissfeldt ("Der Kanaanäische El") observed that, according to the Ugaritic texts, El promised land and descendants to his worshipers. And Cazelles (*DBSup* 7:141–56) pointed out that similar promises are found in numerous religious inscriptions from the third to the first millennium B.C.

These considerations prompt Mettinger to argue for the authenticity of the promises of descendants, land, and God's presence. Further, he notes that "In the patriarchal narratives, God's promise has no antithesis: *the word of judgment is notably absent.* This is to be compared with the alternation between judgment and promise that we find in the prophetic writings, for example."

Second, "God's promise to the fathers is freely given: *any condition for the promise is strikingly absent.* Elsewhere in the OT we find a radically different situation, for we see that the divine promise is usually supplied with a 'conditional clause,' which is introduced by the conditional conjunction 'if'" (*In Search of God,* 63).

Mettinger's second point perhaps overdraws the contrast between the unconditionality of the patriarchal promises and later covenantal thinking, for often God's words contain commands as well as promises (e.g., 12:1; 17:1; 22:2). Nevertheless, there is a contrast that suggests that the promises are unlikely to be merely the creation of later editors. But to prove that the content, let alone the formulation of any particular promise, goes back to patriarchal times is quite another matter. For our purpose, it is sufficient to show that the case for the late creation of the promises is unproven and that they may be an early and integral part of the traditions used by the author of Genesis.

History, Theology, and the Commentator

BIBLIOGRAPHY

Alter, R. *The Art of Biblical Narrative.* New York: Basic Books, 1981. ————. *The World of Biblical Literature.* London: SPCK, 1992. **Barr, J.** "The Literal, the Allegorical, and Modern Biblical Scholarship." *JSOT* 44 (1989) 3–17. **Harvey, V. A.** *The Historian and the Believer.* London: SCM, 1967. **Hirsch, E. D.** *Validity in Interpretation.* New Haven: Yale UP, 1967. **Kuhn, T. S.** *The Structure of Scientific Revolutions.* 2nd ed. Chicago: UP, 1970. **Noble, P. R.** "The *Sensus Literalis:* Jowett, Childs, and Barr." *JTS* 44 (1993) 1–23. **Popper, K. R.** *The Logic of Scientific Discovery.* 3rd ed. London: Hutchinson, 1968. **Rad, G. von.** *OT Theology.* Vol. 1. Tr. D. M. G. Stalker. Edinburgh: Oliver and Boyd, 1962. **Ramsey, G. W.** *The Quest for the Historical Israel.* London: SCM Press, 1982. **Sternberg, M.** *The Poetics of Biblical Narrative.* Bloomington: Indiana UP, 1985. **Thiselton, A. C.** *New Horizons in Hermeneutics.* London: Harper Collins, 1992. **Vaux, R. de.** "Is It Possible to Write a 'Theology of the Old Testament'?" In *The Bible and the Ancient Near East.* London: DLT, 1971. 49–62. **Wenham, G. J.** "Contemporary Bible Commentary: The Primacy of Exegesis and the Religious Dimension." *Proceedings of the Tenth World Congress of Jewish Studies* 1 (1990) 1–12. ————. "The Face at the Bottom of the Well: Hidden Agendas of Pentateuchal Commentators." In *He Swore an Oath,* ed. R. S. Hess, P. E. Satterthwaite, and G. J. Wenham. Cambridge: Tyndale House, 1993. 185–209.

Classical critical commentaries, to which this commentary makes constant reference, are chiefly concerned with historical issues. They are concerned with discovering the meanings of words, phrases, and customs mentioned in the text; with the sources of the biblical books, when and how they have been combined and edited; and with clarifying how far the descriptions in the text correspond to the historical reality behind the text. These concerns are obvious in the three preceding sections of this *Introduction*.

However, modern literary studies of the Bible tend to emphasize the final shape of the text. Their focus is on the present text and its composition, its poetic devices, and its themes and ideas. Indeed, for some new critics, it is irrelevant what lies behind the text, the identity of the author, his historical context, or even the events to which the text refers. It is the world created by the text that matters, not the world that created the text. It is the story told by the Bible that concerns us, not the historical events behind the Bible. It therefore makes no difference to us the readers whether the Bible relates fact or fiction: according to Alter, for example, the books of Samuel and Kings are historical fiction, having as much relationship to history as do the plays of Shakespeare.

This emphasis on the final form of the text and its essential fictionality is especially attractive to those who are pessimistic about the historicity of the Pentateuch. It enables them to assert the theological value of these books without having to defend their historical accuracy. With some truth G. W. Ramsey has observed that it is the biblical story that has down the centuries inspired faith, not the bare facts. "It is not the inaugural events which claim and sustain us but the *stories*. . . . Generations have found in these stories (as they are, and not in some critically reconstructed history 'behind' them) affirmations that shaped their understanding of what it meant to live in 900 B.C. or 500 B.C. or A.D. 1600 in the presence of the Lord God" (*The Quest for the Historical Israel*, 124).

Thus, the new literary criticism and popular piety affirm that the central task of the commentator is to explain the meaning of the text as it stands, not its putative sources; it is not the task of the commentator to reconstruct the history of the patriarchs "as it really was." But should we ignore history altogether and just treat Genesis as an ancient novel? Or is it essential to cling to the essential historicity of the narratives?

Four observations about the nature of the biblical narrative in general will put these questions in context. First, biblical writers offer a suprahistorical interpretation of events. They relate events to the mind and purpose of God. Whereas ordinary historians describe events in terms of human agents and their decisions, motives, and plans, the biblical writers profess to give a God's-eye view of events. "The narrators of the biblical stories are of course 'omniscient,' and that theological term transferred to narrative technique has special justification in their case, for the biblical narrator is presumed to know, quite literally, what God knows, as on occasion he may remind us by reporting God's assessments and intentions, or even what He says to Himself" (Alter, *Art of Biblical Narrative*, 157).

At some points, Genesis does not go much beyond putting a religious interpretation on events. A modern believer could say of his successes, "The Lord was with me," in much the same way as Gen 39 says, "The LORD was with Joseph." But often Genesis lets us into the mind of God and portrays the patriarchs as prophets

privy to the secret intentions of God (e.g., 15:13–21; 18:17–19; 49:1–27). Sometimes it lets the reader know even more of God's plans than the patriarchs did themselves, e.g., 22:1, "God tested Abraham." It is this prophetic perspective, this insight into the mind of God himself, that distinguishes biblical writing from modern historical writing and from most ancient Near Eastern historical texts. We might still try to write history from a providential or moralistic perspective today, but we could never write it from God's standpoint as the biblical writers claim to do.

Second, this suprahistorical, or prophetic, interpretation is undemonstrable. Modern historians may explain the causes of the Second World War in terms of Hitler's ideas or upbringing or of the economic plight of Germany in the interwar years, but they can never interpret the war from God's perspective, because they are not prophets. Genesis tells us why God overthrew Sodom, and Kings why he allowed the sack of Jerusalem. But a modern historian cannot discuss events in these terms, because he is not a prophet who knows the mind of God. This means that if the biblical authors are not right in their interpretation of God's motives, we shall never find another path to understanding his ways.

Third, it is the suprahistorical prophetic interpretation that is theologically significant; it is what matters to the biblical writers. They are not interested in events for events' sake. This is well illustrated in Kings. The episodes related serve to illustrate theological points. They show that those kings who did what was right in the eyes of the LORD brought prosperity to the nation, and those who did not brought disaster. The stories demonstrate how God's promises to David never failed. Similarly, the stories of Genesis demonstrate the slow but sure fulfillment of the promises to the patriarchs. It is this theme of the outworking of *God's* plan that gives unity to the book.

Fourth, the details within the stories could be altered without altering the theological message. It would not make any difference to the theology of Genesis if Abraham had left Harran at the age of seventy-four rather than seventy-five. The significance of his call and the promises made to him are quite independent of his age at the time. In other words, the theological and moral points of the story, the suprahistorical interpretation, are largely independent of the details in the story. If the biblical accounts were pure fiction, they would still carry the same message.

These observations have led some to argue that history is quite irrelevant to the interpretation of the OT. If its message is still the same, whether or not the books are historical, why bother with the historicity or factuality of the accounts?

But this will not do. First, ignoring the historicity of the scriptures fails to do justice to the biblical writers' self-understanding of what they were doing. At least in the patriarchal stories in Genesis, it is clear that they believed that they were telling about real people visiting actual places at particular times.

Second, a historical approach is necessary if we are to understand the narratives, as Sternberg, the arch exponent of the new literary criticism, has cogently argued. Even if the OT were fiction, we should still have the problem of understanding Hebrew words and customs. It is not written in late twentieth-century English nor does it reflect modern society, so at the very least we need all the light that historical study can shed to understand what the authors intended. Modern critics have rightly drawn attention to the problem of discovering the original

author's meaning, but unless recovering that meaning remains the goal, biblical interpretation will dissolve in subjectivism.

Third, though historical details in the stories may be marginal to the suprahistorical interpretation, which I have argued is central, they are not ultimately insignificant. It may make no difference whether Abraham was seventy-four or seventy-five when he was called, but if he never existed, the promises could not have been given to him, and the theological heart of Genesis is destroyed. Similarly, it may not matter whether kings like Manasseh reigned fifty or fifty-five years, but if they did not reign long enough to sin, the biblical writer's point that God punished Jerusalem for their sins is invalidated.

Thus we are arguing that the suprahistorical interpretation of events is what matters most and that it is ultimately undemonstrable, for no modern person can check the mind of God. However, this interpretation is also open to disproof, for if the events never occurred, the interpretation of them is vacuous. This may seem a curious position, but in fact scientific hypotheses are similar according to the philosopher of science Karl Popper. To be scientific, a theory must be open to disproof; one must be able to suggest an experiment that could falsify it. A hypothesis that cannot be tested in this way is unscientific. Yet if the experiment works as the theory predicts, that does not prove the theory in an absolute sense. Dropping apples did not *prove* Newton's theory of gravitation. Later, Einstein offered a more comprehensive theory that superseded Newton's. One day a theory superior to Einstein's may be advanced. But both Newton's and Einstein's theories are good scientific ones, because though neither are ultimately demonstrable, experiments may be devised that could falsify them. So it is with the suprahistorical biblical interpretation of history. It is not positively demonstrable, but because it depends on the historicity of certain events, it could be disproved. Similarly, prophecies are open to disproof, if they do not come true; but even if they do come true, that does not necessarily show that the prophet is expressing the mind of God (cf. Deut 13:2–4[1–3]).

A grounding in historical events is important for biblical faith. It differentiates faith from mere human theorizing and protects it from claims that are just the projection of fevered religious brains. "If Christ has not been raised, your faith is futile and you are yet in your sins," said Paul. Perhaps we cannot be quite so dogmatic about the importance of history in the OT; nevertheless, de Vaux was right to insist that the faith of Israel "rested on the interpretation of events in which it saw at work the hand of its God. But if such an interpretation is to command the faith of Israel and my own faith, it must be true and originate from God himself" (*Bible and Ancient Near East,* 57). Sternberg puts it more bluntly: "Were the narrative written or read as fiction, then God would turn from the Lord of history into a creature of the imagination, with the most disastrous results (*Poetics,* 32).

WORD
BIBLICAL
COMMENTARY

Genesis 16–50

The Birth of Ishmael   (16:1–16)

Bibliography

Alexander, T. D. "The Hagar Traditions in Gen 16 and 21." VTSup 41 (1990) 131–48. **Berg, W.** "Der Sündenfall Abrahams und Saras nach Gen 16:1–6." *BN* 19 (1982) 7–14. **Booij, T.** "Hagar's Words in Gen 16:13b." *VT* 30 (1980) 1–7. **Brenner, A.** "Female Social Behaviour: Two Descriptive Patterns within the 'Birth of the Hero' Paradigm." *VT* 36 (1986) 257–73. **Cohen, C.** "Studies in Extrabiblical Hebrew Inscriptions: 1. The Semantic Range and Usage of the Terms אמה and שפחה." *Shnaton* 6–7 (1978/79) xxv–liii. **Conrad, E. W.** "The Annunciation of Birth and the Birth of the Messiah." *CBQ* 47 (1985) 656–63. **Dahood, M.** "The Name *yišmāᶜēl* in Gen 16:11." *Bib* 49 (1968) 87–88. ———. "Nomen-Omen in Gen 16:11." *Bib* 61 (1980) 89. ———. "Eblaite, Ugaritic, and Hebrew Lexical Notes." *UF* 11 (1979) 141–46. **Görg, M.** "Hagar, die Ägypterin." *BN* 33 (1986) 17–20. **Grayson, A. K.,** and **Seters, J. Van.** "The Childless Wife in Assyria and the Stories of Genesis." *Or* 44 (1975) 485–86. **Hackett, J. A.** "Rehabilitating Hagar: Fragments of an Epic Pattern." In *Gender and Difference in Ancient Israel,* ed. P. Day. Minneapolis: Fortress Press, 1989. 12–27. **Irsigler, H.** "Erhörungsmotiv und Ismaelname in Gen 16:11 und 21:17." In *Die Väter Israels: FS J. Scharbert,* ed. M. Görg. Stuttgart: Katholisches Bibelwerk, 1989. 107–38. **Irvin, D.** *Mytharion: The Comparison of Tales from the OT and the Ancient Near East.* AOAT 32. Kevelaer: Butzon & Bercker, 1978. **Janzen, J. G.** "Hagar in Paul's Eyes and in the Eyes of Yahweh (Gen 16): A Study in Horizons." *HBT* 13 (1991) 1–22. **Jepsen, A.** "Amah und Schipchah." *VT* 8 (1958) 293–97. **Kardimon, S.** "Adoption as a Remedy for Infertility in the Period of the Patriarchs." *JSS* 3 (1958) 123–26. **Knauf, E. A.** *Ismael.* Wiesbaden: Otto Harrasowitz, 1985. **Koenen, K.** "Wer sieht wen? Zur Textgeschichte von Gen 16:13." *VT* 38 (1988) 468–74. **Loretz, O.** "Repointing and Redivision in Gen 16:11." *UF* 8 (1976) 452–53. **McEvenue, S. E.** "A Comparison of Narrative Styles in the Hagar Stories." *Semeia* 3 (1975) 64–80. **Mothes, P.** "Le fils de la migrante: note exégétique sur Genèse 16." *ETR* 67 (1992) 67–70. **Naaman, N.** "The Shihor of Egypt and Shur That Is before Egypt." *TA* 7 (1980) 95–109. **Neff, R. W.** "The Annunciation in the Birth Narrative of Ishmael." *BR* 17 (1972) 51–60. **Rouillard, H.** "Les feintes questions divines dans la Bible." *VT* 34 (1984) 237–42. **Schoors, A.** "A Tiqqun Sopherim in Gen 16:13b?" *VT* 32 (1982) 494–95. **Seebass, H.** "Zum Text von Gen 16:13b." *VT* 21 (1971) 254–56. ———. "A titre d'exemple: réflexions sur Gen 16//21: 8–21 et 20:1–18//26:1–33." In *Le Pentateuque en question,* ed. A. de Pury. Geneva: Labor et Fides, 1989. 215–30. **Seters, J. Van.** "The Problem of Childlessness in Near Eastern Law and the Patriarchs of Israel." *JBL* 87 (1968) 401–8. **Trible, P.** "The Other Woman." In *Understanding the Word: FS B. W. Anderson,* ed. J. T. Butler, E. W. Conrad, and B. C. Ollenburger. JSOTSup 37. Sheffield: JSOT Press, 1985. 221–46. **Tsevat, M.** "Hagar and the Birth of Ishmael." In *The Meaning of the Book of Job and Other Biblical Studies.* New York: Ktav, 1980. 53–76. **White, H. C.** "The Initiation Legend of Ishmael." *ZAW* 87 (1975) 267–306. **Zucker, D. J.** "Conflicting Conclusions: The Hatred of Isaac and Ishmael." *Judaism* 39 (1990) 37–46.

Translation

^{1a}*Now Sarai, Abram's wife, had*^{b} *borne him no children,*^{a} *but she had an Egyptian maid named Hagar,* ^{2} *so Sarai said to Abram, "Since*^{a} *the LORD has prevented me from having children,*^{b} *go into my maid. Perhaps I may have sons*^{c} *through her." Then Abram obeyed his wife.*

^{3}*So, ten years*^{a} *after Abram had settled*^{a} *in Canaan, Sarai, Abram's wife, took Hagar, her Egyptian maid, and gave her to Abram, her husband, as a wife.* ^{4}*He went in to*

Hagar, and she conceived. Seeing that she was pregnant, she looked[a] *down on her mistress.*

⁵*Then Sarai said to Abram, "You are to blame for the violence done to me! It was I*[a] *who gave my maid into your arms. Now that she has seen she is pregnant she looks down on me. May the LORD judge between*[b] *you and me!"*

⁶ *So Abram said to Sarai, "As the maid is under your authority, treat her as you see fit." So Sarai humiliated her, and she ran away from her.*

⁷ *Now the angel of the LORD found her*[a] *near a certain*[b] *spring of water in the wilderness, near the spring on the way to Shur.* ⁸*He said, "Hagar, Sarai's maid, where have you come from and where are you going to?" She said, "I am running away from Sarai, my mistress."*

⁹ *The angel of the LORD said to her, "Return to your mistress and submit*[a] *to her."*

¹⁰ *The angel of the LORD said to her, "I shall so greatly multiply your descendants that they will be too many*[a] *to count."*[b]

¹¹ *The angel of the LORD said to her,*

"You are now pregnant[a]
and will give birth[b] *to a son.*
You will name him Ishmael
for the LORD has noticed your oppression.
¹² *But he will be a*[a] *wild ass of a man.*[a]
He will be against everyone,
and everyone will be against him.
And he shall dwell opposite[b] *all his brothers."*

¹³*She called the name of the LORD*[a] *who spoke to her, "You are El,*[b] *who sees me,"*[b] *for she said,* [c] *"Truly here I have seen him who looks after me?"*[c]

¹⁴*For this reason the well is called*[a] *"Well of*[b] *the living*[c] *who sees me." It*[d] *is now found between Qadesh and Bered.*

¹⁵*Hagar gave birth to a son for Abram. Abram called his son, that Hagar bore him, Ishmael.* ¹⁶*Abram*[a] *was eighty-six years old when Hagar bore him Ishmael.*[a]

Notes

1.a-a. Episode-initial circumstantial clause introducing new episode (*SBH*, 80, 87).

1.b. On the appropriateness of the pluperfect translation in a circumstantial clause, see GKC 142a,b.

2.a. For this translation of הִנֵּה־נָא, see Lambdin, 168; WOC, 579. Joüon, 105c, sees it as a way of introducing a polite request.

2.b. מִן + inf constr of יָלד.

2.c. 1 sg impf niph בנה "to build." GKC, 51g suggests it is a denominative from בֵּן "son," but בנה is regularly used for having children; cf. Deut 25:9; Ruth 4:11.

3.a-a. לְשֶׁבֶת. Note the use of לְ to express the gen "of" following a numeral and its pointing with shewa not ā because of "Abram" making שֶׁבֶת a constr (GKC, 102f, 129f).

4.a. Waw consec + 3 fem sg impf qal קלל.

5.a. The independent pronoun אָנֹכִי "I" is emphatic (GKC, 135a; "a sign of self-assertion," *EWAS*, 52).

5.b. SamPent וּבֵינֶךָ for וּבֵינֶיךָ is more usual. In MT the second י has above it one of the fifteen "extraordinary points" in the MT, possibly indicating doubt about the spelling (GKC, 5n, 103o).

7.a. וַיִּמְצָאָהּ. Note the suffix with ā instead of the more usual ē (GKC, 60d).

7.b. The def art on "spring of water" should be translated here "a" or "a certain" (Joüon, 137n; GKC, 127c).

9.a. Waw + 2 fem sg impv hithp ענה.

10.a. מֵן = מְרֹב "from, because of" (Joüon, 170i) + רֹב "multitude," lit., "it [i.e., descendants] will not be countable because of number."

10.b. 3 masc sg impf niph of סֹפֵר "to count." On the potential meaning of niphal "countable," see Lambdin, 177.

11.a. הֹנֵךְ = הֹנֵה + 2 fem sg suffix. הֹנֵה stresses the present immediacy of the action (Lambdin, 169).

11.b. *BHS* and Joüon, 89j, regard this as a mixed form, i.e., a combination of waw + fem sg ptcp יֹלֶדֶת and waw consec + 2 fem sg pf יֹלַדְתְּ "you shall bear." More probably יֹלַדְתְּ is the older form of the participle (GKC, 94f; Gispen 2:127). The same form occurs in Judg 13:5, 7. Especially with הֹנֵה, the participle often has the force of an imminent future (GKC, 116p: "You are about to give birth to").

12.a-a. פֶּרֶא אָדָם. On this construction, a generic gen, cf. GKC, 128l; Joüon, 129f. G paraphrases: "countryman, i.e., rough"; Vg similarly: "wild, rough."

12.b. On this meaning of עַל־פְּנֵי, see Gispen 2:128; cf. 25:18; also BDB, 818b: "with collateral idea of defiance."

13.a. Westermann's conjectured restoration of הָאֵל "the El" has no textual support. Traditio-historical considerations should not influence textual criticism.

13.b-b. רֳאִי may be an abstract noun, "seeing," so BDB, 909a. In which case translate "you are El, [a god] of seeing." But it may be repointed as רֹאִי, i.e., ptcp רֹאֶה + 1 sg suffix, and translated "who sees me." This is the interpretation of G and Vg, and maybe SamPent, רָאָה "he saw," "seeing."

13.c-c. Without emendation, the Heb. is difficult, lit. "Have I really seen hither after he has seen me?" *BHS* and many modern translations emend "hither" (הֲלֹם) to "God" (אֱלֹהִים) and insert וָאֶחִי "and I lived," so that the whole remark reads "Have I really seen God and lived after my seeing (him)?" Cf. Exod 33:20. While Westermann thinks that this probably expresses Hagar's thought, he does not feel it was necessary for her to have expressed herself so explicitly and, while retaining the emendation of "hither" to "God," does not insert "and lived." He reads "Have I really seen God after he has seen me?" (אַחֲרֵי). Another possibility relies on reinterpreting "after(wards)" as "back of," so KB, 34b. This avoids the need to emend הֲלֹם "hither" to "God," for the whole may be rendered "Have I really seen here the back of the one who sees me?" Cf. Exod 33:23, where Moses sees God's back. Schoors, *VT* 32 (1982) 494–95, thinks "back" is a euphemism for "face." This is possible, but preferable is T. Booij's proposal (*VT* 30 [1980] 1–6), which is to accept "hither" and understand it to refer to Hagar coming into the wilderness. Nowhere else does the idiom רָאָה אַחֲרֵי "see after" = "search for" occur. But following other verbs, אַחֲרֵי often has a purposive sense (e.g., 35:5; 44:4), while רָאָה can mean "search," "look for" (e.g., 18:21). Thus we may literally translate Hagar's remarks "Would I have indeed looked hither for the one who sees me?" Koenen, *VT* 38 (1988) 468–74, points out that if אֶל רֹאִי is taken as a ptcp (see n. 13.b-b), "El, who sees me," this is echoed at the end of the verse. Like Booij he takes the question in v 13b as essentially rhetorical and thus translates the whole "You are the God who sees me," for she said, "Truly I have seen him here who sees me."

14.a. קָרָא "he called." 3 masc sg "he" is here used for indefinite "one," here rendered by pass "is called" (GKC, 144d; Joüon, 155d,e.)

14.b. לְ "of" (GKC, 129c).

14.c. חַי "living."

14.d. *Pace BHS*, הִיא "it" may be elided after הֹנֵה when the subj is evident from the context (*EWAS*, 140; cf. 18:9).

16.a-a. Episode-final circumstantial clause rounds off the story (cf. 17:24–25; 25:26; *SBH*, 81).

Form/Structure/Setting

This tale of family strife falls into three scenes, Sarai's scheme of surrogate motherhood (vv 2–6), Hagar's encounter with the angel (vv 7–14), and the birth of Ishmael (v 15). The account of these events is preceded by an introduction (v 1) and followed by an epilogue (v 16).

v 1	Introductory note on Sarai's infertility	
vv 2–6	*Scene 1:* Sarai's scheme	
	v 2a Sarai's proposal	A
	v 2b Abram's response	B

	vv 3–4	Sarai's action and Hagar's reaction	C
	v 5	Sarai's complaint	A¹
	v 6a	Abram's response	B¹
	v 6b	Sarai's action and Hagar's reaction	C¹
vv 7–14		*Scene 2:* Hagar's encounter with the angel	
	v 7	Angel finds Hagar by well	A
	v 8	First speech by angel and Hagar's reply	B
	v 9	Second speech by angel	C
	v 10	Third speech by angel	C¹
	vv 11–13	Fourth speech by angel and Hagar's reply	B¹
	v 14	Name of the well	A¹
v 15		*Scene 3:* Hagar bears Abram a son	
v 16		Concluding note on Abram's age	

In its present form, the tale is a tightly constructed narrative. The paragraph divisions are those suggested by the use of explicit noun subjects within the narrative. Note how the first scene is constructed of two parallel panels, i.e., two similar sequences in 2a, 2b, 3–4//5, 6a, 6b, while the second is constructed palistrophically, A, B, C, C¹, B¹, A¹. The first and third scenes are both set in Abram's camp, while the central scene takes place in the wilderness. This enhances the balance of the narrative. The concluding note on Abram's age, "when Hagar bore Abram Ishmael" (v 16), makes an inclusion with the opening, "Now Sarai, Abram's wife, had borne him no children" (v 1), and also makes a link with v 15, "Hagar gave birth to a son for Abram."

In each scene, women are the principal actors. Sarai takes the initiative in scene 1, while Abram merely agrees to her suggestions. The action in the second scene is prompted by Hagar's flight. Here the angel of the LORD is dominant, and Hagar accepts his orders and his promises, while Sarai does not appear at all. In the third scene, Hagar gives birth, and Abram names the child (v 15). The tale portrays the conflict between two women vying for one man's respect and affection. Though Sarai is portrayed as mistress throughout, not simply exploiting her maid Hagar but also telling her husband what to do, it is apparent that Hagar comes out best in the end. She becomes Abram's wife. She receives divine promises. And eventually she bears a son not for Sarai as was planned (v 2) but, as the narrative says three times (vv 15–16), for Abram.

Van Seters has noted the affinity of this story with that in 12:10–20. In both there are:

a situation of need (16:1; cf. 12:10)
a plan to deal with problem (16:2; cf. 12:11–13)
plan carried out, but with complication (16:3–6; cf. 12:14–16)
unexpected divine intervention (16:7–11; cf. 12:17)
consequences (16:12; cf. 12:18–20)

He therefore describes it as an anecdotal folktale. He argues that 16:13–14 is irrelevant to the story and therefore secondary. However, as our analysis of the structure shows, these verses match vv 7–8 in the second scene and should not be so quickly dismissed. Furthermore, the real resolution of the story is not to be found in the angel's promise in v 12 but in the record of Ishmael's birth in v 15.

The mention of Hagar's pregnancy in v 4 would normally be followed by a re-mark that she gave birth. This is not found until v 15, where it is then mentioned twice. There the initial problem is at last resolved.

According to standard critical theory, this story is mainly J, because "The LORD" is so frequently mentioned (vv 2, 5, 7, 9, 10, 11, 13). Vv 1, 3, 15–16 are generally assigned to P. The grounds for assigning these verses to P are the chronological data in vv 3 and 16, the mention of the "land of Canaan" in v 3 (a P-phrase), and the naming of the child by the father in v 15. These grounds are not strong: "land of Canaan" also occurs in E, e.g., 35:6, and in J, 44:8; and fathers name their children in 4:26; 38:3, both J. The chronological data of Genesis certainly have an important function unifying the material redactionally, but whether this proves they originated in a separate P source should be left open.

More recent critical studies have tended to minimize the presence of P in this chapter. Van Seters argued that without v 1, with its mention of Sarai's barren-ness, the story loses its point. Therefore, it must be part of the original folktale used by J. In this he has been followed by several writers (e.g., Rendtorff [*Problem*], Coats, Tsevat ["Hagar"], Knauf [*Ismael*]), while Westermann frankly acknowledges the force of Van Seters' argument by saying v 1 is common to P and J. Van Seters argues similarly that v 3 is integral to the storyline while admit-ting that the mention of ten years of childlessness could be P. But this too is contested by Tsevat and Rendtorff, while Berg points out that the conjunction of "taking" and "giving to her husband" is very akin to 3:6 (J). The parallel between vv 3–4 and 6b (Sarai's action and Hagar's reaction) is also marred if v 3 is as-signed to a different source. A few writers, e.g., Rendtorff, Tsevat, Alexander, hold that vv 15–16 are not P but belong to the main story; the majority say that these verses are P. But v 15 is the indispensable conclusion to the story: without a men-tion of Hagar giving birth, the story is left in suspense. Similarly, v 16 underlines v 15 and provides a nice inclusion with v 1. So at least in this chapter it is hard to assign any verses to P with confidence. It could all be the work of J.

Attempts to distinguish between J's work and the sources he was using have failed to reach a consensus. The threefold mention of the angel of the LORD speaking has prompted many to suppose that J has inserted extra divine speeches into the narrative, but opinions differ over which one is original and which is secondary. Neff regards v 10 as original, but Tsevat holds it is secondary. While Van Seters regards vv 13–14 as an etiological appendix, Kilian (*Die vorpriesterlichen Abrahamsüberlieferungen*, BBB 24 [Bonn: Hanstein, 1966]) holds it is the core of the narrative. Eliminating any of these points would disturb the present balance of the story (see our earlier analysis). Furthermore, the central scene of the next chapter (17:1–21) also consists of five divine speeches, and this is generally con-sidered a source-critical unity, so perhaps it is superfluous to suppose the presence of four angelic speeches here indicates multiple authorship or redaction (cf. *Form/Stucture/Setting* on chap. 17). However, these observations do not prove that ev-ery point in 16:10–14 is equally original, simply that it is difficult to distinguish source and redaction in this chapter. J's theological reinterpretation of the mate-rial is clearest in v 13, where Hagar calls the deity "El," but the narrator calls him "the LORD who spoke to her." This phenomenon is found elsewhere in the patri-archal narratives (e.g., 28:21), but it is hardly a sufficient criterion for

reconstructing the original form of the story (cf. *Introduction*, "The Religion of the Patriarchs").

Comment

1 This verse gives the background to the whole story. Frequently new episodes are marked by a circumstantial clause as here, "Now Sarai, Abram's wife, had borne him no children" (cf. 3:1; 4:1; 21:1), which sets the scene for the subsequent action. Sarai, the prime mover, is immediately introduced, and then motives for her activity, "no children," are hinted at. The problem of her barrenness was mentioned back in 11:30, but it had been exacerbated by the promises made to Abram in 15:4 that he would have a real son, not just an adopted one. And as Sarai was "Abram's wife," that seemed to imply she would bear a child.

"She had an Egyptian maid named Hagar" spells out the relationship between Sarai and Hagar, the central woman in this story. She is here called a "maid" (שפחה), that is, the servant companion of a rich woman (Ps 123:2). Often such maids were part of the dowry that a rich woman brought with her into her marriage, as Bilhah and Zilpah were (30:24, 29). At any rate, the maid was not merely subject to her mistress but belonged to her as well. That Hagar is under Sarai's control is emphasized in the following story by the personal adjectives, "my maid," "her maid." Sarai gives Hagar to Abram, and even afterwards Abram states, "As the maid is under your authority" (vv 2, 3, 6). In some contexts שפחה "maid" is interchangeable with אמה "slave-girl," the usual feminine of עבד "slave" (e.g., Exod 20:10). However, "slave-girls" usually seem to be answerable to a master as opposed to a mistress. Indeed, they often serve as concubines, second-class wives, either because the master has another wife as well or because the girl's family was too poor to pay a dowry for her (Exod 21:7–11). In this connection, it is interesting that 16:3 states that Hagar was given to Abram as a wife, and in the next episode where she appears, she is called an אמה "slave-girl/wife" (21:10–13). However, on the basis of 32:23(22); 33:1, 2, 6, where Jacob refers to Bilhah and Zilpah as maids (although they are slave-wives who have borne him children), Cohen (*Shnaton* 5–6 [1978] xxv–liii) argues that there is no difference in meaning between the terms: אמה "slave-girl" is used in legal contexts, whereas שפחה "maid" is used more colloquially in narrative.

Since Hagar is described as an Egyptian, it seems more likely that Sarai acquired her in Egypt (cf. 12:16) than that she brought her from Mesopotamia in her dowry. Despite her ethnic origins, her name הגר seems to be Semitic rather than Egyptian (cf. Arabic *hegira*), and it may mean "flight," perhaps anticipating her later actions. The Bible does not make any connection between Hagar and the Hagrites, a people living in northern Transjordan (1 Chr 5:10, 18–22). Ps 83:7(6) mentions them as allies of the Ishmaelites. In Genesis at any rate, "The name 'Hagar' is meant purely as a personal name; suggestions that it may be the name of a people (Gunkel) or an artificial name meaning 'the driving out' (Noth) are unnecessary and improbable" (so Westermann 2:238).

2–6 The first scene is dominated by Sarai and cast in two parallel panels (see above). She gives the orders, and Abram and Hagar simply carry out her wishes.

When Hagar is cheeky, Sarai blames Abram for the problem. He again allows Sarai to do as she pleases.

"Since the LORD has prevented me from having children." Though the term "prevent" (עצר) is used of infertility only here and in 20:18, the idea that it is God who gives or denies conception is commonplace in the OT (25:21; 30:2; Lev 20:20, 21; Deut 28:11; Ps 113:9). It was a serious matter for a man to be childless in the ancient world, for it left him without an heir. But it was even more calamitous for a woman: to have a great brood of children was the mark of success as a wife; to have none was ignominious failure. So throughout the ancient East polygamy was resorted to as a means of obviating childlessness. But wealthier wives preferred the practice of surrogate motherhood, whereby they allowed their husbands to "go in to" (בוא אל) their maids, a euphemism for sexual intercourse (cf. 6:4; 30:3; 38:8, 9; 39:14). The mistress could then feel that her maid's child was her own and exert some control over it in a way that she could not if her husband simply took a second wife. So Sarai here expresses the hope that she may "have sons through her." "The verb as it stands (אבנה) can only mean 'I shall be built up. . . . At the same time, however, it is an obvious word play on בן 'son'" (Speiser, 117).

This practice of surrogate motherhood is attested throughout the ancient Orient from the third to the first millennium B.C., from Babylon to Egypt. Though much has been made of the closeness of certain cases of surrogacy in Nuzi and Assyria to biblical practice, it is unwise to draw any conclusions about the date of the patriarchs or the exact legal background for their conduct. Thompson (*Historicity*, 252–69) has given a full and judicious review of the various cases and convincingly argues that the variations between one text and another are not determined by chronology or geography but by the different concerns of those involved.

Given the social mores of the ancient Near East, Sarai's suggestion was a perfectly proper and respectable course of action. It is therefore understandable when some commentators like Westermann suppose that the author of Genesis approved of her action. Yet a close reading of the text suggests that von Rad and Zimmerli are right to hold that the narrator regards their action as a great mistake. There is first the general consideration that Sarai's proposal seems to be the normal human response to the problem of childlessness in the ancient world, whereas the promise of a real heir in 15:4 suggests something abnormal would happen. Second, the way in which Sarai takes the initiative to solve a problem instead of waiting for the LORD's intervention smacks of Abram's approach in 12:10–20, where in a difficult situation he called Sarai his sister. Third, close attention to the wording of vv 2–3 suggests the narrator's disapproval, for he clearly alludes to Gen 3.

"Abram obeyed his wife." The fact that the phrase "obey," lit. "listen to the voice" (שמע לקול), occurs only here and in Gen 3:17 would be suggestive on its own. But more than that, in both instances, it is a question of obeying one's wife, an action automatically suspect in the patriarchal society of ancient Israel. That this is more than a chance allusion to the fall seems to be confirmed by v 3, where further echoes of that narrative are found.

3 "Sarai, Abram's wife, took Hagar . . . and gave her to Abram, her husband." Note the identical sequence of key nouns and verbs in 3:6: "The woman

[wife] . . . took . . . gave it to her husband." But as Berg points out, it is not merely the terminology that is close here but also the actions involved.

"The actors correspond: in Gen 16:3 the woman takes the initiative as she does in 3:6b. The recipient of the gift is in both texts the man, in Gen 16:3 the husband, in Gen 3:6b the man for whom the woman was created as partner. In both stories the man reacts appropriately to the woman's action. In 3:6b he eats the proffered fruit: in 16:4a he goes in to the offered Hagar. The means (of sin), the fruit/Hagar, is accepted by the man. The sequence of events is similar in both cases: the woman takes something and gives it to her husband, who accepts it.

"This leads to the conclusion. By employing quite similar formulations and an identical sequence of events in Gen 3:6b and 16:3–4a, the author makes it clear that for him both narratives describe comparable events, that they are both accounts of a fall" (W. Berg, *BN* 19 [1982] 10).

"Ten years after Abram had settled in Canaan." This comment may be double-edged. It obviously explains Sarai's concern to do something about their childlessness, but it may also hint that the promise of the land is proving valid. The passing years should strengthen faith as the fulfillment of the promises is seen, but they also test it because that fulfillment is only partial.

"Sarai . . . gave her to Abram, her husband, as a wife." Normally the girl's father gives her to be married, but in the case of a "maid" her mistress gives her away (cf. 29:28 with 30:4).

4 "He went in to Hagar." Note the absence of an explicit subject. In consummating the marriage, Abram and Hagar are simply instruments of Sarai. "And she conceived" leads to the expectation that Sarai's scheme will be a success, but Hagar's reaction, "she looked down on her mistress," provokes so much jealousy on Sarai's part that without divine intervention it would have been a complete disaster. ותקל "looked down" need not imply that she actually expressed her pride in conceiving by "disdaining" (piel of קלל) Sarai. To disdain Abram was to bring oneself under the divine curse (cf. 12:3), and there is no evidence that Hagar is looked on in this way in this story. Her pride and her mistress' antagonism were almost inevitable in a world that put such store by childbearing. Ancient marriage laws envisage the tensions that are liable to arise in such situations and seek to regulate them (cf. Laws of Ur-Nammu 22–23; Law of Hammurabi 146 [*ANET*, 172]; cf. Prov 30:21–23).

5 Her anger roused, Sarai again takes the initiative and blames Abram for the fairly predictable outcome of her scheme (cf. a similar attempt to shift the blame in 3:12–13). Her anger comes through not only in ascribing her troubles to Abram but in calling Hagar's new-found pride "violence" (חמס), a term used elsewhere in Genesis to describe the sins that prompted the flood (6:11, 13) and the vicious retaliation wreaked by Simeon and Levi (49:5; cf. 34:25). Her outburst closes with what is virtually a curse: "May the LORD judge between you and me" (cf. 1 Sam 24:13, 16[12, 15]).

6 Abram tried to mollify his wife by reaffirming her authority over her maid. Whether he was justified in simply reasserting the *status quo ante* is more dubious, for Hagar was now his wife and the mother of his child and therefore worthy of his protection. However, LH 146 allows a concubine who has claimed equality with the chief wife to be reduced to a slave, but it is not clear that Hagar has gone

this far. Rather, it looks as though Abram hoped his soft answer, "treat her as you see fit," would turn away Sarai's wrath.

But it did not. "Sarai humiliated her." The same term (ענה) is used to describe the suffering endured by the Israelites in Egypt in 15:13; Exod 1:12. So intolerable was her suffering that she ran away (ברח), another term used of the Israelites leaving Egypt (Exod 14:5) but very frequently used of people escaping from attempts to kill them (27:43; 35:1; Exod 2:15; 1 Sam 19:12, 18).

Thus the first scene ends in total disaster for all concerned. Hagar has lost her home, Sarai her maid, and Abram his second wife and newborn child.

7–14 The second scene is set in the wilderness on one of the roads to Egypt through the Sinai peninsula. Hagar is making her way to her native land but encounters the angel of the LORD, who sends her back to Sarai. This apparently harsh intervention is viewed by the narrator as an act of divine grace that salvages at least temporarily something from the wreck of human relationships described in the first scene. The scene opens with the angel finding Hagar by a well and closes with the well being named, enhancing the scene's concentric symmetry (cf. *Form/Structure/Setting*).

7 "The angel of the LORD" (מלאך יהוה) is mentioned fifty-eight times in the OT, "the angel of God" eleven times. Angels of the LORD appear either singly as here or in groups. When first seen, they are usually taken to be men, but by the end of the encounter one of them is realized to be God (18:2, 22; Judg 6:11–22; 13:3–22). When, as here, the text simply speaks of a single angel of the LORD, this must be understood as God himself appearing in human form, nearly always to bring good news or salvation. The angel of the LORD appears frequently in Genesis and in the Book of Judges but rarely in the literature dealing with later periods. The exact relationship between the angel and God himself has been the subject of much inconclusive discussion. The Fathers identified him with the Logos. Modern scholarship has seen the angel as a creature who represents God, as a hypostasis of God, as God himself, or as some external power of God. (For further discussion, see *THWAT* 2:900–908; Westermann, 2:289–91; *EM* 4:975–90; G. von Rad, *OT Theology*, 1:285–89.) Within Genesis, the angel of the LORD tends to appear at moments of dire personal crisis (cf. 21:17; 22:11, 15).

This story, like others in which the angel of the LORD appears, presupposes that initially Hagar did not realize to whom she was talking. He was just a man who had come to the well, a typical setting for male/female encounter in OT narrative (cf. 24:11; 29:2). It was only in the course of the conversation that she realized his identity, though to readers who knew the law was given at Sinai, it was perhaps not surprising that divine revelation occurred in this region.

"The way to Shur" denotes the more southerly of the routes from Canaan to Egypt, from Beersheba via Kadesh-Barnea to the Bitter Lakes. "Shur" is also the name of the desert in northwestern Sinai, next to Egypt (Exod 15:22). It may mean "wall" and be named after the frontier fortification of Egypt, "the wall of the ruler," though this is disputed by Naaman, who thinks Shur is located between Gerar and Kadesh, possibly at Tell el-Farah (*TA* 7 [1980] 95–109; cf. *EM* 7:600–602).

8 For the first time, Hagar is addressed by name and is called "Sarai's maid." This may have surprised Hagar. How could a stranger have known about her identity?

The reader, knowing that the stranger is the angel of the LORD, is not surprised. But the question that follows, "Where have you come from?" although sounding quite natural to Hagar, strikes the reader as rhetorical. It is as unnecessary as the LORD asking Adam "where are you?" (3:9) or Cain "where is Abel?" (4:9). This is, in fact, the first time the LORD has asked someone their whereabouts since Gen 4, and it emphasizes the parallel between this story and those earlier ones.

But whereas Adam and Cain prevaricated, Hagar is perfectly honest in her answer, "I am running away from Sarai, my mistress." She admits that she is a runaway slave, and her chosen verb "run away" implies she has very good reason to escape (cf. v 6).

9 The threefold repetition of "The angel of the LORD said to her" has prompted the suspicion that one or more of vv 9–12 are redactional. But it is hard to know which. At any rate, in its present setting this introduction serves to underline the importance of the angelic words and helps to explain how Hagar came to recognize his identity.

"Return to your mistress and submit." Note how the angel reaffirms that Sarai is still Hagar's mistress. This harsh and uncompromising command seems callous, the more so when it is realized that "submit" (hithpael of ענה) comes from the same root as "humiliate" (v 6) and "oppress" (15:13). Hagar is being told to submit not just to her mistress' authority but to suffering at her hand. The reason for this surprising injunction begins to emerge in the subsequent promises.

10 "I shall so greatly multiply your descendants" is a regular ingredient of the promises to the patriarchs (cf. 17:2; 22:17; 26:24). Again the phraseology "I shall greatly multiply" seems to echo Gen 3:16, but there it was part of God's curse; here it is part of divine reassurance. Abram has been told his descendants will be too many to count (13:16; 15:5; cf. 32:13), and now Hagar learns that her offspring are included in that promise. Just as Abram had been told in chap. 15 that suffering and numerous descendants are interconnected, so too is Hagar here.

11–12 The mysterious identity of the one who can make such harsh demands and make such amazing promises is at last apparent when the angel of the LORD gives a birth oracle, an annunciation that was to become a hallmark of angelic prediction in the Bible (cf. 18:9–15; Judg 13:3–7; Isa 7:14–17; Luke 1:31–33).

In the other biblical oracles, the statement about pregnancy usually refers to the near future; here the angel comments on Hagar's present condition. The promise of a son looks to the future as does his name Ishmael. This is a common Semitic name meaning "El [God] has heard" the parents and given them a son, or "May El [God] hear" the boy and help him. The particular interpretation given here is closest to the first, "The LORD has noticed [lit. 'heard'] your oppression." As elsewhere in the patriarchal stories, El/God is identified with the LORD (Yahweh), the God of Israel. עני "oppression" is the noun derived from the verbal root ענה used in vv 6, 9. So although Hagar was not promised relief from oppression, she was reassured that her suffering had been and would be taken note of by God. Similarly, Leah says "The LORD has seen my oppression" in 29:32, as does Hannah in 1 Sam 1:11. It is also used of the sufferings of Israel in Egypt (Exod 3:7; 4:31; Deut 26:7).

12 This verse describes Ishmael's future destiny, to enjoy a free-roaming, bedouinlike existence. The freedom his mother sought will be his one day. The

"wild ass" (פֶּרֶא, *Equus hemoinus hemippus*) lives in the desert, looks more like a horse than a donkey, and is used in the OT as a figure of an individualistic lifestyle untrammeled by social convention (Jer 2:24; Hos 8:9). "He will be against everyone." "Ishmael's love of freedom will bring him into mutual conflict in his dealings with all other men" (Gispen, 2:128). "He shall dwell apart from his brothers" describes the bedouin living on the fringes of a more permanent settlement. עַל־פְּנֵי "apart from," "opposite" suggests the haughty, defiant attitude of Ishmael toward those caught up in a more conventional way of life (cf. 25:18).

13 The scene comes to a climax with Hagar recognizing God's presence in the angel and his mercy toward her. But as usual in such situations, "As man comes to realize the presence of God, as he recognizes Him, God has disappeared" (Tsevat, 65).

"You are El, who sees me." In Scripture when God sees, he cares (cf. 29:32; Exod 3:7). In appearing to Hagar, the LORD has shown he cares for her. Note though that she calls God El, whereas the narrator calls him the LORD, Yahweh, the name of God revealed to Moses (Exod 3:14–15; 6:3). The God who rescued Hagar in the wilderness is the one who redeemed Israel from Egypt.

"Truly here I have seen him who looks after me?" The Hebrew of this half-verse has caused much perplexity and prompted many emendations (see *Notes*). However, Booij and Koenen have plausibly argued that emendation is unnecessary and have suggested a translation that makes a satisfying climax to the narrative. The emendation most commonly adopted (e.g., *BHS*), "Have I seen God and lived after seeing him?" merely expresses astonishment. Booij's rendering expresses not just surprise but a recognition of God's care for Hagar even in the most unlikely situations, a theme most beautifully developed in Ps 139:1–12; cf. Amos 9:2–3.

14 The mention of the well rounds off the scene. Like Ishmael's name, its name stands as a permanent reminder of God's merciful care. "Well of the living who sees me."

However, the precise location of the well is uncertain. Kadesh (cf. 14:7) is well known, but Bered is mentioned only here. Targum Jonathan renders it Halusa, but this may reflect the importance of this town in the Roman and Byzantine period. Another identification is Umm el Bared on the western side of Wadi el-Jerafi (cf. *EM* 2:337; *GTOT*, 368). Delitzsch (2:24) prefers the old traditional site of Muweileh on the caravan route south of Beersheba.

15 The third scene finds Hagar back with Abram bearing him a son Ishmael. The absence of Sarai is noteworthy. The child was intended to be Sarai's, but three times the text says "Hagar gave birth to a son for Abram." In fulfillment of the angelic prediction, he is called Ishmael. So although Sarai's scheme finally succeeded, she seems to have been shut out from enjoying its success. There may also be a hint that Abram is protecting Hagar.

16 The note on Abram's age (cf. 12:4; 16:3) rounds off the story. Eleven years have passed since his arrival in Canaan; another thirteen are to elapse before the promise of a son is renewed (17:1).

Explanation

The opening verse of the chapter, "Now Sarai . . . had no children," explains both its relationship to the other stories about Abram and the particular issues

addressed here. It focuses on Sarai's childlessness, which was discussed in the previous chapter. There it was Abram who had raised the problem. He had been reassured that his descendants would be as numerous as the stars of heaven. And his trust was "counted to him as righteousness."

Abram was apparently content to wait for the fulfillment of the divine promise in the divine time. But Sarai was not. Here ten years after their settlement in Canaan, she grasps the initiative. Blaming God for her infertility and following long-established Near Eastern practice, she proposes that Abram should cohabit with her maid Hagar. For if Hagar had a baby, this could count as Sarai's child. Her husband consents, and Hagar soon conceives. So Sarai's initiative seems vindicated, at least in the short term.

Nevertheless, it is clear from the outset that the narrator does not endorse Sarai's scheme. Her very first words blame her creator for her predicament, suggesting that she is in her own way going to sort out God's mistakes, hardly a model of piety. Then in the deliberate echoes of Gen 3, Abram "obeying his wife," Sarai "taking and giving to her husband," the narrator suggests we are witnessing a rerun of the fall. Though the consequences are not as calamitous as the disobedience in Eden, they were sufficient to abort Sarai's enterprise had not the LORD intervened to salvage the situation.

Once she is pregnant, the social standing of Hagar, though not her legal standing, is transformed. Whereas in Western societies pregnancy is a state that women often try to avoid, in more traditional societies it was and is a most desirable objective, and quite naturally, if unadvisedly, Hagar looks down on her mistress. In angry jealousy Sarai blames her husband for this situation, despite the fact that she had originated it. He, rather weakly, abjures any responsibility for the one whom he has recently made his wife and encourages Sarai to take her feelings out on Hagar. "Treat her as you see fit." That Sarai does with a vengeance. She humiliates and oppresses Hagar (the same term as is used later of the Egyptian slave masters) to such an extent that Hagar fears for her life and flees.

Hagar attempts to return to her native land of Egypt, but beside a spring of water, she meets the angel of the LORD. As usual in such encounters, the human person involved initially fails to realize who the angel of the LORD is. But the dialogue gradually discloses his supernatural knowledge and power. He first orders Hagar to return and submit to her oppressive mistress. But then he goes on to promise Hagar a progeny beyond counting, a son whose name "God has heard" and whose career as a free bedouin will demonstrate divine concern for the oppressed and his desire for their liberation.

As the angel disappears, Hagar realizes to whom she has been talking and therefore gives the LORD a new name, "El-Roi," "God who sees me"; for even in the wilderness he sought her and cared for her. And the well too commemorates that divine concern: *Beer-lahay-roi* means "Well of the living one who cares for me." In her moment of greatest distress, Hagar has discovered God's concern for her.

So strengthened in spirit, she returns to Abram and bears him a son. Nothing is said about the child being Sarai's, which had been the original intention. Ishmael is the child of Hagar and Abram, not of Sarai: it is Hagar who suffers and is vindicated in this story, not Sarai, despite all her authority and scheming. At the end Abram has a son. But is he the son of promise (15:4) or not? The story in chap.

16 leaves us wondering. The fulfillment of the angelic word to Hagar shows that conception and birth are certainly under divine control and may be suggesting that Sarai should hope for her own child. The unhappy circumstances surrounding the conception of Ishmael leave question marks: only time will tell whether he is the child of promise.

In the longer perspective of Genesis, it emerges that Ishmael's birth was a diversion. Indeed, Sarai's anxiety to have a child seems to have delayed the promise's fulfillment some fourteen years. Hasty action springing from unbelief does not forward the divine purpose. Yet human error can be redeemed at least partially by God's grace. Ishmael becomes the much-loved son of Abram (17:18). And in God's protection of Hagar, we see how he is concerned with the afflicted, whoever they may be, particularly downtrodden foreigners living in Israel (Exod 22:21–23). Her experience of suffering as an Egyptian slave of Sarai is a countertype to the suffering of the Israelites in Egypt. "What the Egyptians would later do to Sarai's children, Sarai did to a child of Egypt. But God listened to both; His compassion is with all his creatures" (Ps 145:9; Tsevat, "Hagar," 70). And it was Hagar who was the first to receive an angelic message: "You will give birth to a son and name him Ishmael for the LORD has noticed your oppression." Two thousand years later Mary, handmaid of the Lord, was to be similarly addressed: "Behold, you will conceive . . . and bear a son, and you shall call his name Jesus." Both Hagar and Mary stand as examples of women who obediently accepted God's word and thereby brought blessing to descendants too many to count.

The Covenant of Circumcision   (17:1–27)

Bibliography

Alexander, T. D. "Gen 22 and the Covenant of Circumcision." *JSOT* 25 (1983) 17–22. **Althann, R.** "*mwl*, 'Circumcise' with the *lamedh* of Agency." *Bib* 62 (1981) 239–40. **Berger, P. R.** "Die bisher ältesten keilschriftlichen Äquivalente zu zwei althebräischen Namen?" *UF* 1 (1969) 216–17. **Conrad, E. W.** "The Annunciation of Birth and the Birth of the Messiah." *CBQ* 47 (1988) 656–63. **Cunchillos, J. L.** "Gen 17:20 et *KTU* 2:10:5–7: À propos de *šmᶜl.*" *RB* 92 (1985) 375–82. **Davidsen, O.** "Bund: Ein religionssemiotischer Beitrag zur Definition der alttestamentlichen Bundesstruktur." *LingBib* 48 (1980) 49–96. **Dell'acqua, A. P.** "*ʾel šaddaj*: un nome divino ancora misterioso." *BeO* 22 (1980) 31–54. **Dumbrell, W. J.** *Covenant and Creation.* Exeter: Paternoster, 1985. **Emerton, J. A.** "The Priestly Writer in Genesis." *JTS* 39 (1988) 381–400. **Fokkelman, J. P.** "Time and Structure of the Abraham Cycle." *OTS* 25 (1989) 96–109. **Fox, M. V.** "The Sign of the Covenant: Circumcision in the Light of the Priestly *ʾôt* Etiologies." *RB* 81 (1974) 557–96. **Fuchs, E.** "The Literary Characterization of Mothers and Sexual Politics in the Hebrew Bible." *Semeia* 46 (1989) 151–66. **Gross, W.** "Bundeszeichen und Bundesschluss in der Priesterschrift." *TTZ* 87 (1978) 98–115. **Gruber, M. I.** "The Reality behind the Hebrew Expression כעת חיה." *ZAW* 103 (1991) 271–74. **Hahn, J.** "Textkritisches zu Gen 17:4a." *ZAW* 94 (1982) 642–44. **Hoenig, S. B.** "Circumcision: The Covenant of Abraham." *JQR* 53 (1962–63) 322–34. **Kilwing, N.** "אבל 'ja, gewiss'—'nein, vielmehr'?" *BN* 11 (1980) 23–28. **Kline, M. G.** "Oath and Ordeal Signs."

WTJ 27 (1965) 115–39. **Knauf, E. A.** "El Šaddai—der Gott Abrahams?" *BZ* 29 (1985) 97–103. **Koch, K.** "Šaddaj." *VT* 26 (1976) 299–332. **Külling, S. R.** *Zur Datierung der "Genesis-P-Stücke": Namentlich des Kapitels Genesis 17.* Kampen: Kok, 1964. **Lohfink, N.** "Die priesterschrift-liche Abwertung der Tradition von der Offenbarung des Jahwenamens an Mose." *Bib* 49 (1968) 1–8. ————. "Textkritisches zu Gen 17:5,13,16,17." *Bib* 48 (1967) 439–42. **Neff, R. W.** "The Birth and Election of Isaac in the Priestly Tradition." *BR* 15 (1970) 5–18. **Oliva, M.** "Las revelaciones a los patriarcas en la historia sacerdotal." *Bib* 55(1974) 1–14. **Ronning, J.** "The Naming of Isaac: The Role of the Wife/Sister Episodes in the Redaction of Genesis." *WTJ* 53 (1991) 1–27. **Ska, J.-L.** "Quelques remarques sur Pg et la dernière rédaction du pentateuque." In *Le Pentateuque en question,* ed. A. de Pury. Geneva: Labor et Fides, 1989. 95–125. **Specht, H.** "Von Gott enttäuscht: Die priesterschriftliche Abrahamgeschichte." *EvT* 47 (1987) 395–411. **Weimar, P.** "Gen 17 und die priesterschriftliche Abrahamgeschichte." *ZAW* 100 (1988) 22–60. **Westermann, C.** "Gen 17 und die Bedeutung von Berit." *TLZ* 101 (1976) 161–70. **Wifall, W.** "El Shaddai or El of the Fields." *ZAW* 92 (1980) 24–32.

Translation

[1] *When Abram was ninety-nine years old, the* LORD *appeared*[a] *to him and said: "I am El Shaddai. Walk in my presence and be blameless,* [2]*so that I may make*[a] *my covenant between me and you, and multiply you exceedingly."*

[3]*Then Abram fell*[a] *on his face, and God spoke to him:* [4]*"For my part,*[a] *since my covenant is*[b] *with you, you shall become father*[c] *of a multitude of nations.* [5]*Your* [a]*name shall no longer be Abram, but*[b] *it shall be Abraham, because I have made you father of a multitude of nations.* [6]*I shall make you exceedingly fruitful and make you into nations, and kings shall be descended from you.* [7]*I shall confirm*[a] *my covenant between me and you and your descendants after you throughout their generations for an eternal covenant in order to be your God and your descendants' God.* [8]*I shall give to you and your descendants after you the land* [a]*to which you have migrated,*[a] *the whole land of Canaan, as a permanent holding, and I shall be their God."*

[9]*Then God said to Abraham: "As for you,*[a] *you must observe my covenant,*[b] *you and your descendants after you throughout their generations.* [10]*This is my covenant which you must observe, my covenant between me and you and your descendants after you: all your*[a] *males must be circumcised.*[b] [11]*You must be circumcised*[a] *in*[b] *the flesh of your fore-skin, so that it*[c] *may be a sign of a covenant between me and you.* [12]*All your*[a] *eight-day-old males must be circumcised*[b] *throughout your generations, those born in your household and those bought from foreigners who are not descended from you.*[c] [13]*He*[a] *who is born in your household or bought with your money must be circumcised, so that my covenant may be in your flesh as an eternal covenant.* [14]*An uncircumcised male whose foreskin is not circumcised*[a] *shall be cut off from his relations:*[b] [c]*he has broken*[d] *my covenant."*[c]

[15]*Then God said to Abraham: "As for Sarai your wife,*[a] *do not call her Sarai, but Sarah.* [16]*I shall bless her, and I shall give you a son from her. I shall bless her*[a] *and she will become nations:* [b]*kings of peoples shall come from her."* [bc]

[17]*Then Abraham fell on his face and laughed, thinking "Can*[a] *a hundred-year-old man become*[b] *a father or Sarah,*[c] *a ninety-year-old woman, give birth?"* [18]*And Abraham said to God, "May Ishmael live in your presence."*

[19]*But God said, "Indeed*[ab] *Sarah your wife is going to bear you a son, and you must call him Isaac. I shall confirm my covenant with him as an eternal covenant*[c] *for his descendants after him.* [20a]*As for Ishmael, I have heard you.*[a] [b]*I have blessed him and shall make him fruitful and multiply him exceedingly;* [c]*he will father twelve princes*[c]

*and I shall make*ᵈ *him a great nation.* ²¹*My covenant*ᵃ *I shall confirm with Isaac whom Sarah will bear you this time next year."* ²²*Then he stopped*ᵃ *talking to him, and God went away*ᵇ *from Abraham.*

²³*So Abraham took his son Ishmael, all those born in his household, and all those he had purchased, every male among the men of his household, and he circumcised*ᵃ *their foreskins that very day as God had spoken to him.* ²⁴*Abraham was ninety-nine years old when he was circumcised*ᵃ *in his foreskin.* ²⁵*Ishmael was thirteen years old when he was circumcised in his foreskin.* ²⁶*That*ᵃ *very day Abraham and his son Ishmael were circumcised.*ᵇ ²⁷*All the men of his household, those born in his household and those purchased from foreigners, were circumcised with him.*

Notes

1.a. Cf. n. 12:7a.

2.a. Waw + 1 sg·coh נתן "to give." Coh following an impv "be perfect" expresses "an intention or intended consequence" (GKC, 108d; cf. 19:5; 23:4; 27:4; WOC, 577–78).

3.a. Waw consec + 3 masc sg impf נפל.

4.a. The extraposed אני "I," "for my part" contrasts with ואתה. "As for you" (v 9) spells out the obligations of the two parties to the covenant (*SBH*, 151); cf. 6:17, 21; 9:7, 9.

4.b. For this translation of הנה, see Lambdin, 169. Alternatively, הנה draws attention to the immediacy of the statement and could be rendered "My covenant is *now* with you." Cf. WOC, 676–77.

4.c. Note the unusual constr אב instead of אבי "father" used only here and v 5, probably to rhyme with Abraham (GKC, 96).

5.a. Though SamPent and some MT MSS omit את before שמך, it is quite common to have את before the effective subj of a pass verb (GKC, 121b).

5.b. Following a negative clause, ו before a verb may be translated "but" (GKC, 163a).

7.a. Cf. n. 6:18.a.

8.a-a. מגריך, lit. "your sojourning." The גר was a "resident alien," "immigrant." Hence "land of your sojourning" = "land to which you have migrated."

9.a. Note ואתה "as for you" matches אני in v 4.

9.b. The preverbal position of "my covenant" is unusual except in law (cf. *EWAS*, 40–41). Here it may highlight "my covenant" (cf. GKC, 142f).

10.a. לכם "for you." ל is used to express a gen relationship, to show to whom the verbal action relates (Joüon, 130g). Thus "every male must be circumcised for you" = "all your males must be circumcised." Alternatively, ל may express the agent here. "All males shall be circumcised by you." Cf. v 12; 34:15, 22; Althann, *Bib* 62 (1981) 239–40.

10.b. Inf abs niph מול as an emphatic impv (GKC, 113bb).

11.a. Waw consec + 2 masc pl pf niph מול; on form, see GKC, 67dd.

11.b. את mark of acc, of the part most affected by the action (GKC, 121d; cf. WOC, 181).

11.c. 3 masc sg may be used as here for an action just mentioned (GKC, 144b).

12.a. Cf. n. 10.a.

12.b. 3 masc impf niph מול.

12.c. The resumptive הוא "he" is required in a negative relative clause (Joüon, 158g); cf. 7:2.

13.a. SamPent has ילידי "those born" for MT יליד "he who is born." Lohfink favors SamPent because it matches v 23 (*Bib* 48 [1967] 439).

14.a. SamPent, G add "on the eighth day."

14.b. Though עם most often means "people," as here, it also means a clan, or a member of one's clan (a relative through one's father; KB, 792).

14.c-c. Apposition clause explaining preceding one (Joüon, 170b; *SBH*, 58).

14.d. 3 masc sg hiph pf pause פרר "break."

15.a. "Sarai, your wife" is here *casus pendens* before the main clause "Do not call her Sarai" and "announces the topic of the whole statement to be made" (*EWAS*, 94; cf. WOC, 76).

16.a. SamPent reads וברכתיו "I will bless him" for וברכתה; also S, Vg, but not *pace BHS* by G (Wevers edition). This reading is preferred by Speiser and Lohfink (*Bib* 48 [1967] 439–40), but MT may be retained.

16.b-b. Clause in expository apposition with preceding (*SBH,* 47), therefore no need to begin with "and" (with SamPent, G).

16.c. G, SamPent support MT "her" *pace BHS.*

17.a. הלבן. The doubling of the consonant, here ל, following interrogative ה is unusual (GKC, 100l).

17.b. יולד 3 masc sg impf niph ילד, lit. "will he be born to." For the use of impf to express potential or surprise, cf. GKC, 107t.

17.c. ואם־שׂרה or the following ה are often deleted, because double-barrelled questions usually take the form ואם . . . . ה, not as here, ה ואם . . . . ה (*SBH,* 114). This unusual construction underlines Abraham's disbelief (GKC, 150g).

19.a. On אבל as a strong asseverative, "Abraham's doubt and mistrust are emphatically controverted," see *EWAS,* 129; cf. N. Kilwing, *BN* 11 (1980) 23–28; cf. G ἰδού.

19.b. SamPent inserts הנה after אבל, making phraseology more typical of annunciation; cf. 16:11.

19.c. *Pace* Westermann, it is unnecessary with some G MSS to insert "to be his God."

20.a-a. On the syntax of this clause, cf. J. L. Cunchillos, *RB* 92 (1985) 375–82.

20.b. Possibly "an accidental perfective whereby a speaker vividly and dramatically represents an action both as complete and independent" (WOC, 490).

20.c-c. Clause in apposition specifying number of children (*SBH,* 47).

20.d. Waw + 1 sg pf נתן + 3 masc sg suffix.

21.a. Note ו attached to obj "my covenant," making this clause disjunctive and contrasting it with הנה clause in v 20 (cf. n. 20.b; *SBH,* 180).

22.a. Waw + 3 masc sg impf apoc piel כלה; cf. 2:2.

22.b. Waw + 3 masc sg impf apoc qal עלה; cf. 13:1.

23.a. Waw + 3 masc sg impf qal מול.

24.a. ב + inf constr niph מול + 3 masc sg suffix.

26.a. This time reference is in apposition to preceding clauses, characteristic of epic style (*SBH,* 41); cf. 7:10–16.

26.b. 3 masc sg pf niph מול. On sg verb with pl subj, see GKC, 146f.

Form/Structure/Setting

This chapter is a watershed in the Abraham story. The promises to him have been unfolded bit by bit, gradually building up and becoming more detailed and precise, until here they are repeated and filled out in a glorious crescendo in a long and elaborate divine speech. From this point in Genesis, divine speeches become rarer and little new content is added to the promises, but the fulfillment of these promises becomes more visible.

Gen 12:1–3 promised Abraham a land, descendants, and a covenant relationship. It is worth tracing these three aspects of the promise through the following chapters to see how chap. 17 constitutes a climax.

The land becomes "this land" in 12:7, "all the land which you can see" in 13:15, and "from the river of Egypt to the great river, the river Euphrates" in 15:18. Though the narrator has frequently identified the promised land with Canaan, it is first explicitly promised by God in 17:8, "I shall give to you . . . the whole land of Canaan as a permanent holding."

In 12:2 Abraham is assured he will become a "great nation." In 13:16 he is told his descendants will be as numerous as the dust of the earth; in 15:5 that he would himself father a child and his descendants will be as many as the stars. In chap. 16 Abraham did father a child, whose offspring will be too many to count. But this apparently miraculous achievement is dwarfed by the promises here. Abraham is not merely to father a nation but a "multitude of nations," and "kings shall be descended from you." He is to father a child not simply through a youthful slave-girl but through his elderly wife, who at ninety will bear her first child (vv 4–6, 15–17).

The nature of the covenant relationship is also defined more clearly in chap. 17 than previously. In 12:3 there was a vague guarantee of protection: Abram's blessers will be blessed and his disdainer cursed. But this too becomes more explicit. Chap. 15 predicts Egyptian slavery and exodus, but 17:7 announces an eternal covenant with Abraham and his descendants, "in order to be your God and your descendants' God."

To mark these great promises, the names of Abram and Sarai are changed to the more familiar Abraham and Sarah, and the national rite of circumcision is instituted as a sign of the covenant between God and Abraham's descendants. But the significance of the occasion is marked too with literary devices: five long and elaborate divine speeches set this episode apart within Genesis.

In arrangement, this chapter bears a number of similarities to chap. 16.

v 1a	Introductory note on Abraham's age
vv 1b–22	*Scene 1:* Dialogue between God and Abraham
v 23	*Scene 2:* Abraham circumcises his household
vv 24 –27	Closing note on Abraham and Ishmael's age

The chief similarities with chap. 16 are in the opening and closing time references (1a, 24–27; cf. 16:1, 16) and in the content of the main scene. In chap. 17 this consists of five divine speeches (vv 1b–2, 4–8, 9–14, 15–16, 19–21) with two questions by Abraham (vv 17, 18); in chap. 16 the central scene consists of four angelic speeches (vv 8a, 9, 10, 11–12) with two comments by Hagar (vv 8b, 13). In both chapters some of the introductory "And God/the angel of the LORD said" strike the modern reader as redundant, serving only to break up the speeches. The second scene in chap. 17 is very brief in comparison with the first. But such variation in scenic length is common elsewhere in Genesis; cf. 16:7–14 with 16:15, or 6:13–21 with 6:22.

McEvenue has noted that chap. 17 is arranged both palistrophically and in two parallel panels.

A	Abraham 99 (1a)
B	The LORD appears (1ba)
C	God speaks (1bb)
D	First speech (1bc–2)
E	Abraham falls on his face (3a)
F	Second speech (name-change, nations, kings) (4–8)
G	THIRD SPEECH (9–14)
F¹	Fourth speech (name-change, nations, kings) (15–16)
E¹	Abraham falls on his face (17)
D¹	Fifth speech (19–21)
C¹	God ceases speaking (22a)
B¹	God goes up from him (22b)
A¹	Abraham 99 and Ishmael 13 (24–25)

Alternatively, the chapter may be read as two parallel panels.

A	Yahweh's intention to make an oath about progeny (1–2)
B	Abraham falls on his face (3a)
C	Abraham father of nations (4b–6)

D   God will carry out his oath forever (7)
E   The sign of the oath (9–14)
A¹ God's intention to bless Sarah with progeny (16)
B¹   Abraham falls on his face (17–18)
C¹   Sarah mother of a son, Isaac (19)
D¹   God will carry out his oath forever (19b, 21a)
E¹   The sign of the oath (23–27)

Palistrophic arrangement of material is frequent in Genesis (e.g., chaps. 2–3, 4, 6–9, 18–19, 22); less usual is the use of parallel panels (cf. chaps. 15, 18–19), particularly in conjunction with palistrophic arrangement. The complexity of the literary form used here underlines the importance of the material; note how both structures focus on circumcision, the sign of the covenant, and make implausible any attempt to split the material in the chapter into two sources (McEvenue, 147–48). Westermann (2:255) rightly states "the chapter is carefully thought out right down to the finest detail; it is an artistic composition." On the other hand, Weimar's attempt (*ZAW* 100 [1988] 22–60) to contest this unity and find four layers of redaction within Gen 17 overpresses nuances in the text and is too complicated to be convincing.

Source critics with few exceptions (Jacob, Külling, Alexander) ascribe this chapter to P on the grounds of its distinctive vocabulary. Terminology characteristic of P includes "God" (אלהים); "El Shaddai" (v 1; the LORD, v 1, is either redactional or a scribal error [Skinner, 289]); "put [נתן] or confirm [הקים] my covenant" (vv 2, 7); "very much" (מאד מאד; v 2); "be fruitful and multiply" (פרה ורבה; v 20); and "that very day" (vv 23, 26). The affinity of this language with other passages conventionally ascribed to P is unmistakable, most obviously with 9:1–17, the Noahic covenant, and to a lesser extent with passages looking back to chap. 17, i.e., 28:3–4; 35:11–12; 48:3–4. But the distinctive terminology of these passages may be adequately explained by their subject matter and genre (divine speech about covenants) as by common authorship, so despite the accumulation of distinctive terms, the case for ascribing the material to P is not clear cut.

It should be noticed that this chapter both presupposes what precedes it in Genesis and is presupposed by what follows. The change of Abram and Sarai's names to Abraham and Sarah is recorded nowhere else, yet the narrative always uses the old names before this chapter and the new names after it. Similarly, Abraham's plea "May Ishmael live in your presence" presupposes chap. 16, as do his remarks about Sarah's barrenness. 21:1–5, recording the birth and circumcision of Isaac, looks back to chap. 17, as do 24:36 and the account of his sacrifice in chap. 22, according to Alexander (*JSOT* 25 [1983] 17–22). The demand to circumcise the Shechemites (chap. 34) also presupposes chap. 17 and appears to quote it (see below on chap. 34). So whatever the history of this chapter prior to its incorporation into Genesis, it has been carefully and thoroughly integrated into the present work. And there are signs that the editor responsible for doing this was J. The clearest sign of his work is the opening comment "The LORD appeared to him." Not merely the mention of the LORD (Yahweh) but also the verb "appear" (niphal of ראה) as in 12:7; 18:1; 26:2, 24 marks this as J. Compare too the double mention of the LORD in 21:1, recounting the fulfillment of the promise to Sarah. Westermann (*TLZ* 101 (1976) 161–62) has noted that 17:1–3a with

its command-promise-affirmative response pattern corresponds very closely to 12:1–4a, so that it is "quite clear that P in chap. 17 is working with the Abraham tradition as a whole." Westermann assumes that P is responsible for shaping 17:1–3, but in the light of the other parallels with J material, it is questionable whether this view can be sustained. Further evidence of J's activity is the organization of chap. 16, which is like chap. 17 but largely ascribed to J. Similarly, chaps. 18–19 are structurally similar to chap. 17 yet assigned to J. Thus the centrality of chap. 17 within the overall patriarchal narratives and the evidence of J-like redaction suggest, contrary to dominant critical opinion, that the material is early and that if it comes from P, P antedates J.

The dependence of chap. 17 on chap. 15 is widely supported (e.g., Skinner, von Rad, McEvenue, Westermann, Coats). McEvenue and Westermann also hold that 18:4–15 is the source of 17:15–22. Though there are certain similarities between chaps. 15 and 17 (both concern covenant making and promises of land and descendants), these are not sufficient to outweigh the great differences in covenant ceremonies and to conclude that chap. 17 is simply a reworking of chap. 15. Nor does the promise of a son in chap. 18 have to be the origin of the promise in 17:15–22. Repeating the promise, like the doubling of dreams, shows the certainty of fulfillment (41:32).

As for the immediately following chap. 18, it apparently presupposes chap. 17. The present form of 18:9–15 appears to be formulated in the knowledge of chap. 17. The assumption of the etymology of Isaac and the use of the names Abraham and Sarah introduced in chap. 17 are clear indicators that the writer of chap. 18 knew the substance of the previous chapter. That Abraham expresses no surprise himself at the announcement is also easier to explain if chap. 17 is presupposed. Finally, the restatement of the promise of 18:10 in 18:14 includes the phrase "at the set time" from 17:21, which shows knowledge of that chapter by the compiler of chap. 18.

The parallels between chaps. 17 and 18 may as easily be ascribed to editorial assimilation as to independent traditions of the same event. Thus if Gen 17 was once an independent early tradition, possibly P, it has been reworked by J (cf. *Form/Structure/Setting* on chaps. 5, 10, 11).

Comment

1 "When Abram was ninety-nine years old" indicates that thirteen years have passed since the last episode (cf. 16:16). Thirteen years in which Sarah's inability to bear children has been further demonstrated. Thirteen years in which Abraham's hopes of an heir have focused on Ishmael (17:18). This passing reference to Abraham's age thus sets the frame for the revelation that follows. All aspects of the promises are enhanced in what follows, but none more so than the promise of descendants through Sarah. The mention of Abraham's age obliquely reminds the reader how amazing the divine promise is.

1b–22 The first scene is a divine monologue, once interrupted by Abraham's thoughts and plea for Ishmael (vv 17–18).

1b "The LORD appeared to Abram." Elsewhere the personal name "The LORD" (Yahweh) is not used in this chapter, simply God or El Shaddai, the name by which God was known to the patriarchs according to Exod 6:3. But as in Gen

16:13, the narrative makes the point that the God who revealed himself to the patriarchs as El was the same God who spoke to Moses as the LORD.

"I am El Shaddai." Melchizedek knew God as El-Elyon ("God most high," 14:19–20), and Hagar called God El-Roi ("God who sees me," 16:13). Here another name of God compounded with El, the high god of the Canaanite pantheon, is introduced. Indeed, it is used more often than other epithets of El in Genesis, 28:3; 35:11; 43:14; 48:3. Shaddai on its own appears thirty-one times in Job and occasionally elsewhere. The combination El Shaddai (אל שדי) occurs only in Genesis, Exod 6:3, and Ezek 10:5.

But the meaning and etymology of the epithet Shaddai is obscure (see *Introduction*, "The Religion of the Patriarchs"). However, it is always used in connection with promises of descendants: Shaddai evokes the idea that God is able to make the barren fertile and to fulfill his promises. The LXX sometimes translates it παντοκράτωρ or Vg *omnipotens* "almighty," and the early Jewish etymologizing שׁדי = די "sufficient" + שׁ "which," i.e., "he who is sufficient," may not be too far from the ideas evoked by this title. "El Shaddai is the God who so constrains nature that it does His will, and so subdues it that it bows to and subserves grace" (Delitzsch, 2:32).

"Walk in my presence and be blameless so that I may put my covenant. . . ." In structure and content this opening sentence seems to echo 12:1–2, "Go . . . be a blessing . . . that I may bless."

"Walk in my presence." Enoch and Noah walked *with* God (5:22, 24; 6:9), but the patriarchs walked before/in the presence of God (24:40; 48:15). It is doubtful whether the different preposition makes much difference. Westermann sums up well the meaning of the phrase: "God directs Abraham (who here represents Israel) to live life before him, a life in which every step is taken looking to God and every day of which is accompanied by him" (my translation 2:311; cf. ET 2:259). However, he is wrong to state that this is not a high demand but something quite natural. When shortly before their deaths Abraham and Jacob speak of walking before God, they are claiming to have been devout and pious throughout their lives. And certainly Enoch and Noah are seen as very devout. "Be blameless" (תמים), an extreme demand; cf. *Comment* on 6:9. Abraham is expected to emulate Noah's moral perfection.

2 This verse goes straight to the heart of the topic: "so that I may make my covenant between me and you." נתן "put," lit. "give," is used only here and Num 25:12 with the object "covenant." It is not immediately obvious in what sense God needs to give a covenant to Abraham, as it has already been inaugurated (כרת "cut") in 15:18. But this is clarified later: the chief concern of this chapter is to "confirm" or "ratify" (הקים, vv 7, 19, 21) the covenant, just as the covenant with Noah was confirmed in Gen 9. Whereas inaugurating the covenant was entirely the result of divine initiative, confirming it involves a human response, summed up in v 1 by "walk in my presence and be blameless" and spelled out in the demand to circumcise every male. But even though Abraham is now expected to respond actively to the covenant demands, he is the beneficiary: he will be multiplied exceedingly. The promise of a multitude of descendants is the key theme of this chapter. Note too that the phraseology anticipates his new name, ארבה . . . במאד "I shall multiply . . . exceedingly" is an anagram of Abraham.

3 "Abram fell on his face." Compare v 17 in which Moses fell on his face when shocked by the outrageous blasphemy of the people (Num 14:5; 16:4). Joab prostrated himself before David to show his gratitude (2 Sam 14:22), but prostration is also a proper and appropriate expression of awe before God (Lev 9:24; Josh 5:14; 7:6). Here Abram, in a gesture more powerful than words, shows his humility before God and his willingness to listen.

4–8 The second divine speech picks up terms from the first speech. The covenant (ברית) is mentioned three times (vv 4, 7) again, and now, like Noah's covenant (9:11, 16), it is to be confirmed and made eternal. In v 2 God promised to "make" (נתן) a covenant; now he promises to "make" Abraham a father of nations (vv 5, 6) and to "give" him the land of Canaan as a permanent (eternal) holding. In v 2 Abraham was assured that he would be multiplied במאד מאד "very much/exceedingly." Now the other verb usually paired with "multiply," "make fruitful," is used with the same phrase (v 6).

But this second speech goes well beyond the first. Three times it states that Abraham will father nations (vv 4, 5, 6), that the covenant and its blessings will be not just for Abraham but for his descendants after him (vv 7, 8), and that the ultimate covenant blessing, "I shall be your God" (vv 7, 8), will be his and theirs (cf. Lev 26:12, where this is also seen as the greatest of all divine benefits).

As befits a scene where Abram's name is changed to Abraham, there are several plays on his name, most obviously אב המון "father of a multitude," which almost rhymes with אברהם "Abraham." But several of the other key words in this passage have identical or similar consonants suggesting a play on Abraham's name, e.g., ברית "covenant," רבה "multiply," פרה "be fruitful," and במאד מאד "exceedingly" (Strus, *Nomen-Omen,* 106–7).

4 The tone of the speech is set by the opening word אני "I" "for my part." What God is doing and will do for Abraham is the subject of this speech. Here the promissory aspect of the covenant is all-embracing, particularly the promise of descendants to which this chapter returns time and again. V 2 stated that it was God's intention to "make" his covenant with Abraham. V 4 clarifies this: since there is already a covenant with Abraham, God will make him "father of a multitude of nations." Previously the promise had simply been that Abram should be a great nation (12:2), beyond counting (16:10). This promise goes much further.

5 The magnitude of the promise is marked by the change of Abram's name to Abraham, probably little more than a dialect variant of Abram (cf. *Comment* on 11:26).

But in traditional societies, and particularly in the OT, names were much more important than they are today. If for us personal names are little more than labels, in the OT they express a person's character and destiny, at least as the parents perceive them (cf. 4:1, 25; 5:29; 16:15); usually children are named at birth by their parents. Here, however, and later with Sarah (v 15) and Jacob (32:28), we have God himself dictating a name change in midlife. This makes the name Abraham more than a pious parental hope that the child may or may not fulfill but a divinely guaranteed statement about Abraham's identity and future destiny. His very name guarantees that he will father many nations.

6 "I shall make you exceedingly fruitful." Here the root פרה, regularly paired with רבה "multiply," reappears, linking this verse with v 2. To "be fruitful and multiply" was the first command given to man (1:28) and was repeated to Noah

(8:17; 9:1, 7). Here a similar remark is made to Abraham, who, like Adam and Noah, stands at the beginning of an epoch in human history. God's original purpose for mankind, thwarted by the fall and faltering again in the post-Noah period, is eventually to be achieved by Abraham's descendants. It may be noted that whereas Adam and Noah were simply commanded "be fruitful" (qal imperative), God makes Abraham a promise, "I shall make you fruitful" (hiphil). This change of conjugation suggests that Abraham will be given divine power to achieve this fertility, whereas his predecessors, left simply to themselves, failed.

"Kings shall be descended from you." Kingship was implicit in the promise of great nationhood (12:2), a passage rich in royal ideology. However, here it is made explicit for the first time. Throughout the Pentateuch, it is anticipated that Israel will one day have a king, but rarely is it mentioned (17:16; 35:11; 49:10; Num 24:17; Deut 17:14–20; 28:36).

7   The LORD now adds to the great promise of kingship what are seen in the OT as even more valuable blessings. The covenant is not to be just between God and Abraham but between God and Abraham's descendants after him. Hitherto he has been promised descendants (13:16) and the land has been promised to them (13:15), but this is the first occasion that the covenant is extended to include Abraham's seed. This makes the covenant with Abraham like the Noahic covenant, as do the phrases "I shall confirm my covenant . . . for an eternal covenant" (9:9, 11, 16). Though the land had been promised in perpetuity (13:15), this is the first time that the Abrahamic covenant has been described as "eternal" or that the covenant formula לאלהים לך היה "to be your God" has appeared. This latter phrase, used twice here and not again till 28:21, expresses the heart of the covenant, that God has chosen Abraham and his descendants, so that they are in a unique relationship: he is their God, and they are his people (cf. Exod 4:16; 6:7; Lev 11:45; 26:12, 45).

8   Though the promise of land to Abraham's descendants is not new (cf. 13:15; 15:18), this is the first time its title "Canaan" has been used by God, and the description of it as "the land to which you have migrated" (28:4; 36:7; 37:1) is fresh: its use suggests that Abraham has already lived a long time in Canaan but that he is still an alien there. It will eventually be their עולם אחזת "permanent holding," that is, their inalienable property (cf. 48:4; Lev 25:34). But their tenure of the land is dependent upon the overarching goal of the covenant: "I shall be their God."

9–14   These verses constitute both the central and the longest divine speech in this chapter, dealing with circumcision, the principal human obligation of the covenant. Its key terms are "covenant" and "circumcise," both of which occur six times. "Flesh" occurs three times, and many other words or phrases each occur twice. "There is no need to think of a conflation of sources here, or of additions, as the thought progresses with perfect logic" (McEvenue, *The Narrative Style of the Priestly Writer,* 169). The general principle for observing the covenant is enunciated in v 9. This means circumcision of all males (v 10). This is the sign of the covenant (v 11). It involves circumcising eight-day-old boys and slaves who join the household (vv 12–13). To be uncircumcised is to break the covenant and will lead to divine retribution (v 14).

Excursus on Circumcision

The rite of circumcision, which involves the removal of the foreskin on the penis, is practiced in many parts of the world by different tribes. Only in Europe and Central and East Asia is the custom unknown. In the ancient Near East, the majority of Israel's neighbors practiced circumcision, including the Egyptians, Canaanites, and Arabs (cf. Jer 9:24–25[25–26]). Among Israel's immediate neighbors, the Philistines, frequently disparagingly referred to as the uncircumcised (Judg 14:3), and the Shechemites, who are described as Hivites, were also uncircumcised (Gen 34:2, 14). It also seems likely that circumcision was not practiced in Mesopotamia. This is suggested by Ezek 32:21–24 and by the fact that Abraham was not circumcised until he came to Canaan.

The significance of the rite outside Israel has been much discussed, but since those who practice it often have no explanation save tradition, i.e., this is what our forefathers did, it remains obscure. Philo (*Special Laws,* 1.2–11) lists four reasons given by others for circumcision: (1) for health, to prevent infection, (2) for purification, (3) for teaching the similarity between procreation and thought, and (4) for improving fertility. Then he adds two other reasons of his own that he regards as most important: first, to teach in a symbolic way that a man must remove lust from himself and control his thoughts; second, to teach that no one can achieve perfection if he does not remove every evil from his heart.

Modern suggestions include the idea that circumcision is a preparation for marriage, marks a man's coming of age, or is an offering to the deity. Functionally, it often incorporates a man into society and is a major rite of passage, usually at puberty. Sometimes it has a magical function, for it is believed to avert sickness and bad luck.

These last two observations fit Israelite practice. According to Gen 17, circumcision marks one as a member of the covenant community. Every Israelite male must be circumcised (17:10–11). And those who refuse to be circumcised are warned that they are liable to be "cut off from their relations" (17:14). This sentence of extirpation is often mentioned in Leviticus (e.g., 7:20–21; 17:4) and is a warning that the sinner is liable to suffer a sudden mysterious death (cf. Wenham, *Leviticus* [Grand Rapids: Eerdmans, 1979] 242, 285–86; H. H. Cohn, *ILR* 5 [1970] 72).

But circumcision is more specifically called "the sign of the covenant" (Gen 17:11). A consideration of this key phrase is necessary to understand the idea of circumcision in Scripture. There are three kinds of signs (אות) in the OT. First, proof signs that convince the observer about something. The plagues were intended to persuade Pharaoh and Israel of divine sovereignty (Exod 7:3–5). Second, certain acts, e.g., acted prophecies, are signs in that they resemble the situation announced (e.g., Ezek 4:3). Third, certain signs are mnemonic in that they are reminders of something. Thus the eating of unleavened bread reminds Israel of the exodus and reminds them to keep the law (Exod 13:9; cf. Deut 6:8; 11:18). The altar covering is a sign warning laymen not to offer incense (Num 17:3, 5[16:38, 40]). The sabbath is a sign reminding the people of Israel that they are called to be God's holy people (Exod 31:13). But closest of all to the usage in Gen 17 is 9:12–17, where the rainbow is said to be the sign of the covenant between God and all mankind. The rainbow reminds God of his promise never to destroy the earth with another flood (9:14–16).

On the basis of the close parallels with the Noahic covenant, Fox argues that circumcision, like the rainbow, reminds God of his promise: in this case, that he will multiply Abraham's descendants exceedingly. "We cannot suppose that it is a reminder to the Israelites to fulfill some duty, because this covenant requires nothing of Israel other than circumcision, and circumcision cannot be a reminder of itself" (*RB* 81 [1974]

595). However, unlike the rainbow, it is not said that circumcision reminds God of his promises. And though the covenant with Abraham does have many parallels with that made with Noah, in other respects circumcision is much closer to the other cultic obligations placed on Israel, such as passover and the sabbath, which clearly were intended to remind Israel of its status as the LORD's people and their obligations to keep the law. And despite Fox, it is not true that there are no other duties imposed on Israel. God's speech to Abraham begins "Walk in my presence and be blameless" (17:2). The permanent marking of the body reflects the eternity of the covenant between God and Israel (17:7, 13, 19). The marking of a man's most intimate member with the sign of the covenant coupled with the call to blamelessness may well have prompted prophetic criticism of Israelites as uncircumcised in heart and ears (Jer 6:10; 9:24–25[25–26]). The people of Israel were called to love God with all their heart, soul, and might, and the rite of circumcision reminded them of this. This does not exclude the notion that circumcision may also have reminded God of his promises, but it seems likely that its primary function was manward, to remind the Israelite man to walk blamelessly with God, as Noah and Abraham did.

9 God's side of the covenant promise had been stated in vv 3–8; now Abraham's obligations are stated, "As for you," but the phraseology closely echoes v 7 ("covenant," "generations," "you and your descendants after you"). "Observe my covenant." Though both the verb שׁמר "observe" and the noun "covenant" are very common, this combination is rare, occurring but thirteen times: seven times the LORD is described as observing covenant and steadfast love (e.g., Deut 7:9), and three times (here, v 10, and Exod 19:5) Israel is urged to observe the covenant.

10 Here the command to observe the covenant is repeated, this time in the plural. Plural suffixes are also used on בּין "between *you*" and on ל "all *your* males." The covenant is not just with Abraham but with his whole group and his descendants—"males." Though female circumcision is practiced among some peoples, the OT especially emphasizes the necessity for men to participate in religion (Exod 23:17; 34:23; Deut 16:16). Restricting circumcision to men is of a piece with this attitude.

11 After stating the general principle that all males must be circumcised, the law now goes into specific detail. First, it specifies where it is to be performed: "the flesh of your foreskin," lit. "of your uncircumcision." On "the sign of the covenant," see "Excursus on Circumcision" above.

12 Next, the timing and the subjects of circumcision are defined more precisely. "All your males" (v 10) covers all baby boys eight days old. Ritual acts at weekly intervals (eight days reckoned inclusively is a week) are often prescribed in Leviticus. Circumcision covers all boys born in the household, whether freeborn or sons of slaves. In their case, circumcision is done at eight days. "But in the case of those bought from foreigners," it is implied that they must be circumcised when they join Abraham's household, i.e., when they are purchased. Sarna (125) argues that the OT's insistence that circumcision should normally be carried out eight days after birth, not at puberty or prior to marriage as is commonly the case in other societies, represents the radical reinterpretation of a social custom as a covenantal symbol.

13 This verse underlines that all male members of the household, whatever their origin, must submit to circumcision.

14 Adults may, of course, be reluctant to undergo circumcision, and a warning of the consequences is appended. "An uncircumcised male . . . shall be cut off from his relations." This sentence is often invoked against offenses that tend to be committed in secret, where the threat of divine punishment would be the main deterrent (e.g., Lev 18:29; 19:8; 20:3, 5–6, 17–18). Though it has been supposed to involve excommunication from the community, to be "cut off" seems more likely to be divine punishment resulting in the offender's untimely death. "The threat of being 'cut off' by the hand of God, in His own time, hovers over the offender constantly and inescapably; he is not unlike the patient who is told by his doctors that his disease is incurable and that he might die any day" (H. H. Cohn, *ILR* 5 [1970] 72; cf. W. Horbury, *VT* 35 [1985] 31–33).

"He has broken my covenant." Breaking (הפר) the covenant is the opposite of observing (שמר; vv 9, 10) or confirming (הקים) it (v 7). But whereas God observes and confirms covenants, he never breaks them (Judg 2:1), though man frequently does. When a man breaks a woman's vow, it is made void. When he says nothing, the vow is confirmed or ratified (Num 30). With both vows and covenants, only the superior party may confirm or break them, so as to terminate them. The inferior party may choose to observe or break them, but in this case the covenant is not terminated. The non-observer simply brings on himself the threats built into the covenant, in this case "being cut off" (cf. Deut 28:15; Isa 24:5).

15–16 The fourth speech does not build on the third; it takes an entirely new turn. For the first time, a promise is specifically addressed to Sarai. Hitherto the LORD has promised to bless Abraham (12:2–3) and has promised to give him children, but it has never been made quite clear how this is to be achieved. By referring more than once to Sarah's old age, the narrator has led us to suppose that she is to be the mother of Abraham's child, but this has never been made explicit. Chap. 16 shows that Sarah herself at least supposed surrogate motherhood using Hagar might have been the answer. That indeed provided Abraham with a son and Hagar with promises about his future, but nothing was said about Sarah.

There are close parallels with vv 4–8, the second speech. There the narrative prepared us for the momentously significant name change; here it is sprung without explanation. Sarah is just an alternative pronunciation of Sarai; they both mean "princess." Then comes the explanation. Twice God says "I shall bless her" and "I shall give you a son from her." This may sound quite prosaic, but every word is significant. Back in 15:3 Abraham had complained "You have not given me descendants." Since then the LORD has given him the land (15:18) and a covenant (17:2) but no son except Hagar's. Now there is to be a son for him from Sarah. Indeed, the nations and kings promised to Abraham in v 6 are to be descended from Sarah.

17–18 The promises to Sarah are abruptly, even rudely, interrupted. As Westermann notes, such an interruption is most uncharacteristic of P (2:267). But this break gives a chance for the promises to be reiterated even more emphatically in what follows. And as Abraham voices his incredulity, this allows the reader's own doubts to be raised as well.

17 The narrative makes Abraham's astonishment very clear in three ways. First, "Abraham fell on his face," a gesture of awe, amazement, and gratitude (cf. v 3). In itself, prostration is ambiguous: clearly it indicates that Abraham found

the remarks about Sarah more amazing than his own name change and the command to circumcise his household. But is he showing faith? "And laughed," his second astonished response, indicates the opposite; he is not simply laughing with joy, as Jacob maintains. Sarah's laughter in Gen 18:12–15 clearly expresses unbelief. Yet the very word ויצחק "and laughed" spells "And Isaac." So in laughing at God's promise, Abraham unwittingly confirms it. Third, he is so overcome by the announcement that he can hardly think straight. The way he frames his doubt, "Can a man . . . give birth?" combines two different constructions for a double-barreled question (see n. 17.c.). To smooth his grammar, various emendations have been proposed. However, they are unnecessary. Probably the confused syntax reflects Abraham's inward confusion. He is so overcome by the announcement that he changes the sentence structure in midstream.

From a human perspective, Abraham's doubts, "Can a hundred-year-old man become a father or Sarah, a ninety-year-old woman, give birth?" seem completely justified. Partly for this reason and partly because he had not uttered them aloud, Abraham's thoughts are not rebuked. Indeed, his plea, in which he indirectly expresses his unbelief, "May Ishmael live in your presence!" is treated with great consideration. Superficially, this is just a prayer that God's care and protection will be granted to Ishmael (cf. Hos 6:2), but in not taking up the promise of a son through Sarah, Abraham shows his reservations.

19–21 But God, who knows man's thoughts and hears our unspoken as well as our spoken prayers, addresses Abraham's doubts directly. This final speech has a well-ordered palistrophic structure.

> A   Sarah will bear a son . . . Isaac (19a)
> B   I shall confirm my covenant with him (19b)
> C   Ishmael (20)
> B¹   I shall confirm my covenant with Isaac (21a)
> C¹ Sarah will bear next year (21b)

19 God rebukes Abraham very firmly. His doubt is emphatically contradicted by the opening אבל "indeed" instead of הנה "behold," which is more usual in an announcement scene (Neff, *BR* 15 [1970] 14). It then continues in the standard fashion, giving the child's name, Isaac, and future destiny.

The name Isaac is typical of early second-millennium Amorite names, consisting of a verb in the imperfect and a divine name (cf. Ishmael or Israel). Thus it is usually surmised that the full name of Isaac was Isaac-el, just as the full name of Jacob was probably Jacob-el. If יצחק אל is the correct full name of Isaac, then it may be translated "The god El laughs/smiles/looks with favor" (cf. Berger, *UF* 1 [1969] 216). Like the name Ishmael, it records divine mercy in granting the child's birth. Another possibility is that Isaac is not a shortening of Isaac-el but a name in its own right and refers to the laughter and pleasure of the parents over the child. Hence it could be interpreted "(The father) laughs/smiles." However, as usual with names, the Bible is not interested in a historic etymology so much as in the associations evoked by the name. Wherever the name Isaac is discussed, it is associated with the verb צחק "to laugh" or in the piel "make sport of" and reflects the skeptical laughter of his parents when told of his birth (v 17; 18:12–15) or Ishmael's mistreatment of him (21:9).

Earlier, God had promised that he would confirm his eternal covenant with Abraham and his descendants (17:7). Now this promise is focused on the as-yet-unborn Isaac. "I shall confirm my covenant with him." By implication, this excludes Ishmael.

20 The exclusion of Ishmael from the eternal covenant is now spelled out. But Abraham's prayer for him is answered. Note the play on Ishmael's name, שמעתיך "I have heard you." Furthermore, as the son of Abraham, he is to enjoy the blessing of multiplication and fruitfulness. The order to "be fruitful and multiply" was given to all mankind (1:28; 9:1), but Ishmael is guaranteed divine success in fulfilling this duty. Indeed, he will become "a great nation" just as had originally been promised to Abraham (12:2). In this chapter, of course, Abraham's sights have been set higher: he is to father a multitude of nations, and kings are to be descended from him. Ishmael is to become just a great nation, and twelve "princes" are to come from him. נשיא means "prince" or "tribal leader." Later, of course, Israel was to be divided into twelve tribes headed by "princes" (cf. Num 7), but here the narrative looks forward to the twelve tribes descended from Ishmael (25:13–16).

21 But however splendid the prospect in store for Ishmael, the covenant is to be with Isaac, who is to be born in just a year's time. For twenty-five years the hope of offspring has been dangled intermittently before Abraham, but nothing ever seemed to happen. Abraham has confessed his own despair to God, and now suddenly he is assured that in only a year's time his elderly wife will give birth. God's promises in this chapter have been breathtaking in their scope and serve to give the stories about Abraham a new sense of direction. But this last phrase does more: it raises the tension of the narrative and injects a feeling of suspense and drama into it.

22 To draw attention to God's dramatic exit, the end of his speech is described much more fully than usual. Usually nothing is said about God ceasing to speak or going away: he just stops and the next event is described (cf. 18:33; 35:13). Here it is solemnly stated "he stopped talking to him, and God went away from Abraham."

23 This verse constitutes the second scene in the story of the covenant of circumcision. Its brevity, especially in contrast with the lengthy first scene filled with five divine speeches, is striking. This terseness conveys the new sense of urgency that the last remark, "this time next year," has engendered. Abraham looks forward impatiently to its fulfillment and therefore acts promptly, "that very day." But the listing of all those circumcised carefully echoes v 12 to insist that Abraham's obedience was not merely prompt; it was exact, "as God had spoken to him."

24–27 The epilogue rounding off the story with a note of the age of Abraham and Ishmael is much longer than usual (cf. 16:16; 13:18; 12:9; 21:34). It not only gives this chronological detail but mentions all the other men who were circumcised at the same time. The prolixity of this epilogue counterbalances the compression of v 23, which might lead one to suppose that the act of circumcision was not really important. On the contrary, by repeating the phrase "that very day," the narrator stresses that the day Abraham circumcised his family was one of the turning points in world history, comparable to Noah's entry into the ark or the exodus from Egypt (cf. 7:13; Exod 12:17, 41, 51).

Explanation

This most significant episode in the Abraham cycle begins rather dully with a note about his age, "When Abram was ninety-nine." Yet this remark is important, for it puts the momentous promises that constitute the centerpiece of this episode in context and makes it possible for us to appreciate how amazing they are. They are addressed to a man and his wife well past the age of childbearing in modern and ancient experience (cf. 17:17). The note about Abram's age also links this story with the account of Ishmael's birth in the previous chapter. In the thirteen years that have elapsed since, Abram has, it may be assumed, accepted that Sarai's infertility is incurable and that Ishmael is his sole heir through whom the divine promises will be fulfilled.

In its arrangement, chap.17 closely parallels chap. 16 (see *Form/Structure/Setting*), but this similarity really underlines the way that the promise of Isaac's birth far outstrips the promises about Ishmael in importance. This is at once hinted at by "The LORD appeared," which intimates that something of great import is about to be announced. It was simply the angel of the LORD who had spoken to Hagar (16:9–11); here "the LORD" himself "appears," a remark signaling new or important revelation (cf. 12:7; 18:1; 26:2).

Furthermore, the LORD here introduces himself by the preferred name of the patriarchal era, "I am El Shaddai." Its etymology is obscure, but wherever it is used in Genesis, it is associated with divine omnipotence, his ability to fulfill his promises and especially to make the barren fertile (28:3; 35:11; 48:3). But the power and grace of this God of Abraham is also complemented by his moral demands. "Walk in my presence and be blameless" expresses the expectation that Abram's piety and behavior must match that of the greatest saints of the old covenant, of men like Enoch and Noah who walked with God and were blameless (5:22; 6:9).

"So that I may make my covenant and multiply you exceedingly." This reference to making a covenant surprises in that a covenant has already been initiated with Abram in chap. 15. So too the promise to "multiply very much," an anagram containing Abram's new name, is at first mysterious, for this had also been promised long before (cf. 13:16; 15:5). Yet both the nature of the covenant with Abram and the identity of descendants are the key themes of this chapter, so that this mysterious introduction exactly indicates its contents. But clearly it was the presence of the LORD rather than his opening words that prompted Abram to prostrate himself in humble awe.

The second divine speech goes right to the heart of the matter. Abram is not simply to become a great nation (12:2) but to be the "father of a multitude of nations." His name, given by his parents, is changed to Abraham, "father of a multitude," by God himself as an unforgettable guarantee of the fulfillment of this promise. Furthermore, he is assured "*I* shall make you exceedingly fruitful" (v 6). Abram and Noah had simply been told to "be fruitful" (1:28; 9:1). Here the creator promises to give what he commands. Abraham will be enabled to achieve the impossible through divine aid (cf. Phil 4:13). Furthermore, through him God's plans for humanity, often frustrated by sin, will at length be realized. Indeed, "kings shall be descended from you." Given the ancient concept of nationhood,

the promise that Abraham would father a multitude of nations involved the idea that kings would be descended from him, but here it is made explicit to underline the seriousness of the promises of descendants. It may also suggest that Abraham's offspring will fulfill the other aspect of man's original mandate "to fill the earth and subdue it" (1:28).

Just as important, however, are the fresh remarks about the covenant (vv 7–8). Already implicit in 12:1–3 and explicit in 15:18, it is now defined more precisely with a view to its confirmation or ratification. This covenant is not simply between God and Abraham but between God and Abraham's descendants "after you throughout their generations." It is to be an "eternal covenant." Though "eternal" may simply mean "without predetermined end," comparison of God's promise to Abraham, with that made to Noah, also termed an "eternal covenant" (9:16), shows that a permanent relationship is envisaged, as durable as life itself (cf. 8:20–22; 9:11). Eternal, too, is Israel's tenure of the land of Canaan, here named by God for the first time: Canaan is a region whose political boundaries are clearly defined in thirteenth- and fourteenth-century Egyptian texts; it corresponds roughly to the modern state of Israel together with part of southern Syria and Lebanon. Abraham had migrated to Canaan; it is now ceded to him as a permanent holding. Finally, and most important of all, the essential heart of the covenant is defined: "I shall be their God." I, El Shaddai, the omnipotent creator of the world and redeemer of mankind, will be Israel's God. This nation descended from Abraham is to be unique, because unlike the other nations, Israel enjoys a unique relationship with the only true God. This relationship is the basis of all subsequent divine interventions on the nation's behalf (cf. Exod 6:7; Deut 29:12[13]; Jer 24:7; 32:38; Ezek 11:20; 34:24; Zech 8:8).

These mind-bursting promises demand a response. But by comparison with the obligations God has taken upon himself for the benefit of Abraham's descendants, the duties imposed on Abraham are quite slight (vv 9–14). He is to institute the circumcision of all the males in his household, a practice well-known in the ancient Near East but here invested with a peculiar significance. The ineradicable mark of circumcision reflects the eternity of the covenant, the permanent bond between God and Israel (v 13). It is a sign of the covenant (v 11) that reminds the Israelite of his special spiritual relationship and of his obligation to walk before God and be perfect.

Though circumcision is quite an easy custom to enforce, at least on eight-day-old baby boys, the speech goes into considerable detail, specifying that every male member of the household, slave and freeman, must submit to this rite. Total commitment is required of Abraham and his household. Failure to comply is to "break the covenant." Covenants broken by man are not terminated; rather the covenant sanctions come into play (cf. Isa 24:5–6), here the threat of being cut off: a sudden untimely death hangs over the head of the man who fails to carry out the obligation of being circumcised (v 14).

At this point, one might have anticipated that the LORD would have stopped speaking. Both sides of the covenant have been explained. The natural next step would have been to report Abraham's obedience: how he circumcised his household as God commanded. But instead God goes on talking, and indeed the narrative tension rises dramatically. Suddenly God announces that Sarai's name

must be changed to Sarah. There is no difference in meaning, so the significance of the change is not immediately apparent. God had prefaced his name-change of Abraham by explaining why he was doing it. Abram was to become "father of a multitude of nations . . . kings shall be descended from you" (vv 4, 6). Could this be the reason behind Sarai's new name? The narrative does not leave us in suspense long. "I shall bless her, and I shall give you a son from her." Nations and indeed kings will be descended from her (vv 15–16).

This bombshell stuns Abraham as much as did the original revelation of the LORD. He again falls on his face and laughs, thinking "Can a hundred-year-old man become a father or Sarah, a ninety-year-old woman, give birth?" The omniscient narrator's insight into Abraham's feelings at this moment allows us to identify with his unbelief and to share in the divine reassertion of these amazing promises. He does, however, put his doubts positively in the form of a prayer for his son, "May Ishmael live in your presence."

The LORD is not put off by this. In a final dramatic speech, he emphatically reaffirms that Sarah will have a child to be named Isaac, a name already anticipated by Abraham's laughter (v 17). This yet-to-be-conceived Isaac is going to see the confirmation of the eternal covenant. Ishmael is not forgotten: princes, not kings, will descend from him, and he will become a great nation, but Isaac is the one with whom the covenant will be confirmed. And "Sarah will bear him this time next year." With this final astonishing remark, God left Abraham. More than twenty-five years of childlessness had surely proved Sarah could never conceive. But what Abraham thought is not recorded: the reader is simply left to fill it in for himself.

Though Abraham's thoughts are left unrecorded, his deeds are not. His prompt and total obedience to the divine injunction to circumcise his household is recorded: "that very day." Beginning with his son Ishmael, on whom all his hopes had rested hitherto, Abraham circumcised all the men of his household, including himself. Whatever his doubts about the possibility of Sarah conceiving, they did not prevent Abraham from obeying God's commands. And his obedience as well as the content of the revelation itself make this day one of the greatest days in redemptive history: "that very day" is a phrase used elsewhere to describe the day the flood came and the day Israel left Egypt (7:13; Exod 12:17). Thus from first to last, the narrator indicates the importance of what is recorded here: the covenant promises are the charter for Israel and are enormous in their scope, yet God can fulfill them just as surely as he made good his promise of a son to Abraham.

Within the book of Genesis, the importance of this episode is obvious: the birth of Isaac is the indispensable next step if God's promises are to be fulfilled. The rest of the book tells how indeed Isaac was born within a year and relates the story of his life and his descendants. Without him there would have been no Israel.

But Israel's national character as the people of the LORD who lived in the land of Canaan depended on the eternal covenant between God and Abraham's descendants. The covenant announced here was the basis of the nation's existence. That God made an eternal covenant with Abraham and his descendants is the assumption of the rest of the OT, even though the phrase "eternal covenant" is not all that common (Ps 105:10). On this covenant rested Israel's claim to the

land of Canaan and to a unique relationship with God. So at turning points in their careers God reaffirms these promises to Isaac (26:3–5) and Jacob (28:13–15). It is the motive for the exodus (Exod 6:4–6) and the guarantee of the conquest, as Deuteronomy persistently reiterates (e.g., 9:5). But more than that, even when Israel rebels and disregards the covenant, bringing upon herself the curse of exile, the covenant is not thereby invalidated: national repentance will lead to national restoration, as Lev 26:40–45 and Deut 30:1–10 affirm.

So when the nation lost its freedom and was deported to Babylonia, the prophets spoke encouragingly about the permanence of the covenant relationship (Isa 24:5). In particular they looked forward to a new and eternal covenant: new in that this time Israel, not just the LORD, would observe it loyally (Jer 31:31–37; 32:40; Ezek 16:60; 37:26). Indeed, through this new and eternal covenant, all nations would be blessed (Isa 55:3; 61:8).

The NT, of course, sees these predictions of the new covenant as fulfilled in Christ, and especially by the incorporation of the Gentiles into the people of God (Acts 15:16–18; Eph 3:1–6; Heb 8:8–13). But though the scope and the validity of these promises are extended in the epistles, this reinterpretation does not undermine their old narrow sense, according to Paul. His long discussion of the place of Israel in the divine plan (Rom 9–11) proceeds on the assumption that God's promises to Abraham are still valid despite Jewish unbelief. God has not rejected his people (Rom 11:1), "for the gifts and the call of God are irrevocable" (Rom 11:29). So he anticipates that one day "all Israel will be saved" (Rom 11:26).

The human obligation of this covenant, the rite of circumcision, is, of course, equally fundamental to the OT and to Judaism, but like the eternity of the covenant, it is rarely mentioned. It is simply assumed that all Abraham's descendants will be circumcised (so 21:4; 34:15, 17, 22, 24). More frequent are references to the uncircumcised nations surrounding Israel, which show that it was a custom taken for granted within Israel. It is the sign of the covenant, which reminds its possessor of his obligation to walk before God and be perfect. Submission to it expresses submission to God and humility before him (Lev 26:41; Deut 10:16). Thus the disobedient generation in the wilderness who allowed the practice to lapse had to be circumcised before they could take possession of the land of Canaan (Josh 5:2–7).

Several passages (Lev 26:41; Deut 10:16; 30:6; Jer 4:4) speak of the circumcision of the heart, suggesting that the rite itself expressed faith and obedience to God. And it is this spiritual aspect of circumcision that Paul stresses in expounding the new relationship between God and man inaugurated by the death of Christ (Rom 2–4). "Real circumcision is a matter of the heart, spiritual and not literal" (Rom 2:29). So he argued violently against those in Galatia who wanted to make circumcision an obligation for Gentile converts. Such an idea blurs the truth that salvation is found through faith in Christ, not through works of the law. But this is not to say that Paul regarded circumcision as wrong for Christians of Jewish descent. Just as he regarded the covenant with Abraham as still valid for the Jew, he still regarded it as appropriate for Timothy to be circumcised (Acts 16:3: cf. Gal 2:3). For Paul, the universal applicability of the gospel did not make the old covenant and its obligations redundant for those born into it; rather, its extension to the Gentiles underlines the astonishing mercy of God.

Seventeen hundred years after Paul, Frederick the Great asked his physician for a proof of the existence of God. "Your majesty, the Jews," he replied. Two hundred years later, after the holocaust and the establishment of the state of Israel, readers of Gen 17 even more skeptical than Frederick might be forced to agree.

The Overthrow of Sodom and
Gomorrah   (18:1–19:38)

Alexander, T. D. "Lot's Hospitality: A Clue to His Righteousness." *JBL* 104 (1985) 289–91. **Alston, W. M.** "Genesis 18:1–11." *Int* 42 (1988) 397–402. **Alter, R.** "How Convention Helps Us Read: The Case of the Bible's Annunciation Type-Scene." *Prooftexts* 3 (1983) 115–30. ————. "Sodom as Nexus: The Web of Design in Biblical Narrative." *Tikkun* 1.1 (1986) 30–38. **Andersen, F. I.** "A Short Note on Construct *k* in Hebrew." *Bib* 50 (1969) 68–69. **Balentine, S. E.** "Prayers for Justice in the OT: Theodicy and Theology." *CBQ* 51 (1989) 597–616. **Baumgarten, A.** "A Note on the Book of Ruth." *JANESCU* 5 (1973) 11–15. **Begrich, G.** "Die Freundlichkeit Gottes als Grundform theologischen Redens: Ein Nachdenken über Gen 18:1–16a." *EvT* 49 (1989) 218–31. **Ben Zvi, E.** "The Dialogue between Abraham and YHWH in Gen 18:23–32: A Historical–Critical Analysis." *JSOT* 53 (1992) 27–46. **Blenkinsopp, J.** "Abraham and the Righteous of Sodom." *JJS* 33 (1982) 119–32. ————. "The Judge of All the Earth: Theodicy in the Midrash on Gen 18:22–33." *JJS* 41 (1990) 1–12. **Brueggemann, W.** "'Impossibility' and Epistemology in the Faith Tradition of Abraham and Sarah (Gen 18:1–15)." *ZAW* 94 (1982) 615–34. **Brunner, H.** "Gen 19 und das 'Frauenverbrechen.'" *BN* 44 (1988) 21–22. **Childs, B. S.** "Anticipatory Titles in Hebrew Narrative." In *Essays on the Bible and the Ancient World III: I. L. Seeligman Volume*, ed. A. Rofé and Y. Zakovitch. Jerusalem: Rubinstein's, 1983. 57–65. **Coats, G. W.** "Lot: A Foil in the Abraham Saga." In *Understanding the Word: FS B. W. Anderson*, ed. J. T. Butler, E. W. Conrad, and B. C. Ollenburger. JSOTSup 37. Sheffield: JSOT Press, 1985. 113–32. **Deurloo, K. A.** "Narrative Geography in the Abraham Cycle." *OTS* 26 (1990) 48–62. **Fields, W. W.** "The Motif 'Night as Danger' associated with Three Biblical Destruction Narratives." In *"Shaʿarei Talmon": Studies in the Bible, Qumran and the Ancient Near East presented to S. Talmon*, ed. M. Fishbane and E. Tov. Winona Lake: Eisenbrauns, 1992. 17–32. **Fisch, H.** "Ruth and the Structure of Covenant History." *VT* 32 (1982) 425–37. **Goodman, D.** "Do Angels Eat?" *JJS* 37 (1986) 160–75. **Gruber, M. I.** "The Many Faces of Hebrew פֶּנִים נָשָׂא 'lift up the face.'" *ZAW* 95 (1983) 252–60. **Haag, H.** "Abraham und Lot in Gen 18–19." In *Mélanges bibliques et orientaux: FS M. Henri Cazelles*, ed. A. Caquot and M. Delcor. AOAT 212. Kevelaer: Verlag Butzon & Bercker, 1981. 173–99. **Hattem, W. C. van.** "Once Again: Sodom and Gomorrah." *BA* 44 (1981) 87–92. **Jeansonne, S. P.** "The Characterization of Lot in Genesis." *BTB* 18 (1988) 123–29. **Keel, O.** "Wer zerstörte Sodom?" *TZ* 35 (1979) 10–17. **Kilian, R.** "Nachtrag und Neuorientierung: Anmerkungen zum Jahwisten in den Abrahamserzählungen." In *Die Väter Israels: FS J. Scharbert*, ed. M. Görg. Stuttgart: Katholisches Bibelwerk, 1989. 155–67. **Klein, J.-P.** "Que se passe-t-il en Genèse 18?" *Le point théologique* 24 (1977) 75–98. **Krašovec, J.** "Der Ruf nach Gerechtigkeit in Gen 18:16–33." In *Die Väter Israels: FS J. Scharbert*, ed. M. Görg. Stuttgart: Katholisches Bibelwerk, 1989. 169–82. **Kümpel, R.** "Die 'Begegnungstradition' von Mamre." In *Bausteine biblischer Theologie: FS G. J. Botterweck*, ed. H.-J. Fabry. BBB 50. Köln: Hanstein, 1977. 147–68. **Lasine, S.** "Guest and Host in Judges 19: Lot's Hospitality in an Inverted World." *JSOT* 29 (1984) 37–59. **Loretz, O.** *"kᶜt hyh* 'wie jetzt ums Jahr': Gen 18:10."

Bib 43 (1962) 75–78. **Mafico, T. J.** "The Crucial Question concerning the Justice of God." *JTSoA* 42 (1983) 11–16. **Massignon, L.** "Die drei Gebete Abrahams." *IKZ* 4 (1975) 19–28. **Matthews, V. H.** "Hospitality and Hostility in Gen 19 and Judg 19." *BTB* 22 (1992) 3–11. **Niditch, S.** "The 'Sodomite' Theme in Judges 19–20: Family, Community, and Social Disintegration." *CBQ* 44 (1982) 365–78. **Peacock, H. F.** "Translating 'Mercy,' 'Steadfast Love' in the Book of Genesis." *BT* 31 (1980) 201–7. **Porter, J. R.** "The Daughters of Lot." *Folklore* 89 (1978) 127–41. **Rodd, C. S.** "Shall Not the Judge of All the Earth Do What Is Just (Gen 18:25)." *ExpTim* 83 (1971/72) 137–39. **Rudin-O'Brasky, T.** *The Patriarchs in Hebron and Sodom (Gen 18–19): A Study of the Structure and Composition of a Biblical Story.* (Heb.) Jerusalem: Simor, 1982. **Schmidt, L.** *"De Deo": Studien zur Literarkritik und Theologie des Buches Jona, des Gesprächs zwischen Abraham und Jahwe in Gen 18:22ff und von Hi 1.* BZAW 143. Berlin: de Gruyter, 1976. **Schweizer, H.** "Determination, Textdeixis—erläutert an Gen 18:23–33." *VT* 33 (1983) 113–18. ————. "Das seltsame Gespräch von Abraham und Jahwe (Gen 18:22–33)." *TQ* 164 (1984) 121–39. **Ska, J. L.** "L'arbre et la tente: la fonction du décor en Gen 18:1–15." *Bib* 68 (1987) 383–89. **Stol, M.** "Blindness and Night-Blindness in Akkadian." *JNES* 45 (1986) 295–99. **Tapp, A. M.** "An Ideology of Expendability: Virgin Daughter Sacrifice in Gen 19:1–11, Judg 11:30–39 and 19:22–26." In *Anti-Covenant: Counter-Reading Women's Lives in the Hebrew Bible*, ed. M. Bal. JSOTSup 81. Sheffield: Almond Press, 1989. 157–74. **Turner, L. A.** "Lot as Jekyll and Hyde." In *The Bible in Three Dimensions*, ed. D. J. A. Clines, S. E. Fowl, and S. E. Porter. JSOTSup 87. Sheffield: Sheffield Academic Press, 1990. 85–101. **Uffenheimer, B.** "Gen 18–19, A New Approach." In *Mélanges A. Neher*, ed. E. A. Levy-Valensi. Paris: Librairie d'Amérique et d'Orient, 1975. 145–53. **Vogels, W.** "Lot, père des incroyants." *EgT* 6 (1975) 139–51. **Weisman, Z.** "Ethnology, Etiology, Genealogy, and Historiography in the Tale of Lot and His Daughters (Gen 19:30–38)." (Heb.) In *"Shaʿarei Talmon": Studies in the Bible, Qumran and the Ancient Near East presented to S. Talmon*, ed. M. Fishbane and E. Tov. Winona Lake: Eisenbrauns, 1992. 43–52. **Wenham, G. J.** "Attitudes to Homosexuality in the OT." *ExpTim* 102 (1991) 359–63. ————. "Method in Pentateuchal Source Criticism." *VT* 41 (1991) 84–109. **Wolff, H. W.** "Sodom und Gomorrha: Predigt über 1. Mose 19:1–29." In *Werden und Wirken des Alten Testaments: FS C. Westermann*, ed. R. Albertz. Göttingen: Vandenhoeck, 1980. 131–37. **Xella, P.** "L'épisode de Dnil et Kothar (*KTU* 1:17 [= *CTA* 17] 5:1–31) et Gen 18:1–16." *VT* 28 (1978) 483–88. **Yaron, R.** *"kāʿeth ḥayyah* and *koh lehay."* *VT* 12 (1962) 500–501. **Young, J. B. de.** "The Contributions of the Septuagint to Biblical Sanctions against Homosexuality." *JETS* 34 (1991) 157–77. **Zakovitch, Y.** "Explicit and Implicit Name-Derivations." *HAR* 4 (1980) 167–81. ————. "The Threshing-Floor Scene in Ruth and the Daughters of Lot." (Heb.) *Shnaton* 3 (1978/79) 29–33.

Translation

[1] *The LORD appeared to him at the oaks of Mamre,* [a]*as he was sitting in*[b] *the doorway of his tent in*[c] *the midday heat.*[a] [2] *He looked up and noticed*[a] *three men standing by him. Seeing them, he ran*[b] *from the door of his tent toward them*[c] *and bowed*[d] *himself to the ground.* [3] *He said, "Sir,*[a] *if indeed*[b] *you*[c] *have favored me, please*[b] *do not leave your*[c] *servant.* [4] *Take*[a] *a little water and wash your feet and rest yourselves*[b] *under the tree,* [5] *so that I may fetch*[a] *a bit of food and revive your spirits. Afterwards you can go on.* [b]*For this is why*[b] *you have come, for your servant's benefit." They said, "All right, do as you have said."*

[6a] *Abraham hurried*[a] *into the tent*[b] *to Sarah and said, "Hurry,*[c] *three seahs of best wheat flour, knead*[c] *it, and make*[c] *loaves."* [7a] *Meanwhile Abraham dashed*[ab] *to the cattle, took a fine tender bull, gave it to a*[c] *lad who hurried to make it ready.* [8] *Then he took yogurt and milk and the bull which he had made ready and he set it before them.* [a]*While he stood under the tree waiting*[b] *on them,*[a] *they ate.*

⁹*They said to him,*ᵃ *"Where is your wife Sarah?" He said, "There*ᵇ *in the tent."* ¹⁰*He said, "I shall certainly*ᵃ *come back to you next year,*ᵇ *and Sarah your wife is going to have a son."* ᶜ*Now Sarah was listening at*ᵈ *the door of the tent, which*ᶜ *was behind him.*ᶜ*"* ¹¹*And Abraham and Sarah were old,*ᵃ *well on in years, and*ᵇ *Sarah* ᶜ*was past the menopause.*ᶜ ¹²*So Sarah laughed to herself thinking, "After I am worn*ᵃ *out, shall I have*ᵇ *pleasure?* ᶜ*And my husband is old too."*ᶜ ¹³*Then the* LORD *said to Abraham, "Why*ᵃ *did Sarah laugh, thinking 'Shall I even*ᵇ *I really*ᶜ *give birth as* ᵈ*I am old?'*ᵈᵉ ¹⁴*Is anything too difficult*ᵃ *for the* LORD*? At the set time next year*ᵇ *I shall come back to you, and Sarah will have a son."* ¹⁵*Sarah denied it. "I did not laugh," she said, because she was frightened. But he said, "Not*ᵃ *so,*ᵇ *you did laugh."*

¹⁶*Then the men stood*ᵃ *up there and looked*ᵃ *out over Sodom, and* ᵇ*Abraham was going with them to accompany*ᶜ *them.*ᵇ

¹⁷ᵃ*But the* LORD *thought: "Shall I hide*ᵇ *from Abraham what I am about to do?*ᶜ ¹⁸*For Abraham is indeed*ᵃ *to become a great and powerful nation, and all the nations of the earth will find blessing*ᵇ *in him.* ¹⁹*For I have chosen*ᵃ *him in order that he may direct his children and his household after him that they may observe the* LORD*'s way to do*ᵇ *righteousness and equity so that the* LORD *may bring*ᶜ *on Abraham what he has spoken about."* ²⁰*So the* LORD *said: "The outcry of Sodom and Gomorrah is indeed*ᵃ *great, and their*ᵇ *sin is indeed*ᵃ *very serious.* ²¹*I want*ᵃ *to go down and see if they* ᵇ*deserve destruction*ᵇ *as implied by the outcry*ᶜ *which has come*ᵈ *to me about it,*ᵉ *and if not, I want*ᵃ *to know."*

²²*Then the men turned*ᵃ *from there and went toward Sodom,* ᵇ*but Abraham was still standing before the* LORD*.*ᵇ ²³*Then Abraham approached*ᵃ *and said, "Would you even*ᵇ *sweep away the righteous along with the wicked?* ²⁴*Suppose there are*ᵃ *fifty righteous in the city, would you even*ᵇ *sweep away and not spare*ᶜ *the place*ᵈ *for the sake of the fifty righteous in her?*ᵉ ²⁵*Far be it from your doing*ᵃ *something like this, to put to death*ᵇ *the righteous with the wicked and to treat the*ᶜ *righteous and the wicked the same.*ᶜ *Far be it from you. Shall not the judge of all the earth act justly?"* ²⁶*So the* LORD *replied, "If I find fifty righteous in the town of Sodom, I shall spare*ᵃ *the whole place for their sake."*

²⁷*So Abraham replied*ᵃ *and said, "Since I have undertaken*ᵇ *to speak to my sovereign,*ᶜ ᵈ*though I am but dust and ashes,*ᵈ ²⁸*suppose the fifty righteous are five short,*ᵃ *would you ruin*ᵇ *the whole city for the sake of*ᶜ *five?" He said,* ᵈ*"I shall not ruin it if I find forty-five there."*ᵈ

²⁹*He spoke yet again*ᵃ *to him and said, "Suppose there are forty found*ᵇ *there." He said, "I shall not do*ᶜ *it for* ᵈ*the sake of forty."*

³⁰*He said, "Do not be angry,*ᵃ *my sovereign, so I may speak.*ᵇ *Suppose thirty are found there." He said, "I shall not do it, if I find thirty there."*

³¹*He said, "Since I have undertaken to speak to my sovereign, suppose twenty are found there." He said, "I shall not ruin it for the sake of twenty."*

³²*He said, "Do not be angry, my sovereign, so I may speak just once*ᵃ *more, suppose ten are found there." He said, "I shall not ruin it for the sake of ten."*

³³*Then when the* LORD *had finished speaking to Abraham he left,* ᵃ*but Abraham returned to his place.*ᵃ

¹⁹:¹ *The* ᵃ*two angels*ᵃ *came to Sodom in the evening,* ᵇ*while Lot was sitting in the gateway of Sodom.*ᵇ *Seeing them, Lot stood up to greet them,*ᶜ *then bowed*ᵈ *to the ground.* ²*He said, "Since* ᵃ*you are here sirs,*ᵇ *please come to your servant's house, stay, wash your feet, and early tomorrow*ᶜ *go*ᵈ *on your way." But they said, "Not*ᵉ *so,*ᶠ *we shall stay* ᵍ*in*

the street."ᵍ ³But he pressed them very hard, and they came and entered his house, and he prepared a feast, ᵃbaking them unleavened bread,ᵃ and they ate.

⁴Beforeᵃ they lay down, the menᵇ of the city of Sodom, young and old, the wholeᶜ population, surroundedᵈ the house. ⁵They called out to Lot and said to him, "Where are the men who came into you tonight. Bringᵃ them out to us, so that we may knowᵇ them." ⁶So Lot went out to the entranceᵃᵇ but shutᶜ the door behind him.ᵇ ⁷He said, "Pleaseᵃ do not do evilᵇ my brothers. ⁸Since I have two virgin daughters, let me bringᵃ them out to you and do to them as you see fit: only ᵇdo not do anything to theseᶜ men for they have come under the protection of my roof for this reason."ᵈ ⁹Then they said, "Come on."ᵃ They said, "Will a single immigrant try to be a judge?ᵇ Now we shall do more evilᶜ to you than to them." They manhandled Lot severely and cameᵈ to batter the door down. ¹⁰Then the men put out their hand and broughtᵃ Lot into the house with them, shut the door, and ¹¹struckᵃ the men at the entranceᵇ of the house, young and old, with sudden blindness,ᶜ so they grew tiredᵈ of trying to find the way in.

¹²Then the menᵃ said to Lot, "Who is still here belonging to you? Bring them outᵇ from theᶜ place, sons-in-law,ᵈ your sons, your daughters, and all in the city who are yours, ¹³because we are about to ruinᵃ this city. For their outcry is great in the LORD's presence, and the LORD has sentᵇ us to ruinᶜ it."

¹⁴So Lot went out and spoke to his sons-in-law, who were to marryᵃ his daughters, and said, "Comeᵇ on, leaveᶜ this place, for the LORD is destroying the city." But his sons-in-law thought he was joking.

¹⁵Atᵃ crack of dawn, the angelsᵇ hurriedᶜ Lot saying, "Comeᵈ on, take your wife and the two daughters you haveᵉ lest you are sweptᶠ away in the punishment of the city." ¹⁶But he dallied,ᵃ so the men grabbedᵇ him by the hand and his wife and his two daughters, because the LORD had compassionᶜ on him, and they broughtᵈ them out and putᵈ them outside the city.

¹⁷ᵃAs soon as they had broughtᵇ them outside, heᶜ said, "Escapeᵈ for your life. Do not lookᵉ behind you. Do not stay in the valley. Escapeᵈ to the hills lest you are swept away." ¹⁸But Lot said to them,ᵃ "No, LORD.ᵇ ¹⁹Even thoughᵃ you have been so kind to your servant and have extendedᵇ your kindness in acting to saveᶜ my life, I cannot escapeᵈ to the hills, so that the disaster will catchᵉ me and I shall die.ᶠ ²⁰Since this city is nearby to flee to, and it is little, let me escapeᵃ there. Is it not a little one? So my life will be saved."ᵇ ²¹He then said to him, "Since I have granted your request about this, not to overturnᵃ the city about which you have spoken, ²²be quick,ᵃ escape there, for I cannotᵇ do anything till you enter it." That is why the city is called Zoar.

²³ᵃAs the sun roseᵇ over the land,ᵃ ᶜLot entered Zoar,ᶜ ²⁴ᵃand the LORD rained brimstone and fire on Sodom and Gomorrah:ᵃ it was from the LORD ᵇfrom the sky.ᵇ ²⁵So he overthrew theseᵃ cities, the whole valley and their inhabitants and the vegetation of the soil. ²⁶His wife lookedᵃ behind himᵇ and becameᶜ a pillar of salt.

²⁷Then Abraham wentᵃ early in the morning to the place where he had stood before the LORD. ²⁸He lookedᵃ out over Sodom and Gomorrah and the wholeᵇ area of the valley and sawᶜ the smoke of the area was like the smoke of aᵈ kiln.

²⁹When God ruinedᵃ the cities of the plain, God remembered Abraham, and he sent Lot out of the overthrow, when he overthrew the cities in which Lot lived.

³⁰Then Lot left Zoar and dwelt in the hills with his two daughters, because he was afraid to liveᵃ in Zoar. He and his two daughters lived in aᵇ cave.ᶜ ³¹Then the elderᵃ said to the younger,ᵇ "Our father is old, and there is no manᶜ at all in the area to come

into[d] us as they do in all the world. [32] Come,[a] let us give our father wine to drink[b] so we may lie with him and produce descendants from our father." [33] So they plied[a] their father with wine that[b] night, and the elder went in and lay with her father, but he did not know about her lying[c] or her leaving.[cd]

[34] Next morning the elder said to the younger, "Since I lay last night with my father,[a] let us ply[b] him with wine tonight[c] as well, and you go and lie with him and we shall raise descendants from our father." [35] So that night too they plied their father with wine, and the younger went[a] and lay with him, but he did not know about her lying or her leaving.

[36] Lot's two daughters became pregnant[a] from their father. [37] The elder gave[a] birth to a son, and she named him Moab:[b] he is the ancestor of the Moabites to this day. [38] The younger also gave birth to a son, and she named him[a] Ben-Ammi: he is the ancestor of the Ammonites to this day.

Notes

1.a-a. Circumstantial clause with participle, expressing a state contemporary with main action (GKC, 141e; *SBH*, 82).

1.b. Omission of prep בְּ "in" is frequent (GKC, 118g), especially before פֶּתַח "doorway" (Joüon, 126h; cf. 19:11).

1.c. כְּ "in/at" expresses the concurrence of two events. "The LORD appeared . . . just as the mid-day heat did" (Joüon, 166m).

2.a. וְהִנֵּה lit. "and behold" shows how things looked to the spectator.

2.b. Waw consec + 3 masc sg impf רוּץ.

2.c. לְ + inf constr קְרָא "to meet" (virtually a prep "toward") + 3 masc pl suffix.

2.d. Waw consec + 3 masc sg impf hishtaphel (not used in Heb. except with this root) חוה (KB, 283–84).

3.a. אֲדֹנָי. The MT pointing interprets it as "Lord" (cf. G, Vg), implying Abraham recognized the divinity of the visitor immediately. Context suggests אֲדֹנִי "sir, my lord" is more apt.

3.b. Frequent use of נָא expresses deference and politeness (GKC, 105b).

3.c. SamPent has "you" instead of MT sg "thee/thy." MT implies leading visitor being addressed, SamPent all three as in vv 4–5. Smoothing typical of SamPent (Waltke, 218).

4.a. 3 masc sg juss qal pass לקח (lit. "let a little water be taken").

4.b. Waw + 2 masc pl impv שׁען.

5.a. Waw + 1 sg coh לקח. Simple waw + coh or impf expresses purpose (Lambdin, 119; *SBH*, 112).

5.b-b. כִּי־עַל כֵּן (cf. 19:8.). "A peculiar phrase emphasizing the ground (for an action) pleonastically" (BDB, 475b).

6.a-a. Note the chiasmus with v 7, "Abraham hurried . . . Abraham dashed," used to suggest Abraham doing everything at once (*SBH*, 129).

6.b. ָה suffix directional ending "towards, to (the tent)" (GKC, 90c; Lambdin, 51–52; not as traditionally supposed an old accusative [WOC, 185]).

6.c. 1 fem sg impv מהר (piel)/לושׁ/עשׂה (qal).

7.a-a. Note chiasmus with v 6.

7.b. 3 masc sg pf qal רוּץ.

7.c. Heb. uses def art for something particular but undefined, where English prefers indefinite (cf. 14:13; 15:1; GKC, 126r; WOC, 243).

8.a-a. Circumstantial clause; cf. n. 1.a-a. (*SBH*, 82).

8.b. For this sense of עמד על, cf. Judg 3:19; 1 Kgs 22:19.

9.a. The dots above אֵלָיו are one of fifteen examples of "extraordinary points" in the MT, probably early critical marks (GKC, 5n).

9.b. הִנֵּה can dispense with a subject (*EWAS*, 140; GKC, 147b; cf. Lambdin, 168–69).

10.a. Inf abs in a promise reinforces the assurance (*EWAS*, 86; Joüon, 123de).

10.b. On this phrase, cf. *Comment*.

10.c-c. Circumstantial clause with ptcp; cf. vv 1, 8.

10.d. On omission of ב with פתח, cf. n. 1.b.

10.e. SamPent reads היא "she"; so too does G (see *Comment*).

11.a. Composite subj with nouns of different gender takes *masc pl* predicate (GKC, 146d; Joüon, 148a,d).

11.b. Heb. lacks "and." Clause in apposition specifying aspect of old age, the menopause, relevant to problem (*SBH*, 47).

11.c-c. *BHS* suggests emending to כארח נשים; cf. 31:35. However, F. I. Andersen, *Bib* 50 (1969) 68–69, retains MT, holding כ helps signal the constr relationship.

12.a. Inf constr בלה + 1 sg suffix.

12.b. היתה-לי "pleasure" is the grammatical subj of the verb. Here the question is not prefaced by an interrogative pronoun or particle (GKC, 150a). The use of the pf היתה for the future is quite rare. Joüon (112j) describes it as an astonished question and suggests translating as a fut pf, "Shall I have had?" (cf. 21:7; Num 17:28[13]; Judg 9:9, 11, 13).

12.c-c. Circumstantial clause turning question into virtual negation (*SBH*, 90); cf. v 13.

13.a. Note enclitic זה suggesting surprise in the question "why"; cf. 3:13 (GKC, 136c; *EWAS*, 136).

13.b. On this nuance of אף, see *EWAS*, 141.

13.c. For this translation of אמנם, see *EWAS*, 133, 141.

13.d-d. Cf. n. 12.c-c.

13.e. Pf of stative verb זקן has present meaning (GKC, 106g).

14.a. ה interrogative + 3 masc sg impf niph פלא.

14.b. Cf. n. 10.b.

15.a. SamPent has לה "to her" for לא "not."

15.b. כי "so" according to *EWAS* (163), but GKC (163a) and Joüon (172c) translate it "but" after the negation.

16.a. Waw consec + 3 masc pl impf קום (hiph) / שׁקף.

16.b-b. Circumstantial clause marking end of paragraph (*SBH*, 82).

16.c. Inf constr piel שׁלח + 3 masc pl suffix.

17.a. Vv 17–19 are in effect a complex circumstantial clause (*SBH*, 85).

17.b. Interrogative ה + masc sg ptcp piel כסה.

17.c. Masc sg ptcp עשׂה. This ptcp and the preceding (n. 17.b.) here express imminent future (GKC, 116p).

18.a. Inf abs היה emphasizing verb (GKC, 113n).

18.b. Cf. note and *Comment* on 12:3.

19.a. 1 sg pf ידע "know" + 3 masc sg suffix. SamPent, G, Vg omit suffix.

19.b. ל + inf constr עשׂה here expands and explains observing the LORD's way (Joüon, 124o).

19.c. Inf constr hiph בוא.

20.a. כי here used as emphatic corroboration (GKC, 148d, 159ee; *EWAS*, 162).

20.b. 3 masc pl suffix "their" refers to the inhabitants of the cities. *SBH*, 118, n. 2, suggests suffix is fem dual, referring to the two cities (fem).

21.a. 1 sg coh ירד/ידע. Enclitic נא gives a sense of urgency (Joüon, 114d).

21.b-b. עשׂה כלה is an idiom: "make destruction"; cf. Jer 30:11; 46:28. God is usually the subj. *BHS* suggests repointing כָּלָה "all of it."

21.c. Note dagesh forte in כ following interrogative ה.

21.d. By stressing the penultimate syllable, MT understands הבאה to be 3 fem sg pf qal בוא. *BHS* transfers accent to final syllable, understanding it as fem sg ptcp. WOC, 339, n. 332, concurs.

21.e. 3 fem sg suffix ה "her" probably refers to "the outcry about her sin" (fem). Some MSS, G, Tg read "their."

22.a. Waw consec + 3 masc pl impf פנה.

22.b-b. Circumstantial clause marking end of paragraph. It is the first of the Tiqqune sopherim (ancient scribal corrections) according to which the original reading, "The LORD stood before Abraham," was reversed on grounds of piety. *SBH* (84–85) argues for the originality of this reading, though 19:27 may support MT.

23.a. Waw consec + 3 masc sg impf נגשׁ.

23.b. אף "can be employed in a rhetorical question which . . . often expresses something unexpected, unbelievable, or an exaggerated, extreme case. . . . The particle relates not to the word immediately following, but to the entire clause" (*EWAS*, 141).

24.a. ישׁ expresses existence (Joüon, 154k).

24.b. Cf. n. 23.b.

24.c. 2 masc sg impf נִשָּׂא.
24.d. G paraphrases: "the whole place."
24.e. N.B. מָקוֹם "place" can be fem (GKC, 122l; Joüon, 134m; *pace BHS*).
25.a. מִן + inf constr עֲשֹׂה.
25.b. לְ + inf constr hiph מוּת.
25.c. Note the use of the prep כְּ before both צַדִּיק and רָשָׁע. This usage (cf. Jos 14:11; 1 Sam 30:24) does not say simply that A is like B, or B is like A, but that A is like B and B is like A. "In other words the two terms are declared identical in one respect" (Joüon, 174i).
26.a. On the use of waw + pf in an apodosis of a conditional, see GKC, 112ff; Joüon, 176d.
27.a. Waw consec + 3 masc sg impf עֲנָה.
27.b. 1 sg pf hiph יאל.
27.c. Some MSS read "the LORD."
27.d-d. Circumstantial clause with concessive meaning (*SBH*, 90; Joüon, 171f).
28.a. 3 masc pl impf חסר + paragogic nun (GKC, 47m).
28.b. ה interrogative + 2 masc sg impf hiph שׁחת.
28.c. On use of בְּ prefix, see GKC, 119p.
28.d-d. Note here how the main clause (apodosis) precedes protasis (if clause). This unusual order indicates that the more important aspect is in the apodosis (Joüon, 167v).
29.a. Cf. n. 8:10.b.
29.b. 3 masc pl impf niph מצא + paragogic nun; cf. n. 28.a.
29.c. SamPent reads אשׁחית, assimilating to vv 28, 31, 32 (Waltke, 222); apparently followed by G, Vg.
29.d. Lit. "the forty" as in vv 31b, 33b, "the twenty, the ten." Numbers may be preceded by def art where referring to number already mentioned (GKC, 134k).
30.a. 3 masc sg juss חרה.
30.b. Waw + 1 sg coh piel דבר. On the sequence juss + coh, here with consec force "so that," see GKC, 108d; Joüon, 116b; *SBH*, 118.
32.a. Cf. Exod 10:17; Judg 6:39.
33.a-a. Episode-final circumstantial clause (*SBH*, 81).
19:1.a-a. *BHS* gratuitously emends to "the men"; cf. vv 12, 16.
1.b-b. Circumstantial clause expressing continuing action contemporary with main verb "came" (GKC, 116o, 141e; Joüon, 121f; 166h).
1.c. Cf. n. 18:2.c.
1.d. Cf. n. 18:2.d.
2.a. Note unique pointing of הִנֶּה (GKC, 100o).
2.b. Note pointing of אֲדֹנַי, indicating men, rather than God, being addressed (GKC, 135q).
2.c. Waw consec + 2 masc pl pf hiph שׁכם "do early" (Lambdin, 238–39).
2.d. Pointing in *BHS* follows L. Others offer usual pointing, וַהֲלַכְתֶּם.
2.e. Dagesh in לֹא following unaccented וּ (GKC, 20g).
2.f. Cf. n. 18:15.b.
2.g-g. Putting the adverbial phrase "in the street" before the verb emphasizes it (GKC, 142g; Joüon, 155p). "Emphasis . . . is a feature essentially belonging to lively conversation" (*EWAS*, 43).
3.a-a. Note chiasmus "bread . . . baked" with main clause "prepared . . . meal": different aspects of one action (*SBH*, 128).
4.a. טֶרֶם is followed by impf (GKC, 107c, 152r).
4.b. On the repetition of "men of," see Joüon, 131i.
4.c. מִקְצֶה "in its entirety" (BDB, 892a).
4.d. 3 masc pl pf niph סבב (cf. Joüon, 82h, on the use of niph instead of qal).
5.a. 2 masc sg impv hiph יצא + 3 masc pl suffix.
5.b. Waw + 1 pl coh ידע. For the sequence impv + simple waw + coh of intended consequence, see GKC, 108d; Lambdin, 119.
6.a. SamPent omits directional ה (Waltke, 217).
6.b-b. Circumstantial clause closing paragraph (*SBH*, 81).
6.c. SamPent reads pl "they [i.e., angels] shut."
7.a. Note the polite enclitic נָא (GKC, 105b[1]).
7.b. 2 masc pl impf hiph רעע.
8.a. 1 sg coh hiph יצא.
8.b. רַק introduces important exceptions (*EWAS*, 131).

8.c. SamPent modernizes archaic MT orthography to הָאֵלֶּה.

8.d. On this phrase, cf. n. 18:5.b-b.

9.a. 2 masc sg impv נְגֹשׁ. On pointing, see GKC, 66e.

9.b. Waw consec + 3 masc sg impf + inf abs שָׁפֹט (cf. GKC, 113r).

9.c. 1 pl impf hiph נָרַע.

9.d. Waw consec + 3 masc pl impf נִגְּשׁוּ.

10.a. Waw consec + 3 masc pl impf hiph וַיָּבֹאוּ.

11.a. 3 masc pl pf hiph נִכּוּ.

11.b. On absence of prep before פֶּתַח, cf. n. 18:1.b.

11.c. Note the def art with "blindness"; common with abstract nouns (GKC, 126n; WOC, 246).

11.d. Waw consec + 3 masc pl impf לָאוּ.

12.a. SamPent reads "angels" as in v 1.

12.b. 2 masc sg impv hiph יָצֵא.

12.c. SamPent, G, S read "this" as in vv 13, 14.

12.d. Delitzsch: "an indefinite collective singular"; cf. *JPS*. But Gunkel, Speiser, and Westermann suggest "son-in-law" is an interpolation from v 14. See *Comment*.

13.a. Masc pl hiph ptcp שׁחֵת. Ptcp is used for imminent fut (Joüon, 12e).

13.b. Waw consec + 3 masc sg impf piel שׁלח + 1 pl suffix.

13.c. ל + inf constr piel שׁחֵת + 3 fem sg suffix. Typically, SamPent has hiph for piel (Waltke, 216).

14.a. Ptcp is timeless. GKC (116d) suggests a fut sense would be apt, "were to marry," but "had married" is also possible.

14.b. Here impv קוּם has exclamatory, introductory function (GKC, 120g; *SBH*, 57).

14.c. 2 masc pl impv יְצֵא. Note dagesh in צ following unaccented וֹ; cf. 19:2 (GKC, 20g).

15.a. A poetic term (cf. BDB, 455b–56a).

15.b. *BHS* again conjectures "men"; cf. n. 19:1.a-a.

15.c. Waw consec + 3 masc pl hiph אוּץ.

15.d. Cf. n. 19:14.b.

15.e. ה def art + fem pl niph ptcp מֻצָּא. G inserts "and go out."

15.f. 2 masc sg impf niph סָפֹה.

16.a. Waw consec + 3 masc sg impf hithpalpel מהה.

16.b. Waw consec + 3 masc pl impf hiph חזק.

16.c. ב ("because," Joüon, 170j) + inf constr חמל.

16.d. Waw consec + 3 masc pl impf hiph נוח/יצא.

17.a. וַיְהִי marks major new development (GKC, 111g).

17.b. כ (cf. n. 18:1.c.; Joüon, 166m) + inf constr hiph יצא + masc pl suffix.

17.c. G, Vg, S have pl "they."

17.d. 2 masc sg impv niph מלט.

17.e. 2 masc sg impf hiph נבט.

18.a. *BHS* proposes "to him." Unnecessary.

18.b. *BHS* proposes sg suffix, i.e., "my lord, sir." But cf. *Comment* and n. 18:3.a.

19.a. On this meaning of הִנֵּה־נָא, cf. WOC, 579.

19.b. Waw consec + 2 masc sg impf hiph גדל.

19.c. ל + inf constr hiph חיה; cf. 6:19, 20.

19.d. ל + inf constr niph מלט.

19.e. 2 fem sg impf דבק + 1 sg suffix (cf. GKC, 60d).

19.f. Waw consec + 1 sg pf qal מות.

20.a. 1 sg coh niph מלט.

20.b. 3 fem sg juss חיה. On the sequence coh + juss, cf. GKC, 109f.

21.a. Inf constr הפך + 1 sg suffix.

22.a. 2 masc sg impv piel מהר.

22.b. 1 sg impf יכל.

23.a-a, c-c. Circumstantial clauses to 24.a-a. (*SBH*, 87), suggesting three events in rapid succession (GKC, 164b; Joüon, 166c).

23.b. Sebir and some SamPent MSS have 3 fem sg יצאה, making שֶׁמֶשׁ "sun" fem. Can be either gender (BDB, 1039).

24.a-a. On syntax, see n. 23.a-a. No textual evidence for transposing it after v 26 as *BHS* suggests.

24.b-b. No textual evidence for supposing it a gloss, *pace BHS*.

25.a. Cf. n. 19:8.c.

26.a. Waw consec + 3 fem sg impf hiph נבט.

26.b. *BHS* suggests reading "behind her." MT "him" refers to Lot.

26.c. Waw consec + 3 fem sg impf (apoc) היה.

27.a. Waw consec + 3 masc sg impf hiph שכם "do early." Usually followed by another verb; hence *BHS* suggests inserting "and he went." Probably unnecessary (Gispen, 2:189).

28.a. Waw consec + 3 masc sg impf hiph שקף.

28.b. G omits "whole." For other possible emendations, see *BHS*.

28.c. והנה "and behold" : the scene described from Abraham's perspective (*SBH*, 95).

28.d. Def art is used especially frequently in comparisons (GKC, 126o; Joüon, 137i).

29.a. ב + inf constr piel שחת. SamPent has hiph; cf. n. 13.c.

30.a. Cf. n. 13:6.b.

30.b. Note use of def art in Heb. = "the cave" in this story (GKC, 126r).

30.c. SamPent, G add "with him," assimilating to v 30a.

31.a. בכירה lit. "firstborn." Heb. uses the simple adjective for the comparative and superlative, old, older, oldest.

31.b. Cf. n. 31.a.

31.c. When the subj, "man," precedes אין "is not," it is emphasized (*EWAS*, 104).

31.d. בוא is more usually followed by אל rather than על, but cf. Deut 25:5.

32.a. 2 masc sg impv הלך. Here little more than an interjection; hence lack of concord remedied by SamPent לכי (2 fem sg). MT to be followed (GKC, 69x; *SBH*, 57).

32.b. 1 pl impf (coh) hiph שקה followed by waw + coh (שכב and חיה piel) "in order that" (Lambdin, 119).

33.a. Waw consec + 2 fem pl impf hiph שקה.

33.b. Absence of def art on הוא (cf. SamPent) is for euphony (GKC, 126y) or result of haplography (Joüon, 138h) or double-duty ה on לילה (I. O. Lehmann, *JNES* 26 [1967] 93–101).

33.c. ב + inf constr קום/שכב + 3 fem sg suffix.

33.d. Dot (extraordinary point) over ו perhaps indicates its superfluity.

34.a. G has "with the father."

34.b. 1 pl impf (coh) hiph שקה + 3 masc sg suffix.

34.c. Lit. "the night." Def art often functions as demonstrative = "this night, tonight" with temporal nouns (GKC, 126b).

35.a. Waw consec + 3 fem sg impf קום.

36.a. Waw consec + 3 fem pl impf הרה.

37.a. Cf. n. 4:1.c.

37.b. G adds "from my father," explaining etymology of Moab.

38.a. G inserts Amman and translates Ben-Ammi "son of my race."

Form/Structure/Setting

Chaps. 18–19 constitute a clear unit within Genesis and fall into four main sections:

18:1–15	Isaac's birth announced to Abraham and Sarah
18:16–33	Abraham pleads for Sodom
19:1–29	Lot and his family escape from Sodom
19:30–38	Lot's daughters commit incest with their father

The unity of these stories is shown by the same actors appearing in most of the scenes, most obviously the angels in 18:1–19:23, Lot throughout chap. 19 and by implication in 18:20–32, and Abraham throughout chap. 18 and in 19:29. Furthermore, the storyline in 19:1–22 closely parallels that in 18:1–30 (see further below), encouraging a comparison to be made between the righteous heroes of these chapters, Abraham and Lot.

But the author does not simply compare Lot with Abraham; he is also interested in comparing the destruction of Sodom with the flood. Clearly the theme

is the same: the mass destruction of the world (cities of the plain) and the escape of one righteous man and his family. There are many verbal echoes of the flood story (e.g., "God remembered Abraham," 19:29; cf. 8:1; see further below), and the overall structures of the narratives are similar: in both cases the story of the hero's escape and the destruction of the wicked, told in a carefully worked out palistrophe (6:9–9:17//18:16–19:28), is followed by his intoxication and shameful treatment by his children (9:20–27//19:30–38).

Although these two chapters invite comparison with the story of Noah, they are perfectly at home in the Abraham cycle, presupposing knowledge of what goes before at many points, e.g., Abraham's relationship with Lot, his move to Sodom, Sarah's barrenness, and the promises to Abraham (12:1–3). Particularly striking is the relationship of chaps. 18–19 to chap. 17. The change of names from Abram to Abraham and Sarai to Sarah described in chap. 17 is presupposed in chap. 18. Both begin with the LORD appearing (17:1; 18:1); in quoting the promise of a child, 18:14 echoes 17:21; and both are cast in palistrophes combined with parallel panels (see below).

We must now turn to a more detailed analysis of chaps. 18–19.

The account of the destruction of Sodom and Gomorrah (18:16–19:29) is closely integrated: the action spans less than twenty-four hours and falls into eleven scenes. It is preceded by a reaffirmation of the promise of Isaac (18:1–15) and followed by an account of the birth of Lot's sons, Moab and Ben-Ammi (19:30–38). Analyzing the account of the destruction of Sodom as a series of scenes, like the flood story (cf. Wenham, *Genesis 1–15,* 157), produces the following:

1. Abraham's visitors look toward Sodom (18:16)	(N) Mamre
2. Divine reflections on Abraham and Sodom (18:17–21)	(M) Overlooking Sodom
3. Abraham pleads for Sodom (18:22–33)	(D) Overlooking Sodom
4. Angels arrive in Sodom (19:1–3)	(N/D) Sodom city gates
5. Assault on Lot and his visitors (19:4–11)	(N/D) Outside Lot's house
6. Destruction of Sodom announced (19:12–13)	(M) Inside Lot's house
7. Lot's sons-in-law reject his appeal (19:14)	(N/D) Outside Lot's house
8. Departure from Sodom (19:15–16)	(N/D) Through city gate
9. Lot pleads for Zoar (19:17–22)	(D) Outside Sodom
10. Sodom and Gomorrah destroyed (19:23–26)	(N)
11. Abraham looks toward Sodom (19:27–28)	(N) Mamre
Summary (19:29)	

As frequently in the OT (cf. Gen 2–3, 6–9, 17), the scenes are arranged palistrophically so that the second half of the story is a mirror image of the first. Thus scene 1 closely parallels scene 11; both are narrative (N) descriptions of people leaving Abraham's tent to look (הֵשׁקִיף) toward Sodom. Scene 2 is a divine monologue (M) reflecting on Abraham's character and the alleged character of Sodom and Gomorrah, which it is hinted may merit destruction. Scene 10 is a narrative (N) describing their destruction. Scene 3 is dialogue (D) in which Abraham pleads with the LORD to save "the city" (presumably Sodom), if sufficient righteous people are found in it. Scene 9 is a similar dialogue, in which Lot pleads for Zoar to be spared. Though Lot's intercession is much briefer than Abraham's, there are echoes of the former dialogue in his plea. Abraham said, "Far be it from your doing something like this to put to death the righteous"

(18:25). Lot argues that if he is not allowed to flee to Zoar, "I shall die" (19:19). The LORD promises to spare (נשׂא) the place if some righteous are found in it (18:26). He uses the same verb when telling Lot "I have granted your request" (19:21). In both scenes, the rather colorless verb "do" (עשׂה) is used to describe the destruction (18:17, 25, 29, 30; 19:22).

Scenes 4 and 8 resemble each other in subject matter and form. They both contain a mixture of narrative and dialogue. Scene 4 describes the angels' arrival in Sodom, scene 8 their departure. These are the only scenes in the narrative where they are called angels (מלאך). It is striking that in both scenes there is a great reluctance to follow advice: in scene 4 Lot has to force the angels to stay, "he pressed them very hard" (v 3; cf. same verb "manhandled," v 9), and in scene 8 they have to compel him to leave, "the men grabbed him by the hand" (v 16).

Scenes 5 and 7 are again mixtures of narrative and dialogue, both describing the Sodomites' rejection of the angels and their message. In both, "Lot goes out" (ויצא לוט, only in vv 6, 14) to appeal to them, and in both cases he is rudely rebuffed (cf. v 9 with v 14).

Scene 6 is the central scene in the story, a monologue in which the angels for the first time explicitly declare the cities' fate and advise Lot to prepare to leave, "we are about to ruin this city." As often in narratives cast in palistrophic form (cf. God remembered Noah, 8:1; cf. 3:6), the central scene marks the turning point in the story. Up to this point, Sodom's fate has been hinted at; now it becomes certain, and the narrative unwinds with them leaving the city.

It should also be noted how the scene of the action also moves palistrophically from Mamre (scenes 1–3), to Sodom's city gate (scene 4), to outside Lot's house (scene 5), inside his house in the central scene (scene 6), and then back again outside Lot's house (scene 7), through the city gate (scene 8), outside the city (scene 9), and finally back to Mamre (scene 11). This movement parallels that found in the garden of Eden story, where the action moves from outside the garden to its center before the tree of knowledge and then exactly reverses itself. Similarly, the flood story tells of Noah entering the ark and then coming out.

Finally, the palistrophe that governs the story of Sodom is further enhanced by the outer panels. The narrative begins with the promise of Isaac's birth (18:1–15) and closes with the account of the birth of Lot's sons (19:30–38), thus enhancing the concentric organization of these two chapters.

Similarities between the account of Sodom's destruction and the flood story have often been noted. Both stories are tales of universal destruction brought about by human wickedness, a destruction from which one righteous man and his family are saved by divine grace. Both stories are followed by the hero's intoxication with wine and the disgraceful actions of his children. And as already pointed out, the main story in each case is organized as an elaborate palistrophe.

But besides these thematic parallels, there are many verbal similarities between the accounts. It begins with Abraham "going [הלך qal] with them" (18:16), which evokes 6:9, "Noah walked [הלך hithpael] with God." Like righteous Noah (6:9; 7:1), Abraham teaches his family to do righteousness (18:19), and he bases his whole argument for the sparing of Sodom on the presence of "righteous" in the city (18:23–32). Though Lot is never described as righteous, the fact that he is brought out suggests that he is regarded as relatively righteous at least.

The divine self-reflection in 18:17–21 is akin to that in 6:5–8, the depravity of man in general and the righteousness of one man in particular constituting their common theme. In both stories "ruin" (שחת) is one of the key verbs to describe the destruction (6:13, 17; 9:11, 15; 18:28, 31, 32; 19:13, 14, 29). The angels' action in putting out their hand and bringing Lot into the house resembles Noah's similar action when he put out his hand and brought the dove into the safety of the ark (19:10; 8:9). And maybe their shutting of the door recalls the LORD's shutting Noah in (19:10; 7:16). As in the flood, where God first warns Noah of the need to build and enter the ark before commanding him to enter (6:13–21; 7:1–4), so here the angels warn Lot in the evening (19:12–13) and then make him leave next morning (19:15–16). The list of escapers, Lot, his wife, and his two daughters, recalls that of Noah, his wife, his sons, and their wives. In pleading with angels to allow him to enter Zoar, Lot speaks of "finding favor in their eyes" (19:19), admittedly a common idiom but used in a special sense of Noah in 6:8 so that his life will "be saved" (hiph of חיה), one of the key verbs in the flood story (6:19,20), and later used by his daughters is the expression "to produce descendants" (piel + זרע; 7:3; 19:32, 34). In both accounts the LORD makes it rain (hiph מטר; 7:4; 19:24). Finally, and most clearly, "God remembered Abraham" exactly recalls "God remembered Noah" (19:29; 8:1).

By themselves, some of the resemblances between the two stories might be coincidental, but their number suggests that the parallels between the flood and the destruction of Sodom and Gomorrah are being deliberately exploited by the author of Genesis. And this observation must inform both the interpretation of the narrative and discussion of its unity. It is striking, too, that these allusions to the flood story are drawn from parts conventionally ascribed to P as well as to J, which requires a reassessment of the normal source-critical analysis of the flood story (cf. Wenham, *VT* 41 [1991] 84–109).

Although the narrative in 18:16–19:29 could stand as a literary unit, it does need an introduction to explain why the LORD is speaking to Abraham and where the angels in Sodom have come from. 18:1–15 supplies the necessary background information. But this is not to say it is a tradition independent of what follows; the references to the time of day in 18:1 and 19:1 show it is an integral part of the narrative. Furthermore, as noted by Van Seters, Rudin-O'Brasky, and Alexander, there are many parallels between the two chapters, as the following table shows:

Chapter 18	Chapter 19
"he was sitting in the doorway" (v 1)	"Lot was sitting in the gateway" (v 1)
"seeing them he ran toward them" (v 2)	"Seeing them Lot stood to greet them" (v 1)
"and bowed himself to the ground"	"then bowed to the ground" (v 1)
"He said, 'Sir'	"He said '. . . Sirs' (v 2)
'please do not leave your servant' (v 3)	'please come to your servant's house'
'wash your feet and rest' (v 4)	'stay, wash your feet'
'afterwards you can go on' (v 5)	'tomorrow, go on your way' (v 2)
'for this is why you have come'" (v 5)	'for they have come under my roof for this reason'" (v 8)
"he took yogurt . . . " etc.	"he prepared a feast"
"they ate" (v 8)	"they ate" (v 3)
"Where is your wife" (v 9)	"Where are the men" (v 5)

"Sarah laughed" (צחק qal) (vv 12, 13, 15)	"His sons-in-law thought he was joking" (צחק piel) (v 14)
"The outcry of Sodom is great" (רבה) (vv 20–21)	"their outcry is great" (גדלה) (v 13)
Abraham's plea for Sodom (vv 23–32)	Lot's plea for Zoar (vv 18–22)
"sweep away" (vv 23, 24)	"sweep away"(v 17)
"put to death" (v 25)	"die" (v 19)
"spare [נשא] the whole place" (v 26)	"granted [נשא] your request" (v 21)
"do" = "destroy" (v 25, 29, 30)	"do" = "destroy" (v 22)

The parallels are clearest in the two hospitality scenes (18:1–8; 19:1–3) and in the pleas for the two cities (18:23–32; 19:18–22). But even in the two texts between these two sections there are some interesting similarities. In other words, Gen 18 and 19:1–22 are told in two parallel panels (for this terminology, see McEvenue, *The Narrative Style of the Priestly Writer*). McEvenue drew attention to the use of this technique combined with a broad palistrophe in chap. 17 (see *Form/Structure/Setting* on 17:1–27). It is striking that the same combination of techniques, palistrophe + parallel panel-writing, is found in the successive chapters, although according to traditional source analysis, chap. 17 is nearly pure P, whereas chaps. 18–19 are almost pure J.

More precisely, all of 18:1–19:38 except 19:29 (P) is conventionally ascribed to J. However, doubts have sometimes been expressed about the unity of the material in J (e.g., Kilian; Haag; cf. Rudin-O'Brasky) on the grounds of the variation in the number and identity of the visitors in the story. Sometimes they are described as men, sometimes as angels, and one of them is identified as the LORD. Sometimes the visitors speak and are addressed in the singular, at others in the plural. So attempts have been made to isolate coherent stylistic units within these chapters. But since these units do not make good sense on their own, these attempts are widely rejected by mainstream commentators.

More widely accepted (e.g., Gunkel, Skinner, von Rad, Westermann, Blenkinsopp) is the suggestion (originally Wellhausen's) that Abraham's intercession is a later addition to the story. It is often alleged that the concept of individual responsibility is the invention of prophets like Jeremiah and Ezekiel in the late seventh and early sixth centuries and that since Gen 18:23–32 reflects these ideas, it must come from this period or later (e.g., Westermann, Haag; cf. Van Seters, Kilian). However, it is far from certain that this idea originated with the later prophets: it is found in second-millennium Mesopotamian literature (e.g., GE 11.180) and is an assumption of the wisdom books of the OT. So it seems wiser to see this section as integral to the whole plot of these chapters and the work of J (so Van Seters, Coats), not a later interpolator. The integrity of this section within the narrative is confirmed by our analysis above, which shows Abraham's intercession to be a vital part of both the palistrophe and the parallel panels that are used to organize this story. Indeed, the way in which Abraham is allowed into the secrets of the divine purposes and then intercedes for Sodom shows that he is a prophet, a point made explicitly in 20:7 and implicitly in chap. 15.

That the present narrative is based on earlier tradition is clear, but attempts to reconstruct earlier forms of the tradition are quite speculative (cf. Van Seters, *Abraham*, 210). It may be that chaps. 18–19 originally formed part of an indepen-

dent Lot cycle and that 18:1 once followed 13:18, which also refers back to the oaks of Mamre. On the other hand, "The LORD appeared to him" (18:1) invites comparison with 17:1: "The LORD appeared to Abram." Clearly both verses are redactional, but it is impossible to know how they differ, if at all, from the wording of the original sources.

At the other end of the narrative, 19:29 causes problems. In its present setting, it serves as a summary of the preceding narratives (cf. 16:16; 17:26–27). It is usually assigned to P on the grounds that only here is God, as opposed to the LORD, mentioned in Gen 18–19. As already noted, this usage serves to make the parallel between the destruction of Sodom and the flood unmistakable (cf. 8:1). On this occasion God remembered Abraham, just as earlier he had remembered Noah (8:1). This parallel would seem sufficient explanation of the usage here, since all the other terms in this verse seem to be drawn from the preceding narrative. Another pointer to the antiquity of this verse, whether it be P or editorial, is its summary in Amos 4:11 and Isa 13:19. As Westermann (2:298) points out, this is the only place in Amos where אלהים is used. Because he believes that P is late, he postulates that Amos is quoting a tradition independent of Genesis, but this seems special pleading; it is easier to suppose Amos knew Gen 18–19 in something like its present form.

Comment

1–15 Abraham's hospitable welcome of three visitors forms a charming introduction to the great and serious matter of Sodom. Its two scenes, vv 1–8, the welcome meal, and vv 9–15, the guests' promise, depict an idyllic picture of the ancient Orient. Abraham's exceedingly warm hospitality is rewarded by the reaffirmation of the imminent birth of a son to Sarah.

1–5 These verses describe the arrival of the visitors and Abraham's warm welcome of them.

1 "The LORD appeared to him at the oaks of Mamre" is clearly an editorial comment like 17:1. We have already noted the lack of an explicit naming of Abraham here, which shows it is part of a sequence of narratives.

"The LORD appeared" reflects the narrator's standpoint: the identity of his visitors was not immediately apparent to Abraham. As v 2 makes clear, he at first thought they were simply men. His warm welcome and alacrity in serving them was in no way prompted by his recognizing them. Rather, this comment, "the LORD appeared," functions like 22:1, "God tested Abraham," to make the reader aware from the start of the story of the real nature of the encounter so that we can interpret the narrative more accurately. What we know from the start about the identity of the visitors Abraham only gradually discovers in the course of conversation.

The circumstantial clause "as he was sitting . . . in the midday heat" is the real start of the story. Abraham has finished his morning work and is just preparing for his siesta, which he would take during the hottest part of the day.

2 "He looked up." The pair of verbs "look up and see" indicates that what he sees will prove very significant (cf. 22:4; 24:63). "Noticed three men standing by him." The storyline suddenly switches to describing events through Abraham's

eyes. Where had these men come from? The narrator does not tell us, for Abraham did not know. Perhaps he had dozed off, and that is why he did not notice them coming. Or is this the first hint that the men are not quite what they seem to be? Visitors from the supernatural world suddenly appear and then disappear again in OT narratives describing encounters with them (Judg 6:11–21). There is a gap in the narrative opened by these two possibilities: was Abraham dozing, or are the visitors supernatural? Presumably Abraham works on the former assumption, and this partly explains his eagerness to make amends for not noticing them before. "Seeing them, he ran . . . toward them and bowed himself to the ground." These gestures express both the warmth of Abraham's welcome and his deep respect for his visitors. Elsewhere in Genesis people run to greet long-lost relatives (29:13; 33:4), and they bow down to the high and mighty (23:12; 37:9; 42:6). But unwittingly Abraham is also treating the representatives of the deity in a fitting way, for bowing down (חוה) is also the word translated "worship" when its object is God (24:26; Exod 20:5).

3 His greeting is eloquent, indeed quite long-winded by biblical standards (cf. 19:2) and very deferential. "Sir, if indeed you have favored me" is a conventional, polite opening to an important request (cf. 33:10; 47:29; 50:4), suggesting that Abraham is laying on the charm in his attempt to make them stay, "please do not leave." But again the phraseology suggests Abraham's words are truer than he realizes. "Sir," lit. "my lord," is vocalized in the MT in the way appropriate in addressing God, which in 15:2, 8 was translated "sovereign." And hitherto the only other use of the phrase "to favor," "to find grace" is of Noah, "who found grace in the eyes of the LORD." This unwitting *double entendre* in Abraham's speech is enhanced by his use of the singular in this verse as opposed to the plural in vv 4–5. Evidently, in pressing them to stay, Abraham is addressing the leader of the group, whereas his subsequent remarks are addressed to all three. Yet given the identity of the leader, which the reader knows but Abraham does not, his use of the singular "*thou* hast favored . . . *thy* servant" has an added significance.

4 After his generous welcome, Abraham offers what hot and weary travelers would most appreciate, a drink of water, a wash of their feet (Luke 7:44), and a rest under a shady tree.

5 His offer of "a bit of food" (פת לחם), lit. a "morsel of bread," presumably something like a flat Arab pita roll, sounds quite modest, even mean. But it shows his anxiety to persuade his visitors to stay. Had he disclosed what a feast he was going to put on, they might have felt they were imposing on him and declined his invitation. So he only mentions part of what he will provide. Such understatement is characteristic of generous people in Scripture.

His final plea, "For this is why you have come, for your servant's benefit," stresses Abraham's pleasure at being able to entertain. It is as if he said "It is my pleasure you have come, you have made my day." Yet like some of his earlier remarks in v 3, these too are unwittingly prophetic, for, as the story will soon disclose, it is for Abraham's benefit that the LORD has come.

And Abraham's charm works, for they agree to stay.

6–8 Then suddenly Abraham changes gear. Despite the midday heat, he hurries to Sarah, tells her to hurry, and runs to the lad, who in turn hurries. The feeling of hurry also comes through in the syntax. His commands to Sarah are snapped out

in four clauses: one, "three seahs of fine flour," lacks a verb, and there is only a single "and" linking the clauses. The chiasmus between vv 5 and 6 (see *Notes*) suggests Abraham hurrying to the tent and running to the cattle almost simultaneously.

6 His "bit of food" turns out to be a feast. If a seah is about two gallons (eight liters) (de Vaux, *Ancient Israel*, 202), "three seahs of best wheat flour" would make a great quantity of bread, while to kill "a bull" for just three visitors shows royal generosity: a lamb or a goat would have been more than adequate (cf. 2 Sam 12:4; Luke 15:27–30).

8 The energetic preparations over, the meal is at last served. As is still customary among the bedouin, yogurt or lebben is served with the bread and the meat. Abraham, as the good host, waits discreetly in the background, allowing his guests to enjoy their lavish banquet.

As far as Abraham was concerned, his warm-hearted hospitality was just the proper way to entertain visitors. But is the reader, who knows who they are (v 1), also meant to reflect on how appropriate these offerings are? Elsewhere in the Pentateuch "best wheat flour" (on this rendering, see R. Rendtorff, *Leviticus* [Neukirchen: Neukirchener, 1970] 91–95) is only used in cereal offerings and for making the bread of the presence (Lev 24:5), and the regulations about the sacrifice constantly insist on the necessity of offering only top-quality animals (cf. Abraham's "fine tender bull"). The narrative may be hinting that he is behaving more wisely than he realized.

9–15 Now at last the meal is over; conversation begins, and the purpose of the visit and the identity of the visitors become plain. This scene actually concerns the LORD and Sarah, but as a married woman she apparently stays inside the tent out of sight of the visitors, while the LORD addresses her by talking to Abraham. This change of focus makes this account of the promise of the birth of Isaac rather different from that in 17:15–21. There the promise was made directly to Abraham, apparently unbeknown to Sarah; here the promise is made to her. There Abraham expressed his astonished unbelief by falling down and laughing. Here Sarah simply laughs to herself inside the tent, and Abraham apparently accepts the promise without demurral. In 17:19 the child is named Isaac, "he laughed," as a reminder of his father's doubts; here, although the same verb is mentioned four times, nothing is made of it. Clearly the narrative assumes the etymology of Isaac in the previous chapter and sees no need to repeat it here.

9 "Where is your wife Sarah?" sounds like a straightforward question; certainly Abraham replies directly, "there in the tent." But surely they ought to have realized from the preparation of the meal where she was, so why ask? And if they did not know where she was, how did they know her name? Gunkel and Rudin-O'Brasky (*The Patriarchs*) are right to see this question as the first hint to Abraham that his visitors are no ordinary men: they know the name of a woman they have never met. Like 3:9, "Where are you?" and 4:9, "Where is Abel your brother?" it is not a real question, for the questioner knows the answer. In this case, it rather shows something about the questioner and indicates the real recipient of the message about to be given.

10 "Next year" (כעת חיה) is problematic, occurring only here, v 14, and 2 Kgs 4:16, 17 in a similar context. But the translation "next year" is made probable by

the analogous Akkadian phrase *ana balaṭ* (see *AHW,* 99a; *CAD,* 51–52; see also R. Yaron, *VT* 12 [1962] 500–501; O. Loretz, *Bib* 43 [1962] 75–78, as well as 17:21).

"I shall certainly come back to you" suggests another visit is planned, but the verb is used elsewhere of God's gracious intervention, e.g., Zech 1:3; Ps 80:15(14), and this must be its sense here, as "Sarah your wife is going to have a son" makes plain. Compared with the threefold announcement of the birth in 17:16, 19, 21, this time it is much shorter and briefer. The promise is for Sarah alone here, and the phrasing (והנה) makes its fulfillment sound even closer. It could be rendered "Your wife Sarah now has a son," yet on this occasion we hear of no doubts expressed by Abraham. The attention is now focused on Sarah, full of curiosity, "listening at the door of the tent." Not only is the tent door between her and the messenger, the latter has his back to the tent. SamPent and G "she was behind him" may suggest that she was out in the doorway but he was not facing her. Whichever the correct reading, the important point for the narrative is that the mysterious speaker cannot see her reaction to the news. The promise of a son implies that the speaker is a divine messenger; the fact that he can discern Sarah's reactions without seeing her proves his status and guarantees his message.

11   17:17 has already said that Sarah is ninety, so it seems superfluous to tell us again that she is "old." This repetition is easily explained if chap. 17 comes from a tradition different from that of chap. 18. But in the context of Genesis, ninety is no great age (cf. Noah, who became a father at 500 [5:32]), and 12:11 has said she is very attractive, a point assumed in chap. 20 also. Thus the new piece of information given here, "Sarah was past the menopause," may not have seemed so self-evident to the original readers as it does to us. It certainly underlines the magnitude of the miracle of Isaac's birth: it was not simply that Sarah had long been infertile but that she was well past the menopause too. Conception, let alone birth, was impossible.

12   Knowing these personal details about Sarah, we tend to excuse her laughter, and this is no doubt the writer's intention: he wants to explain why someone who laughed at God's promise suffered so mild a rebuke. It was something very hard to believe. Abraham had apparently laughed aloud but kept his doubts to himself or at least only expressed them indirectly (17:17–18). Sarah keeps all her emotions hidden. "So Sarah laughed to herself thinking, 'After I am worn out, shall I have pleasure?'"

When the narrator spoke of Sarah being past the menopause, he was quite matter-of-fact about her situation. Sarah describes herself as "worn out," a decrepit old woman. She could certainly not expect to enjoy the pleasures of younger women in being a mother or perhaps even of sexual intercourse with her husband, for he too is quite old.

These remarks of Sarah's show us the basis of her doubts. She laughed not out of cocky arrogance but because a life of long disappointment had taught her not to clutch at straws. Hopelessness, not pride, underlay her unbelief. Her self-restraint in not openly expressing her doubts and the sadness behind them go far to explain the gentleness of the divine rebuke.

13   The Lord continues to speak to Abraham, but really to Sarah. If Sarah was astonished at the promise of a child, the Lord professes astonishment that she should not have believed him. The phraseology of the Hebrew (see *Notes* and

Translation) expresses the divine surprise. The way he phrases Sarah's doubts is instructive. The narrator was direct—"past the menopause"; Sarah was pathetic and blamed her husband, "I am worn out and my husband is old," but the LORD is kindly. He does not describe Sarah as "worn out" or her husband as too old; rather, he simply says that Sarah said, "Shall I even I really give birth as I am old?" But what is most significant is that he knows that Sarah had laughed and what she thought even though he had his back to her and she was inside the tent. This proves who he is and is the foundation for his next remark.

14 "Is anything too difficult for the LORD?" is a rhetorical question that demands the answer no. God, this passage teaches, is both omniscient and omnipotent. As Sternberg points out, these beliefs inform the whole of biblical narrative, but rarely are they quite so explicit as here.

"Too difficult" (niphal of פלא) is used elsewhere of lawsuits too difficult for lower judges to handle (Deut 17:8), of the impossibility of Amnon marrying Tamar (2 Sam 13:2), and of the unimaginable future peace of Jerusalem (Zech 8:6). But Jer 32:17 and 27 offer the closest parallels to Gen 18:14. In both, God's almighty power is explicitly affirmed.

"At the set time next year I shall come back to you, and Sarah will have a son." The original assurance of v 10 is repeated. But note the addition of "at the set time" from 17:21, thereby reaffirming both that promise to Abraham and the one just made to Sarah.

15 Sarah's denial is surprising, and the narrator therefore explains that "she was frightened" by the nature of the messenger and by the substance of his message. But if she now recognized that she was dealing with a divine messenger, why try to deny what he knew? Does this reflect an inadequate theology? The gods of the ancient Orient were not all credited with omniscience. Or is she just telling a half-truth, "She had laughed to herself" (lit. "inside herself," v 12), so to say "I did not laugh" was inexact but not absolutely false. Whatever the thinking, her denial allowed her to pronounce, albeit in jumbled form, the name of her future son (*ṣāḥaqtî* "I laughed"; *yiṣḥāq* "Isaac"). In this way, Sarah unwittingly confirms the divine promise and provides a simple reiteration. "Not so, you did laugh" (*ṣāḥaqt*) clinches the discussion. There is no room for doubt. Sarah will have a son, and he will be called Isaac.

18:16–19:29 These verses focus on the destruction of Sodom. As explained in *Form/Structure/Setting*, this section falls into eleven scenes arranged concentrically around the angelic announcement of Sodom's fate in 19:12–13.

18:16 The first scene, like the final scene 19:27–28, tells of Abraham leaving his encampment to "look out" from the hills near Hebron "over" the Dead Sea plain to the city of "Sodom." But "the men looked out over Sodom" is the first hint that they are interested in the city. The discussion after the meal had been about Sarah's future pregnancy, and Abraham accompanied them on their way as a parting act of respect with apparently no inkling of their plans. But their look toward Sodom has already alerted the reader to what is afoot.

17–21 The second scene consists of a divine soliloquy. It begins by describing God's thought about Abraham, thereby making the reader wiser than Abraham at this point, and continues with a statement of God's worry about Sodom and Gomorrah. In subject and style, these divine reflections resemble those

that precede the flood (cf. 6:5–13), and this gives an ominous feel to the whole
scene, although nothing explicit is said about the fate of Sodom.

17 It is characteristic of the true prophet that he is privy to the divine secrets (cf. Amos 3:7). When the LORD asks here "Shall I hide from Abraham what
I am about to do?" the question seems to be directed at the two "men" accompanying the LORD, who are presumably members of the divine council (Jer 23:18).
The point of the question is whether Abraham is going to enjoy the privilege of
access to the divine committee's deliberations that prophets enjoy.

18 This verse gives the reason for such a privilege: the promise made to
Abraham. "For Abraham is indeed to become a great and powerful nation, and
all the nations of the earth will find blessing in him" is a slightly modified version
of 12:2–3. The addition of the adjective "powerful" (cf. Num 14:12; Deut 9:14;
26:5) and the substitution of "nations" for "families" and "clans" seem to enhance
the original promise.

19 "I have chosen [lit. 'known'] him." For the use of ידע "to know" in the
sense to "choose, elect," cf. Amos 3:2; Exod 33:12, 17; Deut 34:10; 2 Sam 7:20. If
the ground of election was God's promise (v 18), its fuller purpose is now stated
for the first time: to create a God-fearing community (v 19). In 17:11 the future
obligation placed on Abraham's descendants appeared to be limited to the duty
of circumcision. But here he is told to command his sons to do righteousness.
The obligation of instructing children is constantly reiterated in the law (Exod
12:25–27; Deut 6:1–3, 6–7, 20–25) and in the wisdom literature (Prov 1:7; 13:1).
In Job 23:11, observing the LORD's way is equated with observing his commands:
here and in Ps 18:22(21), it is identified with doing "righteousness." On this term,
see *Comment* on 6:9b. The terms "righteousness and equity," frequently paired in
the psalms, appear so often in Ezek 18 (vv 5, 19, 21, 27) that they are probably
making allusion to this passage in Genesis. Both passages are dealing with the
question of how far divine judgment operates on individuals and in groups. "So
that the LORD may bring on Abraham what he has spoken about." This clause
makes the fulfillment of the promise contingent on Abraham's obedience, similarly in 22:15–18; 26:5. This pattern of promise-obedience-fulfillment of promise
is ubiquitous in Scripture, so for Gunkel and Westermann to claim that the earliest form of the promise was unconditional seems rash. It is integral to OT covenant
theology (e.g., Exod 19:4–5).

20–21 "The LORD said" suggests that the following words were spoken aloud
so that Abraham heard them. He notes the cities' reputation; "outcry" refers to
the protests of those offended (cf. Prov 21:13). Like the blood of Abel, unpunished sin cries out to heaven for vengeance (cf. 4:10). That the LORD describes
the outcry as great and the sin as very serious is ominous, especially in the light
of the similar phraseology in 6:5, which presaged the flood. "I want to go down"
(coh of ירד) sounds like the "let us go down" (11:7) that preceded God's judgment at Babel. It is not that God needs to go down to confirm what he knows,
but that he is visiting it with a view to judgment. It sounds like a foregone conclusion ("deserve destruction"), but the final "if not" gives a chink of hope,
and on this slender hope Abraham bases his plea. "It is God himself, who wants
intercession made, and Abraham must be the intercessor" (Jacob, 448–49).

22–33 These verses constitute the third scene, in which Abraham intercedes for Sodom. It matches the ninth scene in this sequence (19:17–22), in which Lot pleads for Zoar. Both scenes are dialogues set outside the city of Sodom. Here Abraham puts in a sixfold plea for the city, each time accepted by the LORD. Each time he asks, "Suppose there are x righteous"; every time God accedes to his plea.

Plea	Reply
"Would you sweep away and not spare . . . ? (23–25)	If I find . . . I shall spare" (26)
"Since I have undertaken . . . would you ruin?" (27–28)	"I shall not ruin . . . if I find" (28)
"(Suppose there are forty?)"	"I shall not do it . . . for the sake of" (29)
"Do not be angry my sovereign . . ."	"I shall not do it . . . if I find" (30)
"Since I have undertaken . . ."	"I shall not ruin it . . . for the sake of" (31)
"Do not be angry, my sovereign"	"I shall not ruin it . . . for the sake of" (32)

Threefold repetition is commonplace in biblical narrative; the doubling of the pattern here is significant and gives Abraham's intercession solemnity and weight. Note, too, the elegant repetition and variation in the pleas and replies: "spare"—"spare" (vv 24, 26); "ruin"—"ruin" (v 28); "I have undertaken" (vv 27, 31); "Do not be angry" (vv 30, 32); "If I find . . . " (vv 26, 28, 30); "I shall not ruin" (vv 28, 31, 32); "for the sake of" (vv 29, 31, 32). Based on these patterns, it would seem that there is a progression in both the pleas and the replies. Abraham starts off with a confident appeal in vv 23–25 and ends with a hesitant "Do not be angry, my sovereign." On the other hand, while the LORD in every case accepts his plea, the tone of his acceptance perceptibly cools. He begins with the positive pair of words "If I find . . . I shall spare." He ends with two more ominous pairs, "I shall not ruin it . . . for the sake of." So it is not altogether surprising that Abraham ends his intercession where he does; the tone of God's replies conveys the feeling that he cannot be pushed much further.

22 "Then the men . . . but Abraham was still standing before the LORD." Throughout these chapters, the relationships between "the LORD," "the men," and "the angels" are shrouded in mystery. Initially it is said that "The LORD appeared" (v 1), but Abraham sees three men (v 2); there is also the strange alternation between singular and plural address in vv 3–4, as though Abraham regarded one as the leader. The supernatural nature of the visitors becomes evident in their conversation, and the promise of a son seems to prove that at least one of them speaks for the LORD. Nevertheless, the exact relationship between them is again blurred in vv 16–17 when "the men stood up . . . But the LORD thought." Here at last the identity of the visitors is clarified: one is or represents the LORD; the other two are angelic companions. When they arrive in Sodom, they are called angels (19:1). It is never explicitly said that the LORD entered Sodom; the underlying assumption is no doubt that he could not endure the presence of such sin. Even the angels are most reluctant to stay a night (19:2). Gunkel, Westermann, and Haag see the variation in description of the visitors and the alternation of singular and plural address as proof of the composite nature of the narrative. With Delitzsch, Dillmann, and Jacob, I see these confusions as deliberate: they express the difficulty of human comprehension of the divine world.

23–25 "Then Abraham approached and said" sounds redundant since he was already standing before the LORD. It may, as Jacob suggests, refer to his internal approach, for this is the first time a man in Scripture initiates a conversation with God. But elsewhere in the Pentateuch the words "approach and say" mark the beginning of a request in which the speaker has a special interest (cf. 43:19; 44:18).

"Would you even sweep away the righteous along with the wicked?" The verb ספה "sweep away" is used again in the next verse and in 19:15, 17. On the term "righteous" (צדיק), cf. 6:9; "wicked" (רשע) is the opposite and is often contrasted with the righteous. Ezek 18 gives many examples of the abominable things, flagrant breaches of the law, that characterize the behavior of the wicked. If God should not distinguish between good and bad behavior, that would be a grave affront to morality and piety. Indeed, that he does distinguish and does reward men according to their deeds is a fundamental assumption of ancient religion, and especially of the OT. The law, the prophets, and the wisdom literature all assert it: indeed, the Book of Job is shocking precisely because in allowing Job to suffer, God seems to be flouting his usual principles. "The LORD loves the righteous . . . but the way of the wicked he brings to ruin" (Ps 146:8, 9) is the presupposition of all the OT. Indeed, in the divine reflections on Abraham in v 19, the principle of reward for righteous behavior has just been reasserted. And it is on this principle that Abraham builds his case. Three times he points out the incongruity, even the inconceivability, of treating righteous and wicked alike. Each time Abraham returns to the point, he makes it more sharply. "Would you even sweep away the righteous along with the wicked?" suggests perhaps an oversight on God's part if the righteous are lost with the wicked; but "to put to death" (hiph מות; v 25) with its overtones of judicial sentence (Lev 20:4; Num 35:19, 21) suggests that God's condemnation is deliberate, while the final phrase, "to treat the righteous and the wicked the same" (see note on grammatical construction), makes the point clear beyond doubt. In this case, God would be cold-bloodedly failing to distinguish good from evil. Israelite judges are expected to acquit the righteous and condemn the wicked (Deut 25:1; cf. Exod 23:6–7; Prov 17:15). If these are the standards enjoined on human judges, "Shall not the judge of all the earth act justly?" If God expects those who rule in his name to "love righteousness and hate wickedness" (Ps 45:8[7]), how can he behave differently himself?

26 The LORD accepts Abraham's logic. "Spare" (נשא) was the key word in Abraham's plea (v 24). The verb literally means to "lift up," so to "lift someone's face" (19:21) is to show favor. It is often followed by "sin," "iniquity" as an object, in which case it means "forgive." Moses uses the same term in his great intercession for Israel (32:32), and eventually the LORD declares his character as the one who is "merciful and gracious . . . forgiving iniquity, transgression, and sin" (Exod 34:6–7). Here God's response to Abraham foreshadows his later declaration to Moses.

"Fifty righteous." It is not clear why Abraham began with fifty and worked down to ten. Jacob, relying on Amos 5:3, suggests a small city could field a hundred fighting men; consequently, fifty might represent half the city. So Abraham may be starting from the hypothetical situation of equal numbers of righteous and wicked in the city. It would be unjust to destroy all because half were sinners. He then works down to less obvious cases.

27–28 Note Abraham's polite diffidence, expressed in his formal language, "I have undertaken" (used only here and v 31 in Genesis) and "sovereign," and in only reducing the number by five. Later, he drops it by ten each time. "Ruin" (שחת), here used for the first time, is a key term in this story and in the flood story; also see Exod 32:7 (see *Form/Structure/Setting*). The LORD uses the same term in assenting to Abraham's plea.

29 The third plea is the briefest and most colorless, as if Abraham feels that another five less will not make much difference.

30 But with the second round of three pleas, the tension starts to rise again, as the very conciliatory opening, "Do not be angry, my sovereign," ushers in a request that the speaker regards as most important (cf. 31:35; 44:18; Exod 32:22; Judg 6:39), and then Abraham drops the threshhold for salvation by another ten.

31 Though Abraham's request has the same polite diffidence as in v 27, the reply has a slightly ominous ring. The LORD himself introduces the word "ruin" in his reply to Abraham, whereas on the previous occasion he had used the more colorless "do," perhaps giving a hint that he cannot be pressed much further.

32 Clearly Abraham feels he has reached the limit of what he dare ask. He opens with the conciliatory "Do not be angry" (v 30) and asks to speak "just once more." And again his request is granted, albeit with the same threatening formula as in v 31: "I shall not *ruin* it."

33 As the LORD had hinted in v 21 that he wanted intercession for Sodom, so he now closes the prayer by going on his way. It was not, as often suggested, that Abraham did not have the courage to go further and press his case to the logical conclusion: "Suppose one is found there. . . ." Rather, God himself had hinted that he should go no further (v 31), and he now terminates the conversation. Nevertheless, Abraham put the case so strongly against the indiscriminate slaughter of the righteous that every reader must wonder what God will do if there are fewer than ten righteous in Sodom. The narrator, too, is aware of the problem: the next few scenes, set in the city itself, will show there are no righteous in Sodom at all, except for Lot, who is only a sojourner there, not a full citizen (19:9).

In interceding for Sodom, Abraham is portrayed as fulfilling a role particularly associated with prophets. We have already noted verbal links with Moses' great intercession in Exod 32–34. Samuel (1 Sam 12:23), Amos (7:1–9), and Jeremiah (e.g., Jer 14:7–9, 13; 15:1) also pleaded with God on the nation's behalf. Here Abraham is not praying for his own people (he does not mention Lot) but for Sodom, and this makes this episode unique among prophetic intercessions.

19:1–3 The fourth scene of the Sodom material tells of the angels' arrival in Sodom's city gate. In the palistrophe, it matches their departure through the gate (19:15–16). This scene also invites comparison with the description of their arrival in Mamre and the hospitality Abraham provided there (18:1–8). The account of their arrival at Sodom is somewhat briefer than at Mamre, but this need not be taken to show Lot was less warm in his welcome than was Abraham. The narrator feels no need to repeat all the details; rather, he highlights the differences in the situation.

1 First, it is observed that two "angels" came to Sodom. מלאך "angel" may simply be "messenger" (32:4[3]), as opposed to "angel" = a messenger from God. The translation "angel" seems appropriate here in the light of what we have

discovered about Abraham's visitors in the previous chapters and in view of what they are about to do. Presumably, to Lot they at first seemed just to be men, as they did to Abraham when they arrived in Mamre. But notice that now they are only two; one, presumably the LORD, has not come (cf. 18:22, 33). This clarifies this scene's relationship to the preceding, as does the time reference, "in the evening," i.e., toward sunset. This seems to imply they have spent most of the day with Abraham before transporting themselves to Sodom. The distance between Mamre and Sodom is too great (at least twenty miles) to suppose they actually walked that distance after their leisurely lunch with Abraham.

"While Lot was sitting in the gateway of Sodom." The gateway was the public square of the city where the elders sat, public meetings were held, and legal disputes were adjudicated. That Lot was here suggests that he was a respected member of the community, but it is strange that no elders of Sodom are mentioned. It is characteristic of Bible storytelling to focus on the main actors and to omit reference to other figures of less consequence who are present but passive. Nevertheless, one would have expected others to have greeted the angels, but nothing is said. Does this indicate a lack of hospitality among the Sodomites: only Lot the immigrant welcomes the visitors? Or does Lot's sitting by himself suggest his estrangement from the men of Sodom? The gap in the narrative here will soon be filled. Lot, at least, shows the proper courtesy: "he stood up to greet them and bowed to the ground" (cf. 18:2).

2 Lot's warm welcome is quite similar to Abraham's (cf. 18:3–5). But the different time of arrival makes it appropriate to offer them a bed for the night, rather than just a meal and a rest under a shady tree. But their reply is most unexpected and apparently ungrateful. "Not so, we shall stay in the street." If oriental convention dictated that one should offer strangers a bed for the night, it just as firmly dictated the acceptance of such offers (cf. 24:23, 54; Judg 18:2; 19:4–20), so the angelic reluctance to stay with Lot increases the apprehension that the opening has already aroused by mentioning the arrival of just two angels (why has the third not come?) and by Lot's solitary greeting (why did not the Sodomites welcome the visitors?). Why should angels be afraid of spending the night with Lot? Are they intent on doing something else overnight—inspecting the city? Or are they fearful of the repercussions of staying with Lot? Their unexpected refusal of Lot's invitation creates more gaps and invites the reader to reflect.

3 Whatever the angelic motives, Lot is scared of what may happen if they do not spend the night with him. So scared that "he pressed them" to come in. The verb "press" (פצר) means "to urge, to insist" (cf. 33:11; Judg 19:7; 2 Kgs 5:16). Here and in 19:9 it is intensified by the addition of מאד "very," so that I have translated it "manhandle." Perhaps here "he twisted their arm" would be an equivalent English idiom. But what did Lot think might happen if they stayed outside? The apprehensions already aroused by vv 1–2 are further heightened by Lot's arm-twisting.

But for a moment the narrative allows us to relax, telling how they relented in the face of Lot's pressure and "entered his house." "And he made them a feast." עשה משתה describes the banquets given on special occasions, e.g., the weaning of Isaac (21:8), weddings (29:22; Judg 14:10), and royal entertaining (40:20; 1 Kgs 3:15). "Baking them unleavened bread" probably because that was quick to make

(cf. Exod 12:39; 1 Sam 28:24), and like Abraham, Lot was hurrying to make his guests welcome.

4–11 The fifth scene, like the seventh, takes place in Sodom outside Lot's house. In both, Lot's appeals are rudely rejected. In this scene, the narrative gaps left in the previous scene are filled; that is, the questions raised but left unanswered are now resolved. The angels discover what the whole population of Sodom is like. We learn that the Sodomites are most inhospitable toward visitors, which explains why the angels were so reluctant to enter Lot's house and why Lot insisted they must. But not only does this scene disclose the character of the Sodomites; it also discloses Lot's commitment to his visitors and, indeed, the nature of his visitors. This is essential if Lot is to take their warning seriously.

4 Note the very emphatic insistence that "the whole population," "young and old," were involved in this crime. There are no righteous in Sodom except for Lot, who is only an immigrant. Lot, as soon will be made clear, will leave, so there is no question of divine injustice in the overthrow of Sodom. The righteous will not be swept away with the wicked as Abraham feared.

5 The mob shouts out that Lot's visitors be brought out, "so that we may know them." It is because of this remark and Lot's subsequent comments that homosexuality has been identified as *the* sin of Sodom. But this has been contested. Certainly their wording is not quite so explicit: "that we may know them." Their words stand in ironic contrast to the LORD's expressed intention to know about them (18:21). The mob could mean simply that they want to know who these visitors are, but since the visitors came through the public gateway and were publicly greeted by Lot, this cannot be all they mean. And since ידע "to know" is frequently used in Genesis of sexual intercourse, this seems the likeliest meaning here (cf. 4:1, 17, 25; 24:16). Indeed, it is made inescapable by Lot's reply, in which he describes his daughters as "virgins," lit. "who have not known a man." ידע must here be intended to mean sexual intimacy, and this is recognized by all the major commentators. All homosexual practice is regarded by OT law as a capital offense (Lev 18:22; 20:13; cf. Rom 1:26–27), but the attitude of Israel's neighbors is less clear, for it is not often discussed in their legal collections. It seems likely that they allowed homosexual acts between consenting adults, but here homosexual gang rape is being proposed, something completely at odds with the norms of all oriental hospitality. (See further G. J. Wenham, *ExpTim* 102 [1991] 359–63.)

6 So far Lot has been portrayed as most hospitable and very solicitous of his visitors' welfare. He is now shown to be a man of no mean courage. True to the cardinal principle of oriental hospitality that protecting your guests is a sacred duty, he bravely goes out to face the mob alone. The last clause, "he shut the door behind him," gives a clue to his thinking. By shutting the door, he cut off his own escape and hoped to protect those inside.

7 He begins with polite entreaty: the enclitic נא (see *Notes*) and the phrase "my brothers" suggest Lot hoped that a soft answer would turn away wrath (Prov 15:1).

8 That appeal fell on deaf ears, and presumably in desperation, he offers to sacrifice his virgin daughters to the lusting mob. His offer no doubt shocked the narrator and first audience as much as it does us, so there immediately follows an explanation of his motives: "only do not do anything to these men for they came

under the protection of my roof for this reason." "For this reason" (כִּי־עַל־כֵּן) is almost redundant semantically (cf. n. 18:5b-b.), but it serves here to underline how committed Lot is to protecting his guests. Putting their welfare above his daughters' may have been questionable, but it shows just how committed he was to being a good host.

9 But the unfortunate offer was not accepted. Verbal abuse turns to physical assault. The unruly scene is vividly described, and the hopelessness of Lot's attempts to save his guests is comprehensively demonstrated. His polite appeal, "Do not do evil, my brothers," is rebuffed by a jibe at his immigrant status: "shall a single immigrant . . . we shall do more evil to you than to them." Lot is pushed aside, and despite his care to shut the door, "they came to batter it down."

10 When all seems lost, the visitors reveal their true identity by taking Lot inside and striking his assailants with blindness. "The men put out their hand and brought Lot into the house with them" sounds just like 8:9, "he put out his hand . . . and brought [the dove] into the ark with him." In view of the other parallels with the flood story, this description of the angelic action is no doubt meant to echo Noah's. As Noah cared for his dove, so they rescued Lot. As Noah's power and wisdom exceeded the dove's, so does angelic protection exceed human.

11 What is more, the angels "struck the men with a sudden blindness." The unusual word for "blindness" (סַנְוֵרִים; cf. Akk. *sinlurmā sinnūru* day- or night-blindness; Stol, *JNES* 45 [1986] 296–97) recurs in 2 Kgs 6:18. It may be, as Speiser argues, that the angels emitted a blinding light. As elsewhere in Scripture (Isa 6:10; John 9), this physical blindness is probably symbolic of intellectual or spiritual blindness. The men of Sodom cannot see physically or spiritually where they are going. Lot's sons-in-law will soon show themselves deaf to his invitation to save themselves (v 14).

"They grew tired of trying to find their way in" ends the scene on a comic note: the men fumbling around looking for the door is laughable. Yet in another way it surprises us. Why did they not go home as soon as they were struck with blindness? Is this another hint of how deeply rooted their sin was? Divine judgment is supposed to induce repentance (cf. Amos 4:6–12); here it does not, so yet greater calamities must be expected. Further, it is unexpected that no one in the large mob, even if blind, found his way to the door and summoned others there. Supernatural agency was manifested not simply in the blinding but also in the continued protection of the house until the mob dispersed.

12–13 The central scene set in Lot's house in Sodom is an angelic monologue. The previous scene revealed both the depravity of his neighbors and the identity of his guests so that now Lot is prepared for the message they have brought. Like Noah, he is warned of impending judgment (6:13–21) and advised to lead his family to a place of safety. In both situations, the ominous word "ruin" (שָׁחַת) appears twice, first in the hiphil then in the piel (6:13, 17; 19:13). The same terms appeared in Abraham's intercession, bringing it to an uncertain close (18:28, 31, 32).

Lot is advised to bring out his "sons-in-law, . . . sons . . . daughters." His sons and unmarried daughters would have been under his patriarchal authority, but his "sons-in-law" would not have been. The indefinite singular form, literally "son-in-law," is odd. But this observation does not prove it is a gloss; some mention of

his "sons-in-law" is necessary to explain why Lot went next to urge them to escape. He had no responsibility usually for his sons-in-law as they did not form part of his extended family. In 18:21, the LORD said he wanted to investigate the outcry. The angels now confirm his original verdict (18:20) and pronounce sentence on behalf of the judge of all the earth. "Their outcry is great in the LORD's presence, and the LORD has sent us to ruin it." Note too how this comment finally clarifies the relationship between the LORD and the two angels already implied in 18:22, 33; 19:1.

14 The seventh scene, like the fifth, is set outside Lot's house and tells how the men of Sodom rejected his advice yet again. When offered a way of salvation, they turn it down, proving once more that they fully deserved judgment. "Who had married his daughters" or "who were to marry his daughters." Both translations are possible. If "had married" is the preferred translation, then the refusal of his sons-in-law to leave meant Lot was leaving some of his daughters behind in Sodom. If, on the other hand, "were to marry" is the better interpretation, the attitude of his sons-in-law is more understandable. This talk of judgment was just a device to call off the marriage after the riot outside his house. The ambiguity of the participle (married/to marry) makes both interpretations viable. But whatever the exact relationship, "his sons-in-law thought he was joking." "Joke" is the same stem (צחק) as "laugh" (cf. 17:17; 18:12, 13, 15), the etymology of Isaac, but here the piel stem is used anticipating 21:9. "Joking" or "mocking" the righteous, like "disdaining them" (12:3), is a dangerous pursuit in Genesis.

15–16 The eighth scene reverses the action of the fourth. There the angels arrive at Sodom; here they leave. In the fourth scene, they were forcibly persuaded by Lot to stay ; now it is their turn to use force to make him go. In the flood story, Noah was warned to prepare (6:13–21) and then later was told to embark in the ark he had built (7:1–4), so the initial warning to Lot (19:12–13) is followed up with a command to leave (19:15–16). But here the time scale is much shorter, and there is an urgency not found in the flood story.

This urgency comes through in the narrative: "At crack of dawn," lit. "as dawn rose." שחר "dawn" is the time when the blackness of night starts to lighten before sunrise (cf. v 23; Judg 19:25–26). "Come on" (קום), lit. "arise," is clearly exclamatory in v 14, but it could be literal here: the angels are waking Lot up. The echo of the previous verse suggests Lot too may be reluctant to go.

"You have," lit. "are found," is the same verbal form as used by Abraham in his plea for Sodom (18:29–32), as is the term "swept away" (18:23, 24). Apart from this verbal link with Abraham's intercession, it is unnecessary grammatically to add "you have." The addition probably indicates that Lot had other daughters living elsewhere in Sodom, and this may partially explain his dallying. But the righteous (cf. Noah) are expected to be prompt in obeying divine commands. "Delaying shows indecisiveness and an incapacity to leave everything behind so that he, together with his wife and two daughters, two with each angel, must be led away. J depicts Lot's character as a contrast to Abraham's in masterly fashion: he is fond of good living (13:10ff), soft (vv 7–8, 30ff), indecisive, and anxious" (Procksch, 129). The angel's use of force is an act of mercy; "had compassion" (חמל) often has the nuance of "sparing from death" (cf. Exod 2:6; Deut 13:9 [8]; 1 Sam 15:3, 9, 15).

17–22 The ninth scene matches the third scene closely: earlier Abraham had interceded for Sodom; now Lot pleads for Zoar. But despite the thematic and verbal parallels, their approach is quite different. Abraham is altruistic, but Lot is selfish. Whereas Abraham pleads divine justice, Lot rests his case on his own weakness and convenience. His plea is sandwiched between the repeated commands to escape (vv 17, 22) (מלט niphal). The root "escape" occurs five times in this scene and is doubtless a play on the word Lot (לוט), as if to say "Lot was *let* out of Sodom."

17 The urgent tone is maintained. Note "As soon as they had brought them outside" followed by four brisk commands. "Do not look back" in this context simply expresses the need for haste. But it is expected to be followed literally, as v 26 makes plain. Only one of the angels issues the commands, and it is to him that Lot speaks.

18 "No, Lord." As pointed, אדני is the proper way to address God (cf. 18:3), and Lot's subsequent intercession is directed to God. Whether the narrative is suggesting that the LORD has now rejoined the angels outside the city, or whether Lot is just being very polite, is obscure. Could he really know who he was talking to in the gloom before sunrise? The mystery is probably deliberate.

19 Lot's plea is somewhat involved syntactically, suggesting perhaps his inner confusion and bewilderment. In his self-description, "you have been kind" (מצא חן "find grace"), Lot associates himself with Abraham (18:3) and Noah (6:8). "To save life" (חיה hiph) also echoes the flood story (6:19, 20). But these comparisons hardly redound to Lot's credit as he continues, "Since I cannot escape to the hills, so that the disaster will catch me, and I die." Instead of obeying without question the injunction "escape to the hills," he says he cannot. Furthermore, he doubts God's ability to save him ("the disaster will catch me"), as though the coming judgment was not under divine control.

20 He suggests that he escape instead to a small city nearby, which he hopes God will spare because it is small (cf. Amos 7:2, 5)—not because it contains righteous people—so that *he* can survive. Out of his own mouth, Lot proves himself to be fearful, selfish, and faithless.

21 Nevertheless, the LORD shows his mercy by accepting Lot's plea. He may accept the prayers of his people, even when they are not as blameless as Noah or as believing as Abraham. Divine grace is the ultimate basis of salvation, not human righteousness.

22 But Lot must be quick, for God cannot act till he reaches his chosen city. "Zoar" comes from the root צער "to be small," which was the basis of Lot's appeal. According to 14:8, its earlier name was Bela. It is usually supposed to lie to the southeast of the Dead Sea, but the location of all these cities is problematic (cf. Wenham, *Genesis 1-15,* 309–10).

23–26 The tenth scene describes the judgment on Sodom and Gomorrah adumbrated in the second scene (18:17–21). Little detail is given: the awfulness of the event speaks for itself.

23–24 The syntax suggests that sunrise, Lot's arrival in Zoar, and the fire from heaven coincide. The LORD acts as soon as Lot reaches his place of safety. Lot for his part must have moved quickly, for in the Middle East there is barely half an hour between dawn and sunrise. "Brimstone and fire" are paired in Ps 11:6 and

Ezek 38:22 as agents of divine retribution. The Dead Sea area still reeks of sulphurous fumes, and asphalt deposits are found, but what combination of natural or supernatural agents destroyed the towns remains speculative (see von Rad, 220; Sarna, 138, for some suggestions). The narrator stresses that "it was from the LORD."

25 "He overthrew" (הָפַךְ), already used in 19:21 and again in v 29, reappears in the later standard phrase "like the overthrow of Sodom" (cf. Deut 29:22[23]; Amos 4:11; Isa 13:19; Jer 49:18). But it is doubtful whether it implies an earthquake contributed to the destruction. Here the overthrow of the cities, their inhabitants, and the vegetation is highlighted. Before this destruction, "all the plain . . . was well-watered like the garden of the LORD and the land of Egypt" (13:10). Genesis implies that the present desolate aspect of the Dead Sea plain goes back to this act of divine judgment.

26 It is often surmised that a strange rock formation near the Dead Sea gave rise to the story of Lot's wife turning to a pillar of salt. While such a hypothesis cannot be disproved, the comment here obviously has a different purpose. By looking back, Lot's wife contravened the instruction not to look back in v 17. By disobeying a God-given instruction, she forfeited her God-offered salvation. In looking back, she identified herself with the damned town. Her petrification also explains her absence from the closing episode of the Lot cycle, when his daughters intoxicate him to have intercourse with him. It would be difficult to imagine their ruse succeeding if mother had been around. Finally, it creates sympathy for Lot, both in the light of his less than perfect righteousness displayed in his reluctance to leave Sodom and flee to the mountains and his inebriation about to be related. It is not so much his bereavement that evokes sympathy but the fact that he was a husband who did not enjoy whole-hearted support from his wife. While the narrator does not condone Lot's lapses, he helps the reader appreciate a contributory cause and suggests why his daughters had few scruples about their behavior. Like their mother, they too had imbibed a love of Sodom and its attitudes.

27–28 The final scene of the Sodom palistrophe matches the first (18:16), with Abraham looking down over the Dead Sea plain on the overthrown cities and the pallor of smoke, like the smoke of a kiln, rising on the morning air. Presenting it through Abraham's eyes, the narrator makes us more conscious of the human aspect of the destruction. Abraham had relatives there. What had happened to them? The reader has been told, but Abraham was still unaware of Lot's escape. He had gone back to the place "where he had stood before the LORD" and interceded for the city. What had been the point?

29 This concluding verse, while superficially just a résumé of the story already told in full, answers Abraham's questions and ours. His intercession had been worthwhile, for "when God ruined the cities . . . God remembered *Abraham* and sent Lot out of the overthrow." As already noted, "God remembered Abraham" echoes 8:1, "God remembered Noah." But a more exact parallel to 8:1 would have been "God remembered Lot," for Noah and Lot are the men saved from disaster. The substitution of Abraham for Lot in this sentence makes an important theological point. Lot was not saved on his own merits but through Abraham's intercession. And this makes a good parallel to the conclusion of the flood story, for there the LORD, after smelling Noah's sacrifice, promises never to destroy the

earth again with a flood (8:20–22). There Noah's sacrifice makes atonement for the world; here Abraham's prayer leads to the salvation of Lot.

30–38 The final episode in the Lot story has many points of similarity to the final episode in the Noah story. In both, the heroes drink too much. In both, when their father is drunk, the children sin against him, and this has consequences for future generations.

Yet the differences are just as striking. Lot clearly is much more drunk than Noah, for he never realized what his daughters did, whereas Noah seems to have been aware immediately. Further, Lot's daughters appear much more culpable than Ham. His offense appears to have been accidental; theirs was clearly deliberate. And seeing one's father uncovered is much less grave than incest. Furthermore, here it is daughters, not sons, that are responsible, and the leading spirit is the older daughter, as opposed to the younger son. In every respect, then, the sin of Lot's daughters is much graver than Ham's, and obviously Lot was more heavily under the influence than was Noah.

It is possible to read the story quite differently. It is often surmised that the tale was handed down among the Moabites and Ammonites, who must therefore have regarded their ancestral mothers as heroic. Certainly the names the mothers give to the children, Moab, "from the father," and Ben-Ammi, "son of my people," does not indicate that they felt ashamed of their deed. And Jacob thinks the narrator shared this positive attitude toward their behavior. He points out that Tamar was forced to act similarly toward her father-in-law Judah because he failed to provide her with another husband after she was widowed. The law (Deut 25:5–10) provides for a widow to marry her brother-in-law, which would in other circumstances be regarded as incest. So he suggests that Lot's daughters had been betrothed and, having lost their future husbands in the destruction of Sodom, were now in a similar position. Their solution to their desperate plight may have been irregular, but their ingenuity in face of their father's inertia is to be applauded.

The absence of clear editorial comment on the behavior of the parties means we must read the story with particular care to determine which interpretation is preferable.

30 "Lot left Zoar and dwelt in the hills." At last he fulfills the original angelic order to escape to the hills (v 17). But though this action may seem laudable, the comment "because he was afraid to live in Zoar" shows that his motives were not. Having been reluctant to obey the command in the first place, he now shows that he does not trust the implied divine guarantee that he would be safe in Zoar (v 21). Lot is portrayed as faint-hearted and vacillating and reduced to living in a cave. Caves in the OT are used either as graves (25:9) or by refugees (Josh 10:16; 1 Sam 13:6). Lot, the rich rancher who had so many flocks and herds that he had to separate from Abraham (13:8–11), chose to live in the fertile Dead Sea valley, which has been destroyed and with it all his other relations and property. He and all he has can be accommodated in a cave. His ruin can hardly be more complete. We may be inclined to sympathize with Lot's plight, but it is not so clear that Genesis does.

"If one surveys the stages of (Lot's) career, his succumbing to the attraction of the luxuriant Jordan valley, his inability to assert himself with his offer to the

Sodomites, and his inability to make up his mind even before divine judgment or to entrust himself to the leadership of the messengers and Yahweh's protection, and finally his succumbing in drunkenness to vital forces, it will become clear that the narrator has drawn a very compact picture in spite of being bound to ancient traditions. Having been set on the way to a promise by Yahweh, just as Abraham was (12:4), he turned aside from this way (ch 13), still supported by God's grace, and then finally slipped completely from God's hand, which directs history" (von Rad, 224).

31 The initiative comes from the older daughter, who should be the more concerned for her parents' welfare. "Our father is old" suggests she is so concerned, but the relevance of her remark to her proposal is obscure. Does she think that because he is old he ought to be looking for a husband for her (cf. 24:1), or that his age precludes him from having sexual intercourse (18:12)? The former seems more likely in the light of "there is no man at all in all the area [world] to come into us as they do in all the world [area]." What she is concerned about is the lack of potential husbands for her father to seek out, not his possible lack of virility. At any rate, her remark "there is no man" can hardly be true, whether we translate אֶרֶץ "area" or "world." Presumably, there were at least eligible husbands no farther away than Zoar. But this comment does give an insight into the girl's state of mind: she is desperate to marry, so she exaggerates the effects of the recent catastrophe. "To come into us" is a respectable term for marriage (cf. Deut 25:5), but "as they do in all the world [area]" (lit. "the way of all the world") is a suspect phrase, for it stands in contrast to 18:19, "the LORD's way." It would be even more dubious if we translate אֶרֶץ as "area," for we have seen that the mores of the Dead Sea valley were not in keeping with "the LORD's way."

32 Had she proposed to give her father wine to drink to drown his sorrows, the narrator might have approved her action. "Give . . . wine to those in bitter distress; let them drink and forget their poverty" (Prov 31:6–7). But the motives expressed here, "so we may lie with him and produce descendants from our father," seem less likely to have been cited approvingly. For though "to lie with" sounds like an innocent euphemism for sexual intercourse, it is rare for it to be used except in the contexts of illicit relationships (e.g., 34:2, 7) or female desperation (30:15, 16). "Produce descendants" shows what she really wanted was children, not a husband.

33–35 The execution of the elder sister's scheme goes without a hitch. So simple was it the first night that exactly the same procedure was followed the next evening by the younger sister. On neither occasion did Lot "know about her lying or her leaving." This shows how passive he was and alleviates the blame that attaches to him. It also highlights the slickness of his daughters, in contrast with their father's befuddled ignorance. But there is a pathetic irony. The angels have rescued Lot and his virgin daughters from the Sodom mob; now they sacrifice their virginity and their father's honor when there is no actual danger.

So although the narrator seems to reserve judgment about this incident, it seems unlikely that he approves Lot's daughters' deed. Throughout the ancient Near East, incest between father and daughter was regarded as wrong, and OT law punishes more remote forms of incest with death (Lev 20:12). Since these

bans apply after the death or divorce of one spouse, it seems unlikely that Lot's circumstances justified them being ignored. The fact that his daughters had to make him drunk shows that they were consciously flouting normal conventions. Because of his readers' moral assumptions, the narrator did not feel it necessary to excoriate Lot's daughters' behavior. The facts spoke for themselves. We are just left to pity Lot in his last and most painful loss of honor at the hands of those who should have loved him most.

36 Despite its impropriety, the scheme worked and Lot's daughters became pregnant and bore children. Genesis is very interested in tracing the origins of Israel's neighbors (cf. chap. 10; 25:12–18; 36:1–43), so the birth of Moab and Ammon is a fitting point to end the story of Lot. Despite the dubious origin of these near-neighbors, this was not held against them. Their territories were regarded as God-given (Deut 2:9, 19). Only Moab's and Ammon's lack of hospitality toward the Israelites on their way to Canaan prompted later animosity (Deut 23:4[3]).

37–38 The interpretations of the names Moab, "from the father," and Ammon, "son of my kin," are, typical of biblical etymologies, plays on the names. But here no obvious historical explanation of these names has been proposed. But both words are anticipated earlier in the narrative, before these explanations are given, especially vv 32, 34, "from our father," and v 36, "from their father," both of which begin with the same consonants as Moab, while Ammon is foreshadowed in vv 30, 32, 34, 35, "with him" עמו (Zakovitch, *HAR* 4 [1980] 168–69).

Explanation

No other twenty-four-hour period in Abraham's life is related more fully than that described in Gen 18–19: a midday lunch with three angels that ended with the destruction of Sodom and Gomorrah early next morning. This gives a hint of the importance of this story for the writer of Genesis, a hint that is certainly noted in the rest of Scripture, for the fate of Sodom and Gomorrah becomes a byword in the prophets and the NT and still lingers in popular religious consciousness. Like the flood story, the story of Sodom and Gomorrah's destruction by fire and brimstone is viewed by some as characteristic of the vicious and brutal God of the OT, by others as proof of the heinousness of homosexuality.

But the commentator's first duty is to try to see the significance of the passage in question for the writer of Genesis, before he reflects on how later biblical writers and commentators have read the tale. And this means reading this episode in the light of what precedes and follows it, and relating it to the theme of Genesis as a whole: the partial fulfillment of the promises to the patriarchs, promises of land, descendants, covenant relationship, and blessing to the nations (cf. Gen 12:1–3). This is what the story does in fact relate.

It opens with "The LORD appeared to him," a comment that preceded two other announcements of divine promises (12:7; 17:1). This leads the reader to anticipate some remarkable revelation, but instead we are regaled with an account of Abraham's lavish hospitality toward three visitors, whom he apparently regarded as ordinary men, though, as the text insinuates, the quality of the food and the service Abraham provided (a fine tender bull and bread made of the best wheat flour, vv 6–7) was fit for God. Not until the meal is over do the visitors

begin to disclose their real identity, first showing they know Sarah's name, so recently changed, then promising her a son in a year's time, and finally gently rebuking her despairing unheard laughter. The repetition of this promise of a child for Sarah in succeeding chapters, like the doubling of dreams (41:32), underlines the certainty of the promise's prompt fulfillment. It is not redundant, for apparently only Abraham had been informed about Isaac's impending birth in 17:19, and as yet he had not told Sarah. Here and in 17:17 the future parents of Isaac unwittingly confirm the truth of the heavenly delegation's message by laughing; indeed, Sarah's denial of her laughter, "I did not laugh," is an anagram of her son's name.

The promise of descendants is thus central to chap. 18, but so too are the covenant relationship and the promise of blessing to the nations. The LORD says, "Abraham is indeed to become a great and powerful nation and all the nations of the earth will find blessing. For I have chosen him . . ." (18:18–19). Then in a prayer that is without parallel in the OT, in that six times the LORD grants Abraham's plea for mercy, the intimacy of Abraham with God is disclosed. Here, in the manner of a true prophet, he intercedes for the people of Sodom: other prophets, Moses (Exod 32), Samuel, and Jeremiah, made intercession for Israel, but Abraham here prays for the Canaanites. The narrative hints that the LORD instigated the prayer and, when he had made his final concession to Abraham, brought it to an end.

But this great prayer does not simply show the intimacy of Abraham with God; it also reflects on the promise that "in him all the nations will find blessing," a proposition apparently negated by the disaster that subsequently befalls Sodom. Yet the narrator insists that Sodom has been given every chance to repent and save itself. Back in chap. 14 Abraham had rescued the king of Sodom from the eastern kings and restored all his property and people only to be treated with surly ingratitude. Yet Abraham still prays for them and is assured that if there are just ten righteous persons in Sodom, the whole city will be spared: God's mercy on the few will outweigh his anger with the many (cf. Exod 34).

But as the story makes clear, there were not even ten righteous in Sodom. Only Lot, an immigrant, welcomed the visitors to the town, gave them a splendid meal, and pressed them to stay the night. The failure of other people in Sodom to welcome the strangers fell far short of the expected standards of oriental hospitality. But this was as nothing when compared with the whole population of the town, "young and old," surrounding Lot's house, clamoring to rape the visitors. Homosexual acts between consenting adults, though condemned in the OT as incompatible with the creator's plan, were tolerated in most other societies in the ancient Orient. But homosexual rape was not: in Assyria it attracted the death penalty, and elsewhere it was used as a demeaning punishment for prisoners of war. But Lot's visitors were not prisoners but guests, and all the rules of oriental hospitality demanded their protection, not abuse. The men of Sodom are thus portrayed as transgressing not simply Israelite moral standards but the universal rule of behavior accepted throughout the ancient Orient. Such was the passion of the men of Sodom that even Lot's desperate attempt to buy them off with the offer of his virgin daughters was of no interest to them: without the miraculous intervention of his angelic visitors, the narrative implies, Lot, his household, and

his guests would probably have been assaulted and murdered by the mob. Mob violence is one thing, but were the individuals in Sodom really all so ill-disposed to Lot and what he stood for? Apparently so, for even Lot's sons-in-law refused to leave the city when Lot warned them of its impending doom.

Abraham's character is portrayed in a wholly positive fashion, but the portrait of Lot and his family is more nuanced. Abraham, an old man, hurries to prepare a banquet for unknown visitors at the hottest part of the day and is described as teaching righteousness and equity and shown to be on the most intimate terms with God. Lot, a younger man, is equally hospitable, prepares a banquet for his guests, and persuades them to stay the night in his home. Indeed, his hospitality seems to go too far when he does not simply risk his own life by going out to face the mob alone but offers his daughters to appease their lust. However, when he is told to leave the city, he dallies, and then having left, he pleads merely for his own convenience to take refuge in Zoar rather than flee to the hills. His slowness to obey the divine command suggests his righteousness is less than complete, but his wife and daughters seem even more attached to Sodom than Lot does. Disobeying the express angelic injunction, his wife looks back and is turned to salt, while his daughters resort to sex with their father, suggesting they shared the warped morality of the city from which they had all escaped. Though Lot is not overtly censured for this act, his career is portrayed as a sad one. Leaving Ur with Abraham and sharing his wealth, and by association at least the blessings promised to Abraham, Lot separated from Abraham to enjoy greater affluence in the Jordan valley. But when last seen he has lost his home, his goods, and his wife and is being shamefully treated by his daughters.

That he survived at all is ascribed to Abraham. "When God ruined the cities . . . God remembered Abraham," and he sent Lot out of danger. But this is more than a reference to Abraham's intercession on behalf of the righteous in Sodom, of whom only Lot appears deserving of that accolade; it is a clear echo of and presumably a deliberate comparison with Noah and the flood. When "God remembered Noah," the flood started to abate; when he remembered Abraham, he rescued Lot. This is just one of many allusions to the flood in these chapters. Clearly, Genesis sees the two events as parallel: two cataclysmic acts of divine judgment on outrageously sinful communities, with the only righteous man and his family spared. The flood involved the destruction of the whole human race except Noah and his family; here the destruction involves a group of cities and the saving of one man and his family. Noah is seen as a second Adam from whom all humanity descended; the destruction of Sodom, though not as awesome as the flood, speaks once again of the terrible depravity to which human society can descend and of the need for redemption. So if Noah is seen as a second Adam, Abraham is probably viewed as a third Adam, the new hope of mankind. It was Noah's sacrifice that mollified God's anger after the flood and spared the world another annihilation. Now the narrator suggests that it is Abraham's prayer that saved righteous Lot and that in Abraham all the nations of the earth may hope to find blessing.

But societies that flout standards of decent human behavior and spurn God's messengers, says the rest of Scripture, cannot hope to escape divine judgment, whatever promises were made to Abraham. The Pentateuch suggests that the

destruction of Sodom is a foretaste of the judgment that will befall other inhabitants of Canaan for their sins (Lev 18:3–30; Lev 20:22–23). Even Israel, the very descendant of Abraham, is likened to Sodom and Gomorrah in the prophets and in the Book of Deuteronomy (Isa 1:9; 3:9; Jer 23:14; Amos 4:11; Deut 29:23; 32:32). Indeed, Ezek 16:46–47 says that Jerusalem's sins are worse than Sodom's, and Lam 4:6 declares her "chastisement . . . has been greater than the punishment of Sodom." And the prophets warn that Israel's neighbors can expect a judgment like Sodom's because of their sin (Isa 13:9; Jer 49:18; Zeph 2:9).

Thus the OT seems to view the overthrow of Sodom as a paradigm of divine judgment: any nation, Jewish or gentile, can expect such treatment if it flouts God's standards and spurns his call to repentance. Similarly, Jesus warns that towns that rejected him or his messengers are more to blame than Sodom: "Truly, I say to you, it shall be more tolerable on the day of judgment for the land of Sodom and Gomorrah than for that town" (Matt 10:15; 11:23; Luke 10:12). Indeed, he compares his own coming in judgment to the flood or the overthrow of Sodom (Luke 17:26–32). Yet even in a society as corrupt as Sodom, Scripture affirms, the LORD has his own people, a remnant who attempt, however imperfectly, to live by divine standards (1 Kgs 19:18). The Abraham or Lot of every age "who is vexed in his righteous soul day after day with their lawless deeds" is urged to remain faithful to God and "to show hospitality to strangers, for thereby some have entertained angels unawares" (2 Pet 2:8; Heb 13:2).

Sarah and Abimelek   (20:1–18)

Bibliography

See also *Bibliography* on 12:10–20.

Alexander, T. D. "Are the Wife/Sister Incidents of Genesis Literary Compositional Variants?" *VT* 42 (1992) 145–53. **Biddle, M. E.** "The 'Endangered Ancestress' and Blessing for the Nations." *JBL* 109 (1990) 599–611. **Dahood, M.** "Abraham's Reply in Gen 20:11." *Bib* 61 (1980) 90–91. **Firestone, R.** "Difficulties in Keeping a Beautiful Wife: The Legend of Abraham and Sarah in Jewish and Islamic Tradition." *JJS* 42 (1991) 196–214. **Hoffmeier, J. K.** "The Wives' Tales of Gen 12, 20 and 26 and the Covenants at Beer–Sheba." *TynBul* 43 (1992) 81–99. **McEvenue, S. E.** "The Elohist at Work." *ZAW* 96 (1984) 315–32. **Merwe, C. H. J. van der.** "Hebrew Grammar, Exegesis and Commentaries." *JNSL* 11 (1983) 143–56. **Moran, W. L.** "The Scandal of the 'Great Sin' at Ugarit." *JNES* 18 (1959) 280–81. **Pappas, H. S.** "Deception as Patriarchal Self-Defence in a Foreign Land: A Form-Critical Study of the Wife-Sister Stories in Genesis." *Greek Orthodox Theological Review* 29 (1984) 35–50. **Rabinowitz, J. J.** "The 'Great Sin' in Ancient Egyptian Marriage Contracts." *JNES* 18 (1959) 73. **Ronning, J.** "The Naming of Isaac: The Role of the Wife/Sister Episodes in the Redaction of Genesis." *WTJ* 53 (1991) 1–27. **Seebass H.** "À titre d'exemple: réflexions sur Gen 16//21: 8–21 et 20:1–18//26:1–33." In *Le Pentateuque en question*, ed. A. de Pury. Geneva: Labor et Fides, 1989. 215–30. **Seidl, T.** "'Zwei Gesichter' oder zwei Geschichten? Neuversuch einer Literarkritik zu Gen 20." In *Die Väter Israels: FS J. Scharbert*, ed. M. Görg.

Stuttgart: Katholisches Bibelwerk, 1989. 305–26. **Weinfeld, M.** "Sarah and Abimelech (Gen 20) against the Background of an Assyrian Law and the Genesis Apocryphon." In *Mélanges bibliques et orientaux: FS M. Delcor,* ed. A. Caquot, S. Légasse, and M. Tardieu. AOAT 215. Kevelaer: Butzon and Bercker, 1985. 431–36. **Yeivin, S.** "Philological Notes, XV." *Leš* 42 (1977/78) 60–63.

Translation

[1]*Abraham journeyed*[a] *from there toward the region of the Negeb and dwelt between Kadesh and Shur and settled*[b] *in Gerar.* [2]*Then Abraham said of* [a] *his wife Sarah, "She is my sister."*[b] *Then Abimelek king of Gerar sent and took Sarah.*

[3]*Then God came to Abimelek in a dream by night and said to him,* [a] *"You are about to die*[a] *because*[b] *of the woman you have taken for*[c] *she is married."*[d] [4]*Now Abimelek had not approached her, so he said, "Lord, will you* [a]*kill a nation, a righteous one at that?*[a] [5]*Did*[a] *he not say to me, 'She is my sister,' and did not* [b]*she herself also*[b] *say 'He is my brother'? I did this with total sincerity and innocence."* [6]*God said to him in the dream, "I know too that you did this with total sincerity, and I it was that kept you from sinning*[a] *against me; therefore I did not allow*[b] *you to touch her.* [7]*But now return*[a] *the man's wife, for he is a prophet, that*[b] *he may pray for you so that you may live.*[c] [d]*If you are not willing to return*[d] *her, know*[e] *that you and all yours will certainly die."*

[8]*So early in the morning Abimelek summoned all his servants and told them all these things while they listened, and* [a]*the men were very afraid.*

[9]*Then Abimelek summoned Abraham and said to him,* [a] *"What have you done to us?*[a] *How have I sinned against you that*[b] *you have brought*[c] *upon me and my kingdom a great sin? You have treated me in ways that never ought to be done."*[d] [10]*Abimelek said to Abraham:* [a] *"What did you intend*[a] *that*[b] *you did this thing?"* [11]*Abraham said,* [a] *"Because I thought surely*[b] *there is no fear of God in this place that they would kill me because of my wife.* [12]*And she is in fact*[a] *my sister, my father's daughter though not my mother's, and she became my wife.* [13]*So when God made me wander*[a] *from my father's house,*[b] *I said*[c] *to her, 'This is the favor you must do me: wherever*[d] *we go, say for me, "He is my brother."'"*

[14]*So Abimelek took*[a] *sheep, cattle, slaves, and slave-girls and gave them to Abraham and returned Sarah his wife to him.* [15]*And Abimelek said, "Look, my land is before you. Dwell*[a] *wherever you like."* [16a]*At the same time he said to Sarah,*[a] *"Look, I am giving a thousand silver shekels*[b] *to your brother. That is for you as compensation for all that has happened to you* [c]*and in everything you shall be justified."*[c]

[17]*Then Abraham prayed to God, and God healed Abimelek, his wife, and his slave-wives, and they gave birth,*[a] [18]*for the LORD*[a] *had completely*[b] *closed every womb in Abimelek's household because of Sarah, Abraham's wife.*

Notes

1.a. Cf. n. 12:9a.

1.b. Waw consec + 3 masc sg impf גור.

2.a. For this meaning, "of, concerning, about," for אל, cf. Isa 29:22; 37:21, 33.

2.b. G adds "For he was afraid to say 'She is my wife,' lest the men of the city should kill him because of her," assimilating to 26:7.

3.a-a. הנה + 2 masc sg suffix + masc sg ptcp מות "die." For this construction for an imminent fut, see GKC, 116p.

3.b. SamPent reads עַל־אֲדוֹת, a rarer alternative to עַל. Cf. 21:11, 25.

3.c. וֹ introducing circumstantial clause, here translated "for, because, although" (*SBH*, 90; GKC, 141e).

3.d. בְּעֻלַת בַּעַל fem sg constr pass qal ptcp בָּעַל "marry, rule" + noun בַּעַל "lord, husband." Cf. Deut 22:22.

4.a-a. For MT הֲגוֹי גַּם, *BHS* and some commentators propose הֲגַם and translate "will you even kill a righteous (man)?" However, this is unnecessary despite the unparalleled interpolation of גַּם between a noun and its qualifier; it "is frequently employed when giving an exaggerated, aggravated or extreme case" (*EWAS*, 143).

5.a. Opening הֲלֹא "did not" governs the second question as well (*SBH*, 114). Cf. 44:5.

5.b-b. SamPent reads וְהִיא גַם for וְהִיא־גַם־הוּא. On the construction, cf. *SBH*, 160.

6.a. מִן + inf constr חֲטֹא; for this form, cf. GKC, 75n, 75qq.

6.b. 1 sg pf נתן + 2 masc sg suffix. For the sense "allow," cf. 31:7. On the construction, see GKC, 157b².

7.a. 2 masc sg impv hiph שׁוּב.

7.b. Simple waw + impf = "in order that" (Lambdin, 119).

7.c. Waw + 2 masc sg impv חיה. On pointing, see GKC, 63q; on syntax, see *SBH*, 108.

7.d-d. In conditional clauses, אֵין + suffix + ptcp (here masc sg hiph ptcp שׁוּב) may have the nuance of willingness (Joüon, 154l; cf. GKC, 159v).

7.e. 2 masc sg impv ידע.

8.a. SamPent, G, Vg add "all."

9.a-a. S reads "What have I done to you?"

9.b. כִּי introduces consecutive clause, especially after questions (GKC, 166b; Joüon, 169e).

9.c. 2 masc sg pf hiph בוא.

9.d. 3 masc pl pf niph עשה. On the nuance "ought/must," cf. GKC, 107gw; Joüon, 113m.

10.a-a. *BHS* proposed emendation, "What did you fear," is unnecessary.

10.b. Cf. n. 9.b.

11.a. SamPent adds "Because I feared" (כִּי יָרֵאתִי).

11.b. On this asseverative use of רַק, cf. BDB, 956b; *EWAS*, 131; 1 Kgs 21:25.

12.a. SamPent reads אָמְנָם, same meaning as MT, same spelling as MT in Josh 7:20.

13.a. 3 masc pl pf hiph תעה. SamPent reads sg הִתְעָה. On the use of pl with אֱלֹהִים, see GKC, 145i and *Comment*.

13.b. SamPent adds "and from the land of my family"; cf. 12:1.

13.c. Waw consec + 1 sg impf אמר.

13.d. אֶל כָּל־הַמָּקוֹם. The usual translation with the def art ה is "to the whole place"; here "to every place." This is exceptional according to GKC, 127e.

14.a. SamPent, G add "a thousand silver shekels," assimilating to v 16.

15.a. 2 masc sg impv ישׁב.

16.a-a. Lit. "And to Sarah he said" links sentence chiastically with v 15, suggesting simultaneity (*SBH*, 129).

16.b. The unit of measurement, "shekels," is to be understood (GKC, 134n).

16.c-c. The Heb. is obscure: וְנֹכָחַת = waw + fem sg ptcp niph יכח (pausal form) "be justified." Transferring the waw to the preceding word (כֹּל) and repointing lead to *BHS* renderings, "and with everyone you will be justified" or "and in everything you will be justified."

17.a. Waw consec + 3 masc pl impf ילד. 3 masc pl impf is preferred to 3 fem pl impf (GKC, 145pu).

18.a. SamPent reads "God."

18.b. Inf abs intensifies the verbal idea (*EWAS*, 87).

Form/Structure/Setting

Chap. 20 is dominated by two major dialogues between God and Abimelek (vv 3–7) and between Abimelek and Abraham (vv 9–13). Classification of the remaining material has given rise to a variety of analyses. But applying Gunkel's definition of scenes, "parts of a narrative differentiated by change of actors, situation or activity" (Gunkel, 36), organizes the material quite clearly.

1. Abraham settles in Gerar (1)   N
   2. Abraham's instructions to Sarah (2a)   D
      3. Abimelek "takes" Sarah (2b)   N
         4. God warns Abimelek (3–7)   D
            5. Abimelek warns his servants (8)   N
         6. Abimelek rebukes Abraham (9–13)   D
      7. Abimelek returns Sarah (14)   N
   8. Abimelek speaks to Abraham and Sarah (15–16)   D
9. Abraham prays for Abimelek and his household (17–18)   N

As frequently in Genesis, the scenes are organized palistrophically. Scene 4, the divine warning to Abimelek (vv 3–7), balances scene 6, Abimelek's rebuke of Abraham (vv 9–13), as do scene 3 and scene 7, the taking and the return of Sarah (vv 2b, 14). Gunkel noted the special significance of the middle scene (v 8): "Abimelek's fear is the consequence of all that precedes and the presupposition of all that follows" (222). While scenes 1 and 2 match scenes 8 and 9 rather more loosely, it may be noted how they maintain the alternation of narrative and dialogue (N and D) as elsewhere in this episode.

Traditional source critics ascribed this chapter to E, except for v 18, which is said to be a gloss because it uses the divine name "the LORD" instead of "God" used elsewhere in this chapter (vv 3, 6, 11, 13, 17). There are four main reasons for ascribing chap. 20 to E: the use of the term אלהים for "God," the term אמה for slave-girl (v 17), the use of a dream for revelation (vv 3, 6), and the doublet of this story in 12:10–20, which is ascribed to J.

However, more recent writers (notably Westermann; Coats; Alexander, *VT* 42 [1992] 145–53; Ronning *WTJ* 53 [1991] 1–27) have followed Van Seters (*Abraham*, 171–75) in arguing that chap. 20 is not an independent parallel version of the story in 12:10–20. Rather, this account presupposes the earlier account in chap. 12. Van Seters observes that the remark in v 2, "She is my sister," is quite obscure unless the reader already knows Abraham's motives as explained in 12:11–13. In 20:13, Abraham states, "When God made me wander from my father's house, I said to her." This, Van Seters argues, shows that the narrator of chap. 20 did not simply know the earlier account but knew it in its present setting following the call of Abraham in 12:1. Furthermore, he suggests that chap. 20 is attempting to deal with some of the questions raised by 12:10–20. Why did God punish the Pharaoh who was unaware of his error in taking Sarah? 20:3–7 offers an answer. Another question that this story answers is why Abraham lied about Sarah being his sister. The explanation offered here is that Abraham's story is a half-truth prompted by religious considerations, namely the godlessness of Gerar (vv 11–12). For these reasons, Van Seters argues that chap. 20 is an expansion of the earliest core of Genesis found in passages such as 12:10–20, but antedating the main J redaction of Genesis. Westermann and Coats, while concurring with Van Seters' assessment of the relationship between 12:10–20 and chap. 20, seem to regard the latter as a supplement to J rather than part of J's sources. However, the reference to "the LORD" in v 18, which is typical of J's redactional technique of beginning or closing an episode with a reference to the LORD (cf. 13:18; 15:1, 18; 17:1; 18:1), adds weight to Van Seters' position. Biddle (*JBL* 109 [1990] 599–611), too, has noted that the theology of this story is typical of J.

Certainly the other criteria traditionally adduced in favor of assigning this to an independent E source carry little weight. Dreams are not confined to E as a means of revelation (cf. chap. 15 and M. Lichtenstein, *JANESCU* 1/2 [1968/69] 45–54). The use of אמה "slave-concubine" as opposed to שפחה "slave-girl" (J's supposed equivalent) proves nothing. Not only is the latter term used in 20:14, but as pointed out in the *Comment* on 16:1, the two terms may denote women of different status: they are not exact synonyms. The fairly consistent use of אלהים "God" as opposed to "the LORD" in this story is nevertheless striking. Theology may partially explain it. "The LORD" is the divine name that was specially revealed to Israel, so it may be thought inappropriate to use it when God reveals himself to a non-Israelite (vv 3, 6) or when theology is discussed with them (v 13). There is a similar tendency in the Joseph story to speak of "God," not "the LORD," when talking to the Egyptians (e.g., 41:25, 28). Furthermore, Exod 6:3 implies that the patriarchs did not know the name "the LORD," so this may explain the reluctance of the narrator to allow the patriarchs to use the term. Nevertheless, the greater frequency with which the word "God" instead of "the LORD" appears in chaps. 20–22 may suggest that at some earlier phase the tradition behind these chapters had a history different from other parts of the Abraham cycle.

However, as it stands, the material is well integrated into the Abraham cycle. We have noted the way this chapter presupposes 12:10–20, but there are also many verbal connections with preceding material, especially chaps. 18–19: in v 4, for "Lord" (אדני), cf. 15:2, 8; 18:3, 27, 30, 31, 32; 19:18; for "nation" (גוי), cf. 12:2; 17:4, 6, 16, 20; 18:18; for "righteous," see 6:9; 7:1; 18:23, 24, 25, 26, 28. In v 7, for "live," see 19:20; for "you . . . will certainly die," see 2:17; 3:3, 4. In v 8, for "early in the morning," see 19:27; for "afraid," see 3:10; 15:1; 18:15; 19:30. In v 9, for "What have you done?" see 3:13, 14; 4:10; 12:18; for "sin," see 18:20. In v 11, for "surely" (רק), see 6:5; 19:8; for "place" "wherever" (מקום), see 18:24, 26, 33; 19:12, 14, 27. In v 13, for "favor," see 19:19. In v 15, for "wherever you like" = "good in your eyes," see 19:8. The description of Abraham as a prophet in v 7 is unique and striking, but it sums up exactly the role ascribed to him in chap. 18. There he is admitted to the secrets of the divine council (18:17–18), and he intercedes for Sodom (18:23–32) in the way that prophetic intercessors should. Lexically and conceptually, this chapter is therefore tied quite closely with what precedes. Indeed, the opening "Abraham journeyed *from there*" makes the connection explicit, and an exegesis of this story in the light of the preceding narratives is therefore called for, if we are to be true to the narrator's intention.

Comment

1 "Abraham journeyed . . . settled in Gerar." Note the same pair of verbs in 12:9–10 (נסע and גור) introducing a similar story. On that occasion Abraham went well over the border of Canaan into Egypt; here he stays closer to Canaan, and Sarah does not become quite so entangled in a royal harem. Providence overrules to prevent Abimelek approaching her.

"From there" in context must be Mamre; cf. 18:1. "Kadesh" (cf. 14:7) is near the southern border of Canaan, while "Shur" is usually located farther east, in the desert in northwest Sinai adjacent to Egypt (cf. *Comment* on 16:7). However,

Abraham apparently turned back from this region to settle, to live as an alien (גור) in Gerar. Gerar is, according to 10:19, on the southeastern border of Canaan. The account of Abraham's itinerary is very compressed and does not allow his route to be followed exactly.

2 In 12:11–16, a much fuller account of Abraham's remarks and the royal actions is provided. Without the earlier account, this verse would be cryptic, as the narrative hastens on to its focus of interest, Abimelek's dream and subsequent discussion with Abraham. Abimelek is a Canaanite name. "My father is Milku" (king); a king of Tyre mentioned in the Amarna letters (EA 146–55) bore this name.

3–7 After the very brief opening scenes, the narrative suddenly becomes more expansive as Abimelek's dream is recounted. This takes the form of a trial in which Abimelek is arraigned by God.

> v 3   God's charge
> vv 4–5   Abimelek's defense
> vv 6–7   God's sentence

Abimelek replies to the divine accusation, and his plea is in part accepted by God. But the opening word of the accusation, "You are about to die" (v 3), recurs at the end, "If . . . you will certainly die" (v 7), underlining the threat hanging over Abimelek if he does not repent. Westermann suggests that the night dream is regarded in the Pentateuch as God's preferred method of revealing himself to non-Israelites (cf. 31:24 [Laban]; Num 22:9, 20 [Balaam]). But since he also spoke to Joseph (37:5–10) and Solomon this way (1 Kgs 3:5–15), it seems unlikely that this explains the use of a dream here.

3 "You are about to die." The phraseology here (הנה + participle) is a straightforward prediction (cf. 6:13, 17; 7:4). But the previous two verses have skated over the background events so quickly that this remark is ambiguous. We do not know how much time has elapsed since Abimelek took Sarah. Has he fallen ill and been warned like Hezekiah that his condition is terminal (cf. Isa 38:1), or is he perfectly well? Not till the end of the episode are these questions answered. However, the cause of his plight is quite apparent, "because of the woman you have taken, for she is married." Abimelek is now informed about Sarah's marital status, something the reader has known all along. That adultery merited the death penalty was accepted throughout the ancient world and is, of course, reiterated in the OT (Lev 20:10; Deut 22:22). The latter passage is the only other use of the phrase "she is married" (בעלת בעל lit. "owned by an owner"). A wife is seen as much more than the property of her husband: she is his *alter ego* and one flesh with him (cf. 2:18–24 and *Comment* there); she is at least her husband's most precious possession, and to take her is the worst kind of theft. So although the threat of death is not surprising here, it is unusual for it to come from God. Usually it was the aggrieved husband who demanded it.

4 "Now Abimelek had not approached her." This observation is significant, for the law demands proof that a man has lain with someone else's wife for death to be exacted (Deut 22:22), and it predisposes the reader to view Abimelek's plea with sympathy, a plea that echoes the great prayer of Abraham in chap. 18. "Lord

[cf. 18:27, 30–32], will you kill a nation, a righteous one at that?" God had been prepared to spare a whole town for the sake of just ten righteous (18:31) people in her. Should he now kill one righteous man, who represents a nation? Given our knowledge of God's attitude declared in chap. 18, Abimelek's prayer seems guaranteed to succeed.

The mention of the "nation" here is unexpected and has led many commentators to emend the text (see *Notes*). But as Gunkel (222) points out, "Abimelek takes it for granted that God's wrath will fall not just on the king but on the whole people." The same idea is expressed in vv 7, 8, 9. Similarly, in Lev 4:3, the sin of the high priest brings guilt on the whole people, and in 2 Sam 24 and frequently in 1–2 Kings, the sin of the kings brings judgment on the nation.

5 Abimelek does not deny his action but claims he was misled and acted in total ignorance of the true situation. Both Abraham and Sarah said they were only brother and sister. He therefore acted with sincerity and innocence. Kings are expected to act in "sincerity": תם לבב "completeness/perfection of heart" (1 Kgs 9:4; Pss 78:72; 101:2). Indeed, the associated adjectives תמים and תם are used of some of the outstanding OT saints (e.g., 6:9; 17:1; Job 1:1, 8; 2:3).

6 The divine reply in repeating verbatim part of Abimelek's speech confirms his sincerity, but God insists, "I it was that kept you from sinning against me . . . I did not allow you to touch her." These remarks show that God understood more about the situation than Abimelek had disclosed, so that Westermann's assertion that God is not regarded as omniscient in this story is quite misguided. He is not just omniscient but omnipotent, restraining Abimelek from sinning against *him* (note here as in 2 Sam 12:13; Ps 51:6[4] adultery is viewed as a sin against God, not just against man). How God prevented Abimelek approaching Sarah is not stated, though the parallel in 12:17 and the remark that he should ask Abraham to pray for him that "you may live" (v 7) may well suggest that some sort of disease "plague" has befallen Abimelek and his household. But that the narrator made this point in v 4 and God repeats it twice here shows the importance attached to the fact. It does not simply reduce Abimelek's guilt; it eliminates the possibility of any of Sarah's offspring being illegitimate. In other words, it anticipates the birth of Isaac in 21:1–7.

7 The real test of Abimelek's sincerity is the return of Sarah. Then Abraham, the "prophet" (נביא) will "pray" (התפלל) "for you." These are the only times these common biblical terms are used in Genesis, though Gen 18 has already shown Abraham as a forerunner of great prophetic intercessors such as Moses, Samuel, Jeremiah, and Amos. "Pray" is used particularly of intercessory prayer (e.g., Num 11:2; 21:7; Deut 9:20; Jer 7:16: 11:14), whereas "to call (on the name of)" (קרא בשם) is a less precise term for prayer used quite often in Genesis (4:26; 12:8; 13:4; 21:33; 26:25). On these terms, see Wenham, *Genesis 1–15*, 115–16. Job (42:8) was told to pray for those who sinned against him. "And live" seems to confirm the supposition that Abimelek was sick, eventually said explicitly in v 17; this illness probably explains why he had not approached Sarah.

"You and all yours will certainly die" is phraseology similar to 2:17. God's final word to Abimelek is like his opening one in v 3, "You are about to die." But Abimelek is now offered a choice between life and death as Israel was often offered (see Deut 30:15; Josh 24:15).

8 The central scene shows Abimelek's prompt response to the divine warning: "early in the morning" (cf. 19:27). "The men were very afraid" (cf. 3:10; Jonah
1:10). This comment shows how unjustified Abraham was to allege that there was
no fear of God in this place (v 11).

9–13 This dialogue between Abimelek and Abraham is similar in fashion to
the Pharaoh's address to Abraham in 12:18–19. Both say "What have you done?"
echoing 3:13. But thereafter the speeches and actions diverge markedly. Pharaoh
put all the blame on Abraham; Abimelek admits he is partly to blame. Pharaoh
gave Abraham no chance to reply; Abimelek does. Pharaoh expelled Abraham
from Egypt immediately; Abimelek lets Abraham have the pick of the land. In
short, this story paints quite a sympathetic portrait of Abimelek, to which this
dialogue makes a central contribution. Abimelek's speeches are not simply harsh
condemnation. Rather, they mix moral indignation with a sense of shock, and
Abraham's lame replies tend to increase our sympathy for Abimelek.

9 This verse contains two rhetorical questions and a statement of fundamental moral principle. With "What have you done to us?" cf. 12:18, "What have you
done to me?" Whereas Pharaoh was concerned for himself, Abimelek is worried
about his kingdom, a point reinforced by the second question, "How . . . you
have brought upon me and my kingdom a great sin?" Abimelek is concerned
especially for his subjects' welfare, the mark of a good ruler (cf. LH 1:27–49; 24:1–
78; Ps 72; Isa 11:1–5). Furthermore, whereas Pharaoh just asked Abraham why
he had lied, Abimelek asks "How have I sinned against you?" The very phrasing
implies his moral earnestness. Abimelek suggests he must have behaved terribly
badly to provoke Abraham to make him fall into a "great sin," a well-known Near
Eastern description of adultery (Rabinowitz, Moran). Compared with Pharaoh's
colorless "I took her," Abimelek's "great sin" and "ways that never ought to be
done" (cf. the same usage for flagrant sexual misbehavior in 34:7; 2 Sam 13:12)
again highlight his moral concern.

10 "What did you intend that you did this thing?" makes the same point rather
more temperately and invites Abraham to explain his action. "It is no common
sign of a just and meek disposition in Abimelek, that he allows Abraham a free
defence. We know how sharply, and fiercely, they expostulate, who think themselves aggrieved: so much greater praise, then, was due to the moderation of this
king, towards an unknown foreigner" (Calvin, 1:528–29).

11 Abraham, while explaining his motives, actually condemns himself out of
his own mouth. The narrative up to this point has given the impression that
Abimelek was a just and God-fearing king deeply concerned for morality. More
than this, his servants too "were very afraid" when Abimelek recounted his dream.
For Abraham to say "surely there is no fear of God in this place" shows how badly
he had misread the situation. So within the immediate context of this story, he
stands condemned. But in the broader context of the Abraham cycle, he has even
less justification for his fears. Divine blessing and success have accompanied him
ever since Gen 12:1–3; he has been shown to be capable of defeating kings (Gen 14)
and to be on intimate terms with the Almighty (cf. Gen 17; 18). It is surprising
that he should now take fright, the more so since he had escaped unharmed from
Egypt in quite similar circumstances. Abraham's harking back to this occasion here
and in v 13, while it may mollify Abimelek, has the opposite effect on the reader.

12 Similarly, the disclosure that Sarah is his half sister cuts both ways. Later biblical law banned such unions (Lev 18; Deut 27:22; 2 Sam 13:13), so while justifying his remarks on one level, he condemns himself on another. Witness the attempts of medieval Jewish commentators and Calvin to make Abraham and Sarah cousins. This, though, is an impossible interpretation of the text (see Jacob, 472). His marriage is, rather, one of several examples in Genesis of disregard for the principles of later pentateuchal law that point to the antiquity of the traditions behind Genesis. The patriarchs are not painted as conforming entirely to the models prescribed in the Mosaic law. But whether Abimelek was as surprised as the later reader about the close relationship between Sarah and Abraham is uncertain. Other ancient Near Eastern law does not seem to have been so concerned as the Pentateuch about intermarriage between close relatives. But what is certain is that even if Abimelek may have regarded Abraham's marriage to Sarah as quite legitimate, that did not justify Abraham's failure to mention it.

13 The rest of Abraham's excuse is also weak. It is especially remarkable that he claims that his behavior in Gerar was his general policy: "wherever we go, say for me 'He is my brother,'" for back in 12:12 (presupposed here) this is presented as a device used once only in Egypt. Certainly the intervening episodes never give a hint that Abraham used this story after his expulsion from Egypt. So what are we to make of this discrepancy? Since there is much evidence that the writer of chap. 20 was fully conversant with the preceding material in Genesis (see *Form/Structure/Setting*), we cannot simply explain this as E's view as opposed to J's. Rather, we conclude that either Abraham was not being quite truthful in saying this was his usual policy, when he had in fact only once before pretended Sarah was merely his sister, or that he was telling the truth and that wherever he went he misled people about Sarah's marital status. Neither explanation redounds to Abraham's credit. The first explanation makes him lie just to Abimelek; the second suggests he is a man of little faith who often tried to save himself by misrepresenting the situation. The first view seems the more likely. But both interpretations make him less of a saint than might be concluded from other passages.

"When God made me wander from my father's house" shows that the narrator knows the story of 12:10–20 in its present context following 12:1–3. Abraham here speaks of "God" rather than "the LORD" either because he is addressing a heathen king or because the patriarchs are reckoned not to know the name "Yahweh, the LORD" (Exod 6:3). It is unusual that "God" here takes the plural verb suggesting that "gods" might be a better translation, and this may represent an accommodation to Abimelek's polytheistic outlook. But the majority of commentators see the plural verb as an anomaly.

14 Though readers of Genesis, who know more about Abraham's past history than Abimelek did, may find Abraham's attempts at justification unconvincing, Abimelek acts most positively. He does his best to make amends by giving Abraham a very generous present as the Pharaoh did (12:16). Abimelek did not give Abraham any asses or camels, but he did give an additional thousand shekels, which was an enormous sum of money (see *Comment* on v 16). Furthermore, mentioning these gifts here seems to imply that unlike the Pharaoh's gifts that were given at the time of Sarah's marriage as convention dictated, Abimelek gave these presents after the proposed marriage had fallen through by

way of reparation for his behavior. This interpretation seems to be confirmed by
his giving back Sarah at the same time and by his subsequent remarks (v 16).
Once again Abimelek appears to be a penitent and generous man.

15–16 Abimelek's generosity comes again to expression here. Chaps. 13–14
disclosed that Abraham was a very wealthy sheikh with large flocks and herds, so
that he and Lot had to separate, because there were too many of them to dwell
together (13:6). Yet Abimelek, king of the small city-state of Gerar, allows Abraham
the pick of his land. "Look, *my* land is before you. Dwell wherever you like."

"A thousand silver shekels" (a shekel = 12 grams/0.4 ounces). Fifty shekels was
the maximum ever asked for in bride money (Deut 22:29); the typical old
Babylonian laborer received a wage of about half a shekel a month. This gives an
indication of the scale of Abimelek's compensation. But note the barbed "I am
giving . . . to your *brother*"—not "to your husband." Despite his prompt obedience to God's instructions and his display of magnanimity toward Abraham,
Abimelek still resented Abraham's behavior.

"That is for you as compensation," lit. "covering of eyes." The exact meaning
of this unique phrase is unclear. The gift makes one blind to what has happened
(cf. 32:21[20]; Job 9:24). But it is not clear whether it is Sarah's eyes or other
people's eyes that are covered, in other words, that they no longer look on her as
a compromised woman. The last clause, "in everything you will be justified," seems
to favor the latter, though it is grammatically difficult (see *Notes*).

17–18 The final scene in this episode relates to the happy resolution of the
whole affair and clarifies some of the points that the initial exposition had left
obscure. Vv 1–2 gave no indication of the span of time involved, but because they
are so brief, it is easy to suppose that settling in Gerar, Sarah's abduction, and the
dream occurred in quick succession. Vv 17–18 show that such an interpretation
is wrong. Abimelek had fallen ill after he had taken Sarah; that was why he had
not approached her (v 4). Furthermore, the LORD had closed the wombs of his
household so that none of his wives gave birth. This last-minute revelation casts a
cloud over Abimelek's earlier protestations of innocence. Although he had not
actually committed adultery with Sarah, it was only the grace of God, albeit through
illness, that had prevented him sinning.

"Closed" (עצר). In 16:3 the term is used of Sarah's inability to conceive, in Isa
66:9 of inability to deliver a baby. It could be that both meanings are intended
here. Assuming that Abimelek's illness was related to his wives' problems, it seems
likely that failure to conceive was at least part of the problem. Childlessness is a
penalty for some types of incest according to Lev 20:20–21. For Abimelek to realize that there were problems with his wives' conception suggests that Sarah had
been a member of his household for weeks, if not months, before he had the
dream disclosing his sin to him.

The fact that the LORD "had completely closed every womb in Abimelek's household" underlines yet again (cf. vv 4, 6) that Isaac was not conceived illegitimately.
That Abraham's prayer for Abimelek restored the health of the royal household
shows his effectiveness as a prophetic intercessor (v 7) and reiterates that through
him all the families of the earth find blessing (12:3; 18:18). But it raises more
sharply than ever the question of why the prayers for his own wife are unanswered.
Sarah used exactly the same word, עצר "close, prevent," when she said, "Since the

LORD has *prevented* me from having children" (16:2) as is used in 20:18, "the LORD
had completely *closed* every womb." By this concluding comment on the Sarah-
Abimelek affair, the author alludes to the overriding concern of the Abraham
cycle and raises the expectation that at last the promise of a son will be fulfilled.

Explanation

This is an astonishing episode. It seems incredible that Abraham should make
the same dreadful mistake again: visiting a foreign country, he passes his wife off
as his sister. If perhaps in chap. 12 we may excuse him, because at that stage he
had little experience of God's providential protecting care, now years older and
richer in experiences of deliverance from danger, it is amazing to find Abraham
fearing for his life in Gerar. The righteous prophet who boldly pleaded for the
salvation of Sodom is now discovered to be less than perfect in his trust in God's
safekeeping. Indeed, when challenged by Abimelek, he resorts to lying, claiming
he described Sarah as his sister wherever they went.

Coming straight after the sacking of Sodom and the unfilial behavior of Lot's
daughters, this story disturbs the reader in another way. In the great city of Sodom,
there were not ten righteous, but Gerar had a God-fearing king who ruled a righteous nation (20:4, 8). Not all foreigners were as godless as Sodom. Thus this
incident makes us realize that Abraham is not such a saint as we might have concluded from chap. 18, nor were all the inhabitants of Canaan so depraved as those
who lived in Sodom.

But the author is not attempting merely to modify the characterizations of the
previous chapters; he is, as always, tracing the working out of the promises to
Abraham. Once again he is saved from the full effects of his folly by the mercy of
God, who sent sickness into Abimelek's household, which prevented him having
intercourse with Sarah. Here the promise of covenantal protection is being fulfilled. But God's mercy is not restricted to Abraham's family; it extends also to
the king of a righteous God-fearing nation. Though it emerges that Abimelek
may not have been quite so pure in heart as he professed, he was genuinely mis-
taken about Sarah's status and later made generous amends for his behavior. And
from his point of view, his sickness was heaven-sent to prevent his falling into
worse sin. Abimelek's positive attitude toward Abraham must guarantee him God's
blessing, for "I will bless those who bless you" (12:3). His is a nation that will find
blessing in Abraham, and this is shown by Abraham's interceding for them so
that "God healed Abimelek, his wife, and his slave-wives" (20:17).

However, it is not just the promise of covenantal protection and blessing to
the nations that is partially realized in this episode. Abraham is invited "to dwell
wherever he likes" in Abimelek's land. Admittedly, this is not the same as possessing the land through purchase (chap. 23), but it does represent a stage nearer
that goal. This chapter is also sandwiched between the double promise of Isaac's
birth (17:16; 18:10–14) and the birth itself (21:1–7), yet apparently says nothing
about it. Instead Sarah is separated from Abraham and lives in a royal harem.
That an elderly woman, long past the menopause (18:11–12), should have been
thought attractive enough for intercourse with a king is intriguing. Is something
happening to Sarah that will make pregnancy possible? Is she undergoing some

sort of rejuvenation? The narrator does not say, but he and God insist that Abimelek never had intercourse with Sarah (20:4, 6). Despite this episode, there is no doubt that Isaac's father is Abraham, not Abimelek. Then finally the episode closes with the comment "Then Abraham prayed to God, and God healed Abimelek, his wife, and his slave-wives, and they gave birth, for the LORD had completely closed every womb in Abimelek's household" (20:17–18). Some years earlier Sarah had observed that "the LORD has prevented [lit. "closed"] me from having children" (16:2). The echo of Sarah's comment in 20:18 surely raises the question "Why cannot the LORD open Sarah's womb in response to Abraham's prayer if he can cure the infertility of Abimelek's household?"

So our chapter closes with a glimmer of hope, a hope that will suddenly be realized in chap. 21. But though the narrative reassures us about the reliability of God's promises, it again reminds us of the waywardness and moral weakness of his servants. The sixth-century prayer of Saint Gregory would have been as relevant to Abraham as it is to us:

> Almighty God, who seest that we have no power of ourselves to help ourselves. Keep us both outwardly in our bodies, and inwardly in our souls, that we may be defended from all adversities which may happen to the body, and from all evil thoughts which may assault and hurt the soul, through Jesus Christ our Lord.

(Collect for Second Sunday in Lent,
Book of Common Prayer)

Isaac Displaces Ishmael   (21:1–21)

Bibliography

See also *Bibliography* on 16:1–16.

Cazelles, H. "Abraham au Negeb." In *Die Väter Israels: FS J. Scharbert,* ed. M. Görg. Stuttgart: Katholisches Bibelwerk, 1989. 23–32. **Cogan, M.** "A Technical Term for Exposure." *JNES* 27 (1968) 133–35. **Fensham, F. C.** "The Son of a Handmaid in Northwest Semitic." *VT* 19 (1969) 312–21. **Neff, R. W.** "The Birth and Election of Isaac in the Priestly Tradition." *BR* 15 (1970) 5–18. **Rabinowitz, I.** "Sarah's Wish (Gen 21:6–7)." *VT* 29 (1979) 362–63.

Translation

[1] *The LORD visited Sarah as he had said, and the LORD did for Sarah as he had promised.* [2] *Sarah conceived[a] and bore[b] Abraham a son in his old age at the time which God[c] had promised him.* [3] *Abraham called the name of his newborn[a] son, that Sarah had borne him, Isaac.* [4] *And Abraham circumcised[a] his son Isaac, when he was eight days old, as God had commanded him.* [5] *Now Abraham was a hundred years old, when Isaac[a] his son was born[b] to him.* [6] *Then Sarah said,*

"God has made me laugh:ᵃ
everyone who hearsᵇ it will laugh for me."

⁷She said, "Who would have announced to Abraham,
'Sarah has nursedᵃ sons'?ᵇ
Yet I have borne him a son in his old age."

⁸The child grew and was weaned.ᵃ Then Abraham held a great feast on the day that Isaac was weaned.ᵇ ⁹Sarah sawᵃ the son of Hagar the Egyptian, who had borne a child to Abraham, mocking.ᵇ ¹⁰So she said to Abraham, "Driveᵃ out this slave-wife and her son, because the son of this slave-wife shall not inherit with my son, Isaac." ¹¹And Abraham was very displeasedᵃ for his son's sake by the remark.

¹²Then God said to Abraham, "Do not be displeasedᵃ for the lad and your slave-wife. Obey Sarah in whatever she says to you, because your descendants will be named through Isaac. ¹³But I shall also makeᵃ your slave-wife's son into a nation,ᵇ for he is your descendant."

¹⁴So early in the morning Abraham took bread and a skin of water and gave it to Hagar, putting it on her shoulder, ᵃand the childᵃ and sentᵇ her off. She went and wanderedᶜ in the wilderness of Beersheba.

¹⁵When the water in the skin ran out,ᵃ she dumpedᵇ the child under oneᶜ of the bushes, ¹⁶and she went and satᵃ down by herselfᵇ opposite at about bowshotᶜ range,ᵈ because she thought, "Let me not see my child's death." So she sat down opposite, ᵉraisedᶠ her voice, and wept.ᵉᵍ

¹⁷Then God heard theᵃ voice of the lad, and the angel of God called to Hagar from heaven and said to her, "What is the matter, Hagar? Do not be afraid,ᵇ for God has heard the voice of the lad ᶜwhere he is.ᶜ ¹⁸Go on,ᵃ liftᵇ up the boy and graspᶜ him with your hand, for I shall make him into a great nation." ¹⁹Then God opened her eyes, and she saw a well of water. So she went and filled the skin withᵃ water, and she gaveᵇ the lad a drink.

²⁰So God was with the boy, he grew up, and lived in the wilderness and became an archer.ᵃ ²¹He lived in the wilderness of Paran, and his mother married him to an Egyptian.

Notes

2.a. Cf. n. 4:1.b.

2.b. Cf. n. 4:1.c.

2.c. G has "the LORD."

3.a. As pointed, def art + 3 masc sg pf niph ילד, "to bear." However, it could be masc sg ptcp niph, especially if repointed הנולד (cf. BDB; KB; WOC, 340).

4.a. Cf. n. 17:23.a.

5.a. On את following niph of ילד, cf. n. 4:18.a.; GKC, 121b.

5.b. ב + inf constr niph ילד.

6.a. Either a noun (so BDB) or inf constr צחק (so Joüon, 124c).

6.b. Def art + masc sg ptcp qal שמע.

7.a. 3 fem sg pf hiph ינק "to suck," hiph "to nurse, suckle."

7.b. "Sons," pl "to denote an indefinite singular" (GKC, 124o; Joüon, 136j).

8.a. Waw consec + 3 masc sg impf niph גמל in pause.

8.b. Inf constr niph גמל.

9.a. Cf. n. 3:6.a.

9.b. Masc sg ptcp piel צחק. G adds "with her son Isaac."

10.a. 2 masc sg impv piel גרש.

11.a. Waw consec + 3 masc sg impf qal רעע "be evil."

12.a. Cf. n. 11.a.

13.a. 1 sg impf qal שִׂים + 3 masc sg suffix.

13.b. Sam Pent, G, S, Vg add "great," probably assimilating to v 18.

14.a-a. An awkwardly placed phrase. If the "and" were omitted or the whole phrase transposed as *BHS* and Westermann suggest, it would be clear that "he placed the child on her shoulder." However, the versions do not support such a transposition. Rather, "the child" is object of "he gave." The delay in mentioning the transfer of Ishmael implies Abraham waited till the last possible minute; cf. the delayed mention of Benjamin in 43:15 (Gispen 2:218).

14.b. Waw consec + 3 masc sg impf piel שׁלח + 3 fem sg suffix.

14.c. Waw consec + 3 fem sg impf qal תעה (apoc).

15.a. Waw consec + 3 masc pl impf qal כלה.

15.b. Waw consec + 2 fem sg impf hiph שׁלך.

15.c. On use of אחד with pl nouns, see Joüon, 137v; WOC, 251.

16.a. Waw consec + 2 fem sg impf ישׁב.

16.b. Ethical dative. See GKC, 119s; cf. n. 12:1.a. (*EWAS,* 122).

16.c. כ + masc pl constr pilel ptcp מחה.

16.d. הרחק inf abs hiph רחק.

16.e-e. *BHS* and many commentators emend to "*he* raised *his* voice and *he* wept" on the basis of G, "they lifted up their voice, and the boy cried," which is ill-founded, since Sam Pent, S, Vg support MT, "she . . . her, she." It is also grammatically awkward, since the use of the waw consec would imply Ishmael did not start crying until his mother sat down. An explicit noun subj, e.g.," the child," might also be expected.

16.f. Waw consec + 3 fem sg impf נשׂא.

16.g. Waw consec + 3 fem sg impf בכה.

17.a. Some MSS and SamPent, *Tg. Ps.-J.* read את for אל.

17.b. 2 fem sg impf ירא.

17.c-c. On this phrase, see GKC, 138e. Westermann wishes to transpose this phrase to v 18 after "the boy." See *Comment.*

18.a. 2 fem sg impv קום, here used as introductory exhortation (*SBH* , 57).

18.b. 2 fem sg impv נשׂא.

18.c. 2 fem sg impv hiph חזק.

19.a. Double acc following מלא.

19.b. Waw consec + 3 fem sg impf hiph שׁקה (apoc).

20.a. Lit. "a shooter, an archer." Two hapaxes, occurring only here in the OT. *BHS* proposes רֹבֵה קֶשֶׁת "shooter of a bow."

Form/Structure/Setting

This section covers two main episodes in the birth of Isaac (vv 1–7) and his weaning (vv 8–21): the content clearly defines its beginning and end. The birth is simply chronicled with very little attempt at scenic presentation apart from recording Sarah's amazement in vv 6–7: Birth of Isaac (1–2), Naming (3), Circumcision (4), Abraham's age (5), Sarah's comments (6–7). However, the weaning of Isaac and the consequent expulsion of Hagar and Ishmael are depicted much more dramatically.

v 8	Introduction
vv 9–10	Sarah demands Ishmael's expulsion
v 11	Abraham's anger
vv 12–13	God tells Abraham to agree
v 14	Expulsion of Hagar and Ishmael
vv 15–16	Hagar and Ishmael's desperation
vv 17–18	Angel of God speaks

v 19   Water found
vv 20–21   Conclusion

As they stand, both episodes are an integral part of the Abraham cycle. The birth of Isaac is the long-delayed fulfillment of the repeated promises of a son to Abraham and Sarah (cf. 13:16; 15:4–5; 18:10–15; and especially chap. 17). Similarly, the expulsion of Hagar and her son presupposes the birth of Isaac (vv 8–10). Abraham's reluctance to obey his wife's demand reflects both chap. 16 and 17:18. The divine reassurance (vv 12–13, 18) that this is right echoes 17:19–20. "God has heard the voice of the boy" (21:17) clearly presupposes the name Ishmael, given in 16:11 but not used at all in this chapter. Finally, the remarks about his life in the wilderness appear to fulfill the prophecy of his future destiny in 16:11.

Traditional source critics are divided about the analysis of vv 1–2 and 6–7. For example, v 1a is J according to Skinner, but E according to Procksch; v 1b is P according to Skinner, Coats, and Speiser, but J according to Procksch. A majority tend to regard vv 1–2a as J, v 2b as P, and vv 6–7 as J or E. Vv 3–5, with their strong connections with chap. 17, have usually been assigned to P, while vv 8–21, which have been construed as a doublet to chap. 16, have often been assigned to E. Apart from the divine-names Yahweh in v 1 and Elohim elsewhere, the only clues to guide the source critic are similarities in phraseology with other sources. Since even the divine-names criterion is not regarded as infallible in v 1, this leads to a diversity of views among older commentators. More recent critics, who see E as one of the sources used by J (Van Seters, *Abraham*) or as an expansion of J (Westermann), argue that this is the case with vv 8–21. Coats sees the whole section (vv 1–21) as J or JE (save for 1b–5 P). Westermann regards vv 1–7 as the work of the final redactor, who incorporated J and P (vv 3–5) into his work. "The middle part, vv 3–5, is an untouched piece of P which is really the genealogical conclusion of ch 17; this is set between two J passages, vv 1–2 and 6–7, in such a way as to form a self-contained string of events. Vv 1–2 are common to both J and P" (2:331).

Westermann's analysis does justice to the interconnections between the diverse materials here but is probably too complicated. As elsewhere in Genesis, I prefer to suppose that the main editor J has introduced and arranged earlier materials, conventionally denoted P and E, to fit in with the overall theme of the narrative. J's hand is most clear in the introductory v 1 (note the double mention of the LORD; cf. 17:1) and possibly in the wording of the promises (vv 13, 17–18).

Comment

1   "The LORD visited Sarah as he had said, and the LORD did for her as he had promised." At long last the promise of a child for Sarah is fulfilled. The birth of Isaac is predicted twice (17:16–21; 18:10–15), and here the fulfillment of the promises is mentioned twice. However, as Westermann rightly observes, the duplication hardly demonstrates the presence of two sources; rather, it gives the announcement of Sarah's conception a festive poetic flavor because of its use of synonymous parallelism. This lifts the statement here above a merely matter-of-fact genealogical

report. For the birth of Isaac is not merely a great event for Sarah; it is indispensable for any further fulfillment of the promises to Abraham. Without an heir, he can never become a great nation, let alone inherit the land.

The term "visit" (פקד) also marks the special significance of this birth. When God "visits," it indicates his special interest in a person, whether for judgment on sin (e.g., Exod 20:5; 32:34) or to describe "the LORD's salvific attention to an individual or his people Israel" (W. Schottroff, *THWAT* 2:476; G. André, *Determining the Destiny: PQD in the OT* [Lund: CWK Gleerup, 1980]). Thus it describes God's intervention to save Israel from Egyptian slavery (Gen 50:24–25; Exod 4:31), to end a famine (Ruth 1:6), and to bring the exiles home (Jer 29:10). But the closest parallel to this usage is 1 Sam 2:21, "The LORD visited Hannah, and she conceived."

Note here the emphasis on the fulfillment of the promise: "as he had said . . . as he had promised." This repetition makes the reader "pause in the consideration of so great a miracle. Meanwhile Moses commends the faithfulness of God; as if he had said, he never feeds men with empty promises, nor is he less true in granting what he had promised, than he is liberal and willing in making that promise" (Calvin, 1:538).

2 "In his old age." This phrase (cf. 21:7; 37:3; 44:20), of course, reflects remarks made earlier about the difficulty of Abraham and Sarah's producing children because of their age (17:17; 18:10–12). Yet despite their doubts, the promise was fulfilled precisely as forecast; "at the (appointed) time," the phrase used in 17:21; 18:14, here appears for the last time in Genesis to emphasize the literal fulfillment "which God had promised him."

3–4 God's precise fulfillment of his promise is matched by Abraham's exact obedience. He names his son Isaac as directed in 17:19 and circumcises him on the eighth day as prescribed in 17:12. Note the redundancy, "which was born to him, that Sarah had borne to him." Comparison with 16:15 shows that "which was borne to him" is unnecessary. But the repetition again serves to drive home the miraculous nature of the birth of a son to Sarah.

5 Similarly, the reference to Abraham being a hundred years old at the birth of Isaac emphasizes that what seemed humanly impossible (17:17) has indeed occurred. The frequent reference in genealogies to the age at which a man fathered his first child suggests this was regarded as a most important milestone in his life (cf. 5:3, 6; 11:12, 14, etc.).

6–7 Sarah breaks out into poetry to express her joy and wonder at what God has done for her. Through her words the narrator brings out the emotional impact of the events so dryly recorded in vv 1–5, and through her rhetorical question, "Who would have announced to Abraham?" invites all who hear the story to contemplate God's grace and power.

> "God made me laugh:
> everyone who hears it will laugh for me."

Twice here Sarah uses the root צחק "laugh" found in Isaac's name. Indeed, the second line involves the exact form of his name: "everyone who hears it will Isaac for me." Thus the play on his name is most obvious here, even though it is not drawn attention to in the narrative. Earlier, the name Isaac had been associated

with the laughter of incredulity (17:17–19; 18:12–15); here, though, it is the laughter of joy (cf. Pss 113:9; 126:2).

"Everyone who hears it will laugh for me." Westermann's suggestion (following Budde, Gunkel, Skinner) to transpose this line to the end of v 7 breaks up the poetic couplet and is unnecessary. Some commentators (e.g., Gunkel, Gispen) translate the second line "everyone . . . will laugh *at* me." In other words, those who hear the story will laugh at such an old woman bearing a child or laugh that she doubted the divine promise. Though possible, such an interpretation jars; the context is suffused with an atmosphere of joy and wonder at God's mighty acts. With most commentators, I prefer to see Sarah drawing attention to the universal pleasure her belated motherhood brings.

> "Who would have announced to Abraham
> 'Sarah has nursed sons'?"

The question expects the answer "No one." Abraham never expected anyone to come from the delivery to tell him that Sarah had safely brought forth a boy and was feeding him (cf. Jer 20:15). Through this question, Sarah puts into words the incredulity every hearer of the story experiences. Like Abraham and Sarah beforehand, we tend to regard the birth of Isaac as impossible. Yet, says Sarah, it has happened: "I have borne him a son in his old age." No one would have announced such a thing to Abraham, unless he were God. And, of course, he had announced it beforehand twice (17:16; 18:12–15). Here we see the final transfiguration of Sarah's hopeless despair (cf. *Comment* on 18:12) into joyous praise.

8–21 But Sarah's joy is short-lived, at least in the narrator's perspective. The old animosity between her and Hagar breaks out again, leading to a final parting of the ways; Hagar and her son (never called Ishmael in this section) are driven out into the wilderness to fend for themselves. And this technique of dealing with sidelines to the main story line before resuming the main track is characteristic throughout Genesis. The sons of Cain are dealt with in 4:17–24 before the main line through Seth resumes in 4:25; similarly, the descendants of Japhet and Ham are listed in 10:1–20 before the Shemite line resumes in 10:21–31; 11:10–26. In the Abraham narrative, the histories of Terah (11:27–32) and Lot (chaps. 13, 14, 19) are brought to a conclusion long before strict chronology warrants it. Here the story of Ishmael is tidied up, so that the narrative can concentrate on the main line of Isaac. But though Hagar is mother of the non-elect Ishmael, it is notable how sympathetically she is portrayed here, just as in chap. 16.

8 Breast-feeding in traditional societies often continues much longer than in the West, so that a child may not be weaned until he is three (2 Macc 7:27). The importance of this occasion was marked by a great feast to celebrate it (cf. 1 Sam 1:22–25; see further *TDOT* 1:26–27). In a society where infant mortality was high, to reach the age of two or three would be regarded as a significant achievement, so this in part explains the magnitude of the celebrations. From now on Isaac looks relatively certain to be Abraham's heir.

9–10 But Isaac's status as heir apparent is always at risk while "the son of Hagar . . . who had borne a child to Abraham" is around, so Sarah demands their expulsion.

9 "Sarah saw the son of Hagar . . . mocking." The opening "Sarah saw" indicates that the reader is going to see things from Sarah's point of view. "Mocking" (piel of צחק) is another play on the name Isaac and may give a clue to what "mocking" involved. The translation "mock" implies a negative verdict on Ishmael's behavior, but the qal of צחק means "laugh" and can have very positive overtones as in v 6, as can the piel of שחק (e.g., Zech 8:5). Consequently, some commentators (e.g., Skinner, Speiser, Westermann) take the passage in a quite neutral sense: they follow the LXX and Vg by adding an object and translating "Sarah saw the son of Hagar . . . playing with Isaac her son." "It is the spectacle of the two young children playing together, innocent of social distinctions, that excites Sarah's maternal jealousy and prompts her cruel demands" (Skinner, 322). Such an understanding, of course, puts Sarah in a dreadful light and, indeed, reflects badly on the LORD and Abraham for acceding to her demand, if this is the context.

But it is dubious whether the piel of צחק will bear such an innocent interpretation. It is used absolutely as here only in 19:21, Exod 32:6, and Judg 16:25, each time with nasty overtones, usually of someone being mocked. If, with the LXX and Vg, the phrase "with her son Isaac" is allowed to be authentic, the situation is not greatly altered. The three passages where it is used with an adverbial phrase imply disapproval of the play by its observer (26:8; 39:14, 17). So something like "mock," "jest," "make fun of" would seem an apt English translation.

But what did Ishmael's mocking consist of? The text leaves it open, so speculation has been rampant. The midrash suggested it might involve idolatry (cf. Exod 32:6), sexual immorality (cf. Gen 39:14, 17), or even murder (cf. 2 Sam 2:14 [שחק]). But this seems unlikely, for elsewhere Ishmael appears in a quite positive light. More likely is the view that Ishmael was making fun of Isaac's status or the circumstances of his birth, which were a source of joyous laughter to Sarah (v 6). "The threat of Ishmael throughout the narrative is that he would replace Sarah's son . . . as the heir of Abraham. Now the wordplay so crucial for the whole story sets out the weight of the conflict. It does not imply that Ishmael has done something amiss with Isaac. It suggests on the contrary, that Sarah saw Ishmael *mĕṣaḥēq*, playing the role of Isaac. Indeed, the act implies some disdain on Ishmael's part, perhaps equivalent to the curse of Hagar in 16:4" (Coats, 153; cf. Calvin, Jacob).

10 "Drive out this slave-wife and her son, because the son of this slave-wife shall not inherit with my son Isaac." As Westermann observes, Sarah was not motivated by jealousy or pride so much as by a ruthless maternal concern for her son's future (cf. Rebekah and Jacob). But her language does suggest a mean belittling of Hagar and Ishmael. Note how she avoids using their proper names; instead she speaks of "this slave-wife" (twice) and "her son" in contrast to "my son, Isaac." The term "drive out" (גרש piel) also evokes harshness (cf. 3:24; 4:14; Exod 6:1). The qal participle is often used of divorcees (e.g., Lev 21:7, 14; 22:13), and clearly that is implied here too.

Nevertheless, for all her ruthless competitiveness, she is right on one point: Ishmael "shall not inherit with my son." By evoking the language of the divine promise, "This one [i.e., Eliezer] will not inherit from you, but one who comes out of your loins, he shall inherit from you" (15:4, the only other passage where ירש is used in this sense in Genesis), Sarah gives some religious justification for her apparently harsh demand. And this parallel mitigates to some extent the

reader's sense of shock that God should endorse her request. It is based on principles enunciated much earlier in the narrative.

That children born to slave-wives could inherit with the children of the primary wife is mentioned in LH 170–71 and LI 25 (cf. Fensham, *VT* 19 [1969] 317–21; Thompson, *Historicity,* 263–67). "The key to Sarah's demand lies in a clause in the laws of Lipit-Ishtar where it is stipulated that the father may grant freedom to the slave woman and the children she has borne him, in which case they forfeit their share of the paternal property" (Sarna, 147).

11 And Abraham was very displeased for his son's sake by the remark. In a sentence of just eight words, the narrator sums up Abraham's explosive reaction to Sarah's suggestion. Elsewhere, men explode in anger when they are merely "displeased" (e.g., Num 11:10; 1 Sam 18:8). When God is "displeased" with someone, death often follows (e.g., Gen 38:10; 2 Sam 11:7). Only here is anyone said to be "*very* displeased." Quite what Abraham said and did to express his displeasure is left to the imagination. The narrator is content to give the reason "for his son's sake." Sarah called Ishmael "the son of this slave-wife," distancing herself as far as she could from him. But for Abraham, Ishmael is "his son." This brief sentence gives a glimpse of Abraham's strong paternal affection and particularly his deep love for Ishmael. If he cannot contemplate sending Ishmael away, how much harder will he find the command in 22:2?

12–13 God endorses Sarah's demand. The length of time elapsed between Sarah's demand and the divine endorsement is not stated. But the narrative seems to presuppose ("early in the morning" [v 14]) that God spoke to Abraham in a night vision soon afterwards, though this may just refer to the coolest time of day to set out on a journey.

12 "Do not be displeased for the lad and your slave-wife." Note God's description of Ishmael: he is a "lad." נער "lad" covers any boy from an infant to a grown man. But in Genesis it usually refers to young men capable of taking care of themselves, such as the seventeen-year-old Joseph (37:2), servants (18:7), and those old enough to be morally responsible (19:4). So using the term here is surely designed to reassure Abraham that his beloved Ishmael will cope with the situation. Note, too, "and your slave-wife"; though Abraham was more worried about Ishmael (v 11), this additional comment shows he was also concerned for Hagar.

"Obey Sarah in whatever she says to you." The last time Abraham obeyed Sarah (16:2) was a great mistake (cf. 3:17), so this command answers yet another objection that Abraham raised to expelling Hagar and Ishmael. It was his right to decide family policy, not Sarah's. Now he must submit to her, for her demands fit in with God's plans, "because your descendants will be named through Isaac" (cf. 48:16). The precise sense of this clause is obscure, but the general sense is clear. The elect line of Abraham's descendants will run through Isaac; none of his other children count, a point already made in 17:19 and here reaffirmed.

13 "I shall also make your slave-wife's son into a nation" reiterates the promise made to Abraham about Ishmael in 17:20, "I shall make him into a great nation." If Abraham was worried about the survival and future greatness of Ishmael, he should be reassured by these remarks.

14 "Early in the morning" (cf. 19:27; 20:8; 22:3), "Abraham took bread and a skin of water and gave it to Hagar." He supplies Hagar with the basic provisions for survival: a skin of water, often made of an old goatskin, could hold about fifteen liters (three gallons, thirty pounds in weight). This sounds rather minimal in the light of the injunction in Deut 15:12–18 to give the departing slave a royal send–off. Why? Was it Abraham's secret intention to make sure Hagar could not go too far (Calvin) ? As Gispen observes, this conflicts with his prompt obedience to God's command intimated by "early in the morning." And his use of the name Hagar here rather than "slave-wife" suggests he is treating her with consideration, as does the apposition clause "putting it on her shoulder." "The inclusion of such details brings to attention the compassionate concern of the distressed Abraham" (Jacob, 482).

Many modern commentators argue that the object of "putting on her shoulder" is "the child" and suggest rearrangements of the word order to make this a more probable rendering of the Hebrew (see *Notes*). However, this is unlikely. First, it would be difficult to carry a large water-skin, bread, and a child, however young, on one's back simultaneously. Second, the angel later explicitly tells Hagar to take Ishmael by the hand (v 18). He was evidently old enough to walk. It seems likely then that Abraham put the bread and water-skin on Hagar's back so that she could have her hands free to take Ishmael by the hand (so Jerome, Jacob). Third, 17:25; 21:12 (note the term "lad") imply that Ishmael was well into his teens by this time, in which case it would be most improbable that he rode on his mother's back! This last point is usually countered by assigning chaps. 17 and 21 to different sources (P and E) and using it as an argument for source analysis. But a theory that demands textual emendation *and* a superficial reading of the story is suspect.

Rather, as Dillmann, Skinner, Weinfeld, and Gispen correctly observe, "and the child" depends on "and he gave." The word order delaying the mention of "the child" (note the term "child" chosen to stress his relationship to Abraham) until the last possible moment conveys Abraham's great reluctance to part with Ishmael, a point already made explicit in v 11. It was a costly decision to part with his firstborn son. In this light, one may interpret the sparse provisioning as evoking Abraham's numbness at sending his son away rather than lack of concern or forethought.

"Send her off" (piel שלח) is a softer term than "drive out" (cf. 18:16; 19:29; 3:23). It is used of divorce (e.g., Deut 22:19; 24:1, 3) and the release of slaves with a generous provision (Exod 11:1–2; Deut 15:13). It may be that Abraham blessed his wife and son before they left or gave them other gifts (cf. Jacob, Westermann). But what matters for the rest of the story is the supply of bread and water, so only these items are mentioned explicitly.

"She wandered" shows she was lost (cf. 37:15, Joseph; Exod 23:4, ox; Isa 53:6, sheep) and did not know where to go, and helps us to sympathize with her situation.

"In the wilderness of Beersheba" means "the fairly flat southern part of the Negeb" (Simons, *GTOT*). Assuming Abraham is still living somewhere near Gerar (cf. 20:1), it would appear that Hagar is moving southeastward toward northern Arabia, later inhabited by some of the Ishmaelites (cf. 25:12–18).

15–16 A graphic and poignant scene requiring little comment. Note how Ishmael is here twice called "the child," emphasizing the bond between him and his mother, rather than his potential independence that the word "lad" evokes.

"Dumped" does not imply either that Hagar had been carrying him or that he was a young child. Seventeen-year-old Joseph was "dumped" in a pit by his brothers (37:20, 22, 24). BDB (1021a) notes that the term is especially used of casting dead bodies (e.g., Josh 8:29). M. Cogan (*JNES* 27 [1968] 133) compares Jer 38:6, 9 and suggests it means "abandon to die." The term suggests Hagar was in despair anticipating her son's imminent death.

"Sat down by herself opposite." The use of the pronoun "by herself" (cf. 12:1) draws attention to her inward feelings. "Notions of isolation, loneliness, parting, seclusion or withdrawal are often recognizable" (*EWAS,* 122).

"At about bowshot range, because she thought 'Let me not see my child's death.' " As Jacob observes, there is a contradiction between her action and her comment, for one can see much farther than bowshot range. "That is the touching illogicality of a mother's heart. In reality she sits at a distance, so that she cannot hear the crying of her child which tears her heart, and to allow herself to weep freely" (Jacob, 483).

17–18 "God heard the voice of the boy" is said both by the narrator and by the angel, though hitherto the story has said nothing about him, merely leaving the reader to surmise that he was crying. That such emphasis should be placed by the narrative on the fact that God heard Ishmael rather than Hagar invites reflection. Why? Calvin suggests that Ishmael's prayers may have been more vital than his mother's, because he was more to blame for their plight, and therefore his presumed penitence was the more significant. However, he prefers to explain God's response in terms of his promise to Abraham about Ishmael. Both explanations are possible. Certainly, that "God heard the lad" highlights Ishmael's central role in the narrative. His behavior led to their expulsion and his prayer to their salvation. His mother was a victim of circumstance on this occasion, not the chief culprit as in chap. 16. And as we have already observed, "and God heard" (וישמע אלהים, *wayyišmaʿ ʾĕlōhîm*) includes the name of Ishmael, though this story never uses his name on its own. He is always described as "son," "lad," or "child."

Doubtless this cryptic reference to Ishmael's name is meant to recall its origin, "You shall name him Ishmael, for the LORD has noticed your oppression" (16:11). On that occasion, there was no mention of Hagar praying before the LORD answered. Similarly, here we are not told that Ishmael prayed until God answered. On both occasions, the one who provokes the situation initially has prayer answered. On both occasions, God shows himself willing to rescue the afflicted even though their own behavior has provoked their persecution. Then Hagar commented, "I have seen him who looks after me." Now the truth of her observation is confirmed again in the nick of time. The phrase the angel calls "from heaven" only occurs again in 22:11, 15, whence Jacob concludes that it shows the urgency of the divine intervention: the angel did not have time to descend to earth as usual. But 22:15, where speed is not crucial, suggests that "from heaven" means the message has immediate divine authority.

At any rate, as often in Scripture, the divine messenger introduces himself with a question that need not be asked by one with supernatural knowledge. In 16:8,

he asked, "Hagar where have you come from?" In 18:9, he inquired, "Where is Sarah your wife?" and here, "What is the matter, Hagar?" In each case, the angel discloses his supernatural identity by mentioning a name that a human stranger would not know. Having thus disclosed indirectly who he is, the angel then gives the apposite message. "God has heard the voice of the lad where he is" shows further that the angel knows Ishmael's ("God hears") name, while the clause "where he is" seems to hark back to Hagar's previous experience when she called the god who appeared to her "the God who sees." Then she had learned that the LORD knows what is going on in the world wherever it happens. Here the angel states that God can see a child lying under a bush and respond to his prayers.

The rest of the message builds on this foundation. Renewed faith must lead to renewed action. "Go on, lift up the boy, grasp him with your hand, for I shall make him into a great nation." For Hagar, this last promise may have been a fresh revelation, for although such an assurance has twice been given to Abraham, this is the first time it is given to Hagar (cf. 17:20; 21:13).

19 Not only does God make promises; he makes provision. "God opened her eyes, and she saw a well of water." A well that had been there all the time Hagar now notices for the first time. For similar miraculous eye-openings, see 2 Kgs 6:17, 20, though the closest parallel is in Gen 22:13, where Abraham raises his eyes and sees a ram caught in a thicket.

20–21 After a vivid scenic narrative, the storyteller reverts to summarizing the rest of Ishmael's career. This explains what happened next and resolves issues raised by the obvious dependence of 21:8–21 on chap. 16. As noted, this story knows Ishmael's name, the experiences that gave rise to it, and the promises associated with it, all set out in chap. 16. However, nothing has been said about 16:12, "He shall be a wild ass of a man . . . he shall dwell over against his kinsman." This we suggested was a prediction of his future nomadic lifestyle. 21:20–21 records the fulfillment of this prediction: "He lived in the wilderness and became an archer." His skill as an archer could refer to his hunting ability (cf. 27:3) or to a fondness for fighting. The "wilderness of Paran" (see *Comment* on 14:6) was the name of some of Ishmael's descendants mentioned in 25:18.

"His mother married him to an Egyptian." Normally, of course, it was the father's responsibility to arrange marriage for his son. This last glimpse of Hagar shows her manfully shouldering full responsibility for her son's future welfare. Her love for her son and her faith in the promise enunciated in 21:18 prompted her to assume this task, the parent's final obligation toward a child. This remark, of course, prepares the way for the list of the sons of Ishmael in 25:13–16. It also gives a clue about how Abraham will handle the problem of Isaac's marriage. Hagar looked to her homeland Egypt for Ishmael's wife. Later Abraham will send to his homeland in Mesopotamia for a wife for Isaac. Thus although separated from her husband, Abraham, we find Hagar acting in the best tradition of his faith and practice.

Explanation

At long last Sarah gives birth to a son as God promised. This is the most visible fulfillment of any of the promises so far and also the most central, for without a

son Abraham could never have a multitude of descendants, inherit the land, or be a blessing to all the nations. And the threefold repetition, "as he had said," "as he had promised," "which God promised," which seems unnecessarily repetitive, draws attention to the theological significance of the event of Isaac's birth.

But the stress on the fulfillment of the divine promise is just as vital for another reason. For ancient and modern readers find it incredible that a man aged one hundred should father a child, especially when his wife was only a few years his junior. And those most involved, Abraham and Sarah, thought similarly, according to the repeated witness of Genesis. They both laughed at the idea of Sarah conceiving. And even if she conceived, who would have believed she could have safely delivered?

> "Who would have announced to Abraham,
> 'Sarah has nursed sons'?"

The question expects the answer no. No one but God could have dared to make such a prediction. The birth of Isaac was a divine miracle, not a natural event that might reasonably have been anticipated, least of all by Sarah and Abraham, who knew only too well their age and biological condition.

Yet though they had laughed in disbelief, now Sarah laughs for joy at the birth of their son Isaac, whose name means "he laughs." And Sarah anticipates that her joy will be universally shared.

> "Everyone who hears it will laugh for me."

But as often in human experience, the source of one person's joy can prove the cause of another's jealousy. The occasion was the weaning of Isaac, which probably took place when he was about three. When Isaac had safely survived the dangers of infancy, Abraham held a great feast to celebrate his weaning. Until this point, Ishmael could reasonably have entertained the expectation of being Abraham's sole heir. The conception of Isaac seemed impossible, his birth exceedingly dangerous, and his infancy hazardous. Yet contrary to all expectation he had come through them all, and now Ishmael's right of succession was at risk. So he started to make fun of Isaac's status. The very term "mocking" could be paraphrased "Isaacking." What Ishmael did is left obscure, but his behavior in the light of 12:3, "he who disdains you I shall curse," placed his own position in jeopardy, for Isaac may now be presumed to share in all the promises made to his father Abraham. Admittedly, Abraham had been assured that Ishmael would become a great nation (17:20) and Hagar that he would grow into "a wild ass of a man and dwell opposite all his brothers" (16:12). And in one sense this story shows the fulfillment of these apparently divergent promises; it shows how Ishmael and his mother left the Abrahamic home and came to be an independent nomadic people, how the history of Ishmael fulfilled the promises made to his mother at birth. But it does much more: it gives an insight into the deep affection of Abraham for Ishmael and Hagar. He explodes with anger at the suggestion that he should drive them out; only divine reassurance makes him consent (vv 11–13), while the touching description of their departure shows him holding on to Ishmael until the very last minute. Similarly, the story highlights Hagar's deep

love for her son. Suffering the trauma of divorce, she wanders dazed in the wilderness until their water runs out, and then she dumps her son under a bush sufficiently distant so that she can see him but not so close as to hear his agonized cries as he dies of thirst. Thus the emotional heart of the family, especially the love of Abraham and Hagar for Ishmael, is laid bare in this distressing episode.

If Abraham and Hagar are portrayed most sympathetically, Ishmael, the cause of the conflict, is depicted rather more equivocally. Though his behavior, quite unwise in terms of the social mores of the age and very dangerous in the light of Gen 12:3, fueled Sarah's fiery jealousy, he did pray with penitence when dying of thirst, and as the narrative points out twice, it was his prayer that God answered (vv 17–18). His name Ishmael means "God will hear," and he proved it on this occasion.

Of all the characters, Sarah evokes least sympathy. Her expressions of joy and faith with which the story opens, "'God has made me laugh. / . . . Who would have announced to Abraham, / "Sarah has nursed sons?"'" lead us to expect her to show more tolerance and patience with Hagar and Ishmael. Yet she who "blesses the Lord" one day, "curses men" (cf. Jas 3:9) some time later with words that are cruel and demeaning, "Drive out this slave-wife and her son" (v 10). Nevertheless, her hurtful demand is sanctioned by God, for ultimately it is his will that triumphs in this all-too-human tragedy. Through the pride of Ishmael and the jealousy of Sarah, Ishmael is cut out of the family of Abraham so that his "descendants will be named through Isaac" (v 12), and Ishmael becomes the forefather of desert tribes as first predicted before his birth (16:12; 17:20). But though separated from the family of Abraham, neither Hagar nor Ishmael are beyond the mercy of God. As she discovered on the first occasion, "the LORD" is the one "who sees me," and this time, too, God answers prayer, providing her with reassurance about the future, "I shall make him into a great nation," and water to quench their thirst. And our last glimpse of Hagar shows her loyalty to the customs of the patriarchs: like them she provides a wife for her son from among her own people. So though Ishmael excluded himself and his mother from the blessings associated with Abraham's immediate family, they still experienced God's care and protection and even to some extent maintained the godly marriage custom of that household.

Within the overall plan of Genesis, this account of Isaac's birth and Ishmael's expulsion is of decisive importance in the unfolding of the patriarchal promises. It is to this aspect of the story that Paul refers in Rom 9:7 and in his more extended reference to the role of Hagar and Ishmael in Gal 4:21–31. For Paul, the all-important point is that Isaac was born following God's promise and in that respect anticipates the gentile believers in God's plan, while Ishmael, born through human contrivance, is a forerunner of the Jews who sought salvation through works of the law.

As a story on its own, this narrative, like many other parts of Genesis, illuminates the mixture of faith and doubt, joy and jealousy, love and hatred that characterizes the human predicament. But above all, in it "God proves himself dependable and gracious. He is 'faithful' in performing his promises to each person. Not only does he give Isaac to Abraham and Sarah as their own child, but he hears Hagar and saves Ishmael also, making him—for Abraham's sake (21:13)—

into a great nation, headed by his sons as twelve princes (16:10; 17:20; 21:13, 18; 25:16)" (L. Hicks, *IDB* 2:748).

Covenant with Abimelek (21:22–34)

Bibliography

Matthews, V. H. "The Wells of Gerar." *BA* 49 (1986) 118–26. **McCarthy, D. J.** "Three Covenants in Genesis." *CBQ* 26 (1964) 179–89. **Ray, J. D.** "Two Etymologies: Ziklag and Phicol." *VT* 36 (1986) 355–61. **Sarna, N. M.** "Genesis 21:33: A Study in the Development of a Biblical Text and Its Rabbinic Transformation." In *From Ancient Israel to Modern Judaism: FS Marvin Fox,* ed. J. Neusner, E. S. Frerichs, and N. M. Sarna. Atlanta: Scholars, 1989. 1:69–75.

Translation

[22] *At that time Abimelek*[a] *and his army commander, Phicol, said to Abraham, "God is with you in all that you are doing.* [23] *Now swear*[a] *to me in God's name here that*[b] *you will not deal falsely with me, my* [c] *descendants, or my successors,*[c] *that as I have been kind to you, so you will be kind to me and the land where you have settled."*[d]
[24] *So Abraham said, "I*[a] *shall swear."*[b]
[25] *Now Abraham berated*[a] *Abimelek about the well*[b] *of water which Abimelek's servants had seized.*
[26] *And Abimelek had said, "I do not know who did this thing. You did not tell me. I did not even hear about it till today."*
[27] *So Abraham took sheep and oxen and gave them to Abimelek, and they both made a treaty.*
[28] *Then Abraham put*[a] *seven ewe-lambs*[b] *on their own.*[c] [29] *So Abimelek said to Abraham, "What are these*[a] *seven ewe-lambs which you have put aside on their own?"*[b]
[30] *And he said, "You must take the* [a]*seven ewe-lambs from me so that it may be evidence for me that I dug this well."*
[31] *Therefore that place was called Beer-Sheba because there both of them swore an oath.* [32] *So they made a covenant in Beersheba. Then Abimelek*[a] *and his army commander, Phicol, arose*[b] *and returned to the country of the Philistines.* [33] *And he*[a] *planted*[b] *a tamarisk in Beersheba and called there on the name of the LORD, El-Olam.* [34] *Then Abraham dwelt*[a] *in the land of the Philistines many days.*

Notes

22.a. G inserts here and in v 32 "and his adviser Ohozath," assimilating to 26:26.
23.a. 2 masc sg impv niph שבע + ה (GKC, 51o.)
23.b. On אם to introduce oaths, see GKC, 149a–c.
23.c-c. נכד "successors" is always paired with נין "posterity"; cf. Is 14:22; Job 18:19.
23.d. 2 masc sg pf גור. On spelling, see GKC, 44g.
24.a. Pronoun common in promises (GKC, 135a; Joüon, 146a). Used when "the speaker's self-consciousness is especially deepened" (*EWAS,* 54).
24.b. 1 sg impf niph שבע. On pointing, see GKC, 51p.

25.a. SamPent has ויוכיח instead of MT והוכח waw consec + 3 masc sg pf hiph יכח. GKC, 112rr, suggests MT is frequentative.

25.b. G reads pl, "wells."

28.a. Waw consec + 3 masc sg impf hiph נצב.

28.b. On use of def art here, see GKC, 127e.

28.c. ל + בד + 3 fem pl suffix; cf. 2:18.

29.a. On def art only on אלה, see GKC, 126x, 134l; WOC, 260.

29.b. Cf. n. 28.c., an alternative 3 fem pl suffix; see GKC, 91f. SamPent assimilates form to v 28.

30.a. On use of את before numerals, see Joüon, 125h; WOC, 180.

32.a. Cf. n. 21:22.a.

32.b. Sg verb with pl subj (GKC, 146f).

33.a. SamPent, G, S, Vg, *Tg. Neof.* insert "Abraham."

33.b. Cf. n. 2:8.a.

34.a. Cf. n. 20:1.b.

Form/Structure/Setting

This short tale poses a number of awkward problems. Its chronological and thematic relationship to the surrounding material is obscure and its internal coherence suspect. The opening phrase, "At that time," relates this story to the preceding material in some way, but it is not clear whether the reference is to the birth and weaning of Isaac or to the story in chap. 20, in which Abimelek is the chief character. Nor is it clear how the story relates to the promises of land, descendants, and blessing to the nations. Is it just a filler to separate the climax of the birth from the sacrifice of Isaac, as perhaps the final remark, "Abraham dwelt . . . many days" (v 34), suggests?

The tale itself consists of one scene (vv 22–33) made up of three speeches by Abimelek, Abraham's responses, and some short concluding comments.

v 22a	Introduction
vv 22b-23	Abimelek's first speech: "Let us make an oath"
v 24	Abraham agrees
v 25	Comment about well dispute
v 26	Abimelek's second speech: "I do not know"
v 27	Abraham and Abimelek make a covenant
v 28	Abraham sets aside ewe-lambs
v 29	Abimelek's third speech: "What are these ewe-lambs?"
v 30	Abraham's reply
vv 31–33	Origin of name Beersheba
v 34	Abraham stays in land of Philistines

It is the transition between v 24 and v 25 that is hardest to follow. Do vv 25–27 recount an incident prior to the oath proposed in v 24 or subsequent to that? Or do vv 25–27 or 25–30 expound the content of the oath proposed in v 24? The possibilities are not mutually exclusive, but it is not clear which is correct. Suspicion that more than one source is present is fueled by the apparently diverse explanations of the name Beersheba—vv 28–29 seem to associate it with the "seven" (שבע *šeba*) ewe-lambs, while v 30 links it explicitly with "swearing" (נשבע *nišba*).

This has led to a variety of source analyses. Some (e.g., Dillmann, Speiser, Coats) see the story as essentially a unity from one source (usually E) with possibly a J addendum in v 33 or vv 32–34. Others hold that two sources, possibly E and J,

have been combined. For example, Gunkel (followed by Skinner and Procksch) holds that vv 22–24, 27, 31 (the oath-covenant account) are from E, while 25–26, 28–30, 32–34 (the well dispute, the seven ewe-lambs, and the name Beersheba) come from J. Van Seters argues that vv 25–26, 28–31a (the dispute followed by an oath) are the earliest version of the story and form a sequel to chap. 20, but that vv 22–24, 27, 31b–34 are a later expansion of the story by J. On the basis of the parallel in 26:26–31, Westermann argues as follows. Chap. 26 seems an older explanation of the name Beersheba. 26:32–33 are an expansion of 26:26–31. Similarly, 21:33–34 expand 21:22–32. 21:31b, the explanation of the name Beersheba, is secondary, being derived from 26:32–33. Since 21:25–26, 28–31a have no parallel in chap. 26, they can be viewed as a secondary expansion. Hence the earliest material in chap. 21 consists of vv 22–24, 27, while vv 25–26, 28–31a are an expansion and vv 33–34 are independent and lead into an itinerary.

The diversity of these source-critical analyses reflects the uncertainty of the criteria for analysis that are being employed. Sarna by-passes this debate and suggests that this section is artfully composed and fits well at this point in Genesis. He notes that the names of Abraham and Abimelek both occur seven times each in this story, that Abraham takes seven ewe-lambs, and that one meaning of Beersheba is "well of seven." 21:22–34 "presupposes a knowledge of the previous encounter between Abraham and Abimelech (chap. 20). It assumes that the reader knows who Abimelech is and that he has treated Abraham decently (20:15ff.; 21:33). The account of the stolen well, Abimelech's plea of blamelessness, and the restoration of the property to the patriarch parallels the monarch's kidnapping of Sarah, his protestation of innocence, and her return to Abraham (20; 21:25ff.). Abimelech made Abraham a gift of sheep and oxen, and Abraham reciprocates (20:14; 21:27); the identical formula, 'took and gave,' is used in both cases" (Sarna, 145).

Whichever source-critical approach is correct, we must still attempt to understand how the final author understood the present form of the material. To this we now turn.

Comment

22 "At that time" (cf. 38:1). According to Coats, the period in question is that of chap. 20, on the grounds that this story is related to the earlier one. Jacob believes "that time" means the occasion of Isaac's weaning, since this explains why there is no mention of Abimelek and Phicol coming: they were already present for the weaning feast. Sarna (cf. Calvin) suggests the events occurred soon after Abraham sent Hagar away. The use of the same phrase in 38:1 suggests that it introduces something outside the main sequence of events, so Sarna's view is less likely than Coats' or Jacob's.

"His army commander, Phicol." Various attempts have been made to explain the name Phicol. The most plausible to date suggests that it is of Anatolian origin. Names beginning with $\Pi\iota\kappa$ are common in classical inscriptions, while names ending in $\omega\lambda o\varsigma$ are well known. Unfortunately, no name such as $\Pi\iota\gamma\omega\lambda\lambda o\varsigma$ has yet been discovered. If the name is of Anatolian origin, this would fit in with the later identification of Abimelek and his people as Philistines, since they may well

have come from the Aegean or Anatolia via Crete (see Ray, *VT* 36 [1986] 358–61). That Abimelek is accompanied by his army commander implies that Abraham himself has a considerable retinue and is a force to be reckoned with (cf. chap. 14), and puts Abimelek's statement in context.

"God is with you in all that you are doing." God (the LORD) was with the other patriarchs (עם, 26:3; 28:15; 31:3; 46:4; or את, 39:3), Moses (Exod 3:12), Joshua (Josh 1:5, 17; 3:7), and David (2 Sam 7:3). The presence of God is manifest in a person's success on God-approved missions. What success is being referred to here is obscure: it could be Abraham's intercession (20:17) or the successful birth and weaning of Isaac (21:2, 8). The use of the participle "doing" may suggest continued success, so that neither of these specific achievements is referred to but, rather, the whole tenor of Abraham's life expresses the blessing of God. Hence it appears that in effect Abimelek is blessing Abraham (cf. *Comment* on 12:2) and may be presumed to be quite sincere.

23 "Swear to me." With this verb *šbᶜ* (שׁבע), the first allusion to the name Beersheba appears, as often in the narratives of Genesis, long before the name itself does. Abimelek is going to propose a covenant sealed by an oath. Negatively, this involves a promise not to "deal falsely" (cf. Abraham's behavior in chap. 20) and, positively, a promise to be "kind." In the OT, it is anticipated that kindness will be repaid with kindness. Indeed, it often leads to conclusion of treaties or covenants (cf. *TDOT* 5:44–64). "As I have been kind to you" presupposes some kindly actions by Abimelek, presumably those recorded in 20:14–16.

More striking are Abimelek's remarks about the future. He is concerned not just for himself but for his descendants and for the land in which Abraham dwells. He seems to take for granted the continuing success and strength of Abraham's family. His attitude expresses an implicit faith in the promises addressed to Abraham, however thin a thread, one child, seems to uphold them at the moment. It recalls his assumption that all men will accept certain moral principles, which underlie his rebuke of Abraham in 20:9.

24 Abraham's reply is terse: "I shall swear." It is, of course, another play on the term Beersheba, but why is it so terse when Abimelek's offer was so lengthy and polite? Does not Abraham share Abimelek's confidence in the future? Is he annoyed with Abimelek? The succinctness of Abraham's response raises questions that the unfolding narrative will resolve.

25 "Then Abraham berated." If the MT is to be followed here, its syntax is odd. The word order "And" + "reproved" (perfect) + "Abraham" is unusual in the context of past time.

The literal rendering "Then Abraham used to reprove" could suggest that after tersely accepting Abimelek's request to make an oath, Abraham brought up several times this violation of his expected rights, so I have translated "berated": Abimelek's servants had "seized" a well of water (on גזל "seize," "steal with force," "the forceful tearing away of an object from its owner" by a stronger person usually illegally, cf. 31:31; Lev 19:13; Job 20:19; Mic 2:2; *TDOT* 2:456–58). Note here the first mention of the "well" whose name is later explained.

26 If Abraham did protest at some length about the seized well, as the frequentative suggests, it becomes easier to appreciate Abimelek's heated response. He claims that he is innocent, "I do not know who did this thing," that Abraham

ought to have complained earlier, "you did not tell me," and that he knew nothing about it "till today." Just as in chap. 20, Abimelek is portrayed as a man with good intentions but one not as aware of the situation as a responsible ruler ought to be. Then he was unaware that Sarah was married; now he is unaware of his servants' actions. What he proposed to do about remedying Abraham's grievance is left unsaid.

27 Nevertheless, his assurances were evidently enough to persuade Abraham of his good faith, for Abraham now takes the initiative: "So Abraham took sheep and oxen and gave them to Abimelek, and they both made a treaty." Exchange of gifts was customary when treaties or covenants were made (cf. 1 Kgs 15:19; Isa 30:6; Hos 12:2[1]). That only Abraham gave gifts suggests he is the lesser party and principal beneficiary of the treaty. (On the phraseology כרת ברית lit. "cut a covenant," cf. *Comment* on 15:18; 17:2.) Later laws (e.g., Exod 23:33; Deut 7:2) forbade treaty-making with the inhabitants of Canaan and insisted on strict separation (Lev 20:26). That Abraham acts in ignorance of later legal norms, in this regard as well as in religion and sexual morality, indicates the antiquity of the tradition here.

28–29 The contents of the treaty are not specified. Presumably it provided for continuing mutual cooperation between Abraham and his successors and Abimelek and his successors (21:23) and perhaps confirmed Abraham's right to be an immigrant in the land (20:15). However, it cannot have explicitly covered the question of the disputed well, for Abraham specifically raises the issue by setting aside for Abimelek seven ewe-lambs.

But this gesture is problematic. It is not clear how these seven lambs relate to the sheep and oxen already mentioned. Are they included in the original gift? If so, Abraham is apparently taking back part of his offering. Or are they an extra present for Abimelek? And is there any significance in their number and type: why not two bulls instead? Unfortunately the Hebrew does not permit a clear answer. Though some argue that the use of the definite article with "seven ewe-lambs" means "the seven ewe-lambs" already mentioned, the article may be used prospectively, i.e., "the seven ewe-lambs" about to be mentioned (cf. *Notes*). So grammar does not decide whether extra lambs are being added or some originally given are being set aside. Generally, female animals were regarded as more valuable (they can breed and produce milk, and young females should do this longer than old ones). So it may be that seven, a sacred number, ewe-lambs would appear as a valuable group. But we cannot be sure. Certainly Abimelek could not see what Abraham was saying by this gesture. His question "What . . . on their own?" by its repetition of v 28 draws attention to Abraham's action and his own perplexity. It also repeats the word "seven," a component of the word "Beersheba."

30 Abraham clarifies what he is doing. "You must take" shows that he is giving additional lambs, not just holding back some that he has already presented to Abimelek. He is giving extra animals because he wants more than a general treaty; he wants a specific concession, namely, the guaranteed use of the well that he had dug. For without the right to water, a promise to be allowed to live in the land is valueless—hence Abraham's determination to secure the use of the well.

31   After the repeated references to "swearing" and "seven" (שבע *šbʿ*, vv 23, 24, 28, 29, 30) and to the "well" (באר *bʾr*, vv 25, 30), it comes as little surprise to discover that the name of the place where it was situated was Beersheba. There an oath, an integral part of a treaty, was sworn. Now at last Abraham had a claim to at least one well in the land of Canaan. The location of this well remains uncertain. The town of Beersheba was an important royal city in the first millennium and is to be identified with Tel es-Saba, east of the modern city of Beersheba. Y. Aharoni ("Tel Beersheba," *EAEHL* 1:168) holds that the patriarchal well may be situated at Bir es-Saba within the modern city.

32   The return of Abimelek and Phicol to the land of the Philistines implies not only that Abraham had a legal claim to a well but that he had *de facto* possession of the region near it (cf. 12:6).

"Land of the Philistines" is anachronistic, since the Philistines did not arrive in Canaan till about 1200 B.C. It could be viewed as proleptic, anticipating the later name of the area and its people (cf. Dan in Gen 14:14; Ur of the Chaldeans in Gen 15:7). But K. A. Kitchen *(POTT,* 56) has suggested that the Philistines of Genesis may, like the later real Philistines, have come from the Aegean area, a suggestion that gains added weight if Phicol is identified as an Anatolian name (cf. *Comment* on 21:22).

33   On other occasions, Abraham stayed near oaks (12:6; 13:18; 18:1); here he plants a tamarisk, *Tamarix aphylla,* a stately tree that can reach thirty feet (ten meters) in height. They are common throughout the Negeb, "where they were planted by the desert Bedouin for their shade and their soft branches, which the flocks eat" (Zohary, *Plants of the Bible,* 115). The precise significance of this act is unclear; the OT sees trees, especially evergreens, as symbolic of the life and blessing of God (Ps 1:3; Jer 17:7–8). On other occasions Abraham built an altar, and presumably offered sacrifice, to express his devotion to God (12:7, 8; 13:18). Sarna ("Genesis 21:33") argues that tree-planting is analogous to altar-building and marked the foundation of the great shrine of Beersheba. Such acts (cf. 26:25), like this one, followed God's promising the land, and Abraham usually responded by calling on the name of the LORD. Here he calls the LORD "El-Olam," El of Eternity, an appropriate epithet for the Canaanite high god. The planting of a tree and prayer imply that something of great moment has occurred in this episode. The use of this divine epithet El-Olam suggests that God's long-term faithfulness to Abraham has been revealed through Abimelek's words and actions. In his opening speech he had looked confidently into the future, with his descendants and Abraham's living peaceably together. By granting Abraham rights to a well, Abimelek had made it possible for Abraham to live there permanently and had acknowledged his legal right at least to water. In other words, after so many delays the promises of land and descendants at last seem on their way to fulfillment.

Explanation

The life of the patriarchs was not made up only of excitement and crisis. As in most people's lives, there were long periods of fairly humdrum activity of quiet pastoral and family life. This short story gives a glimpse of the more mundane side of patriarchal existence.

It begins with Abimelek, king of Gerar, already known to us from chap. 20, and his army commander, Phicol, coming to Abraham with the proposal that they should make a long-term non-aggression treaty. For, says the ever-loquacious Abimelek, "God is with you in all that you are doing"; in other words, "your success is so evident that I want to ensure that my successors continue to live in peace and harmony with your descendants." This is a remarkable confirmation by an outsider of Abraham's standing. Abraham has almost "become a blessing" (12:2), a phrase that means that men will say "God make me as blessed as Abraham." More noteworthy to Abraham than his progress toward becoming a blessing as promised is Abimelek's confidence in the future existence of Abraham's family. That all depended on his only son Isaac, if we may assume that Ishmael was already or soon to be expelled from the family. Through the human voice of Abimelek, the divine promises to Abraham are in effect confirmed.

Yet Abraham is grudging in his acceptance of Abimelek's offer of a treaty. He consents, but not with the grace and enthusiasm that Abimelek's generous offer might have led one to expect. He has a grievance, but not until Abimelek has shown his friendliness does he air it. "He berated Abimelek about the well Abimelek's servants had seized." Caught off his guard, Abimelek plunges into a long defense of himself, assuring Abraham that he had nothing to do with his servants' action. He had not even heard of it till Abraham raised it. Why did he not raise it earlier? Reassured at least about Abimelek's sincerity, even if he retains doubts about his competence, Abraham makes a gift of sheep and oxen to Abimelek, and they both make a covenant, presumably along the lines of Abimelek's original proposal. After this general agreement to live in harmony, Abraham seizes the opportunity to deal with the particular issue of the well. By setting aside an extra seven valuable young ewes, Abraham intimates that he wishes to make another request to Abimelek. Puzzled by the gesture, Abimelek asks about the sheep, and Abraham explains that he wants a specific guarantee about the use of the well. Abimelek agrees, and they swear an oath at Beersheba. Its name, "Well of the oath," is a permanent reminder of the agreement they made there.

Both parties are more than satisfied. Abimelek and Phicol return home with the covenant they had sought, and Abraham is granted permanent use of the well he had dug. The fulfillment of the promises to him is becoming ever more evident; he now has at least a well he can call his own in the land of Canaan. Out of gratitude to the LORD for his continuing faithfulness, he plants a tamarisk and worships there. For it was not just through direct revelation but through his interaction with his neighbors, even in a dispute over the most basic natural resource, water, that Abraham was reassured about his future and God's continuing provision for his needs.

So "Abraham dwelt in the land of the Philistines many days." Peace and stability at last! Tranquil old age is a sign of God's blessing (Lev 26:6–12; Zech 8:4). But it is a lull before the storm.

The Testing of Abraham   (22:1–19)

Bibliography

BASIC HISTORICAL, EXEGETICAL, AND LITERARY STUDIES

Alexander, T. D. "Gen 22 and the Covenant of Circumcision." *JSOT* 25 (1983) 17–22.
Auerbach, E. *Mimesis: The Representation of Reality in Western Literature.* Tr. W. R. Trask.
Princeton: Princeton UP, 1953. **Baltzer, K.** "Jerusalem in den Erzväter-Geschichten der
Genesis? Traditionsgeschichtliche Erwägungen zu Gen 14 und 22." In *Die hebräische Bibel
und ihre zweifache Nachgeschichte: FS R. Rendtorff,* ed. E. Blum, C. Macholz, and E. W.
Stegemann. Neukirchen: Neukirchener, 1990. 3–12. **Bovon, R.,** and **Rouiller, G.** *Problèmes
de méthode et exercises de lecture (Gen 22 et Luc 15).* Neuchâtel: Delachaux & Niestlé, 1975.
Childs, B. S. "Anticipatory Titles in Hebrew Narrative." In *Essays on the Bible and the Ancient
World III: I. L. Seeligman Volume,* ed. A. Rofé and Y. Zakovitch. Jerusalem: Rubenstein's,
1983. 57–65. **Coats, G. W.** "Abraham's Sacrifice of Faith: A Form-Critical Study of Gen 22."
Int 27 (1973) 389–400. **Crenshaw, J.** "Journey into Oblivion: A Structural Analysis of Gen
22:1–19." *Soundings* 58 (1975) 243–56. **Davila, J. R.** "The Name of God at Moriah: An Un-
published Fragment from 4QGenExodᵃ." *JBL* 110 (1991) 577–82. **Duhaime, J. L.** "Le sacrifice d'Isaac (Gen 22:1–19): l'héritage de Gunkel." *ScEs* 33 (1981) 139–56. **Fokkelman, J. P.**
"'On the Mount of the Lord There Is Vision': A Response to Francis Landy concerning
the Akedah." In *Signs and Wonders: Biblical Texts in Literary Focus,* ed. J. C. Exum. SBL, 1989.
41–57. **Galy, A.** "Une lecture de Gen 22." *Le point théologique* 24 (1977) 117–33. **Golka, F.
W.** "Die theologische Erzählungen im Abraham-Kreis." *ZAW* 90 (1978) 186–95. **Golling,
R.** "Zeugnisse von Menschenopfern im AT." *TLZ* 102 (1977) 147–50. **Green, A. R. W.** *The
Role of Human Sacrifice in the Ancient Near East.* ASORDS 1. Missoula: Scholars Press, 1975.
Gross, H. "Zur theologischen Bedeutung von *hālak* (gehen) in den Abraham-Geschichten
(Gen 12–25)." In *Die Väter Israels: FS J. Scharbert,* ed. M. Görg. Stuttgart: Katholisches
Bibelwerk, 1989. 73–82. **Hopkins, D. C.** "Between Promise and Fulfillment: Von Rad and
the Sacrifice of Abraham." *BZ* 24 (1980) 180–93. **Kalimi, I.** "The Land of Moriah, Mount
Moriah, and the Site of Solomon's Temple in Biblical Historiography." *HTR* 83 (1990)
345–62. **Kilian, R.** *Isaaks Opferung: Zur Überlieferungsgeschichte von Gen 22.* SBS 44. Stuttgart:
Katholisches Bibelwerk, 1970. **Lack, R.** "Le sacrifice d'Isaac: Analyse structurale de la
couche élohiste dans Gen 22." *Bib* 56 (1975) 1–12. **Landy, F.** "Narrative Techniques and
Symbolic Transactions in the Akedah." In *Signs and Wonders: Biblical Texts in Literary Focus,*
ed. J. C. Exum. SBL, 1989. 1–40. **Lawlor, J. I.** "The Test of Abraham: Gen 22:1–19." *GTJ* 1
(1980) 19–35. **Magonet, J.** "Abraham and God." *Judaism* 33 (1984) 160–70. ————. "Die
Söhne Abrahams." *BibLeb* 14 (1973) 204–10. **Mazor, Y.** "Genesis 22: The Ideological Rheto-
ric and the Psychological Composition." *Bib* 67 (1986) 81–88. **Moberly, R. W. L.** "The Ear-
liest Commentary on the Akedah." *VT* 38 (1988) 302–23. **Pope, M. H.** "The Timing of the
Snagging of the Ram." *BA* 49 (1986) 114–17. **Qoler, Y.** "The Story of the Binding of Isaac."
(Heb.) *BMik* 29 (1983/84) 117–27. **Reventlow, H. G.** *Opfere deinen Sohn: Eine Auslegung von
Gen 22.* BibS 53. Neukirchen: Neukirchener, 1968. **Safren, J. D.** "Balaam and Abraham."
VT 38 (1968) 105–13. **Sarda, O.** "Le sacrifice d'Abraham (Gen 22): le déplacement des
lectures attestées." *Le point théologique* 24 (1977) 135–46. **Saviv, A.** "*yhwh yireh* = The Place
Which He Will Choose." (Heb.) *BMik* 26 (1981) 279–81. **Ska, J. L.** "Gen 22:1–19: essai sur
les niveaux de lecture." *Bib* 69 (1988) 324–39. **Steck, O. H.** "Ist Gott grausam? Über Isaaks
Opferung aus der Sicht des ATs." *Theologie der Gegenwart* 21 (1978) 65–75. **Swindell, A. C.**
"Abraham and Isaac: An Essay in Biblical Appropriation." *ExpTim* 87 (1975/76) 50–53.

Trible, P. "Gen 22: The Sacrifice of Sarah." In *Not in Heaven*, ed. J. P. Rosenblatt and J. C. Sitterson. Bloomington: Indiana UP, 1991. 170–91. **Tsmudi, Y.** "The Internal Struggle in the Story of the Binding of Isaac." (Heb.) *BMik* 30 (1984/85) 382–87. **Veijola, T.** "Das Opfer des Abraham: Paradigma des Glaubens aus dem nachexilischen Zeitalter." *ZTK* 85 (1988) 129–64. **Vogels, W.** "Dieu éprouva Abraham (Gen 22:1–19)." *Sémiotique et Bible* 26 (1982) 25–36. **Walters, S. D.** "Wood, Sand and Stars: Structure and Theology in Gen 22:1–19." *Toronto Journal of Theology* 3 (1987) 301–30. **White, H. C.** "The Initiation Legend of Isaac." *ZAW* 91 (1979) 1–30.

THEOLOGICAL INTERPRETATIONS

Brock, S. P. "Gen 22: Where Was Sarah?" *ExpTim* 96 (1984) 14–17. **Chilton, B. D.** "Isaac and the Second Night: A Consideration." *Bib* 61 (1980) 78–88. **Dahl, N. A.** "The Atonement—an Adequate Reward for the Akedah?" In *The Crucified Messiah and Other Essays*. Minneapolis: Augsburg, 1974. 146–89. **Daly, R. J.** "The Soteriological Significance of the Sacrifice of Isaac." *CBQ* 39 (1977) 45–75. **Davies, P. R.** "The Sacrifice of Isaac and Passover." In *Studia Biblica 1978*, ed. E. A. Livingstone. JSOTSup 11. Sheffield: JSOT Press, 1979. 127–32. ————. "Passover and the Dating of the Aqedah." *JJS* 30 (1979) 59–67. ———— and **Chilton, B. D.** "The Aqedah: A Revised Tradition History." *CBQ* 40 (1978) 514–46. **Elbaum, Y.** "From Sermon to Story: The Transformation of the Akedah." *Prooftexts* 6 (1986) 97–116. **Feldman, L. H.** "Josephus' Version of the Binding of Isaac." SBLSP 21 (1982) 113–28. **Hayward, C. T. R.** "The Present State of Research into the Targumic Account of the Sacrifice of Isaac." *JJS* 32 (1981) 127–50. ————. "The Sacrifice of Isaac and Jewish Polemic against Christianity." *CBQ* 52 (1990) 292–306. **Leaney, A. R. C.** "The Akedah, Paul and the Atonement." *SE* 7 [= TU 126] (1982) 307–15. **Moberly, R. W. L.** "Christ as the Key to Scripture: Genesis 22 Reconsidered." In *He Swore an Oath,* ed. R. S. Hess, P. E. Satterthwaite, and G. J. Wenham. Cambridge: Tyndale House, 1993. 143–73. **Schmitz, R.-P.** *Aqedat Jishaq: Die mittelalterliche jüdische Auslegung von Gen 22 in ihren Hauptlinien.* Hildesheim: Olms, 1979. **Starobinski-Safran, R.** "Sur le sens de l'épreuve (Interprétations juives de Gen 22)." *RTP* 114 (1982) 23–35. **Swetnam, J.** *Jesus and Isaac: A Study of the Epistle to the Hebrews in the Light of the Aqedah.* AnBib 94. Rome: Biblical Institute Press, 1981. **Yassif, E.,** ed. *The Sacrifice of Isaac: Studies in the Development of a Literary Tradition.* Jerusalem: Makor, 1979.

Translation

[1a]*After these things*[a] *God tested Abraham and said to him, "Abraham."*[b] *He said, "Here I am."*[c]
[2]*He said, "Please take your son, your only child, whom you love,*[a] *Isaac. Go by yourself*[b] *to the district of Moriah,*[c] *and offer*[d] *him there as a burnt offering on one*[e] *of the mountains which I shall tell you."*
[3]*So early in the morning Abraham saddled his donkey, took two of his lads*[a] *with him, and his son Isaac, and cut*[b] *wood for the burnt offering. He set out and went to the place which God had told him about.*
[4a]*On the third day Abraham looked up and saw the place in the distance.* [5]*So Abraham said to the lads,* [a]*"You stay*[b] *by yourselves*[ac] *here with the donkey,* [d]*while I and the lad will go*[d] *on there, so that*[e] *we can worship*[f] *and return*[g] *to you."* [6]*Then Abraham took the firewood and put*[a] *it on Isaac his son, and in his hand he took the fire and the knife. So the two of them went together.*[b] [7]*Then Isaac spoke to Abraham his father and said, "My father." He said, "Here*[ab] *I am, my son." He said, "Here*[a] *is the fire and the wood,*

but^c *where is the sheep for the burnt offering?"* ⁸*Abraham said, "God*^a *will provide himself a sheep for the burnt offering, my son." So the two of them went together.*

⁹*Then they came to the place which God had told him about. There Abraham built an altar, arranged the wood, bound*^a *Isaac his son, and placed him on the altar on top of the wood.* ¹⁰*Then Abraham reached out his hand and took the knife to slaughter his son.*

¹¹*Then the*^a *angel of the LORD*^b *called to him from heaven and said, "Abraham, Abraham!" He said, "Here I am."*

¹²*He said, "Do not lay your hand on*^a *the lad, and do not do*^b *anything*^c *to him, because now I know that you do fear*^d *God, for*^e *you have not withheld your son, your only child from me."*

¹³*Abraham then looked up and saw a ram just*^a *caught*^b *in a bush by its horns, so Abraham went, took the ram, and offered*^c *it up as a burnt offering instead of his son.*

¹⁴*So Abraham called that place "The LORD will provide," as*^a *it is said*^b *today, "In the mountain of the LORD he may be seen."*^c

¹⁵*Then the angel of the LORD called to Abraham a second time from heaven.* ¹⁶*He said, "By myself I swear,*^a *(declares the LORD) that* ^b*it is because*^b *you have done this thing and have not withheld your son, your only child,*^c ¹⁷*that I shall really bless you. I shall really*^a *multiply your descendants as the stars of heaven and like the sand which is on the seashore, so that you may possess the gate of your enemies.* ¹⁸*And all the nations of the world will find blessing*^a *in your descendants because*^b *you have obeyed me."*

¹⁹*Then Abraham returned*^a *to the lads. They got up and went together to Beersheba. Abraham then lived in Beersheba.*

Notes

1.a-a. ויהי + temporal phrase often marks new section in narrative (GKC, 111g).

1.b. G's repetition of Abraham to match v 11 is inept. Here it is merely address; there it is a summons.

1.c. הנה + 1 sg suffix.

2.a. Pf of stative verbs often has a present meaning (Joüon, 112a).

2.b. Cf. n. 12:1.a.; cf. 21:16.

2.c. The versions seem to interpret the name Moriah rather than simply transliterating it, e.g., G "the high land"; σ´, Vg "land of the vision." For other readings, see *BHS*.

2.d. Waw + 2 masc sg impv hiph עלה + 3 masc sg suffix.

2.e. On use of אחד + pl noun for indeterminate sg, see Joüon, 137v; WOC, 251.

3.a. On this translation, as opposed to "his two lads," see Joüon, 140a; Brockelmann, 73a.

3.b. Waw + 3 masc sg impf piel בקע.

4.a. It is rare for a new paragraph to begin without a conj as here, but cf. 8:5 (*SBH*, 37).

5.a-a. Note the chiasmus between clauses a-a and d-d, "stay . . . yourselves" : "I and the lad go," appropriate for simultaneous action (*SBH*, 134).

5.b. 2 masc pl impv ישׁב.

5.c. On the use of the pron + verb, cf. n. 12:1.a.; also 21:16; 22:2.

5.d-d. Cf. n. 5.a-a.

5.e. The sequence impv + impf/coh indicates purpose (Lambdin, 119).

5.f. Waw + 1 pl impf hishtaphel חוה

5.g. Waw + 1 pl coh שׁוב.

6.a. Waw consec + 3 masc sg impf שׂים. Obj understood; cf. 9:23.

6.b. J. C. de Moor suggests it has the overtones of "without company, protection, assistance" (*VT* 7 [1957] 355).

7.a. On the use of הנה, see Lambdin, 168–69.

7.b. This pointing only here and in 27:18 (Joüon, 102k).

7.c. Adversative waw (*SBH*, 185).

8.a. Subj "God" before the verb "provide" to emphasize the subj (Brockelmann, 48).

9.a. Waw consec + 3 masc sg impf עקד "bind." Used only here in the OT, especially of binding the feet (cf. G).

11.a. Or "an angel" (so Joüon, 139c; Brockelmann, 73a).

11.b. S "God."

12.a. SamPent reads על, possibly presupposed by G, Vg "over."

12.b. 2 masc sg impf (apoc) עשׂה.

12.c. Note unusual pointing. Usually no dagesh in מ; see *BHS*.

12.d. Masc sg constr ptcp ירא, lit. "fearer of" God; cf. GKC, 116g; Joüon, 121c.

12.e. Waw to be translated "for" (Joüon, 170c); "for" or "so that." "It is likely . . . that the choice of coordination as a neutral linkage amounts to double talk that leaves it open to the listener to take it any way he likes" (*SBH*, 118).

13.a. אחר is usually translated "After," which is awkward here, so SamPent reading אחד is widely adopted, e.g., G, S, and many commentators. But אחר sometimes occurs in the OT with the meaning "with" or "immediately after" (e.g., Jer 25:26; Ruth 1:16; Ecc 12:21; cf. Gen 18:5) and also in Ugaritic (Pope, *BA* 49 [1986] 115–17). Hence our rendering.

13.b. 3 masc sg pf niph אחז, here with middle sense (cf. Lambdin, 176). Some MSS (see *BHS*) point נאחז as if ptcp.

13.c. Waw consec + 3 masc sg impf hiph עלה + 3 masc sg suffix.

14.a. On this meaning of אשׁר, see Joüon, 169f, or for "so that," see WOC, 639.

14.b. Cf. n. 10:9.a.

14.c. 3 masc sg impf niph ראה.

16.a. Pf with present meaning, for utterances felt to be past as soon as spoken (Joüon, 112f).

16.b-b. יען an emphatic causal conj. Causal clause as here usually precedes main clause (Joüon, 170f,n).

16.c. SamPent, G, S add "from/because of me," assimilating to v 12.

17.a. Inf abs usually pointed הרבה (hiph רבה) for affirming promises (*EWAS*, 86).

18.a. Waw consec + 3 masc pl pf hithp ברך; cf. discussion on 12:3.

18.b. עקב has the sense "in recompense for" (Joüon, 170g).

19.a. Waw consec + 3 masc sg impf qal שׁוב.

Form/Structure/Setting

The account of the sacrifice of Isaac constitutes the aesthetic and theological summit of the whole story of Abraham. It has long been admired for the brilliance of its narrative technique and for the profundity of its theology, which has inspired so much reflection by Jews and Christians.

From a literary standpoint, it is thoroughly integrated with the preceding narratives about Abraham, which are clearly presupposed at every turn. Most obviously, the reaffirmation of the promises (vv 17–18) of blessing, numerous descendants, inheritance, and blessing to the nations combines the refrains of the earlier chapters (12:2, 3; 17:16, 20; 18:18; 16:10; 17:2, 20; 15:4–5) while introducing another superlative, "like the sand on the seashore," into the promises. The phrases "your son, your only child" (vv 2, 12, 16) presuppose particularly chap. 21 with its account of Isaac's birth and Ishmael's expulsion. In content and outline, the stories in chaps. 21 and 22 run parallel, with Abraham in a role like Hagar's, and Isaac like Ishmael.

God orders Ishmael's expulsion (21:12–13) // God orders Isaac's sacrifice (22:2)
Food and water taken (21:14) // Sacrificial material taken (22:3)
Journey (21:14) // Journey (22:4–8)
Ishmael about to die (21:16) // Isaac about to die (22:10)
Angel of God calls from heaven (21:17) // Angel of the LORD calls from heaven (22:11)

"Do not fear" (21:17) // "fear God" (22:12)
"God has heard" // "You have obeyed (heard) my voice" (22:18)
"I shall make into a great nation" (21:18) // "Your descendants will be like stars, sand,"
etc. (22:17)
God opens her eyes and she sees well (21:19) // Abraham raises his eyes and sees ram
(22:13)
She gives the lad a drink (21:19) // He sacrifices ram instead of son (22:14)

This outline highlights many of the verbal parallels between the stories, but
note too "the lad" (22:5, 12; 21:12, 17–19), "early in the morning Abraham took"
(22:3; 21:14; cf. 18:27), and "shall inherit" (22:17; 21:10; 15:3–4). In certain respects, chap. 22 has close verbal affinities with the other Hagar and Ishmael story
in chap. 16. There the angel of *the* LORD appears too (22:11, 15; 16:7, 9–11); the
promise includes the remark "I shall really multiply your descendants" (22:17;
16:10), and in both ראה "see, provide" is a key word explaining the name of the
well in the first story and "the place" in this (22:8, 14; 16:13–14). The reference
to "the place which God had told him" evokes those other "places" where Abraham
had built altars or met with God (22:3, 4, 9, 14; 12:6; 13:3, 4; 19:27). Finally, the
allusion to the very first command given to Abraham, "Go by yourself . . . to a
land which I shall show you," is unmistakable in "Go by yourself to the land of
Moriah . . . which I shall tell you" (12:1; 22:2). Thus the whole of 22:1–19 re-
verberates with the echoes of earlier parts of the Abraham cycle, and these need
to be borne in mind in discussing its structure, in source analysis, and in exegesis.
   The story divides scenically as follows (cf. Ska, *Bib* 69 [1988] 324–29):

Introduction (1a)	N
1. God's command "Sacrifice your son" (1b–2)	M
2. Departure next morning (3)	N
3. The third day at foot of the mountain (4–6b)	D
4. Journey up the mountain (6c–8)	D
5. Preparation for sacrifice (9–10)	N
6. Angel speaks to stop sacrifice (11–18)	M
Epilogue: Return to Beersheba (19)	N

As often in Genesis, the scenes are ordered palistrophically. Scenes 1 and 6
match each other in style and content. Both are essentially divine monologues,
beginning with a summons of Abraham by name (vv 1, 11), followed by Abraham
responding "Here I am" and ending with God or his angel speaking. These two
speeches represent the last recorded words of God to Abraham, and it is noticeable how they echo very closely his first self-disclosure in 12:1–3 (cf. "Go by
yourself . . . " [12:1; 22:2]; "I shall really bless you . . . nations find blessing
[22:17–18; cf. 12:2–3]; see *Comment* for closer analysis). Scenes 2 and 5 match
each other in being pure narrative without any dialogue and focus on Abraham's
preparation for the sacrifice; note the common vocabulary: "wood," "his son Isaac,"
and "the place which God had told him about." Then scenes 3 and 4 correspond
to each other: both are located between Beersheba and the mountaintop and
consist of discussion about the forthcoming sacrifice. In scene 3, Abraham speaks
to his servants, and in scene 4, with Isaac; note again the vocabulary common to

both scenes. Finally, the introduction (v 1a) and epilogue (v 19) match in being pure narrative.

The narrative climaxes in the long sacrifice scene at the mountain top when at the last minute the angel calls off the sacrifice, a ram is substituted, and the great promises are confirmed and elaborated. The short scenes before the sacrifice spin out the preparations and contribute to the build-up of suspense.

Another device used to highlight the final scene is the way the narrative is built up of three main dialogues with a long angelic monologue that rounds off the story with a great coda. In each, there is a sequence of similar words and phrases, producing four parallel panels:

He said	He said	The angel called from heaven and said "Abraham,	The angel called to Abraham (v 15)
"Abraham" (v 1)	"My father" (v 7)	Abraham!" He said	
He said	He said	"Here I am" (v 11)	
"Here I am"	"Here I am"		
		"Do not do anything"	"You have done this thing"
		"You have not withheld"	"have not withheld"
"your son, your only child" (v 2)	"my son"	"your son, your only child" (v 12)	"your son, your only child" (v 16)
"for a burnt offering"	"for a burnt offering" (2x, vv 7, 8)	"for a burnt offering" (v 13)	
"he went"	"the two of them went together" (v 8)	"he went"	"they went together" (v 19)
"the place which God had told him" (v 3)	"the place which God had told him" (v 9)	"the place . . . as it is said" (v 14)	
"he took . . . the knife" (v 6)	"he took the knife" (v 10)		

Certain key words recur in this story: most obviously "Abraham" (18x), "Isaac" (5x), and "son" (10x). As elsewhere, the use of the words "to bless" (ברך) and "to multiply" (הרבה) (vv 17–18) seems to be a play on Abraham's name, while the words "and he took" (ויקח *wayyiqah*), usually with "Abraham" as subject, and "wood" (עצים *ʿēsîm*) may be plays on the name of Isaac (יצחק, *yishāq*).

But as in all great art, these literary devices and structures are used with such finesse that the ordinary listener is quite unaware of their presence. Though they do enhance the dynamic of the storytelling, the substance of the tale is such that even if it were less finely crafted the listener would be gripped by it.

Source critics have usually assigned at least vv 1–14, 19 to E, on the grounds of its use of אלהים "God" for the deity, the parallels with 21:8–21 (also E), and the nocturnal revelation in vv 1–2. Vv 15–18, which speak of the LORD (vv 15–16), are generally assigned to J or to a later redactor. However, more recent writers have questioned this analysis, particularly the attribution of vv 1–14 to E, because it too does not consistently speak of "God" but also of "the LORD" (vv 11, 14) and

on general stylistic grounds. Speiser (166) noted that "the style of the narrative is far more appropriate to J than to E" and suggested that the references to "God" rather than "the LORD" may be blamed on scribal error. Arguing that the divine names are an inadequate guide to source analysis, more recent writers (e.g., Van Seters, *Abraham*; Coats, *Int* 27 [1973] 389–400; and Alexander *JSOT* 25 [1983] 17–22) have tended to suppose that J is the principal author responsible for drafting the story. But in the light of the numerous allusions to other parts of the Abraham saga, Westermann (cf. Moberly, *VT* 38 [1988] 302–23; Veijola, *ZTK* 85 [1988] 129–64) prefers to ascribe this chapter to a late stage in the composition of Genesis, though he recognizes that the original story may go back to the patriarchal age.

The secondary nature of vv 15–18 has also been challenged by Coats, Van Seters, and Alexander. They point out that without these verses the test of Abraham is apparently purposeless. "It is only with the inclusion, in the second speech, of the divine confirmation of the patriarchal promises, vv 15–18, that the ultimate aim of the testing becomes clear. Because of Abraham's obedience his children will be blessed" (Van Seters, *Abraham*, 239). Westermann simply dismisses this argument on the grounds that vv 15–18 are clearly different in style from what precedes. Moberley is more cautious. He notes that whereas vv 1–14 have a "taut and economic style of telling," "[b]y contrast, the style of vv 15–18 is repetitive and cumulative, with use of synonyms and similes" (*VT* 38 [1988] 307–8). He also argues that what really proves the secondary nature of vv 15–18 is their position: "from the point of view of reading vv 1–19 as an integral unity, it would even improve the flow and coherence of the text to read it in the order vv 1–13, 15–18, 14, 19, for the obviously concluding v 14 would then . . . lead naturally into the final narrative note in v 19" (*VT* 38 [1988] 310).

These observations have some value, but whether they show that vv 15–18 have been simply inserted into an earlier version in vv 1–14, 19 is doubtful. The argument of Van Seters and Coats that the testing of Abraham is purposeless unless it leads to something extra that he would not have had otherwise is telling. Had Abraham not undergone the test, there would have been no risk of losing Isaac's life. For God to spare Isaac's life, which would not have been at risk without Abraham's obedient submission to the test, and then merely to say "now I know you fear God" is somewhat of an anticlimax. Surely God should say more to Abraham after putting him through such a traumatic experience. The stylistic argument, that the narrative is terse while the promises are full, proves little. It is partly a question of genre: promises are often expansive in style (cf. chap. 17), whereas narrative is usually brief. It is also a question of highlighting the importance of something: the repetition in vv 15–18, like the full style of chap. 17, draws attention to the significance of the promises made.

That vv 15–18 cannot simply be identified as a late addition to the original story is shown by the parallels between 22:1–19 as a whole and preceding parts of Genesis. For example, the close parallel with 21:8–21 includes a reaffirmation of the promise that Ishmael would become "a great nation" (21:18). It would be extraordinary if this much more traumatic test of Abraham did not contain something comparable, if not much fuller. Vv 15–18 provide just this necessary element. That the angel should speak more than once from heaven is no proof that these

verses are secondary: 16:8–12 has *four* distinct angelic speeches and chap. 17 *five* divine speeches.

Then there is also the striking parallel between chap. 22 and chap. 12, the last and first divine speeches to Abraham. Both begin with a command to Abraham: "Go by yourself to the country/district [אֶרֶץ] . . . that I shall show you" (12:1; 22:2). We are therefore led to expect a reference to the promises that attended that command (12:2–3), and this is precisely what we find in scene 6 (vv 15–18), which, as already pointed out, corresponds closely to scene 1. The echoes of 12:2–3 are as clear in 22:15–18 as those of 12:1 are in 22:2. Now this is not to say that at one stage there may not have been a simpler, shorter account of the sacrifice of Isaac, but to identify the original account with vv 1–14 is too simple, for the author responsible for vv 15–18 has also left his mark on vv 1–14, so that identifying the limits and content of earlier versions of the story is elusive.

Comment

1 The introduction, "After these things God tested Abraham," is of great moment, both from a dramatic and a theological perspective. It serves to cushion the listener from the full impact of the horrific command to Abraham, and it diverts attention from the question whether Isaac will be sacrificed to whether Abraham will stand up to the test. "After these things" suggests that some time has elapsed between this trial of Abraham and the events recorded in chap. 21 (cf. 21:34, "Abraham dwelt . . . many days"). It may well be that Isaac is now to be envisaged as at least a teenager, just as Ishmael was when expelled from Abraham's household; in both narratives they are called "lads" (נַעַר; cf. 22:12; 21:12).

"God" (here and in vv 3, 8 with the definite article). It is unusual that this story begins with this generic form rather than with his personal name, "the LORD." Frequently in Genesis where the body of a story speaks of "God," the narrator prefaces it by a comment, using his proper name (e.g., 17:1; 21:1). Here the term "God" is used in vv 1, 3, 8, 9, and "the LORD" first appears in v 11 when "the angel of the LORD" calls from heaven. If we assume that this variation is more than a literary whim, it may be that "God" is used to avoid the anachronistic implication that Abraham knew him by the name "the LORD" (v 8; cf. Exod 6:3). But since, contrary to his usual practice, the narrator also avoids using "the LORD" to introduce the narrative, Delitzsch may be correct to see a theological motive behind the variation. "He who requires from Abraham the surrender of Isaac is God the creator . . . but it is Jahveh in his angel who forbids the extreme act, for the son of promise cannot perish" (Delitzsch, 2:91). In Gen 2–3, the covenant creator is consistently termed "the LORD God," but in the temptation scene, where alienation between deity and humanity becomes evident, the word "God" appears by itself (3:1–5). Similarly, here in the first half of the story where God is acting in a strange, remote, and inexplicable way, he is called אֱלֹהִים, but when he is revealed as savior and renews the covenant promises, his personal name, "the LORD," is appropriate and is reintroduced.

"Tested" (נסה). "Testing" shows what someone is really like, and it generally involves difficulty or hardship. The queen of Sheba tested Solomon with riddles

(1 Kgs 10:1); Daniel and his companions were tested by being put on a simple diet (Dan 1:12, 14). God is often said to test Israel through hunger and thirst in the wilderness (Exod 15:25; 16:4; 20:20; Deut 8:2, 16), through false prophets (Deut 13:4[3]), or through foreign oppression (Judg 2:22; 3:1, 14). The purpose of such trials is to discover "what was in your heart, whether you would keep his commandments or not" (Deut 8:2; cf. Exod 16:4), "to humble you . . . to do you good in the end" (Deut 8:16; cf. Heb 12:5–11). The use of the term here hints that Abraham will face some great difficulty but that he will ultimately benefit from it. This is the only time God is said to have tested an individual, but *pace* Westermann, this is no proof of the lateness of this text. Early non-religious usage (e.g., 1 Kgs 10:1) certainly covers individuals.

1b–2 Scene 1: A divine monologue matching scene 6, with clear echoes of Gen 12:1. "Abraham . . . Here I am." It is not really necessary to preface the command with the two brief speeches found here; the narrative could simply begin "Abraham, please take . . . " (cf. 12:1; 15:1; 16:8; 17:2). Yet this prolongation is suggestive. Is God hesitating before giving his awful order? The text does not say so, but the break in the address raises such questions. And it certainly allows Abraham's attentiveness and potential obedience to come through in his reply, "Here I am." Three times in this story we have the refrain "Abraham (my father)" with its response "Here I am" (vv 1, 7, 11); each signals a tense new development in the narrative.

2 The reader has been alerted by the verb "test" that something difficult is about to be asked of Abraham, while he, of course, is quite in the dark. The way the command is put here tries to soften the blow for Abraham while maximizing our realization of its enormity. "Please take." The use of the enclitic נָא "please" is rare in a divine command and makes it more like an entreaty, another hint that the LORD appreciates the costliness of what he is asking. Then "your son, your only child, whom you love." With this fourfold characterization of Isaac, the whole poignant tale of Isaac so far, the promise, the delay, and the miraculous fulfillment, is summed up. On him all Abraham's hopes are riding. Note particularly the remark "whom you love," the only explicit clue to Abraham's attachment to his son, precluding any reading of the story that would see Abraham as callous and hard-hearted. Far from it—obedience to God and love for his son will tear him in diametrically opposed directions. But thus far, nothing has been said to disturb his peace of mind.

But "go by yourself" sounds ominous. With the very same words the LORD had told Abram to leave all that he had hitherto held most dear—"his country, his clan, and his father's house" (12:1). Already at his wife's behest, confirmed by God, he has expelled his son Ishmael (21:10, 12), of whom he was very fond. Can anything harder be demanded of a loving father than sending his son away? Questions are raised but not directly answered.

Based on 2 Chr 3:15, "the district of Moriah" has been identified with the temple site in Jerusalem; Kalimi argues that this tradition antedates Chronicles (*HTR* 83 [1990] 350). But since Moriah is mentioned only in these two passages, it has been doubted whether it can really be the original reading here. However, the word "Moriah" is integral to the present narrative. As some of the versions (see *Notes*) recognize with their paraphrases "land of vision," the name anticipates

Abraham's experience that "the LORD will provide" (v 14; cf. v 8). ‏רָאָה‎ *rāʾāh* "provide, see" is a key word of the narrative, and here in the name of the place to which Abraham must take his son, there is the first hint of salvation. A similar phenomenon was noted in 6:6, where the first intimation of the universal flood, "he repented" (‏וַיִּנָּחֶם‎ *wayyinnāḥem*) has the letters ‏נח‎ *nḥ* "Noah" in the middle. Salvation is thus promised in the very decree that sounds like annihilation (A. Strus, *Nomen-Omen*, 158–59, 183).

"Offer him there as a burnt offering." God explains what he wants. A burnt offering involves cutting up and burning the whole animal on the altar and was the commonest type of sacrifice. It seems to have expressed at least two ideas: that the offerer is giving himself entirely to God (for the animal represents the offerer) and that the animal's death atones for the worshiper's sin. The usual victims of burnt offerings were birds, sheep, or if the worshiper was very wealthy, a bull. But to offer one's child was quite out of the question for devout orthodox worshipers. "Shall I give my first-born for my transgression, the fruit of my body for the sin of my soul?" asks Micah (6:7), expecting his hearers to reply with an emphatic no (cf. Lev 18:21; 20:2–5). But it was done occasionally in the biblical world, especially in times of dire crisis (Judg 11:31–40; 2 Kgs 3:27; 17:17). In fact, biblical law expects every firstborn son to be dedicated to God but insists that he be redeemed and an animal offered instead (Exod 22:29[30]; 34:20). Later, the Levites by their service were seen as consecrated to God instead of the firstborn in each family (Num 4:45–49). And it is this background of thought that, as Westermann points out, makes the test comprehensible. "Following Ex. 22:29, it is seen as possible that God can demand such a sacrifice. In reality, however, human sacrifice is not possible (Ex. 34:20). It is precisely because of this ambivalence that the command to Abraham is a particularly suitable test" (2:358).

It has often been suggested that this story was originally an etiology explaining why human sacrifice was no longer permissible in Israel. By eliminating certain parts of the existing story, such a reinterpretation is doubtless possible. But it must remain speculative in the absence of any firm criteria for distinguishing a more primitive version of the story. Furthermore, there is no evidence that human sacrifice was ever common in Israel, or that it ever completely died out, at least before the exile, and even then it continued in some neighboring cultures. So it is not possible to identify a marked change in attitude and correlate different layers in Gen 22 with different periods. It is better simply to accept that at all periods an Israelite reader would regard God's demand as extraordinary, not simply morally but theologically, for Isaac was the son on whose survival the fulfillment of all the promises depended. (On burnt offerings, see *IDBSup*, 769; R. de Vaux, *Ancient Israel*, 415–17; G. J. Wenham, *Leviticus* [Grand Rapids: Eerdmans, 1979] 48–66; R. Rendtorff, *Leviticus* [Neukirchen: Neukirchener, 1985] 15–80. On human sacrifice, see *Ancient Israel*, 441–44.)

"On one of the mountains." The narrative does seem to draw attention to this mountain and stress its height. Abraham looks up and sees it in the distance (v 4), and later he is pictured climbing it alone with his son, having left the donkey behind, as it is too difficult for the ass to ascend. The physical difficulty of the ascent surely increases our feeling of the emotional effort involved. But is there more to the reference to the mountain than this? Why should a mountain be

specified? Noah sacrificed burnt offerings on the mountain where the ark landed, but generally Abraham built altars at sites that, though situated in the hill country of Canaan, are not exactly mountains.

In ancient mythology, the gods were often thought to dwell on mountaintops, and the Canaanites are said to have worshiped "on the high mountains" (Deut 12:2). But more pertinent for our study, the Jerusalem temple was built on Mount Zion (Ps 48:2–3[1–2]), and Mount Sinai is preeminently the place of revelation, where God comes down to speak with his people (Exod 19). So clearly, in biblical thought also, a mountain was a suitable place to meet God, a point later established in v 14: "In the mountain of the LORD he may be seen." It is noteworthy that the text speaks of "one of the mountains which I shall tell you," when it could have said more easily "on the mountain which I shall tell you." It may be noted that "the mountains" (ההרים) is an anagram of Moriah (המריה), but whether this is sufficient warrant for the use of the plural "mountains" is unsure. "Which I shall tell you" clearly echoes "which I shall show you" (12:1) and makes the parallel between God's last command to Abraham and his first the more obvious.

3 Scene 2: Departure. Nothing is said about Abraham's inner feelings at this point. The narrator's silence allows the reader's imagination a free rein. He rather concentrates on Abraham's acts, which show him promptly, "early in the morning," obeying, as he did when commanded to expel Ishmael (21:14; cf. 19:27; 20:8).

"Saddled . . . took . . . cut." This sequence of waw-consecutives implies Abraham did one thing after another, so it is surprising that he cut the wood *after* saddling his ass and gathering together his servants and Isaac. It would have been more sensible to cut the wood first. This illogical order hints at Abraham's state of mind. Is he so bemused that he cannot think straight, is he quite collectedly trying to keep everybody in the dark about the purpose of the journey till the last possible moment, or is he trying to postpone the most painful part of the preparation till last (cf. his withholding Ishmael in 21:14)? All these interpretations are possible, indeed are not mutually exclusive, and need to be borne in mind as the narrative unfolds.

But whatever his state of mind, Abraham did what he was told. "He set out and went to the place which God had told him about." The last clause indicates that God had spoken again to Abraham, for the location of the mountain was not revealed at first. Another divine instruction is also implied by Abraham's action in saddling an ass and taking two servant boys with him. How did he know he needed to take them? By omitting the necessary intermediate dialogue that is presupposed, the narrator enhances the impression of Abraham's prompt obedience while nicely adverting to his state of mind by listing his actions prior to departure.

"Place" is here a holy place or sanctuary (cf. 12:6; 13:4; 28:16; Exod 3:5; 20:24).

4–6b Scene 3: Dialogue at the foot of the mountain.

4 "On the third day." Three days is a typical period of preparation for something important (cf. 31:22; 40:20; 42:18). Westermann notes that the mountain of God to which the Israelites sought to travel was three days' journey (Exod 3:18; 5:3). Indeed, the phrase "on the third day" occurs twice in the Sinai pericope

(Exod 19:11[2x], 16). Calvin observes that the delay made Abraham's ordeal the more painful. "God does not require him to put his son immediately to death, but compels him to revolve this execution in his mind during three whole days, that in preparing to sacrifice his son, he may still more severely torture all his own senses" (1:565).

"He looked up and saw." To "look up" before seeing usually intimates that what is to be seen is of great significance (cf. 18:2; 24:63; 33:1, 5; 43:29), in this case "the place." "From afar"; cf. 37:18 and especially Exod 20:18, 21; 24:1, where Israelites stand or worship "from afar" before Mount Sinai. "We are left to imagine the pang that shot through the father's heart when he caught sight of it" (Skinner, 329).

5 Abraham's first words since setting out are perplexing. Why does he not want his servants to accompany him? Is the way too rough for the donkey? Did he not want the lads to see the sacrifice? Did he fear they might interfere? Was a donkey too unclean to take to a sanctuary? Had God simply told him to leave them? All these possibilities are open and remain unresolved. The parallel with the Mount Sinai experience may again be noted: at Sinai only Moses was allowed to come to the top of the mountain; the people had to stay at the bottom (Exod 19:20, 24; 24:1–2).

But the final remarks to his servants are even more enigmatic. Note in passing that Abraham simply calls Isaac "the lad" rather than "my son," which may suggest that Abraham is trying to be detached. He has already mentally given Isaac to God, so that in a sense he is no longer his son. But then he continues: "so that we can worship and return to you." It is notable that Abraham only says "worship" rather than "offer a burnt offering." "Worship" (השתחוה) is a vaguer term than "offer"; it may simply mean "bow down" (cf. 18:2; 19:1). Does this indicate a weakening of resolve or a desire to hide what was to happen from his servants, or is the term chosen simply for brevity? Confusion about Abraham's real meaning is worsened by his final enigmatic "We may return to you," for he might have been expected to say "so that *I* may return to you."

There are at least three ways of taking "we may return to you." First, it could be a white lie to disguise the true nature of the sacrifice. It is clear from Isaac's question in v 7 that Abraham has not been very explicit about the nature of the sacrifice he is undertaking. Evidently he must have said he was going to offer a burnt offering at God's special request but never said who the victim would be. So one could suppose that here he is simply continuing to allow his entourage to continue under the illusion that he intended to make a normal animal sacrifice, albeit at a special site. Second, it could be read as implying that he does not intend to sacrifice Isaac after all, that he cannot see himself going through with it, and that he will disobey God's command. Third, it may be read as an affirmation of faith, that although he has been told to sacrifice Isaac, yet somehow the promises made to him that "your descendants will be named through Isaac" would be fulfilled.

Many commentators do not comment on the problem. Of those who do note it, some prefer to take it as a lie: "The servants are put off with a pretext whose hollowness the reader knows" (Skinner, 329). Jacob tries to exonerate Abraham by pointing out that unwittingly Abraham did speak the truth, while Dillmann

sees it as an expression of "quiet hope" (Dillmann, 292; so also Gross, "Zur theologischen Bedeutung"). Calvin (1:567) suggests "Abraham spoke confusedly." It seems likely that none of these rival interpretations need be ruled out. White lie, prophecy, hope, even disobedience, can surely coexist in the believer, especially in times of acute crisis. The enigmatic ambiguity of "we shall return" perhaps gives an insight into the quite contrary ideas agitating Abraham's mind at this time ("I believe; help my unbelief," Mark 9:24; cf. Matt 14:27–31).

6 But, however he felt, Abraham continued on the path prescribed for him. We see in the deliberate emphasizing of the details of loading the wood off the donkey and onto Isaac and in the first mention of the fire and the knife Abraham's determination to press on. It also implies that the next part of the journey will be the hardest physically and emotionally for both of them. The wood on Isaac's back looks forward to the moment when Isaac will be lying on his back on the wood (v 9), with his father, knife in hand, ready to slay him (v 10). Thus the wording here anticipates the moment of sacrifice itself. *Genesis Rabbah*, the Jewish midrash, comments that Isaac with the wood on his back is like a condemned man, carrying his own cross.

6c–8 Scene 4: Dialogue between Isaac and Abraham climbing the mountain. This most touching scene reveals a little of the feelings of Abraham and Isaac on their way. "The pathos of the dialogue is inimitable: the artless curiosity of the child, the irrepressible affection of the father, and the stern ambiguity of his reply can hardly be read without tears" (Skinner, 329–30). But it is also a gem of OT literary art. Note how the scene is framed by "So they went both of them together" (vv 6, 8), suggesting both their isolation and their companionship as they climb alone up the mountainside.

Furthermore, this remark "lets one suspect that the boy may have broken the oppressive silence only after a while. And after the conversation the statement is repeated. One sees that the final part of the way was traversed in silence" (von Rad, 236), "the most poignant and eloquent silence in all literature" (Speiser, 165).

But, as so often in this story, it is not merely what is said but what is left unsaid that gives it such depth and richness. In the dialogue, the repeated "my father," "my son" draws attention to the deep affection binding father and son. Yet the dialogue itself is ambiguous and open to more than one interpretation. On the face of it, Isaac's question, "Where is the sheep?" suggests a naiveté that makes his future death the more heart-rending. This impression is reinforced by his docile acceptance of Abraham's reply, which shows Isaac trusting entirely his father's good intentions. Or was he sharp enough to see through his father's enigmatic answer and realize that he was the intended sacrificial lamb? If so, his silence is again impressive, for it implies his total obedience to his father. Either way, Isaac is shown to have those qualities of perfection always looked for in sacrificial victims (cf. Lev 1:3). And either way, our appreciation of the trustful love that existed between father and son is enhanced.

However Isaac understood it, we must inquire what Abraham meant by saying "God will provide himself a sheep for the burnt offering." Is this like "we shall return" in v 5, another case of evasiveness, an expression of faith, a prophecy, or a prayer, "May God provide a sheep," for the imperfect could be understood as a

jussive here? It is also possible to read Abraham's response as an explicit reply: "God will provide a sheep for the burnt offering, namely my son." The last suggestion is unlikely in that "my son" is not preceded by the mark of the definite object and because it demands "provide" (ראה) being followed by a double accusative. But the other readings are all possible and contribute to the richness of the narrative. The organization of the story, which makes "God will provide" the turning point of the story (see *Form/Structure/Setting*), does favor a positive reading, i.e., as an expression of hope, a prophecy, or a prayer, though to Isaac it may well have sounded like evasion. Unlike in v 5, there is now no suggestion that Abraham will disobey. Though we might construe "we shall return" that way, "God will provide" does not suggest that Abraham is looking for an escape route.

Calvin comments: "This example is proposed for our imitation. Whenever the Lord gives a command, many things are perpetually occurring to enfeeble our purpose: means fail, we are destitute of counsel, all avenues seem closed. In such straits, the only remedy against despondency is to leave the event to God, in order that he may open a way for us when there is none. For as we act unjustly towards God, when we hope for nothing from him but what our senses can perceive, so we pay Him the highest honour, when, in affairs of perplexity, we nevertheless entirely acquiesce in his providence" (1:568).

9–10 Scene 5: After four short preparatory scenes, the narrative pace suddenly slows for the climactic scenes on the mountaintop.

9 The opening "They came to the place which God had told him about" reminds us that Abraham is obeying God, not acting out his own will. It raises the tension as we await the slaughter of Isaac. Indeed, we are kept in suspense by an unwonted amount of technical detail describing the construction of the altar and other preparations for the sacrifice (cf. 12:7). This postponement of the critical moment may also hint at Abraham's reluctance to come to the point. But at last Isaac is "bound," probably by his hands and feet (עקד; the verb occurs only here in the OT and gives rise to the Jewish term for this story, The Aqedah, i.e., the binding of Isaac), and placed on the altar.

In two respects the procedure Abraham adopts here differs from that prescribed in Lev 1 for the burnt offering of oxen and sheep. Lev 1 does not mention any binding of the animal prior to slaughter, and the slaughtering takes place before the dismembered animal is placed on the altar. It is not easy to explain these differences. Jacob suggests that binding the animal is simply presupposed in Lev 1, as it was done throughout the ancient Orient (see R. Rendtorff, *Leviticus* [Neukirchen: Neukirchener, 1985] 50). So why bother to mention that Abraham bound Isaac? Perhaps it was because Abraham might relatively easily have slit Isaac's throat when he was off guard; that an elderly man was able to bind the hands and feet of a lively teenager strongly suggests Isaac's consent. So this remark confirms that impression given by vv 7–8 that Isaac was an unblemished subject for sacrifice who was ready to obey his father, whatever the cost, just as his father had showed his willingess to obey God to the uttermost.

10 "Reached out his hand." Reaching out the hand often indicates that the next act is of great moment (cf. 3:22; Exod 3:20; 9:15; Deut 25:11). For the second time "the knife" is mentioned to emphasize the horror of the action. "Slaughter" (שחט) is a sacrificial term (Lev 1:5, 11) usually indicating cutting the

throat. "His son." By drawing attention to the relationship of Abraham and Isaac, the full awfulness of the deed is once again underlined. The unthinkable is about to happen.

11–18 Scene 6 matches scene 1 in being largely a divine monologue with strong echoes of Gen 12:2–3.

11 "The angel of the LORD called from heaven." Calling from heaven emphasizes the urgency and importance of what follows (cf. 21:17). Note that here he is called the angel of "the LORD" (cf. 16:9–11), God's covenant name last used in Genesis when the promised Isaac was born (21:1). The strange God who tested Abraham once again shows himself to be the gracious LORD who keeps his promise (Exod 34:6–7).

"Abraham, Abraham." Compare the single "Abraham" of v 1. The urgent double call (cf. 46:2; Exod 3:4) shows "the angel's anxiety that he could be too late" (Jacob, 499).

"Here I am" (cf. 22:1). With the summons to Abraham and his response, we are into the third panel of dialogue (cf. vv 1–2, 7–8).

12 But though the words of the third panel so often echo the first, how different is their thrust! The original order is now explicitly countermanded.

The parallelism, "Do not lay . . . Do not do anything," gives the prohibition a quasi-poetic flavor and emphasizes both its pressing nature and its joy.

"Now I know"; cf. 18:21, where likewise the mention of God knowing is used more in the sense of confirming his knowledge.

To "fear God" or "the LORD" is a very common expression in the OT and means to honor God in worship and in an upright life. Thus Abraham was worried about the behavior of the people of Gerar because he thought they had no fear of God (20:11), while Joseph tries to reassure his brothers that he will treat them fairly because he fears God (42:18). Perhaps the best parallel to this passage is Job 1:1, 8; 2:3, in which Job is described as "blameless and upright, one who feared God, and turned away from evil." Like Abraham, he also underwent a mysterious test of his loyalty to God.

"Withheld"; cf. v 16 and 39:9.

13 Note how the narrative says nothing about Abraham's reply or Isaac's release. Abraham's obedience proved, the story moves straight on to the substitute offering.

This time, as Abraham looks up, he sees not the fateful mountain (cf. v 4) but "a ram just caught in a thicket." The narrative emphasizes what Abraham saw; no sooner had the angel spoken than he looked and noticed the ram being caught. His subsequent action invites comparison with Noah. As soon as Noah left the ark, he offered sacrifice. Similarly, as soon as Abraham had unbound his son, he offered a sacrifice instead of his son. In both instances, the motives of the sacrifice are implied rather than explained. In both, they express devotion and gratitude and assure God's benevolence toward future generations (8:18–9:17). In sacrifice, the animal symbolically represented the offerer whose place it took. Here the ram replaces Isaac, so a full-grown ram, as opposed to a younger lamb, fittingly takes his place.

14 Abraham's surprise at the remarkably convenient timing of the ram's being trapped in the thicket has already been mentioned in v 13; now he speaks for

himself. Whether his "God will provide" (v 8) should be taken as hope, prayer, or prophecy makes no difference. Like Hagar (16:13–14), he has proved that the LORD does provide: she named a well as a perpetual reminder of the LORD's saving concern; Abraham named the mountain. As already noted, the name Moriyyah (v 2) is here alluded to in the name of the mountain (יהוה יראה‎ *Yahweh yireh*). "In the mount of the LORD he may be seen." Here the same root, ראה‎ "see, provide," is used in the niphal, which is regularly used of the LORD appearing to men (cf. 12:7; 17:1; 18:1), thus making a link backward with Abraham's past experience and forward to Israel's future experiences on the mountain of God (Exod 3:1–2, 16; Lev 9:4, 6, etc.).

15–18 As already observed under *Form/Structure/Setting,* these verses are vital to the narrative. Without them, Abraham's ordeal, unlike Hagar's or Job's, would have done him no good. It would have been purposeless suffering with nothing to show for his willingness to sacrifice his son. Had Abraham flatly refused to obey, Isaac would have remained alive. Are we to envisage him returning home with nothing to show for it? Noah received great assurances about his descendants' future after his sacrifice, and Job's property was doubled after his trial, while Hagar was promised that her unborn son would father descendants without number. To excise vv 15–18 as a late addition makes the supposed original of Gen 22 fall quite flat when compared with these other biblical accounts. But as I have tried to show above, vv 15–18 cohere well with the literary structures that undergird the narrative. They complete the palistrophe and constitute the fourth and final panel of dialogues. What is more, they are the last and most emphatic statement of the promises given to Abraham. Without these verses, the last time in the Abraham cycle that God affirms his promise is to Hagar in 21:18 and that concerns Ishmael rather than Isaac. For all these reasons, vv 15–18 should be regarded as integral and indeed central to this narrative in particular and to the Abraham cycle in general.

15 A second angelic summons "from heaven" (cf. Hagar's single call, 21:17) underlines the importance of what is about to be said.

16 "By myself I swear." This is the first and only divine oath in the patriarchal stories, though it is frequently harked back to (24:7; 26:3; 50:24; Exod 13:5; often in Deuteronomy). Note the preceding "by myself," which gives the oath a special solemnity and weight (Jer 22:5; 49:13; Amos 4:2; 6:8; Heb 6:13–18).

"Declares the LORD" (נאם יהוה‎). This phrase occurs 364 times in the OT, mostly in the prophets but only in one other place in the Pentateuch (Num 14:28). This "formula points above all to God's dependability, as the addition in Ezek 37:14 'I have spoken and I shall carry it out.' The same is shown by the twenty-one passages where it underlines an oath of God" (H. Eising, *TWAT* 5:122).

"It is because" (יען אשר‎, only here in Genesis) draws special attention to the cause of God's renewed promise, "you have . . . your only child," here repeating v 12 (cf. v 2). The meritoriousness of Abraham is reaffirmed by the final clause, "because you have obeyed me."

17 "I shall really bless you." The name Abraham is regularly associated with blessing (12:2–3; 14:19; 17:16, 20; 24:1, 35), but this is the only time in Genesis that the infinitive absolute of ברך‎ "really" is used to reinforce the verb, so making the contents of this promise surpass all others.

"I shall really multiply your descendants." That Abraham's descendants would be extremely numerous (17:2; cf. 16:10), indeed, as countless as the stars (15:5), has been said before, but never has their number been compared to "the sand which is on the seashore."

"Possess the gate of your enemies," i.e., conquer your enemies' cities (cf. 24:60). This again is a novelty, a more realistic formulation of the promise of the land than earlier promises (cf. 12:1, 7; 13:15–17; 15:7–8; 17:8), doubtless implying that its fulfillment is now closer than when it was first enunciated.

18 "All the nations will find blessing." Here the hithpael of ברך is used instead of the niphal as in 12:3; 18:18. There may be no difference in meaning (see *Comment* on 12:3), or it may be combining the remark in 12:2, "you shall be a blessing," i.e., people will say "May God bless me like he has blessed Abraham," with 12:3, "All the families . . . will find blessing in him." Here there is another change to the earlier formulation: "in your descendants" instead of "in you." This implies that the world has already been blessed through Abraham, yet more blessing is to come through his descendants. And all "because you have obeyed me."

Moberly rightly remarks that though the promises here have for the most part been spoken before, "the phrases that are familiar elsewhere are used in a uniquely emphatic way" (*VT* 38 [1988] 318). In particular, they focus on the fulfillment of the promises in Abraham's descendants and on the significance of his obedience. "A promise which was previously grounded solely in the will and purposes of Yahweh is transformed so that it is now grounded *both* in the will of Yahweh *and* in the obedience of Abraham" (*VT* 38 [1988] 320). This is analogous to the assumptions underlying intercessory prayer. Here, too, faithful human response to God is taken up and incorporated within the purposes and activity of God. Moberly notes an analogy with Moses' intercession for Israel in Exod 32. After the golden calf incident, "their life as a people depends not only on the mercy of God but also upon the intercession of God's chosen mediator" (R. W. L. Moberly, *At the Mountain of God* [Sheffield: JSOT, 1983] 106). The flood story provides another paradigm of this intermeshing of divine mercy and human obedience. There God delivers righteous Noah, but it is Noah's sacrifice after the flood that prompts God to promise that never again will the earth be destroyed in a flood (8:21–9:17). Here Abraham's willingness to sacrifice Isaac prompts God to reassure Abraham about the future of his descendants. This parallel between the sacrifices of Noah and Abraham and the subsequent divine promises strengthens the case for seeing vv 5–18 as integral to the narrative (cf. Alexander, *JSOT* 25 [1983] 17–22).

19 Conclusion: A typical close to an episode (cf. 12:9; 13:18; 18:33; 21:34). But it leaves so much unsaid; even Isaac is not mentioned though he has been the subject of the promises, and no mention is made about what Sarah felt. Commentators and preachers have often been tempted to fill in the gaps, but in so doing they draw attention away from the central thrust of the story, Abraham's wholehearted obedience and the great blessings that have flowed from it.

Explanation

No other story in Genesis, indeed in the whole OT, can match the sacrifice of Isaac for its haunting beauty or its theological depth. So much is packed into so

few words that our lengthy comments have not done it justice. Here we cannot explore again all the intricacies of this narrative. Rather, I shall simply keep to the main track and indicate how it has continued to inspire reflection by Christians and Jews down to the present day.

The opening "after these things" puts the story into context. It harks back to the momentous developments in chap. 21, when at long last against all human odds the promised Isaac was born. This joyful event was soon followed by one of the most bitter experiences in Abraham's life. Bowing to his wife's will endorsed by God, Abraham had to expel his firstborn son Ishmael. Wandering in the wilderness, Ishmael and his mother had nearly died, but in the nick of time the angel pointed them to a well that saved them from dying of thirst. Meanwhile, Abraham and Isaac had prospered, so much so that earlier inhabitants of the land made a treaty with Abraham guaranteeing him and his descendants water rights in perpetuity.

Against this background of success, the opening comment "God tested Abraham" warns the reader that the coming narrative will strain Abraham's faith and obedience to the uttermost in order to reveal his deepest emotional attachment. Is he willing to love God with all his heart, mind, and soul? Does he trust and obey simply because it pays him to do so: in the words of the Satan of Job, "Does Job fear God for nought? Hast thou not put a hedge about him. . . ? Thou hast blessed the work of his hands, and his possessions have increased in the land" (Job 1:9–10).

But like Job, Abraham was unaware that his trial was a test; for him it was totally real. Though the comment "God tested Abraham" alters the reader's view of what follows, it must not obscure the awful situation Abraham found himself confronted with—torn between his faith in the divine promises and the command that promised to nullify them, between his affection for his only surviving son and heir and his love for God.

God's command is introduced with unusual gentleness, "Please take," and fully acknowledges Abraham's paternal devotion to his son, "your son, your only child, whom you love," and the hopes he had placed in him, for his very name Isaac was a reminder that he was the child in whom and through whom the oft-repeated promises of land, nationhood, and blessing would be fulfilled. By beginning in this vein, God endorses the propriety of Abraham's love for Isaac and his faith in the promises; at the same time it reminds us of the costliness of the command about to be given.

"Go by yourself . . . which I shall tell you." The gentle tone with which God began is suddenly replaced by an uncompromisingly stern command couched in terms that closely echo 12:1: "Go by yourself from your country . . . your father's house to the country that I shall show you." But hard as that command was, it was easy to carry out compared with "offer him there as a burnt offering." On that occasion, the order to break with the past was at least sweetened by promises of a glowing future, of a new land, numerous descendants, and blessing to all nations. Here the command has no such incentives attached to it; indeed, to carry it out would seem to vitiate any chance of these oft-repeated promises ever being fulfilled. The only glimmer of hope in the command is the name of the mountain, Moriah, which Abraham will later discover means "the LORD will provide, or appear," but when he is told to go there, this is completely obscure to him.

But without delay, "early in the morning," Abraham straightway saddles his donkey and calls two of his servant lads and Isaac to leave. Then when they are ready to go, he suddenly goes to cut the wood for the sacrifice—not the most sensible order of proceeding. Can he not think clearly, or was he trying to hide the nature of his journey until the last possible moment to avoid awkward questions from those left behind, such as Sarah? Or is cutting wood the most painful part of the preparations, which he must leave until the last possible moment? His motives are left unexplained; the narrator gives just a hint about how Abraham felt and then reminds us of the main point, his obedience: "He set out and went to the place which God had told him about."

This last comment shows that God has told Abraham more than is recorded here. This is confirmed by what follows: "On the third day Abraham looked up and saw the place in the distance." Evidently he knew what to look out for and what to do when he reached its foot, even though the divine instructions are not recorded. The narrator's terse economy of style, cutting out all unnecessary repetition, matches the single-mindedness of Abraham, whose overriding objective is to do the will of God. But the narrator again hints at his feelings: Abraham did not just see the mountain; he "looked up and saw the place in the distance." Looking up prior to seeing indicates that the thing seen is of special importance. Abraham sees the place "in the distance," reminding us that his agony was long and drawn out.

The last stage of the journey is also to be the hardest and the loneliest. For the final climb to the mountaintop, Abraham and Isaac must go on alone, Isaac now carrying the wood on his back which hitherto the donkey had carried. As Abraham had tried to avoid telling the rest of his household back in Beersheba, he now avoids giving a full explanation to the two most trusted servants who had accompanied him thus far. He simply but enigmatically states, "Stay by yourselves . . . so that we can worship and return."

In the light of the command to sacrifice Isaac, it is odd that he says "*We* shall return." Is this economy with the truth a smokescreen hiding the true plan from the servants and Isaac? Is Abraham perhaps having second thoughts about sacrificing his son? Or does he hope that somehow Isaac will return as a result of divine intervention? His remark leaves us to speculate, and the narrator does nothing to stop us, for in times of crisis wildly incompatible thoughts are liable to succeed each other in quick succession.

But whatever his innermost feelings, Abraham presses on up the mountain alone with his son Isaac in silence. He may have succeeded in concealing the real purpose of the journey from his household and from his servants up to this point, but now Isaac breaks the silence with a question that pierces to the heart of the situation, "My father . . . where is the sheep for the burnt offering?" Its innocent naiveté makes it the more poignant. How can Abraham avoid saying the unspeakable truth? His reply may be construed as a masterpiece of pious evasion, "God will provide himself a sheep for the burnt offering, my son," as an affirmation of faith, as a prophecy, or as a prayer, "May God provide. . . ." It cannot be construed that he is planning to back out, as "we shall return" might have suggested. If Abraham was tempted to disobey, he has now put such thoughts behind him. This remark, "God will provide," is a turning point in the narrative

(see *Form/Structure/Setting*), so it seems meant to be understood as a statement of faith, as prophecy, or as prayer.

To Isaac it must have sounded like evasion, but he said nothing and went on up the mountain. "The two of them went together." We are forced to conclude that he was naive and totally trusted his father, or that he now realized what was planned, yet he continued on up the mountain with his father. Either way he was a perfect, blameless sacrificial victim.

Finally they reach the top, "the place which God had told them about." Lest in the horror of the final scene we forget why Abraham is doing this, the narrator reminds us: he was obeying God. There an altar has to be built, and the wood must be laid on the altar. This was a real sacrifice according to proper ritual procedures, and there was plenty of time for Isaac to realize, if he had not before, what was going to happen and to run away. But he did not. In fact, he allowed himself to be bound before Abraham cut his throat. This action above anything else indicates his consent. The OT nowhere speaks of sacrificial animals having their legs bound before slaughter, and if Isaac had been reluctant to be sacrificed, it would have been easier for Abraham to have cut his throat or stabbed him rather than tie him up first and then place him on the altar. But he was tied, indicating his own willing submission to God's command revealed to his father.

Then at the very last minute with Abraham's hand poised to cut Isaac's throat, the angel of the LORD yells from heaven, "Abraham, Abraham . . . do not lay your hand on the lad." He has passed the test—"Now I know that you fear God"— he has put obeying God above every other consideration, and that, as Proverbs says, is the beginning of wisdom (Prov 1:7). Like Job, he has shown himself to be a man who was "blameless and upright, one who feared God, and turned away from evil" (Job 1:1; cf. Gen 17:1).

But divine endorsement of Abraham's piety is by no means the end of the story. Before the ordeal, the reader has been told that it was but a test, which led us to anticipate Abraham's success in facing it. And Abraham makes no comment himself. Was he just relieved, or had he believed all along that God would somehow rescue Isaac? Or had he no time to say anything?

As often, we are left to speculate. But if the angelic command did not surprise Abraham, the sudden snagging of a ram in the thicket did. He looks on its capture as God's perfectly timed provision. His ambiguous "God will provide a sheep" (v 8) has been fulfilled more completely and exactly than he had anticipated. Now he knows why the mountain is called Moriah: it means "the LORD will provide," or as others have said, "In the mountain of the LORD he may be seen." He has discovered that God draws near those in deepest distress.

But the angel calls again. God's opening injunction quoted his very first command: "Go by yourself to the country . . . that I shall show you" (12:1). Then the LORD had first made the promises of descendants, covenant, and blessing to the nations. But up to this point in Abraham's trial, nothing has been said on these topics. So the angel now, for the last time in Abraham's career, reiterates them with more force than ever before.

For the first and last time in Genesis, the LORD swears an oath in his own name guaranteeing what he is about to say, a guarantee reinforced by the formula "declares the LORD." From now on, the LORD promises that he will not simply bless

Abraham but *really* bless him. His descendants will be so numerous that they will be compared not just to the stars but to the sand on the seashore. And they will not merely inherit the land; they will conquer it, "possessing the gate of your enemies." But more than that, Abraham's descendants, as well as Abraham himself, will be a source of blessing to "all the nations of the world." And all this will happen, "because you have done this thing and have not withheld your son, your only child." "Because you have obeyed me," all the promises first made to Abraham decades earlier are now augmented and guaranteed by the LORD unreservedly. In this way, Abraham's long pilgrimage of faith, which has not been without its lapses from true piety, is brought to a triumphant conclusion. God's test had put Abraham on the rack. Yet torn between his love for his son and his devotion to God, he had emerged victorious with his son intact and his faithful obedience rewarded beyond all expectation.

It is this categoric affirmation of the promises that gives this chapter such an important place, not just in Genesis but in the whole Pentateuch. The oath sworn to Abraham is often referred to subsequently, for it guarantees the success and protection of his descendants and their hope of eventually settling in Canaan (26:3; 50:24; Exod 33:1; Deut 1:8). God's opening words to Abraham in 12:1–3 were a free and unmerited promise of land, descendants, and universal blessing. Abraham's erratic response, sometimes showing faith, sometimes not, had meant that the promises were fulfilled more slowly than might have been anticipated. He had reached old age with only one son to his name and the right to use just one well in Canaan. But this last display of obedient faith was rewarded by an extension and endorsement of the original promises that not only exceeds every previous formulation but every subsequent statement of the promises. From now on, it is merely necessary to refer back to this occasion to say all that can be said about the promise.

These promises look far into the future as they predict Abraham's offspring becoming numerous as the sand, both conquering the land and yet being blessed by and a source of blessing to all nations, thus implying themselves or their fame spreading throughout the world. This story gives other hints, too, that its horizon is not bounded by the career of Abraham.

As elsewhere in Genesis, his actions foreshadow the later history of Israel. They too were called to go a three-day journey to worship God upon a mountain. There the LORD appeared to them and gave them the law and promised blessing to those who kept it. Every father in Israel was expected to dedicate his firstborn son to the LORD and to redeem him by offering a sacrifice. In Exodus, this redemption of the firstborn recalls the passover in which the firstborn sons of Israel were spared judgment. It may be that Genesis itself is implicitly comparing Isaac's rescue to that sparing of Israel's firstborn sons in the Exodus and the ram Abraham offered to the passover lamb. In later Jewish tradition (e.g., the book of Jubilees, 100 B.C.) a connection is made between passover and the sacrifice of Isaac. The verb "tested" also invites comparison with the Exodus experience, for it most frequently occurs in connection with Israel's wilderness wanderings, either referring to God "testing" Israel (e.g., Exod 16:4) or to Israel "testing" God (Deut 6:16).

Furthermore, this is the first detailed account of a patriarch offering sacrifice and, like Jacob's promise to tithe (28:22), doubtless foreshadows later national practice, so it seems likely that Abraham's sacrifice of the ram anticipates the

burnt offering of a lamb every morning and evening in the temple. In this connection, identification of Moriah with the temple mount in 2 Chr 3:1 is particularly significant. In post-biblical Judaism, it was sometimes affirmed that the temple sacrifices were accepted because of the merits of Isaac. His obedience was recalled each time an animal was sacrificed, so that the atoning value of sacrifice really depended on Isaac's willingness to suffer, not the death of the animal. However, it is dubious whether such ideas circulated before the Christian era. The emphasis in the biblical account is certainly on Abraham's obedience.

In other ways, the role of Abraham here anticipates the role of later national religious leaders. In chap. 18, 20, he appeared as a prophetic intercessor. Here he acts more like a priest, especially like Moses, who ascended the mountain to worship God. In another way, he appears as the archetypal wise man of the Psalms and Proverbs who "fears God." More exactly, he is an example of the righteous suffering like Job, "who feared God and turned away from evil." The story of Job is the story of Gen 22 writ large. Job actually loses his children and is pushed to the limits of human endurance by sickness and his friends' unsympathetic advice, but eventually he meets God face to face, is reassured, and has his children replaced and his herds doubled. Finally, the suffering servant of Isa 53 seems to combine in his person images drawn from Gen 22 with those of Job. Like Job, the servant's physical disfigurement makes his contemporaries conclude he is a sinner. Like Abraham the servant makes an offering and sees his offspring (Isa 53:10). But like Isaac, who silently consented to being sacrificed, he was "like a lamb that is led to the slaughter, . . . [yet] he opened not his mouth" (Isa 53:7). And like Isaac he offered himself, rather than anyone else. But unlike Abraham, Isaac, or Job, the servant actually died (Isa 53:8).

The NT writers develop this imagery in a very striking way. For them Abraham and Isaac are types of God the Father and Jesus. But whereas Abraham did not quite sacrifice Isaac, Jesus did actually die. So his death is a perfect and fully effective atoning sacrifice, whereas Isaac's near sacrifice merely prefigured our Lord's and could not redeem mankind. This typology is very widespread in the NT and therefore must be extremely early and probably reflects Jesus' own self-interpretation of his mission. When Paul says, "If God is for us, who is against us? He who did not spare his own Son but gave him up for us" (Rom 8:31–32), the echoes of Gen 22:12, 16, "you have not withheld your son, your only child," are obvious. John 3:16, "For God so loved the world that he gave his only Son," makes the same comparison. John the Baptist's cry, "Behold, the Lamb of God, who takes away the sin of the world!" may well be making a similar connection, for whether the primary reference is to the lambs for the daily burnt offering or to the passover lamb, Gen 22 seems to associate both with the sacrifice of Isaac. The heavenly voice at Jesus' baptism and transfiguration says, "This is my beloved son." Though this terminology could be linked with Isa 42:1; Ps 2:7, it is even closer to Gen 22:2, 12, 16 in wording, for the LXX translates "only" by ἀγαπητός "beloved." Peter's reference to Christ as "a lamb without blemish," "destined before the foundation of the world" may be another example of using the imagery of Genesis to explain the crucifixion (1 Pet 1:19–20).

James cites Abraham's faithful obedience to show that this is integral to true discipleship. "Was not Abraham our father justified by works, when he offered

his son Isaac upon the altar? You see that faith was active along with his works, and faith was completed by works, and the scripture was fulfilled which says 'Abraham believed God, and it was reckoned to him as righteousness'" (Jas 2:21–23). Heb 11:17–19 offers Abraham as an example of someone who believed in God's promises even when the death of Isaac looked certain. "By faith Abraham, when he was tested, offered up Isaac, and he who had received the promises was ready to offer up his only son, of whom it was said, 'Through Isaac shall your descendants be named.' He considered that God was able to raise men even from the dead; hence, figuratively speaking, he did receive him back" (Heb 11:17–19).

James and Hebrews thus use the account of Isaac's sacrifice not just to shed light on the atonement but on the kind of behavior the pious should imitate. Crises that test faith and obedience to the uttermost are still part of the disciple's lot. The disciple too must be ready to take up the cross and follow. And those who endure to the end may hope to hear the Lord's commendation: "Well done, good and faithful servant; enter into the joy of your Lord."

The Genealogy of Rebekah   *(22:20–24)*

Bibliography

Sternberg, M. *The Poetics of Biblical Narrative.* Bloomington: Indiana UP, 1985. 132–33.

Translation

²⁰*After these things, Abraham was told*ᵃ ᵇ*Milcah too*ᶜ *has borne sons for your brother Nahor:* ²¹*Uz his firstborn, and Buz his brother, and Qemuel,* ᵃ*the father of Aram,*ᵃ ²²*Kesed, Hazo, Pildash, Yidlaf, and Bethuel.* ²³ ᵃ*(Now Bethuel was the father*ᵇ *of Rebekah.)*ᵃ ᶜ*These*ᵈ *were the* ᵈ*eight that Milcah bore to Nahor, Abraham's brother*ᶜ ²⁴*His concubine,*ᵃ ᵇ*named Reumah,*ᵇ ᶜ*also bore him children,*ᶜ *Tebah, Gaham, Tahash, and Maacah.*

Notes

20.a. Waw consec + 3 masc sg impf hoph נגד.

20.b. הנה here expresses surprise and the fact that Abraham has just heard (cf. *SBH*, 94–95; Lambdin, 169).

20.c. גם־הוא links Milcah's childbearing with presumably Sarah's. Cf. 4:4, 22, 26; 19:38; *SBH*, 157.

21.a-a. *BHS* suggests this is a gloss.

23.a-a. *SBH*, 88, takes this as a pseudo-circumstantial clause, "then Bethuel fathered Rebekah," common in genealogies; cf. 4:18; 10:8, 13.

23.b. SamPent typically substitutes hiph הוליד for MT qal.

23.c-c. Apposition clause concluding paragraph (*SBH*, 54).

23.d. Demonstrative pronouns with numerals do not require def art (GKC, 134k; Brockelmann, 85b); cf. 9:19.

24.a. There is no need to emend MT פִּילַגְשׁוֹ "his concubine" to פִילֶגֶשׁ לוֹ "he had a concubine" with *BHS*. MT "his concubine" may be understood as subject of the adjunctive clause c-c; so *SBH*, 93.

24.b-b. On this construction in naming clauses, see *SBH*, 31.

24.c-c. Cf. n. 22:24.a.

Form/Structure/Setting

This short genealogy listing the twelve sons of Nahor and one of his grand-daughters falls into two parts:

vv 20b–23	Milcah's sons
v 24	Reumah's sons

The list of Milcah's sons is expressed as news given to Abraham; cf. v 20a, "Abraham was told . . . ," whereas v 23b is clearly editorial comment, "These . . . Abraham's brother." The comment about Rebekah may or may not be part of the report he received, and v 24 is apparently not.

On the face of it, this genealogical snippet is unexpected, sitting uneasily between the account of Isaac's sacrifice and his mother's burial (chap. 23). However, the opening, "After these things," does connect it chronologically with the preceding material, while "Milcah too has borne sons" makes an explicit connection with 21:1–7, the account of Isaac's birth. On the other hand, the mention of Rebekah in v 23 clearly anticipates her fuller presentation in chap. 24. For this reason and because of its style, most obviously the use of the qal יָלַד for fathering in v 23, this passage has usually been assigned to J. It is seen as the vital stepping stone between the accounts of Isaac's birth and his betrothal.

Westermann is not so sure that this genealogy is J, but he does think that it is one of the earlier parts of the Abraham cycle that originally concluded with 21:1–7; 22:20–24; 25:1–8. The rest of 21:8–25:18 is, according to Westermann, later expansion.

However, this fails to do justice to the careful arrangement of material in Genesis. Abraham had two sons whose careers ran in parallel with each other. After their birth late in Abraham's life, Ishmael's career is summarized first. As a lad, he faced death and was rescued by an angel, who promised to make him a great nation. Subsequently, he married one of his mother's people, an Egyptian (21:9–21). In 22:1–19, Isaac's career has passed through a similar series of stages, climaxing with a tremendous assurance about his descendants, but the last stage, Isaac's marriage, is missing. The reader expects something at this point, but the editor tantalizes him with a mere genealogy. But buried within it is the mention of one grandchild, who is also a girl. This surely raises expectations.

From a formal point of view, Westermann has noted that this genealogy matches the genealogy of 11:27–32. I observed that 22:1–19 echoes in substance and style 12:1–3. Thus, putting in this genealogy of Nahor enhances the overall palistrophic arrangement of Gen 11:27 to 22:24. (See Wenham, *Genesis 1–15*, 263.)

Finally, it may be noted that the stories of Abraham, Isaac, and Jacob all conclude with a similar sequence: promise (22:15–18; 35:9–14; 48:4), journey (22:19; 35:16; 48:7), birth of children (22:20–24; 35:17–18; 48:5–6), and death and burial of patriarch's wife (chap. 23; 35:18–20; 48:7). For further discussion of parallels,

see *Form/Structure/Setting* on chap. 35, chaps. 48–50. These parallels show that
the author of this material worked according to a coherent scheme.

Comment

20 "After these things" (cf. 22:1; 15:1). It is not clear how long after the sacrifice
of Isaac news about his brother's family reached him, but in the time span of
Genesis, it is likely to have been years rather than weeks. "Abraham was told," as
Procksch surmises, by some passing caravan.

"Milcah too has borne sons for your brother." The introductory הנה, left
untranslated here, indicates that this is Abraham's perspective (note "your
brother") and suggests how the news just reached him and maybe his surprise.
Presumably Nahor's children were born before Isaac. The comparison "Milcah
too" is with Sarah (21:2), who had but one son, as opposed to Milcah's eight. On
Milcah, see 11:29.

21 "Uz"; cf. 10:23, where Uz is a descendant of Aram, and 36:28, a descendant of Edom. Clearly Genesis regards these places named Uz as distinctly
different, but how they were related in prebiblical tradition is obscure. Job lived
in Uz, apparently somewhere east of Canaan.

"Buz," mentioned only here (1 Chr 5:14, a son of Gad) and in Jer 25:23, associated with Dedan and Tema, suggests Buz may also be a place in Arabia. Elihu
came from Buz (Job 32:2). The land of Bâzu was conquered by Esarhaddon in
676 B.C. and was described by the Assyrians as dry and thirsty, swarming with snakes
and scorpions. Some place it in Nejd in Arabia, others in Persia. A land of Bâzu is
also mentioned in the Mari letters (*EM* 2:40).

"Qemuel" is a personal name later borne by an Ephraimite (Num 34:24) and
a Levite (1 Chr 27:17).

22 "Kesed" occurs only here in the OT and has been linked to כשדים "the
Chaldaeans." It may be that Kesed is regarded as their forefather. Personal names
phonetically similar to Kesed are found in southwest Semitic (*EM* 4:365).

"Hazo," "Pildash," and "Yidlaf" occur only here in the OT.

"Bethuel," like "Qemuel," appears to be a theophoric name of "El," but the
meaning of the first element is obscure. Though mentioned again in 24:15, 50,
he takes little part in the negotiations for Rebekah's marriage there, suggesting
he is already in retirement.

23 "Now Bethuel was the father of Rebekah." It is not clear whether this continues the report given to Abraham about his brother's children beginning in v
21, or whether it is part of the editor's summary in v 23b. In other words, it is
uncertain whether Abraham knew about Rebekah before he sent his servant to
find a wife for Isaac.

The mention of Rebekah in this short genealogy sticks out. She is the only
female descendant of Nahor listed here among twelve males. Her future as the
most dominating of the patriarchal wives is already hinted at in this first mention
of her existence.

The traditional interpretation of Rebekah is that it means "heifer." But this is
doubtful. It may be related to a common Semitic root meaning "to tie a sheep or
cow with a cord." Even more attractive is to relate it to Akkadian *rabāku* "to be

soft or springy." In other words, "Rebekah" means "soft," "supple"; cf. *EM* 7:321–23. No etymology of her name is given in the OT, but in Gen 24:60–66; 27:1–17 her name is associated with "blessing" (ברכה *běrākāh*). Since she is portrayed as the female counterpart of Abraham, who embodies blessing in his name and in his person, this play on her name is very apt.

"These were the eight. . . ." Adding the four sons by his concubine Reumah, Nahor had twelve sons, like Jacob (29:32–30:24), Ishmael (25:13–16), and Esau.

24 "Concubine" (פילגש) is a word of Indo-European origin perhaps borrowed by Hebrew from the Philistines. Terms from the same root are found in Greek and Latin. A concubine was a second-class wife, probably acquired without payment of bride-money (מהר), who had fewer legal rights than did an ordinary wife. Bilhah is called both concubine and slave-wife (אמה), so Exod 21:7 may set out some of the rights of concubines (see *EM* 6:456–67).

Three of Reumah's sons, Tebah, Tahash, and Maacah, appear to be connected to kingdoms or towns in the area today called Lebanon or Syria. So it has been surmised that Reumah may have been the name of a league or alliance to which they all belonged. Tebah (possibly "slaughter," "bright light") is mentioned in second-millennium Egyptian texts. According to N. Naaman (*EM* 8:521), Tebah may be located in the southern Beqa of Lebanon, Tahash lay near the upper Orontes, and Maacah is situated in the Litani Valley. It is mentioned also in Josh 13:11; 2 Sam 10:6, 8 as well as in the Mari texts (cf. also *EM* 3:363; 5:192–93; 7:295). But whatever the relationship between these names and Aramean tribes or political groups, in the present context they are simply the names of Nahor's sons.

Reumah is mentioned only here. According to Coote (*JBL* 90 [1971] 207), it means "beloved." *EM* 7:129 relates it to ראם "wild ox" (Num 23:22; 24:8).

Explanation

A genealogy of Nahor seems rather an anticlimax after the high tension of the sacrifice of Isaac. But it is not as irrelevant to the story line as it appears on first sight. The angelic promise of vv 16–18 assured Abraham that his descendants would be as numerous as the sand of the seashore. This inevitably implies that Isaac must marry, a conclusion reinforced by the analogous developments in the Ishmael story. He too was at death's door, was rescued by an angel, was promised numerous descendants, and eventually married (21:15–21). Isaac should surely marry too. But that development is delayed to chap. 24.

Instead we have here a list of the twelve sons of Nahor, which makes Abraham's fathering of just Ishmael and Isaac look modest. But the genealogy also mentions one of his granddaughters. Surely Rebekah must have been quite a character to be the only girl listed alongside her father and uncles. Then the genealogy closes, leaving the reader to wonder what the point of it is and whether Abraham had learned of Rebekah's birth or only of her uncles. Here are seeds from which the story will grow further.

Purchase of Burial Ground   *(23:1–20)*

Bibliography

Brink, H. van den. "Gen 23: Abraham's Koop." *Tijdschrift voor Rechtgeschiedenis.* 37 (1969) 469–88. **Emerton, J. A.** "The Priestly Writer in Genesis." *JTS* 39 (1988) 381–400. **Gottstein, M. H.** "נשׂיא אלהים" (Gen 23:6)." *VT* 3 (1953) 298–99. **Lehmann, M. R.** "Abraham's Purchase of Machpelah and Hittite Law." *BASOR* 129 (1953) 15–18. **Licht, J.** *Storytelling in the Bible.* Jerusalem: Magnes, 1978. 20–23, 55–69. **Perrin, B.** "Trois textes bibliques sur les techniques d'acquisition immobilière (Gen 23; Ruth 4; Jer 32:8–15)." *Revue historique de droit francais et étranger* 41 (1963) 5–19, 177–95, 387–417. **Petschow, H.** "Die neubabylonische Zwiegesprächsurkunde und Genesis 23." *JCS* 19 (1965) 103–20. **Rabin, C.** "L- with Imperative (Gen 23)." *JSS* 13 (1968) 113–24. **Reviv, H.** "Early Elements and Late Terminology in the Descriptions of Non-Israelite Cities in the Bible." *IEJ* 27 (1977) 189–96. ————. *The Elders in Ancient Israel.* Jerusalem: Magnes, 1989. 147–52. **Shilar, E.** *The Cave of Macpelah.* (Heb.) Jerusalem: Ariel, 1976. **Speiser, E. A.** "'Coming' and 'Going' at the 'City' Gate." *BASOR* 144 (1956) 20–23 (also in *Oriental and Biblical Studies* [1967] 83–88). **Sternberg, M**. "Double Cave, Double Talk: The Indirections of Biblical Dialogue." In *Not in Heaven,* ed. J. P. Rosenblatt and J. C. Sitterson. Philadelphia: University of Pennsylvania/Bloomington: Indiana UP, 1991. 28–57. **Tucker, G. M.** "The Legal Background of Genesis 23." *JBL* 85 (1966) 77–84. **Westbrook, R.** "The Purchase of the Cave of Machpelah." *ILR* 6 (1971) 29–38.

Translation

[1] *Now Sarah's life*[a] *lasted one hundred and twenty-seven years.* [2] *Then Sarah died*[a] *in Kiryat Arba*[b] *(that is Hebron), in the land of Canaan. Then Abraham came to mourn for Sarah and to weep*[c] *for her.*

[3] *Then he rose up from before his dead wife*[a] *and spoke to the Hittites as follows:* [4] *"As I am just a resident immigrant with you, give*[a] *me a burial plot with you so that I may bury*[b] *my dead wife properly."*[c] [5] *The Hittites replied to Abraham as follows: "Do*[a] [6]*listen*[a] *to us, sir. As you are a mighty prince among us, bury your dead in the pick of our graves. None of us would withhold*[b] *his grave from you to prevent*[c] *you burying your dead."*

[7] *Abraham stood up and bowed to the people of the land to the Hittites.* [8] *He spoke with them as follows: "If it is your will that I should bury my dead properly, listen to me and persuade Ephron the son of Sohar,*[a] *for me,* [9]*that he may give me the cave of Macpelah*[a] *which he owns and is at the edge of his property.* [b]*For* [c]*the full price let him give*[d] *it to me for a burial plot among you.*[b]

[10] [a]*Now Ephron was sitting with the Hittites,*[a] *so Ephron the Hittite answered Abraham out loud before the Hittites before*[b] *all those entering the gateway of his city, as follows:* [11] *"Do,*[a] *sir, listen to me. I hereby give*[b] *you the land, and the cave which is in it I give*[b] *you. Before all my people I give*[b] *it to you. Bury your dead."*

[12] *Then Abraham bowed before the people of the land.* [13] *He spoke to Ephron out loud before the people of the land,* [a]*"But if you . . . , do listen to me,*[a] *I shall give*[b] *money for the field. Accept it from me so that*[c] *I may bury my dead there."* [14] *Then Ephron replied to Abraham as follows: "Do,*[a] [15]*sir, listen to me. The land is worth four hundred shekels. What is that between me and you? Bury your dead."*

[16] *So Abraham agreed with Ephron, and Abraham weighed out for Ephron the money he had publicly stated before the Hittites, four hundred shekels of silver at the merchants' rate.* [17] *So the land of Ephron in Macpelah east*[a] *of Mamre, that is, the land, the cave in it, and all the trees that fall within its boundary, was transferred* [18] *to Abraham by purchase witnessed by the Hittites and all those who entered the gate of his city.*

[19] *Afterwards Abraham buried Sarah his wife in the cave of the land of Macpelah east of Mamre, that is, Hebron in the land of Canaan.*

[20a] *So the field and the cave which is in it were transferred*[a] *from the Hittites to Abraham as a burial plot.*

Notes

1.a. Note the similar construction in 47:28 with its double "days of Jacob . . . years of life." Here "life of Sarah . . . years of Sarah's life." G, Vg omit the last phrase here.

2.a. Waw consec + 3 fem sg impf מות.

2.b. SamPent inserts אל עמק "to (the) valley"; cf. G.

2.c. Waw + ל + inf constr qal בכה + 3 fem sg suffix.

3.a. Masc sg ptcp qal מות (+ 3 masc sg suffix) may be used for female corpses (GKC, 122f); cf. vv 4, 6, 8, etc.

4.a. 2 masc pl impv נתן.

4.b. Waw + 1 sg coh קבר. For the sequence impv + coh with sense of purpose, "so that," see WOC, 577–78; *SBH*, 112.

4.c. Lit. "from before me."

5.a. The concluding לו is problematic following לאמר "saying, as follows"; cf. vv 11, 13, 14. SamPent has לא "not"; so too does G, *Mń*. *BHS*, with many commentators, prefers to repoint לו and make this the opening remark of the Hittites as in vv 11, 14. This could convey the great politeness of both sides. This usage of the emphatic lamed is well-attested in other Semitic languages but poorly attested elsewhere in the OT (cf. *EWAS*, 115–16). Rabin suggests that the three different vocalizations (לו/לו/לא) in vv 5, 11, 13, 14 represent attempts to render a non-vowel in the language of the Hittites (possibly Hurrian), which used an infix *el/ol* to mark the imperative. Thus the use of לו or לו before the imperative "listen to me" suggests the Hittites spoke Canaanite with a foreign accent (H. Rabin, *JSS* 13 [1968] 113–24).

6.a. 2 masc sg impv שמע + 1 pl suffix.

6.b. 3 masc sg impf כלא; note assimilation of III א to III ה form (GKC, 75qq).

6.c. On this use of מן following verbs of restraining, see GKC, 119x.

8.a. SamPent adds "the Hittite."

9.a. If Macpelah is derived from כפל "to fold double," this would explain G, Vg rendering "the double cave," but v 17 seems to count against this explanation.

9.b-b. Clause in apposition to v 9.a and clarifying it (*SBH*, 46–47).

9.c. ב of price (GKC, 119p).

9.d. 3 masc sg impf נתן + 3 fem sg suffix referring to "cave" (fem).

10.a-a. Circumstantial clause introducing new actor (*SBH*, 79).

10.b. On this use of ל, cf. GKC, 143e; Joüon, 125l.

11.a. With Rabin (cf. n. 5.a.), understanding לא as a "Hittite" (?Hurrian) displaced infix to mark the impv.

11.b. Here the pf is used for an action that, though fut, is understood to be complete when the word is uttered, a performative pf (Joüon, 112g; GKC, 106m; WOC, 489).

13.a-a. Rabin (*JSS* 13 [1968] 115–16) sees this as a kind of anakolouthon. Abraham, with a protasis "But if you . . ." (cf. v 8), then switches to "Hittite" idiom: "do listen to me."

13.b. Cf. n. 11.b.

13.c. Cf. n. 4.b.

14.a. Cf. n. 5.a.

17.a. SamPent reads על פני instead of לפני, probably assimilating to v 19 and 25:9.

20.a-a. Here the waw consec ויקם sums up the preceding narrative (GKC, 111k; Joüon, 118i; WOC, 550).

Form/Structure/Setting

Chap. 23 combines a report of Sarah's death and burial (vv 1–2, 19) with a much fuller scenic account of Abraham's purchase of land for her burial (vv 3–18, 20).

> Sarah's age (1)
> Sarah's death and Abraham's mourning (2)
> Negotiations for grave plot (3–15)
> 1. Abraham's initial request (3–4)
>   Hittites' reply (5–6)
> 2. Abraham requests Ephron's cave (7–9)
>   Ephron agrees (10–11)
> 3. Abraham offers to pay (12–13)
>   Ephron names price (14–15)
> Abraham pays; land transferred (16–18)
> Sarah buried (19)
> Summary (20)

The negotiations for the purchase of the cave and the surrounding land dominate this episode to such an extent that the mourning for and burial of Sarah occupy a very minor place in the telling, although it is her death that prompts the land purchase. It may be noted that the negotiations consist of three pairs of speeches, a triadic arrangement often used in Hebrew storytelling. Though the purchase of the cave of Macpelah is mentioned later in Genesis (25:9–10; 49:29–32; 50:13), this episode appears somewhat isolated in the Abraham cycle. It is apparently a quite secular story (it makes no reference to God save as a superlative in v 6: "great prince" = "prince of God"), and it does not obviously relate to the promises or their fulfillment. Simple biographical interest seems to dictate its inclusion.

It is generally held to derive from the P source, though it is almost as widely admitted to be unlike other parts of P in its style and content. Rendtorff (*Problem*, 128–30; cf. T. D. Alexander, "A Literary Analysis of the Abraham Narrative in Genesis," Diss., University of Belfast, 1982) has trenchantly exposed the self-contradictory arguments of many writers. Here it is alleged that the chronological notice (v 1) shows that the whole story belongs to P, whereas usually such introductory notices are separated from the succeeding story, as from a different source. Anyway, the word "hundred" here is in the construct (מאת), whereas elsewhere in P it is in the absolute form (מאה). There are some words, e.g., "Hittites," "prince," "holding" (אחזה), that are occasionally found in other P passages, but that might be because of common subject matter rather than common authorship. In other respects, this chapter's style is quite unlike other P passages. Skinner noted "its markedly secular tone" (335). S. E. McEvenue (*Narrative Style*, 22) noted that "the chatty, colloquial, style of Gen 23 seems untypical of P." Speiser argued that v 1 was "unmistakably from P. As a whole, however, the story betrays a different hand. With a few deft strokes, the author makes us aware not only of the solemnity of the occasion and the high stakes involved, but also of the humorous aspects of the situation. All of this points strongly to J . . ." (173). Similarly, von Rad suggests that here P "incorporated an older narrative pretty well unmodified into his narrative" (249). So Rendtorff concludes, "I see no sufficient reasons for the

assumption that Gen 23 constitutes part of a P-narrative, but many reasons against it" (*Problem*, 130).

In an attempt to date the material within the chapter, various extrabiblical parallels have been cited to prove its antiquity or its modernity. Lehmann (*BASOR* 129 [1953] 15–18) suggested that certain features of Gen 23, in particular the Hittites' desire to sell the land as well as the cave and the mention of the trees on the land, were explicable in terms of Hittite Law. This reads too much into the negotiations. Tucker (*JBL* 85 [1966] 77–84) and Petschow (*JCS* 19 [1965] 103–20) argued that certain features of the text closely paralleled neo-Babylonian dialogue documents of sale. But Thompson (*Historicity*) correctly insists that these parallels also give no unambiguous clues to the date of Gen 23. They reflect customs practiced over a wide area and a long time span whose evolution we cannot precisely chart. Subsequently, Westbrook pointed out that three parties, Abraham, Ephron, and the Hittites, appear to be involved in the transactions here, which parallels arrangements in mid-second-millennium Ugarit, Boghazköi, Mesopotamia, and Elam. He concluded that "the 'double transfer' fiction discussed above points to an authorship of considerably greater antiquity" (*ILR* 6 [1971] 38) rather than to an exilic P. Similarly, on the grounds of the unique linguistic features of this chapter (cf. *Notes* on vv 5, 11, 15), Rabin argues for "an early dating of the chapter as written" and "against its inclusion in source P" (*JSS* 13 [1968] 115). Similarly, Reviv (*IEJ* 27 [1977] 189–96) pointed to the term used for the city elders, "those who go in at the gate," as premonarchic.

Given our still limited knowledge of changes in Near Eastern legal practice and the development of Hebrew, it would be unwise to be dogmatic about the dating of this chapter. However, there is nothing in it that demands a late date or associates it unequivocally with P. I prefer to see it as based on early tradition utilized by the final editor of Genesis. It is difficult to be more precise about the history of its transmission prior to its incorporation by J.

Comment

1 "Now Sarah's life lasted one hundred and twenty-seven years." Sarah was last mentioned in 21:12, when she ordered Ishmael's expulsion, but her part in and reaction to the momentous events in 21:22–22:24 are passed over in silence, according to the narrative a period of nearly thirty-five years. Suddenly, however, her total lifespan (cf. 5:5, 11) and her death are mentioned. The phraseology of this verse is unique (cf. 5:5; 47:28) and has prompted some conjectural emendations, but Sarah is the only patriarch's wife whose age at death is recorded. Whether her age is supposed to be taken literally is unclear. The midrash saw symbolism in it: 100 stands for great age, 20 beauty, and 7 blamelessness. The number 127 also lends itself to easy arithmetic analysis like the patriarchal ages: $127 = 2 \times 60 + 7$ (see *Introduction*).

2 "In Kiryat-Arba (that is Hebron)." Kiryat-Arba is nearly always glossed as Hebron. Hebron (confederation?) seems to be the Israelite name of the city earlier (Judg 1:10) called Kiryat Arba, either "city of Arba" (so Josh 14:15) or "city of four," and lies about twenty miles (thirty-five kilometers) south of Jerusalem on the way to Beersheba (22:19). It is also very close to Mamre (13:18; 14:13, 24;

18:1; 23:17, 19), where Abraham received the great bulk of the promises recorded in Genesis. The association of Hebron with the promises probably explains the otherwise unnecessary "in the land of Canaan."

"He came in to mourn for Sarah and weep for her." The first term (ספד) is used almost exclusively for "bewailing" the dead, while the second (בכה) may cover weeping for joy (33:4; 45:14) as well as in sorrow. But when, as here, בכה is followed by the accusative, it refers always to sorrow prompted by death. The use of both terms together suggests that Abraham did not just weep aloud but carried out other traditional mourning customs, such as rending his garments, disheveling his hair, cutting his beard, scattering dust on his head, and fasting (Lev 21:5, 10; 2 Sam 1:11, 12; 13:31; Job 1:20; 2:12; cf. "Burial and Mourning," *NBD*, 170–72). These rites were carried out in front of the corpse, hence the opening "he came in," i.e., to the tent or part of the tent where Sarah lay; cf. v 3, "he rose up from before his dead wife."

3–15 The negotiations between Abraham and the Hittites proceed in three stages. Each time, Abraham makes a proposal that the Hittites then accept. First, he asks if he may have somewhere to bury Sarah. Then, he asks if he may buy the cave of Macpelah. Finally, he insists that its owner Ephron name the price. This three-stage development is typical of narrative style (cf. Licht, *Storytelling in the Bible*, 55–69).

The outstanding characteristic of this account is the courtesy and deference each side shows in the negotiations. Abraham rises and bows to the Hittites before making a request (vv 3, 7, 12). For their part, the Hittites are very polite, calling Abraham "a mighty prince" (v 6), repeatedly protesting their sincerity, "Do listen to us, sir" (vv 6, 11, 13), and offering Abraham exactly what he wants for nothing. This last point may well be typical oriental exaggeration, but it does show the Hittites' goodwill. Finally, the repeated emphasis on the public nature of the negotiations is evident (cf. vv 10, 11, 13, 16, 18). This was clearly of great importance to make Abraham's claim to the land clear beyond dispute.

3 "The Hittites," lit. "sons of Heth." Heth was a descendant of Canaan, according to 10:15. Their Canaanite affiliation is corroborated in that all Hittites named in the OT have good Semitic names, e.g., Ephron, Sohar, Uriah. "Apart from the expression 'the land of the Hittites,' which sometimes denotes Syria, all other references to 'Hittites' in the OT are to a small group living in the hills during the era of the Patriarchs and descendants of that group" (H. A. Hoffner, *POTT*, 213–14). The biblical Hittites have no obvious connections with the better-known Hittites of Asia Minor.

4 "I am just a resident immigrant with you." Abraham introduces himself with a simple factual statement about his legal situation, which at the same time exposes his vulnerability and need. He is just an "immigrant." Here the Hebrew has two terms, גר "sojourner" and תושב "resident." The former term is much more common. It denotes foreigners living in an alien land potentially permanently, such as the Israelites in Egypt (cf. 12:10). Such immigrants, being separated from their own people, were particularly prone to exploitation, and Israel is frequently urged to protect them (Deut 14:29). "Resident" is a rarer term than "sojourner" and is often used alongside it, so that they appear virtually synonymous (cf. Lev 25:23; Ps 39:13[12]). However, while circumcised "sojourners" could participate

in the passover, "residents" could not (Exod 12:19, 45–49), so they were even more on the fringe of society than sojourners. Here the distinction is not important; what the two have in common is stressed by coupling them, "just a resident sojourner," particularly their lack of land (cf. *TDOT* 2:439–49).

So Abraham asks, "Give me a burial plot with you" (אֲחֻזַּת־קֶבֶר "burial plot," lit. "holding of a grave"). Abraham's use of the term "holding" (אֲחֻזָּה) is probably significant here. It is used in 17:8; 48:4 of Israel's eternal possession of Canaan, so it seems that Abraham is asking for ownership of a piece of land for his permanent use as a burial ground (cf. G. Gerleman, *ZAW* 89 [1977] 313–25).

"So that I may bury my dead wife properly." His demeanor and garb no doubt showed that he was in mourning, but now Abraham gives the reason for his request, which no humane person could refuse.

5–6 The Hittites reply with a warmth that shows their sympathy with the bereaved Abraham. They begin with an assertion of their sincerity, "Do listen to us, sir," in their own local dialect (see n. 5.a.). They continue: "(You are no mere immigrant) you are a mighty prince among us." It should be noted that they speak of Abraham as a "prince," while he described himself as an immigrant, and they change Abraham's "with you" into "among us." Their preposition suggests Abraham is almost one of them. The term "prince" (נָשִׂיא) is most often used for a tribal chief (e.g., 17:20; 25:16; Num 7:2). Here he is called "mighty," lit. "of God"; this may be a mere superlative (cf. D. W. Thomas, *VT* 3 [1953] 215–16), but it could be an acknowledgment that God has evidently blessed Abraham and made him successful (cf. 21:22).

So they continue: "Since you are like one of our chiefs, of course we grant your request." They echo his own terminology exactly in their double reply: positively they say, "Bury your dead [A] in the pick of our graves [B]"; negatively in chiastic apposition they add, "None of us would withhold his grave [B] from you to prevent you burying your dead [A]." Their warm and generous reply apparently gave Abraham all he wanted, but permission to bury Sarah was only part of what he had requested. He had asked for a burial plot, not simply for the use of one of their graves. Despite the warmth of their reply, the Hittites, by omitting any mention of this point, probably indicate their reluctance to transfer land to Abraham, for then he would no longer be a landless sojourner.

7 Encouraged by their positive attitude, Abraham "stood up and bowed." Negotiations were conducted sitting down (cf. v 10; Ruth 4:1–4), so Abraham's elaborate gestures intimate that he is about to make an important request (cf. his standing before the LORD to intercede for Sodom, 18:22). "The people of the land" may be a group of leading citizens within the population, possibly roughly akin to the elders, though more probably it means the free citizens of the country, in contrast to foreign immigrants like Abraham (cf. de Vaux, *Ancient Israel*, 70–72). Perhaps the term is introduced here to emphasize that the Hittites own the land and that Abraham is concerned to buy some land from them.

8–9 Abraham's second request begins with making specific what the Hittites have already in principle conceded. They had said, "none of us would withhold his grave," so Abraham asks for Ephron's cave.

8 "If it is your will"; cf. the similar construction in 2 Kgs 9:15. "Listen to me" seems to be Abraham's attempt to reproduce the Hittites' unusual phrase "Do

listen to us" (v 6). In v 13, Abraham uses it again, but still not quite in the form they use. Rabin sees this as Abraham trying to speak the local idiom (*JSS* 13 [1968] 116). "Persuade" (פגע) is used for someone pleading on someone else's behalf (Jer 7:16; 27:18). "Ephron" and "Sohar" are good Semitic names (cf. Josh 15:9; Gen 46:10).

9 "Macpelah" seems to be the name of the area in which the cave was located (cf. v 17), but from the LXX to KB many hold that it describes the cave, as a double cave from the root כפל to "fold" or "double." Long tradition, going back to Josephus in the first century, identifies the site of Macpelah with the area now covered by the large mosque Haram El-Khalil in the town of Hebron. As remains of Herodian masonry are visible in the mosque, this corroborates Josephus' comments that the tomb of the patriarchs was located there in his time.

"Which is at the edge of his property." Abraham points out that only a small piece of Ephron's property need be transferred to him.

"For the full price" (cf. 1 Chr 21:22, 24 and the Akk. *kasap gamirtu*). "For a burial plot." By using this phrase (cf. v 4) and mentioning payment, Abraham insists that he is not merely interested in the right to bury his dead, a point already conceded by the Hittites, but in owning the land, something they had conspicuously omitted to consent to when they replied to his opening remarks.

10–11 Ephron's response is almost as warm as the remarks made earlier by his colleagues, the Hittites (v 6). Three times he offers to "give" to Abraham the cave *and* the land. At least he makes no mention of payment. This may simply be a matter of oriental courtesy—offering to give when really he is proposing a sale. Or he may simply be reiterating the former offer that Abraham can use his grave but implying that he does not intend to sell the land in perpetuity. Land merely "given" is land on loan. A gift, as opposed to a sale, places the recipient under obligation to the donor. So if Abraham accepted the cave and land as a free gift from Ephron, he could find himself indebted to him in other ways. Ephron's remarks are ambiguous: it is not clear whether he is ready to sell or merely to "give" the land to Abraham. However, the narrative does emphasize the public nature of his response: "Ephron . . . answered Abraham out loud before the Hittites before all those entering the gateway of the city." According to Reviv (*IEJ* 27 [1977] 190–91), "those entering the gateway of the city" is a technical term (Akk. *amîlû ša bābi*) for the elders of the city, who conducted legal affairs in the city gate. And Ephron himself draws attention to the public character of his offer, "Before all my people I give it to you."

12–13 Again expressing his gratitude and politeness, Abraham bows to "the people of the land" (cf. v 7). He too is aware of the importance of any agreement being public and attested by witnesses, so he too "spoke to Ephron out loud before the people of the land."

Whether or not Ephron's offer to give the land was an offer to sell, this is how Abraham takes it. In a rather confused sentence, "But if you . . . , do listen to me," apparently combining his usual opening formula with the Hittite formula (see n. 13.a-a.), Abraham insists on paying for the field, which Ephron had offered to give with the cave.

14–15 At last forced to commit himself, Ephron names a price for the field: "four hundred shekels." But as if ashamed to stoop so low as to mention a price,

he minimizes its significance: "What is that between me and you? Bury your dead." This is as if to say "We are both so rich that we need not worry about the price; you just go ahead and bury Sarah." Probably this is another example of oriental courtesy, rather than seriously meant. "The bargain which is here made between Ephron and Abraham, is to this very day repeated in that country. In Damascus, when a purchaser makes a lower offer than can be accepted, he is answered: What, is it a matter of money between us? Take it for nothing, friend, as a present from me; don't feel under any kind of constraint! Dieterici had a similar experience in Hebron: 'In our excursions we had noticed a fine grey horse belonging to the Quarantine inspector. Mr Blaine, my fellow-traveller, had appeared to wish to buy the animal. It now made its appearance at our tents. We inquired the price, and our astonishment may be conceived, when the dirty Turk offered us the animal as a present. Mr Blaine declared that he by no means intended to take it as a present, when the Turk replied: What then are five purses (£25 sterling) to thee?' Similar experiences take place every day in Egypt" (Delitzsch, 2:99–100).

16   Certainly Abraham takes it as Ephron's price and without quibble or demurral pays the full asking price of "four hundred shekels." We know too little about the price of land in Israel to make a guess about the amount of land involved. (For other land purchases, cf. 2 Sam 24:24; Jer 32:9; 1 Kgs 16:24.) So it seems likely that Ephron's field was substantial, unless he greatly overcharged Abraham. However, his opening "Sir, listen to me" may well protest his sincerity, that he was asking a reasonable price.

Fair or not, Abraham agreed to the price asked. "He makes no attempt to beat down the price. The reporter is aware that it is so important for Abraham to gain unimpeachable possession of the burial place that he will pay any amount for it" (Westermann, 2:375). Again the repeated insistence about the public nature of the transaction is to be noted: the price was "publicly stated before the Hittites," and the whole transaction was "witnessed by the Hittites and all those who entered the gate of his city" (v 18).

17–20   In precise detail, the deal between Abraham and the Hittites is recorded. Note how the exact location of the land "east of Mamre," the property associated with it, "the cave . . . and all the trees," the names of the seller, "Ephron," and the purchaser, "Abraham," and the witnesses are all mentioned.

With the purchase completed, "Abraham buried his wife . . . in the land of Canaan." She died and was buried in the land of promise in "a burial plot" that was to be the resting place also of her husband, son, and grandson and their wives.

Explanation

After Eve, Sarah is the first woman of importance to tread the stage of Genesis. From Cain to Babel, the primeval history preserves an almost exclusively male orientation; women are rarely mentioned except as adjuncts to their husbands. But with Sarah we meet a woman of heroic proportions, worthy grandmother of the nation of Israel. Her life was far from easy. She suffered the shame of childlessness till she was ninety. Twice she was trapped in a foreign king's harem by her husband's unbelieving folly. Twice she was provoked beyond the

breaking point by her slave-girl Hagar or her son Ishmael. Once she had seen her own son leave to be sacrificed by his father. From the way her husband treated her sometimes, one might wonder whether he really cared about his wife at all. Was he not most interested in preserving his own skin, and sometimes in serving God? The stories of the expulsion of Ishmael and the sacrifice of Isaac highlighted Abraham's deep affection for his sons. So this story makes plain Abraham's sincere love for Sarah and the honor he bestowed on her.

Abraham mourned for his wife in the conventional way, but he went much further. With great skill and determination, he purchased a large and expensive piece of land in which to bury Sarah. The business negotiations with the Hittites dominate this chapter to such an extent that it is easy to lose sight of Abraham's motives, his determination that his wife must be buried in an inalienable family grave where she may enjoy undisturbed peace.

The negotiations proceed in three stages. First, he asks the native inhabitants of Hebron, the Hittites, whether they as a body will allow him, a mere foreigner, to have a burial plot for his wife. With a great show of sympathy and open-heartedness, they invite him to use whichever of their graves he fancies to bury his wife. However, they did not actually offer to sell him land for a grave plot.

But deliberately overlooking this small point, Abraham takes up their willingness to allow him the use of their graves and asks if Ephron would sell him the cave of Macpelah, so he can use it for a burial ground. Ephron responds with apparent warmth to this suggestion, offering to give Abraham not just the cave but the surrounding land. Maybe this was more than Abraham wanted, but in one sense it was less. For land merely given, as opposed to bought, might be taken back or impose on the recipient other unwanted obligations.

So Abraham astutely takes the offer to give as an offer to sell, which may well have been Ephron's intention anyway, and he insists that he name his price. At last Ephron does, and the heavy price of four hundred shekels is paid. Even if Ephron did overcharge Abraham, the price paid suggests Sarah's burial ground was quite extensive. As befits the mother of the nation, her grave was impressive, a worthy memorial to a great woman.

Furthermore, it was in a place associated with some of her happiest memories. It was at Mamre that the LORD had promised her that she would give birth to a child within the year (18:1–15). Indeed, most of the great promises of land, descendants, and covenant blessing seem to be associated with their years in Mamre, according to 13:14–18:15. And in a sense the purchase of the plot of land at Macpelah was a first step toward Abraham and his descendants' acquisition of the whole land of Canaan. For this reason, Genesis draws attention twice to the rather obvious point that Hebron is in the land of Canaan (23:2, 19) and repeatedly insists that the negotiations and payment for the land were conducted publicly before the elders of the city (vv 10, 13, 16, 18). There was no doubt that this part of Canaan justly belonged to Abraham and his heirs.

This story of the purchase of the cave of Macpelah well illustrates Clines' contention that the theme of the Pentateuch is the partial fulfillment of the promises to the patriarchs (*The Theme of the Pentateuch*). Here Abraham acquires a very small part of Canaan, but that reminds us how much was still to become his. And most probably it was faith in the eventual fulfillment of this promise as well as a sense

of family solidarity that led to Abraham himself and his son Isaac and his daughter-in-law, as well as his grandson Jacob and his first wife Leah, being buried in the same grave (49:29–32).

Their attitude, declares Heb 11:13–16, is an example to all believers who should look forward to the eventual fulfillment of God's promises. "These all died in faith, not having received what was promised, but having seen it and greeted it from afar, and having acknowledged that they were strangers and exiles on the earth [cf. Gen 23:4]. For people who speak thus make it clear that they are seeking a homeland. . . . They desire a better country, that is, a heavenly one."

The Betrothal of Rebekah   *(24:1–67)*

Bibliography

Aitken, K. T. "The Wooing of Rebekah: A Study in the Development of the Tradition." *JSOT* 30 (1984) 3–23. **Allen, C. G.** "'On Me Be the Curse, My Son.'" In *Encounter with the Text: Form and History in the Hebrew Bible,* ed. M. J. Buss. Philadelphia: Fortress, 1979. 159–72. **Anbar, M.** "Les bijoux compris dans la dot du fiancé à Mari et dans les cadeaux de mariage dans Gen 24." *UF* 6 (1974) 442–44. **Ben–Reuven, S.** "*ʿelem* and *ʿalma* in the Bible." (Heb.) *BMik* 28 (1982/83) 320–21. **Diebner, B.,** and **Schult, H.** "Alter und geschichtlicher Hintergrund von Gen 24." *DBAT* 10 (1975) 10–17. **Driver, G. R.** "Problems of Interpretation in the Heptateuch: 1. Isaac's Meditation (Gen 24:63)." In *Mélanges bibliques rédigés: FS A. Robert.* Paris: Bloud and Gay, 1957. 66–76. **Freedman, D.** "A New Approach to the Nuzi Sistership Contract." *JANESCU* 2 (1970) 77–85. **Freedman, R. D.** "'Put Your Hand under My Thigh': The Patriarchal Oath." *BAR* 2.2 (1976) 3–4. **Gordis, R.** "A Note on Gen 24:21." In *The Word and the Book.* New York: Ktav, 1976. 335–36. **López, F. G.** "Del 'Yahwista' al 'Deuteronomista': Estudio critico de Gen 24." *RB* 87 (1980) 242–73, 350–93, 514–59. **Malul, M.** "More on *paḥad yiṣḥaq* (Gen 31: 42, 53) and the Oath by the Thigh." *VT* 35 (1985) 192–200. **Meier, S. A.** *The Messenger in the Ancient Semitic World.* HSM 45. Atlanta: Scholars, 1988. **Rabinowitz, L. I.** "The Study of a Midrash." *JQR* 58 (1967) 143–61. **Rofé, A.** "The Betrothal of Rebekah (Gen 24)." (Heb.) *Eshel Beer-Sheva* 1 (1976) 42–67. ———. "La composizione de Gen 24." *BeO* 23 (1981) 161–65. ———. "An Enquiry into the Betrothal of Rebekah." In *Die hebräische Bibel und ihre zweifache Nachgeschichte: FS R. Rendtorff,* ed. E. Blum, C. Macholz, and E. W. Stegemann. Neukirchen: Neukirchener, 1990. 27–39. **Roth, W. M. W.** "The Wooing of Rebekah: A Tradition–Critical Study of Gen 24." *CBQ* 34 (1972) 177–87. **Savran, G.** "The Character as Narrator in Biblical Narrative." *Prooftexts* 5 (1985) 1–17. **Wernberg-Möller, P.** "A Note on בשדה לשוח in Gen 24:63." *VT* 7 (1957) 414–16.

Translation

[1a]*Abraham was old and a good age, and the* LORD *had*[b] *blessed him in every way.*[a] [2]*So Abraham said to his slave, the most senior*[a] *in his household, who was in charge of all his affairs, "Please*[b] *put*[c] *your hand under my thigh,* [3a]*so that I can make you take an oath*[a] *by the* LORD, *the God*[b] *of heaven and earth, that you will not marry my son to*

one of the Canaanite girls among whom I live. [4]But[a] you must go to my country, to my clan, and take a wife for my son Isaac."

[5]The servant replied: "Suppose the woman is not willing to go with me to this land, [a]shall I really take[a] your son back to the land which you came from?" [6]Abraham replied, "Take care[a] that[b] you do not take my son back there. [7]The LORD, the God of heaven[a] who took me from my father's house and from the land of my clan, and promised me with an oath, 'To your descendants I shall give this land,' it is he[b] who will send his angel before you, and you shall take a wife for my son from there. [8]But if the woman is not willing to go with you, then you shall be free[a] from this[b] oath of mine: only[c] do not take[d] my son back there." [9]So the servant put his hand under the thigh of his master Abraham, and he took[a] an oath with him about this matter.

[10]Then the servant took ten of his master's camels and went[a] with all[b] sorts of his master's wealth. He set off and went to Aram-Naharaim to the city of Nahor. [11]He made the camels kneel[a] outside the city by[b] a well of water at evening time when women go out to draw[c] water.

[12]Then he said, "O LORD, God of Abraham my master, please guide[a] me today and keep faith with my master Abraham. [13]I am now[a] standing[b] by a well, and daughters of the townsmen are coming out to draw water. [14]Let the girl[a] to whom I say 'please let[b] down your jar for[c] me to drink' who replies, 'Drink and let me also give your camels water,' let her[d] be the one you have appointed[e] for your servant Isaac. By this[f] I shall know that you have kept faith with my master."

[15]Before[a] he had finished speaking,[b] he noticed[c] Rebekah coming[d] out—the daughter of Bethuel, who was the son of Milcah, the wife of Abraham's brother Nahor— with her water pot on her shoulder. [16a]The girl was very good looking, of marriageable age, and a virgin.[a] She came down[b] to the well, filled her water pot, and she came[c] up. [17]The servant ran[a] to greet[b] her and said, "Please give[c] me a sip of water from your jar." [18]She said, "Drink, sir," and she quickly[a] let[b] down her jar into her hand and let him drink.[c] [19]When she had finished[a] letting him drink,[b] she said, "Let me also draw water for your camels until[c] they have had enough to drink." [20]So she quickly emptied[a] her jar into the drinking trough and ran back to the well, and she drew water for all his camels. [21a]The man stared[b] at her silently wondering[c] if[d] the LORD had made his journey successful or[d] not.[a]

[22]When the camels had finished drinking, the man put[a] a gold nose ring of half a shekel in weight[b] and two gold bracelets each weighing ten shekels on her wrists. [23a]He said, "Please tell[b] me, whose daughter are you? Is there room in[c] your father's house for us to stay?"[d] [24]She replied, "I am Bethuel's daughter: he is the son of Milcah and Nahor." [25]She continued, "There is both[a] straw and[a] plenty of fodder with us, and there is also[a] room to stay with us." [26]The man bowed[a] down and prostrated[b] himself before the LORD. [27]He said, "Blessed is the LORD, the God of my master Abraham, who has not forsaken his faithful loving-kindness toward my master. It was I[a] that the LORD led[b] on the way to[c] the house of my master's brothers."[d] [28]The girl ran and told[a] her mother's[b] household about these things.

[29]Now Rebekah had a brother called Laban, [a]so he ran out to the man by the well.[a] [30]As soon[a] as he [b]saw the ring and the bracelets on his sister's wrists and heard his sister's report, "The man said this to me," he came to the man, and there[c] he[d] was standing by the camels at the well. [31]He said,[a] "Come in, blessed[b] by the LORD. Why do you stay standing[c] outside, when I have tidied[d] the house, and there is room for your

camels." [32] *So* [a]*the man came* [a] *into the house. They* [b] *unharnessed the camels, gave them straw and fodder, and water to wash his feet and those of the men with him.*

[33] *Food was put* [a] *before him, but he said, "I shall not eat until I have said* [b] *my piece." So he* [c] *said, "Speak on."* [34] *He said, "I am Abraham's servant.* [35] *The* LORD *has blessed my master tremendously, and he has become a great man. He has given him flocks and herds, silver and gold, slaves and slave-girls, camels and donkeys.* [36] *And Sarah, my master's wife, bore a son for my master* [a]*after she had become old,* [a] *and he has given him all he has.* [37] *My master made* [a] *me take an oath, 'Do not marry my son to any of the Canaanite girls in whose land I live.* [38] *But* [a]*you must go to my father's house, to my clan, and take a wife for my son.'* [39] *And I said to my master, 'Suppose the woman will not come with me.'* [40] *He said to me, 'The* LORD *before whom I have walked will send his angel with you and will make your journey successful, and you must take a wife for my son from my clan and my father's house.* [41] *Then you will be discharged* [a] *from my oath. If* [b] *you go to my clan, and if* [b] *they will not give her* [c] *to you, you will be clear from my oath.'* [42] *So I came here today to the well and I said, '*LORD*, God of my master Abraham, if you are really* [a] *making a success of my journey which I am undertaking,* [43] *I am now standing by a well, let the maiden who comes out to draw water to whom I say, "Please give me a little water to drink* [a] *from your pot"* [44] *who replies, "You* [a] *drink and let me draw for your camels as well," let her be the woman whom the* LORD *has appointed for my master's son.'* [45] *Before* [a] *I had even* [b] *finished praying,* [c] *I noticed Rebekah coming out with her water pot on her shoulder, and she went down to the spring and drew water. So I said to her, 'Please give me a drink.'* [d] [46] *Then she quickly put down the water pot she was carrying and said, 'Drink and let me also give your camels a drink.' So I drank,* [a] *and she also watered the camels.* [47] *Then I asked her and said, 'Whose daughter are you?' She replied, 'The daughter of Bethuel, the son of Nahor and Milcah.' Then I put* [a] *a ring in her nose and bracelets on her wrists.* [48] *I bowed down* [a] *and worshiped the* LORD *and blessed the* LORD*, the God of my master Abraham, who had guided* [b] *me reliably on the way to take the daughter of my master's relative for his son.* [49] *Now* [a] *then if you are going* [b] *to treat my master with kindness and loyalty, tell me; and if you are not, tell me, so that I may look elsewhere."* [c]

[50] *Then Laban and Bethuel* [a] *replied,* [b] *"This thing comes from the* LORD*.* [c]*We cannot contradict anything you say.* [c] [51] *Here is Rebekah; take her* [a] *and go that* [b] *she may marry your master's son, as the* LORD *has promised."* [52] *When Abraham's servant heard their words, he fell down* [a] *and worshiped the* LORD*.* [53] *Then the servant brought out* [a] *objects of silver and gold and garments and gave them to Rebekah.* [b]*At the same time he gave beautiful presents* [b] *to her brother and mother.*

[54] *Then he and the men with him ate and drank and stayed the night. In the morning they rose, and he said, "Send* [a] *me* [b] *to my master."* [55] *But her brother and mother said,* [a] *"Let the girl* [b] *stay with us a year* [c] *or so.* [d] *Afterwards she may go."* [56] *But he replied to them, "Do not delay* [a] *me,* [b]*since the* LORD *has made my journey successful.* [b] *Let me go so that* [c] *I may return to my master."* [57] *So they said, "Let us call* [a] *the girl* [b] *to* [c] *ask her opinion."* [58] *They called Rebekah and said to her, "Will* [a] *you go with this man?" and she replied, "I will* [ab] *go."*

[59] *So they sent off Rebekah their sister and her nurse and Abraham's servant and his men.* [60] *They blessed Rebekah* [a] *and said to her,*

"May you, our sister, become [b] *thousands of ten thousands;*
May your descendants possess the gate of their enemies."

⁶¹*Rebekah and her girls rose* ᵃ *and mounted the camels and followed the man. The servant took Rebekah and went.* ᵇ

⁶²*Isaac* ᵃ*returned from visiting* ᵃ *Beer-Laha-roi, for* ᵇ*he was living in the Negeb.* ᵇ ⁶³*Toward* ᵃ *evening he went into the country to meditate,* ᵇ *looked up and noticed* ᶜ *camels coming.* ⁶⁴*Rebekah looked up and saw Isaac, so she jumped down from her* ᵃ *camel.* ⁶⁵*She said to the servant, "Who is that* ᵃ *man there walking in the country toward us?" The servant said, "That is my master"; so she took her* ᵇ *veil and covered* ᶜ *herself.*

⁶⁶*The servant related* ᵃ *to Isaac all the things that he had done.* ⁶⁷*So Isaac brought* ᵃ *her into the tent of* ᵇ*Sarah his mother,* ᵇ *took and married her, and he loved* ᶜ *her. So Isaac was consoled* ᵈ *after* ᵉ*his mother's death.* ᵉ

Notes

1.a-a. Episode-initial circumstantial clauses (*SBH*, 80, 101).

1.b. On the pluperfect "had blessed," see GKC, 142b.

2.a. Constr sg of זָקֵן "old." Here, as often, the ordinary form of the adjective, e.g., "old," is used for the superlative "oldest."

2.b. The enclitic נָא makes a request more courteous (GKC, 110d).

2.c. 2 masc sg impv שִׂים.

3.a-a. Simple waw ("so that"; cf. Lambdin, 119) + 1 sg impf hiph שׁבע + 2 masc sg suffix.

3.b. Note the repetition of the noun in the constr "God of" (GKC, 128a; Joüon, 129b).

4.a. SamPent has כי־אם, but כי may be adversative (*SBH*, 184).

5.a-a. הֶהָשֵׁב אָשִׁיב. Interrogative ה + inf abs hiph שׁוב + 1 sg impf hiph שׁוב. Inf abs here strengthens the question (GKC, 113q).

6.a. 2 masc sg impv niph שָׁמֶר. On the shortening of final vowel *ē* > *e*, see GKC, 51n; Lambdin, 208.

6.b. On use of פֶּן, see GKC, 152w.

7.a. G adds "and the God of earth."

7.b. הוּא, the resumptive pronoun, probably gives a slight emphasis or contrast (*EWAS*, 99; GKC, 135c).

8.a. Waw consec + 2 masc sg pf niph נקה. On pointing, see GKC, 75x.

8.b. זֹאת without def art is normal after suffixed noun, "my oath" (GKC, 126y; WOC, 310).

8.c. On this use of רק, cf. *EWAS*, 131; *SBH*, 171, 177.

8.d. 2 masc sg juss hiph שׁוב. SamPent has impf תָּשִׁיב. The impf would be more usual. The MT (juss) may be defective spelling of impf (so Joüon, 114l) or for rhythm (GKC, 109d).

9.a. Waw consec + 3 masc sg impf niph שׁבע.

10.a. Omitted by G.

10.b. כל may mean "all kinds of" (GKC, 127b); cf. 2:9; 4:22.

11.a. Waw consec + 3 masc sg impf hiph ברך.

11.b. SamPent has על for MT אל.

11.c. Def art + fem pl act qal ptcp שׁאב.

12.a. 2 masc sg impv hiph קרה.

13.a. The function of הנה is problematic. *SBH*, 115, sees it governing both clauses, "I am standing . . . daughters . . . are coming"; *EWAS*, 139, as emphasizing the subj of the sentence. Most probably it reports the events through the eyes of the servant and draws attention to the vivid present reality of them (cf. Lambdin, 169).

13.b. Masc sg ptcp niph נצב.

14.a. נערה "girl" is usually spelled without the final ה in the MT Pentateuch. This is one of the perpetual qeres, perhaps reflecting older orthographic practice (GKC, 17c). Regularized by SamPent (Waltke, 214).

14.b. 2 fem sg impv hiph נטה.

14.c. "so that I may drink"; simple waw + impf expresses purpose (Lambdin, 119).

14.d. The preverbal position of אֹתָהּ makes it emphatic (*EWAS*, 152).

14.e. 2 masc sg pf hiph יכח.

14.f. בה; 3 fem sg suffix "it" refers to the verbal idea in preceding clause (GKC, 135p; WOC, 110, 305).

15.a. טרם is usually followed by impf (cf. v 45, not pf as here; hence *BHS* proposed emendation יכלה).

15.b. SamPent, G, Vg assimilate to v 45 by adding "to his heart."

15.c. הנה gives servant's perspective (*SBH*, 95).

15.d. Fem sg ptcp יצא.

16.a-a. Circumstantial clauses, a parenthesis within the main action (Joüon, 159f; Lambdin, 164; cf. *SBH*, 117).

16.b. Waw consec + 3 fem sg impf ירד.

16.c. Waw consec + 3 fem sg impf qal (in pause) עלה. Alternatively it could be hiph, "she brought (it) up."

17.a. Cf. n. 18:2.b.

17.b. Cf. n. 18:2.c.

17.c. 2 fem sg impv hiph גמא + 1 sg suffix.

18.a. Lit. "she hurried and." Heb. often uses two verbs where English prefers a verb + adverb (GKC, 120d; Lambdin, 238–39).

18.b. Waw consec + 3 fem sg impf hiph ירד.

18.c. Waw consec + 3 fem sg impf hiph שקה + 3 masc sg suffix.

19.a. Waw consec + 3 fem sg impf piel (apoc) כלה; on construction, see GKC, 164b.

19.b. ל + inf constr hiph שקה + 3 masc sg suffix.

19.c. On construction, see GKC, 106o; Joüon, 112i.

20.a. Waw consec + 3 fem sg impf (apoc) piel ערה. SamPent reads ותורד "she let down" as in v 18.

21.a-a. Episode-circumstantial clause (*SBH*, 81).

21.b. Masc sg constr hithp ptcp שאה probably alternative to שעה. On use of hithp here, see WOC, 428. On use of constr before ל, see GKC, 130a.

21.c. Masc sg hiph ptcp חרש "be silent."

21.d. Interrogative ה in disjunctive question may be followed by אם־לא (GKC, 150i; *SBH*, 148).

22.a. Lit. "took."

22.b. SamPent adds "and put (it) on her nose"; cf. v 47.

23.a. G adds "And he asked her"; cf. v 47.

23.b. 2 fem sg impv hiph נגד.

23.c. ב "in" is often omitted before בית (GKC, 118g).

23.d. Inf constr is usually לון. Joüon (81b) suggests this form is chosen here to avoid the sequence of vowels *a-u* twice.

25.a. On the repeated intensive use of גם, see GKC, 154a[1]; Joüon, 177q; *SBH*, 155.

26.a. Waw consec + 3 masc sg impf qal קדד.

26.b. Cf. n. 18:2.d.

27.a. The pleonastic pronoun "I" is emphatic (GKC, 135e; *EWAS*, 97).

27.b. 3 masc sg pf נחה + 1 sg suffix.

27.c. Acc of direction (GKC, 118f).

27.d. *BHS* prefers the sg אחי "brother of" to MT "brothers of." So G, S, Vg.

28.a. Waw consec + 3 fem sg impf hiph נגד.

28.b. S reads "father's."

29.a-a. *BHS*, with many commentators, transposes this to after 30a. But this has no support in SamPent or versions.

30.a. כ + inf constr ראה indicates simultaneity (Joüon, 166m).

30.b. SamPent adds 3 masc sg suffix ו.

30.c. הנה shows the scene through Laban's eyes (*SBH*, 94–95).

30.d. The subj often omitted after הנה (GKC, 116s; Joüon, 146h, 154c).

31.a. G, S, Vg add "to him."

31.b. Constr pass ptcp qal ברך (cf. GKC, 116l; Joüon, 121p).

31.c. Impf here for continuing action in the present (GKC, 107f; Joüon, 113d).

31.d. 1 sg pf piel פנה.

32.a-a. Vg "he brought him in" seems to take ויבא as hiph.

32.b. Lit. "he unharnessed," indefinite 3 masc sg; cf. WOC, 71.

33.a. Probably read with Qere, SamPent וַיִּשֶׂם: waw consec + 3 masc sg impf hoph (or qal passive; cf. GKC, 73f; WOC, 1375, n. 32) שים.

33.b. Here pf has future pf meaning, "I shall have said" (Joüon, 112i).

33.c. SamPent, G, S have pl "they said." Probably another indef 3 sg; cf. n. 32.b.

36.a-a. Lit. "After her old age" זִקְנָתָהּ + 3 fem sg suffix, "her." SamPent, G read "his"; cf. 21:7.

37.a. Cf. n. 3.a-a.

38.a. אִם־לֹא a strong antithesis (*SBH*, 184; P. A. H. de Boer, *VT* 16 [1966] 289) or introduces the contents of an oath (GKC, 149c). SamPent כִּי אִם and G ἀλλ᾽ support the former view.

41.a. 2 masc sg impf niph נָקֵה.

41.b. כִּי introduces major condition; אִם subclause (GKC, 159bb).

41.c. Pronominal object, e.g., "her," often omitted after נתן (GKC, 117f).

42.a. יֵשׁ + suffix + ptcp is rare in OT. They "indicate that a state of affairs or behaviour . . . is actually as one wants or expects it to be. . . . used when one wants to ascertain and confirm what one is half sure about" (*EWAS*, 77–78, 81; cf. v 49). The addition of enclitic נָא makes the prayer "more humble" (GKC, 159v).

43.a. 2 fem sg impv hiph שְׁקִי + 1 sg suffix.

44.a. On use of גַּם to link clauses, see *SBH*, 159, 160; GKC, 154a[1], 162b.

45.a. טֶרֶם is normally followed by impf.

45.b. The pronoun "I" אֲנִי before טֶרֶם conveys the servant's excitement at his experience, according to *EWAS*, 50.

45.c. Lit. "speaking to my heart."

45.d. SamPent, S add "a little water from your pot." Typical assimilation to the parallel v 17 (Waltke, 222).

46.a. Waw consec + 1 sg impf (apoc) שְׁתֵה.

47.a. Waw consec + 1 sg impf שִׂים.

48.a. Cf. n. 26.a.

48.b. 3 masc sg pf hiph נחה + 1 sg suffix.

49.a. וְעַתָּה introduces the request to which previous remarks are a preamble (H. A. Brongers, *VT* 15 [1965] 293–94).

49.b. Cf. n. 24:42.a.

49.c. Lit. "on [עַל] right or on left." SamPent has אֶל for עַל, but the MT represents the usual idiom.

50.a. Because Bethuel is inactive elsewhere in the story, some commentators and *BHS* suggest it is a mistake for וּבֵיתוֹ "and his household"; others that it is an interpolation. However, there is no textual support for supposing the mention of him here to be an error. See *Comment.*

50.b. Sg verb, "he replied," with multiple subj, "Laban and Bethuel," quite frequent (GKC, 146f).

50.c-c. The sentence in apposition to the preceding is linked by an unspoken "therefore" (*SBH*, 58).

51.a. Note "her" omitted, as in v 41; cf. n. 41.c.

51.b. Sequence impv + impf (juss) may have final sense (cf. GKC, 109f; Joüon, 116d).

52.a. Lit. "to the ground."

53.a. Waw consec + 3 masc sg impf hiph יצא.

53.b-b. Note chiasmus with previous clauses, "he brought out [A] objects of silver [B] etc., beautiful presents [B] he gave [A]," suggesting unity of actions described (*SBH*, 128).

54.a. 2 masc pl impv piel שׁלח + 1 sg suffix.

54.b. G, Vg add "that I may go," assimilating to v 56.

55.a. Sg verb, "he said," with composite subj, "her brother and her mother"; cf. n. 50.b. SamPent has pl verb, typical correction (Waltke, 218).

55.b. Cf. n. 14.a.

55.c. יָמִים may mean "a few days" (GKC, 139h).

55.d. Lit. "ten days." SamPent has חֹדֶשׁ "a month" and presumably understands יָמִים to be "a year"; cf. WOC, 654.

56.a. 2 masc pl impf piel אחר.

56.b-b. Circumstantial clause explaining his reason for not staying (GKC, 142d; Joüon, 159e, 170e; *SBH*, 85, 90; WOC, 651).

56.c. Simple waw in sequence impv + coh = "so that, in order that" (GKC, 108d; Joüon, 116b).

57.a. נִקְרָא is syntactically coh though formally 1 pl impf (*SBH*, 111; Joüon, 114b, n.).

57.b. Cf. n. 14.a.

57.c. וְנִשְׁאֲלָה is simple waw + coh (SamPent has impf וְנִשְׁאַל). The sequence coh + coh may not always have final sense, so we could translate "let us call . . . and let us ask" (Joüon, 143d; *SBH*, 111; Lambdin, 119).

58.a. The impf may have nuance of volition as here, "Do you want to go . . . I want to go" (Joüon, 113n; WOC, 509).

58.b. Affirmative replies are made by repeating key phrase of question (GKC, 150n).

60.a. G, S add "their sister."

60.b. 2 fem sg impv היה.

61.a. On sg verb with composite subject, see GKC, 146g,h.

61.b. Pausal form of וַיֵּלֶךְ.

62.a-a. Lit. "came from coming." SamPent במדבר "in the wilderness"; cf. G. The oddity of the expression has prompted various attempts at conjectural emendation (see Skinner, 347), but none seems obviously correct.

62.b-b. Episode-initial circumstantial clause marking change of scene (*SBH*, 79).

63.a. ל + inf constr פנה "to him." For this idiom, see Deut 23:12(11); cf. Exod 14:27; Judg 19:26; WOC, 607–8.

63.b. ל + inf constr שׂוח. A hapax of obscure meaning.

63.c. והנה indicates Isaac's perspective (*SBH*, 95).

64.a. Def art for possessive pronoun (Joüon, 137f; WOC, 243).

65.a. הלזה a secondary form of זה "this" with strengthened demonstrative force (GKC, 34f).

65.b. Cf. n. 64.a.

65.c. Waw consec + 3 fem sg impf hithp (apoc) כסה.

66.a. Waw consec + 3 masc sg impf piel ספר.

67.a. Waw consec + 3 masc sg impf hiph בוא + 3 fem sg suffix.

67.b-b. *BHS* and many commentators suppose this is a gloss because it is unusual to have a phrase in the gen after a noun with def art and the locale ending. With Ibn Ezra and Jacob, it seems better to regard the phrase as elliptical, "into the tent, the tent of Sarah his mother"; cf. 18:6. For other examples of def art used before gen, cf. Num 34:2; Josh 3:14.

67.c. Waw consec + 3 masc sg impf אהב + 3 fem sg suffix.

67.d. Cf. n. 6:6.a.

67.e-e. Lit. "after his mother." For an analogous use of *arki* = "after the death of" in Akk., see *CAD*, A.2.279; *AHW*, 1469. *BHS*, Gunkel, Skinner, Westermann emend to "after his father's death."

Form/Structure/Setting

The exceptional fullness of this account, the longest of any in Genesis, has prompted some commentators to see it as rather isolated (e.g., Coats). However, it contains so many links with both the Abraham narratives that precede it and the Jacob and Joseph stories that follow it that it should not be dismissed as an erratic boulder within Genesis. The main retrospective references are: v 1, cf. 18:11; 12:2; 22:17; vv 3, 37, cf. 12:6; 13:7; v 4, cf. 12:1; v 5, cf. 15:7; v 7, cf. 22:16; 12:7; 13:15; 15:18; 17:8; v 10, cf. 11:27–29; 22:20; v 35, cf. 12:2, 16; 13:2; v 36, cf. 21:1–7; 25:5; v 40, cf. 17:1; 13:17; v 60, cf. 22:17; v 62, cf. 16:14; v 67, cf. chap. 23. But it also looks forward. Rebekah and Laban are two of the most prominent characters in the Jacob stories (chaps. 25–32), and this scene at the well (vv 11–48) has close parallels with Jacob's encounter with Rachel, also at a well (29:2–14). Other lesser similarities include v 1, 33, cf. 26:29; v 12, cf. 27:20. This episode also has affinities with the story of Joseph, particularly its stress on God's providential overruling of human affairs, but there are specific verbal links as well (v 2, cf. 41:38; 50:7; 47:29; v 9, cf. 47:31; v 28, cf. 39:17, 19; v 36, cf. 39:7–8; vv 42, 56, cf. 43:4; 39:2, 3, 23; v 49, cf. 47:29; v 65, cf. 38:14).

The servant's speeches serve as a prospective obituary for Abraham. His reflections on Abraham's career underline that he has indeed been blessed by the LORD as he was promised. But this episode also shows that the promises will not die with Abraham: the LORD has made full and perfect provision to ensure that

Abraham's son will marry and continue to live in the promised land of Canaan. Indeed, Rebekah's willingness to leave her land and kindred shows that she is, as it were, a female Abraham, who like him will be blessed. Her name, like his, contains the consonants *b* and *r*, which begin the verb "bless" (ברך *brk*), a key word of this chapter (vv 1, 27, 31, 35, 48, 60).

As already mentioned, this episode serves to introduce us to two of the most dominating characters, Rebekah and Laban, in the whole book of Genesis. Reading the subsequent accounts of their activity, it would be easy to conclude that what happened was largely the result of human scheming, but this story shows that such an interpretation would be misguided. It was God who led Abraham's servant to Rebekah and answered his prayers so clearly that no one can doubt that her future career is also under divine control. The very fullness with which this episode is related indicates just how important it was to the author of Genesis.

The narrative falls into four scenes (so López, *RB* 87 [1980] 242–73, 350–93, 514–59; Aitken, *JSOT* 30 [1984] 3–23):

1. Abraham and his servant in Canaan (1–9)
2. Rebekah and the servant by the well (10–28)
3. Negotiations at Rebekah's house (29–61)
   a. Servant's entry (29–32)
   b. Servant explains his mission (33–49)
   c. Proposals accepted (50–53)
   d. Rebekah and servant leave (54–61)
4. Isaac, Rebekah, and servant in Canaan (62–67)

Coats makes the departure of Rebekah (vv 54–61) a separate scene. But though a night separates v 53 from 55, there is no change of place or actors that justifies scenic division. The absence of an explicit nominal subject in v 54b also suggests the narrator did not regard this as the opening of a new scene.

Abraham's key command, "Go and take (a wife for my son)," is eventually answered by Laban and Bethuel's response to the servant, "(Here is Rebekah) take her and go," and fulfilled in v 61, "The servant took her and went," and in v 67, "Isaac . . . took and married her." As often in biblical narrative, there is roughly palistrophic organization of the material. Scenes 1 and 4 correspond in that both are set in Abraham's household in Canaan, whereas 2 and 3 are both set in Aram-Naharaim with Rebekah's family. Indeed, the servant's account of his meeting Rebekah by the well (vv 42–48) matches the second scene most closely. Furthermore, López has noted a certain palistrophic organization within some of the scenes (see *Comment* below).

Opinion about the unity of this chapter has fluctuated. Early critical commentators confidently assumed its unity and assigned it to J. However, on the basis of various repetitions within the account (e.g., Laban twice goes out to the well, vv 29–30) or contradictions (in v 51 Rebekah's relatives agree to her going, but in vv 57–58 she is asked to decide), Gunkel, Skinner, and Procksch argued that two sources had been combined. Gunkel supposed two different J sources had been amalgamated, whereas Procksch and Skinner thought the sources were J and E.

However, subsequent commentators have once again tended to reaffirm the integrity of the chapter and its assignment to J, at least in substance if not in its final shape. Because the present account makes so many connections with other parts of Genesis (see above), Van Seters and, more cautiously, Westermann have argued that it must come from a relatively late stage in the composition of Genesis. Since Van Seters believes J was composed in the sixth century, he can square the J features of the narrative with its other literary relationships without great difficulty. Rofé (*BeO* 23 [1981] 161–65) has argued on grounds of style and content that it cannot have been composed before 500 B.C. He notes linguistic features that are also found in post-exilic Hebrew, e.g., "God of heaven and earth" (vv 3–7), "kneel" (v 11), "empty" (v 20), religious beliefs about the efficacy of prayer and angels, and the insistence on not marrying Canaanites (cf. Ezra and Nehemiah). Though these points of similarity are undeniable, they hardly constitute proof that chap. 24 dates from so late a date. It is just as easy to suppose that later Hebrew writers or reformers are using ancient terminology and recalling old customs as to suppose that all these ideas were invented in post-exilic times.

A very much more refined approach has been adopted by López (*RB* 67 [1980] 242–73, 350–93, 514–59). He argues on the basis of vocabulary that Gen 24 is substantially an early text. Its linguistic affinities are closest to J or L (Eissfeldt's lay-source), so he would date it between the ninth and seventh century. This basic text was then expanded in terminology reminiscent of E or D, probably in the seventh century. Further, a few additions come from the sixth-century deuteronomistic school, and finally, just a handful of additions come from the post-exilic era. Like Rofé, López relies heavily on vocabulary items to determine changes of authorship, and this is in principle questionable. A text's vocabulary is largely determined by its genre and content, not by its authorship.

The approach of Aitken is the most sober. He points out that Gen 24 has an earlier parallel in the Ugaritic tale of Keret, where Keret goes on a military expedition to a foreign land to obtain a wife. And there are still closer analogies in Gen 29 (Jacob and Rachel) and in Exod 2:16–21 (Moses) of OT men meeting their future wives by a foreign well. As far as the OT is concerned, this appears to be a classic situation, what Alter has called a type scene (cf. the patriarchal wife in a foreign harem, Gen 12, 20, 26). Through the unique features of each account, the character of the leading actors comes through clearly. Aitken points out that nearly every feature within the present narrative is required if the plot is to proceed from the initial problem, Isaac's lack of a wife, to his eventual marriage. Very few points appear to be redundant within the story. However, he detects occasional references to wider concerns in Genesis that do not seem germane to the present story, and he suggests that these may reflect the work of the author or redactor bringing out the theological significance of the story. "Vv 62 and 67b are particularly inconsequential within the narrative context. Aside from 1b, the remaining links occur together in a cluster in vv 33–36 in the context of retrospection" (*JSOT* 30 [1984] 17). He suggests that an earlier version of the story may have lacked these remarks and that they have been introduced to link this story more closely with the surrounding narratives. He also suggests that we may

suspect the editor's hand has been at work in vv 34–49, 50–51. These sections are obviously integral to the narrative, but the way they are presented may indicate that the author has slanted the presentation of certain points (e.g., the stress on God's blessing of Abraham, or his leaving his homeland) to make his perspective come across more clearly. Aitken suggests that the story in its original form was a paradigm: it told of the willing bride who left her parents' home to enjoy the blessings of marriage.

In its present form, some also describe it as an example story, but now exemplifying the behavior of an ideal servant who faithfully carries out his master's instructions (Roth, *CBQ* 34 [1972] 177–87; Coats). Others (Van Seters, Westermann) prefer to describe it as a guidance narrative: it demonstrates how divine providence leads men to do his will. All these understandings are valid up to a point, but in the present context of Genesis the overarching purpose of including this story is theological. It reflects on how the divine promises of blessing to Abraham have already been fulfilled and shows that even though he is about to die, they will be yet further fulfilled in the future. A bride is secured for Abraham's son, thus ensuring that his line of descendants will continue. And Rebekah's willingness to leave land and family suggests that she too will enjoy the blessings that her father-in-law experienced.

Comment

1–9   The first scene after an editorial introduction (v 1) consists almost entirely of dialogue between Abraham and his servant. First, Abraham asks his servant to swear that he will find a suitable wife for Isaac from his homeland (vv 2–4). The servant raises a possible difficulty (v 5), and this prompts Abraham to insist once more that only a girl from his own clan must marry Isaac; the LORD who led him out of Ur and promised him the land will surely make this possible (vv 6–8). So the servant swears (v 9).

This first scene contains the last recorded words of Abraham. So although 25:1–11 may indicate that Abraham lived a good few years after this, this scene is analogous to the deathbed scenes of Jacob and Joseph (47:29–31; 50:25). But there are interesting differences. In the latter cases, the patriarch makes his sons swear; here, Abraham makes his will known to his servant. The absence of Isaac is notable and suggests his passivity. And whereas Jacob and Joseph's last words concern their burial in the land of promise, Abraham is most worried about a wife for his son, for without offspring none of the promises will be fulfilled. Abraham enters history through the divine promises (12:1–3, 7); he passes out of history with this promise on his lips.

1   "Abraham was old and a good age." This phrase typically prefaces the last deeds or words of some great man (cf. Josh 13:1; 23:1; 1 Kgs 1:1), though it has already been said of Abraham and Sarah in 18:11. "The LORD had blessed him in every way." Though Abraham was often promised that he would be blessed, and Melchizedek greeted Abram as "blessed" (14:19), and the narrative shows the blessing gradually being realized, this is the first time that the narrator explicitly comments that he has been blessed. It anticipates the servant's observation in v 35.

2 This servant, unlike Eliezer (15:2), is not named, for it is his relationship to Abraham that is all important. Abraham's total confidence in him is underlined by the comment that "he was in charge of all his affairs." Compare Joseph's relationship to Potiphar (39:4, 6) and the pharaoh (41:41; 42:6). Now he entrusts him with the most important and delicate task in his career as Abraham's servant. The sacredness of this duty is underlined by the oath he is invited to swear. Note the "please" (בָ) that precedes the imperative "swear." It is no ordinary request that Abraham is making, so he couches it with some delicacy. By putting his hand under Abraham's thigh, the servant was touching his genitals and thus giving the oath a special solemnity. In the ancient Orient, solemn oaths could be taken holding some sacred object in one's hand, as it is still customary to take an oath on the Bible before giving evidence in court. Since the OT particularly associates God with life (see the symbolism of the sacrificial law) and Abraham had been circumcised as a mark of the covenant, placing his hand under Abraham's thigh made an intimate association with some fundamental religious ideas. An oath by the seat of procreation is particularly apt in this instance, when it concerns the finding of a wife for Isaac. Malul, while pointing to the appropriateness of an oath by the genitals to ensure perpetuity of the family, more problematically suggests that the ancestral spirits were also being invoked to guarantee the oath is carried out (*VT* 35 [1985] 192–200).

3 The servant is asked to swear by "the LORD, the God of heaven and earth," i.e., by the God of the covenant and the creator. The terminology echoes the opening chapters of Genesis, but the whole phrase is unique to this chapter. The closest parallel is 14:22, where Abraham says, "I solemnly swear to the LORD, to El-Elyon, creator of heaven and earth." To argue, with Gunkel, Westermann, Rofé, and López, that the whole phrase "God of heaven and earth" must be late, because "God of heaven" or "God of earth" appears more often in post-exilic literature, is unjustified. As already noted, this particular combined phrase is unique but has its closest parallel in 14:22, an undoubtedly old text. It may also, as Jacob suggests, reflect the custom of calling heaven and earth to witness legal acts such as covenant-making (Deut 30:19; Isa 1:2), a tradition that long antedates the OT (D. R. Hillers, *Treaty Curses and the OT Prophets* [Rome: Pontifical Biblical Institute, 1964] 4).

The insistence on not marrying Canaanites is echoed repeatedly in the law (Exod 34:16; Num 25; Deut 7:3). Here Abraham enunciates the principle for the first time, and later Isaac sends Jacob back to his father's house to find a wife (28:1–2).

4 But Abraham is somewhat vaguer in his instruction. He simply sends the servant to "my country, my clan." This could, as Sternberg (*Poetics*, 134) notes, be hendiadys for "my clan's country," as in v 7. The clan is intermediate in size between "the father's house" (the extended family) and the tribe (see *Comment* on 12:1). Whereas Abraham was just looking for a girl from the right clan or homeland, in fact the servant did much better than asked in finding a close relative, Isaac's cousin, as his wife.

5 However, the servant was not at all sure that he could achieve even Abraham's minimum requirement. So he raises the most obvious difficulty: what if the girl refuses to leave her homeland? Is it more important for Isaac to marry, or must she also be prepared to live in this land?

6 "Take care" (לֹךְ הִשָּׁמֶר) often refutes a shocking or unworthy idea (cf. 31:24, 29; Exod 34:12; Deut 4:9). "Shocked Abraham rejects and forbids it. In no circumstances. God cannot be so inconsistent. He would thereby endanger and be false to his whole plan of salvation to date" (Jacob, 515).

7 So he recalls his own experience in terms that echo 12:1. "Go from your country, your clan, and your father's house to the country that I shall show you," and he quotes exactly the first promise of the land in 12:7: "To your descendants I shall give this land." What is more, the LORD had not simply promised the land to Abraham and his descendants; he had confirmed it with "an oath" (22:16). This oath is partially quoted by Rebekah's family in 24:60.

As the LORD proved his care of Abraham and his family in the past by sending an angel (16:7–13; 19:1; 21:17; 22:11, 15), so Abraham is confident that the same will be proved true again. "He will send his angel before you" (cf. Exod 23:20; 32:34; 33:2). With these emphatic declarations, Abraham declares his faith that the LORD will provide.

8 However, he recognizes that his servant may not share his faith, and so he allows him an escape clause if things do not work out as he hopes. "If the woman is not willing to go [note the key word הָלַךְ again] . . . you shall be free." However, under no circumstances must the servant attempt to salvage the situation by taking Isaac to Mesopotamia. He must stay here.

9 With this clarification of how he will be absolved from responsibility if the chosen girl refuses to go, the servant swears the oath.

10–28 The second scene is set beside a well in Aram-Naharaim and involves just three actors, Abraham's servant, Rebekah, and the LORD. Here God is not actually on stage, but the servant prays to him at the beginning and the end of his meeting with Rebekah, and the whole action and dialogue in vv 15–25 are such a palpable answer to the servant's prayer that we feel God is just behind the curtain pushing Rebekah on stage right on cue. The scene may be analyzed as follows:

vv 10–11	Servant journeys to well
vv 12–14	Servant prays
vv 15–25	Prayer answered
vv 15–16	Rebekah appears: description of her and her actions
v 17	Servant asks for a drink
v 18	Rebekah agrees and gives drink
vv 19–20	Rebekah offers to water camels and does
vv 21–22	Servant's reaction: thoughts and deeds
v 23	Servant asks Rebekah about family and house
v 24	Rebekah identifies herself
v 25	Rebekah describes her house
vv 26–27	Servant worships
v 28	Rebekah goes home

The scene is nicely balanced. Both remarks by the servant elicit a double reply from Rebekah (vv 17–19, 23–25). The description of Rebekah's character and action corresponds to the servant's thoughts and deeds (vv 15–16, 21–22), and the whole is framed by the servant's prayers (vv 12–14, 26–27).

10 This verse describes the servant's departure with various details whose relevance only appears later in the story. In this era "camels" were relatively

rare, and to take "ten" suggests Abraham's great wealth (cf. *Comment* on 12:16). It also makes us appreciate Rebekah's magnanimity and energy in watering them (vv 19–20). "All sorts of his master's wealth." Betrothal was marked by presenting large gifts to the bride's family, so the servant went prepared, as vv 22, 53 show.

"The servant took . . . and went" echoes the key command to "go . . . and take" (v 4). Abraham had instructed him to "go to my country, my clan." When last heard of, they were living in Harran (11:31), which was within the region called "Aram-Naharaim," i.e., Aram of the two rivers, roughly the area bounded by the Euphrates on the west and river Habur on the east. The term "Aram-Naharaim" is also found in Deut 23:5(4); Ps 60:2(0); 1 Chr 19:6 and is apparently identical with *Naḥrima* of the El-Amarna letters and *Nhrn* of sixteenth- to twelfth-century Egyptian texts.

"The city of Nahor." Though this could be circumlocution for Harran (Westermann, Gispen), there was also the city called Nahor (*Naḥur*) (first mentioned in the twentieth-century Kanish texts and later in the Mari letters and neo-Assyrian texts) that was near Harran (*EM* 5:805–9). Usage elsewhere in the OT (cf. *Comment* on 33:18) tends to favor the former view.

11 The long journey from Canaan to the city of Nahor is barely described. The fatigue of the riders and camels is merely alluded to: "he made the camels kneel down" to give them rest, but he does not bother to water the camels. It was customary for women, particularly unmarried girls, to be responsible for drawing the water and herding the flocks (cf. 29:10; Exod 2:16; 1 Sam 9:11) but, as the actions of Jacob and Moses show in a similar situation, quite in order for men to water the animals. But Abraham's servant is weary and needs refreshment himself before he can water his beasts.

12 The servant's prayer is an appeal for God to "keep faith with my master Abraham"; the closing clause thus makes an inclusion with the opening. Within the parameters of OT theology, it is hard to imagine a more powerful basis for prayer, for חסד "loving-kindness, faithfulness, mercy" is one of the most frequently cited attributes of God (cf. Ps 136). The LORD keeps faith (shows steadfast love) to thousands of those who love him (Exod 20:6; Deut 5:10). (On חסד, see *TDOT* 5:44–64; *THWAT* 2:600–621.) But most especially the LORD has demonstrated his love for Abraham and made unconditional promises to benefit him (18:18–19; 22:16–18). The servant asks that the LORD will "guide" him, lit. "make it happen in front of me." The root קרה "happen" occurs several times in the qal in the Joseph story (42:29; 44:29; cf. 42:4, 38) but only here and 27:20 (Jacob's explanation of how he was able to prepare the meal so quickly) in the hiphil. The hiphil expresses God's providential overruling of all events.

13–14 Wanting the best for Isaac, the servant devises "a shrewd character test. What touchstone could be more appropriate than the reception of a wayfarer to determine a woman's fitness to marry into the family of the paragon of hospitality? And it is a stiff test, too, since it would require far more than common civility to volunteer to water 'ten' thirsty camels" (Sternberg, *Poetics*, 137).

The girl who passes this test is the one "appointed" (יכח hiphil is used with this meaning only here and in v 44) for Isaac. And by this means God's will is made known to the servant.

15 "Before he had finished speaking." Cf. "Before they call I will answer, while they are yet speaking I will hear" (Isa 65:24) and the ancient prayer, which begins "Almighty and everlasting God, who art always more ready to hear than we to pray, and art wont to give more than either we desire or deserve." "He noticed Rebekah coming out, the daughter of Bethuel." Although the phraseology "he noticed" (והנה) gives us the impression that we are seeing Rebekah through the servant's eyes, the narrator lets us know much more about the girl than was apparent to the servant: her name, her family, and her marital status. Having already met her name in the genealogy in 22:23, we suspect at once that Rebekah is the appointed bride. If she passes the test, that will clinch the issue, but as yet the servant is totally in the dark.

16 The description of Rebekah's credentials as a potential bride becomes ever more attractive. She is a "girl" (נערה); almost any female under about forty would fit this category; "very good-looking" (an important consideration, especially for someone who would marry Sarah's son); of "marriageable age" (the term בתולה denotes a girl's age range, approximately a teenager, rather than her virginity; see G. J. Wenham, "Betulah," *VT* 22 [1972] 326–48; *ISBE* 4:989–90). Her virgin status is affirmed by the next remark, lit. "whom no man had known." It may well be that her virgin status was obvious from her dress, but it could be that the reader is again being vouchsafed information that was not so immediately obvious to the servant (cf. v 15). "She came down to the well . . . and she came up" seems to imply there were quite a few steps down to the spring and underlines the magnitude of the task of watering the camels.

17–20 The differences between the servant's prayer and Rebekah's actions need close observation.

17 Note the eagerness of the servant running to ask Rebekah for a drink: he hopes she is the answer to his prayer. Yet in asking, he is most polite: "Please give me a sip of water from your jar" is less demanding than "Please let down your jar that I may drink" (v 14).

18 However, Rebekah is more forthcoming than he had prayed for—"She quickly [lit. 'she hurried' (ותמהר)] let down her jar."

19 But will she do any more? "When she had finished letting him drink" delays the action and adds suspense. Then unprompted she makes just the offer the servant had prayed for. But whereas he had prayed that she would say, "Let me give your camels water," she offered, "Let me also draw water for your camels *until they have had enough to drink.*"

20 And she fulfills her offer with unexpected alacrity. "She quickly emptied her jar . . . and ran back to the well." Her enthusiastic hospitality reminds us of Abraham scurrying hither and thither when preparing food for his visitors: the same verbs (מהר "hurry" "quickly" and רוץ "run") are used here and in 18:2–7.

When seen as a whole, all the variations between the servant's prayer and Rebekah's actions "dramatize a single point: that the young woman's performance surpasses even the most optimistic expectations" (Sternberg, *Poetics,* 138).

21 This aside, by delaying the action, helps the reader to appreciate just what a lengthy job it was to water ten camels and the energy of the girl who did it. It also reminds us of the servant's viewpoint as, unlike us, he is not sure whether

Rebekah is the bride he is seeking. He wonders if "the LORD had made his journey successful or not." הצליח "make successful" is a key term in this story (vv 40, 42, 56; cf. 39:3, 23 of Joseph). Though we know that his journey is a success, the servant is still uncertain.

22 These gifts were a handsome reward for a task freely undertaken. A shekel is about twelve grams (0.4 ounces). They confirm that the servant has a wealthy and generous patron, an important consideration in the subsequent negotiations.

23 Having put himself in the girl's debt by his lavish bounty, the servant now asks an even greater favor, the name of her father and whether he would be able to stay the night.

24–25 Rebekah answers the servant precisely; she does not volunteer her own name. She simply says she is the daughter of Bethuel, who was one of the sons of Nahor and Milcah. Nahor was Abraham's brother, and Milcah was the daughter of his other brother, Haran. It is surprising that she mentions the name of her grandmother, Milcah, but not her mother's name. Jacob suggests the marriage of Nahor and Milcah was especially famous in that area, a marriage between "an uncle and orphaned niece, whereby Nahor had fulfilled his loving duty towards his dead brother Haran" (521). Whether this marriage (cf. 11:29) was particularly celebrated is unclear, but it certainly shows that Rebekah is closely related to Abraham. Her father is descended from both of Abraham's brothers. Once again the story shows how things are working out much better than anticipated. Abraham had sent the servant to find a wife from his clan (v 4); the servant had actually met a close cousin of Isaac's!

Rebekah then goes on to answer the servant's question about lodging. He had not mentioned feeding the camels, but she mentions that they have plenty of supplies, indirectly indicating her family's wealth, and that there is room for visitors. However, very properly she does not offer that, for that is not hers to offer. But she does run home (v 28), which shows her enthusiastic goodwill.

26–27 The servant's first act at the well was prayer, and so also was his last. "The man bowed down and prostrated himself." The use of this pair of words (cf. v 48; 43:28; Exod 4:31; 34:8) seems to indicate how overwhelmed he felt at the way his first prayer had been so quickly and completely answered. Certainly his prayer makes this point. He had asked the LORD to keep faith with his master (v 12); now he acknowledges that "the LORD has not forsaken his faithful loving-kindness toward my master." Moreover, he has led him specially (the pronoun "me" here is emphatic; see *Notes*), not just to his master's clan but "to the house of my master's brothers." As Rebekah had indicated, Bethuel was son of Nahor and grandson of Haran, Abraham's brothers. A more perfect answer to his prayer could not have been envisaged.

28 Meanwhile, Rebekah dashes home, indicating more than mere goodwill, closing one scene and heralding the next. The reader is sure and the servant is sure that she is Isaac's appointed bride, but will the family see it the same way? Already we sense complications when we hear she goes to her "mother's household." Will the unnamed mother be as well-disposed toward Abraham as Bethuel would be?

29–32 The entry of the servant to Rebekah's house is described in more detail than is customary and, as Sternberg observes, allows a glimpse of the characters of those involved in the forthcoming negotiations, particularly Laban.

29 "A brother called Laban." Laban is a name known in many texts and periods (לבן means "white"). It may have something to do with the moon god Sin worshiped in Harran (לבנה means "full moon" in Hebrew; cf. KB, 492; *EM* 4:421).

"He ran out to the man" suggests Laban is as enthusiastic and welcoming as his sister Rebekah and his great-uncle Abraham (cf. 18:2–8).

30 This verse dispels such ideas. Laban's actions are motivated by greed, not pure hospitality. His sister's virtue in this regard stands out the more clearly in contrast with Laban's grasping materialism. The warmth of his welcome is prompted, the narrator implies, by the prospect of further enrichment by the as-yet-unidentified stranger. Laban's motives are underlined by the final comment, showing what Laban noticed about the servant: "there he was standing by the *camels.*" Camels were in this period a rare and luxurious type of transport. There may also be a hint of Laban's relief that this wealthy visitor had not already left.

31 "Come in, blessed of the LORD." Laban does not yet know the identity of the servant, so the phrase "blessed of the LORD" is just a polite greeting to a rich man, riches being a sign of divine blessing. But as often in Scripture, the words are truer than the speaker realizes. That the LORD has blessed Abraham and his household is the starting point of the story (vv 1, 35), and on his very first encounter with the servant Laban acknowledges this fact.

32 So at last the servant comes to Rebekah's house, where all the customary hospitalities are provided for his considerable retinue.

33 The climax of such entertainment was, of course, a meal, and then serious discussion would begin (cf. 18:1–15). The servant, who had been too tired to drink or water his camels (v 14), now insists that his mission is so important that he must speak before he eats. We again admire his devotion to duty, that after a long journey he would put fulfilling his duty to Abraham before satisfying his hunger.

34–49 The servant's long speech goes over the events already related in vv 1–27. But this is not mere repetition for the sake of repetition; Hebrew storytellers are usually very sparing with their words, so the fullness of the servant's recapitulation of events shows it has a most important function. The first account shows how the servant discovered Rebekah and became convinced that she was Isaac's chosen bride. But now he has to persuade her family that it is right for her to marry Isaac. His whole approach is pitched with this end in view, and it is important to read the second account in the light of the first to see how the servant appeals to the interests of Laban, in particular to convince him that Isaac is a worthy match for Rebekah. The whole account builds toward his final appeal, "Now then if you are going to treat my master with kindness and loyalty, tell me" (v 49). And in convincing Laban of the rightness of the marriage, the narrator at the same time confirms in our minds that God is indeed in control, answers prayer, and fulfills his promises.

34 He begins by introducing himself, for as yet Rebekah's family do not know who he is. But he does not give his own name; he just describes himself as "Abraham's servant," thereby implying that his wealth is not his own but Abraham's. Indeed, his self-introduction must have prompted Laban to wonder, "If a mere servant has so much money to throw around, what must Abraham be like?"

35 The servant's next remark supports such an inference: "The LORD has blessed my master tremendously." מאד "tremendously, very, exceedingly," though a common word, is used only here to modify "bless." The reader knows that Abraham has been blessed, and the list of Abraham's assets recalls similar lists in 12:16; 13:2; 20:14, but this is more comprehensive than others. Sternberg (*Poetics*, 146) notes how "the items in full view ('gold,' 'manservants,' 'camels') are so interspersed as to command belief in their unseen mates" (v 12, silver, slave-girls, and donkeys).

36 Having established his relationship to Abraham and Abraham's great wealth, the servant now gives some interesting family news. But even this is cannily presented with a view to interesting greedy Laban in a potential marriage alliance with a very eligible bachelor. The birth of a son to Abraham confirms God's blessing on Abraham, as does the remark "after she had become old." But the last comment also serves to suggest that perhaps Abraham's son may still be young enough to marry Rebekah, who genealogically was a generation younger than Isaac (v 24).

And most important, "he has given him all he has." Here the servant anticipates Abraham's intention actualized in 25:5. "But since the present company cannot know, the intention may pass for the deed.

"The man's art lies not so much in the slight stretching of the facts as in their thorough insinuation. And to mask his drift, the persuader varies his technique from the first step to the second. Abraham's riches can be safely painted in the most glowing colors, under the cover story of 'You will be happy to learn that . . . .' But when it comes to his deficiency of children, that pretext would hardly serve. Therefore the speaker so wraps up the topic as to invite the deduction that the parent's misfortune is the son's good fortune: to let the thought 'What a catch!' steal into the audience's mind before they find him actually offered to them on a hard condition" (Sternberg, *Poetics*, 146).

37–41 Up to this point, the servant has been a little more long-winded than the narrator (cf. vv 34–36 with v 1), because Laban must be put in the picture. Now, however, the servant abbreviates Abraham's original commands (vv 2–8) a little, with a view to putting the most attractive slant on them. Note how the servant underlines Abraham's positive motives in looking for a wife for Isaac from his relations, rather than his aversion to acquiring a Canaanite daughter-in-law. Abraham sent the servant to "my country, my clan." Having actually found an eligible bride much more closely related than anticipated, the servant reports Abraham as saying, "Go to my father's house . . . take a wife for my son from my clan and my father's house" (vv 38, 40). The servant puts into words Abraham's deepest hopes, that his son would marry within the extended family, though Abraham himself had not dared to be so specific.

By playing up the kinship aspect between Isaac and Rebekah, the servant minimizes the pain of her separation from her family. He also plays down the possible resistance that the bride might feel about leaving home. Whereas he had asked Abraham what he should do if "the woman is not *willing* to go with me to this land" (vv 5, 8), in the retelling the potential reluctance of the would-be bride is played down; he simply asks, "Suppose the woman will not come with me" (v 39), and later the onus is shifted to her family, "if they will not give her to you" (v 41).

And the possibility that Isaac might leave home, which is raised by the servant and twice rejected by Abraham (vv 5–6, 8), is now carefully omitted. Just to mention it might put ideas into the family's head!

The servant also adopts a slightly different theological tack from Abraham. Whereas his confidence in the success of the servant's mission rested primarily on the divine promises made to him and secondarily on the prevenient angel (v 7), only the latter is mentioned to Rebekah's relatives (v 40). Clearly the servant judges that the partial fulfillment of the promises so far is less likely to persuade his hearers than the remarkable way in which his prayer for guidance was answered. That surely proves the angel of the LORD was with him, making his journey successful.

42–48 So having set out the basic desirability of a marriage between Isaac and Rebekah, he now relates what happened at the well. Here the servant's re-telling runs much closer to the narrator's original version. The facts, as it were, speak for themselves. The servant has no need to embellish them or downplay any of them in his efforts to win the family's assent. A simple account should suffice to persuade the open-minded that God has indeed guided him to Rebekah in a remarkable way. Such abbreviation as here (e.g., no description of Rebekah, v 16) is mainly dictated by his audience, for whom that would be superfluous. But he also fails to mention his moments of doubt (v 21), which are no longer relevant. He also alters his original very polite "Please give me a sip of water" (v 17) to "Please give me a little water to drink." This change not only takes the focus off his civility but also it emphasizes the correspondence between his prayer and its answer.

The one substantial difference between the two accounts occurs at the end. The servant gave the nose ring and bracelets to Rebekah before asking her father's name and whether there was room in her house to stay. In retelling, he omits the inquiry about accommodation, no doubt for reasons of tact, but he says he asked her father's name before giving the jewelry. The servant's motives here are not clear. Maybe having insisted that Abraham had sent him to find a bride from his father's house, he felt he should not have presented Rebekah with anything unless she came from the right family. Perhaps he felt that Laban would have misinterpreted such a gesture of generosity to a girl whose identity he did not yet know. Whatever his motive in rearranging the account, it serves to underline the correspondence between Abraham's wishes and the meeting with Rebekah. It was clear to the servant at any rate that the LORD had guided him reliably to the daughter of his master's relative, lit. "brother" (here used in the broader sense of "relative," for Bethuel was Abraham's nephew).

48 "Reliably" (אמת) is one of the key terms in this narrative. Three of its six occurrences in Genesis are found in this chapter (v 27, "his *faithful* loving kindness"; v 49, "reliability"). "It denotes the nature of the man who is said to be faithful to his neighbor, true in his speech, and reliable and constant in his actions . . . . [T]he meaning of the OT assertion that God is *'emeth* is that Yahweh is the God in whose word and work one can place complete confidence" (*TDOT* 1:313).

49 This story illustrates God's "kindness" (חסד; see v 12) and "reliability" (אמת) to such a degree that the servant appeals to Rebekah's family to show similar qualities in dealing with Abraham. "Now then if you are going to treat my master

with kindness [חֶסֶד] and loyalty [אֱמֶת], tell me." The servant could have put it more simply, "now if you agree, tell me," but as Sternberg observes, "the phrasing is so loaded and slanted as to deter non-compliance. On the one hand the allusion to the recent divine guidance 'by the true way' (= reliably) insinuates the meaning 'If you will do as God has done' or even the more threatening rhetorical question 'Will you go against God?'" And last of all the servant's closing comment is "calculated to brand refusal as an offense against morality . . . if they do refuse, 'I will turn to the right or the left (= I may look elsehere): I will take my suit elsewhere, to relatives more mindful of God and humanity, kinship and wealth'" (Sternberg, *Poetics*, 151).

50–53 "Small wonder, then, that Laban and Bethuel declare in response that 'the thing issues from the Lord; we cannot speak to thee bad or good.' Where God has 'spoken' through the design of events, there remains little room for human speech. Nor is it surprising that, though the material and familial considerations must have had some effect, the narrator makes the kinsmen single out the act of providence. Their world picture falls short of the monotheism common to all the Hebrew observers; their morality leaves something to be desired; their knowledge, thanks to the servant's inventiveness, is certainly deficient; and the consent wrung from them, as their subsequent dilatoriness shows, not quite wholehearted even after the event. . . . Yet . . . like all the other limited participants—the reader included—the Mesopotamians undergo a process of discovery that brings home to them God's management of the world" (Sternberg, *Poetics*, 151–52).

50 The mention of "Bethuel" in this verse is surprising, since up to this point Laban has been the dominant male in the family and all the subsequent negotiations are conducted by Laban and his mother (vv 53, 55). It is therefore often conjectured that "and Bethuel" is either a gloss or a corruption of "and his household." However, there is no other evidence of textual corruption and no reason to suppose Bethuel must have died. His inactivity elsewhere in the story suggests he is either too old to take part in tough bargaining or that he is under his wife's thumb just as Rebekah was later to "organize" Isaac. But he was sufficiently alert to indicate his assent to the proposal of marriage.

"We cannot contradict anything you say," lit. "We cannot say to you evil or good." For this idiom, cf. 31:24, 29; 2 Sam 13:22.

51 "Take her and go that she may marry your master's son." Their vital words of consent echo Abraham's original command, "you must go and take a wife for my son." They have conceded the principal point, that Rebekah should leave home to marry Isaac. Now follow the detailed negotiations about bride-money, hinted at in v 53, and the timing of the wedding (vv 54–58).

52 Note again the emphasis on the servant's piety (cf. vv 12–14, 26–27, 42–44, 48). While we may admire his skillful and successful presentation of Abraham's case, the servant thanks God for its acceptance.

53 Betrothal was customarily effected in the ancient Near East by large capital transfers from the bridegroom's family to the bride's family. Deut 22:29 places a limit of fifty shekels on such bride money (מֹהַר), which would be equivalent to several years' wages for an ordinary paid laborer (cf. Gen 29:18–20). It appears that the "beautiful presents" given to Laban and his mother probably were equivalent to the bride-money. Usually this bride-money was later passed on to the bride

by her family when she married as part of her dowry. (For summaries of wedding customs, see *IDBSup*, 575.) However, here Abraham's servant gave Rebekah herself "silver and gold and garments," items that figure frequently in dowry lists. Whether this was a mark of sheer goodwill or he feared that Rebekah's grasping brother would not give her an adequate dowry is not said.

54 Only after all this presumably lengthy discussion did the servant relax and enjoy his meal and a well-earned rest.

54b–61 But the servant did not relax for long. Without even so much as another explicit noun subject to indicate a break between his rest one night and his rising the next morning, the narrator records his first waking words as "Send me to my master." The man who showed himself such a charming diplomat when he first met Rebekah, "Please give me a sip of water," is here quite blunt. He demands—note the absence of נא "please"—rather than requests to take his leave. So there follows a tense exchange as Rebekah's mother and brother attempt to stall his departure and the servant insists on leaving. The impasse is finally broken by inviting Rebekah to say what she wants to do.

55 "A year or so," lit. "days or ten." The plural "days" may mean "a year"—certainly it does in Lev 25:29 and maybe in 4:3 (cf. *Comment*). So *Tg. Onq.*, Rashi, and Jacob understand the phrase, "a year or ten (months)"; SamPent replaces "ten" by "month," evidently understanding the whole phrase to mean "a year or a month." Gunkel would repoint "days" as a dual ימים "two days." In that the SamPent evidently thinks in terms of a long delay, this possibility must be taken seriously, though it does seem hard to envisage Abraham's servant ever contemplating staying so long, hence the more modern suggestions.

56 Whatever the timespan suggested by Laban and his mother, it was too long for Abraham's servant. His reason for insisting on a prompt return, "since the LORD has made my journey successful," is hardly convincing. Did he fear that if he did not take Rebekah at once, she might never be allowed to go? Or was he worried that Abraham might not live to see his daughter-in-law if she did not go soon? In either case, it would have hardly been diplomatic to make these points to Rebekah's family.

57 At any rate, the servant failed to convince Laban and his mother of the need for a speedy leavetaking. As a way out, Rebekah is invited to say whether she is prepared to go immediately. Presumably, Laban calculated that attachment to home and respect for her mother's opinion would surely make her ask for a delay.

58 So the story reaches its final climax, and the reader waits with baited breath to hear how Rebekah will reply to the fateful question, "Will you go with this man?" Her simple "I will go" is, next to Laban's "Take her and go," the most decisive remark in the narrative. Like Laban, she echoes Abraham's initial opening command, "You must go" (v 4). Indeed, it aligns her with Abraham, who was told to "Go . . . from your father's house" and "went" (12:1, 4).

59 "They sent off Rebekah their sister." Though the use of the term "sister" would suggest that only her brothers and sisters joined in saying farewell and that her parents absented themselves (cf. the maternal opposition in v 55), it seems more likely that "sister" here simply means "female relative" just as "brother" often means "male relative." "Her nurse," the nanny who has looked after her from childhood, joins the party; she was called Deborah, according to 35:8.

60 "They blessed Rebekah." Rebekah's name sounds even more like a play on the root "to bless" (ברך) than does Abraham's, and this connection is here made explicit. The blessing itself, "May you become thousands of *ten thousands*," contains another play on her name, according to Gunkel and Strus (*Nomen-Omen*, 165) for ten thousand is רבבה *rĕbābāh*, again quite similar to Rebekah's own name. It also links up with the frequent command and promise about multiplying (רבה; cf. 1:28; 9:1, 7; 17:2; 22:17). It is through Rebekah that the promise of a multitude of descendants for Abraham will begin to be realized.

"May your descendants possess the gate of their enemies" repeats almost word for word the promise made to Abraham in 22:17. It is widely surmised that this farewell blessing reflects a common blessing bestowed on brides (cf. Ruth 4:11–12).

61 Eventually they leave; no doubt it did not happen quite as quickly as the servant hoped. Note that the chronological framework allows three years between Sarah's death and Isaac's marriage, though they immediately follow each other in the narrative (23:1; 25:20). The party includes Rebekah's "girls"; evidently her family presented her, like Rachel and Leah later, with slave-girls as part of her dowry (29:24, 29). To take this party back to Canaan, the servant needed his ten camels. "The servant took Rebekah and went" is on the face of it redundant, but it reminds us that the servant has done exactly what Abraham asked him to do: he *went* and *took* a wife for Isaac (v 4).

62–67 The fourth and final scene describes the meeting of Isaac and Rebekah. It shows Isaac accepting the bride chosen for him and Rebekah taking Sarah's position as leading woman in the clan. The main thrust of this scene is therefore clear. It does, though, raise, and leave unanswered, a number of questions. Why should Isaac be coming from Beer-Laha-roi and living in the Negeb? Where is Abraham? Nothing is said about the servant reporting back to him, only to Isaac (v 66). Indeed, he describes Isaac as "my master" in v 65. Since Abraham's instructions to his servant in vv 2–8 sound like his last will and testament, the most natural reading of the closing scene would suggest that while the servant has been away, Abraham has died. However, a literal reading of the chronological notices in Genesis would preclude such a conclusion. For if Isaac was forty years old when he married Rebekah (25:20), his father was then 140 and did not die until he was 175 (25:7). So one might conclude that Abraham lived another thirty-five years after the events described in this chapter. The resolution of these problems depends partly on the way the chronological data of Genesis are understood. Are they to be understood as exact timespans or have they a more symbolic function? See further discussion in the *Introduction*, "The Chronology of the Patriarchs," and *Comments* on chap. 25. Provisionally, we assume that Abraham died while his servant was away on his mission.

62 When last heard of, Abraham was at Hebron (23:2), so we must either posit a change of residence or surmise that Isaac is now living apart from Abraham, for Beer-Laha-roi must be placed some way southwest of Hebron (see *Comment* on 16:14). Clearly, the servant knew where to find Isaac.

63 שׂוח "to meditate" is of uncertain meaning, and here we simply follow the consensus of the early versions. More modern suggestions do not seem obviously superior. "Looked up and noticed." To look up and see always indicates that what is about to be seen is of great significance (see *Comment* on 22:4). Here the phrase

describes Isaac's first glimpse of his future wife; in v 64, it describes Rebekah's first sight of Isaac.

64 "She jumped down from the camel." As in vv 29–30, the immediate reaction is related before the reason for it is explained. Presumably, Rebekah asked the servant who the man was before she dismounted, but by mentioning that she "jumped down," lit. "fell," from the camel first, the narrator stresses how promptly she dismounted and her deference toward Isaac (cf. 1 Sam 25:23; Josh 15:18). She did not linger staring at him.

65 That the servant now calls Isaac "my master" seems to imply that he has learned on his journey home that Abraham has indeed died.

"She took her veil and covered herself." At her wedding, a bride was presented to her husband veiled (29:23–25). This verse may imply that Rebekah kept her veil on until her wedding.

66 That the servant reports back to Isaac rather than to Abraham seems to confirm that Abraham has died.

67 With the marriage of Isaac, the story has reached its goal. Abraham's wishes have been carried out, the servant has done his duty, and the divine promises can be further fulfilled. Just as Isaac is now head of Abraham's family, so Rebekah steps into Sarah's shoes and becomes the leading woman in the patriarchal household. So she is "brought into Sarah's tent." Clearly, it would have been improper for her to have entered Isaac's tent before he was married, but giving her Sarah's tent straightaway indicated her position in the community.

"Married her and he loved her." In arranged marriages, love follows the union rather than prompts it.

"So Isaac was consoled after his mother's death." If Abraham had recently died, why is no mention made of that? To that end, some would emend this to "after his father's death." But, as Jacob observes, it would have been psychologically impossible for a wife to have replaced his father in Isaac's affections. Rather, it underlines that Rebekah is the new Sarah, just as Isaac is the new Abraham.

Explanation

Chap. 23 recorded Abraham's concern that his wife Sarah should be worthily buried and how in fulfilling his duty in this respect he purchased part of the promised land. This chapter similarly shows him worried about his family and about the fulfillment of the promise.

Apparently on his deathbed, Abraham invites his servant to take a solemn oath that he will go back to his homeland in Mesopotamia and find a wife for his son Isaac. On no account must Isaac marry one of the local Canaanite girls. When the servant asks what he should do if he cannot find a biddable Mesopotamian girl who is prepared to leave home, Abraham declares, "The LORD . . . who took me from my father's house . . . and promised me with an oath, 'To your descendants I shall give this land,' it is he who will send his angel before you, and you shall take a wife for my son from there" (v 7). Dying, Abraham declares his faith in the promises made to him and in God's continuing care for his descendants. The story goes on to tell how, although Abraham did not live to see the outcome of his servant's mission, it was more successful than either of them had

dared to hope. Divine providence led the servant straight to Rebekah, a cousin of Isaac, whose attitudes and deeds show her to be cast very much in the mold of Abraham and a worthy wife for his son.

Arriving at the city of Nahor in northern Mesopotamia, the servant prays that the LORD will make it clear to him which of the girls who come to draw water at the well is the appointed bride. The test the servant suggests might elsewhere in Scripture be described as a sign. It is at the same time a test that is calculated to reveal the characteristics required in a patriarch's wife, who must be energetic and hospitable. So he prays that the girl from whom he asks a drink of water will not just give it to him but volunteer to give his ten camels a drink too. He has not finished praying when the beautiful virgin Rebekah appears. He asks for a sip of water, and then she enthusiastically waters his camels as well. Amazed, he then inquires who her father is and whether he might stay the night. Even more astonishingly, she replies that she is the daughter of Bethuel, who is in turn descended from *both* of Abraham's brothers. Abraham's hopes and the servant's prayers have been answered abundantly, above all that they asked or thought (Eph 3:20).

But to persuade Rebekah's family of the appropriateness of the match could prove more tricky, and the second part of the story shows Abraham's servant deploying all his persuasiveness to convince the family that he should take Rebekah to marry Isaac. While Bethuel, Rebekah's father, might have been expected to be the most important person to win over, it is quickly apparent to the servant that it is her mother and her brother Laban who will have the final say. And from his first appearance on stage Laban is shown to be more interested in material advantage than other considerations. So the servant begins by informing Laban of Abraham's great wealth and that Isaac is his only heir. Then he mentions that Abraham has insisted that Isaac marry within the family, not a Canaanite—hence the servant's journey to Mesopotamia. After appealing to Laban's pocket and his sense of family solidarity, the servant finally addresses his piety, retelling how he prayed at the well, how Rebekah appeared, and how, though she did not know she was doing so, she fully answered his prayer. Laban and Bethuel acknowledge the irresistible force of the servant's arguments, and they say piously, "This thing comes from the LORD. We cannot contradict anything you say. Here is Rebekah; take her and go" (vv 50–51). They have thereby consented in principle to the marriage. But it is one thing to agree and another to act. And next day, egged on by his mother, Laban attempts to stall. "Let the girl stay with us a few days or so. Afterwards she may go" (v 55). The servant's insistence on immediate departure is stymied by the family's insistence that things should be delayed. Eventually Rebekah is invited to break the deadlock; she is asked, "Will you go with this man?" and despite fraternal and maternal opposition, she says, yes, "I will go." In so doing, she behaves like Abraham, who also left home and family for the promised land.

By the time the caravan reaches Canaan, Abraham has died, for Isaac is now head of the clan. So the servant reports back to him, not to Abraham. Rebekah is given Sarah's tent to live in, a sign that she is now the chief woman in the community, and in due time she marries Isaac. The stage is now set for the next act in the drama of the patriarchs

The length and detail of this narrative surpass any in Genesis, and this indicates both its importance and popularity within the book. And like many of the

stories, it was no doubt read and understood on many levels in OT times. Most obviously, it tells how marriages were arranged in Bible times. Isaac is unusually passive in the process, but the bride's lack of involvement during her parents' negotiation of the match was entirely typical. Yet, this story insists that such methods of matchmaking, when undertaken carefully and prayerfully, are under God's control and that the couple can accept the outcome as willingly as Rebekah and Isaac did. Today in South India, v 50, "This thing comes from the LORD," is used on wedding invitations where the parents have arranged the marriage.

The story also makes the point that Abraham's offspring should not marry Canaanites; they should marry within the family. So later Jacob goes back to Mesopotamia to find a wife (28:1–2), and the law (Exod 34:16; Deut 7:3), the historical books, and the prophets are very insistent that the people of Israel should not marry foreigners (Judg 3:6; 14:3; 1 Kgs 11:1–2; Ezra 10; Neh 13:23–27; Mal 2:11). In similar vein, Paul insists that Christians must not marry non-Christians (1 Cor 7:39; 2 Cor 6:14–18).

Also on a moral level this story illustrates how servants should behave, putting their master's interests first and carrying them out loyally to the best of their ability. Many asides in the wisdom literature may be cited that show the exemplary character of this servant (e.g., Prov 10:32; 13:17; 15:29), but here we meet a flesh-and-blood example of the ideal servant, an ideal that informs Jesus' and Paul's picture of the service God looks for in his servants (e.g., Matt 21:34–36; Luke 12:37–48; 16:10–13; 17:10; Eph 6:6; 1 Cor 4:1–3).

However, this story teaches spirituality as well as morality, a spirituality that pervades the OT, though it is rarely made so explicit as in this story. Abraham's servant is a man who prays before he acts, praises when his prayers are answered, and lives ever conscious that the affairs of men are controlled by the hand of God. He describes Abraham as walking before the LORD (v 40), but he does the same himself and indeed remarks that the God of Abraham had guided him reliably in the way. Though this story is unusual for the way it brings out a man's awareness of God's unseen providence, the stories of Joseph, Job, and Nehemiah have a similar flavor. That man should be in constant communion with God through prayer is frequently reiterated in Scripture (e.g., Luke 18:1; 1 Thess 5:17), and that the prayers of the faithful will be certainly and effectively answered is insisted on times without number (e.g., Ps 65:3[2]; Prov 15:8, 29; Matt 21:22; Luke 18:7).

Finally, as always in Genesis, this incident is recorded for the light it sheds on the theme of the Pentateuch—the fulfillment of the divine promises. The LORD promised to bless Abraham (12:2). Here the narrative records that "the LORD had blessed him in every way" (v 1), while the servant states that "the LORD has blessed my master tremendously" (v 35) and points to his great wealth and the child of his old age as proof of that blessing. And Abraham himself refers to his call and to the oath by which he was promised land and descendants (v 7; cf. 12:7; 22:16). It is because of this promise that he is so anxious that Isaac should marry one of the family but not return to Mesopotamia (vv 3–4, 7–8).

Abraham's last recorded words are thus a confession of faith: "These all died in faith, not having received what was promised, but having seen it and greeted it from afar" (Heb 11:13). The reader is more fortunate, for he learns how very

shortly after Abraham's servant had been commissioned to find a wife for his son from Mesopotamia, the servant met Rebekah, who fitted Abraham's specifications more perfectly than he dared hope. In fact, she was descended from both Abraham's brothers, she was beautiful and of the right age, and even her name Rebekah evoked the word for blessing (*bĕrākāh*). And by her generous hospitality and willingness to leave home in response to the LORD's call, she showed herself to be both in faith and deed another Abraham. Her character inspires confidence that the next stage in the fulfillment of the divine purpose is in good hands. Even if Isaac should prove to be somewhat ineffectual, Rebekah, his new wife, will be equal to the call.

Concluding the Life of Abraham (25:1–11)

Bibliography

Knauf, E. A. *Midian: Untersuchungen zur Geschichte Palästinas und Nordarabiens am Ende des 2. Jahrtausends v. Chr.* Wiesbaden: Harrassowitz, 1988. **Montgomery, J. A.** *Arabia and the Bible.* Philadelphia: University of Pennsylvania, 1934.

Translation

[1] *Abraham married again,*[a] *and his wife was called Keturah.* [2] *She bore*[a] *him Zimran,*[b] *Yoqshan, Medan, Midian, Yishbaq, and Shuach.* [3a] *Yoqshan fathered Sheba*[b] *and Dedan.*[a] [c] *Dedan's descendants were*[d] *the Ashurim, the Letushim, and the Leummim.*[c] [4] *Midian's descendants were Ephah, Epher, Enoch, Abida, and Eldaah. All these were descended from Keturah.*

[5a] *Abraham gave* [b] *all that he had* [b] *to Isaac.*[ac] [6a] *But to the sons of Abraham's concubines Abraham gave*[a] *presents and, while he was still*[b] *alive, sent*[c] *them away from his son Isaac eastward to the land of Qedem.*

[7] *These are the days of the years of Abraham's life which he lived,*[a] *one hundred and seventy-five years.*

[8] *Abraham breathed*[a] *his last and died*[b] *in good old age, old and full of days,*[c] *and he was gathered*[d] *to his relatives.* [9] *His sons Isaac and Ishmael buried him in the cave of Macpelah in the field of Ephron, the son of Zophar the Hittite, opposite Mamre.* [10] *The field was the one Abraham bought from the Hittites; there Abraham and his wife Sarah were buried.*[a]

[11] *After the death of Abraham, God blessed his son Isaac, and Isaac lived near Beer-Laha-roi.*

Notes

1.a. Cf. n. 8:10.b.; 18:29.a.
2.a. Cf. n. 4:1.c.
2.b. SamPent זמרון.

3.a-a. Pseudocircumstantial sequential clause; cf. 10:8, 13, 15, 24, 26 (*SBH*, 88).
3.b. G adds "and Taiman."
3.c-c. Missing in 1 Chr 1:32.
3.d. G adds "Ragouel and Nabdeel and."
5.a-a Note chiasmus between vv 5 and 6a: "Abraham gave . . . to Isaac. But to the sons . . . Abraham gave."
5.b-b. Note four words linked by maqqeph (hyphen); GKC, 16a.
5.c. SamPent, G, S add "his son."
6.a-a. Note chiasmus with v 5; cf. n. 5.a-a.
6.b. ב + עוד + 3 masc sg suffix; cf. 18:22; BDB, 728b.
6.c. Waw consec + 3 masc sg impf piel שלח + 3 masc pl suffix.
7.a. Cf. n. 5:5.a.
8.a. On the clause structure in vv 8–11, cf. *SBH*, 42–43.
8.b. Cf. n. 5:5.b.
8.c. With SamPent (cf. G, S), which adds ימים "days" after MT שבע as in 35:28. MT could be translated "satisfied."
8.d. Waw consec + 3 masc sg impf niph אסף.
10.a. 3 masc sg pf pual קבר. On sg verb with pl subj, cf. GKC, 145a; WOC, 421.

Form/Structure/Setting

This section brings together several traditions dealing with:

vv 1–4	Abraham's marriage to Keturah
vv 5–6	The distribution of his estate
vv 7–11	His death

The final comment about God's blessing on Isaac and his dwelling near Beer-Laha-roi anticipates the theme of the next major section, "the family history of Isaac" (25:19–35:29). It is typical of the editor's method to include a trailer for the next section toward the end of the previous one. (For other examples, see 4:25–26; 6:5–8; 9:18–29; see Wenham, *Genesis 1–15*, 97, 156.) Indeed, the mention of an additional birth (vv 1–2) right at the end of a major section closely parallels 4:25–26. At these points, the hand of the editor may be discerned.

Although this section looks like a ragbag of traditions about Abraham that have been appended here because they do not really fit anywhere else, it should be noted that the three major cycles of patriarchal stories, about Abraham, Isaac, and Jacob, all end similarly:

Death and burial of wife	23:1–20	35:18–20	48:7
Son's marriage	24:1–67	35:21–22	49:3–4
List of descendants	25:1–6	35:22–26	49:5–28
Death and burial of patriarch	25:7–10	35:27–29	49:29–50:14
List of descendants	25:12–17	36:1–42	
"This is the family history of . . ."	25:19	37:2	

These parallels suggest purposeful editorial activity. Furthermore, the material here appears to be old and reflects a situation in which Israel enjoyed good relations with her neighbors in Arabia and the desert lands to the east. But, significantly, the passage never calls them Arabs, a term that did not come into use until the ninth century B.C. From the time of the wilderness wanderings through

the period of the judges, the Midianites troubled Israel, but earlier Moses had fled to Midian and married the daughter of a Midianite priest. No trace of the later animosity between Midian and Israel is detectable in this genealogy; this suggests it is old.

It is much more difficult to know what literary sources are being drawn on. Widely divergent critical analyses are offered, especially as regards vv 1–6. According to some (Delitzsch, von Rad, König, Speiser, Van Seters [*Abraham in History*], Vawter, Coats), they come from J. This, it is argued, is proved by v 5 repeating 24:36, by the use of ילד for fathering (v 3), and because v 3 has Sheba and Dedan descend from Yoqshan, not Raamah, as in 10:7. If 10:7 is P, 25:3 must be from a different source. But according to Gunkel, vv 1–6 come from a later J hand, since their perspective differs from chap. 24 where Abraham's death is near and is presumed. Skinner and Westermann argue that these verses presuppose the account of Abraham's death and burial in vv 7–10 and therefore must be even later than P. According to Skinner, "the adjustments were effected during the final redaction of the Pentateuch" (349).

It is widely agreed that vv 7–10 must be associated with P, since these verses contain chronological details (v 7) and an account of a burial in the cave of Macpelah. If chap. 23 is P (see *Form/Structure/Setting* on chap. 23), then it would seem likely that vv 8–10 are either P or editorial.

V 11 is again the subject of disagreement. Most commonly 11a is ascribed to P, since it links back to v 10, whereas 11b, because of its links with 24:62, is J. However, König and Coats ascribe all of v 11 to P, whereas Van Seters *(Abraham in History)* and Westermann believe all of v 11 originally belonged with chap. 24 (late J).

None of the arguments seem very conclusive, but the stance of Skinner, Van Seters, and Westermann, who regard the J-like material (vv 1–6, 11) as later than the P verses (7–10), is most compatible with our view of the composition of Genesis. Elsewhere we have found much evidence that material traditionally associated with P is earlier than J, and the same is true here. The fact that the overall arrangement of material in chap. 25 matches that found in chaps. 35–36, 48–50 confirms that the final editor of Genesis was responsible for organizing it; it is not an ill-considered insert or appendix.

Comment

1–4 These verses give the family tree of Abraham and Keturah:

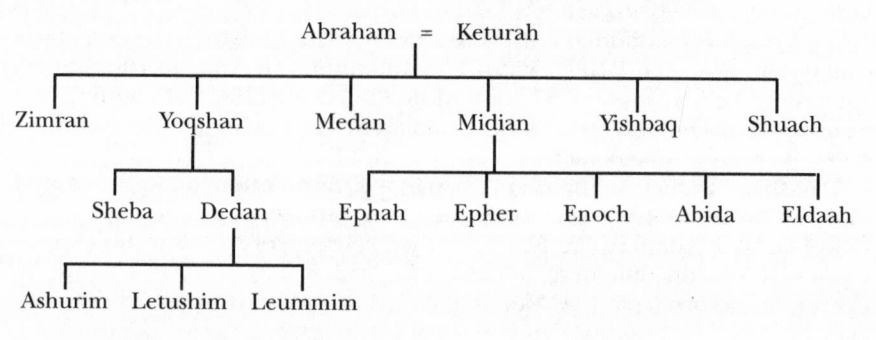

This family tree is of an unusual shape in that only the second and fourth of Keturah's sons have descendants and only the second of Yoqshan's sons, Dedan, has sons of his own.

It is natural to assume that Abraham's marriage to Keturah, coming soon after the account of Sarah's death (chap. 23), mentioned again in 24:67, occurred in the period between Sarah's death and his, which, according to 23:1 and 25:7, spanned nearly forty years. Consequently, Sternberg (*Poetics*, 349) believes that vv 1–4 illustrate the extreme blessedness of Abraham's old age. He who had such difficulty fathering one son earlier in his life now enjoys new procreativity in his latter years.

The majority of commentators, however, believe the text is not to be read sequentially. Speiser points out that if everything in Genesis were arranged in chronological order, the notice of Abraham's death (25:5–6) ought to be placed after the birth of Jacob and Esau (25:19–26), for on a literal reading of 21:5; 25:7, 26, Abraham lived fifteen years after his grandsons' birth. Furthermore, chap. 24 implies that Abraham died while his servant was away in Mesopotamia. "It is thus evident that the various details of this chapter have been grouped in such a manner as to interfere as little as possible with the progress of the narrative" (Speiser, 189). "Abraham married again" (v 1) is "to be understood in a literary not in a biographical sense; its purpose is to associate the names that follow with Abraham; this is done by introducing another wife" (Westermann, 2:395–96).

But at which stage in Abraham's life he married Keturah is not stated, and indeed seems impossible to determine. Calvin (2:35–36) suggested it occurred after Sarah had forced him to divorce Hagar (21:8–21). Jacob puts it even earlier, before chap. 17 or even chap. 14. But such conjecture contributes but little to the understanding of the account. The tradition that Abraham married Keturah had to be mentioned somewhere, and by including it here rather than elsewhere in the narrative, the editor of Genesis was able to keep the focus undistractedly on the promise of Isaac and its fulfillment. Now it is slipped in here to complete the picture and to show how Abraham did indeed become father of a multitude of nations (17:4–6).

1 קְטוּרָה "Keturah" looks like the feminine singular passive participle of קטר "to burn as incense," hence KB's suggested interpretation, "veiled in incense smoke." An association with incense seems probable in that several of her sons seem to be involved in the international spice trade. Although this trade is associated with Arabia in the OT (e.g., 1 Kgs 10:2, 10; Isa 60:6), not all the sons can be located there (see below; cf. *EM* 7:110–11).

2 Zimran is mentioned only here and in 1 Chr 1:32, though there may be a connection with Zimri (Jer 25:25). Pliny mentions an Arabian tribe called the Zamareni (*Natural History* 6.32.158), while Ptolemaeus (6, 7, 5) mentions a town near Mecca called Zambran. South Arabian inscriptions mention an Arab tribe called *ḏmrn*. All these possibilities point to Arabia.

"Yoqshan" (father of Sheba and Dedan, v 3) is mentioned also in 1 Chr 1:32. In 10:28, Sheba is said to be descended from Yoqtan, so some have suggested "Yoqshan" is a variant of "Yoqtan." But the exchange of ש for שׂ is difficult.

"Medan" occurs only here and in 1 Chr 1:32. It may occur in a South-Arabic inscription, according to J. A. Montgomery (*Arabia*, 43–44). It occurs as a personal

name in Ugarit (*UT*, 1431). Simons (*GTOT* §377) links it to the Arab settlement of Badana, mentioned in the annals of Tiglath-Pileser III.

"Midian" is frequently mentioned in texts dealing with the premonarchy period. Midian or the Midianites are a group of tribes inhabiting the deserts surrounding Israel. They were traders (37:28, 36). Moses married a Midianite and later was advised by his Midianite father-in-law somewhere in Sinai (Exod 3:1; 18:1–24). Later, Midianites associated with the Moabites harried Israel in Transjordan (Num 25; 31:1–12). And Gideon drove them back into Transjordan (Judg 7–8).

"Yishbaq" is mentioned in an inscription of Shalmaneser III (*māt Iašbuqi* "land of Yishbaq") and is located in northern Syria (*EM* 3:892–93; cf. *ANET*, 278).

"Shuach." Bildad, one of Job's comforters, "came from Shuach." It is not, as often asserted, in the desert east of Edom. Shuach (Akk. *Sūḫu*) lies on the middle Euphrates between Babylon and Mari. It is first mentioned in the Mari texts (c. 1800 B.C.) and often subsequently. In the first millennium, its inhabitants were mostly Arameans (*EM* 7:532–33; *ANET*, 275, 304, 481).

3 On Sheba and Dedan, cf. 10:7.

"Ashurim" are not the well-known Assyrians but a desert tribe, possibly identical with the Ashur mentioned in Num 24:22, 24 and Ps 83:9(8). Montgomery (*Arabia*, 44) says the name is probably found in a South-Arabic text, where it refers to a district in northwest Arabia.

"Letushim." Various conjectures have been made about them (see *EM* 4:497), but only this passage gives any firm clue that they were part of the league of Dedanite tribes who lived in the west Syrian desert.

"Leummim." No more is known about them than about the Letushim. Their position in this list evidently indicates they had something to do with each other.

4 "Epher" is a personal name meaning "young gazelle" according to Noth (*Personennamen*, 230). Cf. 1 Chr 4:17; 5:24. A town Appani mentioned in Ashurbanipal's record of his campaign against the Arabs may be related (cf. *ANET*, 299).

"Ephah" is linked in Isa 60:6 with Midian and Sheba as bringing gold and frankincense to Israel. It seems likely that Ephah is the name of a nomadic tribe found in northern Arabia, probably the same as the Haippā of the Assyrian inscriptions (*EM* 6:214; *ANET*, 283, 286). It is also a personal name in 1 Chr 2:46.

"Enoch." Cf. *Comment* on 4:17.

"Abida." The name might mean "the father has known (me)" (KB, 4). Many names are formed like this in biblical Hebrew, e.g., Elyada, Jehoiada, Shemida. Van Seters (*Abraham*, 61) suggests Abida may be related to Ibadidi, an Arab tribe mentioned in Assyrian records (*ANET*, 286).

"Eldaah." KB, 49, suggests the meaning "God has called." Montgomery notes (*Arabia*, 43) that two South-Arabian kings were called Abiyada and Yadail.

5–6 In the ancient world, a man divided his estate among his sons before he died (Luke 15:12). Sons of full wives could expect a definite share (Deut 21:15–17; cf. Num 27:1–11). Sons of concubines were completely dependent on their father's goodwill; hence Abraham gives them simply "presents," whereas Isaac received all the rest (v 5; cf. 24:36; cf. Luke 15:31, "All that I have is thine," AV).

6 "Concubines." Though Hagar is described as a "maid" (שפחה) or "slave-wife" (אמה) in Gen 16, 21, she probably could also be described as a "concubine" (פילגש)

as Bilhah is in 35:22 (cf. 30:3, "slave-wife"). 21:8–14, while making clear Abraham's great affection for Ishmael, never mentioned that he gave Ishmael and Hagar anything apart from bread and water, though it is probably implied (see *Comment* on 21:14). This passage shows that he did give Ishmael and his other sons something.

"Qedem." Though קדם may simply be translated "east," here and possibly in 29:1; Num 23:7, it appears to be used more precisely to describe a geographical area. In Egyptian texts from the first half of the second millennium (e.g., the travels of Sinuhe [twelfth dynasty] and one of the pyramid texts [eighteenth dynasty]), it appears to refer to part of the Syrian desert. Later the term is used more loosely to cover those desert areas on the eastern fringes of the land of Israel (*EM* 7:27–28) inhabited by the "people of the east" (e.g., Judg 6:3, 33; 7:12; 8:10; 1 Kgs 5:10[4:30]; Isa 11:14; Job 1:3).

7–8 The more typical concluding genealogical formula would be "All the days of Abraham were 175 years and he died" (cf. 5:8; 9:29). Here the traditional phraseology is greatly expanded to underline the significance of Abraham's career. The death notices of Adam (5:5) and Isaac (35:28–29) offer parallels, but Abraham's is longer still, showing the overwhelming importance of his life.

7 His age at death means he lived one hundred years in Canaan (cf. 12:4).

8 "Breathed his last and died." Cf. *Comment* on 6:17; 7:21. "Was gathered to his relatives." This could just mean that his body now rested with his relatives in the family tomb. But since this is said explicitly in v 9, it would seem more likely that the reference is to the soul of Abraham being reunited with his dead relatives in the afterlife. "It can only denote the union of the soul, the transfigured personality, with the souls of the forefathers" (Jacob, 536).

9–10 On the cave of Macpelah, see chap. 23. The estranged half brothers, Isaac and Ishmael, reunite to bury their father, just as later Jacob and Esau come together to bury their father, Isaac (35:29).

11 "God blessed . . . Isaac" anticipates the theme of the next major section of Genesis, i.e., 25:19–35:29, especially 26:12. Westermann suggests it once formed the conclusion to chap. 24. It is certainly congruent with the techniques of the editor of Genesis (cf. above *Form/Structure/Setting*) to conclude one section of the book with a hint of what will come in the next.

Explanation

It is easy to conclude from the opening remark, "Abraham married again" (v 1), that this section describes the widower Abraham remarrying after the death of his first wife, Sarah. However, the description of Keturah as a concubine (v 6) and a closer examination of the context of this account make this improbable. Were the order of stories in Genesis strictly chronological, the account of Abraham's death should not be mentioned till 25:26 at the earliest. And chap. 24 implies that Abraham died while his servant was away in Mesopotamia. The stories are arranged to describe the careers of the main actors as clearly as possible and to illuminate the fulfillment of the promises. For these reasons, it seems most likely that the editor understood Abraham's marriage to Keturah to have occurred much earlier in his life, but the description of it has been delayed until this point so as not to detract from the main line of the story.

The mention of Abraham dividing his estate among his various sons (vv 5–6) shows he did what was expected when he realized death was imminent. A man assigned his property before he died; it was not left to the executors to carry out the terms of his will. Here Abraham's acts are recorded as an example to future generations. Similarly, Isaac and Ishmael show proper filial piety, despite earlier disagreements, in joining together to bury their father.

The genealogical details of Abraham's sons through Keturah, like the table of nations in chap. 10, define Israel's relationships with some of the neighboring nomadic peoples who inhabited the desert areas on the fringes of Canaan and traded with them. That the descent of these peoples is traced back to Abraham expresses the close affinity Israel felt with these peoples.

Finally, as always in Genesis, the material draws attention to the divine promises. Abram's name was changed to Abraham to assure him that he would be father of a multitude of nations (17:4–6). 25:2–4 lists some of the nations descended from Abraham; implicitly this list reminds us of the fulfillment of the promises. The point is made explicitly in v 11. Now we hear "After the death of Abraham, God blessed his son Isaac." It shows the LORD's "steadfast love to thousands of those who love [him] and keep [his] commandments" (Deut 5:10) and how "his steadfast love endures for ever" (Ps 136:3).

The Family History of Ishmael   (25:12–18)

Bibliography

Harel, M. "'They dwelt from Havilah to Shur which is opposite Egypt.'" (Heb.) *BMik* 17 (1972) 501–2. **Irvine, A. K.** "The Arabs and Ethiopians." *POTT* 287–311. **Knauf, E. A.** *Ismael.* Wiesbaden: Harrassowitz, 1985. ————. "Supplementa Ismaelitica." *BN* 20 (1983) 34–36; 38/39 (1987) 44–49; 45 (1988) 62–79. **Lahav, M.** "Who is the 'Ashurite' (2 Sam 2:9) and 'Ashur' (Ps 83:9)?" (Heb.) *BMik* 28 (1982/83) 111–12. **Malamat, A.** "*Ummatum* in Old Babylonian Texts and Its Ugaritic and Biblical Counterparts." *UF* 11 (1979) 527–36. **Steinberg, N.** "The Genealogical Framework of the Family Stories in Genesis." *Semeia* 46 (1989) 41–50.

Translation

[12]*And this is the family history of Ishmael, the son of Abraham, the son whom Hagar, the Egyptian,*[a] *Sarah's maid, bore to Abraham.*

[13]*These are the names of Ishmael's sons by their names and their clans. Ishmael's first-born son was Nebaiot.*[a] *Then there were Qedar, Adbeel, Mibsam,* [14]*Mishma, Dumah, Massa,* [15]*Hadad,*[a] *Tema, Yetur, Naphish, and Qedemah.* [16]*These are*[a] *the sons of Ishmael, and these are their names by their settlements and encampments: twelve leaders of*[b] *their tribes.*

[17]*These are the years of Ishmael's life, one hundred and thirty-seven years. He breathed his last, died, and was gathered*[a] *to his relatives.*

[18]*They*[a] *dwelt from Havilah to Shur, which is opposite Egypt approaching*[b] *Ashur.*[c] [d]*Opposite all his brothers he settled.*[d]

Notes

12.a. Omitted by G.
13.a. SamPent spells it נבאות.
15.a. Some MSS read הדד, S הדר.
16.a. On the enclitic use of הם "they, these," after אלה "these," cf. GKC, 136d.
16.b. Or "by." On translating ל, cf. BDB, 512b, 516a.
17.a. Cf. n. 25:8.d.
18.a. G, Vg read sg, "he encamped."
18.b. Cf. n. 10:19.b.
18.c. *BHS* would unnecessarily emend to שורה. See *Comment.*
18.d-d. "The apposition clause . . . marks the end of the life of Ishmael" (*SBH,* 42).

Form/Structure/Setting

The Family History of Ishmael (25:12–18) is one of the ten "family histories" into which the book of Genesis is arranged. From Gen 11 onwards, short genealogies of Shem, of Ishmael, and of Esau (11:10–26; 25:12–18; 36:1–43) alternate with the much fuller family histories of Terah, Isaac, and Jacob (11:27–25:11; 25:19–35:29; 37:1–50:26). As is customary in Genesis, the story of the non-elect line, here Ishmael, is dealt with before the history of the chosen line, here Isaac, is described (cf. Esau before Jacob [chap. 36] and Cain before Seth [chap. 4]).

This history of Ishmael also shows the fulfillment of the promises made to his parents about him. Hagar had been assured that her descendants would "be too many to count" (16:10) and that Ishmael would "dwell opposite his brothers" (16:12). To Abraham, the promise was that Ishmael would "father twelve princes and I shall make him a great nation" (17:20). 25:18 thus looks back to 16:12, and 25:13–16 to 17:20.

The family history of Ishmael falls into four distinct paragraphs:

12	Title
13–16	Ishmael's twelve sons
17	Summary of Ishmael's life and notice of his death
18	The territory of the Ishmaelites

According to the usual source–critical theory, vv 12–17 come from P: v 12 because it contains the editorial heading "This is the family history of . . . "; vv 13–16 because they are genealogy and because of their back reference to 17:20 (also P); v 17 because it is a chronological notice, again usually attributed to P. As to the origin of v 18, opinion is more divided. Older commentators (e.g., Dillmann, Gunkel, Skinner, Procksch, Speiser) argued that it came from J because it recounts the fulfillment of 16:12. Indeed, Gunkel suggested that it once formed the conclusion of chap. 16. Westermann (cf. Coats), however, argues that v 18 is a continuation of v 16, denies that there is sufficient evidence to attribute it to J, but says it was an independent tradition adopted by P. Because of the similarity of v 18b to 16:12b, he regards it as a later addition to v 18.

Westermann's attempt to split v 18 seems contrived in that the verb used in 16:12b, שכן "dwelt," is used in v 18a, while the phrase "opposite all his brothers" is found in v 18b. So his attempt to dissociate v 18 from the J material of chap. 16 is weak. It may also be noted that v 12b, "the son of Abraham, the son whom Hagar, the Egyptian, Sarah's maid, bore to Abraham," has the closest verbal affinities with chap. 16 and 21:9, both most probably J. So as in the immediately preceding passage 25:1–11, it appears that P-style material is encased in J-style editorial comment. This is consonant with seeing J as using earlier P material.

Sarna argues that this material must come from an old source because there is no mention of a confederation of Ishmaelite tribes, which this list presupposes, after the time of David. Nor are Ishmaelites mentioned in Assyrian inscriptions dealing with Arab tribes. In later texts, e.g., Isa 60:7 and Assyrian texts, Qedar is the leading north Arabian tribe, but here it is mentioned second to Nebaiot, which may reflect an earlier situation.

Comment

12 "This is . . . Ishmael." For this formula, cf. 2:4; 5:1; 6:9; 10:1; 11:10, 27; 25:19; 36:1; 37:2. "The son whom Hagar, the Egyptian, Sarah's maid, bore to Abraham" recalls all the drama described in chap. 16 and 21:9–21. The introductory formula and the reference to the earlier stories suggest this verse was composed by the editor of Genesis.

13–16 This list is framed by "These are the names of Ishmael's sons" and "These are the sons of Ishmael and these are the names. . . ." This inclusion

appears to mark these verses off as a discrete fragment utilized by the editor. The list names twelve sons of Ishmael. The parallel with Jacob's twelve sons and the fact that many of these sons can be identified with Arab tribes make it likely that the Ishmaelites were once a confederation of tribes like early Israel.

13 "And their clans," lit. "by their descendants." תּוֹלְדֹת is translated "family history of," e.g., 25:12. NAB, von Rad, Speiser, and Gispen, noting the etymology (from ילד "to bear") and the reference to Nebaiot being Ishmael's firstborn, suggest the translation "by the order of their birth." This is possible, but unproven.

"Nebaiot" is also mentioned in 28:9 and 36:3, where it is recorded that Esau married his sister. He may also be regarded as the ancestor of the *Nabayāti*, an Arab tribe conquered by Ashurbanipal in the seventh century and mentioned in Isa 60:7. Whether these *Nabayāti* are to be identified with the well-known Nabateans (fourth century B.C. to fourth century A.D.) is less certain (cf. *IBD* 1043–48; *EM* 5:744–46; *POTT,* 306, n. 19).

"Qedar" is also mentioned alongside Nebaiot in 1 Chr 1:29 and Isa 60:7. Other references to Qedar show that it too was the name of an Arab tribe, or group of tribes (Isa 21:16–17; 42:11; Jer 2:10; 49:28; Ezek 27:21; Ps 120:5). Qedar is also mentioned in Assyrian inscriptions from the eighth and seventh centuries B.C. The Qedarites lived in the desert between Babylon and Transjordan. Qedar's power was greatest from the time of Sennacherib to the fourth century B.C. (*EM* 7:31–33; W. J. Dumbrell, *BASOR* 203 [1971] 33–44).

"Adbeel" (cf. 1 Chr 1:29, the only other biblical mention). Tiglath-Pileser 3 (745–727 B.C.) mentions a tribe *Idibail* living in the northern Sinai peninsula (*EM* 1:90; *RLA* 5:31).

"Mibsam" (cf. 1 Chr 1:29). According to 1 Chr 4:25, a Simeonite had the same name. According to Noth (*Personennamen,* 223), it means "balsam."

14 "Mishma" (cf. 1 Chr 1:30). He is also a descendant of Simeon according to 1 Chr 4:25–26. Jebel Misma, 160 miles east of Tema, may again indicate the Arabian links of this group.

"Dumah" (cf. 1 Chr 1:30). The oracle against Dumah in Isa 21:11–12 seems to make it part of Edom. Sennacherib is said to have conquered a fortress in the desert called Adummat (cf. *RLA* 1:39–40). There is also an oasis east of Petra called Dumat al Ghandal. That is not to say that Duma, Dumah, Adummat, and Dumat should be identified, but these names do confirm the Ishmaelite association with the desert.

"Massa" (cf. 1 Chr 1:30). A king of Massa is mentioned in Prov 31:1. A town *Masʾa* is mentioned in Tiglath-Pileser's annals, where it is associated with Tema and various Arabian tribes.

15 "Hadad" (cf. 1 Chr 1:30). Simons (*GTOT* §121) notes a wadi el-Ḥadad north of Tebuk.

"Tema" is associated with Sheba in Job 6:19, with Dedan in Jer 25:23, and with Dumah, Dedan, and Qedar in Isa 21:14. It is an oasis about 250 miles southeast of Eilat, an important staging post on the trade routes from Arabia to the Mediterranean and to Babylon. In Assyrian times, Tema paid heavy tribute to Tiglath-Pileser 3, and later Nabonidus (556–39), king of Babylon, lived there while his son Belshazzar ruled in Babylon (*EM* 8:522–24).

"Yetur" is also mentioned in 1 Chr 1:31 and 5:19, among those Transjordanians conquered by the tribes of Reuben, Gad, and Manasseh. They may also be the

ancestors of the Itureans (cf. Luke 3:1) who lived in the Antilebanon (*EM* 3:673–74; *NBD*, 590).

"Naphish" (cf. 1 Chr 1:31; 5:19).

"Qedemah" (cf. 1 Chr 1:31, otherwise unknown). The name suggests an association with the east, but whether Qedemah should be identified with the Kadmonites (Gen 15:19; so Simons, *GTOT* §121) or the people of the east (29:1; so Montgomery, *Arabia,* 49) is more doubtful.

16 The terminology used in this verse expresses the wandering lifestyle of the Ishmaelites. They lived in "settlements" (חצר; cf. *ḥaṣārum* of the nomadic settlements at Mari; *CAD* H, 130; also Van Seters, *Abraham in History,* 18) and "encampments" (טיר, i.e., "enclosures," often protected by stone walls; cf. Num 31:10; Ezek 25:4). The word for "tribe" (אמה), used elsewhere only in Num 25:15; Ps 117:1, is a term (Akk. *ummatum*) also found in the texts from Mari and Tell al-Rimah (see Malamat, *UF* 11 [1979] 527–36).

"Twelve leaders" echoes 17:20. Later, Israel also had twelve tribes, each headed by a leader (נשיא).

17 This verse is a typical concluding summary of a patriarch's life (cf. 25:7–8; 35:28–29; 49:33).

18 This verse describes the general area in which the Ishmaelites lived, in the wilderness to the south and east of the land of Israel. "Havilah" (cf. 2:11; 10:7) could well be in Arabia and "Shur" in northern Sinai (16:7; 20:1). "Ashur" was a tribe inhabiting the Sinai peninsula (cf. 10:22; 25:3).

"Opposite all his brothers he settled," a direct quote from 16:12, probably hints at the later antagonism between the bedouin-like Ishmaelites and the more settled Israelites.

Explanation

This short, matter-of-fact family history of Ishmael tidies up the record of Abraham's first son. The reader's curiosity is satisfied by learning what became of Ishmael and his descendants. It also explains how Israel viewed her bedouin-like Ishmaelite neighbors who plied the trade routes in times of peace (cf. 37:25) and pounced on the settlements of Israel in times of war (Judg 8:24). Through all the stories about Ishmael, there runs a schizophrenic streak. On the one hand, these tribesmen are viewed as intimately related to Israel; on the other hand, these tales relate that tension between Israelites and Ishmaelites can be traced right back to the squabbles of Isaac and Ishmael in Abraham's household.

But as elsewhere, Genesis is not interested in sociological observation or historical anecdote for its own sake but in theology, in the fulfillment of the promises made to Abraham. At first blush, this family history of Ishmael has nothing to do with this fulfillment theme; Ishmael is, like Cain, Ham, or Esau, one of the cul-de-sacs in divine history, a man who is by-passed in the unfolding of God's promises recorded in Genesis. Yet he, too, was the subject of divine promises. His mother, Hagar, was assured that he would "dwell opposite all his brothers" (16:12), while his father, Abraham, was assured that he would father twelve princes and become a great nation (17:20). This short family history of Ishmael records the fulfillment of both these promises (25:16, 18). If the LORD fulfilled these rather minor

promises, he will surely fulfill his much greater promises through the chosen line of Isaac. This section therefore encourages the reader to follow with eager anticipation the family history of Isaac that is about to begin. If God did not overlook his promises to Ishmael, how much more certainly will he fulfill those guaranteed by oath to Abraham about Isaac and his descendants.

The Story of Isaac   (25:19–35:29)

Bibliography

Blenkinsopp, J. "Biographical Patterns in Biblical Narrative." *JSOT* 20 (1981) 27–46. **Blum, E.** *Die Komposition der Vätergeschichte.* WMANT 57. Neukirchen: Neukirchener, 1984. **Brodie, L. T.** "Jacob's Travail (Jer 30:1–13) and Jacob's Struggle (Gen 32:22–32)." *JSOT* 19 (1981) 31–60. **Fishbane, M.** "Composition and Structure in the Jacob Cycle (Gen 25:19–25:22)." *JTS* 26 (1975) 15–38; reprinted in *Text and Texture: Close Readings of Selected Biblical Texts.* New York: Schocken Books, 1979. 40–62. **Fokkelman, J. P.** *Narrative Art in Genesis.* Amsterdam: van Gorcum, 1975. **Fretheim, T. E.** "The Jacob Traditions: Theology and Hermeneutic." *Int* 26 (1972) 419–36. **Furman, N.** "His Story Versus Her Story: Male Genealogy and Female Strategy in the Jacob Cycle." *Semeia* 46 (1989) 141–49. **Gammie, J. G.** "Theological Interpretation by way of Literary and Tradition Analysis: Gen 25–36." In *Encounter with the Text: Form and History in the Hebrew Bible,* ed. M. J. Buss. Philadelphia: Fortress, 1979. 117–34. **Hendel, R. S.** *The Epic of the Patriarch: The Jacob Cycle and the Narrative Traditions of Canaan and Israel.* HSM 42. Atlanta: Scholars, 1987. **Heuschen, J. M.** "Jacob de genadevolle uitverkiezing." *ETL* 45 (1969) 335–58. **Kirkpatrick, P. G.** *The OT and Folklore Study.* JSOTSup 62. Sheffield: Academic, 1988. **Kuehlewein, J.** "Gotteserfahrung und Reifungsgeschichte in der Jakob-Esau-Erzählung: Ein Beitrag zum Gespräch zwischen Theologie und Tiefenpsychologie." In *Werden und Wirken des ATs: FS C. Westermann,* ed. R. Albertz, H-P. Müller, H. W. Wolff, and W. Zimmerli. Göttingen: Vandenhoeck & Ruprecht, 1980. 116–30. **Lemaire, A.** "La haute Mésopotamie et l'origine des benê Jacob." *VT* 34 (1984) 95–101. **Miscall, P. D.** "The Jacob and Joseph Stories as Analogies." *JSOT* 6 (1978) 28–40. **Moye, R. H.** "In the Beginning: Myth and History in Genesis and Exodus." *JBL* 109 (1990) 577–98. **Oden, R. A.** "Jacob as Father, Husband, and Nephew: Kinship Studies and the Patriarchal Narratives." *JBL* 102 (1983) 189–205. **Otto, E.** "Jakob in Bethel: Ein Beitrag zur Geschichte der Jakobusüberlieferung." *ZAW* 88 (1976) 165–90. ———. *Jakob in Sichem: Überlieferungsgeschichtliche archäologische und territorialgeschichtliche Studien zur Entstehungsgeschichte Israels.* BWANT 110. Stuttgart: Kohlhammer, 1979. **Pury, A. de.** "Le cycle de Jacob comme légende autonome des origines d'Israel." VTSup 43 (1991) 78–96. ———. "La tradition patriarcale en Gen 12–35." In *Le Pentateuque en question,* ed. A. de Pury. Geneva: Labor et Fides, 1989. 259–70. **Roth, W. M. W.** "The Text is the Medium: An Interpretation of the Jacob Stories in Genesis." In *Encounter with the Text: Form and History in the Hebrew Bible,* ed. M. J. Buss. Philadelphia: Fortress, 1979. 103–15. **Schiltknecht, H. R.** "Konflikt und Versöhnung in der Erzählung von Jakob und Esau." *Reformatio* 22 (1973) 522–31. **Scullion, J.** "'Die Genesis ist eine Sammlung von Sagen' (Hermann Gunkel): Independent Stories and Redactional Unity in Gen 12–36." In *"Wünschet Jerusalem Frieden": Collected Communications to the XIIth Congress of IOSOT, Jerusalem, 1986,* ed. M. Augustin and K. D. Schunck. Frankfurt: Lang, 1986. 243–47. **Smith, S. H.** "'Heel' and 'Thigh': the Concept of Sexuality in the Jacob-Esau Narratives." *VT* 40 (1990) 464–73. **Syrén, R.** *The Forsaken First-Born: A Study of a Recurrent Motif in the Patriarchal Narratives.* JSOTSup 133. Sheffield: Academic, 1993. **Terino, J.** "A Text-Linguistic Study of the Jacob Narrative." *VE* 18 (1988) 45–62. **Thompson, T. L.** "Conflict Themes in the Jacob Narratives." *Semeia* 15 (1979) 5–26. **Weimar, P.** "Aufbau und Struktur der priestershriftlichen Jakobsgeschichte." *ZAW* 86 (1974) 174–203. **Weisman, Z.** *From Jacob to Israel.* (Heb.) Jerusalem: Magnes, 1986. **Whitt, W. D.** "The Jacob Traditions in Hosea and Their Relation to Genesis." *ZAW* 103 (1991) 18–43. **Yaniv, I.** "Guide Words in the Jacob Cycle." (Heb.) *BMik* 34 (1988/89) 68–75. **Zucker, D. J.** "Jacob in Darkness (and Light): A Study in Contrasts." *Judaism* 35 (1986) 402–13.

Form/Structure/Setting

The editorial headings 25:19; 36:1, "This is the family history of Isaac (Edom)," define the limits of this unit within Genesis. As in 11:27 and 37:2, it is the father who gives his name to the section, for he is alive and notionally head of the family throughout the period covered. Isaac's death is not recorded until 35:29.

The Jacob story is one of the three major sections of Genesis dealing with the careers of the patriarchs, the others being the stories of Abraham (11:27–25:11) and of Joseph (37:2–50:26). In *Genesis 1–15*, 257–58, I noted some of the parallels between these stories and suggested that the author deliberately highlights some of the parallels in order to encourage comparison between the careers and characters of the patriarchs.

It is often suggested that the Abraham and Jacob stories have more in common with each other than with the Joseph story, which has a distinct character of its own. But it is truer to say that the Joseph story is the sequel of the Jacob story, indeed, that the Jacob-Joseph story has two parts, 25:19–35:29 being part 1 and 37:2–50:26 being part 2. Part 1 begins with the conception of Jacob and his struggles with Esau in the womb of his mother (25:19–22), and part 2 ends with the last words and death of Jacob (47:29–50:17). Thus, over half of the book of Genesis is devoted to describing the life of Jacob. This emphasis on his life is fitting, of course, because Jacob, or Israel, was the forefather of the nation and his sons were the ancestors of the twelve tribes. The unity of the Jacob and Joseph stories is also apparent in the portrayal of the characters in both stories. For example, in both stories the tension between Leah and her sons on the one hand and Rachel and her sons on the other is of crucial importance. There are parallel motifs in both stories too; just as Jacob deceived his father with a kid (27:9–17), so in turn his sons deceive him with a kid (37:31). The Jacob story ends with father Jacob at loggerheads with most of his sons; it is only the Joseph story that describes the healing of the breach within the family. When compared with the preceding chapters of Genesis, the Jacob and Joseph stories excel at characterization and depth of psychological insight. The unity of the stories is indirectly attested by recent source critics, who tend to view both the Jacob and Joseph stories as from mainly one source, usually J.

Nevertheless, the author of Genesis has deliberately split the Jacob-Joseph story into two parts by putting the family history of Esau 36:1–37:1 in the middle. This allows him to alternate the genealogies of the non-elect lines of Ishmael (25:12–18) and Esau (36:1–37:1) with the fuller family histories of the chosen lines of Terah (Abraham) (11:27–25:11), Isaac (Jacob) (25:19–35:29), and Jacob (Joseph) (37:2–50:26) to produce a total of five patriarchal family histories. This matches the five family histories of pre-patriarchal times (see *Genesis 1–15*, xxii).

The way in which the author of Genesis has created three major cycles of patriarchal history by setting the careers of Abraham, Jacob, and Joseph in three great "family histories" suggests that he wants to draw parallels between them and their significance for the history of salvation. These parallels are enhanced by the arrangement of the "family histories." Each begins with "This is the family history of (Terah, Isaac, Jacob)" (11:27; 25:19; 37:2), and each ends with a reference to the death and burial of the major patriarch (25:7–10; 35:29; 50:1–26). But there are other correspondences too.

The theme of the whole Pentateuch, the partial fulfillment of the promises to Abraham of land, descendants, covenant, and blessing to the nations, is set out first in 12:1–3. And all the subsequent stories in Genesis explain the fulfillment of these promises. This statement of the divine promises thus sets the agenda for the whole of Genesis 12–50. But the family histories of Isaac and Jacob do not just develop the main theme of the Pentateuch; they have subthemes of their own.

Like the main theme in 12:1–3, these subthemes take the form of a divine revelation and occur right at the beginning of each "family history." In 25:22–23, Rebekah consults the LORD about her pregnancy and is told, "'Two nations are in your womb. . . . / The older will be a slave of the younger.'" And it is the struggle between Jacob and Esau that dominates the next ten chapters of Genesis. They wrestle in the womb; then Jacob emerges clutching Esau's heel. Later he persuades Esau to part with his birthright and later yet tricks him out of his blessing. Esau's murderous rage forces Jacob to flee to Paddan-Aram, where he has to remain for twenty years before returning to Canaan and a reunion with his brother.

Similarly, the Joseph story begins with a revelation of Joseph's future greatness. This time, God's purposes are made known through a pair of dreams in which Joseph's parents and brothers bow down to him. Eventually, this prophecy is fulfilled in chap. 46, when all the family goes down to Egypt and meets Joseph, the vizier of all Egypt.

This prefacing of each "family history" with a word from God thus serves to highlight that every stage of the patriarchal history was guided by God. Despite the appalling mistakes of these fallible men, God's purposes were ultimately fulfilled.

The Jacob story falls into the following main sections:

25:19–34	First encounters of Jacob and Esau	A
26:1–33	Isaac and the Philistines	B
26:34–28:9	Jacob cheats Esau of his blessing	C
28:10–22	Jacob meets God at Bethel	D
29:1–14	Jacob arrives at Laban's house	E
29:15–30	Jacob marries Leah and Rachel	F
29:31–30:24	Birth of Jacob's sons	G
30:25–31:1	Jacob outwits Laban	F^1
31:2–32:1 (31:55)	Jacob leaves Laban	E^1
32:2–3 (1–2)	Jacob meets angels of God at Mahanaim	D^1
32:4 (3)–33:20	Jacob returns Esau's blessing	C^1
34:1–31	Dinah and the Hivites	B^1
35:1–29	Journey's end for Jacob and Isaac	A^1

In *Genesis 1–15*, 262–63, I discussed the proposals of scholars who suggest the Abraham stories are arranged palistrophically, i.e., in a mirror-image structure. Such an arrangement is much clearer here, as Fishbane (*JTS* 26 [1975] 15–38), Fokkelman (*Narrative Art*), Coats, and Rendsburg (*Redaction*) have observed. The mirror image is particularly obvious in sections C, D, E, E^1, D^1, C^1. In C^1, Jacob bows down to his brother (33:3), acting out the words of the blessing in 27:29, and he says he is giving the blessing to Esau in 33:11. In both D and D^1, Jacob encounters angels of God: on the first occasion he is leaving Canaan, on

the second returning there. The parallels between Jacob's arrival at Laban's house (E) and his departure (E¹) are clear. F (Jacob marries Leah and Rachel) and F¹ (Jacob outwits Laban) are less obviously reflections of each other, but both in fact deal with trickery, how Laban tricked Jacob into marrying Leah and how Jacob tricked Laban into paying him wages. B and B¹ both deal with relationships between Israelites and the Canaanites and make a sharp contrast between the peaceful situation in Isaac's day and the bitter conflict in Jacob's time. A and A¹ have least in common, though they do bring together Jacob and Esau for the first and last time (35:29).

The central scene (G), the birth of Jacob's sons—more precisely, the birth of a son to Rachel (30:22–24)—is the turning point of the story. As soon as this happens Jacob asks Laban for permission to return home (30:25). Though, of course, he prevaricates and uses various excuses to detain Jacob, it is clear that in Jacob's eyes it is the birth of Joseph to the only woman he regarded as his wife that signals it is time for him to go home. The flood story is another prime example of a palistrophe in Genesis (cf. Wenham, *Genesis 1–15*, 156–58). It is noteworthy that both palistrophes have a similar comment at the turning point (God remembered Rachel/Noah, 30:22; 8:1) to emphasize that it is God who controls events and saves his people.

Classical source criticism found the three main documentary sources in these chapters: according to Driver, J is the major source (60%), E is half the length of J (28%), and P is just an eighth of the total (12%). Recent critics have tended to see J or someone like him as even more important and eliminate E entirely (e.g., Westermann), though as in the Abraham story, P elements are usually still assigned to a different source or writer. Discussion of the different proposals as they affect particular chapters will be found scattered through the commentary.

First Encounters of Jacob and Esau *(25:19–34)*

Bibliography

Ahroni, R. "Why Did Esau Spurn the Birthright? A Study in Biblical Interpretation (Gen 25:29–34)." *Judaism* 29 (1980) 323–31. **Kraft, R. A.** "A Note on the Oracle of Rebecca (Gen 25:23)." *JTS* 13 (1962) 318–20. **Kreuter, J. A.** "Warum liebte Isaak Esau? Überlegungen zu *bepīw* in Gen 25:28." *BN* 48 (1989) 17–18. **Kuntzmann, R.** *Le symbolisme des jumeaux au Proche-Orient ancien.* Paris: Beauchesne, 1983. **Luke, K.** Two Birth Narratives in Genesis (Gen 25:19–26; 38:27–30)." *IndTS* 17 (1980) 155–80. **Maher, M.** "The Transfer of a Birthright: Justifying the Ancestors." *PIBA* 8 (1984) 1–24. **Matthews, V. H.** "Jacob the Trickster and Heir of the Covenant: A Literary Interpretation." *Perspectives in Religious Studies* 12 (1985) 185–95. **Rottenberg, M.** "The Interpretation of Rebekah's Question, 'Why am I like this?'" (Heb.) *BMik* 29 (1983/84) 218–19. **Williams, J. G.** "The Comedy of Jacob: A Literary Study." *JAAR* 46 (1978) 208.

Translation

[19] *This is the family history of Isaac, the son of Abraham. Now Abraham had fathered Isaac.* [20] *Isaac was forty years old when he married*[a] *Rebekah, the daughter of Bethuel the Aramean from Paddan-Aram and the sister of Laban the Aramean.* [21] *Isaac interceded to the LORD for his wife because she was childless, and the LORD heeded*[a] *his*[b] *prayer, and Rebekah his wife conceived.* [22] *The children smashed*[a] *each other inside her, so that she said: "If it is like this, why*[b] *am I*[c] *here?" So she went to consult the LORD.* [23] *The LORD said to her:*

"Two nations[a] *are in your womb.*
Two peoples will be divided[b] *even as they come out of*[c] *you.*
One people will be stronger than the other.
The older will be a slave of the younger."

[24] *When the time for her to give birth*[a] *was up, there were indeed*[b] *twins*[c] *in her womb.* [25] *The first came out all reddish,*[a] *like a hairy cloak, so they*[b] *called him Esau.* [26] *Afterwards his brother came out with his hand clutching*[a] *Esau's heel, so they*[b] *called him Jacob. Now Isaac was sixty years old when they were born.* [27] *The boys grew up. Esau became an expert hunter, a real countryman. But Jacob was a quiet man, who lived in tents.*[a] [28] *Isaac loved Esau for his hunting,*[a] *whereas Rebekah loved Jacob.* [29] *Jacob had made*[a] *a stew, when Esau came in from the country exhausted.* [30] *Esau said to Jacob, "Please let me swallow*[a] *some of the red stew, this red stew, because I am exhausted." So he was called Edom.* [31] *Jacob said, "Sell*[a] *at once*[b] *your firstborn's rights to me."*[c] [32] *Esau said, "Here I am about to die. Of what value to me are the*[a] *rights of a firstborn?"* [33] *Jacob said, "Swear to me at once."* [a]*So he swore to him, and he sold his firstborn's rights to Jacob,*[a] [34] [a]*while Jacob gave Esau bread and lentil stew.*[a] *He ate, drank,*[b] *stood up, and went away. So Esau treated*[c] *the rights of the firstborn with contempt.*

Notes

20.a. בְּ + inf constr לקח + 3 masc sg suffix.

21.a. Waw consec + 3 masc sg impf niph עתר. On pointing, cf. GKC, 51n. On this use of the niph, "tolerative," see WOC, 390.

21.b. לו lit. "for, by him." "The efficient cause (or personal agent) is, as a rule, attached to the passive by ל" (GKC, 121f).

22.a. Waw consec + 3 masc pl impf hithp רצץ.

22.b. Enclitic זה makes the question more pointed (cf. 18:13; GKC, 136c).

22.c. BHS suggests inserting חיה "living" on basis of S. Unnecessary.

23.a. With SamPent and Q, read גוים.

23.b. 3 masc pl impf niph פרד.

23.c. On use of מן here, see GKC, 119ff.

24.a. Cf. n. 4:2.b.

24.b. Cf. *SBH*, 95.

24.c. SamPent has the fuller spelling תאומים.

25.a. On syntax, cf. Joüon, 126a.

25.b. G, S have sg, "he called," as in v 26.

26.a. Fem sg ptcp qal אחז.

26.b. Impersonal 3 masc sg "he" = "they." SamPent reads "they called."

27.a. Cf. n. 4:20.c.

28.a. SamPent צידו "his hunting." G, Vg understand it similarly, but MT is adequate.

29.a. Waw consec + 3 masc sg hiph זוד "boil up."

30.a. 2 masc sg impv hiph לעמ + 1 sg suffix.

31.a. 2 masc sg impv מכר + āh suffix (GKC, 48i).

31.b. כיום lit. "today," with the nuance "now, at once, first of all." Cf. 1 Sam 2:16; 1 Kgs 1:51; M. Rottenberg, *Lěš* 48–49 (1983–85) 60–62.

31.c. Note unusual position of לי. Commonly next to the verb. Probably indicates emphasis "to *me*"; cf. *EWAS*, 44–45.

32.a. Note the omission of the def art in a question (Joüon, 137p).

33.a-a. With *SBH*, 135–36, linking these clauses chiastically with the first clause of v 34.

34.a-a. Cf. preceding note.

34.b. Cf. n. 9:21.a.

34.c. Waw consec + 3 masc sg impf apoc בזה.

Form/Structure/Setting

The opening of this section is clear: "This is the family history of Isaac" is one of the ten headings marking a new division within Genesis (cf. 2:4; 5:1; 6:9; 11:27; 25:12). Its ending is not so obvious. Coats suggests 25:26, and Gunkel and Westermann propose 25:28; whereas the majority prefer 25:34. In the light of the parallels with 11:27–12:9, the last view has most in its favor. This section is in essence an introduction to the whole cycle of Jacob and Esau. The narrator offers us glimpses of three episodes in their early years that both determine and illustrate the subsequent course of their careers. In these sixteen verses, we have their future lives in a nutshell. These introductory paragraphs serve as a trailer to the main story, which comprises Gen 26–35.

It may be analyzed as follows:

Heading: "This is the family history" (19a)
Isaac's nearest relations (19b–20)
Episode 1: Pregnancy and Birth of Esau and Jacob (21–26)
            Scene 1. Isaac prays for Rebekah (21)
            Scene 2. Problems of pregnancy explained (22–23)
            Scene 3. Birth of twins (24–26)
Episode 2: Esau and Jacob contrasted (27–28)
Episode 3: Esau sells his birthright to Jacob (29–34)

Much of the information contained in this section is indispensable for understanding the later stories, and all of it contributes to an appreciation of the themes of the unfolding narrative. Vv 19b–20 remind us of Isaac's links with Laban and Paddan-Aram. Laban, Rebekah's brother, is to give his daughters to Jacob in marriage. Indeed, Laban is to dictate virtually twenty years of Jacob's life in Paddan-Aram (chaps. 29–31).

The childlessness of Rebekah links her both with her mother-in-law Sarah and with her daughter-in-law Rachel. But whereas the parallel stories make much of the matriarch's barrenness, here the point is slipped over quickly. The narrative here focuses on the struggles of her sons. Even before birth they are locked in conflict, a feature that will dominate much of the following narratives (chaps. 27,

32–33). And into this conflict will be dragged their parents, as the father favors Esau and the mother Jacob (vv 27–28; cf. chap. 27). Finally, the carelessness of Esau in selling his birthright to Jacob both shows a preliminary fulfillment of the divine promise that "the older will be a slave of the younger" (v 23) and anticipates the much greater victories Jacob will win in the years ahead (vv 29–34; cf. chap. 27; 32–33). In all these ways this opening section introduces the key themes of the Jacob cycle.

However, this section does not merely look forward; it also looks back, particularly to the opening of the Abraham cycle that it closely parallels.

"This is the family history of"	25:19; cf. 11:27
"Abraham fathered Isaac"	25:19; cf. 11:27
"Isaac married Rebekah"	25:20; cf. 11:29
"(Rebekah) was childless"	25:21; cf. 11:30
Journey to oracle (land)	25:22; cf. 11:31
"And the LORD said"	25:23; cf. 12:1
Predictions	25:23; cf. 12:1–3
First fulfillment	25:24–26; cf. 12:4
Age of patriarch then	25:26b; cf. 12:4b
Second fulfillment of predictions	25:27–34; cf. 12:5–9
Wife/sister scene	26:1–11; cf. 12:10–20

These parallels are sufficiently close to suggest that they are not coincidental. The history of Isaac's family is being deliberately compared with that of Abraham. And if this is so, special attention needs to be paid to the divine oracle summarizing the future career of Esau and Jacob in 25:23, for this occupies a position analogous to the promises made to Abraham in 12:1–3. The latter passage is of cardinal importance not just for the Abraham cycle but for the whole Pentateuch whose theme it states. Here 25:23 is similarly programmatic: it announces the God-determined career of Jacob to be one of conflict culminating in ultimate triumph.

Source critics usually assign vv 19–20, 26b to P because of the *toledot* formula and the use of הוליד in v 19, because of its chronological details (vv 20, 26), and because of the mention of Paddan-Aram in v 20. Vv 21–28 are usually assigned to J because they mention the LORD (vv 21, 23). More doubt surrounds vv 29–34. Gunkel and Procksch held it came from E because of its affinity with 27:36, whereas Westermann believes it came originally from an independent source. Most, however, ascribe the passage to J.

Volz (*Der Elohist*, 70–72), Fokkelmann (*Narrative Art*, 86–94), and Blum (*Die Komposition*, 79–80) have all given strong reasons for holding to the substantial unity of vv 21–34 (apart from 26b), and for its ascription to J. But what is to be made of the P fragments (vv 19–20, 26b)? Westermann has pointed out that v 26b, "Now Isaac was sixty years old when they were born," can hardly have stood alone. It presupposes a mention of the birth of Jacob and Esau. Without the material in the preceding verses, we could not identify "they" in v 26b. He has drawn attention to similar hiatuses in 11:27b and 12:5c caused by the standard source analysis. He therefore ascribes both 11:27–12:9 and 25:19–34 in their present forms to the work of the final redactor who combined J and P.

Our analysis of the parallels between 11:27–12:9 and 25:19–34, which comprises material drawn from both the putative sources J and P, supports Westermann's view that 25:19–34 reflects essentially the final editor's hand. Indeed, the parallels suggest a much greater degree of unity within both passages than is usually admitted. But whereas Westermann wants to distinguish between J and the final redactor, I regard the evidence as insufficient to distinguish two hands here and would prefer to believe it all reflects the hand of J.

Comment

19 "This is the family history of Isaac." On this standard heading, see Wenham, *Genesis 1–15*, 268–69. Isaac barely appears in the story after chap. 27, yet this heading covers all of 25:19–35:29, because these chapters span the whole period in which Isaac was nominally head of the family, so that his sons' deeds are in some sense part of his story.

"The son of Abraham. Now Abraham had fathered Isaac." It is quite unusual for the *toledot* formula, "This is the family history of X," to be followed by a reference to X's father; it is usually followed by a reference to X's descendants. The retrospective reference to Abraham here and in 25:12 reminds the reader both of the drama surrounding Isaac's birth and of the promises that will find fulfillment through him.

20 This verse summarizes the story of Isaac's marriage to Rebekah and looks forward to Jacob's future journey to Paddan-Aram and his dealings with his uncle Laban (Gen 29–31). It is this forward glance that explains the otherwise unnecessary reference to Laban. Only here is Isaac's age at his marriage given. If the chronological details in the patriarchal story are to be taken literally, this would put Isaac's marriage some thirty-five years before Abraham's death, but see *Comment* on 24:62–67. Taken in conjunction with the other remark about Isaac's age in 25:26, this comment puts the pregnancy of Rebekah in a different light.

"Paddan-Aram" occurs only in Genesis (28:2, 5–7; 31:18; 33:18; 35:9,26; 46:15; 48:7). It is the homeland of the family of Bethuel, Rebekah, and Laban, somewhere in the northern Mesopotamia, probably in the vicinity of Harran (cf. 11:31). The meaning of Paddan is uncertain. It may be the equivalent of "field," as in Hos 12:13(12). Alternatively, it may be connected with Akk. *paddānu* "road" (cf. *AHW*, 807) and could be an alternative name for Harran.

"The Aramean." Why the text should so clearly emphasize the ethnic identity of Bethuel and Laban is uncertain, but this aspect of Israel's origin is echoed later (Deut 26:5).

21–26 The first episode in Jacob's life is antenatal and falls into three scenes:

v 21   Isaac's intercession
vv 22–23   Rebekah's pregnancy
vv 24–26   The birth of twins

21 "Isaac interceded to the LORD for his wife." Throughout Genesis, Isaac appears as a rather passive figure, liable to be imposed on by his father, his wife, his children, and foreigners. But here for the first time he is presented as taking an initiative by interceding for his wife. Elsewhere this term עתר involves a request

to remove some serious ill; it occurs most frequently in Exodus of Moses entreating God to send away the plagues (8:4, 5, 24, 25, 26 [8, 9, 28, 29, 30]). "עתר here designates the powerful pacifying influence of a man of God on God" (R. Albertz, *THWAT* 2:386).

"For she was childless." The initial barrenness of the matriarchs is a recurrent theme in Genesis; cf. *Comment* on 11:30.

"The LORD heeded his prayer, and Rebekah his wife conceived." The absence of any reference to time enhances the impression of Isaac the powerful intercessor. Like those of his father Abraham, his prayers for barren women are answered by God (cf. 15:2; 20:17; 21:1–2). Only later do we learn of Isaac's great persistence in prayer.

22–23 Isaac's prayer is answered by a multiple pregnancy, which, though a tribute to the efficacy of his prayer, is extremely painful for Rebekah. "The children" (number unspecified) "smashed themselves inside her." The verb רצץ "smash, crush" is most frequently used figuratively of the oppression of the poor. Literally, it is used to describe skulls being smashed (Judg 9:53; Ps 74:14) or reeds being broken (e.g., Isa 36:6). The use of such a term here vividly indicates the violence of the struggle within Rebekah's womb.

22 "If it is like this, why am I here?" The pregnancy is so painful that she wonders if there is any point going on living. After they had grown up, Rebekah had similar thoughts (27:46; cf. Job). "What a unique conflict we have here! A conflict of twins which rages even in the womb and so vehemently that their mother is driven to despair. 'Behold, how good and pleasant it is when brothers dwell in unity' a psalmist says, but to Jacob and Esau any room is too small when they are together. Their first battlefield is their mother's womb. How cruelly the sweet expectations of children, the greater after twenty years of hope and despair, are dashed for Isaac and Rebekah! As early as the pregnancy their parental happiness is threatened. 'What shall I do' Rebekah wonders in despair" (Fokkelman *Narrative Art*, 88).

"She went to consult the LORD." Elsewhere this involves consulting a prophet; cf. Exod 18:15; 1 Sam 9:9; 1 Kgs 22:8. Further details of this consultation are not given, since they are not relevant, but the prophetic message is given.

23 "Two nations are in your womb.
    Two peoples will be divided even as they come out of you.
    One people will be stronger than the other.
    The older will be a slave of the younger."

The oracle is cast in two pairs of lines. In typical poetic style, the second half of each couplet develops and intensifies the ideas in the first half.

Abraham and Sarah had been promised that many nations would be descended from them (17:4–6, 16), so the first line hardly says anything fresh. It is little more than an affirmation of the older promise and need not even imply a twin birth. But the second line, "Two peoples" (לאם is a term found only in poetry) "shall be divided even as they come out of you," does suggest at least twins. But again Rebekah must have wondered whether it was to be taken literally, for can newborn infants be described as "peoples"? So in what way should division from birth be understood?

The second couplet exhibits the same development from the general, "One people will be stronger than the other," to the more precise and definite, "The

older will be a slave of the younger." But again, by itself this is a perplexing oracle. If Rebekah has twins, how can one be older than the other? In the light of the rest of the story, its meaning is clear. It points forward to Jacob's domination of Esau, to Israel's subjugation of Edom. Their names may indeed, as Strus (*Nomen-Omen*, 60, 135) suggests, be alluded to in this cryptic saying. יעבד "be the slave of" not only rhymes with יעקב "Jacob" by having the same vowels but has three consonants in common too. And "younger" צעיר seems to be a play on "Seir" שעיר, an alternative name for Edom or Esau (e.g., Gen 32:4[3]; 33:14, 16). But to Rebekah this can have been far from apparent; she must have returned from the prophet little the wiser.

The term used here for "older" (רב *rab*) occurs also in Akkadian texts of the mid-second millennium B.C. from Nuzi, Alalah, Ugarit, and Assyria with the same meaning. Later texts use slightly different terminology, such as *aplu rabû* or *māru rabû*. So Selman suggests this is an indication of the antiquity of this text ("Comparative Customs," in *Essays*, 126).

24 At last the enigmatic prophetic saying is confirmed and clarified; והנה "there were indeed twins" draws attention to the family's viewpoint. What the prophet meant by two nations in her womb is now clear, and by implication the longer-range prediction of the older serving the younger is made the more credible.

25–26 The very manner of their birth seems to be an omen visibly underlining the prophetic oracle.

25 "Reddish." The adjective also describes David in 1 Sam 16:12; 17:42. Translation of color terms is notoriously difficult, so it is uncertain what color is intended and whether it describes the color of Esau's hair or his skin. However, there is undoubtedly a play on Esau's other name Edom (אדם) in the term "reddish" (אדמוני).

"Like a hairy coat." Here there is word-play with the term "Seir," the name of the territory of Edom, which contains the same root consonants (שער) as "hair" and in turn anticipates the word "Esau" (עשו). Esau's shaggy hairiness has often been compared to Enkidu, a wild uncivilized man in the Gilgamesh epic, whose "whole body is covered with hair" (GE 1.36). Vawter observes "Hairiness or shagginess seems to have been *eo ipso* a mark of incivility. . . . Similarly, there was a prejudice against a . . . redheaded person, which existed not only in the ancient Near Eastern world but well into the time of Western Christianity as well. Judas Iscariot was depicted in mediaeval art as a redhead! . . . In respect to Esau, therefore, the author's word-plays go beyond mere cleverness and insinuate a bias against him from the beginning" (288). Sarna, on the other hand, thinks a ruddy complexion is intended, which in Crete, Egypt, and Ugarit was associated with heroes.

"Esau" the name is unknown elsewhere in the ancient Orient, and its etymology is uncertain. Arabic *ġašiya* "covered," "hidden" has been suggested. Another less likely possibility is that the name is connected with Ousoos, a hunter in Phoenician mythology (Eusebius, *Praeparatio Evangelica* 1.10.9–10). Certainly the OT offers no explicit etymology but here simply associates his name with hairiness.

26 The name Jacob, on the other hand, is well known. It is usually regarded as a shortened form of יעקב־אל *ya' qob-el* "may El protect, reward" (the meaning of the verb is unsure) and is a typical Amorite name of the early second millennium. It is found in inscriptions from Chagar Bazar (1800 B.C.), Qatuna (c. 1700 B.C.), and occasionally in second-millennium Egyptian texts.

However, as usual, the Bible is not interested in a historic etymology but in the events associated with the birth that led the parents to choose this name. The baby emerged clutching Esau's heel (עָקֵב ʿāqēb) so he was called יַעֲקֹב "Jacob"— "he clutches the heel." The symbolism is everything. Here the second twin is seen trying desperately to catch up with the first. The struggle in the womb is obviously going to continue outside. The pattern for the rest of the story is set.

"Now Isaac was sixty years old when they were born." The birth of the first child was a most significant event in a man's life, so his age at the time is often recorded (5:3, 6, 9, 32; 11:26; 16:16; 21:5). It also shows, contrary to one's initial impression on reading 25:21, how long a period elapsed between Isaac's intercession and Rebekah's conception. It further implies that their joy outweighed all the forebodings evoked by the pregnancy and ominous delivery. Esau and Jacob were the answer to persistent prayer and the fruit of a harrowing pregnancy. Isaac and Rebekah's joy at the twins' safe arrival must have been correspondingly great.

27–28 But as the boys grow up, the different characters already suggested at birth begin to emerge. Esau, the rough and hairy child, becomes the great hunter, the man of the open spaces, whereas Jacob is the quiet stay-at-home. The word translated "quiet" (תָּם) is most problematic. Usually it means "perfect" and is a term of highest moral approbation (e.g., Job 1:1, 8; 2:3; cf. Gen 6:9). However, such a moral sense is inappropriate here, but it is not obvious in what way Jacob is perfect. Perhaps the sense is suggested by the cognate verb תָּמַם "to complete"; Jacob, unlike his outgoing activist brother, is a self-contained, detached personality complete in himself, hence "quiet."

"Who lived in tents" contrasts him with his wild hunting brother and may well suggest he would become a herdsman (cf. 4:20) like his father and grandfather (cf. 13:5).

28 "Isaac loved Esau for his hunting." Now another side of Isaac's character emerges. He is not only a passive, peaceable man of prayer but a gourmand who loves his food. And this exacerbates the tension between the rival brothers, the more so because Rebekah favors Jacob. The reason for her favoritism is not stated; it is left to our surmise. Was it his lifestyle, that he was easier to manipulate than his brother, that he was more often at home? Whatever her motives, the scene is now set for chap. 27, where Rebekah uses her husband's appetite and Jacob's tractability to acquire the blessing for the son she loves, yet thereby losing him. The brothers are already moving inexorably toward realizing the prophetic announcement of their division.

29–34 If the previous episode shows the division between the brothers deepening as predicted, this one shows how the younger starts to make a slave of the older, how Jacob the heel-catcher deserves his name.

29 "Jacob had made a stew." How, when, and why is not stated. Even its contents are not described. The significant thing is that the strong hunter came in "exhausted" (עָיֵף). Exhaustion is in the Near East more likely caused by exertion and thirst than by hunger (cf. Judg 8:4; Isa 29:8; Job 22:7). So what Esau most needed was a drink and a rest.

30 Certainly his remarks, "Please let me swallow some of the red stuff, this red stuff, because I am exhausted," do not suggest he is quite as weary as he professes. He does manage to say "please," to use high-flown language ("swallow"),

and then implicitly, if rather uncouthly, to praise the quality of the stew—"the red stew, this red stew." Surely this description suggests a rich meaty stew such as a hunting man like Esau would relish. In passing, it is explained that this is why Esau is also called Edom, for the word sounds almost like the word "red," אדם *ʾĕdōm*, the third play on the names of Esau in this opening section (cf. 25:23, 26).

31   Whereas Esau drools over the mouth-watering stew and babbles on, Jacob's reply is brusque. "Sell at once your firstborn's rights to me." Note the omission of "please," the use of "at once," and the emphatic position of "to me." The way Jacob states his demand suggests long premeditation and a ruthless exploitation of his brother's moment of weakness.

בכרה "firstborn's rights." The first son in the family was held in especial esteem in Israel; he was regarded as the first fruits of his father's strength (49:3) and dedicated to God (Exod 22:28[29]). He was in turn specially privileged during his lifetime (Gen 43:33) and when the inheritance was divided up. Deut 21:17 (like MAL B1) provides that the firstborn shall receive a double share, that is, twice as much as any other brother, of his father's property. Similar customs are known in other parts of the ancient Near East, but since it was not universal practice, we cannot be sure that it is presupposed here. However, whatever advantages Esau enjoyed as the firstborn he is now invited to sell for a bowl of stew. "Esau sold this portion and nothing else just as in Old Babylonia and in Nuzi inheritances are the object of buying and selling among brothers. Esau's rank and position are not affected by this transaction as chap. 27 shows quite clearly" (M. Tsevat, *TDOT* 2:126). It may also be significant that בכרה "rights of firstborn" is an anagram of ברכה "blessing," the subject of chaps. 26–27 and a key theme in Genesis. What Esau is prepared to forfeit here will pave the way to his greater loss, the loss of the blessing, in chap. 27.

32   Esau prattles on, showing he is far from being on the point of death and exhibiting a careless indifference to a privilege that the ancient world held dear: "Of what value to me are the rights of a firstborn?"

33–34   Jacob's curt three-word reply, "Swear/to me/at once," confirms that he is cold and calculating, determined to cash in on his brother's folly.

The chiastic structure of vv 33b–34a, "He sold to Jacob while Jacob gave to Esau," highlights the two-sided nature of the deal and draws attention to the inequity of the arrangement, "Esau sold—but Jacob gave." And what was it he gave? Not a rich meaty stew, that the word "red" back in v 30 suggested, but only a dish of lentils. With this last-minute revelation we should be stunned. Fancy trading all those treasured rights of inheritance for a mere bowl of lentil soup. We are left to admire Jacob's sharpness and wonder at Esau's folly. The four verbs, "he ate, drank, stood up, and went away," allow us a chance to reflect on his behavior. After his earlier loquaciousness, Esau's silence is eerie. Does he really care about his birthright, or is bitterness already making it impossible to talk to his brother? The final comment of the narrator, "So Esau treated the rights of the firstborn with contempt," is important, because explicit moral commentary is rare in the Bible. It emphasizes, as has already emerged in the dialogue, that Esau has treated with flippancy something of great worth. Though Jacob has been portrayed as heartlessly exploitive, the narrator finds it unnecessary to comment on that aspect here. The subsequent stories will show how Jacob had to pay for the enmity he had

stirred up. Here the most decisive aspect is mentioned. "By his irresponsible behavior toward the choice Jacob offered him, actually Esau despises himself and
also Yahweh; therefore he must change places with Jacob" (M. Görg, *TDOT* 2:63).

Explanation

This section serves as overture to the family history of Isaac. Some characters
are already familiar to the reader, Isaac, Rebekah, and Laban, but the two principal actors in this new stage of the drama, Esau and Jacob, have not been introduced
before. And what is said about them here, particularly in the prophetic oracle,
"The older will be a slave of the younger," will determine their whole career.

Chap. 24 introduced Rebekah, the dynamic bustling daughter of Bethuel. Energy and enthusiasm bubbled out of her as she willingly agreed to go with
Abraham's servant to the land of Canaan to marry Isaac. That same story showed
unambiguously how God controlled events and answered the servant's prayer, so
that immediately he found an even better bride for Isaac than he expected. And
Rebekah had left home with the blessing ringing in her ears, "May you, our sister,
become thousands of ten thousands" (24:60).

But as 25:21 resumes the story, we learn that Rebekah's situation has turned
out very differently; she is childless, and that, as chaps. 12–20 showed, is a miserable condition for any woman in ancient society, let alone one who has been
promised a multitude of children. For nearly twenty years she suffered until the
LORD heeded her husband's prayers and she conceived. But the happiness of
motherhood was clouded by the agonies of carrying twins, so that she wondered
if life was worth living.

Consulting a prophet, she is told that "two nations are in your womb." Though
this is not an unambiguous diagnosis that she has twins, it does suggest that her
offspring will survive and multiply sufficiently to become nations. In this way, the
ancient promises to Abraham are reaffirmed. Further, she is told that from birth
they will be divided, which not only suggests that they are twins but that they will
be quarreling from childhood. Then, finally, she is told that "the older will be the
slave of the younger," another enigmatic pronouncement in the context of a
multiple pregnancy.

But the birth clarifies the issues. Twins are indeed born, and the second emerges
trying to catch the heel of the first. The struggles inside her womb are all set to
carry on outside. Sadly, the conflict is aggravated by the parents' partiality. Isaac,
the passive man of prayer, is also shown to be a man of appetite, and this causes
him to favor his hunting son Esau, who brings him the game he enjoys. But
Rebekah, the maternal activist, prefers her quiet, reserved son, Jacob, who is set
to become a herdsman like his father and grandfather. So already the truth of
the prophetic oracle is beginning to be realized.

More evidence of its truth is shown by the red stew incident. Returning weary
from the hunt, Esau begs his brother for a portion of the red stew he has prepared. Brotherly affection would surely demand that Jacob freely meet Esau's
needs. But with callous calculation, Jacob insists that Esau exchange his firstborn's
inheritance rights for the stew, that he should surrender precious long-term goods
for the immediate appeasement of his hunger. Amazingly, Esau consents, and

Jacob acquires the firstborn's right of inheritance. Already the elder is becoming slave of the younger. But the seeds of deadly animosity between the brothers have been sown, and as they germinate and grow, the whole family will burst apart yet further fulfilling the prophetic prediction that "they will be divided even from your womb." The account of the bitter feud and its consequences will take up most of chaps. 27–33.

But the story of the conflict between Jacob and Esau does not end with Genesis. As their names and the oracle make apparent, Jacob and Esau are the forefathers of two nations, Israel and Edom, who were bitter rivals throughout the OT period. Edom's traditional home was south and east of the Dead Sea. When Israel wandered through the wilderness on the way to Canaan, they had to skirt the land of Edom because of their refusal to allow the Israelites to pass through their territory (Num 20:14–21). Throughout the monarchy period there was conflict between Edom and Israel. Sometimes Edom was incorporated into the Israelite empire (1 Sam 14:47; 2 Sam 8:14); sometimes it enjoyed independence and used every opportunity to assert itself against Israel (2 Kgs 8:20, 22). At the fall of Jerusalem, Edom sided with the Babylonians and helped cut off those Judeans trying to escape from the Babylonians. This unbrotherly action is recalled bitterly in the prophets (e.g., Ezek 25:12–14; Obad 10–14; Ps 137:7). It is, therefore, predicted that Edom will be destroyed once and for all and incorporated into the kingdom of Israel (e.g., Obad 18–21; Mal 1:4). That would represent the ultimate fulfillment of the prediction that "the older will be slave of the younger."

But the reverberations of this age-old conflict are not forgotten in the NT. As often, the book of Hebrews points to the patriarchal stories to draw points for the present. Its readers were probably Jewish Christians tempted to avoid persecution by reverting to Judaism. Like Esau, they were ready to swap long-term blessing for immediate relief, so Hebrews warns "See to it . . . that no one be immoral or irreligious like Esau, who sold his birthright for a single meal. For you know that afterward, when he desired to inherit the blessing, he was rejected, for he found no chance to repent, though he sought it with tears" (Heb 12:15–17).

Hebrews thus sees Esau as a type of the backslider or unbeliever. So does Paul in his use of the key verse in our section:

> "Two nations are in your womb . . .
> The older will be the slave of the younger."

As already noted, this verse is programmatic: it explains the whole Jacob and Esau story in much the same way that 12:1–3 illuminates the Abraham story. It is an announcement that, contrary to natural expectation, Esau the oldest will lose his rights to inheritance and blessing, which will be usurped by Jacob. For Paul, this is an example of the mystery of election. Why is it, he asks in Rom 9–11, that the Jews have failed to recognize Jesus as the Christ when they have all the spiritual resources enshrined in the Old Covenant. He begins his discussion by citing various examples from the OT where God's choice has nothing to do with human merit: "[W]hen Rebecca had conceived children . . . though they were not yet born and had done nothing either good or bad, in order that God's purpose

of election might continue, not because of works but because of his call, she was told, 'The elder will serve the younger'" (Rom 9:10–12).

Certainly, here Paul seems to have caught well the spirit of Genesis. There is no disguising the failures of the chosen line. Noah stumbles. Abraham goes astray more than once. Isaac and Rebekah are partisan. Jacob is at times positively obnoxious, and the author of Genesis does not disguise his disapproval of such conduct. Yet despite all their sinfulness, God's chosen are preserved and blessed. God's saving purpose is not thwarted by human weakness, though it may be delayed. God chooses the patriarchs not because they are particularly loveable characters but because of his declared intention that in them all the families of the earth should find blessing. So the patriarchs emerge from Scripture not as lily-white heroes but as real men of flesh and blood, red in tooth and claw. And with them and their failings everyone can identify.

> "Though justice be thy plea, consider this—
> That in the course of justice none of us
> Should see salvation." (*Merchant of Venice*, IV.i)

Portia might have been describing the situation of the patriarchs, but her words apply to all. And the fact that God was able to use men like Jacob to forward his purposes may shock us, but it should surely encourage us, too, for at times we fall as badly as he did. If God could use him, may he now graciously use us.

Isaac and the Philistines   (26:1–33)

Bibliography

See also *Bibliographies* on 12:10–20; 20:1–18; 21:1–21; 21:22–34.

Cornelius, I. "Gen 26 and Mari: The Dispute over Water and the Socio-Economic Way of Life of the Patriarchs." *JNSL* 12 (1984) 53–61. **Eichler, B. L.** "'Please say that you are my sister': Nuzi and Biblical Studies." (Heb.) *Shnaton* 3 (1978/79) 103–15. **Exum, J. C.,** and **Whedbee, J. W.** "Isaac, Samson, and Saul: Reflections on the Comic and Tragic Visions." *Semeia* 32 (1984) 5–40. **Gispen, W. H.** "A Blessed Son of Abraham." In *Von Kanaan bis Kerala: FS J. P. M. van der Ploeg,* ed. W. Delsman and J. Nelis. AOAT 211. Kevelaer: Butzon & Bercker, 1982. 123–29. **Görg, M.** "Die Begleitung des Abimelech von Gerar (Gen 26:26)." *BN* 35 (1986) 21–25. **Luke, K.** "Esau's Marriage." *IndTS* 25 (1988) 171–90. **Martin-Achard, R.** "Remarques sur Gen 26." *ZAW* 100 Sup (1988) 22–46. **Miscall, P. D.** "Literary Unity in OT Narrative." *Semeia* 15 (1979) 27–44. **Nicol, G. G.** "Studies in the Interpretation of Gen 26:1–33." Diss., Oxford, 1987. **Safren, J. D.** "Ahuzzath and the Pact of Beer-Sheba." *ZAW* 101 (1989) 184–98. **Schmitt, G.** "Zu Gen 26:1–14." *ZAW* 85 (1973) 143–56. **Zwickel, W.** "Rehobot-Nahar." *BN* 29 (1985) 28–34.

Translation

¹ *There was another famine in the land besides the first famine that occurred in the days of Abraham. So Isaac went down to Gerar to Abimelek,*ᵃ *the king of the Philistines.* ² *Then the LORD appeared*ᵃ *to him and said, "Do not go down*ᵇ *to Egypt. Camp in the country which I shall tell you.* ³ *Settle in this country, so that*ᵃ *I may be with you and bless you. For it is to you and your descendants*ᵇ *that I shall give* ᶜ*all these*ᵈ *lands,*ᶜ *and I shall confirm the oath which I swore to your father Abraham.* ⁴ *I shall multiply your descendants as the stars of heaven, and I shall give to your descendants* ᵃ*all these lands,*ᵃ *and in your descendants all the nations of the earth shall find blessing.* ⁵ *This is because Abraham*ᵃ *obeyed me, kept my instructions, commandments, statutes, and my laws."*

⁶ *So Isaac lived in Gerar.*

⁷ *Then the men of the place asked about his wife. So he said, "She is my sister," because he was afraid to say "*ᵃ*My wife, lest the men of the place kill*ᵇ *me because of Rebekah for she is beautiful to look at."*

⁸ *When he had spent a long time there, Abimelek, king of the Philistines, looked*ᵃ *through a window and saw*ᵇ *Isaac playing*ᶜ *with his wife Rebekah!* ⁹ *So Abimelek summoned Isaac and said, "So then*ᵃ *she really is your wife. Why did you say, 'She is my sister'?" Isaac said to him, "Because I thought that I might die because of her."* ¹⁰ *Abimelek replied, "What*ᵃ *have you done to us? Almost any of the people* ᵇ*could have lain*ᵇ *with your wife and brought*ᶜ *great guilt upon us."* ¹¹ *Then Abimelek issued*ᵃ *an order to all the*ᵇ *people. "Anyone who touches this man and his wife shall certainly*ᶜ *be put*ᵈ *to death."*

¹² *Isaac sowed seed in that land that year, and he harvested a hundredfold,*ᵃ *and the LORD blessed him.* ¹³ *The man prospered, and* ᵃ*he went on prospering*ᵃ *until he was exceedingly well off.* ¹⁴ *He acquired flocks and herds and many slaves, so that the Philistines were jealous*ᵃ *of him.* ¹⁵ ᵃ*All the wells which the servants of his father had dug in Abraham's times the Philistines had sealed*ᵇ *and filled them with earth.*ᵃ ¹⁶ *So Abimelek said to Isaac, "Leave us for you have become much too powerful for us."* ¹⁷ *Then Isaac went from there, made his encampment*ᵃ *in the valley of Gerar, and dwelt there.*

¹⁸ *Then Isaac had redug*ᵃ *the wells of water which* ᵇ*had been dug*ᵇ ᶜ*in Abraham's time*ᶜ *and the Philistines had sealed after Abraham's death. He had called them by the same names that his father had.* ¹⁹ *Then Isaac's servants dug in the valley*ᵃ *and found there a spring of flowing water.* ²⁰ *Then the shepherds of Gerar disputed*ᵃ *with Isaac's shepherds saying, "The water belongs to us."*ᵇ *So the well was called "Quarrel" because they quarreled*ᶜ *with him.* ²¹ ᵃ*Then they dug another well and disputed over that as well, so it was called, "Hostility."* ²² *Then he moved*ᵃ *from there and dug another well, and they did not dispute about that. So he called its name "Open spaces" and said, "because now the LORD has made space for us and we shall be fruitful in the land."*

²³ *He went up*ᵃ *from there to Beersheba.* ²⁴ *In that night the LORD appeared to him and said to him, "I am the God of Abraham your father. Do not be afraid,*ᵃ *for I am with you and I shall bless you and multiply your descendants for the sake of my servant Abraham."* ²⁵ *He then built an altar there and called on the name of the LORD. He pitched*ᵃ *his tent there, and Isaac's servants dug*ᵇ *a well there.*

²⁶ ᵃ*Then Abimelek went from Gerar to him,*ᵃ *and also Ahuzzat his police chief and Phicol the commander of his army.* ²⁷ *Isaac said to them, "Why*ᵃ *have you come to me,* ᵇ*since you hate me and have expelled*ᶜ *me from being with you?"*ᵇ ²⁸ *They said, "We have seen ourselves*ᵃ *that the LORD is with you, so we said 'Let there be*ᵇ *an oath between*ᶜ *us,*

between ^dus and you, so that^e we may make a treaty with you. ²⁹(Promise)^a that you will not do^b evil to us, just as we have not touched^c you, as we have only done good to you and sent you away in peace. Blessed are you now by^d the LORD."

³⁰So he made a feast for them, and they ate and drank. ³¹In the morning they arose,^a and each swore to each other. Isaac accompanied them, and they went away from him peacefully.

³²The same^a day Isaac's servants came and told^b him about the well which they had dug. They said to him,^c "We have found water." ³³So he called it "Oath," so the name of that city is Beersheba till this day.

Notes

1.a. Codex Leningrad, which *BHS* reproduces, has a dagesh in מ of Abimelek, which is unusual. E. A. Knauf (*BN* 10 [1979] 23–35) suggests it is to distinguish this Abimelek from the earlier one; cf. 20:2–4.

2.a. Cf. n. 12:7.a.

2.b. 2 masc sg impf ירד.

3.a. Weak waw + impf following impv or juss has final force. Cf. n. 12:2.a.; Joüon, 116b; Lambdin, 119.

3.b. Placing indirect obj, "you and your descendants," before verb may be emphatic (GKC, 142g; cf. *EWAS*, 38–39, 43–44).

3.c-c. G has "all this land."

3.d. SamPent has more usual spelling אלה instead of MT אל.

4.a-a. G, SamPent as in v 3; cf. nn. 3.c-c., 3.d.

5.a. G, SamPent add "your father."

7.a. G, SamPent add "She is."

7.b. 3 masc pl impf הרג + 1 sg suffix.

8.a. Cf. n. 19:28.a.

8.b. והנה shows what is seen through Abimelek's eyes and suggests his surprise (*SBH*, 95).

8.c. Cf. n. 21:9.a.

9.a. On the translation of אך "so then," cf. N. H. Snaith, *VT* 14 (1964) 225, who argues that wherever the term is used there is "an idea of contrariness, exception, restriction, even contradiction," in this instance "Contrary to what you have said, it is plain that she is your wife." Cf. *SBH*, 177.

10.a. Note enclitic ואת making the question more shocked (cf. n. 3:13.a.).

10.b-b. Use of pf to express possible actions in the past (GKC, 106p; WOC, 494).

10.c. Cf. n. 20:9.c.

11.a. Cf. n. 2:16.a.

11.b. G, SamPent read "his people."

11.c. Inf abs qal מות.

11.d. 3 masc sg impf hoph מות.

12.a. G, S read שערים "barley."

13.a-a. Note use of inf abs הלך + verbal adjective גדל (adjective usual with stative verbs, Joüon, 123s). "The idea of long *continuance* is very frequently expressed by the verb הלך *to go*, along with its infinitive absolute. . . . The action itself is added in a second infinitive absolute or sometimes in a participle or verbal adjective" (GKC, 113u).

14.a. On the omission of dagesh from piel form קנא, see GKC, 52d.

15.a-a. On this type of clause, see *SBH*, 92–93; *EWAS*, 93–97.

15.b. 3 masc pl pf piel סתם + 3 masc pl suffix. Masc suffix refers to wells (f). For possible reasons, see GKC, 60h, 135o; WOC, 302.

17.a. Waw consec + 3 masc sg impf חנה.

18.a. On use of שוב + another verb (here "dig") = "do . . . again," see GKC, 120d; Lambdin, 238. On the pluperfect sense "*had* redug," see *Comment;* Jacob, 551–52; cf. 8:1.

18.b-b. Lit. "they dug." On use of 3 masc pl "they" for indefinite personal subj "one," cf. GKC, 144f. For pluperfect "had dug," cf. GKC, 111q.

18.c. For "in days of Abraham," SamPent, Vg, S read "servants of Abraham," so that the whole clause reads "which the servants of Abraham had dug," a smoother but not necessarily superior reading. G combines both readings: "which the servants of his father dug in his father's time."

19.a. G adds "of Gerar."

20.a. Waw consec + 3 masc pl impf ריב.

20.b. "To us" precedes the subj "water" in Heb., probably emphasizing their claim to ownership (GKC, 141m; cf. *EWAS*, 14).

20.c. 3 masc pl pf hithp עשׁק.

21.a. G adds, as in v 22, "Having moved from there."

22.a. Cf. n. 12:8.a.

23.a. Cf. n. 13:1.a.

24.a. Cf. n. 15:1.b.

25.a. Cf. n. 12:8.c.

25.b. Waw consec + 3 masc pl impf כרה.

26.a-a. Episode-initial circumstantial clause; see *SBH*, 79.

27.a. On difference between מדוע and more usual למה, see J. Barr, *JTS* 36 (1985) 1–33. Here מדוע may be prompted by use with the verb בוא "come" (Barr, 25–27).

27.b-b. Here linked circumstantial clauses used to introduce an antithesis to original question, "Why have you come?" (GKC, 142d; *SBH*, 90).

27.c. Waw consec + 2 masc pl impf piel שלח + 1 sg suffix.

28.a. Inf abs of ראה. On form, see GKC, 75n. Used here to stress "that the writer or speaker has especially intense interest in . . . what he expressed by the verbal form . . ."; so this clause should be translated "something like 'we tell you, we have seen'" (*EWAS*, 88; cf. 31:30; 37:8, 10).

28.b. Cf. n. 13:8.a.

28.c. Note בינות + suffixes means "between, among" when more than one party within a group. "Us" in first instance = Isaac + Abimelek, etc.

28.d. But בין + suffixes means "between" when one party is involved, so "us" in second case = Abimelek, and "you" = Isaac (GKC, 103p¹; Joüon, 103n).

28.e. Cf. n. 26:3.a.

29.a. אם often introduces an oath (GKC, 149c).

29.b. On pointing, cf. GKC, 75hh.

29.c. On pointing, cf. GKC, 65h.

29.d. Lit. "blessed of the LORD." On the use of the constr state to express agency, see Joüon, 121p.

31.a. Lit. "they acted early" (cf. n. 19:27.a).

32.a. Lit. "that day" with the meaning "the same day" (Joüon, 143j).

32.b. Waw consec + 3 masc pl impf hiph נגד.

32.c. G apparently read לא "not" instead of לו "to him," i.e., "We have not found water."

Form/Structure/Setting

The limits of this unit are clearly defined. V 1, "There was another famine . . . ," clearly introduces a fresh section with its back reference to the earlier famine described in 12:10. It ends with the naming of Beersheba in v 33 (cf. 21:31–32). Vv 34–35 with their comment on Esau's marriages introduce a topic quite foreign to the rest of chap. 26 and indeed form part of the frame (cf. 27:46–28:9) of Jacob's deception of Isaac in chap. 27.

26:1–33 falls into seven episodes:

vv 1–6	Divine promises to Isaac in Gerar
vv 7–11	Isaac and Abimelek in Gerar
vv 12–17	Isaac blessed in Gerar and therefore expelled by Abimelek
vv 18–22	Isaac digs wells in the valley of Gerar
vv 23–25	Divine promises in Beersheba

vv 26–31   Isaac and Abimelek make peace in Beersheba
vv 32–33   Isaac digs well at Beersheba

It may be noted how the episodes set in Beersheba echo the earlier ones in Gerar.

vv 1–6	//	vv 23–25	Promises
vv 7–11, 12–17	//	vv 26–31	Isaac and Abimelek
vv 18–22	//	vv 32–33	Wells

The promise in v 24 briefly sums up the fuller promise in vv 2–5. Similarly, the negotiations between Isaac and Abimelek in Beersheba in vv 26–31 make frequent and explicit allusion to their earlier dealings in Gerar (cf. v 27 with v 16; v 28 with vv 3, 12; v 29 with vv 10–12). And the parallel between the well-digging at Beersheba (vv 32–33) and in the valley of Gerar (vv 18–22) is also obvious. Though some earlier scholars (cf. Gunkel, Noth [*History of Pentateuchal Traditions,* 104]) regard this chapter as a collection of originally independent traditions, more recently there has been a greater willingness to acknowledge the coherence of the material. Van Seters (*Abraham in History*) argued that within chap. 26 each episode presupposed what preceded it (e.g., vv 12–16 presuppose vv 1–11; vv 17–22 presuppose v 16, whereas vv 26–31 presuppose vv 7–17). His argument is partially accepted by Westermann and Coats, though Westermann thinks the present unity is compiled from an account of Isaac's dealings with Abimelek (vv 12–17, 26–31) with details about wells and journeys. Coats, on the other hand, thinks a tale of a threat to the ancestress in vv 1–17 has been combined with a well itinerary in vv 17–33. Blum (*Die Komposition*) and Nicol ("Studies in the Interpretation") much more confidently affirm the coherence of all the material in vv 1–33. Blum describes it as an "extraordinarily tightly composed narrative unity" (302). He points to the way the second half of the chapter makes frequent reference to remarks in the first. He sees two themes uniting the material in this chapter, Isaac's relations with the Philistines and the LORD's blessing of Isaac. Nicol similarly points out that "each unit demands a certain amount of tacit knowledge which must be derived from the previous unit(s)" (63), that there is no evidence that any of the episodes in chap. 26 ever existed independently as oral stories (23), and that all the material in vv 1–33 relates coherently to the promises made to Abraham, of land, descendants, and blessing to the nations. The promise to the nations is, according to Nicol, the most important aspect of the promises as far as this chapter is concerned (18–30). The chapter relates how the blessing of Isaac is at first seen as a threat by the Philistines so they expel him (v 16), but later, acknowledging its God-given origin, they return to Isaac and thereby enjoy a share of it (vv 26–32).

But the biggest problem posed by this chapter is not its inner coherence but its relationship to the surrounding material. On first sight, 26:1–33 looks quite out of place in the cycle of Jacob and Esau stories, which began in 25:20–34 and immediately resumes in 26:34. Though the birth and early years of Jacob and Esau have been recounted in the previous chapter, there is no sign of them in 26:1–33. How could the Philistines have failed to realize that Rebekah was married if she was accompanied by twin boys of whatever age? "The whole passage

(26:1–33) proceeds as if Isaac were unencumbered by the presence of children, had not yet received Yahweh's blessing, and possessed little personal wealth." So Nicol argues that this chapter relates to "events in Isaac's life prior to the birth of his sons" (Nicol, "Studies in the Interpretation," 15). While suspending judgment about where this narrative fits chronologically in Isaac's biography, we must explore further its position within the Jacob cycle. Is there any literary logic to its being placed here in that cycle, rather than right at the beginning? Or must we concur with Skinner (355) that it is "a misplaced appendix to the history of Abraham"?

It is now widely agreed, following the work of Fishbane (*JTS* 26 [1975] 15–38) and Fokkelmann (*Narrative Art*), that the entire Jacob cycle is cast roughly palistrophically; it begins with strife between the twins, leading to Jacob leaving home and living for twenty years in Syria, and then to his return and eventual reconciliation with Esau. (For fuller discussion, see *Form/Structure/Setting* on 25:19–35:29.) However, two large blocks of material, chaps. 26 and 34 (the rape of Dinah), on first sight have nothing to do with this palistrophic arrangement. It may also be noted that the Joseph story (chaps. 37–50) shortly after it begins has a chapter, 38, devoted to a topic (Judah and Tamar) apparently unconnected with the main theme. And when the concluding chapters of the Abraham cycle are examined carefully, chap. 24 with its account of the betrothal of Rebekah stands out; on chronological grounds at least, chap. 24 would be placed better after 25:1–6 instead of before it. So the problem of chap. 26 is by no means an isolated one within the book. There are other passages that a modern editor might have been tempted to place elsewhere. But we must inquire why the ancient editor chose to put chap. 26 at this point.

Fishbane's observation that chap. 26 balances chap. 34 in the Jacob cycle is helpful. "Without chapter 26, Gen 25 and 27 would be more harmoniously joined. . . . In a parallel manner Gen 34 interrupts Gen 33 and 35.

"The symmetry between Genesis 26 and 34, together with their parallel functions as interludes, thus preclude any assumption of a haphazard editorial arrangement. Moreover, they are linked to each other and to their respective contexts by the common themes of deception and strife. The first section of chapter 26, in which Isaac deceives Abimelekh with regard to Rebekkah (v. 7), involves a case of strife wherein a wife is called a 'sister' (ʾahot) and there is fear of intercourse (stem: *shakhav*) with a member of an uncircumcised ethnic group. In its second section, in which Isaac charges the Philistines with deception (v. 27), there is a case of strife among the shepherds (v. 20) as well as an issue of covenantal malfeasance in which the treaty partners are called 'brothers' (ʾahim). In a parallel way, Genesis 34 also reports an event involving deception (*mirmah*, v. 34; cf. 27:35; and 29:25)—but now because of an actual case of intercourse (stem: *shakhav*) between the 'uncircumcised' Schechem ben Hamor and Dinah, the sister (ʾahot) of Simeon and Levi. The deception also involves covenantal malfeasance (v. 10) and considerable strife" (Fishbane, *Text and Texture*, 47).

Rendsburg (*Redaction of Genesis*, 58) has underlined Fishbane's observations by pointing to a number of words or roots both chapters have in common: hiphil of רבה "multiply" (26:4; 34:12); הרג "kill" (26:7; 34:25–26); מקנה "flock" (26:14; 34:5, 23); רחב in "make space, Rehobot" (26:22); cf. רחבת "expanse" (34:21); and שלם "peace, peaceful" (26:29, 31; 34:21). Thus two chapters that at first apparently

have little to do with the main story line of the Jacob cycle can be seen on closer study to be closely related to each other in terminology and theme; both discuss the patriarchs' relations with the indigenous inhabitants of Canaan. We shall also argue below that they serve to enhance the telling of the main plot of the Jacob cycle.

However, this chapter also serves to link the Jacob cycle with the Abraham cycle. It contains eight explicit references to him (26:1, 3, 5, 15, 18[2x], 24[2x]) compared with fifteen in all of chaps. 27–50. But besides this explicit recall of the Abraham story, topics covered in chap. 26 parallel those early in the Abraham cycle as well as some later on. Above (p. 173) it was observed that the sequence of material in 25:19–34 paralleled 11:27–12:9. This continues in chap. 26.

26:1–11	//	12:10–20	Famine and the wife/sister
26:12–22	//	13:2–10	Wealth prompts quarrels between patriarch's herdsmen and others
26:23	//	13:11–12	Separation
26:24	//	13:14–17	Divine promise of descendants
26:25	//	13:18	Altar built, patriarch encamps
26:26–31	//	chap. 14	Good relations established with foreigners
26:29	//	14:19–20	Patriarch blessed by foreign king

Taken in conjunction with the parallels between 11:27–12:9 and 25:19–34, this table suggests that the position of chap. 26 is not so capricious as appeared at first. Rather, a conscious effort is being made to compare the career of Isaac with that of his father Abraham.

Other parallels emerge toward the close of the Abraham cycle, which also records incidents that involve Abimelek, king of Gerar, so making the parallels even more obvious.

26:1–11	//	20:1–18	The wife/sister
26:15–21	//	21:25	Disputes about wells
26:26	//	21:22	Abimelek and Phicol
26:28	//	21:22	"The LORD has been with you"
26:28	//	21:23	Let there be an oath
26:30–31	//	21:24–31	Treaty made
26:32–33	//	21:31	Well of Beersheba named

It is noteworthy that it is precisely the material that does not mention Abraham's children, Ishmael and Isaac, that parallels 26:1–33 most closely. Similarly, most of the Jacob cycle concerns the deeds of Isaac's sons, Jacob and Esau, but here there is no mention of them, only of their parents, Isaac and Rebekah, and foreigners. The parallels with the Abraham story thus show that though the arrangement of material in Gen 25–26 may well be unchronological at points, chap. 26 at least is hardly misplaced. Indeed, it serves a most important function, locking together the Abraham and Jacob cycles and highlighting the parallels between Abraham and his son. Its position and content invite the reader to reflect on the similarities and differences between the careers of Abraham and of Isaac.

Within the Jacob cycle, it has an equally important role. After the turbulent beginning to the story, with Jacob and Esau wrestling in their mother's womb

and Jacob seizing the first opportunity to obtain his brother's rights, this chapter presents us with an interlude. We see Isaac as a timid, peace-loving man who avoids conflict with his neighbors wherever possible, such a contrast to his contentious sons, who are forever squabbling. This chapter therefore serves to heighten our appreciation of the unnaturalness of the intrafamilial strife that is about to tear apart Isaac's family in the following chapter. Yet Isaac receives the promises (26:2–5) without fighting for them. He is pushed around by the Philistines (26:12–21), yet at the end they come to him asking for a treaty (26:26–32). If Isaac could achieve so much without manipulating people, why do Jacob and Rebekah have to resort to the tactics about to be described. Chap. 26 also underlines what is at issue in Jacob's deceitful acquisition of Isaac's blessing. Here we are reminded of Isaac's great wealth, which both the narrator and the pagan actors within the story ascribe to the LORD (26:12, 28–29). If the source of blessing was obvious to foreigners, how much more so was it to Jacob and Esau. No wonder they fought with such ferocity to make it their own.

Source critics generally ascribe chap. 26 to J because of the unmistakably J phraseology. For example, even Abimelek refers to the deity as the LORD. However, its relationship to other parts of J, especially 12:10–20, has been widely discussed; it has often been maintained that 26:1–11 is the earliest of the three wife-sister accounts (see *Form/Structure/Setting* on 12:10–20). Recently though, following the observations of Van Seters (*Abraham in History*) of the dependence of 26:1–11 on previous passages in the book, it is now recognized that this chapter represents a late phase in the composition of J (cf. Westermann; Coats; Martin-Achard, *ZAW* 100 Sup [1988] 22–46). Blum (*Die Komposition*) suggests on the basis of 26:5 that the promises reflect deuteronomistic additions to an earlier story, which may date from the period of the monarchy. However, the supposedly deuteronomic phraseology actually finds closer parallels with priestly texts in the Pentateuch (see *Comment*). Westermann and Coats seem inclined to date the basic material earlier. But there are no very cogent arguments in any direction. I shall be content to assume the story comes from J, the principal editor of Genesis.

Comment

1–6 This first episode in the account of Isaac's dealings with the Philistines describes how he came to live among them and records the promises made to him. It is these promises that secretly determine the relationship between Isaac and Abimelek, so they are set out right at the beginning. The wording of the promises here clearly echoes 22:16–18, and the double reference to Abraham (26:1, 5) invites comparison between the careers of father and son.

1 "The first famine" (see 12:10). For the first famine of Genesis, see 41:54–42:3. On the name "Abimelek" and "Gerar," cf. *Comment* on 20:1–2. His territory is called "the land of the Philistines" in 21:32, 23, but here he is called "king of the Philistines." K. A. Kitchen (*POTT*, 56) observes that the description of the Philistines in Genesis does not fit in with what we know of them from extrabiblical sources (the real Philistines did not arrive in Canaan till about 1200 B.C.) nor with their descriptions in Judges and Samuel. "Those in Genesis live around Gerar, and under a king, not in the 'pentapolis' (i.e., Gath, Gaza, Ashkelon, Ashdod,

Ekron) under 'lords' (*sĕrānîm*); they are relatively peaceable, not forever waging wars, despite having an army commander. It is, therefore, more prudent to compare the Philistines of Abraham and Isaac with such people as the Caphtorim of Deut 2:23, and to view the term itself as a thirteenth- to twelfth-century term used of an earlier Aegean group such as the Caphtorim by the narrator." There is ample archeological evidence of Aegean contact with the Levant as early as the third millennium B.C. (E. M. Yamauchi, *Greece and Babylon: Early Contacts between the Aegean and the Near East* [Grand Rapids: Baker, 1967] 26–42), which makes Kitchen's position plausible.

Within the context of Genesis, the reference to the earlier famine invites comparison to Abraham's actions in similar circumstances. Will Isaac, like his father, go down to Egypt? Will he attempt to pass off his wife as his sister? Thus the very opening of this chapter raises the tension and suggests the anxieties that must have been aroused in Isaac's mind by the famine.

2–5 These verses express the first promise made directly to Isaac, but they are replete with echoes of chap. 22, which Isaac may be presumed to have heard.

2 First Isaac is told not to go to Egypt; there is no simple repetition of Abraham's experience. Rather, he is to "Camp in the country which I shall tell you." Here the first and last commands to Abraham are alluded to: "Go . . . to *the country* that I shall show you" (12:1); "Go . . . to the district *which I shall tell you*" (22:2). These allusions make it clear that even if Isaac is not to walk in his father's footsteps geographically, he must follow him spiritually.

"Camp in the country which I shall tell you." Is the country Canaan or Gerar? The majority of commentators assume that Gerar is meant, as v 3 makes plain. However, Nicol ("Studies in the Interpretation," 122) suggests that a contrast is being drawn between vv 2 and 3. He understands v 2 "camp" (שׁכן) to mean " live permanently in the land of Beersheba," which is within Canaan, whereas v 3 means "settle (גור) as a temporary immigrant in Gerar." גור is used in this sense of Abraham's residence in Egypt in 12:10. However, though BDB, 1014–15, suggests שׁכן "camp" means "dwell permanently," the term does not by itself indicate the duration of the dwelling (so A. R. Hulst, *THWAT* 2:906). Elsewhere in the Pentateuch, it almost always denotes dwelling in a tent (Gen 9:27; 14:13; 16:12; 25:18; 35:22), especially of God's dwelling in the tabernacle (משׁכן; e.g., Exod 25:8; 29:45–46; 40:35). It seems also to be a poetic synonym for "dwell" (e.g., Deut 33:12).

3 "So that I may be with you." Though Abimelek observed to Abraham that "God is with you" (21:22; cf. 26:28), this is the first time that the LORD himself makes such a promise, but it is repeated on several occasions to Jacob (28:15; 31:3; 46:4). God's presence is a guarantee of protection and success (cf. 39:2). "Bless you" (cf. 12:2; 22:17; 26:24; 27:7). "For it is to you and your descendants that I shall give all these lands." This formulation is novel. Only once before in 17:8 has the land been promised to *you* and your descendants. Hitherto, the promise has usually been that Abraham's descendants will be given the land. The word order in which the indirect object "you and your descendants" comes before the verb may make his promise especially emphatic. Certainly "all these lands" extends the promise beyond the mere land of Canaan; apparently even countries surrounding Canaan, such as the land of the Philistines, will be given to Isaac and his descendants. Furthermore, the motivation for such divine bounty is fresh:

"I shall confirm my oath which I swore to your father Abraham." Only here does God speak of confirming an "oath" as opposed to a "covenant" (17:7, 19, 21). The oath is that referred to in 22:16 (cf. 24:7), as is shown by the multiple quotations from 22:16–18, the only divine oath in Gen 12–25.

4 This verse virtually quotes 22:17–18a, replacing "that you may possess the gate of your enemies" with "I shall give to your descendants all these lands" (cf. 26:3), perhaps a less bellicose formulation to suit the more pacific Isaac.

5 This verse expands 22:18b, "because you have obeyed me." The additions, "kept my instructions, commandments, statutes, and my laws," reinforce and underline the extent and thoroughness of Abraham's obedience. Though often said to be a typically deuteronomic phrase, in fact, "keep my instruction" occurs only once in Deuteronomy (Deut 11:1) but much more frequently in priestly texts in Leviticus and Numbers. Similarly, "keep my commandments," "keep my statutes," and "keep my laws" are frequent phrases in priestly texts but less typical of Deuteronomy, which never speaks of laws in the plural. Presumably, this text has been ascribed to deuteronomistic editing because it strings together terms, but this is more a feature of rhetorical style than authorship.

It is striking that despite the clear quotation of Gen 22:16–18 here, the merit Isaac inherits is not his own obedience on that occasion but his father's. His own willingness to be sacrificed is not mentioned, only his father's readiness to offer him.

6 "So Isaac lived in Gerar" shows Isaac's obedience. But his presence in Gerar becomes the occasion of his error.

7–11 These verses invite close comparison with the earlier episodes, 12:10–20; 20:1–18, which are presupposed here. Now Isaac is about to mislead his foreign hosts in much the same way that Abraham did by saying that his wife is merely his sister.

7 The brevity of the narrative presupposes knowledge of the earlier accounts. Here the narrative focuses on Isaac's fears. As Abraham before him, he is afraid that he will die because of his wife's beauty; in 24:16 she was described as "very beautiful." This comment does not necessarily show that at this time Rebekah was still childless, though the parallels may suggest this; rather the fact that they could live a long time in Gerar without anyone realizing that they were man and wife indicates that this episode precedes the birth of Esau and Jacob. "The men of the place," as opposed to the men of Gerar or the Philistines, may suggest Isaac's suspicions about them; morally they are an unknown quantity in his eyes, and he has forgotten the promise, "settle in this country . . . so that I may be with you" (v 3).

8 "A long time." That Isaac and Rebekah enjoyed a long unmolested stay in Gerar shows that his fears were unfounded. "Through a window" is too vague to be sure what is meant. Gunkel surmises that the king looked through his palace window across the street through Isaac's window. Dillmann believes that they were in the palace garden. That he saw them "playing" (מְצַחֵק *měṣaḥēq*), clearly a euphemism for intimacy only proper between spouses, is what mattered. Note, too, the play on Isaac's name (cf. 17:17; 18:12–13; 21:9).

9–10 The phraseology of Abimelek's angry interrogation ("summoned") echoes earlier similar scenes in chaps. 3, 4, 12, and 20 (3:9; 12:18; 20:9). "What have

you done to us" (3:13; 4:10; 12:18; 20:9) shows that right lies on Abimelek's side, not Isaac's.

As on the previous occasion, Abimelek shows that he is a God-fearing man who eschews sin. "Any of the people could have lain with your wife and brought great guilt upon us" (cf. 20:9). אשם "great guilt" is rarely used in the abstract as here; most frequently it denotes the guilt offering (cf. Lev 5:15–25 [6:7]), one of the most costly sacrifices demanded for serious sins such as adultery (Lev 19:21–22). Isaac's behavior, Abimelek argues, far from bringing divine blessing on the nations (cf. 26:4), has actually brought him and his people into a most dangerous situation.

11 So Abimelek issues a royal decree under which anyone who molests Isaac or his wife will be subject to the death penalty. For the legal terminology used here, cf. Exod 19:21; 21:12, 15, 17; Lev 20:2, 9–13. So all Isaac's fears for his own life (vv 7, 9) are shown to be without foundation. As he promised, the LORD is with Isaac and is blessing him.

12–17 God's blessing of Isaac is also demonstrated by his material prosperity, but whereas in the previous episode Isaac's folly leads to royal protection, here his affluence prompts deportation.

12 Only here is any one of the patriarchs said to have sown and harvested crops, though it is quite common for bedouin to do this in the Near East. It confirms that the LORD is indeed looking after Isaac; he did not need to enter Egypt to escape the famine (v 1). His hundredfold yield, the best to be expected in Palestine (cf. Matt 13:8), was another sign of divine blessing.

"The LORD blessed him." Though there have been many promises of divine blessing in Genesis, this is only the third time the narrator has noted that the blessing has become a reality (cf. 24:1; 25:11), thus fulfilling the promise to Isaac in 26:3, anticipating Abimelek's recognition of God's blessing on Isaac (26:29), and anticipating the great theme of chap. 27.

13–14 Further proof of divine blessing and presence is the multiplication of Isaac's flocks and herds (cf. 13:2–7; 30:25–43). But as Abraham experienced before and Jacob afterwards, this leads to tension and animosity.

"Were jealous" (cf. 30:1; 37:11).

15–16 Abraham's wells had been seized, but when he protested, Abimelek said he was totally unaware of the problem and returned them. Here the more passive Isaac apparently says nothing, despite the treaty made by his father, and eventually Abimelek expels him merely because "you have become much too powerful for us," a term used only here and in Exod 1:7, 20 of the Israelites in Egypt. The Egyptian Pharaoh would later say, "Get away from me," just as Abimelek said to Isaac.

17 "Made his encampment," apart from 33:18, elsewhere in the Pentateuch always refers to the Israelites' camping in the wilderness (e.g., Exod 14:2; 19:2; Num 33:5–49). Like Abraham's before him, Isaac's life foreshadows the experiences of his descendants. (Cf. *Comment* and *Explanation* on chaps. 12–13.)

18–22 The next episode, after an introduction looking back to vv 12–17, falls into three brief scenes (vv 19–20, 21, 22), each concerning a dispute about a well. The first two Isaac is forced to give up, but the third he can retain. The OT often casts stories in three scenes (J. Licht, *Storytelling in the Bible*, 51–74).

18 As Jacob argues, this section appears to be a flashback to the previous episode before Isaac was expelled from Gerar, hence the translation "*had* redug." The fact that "he had called them by the same names that his father had" underlines the injustice of his expulsion, for according to 21:23–33, the name of one of the wells commemorated a treaty with Abimelek, in which he recognized the right of Abraham and his descendants to use the well.

19–20 However, Isaac's departure from Gerar did not end his harassment. When his servants dug a well, the Gerarites claimed it. "So the well was called 'Quarrel.'" Naming a water source after an unhappy incident that occurred in its vicinity is also a feature of the wilderness wanderings. Three watering holes between the Red Sea and Sinai are named in Exodus (15:22–27; 17:1–7).

22 It is quite uncertain where the first well, "Quarrel," was. If "Open Spaces" (*rĕhōbôt*) lies somewhere in Wadi Ruḥēbe twenty miles southwest of Beersheba, then "Hostility" (*śiṭnāh*) could be Wadi Šuṭein/Šuṭnet, mentioned by Dillmann. The location is less important than the significance: "Now the LORD has made space for us and we shall be fruitful in the land." Experiencing peace at last, Isaac recalls the promises that the land would belong to a multitude of descendants (cf. 26:4). פרה "be fruitful," though used often in Gen 1–11, here appears for the first time in the patriarchal story. Elsewhere in Genesis it is always paired with רבה "multiply," a term already used in 26:4 and about to be used again in v 24. Thus Isaac's expression of faith anticipates the renewal of the promises in the next episode.

23–25 The renewal of the promises in Beersheba is essentially a summary and reaffirmation of those in vv 2–4. However, there are a few small changes. God's self-introduction may be noted: "I am the God of Abraham your father." On this and similar phrases in Genesis, Alt (*Der Gott der Väter*) built a whole theory of patriarchal religion (see *Introduction*). However, here and elsewhere (cf. 24:12, 17, 42, 48) use seems to be closely related to the context. Throughout this chapter there is a very strong emphasis on Isaac's relationship to his father, and this is reflected in this speech as well. Note its conclusion: "for the sake of my servant Abraham."

"Do not be afraid" (cf. 15:1). Fear is mentioned as a motive for Isaac's action only in v 7. The way he is pushed around by Abimelek since then could be construed as a reflection of his peaceable temperament. This remark suggests that timidity may also lie behind his lack of resistance. But whatever Isaac's doubts and fears, he is reassured that the promises still hold "for the sake of my servant Abraham."

25 As Abraham did before him, Isaac expresses his faith in and gratitude for the promises by building an altar, offering sacrifice, and worshiping the LORD (cf. 12:7–8; 13:4, 18; 4:26).

"Pitched his tent" (cf. 12:8; 33:19; 35:21).

"Dug a well." Immediately following the land promise, this looks like an act of faith, but nearly every well dug so far has been the occasion for trouble with the Philistines. Will it prove to be so this time, so that yet again Isaac will be forced into an ignominious retreat?

26–31 The treaty between Isaac and the Philistines brought a happy resolution to years of dissension. There are many echoes of the similar negotiations

between Abraham and Abimelek in 21:22–34; note the same negotiators, Abimelek and Phicol, the same setting, Beersheba, and the same motives, "God is with you" (21:22), "The LORD is with you" (26:28), leading to a non-aggression pact.

26 "Ahuzzat his police chief" is not mentioned in chap. 21. Ahuzzat, "possession," has a form similar to Goliath (גָּלְיָת). מרע "police chief" may be the equivalent of רעה "friend," a title of trusted royal officials (2 Sam 15:37; 16:16; 1 Kgs 4:5). But Safren (*ZAW* 101 [1989] 190–98) plausibly argues that the Hebrew term is equivalent to Akk. *merḫû*, "supervisor of the pastorages," at Mari a powerful official who controlled grazing rights and had a police force to enforce his decisions. That Abimelek is accompanied apparently only by two leaders of Gerar, or at least no band of men is said to accompany him (cf. 33:1), suggests his mission is peaceable.

27 However, Isaac's experiences in Gerar have not been happy, and he bristles with suspicion as he greets them. "Why have you come to me, since you hate me and have expelled me . . . ?" Considering how Isaac has taken their earlier action lying down, this is an abrupt change of tone. Is he now showing real courage and faith, or is this bravado simply because there is no serious threat apparent?

28 Abimelek's reply is, however, irenic and flattering. Here Abimelek acknowledges, as he did with Abraham, that "the LORD is with you," and he proposes a treaty. Whereas Isaac had been, and perhaps still viewed himself as, the weaker party, Abimelek insists that their positions are now reversed and that he wishes to make a treaty with Isaac.

29 Abimelek puts the best gloss he can on his treatment of Isaac. He had issued a decree that "anyone who touches this man and his wife would be put to death" (v 11), so that he could claim "we have not touched you." But to say "we have only done good to you and sent you away in peace" is somewhat of a euphemism.

"Blessed are you now by the LORD" (cf. Melchizedek's blessing of Abram 14:19–20). As promised in 12:2, the patriarch has become a blessing. And by invoking blessing on Isaac, Abimelek is indirectly securing his own blessing (cf. *Comment* on 12:2–3).

30 "So he made a feast for them, and they ate and drank." Oriental hospitality should have dictated such treatment before the speech just recorded (cf. 14:18; 18:3–8; 19:2–3). That there is no mention of a meal till after these compliments have been showered shows the depth of alienation that had to be overcome and indicates that both sides did reach agreement. Meals form a standard part of treaty celebrations, from ancient to modern times (cf. 31:54; Exod 24:11); indeed, it has been said that the Hebrew word for "treaty, covenant" (ברית) derives from the verb to "eat, dine" (ברה; *TDOT* 2:253), though this is not very likely. Whatever the precise significance, the act of eating and drinking indicates reconciliation between the two sides. Indeed, the whole episode illustrates Prov 16:7, "When a man's ways please the LORD, he makes even his enemies to be at peace with him."

31 Whereas Abimelek had speciously claimed to have sent Isaac away in peace (v 29), the terminology is appropriate here. Isaac sets them on their way by accompanying them for a short distance (cf. 18:16).

32–33 This last incident confirms the reversal of roles that had become obvious in the last encounter between Isaac and Abimelek. On an earlier occasion,

every time Isaac's servants had discovered wells they were forced to abandon them (vv 18–21). Now they find yet another well, and he names it "Oath," after the oath he had just sworn to Abimelek. Earlier he had been giving the same names to the wells he had dug as his father had (v 18). Here he does it yet again. Beersheba's name is connected in 21:25–31 with the oath Abraham made that allowed him to use a well nearby. The servants comment, "We have found water," seems superfluous, for all useful wells have water, but here their remark surely reinforces the feeling of security. Isaac had been forced by famine to leave Beersheba for Gerar; now the discovery of a good water supply seems like a pledge of future security in the land. Thus this whole chapter closes triumphantly with Isaac walking confidently in his father's footsteps, experiencing for himself the incipient fulfillment of the divine promises.

Explanation

Isaac spends most of his life in the shadow of other members of his family, either of his father Abraham or of his sons Jacob and Esau. Indeed, after chap. 27 he virtually disappears from the story until the brief mention of his death in 35:27–28. Here and only here within Genesis does he appear as a person in his own right, but even here he seems to have less drive than either his father or his sons. This narrative that tells of his relations with the Philistines portrays him as a rather timid character whom the Gerarites push around. Nevertheless, this somewhat ineffectual man receives yet greater promises and experiences their fulfillment in fuller measure than even his father Abraham did. This narrative thus demonstrates that the power of God can work even through those who by human standards are most unlikely material.

Throughout this narrative, comparisons are being drawn between Isaac and his father. There are proportionately more references within this chapter to Abraham than at any other point in the subsequent chapters. Not only is Abraham frequently mentioned, but the narrator draws attention to the similar situations Isaac and Abraham face. V 1 compares the famine Isaac encountered with that Abraham faced. Like Abraham (20:1), he took refuge in Gerar, between Canaan and Egypt, and he was evidently contemplating going farther (cf. 12:10), for the LORD had to tell him, "Do not go down to Egypt" (v 2).

Prohibited from following his father's example of seeking relief from the famine in Egypt, he is encouraged in language that echoes the first and last great tests of Abraham's life "to camp in the country which I shall tell you" (v 2; cf. 12:1; 22:2). In expectation of his obedience, he is further promised, as was Abraham, that the LORD will be with him and bless him. The promise continues: "to you and your descendants . . . I shall give all these lands, and I shall confirm the oath which I swore to your father Abraham. I shall multiply your descendants . . . and in your descendants all the nations of the earth shall find blessing." This is a full and fairly precise reiteration of the promises made to Abraham after he had shown his willingness to sacrifice Isaac. That this quotation is not accidental is shown by the reference "to the oath which I swore," for it is only in chap. 22 that the promises are described as an oath. The promises in 22:16–18 are more categorical and unconditional than anywhere else in the

Abraham cycle; in the light of Abraham's obedience, the original promises can now be termed guarantees. But now the guarantees of 22:16–18 are enhanced. The promises are now made *to you* and your descendants. It is not merely the land of Canaan that is promised but "all these lands." So although it would be easy to write Isaac off as a second-class character among the patriarchs, the promises made to him here outshine any that his father Abraham received. Indeed, he saw more of the promise fulfilled than his father did.

Yet this can hardly be ascribed to his model behavior. Though Abraham had twice tried to pass off Sarah as his sister and been sternly reprimanded for so doing, explicitly by the Pharaoh and by Abimelek, and implicitly by the narrator, the next episode shows Isaac making exactly the same mistake, because, as Isaac himself tells us, "he was afraid." Despite the pledge of divine presence and blessing that he had received, timidity had the better of him. Like his father before him, Isaac was prepared to sacrifice his wife's honor for his own safety. Happily for all concerned, the real situation was discovered before Rebekah was abducted, but, as Abimelek points out, the sin of Isaac could have led to divine punishment befalling the whole people. Once again the patriarch and his wife are saved from his folly by the mercy of God and the integrity of the foreign king. Abimelek's decree, "Whoever touches this man and his wife shall certainly be put to death," underlines his concern for sexual morality.

Yet despite Isaac's lapse from faith and propriety, he continues to flourish. His hundredfold harvest in the land is unparalleled elsewhere in the patriarchal narrative, but it is clear proof that the LORD had blessed him (v 12), and it shows the worth of the land that has been promised to him, even though his wandering lifestyle precluded his enjoying such harvests regularly. The great promises made to him and his father can and will be fulfilled. His flocks and herds also flourish.

But Isaac's prosperity provokes jealousy, so that just when he appears to be on the verge of inheriting the promise, it slips out of his grasp, at least for a while. Abraham had made an agreement with Abimelek allowing him to use a well near Beersheba. At the time, this had been a momentous step, for this was the first legal title Abraham had acquired in the land of promise. But now even these rights are forgotten and disregarded. Wealthy Isaac is expelled from the territory of Gerar. Abraham's wells, even those redug by Isaac's servants, are seized, and Isaac is forced to move on. Twice this happens; a well dug by Isaac's men is taken over by the shepherds of Gerar, so that they are driven far from Gerar. Finally, at the third well, they are left in peace, so Isaac called it Rehobot, "Open spaces . . . because now the LORD has made space for us and we shall be fruitful in the land" (v 22). Whatever appearances may suggest to the contrary, Isaac has not lost faith in the promise.

And from then on his fortunes improve. At Beersheba, the promises are reaffirmed, "I am the God of Abraham your father. Do not be afraid, for I am with you and I shall bless you and multiply your descendants for the sake of my servant Abraham" (v 24). And like Abraham, Isaac responds in worship, building an altar, offering sacrifice, and calling on the name of the LORD.

But whereas the first promise to Isaac was followed by a test, which Isaac hardly excelled in, this promise is followed by encouragement, indeed partial fulfillment of the promises. No sooner had Isaac's servants dug another well than Abimelek

and his retinue arrive. If Isaac's heart sank at yet another confrontation with the Philistines, he did not show it. In fact, he addresses them with unusual straightness: "Why have you come to me, since you hate me and have expelled me?" (v 27). This time, however, instead of harassing him, Abimelek's delegation sues for peace. Isaac is so powerful, "We have seen ourselves that the LORD is with you," that they want to make a treaty with Isaac. Somewhat disingenuously, they gloss over their former maltreatment of Isaac, and Isaac, "blessed by the LORD," graciously grants their request. The oath is sworn. They leave in peace, and that very day a well with abundant water is discovered. This surely suggests that Isaac's tenure of the land of promise is more secure now than at any time in his career. A treaty with the Philistines means that they have acknowledged his right to stay, while the good well will mean that drought or famine is less likely to affect him and force him to leave the land of promise.

Thus this account of Isaac's dealings with the Philistines portrays Isaac as very much walking in his father's footsteps. He receives similar promises, faces similar tests, fails similarly, but eventually triumphs in like fashion. Indeed, in certain respects he is given more in the promises and achieves more. He is promised "all these lands," and by the end of the story he is securely settled in Beersheba and has a treaty with the Philistines in which they acknowledge his superiority.

But this narrative does not just look backward to Abraham; it looks forward too. Most obviously it looks to the experiences of Israel expelled from Egypt, forced to wander in the wilderness looking for water until they arrive at Mount Sinai, where the LORD speaks to them. Thus just as Abraham's career in chaps. 12–13 foreshadowed Israel's exodus and wilderness experiences (see Wenham, *Genesis 1–15*), so Isaac's does too. And, though there are difficulties with identifying these Philistines of Gerar with the better-known Philistines of David's day, it cannot be ruled out that the treaty with Abimelek and his apparent recognition of Isaac's suzerainty look forward to the day when David would subdue the Philistines (2 Sam 8:1). Certainly the promise, "I shall give to your descendants all these lands," was not forgotten; psalmists, prophets, and the NT look forward to the son of David, who will "have dominion from sea to sea" and rule "all tribes and peoples and tongues" (Pss 2; 47; 72; Isa 2:2–4; 4:2–6; 11:10; 55:3–5; Matt 28:18–20; Rev 7:9–12).

As elsewhere in Genesis, there is hardly any explicit comment on Isaac's behavior described here. Like the other patriarchs, he is portrayed as a man of very mixed character. He is timid, fearful for his own skin; he is prepared to lie and to put his wife at risk to save himself. For this, Abimelek justly censures him, and the very phraseology used shows that the narrator concurs with him. And yet despite Isaac's failings, the LORD is with him, protects him, blesses him, and makes him extremely wealthy. God's gracious promises will be fulfilled despite the frailty of his chosen vessels (Rom 11:29; 2 Cor 4:7). But Isaac's shortcomings must not be overstressed. Though his timidity in some situations led him astray, in others it prompted him to be conciliatory where others might have stirred up strife. There is thus an ambivalence about his failure to stand up to the men of Gerar, who kept seizing the wells dug by his servants. But there is no doubt about the outcome of his behavior; it leads to ever increasing prosperity so that even his hostile neighbors come begging for his goodwill. Ps 37 (Ps 37:3, 11, 39–40; cf. Matt 5:5; 1 Pet 2:19–25; 3:8–12) could be a commentary on this chapter:

"Trust in the LORD, and do good;
   so you will dwell securely, and enjoy security. . . .
But the meek shall possess the land,
   and delight themselves in abundant prosperity. . . .
The salvation of the righteous is from the LORD;
   he is their refuge in the time of trouble.
The LORD helps them and delivers them;
   he delivers them from the wicked, and saves them,
   because they take refuge in him."

Jacob Cheats Esau out of His Blessing   (26:34–28:9)

Bibliography

See also *Bibliography* on 24:1–67.

Ackerman, S. "The Deception of Isaac, Jacob's Dream at Bethel, and Incubation on an Animal Skin." In *Priesthood and Cult,* ed. G. Anderson and S. Olyan. JSOTSup 125. Sheffield: Academic, 1991. 92–120. **Coats, G. W.** "Strife without Reconciliation—A Narrative Theme in the Jacob Traditions." In *Werden und Wirken des ATs: FS C. Westermann,* ed. R. Albertz, H.-P. Müller, H. W. Wolff, and W. Zimmerli. Göttingen: Vandenhoeck & Ruprecht, 1980. 82–106. **Dahood, M.** "Poetry versus a Hapax in Gen 27:3." *Bib* 58 (1977) 422–23. **Fokkelman, J. P.** *Narrative Art in Genesis.* 97–112. **Hemiel, H. Y.** "The Mother of Jacob and Esau." (Heb.) *BMik* 32 (1986/87) 332–44. **Keukens, K. H.** "Der irreguläre Sterbesegen Isaaks: Bemerkungen zur Interpretation von Gen 27:1–45." *BN* 19 (1982) 43–56. **Kselman, J. H.** "Semantic-Sonant Chiasmus in Biblical Poetry." *Bib* 58 (1977) 219–23. **Lang, B.** "Altersversorgnung, Begräbnis und Elterngebot." *ZDMGSup* 31 (1977) 149–56. **Levin, S.** "Isaac's Blindness: A Medical Diagnosis." *Judaism* 37 (1988) 81–83. **Luke, K.** "Isaac's Blessing: Genesis 27." *Scripture* 20 (1968) 33–41. **Schedl, C.** "Worte und Zahlen: Neuer Zugang zu den Genesisquellen." *ZAW* 77 (1965) 259–67. **Schmidt, L.** "Jakob erschleicht sich den väterlichen Segen: Literarkritik und Redaktion von Gen 27:1–45." *ZAW* 100 (1988) 159–83. **Sharp, D. B.** "In Defense of Rebecca." *BTB* 10 (1980) 164–68. **Ska, J. L.** "Sommaires proleptiques en Gen 27 et dans l'histoire de Joseph." *Bib* 73 (1992) 518–27. **Willi-Plein, I.** "Gen 27 als Rebekkageschichte: Zu einem historiographischen Kunstgriff der biblischen Vätergeschichten." *TZ* 45 (1989) 315–34. **Zakovitch, Y.** "Reflection Story: Another Dimension of the Valuation of Characters in Biblical Narrative." (Heb.) *Tarbiz* 54 (1984/85) 165–76.

Translation

[34] *When Esau was forty years old, he married Judith, the daughter of Beeri the Hittite, and Basemath, the daughter of Elon the Hittite.*[a] [35] *And they made*[a] *life miserable for Isaac and Rebekah.*

[27:1] *When Isaac was old and his eyesight was too poor* [a] *for him to see,*[b] *he summoned his elder son Esau and said to him, "My son." He replied, "Here I am."* [2] *He said, "Since*[a]

I have grown old [b] *and I do not know when I shall die,* [b] [3] *now take* [a] *your weapons, your quiver* [b] *and your bow, go into* [c] *the field, and hunt me some game.* [d] [4] *Make me a tasty stew that I love and bring* [a] *it to me to eat,* [b] *so that my soul may bless you before I die."* [5a] *Now Rebekah was listening when Isaac spoke to his son Esau.* [a] *So Esau went out into the country to hunt game to bring* [b] *it in.*

[6] *Then Rebekah said to Jacob her son, "I have just* [a] *heard your father speaking to your brother Esau like this.* [7] *'Bring me game and make me a tasty stew for me to eat, so that I may bless you in the* LORD*'s presence before I die.'* [8] *Now, my son, obey me in what I command you.* [9] *Please go to the flock and take from there two good kids so that* [a] *I may make them* [b] *into a tasty stew* [b] *for your father that he loves.* [10] *Then bring it to your father for him to eat so that he* [a] *may bless you before he dies."*

[11] *Then Jacob said to his mother Rebekah, "My brother Esau is hairy, but I* [a] *am a smooth man.* [12] *Suppose my father touches* [a] *me, I shall seem like a mocker* [b] *to him and I shall bring upon myself a curse instead of a blessing."*

[13] *His mother said to him, "Let the curse on you fall on me.* [a] *Just* [b] *obey me. Go and get it for me."* [14] *So he went, took it, and brought it to his mother. Then his mother made a tasty stew as his father loved.*

[15] *Then Rebekah took her elder* [a] *son Esau's favorite clothes, which she had with her in the house, and dressed* [b] *her younger* [a] *son Jacob.* [16] *The skins of the kids she put on his hands and on the smooth part of his neck.* [a] [17] *She gave the tasty stew and the bread she had made into the hands of her son Jacob.*

[18] *Then Jacob went in to his father, and said, "My father," and he said, "Here I am. Who are you, my son?"* [19] *And Jacob said to his father, "I* [a] *am Esau, your firstborn. I have done as you told me. Come* [b] *on, sit* [c] *up and eat* [c] *of my game in order that your soul may bless me."* [d] [20] *Then Isaac said to his son, "How did you ever* [a] *find it so quickly my son?" He replied, "Because the* LORD *your God made me meet it."* [21] *So Isaac said to Jacob, "Please come* [a] *close so that I can feel* [b] *you, my son. Are you really* [c] *my son Esau or* [d] *not?"* [22] *So Jacob came* [a] *close to Isaac his father, and he felt* [b] *him. Then he said, "The voice is Jacob's, but* [c] *the hands are Esau's."* [23] *But he did not recognize* [a] *him because his hands were hairy like the hands of his brother Esau, so he blessed him.* [24] *He said, "Are you* [a] *really my son Esau?" He said, "I* [b] *am."* [25] *He said, "Bring it close* [a] *to me that I may eat* [b] *from my son's game in order that my soul may bless you." So he served* [c] *him and he ate, and he brought him wine and he drank.* [d]

[26] *Then his father Isaac said, "Please come* [a] *close and kiss* [b] *me, my son."* [27] *So he came close and kissed* [a] *him, and he smelt* [b] *the fragrance of his clothes, and he blessed him and said,*

"Look, my son's fragrance is like the fragrance of land [c] *which the* LORD *has blessed.*

[28] *May God give you of the dew of heaven*
and the richness of the earth
an abundance of grain and new wine.
[29] *May peoples serve you*
and nations bow [a] *down before you.*
Be lord over your brother
and may your mother's sons bow [a] *down before you.*
Cursed [b] *are those who curse you,*
and blessed [b] *are those who bless you.*

[30] *Isaac had finished* [a] *blessing Jacob, and Jacob had just* [b] *come* [a] *out from Isaac's presence, when Esau his brother came in from hunting.* [31] *So he also made a tasty stew*

and brought it in to his father. Then he said, "May my father arise[a] *and eat of his son's game, so that your soul may bless me."* [32]*Then Isaac his father said to him, "Who are you?" He replied, "I*[a] *am your son, your firstborn, Esau."* [33]*Then Isaac was gripped by an uncontrollable trembling, and he said, "Who was it then*[a] *who hunted*[b] *game, brought it me, and I ate it all*[c] *before you came and I blessed him? Yes,*[d] *he will be blessed."* [34a]*As soon as Esau heard his father's words, he let out a loud and very anguished scream, and he said to his father, "Bless me, even me,*[b] *father!"* [35]*Then he said, "Your brother has come with deceit and taken away your blessing."* [36]*He said, "Is he not rightly*[a] *called Jacob? He has cheated*[b] *me these*[c] *two times. My right as the firstborn he took away, and just now he has taken away my blessing." He said, "Did you not reserve a blessing for me?"* [37]*Isaac replied and said to Esau, "Look, I have made*[a] *him lord over you; I have made all his brothers his servants, and I have provided him with grain and new wine. So for you*[b] *then, what can I do, my son?"* [38]*So Esau said, "Don't you have just one blessing for me? Bless me, yes me, father,"*[a]*and he broke down and wept.*[b] [39]*So his father Isaac replied and said to him:*

> *"Your dwelling shall be*
> *away from the richness of the earth*
> *and the dew of heaven above.*
> [40]*You shall live by your sword,*
> *and be subject to your brother, and when you grow*[a] *restless,*
> *you shall tear off his yoke from your neck."*

[41]*So Esau bore a grudge against Jacob because of the blessing with which his father had blessed him, and Esau said to himself, "The days of mourning for my father are drawing close, so that I can kill my brother Jacob."* [42]*Now it was reported*[a] *to Rebekah what Esau, her elder son, had said, so she sent and summoned her younger son, Jacob, and said to him, "Your brother Esau is even now*[b] *consoling himself about you by planning to kill you.* [43]*Now, my son, obey me. Get up, run away by yourself*[a] *to Laban my brother in Harran.* [44]*Stay with him for a few days until your brother's wrath abates,* [45]*until your brother's anger subsides from you and he forgets what you did to him, then I shall send and bring you back from there. Why should I lose both of you together*[a] *in a single*[b] *day?"*

[46]*Then Rebekah said to Isaac, "I loathe*[a] *my life because of the Hittite women. If Jacob marries*[b][c]*some of the Hittite women like these,*[c] *some of the girls of this country, why should I go on living?"*

[28:1]*So Isaac summoned Jacob, blessed him, gave*[a] *him orders, and said to him, "You must not marry any of the Canaanite women.* [2]*Up, go to Paddan-Aram*[a] *to the house of Bethuel, your mother's father, and marry there any of the daughters of Laban, your mother's brother.* [3]*May God Almighty*[a] *bless you, make*[b] *you fruitful, and multiply*[b] *you so that you become a multitude of peoples.* [4]*May he give the blessing of Abraham*[a] *to you and to your descendants with you to inherit*[b] *the land to which you emigrated, which God*[c] *has given to Abraham."* [5]*So Isaac sent Jacob away, and he went to Paddan-Aram, to Laban, the son of Bethuel the Aramean, the brother of Rebekah, mother of Jacob and Esau.*

[6]*So Esau saw that Isaac had blessed Jacob and had sent*[a] *him away to Paddan-Aram to marry there, and that when he blessed him that he had commanded him, "You must not marry any of the Canaanite women,"* [7]*and that Jacob had obeyed his father and mother and gone to Paddan-Aram.* [8]*Then Esau realized that Isaac his father did not*

like Canaanite women. ⁹*So Esau went to Ishmael and married Mahalat. She was a daughter of Ishmael, Abraham's son, and the sister of Nebaiot. He married her as well*ᵃ *as his other wives.*

Notes

34.a. SamPent has הַחֹוִי "the Hivite" (cf. G) instead of הַחִתִּי.

35.a. Waw consec + 3 fem pl impf הָיָה.

27:1.a. Waw consec + 3 fem pl impf כהה "be dim."

1.b. מִן (on this usage, see GKC, 119y; Joüon, 169h) + inf constr רָאה.

2.a. On הִנֵּה־נָא "since," see Lambdin, 170–71; main clause in v 3.

2.b-b. Clause in specifying apposition to first (*SBH*, 47).

3.a. Cf. n. 13:14.c.

3.b. Found only here. SamPent spells it תְלִיתָךְ.

3.c. On the use of the accusative to express direction after verbs of motion, see GKC, 118f; WOC, 170. Cf. 1 Sam 20:11.

3.d. K צֵידָה "a piece of game" (GKC, 122t). Q צַיִד "game" (collective).

4.a. 2 masc sg impv hiph בוא + *āh* ending; cf. Joüon, 48d.

4.b. Waw + 1 sg coh אכל. The sequence impv + coh expresses intention or consequence (GKC, 108d; WOC, 575).

5.a-a. Episode-final circumstantial clause (*SBH*, 81).

5.b. Inf constr hiph בוא. Instead of "to bring it," G has "for his father," possibly equivalent to לְאָבִיו.

6.a. On this nuance of הִנֵּה, see Lambdin, 169.

9.a. Cf. n. 4.b.

9.b-b. On the use of the double acc after עשׂה "make something into something," see GKC, 117ii; Joüon, 125w.

10.a. G, "your father."

11.a. The position of the pronoun "I" within the sentence emphasizes it slightly (*SBH*, 152; *EWAS*, 11).

12.a. 3 masc sg impf משׁשׁ + 1 sg suffix.

12.b. כ + masc sg ptcp pilpel תעע.

13.a. Word order, predicate "on me" preceding subj "curse on you," emphasizes predicate (*EWAS*, 14).

13.b. On use of אך, see *SBH*, 177; WOC, 670.

15.a. Comparatives, e.g., "older, younger," in Hebrew are expressed by the simple adjective, "old, young."

15.b. Waw consec + 3 fem sg impf hiph לבשׁ.

16.a. SamPent has sg, but pl of צואר more common in Genesis (cf. 33:4; 45:14; 46:29).

19.a. The more natural Heb. word order in reply would be "Esau am I." "Jacob . . . betrays himself by the eagerly self-assertive form of the reply he chose" (*EWAS*, 19).

19.b. Impv of verbs of motion often functions merely as hortatory ptcp (*SBH*, 56–57).

19.c. 2 masc sg impv ישׁב אכלו + *āh* ending (cf. n. 4.a.).

19.d. Note suffix on impf joined by *ā* (GKC, 60d).

20.a. Enclitic זה may suggest Isaac's astonishment (GKC, 136c, 148b; WOC, 312, 326; cf. 3:13). But cf. Joüon, 143g; *EWAS*, 134–36.

21.a. 2 masc sg impv נגשׁ + *āh* ending.

21.b. Simple waw ("so that") + 1 sg impf מושׁ + 2 masc sg suffix.

21.c. זה here not only adds liveliness and concern to question, but used here particularly because identification is the issue (*EWAS*, 134–35; cf. n. 20.a.).

21.d. For similar structure of question ה . . . אִם־לֹא, cf. 24:21, which effectively "restricts the YES possibility to hǎ, *is it true that?*" (*SBH*, 148.)

22.a. Cf. n. 18:23.a.

22.b. Waw consec + 3 masc· sg impf משׁשׁ + 3 masc sg suffix.

22.c. On the antithesis, see *SBH*, 181.

23.a. 3 masc sg pf hiph נכר + 3 masc sg suffix.

24.a. SamPent reads הַאַתָּה, but it is quite permissible to introduce question without interrogative ה (GKC, 150a).

24.b. Affirmative reply usually expressed by repeating key word in question (GKC, 150n).

25.a. 2 masc sg impv hiph נגשׁ + *āh* ending.

25.b. On the sequence of tenses impv + coh, see GKC, 108d.

25.c. Waw consec + 3 masc sg impf hiph נגשׁ. On pointing, see GKC, 29e.

25.d. Cf. n. 9:21.a.

26.a. Cf. n. 21.a.

26.b. 2 masc sg impv נשׁק + *āh* ending.

27.a. Waw consec + 3 masc sg impf נשׁק.

27.b. Cf. n. 8:21.a.

27.c. SamPent, cf. G, adds מלא.

29.a. Cf. n. 18:2.d. For the usual pointing, see *BHS* footnotes.

29.b. Note sg predicates, "cursed, blessed," with pl subjs, "those who curse/bless you." Shows that each one is affected individually by the statement "those that curse thee, cursed be every one of them, and those that bless thee, blessed be every one of them" (GKC, 145l).

30.a. On use of two pfs to describe immediately successive actions, see GKC, 164b[1].

30.b. On this nuance of אך, see Joüon, 123k; WOC, 588.

31.a. 3 masc sg juss קום, but unusual pointing (GKC, 72t; Joüon, 80k).

32.a. The initial position of "I" seems to make Esau's reply emphatic; cf. v 19; *EWAS*, 19.

33.a. אפוא "serves to point to the logical question or statement containing it and the foregoing statement with the particle" (*EWAS*, 137).

33.b. Ptcp may have pf meaning (GKC, 116d) and then be followed as here by waw + finite verb (Joüon, 121j; WOC, 561, 631).

33.c. *BHS* proposes emending מכל to אכל (inf abs). Unnecessary.

33.d. גם "also" may sometimes emphasize, but here perhaps just "and, also" (*SBH*, 166; *EWAS*, 145).

34.a. SamPent, cf. G, adds ויהי "and it was."

34.b. Repetition of the pronoun emphasizes Esau's high emotion.

36.a. On use of הכי, see *SBH*, 166; GKC, 150e.

36.b. Waw consec + 3 masc sg impf עקב + 1 sg suffix.

36.c. On use of זה before numerals, see GKC, 136d.

37.a. 1 sg pf שׂים + 3 masc sg suffix.

37.b. Word order ("for you" would not normally come first in clause) and use of אפוא "then" emphasizes this element (GKC, 142g, 150l).

38.a. G adds "But Isaac being stupefied."

38.b. Waw consec + 3 masc sg impf apoc בכה.

40.a. 2 masc sg impf hiph רוד. Meaning is uncertain; hence variation in versions (see *BHS*).

42.a. Waw consec + 3 masc sg hoph נגד. On the construction, a pass verb, "was reported," with direct obj, "words of Esau," see GKC, 121a; Joüon, 128b; WOC, 182.

42.b. On this nuance of הנה, cf. Lambdin, 169.

43.a. On the nuance of לך, cf. n. 12:1.a.

45.a. On this translation of גם "frequently employed when giving an exaggerated, aggravated or extreme case," see *EWAS* 143–44 (cf. GKC, 154a[1]).

45.b. See GKC, 118i.

46.a. 1 sg pf qal קוץ.

46.b. Ptcp used for present or imminent fut (Joüon, 167h).

46.c-c. Omitted by G.

28:1.a. Waw consec + 3 masc sg impf piel צוה + 3 masc sg suffix.

2.a. On the pointing, see GKC, 90i.

3.a. In blessings, God's name often comes first in the sentence, whereas more usually the verb precedes the subj (*EWAS*, 35).

3.b. Waw + 3 masc sg juss hiph פרה / רבה + 2 masc sg suffix.

4.a. Some MSS, SamPent add "your father"; G adds "my father."

4.b. ל + inf constr ירשׁ + 2 masc sg suffix.

4.c. SamPent reads "the LORD."

6.a. The waw + pf is unexpected, so *BHS* suggests emending to waw + impf, which would be more regular. Inconclusively discussed in GKC, 112pp. WOC, 542, suggests that this is regular way of expressing pluperfect.

9.a. For this meaning of על, see GKC 119aa[2].

Form/Structure/Setting

Determining the opening and close of this section is here more problematic than usual; the medieval chapter divisions and modern source-critical theories obscure the issues.

That a new major section within the narrative begins in 26:34 is suggested by the abrupt reappearance of Esau, completely unmentioned in 26:1–33, and by the initial ויהי, lit. "and it was when," which often marks an important new development within a narrative (25:20; 26:1). However, since the subject matter of 26:34–35, Esau's foreign wives, reappears in 27:46 and indeed dominates 27:46–28:9, it seems probable that in the editor's mind 26:34–35 anticipates the conclusion of this section of narrative, so that the account of Isaac's deception is set within the framework of the problems caused by Esau's marriages. These same reasons argue for a close of this story at 28:9, rather than at 27:45. This division of the material is supported by the Jewish lectionary, which begins a new reading at 28:10, and in recent times by Dillmann, Vawter, Coats, and Ross (*Creation and Blessing*), who all recognize that 26:34–28:9 constitutes a coherent unit within the present book of Genesis.

However, it hardly constitutes a freestanding independent tale; it is very much part of the longer narrative of Jacob and Esau. It clearly refers back to the story of the twins' birth and early conflicts (25:20–34). The blessing of Isaac (27:27–29) elaborates and underlines the oracle given in 25:23. Esau refers both to the naming of Jacob (25:26) and to his loss of his birthright (25:28–34) in 27:36. Indeed, the whole story rests on the divided loyalties and preferences of Rebekah and Isaac first mentioned in 25:28. In 28:4, Isaac bestows on Jacob the blessing of Abraham, a key theme of chap. 26, and other phrases in 28:2–4 seem to hark back to the same chapter, e.g., being made fruitful and multiplying (26:22, 24). But, of course, it also looks forward to the rest of the Jacob cycle, anticipating Jacob's sojourn in Paddan-Aram, his marriage to Laban's daughters, and his eventual return. Within the overall palistrophic arrangement of the Jacob cycle, this section corresponds to the great reconciliation between Jacob and Esau, which takes place when Jacob returns (chaps. 32–33).

The material is arranged in five scenes, preceded and followed by reports of Esau's marriages.

26:34–35	Esau marries Hittites
27:1–5	Isaac instructs Esau to prepare to be blessed
27:6–17	Rebekah instructs Jacob to acquire blessing
27:18–29	Isaac blesses Jacob
27:30–40	Esau appeals to Isaac for blessing
27:41–28:5	Rebekah thwarts Esau's revenge; Jacob sent to Paddan-Aram
28:6–9	Esau marries an Ishmaelite

The scenic division is widely agreed among commentators. 27:5, with its reference to Rebekah listening, is transitional and by some is made part of the second scene. However, it seems preferable to regard this circumstantial clause as episode-final and make the second scene begin with v 6. The final scene, 27:41–28:5, is usually split in two, 27:41–45 and 27:46–28:5. However, if change of actors is the criterion, it should really be split in three (cf. Sarna):

27:41–45	Rebekah and Jacob
27:46	Rebekah and Isaac
28:1–5	Isaac and Jacob

But all of 27:41–28:5 in its present context relates to Rebekah's scheme to save Jacob from Esau's wrath, and so I, like Coats, see it as constituting a unit within the narrative.

27:1–40 constitutes a type scene, the death-bed blessing scene. Other examples in the OT include Gen 48–49; 50:24–25; Deut 31–34; Josh 23–24; 1 Kgs 2:1–9; and in the intertestamental literature Tob 4, 14; *T. 12 Patr.* 1. Usually when the great man knows he is about to die, he summons his nearest male relatives and blesses them. But here, as Keukens (*BN* 19 [1982] 43–56) points out, Isaac professes to be ignorant of when he is going to die and then summons only one of his sons for blessing. The whole procedure is thus flawed from the outset.

Traditional source critics assigned 26:34–35 and 27:46–28:9 to P and 27:1–45 to JE, though there was doubt about which verses belonged to J and which to E. It was argued that two sources must be present here, because both J and E know of Jacob's flight to Mesopotamia and because there are doublets within chap. 27, e.g., vv 21–23//24–27a; 30a//30b; 33–34//35–38. Further support for source division rests on the different divine names: "The LORD" in vv 7, 20, 27, but "God" in v 28. However, the consensus among modern source critics, ever since Volz (*Der Elohist,* 61–70) is that the whole passage is a substantial unity from the hand of J (so most recently Westermann; Coats; cf. Blum, *Die Komposition;* only Schmidt [*ZAW* 100 (1988) 159–83] wants to find two sources here). Repetition within the narrative is not evidence of two sources but of the narrator's dramatic skill.

However, ancient and modern source critics are agreed that 26:34–35 and 27:46–28:9 belong to P. But the grounds for this ascription are not weighty. 26:34–35 is assigned to P simply because v 34 contains details of Esau's age and chronological information is automatically ascribed to P, and because 28:9, "as well as his other wives," refers back to 26:34–35. Since 28:1–9 is P, 26:34–35 must be too. But as Delitzsch observes, the fact that the names of Esau's wives in 36:2–3 (P) differ from 26:34–35 and 28:9 suggests that the source here cannot be P. Further, Esau's marriage at the age of forty corresponds to Isaac's (25:20) at the same age, while Rebekah's comment in 27:46 is very like 25:22. We argued above (*Form/Structure/Setting* on 25:19–34) that 25:20–22 reflects the hand of the final redactor, and the same could be the case here. The case for finding P here therefore rests entirely on 28:1–8, which contains a number of terms frequently said to be characteristic of P: "Canaanite women" (vv 1, 6, 8), "Paddan-Aram" (vv 2, 5, 7), "God Almighty," "fruitful and multiply," "multitude of peoples" (v 3), "land to which you emigrated," "God" (v 4), and "the Aramean" (v 5). Despite this impressive list of terms, it proves very little. "Canaanite women" and "multitude of peoples" are only found once outside this passage (36:2; 48:4). "Make you fruitful and multiply you," "Paddan-Aram," and "Aramean" are found in non-P passages (probably J), i.e., 25:20; 26:4, 22, 24; 31:18, 20, 24. This leaves only "land to which you emigrated" and "God Almighty" as possible indicators of P (cf. 17:8; 36:7; 37:1; 17:1; 35:11; 43:14; 48:3). On the other hand, "to you and your descendants with you to inherit the land" is very reminiscent of the promises recorded

in J (e.g., 12:7; 13:15; 15:7; 22:17; 24:7, 60; 26:3, 4) as well as P (17:8). And the mention of the blessing of Abraham and the land God has given to Abraham seems to connect this passage not simply with the Abraham cycle but with chap. 26, where the blessing of Isaac is most frequently associated with that given to Abraham (see *Form/Structure/Setting* on 26:1–33).

Rather than claim that the vocabulary of 28:1–5 is distinctively P or characteristic of J, it would be more accurate to say that it is typical of passages where the promises to the patriarchs are being quoted or mentioned. In short, the terms used are genre-specific not source-specific. They do not show that a different writer is at work, only that promises are the subject matter. Nor is the syntax or word order any more revealing, for as Radday (*Genesis*, 79) has shown, human speech in all three sources is indistinguishable.

It is often said that 28:1–9 knows nothing of the enmity between Esau and Jacob and therefore cannot come from the same source as chap. 27. But this is to equate silence with ignorance. 28:1–9 may well presuppose knowledge of the dispute just described but see no point in discussing it further. Indeed, the comments about Esau going to marry an Ishmaelite after he had heard Jacob being told not to marry a Canaanite does suggest at least rivalry between the brothers. This is confirmed by the comment that "Esau realized that Isaac his father did not like Canaanite women" (28:8). Evidently he did not care what his mother thought (27:46). Conversely, that Isaac fails to mention to Jacob that Bethuel and Laban are related to him as well as to Rebekah surely reflects the fact that Jacob is her son, while Esau is his (28:1–2). Further, 28:5, in relating Jacob's obedience, says that he went to "Paddan-Aram, to Laban, the son of Bethuel." This combines reference to 27:43 with 28:2; Rebekah had told Jacob to go to Laban (27:43), whereas Isaac had told him to go to Paddan-Aram to the house of Bethuel (28:2). Thus, 28:5 appears to know both Rebekah's command and Isaac's. This is confirmed by 28:7, "Jacob had obeyed his father and *his mother.*" To dismiss "and his mother" as a harmonizing gloss (Gunkel) is, as Westermann observes, unwarranted. But it does show that the author of 28:1–9 was aware of 27:41–45 and presumably what led up to it (27:1–40). Furthermore, 28:1–2 "seems to echo" (Gunkel) or "is modelled on" (Skinner) 24:3–4, and similarly "the content of the blessing of Isaac (i.e., 28:3–4) particularly recalls that of 26:2–5, 24" (Strus, *Nomen-Omen*, 112–13). Both chaps. 24 and 26 are usually ascribed to J, so it seems reasonable to conclude that 28:1–9, at least in its present form, also reflects his hand. Hence, I shall assume 26:34–35; 27:45–28:9 come from the same hand as that which composed the rest of the section.

Comment

34–35 The opening verb form ויהי, lit. "and it was" (untranslated here), and the note about Esau's age indicate a major new development in the story. The quiet interlude of 26:1–33, which described Isaac's life before Rebekah conceived, is now forgotten. We reenter the world of the warring twins.

34 This remark about Esau's marriage appears to be mere biographical record. He marries at the same age as did his father Isaac (25:20), but unlike Isaac who married one girl from Abraham's family, Esau marries two Hittite

women. When Abraham's intense concern that Isaac should on no account marry a Canaanite is recalled, it is somewhat unexpected that Esau should marry two. The Hittites of Genesis seem to be a subgroup of the Canaanites (10:15; 36:2; see *Comment* on 23:3). Does this reflect slackness on Isaac's part, that unlike Abraham he did not bother to find Esau a suitable wife, or Esau's deliberate rejection of family tradition? The narrative opens up both possibilities and never decides the issue, so that this opening note casts a shadow over both Esau and Isaac, who otherwise would appear completely exploited in the ensuing tale of deception. But once we realize that neither Esau nor Isaac care about Abraham's principle of not marrying Canaanites, we cannot entirely condemn the way Jacob and Rebekah achieve their goals. Esau's indifference to the law's demands, which Abraham held so dear, suggests that perhaps he does not deserve to inherit Abraham's blessing.

Later, according to 28:9, Esau married Mahalat the daughter of Ishmael and sister of Nebaiot, whereas according to 36:2–3 he married Adah, daughter of Elon, Oholibamah, daughter of Anah, and Basemat, daughter of Ishmael and sister of Nebaiot. How these divergent traditions are to be reconciled is unclear, but these differences do suggest that at some stage the traditions were independent.

"Judith" only used here as a proper name in the OT. In later texts it means a female Judean, i.e., Jewess. "Basemat" means balsam according to Noth, (*Personennamen*, 223).

35 Lit. "and they were bitterness of spirit [מרת רוח] to Isaac and Rebekah." The phrase "bitterness of spirit" occurs only here, but it seems akin to מר נפש "bitter in soul," which denotes an intense anguish such as Hannah and Job experienced (1 Sam 1:10; Job 7:11; 10:1). What their Hittite daughters-in-law did to make life so miserable for Isaac and Rebekah is left unclarified, but already some of the costs of Isaac's indifference and Esau's rebelliousness are becoming apparent.

27:1–5 The opening scene has Isaac and Esau alone, with Rebekah listening in the wings. Here, with minimal detail, the essential points that must be appreciated if the rest of the story is to be understood are set out. Certain words, "old," "bless," surely echo the previous deathbed scene in Gen 24, when Abraham sent his servant to find a non-Canaanite wife for Isaac.

1 "His eyesight was too poor." For this description of failing sight in the elderly, cf. Deut 34:7; Zech 11:17; Job 17:7. It is mentioned here, of course, to explain how Jacob could think of tricking his father into blessing him.

Elsewhere in the OT, it is normal for a dying man to summon all his close male relatives and to bless them publicly and in this way to organize the succession (cf. Gen 49; 50:24–25). It is, to say the least, irregular for Isaac to summon merely one of his sons, especially since Jacob and Esau were twins. It raises questions: Why is Isaac prepared to break with convention? Why does he want to bless Esau and not Jacob, since both were entitled to some blessing (cf. vv 34, 38)?

This departure from convention is the more striking when Abraham's concerns at this point in his life are contrasted with Isaac's. Given the way Esau had flouted family custom by marrying two Canaanites and the distress this action had caused his parents, it comes as a surprise to find Isaac on his deathbed preparing to bless Esau, the more so because at the same point in his life Abraham

was desperately concerned that Isaac should marry only within the clan and because the birth oracle had promised Jacob's ascendancy over Esau (25:23).

2 "I do not know when I shall die." Speiser's attempt to show that this phraseology reflects Hurrian custom is probably misguided (see Thompson, *Historicity*, 285–93). However, he was right to draw attention to the unexpectedness of the remark. In the Bible and until relatively recently, people hoped to know when death was imminent in order to summon the family, make their final farewells, and leave their last instructions (47:29; 50:24; Josh 23:14). Often, indeed, God warns old leaders that they are about to die and to prepare for death (e.g., Num 20:24; 27:13; Deut 31:14). So why does Isaac here say that he does not know when he will die? Is he telling the truth? If so, why is he preparing to give a deathbed blessing? Or does he realize he is near to death and is trying to disguise the fact, so that all sons will not assemble to receive his blessing? However we take these problematic words, they do not reflect well on Isaac's intentions. Clearly, he wants to make sure to bless Esau and to give nothing to Jacob.

3–4 "Go into the field and hunt me some game." We have already been told that "Isaac loved Esau for his hunting," so when he says "Make me a tasty stew that I love," we realize that Isaac's sensuality is more powerful than his theology. Outside this chapter (vv 7, 9, 14, 17, 31) "tasty stew" only occurs in Prov 23:3, 6. Note the qualifying phrase, "that I love," suggesting the old man's bondage to his appetite.

4 "So that my soul may bless you before I die." Isaac does not say simply, "So that I may bless you." The use of "my soul" rather than "I" seems to express Isaac's strong desire to bless Esau (cf. Deut 12:20; 14:26; Ps 84:3[2]; Cant 1:7; 3:1–4). He is quite deliberately prepared to overlook Esau's misdemeanors and the God-given oracle. Isaac's will is pitted against God's and Rebekah's. Thus the stakes are high. Though "Esau went out into the country to hunt game" sounds very matter-of-fact, it is a dramatic exit to those who are aware of the issues at stake. Will Isaac and Esau triumph or Rebekah and Jacob, as the LORD had promised?

6–17 Energy and decisiveness characterized Rebekah in her youth (chap. 24). These traits have not deserted her now as she takes command of the situation. She may well have been angered by Isaac's disregard for conventional propriety in not summoning both sons to be blessed, but was she right to react to his deceitful behavior by perpetrating an even more hurtful ruse on her blind and dying husband? The narrator does not answer the question in so many words, but he does leave some clues to his attitude.

6 Note how Jacob is called "*her* son," whereas in v 5 Esau is called "*his* son," thus reminding us of the rift that divides the family (25:28). It is because of her son's interest that Rebekah takes such decisive action.

7 Rebekah, perhaps surmising that Jacob will need a little persuading to undertake her potentially dangerous scheme, modifies Isaac's words to Esau. Isaac said, "Take your weapons . . . so that my soul may bless you before I die" (vv 3–4). Rebekah omits all the remarks about hunting, which might have put Jacob off, then continues "that I may bless you in the LORD's presence before I die." By changing "my soul" to "I," Rebekah seems to be playing down the strength of Isaac's desire to bless Esau, while by adding "in the LORD's presence," she is emphasizing the importance of what Isaac proposes to do. Through this reporting

of Isaac's remarks, she seems to be insinuating the importance of Jacob acquiring the blessing while minimizing Isaac's determination to bless Esau.

8 It is most unusual for the verb צוה "command" to be used with a feminine subject (cf. Esth 4:5). This is the only example of the feminine participle of the verb in the OT. Here, then, Rebekah is portrayed as exerting all the maternal authority she can muster in order to make Jacob carry out her scheme.

9–10 Note that although Isaac asked Esau to prepare the tasty stew, here Rebekah says she will do that. Jacob has merely to fetch the two goats and carry the stew into his father. Why did she not tell Jacob to prepare the stew? Because she thought he was an incompetent cook, too slow, or because she wanted to do all she could? Maybe all these motives underlie her action.

11–12 Rebekah's scheme faced Jacob with a dilemma: should he follow his mother's command or his father's will? When the OT is compared with earlier ancient oriental practice, it may be seen to be clearly enhancing the authority of the mother, since father and mother are often put together in laws and wisdom (e.g., Exod 20:12; 21:15, 17; Prov 1:8; 6:20). However, undoubtedly the OT expects parents to have a common policy toward their children, so what should be done where father and mother disagree is not so obvious. However, since wives are expected to defer to their husbands (e.g., Num 30), it would seem likely that Jacob, despite being his mother's pet, ought to have had more regard for his father's wishes. But instead of basing his doubts on moral principles, he merely expresses his worry that he may be found out. Evidently he agrees with her aims and is only worried lest her scheme backfire on him.

Note the word-play "hairy" (שָׂעִר *śā'ir*) with the other name for Esau, Seir (see 25:25).

The verbal root תעע "mock," used only here and in 2 Chr 36:16, seems a very strong one. It would certainly be a most inappropriate way to treat a blind man, let alone one's parent (cf. Lev 19:14; Exod 21:17). Indeed, Deut 27:18 invokes a curse on those who physically mislead the blind, so it is quite realistic for Jacob to envisage a curse falling on him for deceiving his blind father.

13 Rebekah's reply is as remarkable for what it does not contain as for what it does. She says nothing about dressing up Jacob in goatskin and his brother's clothes. That might have alarmed Jacob even more. Instead she focuses on the most serious point, that Jacob may be cursed for his efforts. The word order, "Let the curse on you fall on me," emphasizes that Rebekah is the one, not Jacob, who will suffer should Isaac pronounce a curse instead of a blessing. Her remark is hypothetical, for Isaac does not curse Jacob, but it is doubtful whether she could have diverted any curse onto herself by simply saying so. The blessing is not transferable even to Esau for whom Isaac intended it, so how could a curse be diverted? Presumably Rebekah realized this, for her plan depends on the irrevocability of the blessing, so her remark, "Let the curse . . . on me," expresses the ferocity of her desire to make Jacob carry out her plan. Probably, Jacob realized curses could not be transferred either and his submission to his mother's will again underlines his complicity in the scheme. But her closing words, "Just obey me. Go and get it for me," repeating her opening injunction (vv 8–9) somewhat more brusquely, reveal her impatience and urgency. It is a naked appeal to maternal authority.

14–17 These verses describe the completion of the preparation. Notice how Rebekah does nearly everything. All that Jacob did is described in three Hebrew

words, "So he went, took, and brought." The very baldness of this comment, there
is no mention of Jacob running or hurrying, may suggest a lack of enthusiasm on
his part for the plan. But if the narrator has roused our ire by his portrayal of the
Machiavellian matriarch manipulating Jacob to defeat the purpose of her blind
and dying husband, he suddenly reminds us of the other side by the essentially
superfluous comments about the "tasty stew *as his father loved.*" The narrator says
"his father," rather than "her husband" or "Isaac," to remind us of the rift in the
family that has led Rebekah to act in this way, while the comment "as . . . he
loved" draws attention to Isaac's appetite that has resulted in favoritism and division.

But the implied criticism is once again set in the context of Isaac's pathetic
condition. Though Rebekah did not say anything about Isaac's possible detec-
tion of the ruse if he felt Jacob, she took precautions to avoid it by dressing Jacob
in his brother's best clothes and putting hairy goatskins on his arms and neck.
That such a device could deceive Isaac has struck some commentators as absurd.
Yet it is eloquent testimony to the decline in Isaac's powers. He is not merely
blind, but his sense of touch is also failing him. He is as much to be pitied as to
be blamed.

18–29 In this second scene, Jacob and Isaac are the sole actors. Whatever
Jacob's earlier hesitations about taking the part of his brother, he now throws
himself wholeheartedly into it. But he nearly gives himself away by talking too
much and overasserting his identity with Esau. Within this scene, Isaac speaks
eight times and Jacob four times. However, after Isaac says, "The voice is Jacob's,
but the hands are Esau's," Jacob only speaks once to say one word "I (am)" (v
24). It is as though Jacob realizes his voice may betray him, so thereafter he says
as little as possible.

Throughout the scene there is great tension, first as Isaac persistently inquires
who it is who has brought him his meal so quickly. His eyesight may have failed,
but his other faculties seem more alert than Rebekah and Jacob expected, so we
wait with bated breath to see whether their ruse will be unmasked. For even when
Jacob stops talking, the danger of discovery is not over, as Isaac persists in asking
him to "come close" (vv 21, 25, 26). Isaac wants to feel him to see if Jacob is really
Esau. Apparently satisfied, he blesses him, but then surprisingly he asks again,
"Are you really my son Esau?" Jacob's terse "I am" seems to satisfy him, but he
twice more asks him to come close to kiss and embrace him (vv 25–27; cf. 48:10).
Will Isaac's last hug of the quivering Jacob give the game away? It is only when
the words of blessing (vv 27–29) are pronounced that the tension finally relaxes.
The plot has been successful; Jacob has acquired his brother's blessing.

18 The opening "My father," as in 22:7, is a deferential request to say something. It is enough to identify the speaker as Isaac's son, but which son? Isaac's
immediately suspicious reply, "Who are you, my son?" shows that the deception
may be more difficult than Rebekah had hoped.

19 Perhaps taken aback by his father's suspicion, Jacob overreacts in asserting his identity. The normal reply in Hebrew to his father's question is "Esau am
I," but he uses a more assertive form "*I* am Esau" and then rattles on about being
Jacob's firstborn, doing what he has been told, and would his father now please
bless him. The reference to him being the firstborn is like much else in this speech
unnecessary, but it is, of course, a key word in the whole cycle. "Firstborn" (בכר *bkr*)

is an anagram of "bless" (ברך *brk*), and it is the firstborn's blessing that Jacob is after. Although he does obtain it on this occasion, he is paid back later by getting a firstborn (בכירה *bkyrh*) that he does not want (29:26)!

20 Isaac's astonished question, "How did you ever find it so quickly . . . ?" prompts a rather lame reply from Jacob, "Because the LORD your God made me meet it." Though excoriated by commentators for taking God's name in vain and thus sinning even more deeply, Jacob is really on the verge of giving himself away by not offering a more convincing reply to this question. Isaac is not so dim as he thought.

21 With Isaac's request that Jacob come close so that he may feel him, the narrative becomes ever more tense. Will he be discovered or not?

22–23 But the disguise provided by Rebekah is sufficient. Only the voice does not seem to fit. Nevertheless, Isaac is sufficiently persuaded to bless Jacob. "So he blessed him." Since the blessing is not pronounced until v 27, introduced by the same verbal form "and he blessed him," this has occasioned some difficulty. Volz (*Der Elohist*, 66) suggested "so he blessed" is a gloss. Others that it is a mark of different sources. Recently, Westermann has argued for the integrity of the passage, but that the sense of "he blessed" is different here from v 27. Here it refers to the whole action of blessing, i.e., the rite of eating, drinking, kissing, and pronouncing blessing, whereas in v 27 it refers only to the pronouncement. Jacob, however, suggests that in v 23 "bless" has a less specialized sense "to greet, to thank" (cf. 24:31; Josh 14:13; 1 Sam 26:25). In support of this rendering may be noted *THWAT* 1:359: "In everyday Israelite usage *brk* means simply 'greet.'" Alternatively, Keil, Delitzsch, Gispen, Ska (*Bib* 73 [1992] 518–27), NEB, NAB may be correct to take it as proleptic, "so that is why he blessed him."

24–26 The tension again rises as Isaac inquires whether Jacob is really Esau and as he is invited to come close and kiss his father. (Kissing was a regular part of the farewell; cf. 48:10; 50:1.) However, all goes smoothly. The wine not only makes it a celebratory occasion, but it ensures that Isaac's critical faculties will be lulled and that he will not ask any more awkward questions. As long as Esau does not turn up, Jacob is safe and the blessing will soon be his.

27–29 The blessing is in verse (cf. Gen 49; Deut 33). It was, of course, intended for Esau but was pronounced over Jacob. And its contents reflect this hybrid setting. It begins with mentioning "the fragrance of the land." שדה "land" refers to the open uncultivated plain, where flocks may be pastured and men like Esau hunt (cf. *Comment* on 2:5). However, Isaac then prays for "the dew of heaven and the richness of the earth," either heavy rain or the rich harvests such rainfall produces, "an abundance of grain and new wine." These are not the concerns of the nomadic hunter but those of the settled farmer. "Grain and new wine" often occur together in lists of the products of Canaan (e.g., Deut 7:13; 28:51; 33:28; 2 Kgs 18:32; Hos 7:14; Joel 1:10). So this remark is much more appropriate for Jacob than for Esau, looking forward ultimately to the settlement in the promised land.

29 The phraseology of these promises clearly echoes the birth oracle (25:23). לאם "nations/people" occurs only here and in 25:23, and the verb עבד "serve" also links these two passages.

However, the precise meaning of the prayer/prediction, "May peoples serve you and nations bow down before you," is less clear. It may be looking forward to

Israel's victories in the conquest or early monarchy period, or to the lesser-known victories of the Edomites.

"Be lord over your brothers" again echoes 25:23, "The older will be a slave of the other," and, as 27:37, is the key statement of the blessing, which Isaac insists cannot be retracted. גביר "lord" occurs only here and in 27:37. The feminine גבירה means mistress (16:8–9) or "queen-mother" (2 Kgs 10:13).

"May your mother's sons bow down before you." In its immediate context, this is a continuation of the previous line, a prayer that Jacob will be honored by Esau and any other brothers he may have. In the broader context of the Jacob cycle, it may be noted that it is Rebekah's grandsons (Jacob's sons) who in fact bow down to *Esau* (33:3, 6–7). Here again the Delphic nature of the blessing is evident; it has multiple meanings, being intended for Esau but addressed to Jacob. It also anticipates Joseph's experiences, in dreams and in reality, of his brothers bowing down before him (37:7, 9, 10; 42:6; 43:26, 28).

Hitherto this blessing stands quite apart from the normal patriarchal promises. There is nothing explicit about numerous descendants or the gift of the land or blessing to the nations, the standard ingredients of the promises. Two of these appear in the second blessing of Jacob (28:3–4). The omissions here again reflect that this promise is intended for Esau rather than Jacob. Only the last clauses, "Cursed are those who curse you, and blessed are those who bless you," hark back clearly to the Abrahamic promise. But when compared with 12:3, "I will bless those who bless you, and he who disdains you I shall curse," it is evident that 27:29 is a much less personal formulation. It uses the passive participles "cursed/blessed" instead of "I shall bless/curse"; it reverses the order of blessing and cursing; and it implies a multitude of enemies, not just a few, by using "those who curse you" for "he who disdains you." All these changes suggest that the intended recipient of this verse is in a less intimate relationship with God than Abraham was. For fuller discussion, see *Comment* on 12:3.

Nevertheless, the overall thrust of the blessing is extremely positive. It opens with a reference to the LORD's blessing in v 27, and its very last words are "blessers blessed." Since blessing is at the center of this story and indeed of Genesis, it is clearly most significant that Jacob has obtained such a categoric affirmation of his status as the blessed one.

30–40 The poignant pathos of this scene is unsurpassed in Genesis. The dialogue is most moving, and unlike most OT narrative, the intense emotions of the actors are described with some fullness. "Isaac was gripped by an uncontrollable trembling"; "He let out a loud and very anguished scream." But the purpose of this scene is more than dramatic; it underlines the fact that however irregular was Isaac's blessing, it was irrevocable, "Yes, he will be blessed" (v 33), and Esau or Isaac can do nothing to change it.

30 This underlines how close Esau came to stopping the blessing of Jacob. Had he arrived just a few minutes earlier, he might have found Isaac eating and unmasked his brother. But all was quiet in Isaac's tent when Esau returned, so he went off to prepare his tasty stew.

31 No doubt the preparation of the stew took some time, but at last in a very cheerful mood Esau brings it in: "May my father arise and eat of his son's game

in order that your soul may bless me." Contrast the much more deferential opening, "My father," in v 18 and in 22:7. One wonders whether Esau's heartiness in fact transgressed oriental etiquette; should a son really address his dying father with such gaiety? In any case, it shows him flushed with his success and expecting the best from his father.

32 But his humor is suddenly deflated by Isaac's question, "Who are you?" When Jacob had brought in his stew, Isaac had said, "Who are you, my son?" Isaac apparently does not even recognize Esau as his son. So his shocked reply begins "I am your son," and then he makes his claim more specific, "your firstborn, Esau."

33 It is now Isaac's turn to panic: "He was gripped by an uncontrollable trembling," lit. "he trembled a very great trembling." The verb חרד "tremble" expressed intense fear and alarm by itself (e.g., by Joseph's brothers when arrested, 42:28, by the people on Sinai, Exod 19:16, or by Abimelek visited by David, 1 Sam 21:2[1]). Here it is supplemented by the cognate noun "trembling" and superlative adjective "very great." Hebrew can hardly express Isaac's panic more graphically.

At last he explains what happened. He has blessed some unknown, and that blessing cannot be revoked: "Yes, he will be blessed."

34 Once again the Hebrew is remarkable for using a strong verb, "scream," with a cognate noun and superlative adjective. On צעק "scream," cf. *Comment* on 4:10. Isaac's extreme panic is matched by his son's extreme distress. When he at last speaks, his plea is pathetic in its simplicity, "Bless me, even me, father."

35 Isaac now answers his own question, "Who was it then" (v 33), and explains why he cannot now bless Esau. He had thought there was something suspicious about his first caller; now he realizes what has happened: "Your brother has come with deceit and taken away your blessing." The noun מרמה "deceit" and the verb רמה "deceive" both suggest deliberate planning, e.g., by the sons of Jacob (34:13), by the Gibeonites (Josh 9:22), by merchants with unfair scales (Amos 8:5). Later Jacob complains to Laban about his substituting Leah for Rachel, "Why have you deceived me?"—a clear case of do as you would be done by.

36 "He has cheated me these two times." "Cheated" (עקב) is a bitter pun on Jacob's name (יעקב). However, the precise meaning of עקב is unclear as it only occurs here, in Jer 9:3(4), and in Hos 12:4(3) as a description of Jacob's own behavior. On the basis of an Ugaritic cognate, ʿqb "to deceive, impede," KB suggests the verb means "to deceive."

"Did you not reserve a blessing for me?" Had this been a proper deathbed farewell, all the sons should have been invited to receive a blessing, but it was not. Esau alone was summoned because Isaac intended to confer a blessing only on him. He went along with this scheme; now he is left with nothing. In the Hebrew there is a nice alliteration between my "birthright" (בְּכֹרָתִי *bĕkōrātî*) and "my blessing" (בִּרְכָתִי *birkātî*). Note too the repetition of "take" (לקח) in both lines.

37 Isaac reaffirms the contents of the blessing pronounced over Jacob, with one slight change. Instead of "may your mother's sons fall down before you," which could anticipate 33:3, 6–7 (see *Comment* on v 29), he says "I have made all his brothers his servants," which seems to look forward to Israel's conquest of surrounding peoples in the period of the settlement or monarchy. Thus, Isaac interprets his blessing of Jacob in a most disadvantageous way for Esau, and so concludes hopelessly, "So for you then, what can I do, my son?"

38 Esau repeats his pathetic plea (cf. v 34, 36) and then breaks down in sobs of despair (cf. 21:16).

39–40 Whether Isaac's eventual response should be described as a blessing is moot. The first line may be taken in two different ways. "From the richness of the earth and the dew of the heaven above" echoes the blessing of Jacob (v 28). But there the prefixed מִן "of/from" means "some of." But does it carry the same sense here? Medieval commentators said it did, but most modern commentators agree that it here has a privative sense, "away from," because this makes best sense in the context. Esau is being condemned to a wandering existence like Cain or Ishmael, haunting the dry wilderness to the south and east of Canaan. And certainly the traditional area of Edom southeast of the Dead Sea is much more arid than the land of Israel. However, if Esau was clutching at any straw, he may well be presumed to take it in the more optimistic sense, "Of the richness of the earth and dew of heaven."

"You shall live by your sword." Throughout the OT, Edom appears as a militant nation, often hostile to his brother Israel (Num 20:18; 1 Sam 14:47; 1 Kgs 11:14–16; 2 Kgs 14:7–10; Obad; Ps 60:10–11[8–9]). From the time of David, Edom was part of the Israelite empire, but later it regained its independence (2 Kgs 8:20–22) and after the fall of Jerusalem took revenge on Judah (cf. Obad; Ps 137:7). It is perhaps these events to which "when you grow restless, you shall tear off his yoke" refer. Thus, the blessing of Esau does end with a glimmer of hope.

41–28:5 In this final composite scene, the dominating, organizing Rebekah reappears. It is, in fact, her last appearance in Genesis. Once again she manipulates her beloved son Jacob and her husband to do what she wants. But ultimately all her maneuvers are futile. Her efforts on behalf of Jacob lead to his flight from home, so that what she was seeking to avoid, "Why should I lose both of you . . . ?" is what really happens. So the career of the woman whose bright start promised to make her the female equivalent of Abraham eventually ends in shadow.

41 "Esau bore a grudge." The verb used here (שׂטם) is rare and suggests long-term persistent hatred (cf. 50:15; Ps 55:4[3]; Job 16:9; 30:21). "The days of mourning for my father are drawing near." Joseph's brothers also expected him to take vengeance after their father's death. But why did Esau plan to postpone his revenge? Isaac was surely too doddery to punish him physically. Does it reflect his affection for his father whom he did not want to hurt further, or fear that his father might curse him and disinherit him? The text does not say, so both possibilities must be left open. But it does underline the intensity of Esau's hatred by the final word, "so that I can kill *my brother.*" He is bent not just on murder but on fratricide; he is intent on slaying the very one whom he should protect. He is potentially a second Cain.

42 Even more intriguing is the problem posed by the comment, "Now it was reported to Rebekah what Esau . . . had said," when in the preceding verse we were told "Esau said to himself. . . ." Is it that after keeping his ideas to himself for a while, Esau later started bragging about what he planned to do? Or is it that Rebekah only received a distorted account of what Esau had in mind, perhaps that he was going to kill Jacob, but not when? Or does it show Rebekah is a prophet, able to divine her son's thoughts (*Gen. Rab.* 67:9)?

Her injunction to Jacob suggests that either she has received an inaccurate report of what Esau was saying or that she put a slant on them in order to make Jacob act more promptly. The use of הנה and the participle, "even now consoling himself," suggests that Esau is about to take action imminently to kill Jacob. Rebekah says nothing about him waiting till after the death of Isaac.

43 She continues in her most commanding matriarchal tone, employing the same phraseology that she employed to move Jacob before, "Now, my son, obey me" (cf. vv 8, 13). The verb "run away" again underlines the deadly danger Jacob faces if he stays (cf. Exod 2:15; 1 Sam 19:12), but then Rebekah encourages him to go by suggesting he go to his relations in Paddan-Aram, in fact to her brother Laban. As Jacob's uncle, he is bound to offer him protection.

44–46 And anyway, your stay there will be only "a few days" (cf. 29:20, Dan 11:20; the only other occurrences of this phrase). Then you will be able to come home. I shall send and fetch you. But it is essential that you leave now, for your brother is extremely angry: "Until your brother's wrath abates, until your brother's anger subsides from you." This double reference underlines the chief cause of her concern. And if he kills you, I shall lose both of you. You will be dead, and vengeance will taken out on Esau. He will be killed or, like Cain, forced into exile.

This powerful plea by Rebekah with its dire warnings of what will happen if Jacob stays and the rosy prospect she paints of a short and congenial stay in Paddan meet with no immediate response from Jacob. Considering with what alacrity he cooperated earlier, this is strange. Does he no longer trust his mother? Does he know she is exaggerating the immediate danger, or is he afraid to go to Paddan-Aram? Or does he intend to go but not in a hurry? Again the narrator leaves us guessing.

46–28:5 But Rebekah is convinced that Jacob must leave immediately and decides to use Isaac to send him away. Note once again how she skillfully deploys her arguments to persuade Isaac to do what she wants. Isaac was never very fond of Jacob, though he adored Esau, so to inform him that Jacob was under threat from Esau would not have been tactful or likely to have achieved what she wanted. Rebekah had long been partisan toward Jacob, so Isaac would have surely discounted any suggestion from her that Esau might kill Jacob.

Instead, she wisely appeals to what they do agree on, that Esau's wives are awful; 26:35 said that they made life miserable for Isaac and Rebekah. She is even more colorful, "I loathe my life because of the Hittite women." קוץ "loathe" is a very strong term of disgust (cf. Lev 20:23; Num 21:5). But it could be worse. Jacob might do the same! Rebekah does not say any more; her husband might object if she told him what to do. Nor does she actually call them Esau's wives, which might trigger a positive attitude toward them, but simply "the Hittite women."

28:1–2 Happily, Isaac does what Rebekah wanted without her direction. In words very reminiscent of his father Abraham, "Do not marry . . . one of the Canaanite girls" (24:3); "Go to my country . . . and take a wife for my son" (24:4), Isaac bids Jacob leave home and find a wife among his kinsfolk. However, whereas Abraham sent his servant on Isaac's behalf, Isaac sends Jacob himself. For Jacob to take a lead in looking for a wife would seem more typical. Isaac is always portrayed as somewhat passive. However, whereas Abraham's servant was simply told to find a Mesopotamian girl for Isaac, Jacob is more or less told to marry one of

Laban's daughters, so he did not have a very wide choice either! Note how Isaac describes Bethuel as your *mother's* father and Laban as your *mother's* brother, when they were also his cousins. This may well reflect on Jacob's closeness to his mother and shows how Isaac encouraged Jacob to leave home.

3–4 Isaac's blessing on this occasion is very different from that he had planned for Esau (27:27–29). He describes this blessing as the blessing of Abraham. And it largely echoes the promises made to Abraham, for nearly every phrase is found in the Abrahamic promises (cf. 12:2–3, 7; 13:15, 17; 15:7–8, 18; 17:1, 6, 8, 16, 20; 22:17; 24:7) and in their recapitulation to Isaac (26:3–4, 24). However, this is the first time that Jacob has been designated heir of the Abrahamic promises, so it is not surprising that the closest parallels to the whole are in 35:11–12 and 48:3–4; cf. also 28:13, where the first promise made to Jacob is recalled.

5 Jacob had ignored his mother's warning, but he does what his father orders. But there are no verbs suggesting any urgency about his journey. He simply "went to Paddan-Aram" to the house of his relatives. Here the outcome of his journey is briefly anticipated. On the Arameans, cf. *Comment* on 10:22.

6–9 The description of Esau's reaction is surprisingly long-winded and seems to emphasize the connection between the blessing of Jacob and his being sent to find a wife in Paddan-Aram. To marry a relation rather than a Canaanite seemed to ensure parental goodwill, so Esau decides to marry a daughter of Ishmael. That it was only after he had heard Isaac sending Jacob off that he realized his wives were unpopular suggests Esau was rather slow-witted. Note though that the text says "Esau realized that Isaac his father did not like Canaanite women," but nothing about his mother's feelings (26:35; 27:46), another hint of the division in the family. Esau wanted to please his father—not his mother.

9 If the chronological data of Genesis are supposed to be taken literally, Ishmael must already have been dead, in which case "Isaac went to Ishmael" must mean he went to the Ishmaelites (cf. 16:16; 21:4; 25:17; 27:1).

"Mahalat" is of unknown meaning; Noth (*Personennamen*, 249) suggests "intelligence."

On Nebaiot, cf. *Comment* on 25:13.

This remark about Esau marrying an Ishmaelite suggests a close association between the two groups; 16:12 and 27:39–40 certainly suggest they were kindred spirits.

Explanation

The drama of this episode is among the most gripping in Genesis. Will Isaac dislodge Jacob's disguise, as he blindly gropes over the goatskins draped round his neck? Will Esau arrive back from the hunt before Isaac has eaten the special stew and blessed Jacob? We wait to discover whether Rebekah and Jacob will get away with their daring ruse. But as the narrator satisfies our love of the theatrical here, he outrages our moral and theological sense of propriety. How can he suggest that God's intention to bless Jacob could, let alone should, be forwarded by such underhanded tactics? Driver (255) aptly sums up what seems to be the gist of the story as follows: it "tells how, instigated by his ambitious and designing mother, Jacob deceives his aged father, and wrests from his brother his father's

blessing. That the action of Rebekah and Jacob was utterly discreditable and in-defensible, is of course obvious."

Most readers would undoubtedly agree with Driver's feelings, at least on first reading. But it seems unlikely that the writer of Genesis saw his characters in such black-and-white terms. The episode begins by remarking that Esau had mar-ried two Hittite wives, who made life miserable for Isaac and Rebekah. In the perspective of Genesis, bigamy is in itself questionable. God only created one wife for Adam, Lamek the first bigamist was vicious, and Jacob's family was always at loggerheads because he had two wives. If bigamy was doubtful, marrying Hittites, i.e., Canaanites, should certainly have been avoided. Intermarriage with Canaanites was quite out of the question for Isaac; his father Abraham had sent a servant all the way to Harran to find him a suitable wife. Loyalty to family tradi-tion should have dictated that Esau do the same.

Or does Esau's marriage to Canaanites really reflect on Isaac's neglect of duty? After all, before Isaac was forty (25:20), Abraham had arranged his marriage to Rebekah. Why had not Isaac done the same for Esau and Jacob? Throughout Genesis, Isaac is portrayed as rather passive. Indeed, in the previous chapter, his quiet peaceable nature in avoiding confrontation with the Philistines was implic-itly applauded, and he was rewarded by a reaffirmation of the promises and great prosperity. Here, however, his virtue has become a vice; his quiet patience has become lethargy. Failing to find suitable wives for his sons, his life has been made miserable by unsuitable daughters-in-law. But this experience had not taught Isaac to be less partisan, for on his deathbed he again flouts convention and summons just Esau to receive his last blessing, whereas it was customary for a dying man to call all his sons to his side to receive an appropriate blessing. Deliberately, though, Isaac calls only Esau to receive his blessing, and he leaves out Jacob. The reason he gives for only calling Esau is that he makes a "tasty stew that I love." One can-not but be reminded of Esau, who some years earlier had swapped his birthright for a lentil stew. If the narrator expects us to compare this deathbed scene with Abraham's (chap. 24), he implies that Isaac and Esau are both alike in putting appetite before principle, self-indulgence before justice, immediate satisfaction before long-term spiritual values. Initially then, the blame for what follows lies with Isaac and Esau, not simply with Rebekah and Jacob.

Rebekah, when we first met her in chap. 24, appeared to be the perfect wife for Isaac—beautiful, energetic, and, like Abraham, willing to leave home and fam-ily for the land of promise. Her energy complemented her husband's retiring nature. But just as his love of the quiet life led him to neglect of his paternal duties and indifference to ancient propriety, so her dominating nature led her to overstep the bounds of moral behavior.

Faced with the prospect of her favorite son not being blessed at all by his fa-ther before his death, she contrives a daring scheme whereby Jacob will receive all the blessing instead of Esau. And it works brilliantly. After dressing up as Esau, Jacob is given a total blessing and promised the fertility of the land and the sub-jection of his brothers. So complete is the blessing that when Esau arrives, Isaac can find very little to say to him.

It is not clear how far Jacob approved of his mother's scheme. He certainly did what he was told, though not with any alacrity. He raised an objection to it, "Suppose

my father touches me . . . and discovers who I am. . . . " But this objection seems to be based more on fear than scruple, for certainly earlier he had no compunctions about exploiting Esau's hunger for his own gain. So it seems likely that he did inwardly support his mother's aims here, even though he had doubts about their success.

It is also not immediately clear how far the narrator approved of Rebekah and Jacob's tricks. Explicit moral comment within a story is rare throughout the OT, but that does not mean the narrator has no moral values or that the vivid way he recounts the success of Rebekah's ruse means that he wholeheartedly endorsed it. Isaac's comment, "Your brother has come with deceit" (27:35), is the nearest the narrator comes to condemning their behavior. Only subsequently does it emerge that Jacob and Rebekah suffer for their deeds. Jacob, of course, has to flee from home to escape his brother's fratricidal wrath; Rebekah hopes that he will be away only "a few days," but it lasts twenty years, and she never sees her favorite son again. Jacob, the deceiver, is for his part cruelly deceived by his father-in-law Laban, who makes him marry the unlovely Leah, as well as beautiful Rachel. And Jacob never accepted Leah or her sons, and the bitter tensions between them would cloud the rest of his life. Like his mother Rebekah, he would spend most of his latter years mourning the loss of his favorite son. Thus, despite his apparent silence about the morality of the actions of Jacob and Rebekah, the narrator points out that they paid dearly for them.

So why then is this episode related in such detail? How does it relate to the theme of the Pentateuch? Fundamental to the whole story is the conviction of the efficacy of the deathbed blessing; what the patriarch says before he dies determines the destiny of his descendants (cf. Gen 48–49). That is why Rebekah is so desperate to make sure Jacob is blessed instead of Esau. That is why Isaac declares he cannot revoke the blessing once uttered, and why Esau pleads for him to find some blessing for him. Clearly, Genesis sees the deathbed blessing as more than a prayer for the future; it is a prophecy whose fulfillment is certain.

So Isaac here declares the future relationship of Esau (Edom) and Jacob (Israel), that one would live a wandering nomadic existence away from settled agricultural existence, while the other would enjoy the fruits of the earth. Like the birth oracle (25:23), Isaac confirms that Esau, the older, will serve the younger, Jacob. These prophecies, of course, find multiple fulfillment in the history of Israel and Edom. More than that, Isaac reiterates the promises made to Abraham and to himself (28:3–4), indicating that the line of God's choice will now pass through Jacob, not Esau.

By setting this new step forward in the history of salvation in the context of such unprincipled behavior by every member of the family, each self-centeredly seeking his or her own interest, the narrator is not simply pointing out the fallibility of God's chosen, whose virtues often turn into vices, but reasserting the grace of God. It is his mercy that is the ultimate ground of salvation.

Jacob Meets God at Bethel   (28:10–22)

Bibliography

Barth, C. "Jakob in Bethel—ein neues Buch zur Vätertradition." *TLZ* 104 (1979) 331–38. **Couffignal, R.** "Le Songe de Jacob: Approches nouvelles de Gen 28:10–22." *Bib* 58 (1977) 342–60. **Donner, H.** "Zu Gen 28:22." *ZAW* 74 (1962) 68–70. **Dumbrell, W. J.** "The Role of Bethel in the Biblical Narratives from Jacob to Jeroboam." *Australian Journal of Biblical Archaeology* 2/3 (1974/75) 65–76. **Eissfeldt, O.** "Jakobs Begegnung mit El und Moses Begegnung mit Jahwe." *KS* 4 (1968) 92–98. **Griffiths, J. G.** "The Celestial Ladder and the Gate of Heaven (Gen 28:12 and 17)." *ExpTim* 76 (1964–65) 229–30. **Hammann, G.** "Le songe de Jacob et sa lutte avec l'ange (Gen 28 et 32): repères historiques d'une lecture et de ses variations." *RHPR* 66 (1986) 29–42. **Houtman, C.** "What Did Jacob See in His Dream at Bethel? Some Remarks on Gen 28:10–22." *VT* 27 (1977) 337–51. **Husser, J.-M.** "Les métamorphoses d'un songe: Critique littéraire de Genèse 28:10–22." *RB* 98 (1991) 321–42. **Jacobson, H.** "An.zaqar: A Conjecture." *Or* 45 (1976) 269. **Jensen, H. J. L.** "Reden, Zeit und Raum in Gen 28:10–15: Textlinguistische und textsemiotische Exegese eines Fragments." *LingBib* 49 (1981) 54–70. **Marböck, J.** "Heilige Orte im Jakobszyklus: Einige Beobachtungen und Aspekte." In *Die Väter Israels: FS J. Scharbert,* ed. M. Görg. Stuttgart: Katholisches Bibelwerk, 1989. 211–24. **Maxwell-Mahon, W. D.** "'Jacob's Ladder': A Structural Analysis of Scripture." *Semitics* 7 (1980) 118–30. **Millard, A. R.** "The Celestial Ladder and the Gate of Heaven (Gen 28:12,17)." *ExpTim* 78 (1966/67) 86–87. **Oliva, M.** "Visión y voto de Jacob en Betel." *EstBib* 33 (1974) 117–55. **Oppenheim, A. L.** *The Interpretation of Dreams in the Ancient Near East.* Transactions of the American Philosophical Society 46. Philadelphia, 1956. **Otto, E.** "Jakob in Bethel: Ein Beitrag zur Geschichte der Jakobsüberlieferung." *ZAW* 88 (1976) 165–90. **Parker, S. B.** "The Vow in Ugaritic and Israelite Narrative Literature." *UF* 11 (1979) 693–700. **Pury, A. de.** *Promesse divine et légende cultuelle dans le cycle de Jacob: Gen 28 et les traditions patriarcales.* Études bibliques. Paris: Gabalda, 1975. **Rendtorff, R.** "Jakob in Bethel: Beobachtungen zum Aufbau and zur Quellenfrage in Gen 28:10–22." *ZAW* 94 (1982) 511–23. **Richter, W.** "Das Gelübde als theologische Rahmung der Jakobsüberlieferungen." *BZ* 11 (1967) 21–52. **Ross, A. P.** "Jacob's Vision: The Founding of Bethel." *BSac* 142 (1985) 224–37. **Sauneron, S.** "Les songes et leur interprétation dans l'Égypte ancienne." In *Les Songes et leur interprétations.* Sources Orientales 2. Paris, 1959. 17–61. **Schwartz, J.** "Jubilees, Bethel and the Temple of Jacob." *HUCA* 56 (1985) 63–85. **Wyatt, N.** "Where Did Jacob Dream His Dream?" *SJOT* 2 (1990) 44–57.

Translation

[10]*Jacob left Beersheba and went to Harran.* [11]*He stopped in a certain*[a] *place and spent*[b] *the night there because the sun had set. He had taken some of the stones of the place, put*[c] *them round his head, and had gone to sleep in that place,* [12]*when he dreamed that he saw*[a] *a ladder erected*[b] *on the ground with its top touching*[c] *the sky, angels of God going up and down on it,* [13]*and the LORD standing*[a] *over it,*[b] *who said, "I am the LORD, the God of Abraham your father and the God of Isaac.*[c] [d]*The land on which you are lying I shall give to you and your descendants.*[d] [14]*Your descendants will be like the dust of the earth and spread westward and eastward, northward and southward, and all the families of the earth shall find blessing in you* [a]*and in your descendants.*[a] [15]*I am*

*really*ᵃ *with you and will guard you* ᵇ*wherever you go*ᵇ *and bring*ᶜ *you back to this land,
because I shall not leave you until*ᵈ *I have done*ᵉ *for you what*ᶠ *I have promised you."*

¹⁶*So Jacob awoke from his sleep and said, "Truly*ᵃ *the* LORD *is present*ᵇ *in this place,
yet I did not realize it."* ¹⁷*Overawed he said, "How*ᵃ *awesome*ᵇ *is this place.* ᶜ*This is
nothing but a house of God, and this must be*ᵈ *the gate of heaven."*ᶜ

¹⁸*Early in the morning Jacob took a stone which he had put for his head and set it up
as a pillar and poured*ᵃ *oil on top of it.* ¹⁹*So he called the name of that place Bethel, but
the city used to be called Luz.* ²⁰*Then Jacob made*ᵃ *a vow: "If God will*ᵇ *be with me,
guard me on the journey I am undertaking, give me food to eat, clothes to wear,* ²¹*and I
return*ᵃ *in peace to my father's house, the* LORD *will be my God,* ²²*and this stone which I
have set up as a pillar will*ᵃ *be a house of God,* ᵇ*and from everything that you give to me,
I shall give a full*ᶜ *tenth to you."*ᵇ

Notes

11.a. The def art may be used in Heb. where the object referred to is determinate in itself, even
though it is indeterminate to the writer. Hence, the English may translate the def art "a" or "a certain"; cf. 16:7; 19:30 (GKC, 126r; Joüon, 137n).

11.b. Waw consec + 3 masc sg impf qal לין.

11.c. Cf. n. 2:8.b.

12.a.-13.b. Note the string of clauses introduced by והנה + subj ("ladder," "angels," "LORD") + ptcp
("erected," "going up," "standing"). This is characteristic of dream reports; cf. 31:10; 37:6–7, 9; 41:1–
7 (SBH, 95).

12.b. Masc sg ptcp hoph נצב.

12.c. Masc sg ptcp hiph נגע.

13.a. Cf. n. 24:13.b.

13.b. More likely than "over him"; see *Comment.*

13.c. G adds "Do not fear."

13.d-d. This word order, with the obj "land" placed first, may emphasize the obj; cf. n. 13:15.a-a.
(Joüon, 156c). SBH, 92, suggests it is used here to introduce a new topic, and *EWAS,* 96–97, sees it as
merely stylistic.

14.a-a. *Pace BHS,* there are no text-critical grounds for regarding this phrase as a gloss.

15.a. Or "I am now with you." הנה expresses immediacy; cf. Lambdin, 169.

15.b-b. G reads "in all the way wherever you go."

15.c. Waw consec + 1 sg pf hiph שוב + 2 masc sg suffix.

15.d. Clauses introduced by עד or עד־אשר do not always express an absolute time limit, but rather
one that extends beyond the main clause (GKC, 164f).

15.e. Here the pf is used with a fut pf meaning especially common after (אשר) עד "I shall have
done" (Joüon, 112i; cf. GKC, 106o; WOC, 491).

15.f. G reads "all that."

16.a. On the asseverative particle אכן, cf. *EWAS,* 132–33; SBH, 185.

16.b. The particle יש "serves to stress the idea of existence" (*EWAS,* 101).

17.a. On מה to express astonishment, see GKC, 148b.

17.b. Masc sg ptcp niph ירא. On the potential meaning "awesome," "ought to be feared" of niphal,
see Lambdin, 177.

17.c-c. Coordinated clauses in expository apposition to first clause, "How awesome . . . place"
(SBH, 50).

17.d. For this translation, see *EWAS,* 10.

18.a. Waw consec + 3 masc sg impf qal יצק.

20.a. Waw consec + 3 masc sg impf נדר.

20.b. On sequence of tenses in vv 20–21, cf. WOC, 526–27.

21.a. Waw consec + 1 sg pf qal שוב.

22.a. Note lack of concord between 3 masc sg verb ויהי and fem subj "stone." Joüon, 150m, suggests that the masc predicate "house" has influenced verb.

22.b-b. Adjunctive clause suggests tithing is an afterthought (*SBH*, 92–93).
22.c. Inf abs piel עָשׂ֑וֹר. Inf abs with finite verb makes promise more definite (*EWAS*, 86).

Form/Structure/Setting

The beginning and end of this story are very clear. It opens with v 10, a summary of Jacob's journey, linking this episode to the surrounding material in chaps. 27 and 29. It closes with Jacob's vow in vv 20–22, which again looks back to his departure from home and forward to his eventual return.

In that the episode covers both the night of the dream and the morning after, it could be split into two scenes (vv 10–17; 18–22), but it seems better to take it as a single extended scene. If the use of an explicit nominal subject (Jacob) marks a new paragraph, the material divides as follows:

vv 10–15   Jacob's experience at Bethel
vv 16–17   Jacob's first reaction
vv 18–22   Jacob's vow

Fokkelman (*Narrative Art*) has noted how key terms in this narrative are arranged palistrophically; (A) "place" (v 11), (B) "take stones, make a headrest" (v 11), (C) "sky" (v 12), (D) "God" (v 12), (E) "the LORD" (v 13), (E) "the LORD" (v 16), (D) "God" (v 17), (C) "heaven" (v 17), (B) "take stone, make a headrest" (v 17), (A) "place" (v 19). There is also repetition, so that the two halves of the tale fall into parallel panels; most obviously, Jacob's vow (vv 20–22) echoes the divine promises (vv 13–15).

"place"(v 11 3x)	"place" (vv 16, 17)
"stones," "headrest" (v 11)	"stone," "headrest" (v 18)
"I am really with you" (v 15)	"If God will be with me" (v 20)
"guard you wherever you go" (v 15)	"guard me on the journey I am undertaking" (v 20)
"bring you back to this land" (v 15)	"return in peace to my father's house" (v 21)
"I shall not leave you" (v 15)	"and the LORD is my God" (v 21)

Though this is a clear, self-contained unit, it has many links with the preceding and following narratives. V 10 "Beersheba" looks back to 26:23–28:5; "Harran" forward to 29:4–31:54. His dream (vv 11–15) invites comparison with 15:12–21 and 32:14(13)–33(32); vv 13–14 quote 12:3, and 13:14–16 and are in their turn echoed in 32:10–13 (9–12) and 35:11–12. The promise of divine companionship and ultimate return to the land (v 15) recurs again in 31:3, 5, 42; 32:13(12); 35:3. Jacob's erection of a pillar and vow (vv 18–22) are mentioned again in 31:13 and more vaguely in 35:1–7. Within the Jacob cycle, this encounter with God on Jacob's departure from the land matches a similar encounter when he returned, 32:2–3(1–2).

According to the traditional source critics (see de Pury, *Promesse divine*, 34–35), this section comes from J and E. From J come vv 13–16, 19a, that is, the divine promises and the naming of Bethel; from E come vv 11–12, 17–18, 20–21a, 22, that is, the dream, the erection of the stone, and Jacob's vow. There is wide

agreement on this analysis, but no clear consensus about v 10 (either J or E), about 19b (J or redactor), or about 21b (E or redactor). In the fullest recent study on these lines, de Pury argues that v 10 is common to J and E and that 19b is redaction and v 21b is E. However, he points out that it is most unlikely that E's version of the dream ended at v 12. All other ancient Near Eastern dreams directed to the foundation of a sanctuary end with the god himself appearing and speaking. Therefore E must have originally contained something like vv 13, 15. The E version, he holds, was displaced by J's version (*Promesse divine*, 377, 449). Based on the source-critical analysis, it is apparent that the main account is E's, supplemented by J in vv 13–16, 19. This source division was justified by the following observations: there are two names of God, the LORD in vv 13, 16, 21 and God in vv 12, 17, 20, 21, 22; there is a different perspective in v 12, where angels appear, from v 13, where the LORD appears; there is double comment on the sacredness of the place in vv 16 and 17; the story apparently ends in v 19; and the vow in vv 20–22 is incompatible with the promise in vv 13–15, neither of which makes reference to the other.

However, this consensus has recently been rejected by scholars preferring a traditio-historical explanation of the text. Most of the alleged contrasts or duplications are susceptible of simple exegetical explanation. Even the divine name criterion is very weak, as Rendtorff (*ZAW* 94 [1982] 511–23) and Blum (*Die Komposition*) point out. Yahweh, the LORD, is the only name of God in the passage. Elohim, God, is a generic term, and it would be inappropriate to replace Elohim by Yahweh in such expressions as "angels of God" (v 12) or "house of God" (vv 17, 22). So Blum concludes, "Our investigation of the literary-critical proposals has shown the extraordinarily weak basis for the assumption of two parallel sources in Gen 28:10ff. It may be doubted whether this shattering of the narrative would have been seriously discussed, if the divine-name criterion had not been unquestioningly accepted as a primary datum" (*Die Komposition*, 23).

Tradition critics (e.g., Westermann, Rendtorff, Blum) prefer to view the account as a simple narrative that has been subsequently expanded at least twice. For Westermann, the earliest pre-Israelite core consists of vv 11–12, 16–19. This was expanded by J adding v 15, and then a third hand added vv 13–14, 20–22. Rendtorff (cf. Blum) again suggests that the earliest material is found in vv 11–12, 16–19. The divine promises in vv 13–15 were added subsequently to link this story to the rest of the patriarchal narratives. Vv 20–22 constitute an independent account of a vow with expansions in v 22b and later in 21b. Coats, however, suggests that the account is essentially J with Elohistic expansions.

It is doubtful how far these traditio-historical interpretations represent a real break with source-critical methodology. As Whybray (*Making of the Pentateuch*, 210) observes, they merely substitute their "own set of presuppositions for the earlier 'documentary' ones." Certainly Skinner's summary of the situation, "a complete Elohistic narrative with a Yahwistic insertion" (vv 13–16), is a simpler and more apt characterization of the section than Coats'. And Weisman (*From Jacob to Israel*, 57–67) has argued that we have here essentially one account reworked by J. Much earlier, Volz (*Der Elohist*) had cogently argued for the unity of 28:10–22 and its assignment to J. So here, as elsewhere in Genesis, it seems likely that the last major editor of this story is J. His interests are particularly clear

in the promises (vv 13–15) and to a lesser extent in the vow (vv 20–22), but to conclude that J simply added these elements to an earlier account would be rash. De Pury has elaborated a careful case for holding that the promises of land (v 13) and protection (v 15) and the vow (vv 20–22) are integral to the earliest patriarchal versions of the story. He sees just the promises of innumerable descendants and blessing to the nations as J's innovations (*Promesse divine,* 173–85). Among modern critics there is thus a wide diversity of approach to this passage, reflecting their different methodological presuppositions. Though I am in most sympathy with de Pury and Weisman's approach, I am more cautious than they are in distinguishing earlier and later elements within the narrative and will concentrate on seeing this passage in the total context of the Jacob cycle and the work of J.

Comment

10–15 In this first paragraph, the narrator describes Jacob's journey and experiences quasi-objectively. Subsequently, in vv 16–22, Jacob's more subjective reactions to these experiences are described.

10 "Jacob left Beersheba and went to Harran." Beersheba was Isaac's base (cf. 22:19; 26:23, 33). Isaac had told Jacob to go to Paddan-Aram (28:2, 5), whereas Rebekah had said Harran (27:43). Clearly, the same general district is meant (cf. *Comment* on 11:31; 25:20). There is no obvious reason for the use here of Harran rather than Paddan-Aram; it is perhaps the more evocative term, for it is in Harran that the call of Abraham is set and the promises first pronounced (11:31–12:5), promises about to be reiterated to Jacob.

11 Other biblical stories of travelers overtaken by nightfall tell of them being put up for the night by people living in the area (cf. 19:1–3; Judg 19:11–21). That Jacob is forced to bed down under the stars may suggest his distance from human habitation, or his estrangement, or simply affirm that providence overruled the traditional custom of finding lodging in someone's house. The threefold mention of המקום "the place" in this verse and then again in vv 16, 17, 19, culminating in the renaming of the place in v 19, hints at the significance of "the place." The term is sometimes used in a cultic sense as a "place of worship" (e.g., Deut 12:5) or "city" (Gen 18:24, 26), but there is no need to read such a precise meaning into it yet, for Jacob does not recognize its sanctity till the morning (v 17). "He took some of the stones . . . and put them round his head." Because v 18 speaks of one specific stone, it is often surmised that Jacob used the stone as a pillow. However, passages like 1 Sam 26:11–12; 1 Kgs 19:6, where the same phrase, "round his head," appears, suggest the stones were placed round his head to protect him rather than to lie on. There is no suggestion that the stones were particularly large.

12 As elsewhere in the Bible, the dream is described through the dreamer's eyes (cf. 31:10; 41:1–7). Three features of the dream are mentioned here: first, the ladder linking earth and heaven; second, the angels going up and down; and third, the LORD himself. It is not clear whether סלם "ladder" describes a ladder (so Jacob; Gispen; Griffiths, *ExpTim* 76 [1964/65] 229–30) or "a ramp or stairway" (most commentators), or whether there is Egyptian or Babylonian influence on the imagery. What matters is that the "ladder" links earth and heaven and has

been placed on the earth presumably near where Jacob is lying (cf. Houtman, *VT* 27 [1977] 337–51).

"Angels of God going up and down on it." Most commentators regard this as merely underlining the idea that earth and heaven were linked by a ladder. But this overlooks that this is a new verbal clause introduced by והנה, which is evidently adding something strikingly original and fresh. Angels in the OT are conceived of as looking after different nations and their territories and as patrolling the earth (Job 1:6; 2:1; Zech 1:8–17; cf. Deut 32:8). So Rashi suggests that the ascending angels are those responsible for Jacob's homeland and descending ones are those responsible for the foreign land to which he is going. In other words, this vision of the angels is an assurance of God's protection of Jacob even though he is leaving home. This is an attractive idea in that the vision thus anticipates the verbal assurances given in v 15. In a similar way, Abraham's night vision (15:11–12) anticipated the prophecy in 15:13–16.

13 "The LORD standing over it." עליו "over it" could also be translated "over him" (i.e., Jacob). However, the traditional understanding, "over it" (cf. G, Vg, König, Jacob), seems preferable for the following reasons: the suffixes in v 12, "its top," "on it," refer to the ladder; the vision is described through Jacob's eyes, so "over me" might be expected, if Jacob was the referent (cf. 40:9, "before me"); and, finally, the image of Yahweh at the top of the ladder forms a fitting climax to the whole and fits in with the idea that angels report back to him after patrolling the earth (1 Kgs 22:19–22; Job 1:6–8; 2:1–3; Zech 1:10). Though the majority of modern commentators prefer to translate "over him," this is because they see v 15 as the start of a new source, J, which is ignorant of the ladder. Therefore, the suffix must refer to Jacob. But Gunkel, while holding that "over him" is how J understood it originally, admits that in its present context the phrase means "over it." However, this attempt to distinguish sources here is suspect, for, as de Pury has pointed out (*Promesse divine*, 377), it is most unlikely that the dream did not include a vision of God and a message from him. This then is a vision of God, the sovereign ruler of heaven and earth, who is ministered to by angels constantly. This is "the LORD, the God of Abraham . . . and the God of Isaac" who addresses Jacob. This heavenly vision gives the promises that follow a majestic authority and weight.

The divine title "The LORD, the God of Abraham your father and the God of Isaac" occurs nowhere else in the OT. Elsewhere can be found such titles as "the God of Abraham your father" (26:24), "the LORD, the God of your fathers, the God of Abraham, Isaac, and Jacob" (Exod 3:15, 16). Here the combination of "the LORD" with "the God of Abraham" indicates that the God known to the patriarchs was indeed the same God who revealed himself to Moses (Exod 3:6–17; 6:2–8). But more than that, the double title "God of Abraham . . . God of Isaac" recalls the great promises and blessings given to them and anticipates their reaffirmation and reapplication to Jacob.

13b-14 The promise here most closely parallels that found in 13:14–16.

28:13	"The land on which you are lying I shall give to you and your descendants"
13:15	"The whole land which you see I shall give to you and your descendants for ever"
28:14	"Your descendants will be like the dust of the earth"
13:16	"I shall make your descendants like the dust of the earth"

28:14   "Spread westward and eastward, northward and southward"
13:14   "Look . . . northward and southward, eastward and westward"

There are, of course, other passages (12:7; 15:18; 17:8; 24:7) containing the promise of land, but in no other are the terms used so close as between 28:13–14 and 13:14–16. It is noteworthy that both passages are associated with Bethel.

Again, "all the families of the earth shall find blessing in you" quotes 12:3 verbatim, adding merely "and in your descendants," which echoes 22:18; 26:4. Through these remarks, the LORD reveals himself to be the very same God who spoke to Abraham, and what is more, confirms that Jacob is the chosen line, who will henceforth enjoy divine protection. And even more, though he is now fleeing Canaan, he will eventually return there. For what chiefly distinguishes this pronouncement of the promises from the earlier statements is their setting: the promises were first made to Abraham as he was settling in the land, but they are reaffirmed to Jacob as he is fleeing from it.

15 What is implied in vv 13–14 is made explicit here: if the LORD is giving the land to the fleeing Jacob, he will certainly preserve him and bring him back to the land at last. The promise of divine presence, "I am really with you," is characteristic of the Jacob cycle (cf. 28:20; 31:3; 46:4), though it is also found in 26:3, 24. However, in other respects the phraseology is quite untypical; שמר "guard" elsewhere in Genesis occurs in this phrase only in 28:20, and עזב "leave" nowhere else, though both terms are common in the psalms. "Until I have done for you what I have promised" does not mean that God's protection of Jacob will end some day, but that it will outlast all his journeyings (see n. 15.d.).

So with these categorical promises that Jacob will leave the land and then return and yet continue to enjoy the protection of divine providence, the plot of the Jacob story is foreshadowed. Whatever unexpected turns Jacob's career may take, the LORD will be with him, saving him from disaster and ensuring the ultimate triumph of what he had promised.

16–17 The story shows Jacob waking up in two stages. First, described in these verses, comes the feeling of awe as he wakes. Then, when he rises, he solemnly dedicates one of the stones and vows to bring his tithes to the God who dwells in this place (vv 18–22). Throughout Scripture the encounter with God brings fear; when sinful man meets the holy God, he is overawed and often becomes acutely conscious of his sin and unworthiness to stand in the divine presence (3:10; Exod 3:6; 20:15(18); Judg 6:23; 13:22). "House of God" (בֵּית אֱלֹהִים *bêt ʾĕlōhîm*) anticipates the name Jacob is about to give to the place, "Bethel" (v 19). "Gate of heaven" occurs only here in the OT, but the idea that heaven, the divine abode, has one or more entrances is a familiar idea in ancient thought. The etymology of Babylon, "the gate of the god," is similar (cf. *Comment* on 11:9).

18 To show his piety, Jacob takes one of the stones and sets it up as a sacred מצבה "pillar," dedicating it by pouring oil. Stones could be erected as memorials to the dead (35:20; 2 Sam 18:18) or as witnesses to agreements, especially boundary agreements (31:45, 51). Standing stones are frequently mentioned elsewhere in the OT as a feature of Canaanite religion that is to be shunned, "Beside the altar of the LORD . . . you shall not set up a pillar, which the LORD your God hates" (Deut 16:21–22; cf. Exod 23:24; 34:13; 1 Kgs 14:23). Now it may be argued,

as de Pury (*Promesse divine*) and Westermann do, that Jacob's stone is merely a witness, a reminder of Jacob's experience and of his vow. However, the wording of the vow, "this stone will be a house of God," and his pouring oil over it, a gesture frequently associated with consecrating cultic items (Exod 40:9–13; Lev 8:10–12; Num 7:1), makes it likely that the stone is seen as more than a mere witness. It is a cult object endued with divine power and representing God himself (cf. Houtman, *VT* 27 [1977] 343). The eighth-century Sefire treaties speak of the stones on which the treaties are inscribed as *bty ʾlhyʾ* "bethels, houses of the gods" (Sefire 2.C.2–3, 9–10): "Sacred stones sometimes considered as the dwelling of the god or even as the god himself" (J. A. Fitzmyer, *The Aramaic Inscriptions of Sefire*, BibOr19 [Rome: Biblical Institute, 1967] 90). Philo of Byblos much later talks of animate stones, calling them *baitylia*, clearly a Greek transliteration of the Semitic term "bethels." This passage in Genesis provides evidence that this notion of sacred stones long antedates the Sefire inscriptions. Indeed, the discrepancy between Jacob's deeds and later Mosaic injunction is an indication that this tradition does indeed go back to patriarchal times. That patriarchal religious practice does not everywhere conform to later pentateuchal law is one sign of the antiquity of the Genesis tradition (see *Introduction*, "The Religion of the Patriarchs"). Indeed, it is hard to envisage this episode being recorded at all after the late tenth century, when Bethel became a center for the Canaanite-style worship of bull calves. Here, though, it is glorified as a most holy sanctuary owing its foundation to Jacob himself, and this suggests the tradition comes from an era before Jeroboam's schism had sullied Bethel's reputation.

19 Though it might have seemed more natural to put this explanation of the change of Luz's name to Bethel at the end of the account, frequently Genesis prefers to put such etiological notes before the end (cf. 16:14; 22:14; 33:17). Evidently they are seen as incidental to the main story line. On the location of Bethel, cf. *Comment* on 12:8.

20–22 This vow is of great importance within the Jacob cycle, for it is mentioned again at key points (31:13; 35:1–3, 7). But the assertion of Westermann and others that it is a secondary element added later to the narrative is unlikely. It is in fact entirely suitable. Under *Form/Structure/Setting*, it was noted that dreams in the ancient Orient always contained a message from the deity; they were not left uninterpreted. So vv 13–15 are likely to be original. And it is precisely the wording of the promises in vv 15, "I am really with you," "guard," and "bring you back," that are echoed by Jacob in v 20. Furthermore, dreams usually culminate in the foundation of a sanctuary, and this is reported in v 22. Finally, the circumstances in which Jacob makes his vow are entirely fitting. Typically in the OT, a "vow is pronounced in a situation of distress, preferably in the sanctuary, and when the believer's prayer has been answered, the vow is fulfilled in the sanctuary. But the narrative in Gen 28 and the whole Jacob cycle presuppose a situation in which a vow is fully appropriate. Jacob is in a distressed state, running away from home, which is equivalent to being under threat of death. He has just received an unexpected revelation announcing his return to his country and guaranteeing him safety on the journey. What can be more natural than for Jacob to make a vow and pledge himself to worship the deity when the divine promise is fulfilled, that is when Jacob has returned to the sanctuary" (de Pury, *Promesse divine*, 438).

20–21a   As already noted, Jacob's conditions echo the promises made in v 15; only the mention of food and clothing is additional. Jacob's prayer is thus based on the divine promise. To suggest that divine promises make prayer redundant, so that Jacob's vow must come from a different author from the promise, misunderstands the nature of petitionary prayer within Scripture (cf. Luke 11:5–13).

21b–22   Though some rabbinic commentators, e.g., Rashi, regard "the LORD will be my God" as Jacob's final condition/petition, "and if the LORD is my God," this seems less likely than seeing it as the apodosis. In other words, Jacob promises that if the LORD brings him back safely, that (1) he will worship the LORD, (2) venerate this place as holy (here as in vv 17–18, the sacred stone represents the holiness of the whole area), and (3) offer tithes. In making the LORD his God and offering tithes, Jacob is imitating the actions of his grandfather Abraham (cf. 17:7; 14:20). He is also, as father of the nation, setting a pattern for all Israel to follow.

Explanation

Despite a warm paternal send-off (28:3–4), Jacob must have been frightened and depressed leaving home. He, the quiet home-loving boy, had been forced to flee for his life because of the hatred of his brother. Now on the first night away from home, he could not find anyone to give him a bed for the night, and he was forced to lie down under the stars. Doubtless, he must have wondered whether there was anything in his father's pious hopes for his future.

At last, falling asleep, he started dreaming. He saw angels going up and down a stairway between earth and heaven, going out to patrol the earth, so that wherever he went he would be accompanied by divine protectors (cf. 48:15–16). And standing above the ladder he saw the LORD himself, who introduced himself as the God of his father Isaac and grandfather Abraham and assured Jacob that the promises made to them would be true for him as well: he would inherit the land, have descendants as numerous as the dust of the earth, and bring blessing to the nations. But these were old promises looking to the long-term future; they did not deal with Jacob's immediate needs. But these the LORD also addressed.

"I am really with you and will guard you wherever you go and bring you back to this land." Jacob was the first in Bible history to hear the assurance "I am with you," a promise later repeated to many of the nation's leaders, Moses (Exod 3:12), Joshua (Josh 1:5), and Gideon (Judg 6:16); indeed Emmanuel, "God with us," (Isa 7:14; Matt 1:23) speaks of God's continuing presence with all his people, "for he has said 'I will never leave you or forsake you'" (Heb 13:5). More than this, though, Jacob is assured of protection, "I will guard you wherever you go," a sentiment reechoed in the priestly blessing, "The LORD bless you and keep (guard) you" (Num 6:24), and in the Psalms (e.g., 121, 23). It may well be that the angels in the dream are seen as Jacob's invisible bodyguards, for as another Psalm (91:11–12) says,

> For he will give his angels charge of you
>> to guard you in all your ways.
> On their hands they will bear you up,
>> lest you dash your foot against a stone.

Finally, last but not least for the home-lover Jacob, he was assured, "I will bring you back to this land." Little did he suspect that it would be twenty years before he came back, but he never stopped looking forward to that day.

For Jacob, this was his first personal encounter with God; he knew his parents' faith and of their own religious experiences, but now for the first time he has come face to face with God, and he is scared and overwhelmed. He confesses, "Truly the LORD is in this place, yet I did not realize it." So he immediately starts to worship according to the customs of the age. He sets up the stone that had guarded his head as a sacred pillar using the oil he had taken for his journey to consecrate it, and he makes a vow. Vows were often made in Bible times by those in distress, e.g., Jephthah (Judg 11:30–39), Hannah (1 Sam 1:10–28), and Jonah and his sailors (Jon 1:16–2:10[9]). Vows were solemn prayers, usually accompanied by sacrifice, in which the worshiper promised to give God something, e.g., a sacrifice, the child Samuel, or here tithes, when the prayer was answered. Some have questioned Jacob's faith in making a vow contingent on his safe return to his homeland, when this had just been promised by God. But real experience of God must always result in heartfelt worship; here he gave all he had, the stone and the oil, and promised to give a tenth of all his future income when his affairs improved. To pray for a safe return showed faith, not unbelief. Indeed, throughout Scripture the basis of prayer is divine promises; it is because we have been promised food, clothes, and the forgiveness of sins that we pray "Our Father . . . give us this day our daily bread; and forgive us our debts" (Matt 6:9–33; cf. Luke 11:2–13).

Jacob's experience at Bethel reaffirmed the promises yet again and brought their fulfillment one step closer. But more than that, his experience is a model for everyone, reminding us that in our moments of deepest crisis God is still with us and will eventually bring his promises to fulfillment in us if we trust him. Philip Doddridge summed up the significance of this episode for every believer in his hymn:

> O God of Bethel, by Whose hand
> Thy people still are fed,
> Who through this weary pilgrimage
> Hast all our fathers led.
>
> Our vows, our prayers, we now present
> Before Thy Throne of grace;
> God of our fathers, be the God
> Of their succeeding race.
>
> Through each perplexing path of life
> Our wandering footsteps guide;
> Give us each day our daily bread
> And raiment fit provide.
>
> O spread Thy covering wings around,
> Till all our wanderings cease,
> And at our Father's loved abode
> Our souls arrive in peace.

Jacob Arrives at Laban's House (29:1–14)

Bibliography for 29:1–32:3(2)

Frankena, R. "Some Remarks on the Semitic Background of Chapters 29–31 of the Book of Genesis." *OTS* 17 (1972) 53–64. **Morrison, M. A.** "The Jacob and Laban Narrative in Light of Near Eastern Sources." *BA* 46 (1983) 155–64. **Postgate. J. N.** "Some Old Babylonian Shepherds and Their Flocks." *JSS* 20 (1975) 1–21. Sherwood, S. K. *"Had Not God Been on My Side": An Examination of the Narrative Technique of the Story of Jacob and Laban, Genesis 29:1–32:2.* Frankfurt: Lang, 1990.

Bibliography for 29:1–14

Daube, D. and **Yaron, R.** "Jacob's Reception by Laban." *JSS* 1 (1956) 60–62.

Translation

[1]*Jacob picked up his feet and went to the land of the people of the East.*[a] [2]*Then he saw a well in the open countryside and just there three flocks lying around it, for the flocks were watered*[a] *from that well, but there was a huge stone*[b] *over the mouth of the well.* [3]*All the flocks*[a] *used to gather*[b] *there. They would roll the stone from the mouth of the well and water*[c] *the sheep. Then they used to return*[c] *the stone to its place over the mouth of the well.* [4]*So Jacob said to them, "My brothers, where are you from?" They replied, "We come from Harran."* [5]*He said to them, "Do you know Laban the son of Nahor?" They replied, "We do."* [6]*So he said, "Is he well?" They replied, "He is, and here is his daughter Rachel coming with the sheep."* [7]*He said, "Look, it is still full day. It is not time to gather in*[a] *the animals. Water*[b] *the sheep, and then let them out to pasture."* [8]*But they said, "We cannot until all the flocks*[a] *are gathered*[b] *and the stone is rolled*[c] *away from the mouth of the well. Then we shall water the sheep."* [9]*While he was still speaking with them, Rachel came with her father's sheep, for she was a shepherdess.*

[10]*As soon as Jacob saw Rachel, the daughter of Laban, his mother's brother, and the sheep of Laban, his mother's brother, Jacob came*[a] *near and rolled*[b] *the stone from the mouth of the well and watered*[c] *the sheep of Laban, his mother's brother.* [11]*Then he kissed*[a] *Rachel and wept*[b] *aloud.* [12]*Then Jacob told*[a] *Rachel* [b]*that he was a relative of her father and that he was Rebekah's son.*[b] *So she ran*[c] *and told her father.*

[13]*As soon as Laban heard the news about Jacob, his sister's son, he ran out to greet him. He hugged him and kissed him and brought*[a] *him into his home, and he told Laban about all these things.* [14]*Then Laban said to him, "You are truly*[a] *my flesh and blood." So he stayed with him a month.*

Notes

1.a. G adds details of Laban's family echoing 28:5.

2.a. Lit. "they used to water" (3 masc pl impf hiph שקה). Here the impf is used to express repeated action (GKC, 107e; WOC, 474) and 3 pl for impersonal "they," equivalent to a passive (GKC, 144f; WOC, 71).

2.b. SamPent omits def art, but Heb. often uses it where one specific object is referred to (GKC 126r).

3.a. SamPent reads רעִים "shepherds."

3.b. Waw consec + 3 masc pl pf niph אסף. Note the string of waw consec + pf in this verse for repeated action (GKC, 112e, WOC, 527).

3.c. Waw consec + 3 masc pl pf hiph שׁוּב/שׁקה.

7.a. Inf constr niph אסף. On this use of the inf constr, see GKC, 114b.

7.b. 2 masc pl impv hiph שׁקה.

8.a. SamPent, G read "shepherds" (cf. v 3).

8.b. 3 masc pl impf niph אסף.

8.c. 3 masc pl, lit. "they rolled," equivalent to a passive (cf. n. 2.a.).

10.a. Cf. n. 18:23.a.

10.b. Waw consec + 3 masc sg impf qal גלל (cf. GKC, 67p).

10.c. Waw consec + 3 masc sg impf hiph apoc שׁקה.

11.a. Cf. n. 27:27.a.

11.b. Cf. n. 27:38.b.

12.a. Cf. n. 9:22.a.

12.b-b. On this construction, see *SBH*, 116.

12.c. Waw consec + 3 fem sg impf רוץ.

13.a. Waw consec + 3 masc sg impf hiph בוא + 3 masc sg suffix.

14.a. On this meaning of אך, see *EWAS*, 129.

Form/Structure/Setting

Chaps. 29–31, the account of Jacob's relationship with Laban, constitute the centerpiece of the Jacob cycle (viz. Gen 25–35). It is a cycle within a cycle and, like the whole Jacob cycle, is constructed palistrophically. The opening episode (29:1–14), telling of Jacob's arrival in Harran and his entry in Laban's household, is balanced by the closing story of Jacob's departure with his wives from Laban (31:1–32:1[31:55]). The second episode, telling how Laban outwitted Jacob in making him work for his two wives for fourteen years (29:15–30), is matched by the account of Jacob outwitting Laban to obtain the flocks and herds that were his due (30:25–43). At the center is the account of the birth of Jacob's sons, the forefathers of the tribes of Israel (29:31–35).

But though the Jacob-Laban cycle is a well-organized coherent narrative in itself, it is by no means independent or self-contained. For example, within chap. 29 there are many allusions to the preceding stories; v 1, Jacob's journey from home (cf. 28:10–22); vv 2–14, his encounter at the well (cf. 24:11–50); vv 5, 10–14, Rebekah as Laban's sister (cf. 22:23; 24:29; 27:43); and v 13, the mention that Jacob told Laban "all these things" (presumably the substance of chaps. 26–28). In particular, there are clear echoes of chap. 27 in chap. 29. Rebekah told Jacob "to stay a few days" with her brother in Harran (27:44). In the event, Laban invites Jacob to stay with him, and the first seven years seem to Jacob like a few days, 29:19–20. Furthermore, the references (vv 25–26) to Laban deceiving Jacob and his refusal to allow the elder to displace the younger are an ironic comment on Jacob's own behavior earlier (25:23–34; 27:19, 35). Similarly, the closing episode telling of Jacob's departure from Harran anticipates the next stage of Jacob's career, his return to the land of Canaan (31:3, 13, 17). Thus, although the Jacob-Laban stories constitute a distinct entity, there is little evidence that they ever circulated independently of the rest of the Jacob cycle.

Defining the units within this part of the Jacob cycle is problematic because of their close interconnection; each unit leads naturally into the next. Here everyone acknowledges that the unit begins in v 1 and that there is a break after v 14, but do vv 15–30 constitute a new episode or are they a continuation of the opening verses? Most commentators take the latter view, but Speiser and Fokkelman (*Narrative Art*) regard them as distinct units. The long break, of a month, between vv 14 and 15 tends to support the subdivision of the chapter, as does the fact that vv 1–14 constitute a type scene in which the patriarch meets his bride beside a well (cf. Gen 24; Exod 2:15–21). But the arguments are finely balanced and make little difference to the exegesis. Reading vv 1–30 as a unit, we should view vv 1–14 essentially as background to Jacob's marriage. Read as a unit in its own right, it functions also as a sequel to the preceding narratives and makes its own points about Jacob's character and divine providence.

Vv 1–14 fall into three scenes:

1–9	Jacob meets the shepherds of Harran
10–12	Jacob meets Rachel
13–14	Jacob stays with Laban

Source critics are unanimous that this section comes from J. Some have held that v 1 is E, since nowhere else is Jacob said to have gone to the sons of the East. But the very singularity of this comment makes its assignment to a particular source dubious, so most modern critics are happy to see it as part of J.

Comment

1–14 These verses constitute a betrothal type scene (cf. chap. 24), in which the patriarch journeys to a foreign land, encounters his future bride at a well, and waters the flocks. Close attention to those features that distinguish this scene from its parallels sheds light on the character of those involved.

1–9 These verses describe Jacob's encounter with the shepherds of Harran. But first, the situation of three flocks encircling the well is described in some fullness; this helps to impress on us the weight of the stone and the strength of the conventions that Jacob was prepared to flout by watering his uncle's flock. His conversation with the shepherds, more of an interrogation than a chat, helps to convey the idea of a pushy young man in a hurry to achieve his own ends.

1 "Jacob picked up his feet." "To pick up the feet" occurs only here in the Bible, so its precise nuance is unclear. *Genesis Rabbah*, followed by Jacob, suggests it is referring back to Jacob's experience at Bethel, so that he now goes on his way cheerfully; Calvin suggests that the experience has given Jacob faith to continue. Speiser thinks the verb נשא "pick up" used with bodily organs (e.g., voice, 21:16; hands, Hab 3:10) focuses attention on the activity involved (Seeligmann, *VT* 14 [1964] 80).

"To the land of the people of the East." The people of the East, noted for their large flocks and herds and numerous camels (Job 1:3), lived a nomadic life on the eastern fringes of Canaan in Transjordan. They joined forces with the Amalekites and Midianites to attack Israel in the time of Gideon (Judg 6:3, 33;

8:10, 11). Here "land of the people of the East" may just be a way of saying "east-wards" (so Jacob, Westermann).

2–3 As might have been anticipated in the land of the people of the East, the first thing that Jacob notices is a well in the open country with three flocks lying around it. "Open country" (שׂדה) means uncultivated land, more suitable for graz-ing than for crops (see *Comment* on 2:5), so it need not be a long way from settlement (*pace* Westermann). After allowing us a glimpse of Jacob's viewpoint (the two clauses introduced by הנה show us things through his eyes), the narrator then explains immediately the significance of the encamped flocks: they are wait-ing for all the flocks who are watered from this well to gather before the huge stone is rolled away. However, it is some time before Jacob elicits for himself the reason for the encampment by quizzing the shepherds (v 8). It is noticeable how the narrator underlines the size of the stone and the necessity of all the flocks gathering before it was removed. The repetition of various details in v 3 rein-forces our realization of its weight and Jacob's strength.

4–8 This dialogue consists of four questions by Jacob and four rather surly replies by the shepherds, suggesting their suspicion of this young foreigner and his own brash self-confidence. Jacob, the passive puppet in his mother's hand, has now grown up. Having left home and met God at Bethel, he is now a man ready to make his own way in the world. On the other hand, the shepherds' cold response to Jacob serves to accentuate the warmth of his reception by Laban.

4 "My brothers" is a polite and ingratiating form of address to strangers (cf. 19:7).

5 Jacob's primary concern is to find his uncle Laban; note the threefold men-tion of Laban in v 10, as directed by his parents (27:43; 28:2).

6 The shepherds' remark, "Here is Rachel coming with the sheep," has a dual purpose. It provides them with yet another excuse for not talking to Jacob; in effect they say "Here's your cousin, ask her about your uncle." But it also indi-cates the passing of time. With Jacob, we peer into the distance trying to see what Rachel is like, but it does take a while for a flock of sheep to come close.

7 So in his impatience, Jacob asks the shepherds an almost impertinent ques-tion, "Why are you wasting your time waiting to water the flocks when you could water them now and then let them graze?"

8 Jacob's cockiness evidently annoyed the shepherds, for at last they speak at length explaining the convention that only when all the flocks are present can the stone be moved and the watering begin, a point the narrator had already made in v 3. Its repetition here sets Jacob's forthcoming actions in perspective. These shepherds do not explain why they have arrived so early, if they must wait for latecomers before watering their flocks. Gunkel surmises that they worked on the basis of "first come, first served." Thus, the earlier they arrived at the well the sooner their flocks were watered. But Jacob, having been apprised of this conven-tion, does not hesitate to disregard it.

9 Meanwhile, during this long interchange, Rachel arrives. Note the insis-tence on the fact that the sheep belonged to her father.

10–12 The warmth of his greeting of Rachel contrasts sharply with the cool-ness with which the shepherds had received him. His enthusiasm empowers him

to roll away the huge stone that normally required several shepherds to move. And then he waters his uncle's sheep, kisses Rachel, weeps, and finally explains that he is "her father's relative, Rebekah's son." This unusual sequence of actions (surely it would have been expected for Jacob to introduce himself before kissing his cousin and weeping?) portrays a man swept along by the joy of meeting his cousin. But what makes him so joyful? Is it relief at finding a relation in a foreign country, or the pleasure of doing something for his uncle, or has he already fallen in love with Rachel? Though his embrace of Rachel no doubt anticipates their later relationship, and Isaac has already directed him to find a wife from Laban's family (28:2), the narrative seems to play down this interpretation by repeatedly insisting that Jacob watered the sheep, not because they were Rachel's, but because they belonged to Laban, "his mother's brother." There is also no comment yet about Rachel's beauty (contrast 24:16). This suggests that Jacob's prime motive at this stage is to ingratiate himself with his uncle.

13 Jacob's alacrity in watering his uncle's flocks is matched by Laban's in greeting him. Of course Laban had been through all this before. Some years earlier his sister had met Isaac's servant at the well, who had showered Laban's family with wealth in order to persuade them to part with Rebekah. Was his haste this time prompted by the possibility of similar enrichment? If it was, he was quickly disillusioned, for Jacob was a runaway, not a rich emissary with ten camels. And the narrative seems to hint that from their first encounter Laban and Jacob's relationship was flawed by Laban's concern for material gain.

"And he told Laban about all these things." A similar phrase in 24:28 refers simply to the meeting at the well, but here rather more is implied. But how much did Jacob divulge of his past? Did he tell of his tricks to acquire his brother's birthright and blessing, or only of Esau's plot to murder him? Did he tell of his parents' injunction to go and stay with his uncle, or also that they wanted him to marry one of Laban's daughters? The text is vague, and we are left to guess, but it seems likely that Laban discovered plenty about Jacob's past and realized that Jacob had not many financial assets to offer and was very much at Laban's mercy. And this must inform our understanding of his comments.

14 "You are truly my flesh and blood" is more ambiguous than it sounds. It is apparently an open-hearted admission that Jacob is indeed Laban's close relative (cf. *Comment* on 2:23), which the particle אך "truly" reinforces. So it could be taken as a warm welcome to Jacob to stay. However, אך may suggest a rather grudging admission on Laban's part of kinship. "You have convinced me that you are my nephew, so you may as well stay" (cf. Jacob; Ehrlich; Fokkelman, *Narrative Art*). On this view, Laban's double-dealing is already being hinted at, even though Jacob must have understood the comment entirely positively and have been reassured by it.

"He stayed with him a month" echoes his mother's injunction, "Stay with him a few days" (27:44). (The phrase "a few days" is found in 29:20.) It seems therefore unlikely that "stay with" meant that Laban legally acknowledged Jacob as a co-heir (*pace* D. Daube and R. Yaron, *JSS* 1 [1956] 61). Thus staying with his uncle, Jacob has begun to fulfill his parents' instructions. Will he now succeed in marrying one of Laban's daughters and returning home as they had also instructed him?

Explanation

This episode in the Jacob cycle is one of the sunniest. It tells of Jacob's success-ful arrival in his uncle's household in Paddan-Aram. Everything appears to run smoothly for him. The promise that the LORD would be with him and guard him wherever he went (28:15, 20) is here manifestly fulfilled. He arrives at a well in the East and discovers shepherds who know his uncle, and indeed ere long his cousin Rachel appears with her flock. God's overruling providential guidance is as manifest here as in the very similar story in Gen 24, where Abraham's servant met Rebekah at the well. Whereas that servant wore his piety on his sleeve, Jacob's faith is unmentioned, though his confident, almost cocksure, approach to the shepherds perhaps reflects his experience at Bethel.

In Gen 24 it was Rebekah who demonstrated her sterling quality by watering Abraham's camels; on this occasion it was Jacob who did so by watering Rachel's sheep. On both occasions, Laban ran out to greet the stranger; but if he re-called the first, he must have been disappointed by the second, for Jacob brought no great wealth, only his own abilities. On both occasions, the future bride came to the well, but whereas the match with Rebekah was quickly arranged, nothing is said about Jacob marrying Rachel. So this episode ends on a note of uncer-tainty. Jacob has obeyed his parents and found his way to his uncle's house. The LORD has fulfilled his promise of guidance and protection. But there is no sign of him marrying or the fulfillment of the promise of numerous descendants or of his return to the land. He simply stayed with Laban a month. Clearly, the divine program has begun to be fulfilled, but how and when the rest will take place is unclear. Though the first stage has been easy, Jacob will discover that there are many huge obstacles to be rolled away before he can return to his land in peace.

Jacob Marries Leah and Rachel   (29:15–30)

Bibliography

Arum, N. "'For Rachel your younger daughter'—'She is Leah?'" A 'False' Statement of Identity Reflecting a False Situation." (Heb.) *BMik* 30 (1984/85) 541–44. **Diamond, J. A.** "The Deception of Jacob: A New Perspective on an Ancient Solution to the Problem." *VT* 34 (1984) 211–13. **Dresner, S. H.** "Rachel and Leah." *Judaism* 38 (1989) 151–59. **Eissfeldt, O.** "Jakob-Lea und Jakob-Rahel." *KS* 4 (1968) 170–75. **Goldfarb, S. D.** "Jacob's Love for Rachel." (Heb.) *BMik* 21 (1976) 289–92. **Jagendorf, Z.** "'In the morning, behold, it was Leah': Genesis and the Reversal of Sexual Knowledge." *Prooftexts* 4 (1984) 187–92. **Postgate,. J. N.** "Some Old Babylonian Shepherds and Their Flocks." *JSS* 20 (1975) 1–20. **Seters, J. Van.** "Jacob's Marriages and Ancient Near East Customs: A Reexamination." *HTR* 62 (1969) 377–95. **Steinberg, N.** "Alliance or Descent? The Function of Marriage in Gen-esis." *JSOT* 51 (1991) 45–55.

Translation

¹⁵*Then Laban said to Jacob,* ^a*"Are you, although you are my relative, working*^b *for me for nothing?*^a *Tell*^c *me what your pay should be."* ¹⁶*Now Laban had two daughters:* ^a*the elder was called Leah and the younger Rachel.*^a ¹⁷*Leah's eyes were soft, but Rachel*^a *had a beautiful figure and a lovely face.* ¹⁸*Now Jacob loved Rachel. So he said, "I will work*^a *for you seven years for Rachel, your younger daughter."* ¹⁹*Laban replied, "It is better for me to give*^a *her to you than to give*^b *her to someone else. Stay*^c *with me."* ²⁰*So Jacob worked seven years for Rachel, but they seemed like a few days because he loved*^a *her.* ²¹*Then Jacob said to Laban, "Give*^a *me my wife, for my time is completed, that I may go*^b *into her."* ²²*So Laban gathered all the people of the neighborhood and made a feast.* ²³*In the evening he took his daughter Leah and brought*^a *her to him, and he went into her.* ²⁴*Laban had given*^a *Leah Zilpah his maid to be her maid.*^b ²⁵*In the morning there was Leah! He said to Laban, "What*^a *have you done to me? Did I not work for you for Rachel?*^b *Why*^c *have you deceived*^d *me?"* ²⁶*So Laban replied, "It is not done*^a *in our area to give*^b *the younger before the firstborn.* ²⁷*Complete the week of that one,*^a *so that we can give*^b *this one as well to you, provided you work for me for another seven years."* ²⁸*Jacob did so and completed this week, and he gave him Rachel his daughter in marriage.* ^{29a}*Laban had given Rachel his daughter Bilhah his maid to be her maid.*^a ³⁰*So he also went into Rachel, and he loved also*^a *Rachel more than Leah, and he worked with him another seven years.*

Notes

15.a-a. This translation follows Joüon, 161j,k, in seeing the introductory הכי as applying only to the second clause, "should you serve me for nothing." This seems preferable to GKC, 150e, who see הכי introducing a strong assertion, "verily thou art my brother."

15.b. Waw consec + 2 masc sg pf עבד + 1 sg suffix.

15.c. 2 masc sg impv hiph נגד + *āh* ending.

16.a-a. On this construction, see *SBH*, 32–33. On the use of the simple adjectives "great, small" for the comparatives "greater, smaller," see GKC, 133f.

17.a. The preverbal position of Rachel accentuates the contrast with Leah (*SBH,* 152).

18.a. 1 sg impf עבד + 2 masc sg suffix.

19.a. Inf constr נתן + 1 sg suffix.

19.b. As above, prefixed by מן.

19.c. See n. 27:19.c.

20.a. ב + inf constr אהב + 3 masc sg suffix.

21.a. Cf. n. 11:3.a. (Joüon, 75k).

21.b. Waw consec + 1 sg coh בוא. On the sequence of tenses giving a final sense, see GKC, 108d, 165a; Joüon, 116b.

23.a. Cf. n. 2:19.c.

24.a. *SBH*, 88, notes the anomaly of waw consec + impf used in a circumstantial clause, for the giving of Zilpah was contemporary with the marriage, not subsequent to the wedding. Hence, it would be better to see this as equivalent to a pluperfect (cf. v 29).

24.b. SamPent adds ל, which is more normal (cf. v 29).

25.a. For the enclitic זאת, cf. n. 3:13.a.

25.b. In the Heb., Rachel precedes the verb for emphasis (GKC, 142g, *EWAS*, 43).

25.c. Joüon, 177m, suggests that the prefixed ו expresses feeling.

25.d. 2 masc sg pf piel רמה + 1 sg suffix.

26.a. 3 masc sg impf niph עשה. Here the impf of customary action, hence "may not, shall not be, done" (GKC, 107g; cf. Gen 34:7; 2 Sam 13:12).

26.b. Cf. n. 15:7.c.

27.a. For this translation, see Joüon, 143b.

27.b. Understanding the form as waw + 1 pl coh qal נִתֵּן. Alternatively, it may be understood as waw consec + 3 fem sg niph נִתַּן, " Then this one shall be given to you too." SamPent, G, Vg render it "that I may give," which lends support to the first view, but GKC, 121b, inclines to the second.

29.a-a. Cf. n. 29:24.a,b.

30.a. This גַּם is awkward syntactically (*SBH,* 161), so G, Vg do not translate it, but since SamPent also has it, it should be retained ("and he really loved Rachel, more than Leah," so Labuschagne [q. by Gispen]).

Form/Structure/Setting

Does 29:15–30 constitute a separate episode in the Jacob cycle or should it be regarded as a unit with 29:1–14? For the reasons set out in the previous *Form/ Structure/Setting,* I prefer to take the passages as separate, though closely inter-connected, units.

29:15–30 falls into two scenes, each followed by a comment on Jacob's labor for his wife.

vv 15–19	The betrothal of Jacob to Rachel
v 20	Seven years of service for Rachel
vv 21–30a	The wedding
v 30b	Another seven years of service

According to the older source critics, this section is mainly E with P comments in vv 24, 29. The only good reason for holding that the source here is not J, the source in vv 1–14, is the fresh introduction of Rachel in vv 16–17. The alleged differences in vocabulary (e.g., "pay," v 15; "elder/younger," v 16) prove nothing. However, the purpose of vv 16–17 is not to reintroduce Rachel, so much as to say that she had a sister, Leah, who was less attractive than she was, and that Jacob loved Rachel. This information is indispensable, if we are to understand Laban's trickery. So, most modern writers agree that it is unnecessary to ascribe this ma-terial to a source different from J, the author of vv 1–14 (so Speiser; Coats; Westermann; Blum, *Die Komposition*). Most still see a different hand at work in vv 24, 29, though Blum admits it is arbitrary to ascribe these verses to P. Speiser and Vawter, however, note that giving a slave-girl as part of a dowry was traditional in the ancient Orient, so that vv 24, 29 could come from the main source and not be an addition. In fact, these verses are necessary for the understanding of the account of the patriarchal births in 29:31–30:24, so it does not seem necessary to ascribe them to a different source.

Comment

15 Laban's question sounds concerned and friendly, but the very mention of "working" and "pay" introduces a jarring note. It sounds friendly to offer one's destitute nephew wages, but should family relationships be reduced to commer-cial bargaining? The words "work, serve" (עבד) and "pay" (root שכר) are key terms in the subsequent narrative (29:18, 20, 25, 27, 30; 30:26, 29; 31:6, 41; 30:16, 32, 33; 31:7, 41) and are laden with echoes of the exploitation Jacob suffered at Laban's hands. But Laban is canny; he has learned Jacob's motives for coming

(29:13) and in the last few weeks has observed his attachment to Rachel, which he is willing to exploit by inviting Jacob to make an offer.

16–17 This interruption by the narrator supplies some necessary background information about Leah and Rachel that has been withheld hitherto but is necessary for understanding the story. This interruption also serves to heighten suspense. We are forced to wait a little before we hear whether Jacob will bid for Rachel and whether it will be accepted. The name "Leah" may mean "cow," as in Akkadian *littu,* Arabic *laʾātu* "wild cow" (so KB, 487), whereas Rachel is Hebrew for "ewe" (cf. 31:38; 32:15). What makes eyes "soft" (רך) is unclear; most commentators think it means they had no fire or sparkle, a quality much prized in the East. Whether her eyes were the only features that let her down is not said, but the glowing description of Rachel as having "a beautiful figure and a lovely face" suggests Leah was outshone by her sister in various ways.

18 So it is little surprise to be told that "Jacob loved Rachel." What is surprising is the price he was prepared to pay for her hand, seven years labor, undoubtedly indicating the intensity of his affection for her. In the ancient Near East, betrothal was effected by paying a מהר, *tirhatum* (Akk.), "marriage present," "bride price" (Exod 22:15[16]). This was essentially a capital transfer by the groom's family to the bride's family pledging the man to marry. The OT fixes the maximum marriage gift at fifty shekels (Deut 22:29), but typically the gifts were much lower. However, since Jacob could not ask his family to pay, he offered seven years of service instead. Since casual laborers received between one-half and one shekel a month in old Babylonian times (G. R. Driver and J. C. Miles, *The Babylonian Laws* [Oxford: Clarendon Press, 1952] 1:470–71), Jacob was offering Laban a very handsome marriage gift in exchange for Rachel's hand.

19 Laban gladly agrees to this excellent offer. But has he already purposed to cheat? He says, "It is better for me to give *her* to you than to someone else," but he never specifies who "she" is. From the context, it appears that "she" is Rachel. But in the light of Jacob's very precise request to marry "Rachel, your younger daughter," it may be no coincidence that Laban never names the daughter he intends to give Jacob. Maybe he was keeping his options open, perhaps hoping that someone else would come along to marry Leah before Jacob had completed his seven years of service for Rachel.

20 According to later laws (Exod 21:1–6; Deut 15:12–18), single men who entered into service as slaves had to be released after six years. But Jacob served seven years, yet "they seemed like a few days" because of his love for Rachel. The phrase "a few days" echoes 27:44, when Rebekah had told Jacob to stay with Laban "a few days." Now that the time has elapsed, Jacob hopes to marry Rachel and return to his homeland. But this delightful prospect is soon shattered.

21–30 The second scene describes the wedding seven years later.

21 In the previous scene, Laban opened the discussion. Here it is Jacob who says, "Give me my wife. . . ." That Jacob had to take the initiative no doubt expresses his keenness to consummate the marriage, "that I may go into her," but does it also suggest a coolness on Laban's part toward the match? Did he really need reminding that Jacob's years of service were completed? The suspicion of grievance on Jacob's part may be strengthened by the way he demands his rights, "Give me my wife," without so much as a "please." Indeed, in two of the three

other passages in Genesis where the verb יהב "give" appears by itself, there is a distinct note of desperation apparent (30:1; 47:15; cf. 47:16) that would not be out of place here.

22 No reply of Laban is recorded; thus his inner thoughts are left shrouded in mystery, but maybe silence itself indicates his reluctance to arrange the wedding feast. However, he does apparently do the right thing; he invites his neighbors in to celebrate the marriage. Normally, a wedding involved processions to and from the bride's house, a reading of the marriage contract, and a large meal attended by both families and neighbors. The first day's celebration ended with the groom wrapping his cloak around the bride, who was veiled throughout the ceremony (24:65), and taking her to the nuptial chamber where the marriage was consummated. However, the feasting and celebration continued for a whole week (cf. Judg 14:12–18; see further G. J. Wenham, "Weddings," in *Oxford Companion to the Bible,* ed. B. M. Metzger and M. D. Coogan [Oxford/New York: Oxford UP, 1993] 794–95). Clearly, the absence of Jacob's family must have led to the omission of certain parts of the celebration. More important, it made Jacob vulnerable to Laban's machinations.

23 The lateness of the hour, the veiling of the bride, and maybe a little too much drink allowed Laban to substitute the unloved Leah for the promised Rachel.

24 Upon marriage, it was customary for the bride's father to give her a large wedding present, a dowry. Ancient marriage contracts show that dowries typically consisted of clothing, furniture, and money. The dowry served as a nest egg for the wife in case she was widowed or divorced. It is not usually mentioned in the OT unless it included something exceptionally valuable, such as slave-girls (24:61; 29:29) or a city (1 Kgs 9:16). However mean Laban was to Jacob, he still treated his daughters generously by presenting them each with a maid. On שפחה "maid," see *Comment* on 16:1. Thus, from the point of view of subject matter, this verse is entirely apposite. Though it sounds like an afterthought, it is actually included to prepare the way for them to be mothers of the patriarchs. This verse and v 29 do not therefore need to be ascribed to a source different from the rest of the chapter.

25 This verse resumes the main thread of the narrative. Lit. "and behold she Leah." These three words describe Jacob's shock through his eyes. Seven years of working for pretty Rachel, and now he finds he has her ugly sister instead. But as usual in Hebrew narrative, his feelings are hinted at rather than analyzed. However, his words show what he was thinking.

"What have you done?" As in 3:13 (God to Eve), 12:18 (Pharaoh to Abraham), and 26:10 (Abimelek to Isaac), מה "what" followed by the enclitic זאת "this" expresses the questioner's astonishment: the unthinkable has happened!

"Why have you deceived me?" "Why" in Hebrew, as in English, often introduces accusatory questions implying that the person should never have acted in this way. The verb רמה "deceive" is cognate with the noun מרמה "deceit" in 27:35. So already in accusing Laban of deceit, Jacob is in fact condemning himself. The archdeceiver has himself been deceived.

26 Consciously or unconsciously, Laban makes the same point, "It is not done . . . to give (put) the younger before the firstborn." These terms for young (צעיר) and firstborn (בכיר) or words derived from them have been used earlier

in the Jacob cycle to describe the relationship of Esau and Jacob (25:23, 32; 27:19, 32). But Jacob, the younger, had put himself before the firstborn Esau, so there is a certain poetic justice in Jacob's deception. Doubtless there is a barbed underhanded dig in Laban's "It is not done *in our area* to put the younger before the firstborn." It was not supposed to be done in Isaac's family either, yet Jacob had.

However, Laban's attempt to justify his action by local convention is weak. Why did he not make the point earlier, if this was his intention? Or why had he not found a husband for Leah during the seven years Jacob had worked for him? Was it because Leah was too ugly to attract a husband, or had Laban been planning all along to palm her off on Jacob? Either way, Jacob had good reason to be incensed by his father-in-law.

27 But Laban continues urbanely with an apparent show of generosity. "Just complete the wedding celebrations of Leah this week, and then next week you can start a party for Rachel and marry her." However unwilling Jacob may have been to continue celebrating his marriage to Leah, he could not opt out. He was isolated without family support, and he did want to marry Rachel. Realizing he has Jacob trapped, Laban then adds a harsh extra demand: after marrying Rachel "you must work for me another seven years." So much for Jacob's hopes of returning home shortly with his new wife.

28–29 The end of dialogue indicates Jacob's sullen acceptance of Laban's new terms. Outwardly, both do the correct thing: Jacob completes the first week of celebrations, and Laban gives him Rachel, and Rachel, like her sister Leah, is given a maid (cf. v 24). The meaning of Bilhah is unclear. Noth (*Personennamen*, 10) suggests "without care."

30 But while outward decorum may have been restored, the narrator hints at the underlying unhappiness. "He loved Rachel more than Leah" (cf. v 31). Jacob does indeed serve another seven years, but unlike the first, they are not said to have "seemed like a few days" (v 20). They were, rather, days of sorrow and strife within the new family as the account of the patriarchs' births now makes plain.

Explanation

"And they lived happily ever after" is the way traditional fairy-tale romances end. But Jacob and Rachel's love story has no such happy ending. The first scene tells how Jacob, entranced with the beautiful Rachel, offers her father Laban seven years of service in lieu of the normal marriage present given to the bride's family when betrothal occurred. This was a high price to pay, but it shows how taken Jacob was with Rachel, a point underlined by the closing comment that the seven years "seemed like a few days because he loved her."

The second scene opens more ominously with Jacob forced to demand the wedding be celebrated because he has served his time; he wants now to marry his beloved and to return home. The wedding feast is duly organized, and on the first night Jacob joins his wife in the nuptial bed. But in the morning he discovers it is Leah, Rachel's ugly older sister, that he has married.

Jacob expostulates with Laban, but he can do nothing to alter the situation. Laban has him over a barrel. The only concession Laban makes is that Jacob may take Rachel immediately as a second wife, but he must work another seven years

for her. Jacob's bitter resentment at Laban and at Leah is hinted at but not described. We simply hear that "he loved Rachel more than Leah." Few marriages can have had a worse start.

Within the narrative there is no theological comment at all, and the narrator leaves us to reflect on how these events fit in with the promises made to Jacob and the providential overruling of his career. The obvious linkages with the earlier episodes in which Jacob deceived his father (chap. 27; cf. 29:25) and in which the younger Jacob displaced his older brother, Esau (25:27–34; chap. 27; 29:26) surely indicate that, although Jacob is chosen, he does not escape divine justice. Nowhere does Scripture allow that the elect are immune from God's discipline and punishment. "You only have I known of all the families of the earth; therefore I will punish you for all your iniquities" (Amos 3:2). "The LORD disciplines him whom he loves, and chastises every son whom he receives" (Heb 12:5–6; Prov 3:12).

Yet through these experiences God's purposes were advanced. Jacob had been promised he would have a multitude of descendants, and it was through the unloved Leah and her maid Zilpah that eight of the twelve tribes traced their descent. Thus even the deceitfulness of Laban and Jacob can be overruled to bring the divine plan to fulfillment (cf. Hos 12:2). Human sin may have delayed Jacob's return to his homeland, but all other aspects of the promises made to him were advanced by his unhappy sojourn in Mesopotamia.

The Birth of Jacob's Sons   (29:31–30:24)

Bibliography

Andersen, F. I. "Note on Gen 30:8." *JBL* 88 (1969) 200. **Arbeitman, Y.,** and **Rendsburg, G.** "Adana Revisited: 30 Years Later." *ArOr* 49 (1981) 145–57. **Ben-Reuven, S.** "Buying Mandrakes as Retribution for Buying the Birthright." (Heb.) *BMik* 28 (1982/83) 230–31. ————. "David's Struggle with Saul in the Light of the Struggle between Leah and Rachel." (Heb.) *BMik* 32 (1986/87) 152–53. **Bosse-Griffiths, K.** "The Fruit of the Mandrake." In *Fontes atque Pontes: FS H. Brunner,* ed. M. Görg. Wiesbaden: Harrassowitz, 1983. 62–74. **Daube, D.** "The Night of Death." *HTR* 61 (1968) 629–32. **Fowler, J. D.** *Theophoric Personal Names in Ancient Hebrew: A Comparative Study.* JSOTSup 49. Sheffield: Academic Press, 1988. **Lehming, S.** "Zur Erzählung von der Geburt der Jakobsöhne." *VT* 13 (1963) 74–81. **Lipiński, E.** "L'Étymologie de 'Juda.'" *VT* 23 (1973) 380–81. **Millard, A. R.** "The Meaning of the Name Judah." *ZAW* 86 (1974) 216–18. **Nicol, G. G.** "Gen 29:32 and 35:22a: Reuben's Reversal." *JTS* 31 (1980) 536–39. **Richter, H.-F.** "'Auf den Knien eines andern gebären'? (Zur Deutung von Gen 30:3 und 50:23)." *ZAW* 91 (1979) 436–37. **Seters, J. Van.** "The Problem of Childlessness in Near Eastern Law and the Patriarchs of Israel." *JBL* 87 (1968) 401–8. **Strus, A.** "Étymologies des noms propres dans Gen 29:32–30:24: valeurs littéraires et fonctionelles." *Salesianum* 40 (1978) 57–72.

Translation

^{31}*When the* LORD *saw that Leah was unloved, he opened her womb, but Rachel remained childless.* ^{32}*Leah conceived,*[a] *gave*[b] *birth to a son, and named him Reuben, for she said,*[c] *"The* LORD *has seen my oppression, because now my husband will love me."* ^{33}*She conceived again, gave birth to a son, and said: "The* LORD *has heard that I am unloved and has also given this one to me." So she named him Simeon.* ^{34}*She conceived again, gave birth to a son, and she said, "Now this time my husband will be attached*[a] *to me, because I have borne him three sons." So she*[b] *named him Levi.* ^{35}*Then she conceived again, gave birth to a son, and she said, "This time I shall praise*[a] *the* LORD*." So she named him Judah. Then she stopped bearing*[b] *children.*

$^{30:1}$*When Rachel saw that she had borne Jacob no children, Rachel was jealous of her sister, and she said to Jacob, "Give me children, or*[a] *I shall die."*[b] ^{2}*So Jacob was very angry*[a] *with Rachel and said, "Am I in God's place,*[b] *who has prevented your womb from bearing fruit?"* ^{3}*She said, "Here is my maid Bilhah, go into her in order that*[a] *she may give birth over my knees that I may be built*[b] *up from her."* ^{4}*So she gave Bilhah her maid to him as a wife, and Jacob went into her.* ^{5}*Bilhah conceived and gave birth to a son for Jacob.* ^{6}*Rachel said: "God has vindicated*[a] *me and also listened to my voice and given me a son." So she named him Dan.* ^{7}*She conceived again, and Bilhah, Rachel's maid, gave birth to another son for Jacob.* ^{8}*Rachel said, "With divine struggles I wrestled*[a] *with my sister; indeed*[b] *I overcame her." So she named him Naphtali.*

^{9}*When Leah saw that she had stopped having children, she took her maid Zilpah and gave her to Jacob as a wife.* ^{10}[a]*Then Zilpah, Leah's maid, gave birth to a son for Jacob.* ^{11}*Leah said,* [a]*"Luck has come,"*[a] *so she named him Gad.* ^{12}*Then Zilpah, Leah's maid, gave birth to another son for Jacob.* ^{13}*Leah said, "In my happiness,*[a] *for daughters will declare*[b] *me happy." So she named him Asher.*

^{14}*Reuben went out in the time of the wheat harvest and found mandrakes in the countryside and brought them to Leah his mother. And Rachel said to Leah, "Please give*[a] *me some of your son's mandrakes."* ^{15}[a]*She replied to her,*[a] *"Is it not enough that you took*[b] *away my husband that you also want to take my son's mandrakes?" Rachel replied, "For this he shall lie with you tonight in return for your son's mandrakes."*

^{16}*When Jacob came in from the country in the evening, Leah went out to meet him and said to him: "You must come in to me, for I have really hired you at the price of my son's mandrakes." So he slept with her that*[a] *night.* ^{17}*And God listened to Leah, and she conceived and gave birth to a fifth son for Jacob.* ^{18}*Leah said, "God has given me pay, because*[a] *I gave my maid to my husband." So she named him Issachar.* ^{19}*Leah conceived again and bore a sixth son for Jacob.*[a] ^{20}*Leah said, "God has endowed me*[a] *with a good endowment. This time my husband will honor me, because I have borne him six sons." So she named him Zebulon.* ^{21}*Afterwards, she gave birth to a daughter and named her Dinah.*

^{22}*Then God remembered Rachel. God listened to her and opened her womb.* ^{23}*Then she conceived and gave birth to a son, and she said "God has gathered up my shame."* ^{24}*She named him Joseph, saying, "May the* LORD[a] *add*[b] *another son to me."*

Notes

32.a. Cf. n. 4:1.b.
32.b. Cf. n. 4:1.c.
32.c. כִּי here introduces direct speech (GKC, 157b).

34.a. 3 masc sg impf niph לוה.

34.b. So SamPent; cf. vv 32, 33, 35. MT reads "He called him."

35.a. 1 sg impf hiph ידה.

35.b. מן + inf constr ילד.

30:1.a. Cf. *EWAS*, 102.

1.b. The word order (predicate "dying" before pronominal subj "I") emphasizes the predicate (*EWAS*, 15).

2.a. Cf. n. 4:5.b.

2.b. Cf. n. 30:1.b.; predicate "in God's place" before subj for emphasis (*EWAS*, 14).

3.a. Note simple waw following impv to express purpose (GKC, 109f.)

3.b. 1 sg impf niph בנה.

6.a. 3 masc sg pf qal דין + 1 sg suffix. On the form, see GKC, 26g, 58i, 59f; WOC, 517, n. 64.

8.a. 1 sg pf niph פתל.

8.b. גם here serves as an intensive "and" (GKC, 154a[1]; *SBH*, 165).

10.a. G adds "Jacob went into her, and Zilpah conceived." This could be assimilation to vv 4–5.

11.a-a. With Q, S, *Tg.*, reading בָּא גָד. K, G, Vg read בְּגָד "with luck."

13.a. Grammatically obscure. This translation follows BDB, 81a, which understands it as בְּ + אֹשֶׁר + 1 sg suffix. Joüon, 89 l[2], understands it as בְּ "in, with" + אֹשְׁרִי "happiness." Cf. "with luck," v 11a.

13.b. 3 pl pf piel אִשְּׁר + 1 sg suffix. Pf used here because future predicted is certain (GKC, 106n; WOC, 490).

14.a. 2 fem sg impv נתן.

15.a-a. G clarifies by paraphrasing "Leah said."

15.b. Inf constr לקח + 2 fem sg suffix.

16.a. SamPent reads the more usual ההוא for MT הוא. MT could have omitted the def art by haplography or for euphony.

18.a. אשׁר may serve as a weak causal conj (GKC, 158b; Joüon, 170e).

19.a. The dagesh in ליעקב is unusual and not found in the majority of texts.

20.a. Note that the obj "me" is expressed twice, both as suffix on "endowed" and also with independent obj pronoun. This makes obj "me" more prominent (*EWAS*, 152).

24.a. G, S read "God."

24.b. 3 masc sg juss hiph יסף.

Form/Structure/Setting

This episode of the birth of Jacob's sons culminates with the birth of Joseph (30:24), which is the cue for Jacob to return home (30:25). This episode, which in fact spans about seven years, lies right at the center of the Laban-Jacob narrative and of the whole Jacob cycle itself. It presupposes all that has gone before, most obviously Jacob's flight to Harran and his involuntary bigamous marriage to Leah and Rachel. Here the unhappy tensions caused by that relationship are displayed most poignantly; the whole episode is governed by Leah's longing for Jacob's love and Rachel's craving for children. Leah's frequent pregnancies only aggravate Rachel's frustration at her own childlessness. But Leah's success in producing offspring leaves her deeply disappointed, for, far from drawing her husband closer to her, it leads her to be excluded from the marriage bed, so that only Rachel has access to Jacob. These dark passions govern the whole narrative, most obviously in Rachel's appeal to Jacob for children (30:1–2) and in Leah's trading mandrakes for sex (30:14–16), but also in the names given to the children, nearly all of which comment on the relationships between the sisters and their husband (29:32–35; 30:6, 8, 11, 13, 18, 20, 23–24).

While a tightly integrated and powerful narrative on its own, this episode also echoes themes found elsewhere in Genesis, most obviously in other parts of the Jacob cycle. Rachel's struggle to gain the upper hand over her older sister mirrors

Jacob's triumph over Esau, as well as the other stories of younger brothers being preferred to the elder (Cain and Abel, Isaac and Ishmael, Joseph and his brothers). Rachel's desperate appeal, "Give me children, otherwise I shall die," echoes Jacob's demand to Laban, "Give me my wife" (29:21), and Esau's plea for blessing (27:36–38). In proposing that her maid Bilhah should bear children for her, Rachel adopts the same procedure and language as Sarah before her (30:3; 16:2), while Leah's resort to hiring her husband (30:16–18) shows her following her father Laban's example of hiring and selling, where giving would be more fitting (29:15; 30:32–33; 31:7–8, 41). Finally, Rachel's remarks about struggling and prevailing seem to anticipate Jacob's achievement (30:8; 32:29).

Fokkelman (*Narrative Art*) divides the episode into three parts; in each, four children are born.

29:31–35	Leah alone
30:1–13	Leah and Rachel
30:14–24	The mandrakes, Leah and Rachel

However, the following scenic analysis seems preferable: the episode falls into two groups of three scenes:

1. The LORD opens Leah's womb (4 boys born) (29:31–35)
   (note 29:31, "the LORD saw")
2. Rachel's desire for children achieved through Bilhah (2 boys born) (30:1–8)
   (note 30:1, "Rachel saw")
   dialogue vv 1–3: Rachel (v 1), Jacob (v 2), Rachel (v 3)
3. Leah's response: children through Zilpah (2 boys born) (30:9–13)
   (note 30:9, "Leah saw")
4. Leah's desire for intercourse (30:14–15)
   dialogue: Rachel (v 14), Leah, Rachel (v 15)
5. Jacob lies with Leah (2 boys, 1 girl born) (30:16–21)
6. God opens Rachel's womb (1 boy born, another prayed for) (30:22–24)

It should be noted how each of the first three scenes begins "X saw that" (29:31; 30:1, 9), while the last two include the comment "God listened to Leah/Rachel" (30:17, 22). If the first group of these scenes is compared to the second group, it may be observed how both contain dialogues initiated by Rachel in an attempt to overcome her barrenness (30:1–3, 14–15) and how in the very first scene "The LORD opens Leah's womb" matches "God opens Rachel's womb" (29:31; 30:22) in the last, thus giving the whole episode a loose palistrophic structure. Indeed, by the end, both major problems seem to have been addressed: Leah's alienation from Jacob (30:16–21) and Rachel's childlessness. Forgetting the stormy past, Rachel looks with hope to the future as she prays, "May the LORD add another son to me" (30:24). In short, this episode combines psychological insight and dramatic pathos to produce a well-integrated narrative.

But traditional source critics speak of the "extraordinary literary compositeness" of this passage . . . composed of small parts, in places very small fragments, of J and E" (von Rad, 293). Put simply, 29:31–35; 30:9–16 are ascribed mainly to J, while 30:1–8, 17–24 mainly to E. The grounds for this division are the two divine

names (Yahweh in 29:31–33, 35; 30:24; Elohim in 30:2, 6, 8, 17, 18, 20, 22, 23); two different words for maid (אמה, 30:3; שפחה, 30:4, 7, 9, 10, 12, 18), the first usually regarded as an E word, the latter a J word; and finally the twofold explanations of some of the names, suggesting two sources are present (29:32, 33; 30:6, 18, 20, 23–24). However, once these criteria are applied, it becomes apparent that, in chap. 30 at least, not all of vv 9–16 can be pure J; nor can all of vv 1–8, 17–24 be pure E. Thus, according to Gunkel, v 1a must be J because it parallels 29:31 and 30:9; 3b is J because it parallels 16:2. V 7 is an expansion because it uses the term שפחה, J's term for maid. Thus, the basically E section vv 1–8 has J fragments in it. Likewise, the J section vv 9–16 has v 9b from P and part of 13b (double etymology) from E. Similarly, the E section vv 17–24 contains the following J insertions: vv 20a, 24b (dual etymologies), and v 22b (parallel with 29:31). More recent source critics have worked on similar principles but are much less sanguine about their results. Speiser admits "the boundaries between J and E are sometimes indistinct" (232), while Vawter is even more candid: "The distinction is admittedly quite chancy when it comes to deciding which verses belong to whom: all that we really know is that a distinction has been made somehow" (324).

Westermann, however, drops the JE analysis entirely. He regards the narrative as essentially a J story, 29:31–32; 30:1–6, 14–18, 22–24 with later genealogical expansions, i.e., 29:33–35; 30:7–13, 19–21. This later reviser also modified 29:32; 30:6, 17–18, 22–24. While this approach does more justice to the integrity of the narrative than the traditional source analysis does, it does not match the scenic division satisfactorily. Casting narratives into three scenes or groups of three is a classic device of prose style. But more significantly, it fails to appreciate the genealogical elements and especially the etymologies that have no point without the narrative framework. The names given to all the children are barbed and poignant comments on their mothers' situations and express their deep and passionate longings. These names reflect the twin themes of this narrative, Rachel's longing for children and Leah's yearning to be loved. Without the narrative, the names and their explanations become little more than antiquarian information. Thus Blum describes the narrative as "unified in conception and well constructed" (*Die Komposition*, 111). He suggests that the double etymologies of Issachar, Zebulon, and Joseph all have a part to play in the narrative—the last in particular because it looks forward to the birth of Benjamin. According to Blum, only 30:21, the birth of Dinah, is not integral to this episode. Not only is she the only girl mentioned, but she has no etymology, nor is she mentioned in 32:23(22). Rather, 30:21 must have been added later to prepare for chap. 34. Now certainly the birth of Dinah is unique in this section, but that is not to say it necessarily comes from a later hand. There is a similar phenomenon in 22:23, where Rebekah is mentioned along with eight male descendants of Nahor; this detail prepares the way for chap. 24, and both sections, 22:20–24 and chap. 24, are usually ascribed to J. Furthermore, Leah says in 30:13, "*daughters* will declare me happy," so it is appropriate for one of her daughters to be mentioned by name here. For these reasons, it seems simplest to regard all of 29:31–30:24 as deriving from J, the main editor of Genesis. As elsewhere, it is very difficult to know what sources he had access to and drew on.

Comment

29:31–35 In this scene, Leah is the sole speaker; indeed, apart from v 31, which supplies background information for understanding her comments, Leah is the only actor. Her soliloquies after the birth of each child underline her isolation and her longing for Jacob's affection.

31 "When the LORD saw" (cf. 30:1, 9). When the LORD sees, he intends to act decisively, often in defense of the weak and oppressed (cf. 6:5; 7:1; 18:21; 31:12; Exod 2:25; 4:31). "Unloved" (pass ptcp שְׂנוּאָה), lit. "hated," appears here in poignant contrast to "(Jacob) loved Rachel." For this use of "hate" meaning "to love less," cf. Deut 21:15; Mal 1:3. "He opened her womb" (cf. 30:22). Throughout the OT, and in most traditional societies, motherhood is perceived as the crowning joy of a woman's life. But the LORD's consolation of Leah did not satisfy her, because it failed to win her husband's love, and it served instead to make Rachel bitterly jealous, for like Sarah and Rebekah before her (11:30; 25:21), she "remained childless."

32 This verse describes the birth of the first of Jacob's twelve sons. Reuben's name sounds like רְאוּ בֵן lit. "see a son." Though Westermann suggests this may be an earlier explanation of the name, this is speculative. The etymology given in the existing text refers more directly to Leah's misery, "The LORD has seen [*r'h*] my oppression [*bᵉnyy*]." Here the play is simply on the consonants of the name, as is typical with the popular etymologies in the OT (cf. Strus, *Nomen-Omen*, 60). The phrase "The LORD has seen my oppression" seems to echo the similar remark addressed to the persecuted Hagar (16:11) and to foreshadow 31:42 (Laban's treatment of Jacob) and Exod 3:7; 4:31 (the Egyptian oppression of Israel). "The LORD." The names of Reuben, Simeon, Judah, and Joseph, the chief actors in the Joseph story, are all explained with reference to the divine name.

"Because now my husband will love me" is another loose poetic etymology of Reuben, for "will love me" has three consonants in common with Reuben (', *b, n*). It also links back to the key word in the previous episode, "love" (vv 18, 20, 30). Jacob "loved Rachel more than Leah." Leah hoped the birth of Reuben would remedy the situation. But it did not.

33 As with Reuben, Leah gives a twofold explanation of the name Simeon. Just as in v 32, the first, a fairly historical etymology, focuses on what the LORD has done; the second is a looser more poetic etymology reflecting on the relationship of Leah with her husband. In other Semitic languages, words ending in *an* (*on*) include abstract nouns, adjectives, and diminutives. Simeon could be a diminutive derived from שְׁמַע "to hear." Or it may be a theophoric name, "The god On has heard," for a god *ᶜon* appears in Ugaritic texts (Strus, *Salesianum* 40 [1978] 64–65; rejected by Fowler, *Personal Names*, 167). In this case, Leah's comment, "The LORD has heard," is very apt. Within Genesis it echoes 16:11, but its continuation, "that I am unloved," shows her bitter disappointment at Jacob's failure to accept her despite the birth of Reuben. "Unloved," lit. "hated" (cf. 29:31), is another free poetic play on the name Simeon; the consonants *ś, n* of "unloved" relate to *š, m, n* of Simeon, as do the sounds *an, no* in אָנֹכִי "I."

34 Levi may mean "attached, joined." Here Leah again explains her choice of name in terms of her forlorn hope that her husband will love her.

35 "Judah" may mean "praise" or be understood as a verbal form, "He (i.e., God) shall be praised." Or it may be an abbreviation of יהודיה or יהודאל, "May God be praised" (so A. R. Millard, *ZAW* 86 [1974] 216–18; see also *TDOT* 5:483–85; Fowler, *Personal Names*, 165). Like the names of her first two sons, Reuben and Simeon, Judah is a name that acknowledges the LORD's mercy to her, but here she makes no mention of her hope for improved relations with her husband. Has she at last come to terms with her plight? She may not enjoy her husband's affection, but God has given her four sons, and she must be thankful for that. "This time I shall praise the LORD"; here, as in the psalms, lament turns to praise.

"Then she stopped bearing children." Why? The narrative does not immediately explain. The most obvious explanation is that she became temporarily infertile, but it could be that marital intercourse now ceased. And if this was the case, was it Jacob's or Leah's decision? Does it represent a worsening of relations between them, or is Leah acknowledging that intercourse without love is pointless? The narrator by his brevity leaves these various possibilities open.

30:1–8 The second scene, like the first, begins with seeing, "When Rachel saw" (cf. 29:31). When the LORD saw Leah's situation, he acted in mercy. But Rachel's reaction to divine kindness is jealousy, and like Sarah (16:2), she adopts the desperate expedient of having children through her maid in an attempt to be even with her sister.

1–2 "To think that after the beautiful, gentle love story of 29:1–20 this angry exchange is our first and only experience of their marriage!" (Westermann, 2:474). The desperate desire of women for children is often expressed in the OT (cf. 1 Sam 1:6–8, 15–16; Prov 30:16), but nowhere so vehemently as here. "Give me children, or I shall die." Sarah's and Rebekah's reactions in similar situations are mild by comparison (cf. 16:2; 25:21), even though they had waited many more years than Rachel. To blame her husband for her plight also smacks of impiety, for the OT regards children as the gift of God, not of man (e.g., Ps 113:9). Prayer, not protest, should have been Rachel's reaction, as Jacob implies in his heated response, "Am I in God's place, who has prevented your womb from bearing fruit?" Rachel demanded sons; Jacob describes children as "fruit of the womb," thereby underlining their God-givenness (cf. Deut 7:13; 28:11; Ps 127:3). "Am I in God's place?" said the king of Israel when faced with another impossible demand (2 Kgs 5:7).

3 But despite Jacob's rebuke, Rachel is set on solving her problem by her own devices and not waiting for God to act. On the custom of surrogate marriages in the ancient Near East and Genesis' view of them, see *Comment* on 16:1–6. Rachel, in fact, quotes Sarah's words in asking Jacob to follow this custom, "that I may be built up from her" (16:2).

The phrase "to give birth over my knees," used only here and in 50:23, is a picturesque way of stating that the baby will be adopted. Richter (*ZAW* 91 [1979] 436–37) suggests that the phrase should be translated, "she will bear, instead (on behalf) of my womb."

Perhaps anticipating Bilhah's new role as Jacob's slave-wife, Rachel calls her my "slave-girl" (אמה). Usually this term defines a slave-girl's position vis-à-vis a master, who is also her husband, whereas שפחה "maid" usually defines the relationship between a maid and her mistress. Cf. *Comment* on 16:1.

4–5 At any rate, whether moved by local convention, grandpaternal precedent, or pity, Jacob complies with Rachel's request. Here, unlike 16:2, "Abram obeyed his wife," Jacob's compliance is mentioned in an uncondemnatory way: "Jacob went into her." And Bilhah apparently easily conceives and gives birth.

6 Unlike Sarah (cf. 16:5–6; 21:9–13), Rachel is delighted by the new baby. This is divine vindication; "God has vindicated me" (*dananni*) is a play on the boy's name Dan. Historically, the name Dan, lit. "he has judged, vindicated," is probably an abbreviation of Danilu, or Daniel, "The god El has judged/is my judge" (cf. Akk. names *Shamash idannani, idin Enlil*). So Rachel's first explanation of the name, "God has vindicated me," is here quite close to the historical. Dan is the perfect of the verb דין "to judge, vindicate," which according to Liedke (*THWAT* 1:446), denotes "the authoritative binding decision in a trial." Often God is described as judging the nations (15:14; Ps 7:9[8]; 9:9[8]; 96:10) or vindicating the poor and needy (Pss 68:6[5]; 140:13[12]).

"Listened to my voice" indicates that Rachel has indeed prayed, although nothing has been said about her prayer up to this point. She saw the birth of Dan as an answer to prayer, but whether the narrator would have agreed is dubious in view of his attitude to surrogate marriage in chap. 16. It is not until v 22 that he says "God listened to her."

"And given me a son." In her second explanation of the name Dan, there is another play on the name. נתן "give" contains both the consonants *n* and *t*, which is close to *d*. Note how Rachel regards Dan as indeed her son, whereas Sarah rejected Ishmael, whose birth she had organized in a similar way (cf. 16:1–7).

8 The rarity of the noun and verb here translated "wrestle, wrestlings" has perplexed interpreters from the LXX to the present. פתל in the niphal elsewhere means "to be deceitful" (e.g., Prov 8:8) but only here "to wrestle," while the noun נפתולי "struggles" is a hapax. It is the following comment, "I overcame her," that has led to the conclusion that these rare words are speaking of struggle (cf. 32:29[28]). The noun נפתולי "struggles" is here qualified by אלהים "of God," hence our translation "divine struggles." But how can competing with her sister be construed by Rachel as a struggle with God? For this reason, many English translations have taken "of God" as equivalent to a superlative: "mighty wrestlings" (AV, RSV), "fine trick" (NEB), "fateful struggle" (NAB). But it is doubtful whether אלהים "of God" should be stripped of its religious content, as such translations would imply to a secularized modern reader. In some sense, Rachel saw her struggle with Leah as a contest in which God was involved, for he had opened Leah's womb but shut hers (29:31; 30:22). So to what is Rachel referring in speaking of "divine struggles"? Suggestions include "struggles in prayer" for God's grace and blessing (Delitzsch; Dillmann; Fokkelman, *Narrative Art*; Andersen, *JBL* 88 [1969] 200); struggles that result in the divine vindication of Rachel (e.g., Procksch). Strus (*Salesianum* 40 [1978] 66) thinks Genesis regards Naphtali as a shortened (hypocoristic) form of *nptly-ʾl* "wrestlings of El."

Whatever the precise meaning of the name Naphtali, it is clear that the etymology offered by Genesis is a typically poetic one. It reflects both on the mother's relationship with God (cf. 29:32, 33, 35; 30:6) and upon the struggle between the sisters for Jacob's affection (29:32, 33, 34; 30:6). This double interest is characteristic of the etymologies in this narrative. Finally, "I overcame" seems to anticipate

32:29(28). Jacob was to struggle with the angel of God and overcome him. Here Rachel has struggled with God and her sister and overcome. Rachel, like Jacob, is the younger child who displaces the older, much to the latter's distress. This similarity in their careers also extends to their struggles with God.

9–13 Tit for tat. Rachel's triumph is short-lived. Anything she can do, Leah can do better. Leah can bear children herself and through her maid Zilpah. Note how this scene, like the previous two, opens with "When Leah (the LORD/Rachel) saw."

11 Leah's explanation for her choice of name is somewhat shorter than previously, with less obvious reference to God's intervention or her yearning for her husband. "Gad" means "good luck, fortune." It was also the name of a Semitic deity (cf. Isa 65:11), as in the Assyrian name *gadilu* or Ugaritic *godya* (Strus, *Salesiamun* 40 [1978] 67, n. 29). Though Schunck (*TDOT* 2:382–84) argues that Gad was originally a secular word meaning "good luck" that was later personified as a deity, it seems more likely, with Noth (*Personennamen*, 126–27) and Strus, that the evolution was the other way. The etymology offered here, "Luck has come" (the qere reading) or "Good luck" (ketib reading), apparently takes the name Gad just as an observation or as a wish. But, with Strus, it seems likely that the name and its explanation have religious overtones.

13 The name Asher, again, may have a religious origin. Asherah was wife of El, head of the Canaanite pantheon. Alternatively, a connection with Ashur of Assyria might be posited. Or it could be an abbreviation of a name like Asarel, "El has filled with joy" (cf. Arabic *ašira* "to fill with joy"; cf. Fowler, *Theophoric Names*, 96, 135). Leah explains it as "In my happiness" and follows it by the comment "daughters will declare me happy," because she is the mother of so many children. Leah's mention of daughters looks forward to the birth of Dinah in v 21 (cf. chap. 34). For the general sentiment, compare Prov 31:28, "Her children rise up and call her blessed" (cf. Cant 6:9); Luke 1:48, "For behold, henceforth all generations will call me blessed."

14–15 This short scene brings into the open the dispute that has long been simmering between Rachel and Leah. Leah's yearning for Jacob's love has come out repeatedly in the names she gave to her children, while Rachel's desperate desire for her own children led to her resorting to surrogate motherhood. Now there is public confrontation.

14 Reuben, Leah's firstborn, may have been five or six years old at this time, if the chronology of Genesis is to be taken as exact. The story itself suggests he may have been somewhat older, Leah having had four children at probably two-year intervals and then being infertile for a while. Whatever his age at "the time of the wheat harvest" (May), he found דוּדָאִים, which have since the Septuagint translation (third century B.C.) been understood as "mandrakes." The mandrake (*Mandragora autumnalis*) is a perennial Mediterranean plant that bears bluish flowers in winter and yellowish plum-sized fruit in summer. In ancient times, mandrakes were famed for arousing sexual desire (cf. Cant 7:13) and for helping barren women to conceive. These properties are certainly presupposed here and in Cant 7:13. Indeed, the word translated "mandrakes" here is almost the same as דוֹדִים "love" (Prov 7:18; Cant 1:2; 4:10; 5:1). However, M. Zohary (*Plants of the Bible*, 188) doubts whether the mandrake is meant here, for it "has never grown

in Mesopotamia," where Jacob, Leah, and Rachel lived. However, Delitzsch (2:177) notes it is found in Syria, and it does not seem out of the question that the plant may somewhat unusually have been found near Paddan-Aram. But whatever the plant Reuben brought home, it seems clear that Rachel and Leah valued it as a fertility drug, Rachel because she had never conceived, Leah because she had become infertile.

Rachel at least asked her sister politely, "Please give me some of your mandrakes"; compare her fierce "Give me children" (30:1) to Jacob.

15 But this request triggered a sharp and bitter response from Leah: "Is it too little for you . . . ?" Direct questions introduced by המעט usually express great exasperation by the speaker (Num 16:9; Josh 22:17; Isa 7:13; Ezek 34:18). Here Leah's reason is understandable; she is aggrieved not simply that she has stopped bearing children but that Jacob "*my* husband" rarely sleeps with her, preferring Rachel's bed. Suspension of conjugal rights can, according to the usual interpretation of Exod 21:10, be grounds for divorce.

Recognizing the justice of Leah's grievance, Rachel makes an offer: "He shall lie with you tonight in return for your son's mandrakes." So Rachel trades one night's conjugal rights for some of the mandrakes. This one remark is an eye-opener. We are shown just how much Jacob is favoring Rachel over Leah, that she is prepared for just one night to give away her mandrakes. But it also shows how desperate Rachel is for children; though Bilhah has borne her children and she has adopted them giving them names that express her sense of triumph, she still really wants a child of her own.

Leah's response to Rachel's offer is unrecorded. Silence indicates her grudging consent.

16–21 This scene portrays at least a degree of reconciliation between Leah and Jacob, even if it was initially secured by the unusual deal with her sister.

16 The use of the imperfect "you must come" is a little less demanding than the imperative "come," but the following infinitive absolute, "I have *really* hired you," shows the intensity of Leah's desire. The word שׂכר "hire" is a key term in the Jacob story (29:15; 30:18, 28, 32, 33; 31:7, 8, 41). The whole of his relationship with Laban seems to be reduced to a commercial level; now even his relationship with his wives is up for rent! At the same time Leah's words, "I have really hired you," anticipate the birth of Issachar, whose name is explained in v 18.

17 The comment "God listened to Leah and she conceived" is a little surprising, for surely what Leah most wanted was Jacob's affection, not more children. This comment does two things: First, it shows that though Rachel and Leah may think conception is aided by mandrakes, the text insists that children are God's gift. "He gives the barren woman a home, making her the joyous mother of children" (Ps 113:9). Sarna (209) notes that the narrative dismisses "the notion that such superstitions (about mandrakes) have any validity. Leah, who gives up the mandrakes, bears three sons; Rachel who possesses them, remains barren for apparently three more years." Second, it suggests that a renewal of relations between Leah and Jacob is on the way. See her comments in v 20.

18 Issachar is an Amorite name attested at Mari: *yaskur-il* "May El (God) be gracious" (Strus, *Salesianum* 40 [1978], 68, n. 32). Another less likely possibility is that it comes from אישׁ־שׂכר "man of hire." As often though, the mother's comment

is a poetic, not a historical, etymology. She sees Issachar's birth as a reward for her giving Zilpah to Jacob. In retrospect, she seems to regard this as a costly sacrifice, though at the time, the births of Gad and Asher were joyful occasions (cf. vv 12, 13).

19–20 Leah's explanation of her next son's name, Zebulon, is more upbeat than that of Issachar, but the historical etymology is more obscure. Zabulan is an Amorite name and also seems to be found in Egyptian texts (Strus, *Salesianum* 40 [1978] 69, n. 35). The root (M. Held, "Root ZBL/SBL," in E. A. Speiser Mem. Essays, *JAOS* 88 [1968] 90–96) *zbl* is in Ugaritic often associated with the gods, so Noth's suggestion (*Personennamen*, 159) that it means "habitation of a god" is not impossible. But the meaning of זבל *zbl* is obscure. Gamberoni (*TDOT* 4:29–31) prefers "glory, heaven" as the root idea.

As often in her choice of names, Leah gives a dual explanation of the name, the first focusing on God's mercy. "God has endowed me with a good endowment." The root זבד "endow(ment)" occurs only here as a noun and verb, but it is often found in Israelite names, e.g., Zebediah, Zabdi, Zebedee. The first two consonants of Zebulon are the basis for the paronomasia here. Then she gives a second explanation, emphasizing her relationship with her husband, "This time my husband will honor me because I have borne him six sons" (cf. *TDOT* 4:31). Her phraseology here echoes 29:34, "This time my husband will be attached to me, because I have borne him three sons." Thus the birth of her sixth son finds Leah in a more optimistic mood.

21 This note of triumph is carried through in calling her daughter "Dinah," "judgment, vindication" (cf. Dan v 6). In fact, no etymology is offered for her name, perhaps because it is too obvious or because she was merely a daughter. It is, of course, extraordinary to mention the birth of daughters; it is done only if they are going to have an important role to play later (cf. Rebekah in 22:23). Dinah's appearance does not just make the number of children born to Jacob up to twelve; it signifies that she too will be an actor of note in a tale of judgment and vindication (chap. 34).

22–24 This short scene brings this episode to a happy conclusion. At last, Rachel succeeds in bearing a son, this time not through her maid, not thanks to mandrakes, but through the mercy of God. "God remembered Rachel." This scene does more though. It marks the turning point in the Jacob story; from now on, Jacob's thoughts are on going back to his homeland (30:25).

22 Gunkel (cf. Westermann) assigns each clause to a different hand. In the light of the exact parallel construction in 8:1, "God remembered Noah . . . and God caused . . . and the waters receded," which is conventionally all ascribed to one source (P), it seems ill-judged to hold that this verse is composite. Indeed, 30:22 is parallel to 8:1 not only in grammar but in setting. Both stand at the turning points in their respective stories. It was God remembering Noah that led to the flood waters declining; it was God remembering Rachel that led to her conceiving and Jacob returning to the land of promise. Westermann might have expected "God listened to her" to have preceded "God remembered Rachel," but the present order stresses the priority of God's grace (cf. Isa 65:24).

"He opened her womb" makes a neat inclusion with 29:31. The framework of the story implies that Rachel had to wait at least seven years after marrying Jacob to bear her first child, and fourteen years since their betrothal (29:18, 27).

23–24 As often, a double explanation of the chosen name is offered. The first is poetic; it refers to the effect on Rachel's reputation of becoming a mother: "God has gathered up my shame." Childlessness was regarded as shameful (see Isa 4:1). The second explanation, "May the LORD add another son to me," is a prayer for the future, a prayer that was indeed answered, but only at the cost of Rachel's life; she died giving birth to Benjamin (35:16–19).

It is also very close to the historic etymology of Joseph, which is generally regarded as an abbreviated (hypocoristic) form of יוֹסֵף־אֵל *yosep-il* "May God (El) add (another child)" (cf. Josiphiah, Ezra 8:10). Like many of the patriarchal names, e.g., Isaac, Ishmael, Jacob, and Issachar, Joseph consists of a third person singular imperfect verbal form ("he will . . . ") plus the name of God (usually understood). Here we notice that the personal name "The LORD (Yahweh)" is used to explain the name as in 29:32, 33, 35. At other points in this episode, God (Elohim) is always preferred. It is characteristic of the editor of Genesis to use "The LORD" at the beginning and end of sections and often to use other epithets elsewhere (cf. 17:1; 20:18; 21:1, 33); this may be sufficient explanation here. In 3:1–7, the narrative uses "God" instead of "The LORD God" as elsewhere in chapters 2–3 to draw attention to the alienation between God and his creatures in this scene. The same motive may be present here. After a relatively cheerful start to the marriage (cf. 29:32–35), alienation between husband and wives and between the wives and God creeps in so that they speak of him as "God," not the LORD. Only in this last scene, with her prayers answered, is the more intimate covenantal name "the LORD" invoked again by Rachel.

Explanation

Bigamy is not explicitly condemned in the OT, unless Lev 18:18 refers to it. However, Gen 2 records that the LORD only created one wife for Adam, which implies that anyone who takes an extra wife is going beyond what God intended. Furthermore, all the polygamous marriages of Genesis turn out to be disasters. Lamek's pretty wives, Adah and Zillah, had to cope with a brutal husband. Though it was his first wife, Sarah, who persuaded Abraham to have intercourse with her maid Hagar, thereby promoting her to the status of slave-wife, the narrator in Gen 16 implies that this act was similar to the fall. It certainly sparked bitter jealousy between the women, leading to Hagar and her son's expulsion.

But of all the polygamous marriages, it is Jacob's that is portrayed in most detail. Though Jacob was tricked into marrying Leah as well as Rachel, he seems never to have forgiven her for consenting to deceive him in this way. He always regards Rachel as his wife and treats Leah and her children as inferior. And this discrimination persists throughout Genesis, leading Leah's sons to try to eliminate Joseph, Rachel's firstborn and Jacob's favorite, from the family.

Here the narrator gives us a few snapshots of the first stormy years of Jacob's marriage. The opening verse depicts the plight of the two wives: "Leah was unloved . . . but Rachel remained childless." Both crave what the other has; Leah longs for Jacob's love, and Rachel is desperate for children. The birth of every child is an occasion for the rivals to put their feelings into words: "Now my husband will love me," "This time my husband will be attached to me" (29:32, 34),

says Leah. "With divine struggles I wrestled with my sister; indeed I overcame her," says Rachel (30:8).

We glimpse the underhand tactics both women use to promote their goals. Rachel resorts to surrogate motherhood, a practice already criticized in chap. 16, to produce children for herself. This is countered in turn by Leah using the same technique. Then Leah exchanges an ancient fertility drug with her sister for a night in her husband's bed, from which Rachel had driven her. But none of these attempts to manipulate their fertility achieves anything. As Jacob (30:2) and the narrator insist, it is the LORD who opened Leah's womb and then Rachel's (29:31; 30:22). This is a story of the triumph of God's power over human sinfulness.

It is into this most bitterly divided family that the forefathers of the twelve tribes were born. Fathered by a lying trickster and mothered by sharp-tongued shrews, the patriarchs grew up to be less than perfect themselves. Yet through them the promises to Abraham took a great step toward their fulfillment, showing that it is divine grace not human merit that gives mankind hope of salvation.

Jacob Outwits Laban   (30:25–31:1)

Bibliography

Brenner, A. "*atupim* and *qissurin* (Gen 30:31–42)." (Heb.) *BMik* 24 (1978) 77–80. **Saracino, F.** "Ras Ibn Hani 78/20 and Some OT Connections." *VT* 32 (1982) 338–43.

Translation

[25] *Now as soon as Rachel had given birth to Joseph, Jacob said to Laban, "Let me go,[a] so that[b] I may return to my home and country. [26] Give[a] me my wives and my children, for whom I served you, so[b] that I may go, for you[c] do know all the service I did for you." [27] Laban replied to him, "If it pleases you, I have grown rich,[a] and the LORD has blessed me because of you." [28] So he said, "Name your wages which I owe,[a] that[b] I may give you them." [29] He replied, "You[a] do know how[b] I have served you and how[b] your herds have fared with me. [30] For the few that you had before I arrived[a] have teemed and increased, and the LORD has blessed you wherever I have gone.[b] Now when can I too do something for my household?" [31] So he said, "What shall I give you?" Jacob replied, "Do not give me anything, except to do this for me: I shall again[a] shepherd your flock. I shall guard[b] it. [32] I shall go through all your flock to remove[a] from it every speckled and spotted animal and every dark one among the sheep and the spotted and speckled among the goats, and they shall be my payment. [33] My honesty will witness against me in the future, when you check my wages. Any of them which is not speckled or spotted among the goats, or a dark one among the sheep is one stolen by me." [34] So Laban replied, "Fine, [a]let it be[a] as you suggest."*

³⁵ *That day he removed*^a *the striped and spotted he-goats and all the speckled and spotted she-goats, all that had any white in them and the dark ones among the sheep, and he gave them to his sons to look after.* ³⁶ *He put*^a *three days' journey between it*^b *and Jacob, so Jacob was left to shepherd the remainder*^c *of the flock.*^d

³⁷ *So Jacob took branches*^a *of fresh poplar, almond, and plane, and he peeled peelings of poplar, exposing the white which is on the branches.* ³⁸ *He set*^a *up the branches which he had peeled in the water troughs*^b *where the flock came to drink opposite the animals, and they bred*^c *when they came*^d *to drink.* ³⁹ *The flock bred*^a *by the branches, and the flocks gave birth*^b *to striped, speckled, and spotted.* ⁴⁰ *The sheep*^a *Jacob separated and put them facing the flock toward* ^b*the striped and every dark one among Laban's flock, and he made separate flocks for himself, and he did not put*^c *them in Laban's flock.*

⁴¹ *So whenever*^a *the robust*^b *animals bred,*^c *Jacob used to place the branches opposite the flock in the troughs to breed*^d *them with the branches.* ⁴² *When the flocks were feeble,*^a *he did not place them, so the feeble*^b *ones were Laban's but the strong*^c *ones were Jacob's.*

⁴³ *So the man teemed abundantly, and he acquired many*^a *flocks, slave-girls and slaves, camels and donkeys.* ^{31:1} *But he heard what Laban's sons were saying: "Jacob* ^a *has taken away all that belonged to our father and from what belonged to our father has made*^a *all this wealth."*

Notes

25.a. 2 masc sg impv piel שְׁלַח + 1 sg suffix.

25.b. Sequence impv + coh (of הלך) indicates purpose (GKC, 108d).

26.a. 2 masc sg impv qal נְתָן + *āh* ending.

26.b. Cf. n. 30:25.b.

26.c. The use of the personal pronoun "you" with the finite verb draws special attention to the subj, "you are the one who knows." The phrase "you know" is frequently used in requests, where previous knowledge ought to move the one requested to agree. Cf. 31:6; *EWAS*, 53.

27.a. N. M. Waldman (*JQR* 50 [1964] 164–65), and J. J. Finkelstein (*JAOS* 88 [1968] 34, n. 19) link the verb with Akk. *naḥāšu* "become full, wealthy."

28.a. For this nuance of עַל, cf. BDB, 753a; Brockelmann, 110b.

28.b. Cf. n. 30:25.b.

29.a. Cf. n. 30:26.c.

29.b. אֵת אֲשֶׁר "the way in which" (GKC, 157c).

30.a. Lit. "before me."

30.b. Lit. "to my foot," though Gispen, 3:93, suggests that since it contrasts with לְפָנַי "before me" ("before I came"), this phrase means "after I came."

31.a. 1 sg coh qal שׁוּב "I shall return" here placed before "shepherd" without copula to mean "I shall shepherd again" (GKC, 120gh).

31.b. Unusually not linked by copula "and," but *pace BHS* no ground for omission.

32.a. 2 masc sg impv hiph סוּר according to G, Vg, but apparently taken as inf abs hiph סוּר by *Tg. Onq. Neof.*, "I will separate." Our translation follows the targums, but it makes little difference to the sense.

34.a-a. *EWAS*, 116, suggests this expression (לוֹ + 3 masc sg juss הָיָה) could be an Akkadianism reflecting Laban's Mesopotamian background.

35.a. Cf. n. 8:13.b.

36.a. Cf. n. 2:8.b.

36.b. SamPent "them."

36.c. Def art + fem pl ptcp niph יתר.

36.d. SamPent adds a comment based on 31:11–13.

37.a. Here collective sg stands for pl.

38.a. Waw consec + 3 masc sg impf hiph יצג.

38.b. בְּ + constr pl שֹׁקֶת. On pointing, see GKC, 10g. SamPent reads בהשקות.

38.c. Waw consec + 3 fem pl impf qal חמם or יחם (BDB, 328b; KB, 389b). Cf. GKC, 47k.
38.d. ב + inf constr בוא + fem pl suffix.
39.a. Cf. n. 30:38.c. Here 3 masc pl impf. On the lack of concord, probably fem subj ("flocks, i.e., ewes," as in v 38) with masc verb, see GKC, 145p,s.
39.b. Waw consec + 3 fem pl impf ילד.
40.a. Placing the obj "sheep" first in the clause draws attention to it (GKC, 142f; cf. *EWAS*, 38–39).
40.b. *Tg. Onq., Ps.-J.* add כל "all."
40.c. 3 masc sg pf שׁית + 3 masc pl suffix.
41.a. So the versions correctly interpret בכל, but it seems unnecessary to posit the omission of עת from MT, *pace BHS*. On the syntax of verbs, see WOC, 534.
41.b. Def art + fem pl ptcp pual קשׁר "to bind," only here with the meaning "strong, robust" (KB, 1076b, but cf. pass ptcp qal in v 42).
41.c. Inf constr piel יחם.
41.d. ל + inf constr piel יחם + 3 fem pl suffix.
42.a. ב + inf constr hiph עטף.
42.b. Def art + masc pl pass ptcp עטף.
42.c. Cf. n. 30:41.b.
43.a. On the pl adjective with sg noun, see GKC, 132g, 145o; WOC, 257.
31:1.a-a. On this chiastic structure, cf. *SBH*, 130; common at close of section (Longacre, *Joseph*, 103).

Form/Structure/Setting

The episode opens with a temporal clause, "As soon as Rachel," that frequently marks a major break in narrative. It is more difficult to determine its close. Nearly all commentators suppose 30:43 concludes the episode. However, Delitzsch continues it to 31:3, but it seems rather odd to end with a divine command without a mention of a human response. But to suppose that 30:43 is a conclusion and that 31:1 opens a new section is problematic, for the latter contains no explicit nominal subject. Rather, it opens with the subject, Jacob, understood: "he heard what Laban's sons were saying." For this reason, Westermann reorders 31:1–2, putting v 2 before v 1. Though this makes sense of the syntax, it lacks any textual warrant. So it is better to accept that 31:1 goes with what precedes; it cannot be the start of a new section. It is less clear whether 31:2 represents the close of this episode or the opening of the next. In that 31:5 echoes 31:2 so closely, "Laban (your father) has not been regarding me as he did previously," it seems preferable to take the new episode as opening with 31:2, not 31:3. If it seems strange for a totally new theme, the jealousy of Laban's sons, to be broached in 31:1 at the end of a section, it should be recalled that the technique of preview is frequent in Genesis (cf. 4:25–26 previewing chap. 5; 6:1–8 previewing 6:9–9:29; 32:2–3 previewing 32:4–33). It is also a regular feature of Genesis for someone to make a comment on what has just happened toward the close of a scene or episode—here "Jacob has taken away all that belonged to our father" (cf. 28:6, 20–22; 29:29; 30:24; 32:3[2]; 33:20; 34:31). Thus by the conventions of Genesis, 31:1 is a fitting close to the episode.

This episode falls into two extended scenes:

vv 25–36   Negotiations between Jacob and Laban
vv 37–31:1   Jacob breeds his own flock

The first scene consists of six speeches by Jacob and Laban with introduction and concluding comments.

v 25a	Introduction: back reference to birth of Joseph
vv 25b–26	Jacob asks Laban's permission to leave
vv 27–28	Laban stalls and asks Jacob to name his pay
vv 29–30	Jacob reminds Laban how he has prospered thanks to Jacob's efforts
v 31a	Laban again asks Jacob to name his pay
vv 31b-33	Jacob asks for nothing but unborn abnormal animals
v 34	Laban agrees
vv 35–36	Laban removes all the abnormal animals so that Jacob has none

This arrangement into six speeches is frequent in Hebrew, and the quotation formulae used at the beginning of each speech are appropriate.

Having been tricked out of any pay, in the second scene Jacob is portrayed turning the tables on Laban by contriving to breed strong healthy bicolored flocks from those monochrome animals left in his care by Laban.

vv 37–40	How Jacob produced bicolored animals
vv 41–42	How Jacob acquired strong animals
v 43–31:1	Conclusion and preview

This episode is an integral part of the Laban-Jacob cycle. So much is presupposed about their previous relationship that it is impossible to envisage it ever having existed independently: Jacob's serving Laban as a shepherd, his marriage to Laban's daughters, his own lack of resources, and Laban's trickery. Likewise, it relates back to Jacob's earlier existence in Canaan; he wants to return to his home and country (v 26; cf. 27:44–45). It also looks forward to his eventual return (chaps. 31–33). The mention of the LORD's blessing of Laban as a result of Jacob (vv 27, 30) links this episode to the many others in Genesis, where this key term appears (e.g., 1:28; 12:2; 17:16; 22:17; 24:1; 26:12; 27:4, 7, 10, 19, 23, 25, 27, 29–31, 33–34, 38, 41; 28:1, 3, 6; 32:1, 27, 30). Other key items are "serve, service" (vv 26, 29; cf. 25:23; 27:29, 40; 29:15, 18, 20, 25, 27, 30; 31:6, 41) and "wages" (vv 28, 32, 33; cf. 29:15; 30:16, 18; 31:7, 8, 41), and the list of the persons and animals acquired by Jacob (v 43) resembles 12:16. It is therefore clear that this episode cannot be divorced from its present setting; it is integral to the total plot of Genesis. It shows Jacob, so long exploited by his father-in-law, Laban, at last turning the tables and preparing to return to the land of promise.

According to some traditional source critics, the two sources J and E are to be distingushed in this episode, though they often admit some uncertainty about parts of the analysis, but others (e.g., Delitzsch, Speiser, Vawter) believe it derives almost entirely from J. Those who maintain the presence of J and E in this passage divide it as follows: vv 25, 27, 29–31, 32a (part), 35–43 J; vv 26, 28, 32a(part)b, 33–34 E. It was argued that the duplication within the narrative, vv 25//26a; 26b//29a; 28//31a, "And he said" (vv 27, 28), "you do know" (vv 26, 29), shows two sources must be present. Since vv 27, 30 mention "the LORD," this must represent the J source, so the other source must be E.

However, Volz (*Der Elohist,* 88) observed that "no one would have come up with a source division here, unless the theory was already in existence." He showed that the supposed doublets were not doublets and that the narrative could be read as a coherent whole. And his view has convinced most modern commentators (e.g., Speiser, Vawter, Coats). Westermann believes that this section is a

substantial unity from J, because it corresponds in form to Babylonian dialogue contracts and also to Gen 23. He does, however, find expansions in vv 32–33, 35, 40, where the narrator goes into long specific detail about excluding "every dark one among the sheep and the spotted and speckled among the goats." Westermann regards these remarks as too prolix for the style of the passage, though they do express J's understanding quite well. These grounds seem somewhat slight for postulating two layers of material. With Blum (*Die Komposition,* 114–16) I accept the coherence of this narrative; the elaborations are necessary in a story of tricky business dealing and ingenious stockbreeding.

Comment

25a   This opening sentence both introduces the new episode and links it back to the preceding. The birth of a boy to Rachel, Jacob's first love, is the turning point in the cycle. As soon as it occurs, Jacob plans to go home. In fact, it is a little difficult to squeeze the birth of six sons and one daughter to Leah described in 29:31–30:21 and a period of barrenness into the space of just seven years, as 29:20, 27; 31:38 imply, but it may be that these figures are supposed to be taken as round numbers, not as an exact chronology (cf. *Introduction,* "The Chronology of the Patriarchs").

25b–26   In this first speech, Jacob demands permission from his father-in-law to return home with his wives and children. He uses the straight imperative without even a "please" (נא) or any of the milder forms of request. The verbal forms suggest a somewhat aggressive first move on Jacob's part, "Let me go so that I may return." Here Jacob echoes the words of Abraham's servant (24:54, 56), who similarly asked leave of Laban to return to Canaan. As on that occasion, Laban now does his best to delay the departure.

"To my home," lit. "to my place." For this meaning of "place," cf. 18:33; 32:1(31:55).

"My land"; cf. 12:1. On the face of it, Jacob is simply expressing a wish to return to the land of his birth, but there could be another dimension to his description of it as "*my* land." The land is his by promise (28:4, 13), so he must go back to claim his inheritance.

26   According to Exod 21:3–6, a slave who is given a wife by his master must leave her and any children behind when after six years he leaves his master's service. If the slave did not wish to be parted from his wife and children, he had to remain a slave. It is not clear whether the law of Exodus was thought to apply in Jacob's case. Despite Jacob describing himself three times as Laban's slave, "I *served* you," "all the *service I did* for you" (the word serve/service could as well be translated "slave"), 29:15 makes us tend not to view Jacob as a slave, because he was Laban's nephew, who was offered wages. But there does not appear to be any reason why a poor man should not indenture himself to a wealthy relative; because he was his kinsman it was hoped he would treat his slave more kindly (cf. Lev 25:35–36). Certainly 31:43 could imply that Laban looked on Jacob more as a slave than as a son-in-law. But whatever Jacob's legal situation, he wants to have his cake and eat it too; he wants his own freedom and to keep his wives and children. He reminds Laban of "all the service I did for you."

27–28 Laban's response is a model of oriental courtesy and cunning. He very politely rejects Jacob's request to be allowed to leave, at least for the present. "If it pleases you" is an obsequious way of addressing a superior (e.g., 18:3; 19:19; 33:10; 47:29; 50:4), but here he uses it to butter up his enslaved nephew.

"I have grown rich." With Finkelstein (*JAOS* 88 [1968] 34, n. 19), this seems more probable than the traditional interpretation "I have learned by divination" (cf. 44:5), for it is unlikely that Laban would have resorted to divination when he was prospering.

"The LORD has blessed me." That all the families of the earth will be blessed through Abraham and his offspring is central to the patriarchal promises (e.g., 12:3; 22:18; 28:14), and this is one of several incidents where outsiders admit that God's blessing very apparently rests on Abraham's family and those associated with them (14:19–20; 21:22–23; 26:12–16, 28–29; 39:5, 23).

But for Laban, far from this being a reason to accede to Jacob's request, it is an excuse to detain him. How can he afford to lose a man who brings him such wealth? He puts it diplomatically, though. "He said" without any further elaboration suggests the following is said politely (Longacre, *Joseph*, 177). "Name your wages which I owe that I may give them to you." According to the wedding agreement (29:18, 27) Laban owed Jacob nothing, because he already had two wives promised in exchange for his fourteen years of labor. This he had only just completed, so he could not demand anything more at this stage. Therefore, if Jacob wants to go with anything more than Leah and Rachel, he will have to work longer. A neat reply.

29–30 Unabashed, Jacob continues to press very courteously for more than permission to leave empty-handed (cf. Deut 15:12–18). You, Laban, admit that you have prospered greatly since my arrival (v 29), but to say merely that "the LORD has blessed me because of you" (v 27) is an understatement. "The few that you had . . . have teemed and increased, and the LORD has blessed you wherever I have gone" (v 30). Here Jacob alludes to the promise made to him in 28:14 that his descendants would "spread" or "teem" (פרץ). The gist of his remarks is: "If God has done so much for you as the result of my work, surely you can now do something for me, or at least let me do something for my family."

31a Laban's question, "What shall I give you?" sounds reasonable and open, but in fact he has already indicated that he will not give Jacob a farewell present.

31b–33 Jacob therefore makes a very modest suggestion that the mean Laban can hardly refuse. In a flock of sheep and goats, the sheep are mostly all white, the goats all black or dark brown. Multicolored sheep and goats are much rarer. Jacob suggests that all the multicolored animals be his wage and that the pure white sheep and the dark goats be Laban's. What is more, Laban may remove all the multicolored animals to start with, so that Jacob will have only the white sheep and the dark goats to care for, and these will be Laban's. Any multicolored lambs or kids subsequently born in that flock Jacob will have as his own.

As Jacob describes the arrangement, it does indeed look as though he is asking for nothing. Laban might well think that if he removes all the multicolored sheep and goats to start with, few multicolored lambs or kids would be born in the flock. Laban will be able to check easily Jacob's honesty in keeping the agreement. Any white sheep or black goats in his flock will be Laban's; the multicolored will be Jacob's.

34 Not surprisingly, Laban accepts this very favorable deal; he did not anticipate Jacob making much out of it, certainly much less than the typical 20 percent
of newborn lambs or kids that ancient shepherds usually received as their wages
(Finkelstein, *JAOS* 88 [1968] 33–35). The commentator Jacob regards Laban's
remarks as somewhat more equivocal, but despite the unusual use of הן "fine"
"behold" it does seem to represent agreement at last.

35–36 Jacob's remark, "They shall be my payment" (v 32), could be taken to
mean that the multicolored animals in the flock at the moment were to be his.
Indeed, he had volunteered to sort the animals himself, but Laban takes no
chances. A cheat himself, he fears Jacob may pull a fast one on him. So Laban
separates the animals himself, and to make doubly sure that Jacob cannot acquire any multicolored animals, he separates them by a three days' journey from
the pure white sheep and black goats that Jacob has offered to look after. This
precaution rebounds on Laban, for it enables Jacob to indulge in selective breeding to his own advantage and later to slip away from Laban's clutches (chap. 31).

37–42 Some of the details of Jacob's methods are obscure, but two principles
are clear. First, the coloring of lambs and kids is determined by what their parents see during intercourse. If they look at multicolored posts when they mate,
their young will be multicolored. If this seems an odd belief in the light of modern genetics, the second principle is not, namely, that strong animals are liable to
produce sturdy offspring and vice versa (vv 41–42). Sarna (212) suggests that the
production of the multicolored sheep and goats may also be scientifically explicable. The vigorous animals were hybrids, whose recessive coloring genes emerged
when they were bred together. By this means, Jacob secured for himself large
flocks of healthy multicolored sheep and goats, whereas Laban's animals were
weak and either pure black or white.

This passage is characterized by the use of a large number of terms relating to animals,
whose precise meaning has not always been grasped by commentators, leading them to
conclude that the passage is composite or glossed. But this seems unlikely. We list the
terms in order of increasing precision:

צֹאן	"animals, flock"	vv 31–32, 36, 38–41
	i.e., sheep or goats	
שֶׂה	"animal"	vv 32, 35
	i.e., one sheep or goat	
כֶּשֶׂב	"sheep"	vv 32, 33, 40
עֵז	"(she)-goat"	vv 32, 33, 35
תַּיִשׁ	"he-goat"	v 35

It is difficult to be precise about the terms here translated "striped, spotted, speckled." The important point to grasp is that sheep are normally white, whereas goats are
normally black. The terms "striped, spotted, speckled" refer to animals, sheep or goats,
that are not all one color.

With this analysis of the vocabulary, it is hoped that the translation of vv 32–42 becomes easier to follow. However, there are some points that require further comment;
see Fokkelman, *Narrative Art*, 145–50; Blum, *Die Komposition*, 114–16 for a fuller discussion.

37 It is unclear why Jacob should have chosen poplar, almond, and plane branches from which to strip the bark. On these trees, see M. Zohary, *Plants of the Bible,* 66–67, 129, 132. Many trees are white under the bark, so presumably would have served equally well. "Poplar" (לבנה) sounds similar to "white" (לבן), which is also Laban's name (cf. above on 24:29). It is possible that there is a play on his name here, as well as on Jacob's; the word translated "striped" (עקד, vv 35, 39) contains two consonants and two vowels that also appear in "Jacob" (Strus, *Nomen-Omen,* 134–35).

39 The successful climax of Jacob's endeavors. The animals breed, producing "striped, speckled, and spotted" young. Note the full list of adjectives here as befits the episode climax.

40 "Striped, speckled, and spotted" could be construed as simply referring to the goats, so Blum (*Die Komposition*). This verse makes it clear that Jacob also managed to make white sheep produce colored lambs. "The sheep Jacob separated." The next clause is awkward, and various suggestions have been made about emending it or reinterpreting it. Jacob reviews various interpretations and says, "A very difficult verse. We know no satisfactory explanation" (608). Two possibilities seem worthy of consideration. Fokkelman explains v 40 as follows: "In the same way Jacob separated the sheep [into white ones for Laban and colored ones for himself]. He gave the best position among the flock to the striped goats" he had bred and every dark sheep among Laban's flock. In this way he made separate flocks for himself apart from Laban's (Fokkelman, *Narrative Art,* 148). As Fokkelman himself points out, the chief difficulty with his view is that he renders ויתן פני הצאן "he gave the best position among the flock," an unparalleled usage, instead of "he put them facing the flock."

The other suggestion of Speiser, Westermann, and Blum (*Die Komposition*), following an earlier suggestion of Rashbam, is that when the white sheep mated they did so looking at Laban's dark goats. This produced dark lambs, just as mating the goats in front of the stripped branches produced spotted and speckled goats. It may be recalled that Laban had left a flock of black goats and white sheep for Jacob to care for. So Jacob found a means not just of making black goats produce spotted kids but of inducing white sheep to give birth to dark lambs. This solution seems simpler than Fokkelman's. The only difficulty is why the "striped" are mentioned along with the "dark" as part of Jacob's procedure. But if Jewish tradition (Jacob, 603) is correct in understanding עקד "striped" as "flecked in the feet," perhaps with the ankles of different color so that it appears to wear a fetter (so Even-Shoshan, *Lexicon*), it could denote a predominantly dark animal with light stripes.

But whatever the correct interpretation, one thing is clear: Jacob comprehensively outwitted Laban and succeeded in breeding multicolored sheep and goats from monochrome stock and so transferred them into his ownership. What is more, he ensured that the strong kids and lambs were his, and the feeble Laban's (vv 41–42).

43 "So the man teemed abundantly." Here the editor himself draws attention to the fulfillment of the promise made to Jacob in 28:14 (cf. 30:30). Indeed, the phraseology here closely echoes 12:16, "Abram . . . acquired sheep, cattle, donkeys, slaves, slave-girls, she-asses, and camels." Jacob became as rich in exile

in Paddan-Aram as his grandfather Abraham had become in Egypt. Now that Jacob has made his fortune, he is in a much better position to leave than he was at the beginning of the episode. Thus, as often in Genesis, the conclusion of one section prepares the way for the next.

31:1 The narrator's detached summary of Jacob's wealth is followed by the very personal perspective of his brothers-in-law. Jacob's success is their loss: "Jacob has taken away all that belonged to our father and from what belonged to our father has made all this wealth." כבד "wealth" is usually translated "glory," but cf. 45:13; 13:2. Even more clearly than in 30:41, the next episode is adumbrated: trouble is brewing between Jacob and Laban's family, and a difficult parting is in the offing. But as elsewhere in Genesis, there is a repeating pattern: Abraham, Jacob, and Joseph all find themselves wealthy as a result of leaving Canaan and sojourning in foreign lands.

Explanation

With the birth of a child to Rachel, all Jacob's yearnings for home were reawakened. The positive purpose of his sojourn in Paddan-Aram was now fulfilled. As his father had directed, he had taken a wife from Laban's daughters, and she had borne a son as promised (28:2–3). Now the time was ripe to return to the land promised as an inheritance to him and to his descendants (28:4, 13–16). Since the LORD had fulfilled the other promises by protecting him and giving him children, Jacob now looks for the land promise to be redeemed. To describe it as my land (v 25) doubtless represents his recollection of the promise as much as the fact that he was born there.

But returning is more difficult than leaving. He left single; he now has wives and children. Indeed his father-in-law Laban regards him as part of his clan, for Jacob has worked for him for fourteen years and married two of his daughters. So Jacob asks permission to leave. He reminds Laban of the valuable service he has performed for him and that if he is fair and generous, he will let him go (v 26). But Laban, as earlier episodes have made clear (chaps. 24, 29), is both tricky and grasping, and he has no intention of letting such a valuable asset as Jacob leave. But he couches his refusal in a polite, even flattering, way. "If it pleases you . . . the LORD has blessed me because of you" (v 27). Though Laban is boss, he addresses Jacob as though Jacob is. His comment on the LORD's blessing is a backhanded way of saying he cannot afford to let Jacob go.

But he continues, "Name your wages that I owe" (v 28). This sounds like a reasonable, open-handed offer, but addressed to Jacob it offers him precisely nothing. For Jacob had contracted to serve Laban fourteen years so that he could marry Rachel. Now having served just these years, Laban and Jacob were even; Laban owed Jacob nothing. He could take his wives but nothing else, for Laban, unlike Deut 15:13–14, did not propose to give his son-in-law a golden handshake for his fourteen years of loyal service.

Jacob remonstrates that this is unfair. "You admit that everything I have touched, particularly your flocks, have flourished as a result of my work. Surely I ought to do something for my household (v 30). After all, Laban, they are your daughters and grandchildren."

At this Laban appears to relent. "What shall I give you?" he replies. But Jacob knows his mean father-in-law too well. He would never give him anything worthwhile. So he apparently withdraws his request for anything substantial at all. He asks simply for a future share of the kids and lambs born in Laban's flocks. Since he only asks for "the spotted and speckled ones," when goats are usually all black and sheep all white, this does not seem likely to amount to much, especially as Jacob says that all existing "spotted and speckled" animals may be removed from the flock to start with. This modest request pleases Laban, since he calculates that Jacob is likely to profit very little by this request and that in the meantime he will keep his excellent shepherd. Indeed, Jacob may take so long to breed a decent flock of his own that he may never leave. So the deal is done (vv 31–34).

But to make sure Jacob does not cheat, Laban himself sorts the flock, removes all the spotted and speckled animals to a safe distance, and leaves Jacob with a flock consisting only of pure white sheep and pure black goats, which under the agreement are Laban's (vv 35–36). So if Jacob is to acquire any flock of his own, he must discover a way of breeding multicolored animals from monochrome ones. Laban evidently believed it could not be done, at least in any big way, or he would not have consented to Jacob's proposal.

Yet, this is just what Jacob does. He discovers that putting partially stripped tree branches in front of the goats as they mate leads to them giving birth to spotted offspring, which under the agreement are his (vv 37–39). Likewise, putting a black goat in front of white sheep when they mate produces dark-colored lambs, which again belong to Jacob (v 40). However, Jacob did not adopt these procedures indiscriminately; he reserved them for the strongest and healthiest animals in the flock. This ensured that the spotted kids and black lambs were healthier than the black kids and white lambs. Thus his flock of multicolored sheep and goats was not only numerous but also more vigorous than Laban's flock of white sheep and black goats. "So the man teemed abundantly, and he acquired many flocks, slave-girls and slaves, camels and donkeys" (v 43).

This story has always given listeners and readers a great sense of satisfaction. The mean old cheat Laban at last meets his comeuppance at the hands of his nephew Jacob, whom he had so unkindly cheated out of Rachel on his wedding day. This had led to seven years of family strife and sorrow. Laban refuses to compensate Jacob for his sterling service that has been so profitable for him. But, nonetheless, Jacob outmaneuvers Laban, not by trickery but simply by keeping to the terms of an agreement freely negotiated between them. In this world where trickery is prevalent, justice—divine justice—will prevail at last. "He makes a pit . . . and falls into the hole which he has made," says Ps 7:15.

But this story is more than an illustration of the principle that the LORD takes the wise in their own craftiness (Job 5:13; 1 Cor 3:19). It is part of the ongoing account of the fulfillment of the promises made to Abraham and renewed to Isaac and indeed to Jacob just before he left the land of Canaan. All the patriarchs were promised offspring, the land, a covenant relationship, and that through them blessing would come to the nations. With the birth of the ancestors of the twelve tribes in 29:31–30:24, Jacob had seen the promise of offspring abundantly fulfilled. In this story there is again emphasis on God's blessing of Jacob, a blessing so evident that Laban acknowledges it (v 27) and Jacob himself refers to it.

The unusual word "teem," used twice (vv 30, 43), harks back to the specific promise made to Jacob in 28:14; it is found in the Pentateuch only in these three passages in Genesis and in Exod 1:12. As Abraham before him (12:16) and his descendants after him in Egypt, so Jacob flourished in a foreign land because God was with him as had been promised (28:15; cf. 39:3–5, 21, 23). And through Jacob, blessing came to Laban and his household (vv 27, 30), showing again that "all the families of the earth shall find blessing in you and in your descendants (28:14; cf. 12:3; 22:18; 26:4). In all these respects, the story shows the promises being amply fulfilled; only the promise of the land is absent.

But it is precisely the land, called by Jacob "my land," that gives the dynamic to the story. It is Jacob's desire to return there that prompts him to ask Laban to leave (v 25), and it is this that Laban wants to stop, for Jacob is too useful to him. Later, the Egyptians were reluctant to release their slaves, for they too found their "service with which they served" (v 26; cf. Exod 1:14) too much of an asset to forfeit freely. It was the heaven-sent plagues that led to the release of the Israelite slaves from Egypt; here it was the miraculous method of breeding that enabled Jacob to break free of the shackles of his father-in-law and be in a position to return to the land of promise.

Thus, both in itself and as part of the larger patriarchal story, this narrative makes points that were ever relevant in the life of the nation: that God is not frustrated by the cheat, that justice will finally be seen to be done, and that his promises to his people, here personified in Jacob, of land, protection, and blessing to the nations will, despite all opposition, eventually triumph.

Jacob Leaves Laban   (31:2–32:3[2])

Bibliography

Ashbel, D. "Striped, Spotted, and Speckled." (Heb.) *BMik* 10 (1965) 48–52. **Briend, J.** "Gen 31:43–54: Traditions et rédaction." In *De la Tôrah au Messie: Études d'exégèse et d'hermeneutique bibliques offertes à H. Cazelles,* ed. M. Carrez, J. Doré, and P. Grelot. Paris: Desclée, 1981. 107–12. **Finkelscherer, B.** "Der Gilead-Vertrag." *MGWJ* 82 (1938) 22–46. **Finkelstein, J. J.** "An Old Babylonian Herding Contract and Gen 31:38f." *JAOS* 88 (1968) 30–36. **Fuchs, E.** "'For I Have the Way of Women': Deception, Gender, and Ideology in Biblical Narrative." *Semeia* 42 (1988) 68–83. **Garcia-Treto, F. O.** "Gen 31:44 and 'Gilead.'" *ZAW* 79 (1967) 13–17. **Good, E. M.** "Deception and Women: A Response." *Semeia* 42 (1988) 117–32. **Greenberg, M.** "Another Look at Rachel's Theft of the Teraphim." *JBL* 81 (1962) 239–48. **Greenfield, J. C.** "Aramaic Studies and the Bible." VTSup 32 (1981) 129. **Hillers, D. R.** "*Pahad Yiṣḥāq.*" *JBL* 91 (1972) 90–92. **Hoffner, H. A.** "Hittite *TARPIŠ* and Hebrew *TERĀPHÎM.*" *JNES* 27 (1968) 61–68. **Houtman, C.** "Jacob at Mahanaim: Some Remarks on Gen 32: 2–3." *VT* 28 (1978) 37–44. **Huehnergard, J.** "Biblical Notes on Some New Akkadian Texts from Emar (Syria)." *CBQ* 47 (1985) 428–34. **Koch, K.** "*Pahad jishaq*—eine Gottesbezeichnung?" In *Werden und Wirken des ATs: FS C. Westermann,* ed. R. Albertz, H.-P. Müller, H. W. Wolff, and W. Zimmerli. Göttingen: Vandenhoeck & Ruprecht, 1980. 107–15. **Kogut, S.** "The Biblical Phrase יֵשׁ אֵין לְאֵל יָד: On the Interpretations and Development

of a Mistake." *Tarbiz* 57 (1987/88) 435–44. **Kutler, L. B.** "Features of the Battle Challenge in Biblical Hebrew, Akkadian, and Ugaritic." *UF* 19 (1987) 95–99. **Loretz, O.** "Hebräisch *ḥwt* 'Bezahlen, erstatten' in Gen 31:39." *ZAW* 87 (1975) 207–8. **Loewenstamm, S. E.** "אנכי אחטנה." *ZAW* 90 (1978) 410. **Mabee, C.** "Jacob and Laban: The Structure of Judicial Proceedings (Gen 31:25–42)." *VT* 30 (1980) 192–207. **Malul, M.** "More on *paḥad Yiṣḥaq* (Gen 31:42,53) and the Oath by the Thigh." *VT* 35 (1985) 192–200. **McCarthy, D. J.** "Three Covenants in Genesis." *CBQ* 26 (1964) 179–89. **Ottoson, M.** *Gilead: Tradition and History.* ConBOT 3. Lund: Gleerup, 1969. **Paul, S. M.** "Two Cognate Semitic Terms for Mating and Copulation." *VT* 32 (1982) 492–94. **Puech, E.** "'La crainte d'Isaac' en Gen 31:42 et 53." *VT* 34 (1984) 356–61. **Seebass, H.** "LXX und MT in Gen 31:44–53." *BN* 34 (1986) 30–38. **Snaith, N. H.** "Gen 31:50." *VT* 14 (1964) 373. **Steinberg, N.** "Israelite Tricksters: Their Analogues and Cross-Cultural Study." *Semeia* 42 (1988) 1–13. **Toorn, K. van der.** "The Nature of the Biblical Teraphim in the Light of the Cuneiform Evidence." *CBQ* 52 (1990) 203–22. **Utzschneider, H.** "Patrilinearität im alten Israel: Eine Studie zur Familie und ihrer Religion." *BN* 56 (1991) 60–97. **Watson, W. G. E.** "Reclustering Hebrew *l'bd.*" *Bib* 58 (1977) 213–15.

Translation

[2]*Jacob noticed that*[a] *Laban was not*[b]*regarding him as he had*[b] *previously.* [3]*The LORD said to Jacob, "Return*[a] *to the land of your fathers and to your clan that I may be with you."*

[4]*Jacob therefore sent and summoned Rachel and Leah into*[a] *the countryside to his flock,* [5]*and he said to them, "I have been noticing that your father has not been regarding me as he did previously; however, the God of my father has been with me.* [6]*You*[a] *do know that*[b]*with all my strength*[b] *I have served your father.* [7]*But your father has made*[a] *a fool of me and has changed*[b] *my pay ten times, but God*[c] *has not allowed*[d] *him to harm*[e] *me.* [8a]*If he said, 'The speckled shall*[b] *be your pay,' all the flock gave birth to speckled; and if he said, 'the striped will be*[b] *your pay,' all the flock bore striped.*[a] [9]*God*[a] *rescued*[b] *the animals of your*[c] *father and gave them to me.* [10]*At the time the flock bred, I raised*[a] *my eyes and saw*[b] *in a dream the he-goats mounting the flock of striped, speckled, and spotted.* [11]*The angel of God said to me in the dream, 'Jacob.' So I said, 'Here I am.'*[a] [12]*He said, 'Look*[a] *up and see that all the he-goats mounting the flock are striped, speckled, and spotted, for I have seen all that Laban is doing to you.* [13a]*I am the*[b] *God of Bethel, where you anointed a standing stone when*[c] *you made a vow to me there. Arise*[d] *and leave*[e] *this country and return to the land of your clan.'"*

[14]*Rachel and Leah answered*[a] *and said to him, "Do we still have any share or inheritance in our father's house?* [15]*Are we not counted*[a] *as foreigners by*[b] *him, because he has sold us and he has also wasted, yes wasted,*[c] *our money.* [16a]*For the wealth that God*[b] *has rescued from our father belongs to us and to our children.*[a] *Now do*[c] *all that God has told you."*[c]

[17]*So Jacob arose, put his sons*[a] *and wives*[a] *on camels,* [18]*and drove all his herds and all the property*[a] *he had acquired in Paddan-Aram to go to his father Isaac in the land of Canaan.* [19a]*Now Laban had gone to shear his flock,*[a] *and Rachel stole her father's teraphim.* [20]*And Jacob deceived Laban the Aramean*[a]*by not*[a] *telling*[b] *him that*[c]*he was running away.*[c] [21]*He ran away and all who were with him. He set out, crossed the river, and set out toward the hills of Gilead.*

[22]*It was told*[a] *Laban on the third day that Jacob had run away.* [23]*So he took his relatives with him, pursued after him for seven days, and drew*[a] *close to him in the hills*

of Gilead. ²⁴*God came to Laban the Aramean in a dream by night and said to him,* "*Take*^a *care lest you contradict Jacob* ^b*in any way.*"^b

²⁵*Laban caught*^a *up with Jacob, when Jacob had pitched his tent in the hills,*^b *and Laban pitched camp with his relatives*^c *in the hills of Gilead.* ²⁶*Laban said to Jacob,*^a "*What have you* ^b*done? You* ^c*have deceived me, and driven my daughters away like captives of war.*^d ²⁷*Why did you conceal your departure and deceive me, and why did not you tell*^a *me? I could have given*^b *you a joyful send-off with singing, tambourines, and harp.* ²⁸*And why did you not allow me to kiss my children and my daughters? Now you have made a fool of yourself acting*^a *like this.* ²⁹*It is in my power*^a *to harm you,*^b *but the God*^c *of your*^b *father said to me yesterday, 'Take care not*^d *to contradict Jacob at all.'* ³⁰*But now you have actually*^a *gone because you yearned*^b *so much*^a *for your father's house, why did you steal my gods?*"

³¹*Jacob retorted to Laban,* ^a"*Because I was afraid,*^a *for I thought you might rob me of your daughters.* ³²*Whoever*^a *you find has your gods shall not live. In the presence of our relatives identify*^b *for yourself*^c *what I have and take it for yourself.*" *But Jacob did not know that Rachel had stolen*^d *them.*

³³*So Laban entered*^a *Jacob's tent, and Leah's tent, and the tent of the two slave-wives, and he did not find them. He came out of Leah's tent and entered Rachel's.* ^{34a}*Now Rachel had taken the teraphim*^a *and put*^b *them in the saddle pouch of the camel and sat*^c *on them.* ^d*So Laban rummaged through all the tent and did not find them.*^d ³⁵*She said to her father, "May it not offend*^a *my lord that I cannot get up for you because the way of women is on me."* ^b*So he searched*^b *but did not find the teraphim.*

³⁶*Jacob became angry*^a *and argued*^b *with Laban. Jacob answered Laban, "What is my crime? What*^c *is my sin that you have so hotly pursued after me?* ³⁷*You have indeed rummaged through all my things. What have you found that belonged to your household? Place it here before my relatives and yours, so they may judge*^a *between us two.* ³⁸*Twenty years*^a *now*^b *I have been with you.* ^c*Your ewes and she-goats*^c *have not miscarried. I have not eaten* ^d*the rams of your flock.*^d ^{39a}*The torn beast*^a *I have not brought*^b *to you. I had to make*^c *up the loss of it myself.* ^d*Whether it was stolen*^e *by day or night, you used to require*^f *it* ^g*from my hand.*^{dg} ⁴⁰*It was I*^a *who suffered*^b *from the heat in the day and the cold at night and was deprived*^c *of sleep.* ^{41a}*Yes for me it's* ^b*twenty years*^a *I have been a slave in your household,* ^c*fourteen for your two daughters and six for your flock,*^c *and you have changed my pay ten times.* ⁴²*If the God of my father Abraham and the fear of Isaac had not been with me, you would certainly*^a *have now sent me away empty-handed,*^b *but my oppression and the toil of my hands*^c *was seen by God and he vindicated*^d *me last night.*"

⁴³*Laban replied to Jacob, "The daughters are my daughters.*^a *The children are my children.*^a *The flock is my flock.*^a *Indeed everything you see belongs to me and my daughters. What can I do for them today or for their children which they have borne?* ⁴⁴*Now then come,*^a *let us make a covenant, you and me,*^b *and it shall be a witness between you and me.*"^c

⁴⁵*So Jacob took a stone and erected*^a *it as a pillar.* ⁴⁶*Jacob*^a *said to his relatives, "Collect stones." So they took*^b *them and made a cairn, and they ate there beside the cairn.*^c ^{47a}*Laban called the cairn "Yegar sahadutha," and Jacob called it "Cairn of witness."*^a ⁴⁸*Laban said, "This cairn is a witness between you and me today." That is why it is called "Cairn of witness."* ⁴⁹*It is the Mispah,*^a *as it is said, "May the* LORD^b *keep watch*^c *between me and you even when we are hidden*^d *from each other.* ^{50a}*You must not oppress*

my daughters or take any extra wives besides my daughters. Even when there is no one else with us, look,[b] *God is a witness between you and me.*"

[51] *Laban said, "See this pile and this pillar which I*[a] *have erected between me and you.* [52] *This pile is witness and the pillar is a witness, that*[a] *I myself shall not*[a] *go*[b] *beyond this pile*[b] *toward you, and that you yourself will not go beyond this pile and this pillar toward me with evil intent.* [53a] *Let the god*[b] *of Abraham and the god*[b] *of Nahor*[a] *judge*[b] *between us,* [c]*the god*[b] *of their father.*"[c] *So Jacob swore an oath by the fear of his father Isaac.* [54] *Jacob offered a sacrifice in the hills and summoned his relatives to eat, and they spent the night in the hills.*

[32:1] *Early*[a] *in the morning, Laban kissed his grandsons and his daughters and blessed them, and Laban went and returned home.*

[2a] *But Jacob went on his way,*[a] *and angels of God met him.* [3] *So Jacob said when he saw*[a] *them, "This is an encampment of God." So he named the place Mahanaim.*

Notes

2.a. והנה "that," "behold" following the verb "see" shows a scene from the participant's perspective (*SBH*, 95).

2.b-b. Lit. "the face of Laban, he not [איננו] with him." Since "face" is a pl noun, SamPent reads אינם "they not."

3.a. Note the sequence of tenses "return" (שוב) impv followed by simple waw + impf (היה) "that I may be with you" giving a final or consecutive sense (GKC, 108d). Note the same sequence in 12:1–2.

4.a. Cf. n. 27:3.c.

6.a. The use of the personal pronoun "you" with finite verb "you know" "may be viewed as motivated by the desire to call special attention to the addressed, especially when the speaker requests something on the basis of the knowledge of the addressed or seeks his agreement" (*EWAS*, 53; cf. GKC, 135a, Gen 30:26, 29).

6.b-b. Placing this adverbial phrase first in the sentence gives it special emphasis (*EWAS*, 43).

7.a. 3 masc sg pf hiph תלל. On pointing, see GKC, 67w.

7.b. Waw consec + 3 masc sg pf hiph חלף. Frequentative use of waw consec + pf (GKC, 112h); SamPent has impf. But WOC, 540, regards it as hendiadys: "he has made a fool of me by changing my pay."

7.c. SamPent "the LORD."

7.d. 3 masc sg pf נתן + 3 masc sg suffix.

7.e. ל + inf constr hiph רעע.

8.a-a. On sentence structure, see GKC, 159r,s.

8.b. Sg verb with pl subj, "spotted, striped," because of sg predicate "pay" (GKC, 145u; Joüon, 150m).

9.a. SamPent "the LORD" as in v 7.

9.b. Waw consec + 3 masc sg impf hiph נצל.

9.c. 2 fem pl suffix often displaced by 2 masc pl suffix (GKC, 135o; Joüon, 149b). But SamPent corrects to אביכן.

10.a. Waw consec + 1 sg impf qal נשא.

10.b. Waw consec + 1 sg impf (apoc) qal ראה.

11.a. Cf. n. 22:1.c.

12.a. Cf. n. 13:14.c.

13.a. Putting the pronominal subj before the predicate shows that there is "emphasis or stress placed upon the subject" (*EWAS*, 12).

13.b. This use of the def art with noun אל in constr is unexpected, but see GKC, 127f. G, *Tg.* gloss "the god, who appeared to you in Bethel." This looks like an interpretative attempt to avoid speaking of a localized God of Bethel. MT is supported by SamPent.

13.c. SamPent, G, smooth the asyndetic construction by adding "and."

13.d. Cf. n. 13:17.a.

13.e. 2 masc sg impv יצא.

14.a. Waw consec + 2 fem sg impf qal עֲנֻה. Note sg verb though composite subj, "Rachel and Leah," follows, but "said" is pl verb. Where verb comes before composite subj, it may be sg, but where it follows, it must be pl (GKC, 146g,h; Jouön, 150p,q).

15.a. 1 pl pf niph חֹשַׁב.

15.b. לְ for the agent of a pass verb (Jouön, 132f; WOC, 210).

15.c. For this emphatic use of inf abs, see EWAS, 88; WOC, 586.

16.a-a. The word order in this clause emphasizes the predicate. Lit. "Ours is the wealth . . ." (EWAS, 17, 75).

16.b. SamPent "the LORD."

16.c-c. The obj in preverbal position as here is emphatic (EWAS, 38).

17.a. SamPent, G, reverse the order: "wives, . . . sons."

18.a. Though, according to BHS, G has omitted the difficult אֲשֶׁר רכשׁ מקנה קנינו, this is dubious since it adds after Mesopotamia "and all that he had" (cf. Gispen 3:109).

19.a-a. Episode-initial circumstantial clause, so verb translated by a pluperfect (GKC, 106f; SBH, 80).

20.a-a. On this unusual conj, see GKC, 152t; 158b; pace BHS, no need to emend.

20.b. Cf. n. 3:11.a.

20.c-c. On the word order in this clause, see EWAS, 27.

22.a. Cf. n. 22:20.a.

23.a. Waw consec + 3 masc sg impf hiph דבק.

24.a. Cf. n. 24:6.a.

24.b-b. G, Vg translate the sense of the phrase "Do not speak evil" or "do not speak against" rather than literally reading "either good or evil."

25.a. Waw consec + 3 masc sg impf hiph נשׂג.

25.b. BHS inserts "of Mispah" without textual support.

25.c. BHS reads "his tent" instead of "with his relatives" without textual support.

26.a. On the string of questions in vv 26–28, see SBH, 114–15.

26.b. S reads "What have I done to you"; MT more likely (cf., e.g., 4:10; 12:18).

26.c. On use of waw + impf here, see WOC, 552.

26.d. כְ + fem pl pass ptcp qal שׁבֻה.

27.a. Cf. n. 12:18.b.

27.b. Waw consec + 1 masc sg impf piel שׁלח + 2 masc sg suffix. Here waw consec + impf has consecutive sense, "so that I could have . . ." (GKC, 111m; Jouön, 118h).

28.a. Inf constr עשׂה. On this, see GKC, 75n. SamPent substitutes the more usual form עשׂות.

29.a. Watson, Bib 58 (1977) 213–15, suggests redividing יֶשׁ לְאֵ לידי, understanding לֹא as noun "power." R. Frankena, OTS 17 (1972) 61, thinks the phrase means "my protective deity."

29.b. G, SamPent read sg.

29.c. It is unusual for the subj to precede the verb. EWAS, 35, notes that this is a feature of sentences with God as subj in Genesis (cf. 28:3; 31:53; 43:14, 29; 44:16; 48:3, 16).

29.d מִן + inf constr piel דבר. Here מִן + inf is equivalent to negative final clause (GKC, 165c).

30.a. Note the use of the inf abs to show speaker's interest in verbal idea (EWAS, 88; GKC, 113p).

30.b. Inf abs niph + 2 masc sg pf niph כֹסף.

31.a-a. G omits "Because I was afraid . . ." and adds at the end "and all that is mine."

32.a. Putting the prep עַם before the pronoun אֲשֶׁר is unusual. More typical word order occurs in 44:9 (GKC, 138f; Jouön, 158m). אֲשֶׁר rarely used as indefinite (WOC, 334, n. 13).

32.b. 2 masc sg impv hiph נכר.

32.c. Note the use of the ethical dative emphasizing "the significance of the occurrence in question for a particular subject" (GKC, 110o; cf. 37:32; 48:25; EWAS, 122).

32.d. 3 fem sg pf גנב + 3 masc pl suffix.

33.a. SamPent, G add "and searched." G also rearranges the order of searches.

34.a-a. Circumstantial clause giving background information, hence waw + subj + verb (pf) with pf translated by pluperfect (SBH, 85; Jouön, 118d).

34.b. Waw consec + 3 fem sg impf qal שׂים + 3 masc pl suffix. Here waw consec carries on pluperfect sense (GKC, 111q; WOC, 556).

34.c. Cf. n. 21:16.a.

34.d-d. Omitted in G, but cf. n. 35.b-b.

35.a. Cf. n. 18:30.a.

35.b-b. G reads "So Laban searched the whole house," paraphrasing the omitted v 34b.

36.a. Cf. n. 4:5.b.

36.b. Waw consec + 3 masc sg impf ריב.

36.c. *Pace BHS* and versions, no need to add "and." On clauses in apposition, cf. *SBH*, 38.

37.a. Waw + 3 masc pl juss hiph יכח with final sense (GKC, 109f).

38.a. Putting adverbial phrase "twenty years" first in sentence emphasizes it (*EWAS*, 43).

38.b. זה "now," lit. "this," often with numerals as a virtual enclitic (GKC, 136d).

38.c-c. Subj before verb for emphasis (*EWAS*, 33).

38.d-d. Obj before verb for emphasis (*EWAS*, 38).

39.a-a. Cf. previous note 31:38.d-d.

39.b. 1 sg pf hiph בוא.

39.c. Usually supposed to be 1 sg impf piel חטא (On sense, see WOC, 509; on the elision of א, see GKC, 23f; 74k) + 3 fem sg suffix. But Loretz, *ZAW* 87 (1975) 207–8, and Loewenstamm, *ZAW* 90 (1978) 410, suggest 1 sg impf qal of חוט or חים + suffix.

39.d-d. Second half of verse in apposition to first. First gives Jacob's perspective; second, Laban's (*SBH* 44).

39.e. Fem sg ptcp pass qal גנב. On the final י, see GKC, 90k,l; WOC, 127–28.

39.f. 2 masc sg impf piel בקש + 3 fem sg suffix.

39.g-g. This phrase in the Heb. occurs at the beginning of the clause for emphasis; cf. n. 31:38.a.

40.a. Lit. "I was." On this unusual construction, see GKC, 143a, n. 2.

40.b. Lit. "it ate me."

40.c. Waw consec + 3 fem sg impf qal נדד.

41.a-a. Fronting of adverbial phrase for emphasis (cf. n. 31:38.a.).

41.b. Enclitic use of זה (GKC, 136d; cf. n. 31:38.b.)

41.c-c. Two conjoined clauses in apposition explaining how twenty years are made up (*SBH*, 50).

42.a. "The absolute certainty with which a result is to be expected is frequently emphasized by the insertion of כי" (GKC, 159ee).

42.b. Cf. n. 31:38.a.

42.c. Cf. n. 31:38.d-d. To bring out the emphasis on "my poverty . . . ," I have put the sentence into the pass in English.

42.d. Waw consec + 3 masc sg impf hiph יכח.

43.a. The word order emphasizes the predicate in each clause (*EWAS*, 17, 75; cf. n. 31:16.a-a.).

44.a. On use of לכה as exhortation, cf. Joüon, 105e; *SBH*, 56.

44.b. Many commentators conjecturally insert "let us make a heap" to provide a masc subj for "it shall be a witness."

44.c. G adds "And he said to him, 'Behold no one is with us, behold God is witness between me and you.'" *BHS* favors following G.

45.a. Waw consec + 3 masc sg impf hiph רום + 3 fem sg suffix.

46.a. Old Latin reads "Laban."

46.b. G "collected" could suggest וילקטו (so *BHS*); but it may just reflect translator's freedom.

46.c. G here inserts "Laban said to him, 'This heap shall be a witness between you and me today.'" Cf. MT v 48.

47.a-a. Note chiasmus "called . . . Laban . . . Jacob . . . called."

49.a. SamPent מצבה "pillar" misses the play on the verb צפה "keep watch."

49.b. G "God."

49.c. 3 masc sg juss צפה.

49.d. 1 pl impf niph סתר.

50.a. On אם to introduce an oath, see GKC, 149a.

50.b. Westermann's repointing of ראה as ptcp "seeing" is unlikely, since it goes with what follows, not with the preceding clause. Cf. Joüon, 105d.

51.a. SamPent "you."

52.a-a. אם־לא normally introduces a positive oath. So here the translation would be "I myself (you yourself) will go. . . ." For this reason, *BHS* would omit לא as in v 50. Preferable is the understanding of GKC, 167b; 149c. This is a case of anakolouthon. Laban begins with the oath formula אני־אם and then switches to the usual strong prohibition לא + impf.

52.b-b. Omitted in G.

53.a-a. On word order with subj before verb, cf. n. 31:29.b.

53.b. It is not clear whether אלהים should be translated sg or pl. The verb "judge" here is pl, suggesting Laban was polytheistic. For obvious reasons G, SamPent, Vg, S prefer the sg verb. But elsewhere in conversations with foreigners, gods are spoken of in the pl, e.g., 20:13; GKC, 145i.

53.c-c. Omitted in G, SamPent "God of Abraham."

32:1.a. Cf. n. 19:27.a.

2.a-a. *Pace SBH*, 80–81, this seems more likely to be an episode-final than an episode-initial circumstantial clause.

3.a. 3 masc sg pf רָאָה + 3 masc pl suffix.

Form/Structure/Setting

The majority of commentators accept that chapter 31:1–32:1(31:55) constitutes a distinct section and that 32:2–3(1–2) either constitutes a separate episode or the start of a new section, 32:2–33. But in the previous *Form/Structure/Setting*, it was argued that the previous episode ends with 31:1, not 30:43. So here I shall focus on the terminus of this section. Is it 31:54 (Keil; Volz, *Der Elohist*; Speiser; Westermann), 32:1 (Delitzsch; Driver; Gunkel; Skinner; von Rad; Fokkelman, *Narrative Art*; Coats; Gispen), 32:2a (Blum), or 32:2 (Dillmann, Jacob, Sarna, Vawter)?

This diversity of opinion shows that it is not easy to determine where this episode ends. Since a night separates 31:54 and 32:1(31:55), 32:1(31:55) must constitute a new scene, but not necessarily a new episode. But without 32:1(31:55), the previous section is incomplete; it tells of the flight of Jacob and his pursuit by Laban, and some reference to Laban's return home is surely to be expected. Thus 32:1(31:55) makes a more apt conclusion to this episode than does 31:54.

But since Jacob is the chief actor in this episode, a mention of him right at the end might well be expected. Indeed, the chiasmus between 32:1, "went . . . Laban," and 32:2, "But Jacob went," ties these two verses very closely together. This prompts Blum (*Die Komposition*) to make 32:2a the conclusion of the episode. However, 32:2b, "and angels of God met him," hardly sounds like the start of a new episode. For although it contains an explicit noun subject, "angels of God," "him" refers back to the previous clause. And v 2b clearly belongs with v 3. The main reason for supposing that vv 2b–3, despite grammatical indications to the contrary, do not belong with the preceding episode, is that their content recounting Jacob's meeting angels has nothing apparently to do with his flight from Laban. Indeed, the phraseology of 32:2b–3 seems to anticipate the rest of chap. 32 in various respects. Jacob sends out messengers (מַלְאָךְ; vv 4, 7, which is the word translated angels in v 2). He divides his party into two camps (32:8, 9, 11, 22; 33:8), the literal meaning of Mahanaim (32:3), and of course, he himself wrestles with a supernatural "man" near the Yabbok (32:23–33).

Now these points of connection could argue for a new episode beginning in 32:2. However, they could equally be cited as an example of Genesis' technique of ending one section with a trailer for the next. There are many examples of this in the primeval history, in the Joseph story, and in the immediately adjacent episodes (31:43–31:1 previews 31:2–32:3; 33:18–19 previews chap. 34). It is also typical for a section to conclude with some vocal comment as here, "This is an encampment of God" (cf. 30:24; 31:1; 34:31). For these reasons, I follow Dillmann, Jacob, Sarna, and Vawter in making this episode end at 32:3(32:2).

The episode falls into seven scenes, reaching its climax in the confrontation between Jacob and Laban, seen by some commentators as the peak of the Jacob cycle (vv 25–44).

Introduction: Jacob notes change in Laban's attitude (2)
Scene 1:   The LORD tells Jacob to return home (3)
Scene 2:   Jacob obtains wives' agreement to leave (4–16)
            Jacob's speech (5–13)
            Rachel and Leah's reply (14–16)
Scene 3:   Departure (17–21)
Scene 4:   Laban's pursuit (22–24)
Scene 5:   Confrontation between Jacob and Laban (25–44)
            Tents pitched (25)
            Laban's accusations (26–30)
            Jacob's reply (31–32)
            Tents searched (33–35)
            Jacob's protests (36–42)
            Laban's reply (43–44)
        Oath between Laban and Jacob (45–54)
            Jacob erects pillar (45)
            Jacob proposes heap be built (46a)
            Heap built, meal eaten (46b)
            Laban and Jacob name heap (47)
            Laban specifies content of oath (48–53)
            Jacob assents, sacrifice and meal (53–54)
Scene 6:   Laban returns home (32:1)
Scene 7:   Conclusion and Preview: Jacob goes on and meets angels (32:2–3)

This episode is an integral part of the story of Laban and Jacob. On the one hand, it cannot be understood on its own, for at nearly every point it presupposes what has been told before, e.g., Jacob's marriage to Leah and Rachel (vv 4–17, 26–50), his service to Laban (vv 6–13, 37–42), his distance from home (vv 3, 18, 30, 49, 52–32:2). On the other hand, it cannot be excised without leaving the earlier story prematurely truncated. It is part and parcel of the Jacob-Laban story; indeed, in the palistrophic arrangement of the narrative, this episode describing Jacob's departure from Laban's household matches the description of his arrival in chap. 29. "The incident of deception found in Genesis 29, during Jacob's early settlement in Aram, is balanced by those presented in Genesis 31. . . . Not only does Jacob refer to Laban's earlier deceits (stem: *talal*, v 7), but the departure is itself redolent with new acts of deceit underscored by the dense repetition of the stem *ganab* 'to steal,' in its several nuances" (vv 19, 26, 27, 30, 39; cf. v 31; Fishbane, *Text and Texture*, 55–56). Other key words in both chapters include "kiss" (29:11, 13; 31:28; 32:1) and "wages" (29:15; 31:7, 41). In both chapters, stones are important. In 29:3, 8, 10, Jacob rolls (גלל) a stone. In 31:45–46, he erects a stone as a pillar and makes others into a mound (גל), and this mound he calls Galed, "mound of witness" (vv 47–48). In the overall palistrophic arrangement of the Jacob cycle, the incident at Mahanaim (32:2–3, where Jacob meets angels of God, declares that this is an encampment of God, and names the place) parallels his experience at Bethel (cf. 28:12, 17, 19).

But though this chapter primarily relates to the Jacob-Laban cycle, it looks beyond; there are clear cross-references to the Jacob-Esau saga. Most obviously v 13, "I am the God of Bethel, where you anointed a standing stone when you made a vow to me," refers back to 28:10–22. But the repeated comments that "God has

been with him" hark back to this, too, for that is the distinctive feature of the
promise to Jacob (vv 3, 5, 29, 42, 53; cf. 28:15, 20). Furthermore, the whole narrative is based on the premise that Jacob is returning to his homeland and to his
father Isaac (vv 3, 18, 30, 49, 52–32:2). This invites the comparison of this episode with chap. 27. "Both Jacob and Rachel deceive their fathers and flee from
home. Rachel deceives Laban by misappropriating his household gods, which
represent the patriarchal blessing and inheritance. She also lies to him when,
having caught up to her, he "felt" (stem: *mashash*; vv 34, 37) for them like a blind
man. It will be recalled that precisely the same verb is used in 27:22, when Isaac
felt Jacob's hands during the latter's attempt to misappropriate the patriarchal
blessing" (Fishbane, *Text and Texture*, 56).

Finally, this chapter also relates to the wider context of the patriarchal narratives. In Paddan-Aram, in roughly the same region as Harran, Jacob receives a
call somewhat like his grandfather's, "Return to the country of your fathers
and to your clan that I may be with you." Syntactically his call resembles
Abraham's, it is an imperative followed by a final clause, and the terms used within
it too are similar: "Go . . . from your *country*, your *clan*, and *your father's* house
to the *country* that I shall show you." The major difference, of course, is that for
Jacob it was a return, but for Abraham it was a step into the unknown. This chapter also invites comparison with chap. 24, when Rebekah left her father Bethuel
and her brother Laban to go and live in Canaan. In both situations, Laban did
his best to prevent his womenfolk leaving. This is the last story in which Laban
appears in Genesis, and from his first appearance in chap. 24 to this his last he is
portrayed as a man governed by financial considerations. But in the repeated
insistence in this chapter that God has been with Jacob in his time abroad (vv 5,
9, 42), there is a refrain that is later taken up in the Joseph story (39:2, 21, 23).
And the search for Laban's teraphim has similarities with the search for Joseph's
cup (44:1–3). In all these respects, 31:2–32:3 is perfectly at home in the patriarchal narratives.

Traditional source critics ascribe most of the material to E, with a few insertions from J, and one (v 18) from P, but there are wide differences of opinion as
to how much should be ascribed to J, especially in the latter part of the chapter.
The grounds for supposing the main source to be E are: the term אלהים "God"
(vv 7, 9, 11, 16, 24, 19, 42; 32:2, 3), the revelation through dreams (vv 10, 11, 24),
and the reference to the vow at Bethel (v 13; cf. 28:18, 20–22). That J is also
present is supported by the use of the divine name "the LORD" in vv 3, 49 and
some repetition and redundancy that allow the latter part of the story (vv 44–54)
to be split into two. However, within this broad approach, there are several variations. Driver and Speiser ascribe only 31:3, 46–50 to J and nearly everything else
to E. At the other extreme, Gunkel and Skinner ascribe considerably more to J
(i.e., 31:3, 19a, 21, 25, 27, 31, 36a, 38–40, 44, 46, 48, 51–53a), and Vawter includes even more, adding vv 17, 22–23, 30, 47 to J and omitting vv 21, 44. Whereas
most commentators suppose that v 49 belongs to J because it mentions "the LORD,"
the last three commentators adopt the LXX reading "God" and maintain that it
is part of E.

However, more recent tradition critics, following Volz (*Der Elohist*), have argued
that chap. 31 is an integral part of J. All the references back to earlier chapters of

Genesis (see above), which are predominantly J, make this position much more plausible than to suppose it is E. The different emphasis within this chapter, e.g., on God's part in Jacob's enrichment as opposed to Jacob's intelligence being the source of his wealth, may be explained by the different perspective of the chapter. The fullness of the narrative style in this chapter reflects the drama of the occasion, not the presence of multiple sources, and the use of God as opposed to "the LORD" in the conversations within the narrative reflects the fact that Jacob's wives come from a pagan environment.

Thus Westermann holds that "the narrator here is the Yahwist . . . there is no Elohistic source to be found in Gen 31" (2:490). He believes there are certain expansions discernible in vv 4–16 and 43–54, for the Yahwist does not tend to such prolixity. This, however, rather begs the question. It is characteristic of Hebrew narrative style to be expansive at points of high drama (e.g., Gen 7, 17, 24; 1 Sam 17), and this chapter is generally regarded as the climax of the Jacob story (cf. Longacre, *Joseph*, 34). Coats is more circumspect than Westermann: he too regards Gen 31 as essentially J with a few minor expansions, which he does not identify (Coats, 221). Blum (*Die Komposition*) likewise dismisses the idea that two sources are present in chap. 31. Laying heavy emphasis on the interconnections between chap. 31 and the preceding chapters, he insists that this shows that the editor of chap. 31 was fully aware of the preceding material and that it cannot come from an independent source. Rather, vv 1–44 represent later reflection on the story of Jacob's craft in chap. 30, explaining his success in terms of divine blessing rather than human skill. The account of the covenant-making (31:45–32:2) he regards as representing an earlier stage in the tradition. While Blum is right in regarding 31:2–44 as a sort of commentary on the preceding episode, this does not necessarily show that it comes from a different hand; the writer may have seen both accounts as complementing each other. And the whole set of stories would end rather lamely if the account of Jacob's flight, Laban's pursuit, and the subsequent row were omitted. Vv 2–44 should therefore be regarded as an integral part of the Jacob-Laban cycle.

Comment

2 The previous verse gave a glimpse of the trouble brewing for Jacob: "Laban's sons were saying, 'Jacob has taken away all that belonged to our father.'" This comment put all Jacob's success as a sheepbreeder under a cloud, but the full consequences were not drawn out. Now Jacob realizes that the remarks of his brothers-in-law are indeed having an effect on his father-in-law, Laban—not surprising in that from first to last Laban is portrayed as a man governed by avarice. Again, the narrator does not spell out exactly the effect of Jacob's wealth, leaving it to our imagination to fill in the details. The important thing is that "Jacob noticed" it: הנה "that" shows us the situation through Jacob's eyes. He realized he was *persona non grata* with both his father-in-law and his brothers-in-law, and with no member of his own family nearby to support him, he senses his exposure and weakness.

3 But as earlier in his career, when on the run from Esau (chap. 28), the LORD appears to him. Perhaps his own awareness of need made him receptive to

God's voice. Certainly there is no need to postulate a change of source between vv 2 and 3 as traditional critics do.

Syntactically and lexically (see *Form/Structure/Setting*), "Return to the land of your father and to your clan that I may be with you" closely resembles God's first word to Abraham, "Go to the country . . . I will make you" (12:1–2). In both instances, the command is followed by a promise. This promise of God's presence was given to Jacob years earlier at Bethel (28:15). Here it is reaffirmed on condition that Jacob obey by returning home. This pattern of promise-command-renewed promise is characteristic of biblical theology. Grace responded to in obedience leads to more grace (cf. G. J. Wenham, "Grace and Law in the Old Testament," in *Law, Morality and the Bible*, ed. B. N. Kaye and G. J. Wenham [Leicester: IVP, 1978] 5–7).

4–16 The second scene consists of dialogue between Jacob and his wives; their speeches are long by biblical standards, indicating the great importance of this discussion. With Laban's family ganging up against him, Jacob must be sure that his wives will side with him, not with their father. So here in a long and detailed speech he does his utmost to persuade them to support him. At various points, his account of his actions and motives differs from what has been said earlier. Is he merely supplementing earlier summary statements or is he giving a distorted picture in order to win over his wives to his point of view? Jacob must convince his wives of the justice of his case if he is to persuade them to leave and go to Canaan, from which he had fled some twenty years earlier in fear of his life. No doubt they have learned the full story of that from Jacob himself; can he now persuade them that to go there will not be jumping out of the frying pan into the fire? These are the issues that Jacob is addressing here.

4 The setting of Jacob's discussion is unusual; "the countryside" is probably chosen to ensure secrecy. In the countryside, it would be much more difficult to eavesdrop on their conversation (cf. Deut 22:25; cf. 23). Note here and in v 14 the order of names, "Rachel and Leah": Rachel is still first in Jacob's affection.

5–13 Jacob's address consists of comparing three times what Laban has done for him with what God has done and then concluding with his description of what God has told him today. Thus:

v 5	Laban's changed attitude	but God with Jacob
vv 6–7	Laban the unreliable	but God prevented him harming Jacob
vv 8–9	Laban's wages	but God gave herds to Jacob
vv 10–13	Vision	

5 Jacob starts by stating something that must have been as obvious to his wives as it was to him: "your father has not been regarding me as he did previously." This could have been Jacob's fault, so it was not necessarily a criticism of Laban. He then mentions that "the God of my father has been with me," which tends to suggest that Laban may indeed bear some blame, but more importantly that God is on Jacob's side.

6 Having established common ground with his wives, Jacob now becomes more open in criticizing his father-in-law. He appeals first though to their own experience, "You (do) know that with all my strength I have served your father." Again he puts his own behavior in the best possible light, before giving explicit criticism.

7 "But your father has made a fool of me." תלל (hiphil) "make a fool of" is a rare term. It involves deceiving someone so that their public reputation suffers as a result (Exod 8:25[29]; Judg 16:10, 13, 15). Here it refers to Laban's habit of making promises to Jacob and then reneging on them: "he has changed my pay ten times." "Pay" (משׂכר) is a key root in these stories about Jacob and Laban (29:15; 30:16, 32, 33; 31:7, 41). "Ten times" is hyperbole for many times. Yet "God has not allowed him to harm me." Note how once again Jacob pits Laban against God.

8 Tactfully, Jacob does not mention the occasion on which Laban really made a fool of him, at his wedding: he wants the support of both his wives now. So he concentrates on Laban's most recent treachery. Here, though, his account of what happened is different from that in 30:31–42. There the Genesis narrator deals with both sheep and goats; here Jacob mentions only goats. There the account only mentions what Jacob did; here Jacob ascribes the breeding entirely to God. The narrator in Gen 30 seems to envisage a single agreement, that any multicolored animals bred by Jacob should be his; but here Jacob mentions two agreements with Laban: first that Jacob should have the speckled, and then that he should have the striped.

As Blum notes (*Die Komposition*, 122), it would be difficult to follow the description of Jacob's action and his agreement with Laban in 31:9 if we did not have the fuller account in chap. 30. The writer here presupposes the previous story. This makes it less likely that a different course of events is being described; rather, the same events are being viewed from two different perspectives. There, it was the author's viewpoint; here, it is Jacob's perhaps somewhat tendentious account designed to impress his wives that God is really with him. This is why he emphasizes that however Laban switched the agreement, fate minutely followed him: speckled and striped differ by only one letter in the Hebrew. No doubt there would have been times in the six years that Jacob was stock-breeding for Laban to change the agreement in the hope of doing better out of it. So it seems unlikely that the details here are incompatible with the version in 30:25–31:1.

9 The details in Jacob's story emphasize that "God rescued the animals of your father and gave them to me." Laban's sons had complained that "Jacob had taken away what belongs to our father." Jacob uses the more colorful term "rescue." Apart from v 16, this verb "rescue" (הציל) is used three times of saving someone from the danger of death (32:12[11]; 37:21–22). It is used in Exodus of the deliverance from slavery (3:8; 5:23; 6:6). In other words, God has not simply transferred the herds from Laban to Jacob; he has done them a favor, giving them a much better life!

10–13 Jacob's description of his vision is fuller than the summary of its main point in v 2, "Return to the land of your fathers and your clan that I may be with you," and these differences cause problems. Is this fuller account true, or does it represent embellishment by Jacob in order to persuade his wives to go? And within the account of the vision, the significance of the goats mounting the multicolored flock is not made clear. Finally, v 13, the climax of the vision, where God introduces himself as God of Bethel, might be expected to have come earlier. For these reasons, vv 10, 12 have often been thought to be an expansion of an earlier narrative that consisted of vv 9, 11, 13. The expansions were seen as developments within E, not an independent source. Westermann regards vv 10–13 as a

combination of originally independent accounts of two visions: vv 10–12a and vv 11, 12b, 13.

However, these source-critical analyses serve merely to excise a difficulty; they do not explain how the editor of Genesis or an earlier source understood the material. With Blum (*Die Komposition*,120), it seems unnecessary to postulate sources or different layers of tradition within this passage. The present arrangement of material corresponds to accounts of other dreams that contain oracles, and it also serves to maximize the impact of the command to leave for Canaan.

v 10	"saw in a dream and behold" (הנה)	cf. 28:12a	15:12a
	vision (he-goats mounting)	28:12b–13a	15:12b, 17
vv 11–12	Explanation of vision	28:13b–15	15:13, 15, 18–21
v 13	Consequent command	cf. 28:20–22	

The parallel with Jacob's dream at Bethel is particularly striking; even the verb "mounting"/"going up" (28:12) is the same.

10 "At the time the flock bred" seems to put the dream back some years, whereas 31:3 puts the command to leave just before Jacob decided to speak to his wives. "I raised my eyes" is a cue in Genesis that what is about to be seen is very significant (cf. 22:4; 24:64). According to the vision, multicolored he-goats (of which there were none in Jacob's flocks, according to 30:35) were mounting the flocks.

11 "The angel of God" also appears in 21:17; 28:12; 32:2. More frequently Genesis speaks of "The angel of the LORD."

12 The angel's words simply repeat what Jacob has himself seen without explicitly explaining what the vision means. But v 8 recorded that the flocks produced all speckled or all striped goats; that Jacob saw this in a vision proves the point he made earlier (v 9), that it was God who rescued the animals and made them his. "Because I have seen all that Laban is doing to you" sounds like a *non sequitur.* But when God sees his people oppressed, he intervenes to save (16:13–14; 29:32; 31:42; Exod 2:25; 3:7, 9, 16). So the obscure vision shows that God is behind Jacob's selective breeding techniques.

13 At Bethel, Jacob had vowed that if the LORD protected him and brought him back to his homeland, the LORD would be his God and he would worship there. Now out of the blue he is reminded of his vow and commanded to return to his homeland. God has so obviously protected him outside his homeland that to return is obligatory on one who has made such a vow and has received a guarantee of even greater blessing in the future. With this powerful argument, Jacob concludes his plea to his wives.

14–16 His appeal clearly moves them, for they respond with alacrity and vigor. "Answered and said." This apparently tautologous collocation often seems to precede a significant remark (e.g., 18:27; 23:5, 10, 14; 24:50; 27:37, 39; 40:18). Sometimes when anger is mixed with the statement, it might be paraphrased "retort" (31:31, 36, 43).

"Share or inheritance." This phrase is a hendiadys and usually refers to the share of land that belongs to every Israelite family except the Levites (cf. Deut 10:9; 12:12; cf. 2 Sam 20:1; 1 Kgs 12:16). Normally, daughters did not inherit property from their fathers; it was shared among the sons (cf. Num 27:1–11). However, they did expect to receive a dowry from their father when they married.

15 Here they seem to refer to the dowry given to daughters by rich fathers when they married. Poor families might sell their daughters to be slave-wives (cf. Exod 21:7–11), in which case no dowry would be given. However, it is clear from the story that both Leah and Rachel received handsome dowries, for they were given slave-girls on their marriage. So what are they referring to when they insist, "He has also wasted, yes wasted, our money"? Commentators often surmise that it was the marriage present given by the bridegroom to the bride's father, which might later be passed on to the bride in her dowry. But Jacob's marriage present was his fourteen years of service, so what they are referring to is elusive. It seems, rather, that they are agreeing that their father has indeed cheated their husband of his due and thereby has cheated them.

16 So they agree with Jacob that God has rescued the money that belongs to them and given it to Jacob.

17–21 Jacob's flight from Laban is quickly told. We are not even told how long he waited. The narrative gives the impression of haste. As soon as his wives said yes, he put them and his children on camels and off they set.

18 This long catalogue of all his retinue, however, slows the narrative down drastically. It suddenly reminds us that this move was a major undertaking. Jacob had become very wealthy, so fleeing from Laban was more difficult than fleeing from home. The terminology used here, particularly "property which he had acquired," reminds us of Abraham's great move from Harran to Canaan (12:5). Later, the same term is used in describing his move to Egypt (46:6) and the exodus (15:14). It was Isaac who had sent him to Paddan-Aram; now as he returns home the same geographical term reappears. Because these words are found in passages generally ascribed to P, v 18b is also often ascribed to P. But Rendtorff (*Problem,* 16–19) has shown the circularity of such arguments. Rather, it seems sufficient explanation of the terms used here to regard them as making a connection with other significant journeys of the patriarchs.

19 This little aside explains how Jacob was able to escape without Laban knowing; he was away shearing his sheep, a very busy time for sheep farmers. It also mentions Rachel's theft of her father's teraphim, something that nearly costs her her life (vv 32–35). What were the teraphim, and why did Rachel steal them? The word "teraphim" occurs fifteen times in the OT and may come from the Hittite word *tarpiš* (Hoffner, *JNES* 27 [1968] 66–67). It is sometimes translated "household gods"; later in this chapter they are simply referred to as "gods" (vv 30, 32). It is usually supposed that they were images of the gods that protected a family and were worshiped by its members. But van der Toorn (*CBQ* 52 [1990] 203–22) plausibly suggests that they were images of the ancestors, whom the living were expected to honor and consult. These images could be quite small, as here, small enough to be hidden in a camel's pouch (v 34), or they could be about as large as a man (1 Sam 19:13, 16). In pagan societies, and evidently sometimes in Israel, family piety was centered on the teraphim (cf. Greenberg, *JBL* 81 [1962] 239–48), but in the OT they are frequently assocated with divination. Evidently they were regarded as capable of predicting the future.

But why should Rachel have stolen the teraphim? A much-favored explanation relates it to Nuzi practice, where according to some interpreters, ownership of the ancestors' images involves inheritance rights (e.g., Speiser, 250–51; cf.

Huehnergard, *CBQ* 47 [1985] 428–31). However, even if this were the case, which is questionable (Greenberg, *JBL* 81 [1962] 239–48), it would not seem likely that stealing the symbols of inheritance would actually convey the property itself. Josephus (*Ant.* 18.9.5) mentions that "it is the custom among all the people of that country to have objects of worship in their house and to take them along when going abroad." Normally one must suppose that a father would have supplied his daughters with copies of the household gods to take with them, and according to Gen 35:2–4, others in Jacob's party had their own gods. But in this case, because of the hurried departure, Rachel took Laban's teraphim. But what was the point of taking them? Greenberg suggests it was to ensure fertility (*JBL* 81 [1962] 247). It might also be that she was rather less confident about leaving home than she sounded (vv 14–16). The teraphim were thus a Saint Christopher for her.

20   "Jacob deceived," lit. "stole the heart of." This phrase occurs only here and in v 26. In 29:25 the verb רמה is used instead, a term that, Strus (*Nomen-Omen*), notes, is a play on "the Aramean" used here and in v 24; 25:20; 28:5. The pun implies that Laban is the arch deceiver and thief. The terminology here at the close of the Jacob-Laban struggle mirrors usage in the opening scenes. This is reinforced by the use of the word "run away" (ברח) in vv 21, 22, 27 and in 27:43.

21   "The river" is the Euphrates. Harran and, presumably, Paddan-Aram lie north of the Euphrates; Gilead to the south. "Gilead" is the region east of the Jordan between the Sea of Galilee and the Dead Sea.

22–24   Jacob has a three-day start on Laban. So it is ten days before Laban catches up with him. "Drew close" (דבק hiph) is used in other contexts of hostile pursuit (Judg 18:22; 20:42, 45; 1 Sam 14:22; 31:2; 2 Sam 1:6). From the Euphrates to Gilead is some three hundred miles, which would be too far for herds to cover in ten days, so we must be dealing with rough approximations here.

24   It seems high-handed of Westermann to dismiss this verse and v 29 as later additions because he sees no function for them in the narrative. But as Gunkel observes, it is precisely God's intervention that prompts Laban's leniency later on in the scene. It also fits well with the earlier refrain in Jacob's speech that God has always protected him, especially from Laban (vv 5, 7, 9). Here the narrative confirms that claim. "Take care" (cf. *Comment* on 24:6) "lest you contradict Jacob in any way" (cf. *Comment* on 24:50). Despite this very stern divine warning, the following diatribe is one of the fiercest and longest in Genesis.

25–54   In the judicial dispute that constitutes the substance of this long scene, the relative standing of Laban and Jacob changes fundamentally. At the outset, Laban as *pater familias* arraigns Jacob, his nephew and son-in-law, who is under his authority (vv 26–30). At the end, Jacob and Laban make a treaty showing that they are now on a more equal footing; Jacob is head of his own household (vv 45–54).

26–30   The burden of Laban's complaint is twofold: first, that Jacob has not observed the proper formalities for leaving his father-in-law (vv 26–30a) and second, that he has stolen from him (vv 27a, 30b).

"This speech is a psychological portrait of thirteen sentences, in which rage and resignation, castigation and sweetness contend for mastery and eventually achieve an unstable equilibrium. Honest indignation here enframes the whole, v. 26

(first two words) and 30b. But as early as v. 26a it passes into feigned indignation, which is more like anger at having been taken in (26b, 27a). Laban continues with pure hypocrisy: he would have loved to have given him a festive send-off with music, etc. (just as in Gen 24), 27b. In v. 28a, he mixes these sweet words with a reproach that would have been sincere from a genuine father, 'I could not kiss Rachel and Leah farewell.' Then, with a shake of his head, he comes to a denunciation ('you have done foolishly,' v. 28b), which inclines towards anger: v. 29a is a threat which is undermined in the nick of time by a report (29b) on the Mighty One of Jacob, who calls things to a halt. Laban tries to resign himself to it and forces himself (30a) for the first and last time to understanding; he 'tries to realize' Jacob's position. . . ! Then he stops short with the perplexed reproach: 'why have you stolen my gods?' The accusation is genuine; that he is addressing the wrong person Laban cannot possibly know.

"The inner contradiction of this speech can be indicated quite precisely on two points. It is demonstrated by the reversal of sounds in Laban's third and fourth sentences: ḥ-r-b becomes b-r-ḥ. First Jacob is accused of pursuing his own ends with the sword, and then he appears to be a fugitive! The combination is absurd!

"This is proved simultaneously a second indication of the inner contradiction in Laban's position, one of which *ḥrb* is a part. Laban accuses Jacob of carrying away 'my daughters' (not 'your wives' of course!) as prisoners by the sword (they are *kišbūyōt ḥareb*). But if anyone, it was Laban himself who detained Leah and Rachel, as well as Jacob (29.25!), who kept them for another six years and made jealousy and hatred wreak their devastating effect upon their family-life. What Leah and Rachel think of this they have said unambiguously in 31.14–16; and in v. 31 Jacob returns the ball. In short, Laban commits what might be termed a Freudian Fehlleistung, accusing Jacob of that which he himself would love to, but is restricted from doing" (Fokkelman, *Narrative Art*, 166–67).

26 "What have you done?" often opens an accusation, where the accuser feels the accused has acted quite unreasonably. Note the irony in that those were the very words Jacob spoke to Laban the morning after his wedding (cf. 29:25; cf. 3:13; 4:10; 12:18; 20:9; 26:10). Westermann's suggested emendation to "what have I done" is therefore unlikely.

"Captives of war" (cf. Deut 21:10–14).

30 "Yearn." This strong term, used only in this form in Ps 84:3(2) apart from here, is made even stronger by the use of the infinitive absolute.

"Why did you steal my gods?" The most serious charge of all. Whereas Laban's other accusations amounted to lack of courtesy and respect, stealing household gods was an aggravated form of theft.

31–32 Jacob's fierce reply heightens the tension. He does not contest that his flight was a breach of etiquette but instead launches a counterattack. He accuses Laban of wanting to rob him of his daughters. The verb גזל "rob" means "to steal using force" (cf. *Comment* on 21:25). And as for the charge that he has stolen the household gods, he is so convinced of the innocence of all his party that he pronounces the death penalty on anyone found guilty. In view of the seriousness of the charge, Jacob invites "our relatives," presumably those who had come with Laban (vv 23, 26), to "identify," used here and in 37:32–23; 38:25–26 in a judicial sense, the stolen property. Whether under normal circumstances theft of the

household gods warranted the death penalty is doubtful, though the laws of
Hammurabi (LH 6) do prescribe capital punishment for stealing temple property. But what Jacob has unwittingly done is to pass a death sentence on his favorite
wife, and so for the reader who, unlike Jacob, knows that Rachel has the teraphim,
the story reaches its dramatic high point.

33–35 Here at the peak of the story, the pace slows to increase suspense (cf.
7:18–24; 22:9–10; 44:12). "The narrator is master of his trade. Quickly he has
increased the tension with the statement, 'Jacob did not know that Rachel had
stolen them' nor does he let the suspense fade away. On the contrary, he adeptly
lets it grow, by gaining time and delaying the solution as long as he can. With v.
33a he carries suspense to extremes: first he has Laban examine all those tents in
which we know the terafim will not be found, so that subsequently the fatal discovery seems inevitable. Trying our nerves the narrator says threateningly, 'then
he entered Rachel's tent.' He has avoided telling us until the last possible moment, that Rachel has made a provision against discovery. Now, v. 34a, he can
delay no longer. Suspense turns into malicious pleasure at the deadly fun made
of the *terafim:* they are only to be 'saved' by a menstruation. This means that they
are as unclean as can be, in this new position they come near functioning
as . . . sanitary towels.

"What Laban does is 'feel all things, one by one.' An effective choice of words,
this iterative *pi‘el* of *mšš* (vv. 34, 37), because the verb had already been used in
Gen. 27. There, Jacob's father was trying to learn the truth about his son
by . . . feeling, but in vain because of a trick of Jacoba's. Thus Jacob received
the blessing; it could not be taken from him anymore. Here Jacob's uncle is re-
trieving his own 'truth,' feeling, frisking, house-searching, and now a trick of
Jacoba's renders this search vain. Thus Jacob can retain the blessing and leave
with his most precious 'asset.'

"Laban is the great loser, for he cuts a foolish figure. His rage seems ridicu-
lous, now that his only dangerous accusation 'seems' to be utterly unfounded.
Laban is perplexed, he 'is nowhere.' The text indicates that with a three-fold *lō
māṣā"* (he did not find) (Fokkelman, *Narrative Art,* 170–71).

36–42 Feeling completely vindicated, Jacob hits back at Laban with his own
string of grievances. He might have used them in his own defense in v 31, but he
held back. At this point in the dialogue they come over with much greater force
and indignation. Indeed, here we have the climax of the whole Jacob-Laban story
with v 42 being the authoritative word about its significance: "You would have
sent me away empty-handed . . . but God vindicated me." His speech is replete
with parallelism and balanced lines:

> "What is my crime?
> What is my sin . . . ?" (v 36)

> "I have not eaten the rams of your flock.
> The torn beast I have not brought to you." (vv 38–39)

This has led some commentators, most recently Fokkelman, to describe this speech
as a poem. But this is going too far. As J. L. Kugel (*The Idea of Biblical Poetry* [New
Haven: Yale UP, 1981]) has insisted, parallelism is also a feature of Hebrew prose,

especially elevated rhetorical prose. And this seems to fit this situation. Here twenty years of angry frustration burst out in a diatribe of ferocious intensity.

36 "Argued," from the verb ריב "to argue," "to conduct a lawsuit." Though this verb and noun sometimes have the precise meaning "lawsuit" and some commentators regard Jacob's protests that follow as part of a legal suit, it seems unnecessary to give the verb such a meaning anywhere in the Pentateuch.

"What is my crime? What is my sin?" The same pair of words is used in 50:17 to describe the offense of Joseph's brothers in selling him into slavery into Egypt. "Crime" (פשע) refers in the first instance to property offenses (e.g., Exod 22:8[9]), but it is also used much more broadly of a variety of heinous offenses (e.g., Amos 1:3, 6, 9, 11, 13) that no civilized people should commit. Here and in Gen 50:17 it seems also to have strong overtones. You must think I have done something dreadful to pursue after me in such hot anger. דלק elsewhere means "to burn," and in this sense "hotly pursue" is used only in contexts of soldiers pursuing their defeated enemies (1 Sam 17:53; Lam 4:19).

37 Not only have you, Laban, not found the household gods which you accused me of stealing, but you have not found anything that belonged to you among my goods.

38 In fact, the more I think about it, the more you seem to be the one guilty of stealing from me. For twenty years, your flocks have flourished under my management, as you yourself admitted (30:27). Very few of the lambs or kids died at birth, and I have not eaten the full-grown animals.

39 Under traditional ancient Near Eastern law, the shepherd was not held responsible for any losses incurred from the attacks of wild beasts and in some cases of theft.

"If a visitation of god has occurred in a sheepfold or a lion has made a kill, the shepherd shall prove himself innocent in the presence of god" (LH 266). Similarly, Exod 22:12(13) states, "If (an animal) is torn by beasts, let (the herdsman) bring it as evidence; he shall not make restitution." Likewise Exod 22:9–11(10–12) insists that a shepherd should not be held liable for thefts from the flock, if he is prepared to swear he has not stolen the beasts himself. Finkelstein (*JAOS* 88 [1968] 36) speculates that in some places the shepherd might be held liable for losses incurred during the day but not for those at night. But with Jacob and Laban things were different. All losses incurred were footed by Jacob the shepherd; Laban the owner suffered no loss at all. It is Jacob who has been cheated of his wages by Laban, not vice versa.

40 This verse reflects accurately the difference between the baking day-time temperatures and the cold of the night in Middle Eastern countries, especially away from the moderating influence of the sea. When he was in love with Rachel, seven years seemed but a few days (29:20), but they were tough times. And this verse makes us aware that Jacob has been toughened up away from home. The soft homebound pet of Rebekah has been hardened; the smooth young man who fled from his hairy open-air brother is now much more of a match for Esau.

41 Now Jacob makes the same charge to Laban's face as he had made behind his back in v 7. He has changed his pay ten times.

42 But here he fills out his earlier statement, "But God has not allowed him to harm me," considerably. God saw Jacob's plight and ensured he was given a fair deal. The phraseology used here has strong associations with other key episodes

in Israel's history. "Send away" (שלח piel) is the verb most often used to describe
Pharaoh sending Israel away from Egypt (e.g., Exod 3:20). Indeed, when the exodus was first promised, Moses was assured that Israel would not leave
"empty-handed" (Exod 3:21). The same collocation of "send away . . . empty-
handed" is found in Deut 15:13–14, which insists that after six years' service a
slave shall not be sent away empty-handed, but "you shall furnish him liberally
out of your flock . . . ; as the LORD your God has blessed you, you shall give to
him." Here Jacob's experience of release from slavery and divine bounty anticipates his descendants, who in turn must imitate God by treating their slaves
generously when they are released.

Phraseology anticipating the exodus pervades the next comment, "my oppression was seen by God" (cf. Leah's comment in 29:32). But Exod 3:7 and Deut
26:7 are the only other uses of this phrase in the Pentateuch, both of the Egyptian oppression (cf. Neh 9:9). It is, of course, used in the psalms of an individual's
plight (9:14[13]; 25:18; 31:8[7]; 119:153) and in Lamentations of the fall of Jerusalem (1:9; 3:1, 19), but rarely in other contexts.

With this concentration of phraseology associated with the exodus, and especially with the call of Moses in Exod 3, the designations "God of my father Abraham
and the fear of Isaac" seem particularly at home (cf. Exod 3:6, 15, 16; 4:5); and to
suggest, as Westermann does, that "the God of Abraham, and the fear of Isaac" is
a later addition seems misguided. This combination of divine titles resembles
28:13, "I am the LORD, the God of Abraham your father and the God of Isaac,"
used in his self-revelation at Bethel to Jacob fleeing from Esau. There he had
promised, "I am really with you and will guard you wherever you go." Now Jacob
himself uses the title as if he recalls the LORD's providential protection, not least
in the vision he gave to Laban the night before.

"The fear of Isaac." This title of God occurs only here and in v 53. It has been
the subject of much discussion. Does פחד really mean "fear"? Modern writers
have proposed alternatives, such as "kinsman of Isaac" (W. F. Albright, *From the
Stone Age to Christianity*, 2nd ed. [Baltimore: Johns Hopkins, 1957] 248) or "thigh
of Isaac" (Malul, *VT* 35 [1985] 192–200). But the evidence for this seems flimsy
(see Hillers, *JBL* 91 [1972] 90–92). Less difficult is Westermann's suggestion, "refuge of Isaac." But on the whole the traditional rendering, "fear, dread of Isaac,"
does not seem out of place here, for it is precisely his experience of this God that
has scared Laban and discouraged him from wreaking revenge on Laban. Pointing to names like Zelophehad (Num 27:1), a thirteenth-century cup mentioning
ypthd from Cyprus, perhaps originating in Canaan, and similar glosses in the
Amarna letters, Puech (*VT* 34 [1984] 356–61) argues for the traditional meaning, "fear of Isaac," and its antiquity.

This last remark of Jacob's is much more than the decisive climax to his speech
of self-justification. It is the summary of the whole story of Jacob's life, at least in
Harran. It invites comparison with 45:5, when at the peak of the Joseph story,
Joseph himself explains the meaning of his career: "you sold me here; God sent
me before you to preserve life" (cf. 45:7; 50:20). Here Jacob confesses that his
preservation and his wealth are all due to God's power overriding the meanness
of his uncle Laban; the LORD is a God who enriches his people even in their
oppression.

43–44 "Laban cannot reply. The fox is in the trap. He must let everything go, women, children, flocks, although it all belongs to him. These words, which must greatly amuse the listeners, are not a snobbish outburst but, as what follows shows, a pitiful complaint. . . . Laban's emotion is seen in the fourfold 'my.' Particularly distressing to him is the thought that he must surrender his daughters and their children into the hands of a foreigner, when he does not know how he will treat them" (Gunkel, 350).

44 When foreigners seek to make covenants or oaths with the patriarchs, it is an acknowledgment of the latters' superiority. Cf. 21:22–24; 26:26–31. Laban now feels he must protect himself from the power and blessing that evidently rest on Jacob; hence, he asks for a covenant. "It shall be a witness between you and me." The subject of this sentence is unclear. To what does "it/he" refer? It cannot be "covenant," for that is feminine while the verb is masculine. So the subject may be "God" (so Rashi), or the erection of the stone (so Ramban), or it may be that something has been omitted such as "let us make a pillar or a heap" (so Dillmann and recently Westermann).

45–54 This description of a covenant-making ceremony is difficult. Its repetitiousness has led many commentators to conclude that there is more than one source here, but there is no consensus on the division between the sources (see *Form/Structure/Setting*). And tradition-critical solutions are equally diverse. Westermann thinks an original account of a family agreement between Jacob and Laban has been later expanded by the account of a boundary agreement between Israel (Jacob) and Syria (Laban). But Blum (*Die Komposition*) thinks that the border agreement is primary and the family agreement is secondary. However, Hittite treaties sometimes contain stipulations both about treating the king's daughters (marriage between treaty partners was common; cf. 1 Kgs 9:16; Blum, *Die Komposition*, 135) and about borders. So the combination of these elements need not indicate a plurality of sources or editors. The erection of stone cairns and their naming are the more perplexing aspects of this narrative. With Fokkelman (*Narrative Art*), Westermann, Koch ("*Paḥad jiṣḥaq*"), and the oldest commentators, we shall endeavor to make sense of the narrative as it stands, while recognizing that the text probably has a complex and irrecoverable history.

45 Jacob had erected a stone as a pillar at Bethel (28:18) and would do so again there as a memorial to Rachel (35:14, 20). The three great turning points in his life are marked by these pillars. "Pillar" (מצבה) anticipates one of the key words in this section, "Mispah" (מצפה), from which it differs by one letter. In the present context, the pillar seems to serve as a witness to the agreement Laban has just called for.

46 Elsewhere in OT, stone cairns are used to mark graves (Josh 7:26; 8:29; 2 Sam 18:17). Absalom was commemorated by a cairn and a pillar (2 Sam 18:18). It seems unnecessary to erect two witnesses to the proposed agreement, but this cairn is central to the account, being mentioned eight times in total in vv 46–52. The word "cairn, heap" (גל) is a play on the word Gilead, which is explained as meaning "cairn of witness" (vv 47, 48). The pillar and cairn are both witnesses in vv 51–52. So we must ask why there are two. Duplication and repetition of symbols, gestures, and words always indicate that something is regarded as most important (cf, Gen 41:32). The OT insists that two witnesses are needed for conviction

(Deut 19:15). It is characteristic of ancient legal texts to summon a multitude of
witnesses, sun, moon, and gods, to witness treaties. So it is not inappropriate for
Jacob to want more than one witness of this important treaty. Laban was, after all,
a somewhat unreliable partner. The explicit mention of "his relatives," more likely
Jacob's than Laban's, shows that this agreement was not just between Jacob and
Laban as individuals but between their clans (cf. Lev 24:14, 16, 23; Deut 21:21).
"They ate there" probably anticipates the sacrificial meal that concluded the cov-
enant ceremony (v 54; cf. Exod 24:11).

47   This verse is an aside commenting on the Aramaic name *Yegar sāhadûthā*
(יְגַר שָׂהֲדוּתָא) and the name "Galed," both of which mean "cairn of witness." The
Syrians in whose area Laban lived spoke Aramaic, and this is the clearest of several Aramaisms within this chapter (for others see Greenfield, VTSup 32 [1982]
129), reflecting Laban's presumed mother tongue.

48   This verse continues the main narrative. First, Laban explains the meaning of the cairn: it is to serve as a witness between him and Jacob.

49   The SamPent reads, instead of "The Mispah," "the watch post," "the
Massebah," i.e., "the pillar." Since the text goes on to make a pun on Mispah,
"May the LORD keep watch" (יִצֶף *yiṣep*), most commentators regard Mispah as
original here and suppose that a place name in northern Gilead is being explained.
This may be so, but in context it is apparent that Laban is referring to the stone
erected as a pillar. Standing stones were sometimes regarded as a dwelling place
of the gods (cf. 28:17–18 and *Comment*). Here Laban plainly speaks of the LORD
watching over their behavior.

50   "Oppress"; cf. 16:6; Exod 22:21–22(22–23) for the oppression of women.
The same root is found in v 42. Laban tries to throw Jacob's accusation back.
There is an element of irony in his demand that Jacob should not take any extra
wives besides his daughters. For though this is a frequent stipulation in marriage
contracts and in some treaties, it was Laban who had forced bigamy upon Jacob
in time past!! "Do as I say, not as I did" is Laban's advice.

"God is a witness." That God protects the rights of the defenseless, especially women,
is often mentioned in the OT (cf. 16:7–14; 21:8–21; Exod 22:22–23[23–24]).

51   Here Laban mentions both pillar and cairn as witnesses (cf. *Comments* above
on v 46.) Laban says here that he erected it, showing that he agreed with Jacob's
initiative in vv 45–46.

52   Now Laban mentions that the pillar and cairn are guarantors, not only of
his daughters' safety but of his territorial integrity. "I myself shall not go beyond
this cairn . . . with evil intent." Grammatically, this formula is unexpected (see
Notes), but it may be translated as we have. Another possibility is that לְרָעָה could
be understood "in an evil situation, i.e., in case help is needed" (so the old Jewish
commentators Chiskuni and Abrabanel, quoted by Jacob, 609). Then the oath
would run "You will pass this cairn toward me (in case of need), and I shall pass
this cairn and this pillar to you in case of need." This would constitute a real
treaty offering mutual assistance. However, there is no parallel to such a use of
לְרָעָה. But both seem easier than Westermann's complicated hypothesis of the
fusing of two traditions or readings.

53   That Laban was a polytheist is suggested by his invocation of at least two
gods, "the god(s) of Abraham and the god(s) of Nahor," which are followed by

a plural verb, whereas Jacob swears by just one: "the fear of Isaac" (cf. *Comment* on v 42).

54 As was customary in the ancient world, the covenant was concluded by the offering of sacrifice and a communal meal (cf. Exod 24:5–11; Deut 27:6–7).

32:1(31:55) Reconciliation is followed by peace. The angry chase ended in a covenant guaranteeing respect for each other's family and territory in the future. Now there is an amicable parting with the traditional kissing (cf. 31:28) and blessing (cf. 24:60; 28:1), and Laban returns home.

2–3(1–2) This final scene shows Jacob pressing on toward Canaan. His experience at Mahanaim both epitomizes his whole experience with Laban and anticipates his encounter with Esau. Throughout this episode it has been stressed that God has been with Jacob (vv 3, 5, 9, 42). It begins with the LORD assuring Jacob that he would be with him; it ends with him re-experiencing this in a new vision, similar in many ways to that at Bethel. Both speak of meeting (פגע; 28:11) and of "angels of God" (28:12). Both visions coincide with his entry to or departure from Canaan. In both, the place is named because of the experience. "Mahanaim" means "two camps" and was, according to Josh 13:26; 21:38, a levitical city in Gad, later the capital of Ishbosheth's kingdom (2 Sam 2:8–9) and the refuge of David during Absalom's rebellion (2 Sam 17:24). Its location is uncertain. This passage and the others cited require it to be a little north of the Yabbok river. Aharoni (*EM* 4:805–8) thinks western Tulul edh-Dhahab is the likeliest candidate.

Unlike his vision at Bethel, no divine word is recorded at Mahanaim, so what the Mahanaim vision meant to Jacob is left obscure. "Two camps" sounds military, and it may be that Jacob saw armies of angels (2 Kgs 6:15–17), but why two? And were they on Jacob's side (cf. Josh 5:13–15)? The most natural assumption is that they were friendly, so that this experience encouraged Jacob just before he encountered Esau, but the failure to be more precise leaves open the possibility that they might be hostile (32:23–31). There is no doubt, however, that Jacob is still being accompanied by God.

Explanation

Delay and disappointment dogged Jacob's stay in Paddan-Aram. He had planned to stay "a few days" (27:44). These few days had lengthened into seven years as he worked for Rachel's hand in marriage. Then, cheated by his father-in-law, he had to work another seven years until Rachel bore her first son, Joseph. As soon as this happened, Jacob again requested permission to leave, but Laban refused to give him the traditional golden handshake due a faithful slave on his release. So Jacob had to work another six years to acquire enough property of his own to make the break and return to his homeland.

Now twenty years after leaving home, he at last manages to set out. But it is not just his heart that pulls him home. The jealousy of Laban and his sons at Jacob's successful breeding of his own flocks and a divine call akin to grandfather Abraham's "Return to the land of your fathers and to your clan" prompt him to depart.

But would his wives agree? Maybe they would prefer to stay with their father, especially Leah, whose marriage to Jacob was so unhappy. Discreetly "in the

countryside," i.e., out of earshot of other members of the household, he sounds them out. He reminds them of his loyal service to their father and how he "changed my pay ten times," yet "the God of my father has been with me" (v 5). It was God who prevented Laban from harming Jacob (v 7), who "rescued the animals of your father" by showing Jacob how to breed them selectively, who told Jacob to "leave this country and return to the land of your clan."

In appealing to his wives, Jacob noticeably omits any mention of the most embarrassing episode in his dealing with Laban, the substitution of Leah for Rachel on his wedding night, or the reason he had fled from home, Esau's deadly hatred, for these points might have discouraged Leah and Rachel from coming with him. Instead, he stresses God's overruling protection of him and his interests. Though we may doubt the complete candor of Jacob's apologia, the narrator certainly regarded it as a valid theological explanation, and his wives were also convinced and agreed to go.

To escape Laban's clutches was another matter. He had procrastinated when Abraham's servant wanted to take Rebekah to Canaan. He had delayed Jacob's return home by nearly twenty years. Doubtless had Jacob sought Laban's agreement to leave, he would have found yet another sound reason for him to stay. So Jacob decided to abscond.

He chose the busiest time in the herdsman's calendar to quit, sheep-shearing, when all Laban's men would have been working from dawn to dusk. This gave him a few days' lead in fleeing from Laban. Eventually Laban catches up with Jacob and in high dudgeon berates him for his behavior. "What have you done? You have . . . driven my daughters away like captives of war . . . why did you steal my gods?" Tucked away in this angry tirade is a little comment that "the God of your father said to me yesterday, 'Take care not to contradict Jacob'" (v 29). Even Laban is forced to admit that God is ultimately on Jacob's side and he cannot touch him.

Then the tables are turned. Laban's abortive attempt to discover his household gods, related with more than a touch of humor, allows Jacob to go on the offensive and remind Laban of all the wrongs he has suffered at his hands, concluding, "If the God of my father Abraham and the fear of Isaac had not been with me, you would certainly have now sent me away empty-handed" (v 42).

So with one last protest, "The daughters are my daughters . . . the flock is my flock" (v 43), Laban at last concedes Jacob the right to be treated as an equal: "Come let us make a covenant" (v 44). The covenant seems unnecessary. That Laban should insist that Jacob should not marry any extra wives is laughable, when he himself had inflicted bigamy on his reluctant nephew. Nor had Jacob any intention of invading Laban's territory; he was intent on returning to Canaan. But the covenant mollified Laban, so Jacob accepted it, and they parted peaceably.

This story, like many in Genesis, illustrates God's sovereign protection of his chosen. Despite Jacob's tactlessness and self-seeking, God has kept his promise made at Bethel that he would be with Jacob and guard him wherever he went (28:15). Having reached Gilead, Jacob was within sight of Canaan and must have wondered about his likely meeting with Esau. Would he really succeed in returning to the land promised to him at Bethel? No verbal reassurance was given him; instead, "angels of God met him." What they looked like or did is not described,

but they surely must have reminded Jacob of his Bethel experience and given him the confidence to press on, knowing God was with him and protecting him.

With his return to Canaan, another chapter in Jacob's life closed, a chapter in which frustration and disappointment outweighed joy. But God was with Jacob even then, and he persevered, so that eventually he saw the fulfillment of what had been promised him. He returned with his wife and children to the land of promise. His escape from the clutches of Laban, who had treated him more like a slave than a nephew or son-in-law, prefigured his physical descendants' escape from Egypt. May his faith in the promises and his endurance inspire his spiritual descendants to run "with perseverance the race that is set before us" (Heb 12:1).

Jacob Returns Esau's Blessing   (32:4–33:20)

Bibliography

Anbar, M. "La 'reprise.'" *VT* 38 (1988) 385–98. **Loretz, O.** "Die Epitheta *ʾlʾlhj jśrʾl* (Gen 33:20) und *ʾlʾlhj ʾbjk* (Gen 46:3)." *UF* 7 (1975) 583. **Puech, E.** "Fragment d'un rouleau de la Genèse provenant du désert de Juda." *RevQ* 10 (1980) 163–66. **Schenker, A.** "*Kōper* et expiation." *Bib* 63 (1982) 32–46. **Schreiner, J.** "Das Gebet Jakobs (Gen 32:10–13)." In *Die Väter Israels: FS J. Scharbert*, ed. M. Görg. Stuttgart: Katholisches Bibelwerk, 1989. 287–303. **Wächter, L.** "Salem bei Sichem." *ZDPV* 84 (1968) 63–72. ———. "Zur Lokalisierung des sichemitischen Baumheiligtums." *ZDPV* 103 (1987) 1–12.

Translation

[4]*Jacob sent messengers ahead to his brother Esau to the land of Seir, the country of Edom.* [5]*He instructed*[a] *them as follows: "You shall speak to my lord Esau. Your servant Jacob says: 'It is with Laban that I have been staying, and I have waited*[b] *until now.* [6]*I have acquired*[a] *cattle, donkeys,* [b]*flocks, slaves and slave-girls, so I have sent*[c] *to let you know*[d] *in order to find favor with you.'"* [7]*The messengers returned to Jacob saying, "We came to your brother Esau, and he*[a] *is coming to meet you, and there are four hundred men with him."*

[8]*Then Jacob was very frightened and distressed.*[a] *So he split*[b] *the people who were with him and the flocks, herds, and camels*[c] *into two groups.* [9]*He thought, "If Esau comes to the first*[a] *group and kills*[b] *them, the surviving group may be able to escape."* [10]*Jacob said, "O God of my father Abraham, and God of my father Isaac, O LORD,* [a]*who said*[a] *to me, 'Return to your country and to your clan, that* [b]*I may do good*[b] *for you.'* [11]*I am not worthy of all your mercies and faithfulness which you have shown your servant. For I crossed this Jordan* [a]*just with a staff,*[a] *and now I have become two camps.* [12]*Please rescue*[a] *me from the hand of my brother, from Esau, for I am afraid he will come and kill*[b] *me, and the mother with*[c] *her children.* [13]*It is you*[a] *who have said that* [b]*I shall indeed do good*[b] *for you and make your descendants as numerous as the sand of the sea, which cannot be counted."*[c]

[14]*So he stayed*[a] *there that night and took some of his income as a present for Esau his brother,* [15]*two hundred she-goats and twenty he-goats, two hundred ewes and twenty rams,*

[16] *thirty milch*[a] *camels and their*[b] *young, forty cows and ten bulls, twenty she-asses and ten he-asses.*[c] [17]*He put each flock*[a] *separately in charge of his servants, and he told his servants, "Go over ahead of me, and put a space between each flock."* [18]*He instructed the first, "When my brother Esau meets*[a] *you, and asks*[b] *you, 'Who do you belong to and where are you going, and whose are these ahead of you?'* [19]*You shall say, 'To your servant Jacob. It is a present sent to my lord Esau. And he himself*[a] *is*[b]*on his way*[b] *after us.'"* [20]*He instructed the second group, also a third group, in fact all those going with the animals, "This is what you shall say to Esau, when you find*[a] *him.* [21]*You must say too, 'Your servant Jacob is*[a] *on his way after us,'" for he thought, "I shall mollify*[b] *him with the present ahead of me, and then afterwards I shall see him face to face. Perhaps he will accept me."* [22]*So he made the present go ahead of him,* [a]*while he spent that night in the camp.*[a]

[23]*He rose that*[a] *night, took his two wives, two slave-girls, and eleven sons and crossed the ford of the*[b]*Yabbok.* [24]*He took*[a] *them and made them cross the wadi, and he sent over all*[b] *that belonged to him.*

[25]*And Jacob was left*[a] *on his own, and a man struggled*[b] *with him till dawn broke.*[c] [26]*He realized that he could not win, so he touched*[a] *his hip socket, and Jacob's hip was dislocated*[b] *as he struggled*[c] *with him.* [27]*He said, "Let me go, for the dawn has broken." He said, "I shall not let you go, unless*[a] *you bless me."* [28]*He said to him, "What is your name?" and he replied, "Jacob."* [29]*He said, "You shall no longer be called*[a] *Jacob, but*[b] *Israel, for you have struggled with God and with men and have overcome."*[c] [30]*So Jacob asked, "Tell*[a] *me*[b] *please your name." He said, "Why do you ask my name?" Then he blessed him there.* [31]*So Jacob named that place Peniel, because "I have seen God face to face and yet*[a] *my life was rescued."*[b]

[32]*Then the sun rose as he passed on from Penuel, and he went limping on his thigh.* [33]*For this reason to this day Israelites do not eat the sinew of the thigh which is on the hip socket, because he touched the socket of Jacob's hip on the sinew of the thigh.*

[33:1]*Then Jacob raised*[a] *his eyes and saw Esau coming and with him four hundred men. So he divided*[b] *the children among Leah, Rachel, and the slave-girls.* [2]*He put the slave-girls with their children at the front, Leah and her children next,*[a] *and Rachel and Joseph at the back.* [3]*He himself went on ahead of them and bowed down*[a] *seven times until he reached*[b] *his brother.*

[4]*Then Esau ran*[a] *to meet him, hugged him, fell on his neck, kissed*[b] *him, and they*[c] *wept.* [5]*Then he raised his eyes and saw the women and children, and he said, "Who are these with you?" He said, "The children with whom God has favored your servant."* [6]*Then the slave-girls drew*[a] *near, they and their children, and they prostrated*[b] *themselves.* [7]*Then Leah and her children also approached,*[a] *and they prostrated themselves. Afterwards Joseph and Rachel approached*[b] *and prostrated themselves.* [8]*He said, "What*[a] *is all this camp that I have encountered?" He said, "To find favor with my lord."* [9]*Esau replied, "I have plenty, my brother. Let yours remain yours."* [10]*But Jacob said, "Please, no. If I have found favor with you, you shall take my present from me, for*[a] *I have seen your face, which is like seeing the face of God, and you have accepted me.* [11]*Please take my blessing which was brought*[a] *for you, because God has been good to me and because I have all I need." So he pressed him and he took it.*

[12]*He said, "Let us travel and go, so I may go in front of you."* [13]*He said to him, "My lord knows that the children are weak and the herds and flocks are giving*[a] *suck, so that if* [b]*they are driven*[b] *hard for just one day all the flock will die.* [14a]*Let my lord go on ahead*

of your servant, and I shall journey[b] *on*[a] *slowly at the pace of the property ahead of me and at the pace of the children, until I come to my lord in Seir.*" [15] *So Esau said, "Please let me station*[a] *with you some of the people who are with me." He replied, "Why*[b] *should it be? Let me find favor with my lord!"*

[16] *So that day Esau returned his own way to Seir.* [17] *But Jacob journeyed on to Succoth and built himself a house and made booths for the animals. That is why the place is called Succoth.*

[18] *Then Jacob came to Salem*[a] *to the city of Shechem, which is in the land of Canaan. When he came from Paddan-Aram, he encamped*[b] *facing the city.* [19] *He bought*[a] *a*[b] *plot of ground where he had pitched his tent from the sons of Hamor, father of Shechem, for a hundred qesita.* [20] *There he erected*[a] *an altar*[b] *and called it, "El, God of Israel."*

Notes

5.a. Cf. n. 2:16.a.

5.b. Waw consec + 1 sg impf qal אחר.

6.a. Lit. "it was to me." On the pl subj ("cattle," etc.) with sg verb, see GKC, 145o.

6.b. SamPent adds "and."

6.c. Waw consec + 1 sg coh qal שלח. On the use of the coh here, see GKC, 49e.

6.d. ל + inf constr hiph נגד.

7.a. On the omission of the pronoun, see GKC, 116s.

8.a. Waw consec + 3 masc sg impf qal צרר.

8.b. Waw consec + 3 masc sg impf (apoc) qal חצה.

8.c. To omit "and camels" with G, so *BHS* and Westermann, seems unnecessary.

9.a. SamPent reads masc אחד. MT probably aural error.

9.b. Waw consec + 3 masc sg pf hiph נכה + 3 masc sg suffix.

10.a-a. On the use of the ptcp to describe past actions, see GKC, 116o.

10.b-b. Waw consec + 1 sg coh hiph יטב. On the sequence impv + coh "in order that," see GKC, 108d.

11.a-a. In the Heb. this phrase stands first to contrast his present prosperity with his former poverty (*EWAS*, 43).

12.a. 2 masc sg impv hiph נצל + 1 sg suffix.

12.b. Waw consec + 3 masc sg pf hiph נכה + 1 sg suffix.

12.c. GKC, 119aa, n. 2, suggests this phrase is proverbial.

13.a. Independent personal pronoun for emphasis (GKC, 142a[1]; cf. *EWAS*, 47–59).

13.b-b. Inf abs + 1 sg impf hiph יטב.

13.c. Cf. n. 16:10.b.; GKC, 107w.

14.a. Cf. n. 28:11.b.

16.a. Fem pl ptcp hiph ינק.

16.b. Though fem pl suffix might be expected (cf. *BHS*), the masc often does duty for the fem (GKC, 135o).

16.c. On the pointing of this word, see GKC, 28b.

17.a. On this construction, see GKC, 123d.

18.a. On the pronunciation of this word, see GKC, 9v, 10g.

18.b. On this form, see GKC, 64f.

19.a. For this nuance of גם, see *SBH*, 166.

19.b-b. הנה often stresses the immediacy and present reality; cf. Lambdin, 169.

20.a-a. ב + inf constr מצא + 2 masc pl suffix. On the unusual punctuation, cf. GKC, 74h, 93q.

21.a. SamPent, G, *Tg. Onq. Neof.* insert "coming." This is a correct interpretation of the text, but it is unnecessary to suppose MT has omitted בא, for the clause is a variant of v 19d, which also lacks a verb (*SBH*, 96).

21.b. 1 sg coh piel כפר. Coh for self-encouragement (GKC, 108b).

22.a-a. Episode-final circumstantial clause (*SBH*, 81).

23.a. On the absence of ה (def art) on הוא, cf. n. 19:33.b.

23.b. SamPent has def art before Yabbok.

24.a. Waw consec + 3 masc sg impf לקח + 3 masc pl suffix.

24.b. With SamPent and versions, read כל "all that." MT "what."

25.a. Waw consec + 3 masc sg impf niph יתר.

25.b. Waw consec + 3 masc sg impf niph אבק.

25.c. Inf constr qal עלה.

26.a. Waw consec + 3 masc sg impf qal נגע.

26.b. Waw consec + 3 fem sg impf qal יקע.

26.c. ב + inf constr niph אבק + 3 masc sg suffix.

27.a. On this construction, see GKC, 163c.

29.a. Cf. n. 10:9.a.

29.b. כי־אם for a marked antithesis (Joüon, 172c; *SBH*, 184).

29.c. Waw consec + 2 masc sg impf יכל.

30.a. 2 masc sg impv hiph נגד.

30.b. "Me" must be understood, as G, S, Vg do. But this does not mean לי was in the Heb.; there are other examples of "tell" not being followed by an indirect obj (e.g., Job 38:4, 18).

31.a. The waw consec here marks a weak contrast (GKC, 111e).

31.b. Waw consec + 3 fem sg impf niph נצל.

33:1.a. Cf. n. 13:10.a.

1.b. Cf. n. 32:8.b.

2.a. *BHS* conjecturally emends "after them."

3.a. Cf. n. 18:2.d.

3.b. Inf constr נגש + 3 masc sg suffix.

4.a. Cf. n. 18:2.b.

4.b. Waw consec + 3 masc sg impf qal נשק + 3 masc sg suffix. The dots around the word are "extraordinary points" (see GKC, 5n).

4.c. *BHS* gratuitously emends the text to the sg "he wept."

6.a. Waw consec + 3 fem pl impf qal נגש.

6.b. Waw consec + 3 fem pl impf hishtaphel of חוה (cf. n. 18:2.d.).

7.a. On sg verb with pl subj (Leah and her children), see GKC, 146g.

7.b. 3 masc sg pf niph נגש. The use of the masc sg for the verb with composite masc and fem subj suggests the word order of MT, SamPent, Vg, "Joseph and Rachel," is to be preferred to G, S, "Rachel and Joseph," which is an assimilation to 33:2 (GKC, 146f).

8.a. Lit. "who?" (מי) is used occasionally for "what" "when the idea of a person is implied" (GKC 37a, 137a).

10.a. On this conj, see GKC, 158b[1].

11.a. 3 fem sg pf hoph בוא. SamPent and versions read הבאתי "I have brought."

13.a. Fem pl qal ptcp עול.

13.b-b. Waw consec + 3 masc pl impf qal דפק + 3 masc pl suffix (on the masc instead of fem suffix, see GKC, 60h), lit. "they will drive them." Here "they" is used impersonally. SamPent and versions rephrase "and I shall drive them."

14.a-a. Chiasmus linking clauses "go ahead, my lord: I, journey on" minimizes contrast between their different actions (*SBH*, 134).

14.b. 1 sg coh hithp נהל.

15.a. 1 sg coh hiph יצג.

15.b. The enclitic זה makes the interrogative "why" more lively (*EWAS*, 134–36).

18.a. SamPent reads שלום "peace," but versions take it as place name Salem.

18.b. Cf. n. 26:17.a.

19.a. Waw consec + 3 masc sg impf apoc qal קנה.

19.b. On the use of the def art here, see GKC, 127e.

20.a. Cf. n. 21:28.a.

20.b. *BHS*'s restoration, "pillar," is conjectural.

Form/Structure/Setting

It is difficult to be sure exactly where this section begins and where it ends. In the preceding *Form/Structure/Setting*, we gave reasons for believing that the new

section begins at 32:4(3) not 32:1(31:55), the most commonly accepted alternative. Here I concentrate on determining the close of the section. Gunkel takes 33:16 as the close and makes 33:17–20 a separate unit. But this is improbable, since v 17 clearly goes with v 16: Jacob's coming to Succoth balances Esau's arrival in Seir. For this reason, other commentators either regard v 17 (so Dillmann, Delitzsch, Vawter, Westermann, Coats, Blum [*Die Komposition*]) or v 20 as the close (Driver, Skinner, Jacob, Speiser, von Rad, Fokkelman [*Narrative Art*]).

The heart of the problem is thus vv 18–20. Do they constitute the conclusion of the previous episode, or do they open a new episode centered on Shechem? V 18 is formally part of an itinerary, with vv 19–20 constituting an expansion typical of an itinerary (cf. 12:6–9; 35:16–22). Now while vv 18–20 are transitional and certainly set the scene for chap. 34, they do seem to make an odd beginning to a new episode. As in 12:6–9 and 35:16–22, this note does bring Jacob back to the promised land of Canaan, the goal of his wanderings (27:45; 30:25; 31:3, 13), Salem being clearly within Canaan and Succoth probably outside. It also brings him back to Canaan in peace, something for which he had prayed in his vow at Bethel (28:21). To leave him outside the land of promise at Succoth is in the theological geography of Genesis somewhat anticlimactic. But that his return is momentous is indicated by his building an altar and praying, something that Abraham had done as soon as he arrived in Canaan (cf. 12:5–9; 13:3–4). Similarly, his purchase of Canaanite real estate seems to echo Abraham's purchase of a burial ground for Sarah (chap. 23). Understood this way, these three apparently unexciting verses (vv 18–20) make a fitting and impressive conclusion to the story of Jacob's return to his homeland. That they also anticipate the next episode set in Shechem is no ground for making them the start of that episode, for as we have frequently observed, it is characteristic of Genesis to have a trailer for what follows at the close of the previous section (e.g., 4:25–26; 9:18–29; 32:2–3[1–2]).

These chapters fall into seven scenes:

Scene 1: Jacob's embassy to Esau (32:4–7)
Scene 2: Jacob prepares to meet Esau (8–22)
          Jacob's fears (8–9)
          Jacob's prayer (10–13)
          Jacob's gifts (14–22)
Scene 3: Jacob and wives cross Yabbok (23–24)
Scene 4: Jacob wrestles with a "man" (25–33)
Scene 5: Jacob and Esau reunited (33:1–15)
          Jacob approaches (1–3)
          Greetings exchanged (4–11)
          Esau's invitation turned down (12–15)
Scene 6: Jacob and Esau part (16–17)
Scene 7: Conclusion and Preview: Jacob settles in Canaan (18–20)

This sevenfold scenic division is very similar to that of the previous section:

	Chapter 31	Chapters 32–33
Scene 1:	Instructions to leave	Planning to meet Esau
Scene 2:	Preparations to leave	Preparations to meet Esau
Scene 3:	Departure and Crossing of Euphrates	Crossing of Yabbok

Scene 4:	Pursuit by Laban	Struggle with man
Scene 5:	Confrontation	Confrontation
Scene 6:	Parting of Laban and Jacob	Parting of Esau and Jacob
Scene 7:	Conclusion/Preview	Conclusion/Preview

Though the parallels between scenes 1 and 2 are not very clear, those between scenes 3–7 in both episodes are striking. Note particularly how the climax to each episode occurs in scene 5.

It is not just in arrangement that chaps. 32–33 cohere well with the preceding material; in theme and content there are close links as well. 32:4 mentions "Esau his brother," presupposing the earlier story in chaps. 25 and 27, and 32:5 presupposes his long sojourn with Laban, the subject matter of chaps. 29–31. V 6 is an even more explicit reminder of the wealth Jacob acquired while away from home. Vv 7–9, describing Jacob's terror at the news of Esau's coming with four hundred men, presupposes Esau's intention of killing Jacob (27:41–45). V 10 recalls God's command to return to Canaan (31:4, 13; cf. 28:13–15), v 11 his original poverty (chap. 28) and his subsequent prosperity (chaps. 30–31), and v 13 the Bethel promise (28:13–14) and possibly Isaac's blessing (28:3–4) as well. The elaborate preparation of large presents for Esau to "mollify him" (vv 14–22) shows the magnitude of the offense for which he is trying to atone (cf. chap. 27). 32:23 and 33:2–3, with their listing of Jacob's wives and children, refer back to 29:15–30:24, while the prostration of Jacob before his brother is an allusion to 27:29, "may your mother's sons bow down before you." Here, in fact, Israel's blessing of Jacob apparently works for Esau; indeed, all through this episode Jacob describes himself as Esau's servant, whereas Isaac had said "May peoples *serve* you. . . . Be lord over your brothers" (27:29). In wrestling with the angel, Jacob shows himself still very anxious to obtain blessing (32:27, 30), but when he speaks to Esau, he describes his present as "my blessing which was brought for you" (33:11). With a slip of the tongue, Jacob attempts to return the blessing out of which he had cheated his brother twenty years earlier (27:35). The use of the term Seir in 33:16 echoes 27:11, 23, where Esau is described as "hairy" (שֵׂעָר *śā ʿir*) and anticipates 36:8–9, where he is said to live in Seir. Canaan and Paddan-Aram (33:18) look back to Isaac's farewell to Jacob in 28:2, 5–7 and recall his motive for returning (31:18) and look forward to 35:6, 9. 33:20 anticipates 35:1, 3, 7, where at Bethel he builds and names another altar. All these cross-linkages show that with this episode the end of the Jacob story has been virtually reached; there are just a few loose ends to tie up.

Within these chapters there are also many overt and hidden plays on key words. This is a frequent enough device in Hebrew prose, but the phenomenon is here more conspicuous than usual. The proper names Jacob, Peniel, Yabbok, all are the subject of punning. Jacob (יעקב *yʿqb*) struggles (אבק *ʾbq*, 32:25–26) near the river Yabbok (יבק *ybq*, 32:23). There his name was changed to Israel, "because you have struggled [שׂרה *śārāh*] with God" (32:29). Peniel means literally "face of God" (32:31–32), and since Esau's face is compared to God's in 33:10, presumably 32:21 anticipates Peniel too. It is also likely that Jacob's frequent description of himself as "your servant" is a play on his own name (32:5, 11, 19, 21;

33:5, 14; Strus, *Nomen-Omen,* 135). Another key word in the whole episode is "grace," "favor" (חן *ḥn;* 32:6; 33:8, 10, 15) and the associated verb "be gracious" (חנן *ḥnn;* 33:5, 11) and the noun "present" (מנחה *mnḥḥ;* 32:14, 19, 21, 22; 33:10), of which "camp," "group" (מחנה *mḥnḥ;* 32:8, 9, 11, 22; 33:8) is an anagram.

As already noted in the palistrophic arrangement of the Jacob story, chaps. 32–33, recounting the reconciliation of Jacob and Esau, correspond to chap. 27, the account of their quarrel. Fishbane (*Text and Texture*) and Rendsburg (*Redaction*) have drawn attention to other reversals in chaps. 32–33 of motifs in chap. 27. In 27:19–29 Jacob cheats Esau of his blessing; in 33:11 he offers it back to Esau. In 27:29 Isaac predicts that Jacob's brothers will fall down before him; in 33:3 it is Jacob who prostrates himself before Esau. Often it is suggested that Jacob's dream at Bethel (28:11–22) matches his struggle with the angel at Peniel (32:23–33), but as already pointed out, there are closer verbal links between the Mahanaim incident (32:2–3) and the Bethel incident than between Mahanaim and Peniel. Besides the obvious inversions already mentioned, there are numerous verbal links between chaps. 27 and 32–33 (see Rendsburg, *Redaction,* 59–63, and our *Comment* below) that show the careful integration of these chapters with the preceding material.

According to the oldest source critics, e.g., Driver and Wellhausen, the great bulk of 32:4–33:20 derived from J. Driver assigned only 33:18–20 to other sources, mostly E, while Wellhausen (*Komposition* 46) also ascribed 32:14b–22 to E. Subsequent source critics tended to find somewhat more E in these chapters. The references to "God" in 33:5, 10, 11 suggest that 33:1–17 might have been expanded by E. But Skinner (412) admits "The documents are so deftly interwoven that it is scarcely possible to detect a flaw in the continuity of the narrative." Similarly, 32:31 led many to argue that 32:23–33 was composed of E and J, though different analyses were offered, even by the same commentator in different editions. More recently the fashion has swung back to regarding 32:4–33:17 as all from the hand of J (so Volz, *Der Elohist;* Elliger, *ZTK* 48 [1951] 1–31; Speiser; Westermann, who allows for a few post-J expansions in 32:23–32; and Coats).

Among older commentators there was at least a broad consensus that vv 18–20 were not from the hand of J. It was held that they must be mostly the work of E, for 35:1–5 (E) presupposes Jacob's presence in Shechem, while the reference to arriving in Canaan from Paddan-Aram in 33:18 came from P. However, once it is allowed that the term "God" is not necessarily restricted to the sources E or P, it is no longer obvious that 35:1–5 belongs to E, so it may well be that 33:18–20 do not belong to it either. Hence Westermann regards these verses as mostly old independent fragments, whereas Volz (*Der Elohist*), de Pury (*Promesse divine*), and Coats more parsimoniously ascribe them to J. Certainly the phraseology of "camping," "building altars," and "naming" in the context of itineraries is quite typical of J (cf. 12:7, 8; 13:18; 22:9; 26:17, 20–22, 25). Also, the way in which these verses serve as both conclusion and review is typical of the redactor's method in Genesis and reinforces the supposition that they belong to J. The clause often ascribed to P in 33:18, "which is in the land of Canaan when he came from Paddan-Aram," is so short that we concur with Rendtorff (*Problem*) that it is high-handed to ascribe it to a different source. Further, to omit it is to diminish the vital theological point that Jacob has now arrived back in Canaan.

Comment

4–7   The first scene tells of Jacob's first attempt to make contact with his brother.

4   On Seir, see 14:6; *EM* 8:323–25.

5   Note the very deferential language used by Jacob in addressing Esau: "my lord . . . your servant." Even oriental courtesy would not lead to such extravagant humility toward a twin brother. Jacob's opening words thus hint at his fearfulness and guilty conscience, or at least constitute an attempt to reverse the relationship in which Esau would be Jacob's servant (25:23; 27:40).

6   The list of Jacob's acquisitions resembles 12:16; 30:43. He is not boasting but seeking to impress his brother, "in order to find favor with you." Here the key word "favor," "grace" (חֵן) makes its first appearance in this episode (33:8, 10, 15; cf. the associated verb "grant" "be gracious," 33:5, 11). Jacob's great desire is to make peace with his brother, and the narrative keeps us in suspense waiting to see whether his hopes will be fulfilled.

7   The messengers' return is eerie, for they bring no reply from Esau but simply report that he is on his way with four hundred men. The brevity makes for ambiguity. Is Esau coming to wage war or to receive his brother royally? If he is planning an attack, why allow the messengers to return unharmed, allowing Jacob to prepare himself? Or does Esau feel so superior that he is prolonging Jacob's agony before striking the final blow? The suspense is heightened.

8–21   The second scene shows Jacob fearing the worst and making every effort to avert catastrophe and win his brother over. He first takes defensive measures (vv 8–9), then prays (vv 10–13), and finally sends the most lavish series of presents to appease his brother (vv 14–22).

8–9   The Bible more often allows human feelings to be surmised than described. Here reticence is thrown aside as Jacob's reactions are portrayed: "Jacob was very frightened and distressed." This last phrase is unusual and is used for people in dire straits, e.g., when facing defeat (Judg 2:15; 10:9; 1 Sam 30:6; cf. 2 Sam 13:2). But fear does not paralyze Jacob; he acts decisively in an attempt at least to salvage something should Esau attack. Splitting his party into two camps may at least allow the rear one to escape. But the mention of two camps recalls the place he has just been to, "Mahanaim," lit. "two camps" (32:2–3[1–2]). There he had met angels evidently accompanying him. And the word "camp" (מַחֲנֶה) contains the consonants *ḥn* that spell "grace, favor" (חֵן), thus hinting that however fearful Jacob was, he was still accompanied by the protecting and gracious hand of providence.

10–13   Jacob's prayer. In prayer the worshiper's deepest feelings are revealed, so these verses are rightly regarded as most important for the understanding of this narrative. Indeed, Westermann regards it as the climax of Gen 31–33, even though he holds that it is largely a late insertion into the story. He finds the oldest part of the prayer in v 12 and considers vv 10–11, 13 to be expansions. However, his arguments for distinguishing older and later elements are not irresistible. He regards "Jacob said" as a poor introduction to a prayer and therefore redactional. But as Longacre (*Joseph*, 181–82) points out, this sort of quotation formula often introduces an emotional outburst, such as this prayer. Nor do the references to

the promises in vv 10, 13 suggest they are from a later hand than the main editor, for the promises are integral to the main theme of Genesis.

10 Jacob's earnestness is shown in his address to God. He invokes the "God of my father Abraham, and God of my father Isaac, O LORD," almost the same as the LORD's self-disclosure at Bethel (28:13). But usually such lengthy titles are avoided in human speech about God (cf. 28:20). By using this full title, Jacob seeks to recall all that God has done for his father and grandfather. Then he reminds the LORD that his present predicament is the result of obeying the divine command. "Return to your country and your clan" is an almost exact quote from 31:3 with the final clause "that I may be with you" paraphrased as "that I may do good for you."

11 Having implicitly recalled God's goodness to Abraham and Isaac, he now explicitly mentions what the LORD has done for him personally. Setting out with nothing, "just a staff," he has now become a very wealthy man having "two camps." "I am not worthy of all your mercies and faithfulness." The sentiments are characteristic of OT prayer (cf. 2 Sam 7:19; Gen 19:19; 24:12, 14; frequently in the Psalms).

12 If God has given Jacob so many good things in life to enjoy, are they now to be brought to nothing by the loss of life itself? So the heart of his petition is "Please rescue me" (on this term, see *Comment* on 31:9) "from my brother." The idea that brother should kill brother should fill God with horror (cf. 4:2–14), and even more so that defenseless women and children should suffer (a perennial concern of the law and the prophets: Exod 22:21[22]; Deut 14:29; Hos 10:14; Mal 3:5). To allow such slaughter would be incompatible with God's moral character.

13 But even more pertinent is that for God to allow it would be to renege on his promises. God has not simply promised to be with Jacob but to make his descendants very numerous (28:14). Indeed, Jacob harks back to the occasion when the LORD intervened to save Isaac's life and guaranteed that his descendants would be as numerous "as the sand of the sea" (22:17).

To regard this final plea of Jacob as an anticlimactic afterthought (so Westermann) is, as Delitzsch said, to misunderstand the nature of prayer. "To keep to His word the God who keeps His word is the way of all true prayer. Upon what else can Jacob rely but upon the promise of God, and how else can he do so but by praying?" (Delitzsch, 2:202).

14–22 These verses describe the urgent steps that Jacob took, apparently during the night (cf. vv 14, 22), to send a series of presents for Esau. Quite how his action is to be interpreted is unclear. To send a present to a great man before meeting him was a conventional courtesy in the ancient Orient (cf. 43:11). It could be that Jacob was, through this gesture, declaring himself Esau's vassal (cf. 2 Kgs 17:3; Hos 10:6; so Jacob), or even that he was symbolically returning the blessing he had stolen from Esau (cf. 33:11; cf. Josh 15:19; Judg 1:15). But whatever the symbolism, Jacob's motive was quite clear: "to mollify him. . . . Perhaps he will accept me" (v 21).

How does this frenetic activity square with his very pious prayer? Does it show he has little faith in God's power to save, or is it, as Calvin argues, a sign of his faith that Jacob did not sit back and do nothing (cf. Deut 20:3–4). The narrative leaves the question unanswered, allowing the possibility that Jacob's emotions were a mixture of faith, fear, and doubt. Cf. *Comment* on 22:5.

14 Jacob calls his gift a "present" (מנחה). That this word contains the consonants חן "favor, grace" has already been noted. In secular contexts, a present is
often a "gift that ingratiates," "a sweetener" (cf., e.g., 43:11; Judg 3:15), and, as Jacob
says, he was aiming to find favor with his brother (32:6; 33:8, 10). But מנחה is also
the term for a sacrifice, usually translated "the cereal offering" (Lev 2:1–14; cf. G.
J. Wenham, *Leviticus* [Grand Rapids: Eerdmans, 1979] 67–71). And it is noticeable
here that Jacob speaks in quasi-sacral terms of this present. It is designed to "mollify" "make atonement" (כפר) for him, so that he may be "accepted" (רצה; v 22),
which are both key terms in sacrificial texts (e.g., Lev 1:4). Finally, Jacob comments, "I have seen your face which is like seeing the face of God." Clearly, for Jacob
to make peace with his brother is to make peace with God (cf. Matt 5:24; 1 John
4:20).

15–16 Jacob made five herds of goats, sheep, camels, cattle, and donkeys—
in total, 550 animals, a princely present.

17–20 Each herd of animals is entrusted to servants. And each group of servants is given the same message: that they are a present "from your servant
Jacob . . . to my lord Esau." Evidently, Jacob hoped that after Esau had heard
this message five times, he might feel more kindly disposed toward him!

21 The sacrificial overtones of "mollify" and "accept" have already been noted.
Their exact meaning in sacrificial texts has been much discussed and is not of
great moment here. Probably "mollify" (piel of כפר) is related to the noun "ran-
som" from the same root. In OT law, some capital crimes could be commuted by
payment of a ransom (e.g., Exod 21:30). So the implication here may be that
Esau's deadly anger will be turned away by the payment of this handsome ran-
som. (For discussion of the term כפר, see *THWAT* 1:842–57; *TWAT* 4:303–18;
Wenham, *Leviticus,* 57–61; B. Janowski, *Sühne als Heilsgeschehen* [Neukirchen:
Neukirchener, 1982]; N. Kiuchi, *The Purification Offering in the Priestly Literature,*
JSOTSup 56 [Sheffield: JSOT, 1987] 87–109).

22 This scene ends with another mention of the "present" (מנחה) and the
"camp" (מחנה) with which it opened, vv 8–9, 14. Will it be peace or war? The very
words convey the uncertainty with which Jacob went to sleep.

23–24 This short scene describes how Jacob brought all his family across the
Yabbok (Arabic *ez-Zerqa*), a fast-flowing tributary of the Jordan, which flows westward to join the Jordan about twenty-five miles north of the Dead Sea. Evidently,
the herds had already crossed; only Jacob and his wives and children were left.

Two things are puzzling about this episode. Why did Jacob rise in the night
and cross the river at night? It would surely have been more sensible to do it by
day. And why, having taken his wives and children over, did he apparently return
to the other side, which seems to be implied by v 25, "And Jacob was left on his
own"? In the absence of any explanation in the text, we are left to conjecture. It
may be that his irrational actions represent his disturbed state of mind: he was
too worried to sleep, so he just decided to press on.

Sub-Bibliography on 32:25–33

Anderson, B. W. "An Exposition of Gen 32:22–32." *AusBR* 17 (1969) 21–26. **Barthes, R.**
"La lutte avec l'ange: analyse textuelle de Gen 32:23–33." In *Analyse structurale et exégèse*

biblique, ed. R. Barthes, F. Bovon, et al. Neuchâtel: Delachaux et Niestlé, 1971. 27–39. **Bauer, J. B.** "Jakobs Kampf mit dem Dämon (Gen 32:23–33)." In *Die Väter Israels: FS J. Scharbert,* ed. M. Görg. Stuttgart: Katholisches Bibelwerk, 1989. 17–22. **Blum, E.** "Die Komplexität der Überlieferung: Zur diachronen und synchronen Auslegung von Gen 32: 23–33." *DBAT* 15 (1980) 2–55. **Bodéüs, R.** "Parallèle pour l'interprétation du 'combat de Jacob.'" *OLP* 4 (1973) 135–40. **Brodie, L. T.** "Jacob's Travail (Jer 30:1–13) and Jacob's Struggle (Gen 32: 22–32): A Test Case for Measuring the Influence of the Book of Jeremiah on the Present Text of Genesis." *JSOT* 19 (1981) 31–60. **Butterweck, A.** *Jacobs Ringkampf am Jabbok, Gen 32:24f in der jüdischen Tradition bis zum Frühmittelalter.* Frankfurt: Lang, 1981. **Coote, R.** "The Meaning of the Name *Israel.*" *HTR* 65 (1972) 137–46. **Couffignal, R.** "Jacob lutte au Jabboq: Approches nouvelles de Gen 32:23–33." *RevThom* 75 (1975) 582–97. **Curtis, E. M.** "Structure, Style and Context as a Key to Interpreting Jacob's Encounter at Peniel." *JETS* 30 (1987) 129–37. **Diebner, B.** "Das Interesse der Überlieferung an Gen 32:23–33." *DBAT* 13 (1978) 14–52. **Dommershausen, W.** "Israel: Gott kämpft. Ein neuer Deutungsversuch zu Gen 32:21–33." *TTZ* 78 (1969) 321–34. **Durand, X.** "Le combat de Jacob (Gen 32:23–33): pour un bon usage des modèles narratifs." *Le point théologique* 24 (1977) 99–115. **Eissfeldt, O.** "Non dimittam te, nisi benedixeris mihi." *KS* 3. 412–16. **Elliger, K.** "Der Jakobskampf am Jabbok: Gen 32:33ff. als hermeneutisches Problem." *ZTK* 48 (1951) 1–31. **Eslinger, L. M.** "Hos 12:5a and Gen 32:29: A Study in Inner Biblical Exegesis." *JSOT* 18 (1980) 91–99. ———. "The Case of an Immodest Lady Wrestler in Deut 25:11–12." *VT* 31 (1981) 269–81. **Fass, D. E.** "Jacob's Limp?" *Judaism* 38 (1989) 143–50. **Floss, J. P.** "Wer schlägt wen? Textanalytische Interpretation von Gen 32:23–33." *BN* 20 (1983) 92–132; 21 (1983) 66–100. **Geller, S. A.** "The Struggle at the Jabbok: The Uses of Enigma in a Biblical Narrative." *JANESCU* 14 (1982) 37–60. **Gevirtz, S.** "Of Patriarchs and Puns: Joseph at the Fountain, Jacob at the Ford." *HUCA* 46 (1975) 33–54. **Hermisson, H.-J.** "Jakobs Kampf am Jabbok (Gen 32:23–33)." *ZTK* 71 (1974) 239–61. **Holmgren, F. C.** "Holding Your Own against God! Gen 32:22–32 (In the Context of Gen 31–33)." *Int* 44 (1990) 5–17. **Kodell, J.** "Jacob Wrestles with Esau (Gen 32:23–32)." *BTB* 10 (1980) 65–70. **Lund, J. A.** "On the Interpretation of the Palestinian Targumic Reading *wqht* in Gen 32:25." *JBL* 105 (1986) 99–103. **McKay, H. A.** "Jacob Makes It across the Jabbok: An Attempt to Solve the Success/ Failure Ambivalence in Israel's Self-Consciousness." *JSOT* 38 (1987) 3–13. **McKenzie, J. L.** "Jacob at Peniel: Gen 32:24–32." *CBQ* 25 (1963) 71–76. **McKenzie, S.** "'You Have Prevailed': The Function of Jacob's Encounter at Peniel in the Jacob Cycle." *ResQ* 23 (1980) 225–31. **Martin-Achard, R.** "Un exégète devant Gen 32:23–33." In *Analyse structurale et exégèse biblique,* ed. R. Barthes, F. Bovon, et al. Neuchâtel: Delachaux et Niestlé, 1971. 41–62. **Meier, S. A.** *The Messenger in the Ancient Semitic World.* HSM 45. Atlanta: Scholars, 1988. **Pury, A. de.** "Jacob am Jabbok, Gen 32:32–33, im Licht einer alt-irischen Erzählung." *TZ* 35 (1979) 18–34. **Ross, A. P.** "Jacob at the Jabbok, Israel at Peniel." *BSac* 142 (1985) 338–54. **Roth, W.** "Structural Interpretations of 'Jacob at the Jabbok.'" *BR* 22 (1977) 51–62. **Shearman, S. L.,** and **Curtis, J. B.** "Divine-Human Conflicts in the OT." *JNES* 28 (1969) 231–42. **Tsevat, M.** "Two OT Stories and Their Hittite Analogues." *JAOS* 103 (1983) 321–26. **Utzschneider, H.** "Das hermeneutische Problem der Uneindeutigkeit biblischer Texte—dargestellt an Text und Rezeption der Erzählung von Jakob am Jabbok (Gen 32:23–33)." *EvT* 48 (1988) 182–98. **Weber, B.** "Nomen est Omen: Einige Erwägungen zu Gen 32:23–33 und seinem Kontext." *BN* 61 (1992) 76–83. **Weimar, P.** "Beobachtungen zur Analyse von Gen 32:23–33." *BN* 49 (1989) 53–81; 50 (1989) 58–94. ———. "'O Israel, Erstling im Morgengrauenkampf' (Nelly Sachs): Zu Funktion und Theologie der Gotteskampfepisode Gen 32:23–33." *MTZ* 40 (1989) 79–113. **Weis, R. D.** "Lessons on Wrestling with the Unseen: Jacob at the Jabbok." *Reformed Review* 42 (1989) 96–112.

Form/Structure/Setting on 32:25–33

32:25–33 constitutes the fourth, and therefore the central, scene in the sequence of seven that describe the return of Jacob to Canaan. Its mysteriousness and the critical problems it poses have led to much discussion.

First, it should be noted with, most recently, Geller (*JANESCU* 14 [1982] 37–60), Blum (*Die Komposition*), Coats, and Westermann that this episode is an integral part of J's account of Jacob. It includes the key words "cross" (עבר) and "face" (פנים), which appear frequently in this context (32:17, 21–24, 31–32; 33:3, 10, 14). The theme of blessing (32:27, 30) is another key word of the Jacob cycle. In chap. 27, Jacob obtains a blessing from his father; here, it comes from God himself. Also, as already noted, the encounter with the "man" (i.e., God) anticipates Jacob's meeting with Esau ("I have seen your face which is like seeing the face of God," 33:10; cf. 32:31). And the transformation of Jacob into Israel, the father of the nation, that takes place here is momentous. The man who cheated his brother out of his blessing is now concerned that he is about to meet that brother again and prays to God not to leave him in the lurch. "The night attack, the life and death struggle, and finally the unexpected conclusion, the gracious blessing and bestowal of a new name, that is . . . God's answer to the deceiver Jacob . . . , whereby God's sovereignty and faithfulness to his promise despite all human unworthiness is demonstrated. Jacob is no longer the strong victorious controller of the divine but Israel who is totally dependent on God's grace and lame" (de Pury, *TZ* 35 [1979] 18).

Contrary to many earlier critics who attempted to distinguish two sources, it is now recognized following the work of Barthes that the tale is a substantial unity conforming to the outline of many folk tales, with perhaps a few later additions.

Barthes ("La lutte," 35) points out that the central part of the scene consists of a dialogue in which new names are given:

v 28, God asks Jacob's name—Jacob's reply—v 29, Name changed
v 30, Jacob asks God's name—Indirect reply—v 31, Place name changed to Peniel

Furthermore, Barthes (38) observed that the whole story contains many of the features of the typical folk tale as distinguished by Propp:

Move to new place	cf. 31:17, Jacob moved from Paddan-Aram
Struggle between hero and antagonist	cf. 32:25–28
Hero receives bodily wound	cf. 32:26–33, Jacob's limp
Victory of hero	cf. 32:27
End of bad luck or need	cf. 32:32, Jacob passes Peniel and reaches Shechem in Canaan (33:18)

De Pury (*TZ* 35 [1979] 18–34) has noted how many of the features of this story correspond to an old Irish (pre-Christian) story, which make it plausible to suppose the substantial integrity of 32:25–33, and that any later additions must be quite minor. A similar suggestion has been made about a Hittite text by Tsevat (*JAOS* 103 [1983] 321–22).

The scene falls into three parts:

vv 25–26	Description of the fight
vv 27–31	Dialogue
	Naming Israel (27–29)
	Naming of Peniel (30–31)
vv 32–33	Departure and Etiological comment (33)

This analysis shows that the emphasis of the story is on the names Israel and Peniel.

Much speculation has been devoted to reconstructing earlier forms of the tradition. Parallels with other tales of night attacks by river demons are often cited to explain the origin of the story. But as Eissfeldt (*KS* 3, 414–16) has pointed out, Jacob does not encounter a localized deity but El, supreme creator God in the Semitic pantheon (32:31; 33:20). Nor is the nature of Jacob's experience very clear. It does not seem to have been just a dream, nor can it be spiritualized into wrestling in prayer; it does appear that a real fight was involved, for Jacob went on his way limping (32:32). But having said that, the nature of the experience still remains mysterious, as all encounters with God must necessarily be.

Comment

25–26 The brief account of the fight is tantalizingly obscure, raising as many questions as it answers.

"Jacob was left alone." It is not clear why Jacob should have brought his family across the Yabbok and then returned to the northern side alone. Was it duty, or anxiety, or simply to inform us that there was none of his party with him when he was attacked?

"A man struggled with him" describes the attack from Jacob's point of view; he is assaulted by an unidentifiable male and has to fight for his life. The verb "he struggled" (ויאבק) occurs only here and in v 26 and is clearly a play on the name Yabbok (יבק), and probably Jacob too (יעקב). So we could paraphrase it "he Yabboked him" or "he Jacobed him"! The form the struggle took is left unspecified. אבק is often said to be a by-form of חבק "to embrace" (cf. 29:13; 33:4), a friendly gesture, but there is nothing friendly about this encounter.

Gunkel, von Rad, and Westermann are among those who suggest that originally this was an account of Jacob's encounter with a Canaanite river god. And this they hold is confirmed by the "man's" desire to depart before dawn, a regular feature of folk tale. However, as Eissfeldt (*KS* 3, 412–16) observed, the story actually identifies the opponent as El, the supreme Canaanite creator god, while in other dangerous encounters with the divine (by Moses, Exod 4:24–26; Balaam, Num 22:22–35; Josh 5:13–16), the unrecognized foe is the LORD or his angel, and often in Genesis the LORD is equated with El (See *Introduction,* "The Religion of the Patriarchs"). The reference to dawn indicates first that the struggle continued a good while, and second explains why Jacob was unaware of his foe's identity and indeed took him on. Had he realized that his enemy was divine, he would never have engaged him in a fight.

26 The absence of explicit subjects and objects has confused some readers, but this verse may be expanded as follows: "The man realized that he could not win, so he touched Jacob's hip socket." For the Israelite reader knowing the man's

identity, the first clause, "he could not win," must have sounded astonishing. For Jacob, it was amazing that his opponent merely by touching his hip could dislocate it, or numb it. Lund (*JBL* 105 [1986] 99–103) notes "numb" is the translation preferred by the versions. Westermann regards the clause "and Jacob's hip was dislocated . . ." as a later addition. But there are no grounds for the supposition, save that Jacob continues to fight in the next verse. Rather, this clause gives an insight into Jacob's situation. A touch that dislocates indicates an opponent with superhuman power (cf. Isa 6:7). But that apparently gives Jacob yet more determination to fight on; indeed, he forces his opponent into speaking and disclosing something of his identity.

27 Why did the "man" demand to be let go before dawn broke? The midrash says the angel wished to keep his appointment to sing in the heavenly choir. Modern commentators generally note the similar request made by Jupiter: "Why do you hold me? It is time. I want to get out of the city before daybreak" (Plautus, *Amphitryon* 532–33). Both these ideas seem to read too much into the words, while the commentator Jacob (following Rashbam, Hiskuni, and Abrabanel) seems to see too little when he paraphrases, "Let me go, for it is time for you to give up." Rather, it indicates a desire to continue to hide his identity. It may also hint at the idea that no man can see God and live (cf. v 31; Exod 33:20). At any rate, it is another hint to Jacob of the supernatural character of his opponent. So as always, Jacob, the man supremely interested in blessing, demands one here; otherwise, he will not let go.

28 To bestow a blessing, the blesser must know who he is blessing. But for an angel to ask Jacob's name is superfluous. However, by divulging his name, Jacob also discloses his character. It is here a confession of guilt; as Jeremiah puts it, "Every brother Jacobs [RSV, is a supplanter]" (Jer 9:3[4]). In uttering his name, Jacob admits he has cheated his brother; cf. "Is he not rightly called Jacob? He has tricked me these two times" (27:36).

29 But instead of merely blessing him, his opponent changes Jacob's name, thus announcing Jacob's new character and destiny. Similarly, Abram's name was changed to Abraham and Sarai's to Sarah to presage the long-awaited fulfillment of the promise of the birth of a son (17:5, 15). Here Jacob's rebaptism as Israel is equally significant, for Israel is of course the name of the nation, and in granting it, Jacob's opponent reveals the true import of the encounter, "for you have struggled with God and with men and have overcome."

The etymology of Israel offered by the text relates יִשְׂרָאֵל "Israel" to the verb שָׂרָה "to struggle, fight." So the word literally means "El (God) fights." This is not exactly the same as "you have struggled with God," but it should be remembered that popular etymologies in the Bible generally take the form of a play on a name rather than a precise historical etymology. It has also been thought that the notion of "God fighting" is incompatible with Israelite theology, so that the real meaning of Israel must be different. So Geller (*JANESCU* 14 [1982] 53), following the Greek translators (LXX, Aquila, Symmachus) and the Vulgate, relates it to שָׂרַר "to rule, be strong," and E. Jacob (*Theology of the OT*, 203) links Israel with יָשָׁר "just, right," comparing the other ancient poetic name Jeshurun (Deut 32:15; 33:5, 26). Albright (*JBL* 46 [1927] 159) suggested it was related to Ethiopic and Arabic stems meaning "to heal"; hence the word means "God heals." R. B. Coote

(*HTR* 65 [1972] 140) relates it to the noun מִשְׂרָה, usually translated "government" (e.g., Isa 9:6[5]); hence he explains the name as "El judges," which is very similar to M. Noth's earlier suggestion (*Personennamen*, 208), "May God rule."

But as Ross observes, "these other suggestions are no more compelling than the popular etymology given in the text of Genesis. . . . The concept of God's fighting with someone is certainly no more of a problem than the passage itself. And the reversal of the emphasis (from 'God fights' to 'fight with God') in the explanation is because of the nature of popular etymologies, which are satisfied with a wordplay on the sound or meaning of the name to express its significance" (*BSac* 142 [1985] 348–49).

His old name, Jacob, recalled his past underhand dealings; his new name, Israel, recalled this incident in which he wrestled with God and prevailed. "Thus his renaming as Israel is not merely an honourable accolade, it is itself a valuable gift, a blessing" (Dillmann, 357). Whenever his descendants heard this name, or used it to describe themselves, they were reminded of its origin and of its meaning, that as their father had triumphed in his struggle with men (i.e., Esau and Laban) and with God, so they too could eventually hope to triumph. Within this episode, of course, his new name is a guarantee of a successful meeting with his brother Esau.

30 The encounter ends as mysteriously as it began. The "man" now implicitly identified with God (cf. v 29) refuses to give his name, lest it be abused (cf. Judg 13:17–18; Exod 20:7), and then he blesses Jacob. Then he disappears in the dark as suddenly as he came.

31 Elsewhere (v 32; Judg 8:8–9, 17; 1 Kgs 12:25) Peniel is called Penuel. The form Peniel may be used here because it sounds more like "face of God." Its location is uncertain, save that it lies close to the southern bank of the Yabbok somewhere between Mahanaim and Succoth. That it lies between these other towns is confirmed by the passages in Judges and by Shishak's list of conquered towns. In Jeroboam I's time it was an important administrative center. The likeliest candidate for Penuel is Tel edh-Dhahab a Shaki (B. Oded, *EM* 6:509–11), which stands on the bank of the Yabbok opposite western Tel edh-Dhahab (= Mahanaim) (cf. Lemaire, *VT* 31 [1981] 50–52).

But for Jacob the most important aspect of the encounter is that "I have seen God face to face, and yet my life was rescued." Seeing God puts man in mortal danger (cf. Exod 33:20; Isa 6:5). The phrase "was rescued" harks back to v 12, and so Jacob confesses that his prayer for deliverance from Esau is answered. If he has survived meeting God, he will survive his meeting with Esau.

32 The rising of the sun (cf. vv 25, 27) marks the passing of the time and the dawn of a new era in Jacob's career. But he limps past Penuel, witnessing to the reality of his nocturnal encounter and showing that although in one sense he was victorious, God had left his mark on him. He was not totally self-sufficient.

33 Nowhere else in the OT is this custom of not eating the sciatic nerve (*nervus ischiadicus*) mentioned. Nor does it feature in later Jewish law, so Westermann's contention that it is a late insertion into the story is unlikely. But like the rite of circumcision, instituted when Abram's name was changed, and the other food laws (see G. J. Wenham, *Leviticus*, 170), this custom was a reminder of the nation's election. By refraining from eating this sinew, the Israelites were constantly

reminded of Jacob's meeting with God and the promise of ultimate victory and blessing he wrung from God then.

1–15 This great scene describes the long-dreaded meeting of Jacob and Esau. As befits the peak of the story, there is retardation with repetitious detail in vv 1–3 before the sudden rush of verbs describing Esau's warm greeting of his brother in v 4. Then comes a rather stilted discussion between the brothers, reflecting Jacob's uncertainty that he has really been accepted by Esau and his consequent reluctance to trust him entirely (vv 5–15).

1 At last Jacob sees Esau. Note how the narrator signals the momentousness by saying "Jacob *raised* his eyes and saw" (cf. 22:4, 13; 24:64). "With four hundred men" as already so ominously reported in 32:7. "So he divided the children," the same word, חצה "split," as in 32:8. Is Jacob still acting out of craven fear?

2 Is he arranging his family in this order so that those whom he loves most, Rachel and Joseph, may stand the best chance of escape, with himself last of all in the procession so that he can head the flight? This was clearly his motive in 32:8–22. Or is he arranging his family in order of precedence, so that they may be presented to prince Esau in the correct way? We are left to wonder.

3 But "he himself went on ahead of them" shows us the new Israel triumphing over the old fear-dominated Jacob. What is more, "he bowed down seven times until he reached his brother." Sevenfold bowing was the proper act of respect of a vassal to his overlord, as the Amarna letters show (e.g., 137, 244, 250; *ANET* 483–85). The term "prostrate" occurs frequently in Genesis as the proper gesture toward high officials (23:7, 12; 42:6; 43:26, 28; cf. 37:7, 9, 10) and toward God or his angels (18:2; 19:1; 22:5). But here it seems to echo Isaac's blessing of Jacob (27:29), which Isaac meant for Esau.

> "May . . . nations *bow down* before you.
> . . . may *your mother's sons bow down before you*."

In bowing down before his brother, Jacob is doing more than acknowledging Esau's lordship; he is trying to undo the great act of deception whereby he cheated Esau of his blessing. Throughout this scene, he insists on making presents to Esau in an attempt to return to him the blessing (cf. 33:11) that should have been his.

4 And how warmly Esau responds. Now there is no hint of the murderous bitterness with which they parted (27:41–42). Instead, he greets Jacob with all the warmth of a long-lost brother. The terms used here, "running" (24:17; 29:12, 13), "embracing" (29:13; 48:10), falling "on the neck" (45:14), and "weeping" (29:11; 45:14, 15; 46:29), are the normal ways of greeting relatives in the Bible. But note here "and *they* wept." When Jacob joins in weeping with Esau, the ice is broken; the brothers are reconciled, and verbal communication can begin.

5–7 Esau opens the conversation as befits the superior party by asking about Jacob's wives and children. And despite the fact that they are brothers, Jacob maintains his deferential posture by constantly referring to himself as "your servant" and to Esau as "my lord" (vv 5, 8, 13, 14, 15). He introduces his family in groups, who in turn prostrate themselves, thereby once again reversing the blessing of 27:29.

But most striking of all is Jacob's first reply to Esau: "The children with whom God has favored your servant." Here a key word "favor" (חנן, verb), חן in this

narrative, appears for the second time (cf. 32:6; 33:8, 10, 11, 15). It is striking that a third of the seventeen references in Genesis to this term occur in these two chapters on the lips of Jacob. It might rather have been expected that Jacob would have said "the children with whom God has blessed me." Not only is the root "to bless" much more common (88x) in Genesis, but Jacob is preeminently the man who seeks blessing (cf. chap. 27 and 32:27). Yet here he avoids using the word "bless." Westermann suggests that Jacob uses the word "favor" here rather than "bless" because it includes the idea of forgiveness, which is absent from bless. But it may also well be that he wants to avoid any reference to that unhappy day when he cheated Esau out of his blessing. By word and gesture, prostrating himself and giving gifts, he is trying to undo his sins of many years earlier.

8–11 The conversation continues with Esau in jovial mood, whereas Jacob is earnestly deferential. Esau jocularly puns, "What is all this camp (מחנה *mḥnh*) that I have encountered?" Doubtless he realized Jacob was sending him a present (מנחה *mnḥh*; cf. 32:14, 19, 21; 33:10), for Jacob had told his servants to explain that they were a gift (32:19). But the pun touched Jacob, for originally he had divided his possessions into "camps" so that they could escape, should Esau attack (32:8, 9, 11).

So Jacob quietly explains again "to find favor [חן] with my lord."

9–10 Now the exchange becomes more heated; note the introductions, *Esau said/Jacob said*. Jacob finally persuades Esau to accept, because as he says, "I have seen your face which is like seeing the face of God, and you have accepted me." The verb "accept" (רצה) is an important sacrificial term used to describe God's receiving of sacrifice (e.g., Lev 1:4; 7:18; 19:7). Jacob's argument is that since you have received me with forgiveness as God has, so you must accept my "present," a term also used for sacrifice (e.g., 4:3–5; Lev 2:1, 3–7), as God would.

11 Indeed you must receive back the blessing that I stole from you, because God has given me more than enough.

This was too much for Esau, but Jacob insists, for doubtless he felt he could not be sure of Esau's forgiveness if he refused his attempt to make amends. "He pressed him" is a very strong term, as its use elsewhere (19:3, 9; Judg 19:7; 2 Kgs 2:17; 5:16) shows. But eventually Esau gave in: "he took it."

12–15 Esau responds to Jacob's gift of herds by offering him land, by inviting him to come with him to the land of Seir (v 12). But Jacob courteously, note "my lord" (vv 13–15), rejects the offer, ostensibly because his group of children and animals could not keep up with Esau's band of warriors (v 13). But is that his only motive? His refusal, according to von Rad, shows "the mistrust of one who himself has often deceived" (328). Calvin suggests that perhaps Esau's charity would not last, and ere long some new cause of conflict might arise between them. There could be a theological reason too; Jacob is returning at the LORD's instruction to his homeland of Canaan, which does not include Seir (cf. 31:3, 13; 32:10). These different motives are not mutually exclusive, and the uncertainty in which the narrative leaves us is no doubt deliberate. Relations between Israel and Edom were uncertain at the best of times.

14 In the light of Jacob's actual journey, this remark seems somewhat disingenuous. It is clearly a very polite way of saying he is not coming to Esau's place now; "until I come to my lord in Seir" leaves his time of arrival quite indeterminate.

Indeed, the use of singular "I" could be construed as implying that not all the party will come there anyway.

15 Even Esau's offer of a bodyguard is politely turned down, whether out of fear or faith (God had often promised to be with Jacob, e.g., 31:3; 32:10) being again left open. What matters is that he has found "favor."

16–17 On this very positive note, they go their own ways (cf. 32:1–2). Seir is the traditional homeland of the Edomites (cf. 36:8 and *Comment* on 14:6).

17 According to the Jerusalem Talmud (*t. Šeb.* 9.2), Succoth is to be identified with Tell Deir ʾAlla. An alternative is Tell Ekhsas, which literally means "booths." Both sites are in the eastern Jordan valley and just over a mile apart, north of the Yabbok. This is perhaps surprising in that the text says nothing about Jacob recrossing the Yabbok, so it could be that neither of the sites is correct (cf. Jacob). However, it is said that Jacob built a house there, which may suggest that he spent a good while there (certainly by chap. 34 his children have grown up), so the itinerary may be rather compressed. Succoth is also mentioned in Josh 13:27; Judg 8:5–6, 8, 14–16; Pss 60:8(6); 108:8(7). Here the main point of the comment is etiological, to explain the origin of the name Succoth and to note its connection with the patriarch.

18–20 As already noted in *Form/Structure/Setting*, these verses form both the conclusion to chaps. 32–33 and a prelude to chap. 34. They constitute an expanded itinerary, as in 12:5–9; 13:1–4; 26:22–25. And though the comments seem mundane, they are of immense significance, for they record that eventually Jacob did reach Canaan after returning from Paddan-Aram. He also bought land there and built an altar. Throughout the whole Jacob cycle, the return to Canaan from Paddan-Aram has always been the goal; now it has been reached, so the promises have been fulfilled—a most fitting end to his wanderings (28:2, 5–6, 15; 30:25; 31:3, 13, 18; 32:10[9]). But as the mention of Shechem hints, things are not to work out quite as smoothly as he might have hoped.

18 "Then Jacob came to Salem, the city of Shechem." Here Shechem is to be understood as a personal name, not the city called Shechem mentioned elsewhere (e.g., 12:6; 35:4). However, many commentators following the Samaritan Pentateuch translate this sentence "Then Jacob came in peace to the city called Shechem," seeing this as the fulfillment of Jacob's prayer in 28:21. Now while Hebrew שלם "to Salem" could be translated "in peace," nowhere else in the OT is it used in this way as an adverb qualifying a verb. And elsewhere in the phrase "the city of X," X is usually the name of someone who lives in the city, such as its king, rather than the name of the city itself (e.g., 24:10; Num 21:26–27; 22:36; 1 Sam 15:5). Finally, the ancient versions all regard "Salem" as a place name, and it may be identified with the modern village of "Salim" about three miles east of Tel Balata (biblical Shechem). Nevertheless, in that Genesis often plays on proper names, there may be a hint of irony in this comment. The city called "peaceful" was to be the scene of the bitterest strife in the patriarchal narrative (34:30; cf. a similar irony in Noah's name, 5:29; 6:6–8, and *Comments*).

19 This verse reinforces the atmosphere of peaceful security suggested by the name "Salem." Whereas Abraham bought land from the "sons of Heth" only after tense negotiations for humanitarian purposes, the burial of his wife, Jacob bought land (the same root קנה in 25:10; 49:30; 50:13) just to camp on, not for

four hundred shekels (23:15) but for one hundred qesita from the "sons of Hamor." These points of similarity and difference are significant. They do suggest good relations between Jacob and the sons of Hamor. Unfortunately, we do not know the relative worth of the shekel and qesita. If the qesita was smaller than the shekel, it would suggest greater generosity on the part of the Hamorites. If, on the other hand, it was worth considerably more, and Job 42:11 may support this, it would show the greater wealth of Jacob and imply he acquired even more land from the Canaanites than his grandfather had.

20 At any rate, his arrival in the promised land and his purchase of substantial real estate there prompted him to worship just as his forefathers had done (12:7–8; 13:18; 26:25; 35:7).

"He erected an altar." Elsewhere the verb usually used of altar construction is בנה "to build," whereas the word used here, הציב "erect," is twice used in Genesis of setting up sacred pillars (e.g., 35:14, 20). This hardly proves (*pace* Westermann) that the text originally spoke of Jacob erecting a pillar, for this verb is also used of erecting a pile of stones (2 Sam 18:17), but it may allude to those other great moments in his career when Jacob did erect such standing stones (cf. 28:18; 35:14, 20).

In calling the altar "El, the God of Israel," Jacob acknowledges that the creator God who had changed his name at the Yabbok to Israel was now his God, and by implication his descendants' God too. He had vowed at Bethel that if the LORD brought him back to his father's house in peace, "the LORD will be my God" (28:21). He has yet to reach Bethel, where he will fulfill the rest of the vow, but by naming this altar he is reaffirming his allegiance to El and declaring that El is Israel's God.

Explanation

This account of Jacob and Esau's reconciliation is another high point in Genesis. It is tense and dramatic; it is also puzzling and enigmatic. It apparently brings the sad story of fraternal strife to a happy and joyful resolution. It brings the exiled Jacob back to his homeland, the promised land of Canaan. Jacob's new name Israel presages a new character at peace with God and man. But as the closing scenes suggest, his relations with Esau remain uneasy, and the friendly Canaanites will soon prove to be the cause of Jacob's greatest shame. As often in Genesis, the narrative illustrates the triumph of the divine promises despite human folly and fallibility.

The first scene (vv 4–7) shows Jacob attempting for the first time in twenty years to make contact with his brother Esau, now living in Seir, in southern Transjordan. His message, couched in excessively deferential language, "my lord Esau, your servant Jacob," suggests a guilty conscience and his fear of possible revenge. He deliberately omits any reference to the reason for his long sojourn with Laban, simply suggesting that it was because he was doing so well in business there. Now, after his absence, he wishes to find favor with Esau. But the embassy returns with no certainty about Esau's intentions, simply that he has four hundred men with him.

Realizing that mere words may not be enough to mollify his brother, Jacob now adopts desperate measures to win him over. The second scene (32:8–21)

shows Jacob in a panic, first taking immediate defensive measures to protect his party (vv 8–10), then praying earnestly (vv 10–13), and finally sending a series of generous presents to Esau (vv 14–22) to appease him. Jacob's prayer, one of the longest in Genesis, highlights many of the theological emphases that recur in the book. It is God who has put him in his present predicament, "who said to me, 'Return to your country,'" and promised to care for him "that I may do good for you." He recalls the LORD's past goodness both by calling him "the God of my father Abraham" and by listing the ways he has flourished and prospered since he left home. But now everything could come to a sorry end, so he pleads, "Please rescue me from the hand of my brother"—do not let him kill me as Cain murdered Abel or even worse "kill the mother with the children" (v 12). Thus Jacob appeals to God's compassion, but finally he reverts to God's promise, for "it is *you* who have said that I shall indeed do good for you and make your descendants as numerous as the sand of the sea." Jacob's prayer, with its appeal to God's mercy and promises, is typical of prayers in Scripture (Exod 32:11–13; Josh 7:6–9; Neh 1:5–11; 9:6–37), not least in the so-called psalms of lament (e.g., Pss 7, 17, 22, 26).

Neither paralyzed by fear nor made complacent by faith, Jacob now acts decisively to appease his brother's wrath. He sends five different herds or flocks ahead as gifts to his brother. He describes them in religious terms, as "a present" (a type of sacrifice) designed to "mollify" Esau so that "he will accept me"; the use of these key terms drawn from the language of sacrificial worship shows Jacob's keenness to make peace with his brother and to atone for his past misdeeds (vv 14–22).

But will his prayers be answered or his presents accepted? Jacob's great anxiety is hinted at by the comment in the next short scene (vv 23–24), "he rose that night." Before the age of artificial lighting, it was extraordinary to undertake something as risky as a river crossing by night. But Jacob does; he cannot bear the strain of waiting any longer. He must press on to meet his brother. He crosses the Yabbok.

Then the unexpected strikes. Having safely brought his family across the fast-flowing Yabbok, he finds himself alone struggling single-handedly with an unknown man. The darkness of the scene is matched by the opacity of the narrative. The reader is allowed to see no more than Jacob. The identity of Jacob's unknown opponent is as obscure to modern readers as it was to Jacob. At first he just thought he was fighting a man, for he seemed to be winning. But when the man touched his hip socket and dislocated it, Jacob began to wonder. Despite his injury or because of it, he determined to fight on, even when his strange opponent asked to be let go, "for the dawn has broken." Jacob, as quick as ever to make spiritual profit out of other people's difficulty (or was it because he sensed his adversary's supernatural power?), insists on receiving a blessing before he will let his enemy go. Throughout his career, Jacob had been determined to acquire blessing by fair means or foul; he had deprived his brother Esau of both his birthright and his blessing. And now on the eve of his first meeting with Esau since that fateful episode (chap. 27), Jacob is portrayed as still anxious to acquire blessing: he does not seem to have changed.

But instead of simply acceding to his demand, the adversary asks his name. "Jacob" he replies, thereby admitting his grimy past. From the womb he clutched his brother's heel (25:26). And later Esau ruefully commented, "Is he not rightly called Jacob? He has cheated me these two times. My right as the firstborn he

took away and just now he has taken away my blessing" (27:36). Now, instead of Jacob, he is renamed Israel, "God fights" or "God rules," "for you have struggled with God and with men and have overcome." Names throughout Scripture are significant, but changes of name in midlife are specially so (cf. Abram/Abraham and Sarai/Sarah in 17:5, 15). Here Jacob's new name was to become the nation's name, and it is fraught with significance.

As often in the Bible, the historical etymology of a name does not exactly match the significance assigned it by the biblical writers. Israel, "God fights or rules," is here reinterpreted as a reference to *Jacob's struggle with God*. Yet this reinterpretation captures the paradox of Jacob's struggle precisely. For while Jacob struggled with God, it was God who allowed Jacob to triumph in the fight. In a similar way, the LORD tested Abraham yet provided a ram for the burnt offering (22:1–14). Later, Moses' deadly encounter with the LORD prefigured the divine deliverance from Egypt (Exod 4:24–26). Jacob's experience at the Yabbok, wrestling with God and yet surviving, was in later times seen as prefiguring the national experience (Hos 12:5). Running through the psalms of national lament there is a similar conviction that the nation's trials are heaven-sent; yet only from heaven can they look for deliverance (e.g., Pss 74, 79, 80, 83). So this story of Jacob's struggle with God summed up for Israel their national destiny. Among all their trials and perplexities in which God seemed to be fighting against them, he was ultimately on their side; indeed, he would triumph, and in his victory, Israel would triumph too.

The church, too, faces testing and struggle. Indeed, we pray, "Lead us not into temptation, but deliver us from evil," thereby acknowledging that God may allow us to be put in testing situations, but through his grace we may overcome them. So Calvin (2:196) aptly comments on the parallels between our experience and Jacob's: "What was once exhibited under a visible form to our father Jacob is daily fulfilled in the individual members of the church, namely in their temptations it is necessary for them to wrestle with God. He is said, indeed, to tempt us in a different manner from Satan; but because he alone is the Author of our crosses and afflictions, . . . he is said to tempt us when he makes trial of our faith . . . . He having challenged us to this contest at the same time furnishes us with means of resistance, so that he both fights *against* us and *for* us. In short, such is his apportioning of this conflict that while he assails us with one hand, he defends us with the other; yea, in as much as he supplies us with more strength to resist than he employs in opposing us, we may truly and properly say, that he fights *against* us with his *left* hand, and *for* us with his *right* hand. For while he lightly opposes us, he supplies invincible strength whereby we overcome."

The stranger's explanation of the name Israel, "you have struggled with God and with men and have overcome," prompts Jacob to inquire about his identity. But he refuses to disclose it. Instead, he blesses Jacob. Then Jacob realizes that he has been wrestling with God, and his demanding pushiness turns to awe, "I have seen God face to face and yet my life was rescued" (v 31). Earlier he had prayed to be rescued from his brother Esau (v 12); now he gives thanks that he has survived the much more dangerous encounter with God, for as the OT repeatedly shows, meeting God unprepared is often fatal (Lev 10; 2 Sam 6). And as perpetual reminders of his experience, Jacob names the place Peniel, "face of God," and decrees that from henceforth his descendants should not eat the sciatic nerve.

The Peniel episode has delayed the climax of the narrative, the reunion of the brothers, but has at the same time prepared the way for it. Jacob is now a new man, Israel; his encounter with God has prepared him to meet Esau, as Jacob himself stresses by comparing Esau to God (vv 10–11). The new character of Israel is soon apparent. Courage replaces cowardice as Jacob himself strides ahead of his family to meet Esau (v 3). Humility takes the place of arrogance as he bows down seven times before his brother (v 3). And penitence prompts him to attempt to give back the blessing out of which he had cheated Esau (vv 10–11). Through his Peniel experience, Jacob has been reborn as Israel.

Esau, too, has changed. When last heard of, he had been waiting for his father to die, so that he could take his revenge on Jacob and kill him. But here, completely unexpectedly, "he ran to meet Jacob, embraced him, fell on his neck, kissed him, and they wept" (v 4). He is most reluctant to accept Jacob's gifts, arguing that he has more than enough to keep him happy (v 9). He warmly invites Jacob to come and live with him in Seir (vv 12, 14–15). Such warmth after so many years of hatred makes this scene one of the most beautiful in Scripture. The full and free forgiveness that Esau displays toward his deceitful brother is, as Jacob himself recognizes, a model of divine love, "for I have seen your face, which is like seeing the face of God, and you have accepted me" (v 10). Indeed, Jesus seems to allude to this scene when he describes the father of the prodigal son greeting his return, "his father ran and embraced him and kissed him" (Luke 15:20), a theme taken up by Paul in commenting on God's work of reconciliation in Christ (2 Cor 5:16–21). And, of course, the duty of making peace with your brother is stressed throughout Scripture (Lev 19:17–18; Ps 133; Prov 17:9, 17; Matt 5:21–26; 1 John 4:12–21).

But his new birth at Peniel did not obliterate the past or completely change Jacob's character; the new Israel still had features of the old Jacob. He does not seem entirely to trust Esau's warmth; the old fears and suspicions still lurk there, as he refuses to accompany him immediately to Seir. More charitably, one may surmise that in obedience to God Jacob may have felt obliged to return to Canaan (cf. 31:3; 32:10), but the way he justifies his refusal (vv 13–15) suggests his motives are not entirely pure. But, for whatever reasons, Jacob returns to Canaan, makes his home there, buys land, and worships El, the God of Israel. At last, he and the narrative have reached their destination; Israel has settled in Canaan, the land promised to his forefather Abraham. This seems the right place to end the story of Jacob, but as so often in Genesis, what promises to be the ultimate resolution proves to be the making of another crisis.

Dinah and the Hivites   (34:1–31)

Bibliography

Caspi, M. M. "'And his soul clave unto Dinah' (Gen 34): The Story of the Rape of Dinah, the Narrator and the Reader." *AJBI* 11 (1985) 16–53. ————. "The Story of the Rape

of Dinah: The Narrator and the Reader." *HS* 26 (1985) 25–45. **Collins, J. J.** "The Epic of Theodotus and the Hellenism of the Hasmoneans." *HTR* 73 (1980) 91–104. **Diebner, B. J.** "Gen 34 und Dinas Rolle bei der Definition 'Israels.'" *DBAT* 19 (1984) 59–76. **Fensham, F. C.** "Gen 34 and Mari." *JNSL* 4 (1975) 87–90. **Fewell, D. N.,** and **Gunn, D. M.** "Tipping the Balance: Sternberg's Reader and the Rape of Dinah." *JBL* 110 (1991) 193–211. **Fischer, G.** "Die Redewendung דבר על-לב im AT: Ein Beitrag zum Verständnis von Jes 40:2." *Bib* 65 (1984) 244–50. **Geller, S. A.** "The Sack of Shechem: The Use of Typology in Biblical Covenant Religion." *Prooftexts* 10 (1990) 1–15. **Kass, L. R.** "Regarding Daughters and Sisters: The Rape of Dinah." *Commentary* 93 (1992) 29–38. **Kessler, M.** "Gen 34: An Interpretation." *Reformed Review* 19 (1965/66) 3–8. **Kevers, P.** "Étude littéraire de Gen 34." *RB* 87 (1980) 38–86. **Klein, H.** "Natur und Recht: Israels Umgang mit dem Hochzeitsbrauchtum seiner Umwelt." *TZ* 37 (1981) 3–18. **Pummer, R.** "Gen 34 in Jewish Writings of the Hellenistic and Roman Periods." *HTR* 75 (1982) 177–88. **Pury, A. de.** "Gen 34 et l'histoire." *RB* 76 (1969) 5–49. **Reviv, H.** "Early Elements and Late Terminology in the Descriptions of Non-Israelite Cities in the Bible." *IEJ* 27 (1977) 189–96. **Salkin, J. K.** "Dinah, the Torah's Forgotten Woman." *Judaism* 35 (1986) 284–89. **Schmitt, G.** "Der Ursprung des Levitentums." *ZAW* 94 (1982) 575–99. **Segal, N.** Review of *The Poetics of Biblical Narrative,* by M. Sternberg. *VT* 38 (1988) 243–49. **Smitten, W. H. in der.** "Gen 34: Ausdruck der Volksmeinung?" *BO* 30 (1973) 7–9. **Speiser, E. A.** "The Verb *shr* in Genesis and Early Hebrew Movements." *BASOR* 164 (1961) 23–28. **Sternberg, M.** "Biblical Poetics and Sexual Politics: From Reading to Counter-Reading." *JBL* 111 (1992) 463–88. ————. *Poetics.* 445–75. **Wyatt, N.** "The Story of Dinah and Shechem." *UF* 22 (1990) 433–58.

Translation

[1]*Dinah, the daughter Leah had borne to Jacob, went out to visit the girls of the region.* [2]*Shechem, the son of Hamor, the Hivite,[a] the prince of the region, saw her, took her, laid her,[b] and shamed[c] her.* [3]*He became very attached[a] to Dinah, Jacob's daughter; he loved[a] the girl[b] and spoke[a] reassuringly to her.* [4]*So Shechem said to his father Hamor, "Get this child for me to marry."*

[5a]*Now Jacob had heard that his daughter Dinah had been defiled, when his sons were out in the countryside with the flocks, and he had remained[ab] silent until they returned.[c]* [6]*Then Hamor, Shechem's father, came to Jacob to discuss with him.* [7]*Meanwhile, Jacob's sons[a] had returned from the countryside as soon as they had heard,[b] and the men were indignant and very angry[c] because a disgrace had been done in Israel by lying with Jacob's daughter, which ought[d] never to be done.* [8]*So Hamor spoke with them as follows: "You know my son Shechem;[a] he has fallen in love with your daughter. Please let him marry her.* [9]*You shall intermarry[a] with[b] us; you can give[c] your daughters to us, and you may take our daughters for yourselves.* [10]*You may live with us; the land is yours, stay here, travel[a] freely in it, and acquire possessions[b] in it."* [11]*Shechem said to her father and brothers, "Let me be favored[a] by you, and I shall give whatever you say to me.* [12]*Impose[a] on me a very large marriage present and gift, and I shall give as much[b] as you say to me. But let me have the girl to marry."* [13]*Then the sons of Jacob responded deceitfully[a] to Shechem and his father Hamor as they discussed, because[b] he had defiled Dinah their sister.* [14]*They[a] said to them, "We cannot do this to allow our sister to marry a man who is uncircumcised, for that would be a disgrace to us.* [15]*Only on this condition[a] will we consent[b] to you, if you will become like us and let all your males be circumcised.[c]* [16]*Then we shall give our daughters to you, and we shall marry your daughters; we shall*

live with you and become one people. [17]*But if you do not agree with us to be circumcised,*
we shall take our daughter and be off."

[18]*Their reply seemed very good to Hamor and to Shechem, Hamor's son.* [19]*So he did*
not delay[a] *accepting this idea, because he was infatuated with Jacob's daughter, and he*
was the most important in his father's household.

[20]*Hamor and his son Shechem came*[a] *to the gate of their city and discussed with the*
men of their town as follows. [21]*"These men are peaceably disposed toward us. Let them*
live[a] *in the land, travel freely in it. Look, the land is big enough for them. Then we shall*
marry their daughters,[b] *and we shall give our daughters*[b] *to them.* [22]*But only on this*
condition will the men consent to live with us and become one people, when all our males
are circumcised[a] *as they are.* [23]*Their flocks, their possessions, and all their herds, will*
they not be ours? Let us just agree with them and let them live with us."

[24]*All those who came to the city gate agreed with Hamor and his son Shechem,* [a]*and*
every male among all those who came to the city gate was circumcised.[a]

[25]*On the third day, when they were*[a] *still sore, two sons of Jacob, Simeon and Levi,*
brothers of Dinah, each took a sword, entered the city which felt secure, and killed all
the males. [26]*They even*[a] *slew Hamor and his son Shechem with the sword, took Dinah*
from Shechem's house and left. [27a]*The sons of Jacob entered over the slain,*[b] *plundered*[c]
the city because their sister had been defiled.[d] [28a]*They took their flocks and cattle and*
their donkeys, whatever was in the town and in the countryside.[a] [29]*They took captive*
their wealth, all their young children, and their wives, and they plundered everything
in their houses.

[30]*Jacob said to Simeon and Levi: "You have brought ruin on me by making me stink*[a]
among the inhabitants of the land, the Canaanites and the Perizzites. I[b] *am just a*
small group, but they will band[c] *together, attack*[d] *me, and destroy me, both me and my*
household." [31]*But they said, "Should*[a] *he treat our sister*[b] *like a prostitute?"*[b]

Notes

2.a. G has "Horite" instead of Hivite.
2.b. *BHS* points אִתָּהּ "with her" instead of אֹתָהּ "her" following G, S. However, this is unwarranted; שכב followed by direct object, e.g., "her," often implies forcible illegitimate intercourse (Num 5:13, 19; Ezek 23:8; cf. Gen 34:7; 19:34; 26:10).
2.c. Waw consec + 3 masc sg impf piel ענה + 3 fem sg suffix.
3.a. Note three consecutive verbs describing the intensity of Shechem's passion (*SBH*, 42).
3.b. On spelling of הנער, cf. n. 24:14.a.
5.a-a. On the string of circumstantial clauses beginning an episode, cf. *SBH*, 79, 87.
5.b. Waw consec + 3 masc sg pf hiph חרש. Though waw + pf is unusual here, it is not unparalleled (cf. GKC, 112ss; Joüon, 119z) and does not warrant *BHS*'s proposed emendation.
5.c. Inf constr בוא + 3 masc pl suffix.
7.a. On the preverbal position of the subject, see *EWAS*, 36.
7.b. כ + inf constr שמע + 3 masc pl suffix.
7.c. Cf. n. 6:6.b.
7.d. Cf. n. 29:26.a.
8.a. On the use of *casus pendens,* here highlighting the subj of the sentence, Shechem, see *EWAS,* 93–95; Joüon, 156b; 157d, n.
9.a. Waw + 2 masc pl impv hithp חתן.
9.b. GKC 117w, *BHS* would repoint אֹתָנוּ instead of MT אִתָּנוּ "us." It is certainly unusual for a hithp to be followed by a direct obj.
9.c. 2 masc pl impf qal נתן.
10.a. Waw + 2 masc pl impv qal סחר + 3 fem sg suffix.

10.b. Waw + 2 masc pl impv niph אֵחֲזוּ. SamPent has qal.

11.a. Coh in mood though not in form (so Joüon, 114b, n.).

12.a. 2 masc pl impv hiph רְבָה.

12.b. On this use of אֲשֶׁר, cf. Joüon, 174a.

13.a. MT's word order makes בְּמִרְמָה "deceitfully" modify "responded," but *BHS*, following S, would place it after "discussed."

13.b. On this meaning of אֲשֶׁר, see GKC, 158b.

14.a. G inserts "Simeon and Levi, the brothers of Dinah, the sons of Leah."

15.a. On this use of *beth pretii*, see GKC, 119p.

15.b. 1 pl impf qal (so GKC, 72h) niph (BDB, KB) אוֹת.

15.c. לְ + inf constr niph מוּל.

19.a. 3 masc sg pf piel אִחַר.

20.a. Sg verb with composite pl subj (GKC, 146f).

21.a. SamPent omits waw יָשְׁבוּ smoothing the syntax (cf. *EWAS*, 75, n. 27).

21.b. Preverbal position of the object "daughters" serves to contrast them.

22.a. Masc pl ptcp niph מוּל.

24.a. To avoid the repetition with the first part of the verse, G rewords "and they were circumcised in the flesh of their foreskin, every male."

25.a. Cf. n. 4:8.b.

26.a. The preverbal position of the obj, "Hamor and . . . Shechem," suggests emphasis on them, hence the translation "even" (cf. *EWAS*, 38–40).

27.a. SamPent, S, (G?) read וּבְנֵי "and the sons."

27.b. *BHS*, Gunkel, and Westermann propose הַחֹלִים "the sick, wounded." An unnecessary emendation.

27.c. Waw consec + 3 masc pl impf בֹזוּ.

27.d. Here 3 pl "they had defiled" used impersonally for a pass (GKC, 144g).

28.a-a. Chiastic apposition between vv 27 and 28 is characteristic of epic style according to *SBH*, 40.

30.a. לְ + inf constr hiph בָאֵשׁ + 1 sg suffix.

30.b. Word order puts a slight emphasis on pronominal subj "I" (*EWAS*, 11).

30.c. Waw consec + 3 pl pf niph אָסַף.

30.d. Waw consec + 3 pl pf hiph נָכָה + 1 sg suffix.

31.a. On this nuance of the impf, see Joüon, 113m; WOC, 509.

31.b-b. In the sentence this phrase comes first, giving it unmistakable emphasis (*EWAS*, 43).

Form/Structure/Setting

Though some scholars have argued that this episode begins in 33:18, we have already accepted the view that 33:18–20 is the close of the preceding episode, which at the same time anticipates chap. 34 (see *Form/Structure/Setting* on 32:4–33:20). 34:31, with its powerful rhetorical question "Should he treat our sister like a prostitute?" makes a fitting close to the story (for similar dramatic closures, cf. 27:45; 29:14; 30:24; 37:35; 42:38; 45:28). 35:5 clearly looks back to chap. 34, but this is not sufficient warrant to make 35:5 the close of the narrative as Westermann does.

The chapter falls into four scenes:

Scene 1: Shechem rapes Dinah and seeks to marry her (1–4)
           Speech to father: "Get this child for me to marry" (4)
Scene 2: Hamor and Shechem propose a marriage alliance with Jacob's family (5–19)
           Hamor's speech (8–10)
           Shechem's speech (11–12)
           Jacob's sons' speech (14–17)
           Hamor and Shechem consent (18–19)

Scene 3:   Hamor and Shechem put terms for marriage alliance to townsfolk (20–24)
                 Hamor and Shechem speak (21–23)
                 Townsfolk consent (24)
Scene 4:   Jacob's sons rape the town
                 Speech to father: "Should he treat our sister as a prostitute?" (31)

Sternberg (*Poetics*) and Kevers (*RB* 87 [1980] 38–86) have already noted how the terminology used toward the end of the narrative echoes that used at the beginning, e.g., "go out" (יצא; vv 1, 26); "take" (לקח; vv 2, 4, 25, 26, 28). But the above scenic analysis makes the symmetry of the story even more striking. Scenes 1 and 4 are both largely narrative. Scene 1 describes the rape of Dinah and her subsequent detention by Shechem and then concludes with Shechem demanding that his father arrange a marriage with her (v 4). Scene 4 describes the slaughter of the men of Shechem by Jacob's sons and their capture of the women, children, and flocks of the town and concludes with a brusque justification of their action to their father Jacob (v 31). Scenes 2 and 3 are both largely dialogues about the terms on which the Shechemites will marry the Israelites. Here the parallels are verbal as well as ideological. Both scenes conclude with the listeners accepting the terms of the intermarriage agreement (vv 18–19, 24).

Though chap. 34 is well constructed in itself, it is not immediately apparent why it should be included in the Jacob cycle at all; it does not seem to relate to the theme of Genesis. By 33:20, Jacob has been reconciled to Esau and has returned to Canaan. 35:1–16 recounts how he finally reaches Bethel, the starting point of his journey. But chap. 34 seems to be a digression, contributing very little to the plot. What is its place and function within the Jacob cycle?

Before discussing how chap. 34 relates to the theme of Genesis in general, and the Jacob story in particular, its inseparability from its context needs to be pointed out. It is no stray boulder that just happens to have come to rest here, but it presupposes what precedes and is assumed in the material that follows. Its geographic setting in Canaan presupposes Jacob's return there. The family relationship of Jacob marrying Leah who bore him six sons and a daughter is obviously assumed. Less obvious, but even more significant for understanding the emotions of the actors in the story, is the fact that Jacob was never very fond of Leah and her children. Jacob's indifference to his daughter's humiliation here stands in sharp contrast to his passionate attachment to Joseph and Benjamin, the sons of Rachel his favorite wife, displayed in the Joseph story. And it seems likely that it is Jacob's indifference to Dinah's plight that prompts the violent overreaction of her brothers in this story. Central too to this narrative is the necessity of circumcision for inclusion within the Israelite community, a principle spelled out in chap. 17. Indeed, the phraseology of 34:15, "let all your males be circumcised," seems to be a direct quote from 17:10, and the other passages about circumcising the males in 34:17, 22, 24 also seem to echo 17:10, 12.

These general observations show that chap. 34 presupposes the earlier narratives in Genesis, but there are also explicit links within the surrounding material that show that the editor viewed this narrative as integral to Genesis. In 30:21, the birth of Dinah is mentioned, the only daughter of Jacob to have her arrival recorded. Usually the birth of girls is not recorded, since the family line was traced through the sons, who inherited the family land. The birth of a daughter is

mentioned only if she is to figure prominently in the subsequent narrative. In this respect, 30:21 parallels 22:23, where Rebekah is the only girl in an otherwise all-male genealogy. 22:23 thus anticipates chap. 24 just as 30:21 anticipates chap. 34. Similarly, it is customary in Genesis for the end of one episode to include a trailer for the next one. This is exactly what is found here. 33:18–19 records Jacob's arrival at Salem, the city of Shechem, and his purchase of land from the sons of Hamor. This sets the scene for the events of chap. 34. Then Jacob's fearful comment in 34:30, "You have brought ruin on me . . . they will band together, attack me, and destroy me," anticipates his journey on to Bethel recorded in 35:1–5, especially 35:5, "Divine terror fell on the surrounding towns so that they did not pursue the sons of Jacob." Finally, Jacob condemns Simeon and Levi's slaughter of the Shechemites in his farewell speech, usually called the blessing of Jacob (49:5–7). These points all indicate that as far as the final editor of Genesis was concerned, chap. 34 is integral to the plot and must somehow relate to the theme. But most studies fail to address this problem.

Fishbane (*Text and Texture*), Fokkelman (*Narrative Art*), and Rendsburg (*Redaction*) have all noted that there is a certain correspondence between chap. 26 and chap. 34 within the Jacob cycle. On first sight, neither chapter relates very closely to the surrounding material or to the theme of Genesis. Both chapters involve dealings with the inhabitants of the land: the Philistines in chap. 26, the Shechemites in chap. 34. In 26:7–11, Rebekah is nearly taken by the Philistine king; in 34:1–26, Shechem actually takes Dinah. In both cases the patriarch shows little courage in protecting his wife or daughter, but ultimately he escapes unharmed and not a little richer (26:31, 13; 34:28–29; 35:5). This too had been Abraham's experience on two occasions (12:10–20; 20:1–18). For further verbal links between chaps. 26 and 34, see *Form/Structure/Setting* on chap. 26.

The ideological parallels between chaps. 26 and 34 probably give the clue to the editor's purpose in including chap. 34 in the Jacob cycle. Its program is summed up in 28:13–15, which reaffirms the familiar Abrahamic promises of land and descendants but adds, "I am really with you and will guard you wherever you go and bring you back to this land, because I shall not leave you until I have done for you what I have promised you" (28:15). Then Jacob made a vow that if God would do this and bring him back "in peace to my father's house, the LORD will be my God" (28:20–21). By the end of chap. 33, Jacob has enjoyed divine protection in Mesopotamia, gained descendants, and bought land in Canaan, but has not quite reached his destination in Bethel. Here, on the verge of the total fulfillment of the promise and his vow, Canaanite lust, his own cowardice, and his sons' folly all combine to destroy the prospect of Jacob's return to his father's house in peace. Yet he does make it; as often in Genesis, the invincibility of the promises is once again demonstrated. Divine grace triumphs despite human sin.

Source critics have found this a tricky section to handle; indeed, Meyer (quoted by Volz, *Der Elohist*, 124) described it as "possibly the most difficult in the whole hexateuch." The starting point of the analysis was the awkward transition between v 26 and v 27, and the observation that at some points Hamor spoke, at others Shechem, and that in some passages it was Jacob, at others his sons, and yet others Simeon and Levi who react to the Shechemites. Hence, two main sources were distinguished, source A (1–2a, 4, 6, 8–10, 13–18, 20–25, 27–29) as the Hamor

source and J (2b–3, 5, 7, 11–12, 19, 26, 30–31) as the Shechem source. Though there was general agreement between early critical commentators about the analysis, there were very different opinions about the attribution of source A, which is clearly the major source into which elements of J have been worked. Delitzsch, Dillmann, Driver, and Procksch identified source A with P, because of its clear affinities with P. 34:15, 22 quotes 17:10, 34:24 echoes 23:10, 18, and other terms are typically P. However, Wellhausen (*Komposition*, 49), Gunkel, Skinner, and others reluctant to concede that P antedates J tended, with very little evidence, to ascribe source A to E. For the same reason, Noth (*History of Pentateuchal Traditions*, 30) proposed that the J material had been expanded by later additions, which he identified as vv 4, 6, 8–10, 15–17, 20–23, 27 as well as the mention of Hamor in vv 13a, 18, 24, 26. Later writers have tended to simplify Noth's traditio-historical approach, giving more to J and less to the later expander (e.g., de Pury, *RB* 76 [1969] 5–49; Kevers, *RB* 87 [1980] 38–86; Blum, *Die Komposition*). Speiser and Coats indeed ascribe the whole episode to J. Westermann has reverted to a two-source hypothesis, like that of Dillmann and Driver, but he does not think either is to be identified with J or P. The variety of views propounded shows the uncertain basis on which the analysis rests. Radday's statistical tests (*Genesis*) give no support for distinguishing this material from J. The kinship of this material with P material in chaps. 17 and 23 could be explained by supposing either that these chapters are by J or that J is a later source or editorial layer than P (see *Form/Structure/Setting* on chaps.17, 23). But our scenic analysis cuts across all the suggested source divisions in chap. 34, making it simplest to suppose that there is but one source here, which, in view of its connections with the main plot of the Jacob cycle, should presumably be identified with J.

Comment

1–4 Though the whole chapter is often subtitled the Rape of Dinah, this topic only constitutes scene 1, which gives the background to the vengeance wrought by her brothers on her attacker.

1 "Dinah, the daughter Leah had borne to Jacob." This long definition of Dinah's relationship to her parents is unusual and probably indicates the emotional dynamics of the situation. She is daughter of Jacob's unloved wife Leah, hence Jacob's relative unconcern at her disgrace. She is also the full sister of Simeon and Levi, who, as the result of their father's apathy, take the law into their own hands. However, *Genesis Rabbah* sees the comment about her being Leah's daughter as being condemnatory. Leah "went out" to allure Jacob (30:16), and here Dinah is copying her mother's example. Though "went out to visit the girls of the land" sounds perfectly innocent, the terms used may suggest Dinah's imprudence, if not impropriety. In LH 141 the cognate Akkadian verb *waṣû* describes a housewife who conducts herself improperly outside her home, and the targums translate "cult prostitute" as "one who goes out in the countryside." Furthermore, Genesis regularly condemns all intermarriage with women of the land (Gen 24:3, 37; 27:46; 28:1, 6, 8), so it may be doubted whether it totally approves of Dinah meeting the girls of the land, for they might have introduced her to one of the boys. Dinah was at least sailing close to the wind!

2 On "Hivite," cf. *Comment* on 10:17. On "prince," cf. *Comment* on 17:20. Reviv (*IEJ* 27 [1977] 192–93) sees it as the title of a hereditary ruler of a Canaanite city. "Laid her" instead of the more usual "lay with her" implies forcible illegitimate intercourse (cf. n. 34:2.b.). "Shamed her" is another term always used to describe intercourse without marriage (e.g., Deut 21:14; 22:29; 2 Sam 13:12). The duplication of very negative terms shows the author's strong disapproval of Shechem's behavior. Had the law of Deut 22:28–29 been applicable, Shechem would have been compelled to marry Dinah and pay fifty shekels, an unusually large marriage present, to her father.

3 However brutal the act, at least Shechem did not treat Dinah as Amnon did Tamar after raping her, who "hated her with very great hatred" and expelled her from his room (2 Sam 13:15–17). Instead, "he became very attached" to Dinah, lit. "his soul stuck to Dinah," precisely the right bond between a married couple (cf. 2:24); he "loved the girl, and spoke reassuringly to her." For the idea of reassurance in this phrase, lit. "to speak over the heart," cf. 50:21; Judg 19:3; 2 Sam 19:7; 2 Chr 30:22; Isa 40:2. So having unequivocally condemned Shechem for assaulting Dinah, the narrator now reveals other facets of his behavior that evoke much more sympathy for him. He evidently did want to marry her properly.

4 Having seen Shechem at his most charming in v 3, we now see another aspect of his character, as he brusquely demands of his father, "Get this child for me." Not only does he use the bluntest form of imperative without even a "please," but he describes Dinah rather disparagingly as "this child."

5–19 This, the longest scene, is almost entirely dialogue and relates the negotiations between the Shechemites and the Israelites. As befits diplomatic negotiation, everything on the surface is very polite, but to appreciate what is really going on, two things must be understood: first, that the Israelites spoke deceitfully (v 13) and, secondly, that the Shechemites held Dinah—she had not returned home (vv 17, 26).

5 This verse sets the scene by giving an insight into Jacob's attitude. "Now Jacob had heard that his daughter Dinah had been defiled." Note how the narrative stresses the relationship between Jacob and Dinah, she was "his daughter," and the seriousness of her treatment, "had been defiled." This leads us to expect a fierce reaction on Jacob's part, like David who on hearing of Tamar's rape was "very angry" (2 Sam 13:21). Instead, he does nothing about it till his sons' return; indeed "he remained silent" (cf. 24:21; Num 30:5[4]). Though silence may be right in some circumstances, the observation of the narrator here reflects badly on Jacob. He does not seem to care about his daughter's honor.

6 Meanwhile, Shechem and Hamor arrive to discuss matters with him, but at this stage only Hamor is mentioned, as if to contrast the two fathers. Hamor does all he can to forward his son's suit, whereas, until others came to him, Jacob kept quiet about his daughter's plight.

7 How differently Dinah's brothers react. They are outraged by the events. For the term "indignant" (עצב), cf. *Comment* on 6:6. They rush home "as soon as they heard." This reading may at least suggest Jacob sent word to them about it. But the syntax is ambiguous, and it may be that Jacob never bothered to let them know. They only discover what has happened when they arrive home. This is to take "as soon as they heard" not with "returned" but with "they were indignant."

The sentence would then be translated, "Now the sons of Jacob had returned from the countryside. As soon as they heard, the men were indignant." Whichever way the sentence is read, it puts the sons in a much more favorable light than the father. "Because a disgrace had been done in Israel by lying with Jacob's daughter, which ought never to be done." It is not clear whether this is the sons' opinion, or the narrator's, or both. With Sternberg (*Poetics*) it seems likely that the last is the most likely option. Narrator, reader, and sons are expected to agree that Shechem's act is a "disgrace" (a term used elsewhere of crimes warranting the death penalty; Deut 22:21; Josh 7:15; Judg 19:23–24; 20:6; 1 Sam 25:25; 2 Sam 13:12). "In Israel . . . Jacob's daughter's." This combination of Jacob's old and new names heightens our surprise that Jacob is so passive and suggests that his sons are as much concerned for his honor as for their sister's. The use of "in Israel" surely suggests that the brothers' view of what is right and proper has abiding validity in national life. Such a thing "ought never to be done."

8 Hamor addresses Jacob courteously, but without apology. There is no mention of what Shechem has done to Dinah, or to the fact that she is still in Shechem's house; he simply asks for her hand in marriage. "He has fallen in love" is a similar but rarer expression than that used in v 3, "became very attached to," suggesting Shechem's free choice of Dinah (cf. Deut 7:7; 10:15; 21:11).

9 Hamor goes even further, proposing full intermarriage between the Israelites and Shechemites. It sounds a generous proposal, but it is just such an arrangement that Deut 7:3 prohibits: "You shall not make marriages with them, giving your daughters to their sons or taking their daughters for your sons," a stance later endorsed by Josh 23:12; Ezra 9:14.

10 Hamor urges them to consider the economic advantages of such an arrangement. "Travel freely in it" seems to be the basic sense of סחר (cf. 34:21; 42:34; Jer 14:18; Speiser, *BASOR* 164 [1961] 23–28), though the participle usually has the more specialized sense of "trader" (cf. 23:16; 37:28). "Acquire possessions in it" (cf. 47:27; Num 32:30; Josh 22:9, 19) is the verb from the noun אחזה used in the divine promise of the land in 17:8; 48:4. Hamor, in effect, offers what God has promised.

"These overtures sound conciliatory and appealing, nor can they be dismissed as insincere . . . [but] the soft-spoken Hivites negotiate from a strong position unfairly obtained. Another of the things unsaid by the two is the crucial fact discovered by the reader only in retrospect, after the massacre, but obvious to the parties concerned: that they have detained Dinah in their house. No explicit mention need ruffle the smoothness of their approach, since the leverage given by the possession of the bride is clear to all" (Sternberg, *Poetics*, 456). In fact, we do not know whether Dinah was detained or staying voluntarily with Shechem, but doubtless her brothers assumed the worst: that Shechem was keeping her against her will.

11–12 Hamor's proposals of intermarriage and settlement are major issues and deserve long discussion, but Shechem is impatient, and he brings them back to the main point with an impassioned outburst, inviting Jacob and his sons to suggest whatever figure they like so that he can marry Dinah. Marriage was always preceded by betrothal, in which the bridegroom's family paid a מהר "marriage present" to the bride's family (1 Sam 18:25). In cases of premarital intercourse,

this still had to be paid to legitimize the union, and the girl's father was allowed to fix the size of the marriage present (Exod 22:15–16[16–17]; limited by Deut 22:29 to a maximum of fifty shekels). So Shechem invites them to name their price for the marriage present and "gift." The nature of the gift is obscure. Upon marriage, a bride received a dowry from her father. In Mesopotamia, she might also receive an endowment from her new husband (*nudunnûm,* LH 171–72) to support her in case she were ever widowed or divorced. Gen 25:6 speaks of "gifts" in this sense, but Jacob (653) on the basis of 24:53 suggests the "gift" was given not to Dinah but to her family. Here it seems likely that Shechem is offering both a "marriage present" to Jacob and "a gift" to Dinah.

13 Shechem's passionate intervention prompts Jacob's sons to "respond" vigorously (on this nuance of ענה, see 31:14), indeed "deceitfully" (cf. 27:35), but it is not immediately clear in what way their words were deceitful; that emerges later. However, this comment "deceitfully" does signal that their words do not mean quite what they seem and serves to mitigate a little the reader's sense of shock at the massacre they perpetrate. We have been warned that Dinah's brothers will not play fair.

"Because he had defiled Dinah their sister." Given the position of this clause in the sentence, it seems best to translate the conjunction אשר as "because." However, it could be translated by the relative pronoun, "who had defiled Dinah their sister," referring back to Shechem. Whichever way the clause is taken, it helps to soften the impact of "deceitfully." The man is being addressed deceitfully because he is the one who has defiled Dinah. Note that she is here called "*their* sister," emphasizing why they have a particular reason to deceive him.

15–17 Whereas Hamor stressed the economic advantages of intermarriage, the brothers emphasize the religious impediments to marriage. To marry an uncircumcised man would be a "disgrace" (חרפה), i.e., something that would make one the butt of adverse comment and ridicule (e.g., childlessness, 30:23; slavery, Josh 5:9; military weakness, 1 Sam 17:26; adultery, Prov 6:33; cf. *TDOT* 5:203–15).

15 They then cite the key stipulation of the Abrahamic covenant: "all your males must be circumcised" (17:10).

16 Only then will intermarriage be possible, leading to Israelite settlement in the land and their union with the Shechemites so that they become "one people" (cf. v 22). "People" (עם), as opposed to nation, is a group that sees itself primarily in terms of common descent, a super tribe or overgrown family (cf. *Comment* on 11:6; 12:2). In other words, Jacob's sons insist that money has nothing to do with marriage; it is a question of religious identity. If the Shechemites satisfy them on this ground, there will be no problem about full union between them.

17 But if they do not comply, then the position will be very different: "we shall take," probably implying forcible seizure of Dinah (cf. v 2), and "be off." With this veiled threat, there is a hint of the brothers' true feelings and a hint of what may happen eventually.

18–19 It is not clear whether Jacob's sons expected Hamor and Shechem to accept their terms; they may well have expected them to balk at such uncomfortable conditions (cf. 1 Sam 18:25), which would have given them grounds for using force. But Hamor and Shechem willingly comply, "because he was infatuated with Jacob's daughter." חפץ suggests a more intense degree of attachment

than "attached," "loved" (v 2), "fallen in love" (v 4), as is apparent from other
passages where this term is used of love between the sexes (Deut 21:14; 25:7–8;
Esth 2:14; *TDOT* 5:95–96). "For he was the most important man in his father's
house" explains why his view would carry so much weight in the community.

20–25 The third scene, like the second, vv 5–19, is essentially dialogue in
which Hamor and Shechem present the terms for an alliance between them and
the Israelites. However, though they go over much the same ground as in the
dialogue with Jacob's sons, the subject is presented quite differently in order to
persuade them to accept the plan.

20 Hamor, the ruler of the city, raises the issue in the public area just inside
the city gate, the typical place for meetings in Bible times (cf. Deut 22:15, 24; Jer
7:2; Amos 5:10, 12). Here he addresses his remarks to the "men of their town."
This, according to Reviv (*IEJ* 27 [1977] 192), corresponds to "the popular assem-
bly of the free and permanent members of the city," a body mentioned in many
Mesopotamian and Canaanite (i.e., from Ugarit and El-Amarna) documents of
the second millennium B.C. This was a broader body than the elders of the city,
since the granting of land rights was "a matter of wide public interest that neces-
sitated the gathering of the people of the land."

21–23 A comparison of this speech with those in vv 9–12, 14–17 is revealing.
In addressing their fellow townsmen, Hamor and Shechem adopt a quite different line from that taken in earlier negotiations. They say nothing about their
own personal involvement in the matter, that Shechem wants to marry Dinah;
rather they begin by insisting on the advantages of intermarriage for the whole
town (v 21). Then they mention the need for circumcision (v 22), and finally they
return to the economic advantages of intermarriage. Whereas they had promised to
the Israelites that "they could acquire possessions in it" (v 10), they say nothing
about that to their own people; instead they say "their flocks, their possessions,
and all their herds, will they not be ours?" Hamor and Shechem also fail to mention the threat to seize Dinah with which Jacob's sons ended their negotiations.

Now some of these changes could be construed as merely diplomatic, for
Hamor had to emphasize the economic advantages for the Shechemites if they
were ever to be persuaded of the value of circumcision. Nevertheless, failing to
mention the land concession and claiming that the Israelite animals would be
theirs verges on deceit. They are either tricking their townsmen, or if they are
being frank with them, they must have been dishonest in their negotiations with
Jacob and his sons. Calvin comments with typical trenchancy, "[Hamor and
Shechem] then enumerate other advantages; meanwhile, they cunningly conceal
the private and real cause of their request. Whence it follows that all these pre-
texts are fallacious. But it is a very common disease, that men of rank who have
great authority, while making all things subservient to their own private ends,
feign themselves to be considerate for the common good, and pretend a desire
for the public advantage" (2:224).

Certainly this disclosure of Hamor and Shechem's double-dealing and the avarice of their fellow citizens tends to reduce our shock at the fate that is about to
overtake them. Indeed, there is an element of dramatic irony in their words. They
describe the Israelites as "peaceably disposed toward us" (v 21), little suspecting
what they were planning. They ask, "Their flocks, their possessions . . . will they

not be ours?" (v 23). But in a few days the situation will be reversed, with the Israelites plundering all their possessions (vv 28–29).

24 But whatever their true motives, the townsfolk agree to circumcision as readily as Hamor and Shechem had (vv 18–19).

25–31 The final scene matches the first formally in being mainly narrative and in concluding with a word from the sons to their father (cf. v 4 and v 31), and it matches it in content by portraying an act of revenge wrought by Dinah's brothers on her ravisher and his associates. The idea of talionic retribution ("eye for an eye") is hinted at in the words used. Simeon and Levi "took" a sword, just as Shechem "took" Dinah. Dinah "went out" in the first scene to the girls of the region, in the last scene from the house of her captivity. But though there is an element of justice in their revenge, it is clearly disproportionate, as the narrative makes clear. No one in this tale escapes the narrator's implied censure.

25 The Shechemites had submitted to circumcision to become "one people" with Israel. For the latter to attack when they were still suffering the aftereffects of the operation was treacherous, as the little comment "which felt secure" underlines. For this sense of בטח "feeling secure," see Deut 33:28; Judg 8:11; cf. Judg 18:7. Even if the Shechemites had not shown such trust in Israel, biblical law gives no warrant for such a terrible act of vengeance. A massacre of all the men of the city for one man's sin was as shocking to the narrator as it is to modern ears. Yet, he does subtly draw attention to the motives of Simeon and Levi, by noting that they are not just Jacob's sons but "brothers of Dinah." It was Jacob's failure to act that provoked them to behave in such an extreme way. He had not loved Leah, or her daughter Dinah, but they did.

26 The narrator also reveals another fact, just at the moment we are most shocked by Simeon and Levi's behavior, that all this time Dinah had been staying, perhaps held hostage, in Shechem's house. They "took Dinah from Shechem's house and left." Clearly her detention was known to all the actors in the story throughout the action, but now it is revealed to the reader for the first time. And this puts a different complexion on the affair. Jacob's sons had felt all along that they had been negotiating under duress.

[The Hivites] have largely brought down that violence on themselves by seeking to impose their will on Jacob's family. With Dinah in Shechem's hands, the option of polite declining is closed to her guardians. And once the brothers refused to submit to the Hivite version of a shotgun wedding, they were left no avenue to the retrieval of their sister except force. Hence also the need for "deceit." Considering the numerical superiority of the troops behind the 'prince of the land'—'two of Jacob's sons' faced a whole city—no wonder the brothers resorted to trickery to make odds more even. And the order of presentation supports the reading of the slaughter as an act enforced and purposive rather than expressing blind fury. First comes the attack on the townsmen, next the killing of Hamor and Shechem, and only then the extrication of Dinah: to rescue their sister, this orderly movement implies, they had to deal with all possible resistance, let alone future retaliation. (Sternberg, *Poetics*, 468).

27–29 If Simeon and Levi's motives can at least be construed as honorable, though their actions were reprehensible, no such considerations can excuse Jacob's other sons' pillaging the dead. According to Sternberg, opportunistic greed

motivates them. It is true that the phraseology here, "plunder" (בזז), "took captive" (שבה), is the language of war (cf. Num 31:9; Deut 2:35; Josh 8:2, 27; Gen 31:26; 1 Sam 30:2). And it could be that the back reference "because their sister had been defiled" is ironic, contrasting "the brothers' fine words and their ugly deeds, between idealistic facade and materialistic reality, between deceit as sacred rage and as unholy calculation" (Sternberg, *Poetics*, 472). On the other hand, it is noticeable that many of the same terms are found in the account of the Israelites' revenge on Midian in Num 31. The Midianites had seduced the Israelites, and Phineas, son of Aaron of the tribe of Levi, had killed the guilty man and woman (Num 25). Later, vengeance is wreaked on all the Midianites as directed in 25:17 by all the tribes of Israel. They slew every male (Num 31:7; cf. Gen 34:25); then they slew the Midianite kings (Num 31:8; cf. Gen 34:26; Hamor was prince, i.e., local king, according to Gen 34:2). Then Num 31:9 repeats Gen 34:29 almost word-for-word in reverse order.

These parallels between Gen 34:25–29 and Num 25 and 31:1–9 show, first, that the postulated source division of 34:25–29 (see above on *Form/Structure/Setting*) is unlikely. In Num 25 vengeance is first taken by Phineas the Levite, then by all Israel (25:17; 31:4–7), just as Levi's action here (34:26) is followed by his brothers (34:27–29). Second, these parallels suggest that the brothers' action here is not viewed as unequivocally evil, for the later action of Phineas is seen as extremely meritorious, and the follow-up attack by all Israel is expressly commanded by God. As Jacob's sons here foreshadow the actions of their descendants, this seems to imply the narrator's qualified approval. "Because they had defiled their sister" is thus another reminder that it was primarily the sexual offenses of Canaan that were to lead to its conquest by Israel (cf. Gen 19; Lev 18:3; 20:23).

28 This list of booty is similar to 12:16, another occasion on which a patriarch was enriched despite his own sin.

30–31 This heated exchange between Jacob and his sons brings the scene and episode to a dramatic close. He accuses them of "bringing ruin." עכר "bring ruin" always seems to involve personal or national disaster. The traditional translation, "trouble," is too weak (Josh 7:25; Judg 11:35; 1 Sam 14:29; Prov 11:17, 29; 15:27). "Made me stink" (cf. Exod 5:21; 1 Sam 27:12). His strong rebuke springs from a faint heart; he fears that "the Canaanites will . . . attack me and destroy me." He had said much the same in 32:12(11). "Esau . . . will kill me." Here, despite his experiences at the Yabbok and his successful reunion with Esau, he is showing the same abject fear as before. Of course, fear is natural in such a situation, but the reasons Jacob gives for damning his sons betray him. He does not condemn them for the massacre, for abusing the rite of circumcision, or even for breach of contract. Rather, he protests that the consequences of their action have made him unpopular. Nor does he seem worried by his daughter's rape or the prospect of intermarriage with the Canaanites. He is only concerned for his own skin.

> Whatever its force elsewhere, therefore, Jacob's argument sounds shabby in the Bible's court of conscience. The ending rubs in the point by having his wordy and terror-driven onslaught countered by Simeon and Levi's proud and epigrammatic "Should he treat our sister like a harlot?" The voice of egocentricity and self-preservation finds itself opposed by the voice of idealism. Damn the consequence, they say, and their response vibrates with the sense of injury that drove them to seek redress in the sword. Shechem

treated Dinah like a whore not only by his cavalier way with her virtue but also by his subsequent offer of "gifts" to her protectors. (Sternberg, *Poetics*, 474)

Note how Simeon and Levi refer to Dinah as "our sister," once again reminding us of the tensions within the family. They do not speak of her as "your daughter," as would be appropriate in addressing Jacob. "They in effect wrest her out of the father's guardianship: she may not be your daughter, but she certainly is 'our sister' and no one will treat her like a whore" (Sternberg, *Poetics*, 474–75). Indeed, their remark "Should he treat her like a prostitute?" could be referring not just to Shechem's treatment of Dinah, but also to Jacob's. It may have been said in private afterwards. To do nothing about the rape and then to be willing to accept gifts after the event is to act like a pimp. These two readings of the brother's reply are not mutually exclusive; it may well be that this last word is intended to be read as a condemnation of both Shechem and Jacob.

Explanation

The account of Dinah's rape and of the terrible revenge exacted by her brothers on the rapist and his town is one of the most dramatic and disturbing in Genesis. It is also remarkable for the subtlety with which it handles character and motivation. Within a firm moral framework sure of what constitutes right and wrong, the narrative hints at the multidimensional aspects of conduct, at the mixed motives that make it impossible either to condemn any of the actors absolutely or to exonerate them entirely.

"Dinah went out to visit the girls of the region" sounds on the face of it entirely innocent. Had we been told she had visited the boys of the area, her action would certainly have been condemned, for intermarriage with Canaanites was always regarded as wrong. But for women to "go out" is in the world of the Bible a little less than proper, and who is to say that one of the girls of the land might not have introduced her to one of the boys? So already the story has suggested that if her actions were innocuous, her motives may have been suspect.

However, Shechem was quite wrong to rape her. The verbs used to describe his action, "took, laid, shamed," bespeak the narrative's unequivocal condemnation of his action, an offense that in OT law would have been punished at least by the payment of large damages and possibly by forced marriage as well. Yet we learn that Shechem was not your callous anonymous rapist, so dreaded in modern society, but an affectionate young man, who "loved the girl and spoke reassuringly to her." Indeed, he insisted that his father obtain Jacob's consent to their marriage.

Now the other members of Dinah's family appear on the scene, and we are immediately made aware of the tensions within the family. Jacob was never fond of his first wife, Leah, and it seems that his coldness spilled over to her six sons and her daughter Dinah. So he took no action about her rape and abduction, whereas her brothers were incensed by it. Thus when Hamor and Shechem arrive to negotiate marriage between Dinah and Shechem, they start by addressing Jacob, but ere long they find that they must really deal with his sons, for it is they who object to the proposed match.

The negotiations apparently proceed smoothly, with Hamor and Shechem ready to grant full intermarriage between them and the Israelites, the right to free movement and to acquire land. Shechem offers to pay whatever marriage present and endowment they see fit to ask. In return, Jacob's sons insist that there is only one obstacle to this arrangement, the Shechemites' failure to practice circumcision. This, the narrator advises, was deceitful, for they had more serious objections to intermarriage than they had intimated. Nevertheless, Hamor and Shechem surprised them by agreeing to the condition. Thus the Hivites appear to be very obliging, reasonable men.

But as the story unfolds we realize this is not the whole truth. Hamor and Shechem had been negotiating from a position of strength, since Dinah was in their house, and, as they reveal in persuading their fellow citizens to accept the arrangement, they hoped to profit financially from the arrangement: "Their flocks, their possessions, and all their herds, will they not be ours?" (v 23).

Three days later the real intentions of Dinah's brothers are unmasked as they attack the unsuspecting Shechemites laid low by the rite of circumcision. All the men of the city, including Hamor and Shechem, are killed, Dinah is rescued, and the women, children, and animals are taken captive. The rape of Dinah has led to war. Jacob is dismayed, but again it is not because of what his sons have done, or what has been done to his daughter, but because of the dangerous consequences: he fears he too may now suffer revenge at the hands of the Canaanites. But when he rebukes his sons, they retort in fierce moral tones: "Should he treat our sister like a prostitute?" (v 31). The family tragedy has not led to reconciliation but to a deepening of the rift between Jacob and his sons.

In this perspective, chap. 34 makes an interesting and instructive sequel to chaps. 32–33. There we learned how the fearful and alienated Jacob was changed into the new Israel, who boldly returned to Canaan and made peace with his brother Esau, whom he had struggled with and cheated since birth. But this story shows Jacob's old nature reasserting itself, a man whose moral principles are weak, who is fearful of standing up for right when it may cost him dearly, who doubts God's power to protect, and who allows hatred to divide him from his children just as it had divided him from his brother.

Looking ahead, this story provides an interesting backdrop to the story of Joseph and his brothers. There the same underlying division between Leah and her sons on the one side and Jacob and Rachel and her sons, Joseph and Benjamin, on the other is both the starting point and the conclusion of the story. It is Leah's sons' hatred of Joseph that leads them to sell him into Egyptian slavery. This almost breaks Jacob's heart, whereas Dinah's rape seems to have left him unmoved. And the Joseph story goes on to tell how this great gulf within Jacob's family is eventually spanned. As Jacob and Esau were eventually reconciled, so Joseph and his brothers eventually forgive each other.

But that is to look ahead. Here we see that despite Jacob's lack of affection, moral principle, and courage, he survives. Indeed, he prospers in an unexpected way from his sons' fierce anger. He is greatly enriched by the seizure of the Shechemites' flocks, herds, wives, and other properties. His grandfather, Abraham, and his father, Isaac, had both failed to protect their womenfolk because they feared for their own skin (12:10–20; 20; 26:6–14), yet they had prospered greatly.

Here Jacob has a similar experience. The promise made to Abraham, that "he who disdains you I shall curse," is once again demonstrated despite fear and unbelief. And the next episode will show the specific promise to Jacob that he would return to his father's house in peace (28:15, 21) also being fulfilled. The covenant promises come true despite human frailty.

Undoubtedly, the heroes of this story, though they are the villains of the Joseph story, are Dinah's brothers, particularly Simeon and Levi. Here they are portrayed as fiercely opposing intermarriage with the Canaanites of the land and taking up the sword to avenge sexual misconduct. Num 25 shows Phineas, a descendant of Levi, acting similarly by killing a Midianite princess and a Simeonite having intercourse together. Later all the tribes join in a war against Midian, killing the males and taking the women, children, and herds captive (Num 31:1–12). Throughout the OT, intermarriage with non-Israelites is looked on with disfavor and often banned altogether (Gen 24:3; 27:46; Deut 7:3; 1 Kgs 11:1–3; Neh 13:23–27), for it is seen as likely to lead to apostasy from the LORD (Deut 7:4; 1 Kgs 11:4–5). For a similar reason, the NT discourages believers from marrying pagans (2 Cor 6:14–18). Gen 34 traces this concern for purity of line back to Simeon and Levi, forefather of the Israelite priestly tribe.

Journey's End for Jacob and Isaac   *(35:1–29)*

Bibliography

Burchard, C. "Gen 35:6–10 und 36:5–12 MT aus der Wüste Juda." *ZAW* 78 (1986) 71–75. **Eissfeldt, O.** "Jakob-Lea und Jakob-Rahel." *KS* 4 (1968) 170–75. **Keel, O.** "Das Vergraben der 'fremden Götter' in Gen 35: 4b." *VT* 23 (1973) 305–36. **Klein, M. L.** "'Not to be translated in public.'" *JJS* 39 (1988) 80–91. **Lombardi, G.** "H Fārāh—W. Fārāh presso Anātôt e la questione della tomba di Rahel." *Studii Biblici Franciscani: Liber Annus* 20 (1970) 299–352. **Nicol, C. G.** "Gen 29:32 and 35:22a: Reuben's Reversal." *JTS* 31 (1980) 536–39. **Rendsburg, G. A.** "Notes on Gen 35." *VT* 34 (1984) 361–66. **Shaanan, J.** "'And His Father Called Him Benjamin (or Benjamim)?'" *BMik* 24 (1978/79) 106. **Soggin, J. A.** "Die Geburt Benjamins, Gen 35:16–20(21)." *VT* 11 (1961) 432–40. ――――. "Zwei umstrittene Stellen aus dem Überlieferungskreis um Schechem." *ZAW* 73 (1961) 78–87. **Vogt, E.** "Benjamin geboren 'eine Meile' von Ephrata." *Bib* 56 (1975) 30–36. **Zakovitch, Y.** "The Tendenz of the Incident of Hiding the Idols in Shechem (Gen 35: 2, 4)." (Heb.) *BMik* 25 (1979/80) 30–37.

Translation

[1] *God said to Jacob, "Up,[a] go up to [b]Bethel and stay there; make an altar there to the God who [c]appeared[c] to you when you fled[d] from your brother Esau." [2]So Jacob said to his household and to all those who were with him, "Put[a] away the foreign gods that are with you, purify[b] yourselves, and change[c] your outer garments, [3]so that we may rise up, go up to Bethel and make an altar there to the God [a]who answered me in my time of crisis and has been with me[a] on the journey I have undertaken." [4]So they gave Jacob all the*

foreign gods which they possessed and the earrings in their ears, and Jacob hid them under the terebinth which is near Shechem.[a] [5]*Then they journeyed,*[a] *and a divine terror fell*[b] *on the surrounding towns, so that they*[c] *did not pursue the sons of Jacob.*

[6]*So*[a] *Jacob and all the people with him came*[a] *to Luz (that is Bethel), which is in the land of Canaan.* [7]*There he built an altar, and he called the place,* [a]*El of Beth-El,*[a] *for there God had revealed*[b] *himself to him when he fled from his brother.* [8]*Then Deborah, Rebekah's nursemaid,*[a] *died,*[b] *and she was buried*[c] *below Bethel, under an*[d] *oak, so it*[e] *was called "Oak of weeping."*

[9]*God had appeared*[a] *to Jacob again, when he was returning from Paddan-Aram, and he*[b] *had blessed him.* [10]*God had said, "Your name is Jacob, but it shall not be called Jacob any more, but your name shall be Israel." So he was named Israel.* [11]*God said to him, "I am God Almighty. Be fruitful and multiply, and may a nation and a multitude of nations come from you and kings come out of your loins.* [12]*The land*[a] *which I gave to Abraham and Isaac I shall give*[b] *to you, and to your descendants after you I shall give the land."*

[13]*Then God went away from him* [a]*at the place where he had spoken to him.*[a] [14]*So Jacob erected*[a] *a pillar in the place where he had spoken to him. It was a pillar of stone, and he had poured*[b] *over it a libation and poured*[c] *oil on it.* [15]*Then Jacob named the place where God had spoken to him Beth-el.*

[16]*They then journeyed from Bethel, and when they were still about two hours' distance from Ephrata, Rachel went into labor, and it became difficult.*[ab] [17]*When her labor was at its hardest,*[a] *the midwife*[b] *said to her, "Don't be afraid, for this is another son for you."* [18]*And as her soul was going*[a] *out of her, for she was dying,*[b] *she named him Ben-Oni, but his father called him Benjamin.* [19]*So Rachel died and was buried on the way to Ephrata, which is Bethlehem.* [20]*Then Jacob erected a pillar over her grave: it is the pillar at Rachel's tomb until the present day.*

[21]*Israel then journeyed and pitched his*[a] *tent farther on toward Migdal-Eder.* [22]*While he was staying in that area,* [a]*Reuben went and lay with Bilhah, his father's concubine,*[a] *and Israel heard about it.*[b]

Now there were twelve sons of Jacob. [23]*The sons of Leah: Reuben, Jacob's firstborn, Simeon, Levi, Judah, Issachar, and Zebulon.* [24a]*The sons of Rachel: Joseph and Benjamin.* [25]*The sons of Bilhah, Rachel's slave-girl: Dan and Naphtali.* [26]*The sons of Zilpah, Leah's slave-girl: Gad and Asher. These are the sons of Jacob, who were born*[a] *to him in Paddan-Aram.*

[27]*Jacob came to Isaac his father in Mamre, in* [a]*Kiryat-Arba*[a] *(which is Hebron), where Abraham and Isaac had been immigrants.* [28]*Isaac lived a hundred and eighty years.* [29]*Isaac expired and died and was gathered to his relations, old and full of years. And his sons Esau and Jacob buried him.*

Notes

1.a. On the use of קוּם as introductory exclamation, see *SBH*, 56–57.
1.b. G adds "to the place of."
1.c-c. On the use of ptcp for relative clause in past time, see GKC, 116o.
1.d. ב + inf constr qal בּרח + 2 masc sg suffix.
2.a. 2 masc pl impv hiph סוּר.
2.b. Waw + 2 masc pl impv hithp טהר.
2.c. Waw + 2 masc pl impv hiph חלף.
3.a-a. Note how the ptcp ("answered") in the relative clause is continued by finite verb ("has been") (GKC, 116o,x; WOC, 561, 631).

4.a. G adds "and he destroyed them unto this day."

5.a. Waw consec + 3 masc pl impf qal נסע (pausal form).

5.b. Masc verb with fem subj ("fear"); cf. GKC, 145o-q.

5.c. Indefinite subj (GKC, 144f).

6.a-a. On this construction, see *EWAS,* 63.

7.a-a. G, S, Vg read simply "Beth-El."

7.b. 3 masc pl pf niph נגלה. SamPent has sg נגלה. Though the versions also have a sg verb, the Vorlage of their reading is uncertain. On the use of the pl verb after "God," cf. 20:13 and GKC, 145i.

8.a. Fem sg hiph ptcp יִנֵק.

8.b. Cf. n. 23:2.a.

8.c. Waw consec + 3 fem sg impf niph קבר.

8.d. On the use of def art, see GKC, 126d.

8.e. 3 sg masc used for indefinite subj (GKC, 144d).

9.a. Cf. n. 12:7.a.

9.b. SamPent, G read "God."

12.a. Cf. n. 13:15.a-a.

12.b. Cf. n. 13:15.b.

13.a-a. Untranslated by Vg.

14.a. Cf. n. 21:28.a.

14.b. Waw consec + 3 masc sg impf hiph נסך.

14.c. Cf. n. 28:18.a.

16.a. Waw consec + 3 fem sg impf (apoc) piel קשה.

16.b. ב + inf constr qal ילד + 3 fem sg suffix.

17.a. ב + inf constr hiph קשה + 3 fem sg suffix.

17.b. Def art + fem sg piel ptcp ילד.

18.a. ב + inf constr יצא.

18.b. As pointed with stress on first syllable, 3 fem sg pf qal מות "she died," but *BHS* prefers stress on second syllable to make it ptcp "dying."

21.a. Old orthography of 3 masc sg suffix ה instead of ו (Joüon, 94h).

22.a-a. The double set of accents on this part of the verse, "intended for public reading, aims at uniting vv 22 and 23 into *one,* so as to pass rapidly over the unpleasant statement in v 22" (GKC, 15p).

22.b. G adds "and it seemed evil to him."

24.a. SamPent, G, S have "And" as in vv 25, 26.

26.a. 3 masc sg qal pass ילד. Here the pass is construed impersonally; hence, concord between sg verb and pl "sons" is unnecessary (GKC, 121ab), though SamPent has pl verb.

27.a-a. *BHS* redivides word "toward Kiryat-Arba."

Form/Structure/Setting

After the full, dramatic, and well-integrated narratives that make up the rest of the Jacob cycle, the miscellaneous collection of very diverse materials in this chapter comes as a surprise to the reader. On first reading it is hard to see how they fit together or much reason for their inclusion. They all relate apparently to Jacob's final steps back to Canaan, shortly before the death of his father Isaac. But first impressions may be misleading. After outlining the contents of this chapter, I shall endeavor to show that its arrangement is consonant with patterns of editorial method discernible elsewhere in Genesis.

v 1	Divine call to go to Bethel
vv 2–8	Jacob's obedience
vv 9–12	Reaffirmation of the promises
vv 13–15	Jacob's worship at Bethel
vv 16–20	Birth of Benjamin: Death and burial of Rachel
vv 21–22a	Reuben's shameful act

vv 22b–26   Jacob's sons
vv 27–29   Death and burial of Isaac by his two sons

Throughout this section there are numerous references to earlier parts of the Jacob story (vv 1, 3 refer to chap. 28; vv 2, 4 to 31:19, 34–35; v 5 to 34:30–31; v 7 to 28:11–22; v 8 to 24:59; v 9 to 33:18; v 10 to 32:25–33; vv 11–12 to 28:3–4, 13–15, 20–21; v 14 to 28:18, 22; v 15 to 28:17; v 16 to chaps. 29–30; v 17 to 30:22–24; v 18 to 30:1; v 21 to 33:19; v 22 to 29:32; 30:3–8; vv 22b-26 to 29:31–30:24; v 27 to chap. 23; vv 28–29 to 25:7–10). It is clear that this chapter presupposes most, if not all, of the other Jacob stories contained in Genesis, and this is significant for the interpretation of the chapter.

The backbone of Genesis consists of three long cycles about Abraham, Jacob, and Joseph. Each begins with a heading "This is the family history of X" (11:27; 25:19; 37:2) and closes with a description of the death and burial of X and/or X's son by his sons (25:7–10; 35:28–29; 49:33–50:26). Westermann has observed that itineraries and genealogical details seem to cluster toward the beginnings and ends of these cycles, e.g., 11:27–12:9; 25:1–11; 37:2–36; 46:1–50:14. Indeed, chap. 35 could be described as an expanded itinerary. Jacob moves progressively southward, from Shechem in the north to Hebron in the south.

vv 1–4   Command to move
vv 5–6   Journey to Luz (Bethel)
v 16   Journey to Ephrata
v 21   Journey to Migdal-Eder
v 27   Journey to Hebron

For this reason, Westermann (2:549) affirms "One cannot say with H. Gunkel and others that Gen 35 is a heap of blocks. Rather it follows a carefully conceived plan."

But this chapter is more than an expanded itinerary, for the expansions within it follow a sequence that is also found toward the ends of the Abraham and Joseph cycles. Most obvious is the death and burial scene that is to be found at the end of each cycle. But most of the material in chap. 35 has parallels in the other two cycles in roughly the same sequence:

Divine call to journey	22:1–2	35:1	46:2–3
Obedience	22:3–14	35:2–8	46:5–7
Divine promise reaffirmed	22:15–18	35:9–14	48:4
Journey	22:19	35:16	48:5
Birth of sons	22:20–24	35:17–18	48:5–6
Death and burial of wife	23:1–20	35:18–20	48:7
Son's marriage	24:1–67	35:21–22	[48:8ff.] 49:3–4
List of descendants	25:1–6	35:22–26	49:3–28
Death and burial	25:7–10	35:27–29	49:29–50:14

These parallels suggest that the same editorial methods have been followed in the composition of all three cycles. It underlines the similarity between the career of Abraham and that of Jacob and the principle of typology apparent at other points in Genesis too. And to appreciate the writer's intention fully requires that these parallels be borne in mind in the exegesis.

Older source critics generally discerned the presence of the sources J, E, and P in this chapter as well as the hand of the redactor. A typical older analysis by Skinner ascribed vv 1–8, 14, 16–20 to E, 21–22a to J, and the rest, vv 9–13, 15, 22b-29, to P. Driver, however, ascribed vv 14, 16–20 to J instead of to E. Most modern critics find no E material at all. Westermann ascribes vv 1–7 to the redactor, vv 8, 14–22a to J, and the rest, vv 9–13, 22b-29, to P. Coats ascribes it all to J save for vv 9–14, 22b-26 (P). This shows the wide diversity of opinion among commentators. The only passages consistently ascribed to a certain source are vv 9–13, 22b-26 to P and 21–22a to J. But even here the arguments are hardly decisive. It is strange, for example, that v 22 calls "Bilhah" a concubine (פילגש), whereas other passages call her a "slave-girl" (שפחה) if they are both from the same source, J. Conversely, the list of Jacob's sons in 22b–26 is hardly unique to P. Certainly the promise terminology of v 11, "God Almighty," "fruitful," "multiply," has parallels in other passages conventionally ascribed to P (e.g., 17:1–6), but if any of the parallels is ascribed to another source, the argument for identifying this passage with P would also fall. This means that identifying the sources used by the editor is problematic. However, the heterogeneity of the material does make it likely that he has utilized several sources here, but the close parallels in the arrangement of material with 22:1 to 25:10 and 46:2 to 50:14 make it reasonable to hold that the final editor has shaped it all into what he regarded as a coherent and intelligible whole.

Comment

1–7 These verses tell how Jacob returned to Bethel, the place where God had appeared to him when he was running away from his brother's sword. At Bethel he had made a vow, promising in effect to return and worship God there. Now at last he fulfills his vow, and the final stage of his journey back becomes a religious pilgrimage.

1 After tricking Esau, his mother and his father both told him to "up and go" (27:43; 28:2) and indeed "stay" with his uncle (cf. 27:44; 29:19), so the very terms used here echo the beginning of the story as does the explicit reference to "when you fled from Esau your brother." However, the verb "go up" (עלה) is different from that used in earlier passages; it has overtones of pilgrimage. One "went up" to the feasts at Jerusalem (Ps 24:3). So here Jacob is being reminded of his religious obligations. "Build an altar." This is the first time a patriarch has been commanded to build an altar, but its setting at this stage in Jacob's career invites comparison with God's command to Abraham "to offer a burnt offering" (22:2). That was a great test of obedience. By comparison, Jacob's test was easy, yet if he was scared to travel because of Canaanite hostility (cf. 34:30), it may have taken more courage than it seems.

2 But Jacob was as prompt as Abraham (cf. 22:3), and he immediately instructs them to prepare for pilgrimage. Worship of other gods was always incompatible with serving the God who said, "You shall have no other gods before me" (Exod 20:3). Ps 24:3–4 asks, "Who shall ascend the hill of the LORD?" and answers, "He who has clean hands and a pure heart, who does not lift up his soul to what is false" (i.e., idols).

And other texts record the putting away of foreign gods in the context of renewed devotion to God (Josh 24:14, 23–24; Judg 10:16; 1 Sam 7:3–4). Worship, which
brings one into the presence of a holy God, demands inward and outward purity,
the latter being seen as an expression of the former. Purification usually took the
form of bathing the body, washing the clothes, and shaving (Lev 14:8–9; Num 8:7).
Before the Sinai revelation, all the people were told to wash their clothes and ab-
stain from sexual intercourse (Exod 19:10–15). Here Jacob insists that they change
their "outer garments," the poncho-type wrapper used as coat and blanket (Exod
22:25–26[26–27]). Their change of clothes represents a new and purified way of life
(cf. 41:14). Elsewhere in the Pentateuch, sexual intercourse and the spilling of blood
in war are seen as polluting (Num 31:19; Lev 15:18; 18:24–29). So this command to
purify themselves probably looks back to the pollution produced in chap. 34.

3 "My time of crisis" is a common phrase, especially in the Psalms (e.g.,
20:2[1]; 50:15). Here Jacob is harking back to his flight from Esau, as the reference to the vow he made then, "If God will be with me, guard me on the journey
I am undertaking" (28:20), makes clear. When the prayer offered as a vow was
answered, the votary was duty bound to fulfill the promise he had made. Now
Jacob implies he is about to do that.

4 The family members respond as requested, putting away their foreign gods
and also their earrings. The significance of this last point is elusive. On two later
occasions, earrings were used to make objects of idolatrous worship, the golden calf
and an ephod (Exod 32:2–4; Judg 8:24–27). It could be that burying the earrings
along with the foreign gods expressed their complete determination to dispose
of the idols and also any material that could be used to replace them. A comparison with Num 31:48–54 suggests a quite different possibility. After the battle with the
Midianites, the Israelites had to purify themselves (Num 31:19–20). Part of their
purification process included donating to the sanctuary booty consisting of "articles
of gold, armlets and bracelets, signet rings, earrings, and beads, to make atonement
for ourselves before the LORD" (Num 31:50). This suggests that the rings removed
by Jacob's sons may well have been part of the booty captured by them from the
Shechemites; indeed it is possible that the outer garments and the foreign gods
(gold-plated idols?) were part of the spoil (cf. Num 31:20; Josh 7:21; Deut 7:25).
We have already noted the close parallels between Gen 34 and Num 31:1–9 (*Comment* on 34:27–29). These further parallels strengthen the case for reading all of
35:1–4, not merely v 5, in the light of chap. 34. 35:5 is not a late gloss or extract
from a different source, but it flows naturally out of the preceding verses.

"Terebinth" (אלה): probably the Atlantic terebinth according to M. Zohary
(*Plants of the Bible*, 110–11).

5 At last, Jacob steps out in obedience to God's call. He had stayed longer
near Shechem than he had intended because of the massacre perpetrated by his
sons, which had made him feel insecure (34:30). But his family's readiness to
dedicate themselves solely to their father's God is rewarded, and the divine promise
of protection cited in v 2 is again vindicated. Jacob may have had his fears, but
"divine terror" struck the surrounding cities so they did not pursue the Israelites.
Once again, Jacob's experience anticipates that of his descendants when they
conquered the land (Exod 23:27; Deut 7:20–24; Josh 2:9–11; cf. Exod 34:24).
Confronting Jacob and Joshua, the Canaanites were paralyzed with fear.

6 The mention of Luz, the old name for Bethel, seems unnecessary here, since the change of name has been already noted in 28:19. It parallels the second mention of the change of Jacob's name to Israel in 35:10 and 32:28–29(27–28). Though postulating multiple sources may partially explain the duplication of traditions, it does not explain why the editor chose to include both. Repetition is used in Genesis to stress the importance or certainty of events (e.g., the birth of Isaac, 17:19; 18:10, and the paired dreams in the Joseph story, 37:6–10; 40:5–19; 41:1–7, 32). Here, the narrative is emphasizing that the changed name of Bethel shows that God had revealed himself or spoken there (cf. vv 7, 13–15).

7 This verse records the fulfillment of the command given in v 1. Whether Jacob fulfilled his vow (28:20–22) is not stated, but the ensuing divine revelation probably implies he did keep his promise.

"El-Bethel." It would be easier to accept the versions reading "Bethel," but a similar title, "*Ilu-bayt-ilî*," is found in an Assyro-Tyrian treaty according to Speiser (244). Jacob's paraphrase (662) "El is in Bethel," though attractive, is rather free.

נגלה "revealed himself" is a term associated with prophetic experience (cf. 1 Sam 3:7, 21), perhaps suggesting that Jacob, like Abraham, was a sort of prophet.

8 This is the first of three deaths mentioned in this chapter. This is the only time Rebekah's nurse is named (cf. 24:59). It is strange that her death is recorded but Rebekah's is not. Perhaps it is understood that Rebekah died when Jacob was in Paddan-Aram. Despite her hopes, she never saw her favorite son again (27:45). Presumably "the oak of Deborah" was a well-known tree near Bethel. On the different varieties of Palestinian oak, see M. Zohary (*Plants of the Bible*, 108–9).

9–12 Just as Abraham's three-day pilgrimage to sacrifice on Mount Moriah climaxed in the most categorical reaffirmation of the promises in his career, so, too, Jacob's sacred journey is crowned with the strongest statement of the promises that he ever heard, summing up and adding to what had been said to him on earlier occasions. And it is to this revelation that Jacob looked back at the end of his life when he blessed Ephraim and Manasseh in 48:3–4.

10 Jacob was given the new name of Israel after wrestling with God at the Yabbok (32:29[28]). The revelation begins by reaffirming his new status embodied in the change of name, but here there is no explanation of the change. That the new name is left unexplained confirms that the reader is supposed to know the previous story: this is not an independent account.

11 This verse echoes both Isaac's blessing of Jacob in 28:3–4 and the covenant ratification with Abraham in chap. 17. Isaac said, "May God Almighty bless you, make you fruitful and multiply you." Here God himself says, "I am God Almighty. Be fruitful and multiply" (cf. 17:1, 2, 6). "May a nation" echoes the oracle before Jacob's birth, "Two *nations* are in your womb" (25:23), while "a multitude of nations" echoes Isaac's prayer, "so that you become a multitude of peoples" (28:3), and rather less closely 17:4, 5, 6. But never before had Jacob been promised "kings shall come out of your loins," though Abraham had been promised rather less vividly "kings shall come out of you" (17:6). Possibly, the phraseology here reflects Jacob's experience at the Yabbok when his thigh was touched.

12 Finally, the promises of land combine elements of Isaac's prayer (28:4) and Jacob's dream at Bethel (28:13), and more loosely 17:8. "The land which I gave to Abraham [cf. 28:4] and Isaac I shall give to you, and to your descendants" (cf. 28:13).

Thus, in a few short sentences all the long-range promises made to Jacob at various points in his life are here summed up. Of course the short-term promises of protection and return to the land (28:15, 20–21) have already been fulfilled, so there is no point in repeating them. But there is a new feature; the promise of royal descendants is here given for the first time to Jacob, though such a promise had been made to Abraham (cf. 17:6, 16).

13 For a similar close to a theophany, cf. 17:22.

14–15 If God's first revelation of himself to Jacob at Bethel warranted such acts of piety as erecting a pillar of stone, pouring a libation, and calling the place Bethel, house of God, how much more did the reaffirmation of the promises. The place fully deserved to be called Bethel (cf. 28:18–20).

16–22 But spiritual elation is followed by family tragedy. First, Rachel, Jacob's favorite wife, dies giving birth to a second son; then Jacob's eldest son, Reuben, dishonors both Jacob his father and his father's wives by committing incest. Jacob's joy is turned to sorrow and then to anger.

16 "About two hours' distance." This is a problematic phrase found only here and in 48:7; 2 Kgs 5:19. This translation of כברת equates Hebrew ברה with Akk. *bēru*, the distance traveled in two hours, roughly eleven kilometers or seven miles (E. Vogt, *Bib* 56 [1975] 30–36; *EM* 4:11–12). "Ephrata" seems to be the name of a region inhabited by Ephrathites, a Judean clan (1 Chr 2:19), of which Bethlehem and Kiriath Jearim were the best-known villages (1 Chr 2:50–52).

The story describes Jacob traveling southward along the main north-south route through the hills from Bethel to Hebron. So this comment places the birthplace of Benjamin and the grave of Rachel somewhere north of Jerusalem. This fits in with Jer 31:15, 1 Sam 10:2, and Josh 18:25, which imply Rachel wept for her children near Ramah in the territory of Benjamin. This Ramah may be identified with Er-Ram about eight kilometers (five miles) north of Jerusalem. This would be, according to Vogt (*Bib* 56 [1975] 36), about thirteen kilometers from the valley of Ephrata around Bethlehem. The modern tomb of Rachel, about a mile from the village of Bethlehem, presumably arises from a failure to understand the phrase here translated "about two hours' distance." Already the LXX merely transliterates, showing it does not understand the phrase. For Genesis it is doubtless significant that Benjamin was born in what was subsequently land belonging to his tribe. It gave him title to it.

17 "Her labor was at its hardest." Speiser (273) appropriately suggests that this is an elative use of the hiphil. "The midwife" here performs her traditional role of encouragement. Her comment, "Don't be afraid, for this is another son for you," is conventional, doubtless reflecting a preference for boys, for the midwife in 1 Sam 4:20 says the same. But in Rachel's case the comment is peculiarly apt, for at the birth of Joseph she had prayed, "May the LORD add another son to me!" (30:24). Now in her dying moments she sees the fulfillment of her prayers.

18 Death in childbirth was, till recently, tragically common, so doubtless Rachel's death did not have quite the same pathos for the ancient reader as it does for us. Yet it was undoubtedly tragic, for it was Rachel who had cried in desperation to Jacob, "Give me children, or I shall die" (30:1). It was ultimately the gift of children that killed her. And her choice of name, Ben-Oni, "son of sorrow" (cf. Ichabod in 1 Sam 4:21–22), reflects this. אוני "sorrow" is used of mourning for

the dead in Deut 26:14; Hos 9:4. But for Jacob, the child was the son of his favorite wife, so he "called him Benjamin," son of the right, the right-hand side being the favored lucky side (e.g., Deut 27:12–13; Matt 25:33). The tribe of Benjamin has often been associated with a tribe at Mari called the Dumu-*yamina*, "sons of the south," especially when the logogram Dumu was read phonetically as *banû*, rather than the more probable *mārū*. It is possible that Benjamin also means "son of the south," but any direct connection between the Hebrew Benjaminites and the Mari "sons of the south" is unproven. However, Benjamin is known as a personal name at Mari, which demonstrates the antiquity of the patriarch's name (cf. *IDBS*, 95–96; *EM* 2:263–81; A. Malamat, *Mari and the Early Israelite Experience* [Oxford/New York: Oxford UP, 1989] 31, 35).

For נֶפֶשׁ "soul" or "life," see *Comment* on 2:7.

19 "Which is Bethlehem" identifies which part of Ephrata is meant. It is not saying that Rachel's grave is in or even very near Bethlehem, simply that Jacob was traveling toward Bethlehemite Ephrata when she died.

20 For fuller discussions of Rachel's grave and its location, cf. Vogt (*Bib* 56 [1975] 30–36), Lombardi (*Studii Biblici Franciscani* 20 [1970] 299–52), and *EM* 7:360–63. For the custom of erecting tombstones, cf. 2 Sam 18:18. "Until the present day," i.e., that of the writer. 1 Sam 10:2 and Jer 31:15 show that the site of her tomb was known as late as Jeremiah's time.

21–22a The extreme brevity with which this episode is related reflects the writer's horror at it (cf. *Comment* on 9:21); while never glossing over wickedness, Scripture does not pander to the prurient by going into sensational detail.

21 "Migdal-Eder," lit. "tower of the flock." The context here implies that Migdal-Eder was a well-known place, but this passage is the only one that gives any clear clues to its location, somewhere between Bethel (v 16) and Hebron (v 27). If "tower of the flock" in Mic 4:8 is a proper name, it could be near Jerusalem. This would fit with locating Rachel's grave north of Jerusalem at Er-Ram. Late Jewish tradition (e.g., *m. Šeqal.* 7:4 and *Tg. Ps.-J.* on this passage) states that the Messiah will reveal himself at Migdal-Eder. So it has been suggested that Migdal-Eder could be Hurvat al-Bireh near the pools of Solomon about three miles southwest of Bethlehem. Christian tradition (Jerome) located Migdal-Eder at the Shepherds' Fields (Diyar el-Ghanam) a mile and a half east of Bethlehem (*EM* 4:37).

22 It seems likely that Reuben's motives were more than sensual. By his act, he hoped to prevent Rachel's maid succeeding Rachel as his father's favorite wife. Reuben resented that Jacob did not honor his mother Leah. Also, it was a claim to authority over his father (cf. Abner lying with Saul's concubine, 2 Sam 3:7–8); as firstborn he was asserting a claim to his father's estate. But these motives do not mitigate Scripture's condemnation. This kind of incest is categorically condemned in Lev 18:8, and according to Lev 20:11, it warrants the death penalty and God's curse, according to Deut 27:20. Within Genesis, it evokes the sins of Ham (9:22–27) and Lot's daughters (19:33–38), and outside Genesis it foreshadows the ultimate act of hybris in Absalom's rebellion, when he went into his father's concubines (2 Sam 16:21–22). This act was a turning point in the rebellion; thereafter everything started to go wrong for Absalom. Similarly, the legal texts show that such an act, which is an offense against both filial piety and sexual propriety, cannot go unpunished. Yet here, as in chap. 34, Jacob is strangely silent. He just "heard about it" (cf. 34:5).

What does he think? By failing to report any reaction on Jacob's part, the narrator has left a gap that no one can miss. Is Jacob as indifferent to Bilhah's abuse as he was to Dinah's, despite her being his dearest Rachel's maid? Or does he care but is now incapable of exercising authority over his oldest son? These great questions are posed just before the Joseph story begins, and they are doubtless intended to color our reading of chaps. 37–50. This episode suggests that there is tension not only between Jacob and his sons descended from Leah but also between the sons of Bilhah and Rachel on the one hand and the sons of Leah on the other. Furthermore, though Reuben appears throughout the Joseph story in quite a humane light, trying to rescue Joseph and so on, this episode shows the dark side of his character. But not until 49:2–3 does Jacob show his deep anger at Reuben's behavior, when the firstborn's blessing turns into a curse.

22b–26 This list of Jacob's sons appears "totally isolated in its context" (Coats, 243), and to ascribe it to a different source from the preceding material does not explain why a redactor should have put such a list here. Yet, as pointed out under *Form/Structure/Setting*, this arrangement of material has good parallels elsewhere in Genesis. Gen 24 tells of Isaac's marriage (cf. 35:21–22a), 25:1–6 lists Abraham's sons (cf. 35:22b–26), and then 25:7–11 records Abraham's death and burial (cf. 35:27–29). Similarly, the Joseph story closes with a mention of Reuben's sin (49:4; cf. 35:21–22a), lists all Jacob's sons (49:3–27), and recounts his death and burial (49:29–50:14). So it could be that this list of Jacob's sons in 35:22b–27 is, like the previous verses (21–22a), preparing the way for the Joseph story, reminding us who they are and which side they are on by arranging them strictly according to their mothers. The two other lists of Jacob's sons, 29:32–30:24 and 49:2–27, do not follow a genealogical arrangement by mothers so strictly. If we are right to see this list as in some sense anticipatory of what follows, this would fit in with Genesis' method elsewhere, for often the end of one section is a trailer for the next (e.g., 4:25–26 for chap. 5; 9:20–27 for chap. 10).

26 "Who were born to him in Paddan-Aram." In the light of vv 16–19, this comment does not cover Benjamin, the youngest son.

27–29 Eventually, Jacob reaches his father's house (cf. 28:21). Isaac has moved north from Beersheba, where he was last heard of, to Mamre in Kiryat-Arba (which is Hebron). On these terms, cf. *Comments* on 13:18; 23:2. Such detailed specification, though seemingly redundant, emphasizes the significance of the place, which was where some of the greatest promises had been made (13:14–18; chaps. 15–18) and where Abraham had first purchased land in Canaan (chap. 23) even though he and Isaac had only been immigrants.

28–29 These verses echo 25:7–9 very closely. As the estranged brothers, Ishmael and Isaac, joined together to bury Abraham, so the reconciliation of Jacob and Esau (chap. 33) is reaffirmed in this final act of jointly burying their father. The text implies that Isaac was buried in the ancestral grave at Macpelah, but this is not made explicit until 49:29–32.

Explanation

After the series of dramatic episodes that make up the Jacob cycle, this chapter comes as rather an anticlimax. It appears to be a hodgepodge of biographical

anecdotes thrown together to round off the story of Jacob's return to his home. But first impressions are deceptive. Though these closing narratives are worded more briefly than most of the preceding, they are not without theological depth, especially when they are set in context and in relationship with each other.

Chap. 34 ended with Jacob paralyzed by the prospect of the vengeance the Canaanites might try to wreak on him for the massacre perpetrated by his sons. Now God again speaks to him, reminding him of the last time he fled to save his life, from his brother Esau (v 1). Jacob is told to go back to Bethel, where he had met God before, the God who had promised to protect him and bring him back to his father's house in peace. It was at Bethel that Jacob had vowed to worship the LORD when he returned to Canaan. So far, Jacob had not fulfilled that vow, so he is told that notwithstanding his fears, he must "go up to Bethel," go on pilgrimage to the town that was holy to him.

Without hesitation he complies, directing his household to prepare themselves to go on pilgrimage. Encounter with God demands purity in the worshiper (cf. Lev 14; Deut 23:15[14]; 26:14; Ps 24:3–4), and the whole family is defiled both by Dinah's rape (34:5) and by the massacre that ensued (34:25–29; cf. Num 31:19–24). So he directs them to "put away the foreign gods"; we are not told whether these were recently acquired as booty or are longer-term possessions (cf. 31:30–35). He also tells them to "purify themselves," i.e., wash and maybe shave, and "change their outer garments," because they had been polluted in the battle or captured from the Shechemites. This, says Jacob, will enable me to return to Bethel and worship the God who has protected me throughout my wanderings as he promised (v 3; cf. 28:15, 20–22). Just as promptly, his household obeys, and like their later descendants (Num 31:50), they hand over their earrings as part of their purification. As there was no approved priest to receive them in Jacob's time, they are simply hidden under the terebinth near Shechem. It could be that this gesture is seen not merely as purificatory or expiatory, as in Num 31:50, but as a fulfillment of Jacob's vow to give "a full tenth" of "everything you give me" (28:22).

Prompt obedience is promptly rewarded. As the later Israelites were to experience when they entered Canaan to capture it (cf. Josh 2:9), "a divine terror fell on the surrounding towns" (v 5), so that Jacob proceeded to Bethel unmolested, once again demonstrating that "I am really with you and will guard you wherever you go." In obedient gratitude, Jacob builds an altar and once again calls the place "El of Bethel."

In the story of Abraham, the journey to and sacrifice on Mount Moriah constitute the final test of his faith. Because God revealed himself there, he called the place "The LORD will provide" (22:14). Similarly, for Jacob this risky journey to Bethel was a great test. He too survived and, like Abraham (22:15–18), subsequently received a powerful reaffirmation of the promises (35:9–12)—a revelation that was to uphold him to his dying day (48:3–4). Once again he was reminded of his new name, Israel, for yet again he had struggled with God and had overcome (32:29[28]). He was reassured that he would have a multitude of descendants, some of whom would be kings, and that his land would be theirs for ever. Here, more strongly than ever before, the great promises that have sustained Jacob throughout his career are endorsed and enlarged.

But as ever within the Pentateuch, the fulfillment of these promises is always partial. Sorrow soon follows joy. Rachel had prayed, "May the LORD add another son to me" (30:24). But when at last her prayer is answered, she dies giving birth, naming him "Son of sorrow." Jacob more optimistically calls him "Benjamin," "Son of the right," "Son of good fortune." But as the Joseph story will reveal, Rachel's name for Benjamin proves more apt than Jacob hoped.

Even worse for Jacob is to follow. In complete contempt of his father, Reuben lies incestuously with his father's concubine, Bilhah. The sons of Leah had protested strongly enough about their sister's rape "being a disgrace in Israel"; now his firstborn commits an even more shameful deed against Israel himself. The self-righteous Reuben is exposed as a hypocrite, and future relations between Jacob and his sons through Leah are overhung by a dark cloud. The ominous comment "Jacob heard about it" (v 22) leaves us in suspense, wondering how and when the storm will break. The list of Jacob's sons, arranged not chronologically but by maternal descent, indicates the divisions within the family that will prove to be so important in the story of Joseph.

Yet that same list of sons (vv 22–26) is a reminder that the promise of a multitude of descendants (v 11) is being fulfilled. One day there will be a nation. One day there will be kings (v 11; cf. 36:31). So, too, the burial of Isaac by his reconciled sons Jacob and Esau has a hopeful side. Isaac is buried in the only real estate acquired by Abraham in Canaan, at Mamre in Kiryat-Arba, a place where the promises to Abraham had been most fully revealed. So the death and burial of Isaac in ripe old age in Mamre is a pledge of Israel's ultimate possession of the land.

Throughout Genesis, the promises look beyond the patriarchal era for their fulfillment. Abraham, Isaac, and Jacob see them only partially fulfilled. And this is very true here too. The only aspect of the promise to Jacob totally fulfilled was the promise of divine protection: after all the vicissitudes of his journey to Paddan-Aram and back, he arrives safe and sound near Shechem. But the last stage from Shechem to Bethel is risky. Nevertheless, he makes it, for the divine terror falls on the surrounding cities. But the longer-term hopes of nationhood and settlement throughout Canaan are still far from realized.

Yet Jacob's experiences here do not just look back to Abraham's; they also look forward and indeed anticipate his descendants' actions. Chap. 34 showed his sons butchering the Canaanites for their sins. Chap. 35 depicts them purifying themselves from the impurity thereby contracted, laying aside the booty they had taken, and describes the divine terror paralyzing their foes. In this way, they set a precedent later followed by the Israelites in their wars of conquest (Num 31; Deut 7; Josh 7). For Jeremiah, Rachel could still be heard weeping at Ramah, not over her own death, but over the death of her children (Jer 31:15). And Matthew develops this idea still further, applying it to the mourning of the mothers of the Bethlehem region at the slaughter of their children (Matt 2:16–18).

Thus, throughout this chapter, as elsewhere in the Jacob cycle, there is a tension between the present reality and future hope. The partial fulfillment of the promises in the patriarchal era makes the reader look beyond that era to his own time to see how much more fully the promises had come true in his own time than then. "These all died in faith, not having received what was prom-

ised, but having seen it and greeted it from afar, and having acknowledged that they were strangers and exiles on the earth. . . . All these, though well attested by their faith, did not receive what was promised, since God had foreseen something better for us, that apart from us they should not be made perfect" (Heb 11:13, 39–40).

The Family History of Esau   (36:1–37:1)

Bibliography

Bartel, A. "Studies in the Lists of Gen 36." (Heb.) *BMik* 32 (1986/87) 364–72. **Bartlett, J. R.** *Edom and the Edomites.* JSOTSup 77. Sheffield: Academic, 1989. ————. "The Edomite King-List of Gen 36:31–39 and 1 Chron 1:43–50." *JTS* 16 (1965) 301–14. **Beeston, A. F. L.** "What Did Anah See?" *VT* 24 (1974) 109–10. **Bennett, C. M.** "Excavations in Tawilan in Southern Jordan 1982." *Levant* 16 (1984) 1–23. **Driver, G. R.** "Gen 36:24: Mules or Fishes?" *VT* 25 (1975) 109–10. **Horwitz, W. J.** "Were There Twelve Horite Tribes?" *CBQ* 35 (1973) 69–71. **Kitchen, K. A.** "The Egyptian Evidence on Ancient Jordan." In *Early Edom and Moab: The Beginning of the Iron Age in Southern Jordan*, ed. P. Bienkowski. Merseyside: Collis, 1992. 21–34. **Knauf, E. A.** "Alter und Herkunft der edomitischen Königsliste Gen 36:31–39." *ZAW* 97 (1985) 245–53. ————. "Supplementa Ismaelitica." *BN* 38–39 (1987) 44–49. **Kornfeld, W.** "Die Edomiterlisten (Gen 36; 1 Chron 1) im Lichte des altarabischen Namensmateriales." In *Mélanges bibliques et orientaux: FS M. Delcor,* ed. A. Caquot, S. Légasse, and M. Tardieu. Kevelaer: Butzon & Bercker, 1985. 231–36. **Luria, B. Z.** "He Is the Anah Who Found the *yemim* in the Wilderness (Gen 36:24)." (Heb.) *BMik* 30 (1984/85) 262–68. **Prewitt, T. J.** "Kinship Structures and the Genesis Genealogies." *JNES* 40 (1981) 87–98. **Renaud, B.** "Les généalogies et la structure de l'histoire sacerdotale dans le livre de la Genèse." *RB* 97 (1990) 5–30. **Wilson, R. R.** *Genealogy and History in the Biblical World.* New Haven: Yale UP, 1977. 167–83. **Zeron, A.** "The Swan Song of Edom." *JJS* 31 (1980) 190–98. **Zwickel, W.** "Rehobot-Nahar" *BN* 29 (1985) 28–34.

Translation

[1] *This is the family history of Esau, that is Edom.*

[2] *Esau married Canaanite wives, Adah, the daughter of Elon the Hittite, Oholibamah, the daughter of Anah, daughter[a] of Zibeon the Hivite,[b]* [3] *Basemat,[a] the daughter of Ishmael, the sister of Nebaiot.* [4] *Adah gave birth to Eliphaz for Esau, and Basemat gave birth to Reuel.* [5] *Oholibamah gave birth to Yeush,[a] Yalam, and Korach. These are Esau's sons, who were born[b] to him in the land of Canaan.*

[6] *Esau took his wives, sons, and daughters, all the persons that belonged to his household, his livestock, all his herds, and all his property which he had acquired in the land of Canaan and went[a] out to a land[a] away from his brother Jacob,* [7] *because their possessions were too numerous for them to dwell[a] together. For the land to which they had migrated was unable to sustain[b] them because of their livestock.* [8] *So Esau settled in the mountain of Seir. Now Esau is Edom.*

[9] *This is the family history of Esau, the father of Edom, in the hill country of Seir.*

[10] *These[a] are the names of Esau's sons. Eliphaz, the son of Adah, Esau's wife. Reuel, son of Basemat, Esau's wife.* [11] *Eliphaz's sons were Teman, Omar, Zepho, Gatam, and Kenaz.* [12] *Now Timna was a concubine of Eliphaz, the son of Esau, and she gave birth to Amalek for Eliphaz. These are the sons of Adah, Esau's wife.* [13] *These are the sons of Reuel, Nahat, Zerach, Shammah, and Mizzah. These were the descendants of Basemat, Esau's wife.* [14] *These are the sons of Oholibamah, daughter of Anah, daughter[a] of Zibeon, wife of Esau. And she gave birth to Yeush,[b] Yalam, and Korach for Esau.*

[15] *These are the chiefs of Esau's sons; the sons of Eliphaz, Esau's firstborn, chief Teman, chief Omar, chief Zepho, chief Kenaz,* [16a] *chief Korach,[a] chief Gatam, chief Amalek. These*

are the chiefs of Eliphaz in the land of Edom. These are the sons of Adah. [17]*These are the sons of Reuel, Esau's son: chief Nachat, chief Zerach, chief Shammah, chief Mizzah. These are the chiefs of Reuel in the land of Edom. These are the sons of Basemat, Esau's wife.* [18]*Now these are the sons of Oholibamah, Esau's wife: chief Yeush, chief Yalam, chief Korach. These are the chiefs of Oholibamah, the daughter of Anah, Esau's wife.* [19]*These are the sons of Esau. These are their chiefs, that is Edom.*

[20]*These are the sons of Seir the Horite, the inhabitants of the land: Lotan, Shobal, Zibeon, Anah,* [21]*Dishon, Etzer, and Dishan. These are the chiefs of the Horites, the sons of Seir in the land of Edom.* [22]*The sons of Lotan were Hori and Heman, and the sister of Lotan was Timna.* [23]*These are the sons of Shobal: Alvan, Manahat, Ebal, Shepho, and Onam.* [24]*These are the sons of Zibeon:* ª*Ayyah and Anah. It was Anah who found the springs*ᵇ *in the wilderness when he was looking after the donkeys for Zibeon, his father.* [25]*These are the sons of Anah: Dishon and Oholibamah, she was Anah's daughter.* [26]*These are the sons of Dishon:*ª *Hemdan, Eshban, Yitran, and Keran.* [27]*These are the sons of Etzer: Bilhan, Zaavan, and Akan.* [28]*These are the sons of Dishan: Utz and Aran.*

[29]*These are the chiefs of the Horites: chief Lotan, chief Shobal, chief Zibeon, chief Anah,* [30]*chief Dishon, chief Eser, chief Dishan. These are the chiefs of the Horites by their chieftainships*ª *in the land of Seir.*

[31]*These are the kings who reigned in Edom before there were kings for the Israelites.*ª [32]*Bela, son of Beor, reigned in Edom, and his town was called Dinhabah.* [33]*Bela died and Yobab, son of Zerach, from Bozrah reigned instead of him.* [34]*Yobab died, and Husham from the land of Teman reigned instead of him.* [35]*Husham died, and Hadad, son of Bedad, who defeated*ª *Midian in the area of Moab, reigned instead of him. His town was called Avit.* [36]*Hadad died, and Samlah from Masreqah reigned instead of him.* [37]*Samlah died, and Shaul from Rehobot-Hannahar reigned instead of him.* [38]*Shaul died, and Baal-Hanan, son of Akbor, reigned instead of him.* [39]*Baal-Hanan, son of Akbor, died, and Hadad*ª *reigned instead of him. His town was called Pau, and his wife was Mehetabel; she was the daughter of Matred, the daughter*ᵇ *of Mezahab.*

[40]*These are the names of the chiefs of Esau by their clans, areas, and names: chief Timna, chief Alva, chief Yetet,*ª [41]*chief Oholibamah, chief Elah, chief Pinon,* [42]*chief Kenaz, chief Teman, chief Mibsar,* [43]*chief Magdiel, chief Iram. These are the chiefs of Edom by their settlements,*ª *in the land of their possession, that is Esau, father of Edom.*

[37:1] *Now Jacob settled in the land to which his father had migrated in the land of Canaan.*

Notes

2.a SamPent, G, S read "son of."

2.b. *BHS* conjecturally emends to "the Horite" to match v 20.

3.a. Here and in vv 4, 10, 13, 17 SamPent has Mahalat instead of Basemat to harmonize with 28:9.

5.a. עשׂו with Qere, SamPent, and versions and MT v 18.

5.b. 3 pl pf qal pass ילד (cf. 6:1).

6.a-a. This expression is unusual. S "to the land of Seir" and *Tg. Onq. Neof.,* Vg "to another land" are simply smoothing the MT. SamPent, G "out of the land of Canaan" could be a similar attempt at smoothing, but the antiquity of this reading gives it a strong claim.

7.a. מִן + inf constr qal ישׁב.

7.b. לְ + inf constr qal נשׂא.

10.a. SamPent G, S, Vg "And these."

14.a. Cf. n. 36:2.a.

14.b. Cf. n. 36:5.a.

16.a-a. Not in SamPent.

24.a. Omitting the וֹ with SamPent and most versions.

24.b. On this word, see *Comment*.

26.a. 1 Chr 1:41, SamPent, G, S read "Dishon." MT "Dishan."

30.a. This is the sense of the passage (cf. G). *Pace BHS*, this does not warrant repointing MT.

31.a. G paraphrases "in Israel."

35.a. Def art + masc sg hiph ptcp נכה. For use of ptcp to express past, see GKC, 116o.

39.a. SamPent, G, S, Vg, 1 Chr 1:50, 51 read "Hadad." MT "Hadar."

39.b. G, S read "son."

40.a. G reads "Yether," but other versions support MT.

43.a. SamPent "clans."

Form/Structure/Setting

This section has a clear title in v 1, "This is the family history of Esau, that is Edom." Each major section of Genesis has this type of heading (e.g., 2:4; 11:27; 25:12, 19; 37:2). The repetition of almost the same title in 36:9 is unparalleled, though, and requires explanation. The next major heading, "This is the family history of Jacob," comes in 37:2, which makes it likely that 37:1, "Jacob settled in the land . . . of Canaan," is the conclusion of this section. Indeed, it echoes 36:8, "So Esau settled in the mountain of Seir," the two comments balancing each other.

The section falls into the following subsections:

v 1	Title
vv 2–5	Esau's marriages
vv 6–8	Esau's move to Seir
vv 9–14	Esau's sons and grandsons
vv 15–19	Chiefs descended from Esau
vv 20–28	Descendants of Seir the Horite
vv 29–30	Chiefs descended from Seir
vv 31–39	List of Edomite kings
vv 40–43	List of chiefs
37:1	Note about Jacob

Within this chapter there is both diversity and repetition of material. Vv 2–5 tell of Esau's three wives and five sons. Vv 9–14 go over the same ground but add the birth of grandsons to his first two sons. Vv 15–19 say the same but describe Esau's grandsons and his sons by his third wife as "chiefs." Vv 20–28 list the seven sons and twenty grandchildren of Seir, vv 29–30 the chiefs of Seir. As in the previous section, the sons of Seir are now called "chiefs." Vv 31–39 list eight Edomite kings, and vv 40–43 eleven chiefs of Esau.

It is difficult to see the rationale for this collection of materials about Edom, save that Edom was viewed as Israel's closest neighbor and was for a while under Israelite rule. However, within the schema of Genesis, "a family history of Esau" is certainly expected at this point. "A family history of Ishmael," Abraham's older but non-elect son (25:12–18), precedes the much longer "family history of Isaac," the chosen younger son (25:19–35:29). So here a fairly brief history of Esau, the non-elect elder twin, precedes the "family history of Jacob," the elect younger twin (37:2–50:26). Thus a section such as chap. 36 is certainly appropriate here.

The diversity of materials makes it probable that a variety of sources have been drawn on for the chapter, but it is not clear at what stage they have been brought together, nor whether what appears to the modern reader as incompatibilities within the material would have been so perceived by ancient authors and readers. R. R. Wilson has suggested that Gen 36 represents "the Edomite lineages functioning in different spheres." If this correct, it has the following consequences. "First, the different versions of Edomite genealogy need not have come from different historical periods. . . . The genealogies would not have been considered contradictory by the people who used them, for they would have recognized that each genealogy was accurate when it was functioning in its own particular sphere. Second, we need not assign the contradictory genealogies to different literary sources or even to different oral traditions. Because the genealogies may have been in use during the same historical period, they may have been preserved in the same oral or written source" (R. R. Wilson, *Genealogy and History,* 180–81).

These important caveats need to be borne in mind when the questions of source criticism are discussed. Headings, such as "This is the family history of," lists, and genealogies are generally assigned to P. The diversity of the material has deterred critics from assigning the whole chapter to P without qualification, for not only is it not homogeneous in itself, but Esau's wives have different names in 26:34 and 28:9, passages which are also usually assigned to P. So two main solutions to these problems have been advanced: either that 36:9–43 reflects sources used by P or that these verses represent a later (post-P) addition to the book. It is not easy to decide between these options, because there are no obvious divisions within the material. Wilson (*Genealogy and History,* 175) argues that vv 9–43 represent a later editorial attempt to harmonize 36:9–43 with 26:34 and 28:9. The editor of vv 1–5 took the names of Esau's wives, Adah, Basemat, and Oholibamah, from vv 10–18. He then took the gentilic epithets "The Hittite" from 26:34 and "daughter of Ishmael" from 28:9 and permuted the names and epithets to produce 36:2–3, "Adah, the daughter of Elon the Hittite, Oholibamah, the daughter of Anah, daughter of Zibeon the *Hivite,* Basemat, the daughter of Ishmael." It is possible that a redactor worked in such a muddled way as Wilson proposes, but it would be simpler to accept that chap. 36 and 26:34; 28:9 represent different traditions of Esau's marriages.

Furthermore, it does look as though 36:9–43 is an insertion into a discrete section (36:1–8; 37:1), for 37:1, "Jacob settled in the land to which his father had migrated in the land of Canaan," matches and echoes 36:7–8 so clearly. Thus almost all commentators conclude that at an earlier stage in the history of the book, 37:1 followed immediately after 36:8. That 36:9–43 is a secondary insertion into the book seems to be confirmed by the second title, "This is the family history of Esau," which is without analogy in the rest of the book. Each of the other nine formulae, "This is the family history of," occurs but once, suggesting that the reduplication here represents an addition to the book, which once had only ten such titles. In this case, 36:9–43 would represent the last part of Genesis to be written.

Westermann (2:561) has suggested that these verses came from the royal archives of Edom, which were taken over by Israel when David subdued the Edomites and incorporated their territory into his empire. Such a hypothesis is speculative,

but Knauf's arguments (*ZAW*97 [1985] 245–53) for a later date are even flimsier. The generally positive attitude toward Esau and the Edomites throughout Genesis fits a period long before the exile, when relations between Israel and Edom became very bitter (cf. Obad; Ps 137:7–9).

Finally, it should be noted that vv 9–43 appear to be a carefully redacted unit in its own right.

Title	"This is the family history of Esau, the father of Edom"	v 9
Subtitle	"These are the names of Esau's sons" (List A)	vv 10–14
Subtitle	"These are the chiefs of Esau's sons" (List A)	vv 15–18
Colophon	"These are the sons of Esau. These are their chiefs, that is Edom"	v 19
Subtitle	"These are the sons of Seir the Horite, the inhabitants of the land"	v 20
	(List B)	vv 20–21
Colophon	"These are the chiefs of the Horites, the sons of Seir in the land of Edom"	v 21
Sub-subtitles	"These are the sons . . ." (List B)	vv 22–28
Subtitle	"These are the chiefs of the Horites"	v 29
	List B (chiefs)	vv 29–30
Colophon	"These are the chiefs of the Horites by their chieftainships in the land of Seir"	v 30
Subtitle	"These are the kings who reigned in Edom"	v 31
	List of kings	vv 32–39
Subtitle	"These are the names of the chiefs of Esau"	v 40
	List of chiefs	vv 41–43
Colophon	"These are the chiefs of Edom by their settlements, in the land of their possession, that is Esau, father of Edom."	v 43

Thus this section falls into three parts, each consisting of a list of sons (or kings) followed by a list of chiefs: vv 10–14//15–18; vv 20–28//29–30; vv 32–39//41–43. And the opening title, "the family history of Esau, the father of Edom" (v 9), is resumed in the final colophon, "in the land of their possession, that is Esau, father of Edom" (v 43). These redactional features do not prove that the whole section has been lifted as it stands from the Edomite archives, which is what Westermann (2:561) suggests. But they do at least make it likely that vv 9–43 were added to Genesis all at once and not in a series of expansions.

Comment

1 This is the standard title for the major sections of Genesis (cf. 6:9; 11:27; 25:12, 19). On the identification of Esau and Edom (cf. Jacob and Israel), see 25:25.

2–5 This brief genealogy lists Esau's three wives and five grandsons born to him in Canaan from Canaanite wives.

As already noted, this list does not match that in 26:34 and 28:9. There, Basemat is called the daughter of Elon the Hittite. Here, Adah is said to be his daughter and Basemat the daughter of Ishmael, whereas in 28:9 Mahalat is Ishmael's daughter. Oholibamah is mentioned here, but Judith in 26:34. That these represent different traditions is obvious, but it is not clear how they are to be related. Possibly Esau had more than three wives, or his wives' names changed.

2 "Adah"; cf. *Comment* on 4:19. "Elon" = "Oak" (cf. 35:8). "Oholibamah" is of uncertain meaning, possibly a Hurrian name (cf. *EM* 1:126–27). "Anah" is an element found in various names from Cappadocia (Puzur-Ana) to Tel-Amarna (Bin-Ana). It could be the name of an Anatolian deity (*EM* 6:307–8). "Daughter of," unless the variant "son" is followed, here has the sense of "granddaughter." "Zibeon" = "Hyena." "The Hivite"; cf. *Comment* on 10:17. Since Adah and Zibeon are termed Horites in v 20, it is possible that "Hivite" is a textual error for "Horite" here.

3 "Basemat"; cf. *Comment* on 36:34. "Nebaiot"; cf. *Comment* on 25:13.

4 "Eliphaz" possibly means "the god El conquers," "my god is Paz," or "the god is strong." "Eliphaz," Job's comforter (Job 2:11), is described as a Temanite. Teman is both a place name and Eliphaz's firstborn according to 36:11. "Reuel" means "friend of El (God)" or "El is a friend" and was a name also used by Israelites (Num 2:14: 1 Chr 9:8).

5 "Yeush" is usually understood as "may (God) help." For other suggestions, see *EM* 3:709. It is also an Israelite name (1 Chr 7:10; 8:39). "Yalam" is of uncertain meaning, perhaps related to עלם "youth" or יעל "mountain goat." "Korach" is usually supposed to mean "Baldhead," but this is doubted by *EM* 7:255. Other Korachs are mentioned in Num 16:1; 1 Chr 2:43; Ps 42:1.

6–8 These verses terminate the story of Esau's life by describing his move from Canaan to Seir. The vocabulary used here is typical of passages describing major moves of clans, especially of clans splitting up (e.g., 12:5 [Abram from Terah]; 13:5–6 [Lot from Abram]; 31:18 [Jacob from Laban]). Note particularly v 7, "because their possessions were too numerous for them to dwell together. For the land . . . was unable to sustain them," echoes 13:6, "[T]he land would not sustain them, dwelling together, because their possessions were too numerous for them to dwell together." Yet in 34:21 Hamor had said, "Let them live in the land . . . look the land is big enough for them," which suggests that however much property Esau really had, there would have been enough room for both Jacob and Esau. But like Lot before him, Esau moves out of the land of promise and out of the record of saving history. Probably 37:1 originally followed 36:8, deliberately contrasting Esau's exit from Canaan with Jacob's staying put and thereby inheriting the promise.

8 "The mountain of Seir"; cf. 33:14, 16; *Comment* on 14:6.

9 This heading, virtually repeating 36:1, betrays what follows as a later insertion into Genesis (see above, *Form/Structure/Setting*).

10–14 These verses fill out the genealogy of vv 2–5 by including Esau's grandsons. Wilson suggests that vv 10–14 give a clue to the different social standings of the Edomite clans. He thinks Amalek, Yeush, Yalam, and Korach were less esteemed than the other clans; Amalek, because his mother is said to be a concubine, and Yeush, Yalam, and Korach, because their mother Oholibamah was probably of Horite descent (cf. *Comment* on v 2). "This fact might also indicate that Horites who had been incorporated into the Edomite social structure were assigned an inferior status" (R. R. Wilson, *Genealogy and History*, 181).

11 "Teman" ("South") is described elsewhere as a district of Edom (Jer 49:20; Ezek 25:13), as famed for its wisdom (Jer 49:7), and as the home of Eliphaz, Job's comforter. On its location, see *EM* 8:524–25. "Omar" perhaps means "eloquent" (BDB), or "lamb" (KB). "Zepho" possibly means "view," "fortune," or "ram."

"Gatam" may mean "thin." "Kenaz": whether this group is related to the Kenizzites mentioned in 15:19 or the Judean clan of Num 32:12 is uncertain.

12   Amalek is well known as one of Israel's most bitter foes, but usually it is not viewed as part of Edom (e.g., Exod 17:8–15; Num 24:20). That this text traces Amalek's ancestry to Esau through a concubine rather than through a full wife may indicate that Amalek joined the Edomite league relatively late and was despised by the Israelites (cf. the unsavory story of Moab and Ammon's origins in 19:32–38).

13   "Nachat," possibly "pure" (Noth, *Personennamen*, 228) or "rest" (KB), is also an Israelite name (1 Chr 6:11[26]; 2 Chr 31:13). "Zerach" may be a shortened theophoric name, "God has shone," or it may mean "brightness, dawn." It is also a common Israelite name (38:30; Josh 7:1; Neh 11:24; *EM* 2:941–42). "Shammah" is a shortened theophoric name, "(God) has heard" (Noth, *Personennamen*, 39, 185). The meaning of "Mizzah" is obscure.

15–19   This list of Edomite chiefs is almost identical to the list of the sons of Esau in vv 10–14. אַלּוּף "chief" occurs forty-two times in this chapter and fourteen times in the parallel in 1 Chr 1:51–54, but elsewhere only four times. Exod 15:15, "Now are the chiefs of Edom dismayed," suggests that "chief" is an Edomite term. In Zech 9:7; 12:5–6, it is used in an archaizing way of Judeans. Jacob and some commentators translate אַלּוּף "clan." Though this translation is contextually possible, the fact that a similar term *ulp* is found with the meaning "leader" at Ugarit (*UT*, 359) and its consistent translation by the versions as "leader" make this interpretation unlikely. It seems that אַלּוּף is the "chief" of an אֶלֶף "thousand, clan." It is hard to be sure why this list of chiefs is included next to the list of Esau's sons. Wilson (*Genealogy and History*, 179) suggests that "the genealogy in 36:15–19 would represent the configuration of the political lineages functioning in the political sphere."

16   "Korach" is the only addition to the names in vv 10–14. SamPent omits it here, so it could be a scribal error or a gloss saying that the Korach of v 18 really counted as a son of Eliphaz. As Dillmann (380) observes, it is certain that two tribes did not have the same name.

20–30   As the previous section, vv 9–19, falls into two repeating sections—a list of sons and grandsons, vv 9–14, and a list of chiefs—so does this: vv 20–28 list sons and grandsons; vv 29–30 list chiefs. But whereas vv 9–19 deal with Esau's sons, this section deals with "the sons of Seir the Horite." Here Seir is both the name of the area inhabited by the Edomites and the eponymous ancestor of its former inhabitants. According to Deut 2:12, "the Horites also lived in Seir formerly, but the sons of Esau dispossessed them, and destroyed them from before them." To judge from Gen 36, Deut 2:12 has somewhat simplified the historical picture. When the Edomites entered Seir, not all the Horites were destroyed; several clans survived and indeed intermarried with the Edomites. Whereas vv 9–19 list the predominantly Edomite clans, vv 20–30 list the predominantly Horite clans.

20   "Horite." These Horites are not to be identified with the well-known Hurrians, for these Horites have Semitic names (cf. *Comment* on 14:6). Speiser and Westermann favor the old etymological explanation of Horite as "cave-dweller," but this is uncertain.

"Lotan" may a longer form of the name Lot. Noth (*Personennamen,* 226) rather improbably suggests that "Shobal" means "basket." It was also a Judean name (1 Chr 2:50, 52; 4:1–2). For "Zibeon" and "Anah," see v 2.

21 "Dishon" is a kind of antelope (Deut 14:5; RSV "ibex"), possibly *Addax nasomaculata* (*EM* 2:655). The meanings of "Etzer" and "Dishan" are unknown.

22 The meaning of "Heman" is uncertain. For "Timna," see v 12.

23 The meanings of "Alvan" and "Ebal" are uncertain. "Manahat" possibly means "resting place" (cf. 1 Chr 8:6). "Ebal" is also the name of a mountain (Deut 27:13). "Shepho" = "bald" according to Gispen. "Onam" may mean "vigorous" (cf. the similar "Onan" in 38:4).

24 "Ayyah" is the name of an unclean bird of prey (Lev 11:14), possibly the kite (G. Bare, *Plants and Animals of the Bible,* 36). "Anah" is distinguished from his uncle of the same name (vv 20, 25) by a comment. Similar comments are found in Gen 4 and 5 to distinguish the two Lameks and two Enochs (4:17–24: 5:21–24, 28–31). So probably not too much should be read into "who found the springs in the wilderness." הימם: "springs" is the translation preferred by modern commentators following the Vg "hot springs" (Luria, *BMik* 30 [1984/85] 266, "geyser"). But the term may be a simple metathesis of המים "water" (cf. 26:19, 32). The main Jewish tradition is that it means "mules," but *Tg. Onq.* suggests "giants" (for fuller discussion, cf. Jacob, 685–86; Beeston, *VT* 24 [1974] 109–10; and Driver, *VT* 25 [1975] 109–10).

25 "Dishon" is another grandson of Seir with the same name as his uncle (vv 21, 26). "Oholibamah": this daughter is mentioned because she married Esau (vv 2, 14).

26 The meanings of "Hemdan" and "Eshban" are uncertain. "Yitran." The *ān* ending is characteristic of this group of names, so it is possible that Yitran has the same meaning as Yeter ("remainder," according to Gispen). "Keran" may mean "vineyard" (*EM* 4:329).

27 The meaning of "Bilhan" is uncertain (cf. "Bilhah," 29:29). The meanings of "Zaavan," and "Akan" are uncertain.

28 "Utz"; cf. 10:23. "Aran": KB suggests "ibex"; cf. Syriac *arhām* and Akk. *armû* "gazelle."

29–30 This list of chiefs is the same as the list of Seir's sons in vv 20–21. See *Form/Structure/Setting* above.

31–39 The third major section of the Edomite insertion begins with a list of "kings who reigned in Edom before there were kings for the Israelites." According to Num 20:14, there were kings in Edom when the Israelites led by Moses passed through Transjordan, so this list could be referring to pre-Mosaic kings of Edom, as Jacob argues. However, most commentators, taking their cue from "before there were kings for the Israelites," argue that the list comes from the period of the Israelite monarchy, possibly the time of David, who conquered Edom (2 Sam 8:13–14). The fact that the last Edomite king listed in Gen 36 may be Hadad and that Hadad, an Edomite prince, led a revolt against Solomon (1 Kgs 11:14–22) enhances the plausibility of this suggestion, although it is by no means proven.

But it is clear from this list that there was no dynastic succession in Edom in the period to which it relates; there is no father-son succession, and the capital city changes with the king. This arrangement invites comparison with the situation

in the book of Judges, when national rulers arose to lead the nation in the hour of crisis. But this list gives too few details to push the analogy with Israelite practice very far.

32 "Bela" possibly means "eloquent" or "glutton" (*EM* 2:133). The city of Zoar was also once called "Bela" (14:2), and it is also the name of Benjamin's eldest son (46:21). His patronymic, "son of Beor," is the same as Balaam's (Num 22:5), but this is insufficient to prove their identity. "Dinhabah" is otherwise unknown.

33 "Yobab"; cf. 10:29. "Bozrah" is one of the Edomite towns most often referred to (e.g., Isa 34:6; Amos 1:12) and is usually identified with Buseira. The absence of settlement before the ninth century at Buseira does not prove the lateness of this king list (*pace* Knauf, *ZAW* 97 [1985] 245–53, and Bartlett, *Edom and the Edomites*), as this verse need not presuppose permanent settlement at Bozrah.

34 "Husham": KB compares Arabic "broadnosed." "Teman": cf. v 11.

35 "Hadad" is the name of the Semitic storm god. Hadad may be a shortened form of a name such as "Hadadezer," "Hadad is a helper." "Who defeated Midian in the area of Moab." Some have speculated that this coincided with Gideon's defeat of the Midianites (Judg 7), but this is without proof. This little historical detail may be included to distinguish this Hadad from the one mentioned in v 39 (cf. *Comment* on v 24). The location of "Avit" is unknown.

36 "Samlah" (KB; cf. Arabic "protection"). "Masreqah" could be related to the noun שׂרק "vine," and so it could be a vine-growing area. Gebel Mushraq, southwest of Maan, is a possibility (*EM* 5:641).

38 "Shaul" ("requested"), usually transliterated Saul in English, was also the name of Israel's first king. The location of "Rehobot-hannahar" ("open spaces of the river") is uncertain.

38 "Baal-Hanan" means "Baal is gracious"; "Akbor" means "mouse."

39 "Hadad"; cf. n. 39.a. and *Comment* on vv 31–39. For "Pau," 1 Chr 1:50 has "Pai," which could point to Wadi Fai on the south bank of the Dead Sea. "Mehetabel" means "El does good." "Matred" perhaps is a shortened theophoric name, "(God) expels (his enemies)." "Mezahab" means "waters of gold."

40–43 A list of chiefs follows the king list, just as lists of chiefs (vv 15–19, 29–30) follow the genealogies of Esau (vv 9–14) and Seir (vv 20–28). But whereas in the previous cases the lists of chiefs were almost identical with the preceding lists of sons, this is not so here. There is no apparent overlap of kings and chiefs. It has been suggested that this is a list of the administrative districts of Edom, since some of the names are place names.

40 The meanings of "Timna" (cf. vv 12, 22), "Alvah" (cf. Alvan, v 23), and "Yetet" are all unclear.

41 "Oholibamah"; cf. v 2. "Elah" means "terebinth"; any link with Elat, the port in southern Edom, is unclear (cf. *Comment* on 14:6). "Pinon," meaning uncertain, may possibly be identified with Punon (Num 33:42–43), modern Feinan twenty miles south of the Dead Sea (*EM* 6:445–46).

42 For "Kenaz" and "Teman," see v 11. "Mibsar" ("fortress") may be mentioned in Ps 108:11(10): "Who will bring me to the fortified city [or the city of Mibsar]? Who will lead me to Edom?" According to Eusebius (*Onomasticon*, 124 20), Mabsara is near Petra. It could be an alternative name for Bozrah (cf. v 33; *EM* 4:612).

43 "Magdiel," "fruit (gift) of El" (KB) or "El is excellence" (Fowler, *Theophoric Personal Names,* 133), is also mentioned by Eusebius. It could be near the village of Majadil four miles (six kilometers) northeast of Tafileh (so *EM* 4:632–33). The meaning of "Iram" is uncertain.

37:1 This verse resumes and completes the "family history of Edom" in 36:1–8. See above on *Form/Structure/Setting* and *Comment* on 36:6–8.

Explanation

Genealogies do not easily inspire theological reflection, but in Genesis they have a most important function. Genesis is concerned with tracing Israel's ancestral line, and in their neighbor Edom, they saw their nearest relative, indeed Israel's twin brother Esau. But why was Jacob chosen while Esau was passed over? Much earlier, the narrative reported the antenatal oracle foretelling that "two nations are in your womb . . . the older will be a slave of the younger" (25:23). And when Isaac blessed Esau, he declared, "You shall live by your sword, and be subject to your brother" (27:40).

As is customary with the subordinate non-elect line in Genesis, Esau's "family history" is given before Jacob's (37:2–50:26) and much more briefly. The double title, "This is the family history of Esau" (36:1, 9), makes it probable that originally "the family history of Esau" consisted merely of 36:1–8; 37:1. Later 36:9–43 was inserted, giving a slightly different slant on the fate of Esau.

36:1–8; 37:1 tell of Esau's marriage to Canaanite women (36:2–5), which proved his disrespect for the traditions of his forefathers, for both Abraham and Isaac were anxious that their sons should marry within the lineage descended from Terah (24:3–4; 28:2), a principle later insisted on by the law (Deut 7:3). Esau's disregard for this principle marks him as cutting himself off from the chosen people.

Not only did Esau forsake his family roots; he left the land of promise. Like Lot before him, he decided that he could not live in Canaan with his brother Jacob, because "their possessions were too numerous for them" (36:7). As chap. 34 showed, there was plenty of space in Canaan for Jacob and others to live together. But Esau felt otherwise, and his decision to leave Canaan could ultimately prove as calamitous as Lot's similar decision. However, it did leave Jacob as the unique inheritor of the Abrahamic promise that his descendants would inherit the land of Canaan, "the land to which his father had migrated" (37:1).

Without the long insertion of 36:9–43, this first "family history of Esau" is comparable to the "family history of Ishmael" (25:12–18), which likewise tells how Abraham's first son eventually established himself outside the land of promise, leaving Isaac with sole claim to its possession. Both Ishmael and Edom are viewed without rancor as relatives who have walked out of the line of promise.

But the long insertion of 36:9–43 puts Esau and the Edomites in a different light. If it is right to see this passage as a later addition to Genesis, possibly dating from the time of David when Edom was conquered and incorporated into the Israelite empire, it may represent the hope that the two brothers, Israel and Edom, would indeed be reconciled in one nation. Certainly this long list of names, some of which were familiar Israelite names, stresses the consanguinity and common tradition of the two nations. That Esau became a nation recalls the promise to

Rebekah that she would mother two nations. That Edom became part of the Davidic empire, though it was older, having kings before Israel, shows that the older did serve the younger (25:23). So whenever it was written, 36:9–43 does reinforce the message that the promise was fulfilled, even its less important aspects concerning other nations. So if these points came true, it is reasonable to expect the greater promises made to Abraham, Isaac, and Jacob to be fulfilled as well.

Later history tended to illustrate the divisions between Esau and Jacob rather than reconciliation. Fierce wars between the two sides fed the fires of mutual hatred (2 Sam 8:13–14; 1 Kgs 11:15–16; 2 Kgs 14:7; Amos 1:11–12), culminating in some of the most bitter prayers of the old covenant (Obadiah; Lam 4:21–22; Ps 137:7–9) and summed up in Malachi's pregnant phrase, "I have loved Jacob, but I have hated Esau" (1:2–3).

For Paul, the election of Jacob and the rejection of Esau is a great example of God's free and unfettered choice (Rom 9:10–12). Yet he too looks for a day of ultimate reconciliation, when those who have long rejected the gospel will find mercy (Rom 11:25–32), a day when, as Rev 7:9 describes it, "a great multitude which no man could number, from every nation, from all tribes and peoples and tongues" will stand before the throne and the Lamb. And it is these two themes, the present rejection of Esau and his ultimate reincorporation into the people of God, that Gen 36 juxtaposes.

The Joseph Story (37:2–50:26)

Bibliography

(See also the *Bibliography* for *Introduction*, "The Egyptian Background of the Joseph Story.")

Aberbach, M. "Joseph and His Brothers—in the Light of the History of the Israelite Tribes." (Heb.) *BMik* 32 (1986/87) 114–20. **Ahuviah, A.** "On the Real Joseph." (Heb.) *BMik* 31 (1985/86) 271–80. **Coats, G. W.** "Another Formcritical Problem of the Hexateuch." *Semeia* 46 (1989) 65–73. ————. *From Canaan to Egypt: Structural and Theological Context for the Joseph Story.* CBQMS 4. Washington: Catholic Biblical Association, 1976. ————. "The Joseph Story and Ancient Wisdom: A Reappraisal." *CBQ* 35 (1973) 285–97. ———— "Redactional Unity in Genesis 37–50." *JBL* 93 (1974) 15–21. **Cooper, J. S.** "Sargon and Joseph: Dreams Come True." In *Biblical and Related Studies: FS S. Iwry*, ed. A. Kort and S. Morschauser. Winona Lake, IN: Eisenbrauns, 1985. 33–39. **Dahlberg, B. T.** "On Recognizing the Unity of Genesis." *TD* 24 (1976) 360–67. **Donner, H.** *Die literarische Gestalt der alttestamentlichen Josephsgeschichte.* Heidelberg: Winter, 1976. **Engel, H.** *Die Vorfahren Israels in Ägypten: Forschungsgeschichtliche Überblick über die Darstellungen seit Richard Lepsius (1849).* Frankfurter Theologische Studien 27. Frankfurt: Knecht, 1979. **Fox, E.** "Can Genesis Be Read as a Book?" *Semeia* 46 (1989) 31–40. **Haag, H.** "Der Aufstieg Josef im Haus des Ägypters." In *Fontes atque Pontes: FS H. Brunner*, ed. M. Görg. Wiesbaden: Harrassowitz, 1983. 205–14. **Hensell, G.** "The Joseph Story." *BiTod* 66 (1973) 1201–9. **Hilgert, E.** "The Dual Image of Joseph in Hebrew and Early Jewish Literature." *BR* 30 (1985) 5–21. **Humphreys, W. L.** "Novella." In *Saga, Legend, Tale, Novella, Fable*, ed. G. W. Coats. JSOTSup 35. Sheffield: JSOT Press, 1985. 82–96. **Kaiser, O.** "Stammesgeschichtliche Hintergründe der Josephsgeschichte: Erwägungen zur Vor- und Frühgeschichte Israels." *VT* 10 (1960) 1–15. **King, J. R.** "The Joseph Story and Divine Politics: A Comparative Study of a Biographic Formula from the Ancient Near East." *JBL* 106 (1987) 577–94. **Knipping, B. R.** "Textwahrnehmung 'häppchenweise': Bemerkungen zu H. Schweizers 'Die Josefsgeschichte' und zu seiner Literarkritik." *BN* 62 (1992) 61–95. **Martin-Achard, R.** "Problèmes soulevés par l'étude de l'histoire biblique de Joseph (Genesis 37–50)." *RTP* 105 (1972) 94–102. **Meinhold, A.** "Die Gattung der Josephgeschichte und des Estherbuches: Diasporanovelle." *ZAW* 87 (1975) 306–24; 88 (1976) 72–93. **Naor, M.** "The Story of Joseph the Righteous (Gen 37:28–45:4)." (Heb.) *BMik* 32 (1986/87) 224–34. **Osman, A.** *Stranger in the Valley of the Kings: The Identification of Yuya as the Patriarch Joseph.* London: Souvenir, 1987. **Rad, G. von.** "Josephgeschichte und ältere Chokma." VTSup 1 (1953) 121–27. **Ruppert, L.** "Die Aporie der gegenwärtigen Pentateuchdiskussion und die Josefserzählung der Genesis." *BZ* 29 (1985) 31–48. ————. *Die Josepherzählung der Genesis.* Munich: Kösel, 1965. ————. "Zur neueren Diskussion um die Josefsgeschichte der Genesis." *BZ* 33 (1989) 92–97. **Savage, M.** "Literary Criticism and Biblical Studies: A Rhetorical Analysis of the Joseph Narrative." In *Scripture in Context*, ed. C. D. Evans, W. W. Hallo, and J. B. White. Pittsburgh: Pickwick, 1980. 79–100. **Scharbert, J.** *Ich bin Josef euer Bruder.* St. Ottilien: EOS, 1988. **Schimmel, S.** "Joseph and His Brothers: A Paradigm for Repentance." *Judaism* 37 (1988) 60–65. **Schmidt, L.** *Literarische Studien zur Josephsgeschichte.* BZAW 167. Berlin: de Gruyter, 1986. **Schmitt, H.-C.** "Die Hintergründe der 'neuesten Pentateuchkritik' und der literarische Befund der Josefsgeschichte Gen 37–50." *ZAW* 97 (1985) 161–79. ————. *Die nichtpriesterliche Josephsgeschichte.* BZAW 154. Berlin: de Gruyter, 1980. **Schweizer, H.** *Die Josefgeschichte.* 2 vols. Tübingen: Francke, 1991. **White, H. C.** "The Joseph Story: A Narrative Which 'Consumes' Its Content." *Sem* 31 (1985) 49–69. ————. *Narration and Discourse in the Book of Genesis.* Cambridge: CUP, 1991. **Whybray, R. N.** "The

Joseph Story and Pentateuchal Criticism." *VT* 18 (1968) 522–28. **Wright, G. R. H.** "Joseph's Grave under the Tree by the Omphalos at Shechem." *VT* 22 (1972) 476–86.

Form/Structure/Setting

The heading, "This is the family history of Jacob" (37:2), and the end of the book (50:26) define the limits of this section most securely. By universal consent, the Joseph story is the most closely integrated part of the patriarchal narrative, and it is often referred to as a short story or, in German, *Novelle*.

It consists of the following episodes:

37:2–36	Joseph is sold into Egypt	
38:1–30	Tamar and Judah	
39:1–20	Joseph and Potiphar	A
39:21–40:23	Joseph in Prison	B
41:1–57	Joseph in the Palace	C
42:1–38	First visit of Joseph's Family to Egypt	A'
43:1–45:28	Second visit of Joseph's Family to Egypt	B'
46:1–47:31	Third visit of Joseph's Family to Egypt	C'
48:1–50:26	The Last Days of Jacob and Joseph	

The Joseph story, as already noted above, develops the theme of the Pentateuch by showing the gradual fulfillment of the promises made to Abraham in 12:1–3. In particular, it shows how God blesses the nations through the descendants of Abraham. Joseph's management of famine relief supplies in Egypt saved the lives of many people. This was not due to chance or human wisdom, but God. As Joseph said to his brothers, "God planned it for good . . . to keep many people alive" (50:20). Joseph's role is already foreshadowed at the beginning of the story in the two dreams in which he sees his brothers and parents bowing down to him. This is of course fulfilled in chaps. 42–47. So it is often held that the Joseph story really ends in chap. 47 and that chaps. 38 and 48–50 do not belong to the story. This, though, represents a failure to grasp the author's understanding of his material.

The relationship between the dreams of chap. 37 and their fulfillment in chaps. 39–47 is plain. The first three episodes demonstrate how the LORD was with Joseph. In the first (A), he rises to the post of Potiphar's assistant (39:1–20). In the second (B), he becomes the prison-governor's deputy (39:21–40:23). In the third (C), he is appointed vizier of Egypt, next in authority to the Pharaoh himself, and he is given responsibility for managing Egypt's food supplies (41:1–57). These episodes build to a climax in the third.

They are followed by another three episodes that again build to a peak. In the first (A'), ten of Joseph's brothers come to Egypt and, not recognizing him, bow down to him, thus beginning to fulfill his dreams (42:1–38). In the second (B'), the brothers are joined by their youngest, Benjamin; they bow down, and in a dramatic denouement Joseph identifies himself to his brothers. Finally, in the third episode (C'), Jacob and all the family come down to Egypt, and Joseph appears to them (46:1–47:31). Thus if the fulfillment of Joseph's dreams is the sole theme of the Joseph story, it is natural to suppose that it ends in chap. 47 and that chaps. 38, 48–50 are later additions.

However, this is not the author's understanding of these narratives. He entitles them "The family history of *Jacob*" (37:2). In other words, he is interested in all the sons of Jacob, not simply Joseph. Similarly, the heading "The family history of Isaac" (25:19) indicates that he is interested in both sons of Isaac, i.e., Esau as well as Jacob. His broader interests are most obvious in the Testament of Jacob (chap. 49), in which the dying Jacob pronounces blessings on all his sons. This passage is correctly identified by Longacre (*Joseph*, 54) as the peak of the Joseph story and of the whole book of Genesis. Here "we have a glimpse of the embryonic nation—with the Judah and Joseph tribes destined to have preeminence in the south and the north respectively."

Thus it is not surprising to find one chapter (chap. 38) devoted entirely to Judah before the three chapters (39–41) in which Joseph is the only son of Jacob on stage. Then in the following chaps. 42–46, the two leading actors are Judah and Joseph with Jacob, Reuben, Simeon, and Benjamin in supporting roles. Throughout Gen 37–50 the author shows his interest in the history of the whole family of Jacob, not just in Joseph.

The "Joseph Story" is thus somewhat of a misnomer for these chapters. Earlier I observed that Gen 25–50 (omitting chap. 36) constitutes the biography of Jacob: it begins with his conception in 25:21 and ends with his burial in 50:14. It is a story told in two parts: part 1, "The family history of Isaac" (25:19–35:29); part 2, "The family history of Jacob" (37:2–50:26). The cross-references between the two parts suggest its unity. The comments on Reuben in 49:3–4 recall 35:22, and those on Simeon and Levi in 49:5–7 recall 34:25–31. Indeed, the importance of the Testament of Jacob (chap. 49), with its vision of the tribes settled in Canaan in the Joseph story, matches that of the narrative of their birth (29:31–30:24) in the Jacob story. Interestingly, just four of Jacob's sons' names are given an explanation using the LORD's name in this birth narrative, Reuben, Simeon, Judah, Joseph (29:32, 33, 35; 30:24), and they are the leading actors in the Joseph story. The tension between Leah and Rachel in Gen 29–31 erupts into open warfare between Leah's sons and Jacob in Gen 34 and 35:22. The rifts between the sons and the father and between Joseph (Rachel's son) and his half brothers are deepened in chap. 37 when Joseph is sold to slave-traders. The rest of Genesis relates the reconciliation between the brothers and their father. Though this is apparently complete by 47:12, suspicions that Joseph may seek revenge still linger in his brothers' minds after Jacob's death. Again Joseph allays their fears (50:14–21). Thus the whole of 25:19–50:26 tells the story of the forefather of the nation and the origin of the twelve tribes.

According to classical source criticism, the main sources are J and E in roughly equal proportions, alternating in chapters 37 to 45. In later chapters, 46–50, there is also some of the P source. A variation (e.g., Redford, *Biblical Story of Joseph;* Schmidt, *Literarische Studien*) regards the J material as a Judah source that was supplemented later by a Reuben source–E source. More recently, opinion has swung to seeing the core of the Joseph story (37, 39–45) as an essential unity (e.g., Coats; Westermann; Blum, *Die Komposition*), perhaps by J, with supplements in the later chapters introducing material from other sources, principally drawn from P and the Jacob narrative (i.e., Gen 25–35), which link the Joseph story narrowly defined with the life of his father Jacob. For detailed discussion of these proposals, see the *Form/Structure/Setting* of each chapter.

Joseph Is Sold into Egypt   (37:2–36)

Bibliography

Abramsky, S. "Ishmaelites and Midianites." (Heb.) *EI* 17 (1984) 128–34. **Anbar, M.** "Changement des noms des tribus nomades dans la relation d'un même événement." *Bib* 49 (1968) 221–32. **Becking, B.** "'They hated him even more': Literary Technique in Gen 37: 1–11." *BN* 60 (1991) 40–47. **Brueggemann, W.** "Life and Death in Tenth Century Israel." *JAAR* 40 (1972) 96–109. **Christensen, D. L.** "Anticipatory Paronomasia in Jonah 3:7–8 and Gen 37:2." *RB* 90 (1983) 261–63. **Görg, M.** "Die Amtstitel des Potifar." *BN* 53 (1990) 14–20. **Greger, B.** "Ein Erklärungsversuch zu צר." *BN* 45 (1988) 28–39. **Grintz, Y. M.** "Potifar—the Chief Cook." (Heb.) *Leš* 30 (1965/66) 12–17. **Longacre, R. E.** "Who Sold Joseph into Egypt?" In *Interpretation and History: FS A. A. Macrae,* ed. R. L. Harris, S. H. Quek, and R. Vannoy. Singapore: Christian Life, 1986. 75–91. **Peck, J.** "Note on Gen 37:2 and Joseph's Character." *ExpTim* 82 (1970/71) 342–43. **Plaut, W. G.** "Who Sold to Whom?" *Central Conference of American Rabbis Journal* 15 (1968) 63–67. **Scharbert, J.** "Josef als Sklave." *BN* 37 (1987) 104–28. **Seebass, H.** "Der israelitische Name der Bucht von *Bēsān* und der Name Beth Schean." *ZDPV* 95 (1979) 166–72. **Ska, J. L.** "Sommaires proleptiques en Gen 27 et dans l'histoire de Joseph." *Bib* 73 (1992) 518–27. **Sperber, D.** "A Note on Kommidion and the Gum Trade." *Aegyptus* 53 (1973) 22–27. **Wenham, G. J.** "Lev 27:2–8 and the Price of Slaves." *ZAW* 90 (1978) 264–65. **White, H. C.** "Reuben and Judah: Duplicates or Complements?" In *Understanding the Word: FS B. W. Anderson,* ed. J. T. Butler, E. W. Conrad, and B. C. Ollenburger. JSOTSup 37. Sheffield: JSOT Press, 1985. 73–97. **Willmes, B.** "Objektive Ergebnisse bei textinterner Literarkritik? Einige Anmerkungen zur Subjektivität literarkritischer Beobachtungen in H. Schweizers Studie 'Die Josefgeschichte.'" *BN* 67 (1993) 54–86. **Wright, G. R. H.** "An Egyptian God at Shechem." *ZDPV* 99 (1983) 95–109.

Translation

²This is the family history of Jacob.

Joseph was seventeen years old, and he used[a] *to be a shepherd with his brothers. He had been a servant boy with the sons of Bilhah and Zilpah, his father's wives, and he told tales*[b] *about them to their father.* *³Now Israel loved Joseph more than all his other sons for he was the child of his old age, and he had made*[a] *for him a special tunic.* *⁴His brothers realized that it was he*[a] *that their father loved more than all his brothers,*[b] *and they hated him and were not able to speak*[c] *civilly to him.*

⁵Joseph had a dream, told[a] *it to his brothers, and*[b]*they hated him even more.*[cb] *⁶He said to them, "Please listen to this dream which I have had.* *⁷Imagine, we were binding sheaves in the countryside, and there, my sheaf rose up, yes stood up, and then, your sheaves surrounded*[a] *my sheaf and bowed*[b] *down to it."* *⁸Then his brothers said to him, "Will you really*[a] *reign over us? Or will you really*[a] *rule over us?" So they hated him even more for his dreams and for what he said.*

⁹He dreamed again, and he related the dream to his[a] *brothers and said, "Look, I have had another dream. I saw the sun, moon, and eleven stars bowing*[b] *down to me.* *¹⁰ᵃAnd he related it to his father and brothers.*[a] *His father reprimanded him and said to him, "What is this dream that you have had? Shall I and your mother and your brothers*

really[b] *come and bow*[c] *ourselves down to the ground before you?"* [11]*His brothers were very jealous of him, but his father held on to what had been said.*

[12]*His brothers went to shepherd* [a]*their father's flocks in Shechem.* [13]*Then Israel said to Joseph, "Aren't your brothers looking after the flocks in Shechem? Come, let me send you to them." He said to him, "I am ready."* [14]*He said to him, "Please go and see how your brothers are and how the flocks are, and bring* [a] *me word." So he sent him from the valley of Hebron, and he came to Shechem.* [15]*A man found him wandering in the countryside, and the man asked, "What are you looking for?"* [16]*He said,* [a] *"It's my brothers that I am looking for.*[a] *Please tell*[b] *me where they are shepherding."* [17]*The man said, "They traveled from here, for I heard them*[a] *saying, 'Let's go to Dothan.'" So Joseph went after his brothers and found them in Dothan.*

[18]*They saw him in the distance before he had come close to them, and they plotted to put* [a]*him to death.* [19]*They said to each other, "Look, this*[a] *master dreamer is coming.* [20]*Now, come on, let's kill him, dump him in one of the pits, so we can say, 'A wild animal has eaten him.' Then we shall see what will happen to his dreams."* [21]*Reuben*[a] *overheard this and rescued*[b] *him from their clutches. He said, "We must not take*[c] *his life."* [22]*Reuben said to them, "Don't shed blood. Dump him in this pit in the wilderness, but don't lay hands on him." This was in order to rescue*[a] *him from their hands and return*[b] *him to his father.*

[23]*As soon as Joseph came to his brothers, they stripped off his tunic,* [a]*the special tunic*[a] *which he was wearing.* [24]*They took him, dumped him in a pit. The pit was empty: there was no water in it.* [25]*Then they sat down to eat food. They looked up and saw a caravan of Ishmaelites coming from Gilead. Their camels were carrying gums, tragacanth, storax, and ladanum, bringing them down to Egypt.* [26]*Then Judah said to his brothers, "What's to be gained by killing our brother and covering up his blood?* [27]*Come, let's sell him to the* [a]*Ishmaelites. Let's not lay hands on him for he is our brother,* [b]*our own blood." And his brothers agreed.* [28]*Midianite traders passed by, so they pulled up Joseph out of the pit and sold Joseph to the Ishmaelites for twenty shekels of silver, and they took Joseph to Egypt.*

[29]*Then Reuben came back to the pit and saw Joseph was not there. So he tore his clothes.* [30]*Then he came back to his brothers and said, "The child's*[a] *gone! And I,*[b] *how can I go home?"* [31]*So they took Joseph's coat, killed a kid, and dipped the coat in the blood.* [32]*They sent the coat and brought it to their father and said, "This is what we found. Please identify*[a] *whether*[b] *it is your son's tunic or not."* [33]*He identified*[a] *it. He said, "It's*[b] *my son's tunic. A wild animal has eaten him. Joseph has been torn to bits."*[c] [34]*Then Jacob tore his clothes, put sackcloth on his loins, and mourned for his son many days.* [35]*All his sons and his daughters did their best to console him, but he refused to be comforted. He said, "I shall indeed go down to Sheol in mourning." So his father wept*[a] *for him.* [36]*Meanwhile, the Midianites*[a] *had sold him to the Egyptians, to Potiphar, an official of Pharaoh, captain of the palace guards.*

Notes

2.a. On the use of the verb היה "to be" with ptcp to describe frequentative actions in past time, see Joüon, 121f.

2.b. On the omission of the def art on רעה, cf. GKC, 126z; Joüon, 126a.

3.a. Waw + pf would usually be understood "and he used to make"; cf. SamPent ויעש, G. But MT may be correct because the verb here is supplying background to "and his brothers realized" (Longacre, *Joseph*, 75, 92–93).

4.a. Preverbal position of obj pronoun emphasizes it (GKC, 142f).

4.b. Though SamPent, G read "his sons" instead of "his brothers," the latter emphasizes the centrality of Joseph at this point in the narrative (cf. Longacre, *Joseph*, 144).

4.c. Inf constr piel דבר + 3 masc suffix. This use of the obj pronoun is unusual but not unparalleled (cf. GKC, 115c).

5.a. Cf. n. 9:22.a.

5.b-b. Omitted by G.

5.c. Waw consec + 3 masc pl impf hiph יסף.

7.a. 3 fem pl impf qal סבב.

7.b. Cf. n. 33:6.b.

8.a. The use of the inf abs conveys the utter surprise of the brothers that young Joseph should rule over them (*EWAS*, 88).

9.a. G adds "his father and."

9.b. Masc pl ptcp hishtaphel חוה.

10.a-a. Omitted by G.

10.b. Cf. n. 37:8.a.

10.c. ל + inf constr hishtaphel חוה.

12.a. את has "extraordinary point" because regarded as suspect by punctuators (GKC, 5n).

14.a. Waw + 2 masc sg impv hiph שוב + 1 sg suffix.

16.a-a. Note the unusual Heb. word order: object ("my brothers")–subject ("I")–verb ("Looking for") in response to a question.

16.b. Cf. n. 29:15.c.

17.a. Note the omission of the direct obj ("them"), not unusual (GKC, 117f), but perhaps read with SamPent שמעתים.

18.a. ל + inf constr hiph מות + 3 masc sg suffix.

19.a. Cf. n. 24:65.a.

21.a. *Pace BHS* there is no textual warrant for reading "Judah" (see *Comment*).

21.b. Waw consec + 3 masc sg impf hiph נצל + 3 masc sg suffix.

21.c. 1 pl impf hiph נכה + 3 masc sg suffix.

22.a. Inf constr hiph נצל.

22.b. ל + inf constr hiph שוב + 3 masc sg suffix.

23.a-a. G, S seem to omit, but there is a similar construction in 44:2, "my cup, my silver," and cf. 2 Kgs 25:30 (Joüon, 140b, n.).

27.a. G adds "these."

27.b. SamPent, G, S, Vg add "and."

30.a. Noun ("the child") preceding suffixed אין shows intense emotion (*EWAS*, 104).

30.b. On repeated subj ("I"), see GKC, 143a. "Emphasis is evident" where extraposed personal pronoun is used (*EWAS*, 95).

32.a. 2 masc sg impv hiph נכר.

32.b. On pointing of ה interrogative, see GKC, 100l.

33.a. Waw consec + 3 masc sg impf hiph נכר + 3 fem sg suffix. On pointing, see GKC, 60d.

33.b. English requires a subj (cf. SamPent, G, S), "it," but this is unnecessary in Heb. (*EWAS*, 20). "Several short clauses in apposition create tension and sometimes mount to a climax. Israel's terrible cry in Gen 37:33 consists of three such clauses in apposition. The postponement of the name 'Joseph' heightens the effect" (*SBH*, 45).

33.c. Inf abs + 3 masc sg pf qal pass (GKC, 113w; WOC, 375, n. 31) טרף.

35.a. Cf. n. 27:38.b.

36.a. Note different spelling from v 28 and the suggested correction in *BHS*.

Form/Structure/Setting

The story of Joseph opens with the title in 37:2, "This is the family history of Jacob." It is usual in these titles (cf. 11:26; 25:19) for the father (Terah, Isaac) of the main character (Abraham, Jacob, and here Joseph) to be named. These are the events that took place when Jacob was head of the extended family. Many commentators regard 37:1 as the start of the Joseph story, failing to realize that it

is the close of the story of Esau in chap. 36 (see *Form/Structure/Setting* on chap. 36), but Dillmann, Delitzsch, and Longacre (*Joseph*) correctly note that 37:2 is the start of a new section in Genesis, which closes at 50:26.

This last major section of Genesis is a closely integrated unit, but 37:2–36 constitutes a clear unit within it, since chap. 38 constitutes a distinct interlude between 37:36 and 39:1. Chap. 37 invites comparison with the opening to the story of Jacob, which as here relates two background incidents illustrating the rivalry of brothers before describing more fully the episode that parted them for twenty years in different countries.

Title: "This is the family history . . ."	25:19	37:2
Age	25:20	37:2
First conflict (In womb/Tale bearing)	25:21–26	37:2–4
Second conflict (Birthright/Dreams)	25:27–34	37:5–11
Ultimate cause of division	27:1–45	37:12–36

The threefold refrain, "they hated him" (37:4, 5, 8), culminating in 37:11, "his brothers were very jealous of him," sets the scene for the whole story.

37:12–35 falls into the following scenes:

Scene 1	vv 12–14	Joseph sent to find brothers	
		Jacob/Joseph dialogue	vv 13–14
Scene 2	vv 15–17	Joseph at Shechem	
		Joseph/man dialogue	vv 15–17
Scene 3	vv 18–20	Brothers' plot	
		Dialogue	vv 19–20
Scene 4	vv 21–22	Reuben's intervention	
		Plea	vv 21–22
Scene 5	vv 23–28	Joseph sold	
		Judah's comments	vv 26–27
Scene 6	vv 29–30	Reuben's return	
		His comment	v 30
Scene 7	vv 31–33	Coat brought to Jacob	
		Dialogue	vv 32–33
Scene 8	vv 34–35	Jacob's mourning	
		His words	v 35

It could be argued that vv 12–17 constitute a single scene, "Joseph looking for his brothers," but the change of location may justify it being subdivided. Similarly, vv 18–22 could constitute one scene, but the arrival of Reuben in v 21 (cf. v 29) argues in favor of division. Note that each scene contains words of the actors involved.

According to traditional source critics, the sources J, E, and P are interwoven in this chapter. According to Gunkel (slightly simplified), the sources are as follows: v 2, P; vv 3–4, J; vv 5–11, E; vv 12–13a, J; vv 13b–14a, E; vv 14b–17, J; v 18a, E; v 18b, J; vv 19–20, E; v 21, J; v 22, E; v 23, J; v 24, E; vv 25–27, J; vv 28–30, E; vv 31–33a, J; vv 33b–34a, E; vv 34b–35a, J; vv 35b–36, E. Other older commentators offer similar, though often simpler, analyses. In favor of this source-critical division, it is noted that there is repetition within the narrative. Sometimes Joseph's father is called Israel (vv 3, 13), once Jacob (v 34). Both Reuben (vv 21–22, 29–30) and

Judah (v 26) intervene to rescue Joseph. And Joseph is apparently sold both to Ishmaelites (vv 25, 28) and to Midianites (vv 28, 36).

However, since Whybray (*VT* 18 [1968] 522–28) and Coats (*From Canaan to Egypt*) argued for the intrinsic unity of the Joseph story, this analysis has been given up by most writers. They argue that the narrative is too powerful to be explained as the product of an amalgamation of sources, that the divisions are postulated in order to produce two sources, and that the differences within the narrative can be explained exegetically. Schmitt (*Josephsgeschichte*) argued that the E source represents an expansion of the J material, but Westermann, Coats, White ("Reuben and Judah," 73–97), Humphreys (*Joseph and His Family*), and Longacre (*Joseph*) all suppose that vv 3–36 come from basically one source with possibly a few glosses or expansions.

Their approach is supported by the scenic analysis given above. Each scene consists of narrative and dialogue, but to split the material between two sources undermines the unity of the scenes. Westermann holds that v 2 comes from P, a different source from the following verses, but Coats and Humphreys are more cautious, arguing that v 2 does make a good introduction to the story. Westermann also argues that vv 3–36 are not from J but from another hand. This seems unlikely in that the whole passage, vv 2–36, closely parallels the arrangement of 25:19 to 27:45, which is mostly J.

Comment

2–4 These verses describe two general grudges Joseph's brothers bore him.

2 "This is the family history." Cf. *Form/Structure/Setting*. "Seventeen years old" fits with the price paid for him by the slave traders (see *Comment* on 37:28). "Used to be a shepherd," but in v 12 he is at home while his brothers are away "shepherding." The reason for this change is explained next. "He had been a servant boy [for this nuance of נער, cf. 22:3] with the sons of Bilhah and Zilpah, . . . and he told tales about them to their father." Chap. 34 showed that there was little love lost between Jacob and his sons descended from Leah. Doubtless, he felt even less affection for the sons of his slave-wives, Bilhah and Zilpah. It is not clear whether Joseph's report about his brothers was true or not, but the term דבה "tales" is always used elsewhere in a negative sense of an untrue report, and here it is qualified by the adjective "evil" (cf. Num 13:32; 14:36–37). So it seems likely that Joseph misrepresented his brothers to his father, his father believed him, and his brothers hated him for his lies. If his account was true, it would doubtless have enraged his brothers, especially since their father had never held them in high regard anyway.

3 "Israel loved Joseph more than all his other sons." Favoritism has a long pedigree in Jacob's family. Isaac loved Esau more than Jacob, Rebekah loved Jacob more than Esau, and most pertinently Jacob loved Rachel more than Leah (25:28; 29:30). His old love for Rachel is now transferred to Joseph, Rachel's son. It is therefore hardly surprising that "they hated him," but that it is said three times (vv 4, 5, 8) indicates the intensity of their feelings. Once again, parental attitudes are emerging in the children. Leah is twice described as "hated," so in turn her sons "hate" (29:31, 33).

"Israel." Though Jacob's name was changed to Israel at the Yabbok, both names continued to be used thereafter, unlike Abram/Abraham. The reason for the choice of one name over another in a particular context is not always clear, but within the Joseph story certain preferences are observable. First, Jacob is used more frequently (31x) than Israel (20x). Since Jacob is the normal form, it is the exceptional appearance of Israel that needs to be explained. Second, whereas in prose Jacob always refers to the historical individual, Israel sometimes refers to the people (46:8; 47:27; 48:20). Third, when Israel is used of the individual, it seems to allude to his position as clan head (43:6, 8, 11; 46:1; 48:2), whereas Jacob seems to be used where his human weakness is most obvious (e.g., 37:34; 42:4, 36; 47:9: cf. Longacre, *Joseph*, 149–51). This fits in with the etymology of the names ("Jacob" = "struggler, deceiver" and "Israel" = "prevailer with God") given earlier in Genesis. So Jacob turns into Israel when his strength revives (45:28; 48:2). Finally, in those scenes where Joseph is present, Israel seems to be preferred (37:3, 13; 46:29, 30; 48:2, 8, 11, 14, 20, 21; 50:2).

"Old age"; cf. 21:2, 7; 44:20.

"Special tunic." On "tunic," cf. *Comment* on 3:21. What was "special" about this tunic is uncertain. Apart from this chapter, the term occurs only in 2 Sam 13:18–19 as the robe of a princess. "Many-colored" goes back to the LXX and Vulgate translation. Another possibility based on the cognate Aramaic term פס "palm of hand or foot" is that it was a long garment reaching to the ankles or the wrists, i.e., with sleeves. Speiser compares the Akkadian term *kitū pišannu*, a ceremonial robe with gold ornamentation. But whatever the tunic looked like, it marked Jacob's special affection for Joseph and served as a perpetual reminder to his brothers.

4 Indeed, so deep was their hatred that they could not "speak civilly to him." "Civilly" means lit. "for peace." This remark thus foreshadows the whole story of Joseph and the loss of peace between the members of his family.

5–11 This is the first of three pairs of dreams that are found in the Joseph story (cf. 40:1–41:36), but the only pair that is dreamed by Joseph himself. Joseph's own dreams foretell his own career and particularly look forward to his brothers' coming to Egypt to buy food and their bowing down before the lord of the land, who, unknown to them, is their brother Joseph (42:6; 44:14). Like Pharaoh's two dreams, which are said to be one (41:25), it seems likely that both Joseph's dreams are making a single point, namely that his family will one day bow down to him, not that they will do so on two occasions. The doubling of the dream suggests, rather, the certainty of fulfillment, that "the thing is established by God" (41:32). This is also suggested by the complementarity of the dreams: one is set on earth (reaping in the fields), the other in heaven (sun, moon, and stars).

However, while the later pairs of dreams are offically interpreted by Joseph with God's help (40:8; 41:16, 25, 28), there is no mention of God in 37:5–11. This makes it uncertain whether Joseph's dreams are revelatory or merely the product of his own inflated ego. Clearly this is how his brothers viewed the dreams, so they simply served to fuel their existing hatred of him.

5 "They hated him even more" is one of several plays on Joseph's name in the story, lit. "they added [וַיֹּסִפוּ *wayyôsipû*] to hate him still" (cf. v 8; וַיְסַפֵּר *wayĕsappēr* "related," vv 9–10). By introducing and closing (v 8) the first dream with this comment, the narrator underlines the impact it made on his brothers.

7 וְהִנֵּה "imagine" describes the dream through Joseph's eyes. "Joseph describes the dream in rhythmic, almost choreographic language, regulated by verbs and with a recurrent וְהִנֵּה. He is full of his dream, which compels him to relate it to his brothers" (Westermann, 3:38). "Binding sheaves." Though Jacob's family members were shepherds, this need not rule out occasional sowing and harvesting (cf. 26:12). But since it is only a dream being described, it is uncertain how far it represents their regular practice.

8 Each time Joseph relates a dream, he stirs up opposition—on this occasion from his brothers, on the next from his father (v 10).

"The form of quotation formula used [noun (brothers) + pronoun (to him)] to introduce their reply indicates rank-pulling. Who is this *younger* brother to say such things, and isn't it time to put him where he belongs? Their outraged reply employs infinitive absolutes + finite verbs to convey their ironic disgust in terms of pseudo certainty"; in addition, the use "of a rhetorical question . . . adds the sense of scolding" (Longacre, *Joseph*, 188).

"Will you really reign . . . rule over us?" Here "reign" and "rule" are used almost synonymously. But despite his brothers' incredulity, their words predict exactly what was to happen: Joseph became "ruler of all Egypt" (45:8, 26) and next in power to the king (41:38–44).

9 The second dream uses astral images and has Joseph's parents as well as his eleven brothers bowing down to him. "Eleven stars." While this could be a reference to the signs of the Zodiac (the twelfth presumably being Joseph), it seems more likely just to be ordinary stars.

"Sun, moon" is taken by Jacob to be "I and your mother," which raises the question as to whether Rachel is still alive at this point in the story, even though her death was reported in 35:19. It is clear that Genesis does not relate everything in strict chronological order, especially deaths (cf. *Comments* on 11:32 and 24:65–66; 25:1–4). But the presence of eleven stars seems to imply Benjamin's existence, so it would seem more likely that Rachel is assumed to have died and that the moon is included just to complete the picture of the heavenly bodies (cf. Coats, *Canaan to Egypt*, 14).

10 His father, having been brought into the dream, is moved to comment on it. "Reprimanded" (גָּעַר) is an uncommon word, especially in early prose. It refers most often to God's reaction to the nations, the wicked, or the seas. It is an expression of great authority, often as here tinged with anger (cf. Pss 9:6[5]; 106:9; 119:21). Despite his deep affection for Joseph, Jacob feels that this time he has gone much too far.

11 "Very jealous" (קָנָא). In context, this seems to be a stronger and deeper passion than "hatred" (vv 5, 8). Indeed, in various passages it is a feeling that is liable to spill over into violent action (e.g., Num 25:11, 13), even with God (Exod 20:5). The ritual in Num 5:11–31 is designed to prevent a husband physically punishing his wife for suspected adultery, and Proverbs cautions against allowing such jealousy free reign (14:30; 23:17; 24:1, 19). So the note that "his brothers were very jealous" is ominous, suggesting that they may well seek revenge.

On the other hand, dreams were a recognized means of revelation, so that "Jacob held on to what had been said" just in case there was something in them. Perhaps this comment helps to explain why he was prepared to send Joseph to visit his brothers despite their intense hatred of him.

12–35 These verses describe in eight short scenes how the long simmering hatred at last boiled over to rupture Jacob's family for at least another twenty years.

12 It begins quietly enough with Joseph's brothers traveling north from the Hebron area nearly twenty miles south of Jerusalem to Shechem some thirty miles north. It was in the Shechem area that Jacob's sons had massacred the sons of Hamor (34:24–30), so it is surprising that they ventured back there.

13–14 Why did not Joseph, a shepherd (v 2), go with his brothers on this occasion? Did he choose not to go? Was his father afraid his brothers might harm him? Was Jacob afraid that the area of Shechem might be dangerous? To judge from the conversation in v 13, neither Joseph nor Jacob thought he was in danger from the brothers. Jacob was just worried about how his sons and flocks were. Here the key word שׁלום "peace" is used twice. Jacob, fearing attacks from outside the family, is apparently blind to the lack of peace within. But the narrator, by repeatedly insisting that the brothers hated (vv 4, 5, 8) and were very jealous of Joseph (v 11), has awakened great apprehension in the reader, who cannot but fear for Joseph being sent so far from the range of paternal protection.

15–17 This second short scene reinforces the sense of Joseph's isolation and vulnerability. He "wanders" (תעה) like a lost sheep himself (Isa 53:6; also of Hagar in 21:14; of an ox in Exod 23:4) and has to be redirected by an unidentified stranger to his brothers. He has to travel another fourteen miles farther north to Dothan (Tel Dothan), even farther from home. Thus, this short scene keeps us in suspense by delaying the confrontation of Joseph with his brothers and by heightening our awareness of the danger he faces so far removed from his father Jacob.

18–20 The scene now switches to the brothers' encampment. Through their eyes, we see Joseph approaching in the distance, and we eavesdrop on their conversation.

18 "They plotted," a rare word, never used positively (cf. Ps 105:25). "To put him to death," though often used of judicial execution (cf. 38:7, 10; Num 35:19, 21), is used here for a neutral objective statement of fact. "Before he had come close" suggests that it did not take them long to make up their minds. It also invites the query: how did they recognize him in the distance? Was he wearing something distinctive?

19–20 "This master-dreamer" is no doubt said sarcastically. They plan to prove his dreams wrong by killing him. "Then we shall see what happens to his dreams." Their animosity against Joseph emerges not merely in their sentiments but in their choice of words. They go in for no euphemism; whereas the narrator speaks of "putting him to death," they speak of "killing"; indeed as long as הרג "kill" is not understood judicially, we might paraphrase their comment, "let's murder him," for this verb is generally used of illicit taking of human life (Gen 4:8, 14; 12:12). Indeed, this is what Esau planned to do to Jacob (27:41, 42). History repeats itself, especially in Genesis.

"A wild animal has eaten him." Already planning their cover story, they never use these words themselves, but Jacob does when they produce the blood-stained tunic (37:33).

21–22 This short scene describes Reuben's unexpected intervention. Clearly he turns up after the plot to kill Joseph had been hatched, so that "he rescued him" (on this term, cf. *Comment* on 31:9). The past "he rescued" summarizes the

effect of his action, which is more fully described next. Why Reuben should disagree with his brothers' decision remains undisclosed. Was he just being the
responsible elder brother? Was he trying to atone for his misbehavior with Bilhah
(cf. Sarna)? "We must not take his life." He first states a general principle. הכה
נפש "take life" is a quasi-judicial phrase often found in laws on homicide (cf. Num
35:11, 15, 30; Deut 19: 6, 11; 27:25).

22 "Reuben said to them." According to Longacre (*Joseph,* 161), Reuben is
mentioned again here because Hebrew prose customarily mentions a character's
name twice when first introduced, but the quotation formula (personal name +
verb + pronoun) also emphasizes Reuben's attempt to exert authority (cf.
Longacre, *Joseph,* 167–69). "Don't shed blood." Whereas in "We must not take his
life," Reuben used the לא for an absolute prohibition (cf. the Decalogue), he
now uses אל, which is less binding: "Don't shed his blood for the moment; just
dump him in a pit."

"Lay hands on him" is an idiom often implying a murderous assault (e.g., 1
Sam 22:17; 24:6; 26:23; cf. Gen 22:12). "This was in order to rescue him. . . ."
The narrator discloses Reuben's motives, but he hid them from his brothers or
else they would not have listened to him.

23–28 In this scene, the action reaches its climax as Joseph arrives, is stripped,
is thrown into a pit, and is sold to Ishmaelite traders. As in the previous scenes, descriptive narrative is followed by direct speech, this time with Judah taking the lead.

23–24 The succession of verbs, "stripped, took, dumped, sat down," conveys
the speed and roughness of the brothers' assault on Joseph. "They stripped off [a
term also used for skinning animals, Lev 1:6] his tunic, the special tunic he was
wearing." This unexpected expansiveness slows down the narrative for a moment
and focuses on the piece of clothing that was the mark of his father's affection
and the occasion of his brothers' hatred. Now we understand how they had recognized him in the distance and made up their minds so quickly to kill him. It
also hints at the grief that Jacob will suffer if Joseph does not return home.

24 "Dumped" (like a dead body; cf. *Comment* on 21:15) in a "pit"—probably a
cistern cut in the limestone and used for storing water. Such pits could be very muddy,
as Jeremiah found when he was imprisoned in one (Jer 38:6–13). Without the comment that the pit was dry, we might have wondered whether Joseph drowned.

The narrative is conspicuously silent about Joseph's reaction. It is left to the
reader's imagination. Not until 42:21 do we hear of his appeals for mercy, to which
his brothers were deaf.

25 Instead, they callously sat down to eat, perhaps enjoying delicacies Joseph
had brought from their father (cf. 1 Sam 17:17–18).

"Looked up" always signals that what is to be observed is of great significance
(cf. 22:4). "A caravan of Ishmaelites." Dothan lies close to the main trade route
through Palestine, the Via Maris, which cuts across the plain of Jezreel from the
Sea of Galilee to pass along the coastal plain to Egypt (Y. Aharoni, *Land of the
Bible,* 41–49). "Coming from Gilead," the area east of the Sea of Galilee.

"Ishmaelites" are mentioned again in vv 27, 28, and 39:1, whereas vv 28, 36 call
the traders Midianites. The relationship between the Midianites and Ishmaelites in
this story has been much discussed, and a wide variety of critical theories, glosses,
multiple sources, and redactional changes have been invoked to explain the problem.

However, White ("Reuben and Judah") has shown that these proposals all rest on unanalyzed assumptions of the critics, and choosing one assumption rather than another is quite arbitrary. Rather, it seems better to take Ishmaelites and Midianites as alternative designations of the same group of traders. This must at least be the understanding of the editor of Genesis, as Gunkel (409) pointed out, for 37:36 says the Midianites sold Joseph to Potiphar, whereas 39:1 says Potiphar bought him from the Ishmaelites. And this is confirmed by Judg 8:24, which explains that the Midianites had earrings "because they were Ishmaelites." Longacre (*Joseph*) argues that such an identification is also required on grounds of discourse analysis. In Hebrew, a new actor is usually referred to by name twice before using a pronoun instead. Here the new term Midianites (v 28) should be repeated in the later part of the verse, if they were a group distinct from the Ishmaelites, so that it would have read "and the Midianites pulled up Joseph," whereas "they" implies the brothers pulled up Joseph.

Commentators identifying the Midianites with the Ishmaelites go back as far as Ibn Ezra and most recently White ("Reuben and Judah"), Humphreys ("Novella"), Longacre (*Joseph*), and Sarna. The alternative possibility that the Midianites pulled Joseph out of the pit and then sold him to the Ishmaelites, though favored by many Jewish exegetes, seems less probable.

It is not clear what is the exact difference between Ishmaelites and Midianites; it could be that Ishmaelites is a general term meaning "nomadic traders," whereas "Midianites" is a more specific ethnic designation showing which tribe they belonged to (so Abramsky, *EI* 17 [1984] 128–34; Longacre, *Joseph*; Sarna). Alternatively, Ishmaelites may designate a league of tribes, of which the Midianites constituted one element (cf. *EM* 3:902–6). Such a view is supported by 25:13–17, which lists the sons of Ishmael, several of whom seem to be desert tribes (cf. 17:20).

"Gums, tragacanth, storax, and ladanum." These are rare terms, and the identity of the substances being traded is uncertain, but I have followed the suggestions of M. Zohary, *Plants of the Bible*.

"Tragacanth" gum (נכאת), almost the same word as Arabic *nakaath,* is produced by making incisions on Astragalus shrubs and letting the juice dry out. It has been "used since ancient times in medicine, industry and the manufacture of confections" (Zohary, *Plants of the Bible,* 195).

"Storax" gum (צרי) is a grayish-brown gum containing balsamic acids made by cutting the trunk of the storax tree, *Liquid ambar orientalis.* It is valuable medicinally.

"Ladanum" (לט) is a "resinous substance obtained from some species of *Cistus*" by scraping the leaves of this shrub. It has a strong balsamic smell, a bitter taste, and is used for cough medicine, perfume, and incense (Zohary, *Plants of the Bible,* 194).

All the gums mentioned here seem to have been grown in Gilead. Jacob later sent the same gums as part of his present to the as-yet-unrecognized Joseph in 43:11.

26–27 Reuben's scheme of just dumping Joseph in the pit left the problem unresolved. Would they let him die there, or kill him later, or would he escape with the danger of his reporting back to Jacob? Judah's suggestion of selling him avoids the danger of blood guilt; a murdered man's blood cries to heaven for vengeance (4:10). It also offers a little financial profit, and it is an acknowledgement that "he is our brother, our own flesh" (on the importance of

these concepts for OT ethical thinking, cf. *Comments* on 2:23–24; 4:9–10), so "the brothers agreed."

28 "Midianites"; cf. *Comments* on 25:2–4; 37:25. "Twenty shekels" was the typical price of male slaves between five and twenty years old, both in the old Babylonian period and in Israel according to Lev 27:5 (Wenham, *ZAW* 90 [1978] 264–65). For shepherds who might expect to earn, if employed by others, about eight shekels a year (cf. LH 261), the sale of Joseph represented a handy bonus!

By selling Joseph into Egypt, his brothers have apparently disposed of him for good, but unwittingly they have actually helped the fulfillment of his dreams.

29–30 Evidently, Reuben had wandered off again after dumping Joseph in the pit and knew nothing of the sale. Now he returns, finds him gone, and reveals his deep affection for Joseph and his father. His action, tearing his garment (a common sign of mourning; cf. Lev 10:6; 13:45; 21:10), and his cry foreshadow Jacob's reaction (vv 33–34). "The child" seems to emphasize Joseph's youthful vulnerability (cf. 33:13; 42:22; 44:20). "How can I go home?" lit. "where shall I come in?" It is the prospect of facing Jacob that alarms Reuben.

31–33 Having sold Joseph to the Ishmaelites, his brothers did not have to carry on with their pretense (v 20) that he had been eaten alive. That they did so in spite of Reuben's outburst suggests a callousness toward their father's feelings. There is of course an irony in their choosing their brother's clothing and a kid to deceive their father, for it was with his brother's clothes and a kid that Jacob had deceived his father Isaac (cf. 27:9–17).

32 "They sent and brought" may imply that the brothers did not take the coat themselves but sent it on ahead by messengers. This would imply that they fully realized that Jacob would be very distressed at the news and wished to avoid experiencing it themselves. Or it may be that they did bring the tunic themselves, in which case there is a brazen effrontery about their action. Neither reading puts their feelings for their father in a good light.

33 "He identified it" (נכר) provides another link with 27:23, where Isaac failed to "recognize" the disguised Jacob. Once again, Jacob is finding the sins of his youth being visited on himself in his old age. But whereas he told his father an outright lie, his sons let him come to his own conclusion, "A wild animal has eaten him," which was of course what they had intended (37:20). Jacob's three short comments, "It's my son's tunic. A wild animal has eaten him. He has been torn to bits, Joseph!" convey the strength of Jacob's emotions, climaxing with the mention of his favorite son's name. Cf. David's response to the news of Absalom's death (2 Sam 18:33).

34–35 The final scene describes Jacob's prolonged mourning for his departed son. The mention of three aspects of his grief, tearing of clothes (cf. v 29), wearing of sackcloth (2 Sam 3:31; 1 Kgs 20:31–32; Jon 3:5), and mourning "many days," underline the intensity of his grief. התאבל "mourned" refers to the public display of grief after death. It is "clearly a technical term for all of these customs together that might be observed in case of a death" (*TDOT* 1:45). It includes loud lamentation (50:10; 2 Sam 19:1–4; Esth 4:3), the wearing of mourning clothes (2 Sam 14:2), and not wearing jewelry or cosmetics (Exod 33:4; Isa 61:3; see further R. de Vaux, *Ancient Israel,* 59–61). Normally, such public grief lasted a week (Gen 50:10) for a parent, or perhaps a month as in the case of Moses (Deut 34:8).

But Jacob refused to stop mourning for Joseph despite the entreaties of all his sons and daughters. He would grieve publicly for Joseph until he died; he declares, "I shall indeed go down to Sheol in mourning." Sheol is the place of the dead in the OT, where the spirits of the departed continue in a shadowy and rather unhappy existence (cf. Isa 14:14–20) and where relatives could be reunited with each other (cf. 2 Sam 12:23). Though Sheol is not beyond God's power (Amos 9:2), the psalmists pray for deliverance from Sheol, and it is possible that the OT believer hoped for something better than life in Sheol in the world to come (cf. Pss 16:10; 30:4[3]; 49:16[15]). The catastrophe of losing Joseph may be seen by Jacob as proof of divine judgment that will lead him to go down with the wicked to Sheol (cf. N. J. Tromp, *Primitive Conceptions of Death and the Nether World in the OT* [Rome: Pontifical Biblical Institute, 1969]; *EM* 4:754–63; 7:454–57).

36 Whereas Jacob had given up hope for Joseph, the narrative reminds us that he was in fact beginning a new life in Egypt in the household of Potiphar, a royal official. Potiphar is probably a shortened form of Potiphera, which means "he whom Re (the sun-god) has given" (Egyptian *Pꜣ-diꜣ-PꜣRᶜ*). This form of the name cannot date from earlier than the nineteenth dynasty (thirteenth century B.C.). Kitchen (*NBD*, 951) suggests that Potiphera "may be simply a modernization in Moses' time of the older form *Diꜣdiꜣ-Rᶜ*, with the same meaning, of a name-pattern (*DiꜣdiꜣX*), which is particularly common in the Middle Kingdom and Hyksos periods . . . (c. 2100–1600 B.C.)."

"Captain of the palace guards." The exact function of this office is uncertain, but he was in charge of the prison for royal officials (40:3–4; 41:10, 12). Nebuzaradan, the Babylonian general who sacked Jerusalem, was also dignified with this title (2 Kgs 25:8–12; Jer 40:1–2). Vergote (*Joseph in Égypte*, 35; cf. Kitchen, *NBD*, 658; Grintz, *Leš* 30 [1965/66] 12–17) suggests that the term should be translated "butler," i.e., the head steward in charge of household arrangements, including catering.

Explanation

Joseph is the patriarch with which modern readers can identify most easily. He is the spoiled brat who through adversity develops into a mature and competent leader. He is the unfairly persecuted boy who eventually becomes top man and shows magnanimity to his persecutors. He is the one despised and rejected by his family who ultimately is the agent of their salvation and countless others. More than that, the story of Joseph shows how God's secret providence is behind the darkest deeds of men and works to their ultimate good. It is thus both a very realistic story and also profoundly optimistic. It is little wonder that it has delighted generations of hearers.

But certainly it was not included in the Pentateuch merely to entertain and encourage ancient Israelites. It has a most important theological message and, indeed, is integral to the plot and theme of the Pentateuch. So before examining the specific contribution made by chap. 37 to the Joseph story, we must look at its place within the whole Pentateuch.

First, the story of Joseph links the history of the patriarchs with their settlement in Egypt. It explains how Jacob and his sons, who had been living in Canaan,

came to settle in Egypt, from where centuries later they left to go first to Sinai and then back to the land of promise. Furthermore, the story of Joseph contributes to unfolding the theme of the Pentateuch, which Clines has defined as "the partial fulfillment, which also implies the partial non-fulfillment, of the promise . . . to the patriarchs" (D. J. A. Clines, *The Theme of the Pentateuch,* 29). In the Joseph story, the family of Israel grows from twelve to seventy, and indeed in blessing his sons, Jacob sees each of them as great tribes. Abraham was promised that he would become a "great nation" (12:2), but by the end of Genesis this has not been fully realized. Closer to realization is the promise that his name would be great, for Joseph rises to a position next to the Pharaoh of Egypt. Furthermore, Joseph experiences the blessing of God: this is most evident after his promotion to power in Egypt, for that an imprisoned slave can become lord of all Egypt is spectacular proof of divine overruling. But in his darkest hour, when he was slave in Potiphar's house and then imprisoned on a false charge, the narrative repeatedly comments that "the LORD was with Joseph" (39: 2, 3, 21, 23).

Finally, through Joseph "all the families of the earth" begin to "find blessing." This is first apparent to Potiphar, who noticed that "the LORD caused all that he did to prosper in his hands" (39:3), but even more so when worldwide famine struck, for then "all the earth came to Egypt to buy grain." Through Joseph's efforts, not only was his own family saved from starvation, but also the Egyptians and many neighboring peoples were delivered. So also in this respect the promise to Abraham was partially fulfilled.

But in one respect the story of Joseph marks a great set-back for the promise's fulfillment, for the whole family has to move from Canaan to Egypt, from the land of promise to the land of future oppression. And it is significant that just when Jacob and his sons leave Canaan to settle in Egypt, God speaks for the only time in the Joseph story: "Do not be afraid to go down to Egypt, for I shall make you into a great nation there. I shall go down with you, and it is I that shall surely bring you up again" (46:3–4). Precisely because moving to Egypt appears to be traveling contrary to the promises, Jacob has to be reassured that God will be with him there and that he will return. So on his death bed he insists that he must be buried in the ancestral tomb at Macpelah (49:29–30). Similarly, before Joseph dies, he makes his brothers take an oath: "God will definitely visit you, and you shall bring my bones up from here" (50:25). So the book closes with a clear reaffirmation of the promises on the lips of the patriarchs, but equally clearly these promises are far from complete fulfillment. Genesis requires a sequel.

If the theme of partially fulfilled promises binds the Joseph story to the rest of the Pentateuch, it is also true that it has a minor theme of its own. It is a story of divine providence summed up in 50:20, "You planned evil against me. It was God who planned it for good . . . to keep many people alive." Or as Brueggemann (293) puts it: "The theme of the Joseph narrative concerns God's hidden and decisive power which works in and through but also against human forms of power. A 'soft' word for that reality is *providence.* A harder word for the same reality is *predestination.* Either way God is working out his purpose through and in spite of Egypt, through and in spite of Joseph and his brothers." These themes already come to expression in chap. 37.

If divine overruling is one theme of the Joseph story, human responsibility is its counterpoint, for within the Bible it offers one of the most interesting analyses of the dynamics of family life. Here we see the dire effects of sin on human behavior. Jacob's favoritism turns normal sibling rivalry into deadly hatred, so that Joseph's brothers plot to kill him. And Jacob is blind to the effects of his actions on his sons.

While fratricide is averted, the tragic effects of this hatred blight the life of Jacob's family for more than twenty years. Not until circumstances contrive to make the brothers repent of their mistakes are reconciliation and a new life together possible. At one level, the story appears to lay most of the blame for the tragedy at Jacob's door, for had he not shown such partiality to Joseph, would such animosity toward him have developed? But at another level, the story suggests that Jacob was the victim of his own upbringing. Chap. 37 makes several allusions to chap. 27, the account of Jacob's deception of Isaac. Chap. 37 shows Jacob being deceived by his sons with a kid and their brother's garment, just as Jacob had deceived. What is more, Isaac had shown partiality toward Esau his older son, whereas Rebekah had favored Jacob the younger one. This had led to Esau planning to murder Jacob and to the latter having to flee for his life. Yet despite his past experience, Jacob does something similar, blatantly favoring Joseph over his older brothers, leading them to want to murder him.

The story opens with a brief mention of two things that led to tension within the family: Joseph's indiscretion, if not downright lying, about some of his brothers and Jacob's equally obvious partiality towards Joseph expressed through his gift of a handsome tunic, which to judge from his journey to Dothan (vv 14–17), he wore on any and every occasion. So bad did things become that his brothers "hated him and were not able to speak civilly to him" (v 4).

Relationships seem to have sunk to rock bottom, but Joseph's dreams made them yet worse. Throughout the ancient world, and Genesis is no exception, dreams were viewed as revelatory, as messages from God. So by sending dreams providence seems to be making a bad situation worse, though doubtless Joseph's cockiness in relating them to his brothers and father made their impact even worse than might otherwise have been the case. Certainly the narrator saw these two dreams as prophetic; the sending of two dreams guarantees their fulfillment (41:32). In the visions of the sheaves bowing down to Joseph, and then the sun, moon, and stars bowing down to him, the apogee of Joseph's career is announced when he will be lord over his brothers, indeed over all Israel. But the very thought enraged them still further; twice it is said that "they hated him even more" (vv 5, 8), and once that they were "very jealous," on the brink of violent revenge (v 11).

Swiftly the story moves to its climax. Apparently oblivious to the danger confronting his favorite son, Jacob sends him to visit his brothers shepherding their flocks, some fifty miles from home. Tension rises as Joseph discovers that they have moved yet farther away to Dothan, completely out of range of their father's control.

Then the perspective alters so that the action is described from the brothers' point of view. They see him in the distance, recognize him by his hated tunic, and before he has come close have planned to kill him and tell his father that a wild animal has eaten him. However, before Joseph arrives, Reuben the eldest

returns and persuades them simply to dump him in an empty water cistern, for, as the narrative informs us, he hoped to return him to his father.

So as soon as Joseph greets his brothers, he is pounced on, stripped of his tunic, and thrown into a pit. Meanwhile Reuben wanders off again, and the other brothers sit down to eat a good meal. Then they note some Ishmaelite traders approaching, and Judah proposes the idea of selling Joseph as a slave, for youthful slaves are valuable. This way they can be rid of their hated brother, enrich themselves, and disprove his boastful dreams all in one fell swoop.

When Reuben returns, he is deeply distressed, not apparently so much for Joseph, but because he realizes the grief his apparent death will cause Jacob. But having set out on this scheme, his brothers will not or cannot turn back and present Jacob with the alleged proof of Joseph's death. Jacob, like his father Isaac many years before, was deceived by his sons' scheme. But this father is broken-hearted, so that all his sons' efforts to comfort him prove fruitless. He insists he will mourn publicly for Joseph until his dying day. The brothers may have succeeded in removing the hated Joseph from their sight, but Jacob's gestures will always remind them where his deepest affections lie.

Thus this first episode shows us Jacob's family rent from top to bottom by hatred and grief. The rest of the story will tell of the resolution of this problem. Meanwhile, we are told that Joseph did reach Egypt; he is still alive, so his dreams have not been killed, but it is certainly very difficult to see any way in which they could be fulfilled.

This episode cannot be viewed in isolation. It shows great sympathy for Jacob and Joseph's plight, though it hints that both men partly deserved what happened to them. However, the dreams hint that there is more to it than meets the eye: divine purposes are at work in this family's history. Ultimately it will be seen that "in everything God works for good with those who love him, who are called according to his purpose" (Rom 8:28). Christian exegetes have often seen Joseph as a type of Christ, the innocent man who through his suffering brings reconciliation to his human brethren and life to the world. It is possible to go further and view him as a model for all believers, who like him must die to self, if they are to make peace with their neighbor.

Tamar and Judah   (38:1–30)

Bibliography

Astour, M. C. "Tamar the Hierodule: An Essay in the Method of Vestigial Motifs." *JBL* 85 (1966) 185–96. **Bal, M.** "Tricky Thematics." *Semeia* 42 (1988) 133–55. **Banon, D.** "Exégèse biblique et philosophie." *ETR* 66 (1991) 489–504. **Ben-Reuven, S.** "'I shall answer for it: you may require it from my hand.'" (Heb.) *BMik* 33 (1987/88) 337–38. **Bird, P. A.** "The Harlot as Heroine: Narrative Art and Social Presupposition in Three OT Texts." *Semeia* 46 (1989) 119–39. ———. "'To Play the Harlot': An Enquiry into an OT Metaphor." In *Gender and Difference in Ancient Israel,* ed P. Day. Minneapolis: Fortress, 1989. 75–94. **Biton,**

G. "Some Derivative Meanings of ʿayin." (Heb.) *BMik* 23 (1978) 478–79. **Bos, J. W. H.** "Out of the Shadows: Gen 38; Judg 4:17–22; Ruth 3." *Semeia* 42 (1988) 37–67. **Burden, J. J.** "'n 'Prostituut' doen reg: Die Juda-Tamar-verhaal (Gen 38)." *Theologica Evangelica* 13 (1980) 42–52. **Carmichael, C. M.** "A Ceremonial Crux: Removing a Man's Sandal as a Female Gesture of Contempt." *JBL* 96 (1977) 321–36. ———. "Some Sayings in Gen 49." *JBL* 88 (1969) 435–44. **Cassuto, U.** "The Story of Tamar and Judah." In *Biblical and Oriental Studies.* Jerusalem: Magnes, 1973. 1:29–40. **Coats, G. W.** "Widow's Rights: A Crux in the Structure of Gen 38." *CBQ* 34 (1972) 461–66. **Emerton, J. A.** "An Examination of a Recent Structuralist Interpretation of Gen 38." *VT* 26 (1976) 79–98. ———. "Judah and Tamar." *VT* 29 (1979) 403–15. ———. "Some Problems in Gen 38." *VT* 25 (1975) 338–61. **Fisch, H.** "Ruth and the Structure of Covenant History." *VT* 32 (1982) 425–37. **Gilad, H.** "The Account of Judah and Tamar." (Heb.) *BMik* 21 (1975) 127–38. **Goldin, J.** "The Youngest Son or Where Does Gen 38 Belong?" *JBL* 96 (1977) 27–44. **Hallo, W. W.** "As the Seal upon Thy Heart." *Bible Review* 1 (1985) 20–27. **Luke, B.** "Judah and Tamar (Gen 38)." *Scripture* 17 (1965) 52–61. ———. "Two Birth Narratives in Genesis." *IndTS* 17 (1980) 155–80. **Mathewson, S. D.** "An Exegetical Study of 'Gen 38." *BSac* 146 (1989) 373–92. **Niditch, S.** "The Wronged Woman Righted: An Analysis of Gen 38." *HTR* 72 (1979) 143–49. **O'Callaghan, M.** "The Structure and Meaning of Gen 38: Judah and Tamar." *PIBA* 5 (1981) 72–88. **Rendsburg, G. A.** "David and His Circle in Gen 38." *VT* 36 (1986) 438–46. **Robinson, I.** "*bepetah ʿênayim* in Gen 38:14." *JBL* 96 (1977) 569. **Ska, J. L.** "L'ironie de Tamar (Gen 38)." *ZAW* 100 (1988) 261–63. **Wright, G. R. H.** "The Positioning of Gen 38." *ZAW* 94 (1982) 523–29.

Translation

¹*At that time Judah left his brothers and joined*ᵃ *up with a man from Adullam named Hirah.* ²*Judah saw there the daughter of a Canaanite named*ᵃ *Shua, took her, and went into her.* ³*She conceived, bore a son, and he*ᵃ *called him Er.* ⁴*She conceived again, bore a son, and called him Onan.* ⁵*Once again*ᵃ *she bore a son and called his name Shelah. He*ᵇ *was in Chezib when she bore*ᶜ *him.*

⁶*Judah took a wife for Er, his firstborn, named Tamar.* ⁷*Er, his firstborn, erred in the LORD's eyes, so the LORD let him die.*ᵃ ⁸*Judah said to Onan, "Go into your brother's wife, marry*ᵃ *her, and produce*ᵇ *descendants for your brother."* ⁹*Onan knew that the descendants would not be his, and so whenever*ᵃ *he went into his brother's wife, he used to ruin the ground, so as to avoid giving descendants to his brother.* ¹⁰*What he did offended*ᵃ *the LORD, and he let him die*ᵇ *too.* ¹¹*So Judah said to Tamar his daughter-in-law, "Live*ᵃ *as a widow in your father's house, until Shelah my son grows up," for he thought, "For fear he dies like his brothers." So Tamar went and lived in her father's house.*

¹²*Many days later Judah's wife, the daughter of Shua, died. Judah was consoled and went up to his sheep-shearing at Timnah with his friend Hirah of Adullam.* ¹³*It was told*ᵃ *Tamar, "Your father-in-law is just*ᵇ *on his way up to Timnah to shear his sheep."* ¹⁴*So she took*ᵃ *off her widow's clothes, covered*ᵇ *herself with a veil, and wrapped herself up. Then she sat down on the way into Enaim, which is on the road to Timnah, for she had noticed that Shelah had grown up, but she had not been given*ᶜ *to him.*

¹⁵*Judah saw her and thought she was a prostitute, for she had covered her face.* ¹⁶*So he turned*ᵃ *off the road to her and said,* ᵇ*"Please let me*ᵇ *come into you," for he did not know that she was his daughter-in-law. So she said to him, "What will you give me*ᶜ *to come into me?"* ¹⁷*He said, "I shall send you a goat from the flock." She said,* ᵃ*"If you give*

me a pledge,[a] *until you return it.*" [18]*He said, "What pledge shall I give you?" She said, "Your seal, cord, and the staff which you are carrying." So he gave it to her, went into her, and she became pregnant for*[a] *him.* [19]*But she rose and went away, took off her veil, and wore her widow's clothes again.*

[20]*Judah sent a kid with his friend the Adullamite in order to take back the pledge from the woman, but he could not find her.* [21]*He asked the men of her*[a] *area, "Where is the*[b] *'holy woman' in Enaim by the road?" They replied, "There never was a 'holy woman' in this place."* [23]*Judah said, "Let her take it for herself lest we become a joke, since I sent this kid but you could not find her."*

[24]*At the end of three months Judah was told, "Your daughter-in-law Tamar has been promiscuous, and she is now pregnant through her action." So Judah said, "Bring*[a] *her out to*[b] *burn her."* [25a]*While she was being brought*[b] *out, she sent word*[a] *to her father-in-law, "I am pregnant by the man to whom these things belong." She said, "Please identify*[c] *who this ring, these cords,*[d] *and this staff belong to."* [26]*Judah identified them and said, "She is*[a] *in the right, not I,*[a] *because I did not give her to my son Shelah." But he did not have intercourse*[b] *with her again.*

[27]*When the time came for*[a] *her to give birth,*[a] *there were twins in her womb.* [28]*When she was giving birth, one*[a] *put out a hand and the midwife tied a red cord on his hand saying, "This one came out first."* [29]*But*[a] *as he was pulling back*[a] *his hand, his brother came out, and she said, "Why have you burst upon you,*[b] *Peres." So he*[c] *was called Peres.* [30]*Afterwards his brother came out with the red cord on his arm, and he*[a] *was called Zerah.*

Notes

1.a. Cf. n. 12:8.c.

2.a. G reads "her name," but MT "his name."

3.a. SamPent, *Tg. Ps.-J.* "she called." MT "he called" could be impersonal 3 sg, "one called."

5.a. Cf. n. 4:2.a.

5.b. G "She was."

5.c. Cf n. 35:16.b.

7.a. Waw consec + 3 masc sg impf hiph מות + 3 masc sg suffix.

8.a. Waw + 2 masc sg impv piel יבם.

8.b. Waw + 2 masc sg impv hiph קום.

9.a. אם unusual to introduce temporal clause, but see GKC 164d. Cf. GKC, 112ee, gg; WOC, 539 on frequentative.

10.a. Cf. n. 21:11.a.

10.b. Waw consec + 3 masc sg hiph מות.

11.a. 2 fem sg impv ישב.

13.a. Cf. n. 22:20.a.

13.b. On this nuance of הנה + ptcp, see Lambdin, 168; WOC, 675.

14.a. Waw consec + 3 fem sg impf hiph סור.

14.b. Waw consec + 3 fem sg impf (apoc) piel כסה. On reflexive meaning of piel, see Joüon, 61b. SamPent has hithp ותתכס.

14.c. 3 fem sg pf niph נתן.

16.a. Cf. n. 38:1.a.; 12:8.c.

16.b-b. On this sense of הבה־נא, see Joüon, 105e.

16.c. לי. The dagesh is a feature of Codex Leningrad. Other editions and MSS omit; cf. v 18 .

17.a-a. The main clause, "you may come into me," is understood; cf. GKC, 159; Joüon, 167r.

18.a. Joüon, 132fN, translates ל as "by."

21.a. SamPent, G, S, Tg read "the area" as MT does in v 22.

21.b. SamPent regularizes ההיא, but def art may be omitted from demonstrative (GKC, 126y).

24.a. 2 masc pl impv hiph יצא + 3 fem sg suffix.

24.b. Waw + 3 fem sg impf niph צרך. Sequence impv + simple waw + impf indicates purpose (Lambdin, 119).

25.a-a. On this construction, ptcp for ongoing action + pf for punctiliar action, see Joüon, 121f, 166f; WOC, 625.

25.b. Fem sg ptcp hoph יצא.

25.c. Cf n. 37:32.a.

25.d. SamPent and versions have singular "cord."

26.a-a. On this translation, see GKC, 138b2; WOC, 265.

26.b. ל + inf constr ידע + 3 fem sg suffix; expected pointing ה.

27.a-a. Inf constr ילד + 3 fem sg suffix.

28.a. On this construction, 3 masc sg for impersonal "one," see GKC, 144d.

29.a-a. כ + ptcp (hiph שׁוב) is unusual, so *BHS* emends. However, there is a parallel in 40:10; cf. GKC, 164g.

29.b. SamPent reads "us."

29.c. Impersonal 3 masc sg "he called," but SamPent, S, *Tg. Ps.-J.* read "she called."

30.a. Cf. n. 38:29.c.

Form/Structure/Setting

Chap. 38 is a clear unit within Genesis, with six scenes.

vv 1–5	Judah marries a Canaanite
vv 6–11	Tamar marries Judah's sons
vv 12–19	Tamar traps Judah
vv 20–23	Judah looks for Tamar
vv 24–26	Tamar vindicated
vv 27–30	Birth of twins to Tamar and Judah

At first blush, chap. 38 seems to have nothing to do with the Joseph story. If it were omitted, the narrative would progress from 37:36 to 39:1 very smoothly. It does not appear to be necessary for understanding chaps. 39–50. In a similar way chap. 49, the blessing of Jacob, does not seem to be necessary to the flow of the narrative. But there is a similar phenomenon in the Jacob story. Chap. 26 toward the beginning and chap. 34 toward the end do not seem immediately relevant to the main plot of the narrative, yet on further examination both chapters make a distinctive contribution to the theme. Can the same be said of chap. 38?

Further considerations show that this episode of Judah and Tamar makes an important contribution to understanding the Joseph story. First, its positioning here creates suspense: having told us that Joseph has been sold to Potiphar, the narrator breaks off with this digression about his brother back in Canaan, leaving us wondering how Joseph is coping in a foreign land. Chap. 38 also serves to show that Joseph was separated from his family a long time; there is time for Judah to marry, for his sons to grow up, and for them to marry.

But it does more. As Humphreys (*Joseph and His Family*, 37) notes: "The unit provides a counterpointing commentary on what we have witnessed of this family and a proleptic look at what is yet to come. The effect for the sensitive reader is to bring to awareness certain critical dimensions and themes in the larger novella (= the Joseph story), thereby to shape perspectives for reading what is to come."

The most obvious parallel between the stories of Tamar and Joseph is found in 38:25–26, "'Please identify who this ring' . . . Judah identified them," which precisely echoes 37:32–33, "'Please identify whether it is your son's tunic or not.' He identified it." Just as in the episode of Joseph's tunic, an element of divine justice is apparent. Jacob had deceived his father Isaac. He in turn was deceived by his son Judah, and now Judah himself is deceived by his daughter-in-law. In all three episodes, goats and items of dress are used in the deception.

More generally, this story shows that injustice will be righted and that the perpetrator will admit his errors. As Judah confesses here, "She is in the right, not I" (38:26), so all Joseph's brothers will one day acknowledge their sin against him. "Truly, we are guilty because of our brother, for we saw his distress, when he implored us and we did not listen" (42:21).

Another general principle of Genesis is God's preference for the younger child, Abel not Cain, Jacob not Esau, Joseph not Reuben, Ephraim not Manasseh. This same idea comes to expression twice in chap. 38: the two older sons of Judah, Er and Onan, die, but Shelah survives (vv 3–11), and at the end of the story though Zerah stuck his hand out first, making him technically the firstborn, Peres actually arrives first (vv 27–30). And it is Peres who was the ancestor of David, who was of course the youngest of Jesse's sons. This triumph-of-the-younger-son motif thus looks back to the struggle between Jacob and Esau, but more immediately to Joseph's dreams, in which he saw his brothers bowing down to him. The double reinforcement of this principle in chap. 38 is an assurance that Joseph's dreams will ultimately be fulfilled.

Then there is a glaring contrast between Jacob's inconsolable grief over the "death" of Joseph, described at the end of chap. 37, and the absence of any mourning by Judah when two of his sons died, as described in 38:7–10. Judah seems to be a hard and callous man. He was the one who had suggested selling Joseph into slavery to make money out of him. Presumably, he thoroughly approved of the scheme to deceive Jacob despite Reuben's appeals for consideration. In this story, he not only fails to mourn the death of his two sons but he summarily orders his daughter-in-law to be burned. Yet what a different Judah we meet in 44:18–34. Here he appeals for Benjamin's release with great warmth and tenderness, describing with great love his father's suffering since Joseph's disappearance and foreseeing his sorrowful death if Benjamin is not allowed to return to Canaan. He concludes by offering to stay as a slave in place of Benjamin. Clearly, Judah is a changed man, and this story shows the beginning of the transformation when he admits "She is in the right, not I" (38:26). Without this account of Tamar putting her father-in-law to shame, we should be hard pressed to explain the change in his character. And in its biographical sketches, character change is what Genesis is all about: Abram becomes Abraham; Jacob becomes Israel. Particularly in Jacob's family we see examples of character change: Reuben, violator of his father's concubine, later shows great concern for both Joseph and his father, while the upstart cocky Joseph becomes the wise statesman who forgives his brothers. Thus, this chapter has a most important role in clarifying the course of the subsequent narrative; without it we should find its development inexplicable.

If scholars had taken more seriously the editor's title in 37:2, "This is the family history of *Jacob*," they might not have been so wont to write off this chapter as

irrelevant. Chaps. 37–50 are not just the story of Joseph but the story of Jacob's family. Therefore, to have sections entirely devoted to other sons of Jacob should not be surprising.

Finally, the relationship of this episode to the theme of Genesis must be explored. Again on first sight, this chapter apparently has nothing to do with the promises to Abraham of land, nationhood, and blessing to the nations. But the central problem of chap. 38 is childlessness. Onan dies because he refuses to procreate. He did not want to produce children for his brother, and by implication for his father and great-grandfather. In other words, by his action Onan demonstrates his disregard for the patriarchal promises. On the other hand, Tamar, a Canaanite girl, is most anxious to have children. Despite the deaths of her first two husbands, she is anxious to marry Shelah. And when she is thwarted by her father-in-law, she manages to find a way of having children through him. Such determination to propagate descendants of Abraham, especially by a Canaanite woman, is remarkable, and so despite her foreign background and irregular behavior, Tamar emerges as the heroine of this story. She is like Melchizedek (chap. 14) and Abimelek (chap. 26), one of those foreigners who see God's hand at work in Abraham and his descendants and therefore align themselves with Israel. In the likes of Tamar the promise that "all the families of the earth will find blessing in you" starts to be fulfilled. She is the forerunner of Ruth who said, "[Y]our people shall be my people, and your God my God" (Ruth 1:16), as well as being ancestor of Ruth's husband Boaz.

Most commentators, while acknowledging that this chapter may have an oral pre-history different from the rest of the Joseph story, generally regard it as part of the main source J. Though some commentators, including Westermann, have queried this, suggesting it is a later addition to the main Joseph story, their grounds, as Emerton (*VT* 25 [1975] 346–52) points out, are not strong. By failing to note the narrative and theological linkages between this chapter and its neighbors, they have come to the conclusion that it must be a later addition. But chronologically this material could be included only at this point in the narrative, and it does cohere well with its context, so I follow the consensus in ascribing it to J.

Comment

1–5 These verses are little more than a genealogy sketching Judah's marriage to a Canaanite and the subsequent birth of three sons. Though the narrative does not underline it here, marrying Canaanites was hardly respectable in Israel. Abraham was most insistent that Isaac should not marry a Canaanite (24:3), and Isaac and Rebekah strongly objected to Esau's marriage with Canaanites and forbade Jacob to do so (27:46–28:1). So it may be presumed that Jacob felt similarly about his son's marriage. Yet knowing his father's antipathy, Judah went ahead, showing once again his callous disregard for his father's feelings. Simeon (46:10) also married a Canaanite, and Joseph an Egyptian (41:45), so by marrying a foreigner, Judah anticipates his brothers' actions.

1 "At that time"; cf. 21:22, i.e., soon after Joseph's sale into Egypt. The events of chap. 38 must span at least twenty years, assuming Judah's sons married in

their mid to late teens. This means there is considerable chronological overlap
between this chapter and the succeeding ones, but all the events described here
could be fitted in before Joseph's brothers discovered him in Egypt, some twenty-
two years later according to 37:2; 41:46–47; 45:6 (Cassuto, *Biblical and Oriental
Studies,* 1:32). "Went down." Hebron (37:14), 3040 feet above sea level, is one of
the highest points in southern Canaan, so to go to Adullam (usually identified
with Tell esh-Sheikh Madkhur) in the Judean foothills northwest of Hebron (cf.
1 Sam 22:1; Mic 1:15) would involve a descent. "Joined up with" could be an
abridged form of "pitched his tent" (cf. 12:8), but here it seems to have the same
sense as "turn aside" (38:16). O'Callaghan (*PIBA* 5 [1981] 23) thinks it has overtones of impetuosity. "Hirah," possibly "rock" (so *EM* 3:122), is presumably the
friend in v 20 dispatched to find Tamar.

2 "Judah saw . . . took her." Though "take" is a perfectly proper term for
marriage, the combination of "see" and "take" has in Genesis overtones of illicit
taking (cf. 3:6; 6:2; 12:15; 34:2; cf. Judg 14:1–2), suggesting Judah's marriage may
have been based on mere lust. The fact that his wife's name is not mentioned,
only her father's, "Shua" ("ruler," *EM* 7:568), may point in the same direction.

3–5 The rapid sequence of "conceived," "bore," "called" suggests that the three
boys were born in quick succession. "Er" perhaps means "guard" (KB, 829) or
"watchful" (Noth, *Personennamen,* 228). "Onan" possibly means "vigorous" (BDB, 206).
The name is also known at Mari (KB, 226). "Shelah" may mean "drawn out" (of
the womb). "Kezib" is the same as Akzib (Josh 15:44: Mic 1:14), three miles west
of Adullam (*EM* 1:278). It was later settled by some of the Shelanite clan (1 Chr
4:21–22), which may explain the mention of Judah going there in this passage.

6–11 These verses introduce the heroine of the story, Tamar ("palm tree"),
the wife of the ill-fated Er. Nothing is said about her background, but she would
appear to be a Canaanite. After Er's death, Tamar was left a childless widow, and in
Hebrew law she could then expect to marry her brother-in-law. The purpose of
this second marriage was to produce a son for her dead husband, so that "his
name may not be blotted out" (Deut 25:6). This custom of the Levirate is found in
many traditional societies and among Israel's neighbors, the Assyrians (MAL A30)
and the Hittites (HL 193, 195), and at Nuzi and Ugarit. The responsibility of marrying one's widowed sister-in-law was not always welcomed, and Deut 25:5–10
provides a ceremony whereby a man who refuses to marry his widowed sister-in-
law is put to public shame. But at least he was not obliged to marry her. It seems
that Gen 38 presupposes an earlier stricter stage in the law in which the obligation
was mandatory, and the responsibility for ensuring it was carried out rested with
the widow's father-in-law, in this case Judah (see R. de Vaux, *Ancient Israel,* 37–38).

7 "Er erred," lit. "Er did evil." "Evil" is Er spelled backwards (רע), and I have
attempted to capture the pun by translating "Er erred." The nature of his sin is
not divulged, "But the completely similar sentence and fate suggest a very similar
sin" to Onan's (Jacob, 712). Lev 20:10–20 prescribes death or cutting off, i.e.,
death at God's hand, for a variety of sexual offenses. The main point though is
that Er deserved to die: it was not Tamar's fault. Note that nothing is said about
Judah mourning the loss of his firstborn, in contrast to Jacob (37:34–35).

8 Judah acts promptly to fulfill the levirate obligation, to "produce descendants [זרע] for your brother." Hitherto in the patriarchal narratives the term

"descendants" has been used almost exclusively of the descendants promised to Abraham, who would become a great nation and inherit the land. It seems likely that for the narrator "descendants" has the same connotations here.

9 Onan has to obey his father's injunction but is unwilling to give "descendants to his brother," so he practices *coitus interruptus* whenever they come together. The Hebrew emphasizes that Onan did this on every occasion of intercourse, not just once or twice.

10 "What he did offended the LORD." The terminology is very similar to v 7. Why was God offended by Onan's contraceptive methods? In the light of passages such as 1:28; 8:17; 9:1, 7; Pss 127, 128, it seems unlikely that the OT would approve of systematic contraception, for it frustrates God's purpose in creating mankind in two sexes. But in Onan's case it is specially reprehensible, for God's repeated promise to the patriarchs was that he would make them fruitful and multiply (17:6, 20; 28:3; 35:11; cf. 15:5; 22:17; 26:4; 32:13[12]). Onan is thus deliberately frustrating the fulfillment of those promises. The threefold reference to "descendants" in 38:8–9 must allude to these promises, and Onan's action demonstrates his opposition to the divine agenda. For this reason, the LORD "let him die" (cf. Num 14:27–35).

11 Judah promises to give Tamar his next son but, as the narrator discloses, plans to do nothing of the sort. That he had an obligation to give her Shelah is hinted at by calling Tamar "his daughter-in-law," which is otherwise redundant. Again this tends to put Judah in a bad light, though his fear that Shelah might also die mitigates this impression a little. Nothing is said about Tamar's feelings; she is in no position to argue with her father-in-law.

12–19 "Until this point Tamar has been a passive object, acted upon—or, alas, not acted upon—by Judah and his sons. The only verbs she was the subject of were the two verbs of compliance and retreat, to go off and dwell, at the end of verse 11. Now, a clear perception of injustice done her is ascribed to Tamar (verse 14), and she suddenly races into rapid, purposeful action, expressed in a detonating series of verbs: in verse 14 she quickly takes off, covers, wraps herself, sits down at the strategic location . . . Judah takes the bait—his sexual appetite will not tolerate postponement though he has been content to let Tamar languish as a childless widow indefinitely—and here we are given the only extended dialogue in the story (verses 16–18). It is a wonderfully businesslike exchange. Wasting no time with preliminaries, Judah immediately tells her, 'Let me lie with you' . . . to which Tamar responds like a hard-headed businesswoman, finally exacting the rather serious pledge of Judah's seal and cord and staff, which as the legal surrogate of the bearer would have been a kind of ancient Near Eastern equivalent of all of a person's credit cards.

"The agreement completed, the narrative proceeds in three quick verbs (the end of verse 18)—he gave, he lay, she conceived—to Tamar's single-minded purpose, which, from her first marriage, has been to become the channel of the seed of Judah" (R. Alter, *The Art of Biblical Narrative*, 8–9).

12 "Many days later," perhaps a year, at least a long enough period to show Judah had no intention of allowing Shelah to marry Tamar. "Consoled" again contrasts with Jacob, who refused to be (37:35), and also with Tamar, who was still wearing her widow's garb (v 14).

"Sheep-shearing" was a lively festival (cf. 1 Sam 25:2–37; 2 Sam 13:23–28), when wine was freely consumed. If Judah was already under the influence, it might help to explain why he did not penetrate Tamar's disguise. "Timnah" is a village in the Shephelah on the border of the tribes of Judah and Dan (Josh 15:10), the scene of Samson's exploits (Judg 14:1–5). Z. Kallai identifies it with Tel el Batashi about four miles west-northwest of Beth-Shemesh (*VT* 8 [1958] 145; *EM* 8:598–600). Some commentators hold that another Timnah in the southern part of the tribal territory of Judah (Josh 15:57) is meant, but this does not fit so well with the location of Enayim, here described as on the road to Timnah (38:14), which is in the northern part of Judah's territory (Josh 15:34).

14 While not actually saying that Tamar dressed as a prostitute, the text implies that the dress and posture she adopted made her easily taken for one (cf. v 16; Robinson *JBL* 96 [1977] 569). "On the way into Enayim." Enayim is usually identified with Enam, mentioned in Josh 15:34 (cf. *Comment* on v 12). "For she had noticed" reminds us why she was stooping to this ruse: her father-in-law's duplicity had forced her to it.

16 "For he did not know that she was his daughter-in-law." Whereas consorting with prostitutes was regarded as very foolish (Prov 7), sexual intercourse with one's daughter-in-law was punishable by death according to later law (Lev 20:12). This comment shows that the narrator shares the moral standards expressed more explicitly elsewhere in the OT.

18 "Seal." Judah, a rich man, would have owned his own personally engraved seal. Both cylinder seals, which imprint by rolling, and stamp seals are known from this period in Canaan. They were carried on a "cord" threaded through the middle. "Staff" was a symbol of authority (cf. Num 17:17[2]; Ps 110:2) as well as being practically useful. It had a carved top to mark ownership.

20–23 According to Gunkel and Westermann, one purpose of this episode is to "portray Judah as an honorable man" (Westermann, 3:53), but in reality it does the reverse. Whereas he had reneged on his solemn promise to give his son Shelah to Tamar in marriage, he is very anxious to pay the goat he had promised to a common prostitute. And his concern here seems to have no higher motive than the return of his pledges. Furthermore, the furtive way in which he sends his friend to make the payment, rather than go himself, shows the disreputable status of prostitution. Though not illegal, it is a shady world from which the respectable citizen tries to keep aloof. Even Hirah uses a euphemism, "holy woman," "temple prostitute," for the common prostitute he is seeking, for evidently prostitutes attached to temples were more respectable than common whores in Canaanite culture. Eventually Judah calls off the search, "lest we become a joke" (v 23). בוז "joke" is the contempt of the rich and arrogant for lesser mortals (cf. Ps 123:3–4; cf. Neh 3:36[4:4]). Judah's fear was well founded, for if he was not already a joke, in three months he certainly would be!

24–26 This is the dramatic climax to the story, as Tamar at the last minute forces Judah to admit that he has wronged her.

24 "Your daughter-in-law Tamar has been promiscuous." The noun זנה means "prostitute," but the verb used here is broader in meaning and covers any illicit sexual intercourse (*TDOT* 4:100; cf. BDB, 275–76; KB, 263–64). To translate the verb here "play the harlot" as RSV does, is to provide too precise a rendering of

the information conveyed to Judah. Since she was in effect betrothed to Shelah, she should have had intercourse with no one else. But clearly she has had, so she is in effect guilty of adultery. Hence Judah can legitimately, if in this case unfairly, demand the death penalty (cf. Deut 22:23–24). Deut 22:21 envisages stoning for adultery during betrothal in a case similar to Tamar's. But to demand death by burning was extreme; that is reserved in Lev 21:9 for a priest's daughter, because such behavior by her was particularly disgraceful.

25–26 But then Tamar plays her trump card, and the case against her collapses. Her prosecutor acknowledges that he is the guilty party, not she. On the root צדק, see *Comment* on 18:23–25. In judicial contexts it often has the sense of innocent (e.g., Exod 23:7; Deut 25:1), so here Judah declares her innocence and admits his own guilt.

27–30 This account of the birth of twins runs in parallel with 25:24–26, the birth of Jacob and Esau. In both cases the twins compete to be born first, and in both it is the older twin who later has to take second place. Here Zerah stuck out his hand first, making him technically the older, but somehow Peres emerged first, taking everyone by surprise. His name, "Peres," "break through," recalls the extraordinary circumstance of his birth. Zerah's name, though not explained, means "shining, brightness."

Explanation

The sudden switch of focus from Joseph on his way to Egypt (37:36) to Judah's marriage (38:2) has thrown many readers, who see chap. 38 as an irrelevant digression. This is because they have forgotten that chaps. 37–50 are not headed "This is the story of Joseph" but "this is the family history of Jacob"(37:2). Consequently, it is not surprising that occasionally sons of Jacob other than Joseph should sometimes occupy center stage. And principles of divine providence that are illustrated on a grander scale elsewhere in Genesis, e.g., justice for the deceived, choice of the younger son, are here encapsulated in a short narrative (for further discussion, see *Form/Structure/Setting*). This short story then helps to focus the leading ideas of the whole patriarchal narrative.

It begins rather inauspiciously with Judah leaving his brothers and seeing and taking a Canaanite as a wife (phraseology suggestive of a union based on chemistry rather than principle), who gives birth to three sons. When his eldest, Er, reaches the age for marriage, probably in his late teens, Judah finds a bride for him. Unfortunately he dies soon after marriage for some unspecified sin. As Tamar is childless, it is her father-in-law's duty to give his next son in marriage to her, to perpetuate the dead son's name. But his next son, Onan, while publicly marrying her, secretly contrives to ensure that no children will be conceived. This is not merely an offense against the conventional morality of the day, which insisted on the duty of Levirate marriage, but it disregards the fundamental duty of husbands to father children (Gen 1:28) and shows scant respect for the promises to the patriarchs that they should have descendants beyond counting. So Onan dies too. Once again, since it was the husband who sinned, Tamar has a right to expect to marry the next of Judah's sons. But Shelah, his third son, is too young, and though he promises to give him to Tamar in due course, Judah decides not

to give any more of his sons to Tamar. Tamar is therefore left a widow, but technically betrothed to Shelah. The time passes and Judah's faithlessness becomes evident, for Shelah has grown old enough to marry and yet he is not given to Tamar.

Legal redress for a widow in Tamar's situation was impossible. So one day she seizes the opportunity to produce a child for her departed husband Er. By dressing as a prostitute she succeeds in having intercourse with her father-in-law, Judah, and immediately conceives. By the standards of Leviticus, such an incestuous relationship merits the death penalty (20:12). This is one of a number of sexual relationships banned by Leviticus that occur in the patriarchal narratives, witnessing the different standards of that age. Evidently Genesis regards Tamar's action as at least partially justified, because Judah had failed to let his son marry her as promised.

Eventually, news of Tamar's pregnancy reaches Judah, who fiercely sentences her to death for disregarding her betrothal vow. Infidelity during betrothal counted as adultery, and therefore merited the death penalty (Deut 22:13–21, 23–24). Under OT law, if Tamar was culpable, so was her partner. Consequently, if he but realized it, Judah in sentencing her to death has also condemned himself to the same fate. At the last moment Tamar makes her point, proving that Judah was indeed the father of the child. Judah admits his guilt, "She is in the right, not I" (38:26). She is innocent, he admits, because I forced her to take this action by refusing to give my son Shelah to her in marriage. She, unlike me, was concerned to perpetuate the family line, to produce descendants for Abraham.

So the story closes with another remarkable twin birth, replacing, as it were, Judah's two lost sons, Er and Onan, with Zerah and Peres. The younger, called Peres, headed the Judahite clan from which Boaz came, so that at his marriage to Ruth the elders prayed, "may your house be like the house of Perez, whom Tamar bore to Judah, because of the children that the LORD will give you by this young woman" (Ruth 4:12). Boaz was the ancestor of King David, who in turn was the forefather of "Jesus . . . who is called Christ" (Matt 1: 6, 16). So this story, which at first sight seems to be so marginal to biblical history, records a vital link in saving history. Tamar, through her determination to have children, secured for Judah the honor of fathering both David and the Savior of the world.

Joseph and Potiphar   (39:1–20)

Bibliography

Furman, N. "His Story Versus Her Story: Male Genealogy and Female Strategy in the Jacob Cycle." *Semeia* 46 (1989) 141–49. **Gan, M.** "The Book of Esther in the Light of the Story of Joseph in Egypt." (Heb.) *Tarbiz* 31 (1961/62) 144–49. **Hollis, S. T.** "The Woman in Ancient Examples of the Potiphar's Wife Motif, K2111." In *Gender and Difference in Ancient Israel*, ed. P. Day. Minneapolis: Fortress, 1989. 28–42. **Jacobson, H.** "A Legal Note on Potiphar's Wife." *HTR* 69 (1976) 177. **Ringgren, H.** "Die Versuchung Josefs (Gen 39)." In *Die Väter Israels: FS J. Scharbert*, ed. M. Görg. Stuttgart: Katholisches Bibelwerk, 1989. 267–70.

Translation

¹^a *Now Joseph had been taken^b down to Egypt,^a and an Egyptian, Potiphar, an official of Pharaoh, captain of the guards, had bought him from the Ishmaelites, who had brought^c him down to Egypt.* ²*The LORD was with Joseph so that^a he became successful and stayed in the house of his Egyptian master.* ³*His master noticed that the LORD was with him and that the LORD made everything that he did successful.* ⁴*Joseph pleased his master and he served him, and he put him in charge of his household and entrusted him with all that^a he had.* ⁵*From the time that he put him in charge of his household and all that he owned, the LORD blessed the house of the Egyptian because of Joseph, and the LORD's blessing rested^a on everything he had indoors and outdoors.* ⁶*So he left everything in Joseph's care. He did not worry about anything except the food which he used to eat.^a ^bNow Joseph had a fine figure and a handsome face.^b*

⁷*After these things his master's wife set^a her eyes on Joseph and said, "Lie with me."* ⁸*But he refused and said to his master's wife, "See my master does not know what I have, or what^a is in the^b house, and all that he owns he has entrusted to me.* ⁹*There is no one in this house more responsible than I am, and he has not withheld anything from me apart from you, because^a you are his wife. How can I do this great wrong and sin against God?"* ¹⁰*But whenever she talked to Joseph day after day, he refused to lie beside her, to be with her.*

¹¹*But about this time^a he entered the house to do his work, while there were no men of the household there in the house.* ¹²*So she grabbed his garment saying, "Lie with me." And he left his garment in her hand and fled^a outside.* ¹³*As soon as she saw^a that he had left his garment in her hand and had fled outside,* ¹⁴*she called the men of her household and said to them, "Look, he brought^a a Hebrew man into us to fool with us, to lie with me. So I cried out in a loud voice.* ¹⁵*Then as soon as he heard me shout^a and cry out, he left his garment beside me and fled outside."* ¹⁶*So she put^a his garment aside until his master came back home.*

¹⁷*She spoke to him about these things as follows: "The Hebrew slave came into me, the one you brought^a in to us to fool with me.* ¹⁸*When I lifted^a up my voice and shouted, he left his garment with me and ran outside."* ¹⁹*As soon as his master heard his wife's words which she had spoken to him, "This was the way in which your slave treated^a me," he was furious.*

²⁰*So Joseph's master put^a him in the prison, the place^b where the royal prisoners were imprisoned. And there he stayed in the prison.*

Notes

1.a-a. Episode-initial circumstantial clause (*SBH,* 80).
1.b. 3 masc sg pf hoph ירד. For pluperfect sense, see GKC, 142b.
1.c. 3 masc pl pf hiph ירד + 3 masc sg suffix.
2.a. On this use of the waw-consec to express necessary consequence, see GKC, 111l; WOC, 548.
4.a. Probably insert, with SamPent and Cairo fragment, אשר; cf. v 5.
5.a. ויהי: 3 masc sg verb with fem subj "blessing" is common with ויהי (GKC, 145q; Joüon, 150j).
6.a. Ptcp in past often has frequentative sense.
6.b-b. Closing sentence anticipating next episode (cf. Longacre, *Joseph,* 88).
7.a. Cf. n. 21:16.f.
8.a. SamPent (?G) reads מאמה "anything" (cf. v 6).

8.b. SamPent, G, S, Vg read "his house."

9.a. On this meaning of בְּאֲשֶׁר, see Joüon, 170j.

11.a. The non-elision of the def art is unusual. For this translation, see GKC, 35n.

12.a. Waw consec + 3 masc sg impf qal נוס.

13.a. כ + inf constr רָאָה + 3 fem sg suffix.

14.a. 3 masc sg pf hiph בוא.

15.a. Cf. n. 14:22.a-a.

16.a. Waw consec + 3 fem sg impf hiph נוח.

17.a. Cf. n. 20:9.c.

18.a. כ + inf constr hiph רום + 1 sg suffix.

19.a. The dagesh in עֲשֹׂה is a quirk of L.

20.a. Waw consec + 3 masc sg impf נתן + 3 masc sg suffix.

20.b. Noun in constr before relative clause (GKC 130c; WOC, 155–56, 645).

Form/Structure/Setting

Most commentators accept that the chapter division correctly defines the next section of Genesis. This gives a nice symmetry to the chapter, with one of the darkest episodes in Joseph's life being encased in the reassuring comment that the LORD was with Joseph (39:2, 21). According to Longacre (*Joseph*, 33), 39:21–23 is a typical closing paragraph, which both sums up what has gone before and anticipates the development in the next episode. But Gunkel and Coats argue that the chapter splits into two scenes in 39:20. Scene 1, Joseph in Potiphar's house, consists of exposition (39:1–6) followed by a narration (39:7–20a); scene 2, Joseph in prison, consists of exposition (39:20b–23) followed by narration (40:1–23); and scene 3 (41:1–57) tells of Joseph in Pharaoh's court. The shift from exposition to narration is in both cases marked by the phrase "After these things" (39:7; 40:1). The third scene has no exposition but simply begins with the statement "At the end of two full years" (41:1).

Coats' analysis seems preferable to the standard view that chap. 39 defines the first unit, for Hebrew writers enjoy telling stories in three episodes, or scenes; the first two are typically quite alike, and then the third surprises by its differences (cf. Gen 14:1–16; Lev 8–10; Num 22–24). Here Joseph is said to experience God's presence and blessing: first, by being put in charge of Potiphar's household (39:2–6); second, by being put in charge of the royal prison (39:21–23). But in both cases his hopes are dashed: Potiphar throws him into prison (39:20), and then the chief butler forgets Joseph and leaves him in prison (40:23). The third act opens ominously for Joseph because unlike the previous two occasions there is no exposition in which it is said that the LORD was with Joseph; here it plunges straight into the narration. But on this occasion Joseph rises instead of falling, and instead of being put in charge merely of a rich man's house, or of the royal prison, he is made vizier of all Egypt, next in authority to the Pharaoh, who declares that the spirit of God is in Joseph (41:38). The following exposition, therefore, broadly follows Coats. However, it seems preferable (with Humphreys, *Joseph and His Family*, 59) to end the first section at 39:20b, not 20a, for as Longacre observes of 39:20b: "And there he stayed in prison" makes a good close to an episode (Longacre, *Joseph*, 88). Lacking an explicit noun subject, this clause would not make an appropriate start to a new episode, whereas "The LORD was with Joseph" (39:21) does.

The section divides as follows:

Recapitulation of Joseph's sale into Egypt (1)
Act 1: Prosperity in Potiphar's house (2–6)
Act 2: Repeated Enticement (7–10)
        Potiphar's wife invites (7)
        Joseph declines (8–10)
Act 3: Joseph's Disgrace (11–20)
        Scene 1: Trapped by Potiphar's Wife (11–12)
        Scene 2: Denounced to Servants (13–15)
        Scene 3: Denounced to Potiphar (16–20)

Note how the last three scenes each contain a description of the attempted seduction: first, the narrator's account (v 12), second, the account of Potiphar's wife to the servants (vv 14–15), and finally, her account to her husband (vv 17–18). These repetitions give an insight into the mind of Potiphar's wife.

According to most source critics, all of chap. 39 comes from J, because it begins and ends with several references to the LORD. Westermann's reasons for dissenting from this view have already been discussed and do not convince.

Comment

1 This verse reintroduces the main thread of the story by recapitulating 37:36, "Meanwhile the Midianites had sold him to the Egyptians, to Potiphar . . . ," but looks at the events from a different perspective. Here Joseph is the subject of the sentence, indeed of a passive verb, showing he is now to be the focus of interest. Potiphar is here called "an Egyptian," a designation repeated in vv 2, 5, perhaps suggesting a parallel between Joseph's slavery in Egypt and that of the Israelites some centuries later. On the other terms, cf. *Comments* on 37:25, 36.

2–6 These verses describe Joseph's rise in Potiphar's esteem. First, he was promoted to work indoors, "in the house of his Egyptian master" (v 2), instead of being sent into the fields to work. Next, "he pleased his master" and became his personal attendant (for this sense of "he served him," see *Comment* on v 4). And ultimately, he was put in charge of his household and was entrusted with all his possessions (vv 4–5).

But this paragraph is not just about Joseph's success but also about the reason for that success: because "the LORD was with Joseph." The use of the divine name "the LORD," "Yahweh," is rare in the Joseph story. Apart from 38:7, 10 and 49:18, the name occurs only in chap. 39 (vv 2, 3[2x], 5[2x], 21, 23[2x]), all in passages where the narrator is speaking. "With its theme of Yahweh-with-Joseph (vv. 2, 3, 21, 23) it forms the theological entrance piece to the Joseph story which finds its counterpart at the end with the concluding words of Joseph 'God brought me here' (45:5–8; 50:17–21). Chs. 39–41 are the story of a rise, but a rise made possible because Yahweh was with Joseph. This is what the passages that frame it, 39:1–2 and 21–23, intend to say, and it is to this that the concluding words return (45:5–8; 50:17–21). Ch. 39, then, is a constitutive part of the Joseph story and is in no wise a later addition" (Westermann, 3:62).

2 "The LORD was with Joseph." It is a characteristic feature of the Jacob cycle that God promised to be with Isaac and Jacob (26:3, 24, 28; 28:15, 20; 31:3). Now the same thing is said about Joseph, twice here and twice in the introduction to the next section (39:21, 23). These remarks help to put the unfortunate events into perspective. Despite all the setbacks Joseph was about to face, God was on his side. For a while this was apparent, for he was "successful," a term earlier used to describe Abraham's servant's mission (24:21, 40, 42; cf. *THWAT,* 2:551–56).

3–4 Indeed, so obvious was Joseph's magic touch that his master realized God was with him and promoted him from indoor worker to his personal assistant. שׁרת "served" is close in meaning to עבד "to work (for)," but whereas the latter term can be used for menial jobs often done by slaves (29:15, 18, 20), the former term always implies personal service. Thus Joshua was Moses' servant (Exod 24:13; Josh 1:1), Elisha was Elijah's (1 Kgs 19:21), and prince Amnon had servants (2 Sam 13:17) (*THWAT* 2:1019–22). "Put him in charge of his household," i.e., he was appointed chief manager or steward of his household (cf. Luke 16:1). Such officials (*mer-per*) are often mentioned in Egyptian texts. They were in charge not "just of the house but the whole estate and all the property" (Vergote, *Joseph en Égypte*, 25).

5 Potiphar's trust in Joseph led to great blessing on him and his estate, because God was with Joseph. Here the blessing that Joseph will bring to Egypt and the neighboring nations when he is entrusted with governing all Egypt is evidently being anticipated. On the word ברך "bless," cf. *Comment* on 1:22; 12:2–3. It is one of the key words of Genesis, so it is not surprising to find it twice here, though it is rarely used in the Joseph story outside of chap. 49.

"39:2–6 shows particularly clearly the meaning of blessing in the OT. God's presence and blessing belong together, though they are distinct. Blessing encompasses both men and other creatures. So the narrator simply assumes that the blessing on the one whom the LORD is with can overflow to a foreign people and adherents of a foreign religion because of God's presence with that person" (Westermann, 3:59, ET 63). Thus in Joseph's experience here we begin to see how all the families of the earth are to find blessing (cf. 12:3) in Abraham's descendants.

6 "He left everything in Joseph's care," lit. "in Joseph's hand." This seems a stronger expression than "entrusted all that he had" (v 4); it implies that Potiphar abandoned his interest in what Joseph was doing because he was so convinced that Joseph was doing the best for him (cf. Neh 9:28; Ps 37:33). The phrase is used in a more literal sense in vv 12–13, when Joseph "left his garment in her hand," thus serving as an ominous foreshadowing of the storm about to break.

"Except the food he ate." This may be a euphemism for "his wife" (cf. Prov 30:20), but it seems more likely to be an idiom for "his private affairs."

"A fine figure and a handsome face." Joseph's mother, Rachel, is also described as having a lovely figure and a beautiful face (29:17). They are the only two people in the OT to be awarded this double accolade. This last comment anticipates the next step in Joseph's career; it is common in narrative for the end of one episode to serve as a trailer for the next. Amid Joseph's many blessings, he suffers from one endowment too many, stunning beauty.

7–20 It is often asserted that this story of the attempted seduction of Joseph is based on the thirteenth-century B.C. Egyptian Story of Two Brothers (see *ANET,*

23–25). This relates how an Egyptian farmer was helped on his farm by his younger brother. One day the elder brother's wife tried to persuade her brother-in-law to have intercourse with her. He indignantly refused and promised never to tell his brother about his wife's indiscretion. However, the wife pretended she had been assaulted and persuaded her husband to ambush his brother when he brought the cows in from the fields. However, the cows warned the younger brother that he was about to be attacked, and he ran away. As he was being chased by his brother, a river full of crocodiles suddenly appeared between them. Shouting to each other across this river, the younger brother convinced his brother of his innocence, so that the older brother eventually went home and executed his wife.

Apart from the motif of the unfaithful wife rejected by the faithful single man, there is practically nothing in common between these stories. And despite claims to the contrary, even the dialogue in the seduction scene is quite different. Gunkel pointed out that the motif of the hero spurning a wife's advances is found in many ancient tales, so that dependency of the Hebrew tale on the Egyptian story would only be proved if the two were particularly close. "But that does not seem to be the case" (Gunkel, 422). Similarly, Redford (*Biblical Story of Joseph*, 93) concludes that direct borrowing "seems rather unlikely" (also von Rad, Sarna).

7–10 These verses seem to cover a prolonged period in which Potiphar's wife tries to persuade the glamorous Joseph to lie with her. Her raw lust and his sense of propriety and loyalty are admirably captured by the dialogue. Her peremptory "lie with me" is countered by a long speech by Joseph, showing his own sense of moral shock at the suggestion.

7 "Lie with me." "The brevity of the sexual proposition on the part of Potiphar's wife is a brilliant stylization—for . . . she *must* have said more than that!—of the naked lust that impels her, and perhaps also of the peremptory tone she feels she can assume toward her Hebrew slave" (Alter, *Art of Biblical Narrative*, 73).

8–9 "By contrast, Joseph's refusal is a voluble outpouring of language, full of repetitions which are both dramatically appropriate—as a loyal servant, he is emphatically protesting the moral scandal of the deed proposed—and thematically pointed" (Alter, *Art of Biblical Narrative*, 109). Note how Joseph uses the key words "all, anything" and "house, household," already stressed in vv 3–6. He gives three reasons that the suggestion must be rejected: it is an abuse of the great trust placed in him (v 6); it is an offense against her husband; and it is a great sin against God. Other biblical texts also describe adultery as a great sin (20:9; cf. Ps 51:4[6]), but this attitude was widespread in the ancient Orient (cf. *Comment* on 20:9). Notice that in talking to an Egyptian, Joseph speaks of "God" rather than "the LORD," the uniquely Israelite name of God.

10 "To lie beside her, to be with her." Nowhere else is the preposition "beside" used with the verb "lie." This may suggest that Potiphar's wife was moderating her demands, "let's just be on our own together for a little," in the hope of making him take the first step.

11–20 But exasperated that he would not even make this concession, one day her patience runs out. Within a single day he is plunged from trust and honor into the ignominy of prison. The events are related in three short scenes.

11–12 First, the narrator tells what really happened. Joseph arrived in the house to do his normal duty (Exod 20:9–10). With no other men on the premises to

act as witnesses, she grabbed his garment. The verb תפשׂ "grab" implies violence (cf. Deut 9:17; 22:28; 1 Kgs 11:30). בגד "garment" covers a variety of clothes. The main items of attire in patriarchal times were mid-calf shorts and a tunic, a long T-shirt (cf. 3:21; 37:3; see *EM* 4:1035–37). To pull either of these garments off against the wearer's will must have involved surprise and violence, perhaps suggesting that the woman was working according to a premeditated plan. נוס "fled" is most often used of running away after defeat in battle (14:10) to escape death (e.g., Num 35:6, 11). Note that the narrator says nothing about her shouting at this stage.

13–15 Joseph's rapid exit could easily have compromised the woman, had he used the opportunity to explain matters to the rest of the household. So Potiphar's wife seizes the initiative and gives an account that is a travesty of the facts, but so worded as to elicit maximum sympathy among her slaves.

"Look," she says, waving the garment before them, "he," Potiphar, your heartless boss, deliberately brought a Hebrew man; note the appeal to xenophobia. "Into us." Here she tactfully identifies herself with her slaves and their plight. "To fool with us" is a nicely ambiguous phrase used of sexual intimacy in 26:8 and of insulting behavior in 21:9. "To lie with me." You may have had to endure his insults, but I have nearly been raped. But "I cried out in a loud voice. Then as soon as he heard me shout and cry out, he left his garment beside me and fled outside." "Because she uses precisely the same series of phrases in her speech (verses 14–15) that had been used twice just before by the narrator (verses 12–13) but reverses their order, so that her calling out *precedes* Joseph's flight, the blatancy of her lie is forcefully conveyed without commentary. That blatancy is even more sharply focused through the change of a single word in one phrase she repeats from the preceding narration" (Alter, *Art of Biblical Narrative*, 109). Instead of saying that Joseph left the garment "in her hand" (v 12), she says he left it "beside her," thus insinuating that he had "disrobed quite voluntarily as a preliminary to rape" (Alter, 110).

16–20 When her husband returns, she tells him the story, but once again it is adjusted to make the maximum impact on him. "The arousal of ethnic prejudice ('the Hebrew') again goes with social incitement, but in the reverse direction. With Potiphar now . . . addressee, Joseph is no longer termed 'man' but 'slave' just as 'us' shifts in reference (and solidarity) from the household to the master and mistress. To sting her husband into action, she again throws on him part of the blame, though by another clever adjustment of psychological tactics, in a manner less shrill and more cautious" (Sternberg, *Poetics*, 425). Whereas she had provoked the slaves by saying "He [i.e., Potiphar] brought a man into us to fool with us," she addresses Potiphar more circumspectly, so as not to insult him. "The Hebrew slave came into me" puts the blame fully on Joseph and at the same time reminds Potiphar that he is a mere slave and a foreign one at that. "Came into me" is deliberately ambiguous; it may be taken literally, but it is also a euphemism for sexual intercourse (16:2; 30:3; 38:8–9). Having first accused Joseph, she then implicates her husband, "the one you brought in to us." Finally, she discloses what Joseph has been doing "to fool with me." This is subtly different from v 14, where she had said "to fool with us," which could simply mean "insult"; here Joseph's purpose in coming in to her is said to be sexual intimacy. But the clause could also be read as subordinate to "the one you brought in," in which case she

is not simply blaming her husband for acquiring a foreign slave but implying that Potiphar had acquired him deliberately to harass his wife. "The second reason obviously would be a sharp rebuke to the husband, suggesting that he had perversely invited trouble by introducing such a sexual menace into the household, but the wife is cunning enough to word the accusation in such a way that he will be left the choice of taking it as a direct rebuke or only an implicit and mild one" (Alter, *Art of Biblical Narrative,* 10).

Her account has the desired effect. Potiphar is furious, and Joseph is put in prison. This is a somewhat unexpected punishment, because convicted rapists were executed when both parties were free citizens (Deut 22:23–27). A slave assaulting his master's wife would certainly expect no better fate. But for some reason Joseph escaped the death penalty. Presumably his protestations of innocence, though unrecorded, were sufficient to convince Potiphar that his wife might not be telling the whole truth, so Joseph was given a lighter sentence. But the narrator is not interested in this point, only that Joseph was "put in the prison, the place where the royal prisoners were imprisoned," because it was the contacts he made in prison that led to his eventual promotion. בית סהר "prison," lit. "house of roundness," is found only in this section of Genesis (cf. 39:21–23; 40:3, 5). The term suggests it was a fortress that also served as a prison, several of which are known in Egypt (Vergote, *Joseph en Égypte,* 25–28). It seems to have been managed by Potiphar (cf. 40:3, 7; 41:10).

Explanation

After the short digression about Judah's affairs, the main line of the story resumes with an account of Joseph's first years in Egypt. Evidently he lands on his feet, being bought as slave by a high-ranking royal official named Potiphar. He soon recognizes Joseph's ability, first letting him work indoors, the job of superior slaves, then making him his personal assistant, and finally appointing him manager of his household, entrusting him with total responsibility for all his business affairs. This rapid promotion, we are told, occurred because the LORD was with Joseph. Indeed, God's presence with Joseph was even evident to Potiphar, which was why he promoted him, and he prospered greatly as a result: "the LORD's blessing rested on everything he had."

But Potiphar's wife was attracted by Joseph's stunning beauty; like his mother Rachel, Joseph had "a fine figure and handsome face." So the mistress of the house determines to have sex with him. Day after day she attempts to seduce him, but he repudiates her advances with ethical and theological argument. One day, however, she catches him alone in the house, pulls off his shirt, and runs outside calling to the servants that Joseph has tried to rape her. She repeats a similar tale to her husband, who thereupon throws his trusted servant in jail.

The story of the spurned woman who takes her revenge on the upright male is doubtless a universal one, because such situations recur in every generation in every society. But this tale is no more included to applaud male propriety over female infidelity than the story of Tamar and Judah is inserted to prove the reverse. Genesis is remarkably evenhanded in describing the failings and the virtues of both sexes. Undoubtedly, Joseph is here portrayed as a model, the wise man

who fears God (Prov 1:7), who is totally loyal and dependable, and who thus enjoys "favor and good repute in the sight of God and man" (Prov 3:3–4) and is not
seduced by "the lips of the loose woman" (Prov 5:3), the "adulteress [who] stalks
a man's very life" (Prov 6:26). In a similar way, Potiphar's wife is an example of
the foreign woman whose morals are suspect.

Similarly, Joseph's unfair dismissal and imprisonment may be seen as typical of
the sufferings the righteous often must endure. "For a righteous man falls seven
times, and rises again" (Prov 24:16). Moses, Job, Jeremiah, and the suffering servant
of Isa 53 are examples of this career pattern in the OT, while Jesus is the supreme
model in the NT. And as Peter says, Christians are called to "follow in his steps" (1
Pet 2:21) and to "[h]umble yourselves . . . under the mighty hand of God, that in
due time he may exalt you" (1 Pet 5:6). On a national level, Joseph's slavery in
Potiphar's house foreshadows Israel's Egyptian bondage, an apparent setback to the
people's fortunes that ultimately leads to the fulfillment of the patriarchal promises.

And it is these promises that most illuminate this dark episode in Joseph's career. The LORD had promised to be with his father and grandfather; he manifestly
was with Joseph (39:2, 3) so that the LORD's blessing rested on the house of the
Egyptian. Here we have his career epitomized: through his affliction, God was at
work to preserve the life of many people (50:20). Through him all the families of
the world would begin to find blessing (12:3). In managing Potiphar's house, he was
being prepared to rule all Egypt. But had he remained Potiphar's manager, he might
never have met Pharaoh's cupbearer in the royal prison and been elevated to the
court. His present disgrace was a necessary preliminary to his future glory.

Joseph in Prison   (39:21–40:23)

Bibliography

Anbar, M. "*ʾereṣ ʿibrîm* 'le pays des Hébreux.'" *Or* 41 (1972) 383–86. **Dahood, M.** "Eblaite
ha-rí and Genesis *ḥōrî.*" *BN* 13 (1980) 14–16. **Görg, M.** "Ein eblaitisches Wort in der
Josepherzählung?" *BN* 13 (1980) 29–31, 205–14. **Marcus, D.** "'Lifting up the head': On
the Trail of a Word Play in Gen 40." *Prooftexts* 10 (1990) 17–27. **Redford, D. B.** "The 'Land
of the Hebrews' in Gen 40:15." *VT* 15 (1965) 529–32.

Translation

^{21}*But the LORD was with Joseph and was*^{a} *loyal to him and gave him favor*^{b} *in the
eyes of the prison governor.* ^{22}*The prison governor entrusted Joseph with all the prisoners
in the prison, and for all that was done there he*^{a}*was responsible.*^{a} ^{23}*The prison governor
did not have to worry about anything that he had entrusted him with, for the LORD was
with him and the LORD made everything he did successful.*

$^{40:1}$*After these things*^{a}*the cupbearer and the baker of the king of Egypt*^{a} *sinned against
their lord, the king of Egypt.* ^{2}*Pharaoh was enraged with his two officials, the head cupbearer*

and the head baker. [3] *So he put them in custody in the house of the captain of the guard in the prison, the place*[a] *where Joseph was imprisoned.* [4] *The head of the guards appointed Joseph to be with them, and he served them, and they were a long time*[a] *in custody.*

[5] *Both the cupbearer and the baker of the king of Egypt, who were detained in prison, dreamed; each had a dream in one night, each with its own meaning.* [6] *Joseph came to them in the morning and noticed that they were looking ill.* [7] *So he asked Pharaoh's officials who were in custody with him in the house of his lord, "Why are you looking glum today?"* [8] *They said to him, "We have dreamed a dream, but* [a]*there is no one to interpret it."*[a] *Joseph said to them, "Don't interpretations belong to God? Please tell it to me."*

[9] *So the head cupbearer related his dream to Joseph and said to him, "In my dream I saw a vine in front of me.* [10] *On the vine there were three stems. As it sprouted,*[a] *it blossomed, and its clusters ripened into grapes.* [11] *I had Pharaoh's cup in my hand, so I took the grapes, squeezed them into Pharaoh's cup, and handed the cup to Pharaoh."*

[12] *Then Joseph said: "This is its interpretation. The three stems are three days.* [13] *In another three days Pharaoh will lift*[a] *up your head and restore*[b] *you to your position, and you shall hand Pharaoh his cup as you used to do when you were his cupbearer.* [14a] *Promise that*[a] *you will remember me when you do well, and* [b]*please do me this kindness to mention me*[b] *to Pharaoh and bring me out of this house.* [15] *For I was kidnapped from the country of the Hebrews, and here I have not done anything that I should have been put in the pit."*

[16] *The head baker saw that he had interpreted well, so he said to Joseph, "I too saw in my dream three baskets of white bread on my head.* [17] *In the top basket there were some of all the Pharaoh's foods, baked cakes, and the birds were eating them out of the basket on my head."*

[18] *So Joseph answered and said, "This is its interpretation. The three baskets are three days.* [19] *In another three days, Pharaoh will lift up your head from off you and hang you on a tree, and the birds will eat the flesh off you."*

[20] *On the third day, it was Pharaoh's birthday,*[a] *and he made a banquet for all his servants, and he lifted up the head cupbearer and the head baker among his servants.* [21a] *He restored*[b] *the head cupbearer to his office, and he handed the cup to Pharaoh.* [22] *But he hanged the head baker, as Joseph had interpreted to them.*[a] [23] *But the head cupbearer did not remember Joseph and forgot him.*

Notes

21.a. Cf. n. 12:8.c.

21.b. On the suffix on חן, see WOC, 303.

22.a-a. Lit. "was doing." On the use of היה + ptcp for repeated action in the past, see GKC 116r; Joüon, 121f.

40:1.a-a. Lit. "the cupbearer of the king of Egypt and the baker." For this construction, see Joüon, 129a. A more common construction would be "the cupbearer of the king of Egypt and his baker."

3.a. Cf. n. 39:20.b.

4.a. GKC, 139h.

8.a-a. On this construction, ptcp + אין + pronoun, see *EWAS*, 102 (cf. GKC, 152o; *SBH*, 83).

10.a. כ + fem sg ptcp qal פרח. On this construction, see GKC 164g; n. 38:29.a-a.

13.a. 3 masc sg impf qal נשא.

13.b. Waw consec + 3 masc sg pf hiph שוב + 2 masc sg suffix.

14.a-a. According to GKC, 163d, כי־אם "except" is short for "I desire nothing else except."

14.b-b. On this precative sense of waw + pf, see WOC, 532–33.

20.a. הלדת inf constr hoph ילד (GKC, 69w).

21.a-22.a. Chiastic linkage between sentences; cf. 14:16; *SBH*, 67.
21.b. Cf. n. 14:16.b.

Form/Structure/Setting

Though most commentators regard chap. 40 as constituting a discrete unit
within the Joseph story, in the previous *Form/Structure/Setting* I set out my reasons
for concurring with Humphreys (*Joseph and His Family;* cf. Gunkel and Coats)
that a new section starts with 39:21. According to this reading, 39:2–20 and 39:21–
40:23 run in parallel:

39:2–6	Divine blessing of Joseph	39:21–23
39:7–19	Human maltreatment of Joseph	40:1–22
39:20	Joseph left in prison	40:23

More precisely, 39:21–40:23 divides as follows:

39:21–23	Joseph promoted in prison
40:1–4	Butler and baker imprisoned
vv 5–19	The morning after the dream
	Opening dialogue (7–8)
	Cupbearer's dream related and interpreted (9–15)
	Baker's dream related and interpreted (16–19)
vv 20–22	Dream fulfilled
v 23	Joseph left in prison

As it stands, this episode is well integrated into the Joseph story. As a whole, it
presupposes 39:20, "Joseph's master put him in the prison, the place where the royal
prisoners were imprisoned." The phraseology of 39:2–6, "The LORD was with Joseph"
(39:2; cf. 39:21), "gave him favor" (39:4; cf. 39:21), "successful" (39:2, 3; cf. 39:23),
"served" (39:4; 40:4), "put in charge, appointed" (39:4; cf. 40:4), "entrusted" (39:4;
cf. 39:22), "did not worry about anything" (39:6; 39:23), is clearly echoed in 39:21–
40:4. The pair of dreams (40:8–19) recalls Joseph's two dreams (37:5–10) and
foreshadows Pharaoh's two dreams (41:1–32), and especially Joseph's skill at interpreting dreams (40:8; cf. 41:16). In particular, 40:15 gives a poignant summary
of both chap. 37 and 39:2–20, "I was kidnapped from the country of the Hebrews, and here I have not done anything that I should have been put in the pit."
    According to traditional source critics, 39:21–23 comes from J, while the bulk
of chap. 40 is assigned to E. However, certain J-flavored fragments are usually
discerned (e.g., Skinner; Schmitt, *Josephsgeschichte*) in 40:1, "the cupbearer and
the baker . . . Egypt"; v 3, "the prison . . . imprisoned" (cf. vv 5b, 15b). The
chief reason for assigning these parts of verses to J or to a J-inspired redactor is
that they presuppose or refer back to J's version of the story (40:3b, 5b to 39:21–
23 and 40:15b), while 40:1 uses a word, "sin," characteristic of J and in content
relates closely to 40:3b, 5b. These observations clearly point to a closer connection between chaps. 39 and 40 than the usual division in two sources allows.
Gunkel, for example, argued that chaps. 40 and 39 come from different sources
because in 39:20–23 (J) Joseph was in prison, whereas in 40:47 (E) he is in the

captain of the guard's house; in 39:22(J) he oversees all the prisoners, but in 40:4(E) he serves two royal officials; 37:27(J) says Joseph was sold into slavery, whereas 40:15(E) says he was kidnapped. But these are slim grounds for postulating duplicate sources, when these differences can easily be explained exegetically and in terms of plot development. The parallels between 39:2–20 and 39:21–40:23 and the triptych arrangement of chaps. 39–41 argue for their unity. So with Coats, Donner (*Die literarische Gestalt*), Westermann, and Humphreys (*Joseph and His Family*), I accept that all of chap. 40 comes from one source, most probably J.

Comment

21–23 The second panel of the three-chapter triptych begins like the first (39:2–6) with a comment on divine providence at work in Joseph's life, "The LORD was with Joseph." This statement "implies quite real protection and promotion in the matters of his external life, not, to be sure, protection from distress, but rather in the midst of distress" (von Rad, 367). As already noted, the terminology of vv 21–23 clearly echoes vv 2–6, emphasizing that, despite all appearances, God was on Joseph's side in his deepest humiliations. But there are a few differences in phraseology that require comment.

21 "Was loyal," lit. "extended kindness to" (נטה חסד), occurs only here in the OT, but the noun חסד "loyalty" is an important biblical term (cf. *Comment* on 24:12; 32:11), often used in prayer to describe God's character. It is his loyalty that prompts him to care for his people and answer their prayers (cf. Gen 24:12, 14, 27). Its use here probably hints at Joseph's prayers during his dark moments of despair: "gave him favor" (cf. 39:4).

22 Once again, Joseph's qualities are so apparent that he is given authority in his domain; last time, it was Potiphar who "had entrusted him with all that he had" (39:4); this time, it is the prison governor.

23 Just like Potiphar (39:6), the prison governor had confidence that Joseph would competently manage everything.

40:1–4 These verses set the background for the dreams and Joseph's interpretations.

1 "After these things" probably marks a considerable time lapse (cf. 15:1; 22:1; 39:7; 48:1). The story does not make clear how long Joseph was in prison before the new prisoners arrived, only that the total period of slavery and imprisonment was about thirteen years (37:2; 41:46).

"The cupbearer" may well have done more than open bottles and taste the wine, if his own description of his duties in v 11 is to be taken literally. The Hebrew term מַשְׁקֶה "cupbearer" corresponds to Egyptian *wbꜣ*. "These officials (often foreigners) became in many cases confidants and favourites of the king and wielded political influence" (Kitchen, *NBD*, 283). Nehemiah occupied a similar position in the Persian court (Neh 1:11–2:8).

"Baker" may be identified with Egyptian *retehti* according to Vergote (*Joseph en Égypte*, 37). The nearest equivalent to "head (of the) baker(s)" (v 2) may be *sš wdhw nsw* "royal table scribe" (so Kitchen, *NBD*, 658).

"Sinned." Their offense is not specified since it is not relevant to the story, but doubtless this term is used to draw the contrast between Joseph thrown into prison

for refusing to sin against God (39:9) and these men for actually offending the king.

2 קָצַף "enraged" is a rarer term than the more common חרה אף "be angry." According to Sauer (*THWAT* 2:664), it often denotes "a passion that is quickly roused, powerful, and soon dies away" (cf. Lev 10:16; 2 Kgs 5:11). Perhaps this verse may be rendered "Pharaoh lost his temper."

3 The prison governor (39:21–23) must have been subordinate to the captain of the guard, who had put Joseph in prison (39:20). If the captain of the guard was, as Vergote (*Joseph en Égypte*) suggests (cf. *Comment* on 37:36), the royal butler responsible for catering arrangements, it is not surprising that he is involved in their imprisonment.

4 Whether the captain of the guard was still Potiphar, after the lapse of time implied in 40:1, is unclear. If Potiphar did still hold this position, it could explain why the captain of the guard appointed Joseph to be the personal servant of these two palace officials, for he had occupied this role in Potiphar's household (39:4). But whatever the motive, Joseph is once again becoming known to top palace officials. But will this stand him in any better stead than it did in Potiphar's household?

5–9 These verses are the central scene of the episode in which the dreams are related and interpreted.

5 It is not simply that they dreamed that raised the apprehensions of the cupbearer and baker, but that they both had a different dream the same night and that they were imprisoned alarms them. The apparently redundant comment about their imprisonment underlines the vulnerability of the men. As prisoners, they were trapped and uncertain of their future, so intimations about their fate in the form of dreams were especially important to them.

6 Since Joseph had been appointed their personal attendant (v 4; cf. 39:4), he naturally came to see them in the morning and noticed that they were looking "ill." זֹעֵף "ill" only occurs here and Dan 1:10 with the meaning "looking sickly, emaciated" (*TDOT* 4:111). Elsewhere, the root has the meaning "furious, angry," sometimes of the anger that results from frustration (e.g., 1 Kgs 20:43; 21:4), which might be appropriate here.

7 "Why are you looking glum?" Nehemiah was asked the same question (Neh 2:2). "Human empathy releases the whole of what follows" (Westermann, 3:74). Joseph's expression of concern leads his fellow prisoners to open their hearts to him, which in turn leads ultimately to his release and promotion in the Egyptian court.

8 The Egyptians shared a belief, widespread in antiquity, that "sleep puts us in real and direct contact with the other world where not only the dead but also the gods dwell. Dreams therefore are a gift from the gods" (Vergote, *Joseph en Égypte*, 48). Their interpretation, however, was a complex science entrusted to learned specialists; while a dreamer might have a hunch whether a dream was auspicious or not, he had to rely on experts for a detailed explanation. In prison they had no access to such expertise; yet being prisoners they were most anxious to know their fate—hence, their despondency. According to Joseph, however, it is not learning but inspiration that matters. "Don't interpretations belong to God?" He was later to make the same point to Pharaoh himself: "It does not depend on

me, but God will declare to Pharaoh his well-being." Joseph's attitude is consonant with the OT's rejection of occult practices and its reliance on prophecy as a means of discovering God's will (Deut 18:10–22).

"Joseph's answer, 'Interpretations belong to God,' is completely polemic. It is again one of those splendid statements which our narrator loves and which go far beyond the situation in the programmatic, doctrinal form in which they are spoken. Spoken by a very lowly foreign slave, whom the two prisoners had not dreamed of questioning, the statement contains a sharp contrast. Joseph means to say that the interpretation of dreams is not a human art but a *charisma* which God can grant. . . . The events of the future lay in Yahweh's hand only, and only the one to whom it was revealed was empowered to interpret" (von Rad, 371).

9–13 The cupbearer's dream is told more fully than the baker's. It also contains fewer allegorical features; only the equation of the three branches with three days is clearly allegorical. The mention of his picking and squeezing grapes could be allegorical, if it was not part of the cupbearer's usual duties (cf. *Comment* on 40:1–4).

10–11 Threes dominate this dream: three stems, three stages of growth, sprouting, blossoming, and ripening, and three actions by the cupbearer, taking grapes, squeezing them, and handing the wine to Pharaoh. The speed with which each stage is described may well suggest the imminence of the dream's fulfillment.

12–13 Joseph's explanation is short and sweet. In three days, the cupbearer will be given his job back.

נשׂא ראשׁ "lift up your head" has two main meanings: (1) count heads, i.e., take a census (e.g., Num 1:2; 4:2) or (2) act confidently (e.g., Judg 8:28; Ps 24:9). But here and in 2 Kgs 25:27 (∥Jer 52:31) it has a different sense, "deal kindly with." It is equivalent to Akkadian *našû rêša* "call someone into the presence of the king." However, in v 19 it is used quite literally for the baker's fate.

14–15 After doing his fellow prisoner a favor, Joseph makes a plea on his own behalf, which also underlines his own confidence in his interpretation. "When you are released, please remember me and mention me to Pharaoh." The phraseology used by Joseph is more commonly applied to divine action than to human action in Genesis, e.g., "remember" (8:1; 9:15; 19:29; 30:22; Exod 2:24), "do this kindness" (24:12, 14; Exod 20:6), and "bring me out of this house" (cf. 15:7 and especially Exod 20:2, "I am the LORD your God who brought you out of the land of Egypt out of the house of bondage"). His plea seems to foreshadow the ultimate redemption of all Israel from Egyptian slavery.

"I was kidnapped" (lit. "stolen") is hardly an exact description of what happened to Joseph, but it expresses very vividly Joseph's feelings about the way his brothers had treated him. They had stolen his freedom and sold him into slavery, a crime that, according to Exod 21:16, warrants the death penalty. "From the country of the Hebrews" (the phrase is used only here) contrasts his present abode with his homeland in Canaan. The case for regarding "country of the Hebrews" as an anachronism is unproven. In fact, the term "Hebrews" within the OT occurs almost exclusively in texts dealing with pre-Davidic times (e.g., 14:13; 39:14, 17, "patriarchs"; Exod 1:15, 16; 21:2, "Moses"; 1 Sam 13:3, 7, 19, "Saul"). Also, if as is widely believed, it is related to Akkadian *ḥabiruʾ*, it may be noted that this too is a common term in second-millennium texts all across the fertile crescent, including

Egypt, but it disappears in the first millennium (H. Cazelles, "The Hebrews," *POTT,* 1–28). Finally, Anbar (*Or* 41 [1972] 383–86) has pointed out that a similar phrase, "field/land of the Hebrews," is found in Ugaritic. He argues that it is not a synonym for Canaan but probably refers to part of Canaan north of Shechem.

16–17   Obviously encouraged by Joseph's optimistic interpretation of the cupbearer's dream, the baker now relates his. The Egyptian dictionary "lists 38 kinds of cake and 57 varieties of bread. . . . These facts, while proving that the Egyptians were first-class gourmets, also give a particular significance to the words of the chief baker which may be literally translated, 'There were in the top basket all sorts of foods for Pharaoh, masterpieces of the pastry cook'" (Vergote, *Joseph en Égypte,* 37).

"White bread." Since the term is found only here, its meaning is uncertain. But KB, 339, suggests "pastries made with white flour," and this has been endorsed by M. Dahood on the basis of Eblaite texts (*BN* 13 [1980] 14–16).

18–19   "Joseph answered and said" (cf. *Comment* on 31:14). To "answer and say" may suggest a brusque impatience on Joseph's part and the momentous nature of his comment. Was he annoyed that the baker should imagine that such an inauspicious dream could have a favorable meaning or that a man who deserved death should hope for pardon? The text leaves both possibilities open. In any event, in giving his interpretation, Joseph manages to keep bad news till last, for initially his explanation of the baker's dream is identical to the cupbearer's. But then in the last breath it suddenly diverges: ". . . from off you and hang you on a tree." The expression "lift up your head" may have the very literal sense of decapitation, but we cannot be sure. What Joseph is predicting is an aggravated form of death penalty, execution followed by exposure (cf. Deut 21:22–23; Josh 10:26). The baker will not simply be executed, but his corpse will be impaled and exposed. This treatment was designed to prevent his spirit from resting in the afterlife. The mention of the birds eating his flesh is both gruesome and emphatic, for it shows Joseph's certainty about the baker's fate.

20–22   Amnesties on the birthday of a Pharaoh are occasionally mentioned in late Egyptian texts. More frequently they were granted on the anniversary of his accession, and this could be meant here (so Schmitt, *Josephgeschichte,* 138–39).

21–22   Joseph's words in vv 13, 19 are echoed closely to show their exact fulfillment, which demonstrates he was inspired by God (v 8), indeed that "the LORD was with him" (39:21).

23   But the cupbearer completely forgot Joseph and his plea (v 14). So Joseph is left bitterly disappointed in as hopeless a situation as he was when first cast into prison at the end of the preceding episode (39:20). And there he stays for another two years (41:1), to all appearances forgotten by man and God.

Explanation

As a human story of hopes raised and then dashed, this episode is meaningful to most readers. Unjustly incarcerated, Joseph is noticed first by the prison governor who then puts him in charge of the other prisoners. Later he is appointed personal attendant to two distinguished prisoners and proves his worth by correctly

interpreting their dreams. But the chief cupbearer, on being restored to his post, fails to do anything about Joseph. He is left to languish in jail for another two years.

The narrative gives a few hints about Joseph's state of mind. He appears sympathetic, inquiring of the dreamers "Why are you looking glum today?" and pious, "Don't interpretations belong to God?" (v 8). The statement "the LORD was with Joseph and was loyal to him" (39:21) further hints that he was a man of prayer, whose prayers were partially answered in that he was given promotion within the prison. But his great hope and prayer—to be released from prison where he bitterly reflects he had been most unfairly kept, "I was kidnapped . . . and have not done anything that I should have been put in the pit" (v 15)—was left unanswered. His experience of painful, apparently fruitless waiting is typical of that of the patriarchs looking for children (15:2; 25:21; 30:1), of Job praying for vindication (Job 19:7), and of numberless psalmists who cry, "How long, O LORD? Wilt thou forget me for ever?" (13:1; cf. 22:2[1]). Such periods of desolation were experienced by our Lord (Matt 26:38–42; 27:46) and by Paul (2 Cor 1:8–10; cf. 2 Cor 11:24–29). And Jesus (Matt 5:10–12), Hebrews (12:1–11), and Peter (1 Pet 2:19–21) warn that all Christians should expect to suffer for righteousness' sake. So once again Joseph's experience may be taken as a paradigm for all disciples.

But it is more. The narrative affirms that the LORD was with Joseph (39:21–23) and proves it when he successfully interprets the two dreams. And these two dreams look back to Joseph's two dreams (37:5–10), which forecast his own ascendancy, and forward to Pharaoh's two dreams, which he will successfully interpret (41:1–32). Ultimately, his plea to be remembered will be recalled by the chief cupbearer, and the prison will prove to be a steppingstone to the palace. Then it will be clear that the suffering of one righteous man has proved to be the source of blessing not just to Egypt but "to keep many people alive" (50:20). Through Joseph, the Abrahamic promise that "all the families of the earth will find blessing in you" (12:3) is partially fulfilled.

Joseph in the Palace   (41:1–57)

Bibliography

Barrick, W. B. "The Meaning and Usage of RKB in Biblical Hebrew." *JBL* 101 (1982) 481–503. **Cohen, J. M.** "An Unrecognized Connotation of *nšq peh* with Special Reference to Three Biblical Occurrences." *VT* 32 (1982) 416–24. **Croatto, J. S.** "*ʾAbrek* 'Intendant' dans Gen 41:41, 43." *VT* 16 (1966) 113–15. **Gai, A.** "The Reduction of the Tense (and Other Categories) of the Consequent Verb in North-West Semitic." *Or* 51 (1982) 254–56. **Lash, S.** "La investituro de la biblia Jozefo." *Biblia Revuo* 17 (1981) 102–3. **Layton, S. C.** "The Steward in Ancient Israel: A Study of (*ʾăšer*) *ʿal-habbayit* in Its Near Eastern Setting." *JBL* 109 (1990) 633–49. **Lichtenstein, M. H.** "Idiom, Rhetoric, and the Text of Gen 41:16." *JANESCU* 19 (1989) 85–94. **Niditch, S.,** and **Doran, R.** "The Success Story of the Wise

Courtier: A Formal Approach." *JBL* 96 (1977) 179–93. **Rendsburg, G. A.** "The Egyptian Sun-God Ra in the Pentateuch." *Hen* 10 (1988) 3–15. **Seebass, H.** "Gen 41 und die Hungersnotstele." *ZDMGSup* 4 (1980) 137–39. **Sperling, S. D.** "Gen 41:40: A New Interpretation." *JANESCU* 10 (1978) 113–19.

Translation

¹*At the end of two full*[a] *years, Pharaoh had a dream. He*[b] *was standing by the Nile.* ²*And out of the Nile rose seven cows, shapely and well fattened, and they grazed*[a] *in the reeds.* ³*Then seven other cows rose after them out of the Nile: they looked terribly thin,*[a] *and they stood by the first cows on the river bank.* ⁴*Then the terribly thin*[a] *cows ate the well-proportioned fat cows. So Pharaoh woke up.*

⁵*He fell asleep and dreamed again. Seven good-looking, healthy ears of corn came up on a single stalk.* ⁶*Then seven thin ears of corn*[a] *scorched by the east wind*[a] *sprouted after them.* ⁷*The seven thin ears swallowed the seven healthy full ears. So Pharaoh woke up and realized it was a dream.*

⁸*In the morning his mind was perturbed, so he sent for*[a] *all the diviner-priests and experts of Egypt,*[a] *and Pharaoh related to them his dream.*[b] *But there was no one to interpret them*[c] *for Pharaoh.* ⁹*Then the head cupbearer spoke with*[a] *Pharaoh. "Today I recall my sins.*[b] ¹⁰*Pharaoh was in a temper with his servants, and he put me*[a] *and the head baker in custody in the house of the captain of the guard.* ¹¹*We both had a dream in a single night, I and he; each of us dreamed a dream with its own meaning.* ¹²*With us there was a young Hebrew man,*[a] *a slave of the captain*[a] *of the guard, and we related it to him and he interpreted our dreams: he interpreted each in its own way.* ¹³*And as he interpreted to us, so it turned out. I*[a] *was returned to my office, and he*[a] *was hanged."*

¹⁴*Then Pharaoh had Joseph summoned, and they rushed*[a] *him from the pit; he shaved, changed his outer clothes, and he came into Pharaoh's presence.* ¹⁵*Pharaoh said to Joseph, "I have had a dream, but there is no one to explain it. However I have heard about you that you know how to interpret dreams."* ¹⁶*Then Joseph replied to Pharaoh,* [a]*"Except for God, who can announce Pharaoh's welfare?"*[a] ¹⁷*So Pharaoh spoke to Joseph,* [a]*"There I was in my dream standing*[a] *on the bank of the Nile.* ¹⁸*Then rising out of the Nile I saw seven well-fattened, shapely cows, and they grazed in the pasture.* ¹⁹*Then seven other cows rose after them; they looked awful and thin. I have never seen any as bad as them in the whole land of Egypt.* ²⁰*Then the thin, awful-looking cows ate up the first seven fat cows.* ²¹*They went down inside them, but no one would know*[a] *it, because they looked just as bad as at the beginning; then I woke*[b] *up.*

²²[a]*"I looked*[b] *in my dream and seven ears of grain were coming up on a single stalk; they looked full and good.* ²³*Then seven ears, shriveled, thin, and scorched by the east wind, sprouted after them.* ²⁴*The seven thin ears swallowed the seven good ears. So I told it to the diviners, but no one could explain*[a] *it to me."*

²⁵*Then Joseph said to Pharaoh,* [a]*"Pharaoh's dreams are one:*[a] *God has declared*[b] *to Pharaoh what he is about to do.* ²⁶*The*[a] *seven good-looking cows are seven years, and the seven good-looking ears are seven years, so that makes the dream one.* ²⁷*The seven thin, bad-looking cows coming up after them are seven years, and the seven empty ears scorched by the east wind will be seven years of famine.* ²⁸*This is the matter that I have told Pharaoh: what God is about to do he has shown*[a] *Pharaoh.* ²⁹*Seven years of great abundance are coming in all the land of Egypt.* ³⁰*Then seven years of famine will follow*

them, and all the abundance will be forgotten in the land of Egypt, and the famine will devastate the land. [31]*Afterwards the abundance will not be known[a] in the land because that famine will be very severe.* [32]*Because the dream has been repeated,[a] the thing is established[b] from God, and God is in a hurry to do it.*

[33]*"Now let Pharaoh look[a] out for an intelligent and wise man and put him over the land of Egypt.* [34]*Let Pharaoh also act and appoint officers over the land and [a]organize the land of Egypt in the seven years of abundance.* [35]*Let them collect all the food of these coming good years and pile up grain under Pharaoh's control, food in the cities, so that they keep[a] it.* [36]*The food will be a reserve for the land for the seven years of famine which are to be in the land of Egypt, so that the land is not cut off in the famine."*

[37]*The idea seemed good to Pharaoh and all his servants.* [38]*So Pharaoh said to his servants, "Can we find a man like this in whom there is God's spirit?"* [39]*Then Pharaoh said to Joseph, "Since God has made known[a] to you all this, there is no one so intelligent and wise as you.* [40]*You shall be over my household, and all my people shall kowtow[a] to your instruction. Only as regards the throne will I be more important than you."* [41]*Then Pharaoh said to Joseph, "Look, I have set you over all the land of Egypt."* [42]*Then he removed his ring from his hand and placed it on Joseph's. He clothed him in linen garments and put a[a] gold chain on his neck.* [43]*He allowed him to ride in the chariot of the second man which belonged to him, and they called out before him, "Bow[a] down," and he put[b] him over all the land of Egypt.* [44]*Pharaoh said to Joseph, "I am Pharaoh, but without your permission no one shall lift[a] a hand or foot in all the land of Egypt."* [45]*Pharaoh named Joseph Sapnat-Paneah, and he gave him Asenat, the daughter of Potiphera the priest of On, as his wife, [a]so Joseph went out over the land of Egypt.[a]*

[46]*Joseph was thirty years old when he entered the service of Pharaoh the king of Egypt, and he left Pharaoh's presence and traveled throughout the land of Egypt.* [47]*The land yielded abundantly during the years of abundance.* [48]*Joseph collected all the food [a]for the seven years which befell the land[a] of Egypt, and he put the food in the cities. Food from the countryside around the cities he put inside them.* [49]*Joseph piled up grain like the sand of the sea, a tremendous quantity so that they stopped measuring it, for it was too much to measure.*

[50]*Two boys were born[a] to Joseph before the year of famine by Asenat, daughter of Potiphera, priest of On.* [51]*Joseph named the firstborn Manasseh, "because God has made me quite forget[a] all my toil and my father's house."* [52]*He called the second one Ephraim, "because God has made me fruitful[a] in the land of my oppression."*

[53]*Then the seven years of plenty in the land of Egypt came[a] to an end,* [54]*and the seven years of famine began[a] to happen as Joseph had predicted. There was famine in all the surrounding countries, but in the whole land of Egypt there was bread.* [55]*Then the whole land of Egypt became hungry, and the people cried out to Pharaoh for bread. So Pharaoh said to all Egypt, "Go to Joseph, who will tell you what to do."* [56]*When the famine had descended over the whole land, Joseph opened all [a]the stores of grain that were in them, and he sold[b] grain to Egypt, and the famine became very severe in the land of Egypt.* [57]*The whole world came[a] to Egypt to Joseph to buy grain because the famine was very severe throughout the world.*

Notes

1.a. On this idiom, see GKC, 131d.
1.b. On omission of the subj "he," see GKC, 116s.

2.a. Waw consec + 3 fem pl impf רעה.

3.a. Here and in v 4, SamPent and a few MSS read רקות instead of דקות. Cf. vv 19, 20, 27.

4.a. Cf. n. 3.a.

6.a-a. Pass ptcp in constr followed by cause, "east wind," in abs (GKC, 116l; WOC, 617).

8.a-a. Lit. "all the diviners of Egypt and all its experts"; this is the normal construction when a gen, "of Egypt," governs two nouns (Joüon, 129a; cf. n. 40:1.a-a.).

8.b. SamPent "dreams."

8.c. G "it."

9.a. SamPent "to."

9.b. Obj, "my sins," before the verb for emphasis (*EWAS*, 39n).

10.a. SamPent "them."

12.a-a. Lit. "a slave to the captain." On this construction, see GKC, 129c.

13.a. The contrast between the men's fates is highlighted by placing the obj pronouns, "me . . . him," before the verbs (*SBH*, 68, 152; cf. Longacre, *Joseph*, 102).

14.a. Waw consec + 3 masc pl impf hiph רוץ + 3 masc sg suffix.

16.a-a. Reading בלעדי אלהים מי יענה as suggested by Lichtenstein (*JANESU* 19 [1989] 91). מי omitted by haplography. A similar sense is presupposed (cf. SamPent, G, S; cf. *BHS*): "Without God it is not possible to give Pharaoh an answer about his welfare."

17.a-a. Note use of הנה + suffix + ptcp for vision in past time (Joüon, 121f; *SBH*, 95).

21.a. 3 masc sg pf niph ידע.

21.b. Waw consec + 1 sg impf qal יקץ.

22.a. G, S, Vg insert "I slept again."

22.b. Cf. n. 31:10.b.

24.a. Masc sg hiph ptcp נגד.

25.a-a. On the unusual syntax, see *EWAS*, 18.

25.b. Cf. n. 3:11.a.

26.a. SamPent normalizes the grammar by adding the def art (cf. WOC, 260).

28.a. 3 masc sg pf hiph ראה.

31.a. 3 masc sg impf niph ידע.

32.a. Inf constr niph שנה.

32.b. Masc sg ptcp niph כון.

33.a. 3 masc sg juss qal ראה. On pointing, see GKC, 75p, hh.

34.a. Switch from juss to waw + pf gives resultative sense, "so that he may organize" (Longacre, *Joseph*, 133).

35.a. Cf. n. 41:34.a.

39.a. Inf constr hiph ידע.

40.a. 3 masc sg impf qal נשק "kiss."

42.a. On the use of the def art in Heb. with materials like gold, see GKC, 126n; WOC, 246.

43.a. Apparently an Egyptian loan word from the Semitic root *brk* "bow down, kneel." Cf. Vergote, *Joseph en Égypte*, 135–41; D. B. Redford, *Biblical Story of Joseph*, 226–28; *CAD* IA (1.32–35).

43.b. Inf abs נתן. On inf abs following finite verb, see GKC, 113z; Joüon, 123x; A. Gai, *Or* 51 (1982) 254–56.

44.a. 3 masc sg impf hiph רום.

45.a-a. Omitted by G.

48.a-a. SamPent, G read "for the seven years when there was plenty in the land" (see *BHS*; cf. vv 47, 53).

50.a. Cf. n. 4:26.b. SamPent typically regularizes to 3 masc pl.

51.a. 3 masc sg pf piel נשה + 1 sg suffix. The unusual pointing (*a* instead of *i*) may indicate a play on Manasseh (GKC, 52m; Joüon, 52aN).

52.a. 3 masc sg pf hiph פרה + 1 sg suffix.

53.a. Waw consec + 3 fem pl impf כלה.

54.a. Waw consec + 3 fem pl impf hiph חלל.

56.a. Something seems to have dropped out; *BHS* and many commentators on the basis of G, S suggest אצרות בר "stores of grain."

56.b. The qal normally means "buy grain"; usually the hiph is used for "sell grain" (cf. 42:6).

57.a. The pl verb "came" with fem sg noun subj "world," which stands for "the inhabitants of the world" (cf. 1 Sam 17:46; GKC, 145e; WOC, 109). SamPent, G have pl subj "lands."

Form/Structure/Setting

Chap. 41 concludes the great interlude in the life of Joseph that constitutes Gen 39–41. Separated from his family and struggling to make his way in an unfriendly foreign land, Joseph has twice enjoyed advancement in the service of high Egyptian officials only eventually to be cast aside. Chap. 39 showed him enjoying favor with God and the man Potiphar, only to be cast into prison on a trumped-up charge. Chap. 40 showed him becoming the confidant of the royal baker and cupbearer, only to be forgotten by the latter when he was released. Chap. 41 constitutes the third scene in this great triptych. It starts ominously, at least when compared with the other two, for it says nothing about God being with Joseph. Yet on this occasion God is more evidently with Joseph than ever before, for he is miraculously summoned from prison, interprets Pharaoh's dreams, and is appointed second in the kingdom to Pharaoh himself. And typical of Genesis' storytelling technique, this episode closes with an anticipation of what is to unfold in the following one, with Joseph distributing food to the hungry masses who are making their way to Egypt because of famine. Among these so prompted to visit Egypt will be Joseph's brothers. So the stage begins to be set for the great denouement in chap. 45.

Chap. 41 subdivides as follows:

Scene 1:	Pharaoh's dreams reported (1–7)	A
Scene 2:	Interpreters fail to explain dreams (8–13)	B
Scene 3:	Joseph's audience with Pharaoh (14–46)	
	Joseph summoned (14–16)	C
	Pharaoh's dreams recounted (17–24)	A^1
	Joseph explains dreams (25–36)	B^1
	Pharaoh appoints Joseph (37–46)	C^1
Fulfillment of interpretation (47–57)		
Scene 4:	Joseph's work in seven years of plenty (47–52)	
Scene 5:	Joseph's work in famine (53–57)	

This shows how this chapter divides into three main parts, describing first the dreams (vv 1–13), then their interpretation by Joseph (vv 14–46), and finally their fulfillment (vv 47–57). Within the first two parts, there are close parallels in the general sequence, dream—failed interpretation—Joseph summoned : dream—successful interpretation—Joseph appointed, and very close verbal echoes, especially when Pharaoh recounts his dream in vv 17–24 (cf. vv 1–7).

The whole chapter coheres well with the rest of the Joseph story. Joseph's imprisonment (39:20–40:23) is presupposed (v 14), particularly his contact there with the royal cupbearer (41:9–13; cf. 40:1–23). Pharaoh's paired dreams (41:1–36) recall Joseph's own pair of dreams (37:5–11) and those of the cupbearer and baker (40:5–19). Joseph's successful interpretation of these dreams presages his accurate interpretation of Pharaoh's. Joseph's storing of grain against a future famine in which all the earth would come to him to buy food (41:55–57) anticipates the arrival of his brothers in Egypt to buy supplies (chaps. 42–44). The naming of Joseph's sons, Ephraim and Manasseh (41:50–52), harks back to his origins (chap. 37) and imprisonment (chaps. 39–40) and looks forward to their

future blessing by grandfather Jacob, which was to make them ancestors of two of the great tribes (chap. 48; 49:22–26). Because this chapter is so well integrated into the rest of the Joseph narrative, it is difficult to agree with Westermann that it may have once been independent, though even he admits that in its present shape "the chapter is at the very center of the Joseph story, the structure of which has been thought through to the last detail" (Westermann 3:85).

Traditional source critics have generally agreed that vv 1–32 are from a single source, probably E, continuing the account of chap. 40. However, they disagree about the unity of the rest of the chapter. Some (e.g., Dillmann, Driver, Speiser) hold that the rest of chap. 41 (save v 46[P]) also comes from E; others (e.g., Gunkel; Skinner; von Rad; Schmidt, *Literarische Studien*) that vv 33–57 mix J and E material. Gunkel, for example, finds the following contradictions within vv 33–57 that lead him to posit the existence of more than one source: in v 33(E), one man is to be appointed to oversee the storage of grain, but in v 34a(J), a class of overseers is called for; v 54b(E) has Egypt escaping the famine, but vv 55–56(J) show it suffering from it; vv 35a, 48(J) speak of "collecting food," whereas vv 35b, 49(E) of "storing grain." There is also a certain amount of redundancy, especially in the description of Joseph's promotion. But as Redford has argued, these "discrepancies have, in large part, been read into the text" (D. B. Redford, *Biblical Story of Joseph,* 166). So with most modern studies of this chapter, we are content to accept it as a substantial unity. "This structure, thought through in every single detail, reveals an overall plan for the whole chapter and is proof of its literary unity" (Westermann, 3:86). The discrepancies and repetitions that troubled earlier critics will be discussed further under *Comment.* The use of "God" as opposed to "the LORD" in this chapter (vv 16, 25, 28, 32, 38, 39, 51, 52) is required by the setting of the story in Egypt and is no indication that the main source of Genesis, J, is not present here. Here people living in Egypt are talking about God, whereas 39:2–5, 21–23, where "the LORD" is used, reflects the narrator's standpoint.

Comment

1–7 The first scene recounts Pharaoh's dreams from the relatively detached standpoint of the narrator. Here the dreams are told in the third person. Later Pharaoh will describe them again in the first person, allowing an insight into the psychological impression they made on him.

1 "Two full years," i.e., about the time of Pharaoh's birthday, the second anniversary of the cupbearer's release and Joseph's continued detention (cf. 40:20). Doubtless this date was significant both for Pharaoh and for Joseph. "Pharaoh dreamed." Kings, especially Egyptian Pharaohs, stood very close to the divine realm, and so they are often credited with revelatory dreams in ancient oriental texts. "The Nile" (יְאֹר), a word of Egyptian origin (*yrw*), is both the basis and the symbol of Egypt's power and wealth.

2 "Rose." This describes how they seemed to appear out of the river in Pharaoh's dream.

"Seven cows." Cows were not simply the typical farm animal of ancient Egypt, but they symbolized Egypt, the primordial ocean, and one of the gods, Isis, among

other things. Throughout the ancient world, "seven" was a sacred number, sometimes symbolizing fate.

"The reeds" (אחו) is another term of Egyptian origin describing the vegetation alongside the Nile (cf. Vergote, *Joseph en Égypte*, 59–66).

3 "They looked terribly thin," lit. "evil in appearance and thin of flesh," the opposite of "shapely [beautiful in appearance] and well fattened." Only here and in v 4 is this phrase used, suggesting a uniquely horrible-looking beast, not to mention their cannibalism. No wonder Pharaoh woke up!

5–7 Egypt, breadbasket of the Roman Empire, was as famous for its grain as for its cattle. Yet in another bizarre dream, the Pharaoh sees seven fat ears of grain being eaten by seven thin ones "scorched by the east wind." The effects of the east wind from the desert, which blowing in the spring or autumn, dries up vegetation overnight, are mentioned in Ezek 19:12; Jon 4:8; cf. Isa 40:7–8; Matt 6:30. In Egypt the desert wind blows from the south, but with an Israelite audience in mind, it is still called the east wind here.

7 "Realized it was a dream." The dream had been so vivid that Pharaoh thought it was real, until he woke up.

8–13 These verses constitute the second scene, set the following morning, when the royal dream interpreters fail to understand the dream. Dillmann (405), on the basis of Egyptian symbols known from classical and Christian sources, claims that the interpreters ought to have been able to make a good guess at the dream's meaning. Cf. *Comments* above on vv 1–2. "The seven fat cows mean seven fruitful years and the seven thin ones seven unfruitful years. The position of the seven thin cows after the seven fat cows expresses the immediate succession of the years of famine on the years of plenty." With the wisdom of hindsight, it is thus possible to see how Joseph's interpretation easily fits Egyptian ideas, but the polyvalency of symbols means that it was not easy in practice to be sure how to take the dream.

8 "Perturbed." For this rare word, cf. Ps 77:5(4); Dan 2:1, 3. "Diviner-priests" (חרטם) is an Egyptian loan word (*hyr-tp*) that describes a class of priests especially learned in arcane arts (cf. Vergote, *Joseph en Égypte*, 66–94).

"His dream . . . to interpret them." This fluctuation between the singular "dream" and plural "them" does not require harmonizing as the versions suggest (see *Notes*) but shows that the narrator saw the dreams as essentially one even though the interpreters could not interpret them as a consistent unity. "No one to interpret them for Pharaoh" does not mean they did not make suggestions as to the meaning of the dreams but that none of their ideas satisfied Pharaoh.

9–13 These verses summarize without obvious distortion the story in chap. 40, using much the same terminology.

9 "I recall my sins." Joseph had asked to be recalled to Pharaoh (40:14; cf. v 23), but the cupbearer had forgotten. So although as far as Pharaoh was concerned, the cupbearer was simply recalling the offense for which he was imprisoned, it is possible that the cupbearer is also tacitly confessing his failure to assist Joseph.

12 "A young Hebrew man, a slave of the captain of the guard." *Ber. Rab.* 89:7 sees this as a rather disparaging reference to Joseph. It may be disparaging. Certainly the description is meant to suggest that Joseph was quite insignificant and that therefore it is not surprising the cupbearer had not mentioned him to Pharaoh before. But placed here, this comment accentuates the change in Joseph's

position as dramatically as possible: one minute a forgotten imprisoned slave, the next on his way to the top of Egyptian society.

14–46 These verses, the third scene, constitute the climax of this chapter, indeed, with 45:1–15, one of the major peaks of the whole Joseph story, when he is transformed from a nobody into the Pharaoh's right-hand man.

14 The rush of finite verbs, "summoned," i.e., "sent and called," "rushed," etc., expresses the urgency that Pharaoh felt and the rapidity of Joseph's metamorphosis from slave to courtier. "From the pit," the term Joseph used to describe his prison in 40:15, and also the place where his brothers dumped him (37:20, 22, 24, 28–29), again accentuates the sharp contrast between his humiliation and his exultation.

"Shaved" refers to cutting the beard (e.g., 2 Sam 10:4) or the hair of the head (Num 6:9) or both (Lev 14:9), which is probably what is intended here. Shaving and a change of clothes are often required in the cultic law as a preparation for entry into God's presence in worship (e.g., 35:2; Exod 19:10, 14; Lev 14:8–9), here for an audience with the Pharaoh. Note here that only his outer clothes are changed; שמלה usually denotes the outer poncho-like cloak used as outer garment and blanket (cf. 9:23; Exod 22:26[27]), which again suggests the urgency of the servants' tasks. They simply had to make Joseph look respectable enough for the royal presence.

15 "You know how to interpret dreams," lit. "you hear a dream to interpret it," perhaps means as Dillmann (406) glosses it, "you only need to hear a dream to be able to interpret it straightaway." Since this expression, "hear a dream," only occurs here, its exact meaning is uncertain. It is clear from a comparison with vv 11–13, where the cupbearer reported Joseph's abilities, that the Pharaoh has exaggerated them somewhat.

16 So Joseph immediately corrects him. Note the slightly confrontational "Joseph replied to Pharaoh"; both the use of ענה (cf. *Comment* on 31:14) and nouns as subject (Joseph) and addressee (Pharaoh) suggest this reading.

"Except for God" (cf. 14:24). "Who can announce Pharaoh's welfare." On the slight textual emendation, see *Notes*. Here as elsewhere (40:8; 50:19), Joseph uses an oblique rhetorical question to draw attention away from himself to God. Joseph is as insistent as he was to the cupbearer (40:8) that not his own skill but God will interpret Pharaoh's dream. Though Joseph is thus being humble about himself, he is at the same time offering something better, divine interpretation of the dreams.

17–24 Pharaoh's own recital of his dreams differs significantly from that of the narrator's in vv 1–7. In the narrator's account, the description of the seven fat cows balances that of the seven thin cows, e.g., in the phrases and adjectives used, and similarly that of the seven fat ears corresponds to that of the seven lean ears. But in Pharaoh's telling, more weight is placed on the awfulness of the thin cows and thin ears. Indeed, about the lean cows Pharaoh says, "I have never seen as bad as them in the whole of Egypt" (v 19), and comments that after they had eaten the fat cows "no one would know it, because they looked just as bad as at the beginning" (v 21). These Pharaonic embellishments suggest that he viewed the dreams as threatening. It is also noticeable that Pharaoh always talks about "my dream" in the singular (vv 17, 22; cf. v 15, "it"), which suggests he regarded both dreams as being a warning about the future and therefore that he would be receptive to Joseph's approach to their interpretation.

25–36 Joseph's interpretation of the royal dream is the first longish speech in the Joseph story. It shows him to be both clear-headed and decisive. His speech divides into two parts: vv 25–32, the interpretation proper, and vv 33–36, the action Pharaoh should take in consequence.

The interpretation makes four points. First, both dreams announce the same thing (vv 25–26). Second, the seven cows or ears represent seven years (vv 26–27). Third, seven years of famine will follow seven years of plenty (vv 29–31). Fourth, the duplication of the dream indicates it will be promptly and certainly fulfilled (v 32).

26 Joseph understands the dreams as allegories (cf. 40:12–19), a familiar category of Egyptian dreams (J. Vergote, *Joseph en Égypte*, 52–59). That cows and ears of grain symbolize the harvests of the land is a natural interpretation, given their importance in Egyptian agriculture. A text from Siheil in southern Egypt dating from the second century B.C. tells of a seven-year famine followed by years of plenty in the time of Djoser (c. 2600 B.C.). Whether this is an authentic record of earlier times or a later forgery is disputed, but it shows that the memory of a seven-year-long famine was known in Egypt as in other parts of the ancient Orient. The Gilgamesh epic (6.102–6) threatens "seven years of empty husks," as does the Ugaritic epic of Aqht (1 Aqht 1.42–46), an Aramaic treaty from Sefire (1.A.27–30), and even David's prophet, Gad (2 Sam 24:13), as well as materials from Mesopotamia (D. B. Redford, *Biblical Story of Joseph*, 206–7; C. H. Gordon, *Or* 22 [1953] 79).

28 "What God is about to do he has shown to Pharaoh" (cf. the nearly identical comment in v 25; cf. v 32). Joseph underlines that the dream is heaven-sent, a view of dreams widespread in Egypt (cf. *Comment* on 40:8; J. Vergote, *Joseph en Égypte*, 48–49).

29–31 The interpretation now becomes prophetic announcement as, in language anticipating the prophets, "(Behold) seven years are coming" (cf. the frequent "behold the days are coming"), Joseph predicts a great famine. Abraham is once described as a prophet (20:7) and in several other passages is cast in a prophetic role (15:1–21; 18:17–33; 20:17), as are Isaac (27:27–29) and Jacob (48:15–49:27), so that it is not surprising that Joseph should be cast in a prophetic role. Here he seems to be more like the late court prophets, such as Nathan, who acted as advisers to the king (cf. 2 Sam 7).

The whole weight of Joseph's announcement falls on the forthcoming famine; just one sentence describes the years of plenty (v 29), whereas five clauses describe the years of famine (vv 30–31). This clearly fits in with the Pharaoh's own recognition that his dream threatened disaster (cf. *Comment* on vv 17–24). Indeed, Joseph picks up one of Pharaoh's additional comments, "They [i.e., the fat cows] went down inside them [the thin cows], but *no one would know it*" (v 21), when he comments, "Afterwards the abundance *will not be known* in the land because that famine will be very severe" (v 31). It was a severe famine that drove Abraham to enter Egypt. This severe famine will bring Joseph's brothers and father down to join him in Egypt (43:1; 47:4, 13). Already this remark foreshadows the next stage in the drama.

32 This explanation of doubled dreams is highly significant for the light it sheds on their place in the Joseph story. It shows that "the thing is established" by God; the same terminology is used of clearly proven cases in Deut 13:15(14);

17:4; of the Davidic dynasty (2 Sam 7:26); and of the moon (Ps 89:38[37]). Doubling also shows that "God is in a hurry to do it." In the immediate context, Joseph's remark refers to the forthcoming famine, but in the context of the book as a whole, it has a deeper significance. Some years earlier Joseph had dreamed a pair of dreams announcing that one day his father and brothers would bow down to him. That prophecy too is established, and God is hurrying to do it. So once again the narrative is hinting at the next development within the story.

33–36 Joseph concludes his interpretation of the dream with some practical advice for Pharaoh. "What is theologically noteworthy is the way in which the strong predestinarian content of the speech is combined with a strong summons to action. The fact that God has determined the matter, that God hastens to bring it to pass, is precisely the reason for responsible leaders to take measures!" (von Rad, 376).

33 ועתה "now" often marks the transition between statements of fact and their moral consequence. "Look out for" is used similarly of the call of David (1 Sam 16:1, 17), of Jehu (2 Kgs 9:2), and of a successor to Ahab (2 Kgs 10:3). "Intelligent and wise." These words are regularly paired and designate those qualities most desired in good leaders (cf. Deut 1:13; 1 Kgs 3:12; Prov 10:13; 14:33).

34 "Act." The same verb "do" describes God's actions in vv 25, 28, 32. Joseph urges Pharaoh to imitate God and take action.

"Appoint officers" (cf. 39:4–5). There is no conflict between appointing "an intelligent and wise man" (v 33) and appointing "officers" (v 34). Clearly the wise man will need assistance in his heavy task. Nor is the suggestion compelling that פקיד "officer" is a late word, in the light of Judg 9:28, which also uses the term. "Organize" (so NAB, JPS, Speiser, and Sarna, among recent commentators, and Onkelos, Rashi, and Luzzatto) relates וחמש "and organize" (a verb used only here in the piel) to the participle of the same root "organized for battle" as in Exod 13:18; Josh 1:14; 4:12. Most dictionaries and commentators relate "organize" to חמש "five" and suggest that the verb be translated "take a fifth of the produce of." This then would anticipate 47:24, 26, where Joseph takes one fifth of the produce in tax. There is no clear ground for deciding between these views, but contextually the former is preferable. A general remark about "organizing" the land seems more likely than a specific direction to impose a 20 percent income tax, especially in the light of the fairly general suggestions made in vv 35–36.

36 "Cut off"; cf. *Comment* on 9:11; 17:14.

37–46 These verses describe Pharaoh's appreciation of Joseph's advice and his promotion as vizier (prime minister) of Egypt. Though Joseph had given a gloomy interpretation of the dream, this did not prejudice the Pharaoh against him, for he too had viewed the dream as threatening. And because Joseph had followed up his interpretation with very positive suggestions about how Pharaoh should act to avert the disaster, his ideas were warmly received.

38 "Can we find a man like this in whom there is God's spirit?" This is the second use of the phrase "God's spirit" in Genesis (cf. 1:2). God's spirit equips the skilled workman like Bezalel (Exod 31:3; 35:31), the victorious warrior (cf. Judg 6:34; 14:6), and especially the wise ruler (1 Sam 10:6; 16:13; Isa 11:2; cf. Dan 5:14). Wisdom is frequently seen as one of the gifts of God's spirit, so Pharaoh's question "Can we find . . . God's spirit?" is an invitation to look for someone

"intelligent and wise" and foreshadows his choice of Joseph, whose words have proved God speaks through him (cf. v 16).

39–40 Pharaoh answers his own question and appoints Joseph to be over his house and gives him authority over all Egypt: "all my people shall kowtow to your instruction." The nature of Joseph's office "over my house" is not exactly clear. His job description makes him second only to Pharaoh in Egypt, "Only as regards the throne will I be more important than you, and, v 41, "I have set you over all the land of Egypt." His role seems to match that of the Egyptian vizier described by J. H. Breasted (*Ancient Records of Egypt* [Chicago: Univ. of Chicago Press, 1906–7] 2.§§665–70): "One will see that the vizier is the great supervisor of all Egypt and that all government activities are under his control" (e.g., treasury, judiciary, police, army, navy, agriculture). "In fact there is no important state activity which does not relate to his authority. He is really the equivalent of Joseph and the writer had before his eyes the functions of the vizier in telling the story of Joseph." Among modern Egyptologists, Vergote (*Joseph en Égypte*, 102–14) and Kitchen (*NBD*, 658) agree that Joseph appears to be the vizier. However, the title "over my house" seems to correspond to Egyptian *mr pr* "master of the palace," an official who was responsible for the royal palace or an administrator of the royal domains (cf. Vergote, *Joseph en Égypte*, 98–102), a less powerful official than the vizier. R. de Vaux (*Ancient Israel*, 129–31) suggests a possible resolution of this problem. In Israel "the master of the palace" (1 Kgs 16:9; Isa 22:15, 19–20) was a much more important figure than in Egypt. In fact, the Israelite master of the palace had similar powers and authority to the Egyptian vizier; both were the highest officials in their states. So in calling Joseph "master of the palace," Genesis is thus using the correct Hebrew equivalent for the office of vizier in Egypt.

"All my people shall kowtow to your instruction." The verb here translated "kowtow" literally means נשׁק "kiss." Though the context makes the meaning of the verb quite clear, how "kiss" comes to mean "submit, kowtow to" is more obscure (cf. Ps 2:12). Among the simpler suggestions are that it is short for "kiss the earth" (König, *JBL* 48 [1929] 342; K. A. Kitchen, *ExpTim* 69 [1957] 30; and D. B. Redford, *Biblical Story of Joseph*, 166). Driver (343) and Ehrlich (1:210) suggest that it comes from the root שׁוק "order themselves." J. M. Cohen (*VT* 32 [1982] 420) suggests that נשׁק פה literally means "seal the mouth," hence "kiss" or, as here, "be silent, submit to."

41–46 The installation of Joseph as vizier of Egypt "is an event that we can visualize in all its details as very few others in the Bible. Every detail of the ceremony has been passed down to us in Egyptian representations, even down to the almost transparent linen garments. We can view the rings, the golden chains, and the war chariots in the museums" (Westermann, 3:97); for illustrations, see *NBD*, 659; *IBD*). There are numerous examples of Semites rising to positions of great authority in Egypt from the Middle Kingdom, Hyksos, and New Kingdom periods. One of the most striking parallels from the time of Akhenaten is that of Tûtu, who, among other offices, was appointed "highest mouth in the whole country. This last title meant that he had total authority in the special tasks he was given and was responsible only to the Pharaoh. It is one of the titles that Joseph is supposed to have had. The wall paintings on the tomb at Tell el-Amarna show Tûtu's appointment by the Pharaoh, who is putting the golden necklace of office

around his neck. They also show him leaving the palace, getting into his chariot and riding off as the people prostrate themselves before him in acclamation. This is altogether an excellent illustration of what must have taken place when Joseph was appointed chancellor in Egypt, in charge of the Pharaoh's household (Gen 41:41–43). Similar scenes are illustrated elsewhere, but what is particularly interesting in this case is that the person whom the Pharaoh is honoring is a Semite" (R. de Vaux, *The Early History of Israel* [London: Darton, 1978] 1:299).

41 This is not a duplication of v 40 as is sometimes alleged by source critics: "they cannot be doublets: the imperative 'see!', and the perfect 'I have placed' in vs 41 demand the presence of vs 40 immediately before, and show that 41 is a dependent, though certainly repetitive statement" (D. B. Redford, *Biblical Story of Joseph*, 167).

42 The gift of the royal signet ring symbolized the grant of authority to Joseph (cf. Esth 3:12; 8:8; Vergote, *Joseph en Égypte*, 116–19).

"Linen garments." The Hebrew word שׁשׁ "linen" is an Egyptian loan word. In Egypt, court officials wore garments of top-quality, almost transparent, linen. In Israel, the curtains of the tabernacle and priestly vestments were made of linen (e.g., Exod 26:1; 39:27). Vergote (*Joseph en Égypte*, 121) suggests that this mention of dressing Joseph in "linen garments" may be a reference to him donning the robe of office of vizier, which was a robe, supported by braces, falling straight and unornamented from the chest to the ankles.

"Gold chain." Many Egyptian paintings show the Pharaoh placing a gold chain or collar round the necks of servants he is rewarding. Whether it was an essential aspect of appointment to the office of vizier is not so clear, but clearly Joseph's appointment was at the same time a reward for his dream interpretation and advice.

43 Joseph was given the chariot of the second man in Egypt. For the meaning "second-in-command to the king," cf. 1 Sam 23:17; 2 Chr 28:7; Esth 10:3. On "bow down," see *Notes*.

44 "No one shall lift hand or foot." Though raising one's hand was a gesture associated with swearing an oath (14:22), here the combination "lift hand or foot" probably is more general for "take any action" (cf. Z. W. Falk, *JSS* 12 [1967] 241–44).

45 Giving Egyptian names to Syro-Palestinians is well attested in Egypt. Vergote (*Joseph en Égypte*, 141) cites examples from the thirteenth dynasty (Hyksos period) and also later from the reigns of Rameses II and Merneptah (thirteenth century B.C.). The precise meaning of Joseph's Egyptian name, Sapnat-Paneah, is uncertain. Josephus translates it as though it were "hiding discoverer." Modern commentators have generally followed Steindorff's 1889 suggestion that it comes from *djd pa Nute(r) (e)f ʾankh* "the god has said 'he will live.'" However, Vergote and Kitchen point out that such a name is more fittingly given at the birth of a child than later in life to an adult, that this name is unattested, and that this type of name is attested from 1100 to 500 B.C. So Vergote has proposed that it comes from *p; s nty ʿm.fn3* which he translates "the man he knows" (*Joseph en Égypte*, 145). Kitchen, however (*NBD*, 1353 and more fully in *He Swore an Oath*, 80–84), suggests it comes from *Djad-naf ʾIpʿankh*, "(Joseph) who is called ʾIpʿ ankh." ʾIp-ʿ ankh was a common name in the Middle Kingdom and Hyksos periods.

"He gave him Asenath . . . as his wife." Marriage into one of the top Egyptian families set a seal on Joseph's promotion. On (Heliopolis) lies ten miles northeast of Cairo and was the center of Egyptian sun worship. "The priestly corporations of On/Heliopolis were equalled in wealth only by that of the god Ptah of Memphis and exceeded only by that of the god Amūn of Thebes, during c. 1600–1100 B.C." (K. A. Kitchen, *NBD*, 910).

"Asenat" is a good Egyptian type of name, meaning "she belongs to the Goddess Neit" (*Iw.s-(n)-Nt*) or "she belongs to her father" (*Iw.s-n-²t*) or "she belongs to you" (fem sg, i.e., to a goddess or to her mother, *Iw.s-n.t*). "Such names are well attested in the Middle Kingdom and Hyksos periods (c. 2100–1600 B.C., K. A. Kitchen, *NBD*, 94). On Potiphera, cf. *Comment* on 37:36 (also Vergote, *Joseph en Égypte,* 147–48; K. A. Kitchen, *NBD*, 1012).

"Went out over the land of Egypt." The only precise parallel to the expression "go out over" appears to be Ps 81:6(5), which is a citation of this passage. But in the light of vv 41, 46, which speak of Joseph being "over" Egypt, JPS is probably right to translate "Thus Joseph emerged in charge of all the land of Egypt."

46 Joseph was seventeen when he was sold into Egypt (37:2). It was thirteen years before his ignominy was transformed into glory. But this chronological notice does more than note the passing of the long years of shame and disappointment; it harks back to the previous notice in 37:2 when in the bosom of his family he dreamed of glory. Soon he will meet his family again, and those dreams will be fulfilled.

"Entered the service of," lit. "stood before." "Stand before" has this nuance also in 1 Sam 16:22; 1 Kgs 1:2.

47–57 These verses record the fulfillment of Pharaoh's dreams and Joseph's actions in response to them. Thus they serve to round off this chapter of the story. Vv 47–53 record the seven years of plenty. Repetition serves to underline the frenetic pace of Joseph's activity, while the relative brevity of the description of the seven years of plenty compared with that of the famine helps to create the impression of time flying by in Joseph's life.

47 "Abundantly," lit. "by handfuls." "Handful" (cf. Lev 2:2, קמץ) is only used here in plural. Seforno, quoted by Jacob, suggests that the image is that of each ear of grain filling the hand.

48–49 "Joseph collected food, food in the cities, . . . piled up grain," shows how he implemented his own advice, "Let them collect up all the food . . . and pile up grain . . . food in the cities" (v 35).

"Like the sand of the sea" is an image also used in the promises to Abraham (22:17) and Jacob (32:13[12]). Here it immediately precedes the mention of the birth of Joseph's sons, a further fulfillment of those promises. This tells, against Westermann's contention (3:97), that vv 50–52 are an interpolation interrupting the context.

50–52 Those seven years proved fruitful for Joseph in other ways too. The birth of children and good crops are always seen as marks of divine blessing in the OT (e.g., Deut 28:4).

51 "Manasseh" means "making forget." Presumably a child was so named at birth because he helped his parents forget an earlier loss, of another child or relative. Here Joseph says the birth of Manasseh makes him "quite forget" (נשה,

used here, seems a little more intense than the usual שכח "forget"; cf. Job 39:17; Isa 44:21; Lam 3:17) "all my toil," which probably refers to his work as a slave (cf. Deut 26:7; Judg 10:16). "And my father's house." The very mention of his "father's house" shows that he has not really forgotten his extended family who, unbeknown to him, he will shortly meet again.

52 "Ephraim" perhaps originally meant "fertile land" or "pasture land," certainly an apt description of the land that the tribe of Ephraim would inherit. But Joseph relates Ephraim to the verb פרה "be fruitful," a key term in Genesis (cf. 1:22, 28; 8:17; 26:22; 35:11), especially in the promises (17:6, 20; 28:3; 48:4). It is a little surprising that after the birth of just his second son Joseph should speak of being fruitful, but again there may be an element of prophecy in the choice of name, for Ephraim became one of the largest tribes (Deut 33:17).

Both names, Manasseh and Ephraim, express Joseph's thankfulness to God. "In one God is praised as the one who preserves, in the other as the one who blesses; both confirm the promise 'I am with you' from 39:2–6, 21–23" (Westermann, 3:97). Thus through his choice of names, Joseph is expressing his faith that God has been with him and blessed him.

"In the land of my oppression." עני "oppression" is used in Exod 3:7; 17; 4:31; Deut 26:7 of the Israelite bondage in Egypt. So here Joseph's experience anticipates that of his descendants.

53–57 Seven-year famines were a familiar feature of life in the ancient Near East. See *Comment* on v 36. Inadequate rainfall in the southern Sudan would prevent the Nile from flooding for its usual three months in northern Egypt, and without this annual flood, Egyptian agriculture was doomed. Similarly, failure of the rains in Palestine and Syria led to poor harvests there. No doubt it was unusual for the rains to fail in both Sudan and the Levant in the same year, but this is what occurred in Joseph's time. However, thanks to his foresight, both Egypt and the surrounding countries escaped the worst effects of the famine.

The description of the famine is terse and repetitive to highlight its seriousness. It affected all the surrounding countries (vv 54, 57) as well as all Egypt (vv 55–56). Note the chiastic patterning: "all the surrounding countries" (v 54 [A]), "whole land of Egypt" (vv 54, 55 [B]), "the whole land," "the land of Egypt" (v 56 [B']), "the whole world" (v 57 [A']). The fivefold repetition of the word famine and its description as "very severe" twice (a term only used elsewhere of the famine in Jerusalem just before it fell, 2 Kgs 25:3; Jer 52:6) emphasize the seriousness. The other point made here is that the famine happened "as Joseph had predicted" (v 54) and that he supplied the Egyptians with food from the stores he had laid up. Thus his interpretation of Pharaoh's dreams was completely vindicated. However, the last comment, "The whole world [i.e., the inhabitants of the whole world; see *Notes*] came to Egypt to Joseph to buy grain," hints at the next stage of the drama, when Joseph's own dream of more than twenty years standing will be fulfilled.

Joseph's work as relief distributor was not without precedent in Egypt. "Iti, the treasurer of the town of Imyotru, boasted that he supplied his fellow citizens with barley in years of famine and helped other towns as well. The steward Seneni of Coptus reported in his stela, or inscribed commemorative stone pillar, that 'in the painful years of distress' he had rationed out barley to his town. Ankhtify, 'the great chieftain of Nekhen,' recorded a seven-year famine in which the entire

south of Egypt is said to have died of hunger and people devoured their own children. He took pride in having foreseen the event, caused by a low Nile, and in having been able to rush grain and grant loans of corn to various towns in order to alleviate the situation. Another famine inscription from this period comes from Ameny, a chief in the days of Senwosre I (ca. 1971–1928 B.C.E.), who recalled that in years of famine he had supplied wheat and barley to the people so that no one went hungry 'until the great Nile had returned'" (Sarna, 290).

Explanation

Thirteen bitter years of slavery and imprisonment in a foreign land come to an abrupt and sudden end. Joseph is summoned from the prison into the very presence of the Pharaoh. The external change in Joseph's circumstances is astonishing, but his character has undergone a remarkable transformation as well. He is no longer the brash teenager whose careless chatter annoyed everyone. Now Joseph is intelligent and wise without peer in Egypt. The vale of tears has proved to be the valley of soul making.

But as elsewhere in the Joseph story, Gen 41 is describing the experience not just of everyman but of a particular individual living in a particular country in a particular period. Throughout the Joseph story, the reader is aware of the Egyptian setting, but here the background of Egypt in the early second millennium becomes unmistakable. Joseph is appointed vizier, second man in Egypt, and his clothes of fine linen, his gold chain, and his chariot are all appropriate to one in his position. He is given an Egyptian name and a wife from one of the great priestly families of On (Heliopolis). His plan of grain storage saves Egypt from the worst effects of famine and makes it a center for relief for the whole Middle East.

Above all though, this story describes God's control of human affairs. It begins by God disturbing the smug complacency of the Pharaoh, who doubtless viewed himself as divine, by sending him two ominous dreams, in which fat Egyptian cows were eaten by thin ones and healthy ears of grain by shriveled ears. Pharaoh's anxieties were further heightened by his experts' failure to interpret the dreams, at least to his satisfaction. This jogs the royal cupbearer's memory, who recalls Joseph's success in interpreting his dream some two years earlier. So Joseph is summoned and presented to the Pharaoh.

Immediately he rejects the royal flattery about his skills as a dream interpreter. "Except for God, who can announce Pharaoh's welfare?" he declares (v 16). And again, after he has listened to the dream and offers an interpretation, he insists, "God has declared to Pharaoh what he is about to do" (v 25; cf. v 28), and again, "Because the dream has been repeated, the thing is established from God, and God is in a hurry to do it" (v 32). Here the double mention of God emphasizes the divine origin both of the dream and of its interpretation.

Pharaoh himself acknowledges the divine inspiration possessed by Joseph. He first asks the question, "Can we find a man like this in whom there is God's spirit?" and then he answers it himself, "Since God has made known to you all this, there is no one so intelligent and wise as you. You shall be over my household."

This divine control of history and its corollary that inspired men can predict the future are assumptions shared by the wisdom writers and the prophets. "A

man's mind plans his way, but the LORD directs his steps" (Prov 16:9). "Surely the Lord God does nothing, without revealing his secret to his servants the prophets" (Amos 3:7). And here Joseph, like Abraham and Jacob, is doubtless viewed as a prototype of later prophets, able to predict the future and advise his hearers concerning how to act in the light of that knowledge; his remark "seven years are coming" sounds like the later prophetic "the days are coming." But more than that, Joseph is portrayed as the archetypal king, "intelligent and wise," endowed with the spirit of God (vv 38–39; cf. Isa 11:2), whose perfect rule makes the land to flourish and to enjoy abundant harvests (Ps 72:16; Isa 9:2[3]).

Joseph's experience of release from slavery foreshadows that of his descendants, who later were released from Egyptian bondage. Yet again Christians have seen in Joseph a type of Christ, the greatest prophet and the greatest king. He too, like Joseph, experienced humiliation before exaltation. As all were commanded to bow before Joseph (v 43), so "at the name of Jesus every knee shall bow" (Phil 2:10). And the experience of Joseph and our Lord is a pattern for all Christians, as Peter says, "Humble yourselves therefore under the mighty hand of God, that in due time he may exalt you" (1 Pet 5:6).

But in the immediate context of Genesis, this episode is another vital step in the chain of events leading to the fulfillment of Joseph's own pair of dreams that he had dreamed thirteen years earlier, in which he had seen his brothers bowing down to him. They had tried to frustrate his dreams by selling him into Egypt. But in Egypt Joseph told Pharaoh, "Because the dream has been repeated, the thing is established from God, and God is in a hurry to do it" (v 32). Very quickly the truth of Pharaoh's dream was demonstrated, but what about Joseph's? The last verse, "the whole world came to Egypt to Joseph to buy grain," hints at the next act in the drama.

First Visit of Joseph's Family to Egypt   (42:1–38)

Bibliography

Greenfield, J. C. "The Etymology of אמתחת." *ZAW* 77 (1965) 90–92. **Kutscher, E. Y.** "Life of Pharaoh." (Heb.) In *Hebrew and Aramaic Studies.* Jerusalem: Magnes, 1977. 392–93. **Rowe, A.** "The Famous Solar-City of On." *PEQ* 94 (1962) 133–42. **Selms, A. van.** "*dawqa*—Its Biblical Precedents." *Semitics* 7 (1980) 40–49.

Translation

¹*Now Jacob saw that there was grain for sale in Egypt, so he said to his sons, "Why do you just look* ª *at each other?"* ²*He said, "Since* ª *I have heard that there is grain for sale in Egypt, go* ᵇ *down there, and buy grain for us so that* ᶜ *we may live and not die."*
³*So ten of Joseph's brothers went down to buy grain from Egypt.* ⁴*But Jacob did not send Benjamin, Joseph's brother, with his brothers, for he thought that* ª *an accident might happen to him.* ᵇ

⁵ *So the sons of Israel came to buy supplies among others who were going, because there was a famine in the land of Canaan.* ⁶ *Now it was Joseph*ᵃ *who was ruler over the land; he was the supplier to all the people of the land. Then Joseph's brothers came and bowed*ᵇ *down to the ground before him.* ⁷ *Joseph saw his brothers and recognized*ᵃ *them, but he pretended not to but spoke harshly*ᵇ *to them and said to them, "Where have you come from?" They said, "From the land of Canaan to buy food."* ⁸ *Now Joseph had recognized his brothers, but they*ᵃ *had not recognized*ᵇ *him.* ⁹ *And Joseph remembered the dreams which he had dreamed for them, so he said to them,* ᵃ *"You are spies. You have come to see the weakness of the land."*ᵃ ¹⁰ *They said to him, "No, my lord. Your servants*ᵃ *have come to buy food.* ¹¹ *We*ᵃ *are all sons of one man. We are honest. Your servants are not spies."* ¹² *But he said to them, "No. You have really come to see the weakness of the land."* ¹³ *They said, "Your servants are twelve. We are brothers, sons of one man in the land of Canaan. The youngest one is now with his father today, and*ᵃ *one is no more."*ᵃ ¹⁴ *Then Joseph said to them, "That*ᵃ *is what I said to you that you are spies.* ¹⁵ *This is how you will be tested.*ᵃ *By the life of Pharaoh you will not*ᵇ *leave here unless your youngest brother comes.*ᶜ ¹⁶ *Send one of you to fetch your brother while you are detained*ᵃ *in order to test your words whether there is truth with you. And if not, by the life of Pharaoh, you really*ᵇ *are spies."* ¹⁷ *So he put them in custody for three days.*

¹⁸ *On the third day, Joseph said to them,* ᵃ *"Do this and live.*ᵃ *I am* ᵇ *a man who fears God.*ᵇ ¹⁹ *If you are honest,*ᵃ *just one*ᵇ *of your brothers will be detained*ᶜ *in custody, while you yourselves*ᵈ *go and bring the famine relief to your homes.* ²⁰ *But your youngest brother you must bring to me, so that your words may be believed and you do not die." So they consented.*

²¹ *Then they said to each other, "Truly*ᵃ ᵇ*we are guilty*ᵇ *because of our brother, for*ᶜ *we saw his distress when he implored us and we did not listen. That is why this distress has befallen us."* ²² *Then Reuben interjected, "Didn't I tell you not to sin against the child, and you did not listen. Now his blood is being required."*ᵃ ²³ *Now they*ᵃ *did not know that* ᵇ*Joseph understood them,*ᵇ *for there was an*ᶜ *interpreter between them.* ²⁴ *So he turned*ᵃ *aside from them and wept.*ᵇ *Then he returned to them and spoke with them and took Simeon from them and detained him while they watched.*

²⁵ *Then Joseph gave*ᵃ *orders that their sacks should be filled*ᵇ *with grain and that each man's money should be put*ᶜ *back in his sack and that they should be given*ᵈ *provisions for the journey. So it was done*ᵉ *for them.* ²⁶ *Then they loaded*ᵃ *their supplies onto their donkeys, and they left.*

²⁷ *At an overnight stop, one of them opened his sack to feed his donkey, and he saw his money at the top of his sack.* ²⁸ *Then he said to his brothers, "My money has been returned*ᵃ *and it's*ᵇ *here in my sack." Their hearts sank, and they* ᶜ*turned to each other trembling,*ᶜ *saying, "What has God done to us?"*

²⁹ *Then they arrived back at their father Jacob in the land of Canaan, and they told*ᵃ *him all that had happened*ᵇ *to them.* ³⁰ *"The man, the lord of the land, spoke harshly to us and held*ᵃ *us to be spies.* ³¹ *And we said, 'We are honest. We are not spies.* ³² *We are* ᵃ*twelve, we are brothers,*ᵃ *that is, sons of our father. One*ᵇ *is no longer, and the youngest is today with our father in the land of Canaan.' The man, the lord of the land said to us, 'This is how I shall discover whether you are honest.* ³³ *Leave*ᵃ *one brother of yours with me, but take the relief supplies*ᵇ *to your homes and go.* ³⁴ *Then bring your youngest brother to me so that I shall know that you are not spies, that you are really honest.* ᵃ*I shall give your brother*ᵃ *back to you, and you shall travel freely in the land.'"*

³⁵Now ªwhen they were emptying their sacks, they discoveredª each man's bundle of money in his sack. Both they and their father saw the bundles of money, and they were afraid. ³⁶Then Jacob their father said to them, ª "It's me that you have bereaved.ª ᵇThere is no Joseph, and no Simeon,ᵇ and ªnow it's Benjaminª you want to take. All these thingsᶜ have happened to me." ³⁷Then Reuben said to his father, ª "You may killᵇ my two sons if I do not bringᶜ him back to you.ª Entrustᵈ him to me, and I shall bringᵉ him back to you." ³⁸But he said, "My son shall not go down with you, for his brother is dead, and he is the only one left.ª If an accident should happen to him on the way you are going, you will bringᵇ me down in my old age to Sheol with sorrow."

Notes

1.a. 2 masc pl impf hithp ראה (cf. GKC, 54f; WOC, 431).

2.a. On this use of הנה, see Lambdin, 170; cf. WOC, 677.

2.b. 2 masc pl impv qal ירד.

2.c. Sequence impv + simple waw + impf for final clauses (Lambdin, 119; WOC, 578).

4.a. For this use of פן to express a fear, see GKC, 152w.

4.b. 3 masc sg impf qal קרא + 3 masc sg suffix.

6.a. The use of הוא "he" as copula after the subj emphasizes Joseph's position (*EWAS*, 72–73).

6.b. Waw consec + 3 masc pl impf hishtaphel of חוה (cf. n. 18:2.d.).

7.a. Waw consec + 3 masc sg impf hiph נכר + 3 masc pl suffix.

7.b. On use of fem pl, cf. GKC, 122q; WOC, 104.

8.a. Use of personal pronoun emphasizes the subj (*EWAS*, 32).

8.b. Cf. n. 42:7.a.

9.a-a. The word order in these clauses emphasizes that the brothers are involved in spying (*EWAS*, 15, 43).

10.a. The position of the subj before the verb is a mark of an antithetical sentence according to *SBH*, 180–81, but *EWAS*, 36, thinks it is prompted by the verb of motion "to come." Note the string of four apposition clauses, "Your servants . . . spies" (vv 10–11), in climactic repetition (*SBH*, 45).

11.a. On the unusual form נחנו "we" (GKC, 32d), used here as "an expression of earnest endeavour on the part of poor strangers to convince Joseph of their honesty," see *EWAS*, 71, cf. 15.

13.a-a. The word order here emphasizes the subj "one" (cf. 37:30; 42:36), "always narrated with intense emotion" (*EWAS*, 104).

14.a. On this fairly rare use of masc pronoun הוא to express neuter, see Joüon, 152b; cf. 44:10. The fem is more common (cf. 42:15, "by this" [fem]).

15.a. 2 masc pl impf niph בחן.

15.b. אם to introduce oath formulae (BDB, 50a).

15.c. ב + inf constr בוא.

16.a. 2 masc pl impv niph אסר, the niph impv "to express a distinct assurance" (e.g., in a threat, GKC, 110c).

16.b. On the asseverative use of כי, especially in oaths, see *EWAS*, 161.

18.a-a. Sequence of two impvs, "do . . . live," "serves to express the distinct assurance or promise that an action or state will ensue as the certain consequence of a previous action" (GKC, 110f; Joüon 116f, 117aN, 167u).

18.b-b. Obj before the verb emphasizes it. "To find the knowledge of *the* God in the top Egyptian official must have been no small surprise to his brothers" (*EWAS*, 38, n. 95).

19.a. Putting the predicate "honest" before the subj emphasizes it (*EWAS*, 15).

19.b. On absence of article on אחד, see WOC, 259.

19.c. 3 masc sg impf niph אסר. WOC, 375, n. 31, says it should be understood as a qal pass.

19.d. Use of personal pronoun for emphasis (*EWAS*, 33).

21.a. *EWAS*, 128–29, sees אבל as a particle with asseverative force, but WOC, 671–72, describe it as a restricting adv, which "can mark a reversal in expectations or beliefs." So they translate "Each said to his brother, '[We believed wrongly that we had gotten away with disposing of our brother] *but* we are (now) found to be at fault in the matter of our brother.'"

21.b-b. The word order, predicate "guilty" before subj, stresses the guilt (*EWAS*, 16).

21.c. For this nuance of אֲשֶׁר see Joüon, 170e.

22.a. Masc sg niph ptcp דֹּרֵשׁ (so Even-Shoshan) more likely than pf (so BDB).

23.a. Use of personal pronoun for emphasis (*EWAS*, 32).

23.b-b. On word order, see *EWAS*, 22–24.

23.c. Def art requires no translation in English (GKC, 126r; WOC, 243).

24.a. Waw consec + 3 masc sg impf qal סבב.

24.b. Cf. n. 27:38.b.

25.a. Cf. n. 2:16.a.

25.b. Lit. "and they filled." For construction, see GKC, 120f.

25.c. Waw + לְ + inf constr hiph שׁוב.

25.d. Cf. n. 15:7.c.

25.e. Lit. "and he did." On use of 3 masc sg in impersonal constructions, cf. GKC, 144b; WOC, 71.

26.a. Cf. n. 7:17.b.

28.a. 3 masc sg pf hoph שׁוב.

28.b. On the omission of explicit subj after הנה (cf. SamPent) + הוא, see GKC, 147b; Joüon, 146h, 154c.

28.c-c. On this translation, see GKC, 119gg; WOC, 193, n. 19.

29.a. Cf. n. 26:32.b.

29.b. Def art + fem pl qal ptcp קרה. On the syntax, see GKC, 116f; WOC, 616, 621.

30.a. G adds "in prison" (cf. v 17).

32.a-a. SamPent, G, S read "we are twelve brothers."

32.b. Subj before suffixed אֵין is for emphasis; cf. n. 42:13.a-a.

33.a. 2 masc pl impv hiph נוח.

33.b. *BHS*, following G, ?S, *Tg. Onq.*, suggests inserting שֶׁבֶר as in v 19.

34.a-a. Apposition clause instead of sequential (*SBH*, 59). Versions insert "and" (cf. *BHS*).

35.a-a. On the translation of ויהי + ptcp, see GKC, 111g.

36.a-a. The preverbal position of the objs, "me," "Benjamin," is for emphasis (*EWAS*, 38).

36.b-b. Cf. n. 42:13.a-a. and 42:32 on subj before suffixed אֵין.

36.c. כֹל + 3 fem pl suffix (cf. GKC, 91f, 135p).

37.a-a. Note the unusual order of the clauses, usually the protasis, "if" clause precedes the main clause. Here the inversion contrasts Reuben's sons with Jacob's (cf. Joüon, 167v).

37.b. 2 masc sg impf hiph מות. Here the impf has permissive sense (GKC, 107s; WOC, 508).

37.c. 1 sg impf hiph בוא + 3 masc sg suffix.

37.d. Cf. n. 30:26.a.

37.e. 1 sg impf hiph שׁוב + 3 masc sg suffix.

38.a. 3 masc sg pf niph שׁאר (pause).

38.b. Waw + 2 masc pl pf hiph ירד.

Form/Structure/Setting

Chap. 42 begins a new phase in the family history of Jacob (cf. 37:2). For twenty years, Jacob, with eleven of his sons, has lived in Canaan mourning the loss of his favorite, Joseph. Meanwhile, the latter, after various trials, has risen to head the Egyptian administration and claims that "God has made me quite forget all my toil and my father's house" (41:51). The career of Joseph in Egypt has been told in three acts, each of which paralleled the other and demonstrated that the LORD was with Joseph (39:1–20; 39:21–40:23; 41:1–57). In the first act, Joseph rose to be head of Potiphar's household, in the second to be head of the royal prisoners, and in the third to be vizier of Egypt, deputy of the Pharaoh. This next section of Genesis likewise falls into three acts, each of which describes a journey to Egypt: the first by his hated older brothers (42:1–38), the second by them and his younger brother Benjamin (43:1–45:28), and the third by all his brothers and his father (46:1–47:12), each one more momentous and emotional than the previous one.

This chapter falls into five scenes:

vv 1–4	Jacob sends his sons to Egypt	A
vv 5–17	First audience with Joseph	C
vv 18–24	Second audience with Joseph	C[1]
vv 25–28	Return journey	B[1]
vv 29–38	Sons report to Jacob on their mission	A[1]

The scenes are arranged roughly palistrophically. If, with Humphreys (*Joseph and His Family*), we regard v 5 as an independent scene, "the journey to Egypt," the palistrophic pattern is even more pronounced. The first (vv 1–4) and last (vv 29–38) scenes involve Jacob and his sons and are set in Canaan. Both emphasize Jacob's reluctance to let Benjamin go down to Egypt, lest "an accident should happen to him" (vv 4, 38), an expression found in Genesis only in these two passages and in 44:29. V 5 and the penultimate scene describe the brothers' journey to and from Egypt, while the two central scenes (vv 6–17, 18–24) clearly match each other, both being audience scenes in which Joseph fiercely interrogates his brothers.

The contents of this chapter presuppose what has gone before, and there are frequent back-references, especially to chaps. 37 and 41. The need of Jacob for food and the decision to go to Egypt (vv 1–3) presuppose 41:54–57. Joseph's lordship looks back to 41:41–50. He remembers his dreams (37:5–11) as he sees their fulfillment (vv 6, 9). Joseph's brothers mention his disappearance (v 13), and then they confess their own complicity in it (vv 21–22; cf. 37:14–36). In imprisoning his brothers (v 17), Joseph seems to be giving them a dose of their own medicine (cf. 39:20–40:23). The closing scene with Jacob's bitter outburst—"It's me that you have bereaved. There is no Joseph . . . you will bring me down in my old age to Sheol with sorrow" (vv 36–38)—shows that twenty years later he is still grieving bitterly for the loss of Joseph (cf. 37:33–35). Furthermore, this episode establishes the framework for the development of the plot in the succeeding chapters. Joseph's determination to bring his younger brother down to Egypt is pitted against Jacob's reluctance to let Benjamin out of his sight. By holding Simeon in prison, Joseph appears to have a hostage that will force Benjamin to come, but paternal favoritism means that Jacob will allow Simeon to languish in jail rather than put his precious Benjamin at risk. Thus chap. 42 is an integral part of the Joseph story and can hardly be understood on its own as a discrete unit of tradition (cf. Coats, 287–88).

Traditional source critics fall into two camps in analyzing this chapter: the straightforward, who hold that the whole chapter is E, apart from vv 27–28 (J), and probably v 38 (e.g., Driver, Speiser, Vawter), and the sophisticated, who hold that fragments of J are scattered through the whole chapter (e.g., vv 2, 3a, 4b, 5, 7, 9b, 10–12, 27–28, 38; so Skinner; cf. Dillmann; Gunkel; and Schmidt, *Literarische Studien*, whose analyses all differ from each other slightly). The latter analysis relies heavily on the presence of doublets, which are better seen as characteristic devices of Hebrew prose. The simpler analysis sees the opening of one sack on the return journey (vv 27–28) as a doublet of the opening of all the sacks in Canaan in v 35. And because v 38, like 43:1–10, fails to mention Simeon's detention, it too is assigned to J. However, these arguments are not compelling. It is not surprising that Jacob is unconcerned about Simeon's fate: he was one of Leah's sons, not Rachel's like Joseph and Benjamin. Besides "43:1 is the logical starting point

of a separate section, which cannot be said of the verse before us" (Speiser, 323). Indeed, Jacob's categoric statement of 42:38 makes a fitting end to an episode and is typical of Genesis' technique (cf. 27:45; 29:14; 30:24; 34:31; 37:35; 45:28). Nor is it necessary to view vv 27–28 and 35 as duplicates. V 35 can be viewed simply as a dramatic heightening of the tension in vv 27–28. On the way, one brother finds his money and could therefore be accused of stealing. At home, after the dismal account of their visit, their apprehensions are increased further when all of them find their money. And both incidents foreshadow their arrest on the next journey by Joseph's agent for stealing his cup. As Redford (*Biblical Story of Joseph*) and Westermann argue, it is easier to regard v 35 as an addition to the story than to consider vv 27–28 a later addition. But Coats and Sternberg (*Poetics*) argue that v 35 is integral to the story, for Jacob jumps to the conclusion that the money comes from the sale of Simeon; hence his violent outburst in v 36. However vv 27–28 and 35 are viewed in source-critical terms, it seems simplest to regard chap. 42 as an integral part of the Joseph story, coming from the same source as the preceding chapters.

Comment

1–4 In this scene, Jacob reemerges as a major actor (hence the double mention of his name in v 1; cf. Longacre, *Joseph*, 144), and he takes the initiative in sending his sons on a journey (cf. 37:13). Indeed, he implies that they are being indecisive, "Why do you just look at each other?" when they could be away purchasing food. Here Jacob's authority is apparent: though old, he is still head of the family, and his grown sons do as he bids. His dithering procrastination at the beginning of chap. 43 stands in marked contrast to his decisiveness here. Note that nothing is said here about famine in Canaan; the comments about the famine affecting the whole region in 41:57 are clearly presupposed.

3–4 Note how Jacob's sons are called "Joseph's brothers," thus foreshadowing their role in the next scene. Presumably, as many as possible of the family go to Egypt in order to buy as much food as possible. But Jacob does not go because he is too elderly, nor Benjamin "for he thought an accident might happen to him." אסון "accident," apart from three occurrences in Gen 42:4, 38; 44:29 (of an accident to Benjamin), only occurs in Exod 21:22–23, of an accident to a pregnant woman that could involve anything up to loss of life. Here Jacob is using what may be a vague term to describe a fate like Joseph's befalling Benjamin, who he now believes to be the only surviving son of his dear wife Rachel. So, right at the beginning of this new act in the drama, the narrator reminds us of the emotional bonds. Benjamin is now the apple of Jacob's eye as earlier his brother and mother had been; Leah and her sons still matter less to Jacob.

5–17 These verses describe the brothers' first encounter with Joseph. The narrative underlines the disparity between Joseph and his brothers in various ways. Most obviously, Joseph is ruler over all the land, whereas his brothers are just a small group among the many hungry foreigners coming to Egypt for food supplies. Thus it is remarkable that Joseph and his brothers should ever have met (v 5). But just as significant is the discrepancy in knowledge: whereas Joseph recognizes his brothers, they do not recognize him. And this allows Joseph to interrogate

them and test them, to see whether they are as heartless now as they were twenty years earlier.

5 This verse would more naturally follow 41:57, but the inclusion of 42:1–4 explains exactly who came and why. The absence of Jacob and Benjamin is crucial to understanding Joseph's reaction. "Sons of Israel" or "Israelites" rather than "sons of Jacob" may be mere stylistic variation, but Israel does seem to be the preferred name when the entry into Egypt is in focus (43:6, 8, 11; 45:28; 46:1, 2, 29, 30; 47:27; cf. 45:21; 46:5, 8; 50:25). The entry of the Israelites as a tribal group into Egypt presages their ultimate exodus from Egypt. But from the point of view of the Egyptians, "the Israelites" were just another group of Semites from Canaan seeking to buy food. "There was a famine in the land of Canaan" echoes 12:10; 26:1, two earlier famines that drove Abraham and Isaac toward Egypt for food.

6 שׁלִיט "ruler." Despite its parallels in Eccl 7:19; 8:8; 10:5, this is not necessarily a late word, since the root is a common Semitic one attested in Old Assyrian and possibly in Ugaritic.

"Joseph's brothers came and bowed down to the ground before him" picks up the key word in his dreams (cf. 37:7, 9–10; 41:32). "Because the dream has been repeated . . . God is in a hurry to do it" already intimated that the fulfillment of Joseph's own dreams was imminent. But this fulfillment does not exactly match the original dream, which included his father (sun) and mother (moon) and eleven brothers (stars) coming and bowing down to the ground before him (37:10). Here there are only ten brothers and no parents.

7–8 "Joseph recognized them . . . they had not recognized him." This is another clear echo of chap. 37, for the same term, הכיר, is used: "Please *identify* whether it is your son's tunic or not" (37:32; cf. v 33). It seems likely, too, that התנכר "he pretended" is a play on התנכל "they plotted" (37:18), for the words only differ by one letter (ר and ל). These echoes of chap. 37, by reminding the reader of Joseph's brothers' treachery and their cruel deception of their father, help to put his own behavior, hiding his own identity and speaking harshly to them, into perspective. The brothers fully deserved to be treated so; they were only being paid back in their own coin.

"Spoke harshly" occurs only here and in v 30. Joseph's motives for treating his brothers harshly have been variously explained: "punishment, testing, teaching, and dream fulfillment. Predictably enough, however, each line (of explanation) is wrong because all are right" (M. Sternberg, *Poetics*, 286). By failing to explain Joseph's conduct explicitly, the narrator leaves the reader to surmise and fill the gap himself, and this allows the creation of a multidimensional image of Joseph.

"The entire dialogue between Joseph and his brothers is remarkable for the way that words, creating the fragile surface of speech, repeatedly plumb depths of moral relation of which the brothers are almost totally unaware and which even Joseph grasps only in part. Ostensibly a political interrogation, it is really the first of three climactic dialogues between Joseph and his brothers about their shared past and the nature of their fraternal bond. The ten brothers, of course, are throughout the object of dramatic irony, not knowing what both Joseph and we know" (R. Alter, *Art of Biblical Narrative*, 164).

9 "Now Joseph remembered . . . ." A comment like this on a participant's state of mind is rare in the Bible and is correspondingly significant. The narrator

has prepared the reader for the confrontation of Joseph with his brothers, but he is caught off balance, for some years earlier he had said, "God has made me quite forget . . . all my father's house" (41:51). Now all his memories come flooding back. It was his telling tales to Jacob that made him so unpopular with Jacob's sons. Now he accuses them of coming as spies to Egypt, perhaps in the pay of one of the great powers—the Hittites or Assyria, whom Egypt always feared (cf. Vergote, *Joseph en Égypte*, 160–61). "The weakness [lit. 'the nakedness'] of the land" refers to the weak points in their defenses.

10–11   The brothers' defense consists of four short sentences in apposition, climaxing with an emphatic rebuttal of Joseph's charge, "Your servants are not spies." Note here and in the first sentence the deferential use of the third person "Your servants" (cf. 41:10; 46:34; 47:3–4), which is good Egyptian etiquette (Vergote, *Joseph en Égypte*, 161–62) as well as good Hebrew (1 Sam 3:9; 16:16; 22:15; 27:5). "We are all sons of one man" expresses more truth than they realized, for Joseph was also a son of Jacob. But by affirming their brotherhood, they hope to rebut the charge of spying, for spies would surely not travel together and risk the whole family by one of them being caught. "We are honest" or "honorable" (כֵּן), i.e., they both tell the truth and do what is right (e.g., Num 27:7; 36:5; 2 Kgs 7:9; 17:9).

12   Joseph hammers away at his brothers, repeating the accusation of spying three times (vv 12, 14, 16). "The constant repetition of the accusation is meant to unnerve the accused and break down his resistance" (Westermann, 3:108). Such interrogation techniques are still, of course, used today. "[T]here is nothing new under the sun" (Eccl 1:9).

13   But Joseph is more than a tough professional interrogator; he desperately wants to know about the absent members of his family. So, under pressure, his brothers continue to volunteer details about their family in an attempt to prove their honesty. "The youngest one . . . is now with his father, and one is no more." The final remark is cryptic, though most easily understood as a euphemism for death (44:20), which is not necessarily implied (cf. 5:24); it simply covers up what happened to Joseph. But the mention of the youngest brother is what interests Joseph. If his half brothers treated him so badly, what might they have done to his full brother Benjamin? So he seizes on the mention of Benjamin as a means of verifying their statements.

15–16   To prove they are not spies, Benjamin must be fetched, while nine of his brothers are held in prison. בחן "tested." On this term, see *TDOT* 2:69–72; *THWAT* 1:272–75. "By the life of Pharaoh" is like the Hebrew oath formula "As my lord the king lives" (2 Sam 15:21). Egyptian oath formulae by Pharaoh are discussed by J. A. Wilson, *JNES* 7 (1948) 129–56; Vergote, *Joseph en Égypte*, 162–67; D. B. Redford, *Biblical Story of Joseph*, 233–34, but in so far as the evolution of these formulae is uncertain, it would seem rash to attempt to date the Joseph story by them, especially as the formulation here may simply reflect Israelite practice (so Westermann, 3:109). Kutscher *(Hebrew and Aramaic Studies*, 393) thinks the Hebrew is in fact a misreading of a second-millennium Egyptian oath formula "As the God Ra exists." Here Joseph uses an oath by Pharaoh to scare his brothers and encourage reflection by them.

17   "Custody" is also used of Joseph's imprisonment in 40:3, 4, 7. "Put," lit. "gathered," is only used here of imprisonment. There appears to be a play on

Joseph's name here: "so he put" sounds a bit like "so Joseph." This makes it likely that there is an element of mirroring punishment here: as his brothers' action had led ultimately to Joseph being imprisoned, so he now gives them a brief taste of it.

18–24 The brothers' audience with Joseph is not a mere filler, as Gunkel suggests; rather it allows the changing attitudes to emerge. Joseph now appears as a gentler more sympathetic character, concerned for the welfare of the alleged spies: "Do this and live. I am a man who fears God." He now proposes to detain only one of them and let the others return to his father. Similarly, the brothers are shown to be learning, confessing their guilt in making Joseph suffer and recognizing the justice of their present predicament. The first steps toward reconciliation are being taken.

18 "On the third day." What prompted Joseph's change of plan is not fully explained. Did he just put them all in prison in vengeful pique, or was it merely a ploy to scare them and make them review their situation, or was it a genuine change of plan to hold only one and allow the others to return? Joseph must have calculated that little food could have been sent to Jacob and Benjamin if only one brother was released and that his father would be unlikely to come if nine of his sons had disappeared on a trip to Egypt. Whatever the shrewd calculation behind the release of his brothers, Joseph gives the highest motive for it. "Do this and live. I am a man who fears God." He wants these alleged spies to live. Furthermore, he professes to fear God. To his brothers, these were doubtless surprising statements whose sincerity they must have questioned. Throughout Genesis, the patriarchs are very suspicious of foreigners and their lack of reverence for God. In Gerar, Abraham said, "There is no fear of God in this place" (20:11; cf. 12:12; 34:30). Though Joseph's professions may have sounded hollow to his brothers, the narrator probably regards them as sincere. Joseph's mission is to preserve life (45:7; 47:25; 50:20), while "to fear God" is, according to the OT, the most fundamental of all religious duties (e.g., Prov 1:7; Eccl 12:13; cf. Gen 22:12; Exod 1:17; Lev 19:14, 32; Deut 6:2, 13).

19 The God-fearing man is one who cares for the needy and hungry (cf. Job 29:12–13; Prov 31:20; cf. 30).

20 In detaining just one of his brothers and sending the others back without him to Jacob, Joseph is not simply devising a punishment to fit the crime but making them relive their actions some twenty years earlier. And the brothers realize the parallels and lose their tempers discussing the affair.

21–22 Their discussion is not a mere summary of 37:12–30; we learn about Joseph's reaction to his treatment at his brothers' hands. Chap. 37 says nothing about what he felt or said as he was assaulted and then sold off to slave traders; there it was left to the reader's imagination. But now his brothers graphically describe his appeals for mercy (cf. Deut 3:23; 2 Kgs 1:13) and his distress of soul. צרה "distress" is more common in poetry than in prose and seems to refer to extreme situations (cf. 35:3; Deut 31:17; 2 Kgs 19:3). They equate their present situation with his, then, perhaps overdramatically, but it shows their awareness of divine providence overruling their affairs and requiring restitution.

Reuben rubs in the last point: "Now his blood is being required" (cf. 9:5, which says three times "I shall require" the blood of a murdered man). His remark suggests that Reuben's brothers never told him exactly what had happened to Joseph,

and he still believed his son had been killed (cf. 37:30). Or it could be that, like Exod 21:16, he equates kidnaping with murder as a capital crime.

Reuben's outburst is even more important for Joseph, for now he realizes that his eldest brother had not consented to his sale, and this may be the reason he decides to detain Simeon, the second oldest in the family, rather than Reuben. But Sternberg (*Poetics*, 291) thinks it is because he wanted Benjamin, Rachel's second son, that he held Simeon, Leah's second son, as hostage.

23 Clearly, interpreters must have been used often in Bible times, and his presence here is mentioned just to show the two levels on which Joseph is operating. Officially, he is the Egyptian vizier dealing with foreigners suspected of spying; in reality, he is talking to his brothers, so that although the private row between them was untranslated, he can follow it.

24 He is deeply moved by the signs of their penitence. Joseph's weeping is the harbinger of further tears on their next journey, when he sees Benjamin (43:30), when Judah offers to remain as slave instead of Benjamin and Joseph reveals his identity (45:2), and on the third journey when he is reunited with his father (46:29). For all his apparent harshness toward his brothers, this action proves that he still loves them and that if they continue to show a change of heart, reconciliation will be possible ultimately.

25–28 This short scene describing the journey both mystifies and intensifies the drama. It gives further insights into the minds of Joseph and his brothers.

25 Why did Joseph put their money back in their sacks? Was it out of brotherly kindness to show they were his guests (von Rad), to make them appear as thieves (cf. 44:1–13), or to reproduce the earlier situation when they were happy to exchange Joseph for money? Would they now decide to hold onto their cash and leave Simeon in prison (so Sternberg, *Poetics*)? It may not be necessary to choose between these ideas; Joseph may have had multiple motives (so Westermann).

27–28 The discovery of their money certainly caused consternation among the brothers. They saw the hand of God upon them in judgment. "What *has* God done?" uses the enclitic זֹאת to express their shock at the discovery (cf. n. 3:13.a.; 12:18; 26:10). Clearly, their aroused consciences (cf. v 21) are interpreting every unexpected development as a sign of God's wrath on their deeds.

27–28 "Sack." Two different words for "sack," שַׂק and אַמְתַּחַת, are used in this passage. The former, the same word as English, is used both of sacks and of sackcloth worn by mourners (e.g., 2 Kgs 19:1–2; Jon 3:6, 8), whereas the latter is found only in Gen 42–44, of the sacks used to carry the grain and money. According to J. Greenfield (*ZAW* 77 [1965] 90–92), the word is related to Assyrian *matāḫu* and means a "pack." Sarna suggests the pack was carried inside the sack, but this appears unlikely in 44:1. Rather, it would appear that sack (cloth) was the broader term and "sack, pack" a more specific one. Traditional source critics used the two terms to distinguish two sources, but as Westermann (3:112) points out, the presence of both terms here in a single verse makes this a dubious criterion for source analysis.

"Their hearts sank," lit. "went out of them." The expression is used only here, so its meaning is uncertain. Since "the heart" in Hebrew is the center of thought, Jacob (774) may well be right to see their reaction as one of confusion, "they did

not know what to think," rather than, as we say, "their heart stopped." "Trembling"; cf. 27:33 and *Comment.*

29–38 The last lap of the first journey to Egypt describes Jacob's sons reporting back to him about their trip. To appreciate its flavor, one must compare their report here with the narrator's own version in vv 6–24 and also with their report of the discovery of Joseph's tunic in 37:32–35, for to Jacob the loss of Simeon in Egypt seems like a replay of the loss of Joseph (42:36).

In their report to Jacob, the brothers call Joseph "the man, the lord of the land" (vv 30, 33), emphasizing both their ignorance of his identity and unwittingly that Joseph's dreams have been fulfilled. In reporting back to Jacob, they mention that they protested their honesty before they divulged details of their family, whereas in v 11 the order is reversed. It is as though they wish to break the most sensitive news to Jacob at the last possible moment. Hence, they mention the existence of Benjamin after mentioning the disappearance of Joseph, whereas in talking to Joseph the order was the reverse. "In any case 'one is no more' is the climactic statement for Joseph, while 'the youngest is now with our father' is the crucial revelation for Jacob, and so in each case what touches most deeply the person addressed is reserved for the last" (Alter, *Art of Biblical Narrative*, 169). Furthermore, they tactfully omit the fact that they were all imprisoned for three days, and instead of saying Simeon "was detained in custody" (vv 19, 24), they euphemistically state that he asked them to "leave one brother of yours with me," as though he were being treated as Joseph's honored guest. They also omit Joseph's warning about executing them if they fail to produce Benjamin (v 20), inventing instead a promise that they could "travel freely" or trade in the land (v 34; cf. 34:10). Finally, they say nothing about the discovery of money in their sacks (vv 27–28). This all-too-bland account of their trip to Egypt, designed to allay Jacob's fears, seems to have left him unpersuaded, for no comment by him on their mission is recorded. He must have thought, "Whatever they say, Simeon has not come home and Benjamin is now being demanded too."

35 The syntax of this verse, opening with ויהי and a participial clause, suggests a lapse of time between it and v 34. But why should the discovery of the money in the sack cause such surprise and consternation to both Jacob and his sons? The sons have already discovered money in at least one of their sacks (vv 27–28), so why the great alarm here? Older source critics claimed that vv 27–28 were an insertion by J into an account (E) that originally only mentioned the discovery here in v 35. More recent source critics prefer to see v 35 as the gloss and hold that the story originally told of the discovery in vv 27–28. But as Alter observes, it hardly seems likely that an editor can have regarded the two remarks as contradictory (*Art of Biblical Narrative*, 138–39). How may he have viewed the two discoveries? The commentator Jacob holds that v 35 is the continuation of the sons' report to their father and is in fact describing their discovery en route, as in vv 27–28. But this is an unnatural reading of the text. So is Sarna's idea that this discovery of their money was staged by the brothers. He thinks that after the initial discovery of money in one sack, the others also found money in their sacks and then arranged to open the sacks together in Jacob's presence. But this ingenious idea fails because the text states that "both they and their father . . . were afraid." More interesting is Sternberg's suggestion. The brothers and father are

scared for different reasons. Joseph's brothers are fearful because their further discovery heightens their sense of guilt and divine judgment already expressed in vv 21–22, 28. "Jacob's outburst, I would argue, implies that his fear differs from their uneasy sense of mystery. It is less obscure and more terrible. Two strange disclosures have been sprung on him in quick succession. Simeon's disappearance and the money's (re)appearance—Jacob refuses to accept them as coincidences. A tight causal explanation, clearing up one mystery in terms of another, suggests itself to him: the brothers have sold Simeon into slavery and are now pretending to be dismayed only to cover their tracks and lay the ground for another coup" (Sternberg, *Poetics*, 298).

36 Such a suspicion would be too dreadful to voice aloud, but the narrator gives us clues that suggest this may indeed be the way Jacob's mind was working. It is only he who has been bereaved and upon whom all these troubles have come, not his sons. He equates Simeon's fate with Joseph's. "There is no Joseph, and no Simeon, and you now want to take Benjamin."

37 This accusation that somehow the brothers have contrived the loss of both Joseph and Simeon prompts the reckless and otherwise inexplicable outburst of Reuben. The brothers are trapped by their past lies and their presently aroused consciences. Jacob's accusation admits of no straightforward denial, because it is half true. "How could (Reuben) say, We (or they) have indeed done away with your favorite and lied to you, but this time our hands are clean and our hearts pure?" (Sternberg, *Poetics*, 299). So, to demonstrate his sincerity, Reuben offers that two of his sons be put to death if Benjamin does not return.

38 This offer only raises Jacob's suspicions further. Perhaps Joseph and Simeon have actually been killed by their brothers. He now explicitly refers to Joseph as "dead," and by referring to him as "my son" and Benjamin as "his brother," he effectively denies any fraternal relationship between the sons of Leah and the sons of Rachel. His final comment, "you will bring me down in my old age to Sheol with sorrow," echoes 37:35. "I shall indeed go down to Sheol in mourning" reveals that Benjamin, Rachel's second son, is now as precious to Jacob as her first son, Joseph, once was and reminds his other sons of the grief they caused their father by selling Joseph. The process of contrition must run further before reconciliation is possible.

Explanation

After three chapters focusing on Joseph's twenty years in Egypt, twenty years that have seen him rise from imprisoned slave to Pharaoh's deputy, the narrative suddenly brings Joseph's family back into the picture. His aged father, Jacob, sends most of his sons to Egypt to buy grain to tide them over the famine, and rather remarkably they are there recognized by Joseph. Not so surprisingly, they fail to recognize him. But this encounter is enough to make both sides recall the events that led to the rift within the family twenty years earlier.

Seeing his brothers bowing down to him, Joseph remembers the dreams in which sheaves and the celestial bodies bowed down to him. But he is perplexed, for only one of the dreams appears fulfilled—that of his brothers' sheaves bowing down to his. The second dream was more explicit, with eleven stars,

representing his eleven brothers, and the sun and moon, his parents, falling down before him. Yet here were only ten brothers and no parents. Where was his full brother, Benjamin, let alone his father and his wives? Those he most wanted to see were absent, while those who had planned to kill had come. He wanted to know what had happened to his father and Benjamin. But how was he to discover?

Would his brothers tell him the truth, if he disclosed his identity? How could he be sure that they still did not harbor deadly hatred against him? To discover the real situation, he adopts a harsh and indirect line of interrogation, charging them with spying in order to elicit information about their home background. He thereby discovers that his father and brother are still alive. But this whets his appetite yet further: have his brothers really told the truth, and if they have, what can he do to make his brother and father come to Egypt?

He therefore detains Simeon, who may well have been the ringleader who sold Joseph to the slavetraders, and sends the others back home to fetch their youngest brother. This detention of Simeon serves two purposes. First, he acts as a hostage encouraging the other brothers to produce Benjamin. Second, his detention replicates in some ways Joseph's detention in Egypt. It poses his brothers with a similar temptation. Will they abandon him as they abandoned Joseph?

The analogy is not lost on them. They confess their guilt about Joseph and indeed mention something omitted in chap. 37: "We saw his distress when he implored us, and we did nothing." Indeed, they see God punishing them for their sin: "Therefore this distress has fallen on us" (42:21). Their distress, they acknowledge, is just retribution for their callous treatment of their brother. As Jesus said, "[T]he measure you give will be the measure you get" (Matt 7:2), and Paul said, "God is not mocked, for whatever a man sows, that he will also reap" (Gal 6:7).

Arriving back home, Joseph's brothers relate to Jacob most of what happened in Egypt, though they do leave out some of the more alarming incidents. But Jacob is hardly reassured. To him it all seems like a rerun of the loss of Joseph: "It's me that you have bereaved. There is no Joseph, . . . and now it's Benjamin you want to take" (42:36). And his sons can do very little to reassure him, for their past deceit about their involvement in Joseph's disappearance cannot be revealed if they wish to persuade Jacob to let Benjamin go back with them to Egypt.

Thus nearly all the actors are trapped by their past. The brothers cannot escape the power of their past guilt by being honest now either to Joseph or to their father. They live in fear of provoking a new uncontrolled outburst of paternal sorrow if they take Benjamin and fail to return him. Jacob himself is even more paranoic, suspecting his sons of selling Simeon to raise cash, and above all determined not to let his beloved Benjamin out of his sight. Only Joseph appears to be in control of the situation, but even he is overtaken by emotion as he hears the first contrite comments by his brothers for the way they treated him. And he cannot be sure whether the device of holding Simeon will suffice to bring all his brothers, including Benjamin, back to Egypt. Will his dreams be fulfilled or not?

The actors within the story seem to sense divine intervention in their lives. Joseph remembers the dreams, and his brothers say, "What has God done to us?" But their surmises are not certainties. The dreams do not match present reality, and the brothers do not know how far divine judgment will go. But the narrator

has no such uncertainty. For him just the fact that Joseph recognized his brothers among the many hungry people arriving in Egypt to buy grain suggests divine overruling. And the principle enunciated in the preceding chapter, that doubled dreams show that they are certain and that God will shortly fulfill them (41:32), applies as much to Joseph's own dreams as to those he interprets. The prophetic dreams of his youth will, like all true prophecy, eventually be fulfilled (cf. Deut 18:22; Isa 8:16–17; 41:22; Hab 2:3), so no reader should doubt that ere long both Benjamin and Jacob will also come down to Egypt. But more than that, the signs of penitence of Joseph's brothers hold the promise that full family reconciliation will one day be possible.

Second Visit of Joseph's Family to Egypt   (43:1–45:28)

Bibliography

Muffs, Y. "Two Comparative Lexical Studies: 1. Aramaic ῾*l ᵓl* = Hebrew *baᵓ ᵓel* 'to receive.'" *JANESCU* 5 (1973) 287–94. **Niehoff, M.** "Do Biblical Characters Talk to Themselves? Narrative Modes of Representing Inner Speech in Early Biblical Fiction." *JBL* 111 (1992) 577–95. **Pautasso, L. G.** "Gen 44:18: A Case for the Textual Relevance of the Targumic Tosephta." *Hen* 10 (1988) 205–18. **Rogerson, J. W.** "Can a Doctrine of Providence Be Based on the OT?" In *Ascribe unto the Lord: Biblical and Other Essays: FS P. C. Craigie*, ed L. M. Eslinger and J. G. Taylor. JSOTSup 67. Sheffield: Academic, 1988. 529–43.

Translation

¹ *The famine was severe in the land.* ² *So when they had eaten up the supplies which they had brought*ᵃ *from Egypt, their father said to them, "Go back*ᵇ *and buy us a little food."* ³ *But Judah said to him, "The man* ᵃ*solemnly warned*ᵃ *us: 'You shall not see me again unless*ᵇ *your brother is with you.'* ⁴ *So if you* ᵃ*are really prepared to send*ᵃ *our brother with us, we will*ᵇ *go down and buy food for you.* ⁵ *But if you are not prepared to send him, we shall not go down, for the man did say to us, 'You shall not see me again unless your brother is with you.'"* ⁶ *Then Israel said, "Why did you treat*ᵃ *me so badly by letting the man know*ᵇ *that*ᶜ *you had another brother?"* ⁷ *They said, "The man inquired carefully about us and our clan asking, 'Is your brother still alive? Do you have a brother?' So we told*ᵃ *him about these things. Could we really*ᵇ *know that he would say, 'Bring*ᶜ *your brother down'?"*

⁸ *Then Judah said to Israel his father, "Send the boy with me, so that we can set off and go and live, and not die, both*ᵃ *we, you, and our children.* ⁹ *I myself shall stand surety for him. From me*ᵃ *you may require him. If I do not bring*ᵇ *him back to you and produce*ᶜ *him in your presence, I shall be guilty before you forever.* ¹⁰ᵃ *For if we had not dallied,*ᵇ ᶜ*we could have certainly gone there twice already."*ᵃ ¹¹ᵃ *Then Israel their father said to them, "If it must be so, do this. Take some of the choice produce of the land in your containers and bring a present to the man, a little storax gum, a little honey, tragacanth and ladanum gum, pistachios, and almonds.* ¹² *Take double money with you and*

take back the money that was returned [a] *in the mouth of your sacks. Perhaps it was a mistake.* [13]*Also take your brother,* [a] *and go return to the man.* [14]*May God* [a] *Almighty grant you mercy from the man, so that he sends back your other* [b] *brother and Benjamin. As for me, if* [c]*I lose my children, I lose them."* [c]

[15]*So the men took this present. They also took double money with them and Benjamin. They set out, came down to Egypt, and stood before Joseph.* [16]*When Joseph saw* [a]*Benjamin with them,* [a] *he said to the man in charge of his household, "Bring* [b] *the men to the house, kill a beast, and prepare* [c] *it, because these men are going to eat at noon with me."* [d] [17]*So the man did as Joseph had said, and the man* [a] *brought them to Joseph's house.*

[18]*When the men saw that they had been brought* [a] *to Joseph's house, they said, "It is because of the money which returned* [b] *in our sacks in the beginning. We are being taken* [c] *inside to be assaulted and fallen upon and to be taken as slaves and also our donkeys."* [19]*So they came* [a] *up to the man in charge of the household of Joseph and spoke with him in the courtyard.* [20]*They said to him, "With your permission,* [a] *sir. We came down on the first occasion to buy grain.* [21]*When we came to the night stopping place, we opened* [a] *our sacks and there was each man's money in the mouth of his sack in full weight, so we have brought* [b] *it with us.* [22]*We have also brought* [a] *down extra money to buy grain. We do not know who placed our money in our sacks."* [23]*He replied "That's fine. Your god, the god of your fathers, must have put treasure in your sacks. I received your money." Then he brought* [a] *Simeon out to meet them.*

[24]*Then the man brought the men into Joseph's house and gave them water, and they washed their feet, and he provided fodder for their donkeys.* [25]*They prepared* [a] *the present until Joseph came at midday, for they had heard that he would eat bread there.* [26]*So Joseph came home, and they brought* [a] *to him the present which they had with them indoors and bowed* [b] *down to the ground before him.* [27]*He asked them how they were and said,* [a] *"How is your old father you mentioned? Is he still alive?"* [a] [28]*They said, "Your servant, our father, is well: he is still alive."* [a] *They again bowed* [b] *down and prostrated themselves.* [29]*Then he raised* [a] *his eyes and saw Benjamin his brother, his own mother's son, and he said, "Is this your youngest brother, whom you mentioned to me?" He said, "May God be gracious* [b] *to you, my son."* [30]*Joseph then hurried out, for his affection for his brother boiled* [a] *up, and he was on the verge of weeping, and he went into an inner room and wept there.* [31]*Then he washed his face, went back out controlling himself, and said, "Serve the food."* [32]*So they served it separately for him and them and for the Egyptians, who ate with him separately, for Egyptians were unable to eat food with Hebrews, for that would be disgusting for Egyptians.* [33]*They were seated in order before him, the firstborn in his place and the youngest in his, and they all were stunned by it.* [34]*He had* [a] *portions distributed from his table, and Benjamin's was* [b] *five times larger than any of the others. So they drank and were merry with him.*

[44:1]*He then gave orders to the man in charge of his household, "Fill the sacks of the men with as much food as they can hold* [a] *and put each man's money in the mouth of his sack.* [2]*As for my cup, my silver cup, you must put it in the mouth of the youngest one's sack and the money for his grain." He did just as Joseph said.* [3]*At morning light,* [a] *the men and their donkeys were sent on their way.* [4]*They had left the city but had not gone far, when Joseph said to his butler. "Up, chase after the men. Catch* [a] *them up and say to them, 'Why have you paid me back with evil, not good?* [5]*Isn't this what my lord drinks from and divines with? You have behaved* [a] *very badly doing this.'"*

⁶*So he overtook*^a *them and spoke to them along these lines.* ⁷*They said to him, "Why does my lord speak like this? Your servants would never do a thing like that.* ⁸*Since we brought*^a *back from the land of Canaan the*^b *money we found in the mouths of our sacks, why should we steal from your master's house silver or gold?* ⁹*If it is found in the possession of any of your servants, he shall die, and we shall become your master's slaves."* ¹⁰*But he said, "All right then, it shall be as you say: in whoever's possession it is found, he shall become my slave, but you shall be free."*

¹¹*So each one hurried to let*^a *his sack down on the ground, and each one opened his sack.* ¹²*Then he searched them, beginning*^a *with the eldest and ending with the youngest, and the cup was found in Benjamin's sack.* ¹³*Then they tore their clothes, each one reloaded his donkey, and they returned to the city.*

¹⁴*Then Judah and his brothers entered Joseph's house. He was still there, so they fell down before him on the ground.* ¹⁵*Joseph said to them, "What is this deed that you have done? Don't you realize that a man like me is a good diviner?"* ¹⁶*Then Judah said, "What can we say to my lord? What can we speak? How can we justify*^a *ourselves? It is God who has found out your servants' guilt. Here we are slaves of you, my lord, both we and the one in whose possession the cup was found."* ¹⁷*But he said, "May*^a *I never do a thing like that. Just the man in whose possession the cup was found shall be my slave. You others may go back to your father in peace."*

¹⁸*Then Judah approached*^a *him and said, "With your permission sir, may your servant please have a word in my lord's ear. Don't be very angry*^b *with your servant, for you are just like*^c *Pharaoh.* ¹⁹*My lord asked his servants, 'Do you have a father or brother?'* ²⁰*So we said to my lord, 'We do have an elderly father, and the child of his old age is young. His brother is dead, so that he is the only surviving*^a *child of his mother. And his father loves him.'* ²¹*Now you said to your servants, 'Bring*^a *him down to me, so that I can look after him.'* ²²*But we said to my lord, 'The lad cannot leave his father. If he does leave him, his father will die.'* ²³*But you said to your servants, 'If your youngest brother does not come with you, you shall not see me again.'*^a

²⁴*"So when we had gone back to your servant my father, we told*^a *him what my lord had said.* ²⁵*Then our father said, 'Go back and buy us a little food.'* ²⁶*But we said, 'We cannot go*^a *back. If our youngest brother is with us, we can go back, because we shall not see the man's face if our youngest brother is not with us.'* ²⁷*Then your servant my father said to us, 'You know that my wife bore me two sons.* ²⁸*One of them left me and I said, "Surely*^a *he has been torn*^b *to bits," and I haven't seen him since.* ²⁹*Now you would take even this one away from me. If an accident happens to him, you will bring*^a *down my gray head in sorrow to the grave.'* ³⁰*Now as soon as I arrive*^a *back at your servant my father without the boy, as his life is bound up with his,* ³¹*as soon as he sees*^a *that the boy is not there,*^{bc} *he will die. So your servants will bring down your servant's gray head in sorrow to Sheol.* ³²*Indeed your servant stood surety for the boy with my*^a *father saying, 'If I do not bring*^b *him back, I shall be guilty before my father forever.'* ³³*So now let your servant please stay instead of the boy as my master's slave, and let the boy go*^a *back with his brothers.* ³⁴*For how can I go back to my father without the boy and*^a *see the calamity that will befall my father?"*

^{45:1}*Joseph was not able to contain himself in the presence of all those standing by him, so he called out, "Make everyone leave*^a *my presence." So there was not anyone waiting on him, when he made himself known*^b *to his brothers.* ²*He wept aloud, and the Egyptians and even the palace of Pharaoh heard*^a *about it.* ³*Then Joseph said to his brothers,*

"I ª am Joseph. Is my father still alive?" But they were not able to answer him, for they were dumbfounded by him. ⁴So Joseph said to his brothers, "Please come ª closer." So they came closer. He said to them, ᵇ "I am Joseph, your brother whom you sold into Egypt.ᵇ ⁵Now then don't be distressed or angry that you sold me here, because God sent me before you ªto preserve life.ª ⁶For so far there have been two years of famine in the land, but there are still five more to go when there will be no plowing or harvest.ª ⁷So God sent me in advance of you to make a remnant for you in the land and to preserveª for you a great number of survivors.ᵇ ⁸Now then it was not you who sent me here but God. He made me a father to Pharaoh and lord of all his household and ruler of all the land of Egypt. ⁹Hurry, go back to my father and say to him, 'This is what your son Joseph says: God has made me lord of all Egypt, so comeª down to me. Don't stay! ¹⁰You shall live in the land of Goshen and be near me, you, your sons, and grandsons, your flocks and herds and all that you have. ¹¹I shall provideª you with food there, for there are still five years of famine to come, so that you and your household and all that belong to you do not becomeᵇ poor.' ¹²Now you yourselves and my brother Benjamin see with your own eyes that it is my own mouth speaking to you. ¹³You then shall tellª my father about all the splendor that is mine in Egypt and everything that you have seen. You must bring my father down here quickly." ¹⁴Then he fell on his brother Benjamin's neck and wept,ª and Benjamin wept over his neck. ¹⁵He then kissed all his brothers and wept over them. Afterwards his brothers talked with him.

¹⁶The story reached Pharaoh's palace that Joseph's brothers had come, and he and his servants were pleased. ¹⁷Pharaoh said to Joseph, "Say to your brothers, 'Load your beasts and go to the land of Canaan. ¹⁸Then take your father and your families and come to me so that I may giveª you the best of the land of Egypt, and you shall eat the choicest produce of the land. ¹⁹You are under orders.ª Do this. Take carts for yourselves from the land of Egypt for your youngsters, and wives, and carry your father and come. ²⁰Don't be sorryª about your belongings, for the best of the whole land of Egypt is yours."ᵇ ²¹So the sons of Israel did so, and Joseph gave them carts as Pharaoh directed, and he gave them provisions for the journey. ²²He gave them all a change of cloaks, but he gave Benjamin three hundred pieces of silver and five sets of clothes. ²³For his father, he sent as follows: ten donkeys carrying some of the best produce of Egypt and ten she-asses carrying grain and bread and provisions for his father on the journey. ²⁴He sent off his brothers and they left, and he said to them, "Don't be stirredª up on the way."

²⁵They went up from Egypt and came to the land of Canaan to their father Jacob. ²⁶Then they toldª him, "Joseph is still alive and rules over all the land of Egypt." Then his heart stopped,ᵇ for he did not believe them. ²⁷They then reported all that Joseph had said to them. He saw the carts which Joseph had sent to transportª him, and their father Jacob's spirit revived.ᵇ ²⁸Israel then said, "Enough. Joseph my son is still alive. I willª go down to seeᵇ him before I die."

Notes

2.a. 3 masc pl pf hiph בוא.

2.b. 2 masc pl impv qal שׁוב.

3.a-a. Inf abs + 3 masc sg pf hiph עוד. On the use of the inf abs for emphasis, see GKC, 113n; *EWAS*, 88.

3.b. On בלתי to introduce exceptive clause, see *SBH*, 174; WOC, 643.

4.a-a. שׁ + ptcp expresses more than a willingness to act (so Joüon, 154l); it indicates "that a state of affairs or behaviour . . . is *actually* as one wants or expects" (*EWAS*, 77).

4.b. Coh expresses the will to act (Joüon, 114e).

6.a. 2 masc pl pf hiph רעע.

6.b. Cf. n. 32:6.d.

6.c. ה introducing indirect question (GKC, 150i).

7.a. Waw consec + 1 pl impf hiph נגד.

7.b. Inf abs "used to strengthen a question, especially in impassioned or indignant questions" (GKC, 113q; cf. WOC, 587).

7.c. 2 masc pl impv hiph ירד.

8.a. Note thrice-repeated גם for emphasis (Joüon, 177q).

9.a. Fronting of the adverbial phrase for emphasis (*EWAS*, 43).

9.b. 1 sg pf hiph בוא + 3 masc sg suffix.

9.c. Waw + 1 sg pf hiph יצא + 3 masc sg suffix.

10.a-a. On the construction of unreal conditional clauses, see GKC, 159x; WOC, 494.

10.b. 1 pl pf hithpalpel מהה.

10.c. On use of כי in apodoses, see GKC, 159ee; Joüon, 167s.

11.a. For analysis of grammatical structure of vv 11–14, see *SBH*, 108–10.

12.a. Def art + masc sg ptcp hiph שוב.

13.a. Note precious Benjamin mentioned last in list (*EWAS*, 38).

14.a. Note that the subj "God Almighty" often precedes the verb in blessings (cf. n. 28:3.a.; *EWAS*, 35).

14.b. Omission of article not unusual with אחר (WOC, 260). SamPent, G read האחד "the one."

14.c-c. On construction, see GKC, 106o: "an expression of despairing resignation."

16.a-a. SamPent, G, Vg read "them and Benjamin."

16.b. 2 masc sg impv hiph בוא.

16.c. Waw + 2 masc sg impv hiph כון.

16.d. Initial position of "with me" for emphasis (*EWAS*, 43).

17.a. Omitted by G, S.

18.a. 3 masc pl pf hoph בוא.

18.b. Def art + masc sg ptcp qal שוב. On use in relative clauses, see GKC, 116d; WOC, 623.

18.c. Masc pl ptcp hoph בוא.

19.a. Cf. n. 19:9.d.

20.a. On this expression (בי), cf. Joüon, 105c; J. Hoftijzer, *VT* 20 (1970) 427–28.

21.a. On use of (pseudo)coh here, see WOC, 576–77.

21.b. Waw consec + 1 pl impf hiph שוב.

22.a. 1 pl pf hiph ירד.

23.a. Cf. n. 15:5.a.

25.a. Waw consec + 3 masc pl impf hiph כון.

26.a. On the dagesh in the א, see GKC, 14d.

26.b. Cf. n. 42:6.b.

27.a-a. On word order, cf. *EWAS*, 17; *SBH*, 48.

28.a. SamPent, G add "And he said 'May that man be blessed by God.'"

28.b. Waw consec + 3 masc pl impf קדד.

29.a. Cf. n. 13:10.a.

29.b. 3 masc sg impf qal חנן + 2 masc sg suffix. On punctuation, see GKC, 67n; Y. Lerner, *Leš* 47 (1982/83) 155. On word order, see *EWAS*, 35.

30.a. 3 masc pf niph כמר. On ingressive stative sense of niph, "grew hot," see WOC, 386.

34.a. Lit. "he distributed portions," but obviously done by Joseph's servants (GKC, 144n).

34.b. Waw consec + 3 fem sg impf (apoc) רבה.

44:1.a. Cf. n. 4:7.a.

3.a. Lit. "the morning was light," 3 masc sg pf qal אור.

4.a. Waw consec + 2 masc sg pf hiph נשג + 3 masc pl suffix.

5.a. Cf. n. 43:6.a.

6.a. Waw consec + 3 masc sg impf hiph נשג + 3 masc pl suffix.

8.a. 1 pl pf hiph שוב.

8.b. So SamPent, G; MT omits def art.

11.a. Waw consec + 3 masc pl impf hiph ירד.

12.a. Cf. n. 6:1.b.

16.a. 1 pl impf hithp צדק.

17.a. חלילה to introduce a negative oath (WOC, 608; Joüon, 165k.)

18.a. Cf. n. 18:23.a.

18.b. Cf. n. 18:30.a.

18.c. On כ . . . כ "just like," see Joüon, 154b; 174i.

20.a. Waw consec + 3 masc sg impf niph יתר.

21.a. 2 masc pl impv hiph ירד + 3 masc sg suffix.

23.a. 2 masc pl impf hiph יסף + nun paragogicum; on this, see WOC, 517, n. 61.

24.a. Cf. n. 43:7.a.

26.a. ל + inf constr qal ירד.

28.a. On the meaning of אך, see WOC, 670, *EWAS*, 129.

28.b. Cf. n. 37:33.c.

29.a. Cf. n. 42:38.b.

30.a. כ + inf constr בוא + 1 sg suffix.

31.a. כ + inf constr ראה + 3 masc sg suffix.

31.b. The word order means absence, not non-existence (*EWAS*, 103).

31.c. SamPent, G, S add "with us."

32.a. SamPent "his father."

32.b. Cf. n. 42:37.c.

33.a. 3 masc sg juss qal עלה. On chiastic linkage of jussives, "stay . . . go back," see *SBH*, 134.

34.a. On this use of פן, see GKC, 152w.

45:1.a. 2 masc pl impv hiph יצא.

1.b. ב + inf constr hithp ידע.

2.a. *BHS* suggest G, S read this as niph, "was heard."

3.a. According to *EWAS*, 13, the word order emphasizes "I."

4.a. 2 masc pl impv נגש.

4.b-b. On clause structure, see GKC, 138d; WOC, 334.

5.a-a. Fronting of this phrase in the Heb. emphasizes it (*EWAS*, 43).

6.a. On the unexpected dagesh, see WOC, 22.

7.a. Cf. n. 6:19.c.

7.b. SamPent omits initial ל.

9.a. 2 masc sg impv ירד + *āh* ending.

11.a. Waw + 1 sg pf pilpel כול.

11.b. 2 masc sg impf niph ירש.

13.a. Waw consec + 2 masc pl pf hiph נגד.

14.a. Cf. n. 27:38.b.

18.a. Cf. n. 17:2.a.

19.a. 2 masc sg pf pual צוה; cf. *BHS* suggested emendation "command them."

20.a. 3 fem sg impf qal חוס.

20.b. Word order emphasizes "to you" (*EWAS*, 17, 75).

24.a. SamPent has hithp. Same meaning.

26.a. Cf. n. 26:32.b.

26.b. Waw consec + 3 masc sg impf פוג.

27.a. Cf. n. 36:7.b.

27.b. Waw consec + 3 fem sg impf חיה.

28.a. Coh here expresses speaker's strong resolve (WOC, 573; Joüon, 114c).

28.b. Waw + 1 sg impf qal ראה + 3 masc sg suffix.

Form/Structure/Setting

Chaps. 43–45 describe the second of three journeys to Egypt and include the high point of the Joseph story, his self-disclosure to his brothers. This unit of narrative consists of seven scenes that, as in chap. 42, are arranged palistrophically.

Scene 1:   Jacob sends sons to Egypt (43:1–14)   A
Scene 2:   Arrival in Egypt: Steward and brothers (43:15–25)   B
Scene 3:   Lunch with Joseph (43:26–34)   C

Scene 4: Brothers arrested (44:1–13)   D
Scene 5: Joseph discloses himself to brothers (44:14–45:15)   C¹
Scene 6: Departure from Egypt: Pharaoh and brothers (45:16–24)   B¹
Scene 7: Sons report to Jacob on mission (45:25–28)   A¹

As Coats and Westermann have pointed out, the structure and contents of these chapters echo chap. 42.

42:1–4	Jacob's sons sent to Egypt	43:1–14
42:5	Arrival in Egypt	43:15–25
42:6–16	First audience with Joseph	43:26–34
42:17	Brothers in custody	44:1–13
42:18–24	Second audience with Joseph	44:14–45:15
42:25–28	Departure from Egypt	45:16–24
42:29–38	Sons report to Jacob	45:25–28

At nearly every point in the account of the second journey, there are references back to the first, e.g., 43:27, 29; 44:19–23, or at least implicit comparisons are made between the two journeys: 43:1–2 // 41:57–42:2; 43:3–8 // 42:12–20; 43:11–12 // 42:25–28, 35; 43:14–15 // 42:19, 24, 36; 43:16 // 42:7; 43:18 // 42:28, 35; 43:20–23 // 42:25–28; 43:23b // 42:24; 43:26, 28 // 42:6; 43:27–28 // 42:11; 43:29 // 42:13, 15; 43:30–31 // 42:24; 43:33 // 42:28, 35; 44:1–12 // 42:25–28; 44:14 // 42:6; 44:16 // 42:21; 44:17 // 42:19; 44:18–23 // 42:10–20; 44:24–31 // 42:29–38; 45:1 // 42:24; 45:3 // 42:13; 45:4–5 // 42:21–22; 45:21–23 // 42:25.

There are also references to earlier episodes in the Joseph story: 43:11 refers to 37:25; 43:26 to 37:7, 10; 44:19, 28 to 37:3, 33; 44:31 to 37:35; 45:4–5 to 37:27–28; 45:6 to 41:26–30; 45:8–9 to 41:38–46.

It is therefore clear that, despite the chapter divisions, 43:1–45:28 constitutes a single unit within the Joseph story. A few commentators regard chaps. 43–44 as one block and chap. 45 as another, but this failure to note the obvious connections across the chapters in structure and content rests on the ascription of chap. 45 to a different source (E) from chapters 43–44 (J) and not on rhetorical features.

Traditional source critics see chaps. 43–44 as J's version of the journey to Egypt found in E in chap. 42. Chap. 45, on the other hand, continues the E version with some supplementation by J, though there is less agreement about which verses are to be ascribed to J. More recently, Redford (*Biblical Story of Joseph*) has suggested that the original Joseph story largely represented in this section by E (i.e., chaps. 42, 45) has been expanded by the addition of the J material (i.e., chaps. 43–44). Schmitt (*Josephsgeschichte*) argues for the reverse order—chaps. 43–44 as the primary core expanded by chaps. 42, 45. But these source-critical analyses have missed the intimate connections and patternings that link chapters 42–45. So I concur with recent studies by Coats, Donner (*Josephsgeschichte*), Westermann, Humphreys (*Joseph and His Family*), and Sarna, who recognize the essential unity of this material. Westermann has expressed himself particularly forcefully about the unity of these chapters. Source critics, he says, have read nonexistent differences and tensions into the text. "But if, on the contrary, one regards the sequence of chs 42–45 as rooted in the overall plan of the writer, for whom the mounting tension from the first to the second journey is necessary, then one has no need to

strike out or postulate anything" (3:119). "It is beyond doubt that the narrator intends the contrast between Joseph's reception in chs 42 and 43. The structure of ch 43 shows with utter certainty that the author intends a sequence in chs 42–43" (3:120). "Ch 45 is a particularly obvious example where only a preconception can have led to source division" (3:142).

Comment

1–14 The opening scene of this section matches the opening scene of chap. 42 and describes the family discussion that preceded each visit to Egypt. But here and throughout chaps. 43–44 the dialogues and narrative elements are fuller, thus slowing down the story as it draws near to its climax.

1 Same wording as 12:10 and similar to 41:57.

2 "They." The lack of an explicit noun subject shows that this is a continuation of the previous chapter and not a duplicate. As on the first trip, Jacob asserts his patriarchal authority by suggesting an expedition to Egypt to buy food (cf. 42:1–2). But whereas then he ordered them to go, here he puts it almost diffidently: "buy us a little food," "as though it were a matter of a trip to a nearby market" (Alter, *Art of Biblical Narrative,* 171). He is careful not to anger his sons this time, for he knows that it is his veto that is delaying them (cf. 42:36–38).

3–5 Reuben had earlier tried to persuade Jacob to let Benjamin accompany them to Egypt. His argument had been inept, to say the least (42:37–38), and no doubt it was not helped by his bad standing with his father (cf. 35:22; cf. 49:4). Maybe a similar motive underlay Levi's silence, and of course his companion in crime, Simeon, was in Egyptian custody (34:30; cf. 49:5–7). So Judah, the oldest son in good standing with his father, intervenes and pleads for a change of policy.

Judah begins and ends his plea by recalling Joseph's threat, "You shall not see me again unless your brother is with you" (vv 3, 5; cf. 42:15, 20). "See me," lit. "see my face," characteristically refers to audiences with the great, such as kings (e.g., Exod 10:28–29). But whereas when the brothers last tried to persuade Jacob to let Benjamin go to Egypt, they glossed over Joseph's warnings, this time Judah hints at his threats (42:16, 20). "Solemnly warned," "warn" (hiph of עוד) is used of threats that are not empty (e.g., Exod 19:21, 23; Jer 11:7; Neh 9:26, 29–30). Here the finite verb "warned" is prefaced by the infinitive absolute "solemnly," making the threat even more ominous.

6 It is easy to be wise after the event, and Jacob's grumble about their indiscretion is really just stalling.

7 So all the brothers back up Judah, pointing out that it was impossible to predict the way the conversation would go. 42:10–16 does not record Joseph putting these questions so directly. It rather portrays them volunteering the information, but that is not how this interrogation felt to them. They felt that supplying details about their family background was the only way to clear themselves of the charge of espionage; they sensed that the man wanted to know about their "clan." On this term, see 12:1 (*Comment*); cf. 24:4, 7; 31:3, 13.

8–10 Judah now pushes his father to make a decision by appealing to his paternal instincts. Earlier, Jacob had said that they must go to Egypt to buy grain "so that we may live and not die" (42:2). So Judah now makes the same point and

underlines it with the comment that this will save him "and our children as well." טַף "children" is a term that refers to the dependent and vulnerable younger generation, whom parents have a particular duty to protect (cf. 45:19; 47:12; Num 14:3, 31). Judah then grasps the nub of the problem, offering to stand surety himself for Benjamin. Quite what this would mean in practice, if Benjamin failed to return, is not clear, but standing surety for someone was regarded as very risky and not to be entered into lightly (e.g., Prov 6:1; 11:15). "From me you may require it," though it uses a different verb, sounds like 9:5 and suggests that Jacob could demand Judah's own life if he fails to return Benjamin. At the very least, he would always "be guilty" before him. Having thus offered himself, Judah urges his father to stop dallying (cf. 19:16 and *Comment*) and reminds him of just how desperate the food situation now is: "we could have certainly gone there twice already."

11–14 At last swayed by Judah's appeal, Jacob makes up his mind and tells his sons to go. Facing a crisis like his meeting with Esau (chaps. 32–33), he trusts in decisive action and providence. Despite the famine, he prepares a "present" of the "choice produce of the land" for "the man." Though somewhat smaller than the present he sent to Esau, it was no doubt sent with a similar motive: "for he thought 'I shall mollify him with the present ahead of me, and then afterward I shall see him face to face. Perhaps he will accept me'" (32:21[20]).

"Choice produce of the land" is a phrase found only here. "Choice produce" (זמרה) is lit. "strength," as in Exod 15:2; Isa 12:2; Ps 118:14.

"Storax . . . almonds." The list of the items in the present is similar to that in 37:25 with some extras such as honey, pistachio, and almond nuts. On "pistachio," see Zohary, *Plants of the Bible*, 5. "Honey" is often mentioned as one of the special products of the land that flows with milk and honey. It is often thought to include the syrup produced from dates or grapes, called *dibs* in Arabic (e.g., KB, 204). But in those biblical passages where the origin of the product is clear, honey is produced by bees (e.g., Deut 32:13; Judg 14:8–9; 1 Sam 14:26–29; see *EM* 2:585–6). It is possible that the narrator sees a parallel between this expedition to Egypt and the Ishmaelite caravan that brought Joseph there. Both carried similar products, "gums of tragacanth, storax, and ladanum." From the Ishmaelites, Joseph's brothers received money; now they are carrying money back to Egypt. "The wheel seems to have come full circle. The plot movement that started with a brother leaving home in all innocence to join his brothers, only to find himself the property of a trading caravan bound for Egypt, now presses for closure once the brothers leave home in a caravan to rescue a brother in Egypt" (M. Sternberg, *Poetics*, 300–301).

13 Note how Jacob leaves giving permission for his beloved Benjamin to go until the last possible moment (cf. 22:3).

14 Though briefer, Jacob's prayer invites comparison with his prayer in 32:10–13(9–12): on both occasions, he invokes the God of his forefathers to deliver him and his family from his present predicament. On God Almighty, "El Shaddai," see *Comment* on 17:1 (cf. 28:3; 35:11; 48:3; 49:25). "Grant you mercy"; cf. Deut 13:18(17); Jer 42:12. "Your other brother" in context refers to Simeon, but the narrator may have a greater answer to the prayer in view, for the other brother could be Joseph (cf. Eph 3:20). (This has been observed by some Jewish commentators: "Jacob

prophesied but knew not what he was prophesying; 'your brother' refers to Benjamin, 'another' refers to Joseph," so ⁾*Abot r. Nat.*, quoted by Leibowitz, 480; similar points are made by *Midr. Rab.* 90:3; Rashi; Ramban.) But Jacob obviously doubts whether his prayer will be answered, for he concludes with deep resignation, "If I lose my children, I lose them," a sentiment that echoes that of his mother Rebekah when she heard Esau planned to murder Jacob (27:45; cf. 1 Sam 15:33; Gen 42:36).

15–25 The tension palpably rises as the narrative pace slows to describe the brothers' reception in Egypt, an event that is hardly described in the first journey (42:5). The brothers evidently reach Egypt easily, but then they are taken aback by the unusual interest shown in them by Joseph's steward. Their conscience starts pricking them again as they wait for lunch, anxiously putting the last touches on their present for the great man.

16 "When Joseph saw Benjamin" implies that all Joseph did next was prompted by Benjamin's arrival. But as far as his brothers were concerned, an invitation to dine at Joseph's house was an overreaction; all they hoped for was Simeon's release and fresh food supplies.

17 This verse sums up all the steward's actions that are more fully described in the succeeding verses (vv 18–24). It is common in Hebrew narrative for a summary to be followed by a fuller explanation.

18 The brothers cannot believe the change from their suspicious, hostile reception on their first journey to their present overfriendly welcome can be genuine, so they think they are merely being taken in to be attacked and enslaved. The verbs "assaulted" and "fallen upon" occur only here with this meaning or form.

19 "They came . . . spoke." As elsewhere in the Bible, this collocation generally introduces a request of special importance to the speaker (cf. 18:23; 44:18; Num 32:16; Josh 14:6; 21:1–2). "In the courtyard," lit. "in the opening of the house." As in the ritual texts, פתח "opening" seems to have the sense of a precinct, such as the court of the tabernacle, surrounding a building (cf. e.g., Lev 1:3, 5).

20–22 The brothers' speech is exceedingly deferential and tactful, as they confess how they found their money on the way home. The account of the finding is somewhat simplified compared with 42:27–28, 35, but this is neither dishonesty on their part nor proof that the chapters come from different sources; it simply indicates that the focus of their concern is to show that they did not steal it and have now returned it. They have brought extra money to buy more grain.

23 The steward's reply, while reassuring the brothers who did not know where the money came from, disconcerts the reader, who does know that the steward put the money in their bags. His comment, "Your god . . . must have put treasure in your sacks," while putting the brothers off the track of the human agent, does though express an important theological idea of the narrative, that God's plans are worked out through human agents, as Joseph will say shortly to his brothers, "You sold me here, because God sent me before you to preserve life" (45:5). Here (cf. 41:38–39) even an Egyptian is portrayed as acknowledging the overarching control of human affairs by divine providence.

"He brought out Simeon to them" must have reassured the brothers that the steward was indeed acting in good faith.

24–25 Their worst fears relieved, the brothers now enter Joseph's house and enjoy the normal oriental courtesies of water to wash their feet and fodder for their animals (cf. 18:4; 19:2; 24:32; Luke 7:44). For their part, they do their best to make their "present" look worthy of the great man.

26–34 The third scene here, like the third in chap. 42, is Joseph's audience with his brothers. Both begin with the brothers prostrating themselves before Joseph, and both are dominated by the disparity in power and knowledge between him and his brothers; he knows who they are, but they do not recognize him (cf. 42:7–8). But whereas last time he spoke harshly to them, this time he is friendly.

26 "They . . . bowed down to the ground to him" (cf. 42:6). 42:9 then comments, "Joseph remembered the dreams which he had dreamed for them," implying that he noted the discrepancy between the dream of eleven brothers and his parents bowing down to him and the fulfillment when only ten brothers were present. Now there are eleven, but still no parents.

27–28 So this prompts the questions, "How is your old father you mentioned? Is he still alive?" to which they reply positively. But what Joseph thought about this news or what he proposes to do for his father is not revealed.

29 "He raised his eyes" often indicates that what is about to be seen is most important (13:10; 18:2; 22:4, 13; 33:1, 5; 37:25). "Benjamin his brother, his own mother's son." Hitherto in the audience scene, no relational terms have been used. The brothers are just "the men" and Joseph is "the man," but here suddenly Benjamin is called "brother" and "mother's son" to emphasize the bond between him and Joseph. Joseph asks, "Is this your youngest brother . . . ?" just to preserve the mystery of his own identity. "May God be gracious to you, my son," anticipates the priestly blessing of Num 6:25. On חנן, see *Comment* on 33:5. "My son" expresses friendliness between two unrelated men of unequal status (1 Sam 3:16; 4:16; 26:21, 25).

30 "His affection for his brother boiled up." The same idiom is used in 1 Kgs 3:26 of a mother's feelings for her child at the prospect of its death (cf. Lam 5:10; Hos 11:8). "On the verge of," lit. "he sought to"—for this nuance of בקש, cf. JPS, Sarna.

"He wept there" (cf. 42:24). This action, unseen by his brothers but reported to us, intimates that there is a difference between Joseph's public face and his private feelings. He is determined for some undisclosed reason to continue to hide his true identity from his brothers. Meanwhile, they are being lulled into a false sense of security.

31 "Serve the food." "Joseph hosts a meal for his brothers, who years before had callously sat down to eat while he languished in the pit" (Sarna, 302).

32 The Egyptian aversion to eating with foreigners is well attested in classical sources, such as Herodotus, Diodorus, Strabo listed by Dillmann. Here a very strong term is used: תועבה "disgusting" is often translated "abomination" in religious texts that describe practices totally abhorrent to God (e.g., Lev 18:22, 26, 29). Other customs regarded as "disgusting" by the Egyptians are mentioned in 46:34 and Exod 8:22(26).

33–34 Surprise at being invited to dine with the great man turns to amazement when they find themselves seated in order of seniority. Everywhere else the

verb "stunned" (תמה) describes a strong reaction to something both unexpected and unpleasant, a manifestation of divine judgment (e.g., Job 26:11; Ps 48:6[5]; Jer 4:9). How many of these elements are present here is unclear, but the brothers were certainly disconcerted. The narrative also notes that Benjamin, like his brother Joseph before him, was singled out for special treatment, receiving five times as much as any of the rest. Was this an attempt by Joseph to reproduce the earlier situation to see whether the rest of his brothers would show the same jealousy toward Benjamin as they had to him, or was it just a mark of his affection for his only full brother? However, neither the mystery of the seating arrangements nor the favoritism shown to Benjamin seems to have disturbed the party atmosphere, for plenty of alcohol seems to have put them all at their ease. "They drank and were merry with him" (cf. 9:21).

44:1–13 Hangovers in Scripture and in life are often unpleasant. While the brothers sleep off their banqueting, Joseph and his steward set them up for arrest. Compared with the parallel in 42:17, this scene is related in much greater detail.

1 Initially, Joseph appears generous, filling the sacks with as much grain as they can hold, not simply as much as they paid for, and returning the purchase price.

2 But then his silver cup, generally supposed to be calyx-shaped, though perhaps more like a bowl, according to C. L. Meyers (*The Tabernacle Menorah* [Missoula, MT: Scholars, 1976] 22–33; cf. Exod 25:31, 33–34), is to be hidden in Benjamin's sack. Why he should be picked out remains obscure for the moment.

3 The brothers must at this moment have been congratulating themselves on successfully completing their mission: they had the grain, Simeon, and Benjamin. Little did they realize that the hardest part of the journey was ahead of them.

4–5 "Why have you paid me back with evil . . . ?" The steward begins with a general accusation to produce maximum consternation. "The brothers had been received as guests, they had shared a meal with the master of the house, and now they had shown outrageous disdain for their host!" (Westermann 3:132). The uncertainty about their offense is heightened by the imprecise way in which he continues, "Isn't this what my lord drinks from . . . ?" which assumes that they know what he is talking about when of course they do not.

"Divines with." Divination with liquids, e.g., water, wine, oil, was well known in ancient times, and all types of divination are forbidden in the law (e.g., Lev 19:26; Deut 18:10). It is dubious whether this remark by the steward describes Joseph's practice; it is just a threatening comment to stress the gravity of the offense and to explain why he is sure the brothers are guilty.

7–9 The brothers protest their innocence in the most outspoken terms. They point to their past behavior: their return of the money on their previous trip. Their wild offer, that if any of them is a thief, he should die and the rest of them be enslaved, shows their confidence in their innocence. But in the total perspective of the Joseph story, the punishment of theft with slavery or death has echoes of their treatment of Joseph; the brothers are now offering to suffer as they made him suffer. So they are being fairer than they realize in making such an offer.

10 But Joseph's whole purpose is to single out Benjamin to see whether his brothers will sacrifice him as they did Joseph. Hence, the steward insists that only

the thief will be taken into custody; the others will be "free" (נקי) of guilt and responsibility.

11–12 The brothers' alacrity to dismount and submit to a search shows their own conviction of innocence. The tension of the occasion is neatly summed up in the comment "beginning with the eldest and ending with the youngest." The whole incident invites comparison with an earlier pursuit and search in which most of the brothers were involved. When Jacob ran away, Laban chased after them, overtook them, and searched for his teraphim (vv 4, 6, 12; cf. 31:23, 25, 33, 35), but failed to find them even though they were hidden in Rachel's tent. But this time Rachel's son is not so fortunate: "the cup was found in Benjamin's sack." On that occasion, Jacob had pronounced a death sentence on the guilty person, not realizing that his favorite wife was involved. Now the brothers have done the same. How will they react?

13 They say nothing, but their actions speak louder than words. When Joseph disappeared, it was only Jacob who tore his clothes (37:34); now all the brothers do, the first clear sign of fraternal solidarity. Whereas they had contrived to dispatch Joseph to Egypt, this time they voluntarily return with Benjamin to Egypt.

14–45:16 In this scene, the Joseph story reaches its climax with Judah's great speech prompting Joseph's self-disclosure.

14 "Judah and his brothers" already hints at the decisive part to be played by Judah in the coming interview. "He was still there." The brothers had left very early (v 3), so Joseph was still at his residence. "Fell" implies a more abject submission than 42:6, 43:26, "bowed down."

15 Joseph lays on the psychological pressure, claiming "a man like me is a good diviner." This remark demonstrates the brothers' powerlessness. They and the reader know they are guiltless, yet they have no means of demonstrating their innocence. They can only appeal for mercy, not justice.

16 So Judah does not claim to offer any proof of their innocence. Indeed, "It is God who has found out your servants' guilt" could have been intended to sound like a confession of their responsibility for stealing the cup, and doubtless this is how the ordinary Egyptians understood it. But probably Judah was confessing to the much greater crime of their maltreatment of Joseph, which on an earlier visit they had concluded caused them to be treated so harshly (42:21–23). It is therefore right that they all should suffer, so Judah repeats the previous offer to become Joseph's slaves.

17 But Joseph cannot be certain that they are really sorry for their earlier sin, and he puts them in a situation that replicates their situation twenty-two years earlier as closely as possible. He therefore invites them to return home without Benjamin, who will stay in Egypt as his slave.

18–34 But Joseph's ostensibly generous offer to his older brothers is met with the longest and most impassioned speech in Genesis, "a speech of singular pathos and beauty" (Driver), "the finest specimen of dignified and persuasive eloquence in the OT" (Skinner). On first reading, it may appear to be a simple recapitulation of what has already been said in the preceding chapters, but closer examination shows that this is far from the case. Aspects of earlier dealings that could annoy Joseph are not mentioned, while Judah includes fresh details of his father's reactions that he hopes will soften Joseph's stance; in fact, he mentions his father fourteen times.

The speech falls into three parts:

vv 18–29   Review of past
vv 30–32   Likely consequences if Benjamin does not return   ·
vv 33–34   Judah's offer of himself

The speech begins very formally, "with your permission, sir," and maintains a deferential mode of address, "your servant(s)," until his final appeal when he slips
in a direct personal form: "How can I go back to my father without the boy and
see the calamity that will befall my father?" (v 34).

Alter (*Art of Biblical Narrative,* 174–75) admirably sums up the thrust of this
speech:

> [T]his remarkable speech is a point-for-point undoing, morally and psychologically, of
> the brothers' earlier violation of fraternal and filial bonds. A basic biblical perception
> about both human relations and relations between God and man is that love is unpre-
> dictable, arbitrary, at times perhaps seemingly unjust, and Judah now comes to an ac-
> ceptance of that fact with all its consequences. His father, he states clearly to Joseph,
> has singled out Benjamin for a special love, as he singled out Rachel's other son be-
> fore. It is a painful reality of favoritism with which Judah, in contrast to the earlier
> jealousy over Joseph, is here reconciled, out of filial duty and more, out of filial love.
> His entire speech is motivated by the deepest empathy for his father by a real under-
> standing of what it means for the old man's very life to be bound up with that of the
> lad. He can even bring himself to quote sympathetically (verse 27) Jacob's typically
> extravagant statement that his wife bore him two sons—as though Leah were not also
> his wife and the other ten were not also his sons. Twenty-two years earlier, Judah engi-
> neered the selling of Joseph into slavery; now he is prepared to offer himself as a slave
> so that the other son of Rachel can be set free. Twenty-two years earlier, he stood with
> his brothers and silently watched when the bloodied tunic they had brought to Jacob
> sent their father into a fit of anguish; now he is willing to do anything in order not to
> have to see his father suffer that way again.

18   "Judah approached and said" (cf. *Comment* on 43:19). "Don't be angry"
(cf. 18:30, 32; 31:35).

"You are just like Pharaoh" explains Judah's deference and maybe hints at
Joseph's power to pardon.

19–23   Judah's summary of their first visit to Egypt tactfully omits any reference to the charge of spying, their imprisonment, or the detention of Simeon.
Even the demand to bring Benjamin is softened into "so that I can look after
him" (v 21), lit. "put my eye upon him," a phrase that generally expresses benevolent attention (cf. Jer 24:6; 39:12; 40:4). And Judah slips in more details about
the age of Jacob and his attachment to Benjamin. Jacob is "elderly"; Benjamin is
"young," the "child of his old age"; "his brother is dead" (not just "no more"
[42:13]); and "his father loves him," indeed "will die" if he does not return. The
acknowledgment of his father's favoritism is striking, for it was Jacob's love of
Joseph that caused his brothers to hate him. Now this same favoritism is cited as
ground for mercy; the other brothers, or at least Judah, have accepted that love
for their father must override all other grudges.

24–29   Judah continues to show his sympathy and identification with his father's
perspective as he sums up the discussion at home about whether Benjamin should

be allowed to accompany them to Egypt. Nowhere in 42:29–43:14 does Jacob say, "You know my wife bore me two sons" (44:27), but Judah puts his father's attitudes into words, even though he thereby in effect delegitimizes himself. Then he goes on to tell what Jacob surmised had happened to Joseph: "Surely he has been torn to bits [cf. 37:33], and I haven't seen him since." "Joseph now hears for the first time what happened at home when the brothers came back without him. He hears of his father's lament and grief that still persists; he hears the father's cry 'torn to pieces, torn to pieces!' which still echoes in the brothers' ears" (Westermann 3:136).

30–32 Judah then predicts Jacob's death if Benjamin fails to return. He makes Jacob's words his own, "bring down your servant's gray head in sorrow to the grave" (cf. 42:38). Once again adding a comment of his own, Judah underlines the bond of affection between Jacob and Benjamin: "his life is bound up with his."

33–34 Finally, Judah offers himself to stay behind as Joseph's slave. "Simply, Judah so feels for his father that he begs to sacrifice himself for a brother more loved than himself" (Sternberg, *Poetics*, 308).

To Joseph, of course, the speech again reveals even more than the speaker intended: the official version of his own death ("torn to pieces"), the reason for the delay in the brothers' return, the pain his testing as well as his fate must have given. Most important, if to a listener ignorant of the family situation and record, the brothers' attitude as expressed by their leader would appear admirable, then to one in the know it surely manifests nothing short of a transformation, from subnormal to abnormal solidarity. That the sons of the hated wife should have come to terms with the father's attachment to Rachel ("my wife") and her children is enough to promise an end to hostilities and a fresh start. That the second of these children should enjoy his brothers' affection is amazing. But that Judah should adduce the father's favoritism as the ground for self-sacrifice is such an irresistible proof of filial devotion that it breaks down Joseph's last defences. (Sternberg, *Poetics*, 308)

45:1–7 "Judah's speech in every respect brings the climax to the suspense, both with regard to the brothers' despair and to Joseph's inner emotion. . . . This seething of his emotion coincides precisely with the inner end of the test of the brothers, for Judah's words had shown that the brothers had changed. They obviously intend to treat Rachel's younger son, Benjamin, quite differently from the way in which they had formerly treated the elder son" (von Rad, 397).

1–2 Twice before, Joseph has wept when meeting his brothers but managed to hide it from them (42:24; 43:30). Now he sends out his attendants in order to make this a personal family occasion in which they could speak freely about the past without it becoming public knowledge. Nevertheless, the news soon reached the palace.

3 Tears mark deep emotion of both sorrow and joy, so the change in Joseph's demeanor must have shaken his brothers, but his statement "I am Joseph" left them בהל "dumbfounded," a term used of a paralyzing fear sometimes felt by those involved in war (Exod 15:15; Judg 20:41; 1 Sam 28:21; Ps 48:6[5]). "Is my father still alive?" Were this not such an emotional occasion, such a question would seem odd after Judah's long speech about his father, but it shows Joseph's chief concern now that he is reunited with the rest of the family. Judah had painted such a terrifying picture of the impact on Jacob of the loss of his sons that Joseph was worried.

4   His brothers were too terrified to speak, so Joseph identifies himself again,
"I am Joseph your brother whom you sold into Egypt." This last comment, while
confirming his identity, must have increased their alarm.

5–8   So Joseph hurries on to reassure them that he has no plans for revenge,
that their actions have served to further God's saving purposes. Four times he
makes the point: "God sent me before you to preserve life." "God sent me in
advance of you . . . to preserve . . . a great number." "[I]t was not you who
sent me here but God." "God has made me lord of all Egypt." In these verses we
have summed up the essence or theme of the Joseph story, termed by Longacre
its macrostructure: "Joseph's brothers, meaning to harm him, sold him into Egypt,
but in reality God sent him there so that he could save Jacob's family and many
others from death by starvation" (Longacre, *Joseph*, 43). Each episode in the story,
Longacre argues, relates to this macrostructure.

> Here in the scene of recognition the narrator indicates clearly for the first time what is
> of paramount importance to him in the entire Joseph story: God's hand which directs
> all the confusion of human guilt ultimately toward a gracious goal. After so much has
> been said exclusively about men's actions, it is surprising for Joseph in two statements
> to mention God as the real subject of the whole occurrence; God, not the brothers,
> "sent" Joseph here. Joseph veils the actual event with this alleviating expression. But it
> would be wrong to see only distracting friendliness in Joseph's remarks; rather, Joseph
> wants to state an objective truth, in which, to be sure, the enigma mentioned above,
> the question of how this activity of God is related to the brothers' drastically described
> activity, remains an absolutely unsolved mystery. The matter must rest with the fact that
> ultimately it was not the brothers' hate but God who brought Joseph to Egypt and more-
> over to "preserve life." (von Rad, 398)

5   "Don't be distressed." On this term for the most intense emotion, a mixture of rage and anguish, cf. *Comment* on 6:6.

6   See Pharaoh's dreams and Joseph's interpretation (41:1–57; cf. 8:22).

7   "God sent me . . . to make a remnant for you in the land and to preserve
for you a great number of survivors. שארית "remnant" here has the sense of surviving descendant as in 2 Sam 14:7.

פליטה "survivors" (cf. 32:9[8]; Exod 10:5). Westermann claims that since "remnant" and "survivors" are often paired in the prophets, this remark represents a
late expansion of the text. But the usage of both terms in both 2 Sam 14:7 and
Exod 10:5 makes this less plausible. In fact, the phrase "remaining survivors" (פליטה
נשארת) occurs in Exod 10:5 (cf. Gen 32:9[8]), which suggests the pairing could
be early. "To preserve" (life) is a key phrase in the flood story (6:19–20; cf. 7:3;
50:20), implying that Joseph is like Noah, an agent in the divine saving plan.

8   "A father to Pharaoh," i.e., his chief adviser. In other passages, priests and
prophets are spoken of as "father to" (Judg 17:10; 18:19; 2 Kgs 6:21; 13:14), because like real fathers they instructed their "sons." It is often surmised that the
underlying Egyptian title is *it-ntr* "father of the god" (i.e., Pharaoh), which was
given to a variety of high officials, such as clergy, who advised the crown. "Lord of
all his household" (cf. *Comment* on 41:39–40).

9–13   Joseph is so keen to see his father (cf. his first question in v 3, "Is my father
still alive?") that the gestures of greeting are postponed until later (vv 14–15). He

begins and ends by urging them to hurry (vv 9, 13). He promises them good pasture land near to his residence and plenty of provisions during the next five years of famine (vv 10–11).

10 "Goshen." "Its exact location and extent remain uncertain, but it was certainly . . . in the E Nile Delta" (K. A. Kitchen, *NBD*, 483). This area would have been close enough to the royal court in Memphis or Avaris for Joseph to have contact with his family, and later for Moses to conduct negotiations with his Pharaoh (Exod 7–12).

11 "I shall provide you with food" (cf. 47:12; 50:21; 1 Kgs 17:4, 9). "There are still five years of famine" repeats the point already made in v 6, doubtless because Joseph fears his father will be reluctant to move. "Become poor." In famines, the poor mortgaged their lands or sold their family and even themselves into slavery; some doubtless died (cf. 47:13–26).

12 "You . . . see with your own eyes," lit. "Your eyes are seeing," seems to stress that they are personal eyewitnesses (cf. Deut 3:21; 4:3; 7:19; 10:21; 2 Sam 24:3; Isa 6:5). "My brother Benjamin" is perhaps mentioned because Jacob may not trust his older sons. "My own mouth," that is, without interpreters (cf. 42:30).

13 "My father . . . my father," from first (v 3) to last, Joseph's dominating concern in this speech.

14–15 At last the emotional embrace. But only Joseph and Benjamin are said to have wept, suggesting that the other brothers are too stunned or still too distant from Joseph to weep for joy. But at last they talk to him, ending twenty-two years of noncommunication (37:4).

16–24 The penultimate scene tells of Pharaoh approving of Joseph's family coming to Egypt and making even more generous promises for the future and provision for the journey.

16 Note that not just Pharaoh but his courtiers approve of Joseph's family coming (cf. 41:37).

18 Whereas Joseph offered to let them live in "Goshen and be near me" (v 10), Pharaoh is more generous, "so that I may give you the best of the land . . . and you shall eat the choicest products."

19 He then goes on to make practical provision for the journey; Joseph had just told them to hurry (vv 9, 13). He tells them to take "carts"; probably large, two-wheeled ox-carts are meant (illustrated in C. Aldred, *JNES* 15 [1956] 150–52, plate 17), "for your youngsters, and wives, and carry your father and come." This final comment shows the Pharaoh to be a thoughtful, friendly man.

20 Like Joseph (cf. v 11), the Pharaoh is worried that the family may stay put because they cannot bring all their possessions (cf. 31:37) with them, so he says once again, "the best of the whole land of Egypt is *yours*" (cf. v 18).

22 "Change of cloaks." The phrase is used only here; elsewhere the phrase used is change of clothes (בגד; Judg 14:12–13, 19; 2 Kgs 5:5, 22–23). The cloak is the outer garment used as a blanket at night (Exod 22:26[27]). Judg 14 and 2 Kgs 5 show that fine clothes were a much appreciated gift in biblical times, but here they may also be a gesture of reconciliation, for Joseph's tunic had been the occasion of strife years before. Benjamin, as at the lunch (43:34), is given extra favors.

23 Promises of the "best of the land" (vv 18, 20) are already implemented as Joseph dispatches a caravan of the choicest Egyptian fare to his father Jacob. (She-asses provide milk.)

24 Joseph speaks one last injunction, "Don't be stirred up." Modern commentators see this as admonition not to quarrel, to become involved in recriminations over the past. Prov 29:9 may support this meaning for רגז "stir up." But most often the term describes fear, e.g., Exod 15:14, so many rabbinic commentators see Joseph encouraging them not to be afraid of robbers attacking the well-laden caravan. He could also be encouraging them not to have second thoughts about returning to Egypt for fear of how they may be treated in future. These different interpretations are not mutually exclusive.

25–28 This closing scene offers a marvelous contrast to the two previous occasions when the brothers returned to Jacob. Then he said, "Joseph has been torn to bits . . . I shall go down to Sheol in mourning" (37:33, 35). "There is no Joseph," "he is dead," "you will bring me down in my old age to Sheol with sorrow" (42:36, 38). Now he says, "Joseph my son is still alive. I will go down to see him before I die" (45:28).

26 "His heart stopped," lit. "his heart became weak" (cf. Hab 1:4; Ps 77:3[2]). "Believe" (cf. *Comment* on 15:6).

27 "His spirit revived." This is a unique and unexpected comment since the spirit is regarded as the life-giving element in man (cf. 2:7; 6:17; 7:15, 22). The closest parallels seem to be Ps 22:27(26), "May your hearts live for ever"; Ps 69:33(32), "let your heart revive"; and Isa 57:15, "to revive the spirit of the humble."

28 Jacob's final triumphant comment brings to a fitting conclusion this climactic episode in the Joseph story. To ascribe it to a different source merely because he is here called Israel (on this usage, cf. *Comment* on 37:3) is to truncate a powerful narrative and to spoil the parallels between this and the previous returns of his sons. It is characteristic of the more dramatic episodes of Genesis to end with a trenchant comment by one of the chief actors that often anticipates the next section. "Enough. Joseph my son is still alive. I will go down to see him before I die" perfectly fits this pattern in Genesis (27:45; 29:14; 30:24; 37:35; 42:38).

Explanation

The second journey to Egypt constitutes not the conclusion but the climax of the story of Joseph and his brothers. And within these chaps. 43–45, the appeal of Judah for Benjamin's release followed by Joseph's self-disclosure begins the process of reconciliation of the warring brothers, which leads them all to migrate to Egypt.

All episodes within Genesis may be read on various levels. The personal interaction and psychological development of the characters invite exploration. The place of a particular episode within the plot of the Joseph story also needs examination. And finally the contribution of an episode to the theme of Genesis as a whole requires discussion. We shall therefore look at these different aspects in turn.

The episode begins and ends with Jacob or Israel, the father of the twelve tribes. It is he who suggests at the beginning a trip to Egypt to "buy a little food"; it is he who finally agrees to go down himself "to see my son Joseph before I die" (43:2;

45:28). He is still the patriarchal head of his extended family, who takes the initiative and makes the ultimate decision to send Benjamin and later to move to Egypt, but in other respects he is very much yesterday's man. He is still living in the past, now lavishing all his love on Benjamin as formerly he did on Joseph, still regarding Rachel as his only wife, still mourning the death of Joseph (44:27–30), and still mistrustful of his other sons (43:6; 45:26). Yet eventually he concedes what they request, permission for Benjamin to accompany them to Egypt. Though this concession is wrung out of him reluctantly, he then takes charge, trusting as he did with Esau that a large present and divine grace will make "the man" merciful (43:11–14).

If Jacob's character and outlook seem to have changed little with the passing years, that cannot be said of his sons or at least of their chief spokesman, Judah. In some ways, they too are trapped by their past. In dealing with their father, they are forced to be less than frank, because they cannot confess their sins to him, which makes their pleas to him less than fully effective. Their guilty past, though rarely explicitly referred to, obviously weighs heavily on them. They interpret every setback in Egypt as divine punishment for their treatment of Joseph. On their first journey to Egypt, they said, "Truly we are guilty because of our brother. . . . Therefore this distress has befallen us" (42:21). Their fear when they discover the money in their sacks, their apprehension at being invited to lunch, their shock at being placed in order of age at table, all culminate in the discovery of Joseph's cup in Benjamin's sack, so that they all tear their clothes and return to the city.

There, before Joseph, Judah confesses their corporate guilt. "It is God who has found out your servants' guilt" (44:16) sounds like an admission that they did indeed steal the precious cup, but that is not what Judah means. He means their guilt about Joseph, and he then goes on to show in his plea for Benjamin how completely they have repented of their former sins. Benjamin is now Jacob's darling just as Joseph used to be "the only surviving son of his mother," whose life is bound up with Jacob's, whose disappearance would cause the death of his father. But whereas Judah had been happy to sell Joseph into slavery, make money on the deal (37:27), and disregard his father's distress, now Judah pleads to be allowed to "stay instead of the boy as my master's slave, and let the boy go back with his brothers. For how can I go back to my father without the boy and see the calamity that will befall my father?" (44:33–34). No more moving example of true contrition and repentance is to be found in Scripture, unless it be the parable of the prodigal son (Luke 15).

Apart from chap. 37, which painted Joseph as a precocious and uppity teenager, the Bible generally portrays him as a model, a faithful, chaste, wise, far-sighted, energetic, and, above all, God-fearing man. Yet in this section he appears in a somewhat different light, at least in handling his brothers. He seems bent on revenge, intent on setting them up and arresting them on a completely trumped-up charge. It appears that he only relents when Judah points out the suffering his injustice will cause to the elderly father back home. But though Joseph may have appeared the heartless foreign tyrant to his brothers, the narrator makes it plain that this is not the way he views Joseph's actions nor the view Joseph had of himself. In dealing with his brothers Joseph was deliberately putting

on a hard front, which he could only maintain by sometimes withdrawing to weep (42:24; 43:30), and when at last he is convinced of their change of heart, he weeps freely over them (45:1–2, 14–15). During his slavery and imprisonment, the narrator had said that the lord was with Joseph (39:2, 21, 23). Now Joseph makes the same point himself; four times he describes himself as God's agent: "God sent me before you to preserve life" (45:5; cf. vv 7–8); "God has made me lord of all Egypt" (45:9). Even his steward makes the same point, "Your god . . . must have put treasure into your sacks," even though he presumably knew it had been put there on Joseph's orders (43:23; cf. 42:25).

The statements about God's overruling of human affairs are undoubtedly the key to understanding the whole Joseph story. "It was not you who sent me here but God" (45:8), he says here. Later, after the death of Jacob, he reiterates the point: "You planned evil against me. It was God who planned it for good, . . . to keep many people alive" (50:20). All the episodes in the Joseph story contribute to demonstrating how God's purposes are ultimately fulfilled through and in spite of human deeds, whether or not those deeds are morally right. The apparent secularity of much of the story, which has led some commentators to see wisdom influence, is rather witness to the invisibility of God's actions in human affairs: only in retrospect can man see what God has been doing.

The relationship between divine sovereignty and human responsibility is a theological mystery that is something ultimately beyond human comprehension. Mysteries make us uncomfortable, and thus there is always a temptation to rationalize them, that is, to modify one belief to make it more compatible with the other, in this case to play down divine sovereignty by saying that certain actions fall outside the realm of God's control or, alternatively, to claim that, since all is predestined, man is not really answerable for his acts. But the Joseph story and the rest of Scripture insist that both divine sovereignty and human responsibility are true. The insistence on divine sovereignty is particularly clear here in "it was not you who sent me here but God" (45:8; cf. 50:20). The fulfillment of his childhood dreams, which foretold all his brothers bowing down to him, also showed that God had been in control of his career.

That God is the ultimate author of events is the presupposition of the biblical historians and prophets.

> "Ah, Assyria, the rod of my anger,
>   the staff of my fury!
> Against a godless nation I send him." (Isa 10:5–6)

> "Does evil befall a city,
>   unless the LORD has done it?" (Amos 3:6)

And the same view is maintained in the NT. Jesus says, "your heavenly Father feeds [the birds]" and "clothes the grass" (Matt 6:26, 30), and the apostles pray to the "Lord" who ordered affairs "to do whatever thy hand and thy plan had predestined to take place" (Acts 4:25, 28). It is belief in God's power to control affairs that underlies all intercessory prayer, for if God does not order our affairs, why pray for daily bread, healing, or world peace?

Yet, at the same time, human responsibility is equally strongly affirmed. That God used the brothers' hatred to send Joseph to Egypt does not, according to

Genesis, excuse that hate. The story spends most of its time portraying the cost of this hatred to the whole family: Jacob's unquenchable grief, Joseph's unjust imprisonment, and the brothers' own guilty consciences. Twenty-two years after selling him, they are acutely conscious of divine retribution overtaking them for their sins, "we are guilty because of our brother"; "God . . . has found out your servants' guilt" (42:21; 44:16). Full forgiveness and reconciliation only become possible after Judah has demonstrated in his words and in his willingness to take Benjamin's place a sincere repentance. Though Genesis emphatically states that God uses the sins of Joseph's brothers for good, it nowhere excuses their sins or pretends they can be forgotten; rather, they needed to be acknowledged and repented of.

The rest of Scripture treats human responsibility equally seriously. The king of Assyria may be God's rod, but he will in turn be punished for his boasting and pride (Isa 10:12). God may send evil on cities precisely because he punishes "Israel for his transgressions" (Amos 3:14). Similarly, the NT affirms that while Jesus' death is predestined, Judas bore full responsibility for it. "For the Son of Man goes as it has been determined; but woe to that man by whom he is betrayed!" (Luke 22:22). Thus both divine sovereignty and human responsibility are fully affirmed.

It is divine sovereignty that undergirds the optimism of Genesis. "God sent me to *preserve life,*" says Joseph. "God sent me . . . to preserve for you a great number of survivors" (45:5, 7), and later still "God meant it for good." The God of Genesis is a God of mercy (43:14) and grace (44:29), who answered Jacob's forlorn prayer "May God Almighty grant you mercy from the man, so that he sends back your other brother and Benjamin" (43:14) beyond his wildest dreams. But in so doing, God is not just proving his control of events but keeping his promise to the patriarchs that they should have a multitude of descendants, or as Joseph puts it, "a great number of survivors." Not only do the descendants of Abraham benefit from Joseph's work, but so do Egypt and the other peoples who came to Egypt to buy grain, so that in him some, though not all, the nations of the earth found blessing. Thus, not only does the story of Joseph offer just models of repentance, forgiveness, and reconciliation and illustrate the workings of divine providence in human affairs, but it reports yet another stage in the story of God's saving purpose for the whole world.

Third Visit of Joseph's Family to Egypt (46:1–47:31)

Bibliography

Battenfield, J. R. "A Consideration of the Identity of the Pharaoh of Gen 47." *JETS* 15 (1972) 77–85. **Betser, T.** "*ʾāpēs kāsep* and Its Consequences." (Heb.) *BMik* 28 (1982/83) 177–79. **Chirichigno, G.** *Debt Slavery in Israel and the Ancient Near East.* JSOTSup 141. Sheffield: JSOT, 1993. **Freedman, R. D.** "'Put your Hand under My Thigh.'" *BAR* 2 (1976) 3–4, 42. **Langlamet, F.** "Arithmétique des scribes et texte consonantique: Gen 46:1–7 et 1 Sam 17:1–54." *RB* 97 (1990) 379–409. **Loretz, O.** "Die Epitheta *ʾlʾlhj jsrʾl* (Gen 33:20) and *ʾlʾlhj ʾbjk* (Gen 46:3)." *UF* 7 (1975) 583. **McKenzie, B. A.** "Jacob's Blessing on Pharaoh: An

Interpretation of Gen 46:31–47:26." *WTJ* 45 (1983) 386–99. **Ruppert, L.** "Zur Offenbarung des Gottes des Vaters (Gen 46:1–5): Traditions- und redaktionsgeschichtliche Überlegungen." In *Die Väter Israels: FS J. Scharbert,* ed. M. Görg. Stuttgart: Katholisches Bibelwerk, 1989. 271–86. **Shibayama, G.** "Notes on *Yārad* and *ʿālāh:* Hints on Translating." *JBR* 34 (1966) 358–62. **Steiner, F.** "Enslavement and the Early Hebrew Lineage System: An Explanation of Gen 47:29–31; 48:1–16." *Man* 54 (1954) 73–75; repr. in *Anthropological Approaches,* 1985. 21–25.

Translation

[1] *So Israel and all who belonged to him set* [a] *out and came to Beersheba, and he offered sacrifices to the God of his father Isaac.* [2] *Then God said to him in a night vision,* [a] *"Jacob, Jacob." He replied, "Here I am."* [3] *Then he said, "I am El, the God of your father. Do not be afraid to go* [a] *down to Egypt, for I shall make* [b] *you into a great nation there.* [4] *I shall go down with you there, and it is I that shall surely* [a] *bring* [b] *you up again, and Joseph will put his hand on your eyes."*

[5] *So Jacob arose from Beersheba, and the sons of Israel lifted* [a] *Jacob their father, their youngsters, and their wives onto the carts which Pharaoh had sent to carry* [b] *them.* [6] *They also took their livestock and the possessions which they had acquired in the land of Canaan, and Jacob and all his descendants who were with him entered Egypt.* [7a] *He brought* [b] *with him to Egypt his sons and grandsons who were with him, his daughters and granddaughters, that is, all his descendants.* [a]

[8] *These are the names of the sons of Israel who came to Egypt, that is, Jacob and his sons. Jacob's firstborn, Reuben,* [9] *Reuben's sons, Enoch, Pallu, Hezron, and Carmi.* [10] *The sons of Simeon, Yemuel, Yamin, Ohad,* [a] *Yachin, Zohar,* [b] *and Shaul, the son of a Canaanite woman.* [11] *The sons of Levi, Gershon, Kehat, and Merari.* [12] *The sons of Judah, Er, Onan, Shelah, Peres, Zerah. Er and Onan died in the land of Canaan, and the sons of Peres were Hezron and Hamul.* [13] *The sons of Issachar, Tola, Puah, Yashub,* [a] *and Shimron.* [14] *The sons of Zebulon, Sered, Elon, and Yahleel.* [15] *These were the sons of Leah, whom she gave birth to for Jacob in Paddan-Aram, and also Dinah, his daughter. All these persons, his sons and daughters, came to thirty-three.*

[16] *The sons of Gad, Ziphyon,* [a] *Haggi, Shuni, Ezbon,* [b] *Eri, Arodi, and Areli.* [17] *And the sons of Asher, Yimnah, Yishwah, Yishwi, Beriah, and Serah their sister: the sons of Beriah were Heber and Malchiel. These were the sons of Zilpah, whom Laban gave to his daughter Leah, and she gave birth to them for Jacob, sixteen persons.*

[19] *The sons of Rachel, Jacob's wife, were Joseph and Benjamin.* [20] *There were born* [a] *to Joseph in the land of Egypt Manasseh and Ephraim, whom Asenath, daughter of Potiphera, priest of On, gave birth to for him.* [21] *The sons of Benjamin were Bela, Beker, Ashbel,* [a] *Gerah, Naaman,* [b] *Ehi, Rosh, Muppim, Huppim,* [b] *and Ard.* [22] *These are the sons of Rachel, who were born* [a] *to Jacob, fourteen persons in all.*

[23] *The son of Dan was Hushim.* [a] [24] *The sons of Naphtali were Yahsed, Guni, Yetser, and Shillem.* [a] [25] *These were the sons of Bilhah, whom Laban gave to his daughter Rachel, and she gave birth to them for Jacob, seven persons in all.* [26] *Every person who came to Jacob to Egypt and was descended from him, apart from Jacob's sons' wives, came to sixty-six persons all told.* [27] *There were two sons of Joseph who were born to him in Egypt. Thus all the persons who belonged to Jacob's household who came* [a] *to Egypt amounted to seventy.*

[28] *It was Judah that he sent before him to Joseph to discover* [a] *about the land of Goshen in advance of him. So they* [b] *came to the land of Goshen.* [29] *Then Joseph harnessed his chariot and went up to meet Israel his father at Goshen. Then he appeared* [a] *to him, fell*

on his neck, and wept over his neck again and again. ³⁰ *Then Israel said to Joseph, "I am ready* [a] *to die this time, now that I have seen* [b] *your face, because you are still alive."* ³¹ *So Joseph said to his brothers and his father's household, "Let me go up and tell* [a] *Pharaoh and say to him, 'My brothers* [b] *and my father's household, who were in the land of Canaan, have come to me.* ³² *The men are shepherds because they have flocks and herds, all of which they have brought* [a] *for themselves.'* ³³ *So if Pharaoh invites you and asks you what your work is,* ³⁴ *you shall say, 'Your servants have been owners of livestock from their youth until the present, both we ourselves and our ancestors,' in order that you may dwell* [a] *in the land of Goshen, for any shepherd is an abomination to the Egyptians."*

⁴⁷:¹ *So Joseph came and told* [a] *Pharaoh and said to him, "My father* [b] *and my brothers, their flocks and herds, and all that they have, have come from the land of Canaan, and they are now in the land of Goshen."* ² *So he took* [a] *a selection of five of his brothers and presented* [b] *them to Pharaoh.* ³ *Pharaoh said to his* [a] *brothers, "What is your work?" They said, "Your servants are shepherds, both we ourselves and our ancestors."* ⁴ *They said to Pharaoh, "We have come* [a] *as immigrants in the land,* [a] *because there is no pasture for your servants and because the famine is severe in the land of Canaan. So now please let your servants dwell in the land of Goshen."* ⁵ *So Pharaoh said to Joseph,* [a] *"Your father and your brothers have come to you.* ⁶ *The land of Egypt is yours. Settle* [a] *your father and brothers in the best of the land. Let them dwell in the land of Goshen, and if you know of any able men among them, appoint* [b] *them as chief stockmen over what belongs to me."*

⁷ *So Joseph brought* [a] *Jacob his father and stood him before Pharaoh, and Jacob blessed Pharaoh.* ⁸ *Then Pharaoh said to Jacob, "How many years have you lived?"* ⁹ *Jacob replied to Pharaoh, "My stay has lasted one hundred and thirty years. The years of my life are* [a] *few and bad.* [a] *They have not come* [b] *up to days of the years of my ancestors' lives in their stay."* ¹⁰ *So Jacob blessed the Pharaoh and left his presence.* ¹¹ *So Joseph settled* [a] *his father and his brothers and gave them a holding in the land of Egypt, in the best part of the land, in the land of Rameses, as Pharaoh commanded.* ¹² *Joseph provided* [a] *his father, his brothers, and all his household with as much food as their youngsters needed.*

¹³ *But there was no food in all the land of Egypt, for the famine was very severe, and the land of Egypt and the land of Canaan languished* [a] *because of the famine.* ¹⁴ *So Joseph scraped up all the money which was in the land of Egypt and the land of Canaan through selling grain, and he brought the money to Pharaoh's palace.* ¹⁵ *When the money of the lands of Egypt and Canaan was exhausted, all Egypt came to Joseph saying, "Give* [a] *us food. Why should we die before your eyes because* [b] *money has run out?"* ¹⁶ *Joseph replied, "Give me your livestock, so that I may give* [a] *you food* [b] *for your livestock, if money has run out."* ¹⁷ *So they brought their livestock to Joseph, and Joseph gave them food in exchange for their horses and for their livestock of sheep and goats and cattle and for their donkeys. So he provided them with food that year in exchange for their livestock.* ¹⁸ *When that year ended, they came to him the next year and they said to him, "We cannot disguise from my lord that our money is exhausted, that our livestock and animals belong to my lord. There is nothing left for my lord save our corpses and our land.* ¹⁹ *Why should we die before you, both we and our land? Buy us and our land for food so that we and our land can become Pharaoh's slaves. Give us seed so that we may live and not die and the land not be devastated."* [a] ²⁰ *So Joseph bought* [a] *up all the land in Egypt for Pharaoh, for each Egyptian sold his piece of land, because the famine was so severe, and the land became Pharaoh's.* ²¹ *As for the people,* [a] *he made them into slaves* [a] *from one end of Egypt to the other.* ²² *It was only the priests' land that he did not buy, because the priests*

*had an appointed portion from Pharaoh, and they used to eat*ᵃ *their assigned portion which Pharaoh gave them; therefore they did not sell their land.* ²³*Joseph said to the people, "Since I have bought your land today for Pharaoh, here is seed for you so that you can sow the ground.* ²⁴*When there is produce, you shall give a fifth to Pharaoh, but four parts shall*ᵃ *be yours for sowing your land and for eating by your households* ᵇ*and youngsters."*ᵇ ²⁵*They said, "You have saved*ᵃ *our lives.* ᵇ*May my lord be gracious to us,*ᵇ *and we shall become Pharaoh's slaves."* ²⁶*So Joseph made*ᵃ *a decree, which is still valid today, that the land of Egypt belongs to Pharaoh and he is entitled to a fifth. Only the priests' lands were set apart. They did not belong to Pharaoh.*

²⁷*So Israel settled in the land of Egypt in the land of Goshen. They held*ᵃ *land there and were fruitful and multiplied exceedingly.* ²⁸*So Jacob lived in the land of Egypt seventeen years. The days of Jacob's life came to one hundred and forty-seven years.* ²⁹*Then the time in Jacob's life drew near for him to die, so he called for his son Joseph and said to him, "If I have found favor with you, please place your hand under my thigh and swear you will treat me with kindness and loyalty. Please do not bury me in Egypt.* ³⁰*I shall lie with my forefathers, so you shall carry me up from Egypt and bury me in their grave." He replied, "I shall do as you say."* ³¹*He said, "Swear to me." So he took an oath for him. Then Jacob bent over at the head of his bed.*

Notes

1.a. Cf. n. 12:9.a.

2.a. Pl form "visions" has sg meaning. On the pl of "intensity," see GKC, 124e; on the pl of "generalization," see Joüon, 136j. On the use of def art, see GKC, 126r.

3.a. מ + inf constr ירד. On this form of the infinitive, see GKC, 69m.

3.b. 1 sg impf qal שׂים + 2 masc sg suffix.

4.a. Inf abs qal עלה. On use of qal inf abs with hiphil verb, see GKC, 113w; WOC, 582. Here used to contrast with going down (GKC, 113r).

4.b. 1 sg impf hiph עלה + 2 masc sg suffix.

5.a. Cf. n. 7:17.b.

5.b. Cf. n. 36:7.b.

7.a-a. On use of apposition in 46:6–7, cf. 8:18–19; cf. *SBH*, 40.

7.b. Cf. n. 39:14.a.

10.a. Omitted in Num 26:12; 1 Chr 4:24.

10.b. SamPent צהר; Num 26:13; 1 Chr 4:24 זרח.

13.a. So SamPent, G; Num 26:24; 1 Chr 7:1 read ישׁוב; MT יוב.

16.a. SamPent, G, Num 26:15 read צפן.

16.b. SamPent, S read אצבעון.

20.a. Cf. n. 4:18.a.

21.a. Probably add, with G (cf. 1 Chr 8:3), "And the sons of Bela were . . ."

21.b-b. Possibly read "Ahiram, Shafufam, and Hufam"; cf. Num 26:38–39.

22.a. Cf. n. 4:26.b.; GKC, 121b.

23.a. *BHS* suggests reading שׁוחם with Num 26:42.

24.a. SamPent, 1 Chr 7:13 read שׁלום.

27.a. Cf. n. 18:21.d. As pointed, def art + 3 fem sg pf qal בוא; cf. GKC, 138k.

28.a. ל + inf constr hiph ירה "to instruct." G reads "to meet"; SamPent "to appear before" (cf. *BHS*).

28.b. SamPent, S, Vg "he came."

29.a. Waw consec + 3 masc sg impf (apoc) niph ראה.

30.a. On this use of coh, see GKC, 108b; Joüon, 114c, n.

30.b. Inf constr ראה + 1 sg suffix.

31.a. Waw + 1 sg coh hiph נגד.

31.b. Initial position of subj prompted by verb בוא (*EWAS*, 36).

32.a. Cf. n. 43:2.a.
34.a. 2 masc pl impf qal יָשֻׁב.
47:1.a. Cf. n. 9:22.a.
1.b. On word order, cf. n. 46:31.b.
2.a. SamPent adds "with him."
2.b. Waw consec + 3 masc sg impf hiph יָצַג + 3 masc pl suffix.
3.a. SamPent, G "the brothers of Joseph."
4.a-a. Lit. "to immigrate to the land." On the position of an inf at the beginning of a sentence, cf. GKC, 114g; Joüon, 155r.
5.a. *BHS* proposed emendation unnecessary and not supported by G.
6.a. 2 masc sg impv hiph יָשַׁב.
6.b. Waw + 2 masc sg pf qal שִׂים + 3 masc pl suffix.
7.a. Cf. n. 2:19.c.
9.a-a. Word order here emphasizes "fewness and badness" of Jacob's days (*EWAS,* 15).
9.b. 3 masc pl pf hiph נִשָׂג.
11.a. Waw consec + 3 masc sg impf hiph יָשַׁב.
12.a. Waw consec + 3 masc sg impf pilpel כוּל.
13:a. 3 fem sg impf (apoc) qal לָהָה.
15.a. Cf. n. 11:3.a.
15.b. SamPent adds def art.
16.a. Cf. n. 17:2.a.
16.b. Insert with SamPent, G.
19.a. 2 fem sg impf qal שָׁמַם (Joüon, 82h; GKC, 67p).
20.a. Cf. n. 33:19.a.
21.a-a. So SamPent, G; cf. Vg; see *BHS*. MT reads "he transferred them into cities."
22.a. Cf. GKC, 112l; WOC, 535.
24.a. Fem pl subj (4 parts) with masc sg verb, not unparalleled (cf. Exod 28:7; 30:4; Joüon, 150l).
24.b-b. Not explicit in G.
25.a. 2 masc sg pf hiph חָיָה + 1 pl suffix.
25.b-b. On construction, see Joüon, 114bN.
26.a. Cf. n. 2:8.b.
27.a. Waw consec + 3 masc pl impf niph אָחַז.

Form/Structure/Setting

Chaps. 46–47 describe the third and final journey to Egypt by Jacob and all his sons. Whereas the first two journeys had just been visits to Egypt to buy grain, this final trip describes a long-term move by the whole family to settle there. Thus there are some obvious differences between this journey and the previous two: most noticeable is the absence of a return by the brothers to Canaan; instead Joseph is simply asked to swear that he will take Jacob back to Canaan for burial. In the description of the journey to Egypt, there are three new features: first, the vision encouraging Jacob to go (46:2–4); second, the list of Jacob's descendants who moved to Egypt with him (46:8–27), and third, the devastating effects of the famine in Egypt (47:13–26). All the additional features underline the importance of this move. Though these additions differentiate this journey from its predecessors, they do not obscure the parallels. All the journeys are prompted by Jacob's decision (42:1–2; 43:1–14; 46:1); they all climax with Joseph meeting his family (42:6–24; 43:26–45:15; 46:28–47:12); and they all conclude with Jacob mentioning his death (42:38; 45:28; 47:29–31).

Though we have assumed above that the traditional chapter division between 47 and 48 marks the end of the unit, it is not at all clear that this is correct; only Brueggemann and Longacre (*Joseph*) among recent commentators do this. Some

commentators make a break between chaps. 46–47. However, this truncates the account of Jacob's journey and makes his interview with Pharaoh an incidental extra feature (47:1–10), whereas Pharaoh's solicitude for Jacob's welfare in 45:16–21 surely requires a prompt audience as soon as the family arrives in Egypt. There is more justification for concluding the section at 47:12 or 10, and seeing 47:13–26 (Joseph's famine relief measures) as marking a new section (so Driver, Skinner, Sarna; cf. Longacre [*Joseph*]). Certainly 47:13–26 is a digression from the principal concern of chaps. 46–47—Jacob's move to Egypt. But it hardly begins a new section of its own, for 47:27 resumes 47:11–12. Nor are vv 13–26 quite such an erratic boulder as some commentators suppose, for in speaking to his brothers on their second journey, Joseph repeatedly insisted that the famine was only just beginning and that God had sent him to Egypt to preserve life (45:5–13). Now the truth of his words is demonstrated; indeed the Egyptians themselves say, "You have saved our lives" (47:25). Thus it seems better to regard this section as continuing at least to 47:27.

But does 47:28 mark the start of a new major section as suggested by the parasha division, Dillmann, Coats, and Humphreys (*Joseph and His Family*)? They hold that 47:27, "So Israel settled in the land of Egypt," marks the close of a section. Indeed by comparing 47:27 with 37:1, "Jacob settled in the land . . . of Canaan" (which marks the end of the family history of Esau), Coats argues that the main Joseph story ends here. But this parallel is inexact, for on the analogy of 36:1 (family history of *Esau*) and 37:1 ("*Jacob* settled"), we should expect different people to be referred to in 37:2 (family history of *Jacob*) and 47:27 (*Israel* settled). In fact, a better parallel to 37:1 is 50:22, "Joseph dwelt in Egypt." Thus there is a broad parallel between 36:1 and 37:2, "the family history of Jacob."

36:1	"family history of Esau"	37:2	"family history of Jacob"
36:8	"Esau settled"	47:27	"Israel settled"
37:1	"Jacob settled"	50:22	"Joseph settled"

It may be that the migration of Esau/Edom to Seir is seen as paralleling Jacob/Israel's move to Egypt.

36:2–5	List of Esau's descendants	46:8–27	List of Jacob's descendants
36:6–8	Esau's move to Seir	46:28–47:27	Jacob's move to Egypt
36:8	Esau settled	47:27	Israel settled

According to Westermann, 47:27–28 belongs together so that our section really ends with 47:28; he regards 47:13–26 as an appendage. He makes a new section begin with 47:29. He is justified in linking vv 27 and 28, for there is a similar sequence of verbs and train of thought in 50:22: "Joseph and his father's family *settled* in Egypt, and Joseph *lived* one hundred and ten years." But the grounds for making a break between 47:28 and 29 are slim. Obviously the death of Jacob, the concern of chaps. 48–50, comes into focus in 47:29, but it is already implied in v 28. More significantly, the opening clause of 48:1, "(And it was) after these things," marks a lapse of time and a significant new development (15:1; 22:1; 40:1), which suggests that the new section begins here. Furthermore, the content of 47:29–31 takes up the theme of Jacob's death already mentioned at the end of both previous journeys to Egypt (42:38; 45:28). It also closely parallels the parting words of

Joseph in 50:24–25 which, as already noted, is part of a section running in parallel with 47:27–37 (cf. 47:27//50:22). Finally, as noted many times before, it is characteristic of the editor's method to include in the final scene of a section a trailer for the next one (for example, 4:25–26; 6:5–8; 9:24–27). The arrangement here then conforms perfectly with the patterns employed elsewhere in the arrangement of Genesis.

Chaps. 46–47 thus subdivide as follows:

Scene 1: God appears to Jacob (46:1–4)
Scene 2: Jacob journeys to Egypt (46:5–27)
Scene 3: Joseph meets Jacob (46:28–34)
Scene 4: Joseph's brothers meet Pharaoh (47:1–6)
Scene 5: Jacob meets Pharaoh (47:7–10)
Scene 6: Joseph cares for his family and Egypt (47:11–26)
Scene 7: Jacob prepares to die (47:27–31)

There is a loose symmetry in this section. The first and the seventh scenes are both explicitly concerned with the patriarchal promises and their fulfillment: "Do not be afraid" (46:3; cf. 15:1; 21:17; 26:24; 35:17); "I shall make you into a great nation" (46:3; cf. 12:2; 17:6, 20; 18:18; 21:13, 18); "I shall go down with you" (cf. 28:15, 20; 31:3); "I am the God of your father" (cf. 26:24; 28:13; 32:10); "I shall bring you up again" (46:4; cf. 15:14; 12:1, 7; 13:15); "were fruitful and multiplied" (cf. 35:11; 17:6, 20; 28:3); "I shall lie with my forefathers" (cf. 23:1–20; 25:8–10; 35:29). Scenes 2 and 6 are both long and contain digressions from the main story line: the list of Jacob's sons in 46:8–25 and the description of Joseph's activity in 47:13–26. Scenes 3 and 5 match in both being concerned with Jacob meeting Joseph and Pharaoh, while scene 4 is the centerpiece in which Pharaoh grants the sons of Jacob permission to settle in the best of the land. The whole section presupposes what has gone before. 46:1–4 looks back to Joseph's invitation to come to Egypt and the patriarchal promises. The terminology of 46:5–7 echoes that of other great migrations in Genesis (e.g., 12:5; 31:18; 36:6), while the names of Jacob's wives and children show knowledge of 29:31–30:24; 34:1–31; 35:16–21; 41:45, 50–52. All the details about Joseph, his relationship to Pharaoh, and his job in dealing with the famine (46:29–47:26) hark back to his interpretation of Pharaoh's dreams and his appointment as vizier (41:15–57). These chapters then bring to a rounded conclusion the different facets of the Joseph story, and as Coats says (*From Canaan to Egypt,* 48), constitute "an element in the primary structure of the story."

Traditional source critics broadly agree about the character of the sources present here. The list of Jacob's sons (46:6–27) and the dates in 47:27–28 are P, because P is interested in genealogy and chronology. 47:7–11 is also assigned to P because its account of Jacob's presentation to Pharaoh duplicates that of his sons' presentation in 47:1–6. 46:1–5, Jacob's vision, is generally assigned to E, because it speaks of "God" and "Israel" rather than "the LORD" and "Jacob" (J features) and speaks of a revelation by night (dreams are supposedly a feature of E). The remaining verses of these chapters are assigned to J (i.e., 46:28–47:6, 12–26, 29–31). Coats alters this analysis slightly by assigning 47:7–11 to J instead of P. Westermann holds that in these two chapters the unified core of the Joseph story

(chaps. 37, 39–45) is combined with the two major sources of the Pentateuch, J and P. The core Joseph story is found in 46:5b (cf. 45:25–28); 46:28–47:6, 11–12, 27a. Then there is the end of the Jacob story J present in 46:1–5a; 47:29–31 and P in 46:6–27; 47:7–11, 27b-28, while 47:13–26 is a late appendage.

These analyses are overcomplex and are based on inadequate criteria. As we have seen, the Joseph story recounts three expeditions to Egypt, and chaps. 46–47 record the culminating one, which brought the twelve tribes of Israel there. It is, therefore, an editorial necessity to underline its importance by including various details that at first reading seem superfluous, e.g., the theophany in 46:1–5 and the lists of 46:6–26. As elsewhere in Genesis, there are clear indications that the arrangement of materials is due to the editor and that he should be identified with J. The closing paragraph, 47:29–31, universally ascribed to J, is a trailer for chaps. 48–50, a characteristic editorial device in Genesis. The opening scene (46:1–5) has, as Redford (*Biblical Story of Joseph,* 20), Westermann, and Blum (*Die Komposition,* 246–49, 298–99) have noted, closer parallels with 12:1–3; 15:13–16; 26:23–25; 31:11–18, which are generally regarded by modern critics as J passages. This makes it likely that we have here P material framed by J material and J's own editorial activity. Indeed, the longest section with the strongest claim to be from P, the list of Jacob's sons, (46:6–26) as Skinner pointed out, may well show marks of accommodation to the tradition of J. Note the mention of Dinah (46:15; cf. chap. 34) and the death of Er and Onan (46:12; cf. chap. 38). The whole organization of this list of descendants (46:5–27) and the comments in 46:28–47:27 parallel 36:2–8, which lends weight to the idea that an originally shorter list and a comment on a move and resettlement by Jacob have been expanded by the principal editor of Genesis.

Comment

1–4 The first scene recounts Jacob's sacrifice at Beersheba and the vision that he received there. To emigrate to Egypt was as momentous a move as Abraham's journey from Ur (12:1–3) or Jacob's flight to Paddan-Aram (28:1–22) or his return to Canaan (31:3–54), all of which were encouraged by visions. This revelation occurred at Beersheba, home base for Isaac (cf. 26:23–25), so it is not surprising that echoes of all these passages are found here. Such a move as Jacob is undertaking requires divine sanction, the more so in that to leave Canaan is to retreat from the promised land. Without divine approval, such a move could seem like unbelief.

This vision occurs not simply at a turning point in Jacob's life; it is also the last time God is recorded as speaking to the patriarchs. The next recorded revelation takes place in the time of Moses. This, then, is the culmination of all the promises made to the patriarchs, and it picks up motifs from other great moments of revelation (e.g., 15:1–21; 17:1–21; 22:1–18). God, as it were, reminds Jacob of all the promises made to him in his own lifetime and to his forefathers Abraham and Isaac before him.

1 "Israel" is the preferred name where travel to and from Egypt is concerned (cf. *Comment* on 42:5). "Set out" (cf. 12:9; 20:1; 35:21), presumably from the Hebron area (cf. 37:14). "Beersheba" is some twenty-six miles (forty kilometers)

south of Hebron and marks the practical southern border of the land (cf. "from Dan to Beersheba," 2 Sam 24:2). Beyond Beersheba, cultivation is difficult. The desert prevails until one reaches Egypt. So offering a sacrifice at this point is appropriate (cf. 31:54). Setting out on a major journey, Jacob desired God's blessing and therefore sacrificed (cf. mentions of altar building: 12:7, 8; 13:18; 22:9; 26:25; 33:20; 35:1, 3, 7). זבח "sacrifice" is a general term for sacrifice, often restricted to peace offerings (see Lev 3), which could be offered in making vows, or as acts of thanksgiving. Such motives would be appropriate here. The offering of sacrifice sometimes is seen as a preliminary to prophetic inspiration (Num 23:1, 14, 29; Ps 50:5; Isa 6:6).

2 "Night vision." Westermann, on the basis of Ezek 8:3; 40:2, argues that this is a late phrase. But 1 Sam 3:15 (cf. Num 12:6) shows it can be used in an early text of a purely auditory experience at night. The terminology and content point to Jacob as a prophet (cf. Abraham in chaps. 15, 18). "Jacob, Jacob." He replied, "Here I am" (cf. the summons in 31:11). The insistent repetition of his name recalls 22:11, the climax of Abraham's final test and direct revelation of God. He also responded "Here I am" (cf. 1 Sam 3:4–10). Moses too was summoned—"Moses, Moses"—and replied, "Here I am" (Exod 3:4).

3 "I am El, the God of your father." On El, cf. *Comment* on 14:18 (cf. 16:13; 17:1; 31:13; 33:20; 35:1; *Introduction*, "The Religion of the Patriarchs"). "God of your father" is a particularly frequent epithet in the Jacob stories (cf. 28:13; 31:5, 29, 42, 53; 32:10[9]; cf. 26:24). Not only does this self-description link this occasion with all the previous moments of revelation to the patriarchs, but it looks forward to the next great moment, i.e., the call of Moses: "I am the God of your father, the God of Abraham, the God of Isaac, and the God of Jacob" (Exod 3:6).

"Do not be afraid" is a typical introduction to a prophetic salvation oracle (e.g., Isa 7:4), also used in the closely similar revelations to Abraham (15:1) and Isaac (26:24). "To go down to Egypt." Abraham had been fearful entering Egypt (12:10–13), but Jacob should not have had the same grounds for anxiety, since he had been invited by Joseph, ruler of the whole land, and seems to have set out before receiving this vision. His apprehension must rather be assumed to arise out of the clash between the patriarchal promise of the land and his present necessity and desire to see Joseph. So the vision goes on to reassure him that, despite this apparent conflict with the divine plan, moving to Egypt has God's approval. So the great promises made to Abraham and Isaac in the past are reaffirmed and reapplied: "I shall make you into a great nation." This is closest in terminology to 12:2; 17:20; 18:18; 21:18, but it also sums up the repeated promises of the multitude of descendants Abraham will have. However, there is a new element here; "there" announces that great nationhood will be achieved in Egypt and not in Canaan.

4 "I shall go down with you" reiterates another familiar theme of the patriarchal narratives, God's protecting presence that guarantees blessing (cf. 26:24; 28:15, 20; 31:3, 5, 42; 39:2–3, 21, 23). It is a promise that will later be made to Moses (Exod 3:12) and Joshua (Josh 1:5).

"It is I that shall surely bring you up." The personal pronoun "I" and the infinitive absolute, "surely bring up," make this statement very emphatic. This is not merely a promise that Jacob will be buried in Canaan but, like 15:13–16, the

only comparable statement in Genesis, an announcement of the exodus. Once again this remark harks back to past promises and looks forward to the future exodus (cf. Exod 3:8, 17).

Finally, "Joseph will place his hand on your eyes." "The concluding promise is most unusual and moving" (Westermann, 3:156). It is a promise of a peaceful death at which Joseph will be present to close his eyes (cf. 15:15). From the great national concerns that have dominated the rest of the announcement, God finally deals with Jacob's most immediate and intimate concern. A frail and elderly man is assured that God will grant his dearest wish.

5–27 The second scene is comparatively long, which helps to underline the significance of Jacob's move to Egypt. Most of this passage is taken up with the list of Jacob's descendants, but the opening comments also help to make the point about this journey's importance. Some phraseology echoes key terms from the flood story—"enter" // "bring in" (vv 6–7; cf. 6:18–20), "descendants" (vv 6–7; cf. 7:3)—while "the possessions which they had acquired in the land of Canaan" echoes the descriptions of earlier major migrations (v 6; cf. 12:5; 31:18; 36:6). These parallels implicitly compare Jacob's move to Egypt to Noah's entry into the ark, Abram's migration to Egypt, Jacob's to Canaan, and Esau's to Edom. More obviously, the reference to the carts to carry Jacob (v 5) refers back to Pharaoh's command and Joseph's provision (45:19, 21; cf. 45:27). Finally, the double mention of זרע "his descendants" (vv 6–7), a word used elsewere in the patriarchal narratives of the promised offspring, underlines God's fidelity to his covenant. The presence of seventy promised descendants shows that God keeps his promises and will in due course fulfill the promise of their return to Canaan as a great nation (vv 3–4).

8–27 This list of Jacob's descendants gives an impression of those who entered Egypt at that time with him. That Jacob went down to Egypt with seventy persons is mentioned in Exod 1:5; Deut 10:22. Often seventy seems a round number for a large group or family (Exod 24:1, 9; Judg 8:30; 12:14), and Gen 10 records that seventy nations were descended from Noah. Thus the nation of Israel represents the family of man in microcosm. But here an attempt is made to specify exactly who made up the seventy souls who went down to Egypt. It is evident, as Westermann argues, that an old descendants' list has been used here. It is not a list of tribes or clans but of individuals. This is shown by the character of the names: they fall into three main types, animal names, parts of the body, and theophoric names. "These three groups prove that the names have been given to children on the occasion of their birth" (Westermann, 3:161). That the list is early is suggested by the use of El "God," not Yahweh "the LORD," in the theophoric names (cf. *Introduction*, "The Religion of the Patriarchs") and the parallels with names in the book of Judges. It is possible that originally this was a list of seventy descendants of Jacob, thirty-three descended from Leah, sixteen from Zilpah, fourteen from Rachel, and seven from Bilhah. However, the editor noticed that this list did not correspond exactly to those who went down to Egypt with Jacob, for Er and Onan died in Canaan (38:7, 9) and Joseph's sons were born in Egypt (41:50–52). So he annotated the list to make these points clear (vv 12, 20, 26–27). That means just sixty-six of Jacob's descendants entered Egypt with him (v 26). However, if one includes Dinah (v 15) in the group led by Jacob and views

Joseph's journey to Egypt as part of the movement of the whole clan of Jacob, one can still affirm that in total seventy persons belonging to Jacob's household went down to Egypt (v 27).

8–9 On "Reuben," cf. 29:32; 30:14; 35:22–23. For "Enoch," cf. *Comment* on 4:17. Note that the eldest grandsons of Adam and Jacob have the same name, Enoch. "Pallu" is possibly short for "(God is) a miracle worker" (so Noth, *Personennamen*, 38, 191; *EM* 6:482). "Hezron" is the same name as Judah's grandson (46:12), but its meaning is uncertain (*EM* 3:276). "Carmi," also the name of Achan's father, is most plausibly associated with כרם "vineyard," so Carmi may originally have been a place name or short for "vineyard of (God)" (cf. Isa 5:7; *EM* 4:322).

10 On "Simeon," cf. 29:33. The meaning of "Yemuel" is uncertain (cf. *EM* 3: 700–701). "Yamin" possibly means "lucky" (cf. *EM* 3:701; cf. *Comment* on 35:18). The meaning of "Ohad" is unknown: its absence from parallel lists in Num 26:12; 1 Chr 4:24 perhaps indicates he had no descendants or that they died out (*EM* 1:122). "Yachin" is short for "(may God) strengthen him" (cf. Jehoachin [2 Kgs 24:6] and the temple pillars Jachin and Boaz [1 Kgs 7:21]). "Sahor" is apparently a color, perhaps "white" (cf. KB, 956). "Shaul" is the name of another man in 36:37–38.

11 On "Levi," cf. 29:34. "Gershon": Noth's suggested interpretation (*Personennamen*, 223) that it means "bell" is unproved. "Kehat" is perhaps related to Ugaritic *Aqht* and is of uncertain meaning. De Moor (*BO* 26 [1969] 106) has suggested "obedient." "Merari" probably means "strong" (so KB, 604; *EM* 5:475).

12 Cf. 29:35; 38:3–4, 29–30; 46:9; "Hamul" means "spared."

13 For "Issachar," cf. 30:18. "Tola" may mean "worm," perhaps anticipating this clan's later involvement in the dye trade (*EM* 8:466). "Puah" means "madder" according to Noth (*Personennamen*, 225), possibly another clan involved in dyeing. "Yashub" is short for "may (God) return," i.e., to save or grant another child. "Shimron" is very like the place name "Shomron," i.e., "Samaria."

14 On "Zebulon," cf. 30:20. For "Sered," the meaning is unknown. "Elon" means "oak." "Yahleel" means "may God (El) be kindly" to the child (so Noth, *Personennamen*, 204) or "wait for God" (BDB, 404a).

15 Dinah is mentioned here and in 30:21, because of the story about her in chap. 34. She is not included in the total of "thirty-three" descendants of Jacob listed here, but Er and Onan, despite dying in Canaan, are, and so are "Hezron and Hamul," who were probably born in Egypt (cf. v 12).

15–18 These verses list the sixteen descendants of Zilpah, Leah's maid. Both wives, Leah and Rachel, bear twice as many descendants of Jacob as do their maids: Leah has thirty-three, whereas Zilpah has sixteen. Rachel has fourteen, whereas Bilhah has seven.

16 On "Gad," cf. 30:11. "Ziphyon" is unexplained. "Haggi" is possibly short for "festival of (God)"; a birth on a festival was especially joyous (*EM* 3:27). "Shuni" is unexplained. "Ezbon," KB suggests, is related to Arabic *ʾaṣaba* (verb) "be bald." If the SamPent "Ezbaon" is followed, it may be related to the noun אצבע "finger," a sign of good luck to the family of the new child. "Er" means "watchful" (so Noth, *Personennamen*, 228). The meanings of "Arodi" and "Areli" are uncertain.

17 For "Asher," cf. 30:13. "Yimnah" is probably short for "may (God) allot him (his portion)" (KB, 397; *EM* 3:703) or possibly "luck" (cf. BDB, 412b; Noth,

Personennamen, 224). "Yishwah," "Yishwi" may be alternatives, the meaning of which is unclear (but *EM* 3:894: "proper, suitable"). "Beriah" means "outstanding," according to Noth, *Personennamen,* 224. "Serah" is probably a shortened theophoric name of Elserah, Yisrahel. Serah may mean "cause to flourish" (Noth, *Personennamen,* 180; *EM* 8:391–92). "Heber" means "companion." "Malchiel" means "My king is El."

18 "Sixteen persons" are just fewer than half her mistress Leah's total of thirty-three (v 15).

19–20 Cf. 30:24; 35:18; 41:50–52.

21 The rest of the Joseph story implies that Benjamin was still quite young when he entered Egypt, and it is therefore unlikely that he then had ten sons of his own. This is another clue to the different original purpose of this list. It may well be that the editor realized Benjamin's sons were not yet born when he entered Egypt but that he thought it was right to include them, for as Heb 7:10 puts it, they were "still in the loins of [their] ancestor."

For "Bela," cf. 36:32. "Beker" means "young camel." "Ashbel." The meaning is uncertain, possibly "with a long upper lip" (so Noth, *Personennamen,* 227). "Gera" is short for "Sojourner of some god" (cf. "Germelkart," i.e., adherent of god [Melkart] [*EM* 2:550]). "Naaman," lit. "pleasantness," is also a god's name (BDB, 654; *EM* 5:893). "Ehi," if correct, is short for "Ahi (god's name)" or Ahiram, "My brother (i.e., the god) is exalted of Ram." "Rosh," "Muppim." See *Notes* for possible textual corruption here; "Shupham," as in Num 26:39, means "viper." "Huppim" (or possibly "Huppam"). The meaning is uncertain. "Ard." Noth (*Personennamen,* 227) suggests that this name and Arodi (v 16) mean "hunch-backed," but this is not certain. Alternatively, it may represent a short form of "Ard-god's name," i.e., "servant" of a god.

23 For "Dan," cf. 30:6. For "Hushim," the meaning is unclear (cf. *EM* 3:65–66).

24 For "Naphtali," cf. 30:8. "Yahsed" means "may God (El) grant him a share or be gracious" (so Noth, *Personennamen,* 204). "Guni" perhaps is a partridge (so KB, 176). "Yetser" is probably short for "Yetsarel," i.e., "El (God) has moulded, created" (cf. 2:7; *EM* 3:761). "Shillem" is short for "(God) has rewarded (the mother with a child)" or "(God) has replaced (a dead child)" (*EM* 8:693).

26–27 On the arithmetic of the list, see *Comment* above on vv 8–27. "70 is understood here to be a typological rather than a literal number. It is here used, as elsewhere in the biblical literature, to express the idea of totality" (Sarna, 317). It thus expresses the notion that all Israel entered Egypt when Jacob's family went there (cf. 15:13).

28–34 After the pause in the narrative occasioned by the list of Jacob's descendants, the account of the journey in vv 5–7 resumes to describe the meeting of Jacob and Joseph. Now Jacob's dearest wish is fulfilled, and he pronounces himself ready to die (v 30). Yet apart from this remark and Joseph's weeping, the description is brief and low key—almost an anticlimax. Joseph appears more concerned about his brothers' forthcoming interview with Pharaoh, for which he coaches them carefully.

28 Judah continues to take a leading part in arranging the reunion of Joseph and Jacob (cf. 43:3–10; 44:14–34). It is fitting that as Judah's scheme led to the parting of father and son (37:26–27), so he should oversee their reunion.

"To discover about" is unusual, for this verb should be followed by the object, so the SamPent "to appear before" may be preferable. For "Goshen," cf. *Comment* on 45:10.

29 "Harnessed his chariot." This superfluous detail (cf. 22:3) hints at the importance of the journey. "Appeared to him." Elsewhere in the patriarchal stories this verb is always used of God appearing to man, and its use here draws attention to the overwhelming impression on Jacob of the power, grandeur, and graciousness of Joseph in his own chariot attended by numerous servants. "Fell on his neck . . . wept." It is possible, as Ramban, Jacob, and Leibowitz suggest, that the subject of "fell . . . wept" is Jacob, for sometimes in Hebrew subjects of a string of verbs change without it being made explicit. However, it seems more likely that Joseph weeps over Jacob here, just as earlier he had wept over Benjamin when they met (45:14). Or it could be deliberately ambiguous to indicate that both wept over each other.

30 Jacob's hopeless lament, "I shall indeed go down to Sheol mourning" (37:35; cf. 42:38; 44:29), is at last turned into a tranquil Nunc Dimittis (Luke 2:29). The purpose of his journey is fulfilled (cf. 45:28), and he is ready to die in peace.

31 Joseph's chief concern now is to secure his family's position in Egypt. Pharaoh had encouraged them to come (45:16–20), but he now has to be told they have arrived. As Westermann observed (3:168), this repetitiveness is no sign of different sources, simply a mark of courtly style.

32–34 Heavy emphasis is placed on their occupation as herdsmen and shepherds and that they have brought their livestock with them. This seems to be intended to reassure Pharaoh that Joseph is not about to indulge in a bout of nepotism by filling the Egyptian civil service with his relatives. His brothers have been herdsmen from their youth and intend to continue to look after their flocks in the future. Furthermore, the insistence that they have brought their livestock with them shows that they do not intend to be a burden on the state, but that they do need suitable pastureland. This should encourage Pharaoh to settle them "in the land of Goshen" (v 34). In inviting them, Pharaoh had not specified where they should live (45:16–20), though Joseph himself had mentioned "Goshen" (45:10). On the different terms, מקנה "livestock," צאן "sheep, goats," בקר "cattle," see *Comment* on 4:20.

"For any shepherd is an abomination to the Egyptians" (cf. *Comment* on 43:32). If this was the Egyptian attitude, it seems odd that Joseph should have stressed it so much. Egyptian literature does not disclose a particular dislike of shepherds, though they are rarely portrayed in their paintings. Rather, their antipathy is probably an example of the widespread distrust and fear of nomadic peoples by settled urban dwellers (cf. modern attitudes towards gypsies and hippies; Vergote, *Joseph en Égypte*, 188–89). By drawing attention to their lifestyle, Joseph hoped that Pharaoh would assign them land on the margin of Egypt, e.g., in an area like Goshen. As the next scene describes, his ploy succeeded.

47:1–6 These verses constitute the central scene of this episode, the encounter between Pharaoh and the sons of Jacob, in which he grants permission for them to settle in Egypt. Courtly propriety is suggested rather than described. Joseph announces his brothers first, and after the royal interview with them is over, Pharaoh directs him in lofty stilted tones how they are to be treated.

1 As he promised (46:31–32), Joseph informs Pharaoh of his brothers' arrival. He mentions in passing that they are already in Goshen, planting the idea perhaps that they might be allowed to stay there.

2 Joseph takes just five of his brothers to be formally presented to Pharaoh.

3–4 As Joseph had foreseen, the Pharaoh asks them about their occupation, and they duly give the prescribed reply, "Your servants are shepherds" (cf. 46:34). They continue in deferential manner (suggested by the speech formula "they said to Pharaoh"; cf. Longacre, *Joseph*, 183–84), making the point that they have only come as immigrants because the famine is so severe. The use of the term גור "to be an immigrant" is suggestive. It fulfills the prophecy in 15:13, and ever afterwards the Israelites looked back to their sojourn in Egypt as a period of oppression. Because of their experience of being immigrants, they are often urged in the law to be considerate toward immigrants and their needs (e.g., Exod 22:20[21]; 23:9; Lev 19:34; Deut 10:19).

"The famine is severe in the land"; cf. 12:10; 26:1; 43:1. In an otherwise very succinct account of the audience, this little detail perhaps suggests the chattiness of Joseph's brothers; certainly they exceeded Joseph's brief by actually asking to be allowed to settle in Goshen (cf. 46:34).

5–6 But the audience went well. Pharaoh allowed them to settle in the best of the land of Goshen. Indeed, he offered them jobs as royal stockmen. "This office is mentioned frequently in Egyptian inscriptions since the king possessed vast herds of cattle; Rameses III is said to have employed 3,264 men, mostly foreigners, to take care of his herds. The appointment of some of Joseph's brothers to supervise the king's cattle means that they are to be officers of the crown and thus will enjoy legal protection not usually accorded aliens" (Sarna, 319).

"So Pharaoh said to Joseph." Note that although the brothers spoke to Pharaoh, he replied to Joseph. This is suggestive of courtly decorum: the great Pharaoh makes his decisions known to his chief minister, perhaps after the brothers have left his presence. Indeed, his speech to Joseph is pompous and formal as befits a Pharaoh issuing an important decree.

7–10 After the brothers' audience, Jacob is introduced to the Pharaoh. Whereas the previous scene was stiff and formal, the atmosphere here is more intimate and relaxed. Jacob does not call himself "your servant," as the brothers did (v 3); instead he talks about himself naturally in the first person "my" (v 9). Whereas Jacob's sons had come to Pharaoh requesting favors, here Pharaoh is being done a favor by the old man visiting him. It is Jacob who blesses Pharaoh, i.e., prays for Pharaoh's welfare (on this key term in Genesis, cf. *Comment* on 1:22; 12:2–3), both on his arrival and on his departure. Pharaoh simply asks respectfully, "How many years have you lived?" Jacob's great age demands respect from the all-powerful ruler of Egypt. Jacob's reply, "Few and bad," are hardly expected from a man aged one hundred and thirty whose son has risen to be vizier of Egypt, but they are a poignant comment on Jacob's life, his flight to Mesopotamia, the rape of his daughter, his favorite wife's death, and his favorite son's apparent death. He is now so infirm that he must be carried to court and "stood before Pharaoh." Yet tragic though his earthly life seems to have been, he is deferred to by the Pharaoh, who is twice blessed by Jacob. Jacob, who in his youth cheated to obtain blessing, is now the source of blessing, not just to his family but, as

Westermann observes (3:171), to all the families of the earth. And because the Pharaoh has acknowledged Jacob's special status by receiving him graciously and honoring his sons, he and his countrymen may expect to find blessing through Jacob and his descendants (28:14). The most immediate fulfillment of this blessing is Joseph's rescue of Egypt from the effects of famine (47:11–27).

11–27 The penultimate scene of this section matches the second scene (46:5–27) in being lengthy: in both scenes there is a long digression, which may have originally been separate from the surrounding narrative. In 46:8–25 there is a list of Jacob's descendants, and here in vv 13–26 there is an account of Joseph's relief measures, prefaced (vv 11–12) and concluded (v 27) by a summary of what he did for his family. But though Westermann may be correct to think that 47:13–26 once circulated independently, he is wrong to argue that it is therefore a late appendage. Traditional analysis that regards this passage as integral to J is more appropriate, for it is integral to the narrative's story line and theology. Joseph's great prediction was that Egypt should suffer seven years of severe famine. Thus far there have been passing references to the effects of the famine (e.g., 41:56) but no full-blown description of it, which is at last provided here. Second, this account of Joseph's activity shows him fulfilling the promise that through Jacob's descendants all the world should find blessing (28:14). So this account of his benevolent rule of Egypt is very appropriate here. And the grateful Egyptians themselves acknowledge, "You have saved our lives" (v 25), an expression Joseph himself uses twice to explain his providential mission, "God sent me before you to preserve life" (45:5; cf. 50:20). So this passage is an integral part of the book of Genesis.

11 First, though, Joseph fulfills the Pharaonic command of 47:6. In two small respects the fulfillment deviates from the command. First, Joseph grants his brothers a "holding" (אֲחֻזָּה), i.e., a permanent inheritance in Egypt. On this term, cf. 17:8; 23:9, 20; *THWAT* 1:107–10; G. Gerleman, *ZAW* 89 (1977) 313–25. They thus enjoy more rights than the typical immigrant. Second, he settled them "in the land of Rameses," not the land of Goshen. In fact, the phrase "land of Rameses" occurs only here and is apparently another designation of Goshen, which was near the city of Rameses (Exod 1:14; 12:37), a late name for a town in the area (cf. J. J. Bimson, *Redating the Exodus and Conquest,* JSOTSup 5 [Sheffield: JSOT, 1978]).

12 "Joseph provided his father . . . ," thus fulfilling the promise made to his father in 47:11.

13–26 The primary purpose of this account of Joseph's measures is to show the severity of the famine and the desperate plight of the Egyptians that he alleviated. Three stages in the famine are described:

1. Egyptians exchange money, i.e., silver, for grain (13–14)
2. Egyptians mortgage herds for grain (15–17)
3. Egyptians mortgage land and become royal slaves for grain (18–26)

Thus at the end of the famine all Egyptians, save the priests, were serfs, that is, tenants of royal lands paying one-fifth of their produce to the crown (vv 24–25), a situation that still prevailed in the author's day (v 26).

This account has roused the curiosity of Egyptologists and biblical historians, who have used it to try to date Joseph's career and the period in which the account was written up. But too little is known about Egyptian economic history to give a definitive answer to either question. Vergote (*Joseph en Égypte*) argues that the details of Egyptian life suggest the account came from the nineteenth dynasty, roughly the time of Moses (thirteenth century B.C.); de Vaux (*History of Israel*) surmises on the same basis that it originated in Solomonic times (tenth century), whereas Redford (*Biblical Story of Joseph*) thinks that it comes from Saitic times (seventh century B.C.) or later.

But "although we cannot give a precise date to the story of Joseph on the basis of this description of the Egyptian land system, it cannot be denied that the essential aspects of the outline are correct. Two facts that are established beyond doubt, for example, are the sovereign right of the Pharaoh over the whole land and the extent of the crown domains and of those belonging to the priests, between them covering almost the whole of the land of Egypt. The most striking characteristic of this system was that the principal landowners were institutions and that the right of private ownership was . . . hardly developed at all" (R. de Vaux, *History of Israel*, 306).

It may also be noted that the stages of increasing destitution described here have parallels in the pentateuchal legislation. Debt led first to dependents of the debtor being taken into slavery (Exod 21:2–11; Deut 15:1–18; cf. Gen 47:13–14), further debt to a man mortgaging his land (Lev 25:25–34; cf. Gen 47:20) and ultimately to the slavery of the debtor himself (Lev 25:35–54; cf. Gen 47:21). In Israel, as in Egypt, there were exemptions for priestly (Levitical) land (Lev 25:32–34; cf. Gen 47:22). But whereas in Egypt the land and people belonged permanently to the Pharaoh, in Israel all Israelite slaves and mortgages were released in the year of Jubilee (Lev 25:28, 54). For further discussion, see G. C. Chirichigno, *Debt Slavery*, JSOTSup 141 (Sheffield: JSOT, 1993) 302–43.

13–14 Note the stress on the famine's severity (cf. 41:31) and its impact on Canaan as well as Egypt (cf. 12:10; 47:4). לקט "scraped up" is a term used of gleaning or picking up scraps (e.g., Lev 19:9; Judg 1:7), implying the people bringing every last penny to buy food (cf. v 15). On Joseph's earlier sales, see 41:56–57. "And brought it into Pharaoh's palace" is perhaps mentioned, as Calvin suggests, to show Joseph's honesty.

15 "Give." The same verb in 30:1 has overtones of desperation: "Why should we die?" (cf. 42:2).

16–17 Joseph agrees to exchange their livestock for grain. Animals were an important capital asset in agricultural societies. Whether they were actually exchanged for grain or mortgaged is not clear. As Jacob observes, mortgaging them would be more practical. Note that this is the first mention in the Bible of the horse, the most important beast of burden. The horse arrived in the Middle East at the beginning of the second millennium B.C. and in Egypt by the seventeenth century. Egypt was an important source of horses in Solomon's day (1 Kgs 10:28–29; cf. *EM* 5:105–7).

18 "Next year," lit. "the second year." Where this year fits in the seven years of famine is unclear.

"Our corpses" vividly anticipates their state if Joseph does not provide them with food.

19–20 It is therefore better for them to sell themselves as slaves and their land to Pharaoh. If Joseph gives them grain to eat, they will also be able to sow their land so that it does not revert to desert. He consents, and the land becomes Pharaoh's.

21 "He made them into slaves." Though this sounds harsh, it was in this situation beneficial, for now their food supply was Pharaoh's responsibility. The MT reading, "he transferred them into cities," is difficult to understand, because they needed to stay on their holdings and cultivate them (cf. vv 23–24), even though the land was owned by the crown to whom they paid a fifth of their produce. Nor would they have moved to the cities just to be near the granaries.

22 As already pointed out, most land in Egypt belonged either to the Pharaoh or the temples. Furthermore, they received a portion (פח; cf. Exod 29:28; Lev 7:34; 10:13) from the crown, so they did not need to mortgage their land.

23–24 Having mortgaged their lands and their persons, the Egyptians were now allocated grain to eat and to sow. One fifth of their yield was to be paid to Pharaoh, the rest retained by the grower. This was the basis of the 20 percent income tax in Egypt (v 26).

25 For "Saved our lives," cf. 45:7; 50:20. "Slaves." Memories of the African slave trade color our view of slavery, so that we cannot understand this expression of gratitude. But in ancient society slavery was the accepted way of bailing out the destitute, and under a benevolent master could be quite a comfortable status (cf. Joseph with Potiphar). Indeed, the law envisages some temporary slaves electing to become permanent slaves rather than take the freedom to which they were entitled after six years of service. Ancient slavery at its best was like tenured employment, whereas the free man was more like someone who is self-employed. The latter may be freer, but he faces more risks (cf. Exod 21:5–6; Deut 15:12–17).

26 As royal serfs, the Egyptians were expected to contribute one-fifth of their produce to the king, but the temples were exempt from this obligation. Egyptian texts imply temples were generally free from most taxation. "Still valid today," i.e., in the author's day.

27 "So Israel settled in the land of Egypt" concludes the account of the move to Egypt begun in 46:1 (cf. parallel in 36:2–8). See *Form/Structure/Setting* on chaps. 46–47.

For "held land," cf. 34:10; 47:11. "Were fruitful and multiplied" fulfills the promise and command made to him earlier in his career (28:3; 35:11; cf. 1:28; 9:1, 7) and anticipates the situation that precipitated the exodus: "the descendants of Israel were fruitful and increased greatly; they multiplied and grew exceedingly strong . . ." (Exod 1:7).

28–31 The seventh and final scene: Jacob prepares to die. The clear allusion to the patriarchal promises of numerous progeny in v 27 leads naturally into a reference to the other chief interest of the promises, the land of Canaan. Many commentators, however, view this scene as part of the following section, Jacob's final blessing and farewell to his sons (chaps. 48–50), but this is not justified. "After these things" (48:1) marks a significant new departure in the narrative, and it is entirely typical of Genesis' technique to make the last scene of one section a trailer for the next (cf. 4:25–26; chap. 5; 6:5–8; 6:9–9:29). It may be that 47:28–31 constitutes a proleptic summary of chaps. 48–50, but it may be that

Jacob's actions described here did precede his death by days or months. The close similarity of this scene to 24:1–9, where Abraham makes his servant take a similar oath, is also instructive, for this also takes place some time before the patriarch's death. Similarly, 27:1–40 recounts Isaac making his last will and testament, but this occurs some time before his death (cf. 27:41). Finally, the very last scene of Genesis describes Joseph making his brothers swear that they will bury him in Canaan. For all these reasons, it seems right to regard 47:28–31 as a discrete scene concluding the account of Jacob's journey to Egypt and anticipating, but not describing, his death.

28 Note the similar sequence "settled [v 27] . . . age at death [v 28]" in 50:22. "Seventeen years." Jacob lived in Egypt with Joseph as long as Joseph had lived with him in Canaan (37:2).

29 "If I have found favor" is a surprisingly deferential way for an old man to make a request to an obliging son (cf. 18:3; 33:10; 50:4), suggesting how much it mattered to him. "Place your hand under my thigh" (cf. 24:2, 9). On the significance of the gesture, see *Comment* on 24:2. Jacob appears consciously to be imitating his grandfather here. Both patriarchs' great concern was the fulfillment of the covenant promises: Abraham by securing a wife for his son, Jacob by his burial in the land of promise. "Treat me with kindness and loyalty." Another clear echo of chap. 24; cf. 24:27, 49.

30 On the patriarchal grave, see chap. 23; 25:9; 35:27–29; 49:29–32. On "I shall do as you say," cf. 50:5–14.

31 On "swear to me," cf. 24:7, 9; 50:5–6.

"Jacob bent over." The narrative does not explain exactly why he did. Is it just the weakness of approaching death or a gesture of gratitude or prayer? By its ambiguity, it leaves open all these interpretations.

Explanation

After the high drama of the second journey to Egypt by Joseph's brothers (chaps. 43–45), the account of the third journey in these chapters seems somewhat of an anticlimax as a narrative. But theologically it is the most important, for it brought Israel out of Canaan, the land of promise, to Egypt, the land of slavery, from which they must eventually escape. It therefore raises the question: was the Israelite migration to Egypt a big mistake? In retelling the story, the narrator is acutely aware of this issue and addresses it decisively.

The third journey begins with the only divine vision in the Joseph story, indeed the last in Genesis. Cast in the form of a salvation oracle, it reassures Jacob that it is God's will for him to enter Egypt. "Do not be afraid to go down to Egypt" echoes the great promises made to Abraham and Isaac in the past, and by this the LORD reassures Jacob that these promises will be fulfilled. "I shall make you into a great nation, . . . I shall go down with you, . . . I . . . shall surely bring you up again" (46:3–4). In context, this last remark is particularly important in emphasizing that the family's sojourn in Egypt will only be temporary: Canaan is their ultimate goal.

But having underlined Jacob's prophetic gifts as recipient of these great promises, the narrative draws attention to his present pathetic weakness. The Jacob

who had triumphed over his elder brother Esau and defeated the angel at the Yabbok is now so infirm that his sons have to lift him onto a cart to carry him to Egypt. The promises, we learn, will be fulfilled not through human effort but by divine overruling. Man's power withers like grass, "but the word of our God will stand for ever" (Isa 40:8). And the sustaining power of God's promises is illustrated by the fact that a large group of descendants, seventy is a sacred round number, accompany Jacob into Egypt. Already Israel is in the process of becoming the great nation promised to Abraham (12:2) and just reaffirmed to Jacob (46:3). Most of this long list of Jacob's descendants were fathers of the tribes and clans in later Israel and would have been known as such to the first readers of Genesis, who would have appreciated very clearly the fulfillment of the promises.

But the narrative quickly refocuses on the personal issues involved in Jacob's move to Egypt. First comes the emotional reunion of the father with his favorite son. Jacob is overwhelmed when he sees Joseph in all his glory; he appears to him as if in a vision. But Joseph turns out to be completely real, as he falls on his father's neck and weeps over him again and again. And because Joseph is alive, Jacob's attitude to death is revolutionized. Twice Jacob had declared that the loss of his sons would bring him in mourning to Sheol, the realm of the hopeless dead (37:35; 42:38). Now Joseph's resurrection allows Jacob to die in peace, just as the resurrection of a greater Joseph has allowed many to face death with courage and hope (1 Pet 1:3; cf. Phil 1:21–26).

If for Jacob reunion with Joseph is all that matters, Joseph sees things differently. Having invited his family to emigrate to Egypt, he has the responsibility of securing their future there. So he carefully coaches his brothers for their interview with Pharaoh. They must emphasize that they are full-time herdsmen who have brought their flocks with them. They are neither looking for jobs in Egypt nor food for themselves, just a suitable place to pasture their flocks (46:31–34).

This approach succeeds magnificently. The audience with Pharaoh goes well and concludes with him offering Joseph's brothers the best pastureland in Egypt, in the area of Goshen, and inviting them to become royal stockmen too (47:1–6). Though the narrator makes no comment on the outcome, doubtless he viewed this as another example of divine providence working for his people's good, just as Joseph's earlier successes were proof that the LORD was with him (cf. 39:3, 21, 23).

Then follows Jacob's audience with the Pharaoh; at least that is how it was seen officially. But in reality it was Pharaoh's audience with Jacob. Jacob is carried into the court, is helped to stand by Joseph, and blesses the Pharaoh. Politely, the Pharaoh inquires about the old man's age. Jacob replies, "The years of my life have been few and bad," a comment that at first seems surprising from a man who has lived already to a hundred and thirty and whose son is vizier of Egypt. But what is long life and a successful career when, as in Jacob's case, it has meant running away from his parents, an unhappy marriage, and more recently mourning the loss of his favorite wife and son? Yet despite his deeply unhappy life, Jacob is the bearer of divine blessing: through him and his descendants the promises of God are being fulfilled. So he blesses Pharaoh again and leaves (47:7–10).

Pharaoh's goodwill toward Jacob shown at the audience and afterwards (47:11–12) does of course redound on him and his people, for Isaac had said, "Blessed

are those who bless you." The following episode describing Joseph's relief activities in Egypt shows how divine blessing came to Egypt. Modern readers find it difficult to regard Joseph's measures as benevolent. They look to us like exploitation of the destitute, who are forced to sell or mortgage animals, land, and their own freedom in order to stay alive. Joseph, the cunning agent, makes the most of their plight to enrich the crown. But this is to misread the account's intentions. The OT law itself does not envisage the destitute simply being bailed out by the more well-to-do. Rather, if possible, members of a family should help their destitute relatives, just as Joseph did, by buying their land and employing them as slaves (cf. Lev 25:13–55). This was viewed as a great act of charity, for as the Egyptians say to Joseph, "You have saved our lives" (47:25). It is within this context that Joseph's actions must be judged. In Israel, those who became destitute and sold their land or themselves to a more prosperous relative or friend were given their land or freedom back in the year of Jubilee, which occurred every fifty years. Apparently, the Pharaoh was not so generous; he retained the land and people as his serfs in perpetuity. But Joseph cannot be blamed for that. He saved the Egyptians from famine and so carried out the scheme he had proposed after interpreting Pharaoh's dream and demonstrated his God-given wisdom (42:36). In the longer perspective, Joseph's actions partially fulfill the promise that "all the families of the earth shall find blessing in you and your descendants" (28:14; cf. 12:3; 18:18; 22:18; 26:4).

That Jacob's move helped to fulfill rather than frustrate the promises is reiterated at the close of this section. In Egypt, "they were fruitful and multiplied" (cf. 17:6; 28:3; 35:11). And just as Abraham had been preoccupied before his death with securing a wife for his son so that the promise of descendants could be fulfilled (24:1–9), so Jacob, acting like his grandfather, made his son Joseph swear that he would bury him in the land of promise, not in Egypt. His action showed he believed the word that brought him into Egypt: "I shall bring you up again" (46:4). Jacob, in life too often the cunning schemer who trusted his own wiliness to achieve his ends, now in the face of death shows that his ultimate hope is the promise of God.

The Last Days of Jacob and Joseph (48:1–50:26)

Bibliography

Bartelmus, R. "Topograpie und Theologie: Exegetische und didaktische Anmerkungen zum letzten Kapitel der Genesis (Gen 50:1–14)." *BN* 29 (1985) 35–57. **Ben Zvi, E.** "The Closing Words of the Pentateuchal Books: A Clue for the Historical Status of the Book of Genesis within the Pentateuch." *BN* 62 (1992) 7–10. **Brueggemann, W.** "Gen 50:15–21: A Theological Exploration." VTSup 36 (1985) 4–53. **Gevirtz, S.** "The Life Spans of Joseph and Enoch and the Parallelism *šibʾātayim-šibîm wešibʾāh.*" *JBL* 96 (1977) 570–71. **Kingsbury, E. C.** "'He Set Ephraim before Manasseh.'" *HUCA* 38 (1967) 129–36. **Labuschagne, C. J.** "The Life Spans of the Patriarchs." *OTS* 25 (1989) 121–27. **Lebram, J. C. H.** "Jakob segnet

Joseph's Söhne: Darstellungen von Gen 48 in der Überlieferung und bei Rembrandt."
OTS 15 (1969) 145–69. **Luke, K.** "The Blessing Jacob Conferred upon Ephraim (Gen 48:8–
20)." *IndTS* 14 (1977) 72–90. **Mendelsohn, I.** "A Ugaritic Parallel to the Adoption of
Ephraim and Manasseh." *IEJ* 9 (1959) 180–83. **Merwe, B. J. van der.** "Joseph as Successor
of Jacob." In *Studia Biblica et Semitica: FS T. C. Vriezen.* Wageningen: Veenman, 1966. 221–
32. **Richter, H.-F.** "'Auf den Knien eines andern gebären?' (Zur Deutung von Gen 30:3
und 50:23)." *ZAW* 91 (1979) 436–37. **Schweizer, H.** "Fragen zur Literarkritik von Gen 50:
Diskussionsbeitrag zu R. Bartelmus." *BN* 36 (1987) 64–68. ———— "Literarkritik." *TQ*
168 (1988) 23–43. **Seebass, H.** "The Joseph Story, Gen 48 and the Canonical Process."
JSOT 35 (1986) 29–43.

Translation

[1] *After these things, someone said* [a] *to Joseph, "Your father is now* [b] *ill." So he took with
him his two sons, Manasseh and Ephraim.* [c] [2] *Then Jacob was told,* [a] *"Your son Joseph
has just* [b] *come to you," so Israel pulled himself together and sat up on his bed.* [3] *Then
Jacob said to Joseph, "El Shaddai* [a] *appeared to me in Luz in the land of Canaan and
blessed me."* [4] *He said to me, "I am making* [a] *you fruitful, and I shall multiply you and
make you a multitude of peoples and give this land to your descendants after you as a
permanent holding.* [5a] *Now the two sons which have been born* [b] *to you in the land of
Egypt before I came* [c] *to you in Egypt belong to me: Ephraim and Manasseh shall be mine
as Reuben and Simeon are.* [a] [6] *But your family, which you have fathered* [a] *after them,
shall be yours: they shall be named after their brothers' names in their inheritance.* [7] *As
for me,* [a] *when I came* [b] *from Paddan,* [c] *Rachel* [d] *died to my loss* [e] *in the land of Canaan as
we were on the way about two hours' distance* [f] *from Ephrata. I buried her there on the
way to Ephrata, that is Bethlehem."*

[8] *Then Israel saw Joseph's sons and said, "Who are these?"* [a] [9] *Joseph said to his father,
"They are my sons whom God has given me here." He* [a] *said, "Please bring* [b] *them to me
so I may bless* [c] *them."* [10] *Now Israel's eyes were heavy because of age:* [a] *he could not see.* [a]
So he brought [b] *them to him, and he kissed* [c] *them and hugged them.* [11] *Then Israel said
to Joseph,* [a] *"I never expected to see* [b] *your face;* [a] [c] *now God has just showed me your descendants as well."* [c]

[12] *Then Joseph took* [a] *them from his knees, and he bowed* [b] [c] *face down to the ground.* [c]
[13] *Joseph took both of them, Ephraim in his right hand to Israel's left and Manasseh in
his left hand to Israel's right, and he brought them near.* [14] *Then Israel stretched out his
right hand and placed* [a] *it on Ephraim's head,* [b] *although he was the younger,* [b] *and he
put his left hand on Manasseh's head: he thus crossed his hands,* [c] *even though Manasseh
was the firstborn.* [c]

[15] *Then he blessed Joseph* [a] *as follows:*

> *"May the God, before whom my fathers, Abraham and Isaac, walked,*
> *May the God, who has guided me from then until now,*
> [16] *May the angel,* [a] *who rescued* [b] *me from every evil, bless the lads.*
> *May my name and the name of my fathers, Abraham and Isaac,*
> *be carried on through them.*
> *May they multiply like fish in the earth."*

¹⁷ *Then Joseph noticed that his father had placed his right hand on Ephraim's head, and he was displeased, so he grasped his father's hand to transfer*ª *it from Ephraim's head to Manasseh's.* ¹⁸ *Joseph said to his father, "Not this way, father! This is the first-born. Put your right hand on his head!"* ¹⁹ *But his father refused and said, "I know, my son. I know that he also will become a people, that he too will be great.* ª*Nevertheless, his younger brother*ª *will be greater than he, and his descendants will be full of nations."*

²⁰ *So he blessed them that day,*

*"May Israel pronounce blessings*ª *by you with the words*
'May God make you like Ephraim and Manasseh.'"
So he put Ephraim before Manasseh.

²¹ *Then Israel said to Joseph, "I am about*ª *to die. May God be with you and bring*ᵇ *you back to the land of your fathers.* ²² *I give*ª *you one*ᵇ *shoulder above your brothers, which I have taken from the hand of the Amorite with my sword and bow.".*

⁴⁹:¹ *Jacob summoned his sons and said:*

*"Assemble*ª *that*ᵇ *I may declare to you what will happen to you in the latter days.*
² *Gather and listen, sons of Jacob,*
          Listen to Israel your father.
³ *Reuben, you are my firstborn,*
          my strength and the first fruit of my virility,
          outstanding in majesty and power,
⁴ *frothy*ª *as water, you shall not excel,*ᵇ
          for you went up to your father's bed;
          then you profaned my couch,
          *he*ᶜ *went up to my couch.*
⁵ *Simeon and Levi are brothers.*
          *They are equipped with weapons*ª *of violence.*ᵇ
⁶ *May my soul not enter their circle.*
          *May my reputation*ª *not rejoice*ᵇ *in their company.*
          For when angry, they kill a man;
          And when they please, they hamstring an ox.
⁷ *Cursed be their anger, for it is strong,*
          and their wrath, for it is hard.
          I will divide them up in Jacob
          *and disperse*ª *them in Israel.*
⁸ *Judah, your brothers praise*ª *you.*ᵇ
          Your hand will be on the back of your enemies.
          Your father's sons will bow down to you.
⁹ *Judah is a young lion:*
          My son, you have just left your prey.
          He crouches, he lies like a lion.
          *Like a lion, who will dare rouse*ª *him?*
¹⁰ª *The staff will not desert Judah*
          or the scepter from between his feet,
          until tribute is brought to him
          and the peoples obey him.
¹¹ *He tethers*ª *his*ᵇ *ass to the vine,*

his pure-bred foal[a] to the choice vine.
He washes his clothing in wine,
his[b] garment[c] in the blood of grapes.
[12] His eyes are darker than wine,
and his teeth whiter[a] than milk.
[13] Zebulon lives[a] by the seaside,
and he is a haven[a] for ships,
and his rear reaches Sidon.
[14] Issachar is a strong-boned ass,
lying down by its packs.
[15] He saw a good[a] place to rest
and an[b] attractive land.
So he put[c] his shoulder to carry burdens,
and he was forced to toil as a slave.
[16] Dan will vindicate his people
like any of the tribes of Israel.
[17] May Dan be a snake on the path,
a horned viper on the wayside,
that bites the horse's heels
and makes its rider fall off.
[18] I look[a] for your deliverance, O LORD.
[19] Gad, raiders will raid[a] him,
but he will raid[b] their retreat.
[20] Asher[a] [b]has rich food;[b]
he will produce royal delicacies.
[21] Naphtali was born a free-running doe,[a]
she gives birth to fawns of the fold.
[22] Joseph[a] is a [b]wild [c]ass,[b]
a wild ass beside a spring,
his wild colts beside the wall.
[23] The archers were bitter and shot;[a]
they bore a grudge against him.
[24] Their[a] bow remained[b] firm,
though their[a] hands and arms were agile,[c]
thanks to the strength of the mighty One of Jacob,
thanks[d] to the shepherd of the stone of Israel.
[25] Thanks to the God of your father—may he help you.
Thanks to [a]Shaddai—may he bless you,
with the blessings of heaven above
and the blessings of the deep crouching beneath,
the blessings of the breast and the womb.
[26] The blessings of your father surpass
the blessings of the [a]eternal mountains,[a]
the bounty of the everlasting hills.
Let them be for the head of Joseph,
for the crown of the prince among his brothers.
[27] Benjamin tears like a wolf:

> *in the morning he eats his prey,*
> *in the evening he divides up the spoil.* "

[28] *All these are the twelve tribes of Israel, and this is what their father said to them when he blessed each* [a] *of them with their own special blessing.*
[29] *Then he commanded them and said, "I* [a] *am being gathered to my people.* [b] *Bury me with my fathers in the cave which is on the land of Ephron the Hittite,* [30] *in the cave which is on the land of Macpelah which is opposite Mamre in the land of Canaan, on the land* [a] *which Abraham obtained from Ephron the Hittite for a burial plot.* [31] *There* [a] *Abraham and Sarah his wife* [b] *were buried.* [b] *There* [a] *Isaac and Rebekah his wife* [b] *were buried,* [b] *and there* [a] *I buried Leah,* [32] *there in the land and cave that belongs to it which was acquired from the Hittites."* [33] *Then Jacob stopped giving instructions* [a] *to his sons, gathered his feet to his bed, expired, and was gathered to his relatives.*

[50:1] *Then Joseph fell on his father's face, wept* [a] *over him, and kissed* [b] *him.* [2] *Joseph gave orders to his servants and the physicians to embalm his father. So the physicians embalmed Israel.* [3] *They completed forty days for him, so they finished the period of embalming. Then the Egyptians wept for him seventy days.*

[4] *When the days of mourning for him were over, Joseph spoke to the house of Pharaoh, "If now I enjoy your favor, please speak to Pharaoh.* [5] *'My father made me take an oath* [a] *as follows: "I am about to die. Bury me in the grave which I hewed for myself in the land of Canaan." Now please let me go up to bury my father* [b] *and then return.'"* [6] *Pharaoh replied, "Go up and bury your father as he made you swear."* [7] *So Joseph went up to bury his father. All the servants of Pharaoh went up with him, the elders of the palace and all the elders of Egypt,* [8] *all Joseph's household and his brothers and his father's household: they left only the young children, their flocks, and herds in the land of Goshen.* [9] *There also went up with him both chariots and horsemen. The encampment was very powerful.*

[10] *They came to the Bramble Threshing Floor which is over the Jordan, and they mourned there with a great and solemn lamentation, and he mourned seven days for his father.* [11] *The Canaanite inhabitants of the land noticed the mourning at the Bramble Threshing Floor and said, "This is a serious mourning by the Egyptians." That is why it is called "Abel* [a] *-Misraim" which is beyond the Jordan.* [12] *So his sons did for him as he had instructed them.* [13] *His sons carried* [a] *him to the land of Canaan and buried him in the cave in the land of Macpelah, the land* [b] *which Abraham had acquired for a burial plot from Ephron the Hittite opposite Mamre.* [14a] *After he had buried his father,* [a] *Joseph returned to Egypt, he, his brothers, and all who had gone up from Egypt to bury his father.*

[15] *The brothers of Joseph realized* [a] *that their father had died and said, "Suppose* [b] *Joseph harbors a grudge against us and* [c] *really returns* [c] *us all the evil which we have done to him."* [16] *So they sent instructions* [a] *to Joseph as follows: "Our father directed us before his death as follows:* [17] *'You must say this to Joseph, "Please, please forgive* [a] *your brothers' crime and their sin, for they have done you evil."' Now please forgive* [a] *the crime of the servants of our father's God." So Joseph wept when they spoke to him.* [18] *But his brothers came* [a] *and fell before him and said, "Look, we are your slaves."* [19] *Joseph replied to them, "Do not be afraid. Am I in the place of God?* [20] *You planned evil against me.* [a] *It was God who planned it for good,* [a] *so that it should happen* [b] *as it is today* [c] *to keep* [d] *many people alive.* [21] *Now, do not be afraid. I shall supply* [a] *you and your youngsters with food." So he consoled them and spoke reassuringly to them.*

^{22}*Joseph and his father's family settled in Egypt, and Joseph lived a hundred and ten years.* ^{23}*Joseph saw* ^{a}*Ephraim's grandchildren,*^{a} *also the children of Machir, Manasseh's son, were born* ^{b}*on Joseph's knees.*^{b}

^{24}*Then Joseph said to his brothers, "I* ^{a}*am dying but God*^{a} *will definitely visit you and bring you out of this land to the land which he swore to Abraham, Isaac, and Jacob."* ^{25}*Then Joseph made the sons of Israel take an oath, "God will definitely visit you, and you shall bring my bones up from here."*^{a} ^{26}*Then Joseph died aged one hundred and ten. They embalmed him, and he was put*^{a} *in a coffin in Egypt.*

Notes

1.a. On impersonal use of 3 masc sg, lit. "and he said," see GKC, 144d; Joüon, 155e. *Pace BHS*, it is unnecessary to repoint as niph despite G.

1.b. On this nuance of הנה, see WOC, 675.

1.c. G adds "he came to Jacob."

2.a. Lit. "and he said"; cf. n. 48:1.a. *BHS* repointing unnecessary.

2.b. Cf. n. 48:1.b.

3.a. Note subj "El Shaddai" preceding verb, common in clauses with God as subj (*EWAS*, 35).

4.a. Masc sg hiph ptcp פרה + 2 masc sg suffix.

5.a-a. On the word order in this verse, see *EWAS*, 17.

5.b. Def art + masc pl ptcp niph ילד.

5.c. Inf constr בוא + 1 sg suffix.

6.a. 2 masc sg pf hiph ילד.

7.a. Extraposed personal pronoun "me" is emphatic. "By using extraposition, Jacob talks not of Rachel's death but of his own misfortune" (*EWAS*, 98, n. 16).

7.b. Cf. n. 48:5.c.

7.c. Elsewhere always Paddan-Aram, to which SamPent, G, S correct MT.

7.d. SamPent, G add "your mother."

7.e. On this nuance of על, see WOC, 217; Joüon, 133f.

7.f. On this translation, see *Comment* on 35:16.

8.a. SamPent (cf. G) adds לך "that belong to you."

9.a. G adds "Jacob."

9.b. 2 masc sg impv qal לקח + 3 masc pl suffix. On pointing, see GKC, 58g.

9.c. On pointing, see GKC, 60d.

10.a-a. Note apposition clause emphasizing Jacob's blindness (cf. 27:1; *SBH*, 45).

10.b. Waw consec + 3 masc sg impf hiph נגש.

10.c. Cf. n. 27:27.a.

11.a-a. Word order, obj preceding verb, emphasizes Jacob's astonishment (*EWAS*, 39).

11.b. Unusual inf constr qal ראה (GKC, 75n).

11.c-c. On this surprise clause, see *SBH*, 95, 161.

12.a. Cf. n. 15:5.a.

12.b. Cf. n. 18:2.d. SamPent, G, S read pl, "they bowed."

12.c-c. *BHS*-proposed emendation on the basis of G is unnecessary. The same construction occurs in Num 22:31; 1 Sam 20:41; 2 Sam 18:28.

14.a. Waw consec + 3 masc sg impf qal שית.

14.b-b., c-c. On these concessive clauses, see GKC, 141e, 156d; *SBH*, 90.

15.a. G "them."

16.a. SamPent "king."

16.b. On the use of ptcp in relative clauses dealing with past, see GKC, 116o.

17.a. ל + inf constr hiph סור.

19.a-a. Conj ואולם (Joüon, 172b) and word order, subj preceding verb (*EWAS*, 33), emphasize the contrast here.

20.a. 3 masc sg impf piel ברך; cf. 48:16. G "will be blessed" apparently points יברך as pual (so *BHS*) or niph impf.

21.a. הנה + ptcp for imminent events "near at hand and sure to happen" (GKC, 116p).

21.b. Waw consec + 3 masc sg pf hiph שׁוּב.

22.a. On this nuance of pf, see GKC, 106m.

22.b. On pointing, see GKC, 130g.

49:1.a. 2 masc pl impv niph אָסַף.

1.b. Waw + 1 sg coh hiph נגד "in order that" (Joüon, 116b).

4.a. SamPent פחזת "you were frothy." Though versions also read "you," they may be interpreting MT, not following a reading like SamPent.

4.b. 2 masc sg juss hiph יתר; S *tpwš* leads *BHS* to suggest repointing as niph, "do not be left over."

4.c. G (cf. S, *Tg. Onq., Tg. Ps.-J*) "you went up" could be interpretative, not witness to different text.

5.a. SamPent כלו; cf. G "they completed."

5.b. *BHS* proposes reading "their nets" (cf. Isa 19:8; Hab 1:15) instead of the unique MT form here. See further in *Comment*.

6.a. G apparently repoints כבדי "my liver."

6.b. Reading תֵּחַד 3 fem sg impf qal חדה. MT 3 fem sg impf qal יחד; cf. SamPent יחר "be angry."

7.a. Waw + 1 sg impf hiph פוץ + 3 masc pl suffix.

8.a. 3 masc pl impf hiph ידה + 2 masc sg suffix.

8.b. Extraposed pronoun (אתה) for emphasis (GKC, 135e; *EWAS*, 97).

9.a. 3 masc sg impf hiph קום + 3 masc sg suffix.

10.a. On the textual variants and versional interpretations, see *Comment*.

11.a. י unexplained ending on some constructs (cf. GKC, 90l,m; WOC, 127, 128; Joüon, 93m,n).

11.b. ה archaic 3 masc sg suffix for usual ו.

11.c. SamPent replaces MT's hapax with כסותו "his covering."

12.a. Constr of לָבָן "white" (GKC, 93dd).

13.a. *BHS* emendation unnecessary.

15.a. טוֹב masc, not fem sg as SamPent, perhaps because כי טוב is an idiom.

15.b. On the use of את here, see GKC, 117b1; WOC, 646).

15.c. Cf. n. 12:8.c.

18.a. On this nuance of pf, see GKC, 106g.

19.a. 3 masc sg impf qal גוד + 3 masc sg suffix.

19.b-20.a. Redividing the consonantal text עקבם אשר with G, S, Vg. MT reads "the retreating [lit., 'heel']. From Asher."

20.b-b. Lit. "his food is fat." שמנה "fat" is fem adj, which implies לחם "food" is too, unless "fat" is supposed to be a fem noun. Despite Gevirtz (*VT* 37 [1987] 154–63), it is easiest to accept "food" as fem here.

21.a. *BHS* emendations here and elsewhere in v 21 are probably unnecessary. The rare terms can be understood; see *Comment*.

22.a. On major problems of verse, see *Comment*.

22.b-b. *Pace BHS*, not to be deleted.

22.c. Abs not to be changed to constr, *pace* GKC, 96.

23.a. *BHS* proposes reading impf וירבו. But SamPent (cf. G, Vg) reads ויריבהו "and they strove with him."

24.a. Lit. "his," but probably refers to the archers and not to Joseph; see *Comment*.

24.b. No emendation necessary, *pace BHS*.

24.c. Waw consec + 3 masc pl impf qal פזז. Emendation unnecessary.

24.d. MT lit. "from there." Of various suggested emendations, the easiest involves repointing מִשֵּׁם "from the name of" (cf. S, *Tg. Onq.*).

25.a. Some MSS, SamPent, G, S read ואל "and El" for the awkward MT ואת. However, MT may be retained; see *Comment*.

26.a-a. Emending MT הורי "my ancestors" to הררי־עד (cf. G) "steadfast mountains."

28.a. אשר is awkwardly placed. It would be more natural after כברכתו, so some MSS omit it. *BHS* emends אשר to איש.

29.a. Fronting of personal pronoun, "I," because of Jacob's tenseness facing death, or to contrast with "my people" (*EWAS*, 27).

29.b. *BHS* and some commentators repoint "my relatives."

30.a. Repetition of nominal obj השדה is rare (cf. 50:13, Joüon, 158hl).

31.a. Fronted adverb for emphasis, suggesting "Jacob's nostalgic attachment to the far-away land of his origin" (*EWAS*, 43).

31.b-b. Lit. "they buried" Abraham et al.; 3 masc pl often used for indefinite subj (GKC, 144f).

33.a. לְ + inf constr piel צוה.

50:1.a. Cf. n. 27:38.b.

1.b. Cf. n. 27:27.a.

5.a. SamPent adds "before his death."

5.b. SamPent adds "as he made me swear."

11.a. "Meadow" is the meaning suggested by the MT punctuation. Repointing אָבֵל would mean "mourning of" with G.

13.a. Cf. n. 7:17.b.

13.b. Cf. n. 49:30.a.

14.a-a. Omitted by G as redundant.

15.a. Vg "feared," i.e., vocalizing consonants differently (cf. *BHS*).

15.b. On לוּ with suppressed apodosis, see GKC, 159y.

15.c-c. Cf. n. 24:5.a-a.

16.a. G (cf. S) "and they came."

17.a. Cf. n. 13:14.c.

18.a. *BHS* conjecturally emends to "wept," replacing לְ with בְ. Cf. *Comment.*

20.a-a. Antithetic clause contrasting God's action with your action. Note subj,"God," before verb for contrast. No need to insert "and" with SamPent and versions (*SBH*, 57, 153; *EWAS*, 33).

20.b. Inf constr (unusual form, GKC, 75n) עשׂה.

20.c. The verb "to be" is understood (Joüon, 174d4).

20.d. Cf. n. 6:19.c.

21.a. 1 sg impf pilpel כול.

23.a-a. On this construction, cf. Joüon, 130g. SamPent reads abs בנים "sons" for MT בני "sons of." GKC, 128v, suggests MT's "sons of third generation" means "grandchildren," not "great-grandchildren." SamPent could be understood "Ephraim's sons, grandchildren" (i.e., of Joseph); cf. G.

23.b-b. SamPent "in Joseph's days."

24.a-a. Fronting of subjs for contrast (*EWAS*, 12, 33).

25.a. Some MSS, SamPent, and versions add "with you."

26.a. Possibly 3 masc sg impf qal pass (GKC, 73f). SamPent וַיּוּשָׂם is waw consec + 3 masc sg impf hoph שׂים.

Form/Structure/Setting

Chaps. 48–50 bring to a conclusion the long story of Jacob, which began in chap. 25, and that of Joseph, which began in chap. 37. The opening of a new section in 48:1 is signaled by "After these things," an important structural marker throughout Genesis (cf. *Form/Structure/Setting* on chaps. 46–47), and the close in 50:26 is obvious. Accounts of the last words of the patriarchs figure regularly in Genesis (cf. Abraham, chap. 24, and Isaac, chap. 27), so that it constitutes a type scene (cf. Keukens, *BN* 19 [1982] 43–56), the deathbed blessing scene. When a patriarch is about to die, he summons his nearest male relatives and blesses them. Here, two such scenes are presented in quick succession; the first, 48:1–49:32, is much longer than the second, 50:24–26. Indeed the first, recounting Jacob's death, is the longest in Genesis. And this is fitting, for Jacob is the father of the nation of Israel, so in blessing his sons he is giving an allusive preview of the future of the tribes who are to make up that nation. Jacob's emphatic and repeated insistence that he must be buried with his forebears in Canaan, like the tribal blessings themselves, underlines that Israel's future lies in Canaan, not in Egypt. This, says Jacob, is the land promised by God to us in the past and to which I must be returned when I am dead. Thus, through Jacob's dying words, the author of Genesis is able to sum up the theme of Genesis, to point to the fulfillment of the promises made to Abraham and Isaac about descendants and protection, and to reiterate the hope that one day Canaan will be theirs too, as the LORD had promised.

This long deathbed blessing scene is succeeded by two shorter scenes rein-
forcing the assurance that the promises will eventually be completely fulfilled.
Joseph's brothers, fearing revenge after their father's death, plead for forgiveness. This allows Joseph to reaffirm the key theme of the Joseph story, that through
his brothers' jealousy, God's purpose of salvation was achieved—"God planned it
for good . . . to keep many people alive" (50:20). This, in turn, reflects the promise made to Abraham that in his descendants all the families of the earth would
find blessing (cf. 12:3; 22:18).

Finally, in the short account of Joseph's death, we hear him insisting that one day
"God will definitely visit you, and you shall bring my bones up from here." Like his
father, Joseph wants to be buried in Canaan, but unlike Jacob, Joseph is prepared to
wait for that day when all his people will leave Egypt and settle in the land of promise.

The material may be analyzed as follows:

Scene 1:   Jacob blesses Ephraim and Manasseh (48:1–22)
                 Introduction (1–2)
                 Past promises fulfilled: burial of relatives (3–7)
                 Introduction of Ephraim and Manasseh (8–10)
                 Ephraim blessed more than Manasseh (11–20)
                 Instructions about his own burial (21–22)
Scene 2:   Jacob blesses his sons and dies (49:1–50:1)
                 Introduction (1–2)
                 Tribal blessings (3–28)
                 Instructions about burial (29–32)
                 Jacob dies (33–50:1)
Scene 3:   Jacob is embalmed and mourned (50:2–3)
Scene 4:   Pharaoh grants permission for Jacob's burial in Canaan (50:4–6)
Scene 5:   Jacob buried in ancestral grave (50:7–14)
Scene 6:   Joseph reassures his brothers (50:15–21)
Scene 7:   Joseph's last deeds and words (50:22–26)

This analysis highlights the two main concerns of these chapters: first, that
Jacob should be buried in the patriarchal tomb in Canaan mentioned repeatedly
(48:7, 21–22; 49:29–32; 50:5–14, cf. 25); second, the future destiny of the sons
and grandsons of Jacob, a topic that dominates the two longest scenes (48:8–
49:28). At first sight, it seems odd that there are two deathbed blessing scenes,
first for Jacob's grandsons and then for his sons, but 27:1–28:5 offers a parallel.
There Isaac, who like Jacob has lost his sight, first blesses Jacob and Esau, putting
the younger Jacob before the elder Esau (cf. Ephraim and Manasseh). Protests
by Esau (cf. Joseph) are dismissed by the old man, who subsequently goes on to
pronounce a second blessing.

48:10	Patriarchal blindness	cf. 27:1
48:14–16	Blessing pronounced on younger son	27:27–28
48:17–18	Protest	27:34–36
48:19–20	Reaffirmation of preference	27:37–40
49:2–28	Second blessing pronounced	28:2–6

That this parallel between the two deathbed blessing scenes is not accidental
is confirmed by Jacob's opening remark in 48:3–4, "El Shaddai appeared to me

in Luz," which apparently refers to the promises made to Jacob when he returned from Paddan-Aram (35:9–12), whereas the phraseology that follows, "I am making you fruitful [hiphil פרה] and I shall multiply [hiphil רבה] and make you a *company of peoples,*" echoes most closely his father's blessing in 28:3.

Throughout these closing chapters there are many other references to earlier episodes in the book (e.g., compare 48:5 to 41:50–52; 29:32–33; cf. 48:7 to 35:9, 16–19; cf. 48:9 to 41:50–52; cf. 48:11 to 37:33–35; 45:28; cf. 48:14 to 27:27–28; cf. 48:15 to 13:17; 17:1; 26:3; 28:15, 20–21; cf. 48:22 to 34:25–29; cf. 49:3 to 29:32; cf. 49:4 to 35:22; cf. 49:5 to 29:33–34; cf. 40:5–7 to 34:25–31; cf. 49:8 to 29:35; cf. 49:13 to 30:20; cf. 49:14 to 30:18; cf. 49:16 to 30:6; cf. 49:19 to 30:11; cf. 49:20 to 30:13; cf. 49:21 to 30:8; cf. 49:22 to 30:24; cf. 49:27 to 35:18; cf. 49:29–32 to 23:2–20; cf. 49:31 to 25:9; 35:29; cf. 50:1 to 46:29; cf. 50:4 to 47:1; cf. 50:5–6 to 24:3, 37; 47:31; cf. 50:8 to 45:10; 46:28, 34; 47:1, 4, 6; cf. 50:9 to 41:43; cf. 50:13 to 23:2–20; cf. 50:15 to 27:41; 37:18–35; cf. 50:17 to 31:36; cf. 50:18 to 44:14, 16; cf. 50:20 to 45:5, 7–9; cf. 50:21 to 45:11; 47:12; 37:35; 34:3; cf. 50:24 to 48:21; 50:5; 22:16; 26:3; 35:12; cf. 50:25 to 24:3, 37; 47:31; 50:5–6). This constant harking back to earlier episodes and promises is totally in place in a book whose theme is the fulfillment of promises, a book that regularly uses analogy between episodes as a narrative technique. And at the close of a book it is particularly appropriate to exploit these cross-linkages to the full. It reinforces the sense of completeness and suggests that the story has reached a natural stopping point.

Source critics have argued that these chapters are composed of J (49:1b–28a; 50:1–11, 14), E (48:1–2, 8–22; 50:15–26), and P (48:3–7; 49:1a, 28b–33; 50:12–13). This is Driver's relatively simple analysis. Later source critics (e.g., Gunkel; Skinner; Schmitt, *Josephsgeschichte;* Schmidt, *Literarische Studien*), perturbed by the repetitiveness of chaps. 48 and 50 and the alternation between the names Jacob (supposedly E) and Israel (supposedly J) and the divine names, have put forward more complex and contradictory analyses of these chapters.

Tradition critics, however, see these chapters as an amalgam of the Joseph story and the P version of the Jacob story with various redactional expansions. For example, Westermann holds that 48:1–2, 8–12; 50:1–14 represent the conclusion to the Joseph story, while 48:3–6; 49:1b, 28–33; 50:12–13 come from P. Other passages (48:7, 13–22; 50:15–26) represent yet later expansions. Blum (*Die Komposition*), however, on the basis of the parallels with chap. 27, argues that more of chaps. 48 and 50 form part of the Joseph story (48:1–2, 8–14, 17–20; 50:1–11, 14–21), to which other elements, some from P, have been added by later redactors. Coats, too, argues that 47:28–50:14 is a coherent narrative unit incorporating earlier material such as the blessings in 49:2–27 and material from P (e.g., 48:3–7). To this has been added a recapitulation in 50:15–21 and an appendix in 50:22–26. He seems to regard the narrative framework as originating with J.

Coats offers few arguments in favor of his approach save that the material is coherent and makes sense read as a unity. That he is basically correct is confirmed by examining the parallels to these chapters elsewhere in Genesis, where similar editorial procedures are visible. We have already noted that they constitute a type scene, the deathbed-blessing scene, which is also found in chap. 27. This also includes a double blessing of the son (27:27–28//28:2–6), so that the duplication of Jacob's blessing of his descendants in chaps. 48 and 49 is quite in keeping with

the narrator's style. Similarly, the parallels with the close of the Abraham and Jacob cycles show a similar redactional method.

Divine promise reaffirmed	22:15–18	35:9–14	48:4
Journey	22:19	35:16	48:5
Birth of sons	22:20–24	35:17–18	48:5–6
Death and burial of wife	23:1–20	35:18–20	48:7
Son's marriage	24:1–67	35:21–22	(48:8–9)
			(49:3–4)
List of descendants	25:1–6	35:22–26	49:3–28
Patriarch's death and burial	25:7–10	35:27–29	49:29–50:14

The supposition that 50:14–26 represents a subsequent expansion of the book is unnecessary. Schweizer has incisively argued that it is integral to the story of Joseph. Love for Jacob bound Joseph and his brothers together. With their father's death and very aptly just after the funeral, the brothers start to worry that Joseph may take his revenge, just as Esau planned to do after Isaac's death (27:41–45). A renewed act of reconciliation unmotivated by the father is therefore demanded at this point. "Whoever eliminates this scene really eliminates the climax of Gen 50 if not . . . that of the whole original Joseph story" (Schweizer, *BN* 36 [1987] 68). The subject matter, by recapitulating the main thrust of the Joseph story and the heart of the patriarchal promises, is perfectly congruent with the theme of Genesis as a whole. And as noted earlier, the remark in 50:22, "Joseph . . . settled in Egypt," gives "the family history of Jacob" (37:2–50:26) a closure similar to "the family history of Esau."

36:1//37:2	This is the family history of Esau/Jacob
36:2–5//46:8–27	List of Esau's (Jacob's) descendants
36:6–8//46:28–47:27	Move to Seir (Egypt) by Esau (Jacob)
36:8//47:27	Esau (Israel) dwelt
37:1//50:22	Jacob (Joseph) settled

For these reasons, I prefer to see chaps. 48–50 as a coherent, well-organized unit. This is not to deny the use of earlier material in these chapters; it seems likely that the blessing of Jacob has a long prehistory (see discussion below). It may be that the passages traditionally ascribed to P (48:3–7; 49:28b–33; 50:12–13) had a separate prehistory. But the ascription of these passages to P rests on the ascription of similar passages in chaps. 23 and 35 to the same source. And if, as already argued above, it is uncertain that the earlier passages come from P, the source of the latter passages is also open to question. Even if it were admitted that 23:1–20 and 35:9–14 come from P, it could be argued that the editor of chaps. 48–50 is simply drawing directly from these passages and not from an independent source.

Comment

1–22 The first scene relates how, in their final meeting with their grandfather, Manasseh and Ephraim are promoted to be leaders of tribes on a par with Jacob's sons and how in blessing them Jacob advances Ephraim above his older brother Manasseh.

1 "After these things" marks a significant new stage in the story (cf. 15:1; 22:1, 20; 39:7; 40:1). חלה means "ill" or "weak" (Judg 16:7, 11, 17), since illness often makes one weak. Here, as in 1 Kgs 14:1, 5; 2 Kgs 8:7, it refers to a terminal illness. "Joseph . . . took with him his two sons." All the male heirs were expected to attend the patriarch's deathbed to receive his final blessing; contrast 27:1–4, where Israel deliberately summoned only Esau.

2 "Then Jacob was told." This impersonal form, lit. "one told Jacob," may suggest that Joseph the great man is being announced to his father or that Jacob cannot see who has arrived. "Pulled himself together." For this nuance, cf. 1 Sam 4:9; 1 Kgs 20:22. Similarly, Isaac invigorated himself by eating a hearty meal before pronouncing the blessing.

3–7 Without further prompting, the old man launches into reminiscence, and typical of a dying patriarch, his concern is with the fulfillment of the divine promises. Ostensibly, Jacob refers back to the promises made to him at Bethel when he returned to Canaan after twenty years in exile (35:9–13), but he also echoes the parting blessing given him by Isaac before he died (28:3–4). Just as Isaac's blessing was ultimately fulfilled when Jacob returned to Canaan, so Jacob hopes his last words will come true when his descendants return there. To underline the importance of returning to their ancestral home, he insists that he must be buried there.

3 "El Shaddai appeared to me" summarizes 35:9, 11 (cf. 17:1). On "El Shaddai," cf. 17:1. "Luz" is the old name of Bethel (28:19; 35:6).

4 Jacob says he is quoting what God said to him at Bethel. The gist is certainly the same as in 35:11–12, but some of the phrases, "make you fruitful . . . multiply you [hiphil]" and "multitude of peoples," more closely echo 28:3, whereas "permanent holding" echoes 17:8. By this device of echoing other promise passages, Jacob identifies his convictions about the future of the nation with those of his father Isaac (speaker in 28:3) and Abraham (addressed in 17:8). The divine promises and commands have been given to Abraham, Isaac, and Jacob, so the next generation must loyally carry them out. "Holding" also describes the land allocated to them in Egypt by Joseph (47:11), but unlike Canaan it was not a God-given "permanent holding."

5 Jacob therefore proceeds to adopt his grandsons formally, putting them on a par with his two eldest sons, Reuben and Simeon (cf. 29:32–33). Such adoptions within a family are well attested in the ancient Orient; a text from Ugarit records a grandfather adopting his grandson as his heir. It should be noted that Jacob mentions Ephraim before Manasseh, already anticipating his action in vv 14–20. This act of adoption does not simply make Ephraim and Manasseh Jacob's heirs but makes them the ancestors of tribes on a par with those tracing their origin back to Jacob's own sons, such as Judah and Benjamin.

6 This is the only mention of other sons born to Joseph. In future, they will be incorporated into the tribes of Ephraim and Manasseh.

7 The great experience of Bethel, where the promises were reiterated (35:6–15), was soon followed by Jacob's greatest loss, the death of his beloved wife Rachel in childbirth (35:16–20). This is briefly mentioned again, foreshadowing his own imminent death and burial.

8 "Israel saw Joseph's sons and said, 'Who are these?'" This seems a most surprising question after they had come in earlier (v 2), and Jacob himself has

already referred to them in v 5. For source critics, this is evidence that vv 3–7
come from P, whereas vv 1–2, 8–12 come from E or J. But, as often, this is only a
partial explanation, as it fails to explain how the redactor related the two remarks
or to take account of the parallels in chaps. 22–24, 35 that have a sequence (death
of wife, marriage of a son) similar to 48:7–9. Sarna's proposal (327) that checking their identity is a necessary part of an adoption procedure has greater merit.
Alternatively, older commentators may be right to take Jacob's question "Who
are these?" as genuine, just like his father Isaac's "Who are you, my son?" (27:18).
Both Isaac and Jacob were blind (27:1), or nearly so (48:10), and needed to be
sure who they were about to bless.

9 Joseph's reply does not name his sons, which shows that Jacob knows their
names (cf. v 5). Rather he states, "These are my sons whom God has given me
here." Since throughout the Bible children are seen as God's gift (cf. Pss 127,
128), this comment seems rather a platitude, but despite the promises of offspring, children came slowly to the patriarchs. So Joseph's remark draws attention
to the fulfillment of the promises.

"Please bring them to me so that I may bless them." Reassured of his grandsons' identity, Jacob indicates his intention of blessing them. This key word,
"blessing," is used nineteen times in 27:1–28:9 and nine times in chaps. 48–49
out of a total of thirty-seven times in the life of Jacob (chaps. 27–50). Jacob, who
was so anxious at his father's deathbed to acquire blessing for himself, is now just
as keen to pass it on to his descendants before he dies.

10 This comment on Jacob's failing eyesight may explain his comment in v 8
and Joseph's reaction to the confusion of Ephraim and Manasseh in vv 17–19: he
thought he had mixed them up because he could not see. It also highlights the
parallel with chap. 27 (cf. v 1), as does the remark "he brought them to him and
he kissed them" (cf. 27:26–27, "he came close and kissed him"). Jacob also "hugged
them" as Laban and Esau had earlier hugged him (29:13; 33:4). Sarna sees these
gestures as part of the legal process of adoption.

11 "I never expected" harks back to his earlier belief that Joseph had died
(37:33–35; 42:36; 45:26). But despite his unbelief, God's promise had been fulfilled beyond his bravest hopes, "God has shown me your descendants as well."

12 "From his knees" does not imply that the boys were sitting on the
grandfather's knees. More probably, they had stood by his knees or leaned over
them, perhaps another gesture betokening his legitimation of them as the equals
of his sons.

"He bowed face down to the ground" elsewhere in Genesis is a greeting to
someone of great honor whose favor is being sought (e.g., 24:52; 33:3; 42:6; 43:26).
Though Jacob has intimated that he wants to bless Joseph's sons, Joseph by this
action deferentially requests it.

13–20 Ephraim and Manasseh, having been introduced to their grandfather,
are now positioned by Joseph to receive the appropriate blessing. Manasseh, the
elder, should receive the greater blessing, so Joseph puts him under Jacob's right
hand. Throughout Scripture the righthand side is regarded as the place of honor
and blessing (cf. Deut 11:29; Ps 110:1; Matt 25:33; Heb 1:3). But, unexpectedly,
Jacob crosses his hand, so that Ephraim, instead of Manasseh, receives the
firstborn's blessing.

While Joseph supposes this is just a blind man's mistake and tries to correct Jacob, the latter insists he knows what he is doing. He was deliberately giving precedence to the younger son, something that has happened a number of times already in Genesis: Cain and Abel (4:1–8), Peres and Zerah (38:27–30), and most obviously Jacob and Esau (chap. 27). But whereas in the last case the blind Isaac was tricked into blessing his younger son, this time the blind Jacob deliberately chooses to bless the younger Ephraim. If Isaac's unintended blessing was effective, how much more so the deliberate decision by Jacob to put Ephraim before Manasseh.

15–16 However, the gesture alone points to Ephraim's future ascendancy as both the boys receive the same blessing. Their equality is also implied by the comment "he blessed Joseph."

"May the God, . . . may the God . . . may the angel." This blessing foreshadows the later priestly blessing in its tripartite structure, "May the LORD, . . . may the LORD, . . . may the LORD," and, like the priestly blessing, Jacob's has also been used in Jewish liturgy.

Jacob's blessing recalls God's guidance and protection of himself and his father and grandfather. Once again, it contains clear echoes of Abraham's final words. Abraham *walked before* the LORD who sent his *angel* ahead of his servant to find a wife for Isaac (24:40). On the term "walks before," cf. *Comment* on 5:22; 17:1 of a life lived in the presence of God.

"Who guided me," lit. "shepherded me." The idea that gods shepherd their people was common in the ancient Near East. The image is particularly evocative in the mouths of men like Jacob or David who were once shepherds themselves (Gen 29–31; 1 Sam 16:11; cf. Ps 23:1).

16 "May the angel." The OT speaks of angels who accompany God (e.g., 19:1), but it also speaks of "the angel of God/the LORD" or, as here, of just "the angel" in the singular, who is an appearance of God in human form (cf. *Comment* on 16:7). Typically, he appears at moments of personal (16:7; 21:17; 22:11, 15) or national crisis (Exod 3:2; Judg 2:1). So here Jacob describes the angel as the one "who rescued me from every evil." גאל "rescue" has important connotations in biblical thought. "The rescuer" (*gōʾēl; TDOT* 2:350–55; *THWAT* 1:83–94) was usually the nearest male relative, whose responsibility was to bail someone out if he fell into debt or slavery (Lev 25:22–26, 48–49) or to avenge his death in the case of murder (Num 35:12). But Jacob, who fled from his brother into the clutches of his uncle, had no human rescuer; God himself stepped in and rescued him from his uncle (31:42) and later from his brother (chaps. 32–33; cf. Hos 12:4–5).

"My name . . . be recalled through them." Their future greatness as tribes will make people remember their ancestors Abraham, Isaac, and Jacob.

"May they multiply like fish." The future multiplication of the patriarchs' descendants is a familiar element in the promises (15:5; 22:17; 28:14), but the comparison with fish is new here.

17–18 No sooner are the words uttered, with Ephraim receiving the righthanded blessing, than Joseph attempts to reverse it, just as Esau attempted to reverse the blessing given to Jacob in 27:34–36. But blessings once uttered are irreversible (cf. Num 23:20; Rom 11:29), and Joseph's protest only serves to highlight this. If Isaac's unintentional blessing of Jacob instead of Esau could not

be altered, how much less Jacob's deliberate choice of Ephraim instead of Manasseh.

"Displeased." The phrase implies powerful anger (cf. *Comment* on 21:11, 12; 38:10). In deference to Jacob's age and infirmity, Joseph curbs his feelings, but his attitude is suggested by his action (תמך "grasping" implies a firm hold; cf. Exod 17:12; Isa 41:10; 42:1) and by his rather brusque imperative, "Not this way, father. . . . Put your right hand" (cf. Exod 10:11; 2 Sam 14:4).

19–20 As Esau's protests in 27:34–36 were countered with a reaffirmation of the blessing just pronounced (27:37–40), so here Joseph's attempt to make Jacob change his blessing is rejected. This parallel between the deathbed-blessing scenes tends to show the unity of the material and tells against Westermann's complex redactional hypotheses.

Whereas Manasseh will become a "people," Ephraim's descendants will be "full of nations." This last phrase occurs only here and is difficult to interpret. It certainly promises greater fertility to the Ephraimites and is reminiscent of the promise to Abraham, that he would be the father of a multitude of nations (17:4–6; cf. 35:11).

20 "May Israel pronounce blessing by you with the words 'May God make you like Ephraim and Manasseh.'" Here Jacob's prayer echoes the first promise to Abraham that he would be a blessing (cf. *Comment* on 12:2). Similar blessings using the names of Rachel, Leah, and Peres are used in Ruth 4:11–12, and a curse uses Zedekiah's name in Jer 29:22. Jacob thus clearly predicts that both Joseph's sons will prove to be outstanding examples of divine blessing.

21–22 Though Jacob is dying in Egypt, he has already made his son take an oath not to bury him there (47:29–31). Now he reminds Joseph that God will bring them all back to Canaan. Soon he will instruct all his sons to bury him in the family plot (49:29–32).

22 Mention of Canaan prompts Jacob to recall that he owns part of the land that he now gives to Joseph. Was this a token of his continuing attachment to Joseph, or also a reminder to his most Egyptianized son where his true home lay? The text leaves us to guess. And it is no easier to identify the "one shoulder" that he mentions here. 33:18–19 reports that Jacob bought a piece of land from the Canaanites near the city of Shechem, while chap. 34 describes Simeon and Levi putting that city to the sword. In that the Hebrew for "one shoulder" is literally "one Shechem," it is tempting to equate "which I have taken . . . with my sword and bow" with this episode. Historians suggest that this would explain why Joshua was able to hold ceremonies at Shechem (Josh 8:30–35; 24:1–32) without apparently ever having to fight for it. The main problem with this suggestion is Jacob's disapproval of his sons' treatment of Shechem and his subsequent flight from that area (34:30–35:5). However, it should be noted that Joseph was later reinterred at Shechem (Josh 24:32), in the land Jacob had bought from the Shechemites. Both Jacob and Joseph died in Egypt, and both were eventually buried in Canaan. It therefore seems likely that this explains the otherwise strange transition between v 21 and v 22, Jacob's burial.

Sub-Bibliography on Gen 49:1–33

Aberbach, M., and **Grossfeld, B.** *Targum Onqelos on Gen 49: Translation and Analytical Commentary.* Missoula: Scholars, 1976. **Ahubiah, A.** "'When they please, they hamstring an ox'

(Gen 49:6)." (Heb.) *BMik* 35 (1989/90) 227–29. **Barr, J.** "'ερίζω and ἐρείδω in the Septuagint: A Note Principally on Gen 49:6." *JSS* 19 (1974) 198–215. **Caquot, A.** "La parole sur Juda dans le testament lyrique de Jacob (Gen 49:8–12)." *Sem* 26 (1976) 5–32. ———. "Ben Porat (Gen 49:22)." *Sem* 30 (1980) 43–56. ———. "'Siméon et Lévi sont frères.'" In *De la Tôrah au Messie: FS H. Cazelles,* ed. M. Carrez, J. Doré, and P. Grelot. Paris: Desclée, 1981. 113–19. **Carmichael, C. M.** "Some Sayings in Gen 49." *JBL* 88 (1969) 435–44. **Cohen, M.** "*mekērōtēhem* (Gen 49:5)." *VT* 31 (1981) 472–82. **Criado, R.** "Hasta que venga Silo (Gen 49:10): Recientes explicaciones católicas." *EstBib* 24 (1965) 289–320. **Cross, F. M.,** and **Freedman, D. N.** *Studies in Ancient Yahwistic Poetry.* Missoula: Scholars, 1975. **Dahood, M. J.** "Is *ʾeben yiśrāʾel* a Divine Title?" *Bib* 40 (1959) 1002–7. ———. "*MKRTYHM* in Gen 49:5." *CBQ* 23 (1961) 54–56. **Eissfeldt, O.** "Gabelhürden in Ostjordanland." *KS* 3 (1966) 61–70. **Emerton, J. A.** "Some Difficult Words in Gen 49." In *Words and Meanings: FS D. W. Thomas,* ed. P. R. Ackroyd and B. Lindars. Cambridge: CUP, 1968. 81–93. **Gevirtz, S.** "The Reprimand of Reuben." *JNES* 30 (1971) 87–98. ———. "The Issachar Oracle in the Testament of Jacob." *EI* 12 (1975) 104–12. ———. "Of Patriarchs and Puns: Joseph at the Fountain, Jacob at the Ford." *HUCA* 46 (1975) 33–54. ———. "Adumbrations of Dan in Jacob's Blessing on Judah." *ZAW* 93 (1981) 21–37. ———. "Simeon and Levi in 'The Blessing of Jacob' (Gen 49:5–7)." *HUCA* 52 (1981) 93–128. ———. "Naphtali in 'The Blessing of Jacob.'" *JBL* 103 (1984) 513–21. ———. "Asher in the Blessing of Jacob (Gen 49:20)." *VT* 37 (1987) 154–63. **Giladi, H.** "משפחם." (Heb.) *BMik* 24 (1978/79) 33–44. **Goldfarb, S. D.** "Also Simeon Shall Be Blessed." (Heb.) *BMik* 20 (1975) 227–30. **Good, E. M.** "The 'Blessing' on Judah, Gen 49:8–12." *JBL* 82 (1963) 427–32. **Gordon, R. P.** "Targum Onkelos to Gen 49:4 and a Common Semitic Idiom." *JQR* 66 (1975/76) 224–26. **Gunneweg, A. H. J.** "Über den Sitz im Leben der sogenannten Stammessprüche (Gen 49 Dtn 33 Jdc 5)." *ZAW* 76 (1964) 245–55. **Heck, J. D.** "The Missing Sanctuary of Deut 33:12." *JBL* 103 (1984) 523–29. ———. "Issachar: Slave or Freeman?" *JETS* 29 (1986) 385–96. ———. "A History of Interpretation of Gen 49 and Deut 33." *BSac* 147 (1990) 16–31. **Krebs, W.** "'. . . sie haben Stiere gelähmt' (Gen 49:6)." *ZAW* 78 (1966) 359–61. **Kruse, H.** "David's Covenant." *VT* 35 (1985) 139–64. **Kuboth, J.** "Signifo de la vorto Šilôh en Gen 49:10." *BiblioRevuo* 15 (1979) 24–30. **Kutler, L.** "A 'Strong' Case for Hebrew MAR." *UF* 16 (1984) 111–18. **Levene, A.** "The Blessings of Jacob in Syriac and Rabbinic Exegesis: Studia Patristica, 7/1." *Texte und Untersuchungen* 92 (1966) 524–30. **Lipiński, E.** "באחרית הימים dans les textes préexiliques." *VT* 20 (1970) 445–50. **Luria, B. Z.** "'We shall not forget the northern border." (Heb.) *BMik* 35 (1989/90) 3–19. **Maier, J.** "Bemerkungen zur Fachsprache und Religionspolitik im Königreich Juda: 1. Gen 49:5–7." *Judaica* 26 (1970) 89–105. **Margalith, O.** "*Mekērōtēhem* (Gen 49:5)." *VT* 34 (1984) 101–2. **Margulis, B.** "Gen 49:10 / Deut 33:2–3: A New Look at Old Problems." *VT* 19 (1969) 202–10. ———. "Emendation and Exegesis: A Reply to L. Sabotka. (*Bib* 51 [1970] 225–29)." *Bib* 52 (1971) 226–28. **Martin-Achard, R.** "A propos de la bénédiction de Juda en Gen 49:8–12." In *De la Tôrah au Messie: FS H. Cazelles,* ed. M. Carrez, J. Doré, and P. Grelot. Paris: Desclée, 1981. 121–34. **Miller, P. D.** "Synonymous-Sequential Parallelism in the Psalms." *Bib* 49 (1980) 256–60. **Monsengwo-Pasinya, L.** "Deux textes messianiques de la Septante: Gen 49:10 et Ezek 21:32." *Bib* 61 (1980) 357–76. **Moran, W. L.** "Gen 49:10 and Its Use in Ezek 21:32." *Bib* 39 (1958) 405–25. **Müller, H.-P.** "Zur Frage nach dem Ursprung der biblischen Eschatologie." *VT* 14 (1964) 276–93. **O'Connor, M.** *Hebrew Verse Structure.* Winona Lake: Eisenbrauns, 1980. **Nobile, M.** "Le 'benedizioni' a Giuda e a Giuseppe in Gen 49:8–12 e in Deut 33:7, 13–17, nel quadro della redazione Gen–2 Re." *Antonianum* 64 (1989) 501–17. **Pili, F.** "Possibili casi di metatesi in Gen 49:10 e Salmo 2:11b-12a." *Augustinianum* 15 (1975) 459–71. **Prigent, P.** "Quelques testimonia messianiques: Leur histoire littéraire de Qoumrân aux Pères de l'Église." *TZ* 15 (1959) 419–30. **Rendsburg, G.** "Janus Parallelism in Gen 49:26." *JBL* 99 (1980) 291–93. ———. "Double Polysemy in Gen 49:6 and Job 3:6." *CBQ* 44 (1982) 48–51. **Sabotka, L.** "Noch einmal Gen 49:10." *Bib* 51 (1970) 225–29. **Salo, V.** "Joseph, Sohn der Färse." *BZ* 12 (1968)

94–95. **Sanmartín, J.** "Problemas de textologia en las 'Benediciones' de Moiseés (Deut 33) y de Jacob (Gen 49)." In *El misterio di la Palabra: FS L. Alonso Schökel,* ed. V. Callado and E. Zurro. Madrid: Ediciones Cristiandad, 1983. 75–96. **Schmitt, G.** "Der Ursprung des Levitentums." *ZAW* 94 (1982) 575–99. **Seebass, H.** "Die Stämmesprüche Gen 49:3–27." *ZAW* 96 (1984) 333–50. **Talmon, S.** *"Yad wasem:* An Idiomatic Phrase in Biblical Literature and Its Variations." *HS* 25 (1984) 8–17. **Treves, M.** "Shiloh (Gen 49:10)." *JBL* 85 (1966) 353–56. **Vawter, B.** "The Canaanite Background of Gen 49." *CBQ* 17 (1955) 1–18. **Watson, W. G. E.** "Hebrew 'To Be Happy': An Idiom Identified." *VT* 31 (1981) 91–95. ———. "The Hebrew Word-pair ʾsp//qbs." *ZAW* 96 (1984) 426–34. **Young, D. W.** "A Ghost Word in the Testament of Jacob (Gen 49:5)?" *JBL* 100 (1981) 335–42. **Zobel, H.-J.** *Stammesspruch und Geschichte: Die Angaben der Stammessprüche von Gen 49, Dtn 33 and Jdc 5 über die politischen und kultischen Zustände in damaligen "Israel."* BZAW 95. Berlin: de Gruyter, 1965.

Form/Structure/Setting

Gen 49:1–27, often called the Blessing of Jacob, is more aptly titled the Testament of Jacob, for these last words of the patriarch contain curses as well as blessings. The overall arrangement of chaps. 48–50 has already been discussed (see *Form/Structure/Setting* above), but 49:1–27 requires special discussion in that it is the first long poem in the Bible, whose origin and background have been much discussed, and also because it is often thought that it is out of place in its present setting and that the narrative would run more smoothly without it. So here we shall briefly examine its place within the book of Genesis, compare it with other deathbed sayings, and discuss the order of the tribal blessings, the nature of the poem (is it just a collection of originally independent sayings?), its possible use before incorporation into Genesis, and its date of composition.

Rejecting conventional views of chap. 49, Longacre has insisted on its centrality to the whole Joseph story, indeed to the book of Genesis, possibly constituting its peak. "This chapter, in that it is poetry, seems to be intended to be a high point of the *tōledôt yaʿ ăqōb* (i.e., chaps. 37–50), if not the whole book of Genesis" (*Joseph,* 23). "In this chapter . . . we have a glimpse of the embryonic nation— with the Judah and Joseph tribes destined to have preeminence in the south and north respectively" (*Joseph,* 54). Longacre observes that within the Testament of Jacob, ten of the twenty-five verses refer to Judah (vv 8–12) and to Joseph (vv 22– 26), a ratio that corresponds to their importance in the surrounding narrative, where apart from Joseph, Judah is the leading figure among Jacob's sons (cf. 37:26–27; 38:1–26; 43:3–10; 44:14–34; 46:28). But Longacre's observations may be developed further in that another five verses of the Testament (vv 3–7) concern brothers who are also mentioned by name in the Joseph story, i.e., Reuben and Simeon (37:21–22, 29–30; 42:22, 37; 48:5; 42:24, 36; 43:23), whereas Zebulon, Issachar, Dan, Gad, Asher, and Naphtali, who elsewere appear just in lists, merit only eight verses among them.

But the relationship of the Testament with earlier parts of Genesis is also apparent. First, the order of blessings from Reuben to Benjamin corresponds roughly to their order of birth recorded in 29:32–30:24; 35:18 (the reasons for the minor deviations from this order will be discussed later). Second, Jacob's condemnations of Reuben (v 4), Simeon, and Levi (vv 5–7) refer to episodes related in chap. 34

and 35:22. Finally, it should be noted that it is only the four sons whom Jacob concentrates on here, Reuben, Simeon, Judah, and Joseph, whose names are explained at their birth by reference to the divine name Yahweh (the LORD; 29:32–35; 30:24); by this device these four sons are marked out from birth as the key players in the drama that unfolds in Gen 29–50. Though these points have eluded most modern commentators, they show that chap. 49 is well integrated into the book.

The coherence of 49:1–27 within chaps. 48–50 has already been addressed (see *Form/Structure/Setting* above). There it was noted that the type of material in these chapters closely matched the content and sequence of that in 22:15–25:10 and 35:9–14, the closing sections of the Abraham and Jacob cycles. Furthermore, the repetition of a deathbed blessing occurs in 28:2–6. Outside the patriarchal narratives, the song of Deborah with its roll call of the tribes (Judg 5:14–18), and the blessing of Moses (Deut 33:2–29), with its probable echoes of Gen 49, parallel this section. Within Genesis, Noah's last words (9:25–27), beginning with a curse on Ham for his past behavior and ending with blessings on his other sons, also provide a parallel with 49:1–27, which likewise begins with Jacob cursing three sons for their past conduct before going on to predict a more glorious future for the other sons. In both cases, the comments of the dying patriarch foreshadow the future of their respective sons and their descendants: in Jacob's case the future of the Israelite tribes, and in Noah's the destiny of the nations set out in Gen 10.

Within the Testament of Jacob, the tribal blessings are arranged in roughly the order of the patriarch's birth: first, the sons of Leah (Reuben to Issachar), then the maids' sons (Dan to Naphtali), and finally Rachel's sons (Joseph and Benjamin); cf. 29:32–30:24; 35:18. But among Leah's sons, Zebulon precedes Issachar (contrary to 30:17–20), possibly because Zebulon's destiny (49:13) is better than Issachar's (49:14–15). The order of the maids' sons, Dan, Gad, Asher, Naphtali, does not match 30:5–13, which is Dan, Naphtali (sons of Bilhah, Rachel's maid), Gad, Asher (sons of Zilpah, Leah's maid). Sarna points out that this gives a chiastic order to the list.

Dan	son of Bilhah
Gad	son of Zilpah
Asher	son of Zilpah
Naphtali	son of Bilhah

Dillmann, however, suggested that the order of these tribes reflects their place of settlement from south to north: Dan (cf. Josh 19:40–48), Gad (Num 32:33–36), Asher (Josh 19:24–31), and Naphtali (Josh 19:32–39).

Despite the assumption of some recent writers (e.g., Zobel, *Stammesspruch*; Westermann; Stuart, *Study in Early Hebrew Meter*; Sarna) that the tribal sayings originally circulated independently, the arguments of earlier scholars (e.g., Dillmann, Gunkel, and Skinner and more recently Seebass, *ZAW* 96 [1984] 333–50) for the essential unity of the poem seem cogent. As already noted, the Testament of Jacob consists of a mixture of quite long sayings dealing with Reuben, Levi, Simeon, Judah, and Joseph and quite short sayings about other tribes that pun on their names or compare the tribes to animals. The longer tribal sayings constitute more

than two-thirds of the Testament and are intimately linked to each other and to the wider context of Genesis. All presuppose that Jacob is the speaker (49:3–4, 6, 8–9, 25–26), mention relations between the brothers (49:4, 7, 10, 26), and concern major actors in the Jacob and Joseph stories. This makes it highly likely that these tribal sayings, at least in their present form, all belong together; they make less sense as isolated statements. And this is even more true of the other tribal sayings, e.g., about Gad, Asher, or Naphtali (vv 19–21). In their present context, these tribal sayings make sense, showing Jacob's concern for all his descendants, but it is hard to envisage a situation where remarks such as "Asher has rich food; he will produce royal delicacies" (v 20) would have a place by itself. It therefore seems most likely that this poem was from the start a substantial unity; this is not to rule out the probability that the poem developed with time, but whether the stages of its growth can be identified must be left to exegesis rather than decided in advance.

It is widely agreed that the Testament of Jacob was incorporated first by J in his account of the patriarchal period. Can anything be said about its earlier use or its date of composition? Gunneweg (*ZAW* 76 [1964] 254) has argued that like Deut 33, Gen 49 was used in a national covenant festival marked by a theophany and a gathering of all the tribes. This idea seems more feasible for Deut 33 than this chapter, for Gen 49, unlike Deut 33:2–5, mentions no divine appearance, and it is hard to envisage curses on three tribes (Gen 49:3–7) being regularly repeated at a national festival. Given the constant tradition within Genesis that dying patriarchs pronounce on their descendants' future, it would seem more likely that from the first this testament was associated with Jacob.

Its date of composition is hard to determine. The animal similes or puns on names are undatable, and the curses on Reuben, Levi, and Simeon refer to episodes in the patriarchal period that might have given rise to such reflections at any subsequent time. The only allusions within the Testament that may give a clue to its period of composition are those specifying where the tribes live, i.e., Zebulon (v 13) and possibly Issachar (vv 14–15), the scattering of Simeon and Levi (vv 5–7), and the relative strength of the tribes of Judah (vv 8–12) and Joseph (vv 22–26). This situation roughly mirrors the time of the Judges. By then, the Levites had become a priestly tribe (to which Genesis makes no allusion) and were dispersed in their levitical cities, and probably the tribe of Simeon was well on its way to being absorbed by Judah. But according to Josh 19:10–16, the tribe of Zebulon was allotted inland territory, not coastal territory as Gen 49:13 implies, and Issachar, according to Judg 5:15, was one of the less subservient tribes (*pace* Gen 49:15). Gen 49:10, "the staff will not desert Judah," has long been understood as a prophecy of the rise of the Davidic dynasty or the Messiah, and if it is not, a prediction could point to the composition of at least this part of the Testament in the time of David or Solomon. For these reasons, the common view among critical scholars is that the poem probably dates from the Judges period with some revision in the tenth century B.C. Dillmann, however, observed that if the Testament were so late, it is surprising that it says nothing about the Mosaic era or the kingship of Saul, and he therefore preferred to date the whole poem to the period of the Judges. Seebass (*ZAW* 96 [1984] 333–50) argues similarly, that apart from a few glosses, e.g., vv 7b, 8b-9, 18, the Testament antedates the

song of Deborah (Judg 5) and probably originated in the twelfth century. Delitzsch argued that it indeed originated with Jacob, who on his deathbed was inspired with a vision of the future settlement of the land. He pointed to the inconsistencies between the situation in which the tribes found themselves after the settlement and the vision described here and emphasized the irrelevance of the condemnation of Reuben, Levi, and Simeon in the post-Mosaic era. Here, as often in biblical criticism, it is clear that assumptions are, in the absence of hard evidence, of paramount importance in determining the date of material. But there is universal agreement that here we are dealing with one of the oldest parts of the Bible. Indeed, Gunkel claimed that "for the earliest history of the tribes, Gen 49 along with Judg 5 is the most important chapter in the OT" (Gunkel, 478).

Comment

1–2 These verses introduce Jacob's Testament. קָרָא אֶל "summoned," as in 28:1 (Isaac's farewell to Jacob) and 3:9; 22:11, 15; Exod 19:3, intimates the importance of the message.

בְּאַחֲרִית הַיָּמִים "in the latter days" is a phrase that only appears in prophetic contexts. In some passages it has a clearly eschatological sense (e.g., Isa 2:2; cf. NT "last days"), but elsewhere it seems to have a less technical sense, "in the distant future," after certain other things, which the prophet has just described or hinted at, have happened (cf. Num 24:14; Deut 4:30; 31:29; cf. *TDOT* 1:210–12). Such a sense here would explain why Jacob looks beyond the period of Egyptian slavery and exodus to the era of settlement in Canaan.

2 Note the use of repetition and parallelism, "listen . . . sons of Jacob, listen to Israel your father," giving Jacob the mantle of a wise teacher (cf. Prov 1:8; 4:1) as well as a prophet.

3–4 The Testament of Jacob, like Noah's (9:25), pronounces curses on sons guilty of unfilial conduct. Once again in Genesis the eldest son (cf. Cain, Ishmael, Esau, and Er) loses his privileged position because of his sin. The incident referred to here is briefly related in 35:22, "Reuben went and lay with Bilhah, his father's concubine, and Jacob heard about it." Jacob's long and eerie silence about that episode is now broken in one of the fiercest denunciations in Genesis. Afraid of doing anything to Reuben in his lifetime, Jacob curses him on his deathbed (cf. David and Joab, 1 Kgs 2:5–6).

3 Jacob first sketches the honor and prestige attached to Reuben's status as his firstborn son. Jacob describes him as "my strength and the first fruit of my virility, outstanding in majesty and power." In Bible times, the firstborn son was not simply his parents' pride and joy; he had a special status and legal privileges, which Jacob tricked Esau out of (25:31–32; cf. chap. 27). Deuteronomy 21:15–17 mentions that the oldest boy usually received twice as large a share of his father's estate as his brothers. But it also forbids a father from transferring the rights of the firstborn by his first wife to the eldest son of a second wife, as Jacob clearly did. This is one of several examples of patriarchal practice conflicting with later legal theory and is a pointer to the antiquity of these traditions. Because the firstborn boy was so precious to his parents, the law insisted that, like the first fruits of the crops, he had to be dedicated to God (cf. Exod 13:2; 34:20), a status later

assumed by the tribe of Levi (Num 3:45–51). The phrases "firstborn" and "the first fruit of my virility" recur in Deut 21:17; Pss 78:51; 105:36. The term "first fruits" (ראשית) is common in sacrificial contexts (e.g., Lev 2:12; 23:10; Num 15:20; 18:12; Deut 18:4; 26:10) and suggests the holy calling that Reuben ought to have followed.

For he was "outstanding in majesty and power" are terms that aptly describe Almighty God (cf. Job 13:11; 31:23; Exod 15:2). יתר "outstanding," though used twice here, is rare elsewhere in the OT with this sense (cf. Isa 56:12; Ps 31:24; Prov 17:7; possibly Deut 28:54). But it prepares the way for the word play in v 4, "you shall not excel" (hiphil of יתר), and plays on words are common in this Testament (cf. vv 8, 16, 19, 20, 22).

4 But Reuben's godlikeness has been ruined through most ungodly behavior. "Frothy [פחז] like water" is a very difficult phrase. The noun פחז "froth" only occurs here; a similar noun occurs in Jer 23:32 and a participle from the same root in Judg 9:4 and Zeph 3:4. In two of these passages, it refers to false prophets inventing messages out of their own imagination, while in Judg 9:4 it refers to unscrupulous men bribed to murder. So LXX translates here "You have run riot," "waxed insolent"; Vulgate "poured out"; Tg. Onq. "You followed your own direction." It is clear that Reuben's behavior is reprehensible, but the exact point of the censure "frothy" or the simile "like water" is unclear. Does water's slipperiness suggest Reuben's lack of principle? Or do the images of boiling up in a pot, pouring down in a torrent, and foaming up in a storm, suggest Reuben's passion bubbling up and overflowing? "[T]he wicked are like the tossing sea; for it cannot rest, and its waters toss up mire and dirt" (Isa 57:20).

"You shall not excel." Only here does יתר (hiph) have this meaning. This, though, is the main point of Jacob's remark: Reuben is deprived of his status because of his misconduct. Three times, for emphasis, Reuben's offense is described: "you went up . . . you profaned . . . he went up to my couch." But grammatically the Hebrew of the last two lines is problematic because of the change of person, "*you* profaned . . . *he* went up," and the elision of "my couch" in the third line. Ellipsis is, however, a common poetic device, so it does not seem difficult to suppose it here. The switch from second to third person is more difficult, so it is not surprising that some versions read "you have gone up" (see *Notes*). These problems are avoided by Dahood's repunctuation of the two lines (*Bib* 45 [1964] 282): "ʾāz ḥillaltā yᵉsûᶜē yᵉᶜēlāh, 'You then defiled the couch of the doe,' where the animal-name is metaphorical as in Prov 5:19 . . . for 'wife.'" This is a neat solution, but on balance ellipse seems more likely. In the final colon, "he went up" suggests that Jacob turned from addressing just Reuben to all his sons and then informed them why Reuben had lost his privileges. The switch to the third person, "he went up," prepares the way for the next saying about Simeon and Levi, which is in the third person. "Profaned my couch" is a striking remark, for to profane means to make something that is holy unholy: it is the reverse of sanctifying. Thus, the law speaks of profaning the sabbath, the sanctuary, the name of God, sacrifices, or the priesthood (Exod 31:14; Lev 21:12; 19:12, 8; 21:9). This comment then implies that Jacob's marriage bed is also holy (cf. Lev 19:29; Heb 13:4).

The antiquity of this saying is evident. From the time of the settlement onward, there is no trace of Reuben's original primacy. Having settled in Transjordan

(Num 32), the Reubenites seem to fade out of national history: no prophet, judge, or king came from this tribe (cf. *EM* 7:285–95).

5–7 Like the adjacent tribal sayings, those about Simeon and Levi are fraught with difficulty, and this has led to very diverse interpretations. However, the context does set limits to the interpreter's freedom, at least if we aim to recover the editor's understanding of the text. These verses must be set within the framework of the whole book of Genesis. It is plain then that just as v 4 refers to Reuben's deeds mentioned in 35:22, so these verses must refer to Simeon and Levi's attack on Shechem (chap. 34). To suppose the mention of their hamstringing oxen refers to an entirely different incident is unlikely. So too is the suggestion that by singling out "Simeon and Levi" as "brothers," this saying supposes only the two tribes as blood brothers. From Gen 30 to 50 it is repeatedly made clear that all the tribes are descended from Jacob and therefore brothers. Thus "brothers" here must be understood in a non-literal sense. Finally, the immediate context is important for interpretation. Having demoted Reuben from his primacy, Jacob might have been expected to confer the leadership on his next oldest sons, Simeon or Levi. But they too have disqualified themselves, and Judah is promised supremacy, in the words "Your father's sons will bow down to you" (v 8).

5 "Simeon and Levi are brothers." "Brother" here has the sense of "ally" or "confederate" (cf. 1 Kgs 9:13; 20:32), also used more loosely of someone who makes common cause with another (e.g., Prov 18:9). They were, of course, full blood brothers as well, but so were Reuben, Judah, Issachar, and Zebulon (cf. 29:32–30:19). Here their collaboration in sacking Shechem is in view, as the next remark makes plain: "They are equipped with weapons of violence."

The word translated "They are equipped with" occurs only here and is quite obscure: literally "Their *mekerot* are weapons of violence." What is a מכרה, and how does it relate to their actions in Gen 34? A variety of answers have been given. מכרה means (1) sword, perhaps borrowed from Greek μάχαιρα "sword" (so *Ber. Rab.*, Rashi, Rabin [*EM* 4:1079], and Margalit among others); (2) "circumcision sword" from the root כרה "to cut" (Dahood, *CBQ* 23 [1961] 54–56); (3) "ware" from the root מכר "to sell" (Speiser; Caquot, "'Siméon et Lévi'"; Sarna); (4) "wedding feast," from the Akkadian noun *kirru* (Young, *JBL* 100 [1981] 335–42). All these suggestions are possible, unlike many others that are far-fetched. But they all have their snags. (1) A Greek derivation becomes more difficult the earlier the poem is dated. (2) Though the verb "to cut" is well known in Hebrew, there is no other example of מכרת meaning "circumcision knife." (3) "Ware" "something sold" seems rather a colorless term in the context. (4) "Wedding feast" is the most interesting proposal and deserves further explanation. In the ancient Near East, a marriage feast was a regular component of weddings. According to LE 27, for a woman to cohabit with a man without a wedding feast (*kirru*) or contract was insufficient to make her his wife. Young points out this was Shechem's situation, living with Dinah without having gone through the proper formalities, including a *kirru*. Simeon and Levi demanded the union be regularized, and so Young surmises that we have a reference to these demands here. On his understanding, we should translate this line "Their wedding feasts turned out to be weapons of violence." Attractive though this proposal is, it faces two snags: usually the wedding breakfast took place in the groom's home (cf. LE 27), not the bride's, so why should

the poem speak of "their [i.e., Simeon and Levi's] marriage feast," when it should have been Shechem's? Second, Young posits the prefixed מ before כרתיהם is an enclitic mem. This seems a little cavalier. So this attractive hypothesis remains open but unproved.

חמס "violence" is a strongly condemnatory term, "cold blooded and unscrupulous infringement of the personal rights of others, motivated by greed and hate and often making use of physical violence and brutality" (*TDOT* 4:482; cf. *Comment* on 6:11).

6 Their behavior makes Jacob wish to shun their company (cf. Ps 1:1, 5). The first two lines neatly parallel each other: soul//reputation; enter//rejoice; circle//company. In our translation, we have adopted Gevirtz's proposal to repoint the second verb תחד to read "rejoice" instead of "be joined" (see *Notes*). This is supported by the parallelism of "enter" and "rejoice" in Job 3:6 and by an Akkadian idiom, *kabattu ḫadu* "the belly rejoices" (cf. *CAD* K, H; Gevirtz, *HUCA* 52 [1981] 108). This Akkadian idiom suggests that there is no need to repoint כבדי "my reputation, glory" as "my liver" (see *Notes*). Rather, here and in Pss 7:6(5); 16:9; 30:13(12); 57:9(8); 108:2, כבוד corresponds to Akk. *kabattu* "belly," which like other parts of the body may stand for the whole person. Rendsburg (*CBQ* 44 [1982] 48–55) suggests that these lines were intended to be read in two ways: "Let my soul not enter/desire their council; Let my spirit not be united/rejoice in their company." This depends on pointing both verbs in two different ways. Though the unpointed text could have led readers to interpret it differently, when it was first recited and whenever it was reread aloud, only one interpretation was possible. The modern reader and translator face a similar problem.

"When angry, they kill a man, and when they please, they hamstring an ox." Parallelism is once again used to good effect here (angry//please; kill//hamstring; man//ox) to bring out Jacob's passionate rejection of his sons' actions. Clearly, the first line refers to the massacre of all the men in Shechem's city (34:25–26), but what is the second line with its reference to hamstrung oxen talking about? 34:28 speaks of Simeon and Levi taking away all the Canaanites' flocks and herds, but not of hamstringing, that is, cutting their back tendon to hobble them (e.g., warhorses in Josh 11:6, 9). While not kind to cattle, such a comment is an anticlimax after the mention of homicide in the previous line; this is contrary to the conventions of poetry, where typically the second line develops or says something more important than the first line.

So, not surprisingly, a variety of explanations of the hamstringing of oxen have been put forward. (1) This is a different tradition from that found in Gen 34: another version of the story spoke of oxen being maimed, not captured. Though possible, given that elsewhere in his Testament Jacob seems to comment on the existing stories in Genesis, this type of explanation must be a last resort. It also fails to make the second line a more serious charge than the first. (2) The word translated "ox" (שׁור) could also mean "wall" if pointed שׁוּר, while the word translated "hamstring" twice means "uproot" (Eccl 3:2; Zeph 2:4). The line would then be translated "when they please, they uproot a wall," perhaps a picturesque way of referring to the sacking of the city. But there is no explicit reference to them doing this in chap. 34. (3) "Ox" refers to the leaders of the Canaanites, Hamor or Shechem, slaughtered by Simeon and Levi. "Hamor" literally means "donkey," so

why not refer to his son Shechem as "ox." Describing leaders as "bulls" is well attested in Ugaritic (Vawter, *CBQ* 17 [1955] 4). (4) Another possibility, suggested by Good (*JBL* 82 [1963] 427–32) and Carmichael (*JBL* 88 [1969] 435–44), is that the "ox" refers to Jacob, whose interests in peace and security were put at risk by his sons' deeds. Indeed, he says, "You have brought ruin [עכר] on me" (34:30), and it could be that Jacob here is punning on his earlier comment when he speaks of hamstringing (עקר) oxen. As in chap. 34, Jacob here appears more concerned about his own welfare than that of his daughter or the Shechemites. In short, the third and fourth explanations are preferable to either of the first two, but it is not easy to choose between them.

7 The curse on anger is a curse on those who display it. For the parallelisms anger//wrath, cf. Hos 13:11; Amos 1:11; strong//hard, Cant 8:6; Isa 19:4.

"I will divide . . . I will disperse." Though Jacob is speaking, the saying sounds like a divine oracle of judgment, highlighting Jacob's prophetic role here. To what does this oracle refer? Most commentators hold that it refers to the dispersal of the Levites to forty-eight cities in Israel after the settlement (Josh 21). At that time, Simeon was allocated an enclave within the tribe of Judah (Josh 19:1–9; cf. 15:32–42). But this could hardly be termed dispersal. So Jacob argues that all that is being predicted here is that these two tribes should no longer work together: that in future they will be divided. Num 25:7–14 does tell of Phineas, a Levite, killing a Simeonite, a passage with close affinities with Gen 34 (cf. *Comment* there). However, while such an interpretation may suffice to explain "divide them," "disperse in Israel" does imply both a loss of power and a dispersal of this tribe within the nation. And several texts indicate that this was the fate of Simeon (cf. Num 1:23 and 26:14; 1 Chr 4:38–43; 2 Chr 15:9; 34:6 and *EM* 8:132–36; the absence of Simeon from Deut 33 is often taken to be a sign of the tribe's weakness then).

8–12 The blessing on Judah has provoked more discussion than the whole of the rest of the chapter. Though the general sense is clear, many of the details of interpretation are very difficult. The blessing on Judah consists of three parts:

v 8   Prediction of Judah's supremacy
v 9   Judah like a lion
vv 10–12   Judah's leader

There is a kaleidoscope of images in these few verses, lions, donkeys, scepters, vines, wine, milk, that are hard to interpret and relate to each other. Apart from glorifying Judah, what is the link between these images, if any? Good (*JBL* 82 [1963] 427–32) and Carmichael (*JBL* 88 [1969] 435–44) have argued that, like the sayings about Reuben, Simeon, and Levi in vv 3–7, the blessings on Judah are commenting on episodes in Judah's life related earlier in Genesis. Thus, Judah the lion (v 9) is the wild beast who devoured Joseph (37:33), the staff (v 10) is the one he pledged to Tamar (38:18, 25), his ass (עיר, v 11) stands for Er (ער, 38:6–7), and "washing his garment in the blood of grapes" (v 12) alludes to Joseph's coat being dipped in blood (37:31). Ingenious as this allegorical interpretation is, it fails to carry conviction because the symbolic equations are far from obvious, and it demands Jacob's remarks being understood as criticisms of Judah rather than as praise. This is difficult in the light of the explicitly positive v 8.

Another attempt to understand the unity of the blessing suggests it contains various additions. e.g., v 8 (Gevirtz; Seebass, *ZAW* 96 [1984] 333–50). While it is possible that vv 8–12 are composite, it is unwise to be dogmatic in that several other tribal sayings contain a mixture of animal imagery and comments on their future prosperity (Issachar, vv 14–15; Dan, vv 16–17; Joseph, vv 22–26).

8 "Judah, your brothers praise you." Here the link is an elaborate play on the name Judah with both alliteration and rhyme: in transliteration *yĕhûdāh . . . yôdûkā* "Judah . . . they praise you." Further paronomasia is found in the next line, *yādĕkā* "your hand." Similar word play is found in vv 11, 16, 19, 20, 22. Here the verb "praise" echoes Leah's words at Judah's birth: "This time I shall praise the LORD." Here, quite unusually, a man is being praised; usually God or his name is the object of praise. There are only three other passages where human beings are said to be praised (Job 40:14; Pss 45:18[17]; 49:19[18]); Westermann (*THWAT* 1:674) suggests that the verb for praise (hiphil ידה) here indicates it is achievement rather than essence that prompts this praise. Judah is being praised by his brothers for becoming a leader.

"Your father's sons will bow down to you," just as earlier they had bowed down to Joseph (cf. 37:7, 9; 42:6; 43:26; 43:28).

"Your hand will be on the back of your enemies," a gesture of triumph over them (cf. Exod 23:27; 2 Sam 22:41). Gevirtz (*ZAW* 93 [1981] 23–24), on the basis of an apparent quotation of this verse in 1QM 12:10, suggests that originally this line was a couplet:

> "Put your hand on the necks of your enemies
> and your foot upon the backs of the slain."

This would make the Judah sayings open with a reference to hands and feet and end with mention of "eyes and teeth" (v 12), echoing the talion formula "eye for eye, tooth for tooth, hand for hand, foot for foot" (Exod 21:24). In the absence of manuscripts supporting this reading, this emendation remains conjecture.

9 In a series of images, Judah is likened to a fierce lion that has seized its prey, returned to its den, and there lies daring anyone to challenge it. Elsewhere, similar imagery is applied to Israel (Num 23:24; 24:9), to the tribes of Gad and Dan (Deut 33:20, 22), and by the prophets to Israel's foes (e.g., Nah 2:11–12). Lions are mentioned over 100 times in the OT and were common in Israel (cf. Judg 14:5; 1 Kgs 13:24–25) and the Middle East in Bible times, and kings boast in inscriptions and depict in palace reliefs their prowess in hunting them. They became rare in Palestine after the Crusades, and in 1950, according to *EM* (1:500), only a few were to be found on the Upper Euphrates and in isolated places in the Arabian desert. Historically, the military successes of King David from the tribe of Judah may be seen as the fulfillment of this blessing, which also gave rise to the messianic title "Lion of Judah."

10 In this verse, the imagery changes yet again, but still the message of Judah's future leadership is plain. He will carry the symbols of authority, "the staff" and "the scepter" (cf. Num 24:17; Ps 45:7[6]; Zech 10:11; Num 21:18; Ps 60:9[7]). From this verse alone it is not obvious whether Judah is being invested merely with a tribal leader. However, v 8 makes it likely that Judah is being promised that

their leader will lead all the tribes. "From between his feet." This obscure phrase has attracted much discussion. SamPent's change to "between his standards" does not clarify the text. Skinner pictures the tribal leader sitting in state propping up the scepter with his feet. But more likely is the view of the ancient versions (LXX, Vg, Tgs.; see Caquot, *Sem* 26 [1976] 5–32; Sarna), which apparently, on the basis of Deut 28:57, take this as a reference to Judah's descendants: children come out from "between your feet." "Feet" are a regular euphemism for the private parts (e.g., Judg 3:24; 1 Sam 24:3; Isa 7:20). In other words, a descendant of Judah will always be a national leader.

"Until tribute is brought to him" has been described as the "most famous *crux interpretum* in the entire OT" (Moran, *Bib* 39 [1958] 405). So many suggestions have been put forward that Westermann says (3:231), "The whole discussion has not yet reached even a limited consensus." In order to keep our comments within bounds, we shall concentrate our attention on those suggestions that are congruent with the context and require the minimum of textual emendation. Thus, interpretations that depend on postulating major disruptions of the consonantal text (e.g., Margulis, *VT* 19 [1969] 202–10) or unusual meanings of rare words (e.g., עד "throne" [Sabotka, *Bib* 51 (1970) 225–29] or šēlu Akk. "ruler" [so various scholars]) will be discounted. Within these limits, there are four main ways of understanding this line. First, it may be translated without emendation: "Until he comes to Shiloh," i.e., until a Judean ruler controls Shiloh (so Jacob; cf. Delitzsch; Dillmann; Emerton, "Difficult Words"). Shiloh was for a while in the judges period an important sanctuary some miles north of Jerusalem in the tribal territory of Ephraim and was apparently destroyed by the Philistines (see discussion by D. E. Schley, *Shiloh*, JSOTSup 63 [Sheffield: Academic Press, 1989]). As far as is known, it was not an important center in the period of the united monarchy, when the Davidic dynasty (of Judah) ruled over all Israel. So it is not obviously relevant to that era, though certainly Shiloh was then under Davidic control. A weightier objection to taking this Shiloh as a place name is that it is spelled differently; here it is plene שׁילה, whereas elsewhere the place name is written defectively שׁלה. However, some Hebrew, MT, and the SamPent manuscripts and some of the versions have or presuppose this defective spelling.

But the versions, in reading שׁלה, evidently take it as לה + שׁ "which is to him." The line must then be translated "until he comes whose it is," i.e., "until the owner of the scepter comes." On this understanding, we have at least a reference to the Davidic dynasty, if not to a king superior to that dynasty, i.e., the messiah. Favored by RSV, NIV, REB, Skinner, this view faces two main objections. First, it makes a rather poor poetic line: something better to balance the next line, "the peoples obey him," would be preferable. Second, it is hard to understand why, if שׁלה were the original reading, it should have been changed into שׁילה, the more difficult reading.

The third possibility is that שׁילה means "ruler" or is a corruption of משׁלה "his ruler" (so Westermann, von Rad). The line would then read "Until his (the) ruler comes"; once again this would be announcement of a Davidic king or messianic figure. The supposed Akkadian etymology of שׁילה "ruler" has been demolished by Moran (*Bib* 39 [1958] 405–25), but Seebass (*ZAW* 96 [1984] 346) has suggested that שׁילה may go back to Egyptian *šr* "prince," which is written *šiāra* in an

Akkadian text from Boghazköi. Given the Egyptian setting of the blessing, this etymology cannot be ruled out, but it seems remote. The inner Hebrew explanation posits a double corruption of the consonantal text, which would be better avoided.

The fourth possibility ,"until tribute is brought to him," which we have adopted, requires no alteration of the consonantal text but only some repointing. It has an old Jewish pedigree (Yalkut and Lekaḥ Tov), but in modern times it was proposed by Moran and accepted by Speiser, NAB, Vawter (NEB, Monsengwo-Pasinya (*Bib* 61 [1980] 357–76), JPS, Sarna, Criado (*EstBib* 24 [1965] 289–320). This splits the words and repoints them as follows: לֹה "to him" שַׁי "tribute" יָבֹא "is brought." The advantage of this proposal, aside from its minimal changes in pointing, is that it produces a good poetic line in parallel with the next line, "and the peoples obey him": tribute from foreign nations expresses their submission to the Judean king. Furthermore, these two lines take further the leadership promised in the previous two lines, which spoke of a Judean always heading the nation. "The staff will not desert Judah": now the verse promises rule over foreign nations, who will bring him "tribute," a term used also in Pss 68:30(29); 76:12(11); Isa 18:7 of gifts brought by foreigners to Jerusalem. The idea that the Davidic king was appointed to rule the nations is of course often celebrated in the psalms (e.g., Ps 72:8–11) and the prophets (e.g., Isa 2:2–4). But interestingly, Ezekiel apparently alludes to this blessing of Judah, not only in chap. 19 (n.b. lion and vine) but also in 21:32(27), "until he comes whose right it is." In all these passages, Ezekiel is predicting the reversal of Jacob's blessing on Judah: because of sin, the lion of Judah will be captured and put in a Babylonian zoo, the Judean vineyard will be uprooted, and instead of ruling, the nations will be subject to them.

Whichever of these interpretations is adopted, and, though we prefer the last, we acknowledge that the alternatives are possible, all at least agree that this line is predicting the rise of the Davidic monarchy and the establishment of the Israelite empire, if not the coming of a greater David. And if the primary reference is to David, traditional Jewish and Christian exegetes would agree that like other Davidic promises it has a greater fulfillment in the Messiah.

"The peoples obey him," lit. "the obedience of the peoples." The noun "obedience" is only attested once elsewhere in Prov 30:17, but the verbal root *wqh* "obey" is attested in several cognate languages (KB, 411). "Peoples" (עמים) in the plural probably refers to non-Israelite nations, not just Israelite clans (e.g., 17:16; Exod 15:16; Deut 32:8).

11 "He tethers his ass to the vine." Asses were the mounts of chiefs in the judges period (Judg 10:4; 12:14), and Zech 9:9 declares Jerusalem's king will come

> triumphant and victorious . . . ,
> humble and riding on an ass,
> on a colt the foal of an ass.

Here it is not the king's triumph so much as the fruitfulness of the land that fills the poet's eye. There will be so many vines that the ruler will not worry about his ass eating the choicest vines, as it surely would if tethered to them. The territory of Judah is excellent for viticulture, as the spies found (Num 13:22–24).

"Pure-bred foal," lit. "son of a she-ass" (as RSV, Zech 9:9). M. Noth (*The Laws in the Pentateuch and Other Studies* [Edinburgh: Oliver & Boyd: 1966] 111) compares the similar Akkadian phrase, *mār atānim,* which has this meaning.

"He washes his clothing in wine" is another image of the abundance of wine at this time. There will be such an abundance of grapes that those trampling them in the wine press will not just splash their garments (cf. Isa 63:1–3) but soak them. Or the image may be of such a surplus of wine that people will not worry about using it to wash clothes in!

Throughout the OT, the golden age of future blessing is associated with bumper harvests, including grapes (cf. Lev 26:5; Ps 72:16; Isa 25:6; Joel 2:24; Amos 9:13). It seems likely that this passage was the source of these pictures of the messianic age.

12   "His eyes are darker than wine, and his teeth are whiter than milk" seems to be a reference to the leader's beauty (cf. 1 Sam 9:2; 16:12; cf. LXX, Vg, S, Caquot [*Sem* 26 (1976) 5–32]), but it could be another reference to the abundance of wine and milk under the coming king. In this case, it would be preferable to translate the lines "His eyes are dark with wine and his teeth white with milk." Canaan is often described as "flowing with milk and honey" (e.g., Exod 3:8, 17; Num 13:27; Deut 6:3). In an Arabic proverb, being "red with wine" is metaphorical for being very rich. And Isa 7:21–23 reflects on the erstwhile abundance of milk and vineyards. But the suggestion that his eyes will be "dark with wine" might suggest drunkenness as in Prov 23:29, which prompts the Targums to take the eyes and teeth as metaphors for the mountains and valleys of Palestine (e.g., *Tg. Onq.*).

> "His mountains shall be red with his vineyards;
> His valleys shall be white with grain and with flocks of sheep."

"Dark." The root occurs only here, in Prov 23:29, and in Akkadain *ekēlu* "to be dark" (cf. A. Demsky, "'Dark wine' from Judah," *IEJ* 22 [1972] 233–34; S. M. Paul, "Classification of Wine in Mesopotamian and Rabbinic Sources," *IEJ* 25 [1975] 42–44).

13   Usually Naphtali precedes Zebulon in Genesis. For possible reasons for the reversal here, see *Form/Strucure/Setting.* The saying about Zebulon may combine word-play with animal imagery—word-play in that *yiškōn* "lives" is synonymous with *yizbōl* (cf. Zebulon and *Comment* on 30:20; A. Strus, *Nomen-Omen,* 96) and animal imagery, if Dillmann is right in holding that Zebulon is here pictured as a man or an animal settling down with its face toward the sea and its backside toward Sidon. שׁכן may be used of animals resting (Deut 33:20; Job 37:8; Isa 13:21). Word-play and animal imagery are frequent in the other tribal sayings (cf. vv 8–9, 14, 16–17, 19, 20, 22).

Historians are perplexed by the reference to Zebulon living "by the seaside" (i.e., the Mediteranean) and being a "haven for ships," for the territory allocated Zebulon in Josh 19:10–16 was inland (roughly east of Haifa and Akko). Similarly, Deut 33:19 speaks of Zebulon and Issachar enjoying the affluence of the seas, implying that both tribes profited from seagoing activities. It may be that Zebulon did have an outlet to the sea or that men from this tribe were employed by the Phoenicians in their maritime trade. Or this saying and Deut 33:18–20 may not be envisaging permanent settlement by the seashore at all. Zebulon is said to "live by the seaside," and the word שׁכן "live" is often used of living in tents like

bedouin (e.g., 9:27; 16:12; 25:18), or is applied to clouds settling on the tabernacle or mountaintops (Exod 24:16; Isa 8:18). Hence, it may well suggest transient
residence rather than long-term settlement, which the book of Joshua envisages.

"Sidon," one of the major cities of the Phoenicians (10:15), is here used to
refer to Phoenicia in general. "His rear reaches Sidon" does not mean that the
land occupied by Zebulon reached as far as the city of Sidon, simply that the
tribe lived near Phoenicia.

14–15 The general sense of the saying about Issachar is clear: Jacob predicts
the tribe will settle in a fertile part of the country and there be enslaved by its
neighbors, presumably Canaanites. However, as often, the precise nuances of the
saying are hard to catch, and the historical reality to which it refers is hard to
place. As in the adjacent sayings, there is animal imagery. Issachar is likened to a
"strong-boned ass" (if גרם "strong-boned," as elsewhere, means "bone," e.g., Job
40:18; cf. Heck for other suggestions) and a play on the name: in 30:18 Leah
links the name Issachar with the word śākār "pay" (cf. *Comment* on 30:18). Here
Jacob rather more rudely states that Issachar is not a hired man but a slave.

"Lying down between his packs." The word translated "packs" occurs only here
and in Judg 5:16, and neither passage gives many clues to its meaning. Translators and commentators vacillate between this translation and "pens, sheepfolds"
or "borders." But what is the point of comparing Issachar to a donkey lying down?
Its stubbornness, laziness, or exhaustion from hard work? It is not clear. *Genesis
Rabbah* sees this figure of a recumbent ass as a description of Issachar's tribal
territory with Mount Tabor in the middle and the valley of Jezreel and the plain
of Akeslo on the borders (cf. Aberbach and Grossfeld, *Targum Onkelos*, 294–95).

15 "A good place . . . attractive land" aptly describes the fertile area allotted Issachar, southwest of the Sea of Galilee (Josh 19:17–24).

"So he put his shoulder to carry burdens . . ." Similar terminology (סבל) is
used of the Israelite slavery in Egypt (cf. Exod 1:11; 2:11; Ps 81:7[6]).

"To toil as a slave" (מס־עבד) is the phrase used of the forced labor gangs (corvee)
established by Solomon to undertake public words (1 Kgs 9:21). According to
Josh 16:10 (cf. Judg 1:28, 30, 33), it was Israel that made the Canaanites serve
them in this way, but here Jacob predicts that Issachar will in fact find himself
toiling as a slave, presumably to the Canaanites.

How and when this occurred is difficult to say. But a letter from the king of
Megiddo to Egypt (c. 1400 B.C.) found at El-Amarna mentions that men from
Yapu and Nuribda were working in the corvee at Shunem (*ANET*, 485, Letter *RA*
19, p. 97). Shunem was part of Issachar's territory (Josh 19:18) and Yapu (Japhia)
part of the adjacent territory of Zebulon (Josh 19:12). Hence, de Vaux (*Early
History of Israel*, 664) concludes "the eastern part of the plain of Jezreel must therefore have been colonized by groups of people coming from Zebulon, who chose
to live as serfs on good land rather than as shepherds or herdsmen in a poorer
district." This conflation of the El-Amarna data with this verse of Genesis is open
to question, but it does look as though both texts are reflecting on a similar historical situation in the early settlement period.

16–18 The blessing on Dan, the first of the handmaid tribes, like the preceding blessings, consists of a play on his name (v 16) and a comparison with an
animal (v 17). Unusually, it ends with an invocation of divine help (v 18). Why

this should be placed here and whether it really belongs to the blessing on Dan are unclear and will be discussed below.

16 "Dan will vindicate his people." Dan means "vindicated" or "judge" (cf. Rachel's comment at his birth, "God has vindicated me," 30:6 and *Comment*), so this is a pun on Dan's name typical of these sayings. "His people." Commentators are divided on whether this means "his tribe," i.e., the tribe of Dan, or the nation Israel. In that elsewhere the OT speaks of "God vindicating his people" (Deut 32:36; Ps 135:14; cf. Ps 72:2), the latter seems more likely. In other words, Dan's victories will benefit the whole nation of Israel.

"Like one of the tribes of Israel" is a puzzling phrase. Since the descendants of Dan are always seen as a tribe of Israel, why does Jacob need to draw attention to it? It may be a hint that Dan was not as strong as the other tribes: Judges describes the Danites' forced migration from their original area in the southwest of Canaan to the north. But like those of other bigger tribes, Dan's victories will help all Israel.

17 The idea that Dan is small but potent is certainly conveyed by the image of him as a deadly snake. "A horned viper." The traditional identification is *Pseudocerestes fieldi* a poisonous yellow snake (up to three feet long) with protuberances above its eyes that look like horns. It hides in crevices or burrows in the sand and bites animals that come within range (*EM* 8:249–50). "H. B. Tristram (*The Natural History of the Bible* [1868], 274) states that once whilst he was riding in the Sahara his horse suddenly started and reared, in the utmost terror: he could not discover the cause, until he noticed a Cerastes coiled up two or three paces in front, with its eyes intently fixed upon the horse, and ready to spring as the animal passed by" (Driver, 389).

But what is the point of comparing Dan to a horned viper? In that the other tribal sayings nearly all appear to relate to the experiences of the tribes between the settlement and the rise of the monarchy, it is natural to look for the fulfillment of Jacob's prediction within the Book of Judges. And this is what the Targums do (e.g., *Tg. Neof.*, "The venomous serpent . . . He is Samson bar Manoah"), as do most of the medieval Jewish commentators (see Leibowitz, 548–54). Through his own strength and various tricks, Samson defeated the Philistines on various occasions (Judg 13–16). Later the small tribe of Dan migrated northwards and sacked the unsuspecting town of Laish (Judg 17–18). Yet despite the prominence of Danites in the Book of Judges, modern commentators are strangely reluctant to link these sayings about Dan here with exploits of Samson or his tribe. Only Delitzsch, Dillmann, Driver, and König do so cautiously. Though it is unfashionable, I agree with this linkage.

18 "I look for your deliverance, O LORD." This first-person comment is a reminder that this is a speech by Jacob in which he has a strong personal involvement (cf. "my firstborn," "my soul," "my son," vv 3, 6, 9). It is also the last time God's name "the LORD" is used in Genesis.

But the interjection of a prayer at this point is unexpected, and consequently Westermann is one of several scholars who regard it as a later gloss. However, Ps 119:66, *pace* Westermann, is not "word for word the same," and it seems overdogmatic on the basis of the loose psalm parallels he cites to claim it reflects the hand of an exilic or post-exilic editor. And whether it is original or a gloss, we must ask what it means in its present context.

The collocation "look for deliverance" is unique to this passage, though it is found expanded in Isa 59:11, "we look for . . . salvation" (cf. Prov 20:22). Both terms are poetic, occurring most frequently in the Psalms and Isaiah. קוה "look for, hope, wait for" expresses a positive expectation as in English "look forward to." "God, light, good grapes, justice" are things that the Bible writers "look forward to." ישועה is usually translated "salvation," because it most frequently comes from God. But since "salvation" tends to be understood in English in a narrow spiritual sense, I have rendered it "deliverance," because it covers earthly God-given benefits as well (e.g., victory [Exod 15:2], childbirth [1 Sam 2:1]).

Within the context of a prophecy about the nation's future, this prayer of Jacob seems to be a reflection of the difficulties he sees the tribes facing: he prays to the LORD that he will deliver his descendants in future (cf. 15:11–21 and *Comment* on 22:17). Attached to the blessing of Dan, Jacob's remarks suggest an awareness of the precarious plight of that tribe: despite Samson's spectacular exploits, the Danites were forced to migrate to the north. And though on first reading the book of Judges may sound like a celebration of Israel's glorious heroes, it seems likely that the book is really illustrating the nation's political and moral decline in that era (cf. L. R. Klein, *The Triumph of Irony in the Book of Judges*, JSOTSup 68 [Sheffield: Academic Press, 1988]; B. G. Webb, *The Book of the Judges: An Integrated Reading*, JSOTSup 46 [Sheffield: Academic Press, 1987]). It may be that the Testament of Jacob shares this perspective on the post-settlement era and that this is reflected in Jacob's plea.

19 The saying about Gad is one long pun: four of the six Hebrew words in this verse contain the consonants גד *gd*. It predicts Gad's frequent involvement in war, it being a frontier tribe that settled in Transjordan between modern Amman and the river Jordan (Num 32; Josh 13:24–28). But as the second line, "But he will raid [יגד *ygd*] their retreat," makes plain, they will not lack success (cf. Deut 33:20–21; Judg 11; Mesha Stone, lines 10–13, *ANET,* 320). Gadites were famed for their military prowess, according to 1 Chr 5:18; 12:8.

20 Asher, second son of Zilpah, was so called because he made Leah happy (30:13). Now his descendants are promised a happy and prosperous existence. Asher settled a fertile strip of land running north from the Carmel range (Josh 19:24–31; Deut 33:24–25). Hence Jacob can say, "Asher has rich food." But from earliest times the Asherites lived alongside and doubtless traded with the Canaanites and Phoenicians (Judg 1:32; Ezek 27:17). "He will produce royal delicacies" probably refers to Asher supplying foreign courts. It is not clear whether this remark is a compliment or a rebuke, or simply a comment on Asher's affluence.

21 Naphtali was the second son of Bilhah (30:7–8), and the tribe settled west of the upper Jordan valley beside lake Huleh and the sea of Galilee (Josh 19:32–39; cf. *EM* 5:906–12). So much is clear, but the interpretation of this verse is quite uncertain. Each line can be understood in about three different ways, which has given rise to a great variety of interpretations. The translation offered here requires no emendation or repointing of the text and avoids positing rarely attested senses of the more obscure terms.

"Naphtali was born a free-running doe." אילה "doe" is the female of some kind of deer; *EM* 1:263 suggests one of the *Cervidae* family. "Does" are famed for their beauty and fleetness of foot (Prov 5:19; 2 Sam 22:34). However, apparently the

LXX and a minority of subsequent translators and commentators repoint the word אֵילָה "terebinth," which requires a quite different understanding of the second line. As the rendering "doe" makes sense and requires no repointing, we have followed it.

"Born a free-running" translates שְׁלֻחָה (passive participle of "send"). Here שׁלח has a secondary sense, but what exactly? Most commentators think it means here "release, set free" (cf. 8:7–8; Exod 22:4; Lev 16:22), e.g., RSV, "a hind let loose." This involves taking the qal passive participle as equivalent in meaning to the pual participle. Gevirtz (*JBL* 103 (1984) 518–19) gives many examples of this equivalence but argues that here שְׁלֻחָה means "was born." שׁלח may have this sense in Job 21:11, "they *produce babes in droves*" (REB), and Job 39:3, "are *delivered* of their young." The parallel with "give birth" (נתן) in the next line enhances this possibility. Nevertheless, Gevirtz's proposal is positing an unusual sense for שׁלח, so our translation combines both possible views.

"She gives birth to fawns of the fold." Every word of this line is problematic. First, "she gives birth" (הנתן) is a *masculine* participle, whereas a doe should be followed by a feminine participle, resulting in the proposed emendation נתנה of *BHS* and others. However, Gevirtz (*EI* 12 [1975] 111; *JBL* 103 [1984] 520–21) has argued that poets liked to alternate words of different gender in adjacent lines, and this could be happening here.

But the second and major problem of this line is the phrase אִמְרֵי־שֶׁפֶר, which we have tentatively translated "fawns of the fold." The sense of both words is uncertain. The noun שֶׁפֶר occurs only here, but the verb in Ps 16:6 and in Aramaic means "to be beautiful." Hence, the noun is usually understood to mean "beauty" (hence RSV "comely"; JPS, NAB, REB "lovely"; NIV "beautiful"). אִמְרֵי is most easily understood as the construct plural of אֵמֶר "word." This suggests the translation "who gives words of beauty" e.g., *Tg. Frg. Neof.* "announcing good tidings" (so too *Tg. Onq., Ber. Rab.,* some medieval commentators, and more recently Jacob and hesitantly Sarna). According to this view, "the good tidings" would be those brought by Barak, a Naphtalite, to Deborah about his victory over Sisera (Judg 4–5).

However, most modern commentators regard this as too abrupt a transition from the animal imagery of the previous line. Most therefore suppose that אִמְרֵי is the construct plural of a common Semitic word meaning "sheep" or "lamb" (Akk. *immeru;* Ugaritic *imr;* Aramaic אִמְּרָא). This is the basis of the translation "lovely/comely fawns." But F. I. Andersen (*The Verbless Clause* [1970] 44, 123) and Gevirtz *JBL* 103 [1984] 515–17) have pointed out that the whole phrase אִמְרֵי־שֶׁפֶר has parallels in Ugaritic *imr špr* and Akkadian *immir supūri*, which should be translated "lambs of the fold" or, assuming that אֵמֶר may also refer to the offspring of deer, "fawns of the fold."

According to this reading of the blessing, Naphtali is described as "born a free-running doe," who later "gave birth to fawns of the fold." She exchanged her original freedom for a later more sedentary domesticated lifestyle. This could refer to the process of settlement; the wandering desert-dwellers captured towns like Hazor and inhabited them. Or it could be a veiled criticism that the tribe of Naphtali accommodated itself to the Canaanite population (cf. Judg 1:33). So, like the previous blessing on Asher (v 20), it may be taken either as a straight comment, a compliment, or a mild rebuke.

22–26 The blessing on Joseph is "the longest, most complex, and most obscure" (Caquot, *Sem* 30 [1980] 43) of the tribal sayings in this chapter. Text-critical
issues (the SamPent and LXX offer a quite different version from the MT) inter-
twine with multiple problems in the MT Hebrew to make this an exegete's
nightmare. But as elsewhere in this poem, we shall eschew ingenious, but far-
fetched, suggestions for emendation and interpretation and try to find a coherent
reading of the text consistent with minimal textual changes.

The saying falls into three parts

v 22	Joseph compared to a vine or wild ass
vv 23–24	Joseph's successful self-defense
vv 25–26	Joseph's comprehensive blessing

22 This verse as translated here (cf. JPS, NAB, NIVmg) likens Joseph to a wild
ass. However, the traditional view from the Targums to the majority of modern
commentators is that the comparison is with a vine or some fruitful tree:

> "Joseph is a fruitful bough,
>   a fruitful bough by a spring;
>   his branches run over the wall." (RSV)

I shall therefore first explain this old view of the imagery before explaining why
the new view, while not without problems, is probably preferable.

The image of a righteous man flourishing like a tree planted by a river is well
known in the OT (Pss 1:3; 92:13–15[12–14]; Jer 17:7–8). And since Joseph is portrayed as the most righteous of Jacob's sons, the image of him as a fruitful tree
seems natural. It depends on taking the phrase פרת בן "wild ass/fruitful bough"
as the construct (despite unusual pointing) of בן "son of" + the feminine participle of פרה "be fruitful" or the abstract noun "fruitfulness." To maintain this
image, it is then supposed that the third line, lit. "daughters stride over a wall"
(translated here as "wild colts beside a wall"), refers to the branches of the tree,
its "daughters."

Simple as this traditional understanding may appear at first sight, it faces some
difficulties. If פרת is a participle of פרה, or an abstract noun "fruitfulness," it occurs only here and is an irregular form for a participle. Also, nowhere else is בן
"son" used to refer to a plant (Ps 80:16[15] offers dubious support for identifying a son with a vine), or בת "daughter," "branch" used for part of a plant, or צעד
"stride" used of plant growth. Nor does "strides" singular agree with its plural
subject "daughters." Finally, in the other tribal sayings where some metaphor is
used, the tribe is always compared to an animal, not to a plant (v 9, lion; v 14,
donkey; v 17, snake; v 21, deer; v 27, wolf), so an animal would be more suitable
here.

Perhaps this is what lies behind the comment of *Gen. Rab.* 99:12, "He became
great through kine" (*paroth*). So some modern commentators (Caquot, *Sem* 30
[1980] 44–45) have made various suggestions as to the identity of פרת בן, culminating in Speiser's that פרת is the feminine of פרא "wild ass," an epithet applied
to Ishmael in 16:12 (see Gevirtz, *HUCA* 46 [1975] 38–40 for morphology). This
possibility becomes more probable when the parallel phrase in the next line (בנות

צעדה) is recognized as equivalent to Arabic *banāt saʿadat* "wild asses," a proposal first made by Vater in 1802 (so Caquot, 51).

שור "over a wall." Speiser, JPS, and Sarna paraphrase "hillside" and suggest "The picture . . . is . . . of spirited young animals poised on some nearby elevation." The only other passage to use the word (2 Sam 22:30//Ps 18:30[29]) sees a wall as something to be leaped over, again suggesting vigor and strength. Gevirtz, on the basis of Gen 16:7, 12, which mention a place named "Shur, wall," argues that Gen 49:22 attests the incorporation of Ishmaelites into the house of Joseph, but this seems unlikely. If there is any allusion to Ishmael, it could be to 37:25, 28; 39:1.

Whatever the preferred translation of this verse, it seems likely that "Joseph is a wild ass" (בן פרת) is a pun on the name of his son Ephraim (cf. 41:52), though to Strus (*Nomen-Omen*, 99) it is a play on the title Pharaoh, with the suggestion "Joseph is the successor of Pharaoh."

23 Though modern commentators tend to see this as a prophetic reference to future attacks on the tribes of Manasseh and Ephraim (e.g., Judg 6:3), such attacks are not emphasized elsewhere in the OT. It may therefore be better to accept the view of traditional Jewish commentators, who see this remark as an allusion to the oppositon Joseph faced throughout his career, e.g., from his brothers, the Ishmaelites, Potiphar's wife, the royal cupbearer, and others. Slander is often likened to arrows (Jer 9:2[3], 7[8]; Prov 25:18; 26:18–19). A comment on Joseph's life would be most appropriate here, since the surrounding narrative has largely been concerned with him, and if incidents in the lives of Reuben, Simeon, and Levi appear in the long sayings about them at the beginning of Jacob's Testament (49:3–7), paternal reflections on Joseph's career would be appropriate at the end. The term "bore a grudge" reappears in 50:15, and this makes it likely that the editor saw these sayings about Joseph as dealing with his own life, not the long-term future of his descendants.

24 The general gist of this verse is clear. It tells how the attacks on Joseph failed because of divine assistance. However, the details of the imagery evade certainty, partly because of the rarity of the terms, partly because of the grammar.

> "Their bow remained firm,
>   though their hands and arms were agile"

A more literal translation would be

> "His bow remained firm,
>   and his hands and arms were agile"

and this is adopted by the majority of modern translations. The picture is of Joseph successfully fighting off his opponents: "the bow held steadily in position, while the hand that discharges the arrows in quick succession moves nimbly to and fro" (Skinner, 530).

Appealing though this image is, there is no intimation in Genesis of Joseph's agile verbal self-defense against false accusation. Rather, he appears as the sufferer whose appeals go unheeded. So Speiser's rendering, which we, like the NAB, NEB, and Vawter, have followed, is appealing. He suggests that the "his" in "his

bow . . . hands" is used distributively of the individual archers attacking him.
The firmness of the bow refers not to the enduring courage of the archer but to
its loss of suppleness. Speiser notes other references in Near Eastern literature to
bows losing their resilience. Furthermore, he notes that the LXX, the earliest
translation/commentary on this passage, also understands this comment to be
referring to the bows of Joseph's enemies, not his own. It reads, "And their bows
were broken with strength." In that the SamPent has the same Hebrew text as the
MT, it is unlikely that the LXX presupposes a different text, merely that the bow
mentioned here is not Joseph's. That the LXX is interpreting the MT here is
further suggested by its rendering of באיתן "firm" as "with strength," which the
Targums take as a divine epithet, "the Strong One."

But however this first half verse should be understood, the word-play on Joseph's
name here should be noted. Strus (Nomen-Omen, 93) is right to see full
paronomasia in וַיָּפֹזּוּ wayyāpōzzû "were agile" (2 Sam 6:16) with יוֹסֵף yôsēp "Joseph"
in v 22. Most of the other tribal sayings contain word-play on the name (vv 8, 13,
16, 19; cf. 14–15, 20), but the word-play here has often been overlooked.

"Thanks to the strength of the Mighty One of Jacob." אביר יעקב "Mighty One
of Jacob" seems to be an ancient epithet for God that is echoed in Ps 132:2, 5; Isa
49:26; 60:16; cf. 1:24. It may be compared to the Akkadian divine title bel abāri.

"Thanks to the shepherd of the stone of Israel" is again problematic. As indicated in the Notes, "Thanks to" implies a slight repointing of מִשָּׁם, which as pointed
in the MT, means "from there." Many commentators suggest that at this moment
Jacob pointed up to heaven to indicate the source of blessing. But though מִשָּׁם
occurs nowhere else, the similar expressions מִשּׁוּם in Aramaic and aššum in
Akkadian, and the parallelism with the preceding lines, make this reading probable. "The shepherd of the stone of Israel" may be a conflation of two names of
God: "shepherd of Israel" (cf. Ps 80:2[1]) and "stone of Israel" (this is a unique
variant of the more common divine title "Rock of Israel," 2 Sam 23:3; Isa 30:29).
On the other hand, it may be an allusion to Jacob's Bethel experiences, where
Jacob erected a stone in honor of the God who had shepherded him all the way
to Paddan-Aram and back (28:10–22; 35:1–15).

25 "Thanks to the God of your father—may he help you. Thanks to Shaddai—
may he bless you." Here the old name of God, "El Shaddai," has been split between
the two parallel lines: "God of your father" is literally "El of your Father," a phrase
found only here. This sharing of the epithet El Shaddai between two lines is also
found in Num 24:4, 16 and often in Job (e.g., 8:3, 5). Similarly, the initial preposition מ "thanks to" does double duty, for in the second line ואת is short for ומאת
(so Jacob, following Ibn Ezra).

The title "El Shaddai" (see Comment on 17:1) is consistently associated with
blessing and particularly with Jacob's career (cf. 28:3; 35:11; 43:14; 48:3), so it is
fitting that this prompts the comment "May he bless you." Blessing is one of the key
words of Genesis (cf. Comments on 1:22; 12:2–3), occurring some eighty-eight times
in the book. Here in two verses, like the finale of a fireworks display, the root occurs
six times (verb 1x, noun 5x) making a brilliant climax to the last words of Jacob.
The God-given blessings of the future will far outshine those already experienced.

All the important spheres of human activity will enjoy divine favor. Rain from
heaven and springs from the deep (cf. 1:2) beneath will ensure fruitful agriculture

(contrast 3:17–19), while women will enjoy the blessing of many children (contrast 3:16). In the Hebrew there is alliteration between "heaven" (שָׁמַיִם *šāmayim*) and "breast" (שָׁדַיִם *šādayim*), "deep" (תְּהוֹם *tĕhôm*) and "womb" (רֶחֶם *reḥem*). This deliberate balancing of divine blessing on male and female spheres of interest suggests the completeness of God's promises to all Joseph's descendants, both men and women.

26 Here Jacob, the man preoccupied with acquiring blessing from his earliest days, now reflects on his success. "The blessings of your father surpass the blessings of the eternal mountains, the bounty of the everlasting hills." The green mountain tops of Carmel, Hermon, or Lebanon in a land where other vegetation dries up in summer were an image of God-given life and prosperity (Cant 7:6[5]; Isa 2:13; 35:2). "Bounty," lit. "desirable thing" (cf. 3:6).

Now this abundant blessing is bestowed on Joseph, here described as "the prince among his brothers." נָזִיר "prince" only has this sense here, in the parallel Deut 33:16, and in Lam 4:7. Since kingship is nowhere seen as the prerogative of the Joseph tribes, this presumably is a retrospective comment on Joseph's preeminence among his brothers. In Egypt they often acknowledged his sovereignty as viceroy of the land.

27 Finally and briefly, Jacob blesses his youngest son Benjamin. But the contrast between the defenseless son of Jacob in the preceding narrative and the description of him as a fierce wolf in this saying is striking. Clearly, the future military exploits of the tribe of Benjamin are in view. Judges tells of Ehud the Benjaminite who delivered Israel from the Moabites (3:15–30), of Benjamin's participation in the war against Sisera (5:14), and of their savagery at Gibeah, prompting a civil war (chaps. 19–21). And it was from Benjamin that Saul and his able warrior son Jonathan came (1 Sam 10–14). But that there is no mention of kingship in this saying suggests its antiquity.

28 This editorial comment on the Testament of Jacob reiterates the largely future references of the sayings. Jacob had said he would declare "what will happen to you in the latter days." Here the author makes the point by saying that they concerned "the twelve tribes of Israel," not just the tribes' founding fathers. This is the first mention of the twelve *tribes* in the Bible.

29–50:1 These very last words of Jacob show the same concern as in his poetic Testament, the land. Having foretold the tribes' glorious future in the land of Canaan, he once again insists that he should be buried there. This is the third time that he has made this point (cf. 47:29–31; 48:21–22). Indeed, when he was leaving Canaan, God had assured Jacob: "I shall surely bring you up again, and Joseph will put his hand on your eyes" (46:4). The second half of that promise is about to be fulfilled with Joseph closing his father's eyes in death, but Jacob now wants to make sure his sons will carry out the other part of the promise.

The phraseology here, as in other passages about the patriarchal tomb, is detailed and precise, emphasizing Israel's legal title to the burial ground (cf. 23:17–20; 25:9–10; 50:13).

31 But sentiment, as well as legal title, requires that he be buried there, for that is where his mother Rebekah is buried, as well as his wife Leah, who is also the mother of six of his sons. Earlier in the narrative, the burials of Abraham, Sarah, and Isaac have been mentioned. But this is the only time that the resting

place of Rebekah and Leah is recalled. In life, Rebekah and Leah provoked much division within the family, but Jacob insists on being united with them in death. Fulfillment of the promise of the land goes hand in hand with reconciliation within the family.

33 On the terminology here, cf. *Comment* on 25:8. It is likely that "gathered" (ויאסף) both echoes 49:1, "gather," and is a play on the name Joseph, which consists of the same consonants and similar vowels.

50:1 In this dramatic farewell, unparalleled anywhere else in the OT, we are reminded that the great bond between Jacob and Joseph, which has been the mainspring of the story since chap. 37, is at last broken, and a new era is about to begin. This display of affection does something else too: it fulfills the divine promise that "Joseph will put his hand on your eyes" (46:4), i.e., be present at your dying moments, and is a token that in time all the other promises will be fulfilled as well.

2–3 The OT mentions the mummification only of Jacob and Joseph (v 26), doubtless a mark of their high standing in Egypt. Mummification was a long and complex process, which could involve extracting the brain and internal organs, filling the space with spices, soaking the body in niter, and finally wrapping it in linen bandages. Typically it took seventy days. V 3 speaks of forty days of embalming and seventy days of mourning. Whether these periods are regarded as consecutive or concurrent is unclear. Later, Israel mourned thirty days for Aaron (Num 20:29) and Moses (Deut 34:8), so it is possible that the seventy days of mourning includes forty days for embalming. (For discussions of mummification, see Vergote, *Joseph en Égypte*, 197–200; *EM* 3:215.)

4–6 Having fulfilled Egyptian etiquette by embalming his father, Joseph now proceeds to fulfill Jacob's last wish to be buried in Canaan (cf. 47:29–31). Comparison of the original injunction with Joseph's remark here sheds interesting light on his attitude.

4 Note that Joseph puts his request indirectly to Pharaoh: he speaks to the "house of Pharaoh," i.e., to some of the courtiers. Presumably, some mourning custom prevented his own audience with the king. The very deferential "If now I enjoy your favor" (cf. 47:29) emphasizes the importance of the request to him personally.

5 Joseph tactfully leaves out Jacob's comments about not wanting to be buried in Egypt or that he wants to be buried with his ancestors (cf. 47:29–30). This might suggest a lack of commitment to Egypt. Instead, Joseph stresses that Jacob has already prepared the tomb (cf. 2 Chr 16:14) and that, having buried his father, he will certainly return. But those sensitive to the overtones of Hebrew terms will observe that Joseph speaks of "going up" to Canaan. To "go up" (עלה) is one of the key terms in this chapter (cf. vv 6, 7, 9, 14, 24–25) and very often refers to the exodus from Egypt (e.g., Exod 1:10). Jacob's insistence on being buried in Canaan is a statement of where Israel really belongs. His burial procession from Egypt to Canaan is doubtless seen as a pledge or acted prophecy of the nation's future move (cf. 50:24–25 with Exod 13:19).

7–14 The grandest state funeral recorded in the Bible was given to Jacob. His life-story spans more than half of Genesis and now, as befits the father of the nation, he is laid to rest with all the pomp and ceremony that Egypt could muster. Note the insistence on "all the servants of Pharaoh, . . . all the elders of Egypt" and the armed escort of "chariots and horsemen" that made up the cortege.

Many of the terms and phrases used here, "servants of Pharaoh," "young children," "flocks," "herds," "chariots," "horsemen," "encampment," "very powerful," next recur in the account of the exodus (e.g., Exod 10:7; 11:3; 10:9–10, 24; 14:9, 17–20; 12:38). But whereas now the Egyptians help the expedition, while the children and animals are left behind, then they will oppose it, but the dependents will leave Egypt.

10 "The Bramble Threshing Floor which is over the Jordan." The location of this place is uncertain, and the sense of the qualifying phrase is ambiguous. בעבר הירדן "over the Jordan" may mean "east of Jordan, west of Jordan" or in the Jordan valley, depending on the speaker's situation (B. Gemser, *VT* 2 [1952] 349–55). So the suggested sites are radically different. The traditional location, going back to Eusebius and Jerome, is near Jericho in the Jordan valley. Another modern suggestion is that it is Tell el Ajjul (four miles/seven kilometers) southwest of Gaza, an Egyptian garrison town on the main coast road from Egypt to Canaan. Vv 11–13 make it clear that it was close to Canaan, for the Canaanites comment on the gravity of the mourning. Yet it is Jacob's sons alone who enter Canaan to bury him. This perhaps more easily fits a site in the Jordan valley and, if correct, would imply that the cortege took a route south of the Dead Sea and entered Canaan by crossing the Jordan near Jericho. As long noted (most recently by Bartelmus, *BN* 29 [1985] 35–57), this would suggest that Jacob's return to Canaan took the same route as did his descendants centuries later.

"Mourning." On customs associated with mourning, see *Comment* on 23:2.

"Abel Misraim" or "Abel-Egypt" is one of several place names compounded with Abel (possibly "meadow" or "brook"; cf. Num 33:49; Judg 11:33; 2 Sam 20:15). Here, however, it is linked to the verb אבל "to mourn" and understood to mean "Mourning of Egypt."

12 This verse refers back to 47:30; 49:29–32.

13 Apparently, the main cortege was left at Abel-Misraim, and only Jacob's sons carried his body into Canaan to bury him at the ancestral tomb at Macpelah. As at the internment of Abraham and Isaac, all the sons participated (25:9; 35:29). Reconciliation of formerly warring brothers was expected at family funerals at least.

14 Joseph's return to Egypt fulfills his promise to Pharaoh (v 5).

15–21 This, the penultimate scene of the Joseph story, is aptly called the finale by Sarna, for here the great theme of this story, the tension between Joseph and his brothers, is finally resolved. Joseph's deeds and words (from chap. 45) had shown he wanted to be reconciled to his brothers, but they had never asked for forgiveness, so their feelings of guilt had continued to haunt them. Now with their father dead and the great funeral over, they are gripped by fear that all Joseph has done was motivated by affection for Jacob, not out of real love for them.

As von Rad and Schweizer observe, that the brothers should have felt anxious at this time is "quite realistic psychologically" (von Rad, 431). Westermann's claim that this scene has "no necessary function in the course of the narrative" (3:204) depends on a superficial reading of earlier episodes and a failure to appreciate the psychological dynamics of the situation.

15 With father dead, Joseph may seek revenge just as Esau had planned (cf. 27:41, where the same term, "bear a grudge," is used). Here they acknowledge their own guilt as explicitly as in 42:21–22 and that they deserve to be punished.

16–17 Most traditional commentators who hold that the Testament of Jacob is integral to the narrative argue that, since Jacob makes no clear reference to his sons' treatment of Joseph, he cannot have known what they had done to him. Therefore they suggest that this plea is, in Sternberg's words, a "desperate fabrication" (*Poetics*, 379). In mitigation, it may be said that if Jacob had known, he might have said something like this.

The brothers certainly pull out all the emotional stops in an effort to obtain Joseph's mercy. First, they approach him through an intermediary: ויצוו "they sent instructions." That they did not go in person to start with is implied by v 18, "they came and fell." Second, they say Jacob gave instructions just before his death, a particularly solemn moment. Third, they twice plead for forgiveness. Fourth, they describe their sin in the most comprehensive way, as "crime" (twice), "sin," and "evil," three of the four principal OT terms for wicked deeds (only עוון "iniquity" is missing here; cf. *THWAT* 1:547). Finally, they implore Joseph to act like their father's God, who is one who "forgives iniquity, transgression [crime], and sin" (Exod 34:7; Ps 32:1, 5; Mic 7:18).

"So Joseph wept" (cf. 42:24; 43:30; 45:14–15). "He weeps because they think they need a mediator, because they are afraid of him, because they ascribe to him the attitude of v 15, because he hears his father's voice, because he recalls his youth persecuted by their hate, and because it is they who remind him of this through their submissiveness. These his last tears are really their tears" (Jacob, 940).

18 Their deeds and words continue to recall those earlier occasions. "Fell down" (cf. his dreams and their fulfillment, 37:7, 9; 42:6; 43:26, 28). "We are your slaves." So said Judah when first arrested (44:16).

19–21 "Your fears are groundless," says Joseph, and he recalls what he had said the first time he disclosed his identity to them (cf. 45:5–11). What he promised to them before his father arrived in Egypt he now reaffirms after he has gone. In these two passages we have expressed the key idea that informs the whole Joseph story, that through sinful men God works out his saving purposes.

Von Rad (432) says, "The statement about the brothers' evil plans and God's good plans now opens up the inmost mystery of the Joseph story. It is in every respect, along with the similar passage in ch. 45.5–7, the climax to the whole. Even where no man could imagine it, God had all the strings in his hand. But this guidance of God is only asserted; nothing more explicit is said about the way in which God incorporated man's evil into his saving activity."

21 "Supply you and your youngsters" (cf. 45:10–11); "console" (cf. 37:35); "speak reassuringly" (cf. 34:3).

22–26 A few biographical details from Joseph's later life and an emphatic, indeed triumphant, reassertion of the promise of the land brings his story and the book of Genesis to a close.

22 "Joseph . . . settled in Egypt." As noted in *Form/Structure/Setting*, this formula matches 37:1 and indicates (*pace* Westermann) that this last section has not been tacked on without thought but carefully integrated into the book. "One hundred and ten years" was regarded as the ideal life span in Egypt (Vergote, *Joseph en Égypte*, 200–201).

Jacob comments, "With (this scene) the goal not merely of the Joseph story, but of the whole patriarchal history is reached: the ideal unity of the sons of Israel has been created.

"Abraham had two sons but they did not get on together. Isaac had two sons, but they parted forever. Not until Jacob's twelve sons was the future firmly established. But precisely because they were a large number was there a danger of disunity and division. In the event there was dissension among them, so that they hated and persecuted the best of them. But eventually there was a complete reconciliation, not through the arbitration of a third party, but through the inner transformation of those who hated, for which the sufferer had waited and now in brotherly love acknowledges" (Jacob, 942).

Joshua also reached this age (Josh 24:29). Labuschagne *(OTS* 25 [1989] 126) regards Joseph's age as symbolic. The age of the patriarchs follows a sequence, Abraham $175 = 7$ x 5^2; Isaac $187 = 5$ x 6^2; Jacob 3 x 7^2; Joseph 1 x $(5^2 + 6^2 + 7^2)$. "Joseph is the *successor* in the pattern $(7, 5, 3, 1)$ and the *sum* of his predecessors $(5^2 + 6^2 + 7^2)$."

23 To live to a ripe old age and to see your grandchildren or even great-grandchildren was regarded as a mark of God's favor (Job 42:16). "Ephraim's grandchildren." As n. 50:23.a-a. makes clear, it is not certain whether this is the correct interpretation: they could be Joseph's grandchildren, i.e., Ephraim's sons. "Born on Joseph's knee" implies their adoption by Joseph (cf. 30:3). Machir was one of the clans of Manasseh (1 Chr 7:14–17) that in Judg 5:14 fought alongside the other tribes of Israel.

24–25 Like Abraham, Isaac, and Jacob when they died, Joseph's last concern was the fulfillment of the promise (cf. 24:1–7; 28:1–4; 47:29–31). Joseph predicts "God will definitely visit you" (on "visit," see 21:1) "and bring you out of this land to the land which he swore to Abraham, Isaac, and Jacob." Here the promises that constitute the theme of Genesis are linked to the exodus, which will be the focus of the next book.

To underline the importance of this topic, Joseph repeats the point again, and like Abraham and Jacob, he makes his successors swear an oath to carry out his wishes (cf. Exod 13:19). Here "his brothers," "the sons of Israel" may well be meant in a broader sense of "relatives," "descendants," since all of his brothers except Benjamin in the narrow sense were older than he was.

26 But whereas Genesis goes on to tell of the faithful execution of the wills of Abraham and Jacob, here we simply read that "they embalmed him, and he was put in a coffin in Egypt," the only coffin mentioned in the OT. The story is thus complete and incomplete. The next installment must await the rise of a king who did not know Joseph (Exod 1:8).

Explanation

To modern readers, the last three chapters of Genesis seem to be rather an anticlimax after the high drama of the discovery of Joseph's identity in chap. 45 and his reunion with his father in chaps. 46–47. The accounts of the deaths of Jacob and Joseph strike us as over-detailed, if not morbidly melodramatic.

But such a conclusion mistakes the purpose and interests of the author of Genesis. He is interested in the fulfillment of the promises made to Abraham, promises

of land, descendants, covenant, and blessing to the nations. In the very first chapter, he declares his blessing on mankind. The story of Jacob is dominated by his quest for blessing. Now at the end of his life that quest is completed. He looks back on God's promises to him and declares that "El Shaddai appeared to me . . . and blessed me" (48:3). He observes that he has received more from God than he ever anticipated, "I never expected to see your face; now God has showed me your descendants as well" (48:11). He reflects on the fulfillment of the promises. He and his fathers have acquired a permanent holding in the land of Canaan (48:4), both the burial place at Macpelah (49:29–32; 50:13) and land captured from the Amorites (48:21–23). As for descendants, he has twelve sons of his own and he adopts his grandsons Ephraim and Manasseh too. Similarly, Joseph lives to see his grandchildren (48:12–20; 50:23). After many a close scrape with death he can look back on life in which "God . . . has guided me from then until now" whose "angel . . . rescued me from every evil."

However, the experiences of Jacob and Joseph are merely a foretaste and pledge of the glory to come, just as the believer's experience of the Spirit is a guarantee of a greater inheritance (Eph 1:13–14). Genesis portrays all the major patriarchs, Abraham, Isaac, Jacob, and Joseph, as endowed with the gift of prophecy, but none give on their deathbed such a detailed review of Israel's future, as Jacob does; only Moses, the greatest of the prophets, surpasses Jacob in this respect. In blessing Ephraim and Manasseh, Jacob declares that these two tribes will become "a people" and "full of nations" (48:19). Then in chap. 49 he speaks of what will happen "in the latter days," that is, in the distant future, when the tribes have settled in Canaan and have come into their inheritance there. He mentions the kind of land they will inherit (e.g., suitable for viticulture, or by the sea). He traces the rise of the great tribes of Judah and Joseph (49:8–12, 22–26), the decline of Reuben and Simeon (49:3–7), and the oppression of Issachar, Dan, and Gad (49:14–19). This long prophecy climaxes with the prediction of superlative blessings on Joseph that will ensure his prosperity in every sphere of life "thanks to the strength of the Mighty One of Jacob, thanks to the shepherd of the Stone of Israel" (49:24–26).

Having painted Israel's glorious future in the promised land, Jacob for the second time insists that he must be buried there in the ancestral burial plot (49:29–32; cf. 47:29–30). His son Joseph arranges for him to be buried in the grandest Egyptian manner; indeed, they mourn for Jacob as for a king—seventy days. Then with the Pharaoh's permission, his bier is escorted out of Egypt by chariots and horsemen and by all sorts of Egyptian dignitaries, as well as by Jacob's own sons, of course. The language describing this departure from Egypt, and maybe even the route they took, if they skirted south of the Dead Sea and entered Canaan from the east near Jericho, anticipated the much later exodus. Thus, the very manner of Jacob's dying confirmed his last words about their eventual inheritance. It was itself an acted prophecy that the descendants of Israel would indeed possess the land where he himself was interred. As his son Joseph put it on his deathbed, "God will definitely visit you and bring you . . . to the land which he swore to Abraham, Isaac, and Jacob."

Thus, once again the storyline relates very clearly to the theme of the Pentateuch, the partial fulfillment of the promises to the patriarchs. And for all

their failings, the patriarchs are portrayed preeminently as men of faith who placed their trust in these promises and looked forward to the day of their fulfillment. "By faith Jacob, when dying, blessed each of the sons of Joseph. . . . By faith Joseph, at the end of his life, made mention of the exodus of the Israelites and gave directions concerning his burial" (Heb 11:21–22).

It is not just the great overarching theme of the Pentateuch that this section relates to, but to the Joseph story in particular, that unhappy tale of disastrous sibling rivalry, which was only resolved through the overruling of divine providence and Joseph's magnanimity. Naively we tend to assume that all this dissension came to an end with the great acts of mutual recognition and reconciliation described in chap. 45. But the past is not so easily forgotten, and with their father's death, the brothers start to worry again that Joseph will seek his revenge. For the first time, they frankly confess their sin and plead for forgiveness (50:17). Not for the first time, they fall down before him and offer to become his slaves (50:18). And this gives Joseph a chance to explain what is the purpose of all his sufferings. "You planned evil against me. It was God who planned it for good, so that it should happen as it is today to keep many people alive" (50:20; cf. 45:5–8). The idea that God overrules the plans of the wicked to achieve his own purposes of good is of course an assumption that pervades Scripture (e.g., Prov 16:9; 19:21). Indeed, it seems to be suggested that, through the suffering of the righteous Joseph at the hands of his wicked brothers, life was brought to the world. "God planned it for good . . . to keep many people alive." In Joseph ". . . the families of the earth found blessing" (cf. 12:3): in his career the promises to Abraham of universal blessing to all nations began to see fulfillment. And that God delivers innocent sufferers and secures through them great salvation is the presupposition of many of the psalms of lament, where the psalmist prays for deliverance (e.g., Pss 22, 40, 140). This principle of salvation being brought to all through the suffering of the one finds its clearest expression in the NT in the life, death, and exaltation of our Lord (cf. Mark 10:45).

Yet clearer messianic prospects have universally been recognized in the blessing of Judah, to whom the royal symbols of authority, the staff and the scepter, will be entrusted, to whose descendant "tribute is brought" and whom "the peoples obey" (49:11). If in the short term this prophecy was fulfilled in the reign of David, psalmists and prophets looked for a yet greater Son of David, the lion of the tribe of Judah, the king of kings and lord of lords, before whose throne all tribes and peoples and tongues will fall crying with a loud voice: "Salvation belongs to our God who sits upon the throne and to the Lamb" (Rev 5:5; 7:9–10). To us whose vision has been enriched and enlarged by the witness of the rest of the Bible, Joseph still says, "God will definitely visit you . . . and bring you to the land which he promised."

Index of Authors Cited

Index of Principal Subjects

Index of Biblical Texts

A. Old Testament

B. New Testament